Guillaume
de Machaut

GARLAND COMPOSER RESOURCE MANUALS
VOLUME 36
GARLAND REFERENCE LIBRARY OF THE HUMANITIES
VOLUME 996

GARLAND COMPOSER RESOURCE MANUALS
Guy A. Marco, *General Editor*

STEPHEN COLLINS FOSTER
by Calvin Elliker

JOHANNES OCKEGHEM AND JACOB
OBRECHT
by Martin Picker

HENRY PURCELL
by Franklin B. Zimmerman

CLAUDIO MONTERVERDI
by K. Gary Adams
and Dyke Kiel

CARL MARIA VON WEBER
by Doanld G. Henderson
and Alice H. Henderson

GIOVANNI BATTISTA PERGOLESI
by Marvin E. Paymer
and Hermine W. Williams

CLAUDE DEBUSSY
by James Brisco

G. F. HANDEL
by Mary Ann Parker-Hale

FRANZ JOSEPH HAYDN
by Floyd K. Grave
and Margaret G. Grave

ALESSANDRO AND DOMENICO
SCARLATTI
by Carole F. Vidali

GUILLAUME DE MACHAUT
by Lawrence Earp

EDWARD ELGAR
by Christopher Kent

GUILLAUME DE MACHAUT
A GUIDE TO RESEARCH

LAWRENCE EARP

GARLAND PUBLISHING, INC.
NEW YORK AND LONDON
1995

Library of Congress Cataloging-in-Publication Data

Earp, Lawrence Marshburn.
    Guillaume de Machaut : a guide to research / Lawrence Earp.
       p.   cm. — (Garland composer resource manuals ; 36)
    Discography: p. ***
    Includes bibliographical references and index.
    ISBN 0-8240-2323-4
    1. Guillaume, de Machuat, ca. 1300–1377—Bibliography.
    I. Title. II. Series: Garland composer resource manuals ; v. 36.
Ml134.G956E3 1995
016.841'1—dc20   95-35044
                                                 CIP
                                                 MN

Cover illustration of Guillaume de Machaut composing a lyric, *Remede de Fortune*. BN fr. 1586, fol. 26. Illustration © the Bibliothèque Nationale, Paris. Reproduced by permission.

Printed on acid-free, 250-year-life paper
Manufactured in the United States of America

GARLAND COMPOSER RESOURCE MANUALS

In response to the growing need for bibliographic guidance to the vast literature on significant composers, Garland is publishing an extensive series of research guides. This ongoing series encompasses more than 50 composers; they represent Western musical tradition from the Renaissance to the present century.

Each research guide offers a selective, annotated list of writings, in all European languages, about one or more composers. There are also lists of works by the composers, unless these are available elsewhere. Biographical sketches and guides to library resources, organization, and specialists are presented. As appropriate to the individual composer, there are maps, photographs or other illustrative matter, glossaries, and indexes.

Contents

vii

ix

Preface

Guillaume de Machaut (ca. 1300–April 1377) was the greatest poet and composer of the fourteenth century in France. He influenced two generations of poets, including Chaucer, Froissart, Deschamps, and Christine de Pizan, to name only the most important of his immediate successors, while the style of polyphonic chanson he probably invented remained viable for more than a hundred years after his death. Further, no other poet or musician of the Middle Ages was as careful as Machaut in insuring the survival of his works. Problems of attribution common in this period do not generally arise for Machaut, and we are assured, as is the case for few other figures, that his complete oeuvre is extant.

The first surviving complete manuscript of Machaut's works (Paris, Bibliothèque Nationale, fonds français 1586) dates from a little later than 1350, around the midpoint of his career and may have originally been intended for Bonne of Luxembourg, wife of John, duke of Normandy, the future King John II of France (r. 1350–64). Many other manuscripts, beautifully illustrated books containing Machaut's poetry and music exclusively, were copied in the course of the 1360s and 1370s for rich patrons. A *Prologue* prefacing late manuscripts sums up his entire poetical and musical career and makes it clear that Machaut regarded these large books containing his complete oeuvre—no other poet or musician of the Middle Ages cultivated as many different genres— as unified works of art.

Many of Machaut's narrative and didactic poems (*dits*) were strongly influenced by the *Roman de la Rose*. As in the *Rose* of Guillaume de Lorris, Machaut wrote dream visions and used allegorical figures, and as in the *Rose* of Jean de Meun, he was eager to display his learning. But unlike the *Rose*, Machaut himself figured as a character in his *dits*, and his (pseudo-) autobiographical inclinations grew as his career progressed and his fame spread.

Two important *dits* incorporate lyrical insertions, some of them set to music. The *Remede de Fortune* (1340s) is a Boethian poem of comfort as well as a didactic treatise on the art of poetry that provides examples of each of the lyrical forms, all within the frame of an amorous *dit*. The *Voir Dit* (1362–65), a purportedly autobiographical work, includes in the course of the narrative over sixty lyrical poems, ten of them set to music, as well as nearly fifty prose letters exchanged between the sixty-year-old poet and a fifteen-to-twenty-year-old admirer identified as one Peronne.

In his lyrical poetry—the large collection of lyrics not set to music is labeled *La Loange des Dames* [the praise of ladies] in one late manuscript—Machaut carried on the tradition of *fin' amors* established by the troubadours and trouvères, though formally his statements are couched in the new "fixed forms," mostly ballades and rondeaux.

Machaut was the last major poet to set his lyrics to music, and his manuscripts contain musical settings of a number of ballades, rondeaux, and virelais. Another form Machaut often set to music, the lai, was poetically of a complexity and subtlety to which later poet-musicians did not aspire. A few imitators carried it on as a literary form, but the lai as a musical genre died out in the early fifteenth century. Machaut also wrote isorhythmic motets, the most learned musical form of the late Middle Ages, in the style created by Philippe de Vitry. The largest musical work of Machaut, the Mass, is also his only liturgical work. It is the first known polyphonic setting of all sections of the Mass Ordinary by a single composer.

xi

Guillaume de Machaut: A Guide to Research provides an overview of the current state of research on Machaut up to approximately 1993/94, with the beginnings of a listing for 1995. I have attempted to encompass the broadest range of subjects bearing upon Machaut studies, even though my own area of training and research is restricted to the musicological aspects of his work. Few other figures in the history of artistic endeavor call for the degree of inter-disciplinary inclusion that Machaut does. Forays into fields not my own, including political history, literary history, codicology, and art history, are offered with apologies; my competence in these areas is limited. I nevertheless hope that the book will be of some service to scholars in these fields, even if only to spur on scholarship that will revise the views presented here. Too much specialization sometimes hinders our understanding of Machaut's achievements.

This book is organized, as the title indicates, as a companion to Machaut research, a guide to secondary sources, rather than a conventional bibliography. Yet it has been possible occasionally to offer some new interpretations. Chapter 1, a biography of Guillaume de Machaut, attempts to organize the documentary material from many sources in a fashion that will facilitate further research, and it will be obvious that much remains to be done in this area. Chapter 2 assembles mostly posthumous literary and musical references to Machaut, ground-work for further consideration of his literary and musical influence. Chapter 3 concerns the manuscripts, organized according to the various types of manuscripts in which Machaut's works circulated. Chapter 4 deals with art-historical aspects and includes a concordance of the miniatures in each of the illustrated Machaut manuscripts, with references to published studies and facsimiles. Chapter 5, on the large narrative poems or *dits*, provides a summary of literary scholarship on Machaut and pulls together the research of several literary scholars, not only scholars of medieval France but also a large sampling—by no means exhaustive!—of work on Machaut by Chaucer scholars. Chapter 6 is devoted to the lyrical poems not set to music, the fixed forms and *complaintes* of the *Loange des Dames*, and provides a new comprehensive concordance of these works. I have also collected together scattered bibliographical references concerning the lyrics. Chapter 7 summarizes the directions that musicologists have explored and provides bibliographical references to studies of each of Machaut's musical works. Finally, chapter 8, the discography, provides the most complete listing of Machaut recordings yet assembled and includes critical evaluations of those recordings that I have been able to hear, judged according to recent conceptions of fourteenth-century performance practice.

Author-date references key all of this to the large bibliography, arranged by author. I consider the author-date system easier for the reader than numbered references; in any case, it has allowed additions and revisions up to the last possible moment. The disadvantage is, of course, that the bibliography stands in a single alphabetical series, without division into categories, and thus is not intended for end-to-end reading. Unless the reader wishes to find works concerning Machaut by a specific scholar, access to the bibliography must usually be made through references in the chapters.

I know of only one other published bibliography that is devoted exclusively to Machaut: Hamzaoui 1981. Many of the citations in her work reference survey books little known outside France, and I have not duplicated all of Hamzaoui's entries. For political history I have consulted Chevalier 1905, the *International Medieval Bibliography* (University of Leeds, 1967–), and the *Bibliographie annuelle de l'histoire de France* (Paris: Centre National de la Recherche Scientifique, Institut d'Histoire Médiévale et Contemporaire, 1953–). Literary bibliographies with sections devoted to Machaut include Bossuat 1951 (with supplements published in 1955, 1961, and 1991 as Vielliard/Monfrin 1991),

Holmes 1952, the short introduction in Knight 1982, Switten 1995, and the ongoing bibliographies in *Encomia: Bibliographical Bulletin of the International Courtly Literature Society* (1974–), the *Year's Work in Modern Language Studies* (1931–), and the yearly bibliographies of Klapp (1956–). In addition, the annual *MLA International Bibliography of Books and Articles on the Modern Languages and Literatures* (1956–) is available on CD-ROM.

The influence of Machaut on Chaucer is an area of enormously productive research, and thus bibliographies on Chaucer are also useful to Machaut scholars. I have used volumes by Griffith (1955), Crawford (1967), Baird (1977), Peck (1983; 1988), L.K. Morris (1985), Allen/Fisher (1987), Baird-Lange/Schnuttgen (1988), and the *Year's Work in English Studies* (1919/20–). For music I consulted Hughes 1980 and the yearly bibliographies *Music Index* (1949–), and *RILM* (1967–), now also partly available on CD-ROM. Near the end of my work on this project I ran across John Stinson's on-line bibliographies of fourteenth-century composers (Internet: gopher.latrobe.edu.au 70; World Wide Web: http://www.latrobe.edu.au/music14.html). His Machaut bibliography provided a welcome check for several items, provided some additional ones, and led me to reinstate some items I had previously rejected.

I gratefully acknowledge the help of several scholars. It was Margaret Bent who originally suggested that Garland should entrust me with this undertaking. James I. Wimsatt has been a source of great encouragement over many years, and his critical comments have improved several sections of this book. Many scholars have provided encouragement, advice, and materials, though they may not have known at the time what the result would be, including Lois Anderson, Wulf Arlt, Rebecca A. Baltzer, John W. Barker, Jacques Boogaart, Maureen Boulton, Kevin Brownlee, Alison Bullock, William Calin, Margaret Ehrhart, Paula Higgins, Sylvia Huot, Douglas Kelly, Michael Long, Laurence de Looze, Kumiko Maekawa, Jerome F. Weber, Daniel Leech-Wilkinson, and especially my colleague David Crook. Four graduate students at the University of Wisconsin have helped with this project, Ann Edahl near the beginning, Steven Kurr and Timothy Noonan near the middle, and Jeremy Packer near the end.

I have used the facilities of several libraries along the way, primarily, of course, the library of the University of Wisconsin-Madison (with special thanks to John Dillon, Geraldine Laudati, Alexander Rolich, and Steven Sundell), but also the Princeton University Library, the University of Pennsylvania Library, the Newberry Library, and the Pierpont Morgan Library. In Europe, I have made use of three Parisian libraries, the Bibliothèque Nationale (with very special thanks to François Avril, conservateur in the Département des manuscrits), the Bibliothèque de l'Arsenal, and the Bibliothèque de l'Institut, as well as the marvelous facilities and staff of the Institut de Recherche et d'Histoire des Textes. I have also consulted materials at the Bibliothèque du Musée Condé (Chantilly), the British Library (London), the Bodleian Library (Oxford), the National Library of Wales at Aberystwyth (with thanks to Dr. Cleridwin Morgan), the Bayerische Staatsbibliothek (Munich), and the Staatsbibliothek Preussischer Kulturbesitz and Kupferstichkabinett der Staatlichen Museen (Berlin).

Finally, I gratefully acknowledge grants from the American Philosophical Society (Travel Grant, Summer 1989), and the University of Wisconsin-Madison Graduate School Research Committee (Summers of 1990 and 1991), which generously helped to fund this project.

Lawrence Earp
5 September 1995
Madison, Wisconsin

Abbreviations

LINE NUMBERS for the narrative poems are cited according to Hoepffner 1908–21, unless otherwise indicated. For the *Remede*, I give line numbers both to the Hoepffner edition and to the edition of Wimsatt and Kibler (1988) when they differ. For the *Prise*, Mas Latrie 1877 is cited; for the *Voir Dit*, both line numbers and page numbers of P. Paris 1875 are cited. Line numbers for lyrical poems are cited after Chichmaref 1909. All translations not otherwise attributed are my own.

MINIATURES are through-numbered for each manuscript. Thus, "miniature C1," the first miniature in MS C, introduces the *Jugement Behaingne*, while "miniature Vg1," the first miniature in MS Vg, introduces the *Loange*. Since the concordance of miniatures in chapter 4.4 is arranged according to the order of works in MS **F-G**, it may be necessary first to refer to the index of miniatures and artists by manuscript (chapter 4.2), arranged according to the order of works in each manuscript, to locate a given miniature in the series.

MANUSCRIPT *SIGLA*. See the Index of manuscripts. For the main Machaut manuscripts I have retained the familiar *sigla* that derive mostly from the edition of the narrative poems by Ernest Hoepffner, well known to historians of both literature and music. *Sigla* of musical anthologies derive mostly from Besseler. For manuscripts only briefly mentioned, I employ *RISM sigla*, familiar to scholars of music. These follow a conventional format that abbreviates country, city and library, and shelf number, and can be found in the Index of manuscripts; for instance, *F:Pn 146* indicates the manuscript France, Paris, Bibliothèque Nationale, fonds français 146. For manuscripts containing works of Machaut I frequently refer to a manuscript both by *siglum* and by a number in square brackets, which is keyed to the through-numbered manuscript descriptions in chapter 3. For instance, **Trém** [58] indicates that a full description of this manuscript is found as item number 58 in chapter 3 (pages 122–23).

A. Paris, Bibliothèque Nationale, MS fr. 1584

Alerion. Le Dit de l'Alerion

Ar. Arras, Bibliothèque Municipale, MS 897

Ars. Paris, Bibliothèque de l'Arsenal, MS 683

B. Paris, Bibliothèque Nationale, MS fr. 1585

B–. Ballade set to music, numbered according to editions of Ludwig (1926–54) and Schrade (1956b).

Bc. Barcelona, Biblioteca de Catalunya, MS 8

Bk. Berlin, Staatliche Museen Preussischer Kulturbesitz, Kupferstichkabinett, MS 78 C 2

Bn–. Numbers for the *ballades notées* in Chichmaref's text edition (1909).

C. Paris, Bibliothèque Nationale, MS fr. 1586

CaB. Cambrai, Bibliothèque Municipale, MS B.1328

Cerf Blanc. Le Dit du Cerf Blanc [opus dubium]

Ch. Chantilly, Bibliothèque du Musée Condé, MS 564

Confort. Le Confort d'Ami

Cp–. *Complainte*, numbered according to the edition of Chichmaref (1909).

D. Paris, Bibliothèque Nationale, MS fr. 1587

E. Paris, Bibliothèque Nationale, MS fr. 9221

F-G. Paris, Bibliothèque Nationale, MS fr. 22545–22546

Fa. Faenza, Biblioteca Communale, MS 117

Fonteinne. Le Dit de la Fonteinne Amoureuse

FP. Florence, Biblioteca Nazionale Centrale, MS Panciatichiano 26

Frib. Fribourg, Bibliothèque Cantonale et Universitaire, MS Z 260

Gr 3360. Ghent, Rijksarchief, MS Varia D.3360

H. Paris, Bibliothèque Nationale, MS fr. 881

Harpe. Le Dit de la Harpe

I. Paris, Bibliothèque Nationale, MS n.a.fr. 6221

Iv. Ivrea, Biblioteca Capitolare, MS 115 (CXV)

J. Paris, Bibliothèque de l'Arsenal, MS 5203

Jp. *Le Jardin de Plaisance et Fleur de Rethoricque.* Paris: Ant. Vérard, [1501]

Jugement Behaingne. Le Jugement dou Roy de Behaingne

Jugement Navarre. Le Jugement dou Roy de Navarre

K. Bern, Burgerbibliothek, MS 218

Kr. New York, H.P. Kraus, MS (formerly Phillipps MS 6740)

L. Bern, Burgerbibliothek, MS A 95 (10)

L–. Lai, numbered according to the text edition of Chichmaref (1909) and the music edition of Ludwig (1926–54). Schrade (1956b) edits only lais set to music. Thus, *Qui bien aimme* (L22/16) is no. 22 in the editions of Chichmaref and Ludwig, and no. 16 in the edition of Schrade.

La. Lausanne, Bibliothèque Cantonale et Universitaire, MS 350

Lis et Marguerite. Le Dit de la Fleur de Lis et de la Marguerite

Loange. La Loange des Dames

Lo–. Ballade, rondeau, *chant royal*, or virelai in the *Loange*, numbered according to the edition of Chichmaref (1909).

LoA–. *Sotte chanson*, ballade, or virelai in the Appendix of Chichmaref 1909, vol. 2. I regard all of these lyrics as *opera dubia*.

Lyon. Le Dit dou Lyon

M. Paris, Bibliothèque Nationale, MS fr. 843

M–. Motet, numbered according to the text edition of Chichmaref (1909) and the music editions of Ludwig (1926–54) and Schrade (1956b).

Maggs. formerly London, Maggs Brothers; current location unknown

Marguerite. Le Dit de la Marguerite

Mn. Madrid, Biblioteca Nacional, MS 10264

Mod. Modena, Biblioteca Estense, MS a.M.5.24

Nur. Nuremberg, Stadtbibliothek, MS Fragm. lat. 9 and 9a

P. Paris, Bibliothèque Nationale, MS fr. 2165–2166

Pa. Pennsylvania, University of Pennsylvania Libraries, MS Fr. 15

PadA. Oxford, Bodleian Library, MS Canonici Pat. lat. 229; Padua, Biblioteca Universitaria, MS 658

Pc. Paris, Bibliothèque Nationale, MS fr. 1149

Pe. Cambridge, Magdalene College, Pepysian Library, MS 1594

Pg. Prague, Národní knihovna, MS XI.E.9

Pit. Paris, Bibliothèque Nationale, MS it. 568

Pm. New York, Pierpont Morgan Library, MS M.396

PR. Paris, Bibliothèque Nationale, MS n.a.fr. 6771

Prise. La Prise d'Alexandre

Prologue. Le Prologue

R. Paris, Bibliothèque Nationale, MS fr. 2230

R–. Rondeau set to music, or appearing in the music section of the manuscripts, numbered according to *rondeaux notés* of Chichmaref (1909) and the music editions of Ludwig (1926–54) and Schrade (1956b).

Ra. Paris, Bibliothèque Nationale, MS fr. 20026

Remede. Remede de Fortune

RF–. One of the seven lyrical-musical insertions in the *Remede.* Schrade (1956b) ranges the lai, the two ballades, the virelai, and the rondeau at the end of the series of works in each respective genre.

Rose. Le Dit de la Rose

SL. Florence, Biblioteca Medicea-Laurenziana, Archivio capitolare di San Lorenzo, MS 2211

St. Stockholm, Kungliga Biblioteket, MS V.u.22

Str. Strasbourg, Bibliothèque Municipale, MS M. 222 C. 22

Ta. Turin, Archivio di Stato, MS J.b.IX.10

Trém. Paris, Bibliothèque Nationale, MS n.a.fr. 23190

Utr. Utrecht, Universiteitsbibliotheek, MS 6 E 37 II

V–. Virelai set to music, or appearing in the music section of the manuscripts, numbered according to the music edition of Ludwig (1926–54). Schrade (1956b) edits only virelais set to music. Thus, *Se je souspir* (V36/30) is no. 36 in the edition of Ludwig, and no. 30 in the edition of Schrade.

VD–. Lyrical insertion in the *Voir Dit* (see table 5.3, pp. 224–27).

Vergier. Le Dit dou Vergier

Vezci les biens. Vezci les biens que ma dame me fait

Vg. New York, Wildenstein Collection, MS without shelfmark

Vn–. Numbers for the *chansons balladées notées* in Chichmaref's text edition (1909).

Voir Dit. Le Livre dou Voir Dit

W. Aberystwyth, National Library of Wales, MS 5010 C

Wm. London, Westminster Abbey Library, MS 21

Ys. Paris, Bibliothèque Nationale, MS fr. 1595

Machaut's musical works (with a few works not set to music, but given in the music fascicles of the manuscripts and included in Ludwig's numbering), here arranged by genre according to Ludwig/Schrade numbers, are given short incipits as follows:

Lyrical insertions in the *Remede*:

RF1/L19	*Qui n'aroit* (lai)
RF2	*Tels rit* (complainte)
RF3	*Joie, plaisance* (chant royal)
RF4/B41	*En amer* (ballade)
RF5/B42	*Dame, de qui* (ballade)
RF6/V33	*Dame, a vous* (virelai)
RF7/R22	*Dame, mon cuer en vous* (rondeau)

Lais:

L1	*Loyauté, que*
L2	*J'aim la flour*
L3	*Pour ce qu'on puist*
L4	*Aus amans*
L5/4	*Nuls ne doit*
L6/5	*Par trois raisons*
L7/6	*Amours doucement*
L8	*On parle*
L9	*Amours, se plus (Le Paradis d'Amours)*
L10/7	*Amis, t'amour (Le Lay des Dames)*
L11	*Se quanque Diex (Le Lay du Mirouer Amoureux)*
L12/8	*Un mortel lay (Le Lay Mortel)*
L13	*Maintes fois*
L14/9	*Ne say comment (Le Lay de l'Ymage)*
L15/10	*Contre ce dous (Le Lay de Nostre Dame)*
L16/11	*Je ne cesse (Le Lay de la Fonteinne)*
L17/12	*S'onques (Le Lay de Confort)*
L18/13	*Longuement (Le Lay de Bonne Esperance)*
L19/14	*Malgré Fortune (Le Lay de Plour)*
L20	*Je ne me say (Le Lay de la Souscie)*
L21/15	*Pour vivre joliement (Le Lay de la Rose)*
L22/16	*Qui bien aimme (Le Lay de Plour)*
L23/17	*Pour ce que plus (Un Lay de Consolation)*
L24/18	*En demantant*
RF1/L19	*Qui n'aroit*

Motets:

M1	*Quant en moy / Amour*
M2	*Tous corps / De*
M3	*He! Mors / Fine*
M4	*De Bon Espoir / Puis que*
M5	*Aucune gent / Qui plus*
M6	*S'il estoit / S'Amours*
M7	*J'ay tant / Lasse!*
M8	*Qui es / Ha! Fortune*
M9	*Fons / O livoris*
M10	*Hareu! / Helas!*
M11	*Dame, je sui / Fins cuers*
M12	*Helas! pour quoy virent / Corde*
M13	*Tant doucement m'ont / Eins*
M14	*Maugré mon cuer / De ma dolour*
M15	*Amours qui a / Faus Samblant*
M16	*Lasse! comment / Se j'aim*
M17	*Quant vraie amour / O series*
M18	*Bone pastor / Bone pastor*
M19	*Martyrum / Diligenter*
M20	*Trop plus / Biauté*
M21	*Christe / Veni*
M22	*Tu qui gregem / Plange*
M23	*Felix virgo / Inviolata*

Mass:

Messe de Nostre Dame

Hocket:

Hoquetus David

Ballades:

B1	*S'Amours ne fait*
B2	*Helas! tant*
B3	*On ne porroit*
B4	*Biauté qui*
B5	*Riches d'amour*
B6	*Dous amis, oy*
B7	*J'aim miex*
B8	*De desconfort*
B9	*Dame, ne regardez*
B10	*Ne pensez pas*
B11	*N'en fait*
B12	*Pour ce que tous*
B13	*Esperance*
B14	*Je ne cuit*
B15	*Se je me pleing*
B16	*Dame, comment qu'amez*
B17	*Sans cuer m'en / Amis / Dame*
B18	*De petit po*
B19	*Amours me fait*
B20	*Je suis aussi*
B21	*Se quanque amours*
B22	*Il m'est avis*
B23	*De Fortune*
B24	*Tres douce dame que*
B25	*Honte, paour*
B26	*Donnez, signeurs*
B27	*Une vipere*
B28	*Je puis trop*
B29	*De triste / Quant / Certes*
B30	*Pas de tor*
B31	*De toutes flours*
B32	*Plourez, dames*
B33	*Nes qu'on*
B34	*Quant Theseüs / Ne quier*
B35	*Gais et jolis*
B36	*Se pour ce muir*
B37	*Dame, se vous m'estes*
B38	*Phyton*
B39	*Mes esperis*
B40	*Ma chiere*
RF4/B41	*En amer*
RF5/B42	*Dame, de qui*

Rondeaux:

R1	*Dous viaire*
R2	*Helas! pour quoy se demente*
R3	*Merci vous pri*
R4	*Sans cuer, dolens*
R5	*Quant j'ay l'espart*
R6	*Cinc, un*
R7	*Se vous n'estes*
R8	*Vo dous regars*
R9	*Tant doucement me sens*
R10	*Rose, lis*
R11	*Comment puet*
R12	*Ce qui soustient*
R13	*Dame, se vous n'avez*
R14	*Ma fin*

R15	*Certes, mon oueil*
R16	*Dame, qui vuet*
R17	*Dix et sept*
R18	*Puis qu'en oubli*
R19	*Quant ma dame les maus*
R20	*Douce dame, tant*
R21	*Quant je ne voy*
RF7/R22	*Dame, mon cuer en vous*

Virelais:

V1	*He! dame de vaillance*
V2	*Loyauté vueil*
V3	*Aymi!*
V4	*Douce dame jolie*
V5	*Comment qu'a moy*
V6	*Se ma dame m'a*
V7	*Puis que ma dolour*
V8	*Dou mal*
V9	*Dame, je vueil*
V10	*De bonté*
V11	*He! dame de valour*
V12	*Dame, a qui*
V13	*Quant je sui*
V14	*J'aim sans*
V15	*Se mesdisans*
V16	*C'est force*
V17	*Dame, vostre*
V18	*Helas! et comment*
V19	*Diex, Biauté*
V20	*Se d'amer*
V21	*Dame, le doulz*
V22	*Se Loyauté*
V23/21	*Je vivroie*
V24	*Cilz ha bien*
V25/22	*Foy porter*
V26/23	*Tres bonne*
V27/24	*En mon cuer*
V28/25	*Tuit mi penser*
V29/26	*Mors sui*
V30/27	*Liement*
V31/28	*Plus dure*
V32/29	*Dame, mon cuer emportez*
V33	*Je ne me puis*
V34	*L'ueil, qui est*
V35	*Plus belle*
V36/30	*Se je souspir*
V37/31	*Moult sui*
V38/32	*De tout sui*
RF6/V33	*Dame, a vous*

List of Tables

Guillaume de Machaut

I

Biography of Guillaume de Machaut

1. Introduction

The chronological stages of Machaut's career are recounted below in several narrative segments. Most of these are followed by one or more excursus (in smaller type), which attempt to lay out the documentary, literary, and bibliographical resources of the Machaut biography in an organized fashion, keeping to the facts as they stand at this writing.[1] The reader looking for an overview of Machaut's biography will miss nothing essential by skipping the several excursus.

Although I have been able to assemble material from a variety of sources and have found a few published documents that have not hitherto been noticed by Machaut biographers, the current state of the documentation of Machaut's life remains confused. Planned studies by Anne W. Robertson, Daniel Leech-Wilkinson, and Andrew Wathey promise to set Machaut biography on a stronger foundation, based on a reexamination of the archival sources.[2] I have myself undertaken no new archival studies for this biography.

Older biographies that retain their value as starting points include Hoepffner 1908–21, 1:xi–xliii (still the most readable introduction to the life and works), Chichmaref 1909, 1:vii–lxxi (particularly useful for its incorporation of material from Eastern European sources), and Machabey 1955b (the longest biography up until now, though indifferently documented). The most useful brief survey of Machaut's life in English is by Hoppin (1978b, 396–99).[3]

2. Birth, education

Guillaume de Machaut was born ca. 1300 in Champagne, perhaps in Machault (dépt. Ardennes) or Reims. Nothing is known of his parents, except that they were not members of the nobility (chap. 1.2.3). Literary and archival references tell us something about his younger brother, Jean de Machaut, the only relative of Guillaume to have been identified with certainty. Jean was a simple clerk in the diocese of Reims (perhaps Reims itself) before receiving any ecclesiastical benefices, and since the careers of the two brothers ran very much in parallel, one might assume that Guillaume also began as a young *clerc* in the diocese. His early education was probably accomplished at the cathedral. He then pursued studies at a university, most likely in Paris. He is referred to as *maistre* on several occasions and thus obtained a degree, probably the *maître-ès-arts*.[4] Although he never became a priest, his position as canon of Reims cathedral, beginning in 1340, would likely have demanded the subdeaconate. We can

---

[1] Calin's admonitions concerning the use of literary evidence for biographical information on an author should be constantly borne in mind (Calin 1987a, chap. 2). In addition, see Wathey's discussion of the perils of interpreting historical documents for fact (Wathey 1994).

[2] Some results of new archival studies are seen in studies by Gushee (1980), Wilkins (1983b), Leech-Wilkinson (1990c), and A.W. Robertson (1992).

[3] For other brief surveys and dictionary articles, see chap. 5 n. 26 and chap. 7 n. 23.

[4] For a possible alternative interpretation of *maistre*, see chap. 1.2.8.

glean a few clues to his education in literary and musical matters from the sources utilized for his poetry and music.

1.2.1. MACHAUT'S DATE OF BIRTH. All scholars since Antoine Thomas have retained ca. 1300 as Machaut's date of birth.[5] Before Thomas's discoveries, biographers usually placed Machaut's date of birth early enough to give him a reasonable age for some documents of the early fourteenth century that name a "Guillelmus de Machello" and a "Guillelmus de Macholio."[6] G. Paris (1877) expressed serious doubts about the old interpretations because of the advanced age of a poet born supposedly in 1282 or 1284, most of whose works fall in the period from the 1340s to the 1370s, and on the Latin orthography of the name "Machaut" (which should be rendered "Machaudio"). A. Thomas (1881 and 1884), who found papal documents relating to a noble family "de Machello," from the area around Orléans, as well as to a non-noble family "de Machaudio," from the area around Reims and Machault, definitively clears up the problem.[7]

If Guillaume entered the service of John of Luxembourg in 1323 (chap. 1.5.2) with the degree of *maître* (chap. 1.2.8), he may have been born slightly later than 1300, say ca. 1302, since this degree required a minimum age of about twenty.[8] His career in the church is consistent with a birth date of ca. 1300 to 1302. A canonicate, which was first awarded to Machaut in 1330 (chap. 1.6.1b), required a minimum age of twenty-five (Mollat 1921, 21; but see below, n. 85), and the more advanced age of about thirty is reasonable for a clerk receiving his canonicate as a reward for meritorious service (cf. Millet 1982, 53).

1.2.2. MACHAUT'S HOME PROVINCE. Several small pieces of evidence argue that Machaut was born in Champagne. Most often cited are two literary references, a ballade by Eustache Deschamps (chap. 2.1.1b), and a later reference in the *Livre du Cuer d'Amours Espris* (1457) of René d'Anjou (chap. 2.3.2e). The name "de Machaut" does not necessarily mean that he was born in the town of Machault (dépt. Ardennes); the name is also found in Reims, Attigny, and other towns in the area (Machabey 1955b, 1:14–19).

An incidental bit of evidence that Machaut originated from around Reims is provided by Pope Benedict XII's reform of the abusive multiplication of benefices, especially the expectatives, that had become common under his predecessor John XXII. In reducing the number of a canon's benefices Benedict usually left him with a canonicate in the metropolitan church of his home province (Dricot 1982, 144). In Machaut's case a bull of 17 April 1335 (chap. 1.6.1f) allowed him to retain an expectative at Reims, while at the same time requiring him to sacrifice expectatives at Verdun and Arras.

1.2.3. MACHAUT'S SOCIAL STATION. Early biographers of Machaut argued over his noble or non-noble status.[9] Since Antoine Thomas (1881 and 1884) managed to discount the old documents, we have been left with no clue concerning Machaut's family.[10]

One item may argue against an origin from a bourgeois family at Reims. Desportes (1979, 300–301) notes that it was rare in the fourteenth century for canons of the cathedral of Reims to come from among the bourgeois of the city; the same was true for the chapter at Laon (Millet 1982, 77–78).

---

[5] A. Thomas 1881, 327; 1884, 38; Hoepffner 1908–21, 1:xii; Chichmaref 1909, 1:xi–xiii.

[6] Lebeuf 1753; Caylus 1753a and 1753b; Rive 1780; Tarbé 1849; Fétis 1860–65; Mas Latrie 1877b, etc.; for an overview, see Hoepffner 1908–21, 1:ix–x. P. Paris, who requires a fairly young Machaut in light of his redating of the *Voir Dit* to the years 1363–65, placed his birth between 1311 and 1316; Paris forgets that he had established 1307 as the death date of Machaut's supposed father (P. Paris 1875, xiv–xv).

[7] A. Thomas 1881, 325–28; 1884, 36–40; Chichmaref 1909, 1:vii–xi; Hoepffner 1908–21, 1:xi–xiii; Machabey 1955b, 1:14.

[8] Cf. the ages suggested in Verger 1973, 66 (twenty-one); Millet 1982, 55 (ca. eighteen); and Pycke 1986, 313 (ca. nineteen to twenty).

[9] Of the early biographers, Lebeuf (1753), Caylus (1753a), Tarbé (1849), and P. Paris (1875) argue that Machaut came from a noble family, while Rive (1780) and Mas Latrie (1877b) argue that the family was not noble. See also Machabey 1955b, 1:74–75.

[10] Cf. Hoepffner 1908–21, 1:xii; Chichmaref 1909, 1:ix–xi. The potential relatives discussed by Machabey (1955b, 1:15–19; 1955c, 253 n. 2; 1960, 1392) are purely speculative, as he himself acknowledges.

All that remains for us to judge Machaut's social situation is what he provided in a few literary references in the narrative poems, which lead us to believe that he was placed in his high position with regard to the nobility purely on the basis of his talent and intelligence, something that was possible with an education in the church:

a. *Alerion* (ll. 4812–14). "Par ce verrez tout clerement / Se cils est clers ou damoiseaus / Qui fist ce 'Dit des quatre oiseaus'" (*explicit*) [By this means, you will clearly see / If he's a clerk or a young knight / who write this 'Tale of the Four Birds' (trans. Gaudet/Hieatt 1994, 166)] (an anagram giving the name "Guillaume de Machaut" precedes this passage).[11]

b. *Jugement Navarre* (ll. 4199–4200). "Je, Guillaumes dessus nommez, / Qui de Machau sui seurnommez" [I, the Guillaume named above, / Who has the surname de Machaut (trans. Palmer 1988, 189)].[12]

c. *Confort* (ll. 21–26). "Sire, et se je t'apelle amy, / N'en aies pieur cuer a my; / Car bien sçay que tu es mes sires, / Et je des mieudres ne des pires / Ne suis..." [Sire, if I call you friend, / Please don't be angry with me; / For you know quite well you are my lord, / While I come neither from the very high / Nor the very low (trans. Palmer 1992, 3)].

d. *Fonteinne* (ll. 139–40). "Et comment que je soie clers / Rudes, nices et malapers" [And though I might be a clerk / Who is ignorant, incapable, and inept (trans. Palmer 1993a, 97)]. The adjectives have been cited as evidence of a common origin (Hoepffner 1908–21, 1:xiii), but they are more probably conventional literary attributes of the clerk.[13]

For further discussion of Machaut's social status in relation to his literary works, see Cerquiglini 1984; 1985a; 1985b, part 2 passim, 182, 245; Imbs 1991, 23 and 181.

1.2.4. MACHAUT'S FAMILY. The only well-attested member of Machaut's family is his brother Jean de Machaut, who was a simple clerk from the diocese of Reims before receiving his first benefice in 1333 (chap. 1.11.1a). The dates of the papal documents that refer to the two brothers suggest that Jean's career was a step behind Guillaume's, and thus that Jean was younger than Guillaume.[14]

Two other documents make reference to so-called relatives of Machaut. First, a document of 1371, associated with John, duke of Berry, refers to a "cousin," Person de Suygnon (chap. 1.14.1b). Second, a passage in an anonymous rhetorical treatise, the *Regles de la Seconde Rettorique* (datable between ca. 1404 and 1432) calls Eustache Deschamps a "nephew" of Machaut (chap. 2.1.1c).

1.2.5. MACHAUT'S EDUCATION. Nothing is known of Machaut's early education in literary and musical matters.[15] His early education was probably accomplished at the cathedral.[16] (For

---

[11] The passage is further discussed below (chap. 5.9) in connection with biographical aspects of *Alerion*.

[12] On such passages where Machaut names himself, see Cerquiglini 1985b, 119, 234 n. 25; de Looze 1988a, 205–6.

[13] On this passage see Cerquiglini 1985b, 109–10. Guillaume employs similar adjectives, although without the noun *clerc*, throughout the *Voir Dit*: letter 2 (P. Paris 1875, 19), l. 1239 (55), letter 10 (68), l. 1991 (86), l. 2320 (98), letter 19 (164); cf. also l. 7790 (318). For *Jugement Navarre*, see Calin 1974, 117.

[14] A. Thomas 1881, 329–30; 1884, 42; Hoepffner 1908–21, 1:xxi. Several passing references to Machaut's brother appear in the *Voir Dit*, of which the most specific is the following, in which Machaut's secretary mentions Jean: "Et que diroit vostres bons freres / Qui vous est fils, sires et père / Qui si doulcement vous norrit" (ll. 6966–68, ed. P. Paris 1875, 286) [And what would your good brother say, who is son, lord, and father to you, who so kindly nourishes you]. P. Paris (1875, 286 n. 1) and Imbs (1991, 54) concluded from this that Jean was the older brother, while Machabey (1955b, 1:61) interpreted it to mean that Jean merely took care of daily matters. Other mentions of Machaut's brother in the *Voir Dit* include letter 26 (ed. P. Paris 1875, 195), letter 28 (208), letter 32 (251), letter 35 (262), and letter 41 (314).

[15] Poirion (1965, 193) provides a brief and speculative outline of Machaut's education. See also the remarks in Gauvard 1982, 31–32; Dricot 1982; and Imbs 1991, 179–80. Leech-Wilkinson finds evidence of the influence of Philippe de Vitry on Machaut's education as a motet composer (1989, 1:104, and chap. 2 passim); see also commentary to *Aucune gent / Qui plus* (M5) below, chap. 7.3.

further speculation, see chap. 1.5.2 and chap. 1.6.1a.) The few literary references to Machaut's education in his narrative poems are perfunctory and tell us little:

a. *Voir Dit* (l. 8599, ed. P. Paris 1875, 349). "Je, qui ay esté à l'escole, / Lisi la lettre mot à mot" [I, who was at school, read the letter word for word]. This can be taken as a playful reference to the beginning reader in school.

b. *Jugement Navarre* (l. 605). "De nuit, en estudiant, veille" [by night, studying, he stays awake (trans. Palmer 1988, 29)]. Machaut continued to pursue his studies on his own, attested by the character Dame Bonneürté's playful reference to Guillaume's lucubrations. On the musical side, there are the following references:

c. *Jugement Behaingne* (ll. 1830–31). "Et c'est bien droiz, car elle acquiert grant blame / De muance faire en la fausse game" [and it's quite right to do so, for she earns great blame for changing her key in mid-tune (ed. and trans. Wimsatt/Kibler 1988, 152–53)]. Concerning this passage, see the comments in Daniel Leech-Wilkinson's review of Wimsatt/Kibler 1988.

d. *Remede* (ll. 3999–4002/4001–4). "Et s'i ot des musiciens / Milleurs assez et plus scïens / En la vieus et nouvelle forge / Que Musique qui les chans forge" [And there were musicians more skilled and knowledgeable in both the new and old styles ... than Music, who writes the songs (ed. and trans. Wimsatt/Kibler 1988, 392–93)]. Machaut was doubtless referring here to the musical Ars Antiqua and Ars Nova (S.J. Williams 1952, 330; Günther 1963b, 116).[17]

e. *Confort* (ll. 3993–94). "Mon b mol de be fa be mi / Mis en b dur..." [my B-flat, through B-fa B-mi is turned to B-natural; i.e., I have become obdurate]. In this manner Machaut demonstrates his knowledge of the solmization system (cf. Françon 1947; Sonnemann 1969, 109–10). In the context of the poem, these lines are supposed to have been composed by the king of Navarre, but surely this carefully crafted codetta of twenty-six lines, all on the same rhyme, is by Machaut.

f. *Voir Dit* (ll. 5648–51). "Mais Jubal au son des martiaus / Fist tons et sons, et chans nouviaus / Et notés, et les ordenances / De musique et les concordances"[18] [But Jubal, to the sound of the hammers, made tones and sounds, and new notated songs, and the rules and concords of music].

1.2.6. SOURCES FOR MACHAUT'S POETRY AND MUSIC. Hoepffner discusses the literary sources of Machaut's narrative works in the introductions to his editions. The major sources for the larger poems are as follows (for more details, see the discussion of the literary antecedents for each work in chap. 5): *Vergier* (*Roman de la Rose*; see Hoepffner 1908–21, 1:lvi–lix); *Jugement Behaingne* (*Altercatio Phyllidis et Florae* and related Latin debate poems; see Hoepffner 1908–21, 1:lx–lxi); *Jugement Navarre* (*Ovide Moralisé*; see Hoepffner 1908–21, 1:lxx, lxiii–lxxxv, better demonstrated in De Boer 1914, 342–46); *Remede* (Bible, *Consolation of Philosophy* of Boethius, *Roman de la Rose*, and *Dit de la Panthere* of Nicole de Margival; see Hoepffner 1908–21, 2:xvi–xxxiii; and 1920a); *Lyon* (principally the Arthurian romances of Chrétien de Troyes; see Hoepffner 1908–21, 2:lviii–lxii); *Alerion* (Vincent of Beauvais and oral sources; see Hoepffner 1908–21, 2:lxiv, lxviii–lxx); *Confort* (Bible and contemporary commentaries, Vegetius, Vincent of Beauvais, and *Ovide Moralisé*; see Hoepffner 1908–21, 3:ii–xii; De Boer 1914, 348–50); *Fonteinne* (*Roman de la Rose* and *Ovide Moralisé*; see Hoepffner 1908–21, 3:xxxii–xxxviii; De Boer 1914, 346–48); *Voir Dit* (*Ovide Moralisé*; see A. Thomas 1912 and De Boer 1914, 335–42; see also De Boer 1913).

More recent literary studies have contributed to the foundations laid by Hoepffner and De Boer (B. Harrison 1934; Schilperoort 1936, 51–66; Wimsatt 1968; Calin 1974; Ehrhart 1974; Kelly 1978, 49–50 et passim; Ehrhart 1979; Badel 1980, 28; Ehrhart 1980a; 1980b; 1980c; Kelly 1981; Brownlee 1984; Cerquiglini 1985b; Ehrhart 1987; 1990; 1992); nevertheless, an exhaustive study of this aspect of the sort available for the works of Chaucer (Crow/Olson

---

16 For the cathedral school and other schools at Reims, see Desportes 1975. Desportes briefly mentions Machaut (1975, 116), but specific documentation is lacking. The scholaster, or *scholasticus* at Reims from 1299–1322, the period covering Machaut's possible time of attendance, was Gaucher de Neuville (Desportes 1975, 108 n. 4).

17 On the term "forge" in this passage, see Cerquiglini 1985b, 212; Switten 1989.

18 Cerquiglini (1985b, 213) edits and discusses this passage.

1966; Wimsatt 1968 and 1991b, etc.) is lacking for Machaut. On the *Roman de la Rose* as a source for Machaut, see, besides Hoepffner's introductions, Uitti 1978; Badel 1980; Brownlee 1984; Newels 1989; Huot 1993.

Studies of the development of the lyrical forms cultivated by Machaut include several articles of Hoepffner (1910, introduction; 1911; 1920a; 1920b) (summary in Reaney 1962). Wilkins (1983a, 190–94) and especially Wimsatt (1991b, chap. 2) provide new information and further bibliography on Jean de le Mote, Machaut's most important immediate poetic predecessor.

A systematic study of Machaut's musical sources is also lacking. A few starts have been made, especially by Günther (1972). See also the individual discussions of the following works in chap. 7.3: *Nuls ne doit* (L5/4), *Un mortel lay* (L12/8), *Contre ce dous* (L15/10), *Malgré Fortune* (L19/14), *Aucune gent / Qui plus* (M5), *Hareu! / Helas!* (M10), *Tant doucement m'ont / Eins* (M13), *Amours qui a / Faus Samblant* (M15), *Martyrum / Diligenter* (M19), *Christe / Veni* (M21), *Felix virgo / Inviolata* (M23), Gloria and Credo of the Mass, *On ne porroit* (B3), *N'en fait* (B11), *Pour ce que tous* (B12), *Esperance* (B13), and *Comment qu'a moy* (V5).

1.2.7. THE TITLE *CLERS* (CLERK). Machaut refers a number of times in his works to the title *clers*, a very vague term in the Middle Ages meaning little more than "lettered," a person who obtained some schooling at a church or cathedral school (cf. Verger 1973, 81). It was Machaut's education as a clerk that allowed him to enter a level of society that otherwise would have been closed to him, and gave him a sufficient background in literary and musical matters for his artistic personality to develop. On the attributes given the clerk in contemporary literature, see Cerquiglini 1984; 1985a; 1985b, part 2. Some mentions of *clers* in Machaut's literary works include the following:

a. *Jugement Behaingne* (ll. 1474–75). "S'i ot .i. clerc que nommer ne saroye / Qui li lisoit la bataille de Troye" [and a clerk, whom I cannot name, was reading to him from the Battle of Troy (ed. and trans. Wimsatt/Kibler 1988, 134–35)]. This is an amusing indirect reference to Machaut's duties as a clerk in the service of John of Luxembourg (see Poirion 1965, 194; Pelen 1976–77, 132; Brownlee 1984, 166).

b. *Jugement Behaingne* (ll. 1585–86). "Sire, et cilz clers / Qui me semble gais, jolis, et appers, / Se fu tapis ou jardin et couvers" [Sir, this clerk who seems to me to be gay, merry, and clever was hidden in the park (ed. and trans. Wimsatt/Kibler 1988, 138–39)]. The knight is here referring to the narrator, i.e., to Machaut (see Brownlee 1984, 165–66; Cerquiglini 1985b, 110–11).

c. *Alerion* (ll. 4812–14). See chap. 1.2.3a.

d. *Confort* (ll. 3105–12). "Ne fai pas clers tes consaus d'armes, / Qui doivent prier pour les ames / Et doivent compter et escrire / Et chanter leur messes ou lire / Et consillier les jugemens / Aus consaus et aus parlemens. / Si que tien chascun en son ordre / Si bien qu'il n'i ait que remordre" [Do not make your military counsel of clerics, who are supposed to pray for souls, keep accounts, write, sing or read mass, and give counsel on judgments handed down in conference and court. Let each person keep to his assigned place so that there may be nothing to criticize (trans. Kelly 1978, 128)]. In this manner Machaut advises King Charles of Navarre on the role of the clerk in the service of a prince (cf. Cerquiglini 1985b, 115). He later excused himself for being perhaps too forward with his advice (ll. 3665–67): "Plus n'en di, qu'il n'apartient mie / Que je des seigneurs chose die / Qui leur puist ou doie desplaire" [I'll say no more since it's not fitting / For me to report anything about the great lords / That should or could displease them (trans. Palmer 1992, 191)].

e. *Fonteinne* (ll. 139–40). See chap. 1.2.3d.

f. *Prise* (l. 785). "Je fu ses clers ans plus de trente" [I was his clerk for more than thirty years]. See chap. 1.5.2 on this often-cited passage concerning the king of Bohemia. Also concerning the *Prise*, see Cerquiglini 1985b, 182.

1.2.8. THE TITLE *MAISTRE* (MASTER OF ARTS). The title *maistre*, which Machaut curiously never mentioned in his poetry, would indicate that Machaut had studied at the university, and that he had obtained at least the degree of *magister artium* (master of arts; on this degree see Verger 1973, 65–66). None of the papal documents that record the ecclesiastical graces awarded to Machaut ever mentions a university degree, but Machaut's function as *clerc du roi* may well imply that he had university training (Millet 1982, 87).[19] Three documents, three manuscript rubrics, four literary references, three library inventories, and one music theory treatise give Machaut the title *maistre*[20]: (a) document of 18 August 1352 (chap. 1.7.1f); (b) document of December 1361 (chap. 1.15.1a); (c) document of 15 October 1371 (chap. 1.14.1b); (d) rubric to index of MS E [7], see chap. 6.1; (e) rubric attributing *Confort* to *maistre Guillaume de Machaut* in MS L [34], see chap. 3, n. 61; (f) rubric at the beginning of MS D [11] (chap. 4.4p, miniature D1); (g) Eustache Deschamps's second ballade on Machaut's death (Wimsatt 1991b, 247; below, chap. 2.1.1g); (h) letter of Eustache Deschamps, dated 28 May 1377? (chap. 2.1.1h); (i) lai of Oton de Granson, before 1397 (chap. 2.1d); (j) two references in the *Regles de la Seconde Rettorique*, an anonymous second rhetoric treatise, ca. 1404–1432 (chap. 2.1.1c and chap. 2.3.1a).

Three further witnesses to this title are found in Burgundian library inventories of the fifteenth century, which refer to a book of "Maistre Guillaume de Machaut": (k) the early binding of MS E [7][21]; (l) a lost Burgundian manuscript discussed in chap. 3, MS [8]; (m) another lost Burgundian manuscript discussed in chap. 3, MS [19]; (n) finally, an anonymous Italian music theorist speaks of polyphony composed by "magistro Guillelmo de Mascandio" (Page 1993, 113).

3. Ca. 1320–46. Service of John of Luxembourg, king of Bohemia

Machaut's association with aristocratic patrons began with John of Luxembourg (the Blind), king of Bohemia (b. 1296; r. 1310–1346), regarded by contemporaries as the very epitome of chivalry. The time spent in the service of this great sovereign, both at court and on the cavalcade, was decisive to Machaut's development as a court poet and composer. Machaut probably entered his service around 1323, possibly from Reims.

Several of Machaut's narrative poems provide references to regions of Europe through which John of Luxembourg traveled or to specific historical events in which he was involved. On the basis of the detailed geographical knowledge Machaut displays in these descriptions, we assume that Machaut accompanied the king on many campaigns in central and eastern Europe in the 1320s and early 1330s, traversing Bohemia, Silesia and Poland (1327, 1329), East Prussia and Lithuania (1328–29), and perhaps also Lombardy and Carinthia (1331). The campaigns in eastern Europe during the years 1327–29 are the most significant, and were the most successful for the king. It is fitting that the period of John's most successful campaigns was the one that Machaut recounted in the greatest detail. The campaigns against the infidels of Lithuania were also doubtless the ones that resonated most strongly to fourteenth-century crusading sensibilities.[22]

Through papal documents we can follow Machaut's *cursus honorum* under John of Luxembourg, a career fully typical of the time. Machaut advanced from

---

[19] More than half of the canons at Laon and Tournai, two chapters for which excellent recent studies have been made, had at the very least attained the master of arts degree (Millet 1982, 87–88; Pycke 1986, 68–70). At Laon canons who were familiars of the pope and the king of France might lack a university education, while familiars of other princes and bishops did have a particular university competence (Millet 1982, 142–43).

[20] On indirect literary evidence from *Jugement Navarre*, see Imbs 1991, 265–66 n. 50 (to p. 151).

[21] Ludwig 1926–54, 2:11a*, 40b*; see Barrois 1830, no. 1308 (1467 inventory), and no. 1719 (1487 inventory).

[22] Dembowski (1983, 48–50, 130–49) makes a strong case for the importance of the Teutonic Order and the crusade in Prussia to the chivalric ideology behind Froissart's *Meliador*, and much of what he says is relevant to Machaut's depiction of John of Luxembourg as the ideal prince. See also Cerquiglini-Toulet 1993b, 30–33.

a simple clerk to almoner by 1330, to notary by 1332, finally serving the king as secretary by 1333 (chap. 1.6 and 1.6.1). Campaigns of John of Luxembourg after 1331 are not specifically recounted by Guillaume, and details of the poet's whereabouts before 1340 are unknown. It is possible that by the mid 1330s he was leading a more sedentary life as court poet. Only two documents have come to light that relate to his direct service of John of Luxembourg, one from 1334, the other from 1341 (chap. 1.5.4).

The lavish feasts, tournaments, and court life of John of Luxembourg must have exerted an enormous influence on the formation of the poet. John's main center in the West was Durbuy,[23] described by Machaut in the *Jugement Behaingne* (ll. 1468–71; 1476–85).[24] As Machaut playfully stated (chap. 1.2.7a), one of his duties was reading romances aloud to entertain the king, undoubtedly an important exercise for the aspiring young poet.

Philip of Valois, the future King Philip VI of France, was very attached to John of Luxembourg, and in February 1328, on becoming regent after the death of Charles IV, Philip gave John his former residence in Paris, the Hôtel de Nesle. The hôtel was located on the site of the present Bourse de Commerce near St-Eustache (it is visible east of St-Eustache as the Hôtel de Soissons on the well-known *Plan de Turgot* of 1739).[25] After the death of John of Luxembourg in 1346, the hôtel came back to the crown through his daughter Bonne of Luxembourg, wife of John, duke of Normandy, the future King John II.[26]

4. 1324. Earliest datable work. Possible contact with Philippe de Vitry

The new musical form of the Ars Nova, the isorhythmic motet, was doubtless the vehicle for Machaut's earliest essays into poetry and music. Since the very beginning of the revival of interest in Machaut, scholars have accepted the motet *Bone pastor Guillerme / Bone pastor* (M18) as Machaut's earliest datable work (Lebeuf 1753, 381). The texts of both the triplum and motetus refer to a newly-selected archbishop by the name of Guillaume, and only one archbishop of Reims from this period has this forename.[27] Guillaume de Trie (d. 1334) was nominated 28 March 1324, but it may be possible to place the motet early in 1325, since he did not come to Reims to take the oath of office until 6 January 1325.[28] On the other hand, a motet favorable to Guillaume de Trie may not have been written at Reims at all, since the canons despised him.[29] It would

---

[23] In the Belgium province of Luxembourg, south of Liège on the river Ourthe. See Puymaigre 1892, 408 n. 2.

[24] Machabey 1955b, 1:22–23, 25, 27–28. Documents and literary references to John's court are given in Wilkins 1983b.

[25] Puymaigre (1892, 421–22 n. 6) published the document relating to the gift of the hôtel, but confused the Hôtel de Nesle with the notorious Tour de Nesle. See also Machabey 1955b, 1:23–25; R. Cazelles 1947, 169; 1958, 368; Lehoux 1966–68, 1:5 n. 2.

[26] In 1356 King John II gave the hôtel to Count Amadeus VI of Savoy (*Mémoires* 1756, 262–71; Machabey 1955b, 1:23–25 [chap. 1.15.2c treats Amadeus VI as a patron of Machaut]). In 1388 it passed to Louis d'Orléans. The building was demolished in 1749.

[27] For editions and translations of the texts, see chap. 7.3 under *Bone pastor / Bone pastor* (M18).

[28] According to Hoepffner (1908–21, 1:xv n. 1, citing *Gallia Christiana*), Guillaume de Trie accepted his episcopate in June 1324. Guillaume's brother Mathieu de Trie was at this time marshall of France (Desportes 1979, 295). The house of Trie later provided several royal officers to the crown (R. Cazelles 1958, 55, 85, 288; 1982, 67–69).

[29] Relations between the cathedral chapter and the archbishop had been precarious for some

seem more profitable to seek an occasion that brought Machaut into contact with
the entourage of the French royal court as an occasion for the composition of a
motet celebrating this royal official. One good possibility is an excursion,
discussed below, that John of Luxembourg made with King Charles IV the
Fair.

   Bone pastor was not, however, Machaut's earliest motet. Other Machaut
motets, student works heavily indebted to models by his slightly older
contemporary Philippe de Vitry (1291–1361), must have preceded this effort.
Philippe, who by the age of twenty-five had probably established himself as the
leading composer of the Parisian musical avant-garde, was doubtless the
greatest musical influence on the young Machaut. Although concrete documentary evidence establishing a formal connection between these two figures is
lacking, Leech-Wilkinson (1982–83, 5; 1989, chap. 2) has noted some
references in the text of the motet *Aucune gent / Qui plus* (M5) suggesting that
Machaut was emulating Vitry; he has also discovered a clear structural model
for M5 in Vitry's motet *Douce playsence / Garison.*[30] Vitry's influence on
Machaut's poetic efforts, particularly in the field of lyrical poetry, was also
probably decisive (Earp 1991b).

   Opportunities for Machaut to consult with Philippe de Vitry were frequent in
the early 1320s. John of Luxembourg was at Reims for the coronation of
Charles IV the Fair in 1322; we may speculate that Machaut and Vitry were
there as well. An occasion for a much more extended period of contact between
the two poet-musicians soon presented itself. From the winter of 1323 through
the spring of 1324, John of Luxembourg and a large entourage accompanied
King Charles IV to Toulouse. Unfortunately, the excursion had a sad outcome:
on the way back to Paris, the queen was injured in an accident, and died on 25
March 1324. John of Luxembourg was present as his sister Marie of
Luxembourg was buried at Montargis (dépt. Loiret) on 28 March 1324, the
same day that Guillaume de Trie was named the new archbishop of Reims.

   Charles of Valois, father of of Philip of Valois, the future King Philip VI,
was also present on the excursion to Toulouse of 1323 to 1324. John of
Luxembourg had already cultivated an official association with the house of
Valois, which would provide the kings of France after the death of Charles IV
in 1328. On 8 May 1323 in Paris, in the presence of John of Luxembourg, the
daughter of Charles of Valois, Blanche (Marguerite), became engaged to John
of Luxembourg's son Charles, the future Holy Roman Emperor Charles IV
(they were married in 1329). We may speculate that the young Philip of Valois
and Guillaume de Trie were also among the royal entourage at Toulouse.
Guillaume de Trie was Philip's tutor, and as archbishop of Reims, he would
preside at his coronation as King Philip VI on 29 May 1328 (Machabey 1955b,
1:22 n. 37). John of Luxembourg was of course present at Reims for the
coronation (R. Cazelles 1947, 170).

   In sum, one can without difficulty imagine an occasion near the end of the
extended excursion of 1323 to 1324 that brought together members of the
French court, including Charles of Valois—as well as his son Philip, Philip's
tutor Guillaume de Trie, and Philippe de Vitry—with the entourage of John of

---

time, but the relation between Guillaume de Trie and the canons of the cathedral was
particularly contentious (see Machabey 1955b, 1:37; and especially Desportes 1979, 297 n.
16, 301–2). Kügle (1993, 147 n. 15) proposes a date as late as 1334, for the death of
Guillaume de Trie.

[30] Kügle (1993, 208–14) finds that *Martyrum / Diligenter* (M19) was modeled on the motets
Impudenter / Virtutibus and *Flos / Celsa*, both of which Kügle attributes to Vitry.

Luxembourg, which probably included the young clerk Guillaume de Machaut. Machaut most likely wrote the motet *Bone pastor / Bone pastor*, which celebrates the nomination of Guillaume de Trie as archbishop of Reims, for this occasion.

5. 1320s–30s. Works written under the direct patronage of John of Luxembourg

Although we have no good evidence for the date of Machaut's earliest narrative poem, the *Dit dou Vergier*, it was doubtless written for the entertainment of John of Luxembourg. As Poirion (1965, 194) put it, *Vergier* "is written at the demand of the god of Love; translated: the prince ordered a work from him on an amorous topic."[31] Highly derivative of the *Roman de la Rose*, it dates perhaps from around 1330.

The *Jugement dou Roy de Behaingne,* probably written in the 1330s when Machaut was at Durbuy castle with John of Luxembourg, is the major work of the period of Machaut's direct contact with the king of Bohemia. Extremely popular and influential, *Jugement Behaingne* established Machaut's reputation as a narrative poet. Hoepffner (1908–21, 1:xxix) notes that Machaut used an anagram for the first time in this work, a device that presumes an author has attained a certain notoriety. *Jugement Behaingne* was an important model for Geoffrey Chaucer's *Book of the Duchess*, an early work of ca. 1368. Christine de Pizan (1365–ca. 1430) and Martin Le Franc (b. ca. 1410, fl. ca. 1440) would later take up the same debate. The debate form was also important for Alain Chartier (ca. 1385–ca. 1435).[32]

By the 1330s Machaut's skill as a poet was in great demand, and this fact may explain the apparent small use made of Machaut as an official secretary to the king (e.g., the document of 1334, chap. 1.5.4a). At any rate, the last verses of *Jugement Behaingne* attest to Machaut's activity as a court poet in these years: "Ci fineray / Ma matere, ne plus ne rimeray; / Car autre part assez a rimer ay" (ll. 2052–54) [Here I'll end my account and rhyme no more, for I've enough rhymes to write elsewhere (ed. and trans. Wimsatt/Kibler 1988, 162–63)].

1.5.1. MACHAUT AND THE KING OF BOHEMIA (GENERAL REFERENCES). A review of the extensive bibliography on John of Luxembourg goes well beyond the scope of this overview. For further bibliography not cited in the account that follows, see Jireček 1878; Puymaigre 1892, 391–92 n. 1; Chichmaref 1909, 1:vii–viii n., xxii n. 1; R. Cazelles 1947, 289–92; Seibt 1967, 351–55 (an excellent annotated review of research); Gerlich 1973, 143–46 (with some annotations); Seibt 1974, 470; Wilkins 1983b, 279 nn. 1–2. For a brief account of Machaut's service to John of Luxembourg, see R. Cazelles 1947, 135–37.

Besides Machaut, several contemporary poets praised John of Luxembourg, including Froissart, Deschamps, and Geffroy de Paris (Prioult 1950, 17–18).[33] Modern historians are usually much less kind to John of Luxembourg, although Seibt (1967, 382, 384 n. 21) finds in John a skilled politician who achieved significant and long-lasting results for Bohemia.

Machaut mentioned John of Luxembourg or experiences with John in five of his narrative poems (further discussion of each passage will be found below):

a. *Jugement Behaingne* (ll. 1364–501). Description of Durbuy castle, the king of Bohemia, and his entourage.

---

[31] Davis (1991, 25–31) relates attributes of the god of Love (his blindness and his wings, indicating swiftness) to John of Luxembourg. This hypothesis would call for an unusually late date for *Vergier*. See below, n. 56.

[32] See chaps. 2.1 and 2.3 for references to these later poets.

[33] On Froissart's praise of John, see Dembowski 1983, 164–65 n. 59, 165 n. 62. Hoepffner (1908–21, 3:xi n. 3, xix–xx) believes that Machaut was the inspiration for the passages praising John in Froissart and Deschamps, and thus it was Machaut who made John into the ideal king reflected in contemporary literature and history (see also Calin 1974, 226).

b. *Lyon* (ll. 1271–303; 1444–57). The dangers of travel in the Empire; lands that Machaut may have passed through while in the service of John of Luxembourg.

c. *Confort* (ll. 2923–3086, 3203–12, 3421–32). Detailed examples for the instruction of King Charles of Navarre that praise John of Luxembourg as the ideal prince (Hoepffner 1908–21, 3:xi–xiii; Palmer 1992, lv–lvii).

d. *Fonteinne* (ll. 139–55). Machaut as a cowardly clerk riding beside John of Luxembourg in the Empire (the beginning of this passage is quoted above, chap. 1.2.3d).

e. *Prise* (ll. 975–1379). This long passage concerns Pierre de Lusignan's visit to the Emperor Charles in Prague but seems to call on Machaut's memory of earlier days. Besides this passage, there are general eulogies of John of Luxembourg in ll. 779–92 and 831–38. The passage in ll. 831–38 was mistakenly taken by earlier writers as praise of King John II of France (Hoepffner 1908–21, 1:xxxv).

1.5.2. ENTRY INTO THE SERVICE OF JOHN OF LUXEMBOURG. The magnificent festivities surrounding the coronation of Charles IV the Fair in 1322 provided a likely occasion for a clerk at Reims to have come into contact with John of Luxembourg.[34] Links between the House of Luxembourg and the House of France subsequently became quite solid. King Charles IV married John's sister, Marie of Luxembourg, on 21 September 1322, after having his previous marriage to Blanche of Burgundy nullified for adultery.[35] After a delay that expressly allowed her brother John to be present, Marie of Luxembourg was officially crowned queen of France at the Sainte-Chapelle in Paris on 15 May 1323 (R. Cazelles 1947, 106–10).

Early discussions of the circumstances of Machaut's entry into the service of the king of Bohemia begin with Caylus (1753a, 405), who incorrectly analyzed references in the *complainte A toi, Hanri* (Cp3) as referring to Emperor Henry VII (d. 1313), the father of John of Luxembourg.[36] The date "ca. 1323" for Machaut's entry into John's service is arrived at indirectly: a bull of Benedict XII dated 17 April 1335 (chap. 1.6.1f) states that Guillaume had been a clerk, secretary, and familiar of John of Bohemia for about twelve years, indicating that Machaut entered his service ca. 1323. But this date contradicts a literary reference from ca. 1370 in the *Prise* (l. 785), which states that Machaut had served John of Bohemia for over thirty years (chap. 1.2.7f). This would place the time of Machaut's earliest service in 1316, thirty years before John's death. Many scholars have noted and discussed the seven-year discrepancy.[37]

Yet it would seem possible to reconcile the two dates. Since Machaut apparently did not come from a rich family, a patron such as the king of Bohemia may have provided him with the material means to pursue his studies at the university (cf. Millet 1982, 78). Perhaps it was Machaut's first benefice, the chaplaincy at Houdain (chap. 1.6.1a)—one not demanding care of souls—that paid for Machaut's schooling. If this were the case, Machaut's university training could have started ca. 1316 (the date suggested by the literary reference in the *Prise*), while the beginning of his entry into direct service of the king may be placed ca. 1323 (the date suggested by the 17 April 1335 bull of Benedict XII) (cf. Guillaume de Machaut 1982, 68n.).

1.5.3. CAMPAIGNS OF JOHN OF LUXEMBOURG. Let us begin with the references that are less concrete:

a. *Lyon* (ll. 1444–57). Although this reference is not specifically attached to John of Luxembourg, it provides several place names that recall locations of John's campaigns: Germany, Austria, Bohemia, Hungary, Denmark, Prussia, Poland, Cracovy, Tartary, Lithuania, Livonia, and Lombardy (Prioult 1950, 18).

---

[34] Other commentary on this time period is in Hoepffner 1908–21, 1:xv n. 2; Machabey 1955b, 1:20–21. R. Cazelles (1947, 92–144) provides a more detailed account of John of Luxembourg in the years 1320–24.

[35] Gerlich (1973, 143) gives the date of the marriage as 24 August.

[36] The erroneous discussions of this question by Tarbé (1849), Mas Latrie (1877b), and Puymaigre (1892, 409–10) depend on the error in the Machaut family name discussed above, chap. 1.2.1.

[37] A. Thomas 1881, 329n.; 1884, 41–42; Chichmaref 1909, 1:xii–xiii; Hoepffner 1908–21, 1:xiii–xiv; Černy 1982; Wilkins 1983b, 259 (with reference to S.J. Williams 1952, 38 n. 1); Imbs 1991, 268 n. 70 (to p. 162).

b. *Confort* (ll. 2923–28). Mention of France, Germany, Savoy, Lombardy, Denmark, Hungary, Poland, Russia, Cracovy, Masoria, Prussia, and Lithuania (Prioult 1950, 20).

c. *Fonteinne* (ll. 139–55). A general reference to Machaut's sufferings at the side of the king of Bohemia (see Hoepffner 1908–21, 1:xviii n. 2; Machabey 1955b, 1:26; Cerquiglini 1985b, 124).

d. *Prise* (ll. 875–1623). The detailed knowledge of central Germany that Machaut displayed in this passage may well derive from experiences with John of Luxembourg.[38] The description of the 1364 European tour of Pierre I de Lusignan, king of Cyprus, mentions several place names in central Europe (ll. 1269–76; discussed in Chichmaref 1909, 1:xvi–xviii, xxii, with some additional bibliography in Polish and Czech on this question; see also Zajączkowski 1929 and chap. 1.16). There is also a detailed description of Pierre de Lusignan's entry into Carinthia in 1364 that may draw upon Machaut's personal experiences of events of 1330, when John of Luxembourg was in Carinthia (ll. 1518–19; discussed in Chichmaref 1909, 1:xviii; R. Cazelles 1947, 185). Finally, there is some general mention of the dangers of travel in the Empire (ll. 1044–47; discussed in Hoepffner 1908–21, 1:xviii–xix).

More specific references to various campaigns of John of Luxembourg in Eastern Europe are found in a long passage in the *Confort,* a work datable to 1357.[39] A long passage (ll. 2923–3086) mentions several episodes:

e. *Confort* (ll. 2989–96). In 1310 John put down revolts in Bohemia in order to assure his crown. Machaut, of course, could not have been present on this occasion.

f. *Confort* (ll. 2997–3006). The battle of Esslingen (1316).

g. *Confort* (ll. 3007–16). The battle of Mühldorf (28 September 1322), and the captivity of the Hapsburg duke of Austria, Frederick the Handsome (d. 1330), at John's fortress Bürglitz (*Bruguelis* in Machaut).[40] Machaut stated "Bien le say, car j'y ay esté" (l. 3016) [well do I know, for I was there].

In the following segment (ll. 3021–54), what appear to be personal reminiscences are found, and it seems likely that Machaut was indeed present on the occasions he describes[41]:

h. *Confort* (ll. 3021–29). Campaigns in Poland and Silesia (January-May 1327; see Zajączkowski 1929; R. Cazelles 1947, 152–53; Seibt 1967, 370, 372; Voisé 1982, 52–54). Duke Boleslav (*Boselau* in Machaut) and several other Silesian dukes gave their oath of fealty to John in February 1327 and again at Wrocław in April-May 1329, joining almost all of the Silesian duchies to Bohemia, effectively doubling the size of the Bohemian kingdom.[42] Machaut specifically noted his own presence at Wrocław on this occasion.

i. *Confort* (ll. 3030–50). This passage relates to a crusade of the Teutonic Order and the king of Bohemia against the infidels in Lithuania (December 1328–May 1329) and campaigns in Poland and Silesia (R. Cazelles 1947, 155–63; Seibt 1967, 372). Machaut's description of this expedition specifically notes his own presence, although details of the place names he cites have proved difficult to interpret (Hoepffner 1908–21, 1:xvii–xviii; Voisé 1982, 53; Nikžentaitis 1988).

---

[38] Guillaume exhibited some memory of the German language (at least the word *Frau*) in the *Voir Dit,* with his reference to a *vravelette* (l. 2687, ed. P. Paris 1875, 111).

[39] For a historical perspective on the campaigns in eastern Europe, see Housley 1986, 65–74, and the literature cited there.

[40] See R. Cazelles 1947, 111–15; Seibt 1967, 362, 374 n. 13. Chichmaref (1909, 1:xvi) doubts Machaut's presence on this occasion, perhaps because he felt the date of the battle a bit too early for Machaut's presence in John's service. The castle of "Bürglitz" (Pürglitz) is placed in Bohemia in Hoepffner 1908–21, 1:xvii and Machabey 1955b, 1:23 (see also P. Paris 1875, xv n. 1; Černy 1982, 67 [Bürglitz-Křivoklát]); while Prioult (1950, 16) places "Bruguelis" in Hungary.

[41] For this segment see especially Chichmaref (1909, 1:xix–xxix), who was able to draw upon Polish and Czech secondary sources (1909, 1:vii–viii n., xxii n. 1) to correct the analysis of Puymaigre (1887; 1892). See also Prioult 1950, 21–28; and Machabey 1955b, 1:23, 25–28.

[42] Pustejovsky (1975) provides thorough treatment of the historical situation in Silesia in this period, with a large bibliography.

j. *Lyon* (ll. 1271–82, 1291–1303). An additional pair of literary references apparently recount Machaut's personal impressions of the frigid northern winter of 1328–29 that he experienced during John's Lithuanian campaign (Prioult 1950, 15–20).

k. *Voir Dit* (l. 2101; ed. P. Paris 1875, 90). A reference to the ice floes of East Prussia may well recall the same campaign. John's return to Prague on 25 May 1329, at the age of thirty-two, marked a high point of his fame and power.

l. *Confort* (ll. 3051–69). This passage briefly mentions some later campaigns, although their chronology appears confused. It includes campaigns of 1337 and 1345 in Prussia (Seibt 1967, 380) and Russia. The first campaign in Lombardy (1330–31) is described in greater detail (see R. Cazelles 1947, 181–95; Mollat 1963, 103–10; Seibt 1967, 375–78). Finally, there is brief mention of campaigns of late 1331 in Poland and Hungary (R. Cazelles 1947, 196–98; Seibt 1967, 377).

Machaut provided no specific information on John's military activities after the Italian campaign of 1331 (cf. *Confort*, ll. 3067–69; Machabey 1955b, 1:28–29), and he may not actually have been present on the later expeditions. But John's later efforts were less successful,[43] and perhaps Machaut had wanted to single out only the best moments for use as *exempla* for the king of Navarre in the *Confort*. Hoepffner (1908–21, 1:xviii; followed by Machabey 1930, 432), nevertheless thinks that Machaut was indeed present on these occasions, since the 1330s is the period from which we have papal documents that attest to Machaut's service to the king of Bohemia. Machabey (1930, 435; 1955b, 1:31, 2:172) wonders where Machaut could have been in 1337, when his prebend at Reims was received by procuration (chap. 1.6.1g), if not with John of Luxembourg in Lithuania. But perhaps Machaut was beginning to exploit his talent as a poet and composer, and service on the battlefield at the side of the king was no longer expected.

1.5.4. DOCUMENTS FROM THE TIME OF MACHAUT'S SERVICE TO JOHN OF LUXEMBOURG

a. 1334. Gushee (1980, 148) has published a document that attests to Machaut's service as a secretary of John of Luxembourg, a letter of 1 May 1334, given by John at Noyon, signed "Par le roy, Guillaume de Machau." Unfortunately, the original does not survive, and thus we are denied a look at Machaut's signature. Wilkins (1983b, 259, 279–80 n. 13, 282–84) provides facsimiles of two copies of the document and a transcription.[44]

During this period, John of Luxembourg was active in the Low Countries in a war against Duke John III of Brabant (r. 1312–1355) (R. Cazelles 1947, 224–26). King Philip VI was also present on this occasion at Noyon.

b. 1341. Gushee (1980, 148) also brought to light a document of 1341 dated "Sabbato ante divisionem apostolorum" (i.e., 14 July). The household accounts of the count of Holland at Binche (Hainaut) record 20 *scuta* for the gift of a gilded goblet to "Willelmo de Machau." William II of Avesnes, count of Hainaut, also known as William IV, count of Holland and Zeeland (r. 1337–1345), was at this time an ally of the English. His sister Philippa of Hainaut became the wife of King Edward III of England and patroness of Froissart and Chaucer.

The document gives evidence of Machaut's probable continued service with John of Luxembourg after the time of his settlement in Reims. It is also possible that this occasion had nothing to do with John of Luxembourg. Perhaps Machaut accompanied Jean de Vienne, archbishop of Reims and the representative of King Philip VI, who had come to Binche to arrange a truce with the English.

6. Before 1330–40. Ecclesiastical benefices,
early residence at Reims

As recompense for services rendered to the king of Bohemia, the pope nominated Machaut to several benefices. A benefice is an ecclesiastical office that grants permanent income from revenues of the church to which the clerk is

---

43 For instance, in 1333 John had to renounce his claim to the northern Italian towns that had so readily pledged their loyalty to him in 1331 (R. Cazelles 1947, 217–18; Seibt 1967, 337).

44 Brussels, Archives générales, MSS divers, 20, fols. 82v and 84r; Lille, Archives départementales du Nord, MS B 1583, p. 233.

attached, in return for the performance of sacred functions.[45] Machaut first obtained a chaplaincy, one of the less lucrative benefices. But service with an influential royal personage such as the king of Bohemia guaranteed a more profitable office, a canonicate, which entailed carrying on liturgical services at a church, especially the singing of the daily Offices and Mass. The most coveted reward, a canonicate at a cathedral chapter, was obtained by Machaut in 1337.[46] A prebend (i.e., income) as a canon was part of the normal career of a clerk in the service of a king such as John of Luxembourg. It appears likely that as a canon of Reims cathedral, Machaut would have received a major order, at least the subdeaconate (cf. Desportes 1979, 297; Millet 1982, 43, 49–51; Pycke 1986, 243–47).

Since a pope would be deluged by supplications (i.e., petitions) for such graces, it was common for the actual office and income to be merely "expectative," in anticipation of the decease of the incumbent, especially beginning with the pontificate of John XXII (r. 1316–1334). The resultant multiplication of benefices was reduced under Benedict XII (r. 1334–1342), and henceforth a new pope would annul the expectative graces of his predecessor (Mollat 1921, 32).[47]

Once the pope approved the supplication, the clerk was examined at Avignon for his competence in reading, singing, and writing style. Exceptions were often requested, and some clerks in the protection of powerful patrons were able to obtain a dispensation for the examination at Avignon.[48] After the candidate passed his examination, the official bull of provision was copied, taxes were paid, and the bull was delivered to the new office holder.[49]

In order to obtain his prebend, the clerk would have to present himself to one of the three executors named by the pope in the bull of provision.[50] After examination by one of the executors, the candidate presented himself to the chapter in question for further examination and the official swearing-in ceremony.[51] If the candidate's prebend was merely expectative, the chapter would record the date and purport of the documents in the chapter register, and the candidate would simply have to wait for a vacancy. When a prebend became available, the claimant had a month from the day he found out about the vacancy in which to accept it; prompt action on this point was important in order to prevail against other claimants (Millet 1982, 173–74). If the candidate found himself outside the kingdom of France at the time the prebend became available,

---

[45] R. Cazelles (1958, 383–87) and Millet (1982, 136–38) treat the question of the use of ecclesiastical benefices as payment for services to the king of France. For the account that follows, see Mollat 1921, 39–57; Millet 1982, 165–81; and relevant articles in the *DDC*. Recent works by Starr (1987; 1992) and Haggh (1988) are extremely helpful, providing clear expositions and ample bibliography on the subject.

[46] For an overview of the cathedral chapter at Notre-Dame of Paris, see C. Wright 1989, 18–27. There are detailed studies for Laon (Millet 1982) and Tournai (Pyke 1986). For Brussels, see Haggh 1988.

[47] Expectatives again blossomed under Clement VI (r. 1342–1352), while Innocent VI (r. 1352–1362) and Urban V (r. 1362–1370) were much less generous; after the schism, the problems of expectatives again became acute (Millet 1982, 171–73).

[48] For example, John of Luxembourg obtained such a dispensation in 1343 from Pope Clement VI for a canon of Liège (Berlière 1906, 140 no. 611; cited in Mollat 1921, 46).

[49] A bull is an official papal letter, traditionally sealed with a *bulla,* or lead seal.

[50] On duties of the executors, see Mollat 1921, 50–57; and especially Rudt de Collenberg 1980.

[51] For details on the ceremony, see Millet 1982, 167–68.

a procurator could represent him. This was the scenario when Machaut was finally granted his prebend at Reims in 1337. If the recipient of such a prebend remained in a royal entourage, he could obtain a dispensation of residence from the pope (R. Cazelles 1958, 385). Machaut presumably did not obtain such a dispensation of residence, since he is found at Reims in 1340, and regularly thereafter.

In the fourteenth century, when the pope had control over the collation, or process of conferring, of almost all benefices, it was extremely important for the career advancement of someone not born to privilege to be in the service of an influential personage such as the king of Bohemia. Most often, it was necessary for a clerk—even one with a university degree—to prove himself in the entourage of a prince before becoming a canon (Millet 1982, 189). Royal service guaranteed the clerk the attention of the pope and eventual admission to the security of a cathedral chapter prebend as a sort of retirement pension.[52]

Before obtaining any favors, Guillaume de Machaut probably began his career like his brother Jean, a simple clerk from the diocese of Reims. Through his association with King John of Luxembourg, he obtained several expectative graces from Pope John XXII, later reduced in number by Pope Benedict XII. The papal documents regarding these benefices allow us to follow the advancement of Machaut's secular career under John of Luxembourg, a career fully typical of a royal officer of the time (cf. R. Cazelles 1958, 344–45). He advanced from a simple clerk to almoner by 1330, to notary by 1332, and finally to secretary by 1333.

The combined income from Machaut's canonicate at Reims and his canonicate at St-Quentin, a total of 100 *livres* of Paris per year,[53] gave him a permanent income, which allowed him to leave the immediate service of the peripatetic king of Bohemia. Machaut apparently welcomed the opportunity, for by 1340 he had taken up permanent residence at Reims as one of the seventy-four canons of the cathedral.[54] Because of his association with the king of Bohemia, he had more freedom of movement than canons not attached to princes and certainly could easily have obtained a dispensation from the pope allowing non-residence.[55] Even as a canon in residence at Reims, Machaut would have had five months of free time, without losing the rights of residency (Desportes 1979, 297). Yet his later travels, as far as we know, were by comparison with his early years short and uneventful. We may speculate that Machaut's period of tranquility had a connection to the onset of John's blindness.[56]

---

[52] Eustache Deschamps praised the easy life of the canon as the most desirable of all estates in the ballade *Quant j'ay veu et bien consideré* (ed. Queux de Saint-Hilaire/Raynaud 1878–1903, 7:140–41 no. 1355). Perhaps he was inspired by the example of Machaut, with whom he may have lived for several years (see chap. 2.1.1j).

[53] This figure does not include the daily wages, or distributions, paid to resident canons reciting the daily Offices, which could as much as double a canon's income (Millet 1982, 259–61; Pycke 1986, 204–11; see also Haggh 1988, 131 n. 114).

[54] Some authors list the number as seventy-two; there were seventy prebends and four half-prebends (Desportes 1979, 296).

[55] Cf. Berlière (1906, 218 no. 883) for an example of such a dispensation granted to a secretary of John of Luxembourg in 1345.

[56] It was during the 1337 expedition to East Prussia that John of Luxembourg first experienced problems with his eyes (Chichmaref 1909, 1:xxvi; R. Cazelles 1947, 243; Machabey 1955b, 1:25–26 n. 51; Seibt 1967, 383 n. 16). In 1340 he became completely blind (Machabey 1955b, 1:31–34, 2:172), a humiliating condition for a noble (cf. the interesting comments in Cerquiglini 1984; 1985a, esp. 24 n. 12; and 1985b, 112–13, on the *borgne clerc* as a literary theme). Perhaps this is why mention of John's blindness

1.6.1. MACHAUT'S BENEFICES. A thorough account of the papal politics of John of Luxembourg is beyond the scope of this overview, but we note that John had a good rapport with Avignon after 1322 (R. Cazelles 1947, 110). In the summer of 1330 John was in contact with Pope John XXII regarding the matter of the succession of Carinthia (R. Cazelles 1947, 176–79). Events later in the year 1330 in Italy would turn John XXII away from John of Luxembourg, but only until late March 1331 (Mollat 1963, 103–5).

In the following list of the papal bulls concerning Machaut, I include the names of the three executors. As Rudt de Collenberg (1980) has shown, the executors were chosen by the beneficiary, and one of the three was usually a personal acquaintance. On Machaut's own service as an executor in 1345, see chap. 1.7.1c.

a. by July 1330: chaplaincy at Houdain. Sometime before 30 July 1330, Machaut obtained the perpetual chaplaincy at the Hospital at Sainte-Marie-de-Houdain (diocese of Arras, dépt. Pas-de-Calais).[57] Such a charge could involve the celebration of a Mass or Masses annually or weekly, depending on the stipulation of the foundation, at a certain church or specific altar; alternatively, the chaplain could be charged with assisting the celebration of the daily Offices at a given church. A chaplaincy is not necessarily sacerdotal, that is, the chaplain is not necessarily required to celebrate Mass himself. Machaut's chaplaincy was *sine cura*, i.e., one not demanding care of souls, attested by the documents of 4 January 1333 (below, item d) and 17 April 1335 (below, item f). Machaut thus did not have to reside at Houdain, nor did he have to be a priest.

Perhaps this benefice paid for Machaut's schooling, as suggested above (chap. 1.5.2). It was normal for a prince to facilitate the career of a student who would later enter the prince's service. One of the most effective means of doing this was to obtain a prebend that paid the school expenses of the young clerk (R. Cazelles 1958, 299).[58]

The following document attests the collation of this benefice:

b. 1330: canon of Verdun. A bull of Pope John XXII, dated Avignon, 30 July 1330, granted *Guillelmo de Machaudo* an expectative canonicate and prebend at the Cathedral of Verdun (dépt. Meuse) on the request of the king of Bohemia.[59] Machaut is named as the king's clerk, almoner, and familiar ["clerico, elemosinario et familiari suo domestico"]. The terms *familiaris* and *domesticus* indicate that John admitted Guillaume into his immediate entourage (Hoepffner 1908–21, 1:xvi), a status also supported by the literary testimony of the *Jugement Behaingne* (chap. 1.2.7a).

Presumably the almoner [Fr. *aumônier*] was in charge of the important gift-giving function of the prince (cf. R. Cazelles 1982, 26). This function is supported by the literary testimony of the *Confort* (below, chap. 1.6.2). The almoner also sometimes served as a counselor of the prince (cf. R. Cazelles 1982, 233), or was in charge of his religious services (Delachenal 1909–31, 2:293).

The bull mentions a previous benefice, a perpetual chaplaincy at the Hospital at Sainte-Marie-de-Houdain (above, item a), which Machaut was allowed to retain.

The three executors of this benefice were (1) the abbot of the monastery of Our Lady of Luxembourg (diocese of Trier); (2) the deacon of the collegiate church of St-Sauveur at Metz; and (3) *magister* Petrus de Vigone, canon of Turin.[60]

---

never clouds Guillaume's favorable picture of him. See, however, Davis (1991, 25–28), who relates the blind god of Love in *Vergier* to the king.

[57] For a full discussion of chaplaincies, see *DDC* 1935–65, 3:527–30 s.v. "chapellenie"; cf. also C. Wright 1989, 27; Haggh 1988, 1:24–25, 182–87. On chaplaincies at Reims, see Desportes 1979, 297. The *Capellania Beate Marie de Housdaign* was at the collation of the abbot of St-Rémi of Reims. For more information on this foundation, see Guesnon 1912, 92–93 and the references cited there.

[58] A chaplaincy could pay a maximum of 10–15 *livres* of Tours per year (Guillemain 1952, 56), a generous allowance for a student; cf. Pycke 1986, 283.

[59] See A. Thomas 1881, 328, 330–31 no. 1; 1884, 40, 43 no. 1 (the 1881 publication is more complete). Mollat (1928, 392 no. 50428) provides a shorter summary. Philippe de Vitry was provided with a canonicate in expectation at Verdun in 1323, and by 1327 had received his prebend (A. Thomas 1882, 178–79; Fayen 1912, 152 no. 2031).

[60] The same three executors were named for another grace requested by John of Luxembourg

The king of Bohemia had a strong interest in the control of Verdun, and disputes over this matter with the king of France and the count of Bar went back to 1315 (R. Cazelles 1947, 102–4, 121–22). By 1336 King Philip VI had won the upper hand but ceded protection of the city to John of Luxembourg and the count of Bar when hostilities with England commenced in 1337 (R. Cazelles 1958, 435; H. Thomas 1973, 125–28).

c. 1332: canon of Arras. A bull of Pope John XXII, dated Avignon, 17 April 1332, granted *Guillelmo de Machaudio* an expectative canonicate and prebend at Arras (dépt. Pas-de-Calais) on the request of the king of Bohemia.[61] He was allowed to take possession of it either personally or by procuration. Machaut is named as the king's domestic, familiar, and notary ["domestico, familiari, notario"]. Previous benefices include the canonicate (still in expectation) at Verdun, as well as the perpetual chaplaincy at Houdain.

The three executors of this benefice were (1) the provost of the cathedral of Lavaur (dépt. Tarn), (2) the archdeacon of the church of Avranches (dépt. Manche),[62] and (3) the *official* (i.e., the *official* of the bishop) of the cathedral of Arras.

In this part of the year 1332, John of Luxembourg was in Paris for the marriage of his daughter Bonne to John, duke of Normandy, the future John II the Good. Guillemain (1962, 517) reports that John of Luxembourg was at Avignon in the course of the year 1332.

d. 1333: canon of Reims. A bull of Pope John XXII, dated Avignon, 4 January 1333, granted *Guillelmo de Machaudio* an expectative canonicate and prebend at the cathedral of Reims on the request of the king of Bohemia.[63] Machaut is named as the king's familiar and domestic, notary, and secretary ["familiari et domestico ac notario secretario"]. The promotion of a notary to a secretary was a typical reward for faithful service (R. Cazelles 1982, 344–45), and this document provides the first mention of Machaut as a secretary. Machaut was allowed to retain his expectatives at Verdun and Arras, as well as the perpetual chaplaincy at Houdain, here specifically labeled as *sine cura*.

The three executors of this benefice were (1) the abbot of the monastery of Ste-Geneviève in Paris; (2) the scholaster (*scolasticus*) of the cathedral of Toul (dépt. Meurthe-et-Moselle)[64]; and (3) the *official* of Reims cathedral.

In early 1333, at the time of this appointment, John of Luxembourg was in transit between Paris and Northern Italy.

This and a further papal bull granting Jean de Machaut a benefice (chap. 1.11.1a) have the same date, doubtless because the supplications from the king of Bohemia were copied together on a single *rotulus* and were thus considered and granted by the pope on the same day (cf. Berlière 1906, xv).

e. 1333–35: canon of St-Quentin. The 17 April 1335 document discussed below (item f) indicates that Machaut had obtained a canonicate and prebend at St-Quentin in Vermandois (diocese of Noyon, dépt. Aisne). Nothing further is known of when or how Machaut received this grace, although the fact that it is not mentioned in previous papal documents suggests that he received it after 4 January 1333 (Hoepffner 1908–21, 1:xx). Machabey (1955b, 1:30), taking into account a variety of confusing problems with the documents, proposed that this canonicate could have been obtained in 1325. A document of 1362

---

that was awarded on the same day, doubtless because both requests were entered on the same *rotulus* of supplications (Fayen 1912, 426 no. 2817). Petrus de Vigone, a canon of Novare (Italy) and papal scribe, was a member of the Curia named on several other occasions as an executor for graces awarded by Pope John XXII and Benedict XII.

[61] See A. Thomas 1881, 328–29, 331; 1884, 40, 43–44 (the 1881 version is slightly more complete). Mollat (1930, 176 no. 56947) provides a shorter summary.

[62] Guillaume Pichnon, secretary of John of Luxembourg, at various times canon with prebend at Verdun, Reggio Emilia, Fosses (diocese of Liège), St-Paul beyond the walls of Trier, archdeacon of Avranches, with an expectative canonicate and prebend at Avranches and Coutances.

[63] See A. Thomas 1881, 329, 331–32; 1884, 40, 44. Mollat (1932, 73 no. 59243) provides a shorter summary.

[64] This was *magister* Jacobus de Actis de Mutina, *capellanus pape* and canon at the Cathedral of Cambrai, etc., an official of the Curia named in several dozen papal documents.

indicates that the prebend at St-Quentin brought Machaut an annual income of 40 *livres* (chap. 1.15.1b).[65]

It was Hoepffner (1908–21, 1:xx n. 3) who first noted the connection of the motet *Martyrum / Diligenter* (M19) to St. Quentin.[66] In a forthcoming study Anne W. Robertson will discuss further details surrounding the circumstances of the composition of this work.

f. 1335: adjustments of Benedict XII. A bull of Pope Benedict XII, dated Avignon, 17 April 1335, to *Guillelmo de Machaudio,* canon of Reims, served to regulate the benefices granted by Pope John XXII.[67] Benedict XII sought to reduce the abusive multiplication of benefices, especially the expectatives, which had proliferated under Pope John XXII. On 18 December 1335 all expectative graces granted before the papacy of Benedict XII were revoked (Mollat 1963, 33). Benedict XII usually left canons with their appointments at the metropolitan churches in their home provinces (Dricot 1982, 144), and thus it is significant that he suppressed Machaut's expectatives at Verdun and Arras but allowed him to retain the expectative at Reims. Further, Machaut was required to resign the chaplaincy at Houdain as soon as he should take over the next vacant prebend at Reims. He was allowed to keep the prebend he already had at St-Quentin (item e above), apparently obtained without papal intervention.

Benedict XII stated that the king of Bohemia had made his previous requests to John XXII "for you, hitherto his clerk, secretary, and household familiar, whom he maintains carried on his divine services for twelve years or thereabouts" ["pro te, adhuc clerico suo secretario et familiari domestico, quem asserit duodecim annis vel circa suis obsequiis institisse"]. On the indication of Machaut's twelve years of service in the entourage of John of Luxembourg, see chap. 1.5.2.

The three executors of this benefice were (1) the monks of Ste-Geneviève in Paris; (2) the abbots of the monastery of St-Nicasius of Reims; and (3) the archdeacon of Avranches (dépt. Manche).[68]

g. 1337: collation of Guillaume's prebend at Reims by procuration. Two documents mention the collation of Machaut's prebend at Reims on 30 January 1337 (Thursday after the Conversion of St. Paul), (1) a cartulary called the *Livre rouge du chapitre de Reims,* fol. 54r[69]; and (2) an eighteenth-century copy, probably deriving from the previous document, in *F:RS 1773* (MS Weyen), fol. 284r, copied by Jean Herman Weyen (d. ca. 1732), canon of Reims.[70]

Machaut took over prebend no. 40 (Machabey 1955c, 249–52) at Reims by procuration. Thus, he was not present in Reims at the time. Machabey (1930, 435; 1955b, 1:31, 2:172) suggested that he was in Lithuania with John of Luxembourg. Machaut took personal possession of the prebend by 1340 (below, item h).

The yearly value of the benefice of Machaut's canonicate at Reims was 60 *livres* of Paris, attested by a levy of clerical taxes in the diocese of Reims in 1346 (chap. 1.7.1d).

---

[65] Non-residence entailed a smaller annual income. Machaut would have paid a vicar to cover his sacred duties at St-Quentin (cf. Millet 1982, 224).

[66] See also Machabey 1955b, 2:62, 103. Günther (1963a, 100) tentatively proposes a date ca. 1335 for this motet. Millet (1982, 286) notes that each year a delegate of each chapter of the province of Reims travelled to St-Quentin for an assembly on 8 May; one wonders if perhaps the composition of the motet was related to this event. See further the forthcoming study by A.W. Robertson.

[67] See A. Thomas 1881, 332–33; 1884, 45–46 (the 1881 publication is more complete); Vidal 1903, 77 no. 751.

[68] Namely Guillaume Pichnon, as in item c above.

[69] Modern publication of the document cited in Dricot 1982, 144 n. 10. Leech-Wilkinson (1990c, 2 n. 7) gives the modern shelfmark, AMR 2G 1650, fol. 54r. Varin (1839, 1:clxxi) provides a description of the contents of the *Livre rouge.*

[70] Hoepffner 1908–21, 1:xxi n. 3; and Chichmaref 1909, 1:xxxiii. On the MS Weyen, see Desportes 1979, 548 n. 45; Machabey 1955c. There are some confusing problems of conflicting dates in the MS Weyen, which Machabey (1955c) attempts without success to clear up; see also Leech-Wilkinson 1990c, 2 n. 6.

h. by April 1340: Guillaume occupies his canonicate at Reims. Machaut's final benefice, the canonicate at Reims, had been granted in expectation in 1333, received by procuration in 1337, and officially occupied by 1340. Machaut's presence at Reims is attested by a list of thirty canons who were present as Jean de Vienne (d. 1351) was sworn in as archbishop of Reims on 13 April 1340.[71] Since Machaut is listed last in the document, he was the most recent canon (Machabey 1955b, 1:34; Desportes 1979, 295–96, 297 n. 16). The apparent high degree of absenteeism (forty-four of the seventy-four canons were absent) is not unusual for the time.[72]

i. 1343: canon of Amiens. G.P. Johnson (1991, 253–54) has signaled a document indicating that Guillaume de Machaut was received as a canon of the chapter at Amiens in 1343, that he founded an anniversary service there, even that he had a house in the cloister. Further research is needed.

1.6.2. THE TITLE *ELEMOSINARIUS* (ALMONER). A papal bull of 1330 (chap. 1.6.1b) refers to Machaut as *elemosinarius* [almoner], i.e., the one in charge of charity and the distribution of gifts, a job possibly attested by two passages in the *Confort* that celebrate the prodigal generosity of John of Luxembourg:

a. *Confort* (ll. 2930–33). "Il donnoit fiez, joiaus et terre, / Or, argent; riens ne retenoit / Fors l'onneur; ad se tenoit, / Et il en avoit plus que nuls" [He bestowed fiefs, jewels, land, / Gold, silver, kept nothing / But the honor, treasuring it. / And he had more than anyone else (trans. Palmer 1992, 153)]. Compare *Jugement Navarre* (ll. 1265–78), where a similar listing describes the attributes of Lady *Largesse*, perhaps recalling this quality in John of Luxembourg.[73]

b. *Confort* (ll. 2937–46). "Il ne pooit estre lassez / De donner, et s'avoit assez / Toudis, quel que part qu'il venist. / Et par ma foy, s'il avenist / Qu'il heüst deus cens mille livres, / Il en fust en un jour delivrés, / Qu'a gens d'armes les departoit, / Et puis sans denier se partoit. / Je le say bien, car je l'ay fait / Plus de cinquante fois de fait" [He could never weary / Of giving, and he possessed so much / At all times wherever he went. / And by my faith, if it happened / He had two hundred thousand pounds, / In a single day he'd be rid of them, / Giving everything to his knights, / And then going his way without a penny. / I know this well, for I've seen it happen / More than fifty times, in fact (trans. Palmer 1992, 153)].

While both of the passages cited above serve to characterize an ideal and noble ruler (cf. Dembowski 1983, 15–16), and therefore can be seen as simply conventional, we know for a fact that Machaut is not exaggerating John's generosity by much.[74]

c. *Confort* (ll. 3837–42). Here Machaut counsels giving alms to the poor, though there is no specific reference to John of Luxembourg.

---

[71] AMR 2G 323, no. 13, cited in Goy 1982, 154–55; Leech-Wilkinson 1990c, 3 n. 9.

[72] Millet (1982, 235–46) has studied non-residency of the canons at the chapter at Laon. She estimates that for the period 1272 until 1412, the average daily size of the community was a little more than a quarter of the total (Millet 1982, 238).

[73] "Aprés Prudence se sëoit / Largesse qui riens ne vëoit, / Einsois donnoit a toutes mains, / A l'un plus et a l'autre meins, / Or, argent, destriers, oisiaus, terre, / Et quanqu'elle pooit acquerre, / Contez, duchiez et baronniers, / A heritages et a vies. / De tout ce riens ne retenoit, / Fors l'onneur. Ad ce se tenoit: / Noblesse li avoit apris. / Et avec ce, dont mieus la pris, / Elle reprenoit Advarice / Comme de tout le pieur vice" (ll. 1265–78) [Afterward Prudence seated herself / Near Generosity, who sees nothing, / But rather gives with both her hands, / More to one and less to another, / Gold, silver, chargers, hunting birds, / estates, / And whatever else she might acquire, / Counties, duchies, and baronetcies, / In perpetuity and for life. / Of all this she retains nothing, / Except what honor there is. She keeps to this; / Nobility has taught her to do so. / And even more, wherefore the greater her worth, / She accuses Avarice / Of being the worst vice of all (trans. Palmer 1988, 57, 59)]. See also the literary discussion of *Donnez, signeurs* (B26) in chap. 7.3.

[74] On John's extravagant disbursement of the taxes paid grumblingly by the Czechs back in Bohemia, see, for instance, R. Cazelles 1947, 79–82, 101, 145, 147, 151–52, 214, 237, 253–54.

1.6.3. THE TITLES NOTARY AND SECRETARY. Two papal documents (from 1333 and 1335, see chap. 1.6.1d and 1.6.1f) prove that Machaut did attain the position of secretary, after he had served for a while as a notary.[75] On the distinction between the office of notary and secretary, at least with respect to the organization of the French Royal Court, see Morel 1900, 62–68, 94–97, 395–97. The secretaries, whose office was first mentioned in 1316, were a small group of notaries who were attached directly to the king. Notaries stayed at court, while the secretaries, usually no more than two at a time serving in rotation, accompanied the king on his displacements. The principal function of a notary or secretary was to write acts emanating directly from the king (to date only one has been found signed by Guillaume, chap. 1.5.4a).

It is particularly interesting that notaries and secretaries, as officers of the hôtel, were allowed tax exemptions, at least at the French Royal Court (Morel 1900, 97, 395). Machaut may have been recalling his former rights later when he complained bitterly about the taxes imposed upon him as a canon at Reims (see the discussion of *A toi, Hanri* [Cp3], chap. 6.5). R. Cazelles (1958, 351) noted that Philippe de Vitry, as a notary of the king of France, received six *sous* per day for life. It is not known if Guillaume de Machaut received a permanent income of this sort from the House of Luxembourg.

In his poetry Machaut mentioned the title of secretary twice:

a. *Sire, a vous fais ceste clamour* (Cp7) (l. 6). "Quant secretaire me feïstes" [when you made me secretary]. Most recently, Günther and Cerquiglini have attached this *complainte* to Charles, king of Navarre (chap. 1.12.2 and chap. 6.5).
b. *Prise* (ll. 789–90). "Car j'estoie ses secretaires / En trestous ses plus gros affaires" [For I was his secretary in all of his most important affairs], indicating that Machaut served as John of Luxembourg's secretary and apparently also advisor. This passage in the *Prise* immediately follows that cited above, chap. 1.2.7f.

7. Ca. 1340–46. Works written at Reims in the service of John of Luxembourg

Delachenal (1909–31, 1:17–18) suggests that Machaut was among the many clerks, along with Gace de la Buigne and Philippe de Vitry, who frequented the Royal Court, a part of the intellectual milieu in which the future Charles V was educated. We do not know how often Machaut left his post at Reims, but this would have been perfectly permissible, since he was still in the employ of the king of Bohemia. Hoepffner (1908–21, 1:xxviii) has suggested that by 1342, a date supplied near the beginning of the *Lyon*, Machaut had left the immediate service of John of Luxembourg.[76]

The early career of Philippe de Vitry is in many ways comparable to Machaut's early career. Philippe, however, remained in the royal administration and was rewarded for his service in 1351, late in life, with the bishopric of Meaux, while Guillaume de Machaut soon settled down to his canonicate at Reims, devoting his life to his poetry and music, and was not formally tied to the court of a particular patron (cf. Poirion 1965, 23). The steady support of the church allowed Machaut the peaceful environment and time necessary to the pursuit of his poetic and musical interests, in particular, the composition of lyrical poetry.

Hoepffner argues that no lyrics of Machaut—except of course motet lyrics— can convincingly be placed before the period of his final settlement at Reims, ca. 1340 (1911, 165–66; 1920a; see also Earp 1991b). If this was the case, these early years at Reims saw an enormous productivity, with the establishment of the ballade style in poetry and music, the production of numerous monophonic virelais and lais, and the beginnings of the polyphonic rondeau.

---

[75] On the importance of secretaries in the literary history of this era, see Poirion 1965, 173.
[76] Wilkins (1983b, 259 and n. 15) notes a document of 24 October 1337 suggesting that Machaut's position as the king's secretary had been taken over by one Pierre de Waben.

On the narrative side, the composition of the *Remede* probably falls in this period, while the *Alerion*, to judge from the manuscript transmission, is probably a bit later, after 1345. The stimulus for this burst of poetic and musical activity may lie with the service of an influential lady, Bonne of Luxembourg, the daughter of the king of Bohemia.

1.7.1. MACHAUT AT REIMS IN THE 1340S AND 1350S. For documents of the 1360s and 1370s that place Machaut at Reims, see chap. 1.15.1a–b, 1.15.1d, and chap. 1.18.1a.

a. 1340: the sale of Machaut's horse. A principal goal in the scholarly discussions surrounding Machaut's sale of a horse is to prove that he had taken up residence at Reims by 1340. That the documents actually refer to our Guillaume de Machaut is in dispute, however. Fortunately, an unrelated document, recording Machaut's presence at the swearing in of archbishop Jean de Vienne on 13 April 1340 (chap. 1.6.1h) already proves Machaut's presence at Reims by that date.

Two documents, both excerpts from the municipal accounts of Reims from 1 March 1340 to 21 February 1341 (Varin 1843–48, 2/2:822–44) concern the purchase of a packhorse needed for a journey made by an alderman traveling to see King Philip VI. Document i, probably from June or July 1340, provides us with a glimpse of the early stages of the Hundred Years' War. The destruction of the French navy at Ecluse on 24 June 1340 by the English under Edward III was followed by the unsuccessful Siege of Tournai. Meanwhile, Philip VI was trying to raise money for French military operations. After repeated meetings the king was unable to obtain a tax subsidy from Reims, and probably in June the *arrière-ban* was issued, doubtless a ploy to speed collection of the tax (Henneman 1971, 148–49; see also Desportes 1979, 539–40). Document ii gives a practical example of the consequences of the frequent mutations of the money practiced under Philip VI.

i. *"Item*, xxiii liv. pour un cheval acheteit à G. de Machaut, pour ce que on ne peust recouvrer de cheval à louier, pour porter la male H. le Large,[77] quant il fust en l'ost devant Estantdemire, pour parler au roy, pour le cris qui fust fais en ceste ville que chascuns alast en l'ost" (Varin 1843–48, 2/2:831–32)[78] [Item, 23 *livres* for a horse purchased from G. de Machaut, because a horse to lease could not be found, to carry the trunk of H. le Large, when he was with the army at Estantdemire (*recte* Estaudemire?), in order to speak to the king on account of the proclamation made in this town that everyone was about to be mustered].

ii. *"Item*, xviii s. pour frais de ix double d'or à H. li Large, qui presta pour un cheval acheté à G. de Machau; et ne valoient li doubles d'or que xlviii s. quant lidis Hues les presta; et il contarent l s quant il furent rendus (Varin 1843–48, 2/2:833–34) [Item, 18 *sous* for H. li Large's expenses, who borrowed 9 gold *doubles* for a horse purchased from G. de Machaut; and the gold *doubles* were only worth 48 *sous* when the aforementioned Hues borrowed them, and they were worth 50 *sous* when they were repaid].

Machabey (1955b, 1:34) disputes the connection of the two documents to Guillaume de Machaut, according to a "personal communication of 1928"; his summary chronology (1955b, 2:172) resolves the "G. de Machau" of the documents as "G(uiot) de Machaut." The same municipal accounts do identify a "G. de Machau" as a *cordier* (Varin 1843–48, 2/2:824), but I have not discovered the source for the name "Guiot."

Paulin Paris (1875, 383) associates the two documents concerning the sale of Machaut's horse with the composition of the *complainte A toi, Hanri* (Cp3). Chichmaref (1909, 1:xxxiv–xxxix) agreed with the 1340 dating proposed by Paris, but for different reasons, while Hoepffner (1908–21, 1:xxiii n. 1) disputes the date, proposing May to November 1359, a date near the time of the Siege of Reims. Machabey (1955b, 1:34, 43–44, 51–52,

---

[77] Hues le Large le Jeune de Coursalin (d. 1349) served as an *échevin* (alderman) of Reims at various times, including the period 1339–40 (Desportes 1979, 286 n. 66). He made several journeys concerning the issue of subsidies for the king.

[78] Reims, Archives communales, compte de l'échevinage 1340–41, fol. 25v. Desportes (1979, 13) gives the modern designation, Reims, Archives municipales, Comptes du greffe de l'échevinage, Reg. no. 154. Hoepffner (1908–21, 1:xxii n. 1) gives a significantly different reading of this document in that the initial "G." is silently resolved as "Guillaume"; further, the alderman travels to "Escaudevre" (i.e., Escaudœuvres, Belgium).

2:172–73) also favors the later date for the *complainte*, since, as the amusing argument runs, Machaut still had his horse Grisart in 1349, when, as Machaut narrated near the beginning of the *Jugement Navarre*, he went rabbit hunting, and thus he could not have sold his horse in 1340. The manuscript transmission of Cp3 argues for the later date, and Wimsatt's recent discussion (1991b) confirms this (see chap. 6.5).

b. **1344: Guillaume and Jean de Machaut witness a document.** Guillaume de Machaut, canon of Reims, and Jean de Machaut, canon of Verdun, witnessed a document dated Trinity (30 May) 1344, which reestablished John of Luxembourg's feudal rights over some land belonging to the bishop of St-Rémi of Reims.[79]

c. **1345: Guillaume serves as an executor.** A letter of Pope Clement VI of 4 December 1345 names *Guillelmus de Marchandio*, canon of Reims, as one of the three executors for the expectative grace of one Johannes Arbalistarius (or Arbalestrarius), a clerk in the service of John of Luxembourg, at the collegiate church of S. M. Magdalene in Verdun.[80]

d. **1346: Machaut taxed for his benefice at Reims.** An article in an account of clerical tenths for 1346, in the diocese of Reims, assessed Guillaume de Machaut a tax of 60 S. on a benefice of 60 *livres* of Paris.[81]

e. **1352: Machaut at the archbishop's installation.** Machaut was among the twenty-nine canons (listed second-to-last) present on 1 January 1352 as Hugues d'Arcy (d. 1352) was sworn in as archbishop of Reims.[82] The absence of the majority of the chapter (forty-three of the seventy-four canons) on this important occasion is not anomalous (cf. also item g below, and chap. 1.6.1h).

f. **1352: Machaut is upbraided.** On 18 August 1352[83] *Magistri Michael de Serenofonte*,[84] *Dionysius de Meriaco, et Guillelmus de Machaudio*, three canons of Reims, allowed a younger canon, Hugon de Castellione,[85] to wear the official vestment of a subdeacon, the *almutia* [Fr. *aumusse*, almuce], both within and without the choir,[86] even though he had not yet received a major order, a serious breach of decorum. The provost of the chapter, Etienne de Courtenay, probably absent when the incident occurred, opposed the irregularity in a ruling of 21 August. This document is the earliest that officially refers to Machaut as a *magister* (see chap. 1.2.8).[87]

---

79 Modern publication cited in Machabey 1955b, 1:36 n. 91, 2:172. Leech-Wilkinson (1990c, 3 n. 10), gives the modern shelfmark as Reims, Archives départementales, 56.H.74, pièce A, fol. 30r.

80 Berlière 1924, 644 no. 1736; the corresponding supplication from the king of Bohemia is in Berlière 1906, 243 no. 964; cf. also Berlière 1906, 110 no. 495.

81 AMR 2G 1650, fol. 269*bis* v, cited in Leech-Wilkinson 1990c, 3 and n. 11. Varin (1843–48, 2/2:1024–1124 no. DLI) published the document, dated 25 May–1 November 1346; Machaut is listed on p. 1034. The document is also cited in Tarbé 1849, xii n. 2; Mas Latrie 1877b, xvi; Hoepffner 1908–21, 1:xxv; Chichmaref 1909, 1:xxxvii; Machabey 1955b, 1:42 n. 109.

82 Machabey 1955b, 1:47–48; Desportes 1979, 296 n. 9, 297 n. 16. The document is AMR 2G 323, no. 15, cited in Goy 1982, 154–55; Leech-Wilkinson 1990c, 5 n. 17.

83 The document, AMR 2G 323, no. 415 (Poirion 1965, 193 n. 6), is published in Varin 1843–48, 3:31–32 no. 635; and cited in Chichmaref 1909, 1:xlix; Hoepffner 1908–21, 1:xxv; Machabey 1955b, 1:47. See also Desportes 1979, 542.

84 *Magister* Michaelis de Serenofonte (i.e., Sérifontaine, dépt. Oise), canon of Reims, died before 23 July 1367 (Hayez 1983, 55 no. 25725, 479–80 no. 27564).

85 Berlière (1911, 320–21) publishes a papal document involving Hugon de Castellione (Hugues de Châtillon). He was doubtless an aristocrat under the age of eighteen (on younger canons, cf. Millet 1982, 50–53). In a document of 1372 that mentions Machaut's house (chap. 1.18.1a), we learn that Hugues was a neighbor of Guillaume.

86 Cf. Millet 1982, 279; Pycke 1986, 241–43. The *aumusse* is a fur bonnet that covers the head and shoulders. Machaut is pictured carrying one over his shoulder in the well-known *Prologue* miniature A2 (for references to the many reproductions, see chap. 4.4a).

87 Two further canons are named in this document, Nicolas de Castro-Villano and Therricus de Curvilla.

g. 1353: Machaut absent from Reims. On 2 May 1353, as Dauphin Humbert was sworn in as archbishop of Reims (Desportes 1979, 297 n. 16), twenty canons were present, but Machaut is not listed (Goy 1982, 154–55; Leech-Wilkinson 1990c, 5 n. 17).

h. 1355: Machaut at the archbishop's installation. Machaut was among the twelve canons (listed in fifth place; seven others follow Guillaume) present on 4 November 1355 as Jean de Craon (d. 1373) was sworn in as archbishop of Reims.[88] Machaut's brother Jean, who had recently taken possession of his canonicate of Reims (chap. 1.11.1g), was absent. Perhaps Jean was still in the service of the House of Bar or the House of Navarre.

8. Ca. 1332–49. Service of Bonne of Luxembourg, duchess of Normandy

Machaut maintained his associations with the high aristocracy after the glorious death of John of Luxembourg at the battle of Crécy, 26 August 1346.[89] By then Machaut had probably, already for some time, been in the service of the duchess of Normandy, Bonne of Luxembourg (1315–1349), daughter of the king of Bohemia, who had married John, duke of Normandy (the future King John II "the Good," b. 1319, r. 1350–1364) at Melun (dépt. Seine-et-Marne) on 28 July 1332.[90]

Obscure circumstances surround her death, probably of the plague, on 11 September 1349 at the abbey of Maubuisson near Pontoise (dépt. Val-d'Oise).[91] Rumors were afoot that John, duke of Normandy, notorious for his hot temper, had had Bonne murdered for a liaison with Raoul de Brienne, count of Eu and constable of France.[92] This would explain King John's quick anger, which led to the summary decapitation without trial of the count of Eu on 19 November 1350, soon after the count had returned from England, where he had been a prisoner since July 1346. The Liégeois chronicler Jean Le Bel (writing 1352–61) speaks explicitly of John's revenge for an affair between Bonne and the constable, but other chroniclers are more reticent. The most authoritative recent historian of the period notes that Bonne's alleged adultery is "far from being proven" (R. Cazelles 1982, 45).[93]

---

[88] AMR 2G 323, no. 17, cited in Goy 1982, 154–55; and Leech-Wilkinson 1990c, 5 n. 17; see also Machabey 1955b, 1:49–50 and n. 134.

[89] Froissart recounts the suicidal manner of his death, never mentioned by Machaut (see Leech-Wilkinson 1990c, 3; R. Cazelles 1947, chap. 16). Hearing the noise of the battle, he had his horse attached between the horses of two knights, and the group of them then charged en masse into the melee. All three soon fell.

[90] On the date of the marriage, see Delachenal 1909–31, 1:2; R. Cazelles 1958, 193. Gerlich (1973, 143) gives the date as 28 March 1332. Machabey (1955b, 1:28, 2:172) indicates that John of Luxembourg was at the ceremony at Melun, but places the marriage in May 1332. By July John of Luxembourg may have been responding to new troubles in Bohemia (cf. R. Cazelles 1947, 208–13). In any case, he was present at the magnificent celebration at the Palace on the Ile de la Cité when John of Valois was dubbed the new duke of Normandy early in October 1332 (R. Cazelles 1947, 211–12).

[91] Both Delachenal (1909–31, 1:37) and R. Cazelles (1982, 45) opt for the date 11 September instead of 11 August. On the earlier date, see R. Cazelles 1958, 228; Lehoux 1966–68, 1:13 n. 3.

[92] See the references in Delachenal 1909–31, 1:20, 67–69; Machabey 1955b, 1:42; R. Cazelles 1958, 228, 247–52, 435; 1982, 47, 60, 131, 140. During the Parisian revolution of 1357–58, Charles of Navarre and Robert Le Coq, bishop of Laon, no doubt referred to rumors that King John II had had his wife murdered, in order further to alienate the young regent Charles (the future Charles V) from his father, King John II, then imprisoned in England (Delachenal 1909–31, 1:37, 67–69, 134).

[93] Markstrom (1989, 23–26) discusses these events in the context of a suggested date and occasion for Machaut's motet *Fons / O livoris* (M9).

Rumors of this sort, whether they were true or not, could nevertheless have contributed to Machaut's apparent turn from the House of France to the House of Navarre after the death of Bonne, at the very beginning of the reign of John II (crowned 26 September 1350).

9. Ca. 1340–49. Works written for Bonne of Luxembourg

Little is known about Bonne of Luxembourg, who apparently spent most of her time at Vincennes (Lehoux 1966–68, 1:6–9). Specific references to Bonne in Machaut's work are few and date from the end of his career (*Prise*, ll. 764–71). Even so, recent studies have suggested that Machaut was very devoted to her, and clues in several works can be interpreted as thinly masked references to Bonne. The *Remede*, the most important of Machaut's earlier narrative poems, was probably written specifically for her (Wimsatt/Kibler 1988, 33–36, 53). In this scenario, the lady of the castle in the poem recalls Machaut's direct experience of Bonne and her entourage. Further, the composition of the *Jugement Navarre* was probably begun for Bonne, whom we assume had urged Machaut to review the earlier poem dedicated to her father, with its judgment so unfavorable to women.[94] Bonne's death caused work to be broken off on this new poem, which was later finished for Charles, king of Navarre.

Besides the narrative poems composed for Bonne, a great number of lyrics—with or without music—were probably part of the glitter of her court. These are contained in MS C [1], the first of Machaut's complete-works collections. It is particularly tempting to associate the large repertory of monophonic virelais with Bonne's court. In a scene well described in the *Remede* (ll. 3359–3516), the monophonic virelai *Dame a vous* (RF6) serves as accompaniment to a round dance outside the château. If we agree with Wimsatt and Kibler that the court of Bonne is the locus of the poem, we have a possible venue for the large group of similar monophonic virelais contained in MS C. Kelly (1978, 147–48) notes that a new literary conception of love, first seen in the *Remede*, is prominent among the lais. I have suggested that Machaut's new conception of love is associated with his service to Bonne of Luxembourg (chap. 5.7, "Patron"), and perhaps the lais too were especially prized by this patron.

The final motet in MS C, *Trop plus / Biauté* (M20), the last work in the manuscript, may be Machaut's memorial benediction for Bonne of Luxembourg.[95] The work is easily placed ca. 1350 on stylistic grounds. Rhythms in the upper voices are more advanced than in any other motet of Machaut and resemble experiments then being made in Machaut's settings of secular lyrics, for instance, in the rondeau *Rose, lis* (R10). Perhaps the innovation was allowable in the motet because of the use in this instance of a rondeau tenor.[96] It

---

[94] References to allegorical characters may mask references to specific personages. Poirion cites references to "Bonne amour" in the *Remede*, and to "Bonneürté" in the *Jugement Navarre* to support the association with Bonne (Poirion 1965, 194, 201 n. 28; further bolstered in Wimsatt/Kibler 1988, 33–36, 53; cf. also Earp 1989, 464, 468 n. 16; Wimsatt 1991b, 161 esp. n. 19). Along similar lines linguistically, compare the allegorical reference to "Sens" in the *Roman des Deduis* of Gace de la Buigne, a reference that R. Cazelles (1982, 402–3) related to Guillaume de Melun, archbishop of Sens.

[95] The order of this motet as last in the collection is not in doubt, because the motets form a closed group placed at the end of the completed manuscript (Earp 1983, 140–42). Wilkins connects two rondeaux to Bonne, but this seems doubtful; see the commentary in chap. 7.3 to *Certes, mon oueil* (Lo234=R15), and to *Dame, qui vuet* (R16).

[96] The rondeau tenor, perhaps a refrain but not attested elsewhere, may mask Machaut's feelings for Bonne, a bit *outré*: "Je ne sui mie certeins d'avoir amie, mais je sui loyaus amis" [I am not at all certain of having a lady friend, but I am a loyal suitor].

is significant that the benedictions intoned by the upper two voices both declaim the word "Amen" as the last word of the work, and thus as the last word of the manuscript.[97] In sum, it is likely that MS C was intended for Bonne and later completed for John II in her memory, although, as we have seen, other sources hint that John may not have been so kindly disposed towards his deceased wife.

King Charles V (b. 1338; r. 1364–1380) was only eleven years old when his mother died, but his devotion to her memory was strong. After his own death in 1380, his entrails were buried at the church of the abbey of Maubuisson, beside Bonne of Luxembourg (Delachenal 1909–31, 4:541, 5:430). Perhaps mutual devotion to the memory of Bonne played a role in the warm relation between the dauphin Charles and Guillaume de Machaut in the early 1360s (R. Cazelles 1982, 55; see chap. 1.15).

The artistic patronage of the rather mysterious Bonne of Luxembourg would seem to provide an interesting direction for further research, in particular, the question of a possible connection between Bonne's patronage and Machaut's development of the polyphonic fixed forms, as well as his early cultivation of the monophonic virelai as a dance song. It is also interesting to consider *Lyon* and *Alerion* as works possibly written for Bonne.[98] In the *Voir Dit*, in his response to the first *rondel* sent by the Lady, supposedly an event of the year 1362, the Narrator says that it has been ten, no, rather, more than twelve years since he had loved and served a lady (ll. 229–41, ed. P. Paris 1875, 9–10). Might we interpret this figuratively to mean that Machaut had not served and drawn inspiration from a female patron since the death of Bonne of Luxembourg in 1349?

10. Ca. 1332–64. Machaut and John, duke of Normandy (from 1350 King John II)

A direct connection between Machaut and King John II is surprisingly difficult to establish,[99] yet Machaut must have had a long-standing connection to John through Bonne of Luxembourg and her children. Further, Wimsatt and Kibler (1988, 35–36) have established that the *Remede* is set in the park at Hesdin, a favorite locale for John. Apparently Machaut rarely had much to do with John but rather served Bonne. Shortly after Bonne's death in 1349, John married Jeanne de Boulogne, and it is possible that Machaut's rondeau *Cinc, un* (R6) was written for this occasion (see chap. 1.12a).

There is considerable documentary evidence for John's appreciation of music, although much of it concerns minstrels and thus touches on improvised instrumental music.[100] He enjoyed courtly chansons of the kind composed by Machaut as well, if, as seems likely (C. Wright 1979, 17; Strohm 1984a, 125 n. 23), *Perotus de Molyno* is identical to Pierre des Molins, composer of the rondeau *Amis, tout dous vis* and the ballade *De ce que fol pense*, this latter the most widely circulated musical work of the entire fourteenth century.[101] Surely

---

[97] See, however, the literary analysis of Huot (1987, 266), proposing that "Amen" refers to the death of the poet.

[98] For example, there may be a connection between *Alerion* and attempts to teach Charles (the future King Charles V) falconry (cf. R. Cazelles 1982, 233).

[99] Earlier biographers had spoken of Machaut's service to John II, but these assertions were disproved by Hoepffner (1908–21, 1:xxxiv–xxxvii; see also Chichmaref 1909, 1:xliii; Machabey 1955b, 1:64).

[100] Delachenal 1909–31, 2:295; Lehoux 1966–68, 1:39 nn. 1–2; especially C. Wright 1979, 11–18; R. Cazelles 1982, 44; Wilkins 1983a, 195–97; 1983b, 261–62.

[101] For the earlier view, see Günther 1963c, 84–85.

the chaplains at John's court performed several of Philippe de Vitry's isorhythmic motets.[102]

It is possible that John II paid for the production of MS C, perhaps first as part of Bonne's household expenses, and later as a memorial to her. This would seem to provide a strong link between the king and the poet, although the manuscript gives evidence that Machaut was no longer supervising its final stages of compilation. Further, C may have been among the books seized with King John at Poitiers in 1356 and taken to England, where perhaps Chaucer saw it (Wimsatt/Kibler 1988, 52–54).[103] The disastrous capture of the king at Poitiers affected France profoundly in the late 1350s, although Machaut mentioned the event but little in his poetry.

After the treaty of Brétigny in 1360, King John returned to France. Machaut mentions a 1363 visit of the king to Reims in the *Voir Dit*, but only indirectly. One can contrast the slight attention paid to the king in the *dit* to the warm personal relationship that Machaut enjoyed with the dauphin Charles, soon to become King Charles V.

1.10.1. JOHN II AND MS C. A marginal note dated Ascension (2 May) 1353 in a treasury account of John II for 1349–50 (Delisle 1907, 1:333, 404–5), which Avril (1973, 122) associated with the copying of a moralized Bible for John, duke of Normandy (now *F:Pn 167*), mentions the copying and illumination of "other books in French" ["et aliorum librorum in gallico"]. Günther (1982, 101–2) has plausibly suggested that one of the "other books" was Machaut's MS C. The document thus provides a possible link between Machaut's MS C and John. Although, as mentioned above, MS C was likely begun for his wife Bonne, the duchess of Normandy, John would have paid for the copying of the manuscript. It is further tempting, I find, to connect MS C with a reference of 1349, concerning a *livre de motets* illuminated by Jean de Wirmes.[104] It would seem very unusual in the fourteenth century to have a book of motets illuminated, since such a book would be destined for the chapel library for practical use by the musically literate clerks. But if we interpret the reference as "a book with illuminations that contains music," a possible description of a Machaut manuscript emerges. The date 1349 is not too early for the completion of the first layer of MS C, which would have been broken off on the death of Bonne in November 1349.

In any case, Machaut left or was cut off from royal service after Bonne's death. The curious mixing of genres in the later portion of the music section of MS C, the portion that Günther (1963a, 99; 1982, 97–98) referred to as "CII," corroborates the hypothesis that the author was no longer supervising the compilation of the manuscript. Although the scribes were able to obtain new works that had entered circulation in the early 1350s, the author was not present to direct the ordering of the series of new works in the manuscript.

1.10.2. LITERARY REFERENCES TO JOHN II
a. *Complainte* 3. Wimsatt (1991b, 82) suggests that a reference in *A toi, Hanri* (Cp3, ll. 32–33) to "mon droit dieu terrien" [my true earthly god], whom Machaut "regret souvent en souspirant" [often regrets with a sigh] refers to John II in captivity, but see the discussion of Cp3 in chap. 6.5.

b. *Complainte* 7. Lebeuf associated *Sire, a vous fais ceste clamour* (Cp7) with King John II, while Chichmaref left open the possibility of a connection either to John II or to Charles V. Hoepffner opts for Charles V, as does Fourrier, who dates Cp7 to the first months of 1365. The most recent views associate Cp7 with Charles of Navarre and place it early in 1361 (see chap. 1.12.2 and chap. 6.5 for references).

c. The battle of Poitiers (19 September 1356). Machaut said very little about the military disasters that befell France and her king in the mid-fourteenth century. Not a single line of

---

[102] John's first chaplain since at least 1351 was Gace de la Buigne, who left a famous eulogy of Philippe de Vitry's powers of motet composition in his *Roman des Deduis* (C. Wright 1979, 14), completed in 1377 for Philip the Bold, duke of Burgundy.

[103] On books that John had with him at Poitiers, see Delisle 1907, 1:330–31.

[104] On Jean de Wirmes (Viarmes), see Delisle 1907, 1:133; Avril 1973, 117n., 121n., 122n.; C. Wright 1979, 14; R. Cazelles 1982, 43.

poetry mentions the disaster at Crécy, where John of Luxembourg fell in 1346, and only a backhanded comment about Poitiers is found in *Confort*. Machaut intended to provide consolation to the imprisoned king of Navarre when he asserted that had Charles been at Poitiers, he might have shared the sad fate of King John (l. 2795, "La fu pris li bons roys de France" [there the good king of France was taken]; discussed in Hoepffner 1908–21, 3:xiii–xiv; Gauvard 1982, 29 n. 28; and Palmer 1992, xxix–xxx; a further passage is noted in Hoepffner 1908–21, 3:251, n. to ll. 3122–23). This is an excerpt from a longer passage (ll. 2778–863) that provides an extended eulogy of King John II, in which Machaut compares John to seven of the nine worthies, and to other heros of classical antiquity and medieval epic.

Hoepffner (1908–21, 1:xxxiv, xxxvii) was the first to cite the lai *En demandant* (L24) in connection with the battle of Poitiers, arguing against attribution of the work to Machaut based on its transmission as an *unicum* in the suspect MS E [7]; Chichmaref (1909, 1:xliii) accepts it.[105]

Paulin Paris (1875, 138 n. 2) connects a passage in the *Voir Dit* (ll. 3193–208, ed. P. Paris 1875, 137–38), indicating that a knight should not flee from a battle, to Poitiers. It seems however too general a reference to refer conclusively to a specific battle.

d. King John at Reims. King John visited Reims on at least two occasions after his coronation on 26 September 1350, first from 28 September to 5 October 1354, possibly longer, in order to celebrate the fourth anniversary of his coronation (R. Cazelles 1982, 169), and then again from 30 September to at least 23 October 1363, to celebrate the thirteenth anniversary (Delachenal 1909–31, 2:349 n. 2; R. Cazelles 1982, 440). Four *Voir Dit* letters refer to an interval near the second of these visits:

i. letter 29 (ed. P. Paris 1875, 235), dated 17 September [1363]. Toute Belle writes that her brother had gone to the king.

ii. letter 30 (ed. P. Paris 1875, 239), undated, but probably mid-to-late September 1363 (Leech-Wilkinson 1993b, 122). Guillaume writes that *seigneurs*, perhaps part of the king's entourage, were lodging at his house.

iii. letter 31 (ed. P. Paris 1875, 240), dated 28 September [1363]. Guillaume writes that Toute Belle's brother, perhaps part of the king's entourage, had come to visit him.

iv. letter 33 (ed. P. Paris 1875, 259), dated 9 October [1363]. Guillaume writes that some of the king's entourage ("des gens du roi"), as well as part of the entourage of the duke of Bar, were lodging at his house.

e. King John in the *Prise d'Alexandre*. Finally, in the *Prise* (ll. 679–83, 763, 794) Machaut briefly referred to King John (Chichmaref 1909, 1:xliv). On the passage in ll. 831–38, formerly taken as praise of John II, see chap. 1.5.1e.

11. 1333–72. The career of Jean de Machaut

For the most part, the career of Jean de Machaut runs in parallel with that of his brother Guillaume. Both were clerks who first served John of Luxembourg, and both were repaid for their services with ecclesiastical benefices. Both later had connections to King Charles of Navarre, and both settled down as canons of Reims.[106]

The stages of Jean's career advancement were a few years behind Guillaume's, which may indicate that Jean was the younger brother (chap. 1.2.4). Praised as a familiar and almoner in the household of John of Luxembourg, he was a simple clerk in the diocese of Reims before 1333, when he was granted an expectative benefice at Montebourg in the Cotentin (dépt. Manche). By 1342, when Guillaume was already settled at Reims with a canonicate at the cathedral, Jean was named as a secretary to John of

---

[105] Hoepffner seems to have changed his mind by 1921, since he then accepts the lai as Machaut's (1908–21, 3:xiii n. 2; see also Machabey 1955b, 1:50 and Günther 1982, 101). Earp (1983, 309–10, 326) argues against attribution of the lai to Machaut.

[106] Some references to a Johan de Mascó or Maschó, a jongleur and cornemuse player—not Guillaume's brother—are given below, chap. 2 n. 22.

Luxembourg. In the same year he received a canonicate and prebend at Verdun in addition to the canonicate and prebend at Leuze (Belgium) that he had already obtained at some time between 1333 and 1342. In 1343 Jean was granted an expectative canonicate and prebend at Reims. Doubtless he wished to join his brother Guillaume at Reims as soon as possible, since later patrons renewed the request for a prebend at Reims in 1350 and again in 1354. By 1354 Jean held canonicates and prebends at Leuze, Verdun, Bar-le-Duc, and Toul. He finally took possession of his prebend at Reims in 1355, after a twelve-year wait, and a few later documents attest to his residence there. From August 1356 to August 1358, he served as the chapter's officer of the *anniversaria*. The brothers lived together in the same house, as Machaut reveals in the *Voir Dit* (ll. 6966–68; ed. P. Paris 1875, 286).[107] Perhaps Jean had already resided with Guillaume at Reims at an earlier date, at least occasionally. Guillaume had been a resident at least since 1340, and a document of 1344 places both brothers at Reims (chap. 1.7.1b).

A. *Yolande of Flanders and Philip of Navarre.* Previous biographers have not sufficiently considered the published papal documents concerning Jean de Machaut, which shed light on questions concerning Guillaume's patrons of the 1350s. Most significant is a 1350 supplication (below, chap. 1.11.1e), which shows that by then Jean de Machaut had passed into the service of Yolande of Flanders, countess of Bar and lady of Cassel (d. 1395).[108] Yolande's first husband (married in 1340), Count Henry IV of Bar (r. 1337–1344), a cousin of Count Louis de Male of Flanders, died in December 1344. His testament had cut Yolande off from control of Bar, and she spent the next decade trying to gain control of the county for her two children, Edward (count of Bar 1344–1352) and Robert (count of Bar 1352–1354; duke of Bar 1354–1411).[109]

In 1353 Yolande of Flanders married Philip of Navarre, count of Longueville (d. 29 August 1363), the brother of King Charles of Navarre, and his tireless supporter. Thus, the supplication of 1350 provides for a new possibility, that after the death of Bonne of Luxembourg, Machaut passed into the service of the king of Navarre through his brother Jean de Machaut (cf. R. Cazelles 1982, 88). Previously, the first documentary proof of a relationship between Guillaume de Machaut and King Charles of Navarre had been a papal letter of 1354 (chap. 1.11.1f), since it was assumed that Guillaume was the one who had petitioned the king of Navarre for this grace on behalf of his brother. It now seems more likely that Jean de Machaut obtained the favor on his own merits.

B. *Robert I, duke of Bar.* Jean de Machaut's connection to the House of Bar perhaps provided Guillaume with a second important aristocratic patron. Guillaume mentions the son of Yolande of Flanders, Robert I, first duke of Bar (r. 1354–1411), as a patron in the *Voir Dit* (chap. 1.15.2a). On 1 December 1364 Robert married Marie de France (1344–1404), the second daughter of King John II (Delachenal 1909–31, 3:145–47). Their daughter Yolande (1365–

---

[107] See chap. 1.2.4, and the analysis in Eichelberg 1935, 112–15. On Machaut's house, see chap. 1.18.1a.

[108] On Yolande of Flanders, see Delachenal 1909–31, 3:115–16 and n. 4; she is well known to art historians as the original owner of an important book of hours (*GB:Lbl Yates Thompson 27*)—perhaps commissioned for her marriage to Philip of Navarre—illuminated by Jean Le Noir and his daughter Bourgot ca. 1355 and confiscated by Charles V in 1372 (see Delisle 1907, 1:52, 214–18; Avril 1978, 21 [fig. viii], 22–23, 33 [bibliography to fig. viii]; Sterling 1987, 114–17 [with further bibliography]).

[109] H. Thomas (1973) provides a thorough recent treatment of the historical situation in Bar during this period; see also J. Schneider 1990.

1431), duchess of Gerona and later queen of Aragon, became one of Machaut's most avid readers, as a series of Catalan documents attest (chap. 2.2.1). Indeed, Yolande of Bar may have owned one of the most important extant sources of Machaut's works, the MS **Vg** [3].[110]

C. *Raoul de Vienne, sire de Louppy.* The 1350 supplication (chap. 1.11.1e), by providing an early link with the House of Bar, relates to another aristocratic acquaintance of Guillaume de Machaut. Machaut's ballade *Mes dames qu'onques ne vi* (Lo250) mentions "Monseigneur de Loupy," identified by Hoepffner (1908–21, 1:xl) as Raoul de Vienne, sire de Louppy, governor of the Dauphiné from 1361 until 1369.[111] In 1345, as an official of King Philip VI, Raoul de Louppy was involved in mediating the many conflicts between Bar and Lorrain that followed the death of Count Henry IV of Bar in 1344. He was in the service of Yolande of Flanders in 1349 and 1353. A counselor of King John II in October 1354 (R. Cazelles 1982, 171–72), he became a major player on the side of the nobility in the reform movement of the years 1356 to 1358. In addition, the Sire de Louppy was the brother-in-law of Jean de Conflans, the marshall of Champagne, a trusted official of the dauphin Charles and a partisan of Charles of Navarre, ignominiously murdered 22 February 1358 by the mob surrounding Etienne Marcel in the chambers of the dauphin at the Palais on the Ile de la Cité. His cousin, another Jean de Conflans, was the stepfather of the Peronne that Paulin Paris (1875, xxiii–xxiv) connects to the *Voir Dit* of 1363–65 (R. Cazelles 1982, 90). Raoul de Louppy disappeared after 1379; some details of his distinguished career in the 1360s and 1370s are recounted by Raymond Cazelles (1982, 420–21).

In sum, the new documents allow the possibility that Machaut owed his association with three important patrons, Charles, king of Navarre, Robert, duke of Bar, and Raoul de Louppy, to the prior connections of his brother Jean. Jean died probably in 1372 and was buried in the cathedral of Reims. In 1377 Guillaume was laid beside his brother in the same tomb.

1.11.1. JEAN DE MACHAUT'S BENEFICES. JEAN AT REIMS

a. 1333: expectative benefice at Montebourg. A bull of Pope John XXII, dated Avignon, 4 January 1333, granted *Johanni de Machaudio* an expectative benefice at the abbey and convent of the Benedictine monastery of Our Lady of Montebourg (diocese of Coutances; dépt. Manche), on the request of the king of Bohemia.[112] The income from the prebend is set at sixty *livres* of Tours *cum cura*, and forty *livres* of Tours *sine cura*. Jean is named as the king's familiar, domestic, and almoner ["familiari et domestico eleemosynario"]. Since Jean is addressed as a simple clerk of the diocese of Reims, he presumably had no prior benefices.

The three executors of this benefice were (1) the abbot of the monastery of Our Lady of Montebourg; (2) the scholaster of the same monastery; and (3) the archdeacon of the cathedral of Coutances.[113]

By the 1360s this area of France, the Cotentin, was dominated by partisans of the king of Navarre (Henneman 1976, 237); a 1361 document (chap. 1.12.2) from Charles of Navarre, providing Guillaume de Machaut with the gift of a horse, originated from this region.

---

[110] See the discussion of the date and provenance of MS [3] in chap. 3.

[111] Louppy-le-Château is in the county of Bar, just to the northwest of Bar-le-Duc (dépt. Meuse). Machaut's ballade cannot be dated precisely; judging from manuscript transmission, it may be placed in the 1360s.

[112] See A. Thomas 1881, 329–30, 333; 1884, 42, 46 (the 1881 publication is slightly more complete). Mollat (1932, 73 no. 59242) provides a shorter summary.

[113] Antoine Thomas lists the same executors for this letter as for the letter of the same date involving Guillaume (chap. 1.6.1d), doubtless in error. The executors listed here are those given by Mollat.

b. 1342: canon of Verdun and Leuze. A supplication of 23 September 1342 from the king of Bohemia for a canonicate and prebend at Verdun for Jean de Machaut was approved by Pope Clement VI (r. 1342–1352).[114] Jean is named as the king's clerk, secretary and domestic ["clerici et secretarii sui domestici"]. Previous benefices include a canonicate and prebend in the collegiate church of St-Pierre at Leuze (diocese of Cambrai, now in the province of Hainaut in Belgium).

The three executors of this benefice were the abbots of the monasteries of St-Nicasius at Reims and St-Vitonus at Verdun, and the archdeacon of Bauptois in the cathedral of Coutances.[115]

c. 1343: canon of Reims, requested by John of Luxembourg. A bull of Pope Clement VI, dated 18 April 1343, granted Jean de Machaut an expectative canonicate and prebend at Reims on the request of the king of Bohemia (Klicman 1903, 100 no. 183). Jean is named as the king's clerk and domestic familiar ["clerico et familiari domestico"]. The published summary does not list the executors.

d. 1344: Jean de Machaut at Reims. Guillaume and Jean de Machaut were both present at Reims on 30 May 1344 to witness a document (chap. 1.7.1b).

e. 1350: canon of Reims, requested by Yolande of Flanders. A supplication dated 16 November 1350 from Yolande of Flanders, and approved by Pope Clement VI, requests an expectative canonicate and prebend at Reims for *Johanni de Machaudio*.[116] Jean is named as the countess's familiar ["familiari suo"]. Previous benefices include canonicates both at the cathedral of Verdun and at the church of St-Pierre at Leuze. This is a redundant request, since in 1343 (item c above) John of Luxembourg had already petitioned Pope Clement VI to award Jean de Machaut a prebend at Reims. Nor would this be the last petition for this particular grace.

f. 1354: canon of Bar-le-Duc and Toul; canon of Reims, requested by King Charles of Navarre. Two documents of this year relate to Jean de Machaut. A supplication dated 14 October 1354 from Charles of Navarre to Pope Innocent VI (r. 1352–1362), renewed a request that he had already made to the previous pope, Clement VI, for an expectative canonicate and prebend at Reims.[117] Jean's previous benefices include canonicates at the cathedral of Verdun, at the collegiate church of St-Maxe at Bar-le-Duc (diocese of Toul, dépt. Meuse), and at the collegiate church of St-Pierre at Leuze. The canonicate at Bar-le-Duc has not previously been mentioned in the literature, and was presumably obtained with the favor of Yolande of Flanders between 16 November 1350, when it was not listed (item (e) above), and the present document of 14 October 1354. Jean is declared ready to vacate one or the other of his canonicates and prebends already obtained at Bar-le-Duc or at Leuze in favor of the canonicate at Reims.

The supplication of Charles of Navarre indicates that Jean de Machaut wanted more than anything else a canonicate at Reims cathedral with his brother Guillaume. Even so, the pope signed the petition "Fiat in ecclesia Tullensi," and thus the surviving papal bull of the same day awarded Jean de Machaut a canonicate not at Reims, but instead at the cathedral of Toul (dépt. Meurthe-et-Moselle).[118] Jean de Machaut is listed as a favorite ["dilecto suo"] of

---

[114] Klicman 1903, 63 no. 109, summarized in Berlière 1906, 45 no. 216. Klicman (1903, 64 no. 110) and Berlière (1924, 166 no. 513) summarize the papal letter of collation. Some interesting entries from the accounts of the collector referring to the same event are published in Kirsch 1894.

[115] Geraldus de Magnaco, *capellanus pape* to Clement VI and papal *nuntius*. He served as the executor for several benefices petitioned by the king of Bohemia (cf. Berlière 1924).

[116] See the summary in Berlière 1906, 548 no. 2107.

[117] Berlière 1911, 224 no. 534. Charles was himself at Avignon in November 1354 to meet the duke of Lancaster and English ambassadors; see Delachenal 1909–31, 1:88; Guillemain 1962, 517 (also recording a 1350 visit to Avignon); Lehoux 1966–68, 1:43; R. Cazelles 1982, 168. Pope Innocent VI was readily influenced by Charles of Navarre (Delachenal 1909–31, 1:78).

[118] See Despy 1953, 288 no. 855. A. Thomas (1881, 330n.; 1884, 42n.) gives the main tenor. R. Cazelles (1982, 90 n. 16) erroneously attaches this benefice to Guillaume instead of to Jean de Machaut.

the king of Navarre. Perhaps as consolation for not receiving the actual request, Jean was allowed to retain all three of his previous benefices, at Verdun, Bar-le-Duc, and Leuze. This request for a canonicate at Reims was the third since the original supplication of the king of Bohemia in 1343. Jean would have less than a year to wait for this final grace.

The three executors for this benefice were (1) the abbot of the monastery of St-Denis of Reims; (2) the abbot of the monastery of St-Leo beyond the walls of Toul; and (3) Droco de Rouriis, canon of Soissons (dépt. Aisne).

g. 1355: Jean occupies his canonicate at Reims. Two documents mention that Jean de Machaut took over prebend no. 44 at Reims on 13 September 1355, (1) a cartulary called the *Livre rouge du chapitre de Reims*, AMR 2G 1650, fol. 13r; and (2) *F:RS 1773* (MS Weyen), fol. 291r.[119] It is not known if King Charles of Navarre had had to intervene further on behalf of Jean. In a document of 4 November 1355 (chap. 1.7.1h), Jean was absent from Reims.

h. deacon at the cathedral of Reims. Chichmaref (1909, 1:xi) cites a list of canons and bene- fices of the diocese of Reims published by Varin (1844, 1:106n., the *Livre rouge du chapitre de Reims*, fol. 309r) in which *Johannes de Machau* appears among the deacons of Reims. Chichmaref dates the document ca. 1350 and leaves open the possibility that it refers to the younger brother of Guillaume de Machaut. Varin (1853, 494) indexes the reference with the canon Jean de Machaut, but Daniel Leech-Wilkinson (personal communication) reports that the reference, in a thirteenth-century hand, is not to our Jean de Machaut.

i. 1358: officer of the anniversaries of the Chapter of Reims. A document of 12 February 1358[120] mentions *Johannes de Machaudio* in the context of a dispute between the provost of the chapter, Etienne de Courtenay, with whom several canons were aligned, and the dean of the chapter, with whom several other canons were aligned, on the matter of the annual election of certain dignitaries. The dispute was finally referred to *parlement* through the bailiff of Vermandois, who named two canons to mediate the dispute on 9 September 1357. The two arbitrators decided to return all annually elected offices to the status of 1 August 1357. The offices and dignitaries involved are named, including two seneschals,[121] an officer of the hours, an officer of the anniversaries (Jean de Machaut), two officers of the Fabric,[122] two officers of the hospice [*ad Hospicium*],[123] and two officers of the keys. Thus, Jean de Machaut served from 1 August 1356 to 1 August 1358. Perhaps he was in charge of the services associated with the numerous foundations for deceased canons, or perhaps he supervised the investment and the distribution of the revenues according to the will of the founders.[124]

1.11.2. 1372. DEATH OF JEAN DE MACHAUT. The death of Jean de Machaut before 3 May 1372 is recorded in a letter of Pope Gregory XI (r. 1371–1378), which assigns a canonicate at Reims made available by the death of *Johannes de Machaudio* to *Johannes le Houdain* (Tihon 1962, 84–85 no. 1585).[125] This date conflicts with the one normally given for Jean de Machaut's death, between 1 January and 21 February 1374 (AMR 2G 1650, fol. 13 and *F:RS 1773*, fol. 291r, cited in Leech-Wilkinson 1990c, 10 n. 36). Unfortunately, the MS Weyen, which otherwise would be expected to answer this question, has many ambiguities with regard

---

[119] Hoepffner 1908–21, 1:xxxii n. 2; Machabey 1955b, 1:49; 1955c, 252.

[120] Varin 1843–48, 3:101–3, cited in Chichmaref 1909, 1:xlix; Hoepffner 1908–21, 1:xxxii; Machabey 1955b, 1:13 n. 5, 49.

[121] On their duties, see Desportes 1979, 297 n. 18, 653–54.

[122] On their duties, see Pycke 1986, 192–93; Haggh 1988, 1:25–26.

[123] A charitable duty, perhaps concerning services at the several hospices at Reims (cf. Pycke 1986, 293–95 for the practices at thirteenth-century Tournai).

[124] On anniversary foundations, see Millet 1982, 287–88; Pycke 1986, 211–13, 258–66, 318–20, 354–55; Haggh 1988, 1:338, 354–79.

[125] Machabey (1955c, 253) mentions Lehoudain; for a complete biography, see Tomasello 1983. The documents that include mention of Jean de Machaut are published in Mirot/Jassemin 1935 and Tihon 1962, cited above.

to dates and prebend numbers (Machabey 1955b, 1:69, 2:185; 1955c, 252–53). The weight of the papal documents argues for placing the death of Jean de Machaut in 1372.[126]

12. Ca. 1352–ca. 1360. Navarrese years

The date supplied in the opening segment of the *Jugement Navarre*, 9 November 1349, has been taken as the date of the poem itself, and as proof that Machaut had by then entered the service of Charles II, king of Navarre (b. 1332; r. 1349–1387). Following a suggestion of Poirion (1965, 194), however, it appears likely that the *Jugement Navarre* was begun for Bonne of Luxembourg and only later revised for the new patron. This would allow a later date for Machaut's entry into the service of Charles, let us say around 1352.[127] The circumstances surrounding Machaut's entry into his service are not known, nor do we know in what capacity Machaut served the king.[128]

The *Jugement Navarre*, probably completed in the early 1350s, actually has only the most tenuous connection to Charles. There is nothing of the personal familiarity and local descriptions that connect the *Jugement Behaingne* specifically to John of Luxembourg. It would appear that any king's name could have been substituted for the king of Navarre, with no further changes necessary to the narrative. One wonders if Machaut was seeking the favor of a new patron; surely Charles did not commission the work, and maybe there was some opportunism involved in the dedication of the new poem to the king of Navarre. Perhaps Machaut saw in the dashing young king the promise of a patron more in the mold of the generous John of Luxembourg. As we have seen, it is also possible that Guillaume passed into the service of the king of Navarre on the recommendation of his brother Jean, who had had a connection to the House of Navarre at least from 1353, when his patron Yolande of Flanders married Philip of Navarre, and who had a benefice in a region of Normandy controlled by the king of Navarre.

A. *1352: the wedding of Charles of Navarre and Jeanne of France.* Charles of Navarre married Jeanne de France on 12 February 1352 at Vivier-en-Brie (dépt. Seine-et-Marne).[129] Ursula Günther (1982, 106) has attached the rondeau

---

126 Anne W. Robertson (personal communication) has discovered a published document of 1373 naming a Jean de Machaut serving on a municipal commission in Châlons, but I do not believe it refers to Guillaume's brother: "Commission donnée par les seigneurs temporels de Châlons à Bertrand du Pont et Mathieu Duvivier, chanoines, Nicolas de Plancy, Garnier Petitsaine, Jean d'Aougny, Jean de Machaut, Henri Debar et Jean Sauville pour recevoir le compte des deniers des octrois qui doivent être employés aux fortifications" (Pelicier 1899, 124: G.471 [Seigneurie en partie de la Ville], no. 4 [Châlons, 12 June 1373]).

127 Hoepffner (1908–21, 1:xxxi) cites a suggestion of Suchier, who places the the beginning of Machaut's service in 1353, when Charles of Navarre became the son-in-law of John II (this occurred actually in 1352), but Hoepffner finally opts for the earlier date of 1349 suggested by the opening of the *Jugement Navarre*. Machabey (1955b, 1:43) and Poirion (1965, 24) also places the beginning of Machaut's service in November 1349, when Charles of Navarre would have been only seventeen years old.

128 Machabey (1955b, 1:43, 47) speculates that Charles' interests in his heritage in Champagne brought them together, that Machaut served Charles as a secretary, and even that Machaut served as a kind of informant for Charles on the affairs of Champagne. See also the commentary below, chap. 6.5, concerning the *complainte Sire, a vous fais ceste clamour* (Cp7). Palmer (1992, xvii–xxiv) provides another account of Machaut's Navarrese years.

129 Delachenal 1909–31, 1:61, 81; R. Cazelles 1958, 238; Lehoux 1966–68, 1:25 n. 4; R. Cazelles 1982, 148 (the conflicting date of 1351 [R. Cazelles 1982, 10] is apparently an error). It is possible that John, duke of Normandy, and Bonne of Luxembourg had a hôtel

Cinc, un, trese, wit, neuf (R6) to the wedding, and on stylistic grounds this does provide a reasonable date for the work. Nevertheless, two other possible occasions for the composition of a rondeau to a "Jehan" or "Jehanne" suggest themselves, (1) the February 1350 marriage of the duke of Normandy and Jeanne de Boulogne at Melun (dépt. Seine-et-Marne), an occasion that has the advantage of covering both possible names,[130] and (2) the 8 April 1350 marriage of two twelve-year-olds, the dauphin Charles, the future Charles V, and Jeanne de Bourbon.[131]

B. *"Charles the Bad."* The question of Machaut's association with Charles of Navarre has broad ramifications, which have only begun to be explored (see Gauvard 1982, utilized in Markstrom 1989; Palmer 1992, introduction). Many of the early biographers have been at pains to excuse Machaut's association with Charles, dubbed "Charles the Bad" in the sixteenth century for his traitorous acts against the crown (R. Cazelles 1982, 9). In this scenario, Machaut, after having gone astray for a few years, returned to the fold of the house of France, barely in time to avoid disgrace. Hoepffner (1908–21, 1:xxxiv), for instance, excuses Machaut by asserting that he was not interested in politics and unaware until a late moment of the dangers of his choice of patron. Yet relations between King Charles of Navarre and King John II were cordial in 1350, at the very beginning of the reign of King John (R. Cazelles 1982, 9–10). Lines were very close between the house of Valois and the house of Evreux-Navarre in the early 1350s, and Machaut's association with the king of Navarre was not questionable. It is anachronistic to view Machaut's relation to King Charles of Navarre as in any way dishonorable or unpatriotic.

C. *Supporters of Charles of Navarre.* Raymond Cazelles has studied the very broad support that Charles of Navarre enjoyed.[132] Among his partisans were former officers of John of Luxembourg (including, of course, Machaut), and the families of both wives of King John II, Bonne of Luxembourg and Jeanne de Boulogne. Besides strong support in Auvergne and Normandy, there were many Navarrese in the lands previously belonging to the house of Evreux-Navarre, notably in Champagne and Brie.[133] We have already met the nobleman Raoul de Louppy, who served Philip of Navarre, husband of Yolande of Flanders (chap. 1.11c). Raoul de Louppy was one of the reformers in the period 1356–58 who would go on to lend stability to the government throughout the reign of Charles V (R. Cazelles 1982, 265–67, 418–19, 495). A new member of the governing council of King John II in 1351, Guillaume de Melun, archbishop of Sens, also had strong Navarrese connections for a time (R. Cazelles 1982, 142, 385, 409). He later became the most influential

---

at Vivier-en-Brie (Lehoux 1966–68, 1:8). R. Cazelles (1982, 149) noted that the marriage was celebrated "almost clandestinely," without any chronicler reporting it. Lehoux (1966–68, 1:25–26) also discusses this ceremony.

[130] Lehoux (1966–68, 1:39 n. 1) mentions a payment of the duke of Normandy to Robert de Caveron, king of the minstrels for this occasion; see also C. Wright 1979, 18). On Robert de Caveron, see also Wilkins 1979, 139; Gushee 1980, 142, 150 n. 11.

[131] Delachenal 1909–31, 1:43. Delachenal notes, however, that the ceremony was evidently modest, due to the recent deaths of both Bonne of Luxembourg, first wife of the duke of Normandy, and Jeanne of Burgundy, first wife of King Philip VI.

[132] R. Cazelles 1982, 85–92; see the summary in Henneman 1976, 18–19, and his further characterization of Charles (Henneman 1976, 34–35).

[133] In 1318 King Philip V excluded Jeanne of Navarre, Charles's mother, from her inheritance of the counties of Champagne and Brie in exchange for the county of Angoulême (R. Cazelles 1958, 38–39, 48–52, 205–8).

member of the government during the crisis of 1357–58 after the Battle of
Poitiers and throughout most of the reign of Charles V. Indeed, at one time or
another, almost all of the most trusted officials of the government of King John
II and King Charles V had been partisans of the king of Navarre.

Influential members of the clergy were also in the Navarrese camp.[134]
Through Jean de Vienne, archbishop of Reims (r. 1334–1351), himself long a
servant of the House of Evreux-Navarre, the cathedral chapter of Reims had
become favorable to the king of Navarre (R. Cazelles 1982, 98). And a later
archbishop of Reims, Jean de Craon (r. 1355–1373), spokesman for the clergy
in the December 1355 Estates, was also an important member of the October
1356 Estates, which had called for reform (R. Cazelles 1982, 196–97, 231).
By "reform" intellectuals expressed their desire for an end to currency
fluctuations, for the election of royal officers (i.e., the king's council should
designate officers according to their competence), for the inalienability of the
domain (i.e., the king should live off the revenues of his land rather than
dispensing his patrimony to his favorites), for a distinction between the king's
household expenses and the expenses of government, etc. Reformers that
remained in the government were important elements in the fabled efficacy of
the reign of Charles V. Machaut demonstrated a clear sympathy for such ideals
in his *Confort* (chap. 1.12.1).

Finally among the intellectuals supporting the king of Navarre, we must count
the members of the College of Navarre, founded in 1304 by Jeanne de Navarre,
queen of Philip the Fair. One of the students of that college, Nicole Oresme,
wrote a monetary treatise that strongly influenced the reformers of 1355 and
1356 and was later known for his translations of Aristotle for Charles V (R.
Cazelles 1982, 102).[135] It has been assumed that Johannes de Muris and
Philippe de Vitry were active at the College of Navarre.[136] Many bourgeois also
supported the king of Navarre for a time, the most notorious of whom was the
Parisian provost of the merchants, Etienne Marcel (R. Cazelles 1982, 103–4).

D. *Charles of Navarre imprisoned.* Real difficulties between King John and
King Charles did not begin until the second half of 1353 (R. Cazelles 1982,
155–57) and came to a head with Charles of Navarre's complicity in the murder
of Charles of Spain in January 1354.[137] King John's quick pardon a month
later by the treaty of Mantes was probably more to avoid the potentially
disastrous consequences of an alliance between the English and the king of
Navarre than out of any renewal of trust in Charles of Navarre (Delachenal
1909–31, 1:84–85). Despite the continuing questionable activities of Charles,
there were several reconciliations between him and John II throughout 1354 and
1355 (Delachenal 1909–31, 1:109; R. Cazelles 1982, chap. 25).

The unexpected events precipitated by King John II at Rouen on 5 April
1356, the arrest and imprisonment of the king of Navarre, and the execution
without trial of four of his followers, tended to make a martyr of Charles of
Navarre and ended only in eliciting sympathy for him. Delachenal (1909–31,
1:157) cites Machaut's *Confort* (ll. 1803–14) in support of the assertion that
most people did not know the reasons for John's apparently arbitrary action.[138]

---

134 Delachenal 1909–31, 1:250–57; R. Cazelles 1982, 97–101, 301–3.

135 Oresme was rector of the College of Navarre from October 1356 (R. Cazelles 1982, 303).

136 Fuller (1985–86, 45–46) doubts Vitry's presence there.

137 See Bessen 1985, 47. R. Cazelles (1982, 166) presents a brilliant analysis of the situation surrounding the assassination of Charles of Spain.

138 Delachenal 1909–31, 1:140–57, 159, 262–63. See also Hoepffner 1908–21, 3:xiii–xiv;
Gauvard 1982, 25–26.

In fact, Machaut's evident continuing Navarrese sympathies throughout these years actually speak highly for his intelligence and interest in politics. The most enlightened among the intelligentsia of the mid fourteenth-century in France—both noble and clerical—adhered to the hope that Charles of Navarre would help them to enact their programs of reform.[139] After the disastrous battle of Poitiers (19 September 1356), where King John II was taken prisoner by the English, the Estates of October 1356 called for the release of Charles.[140] Jean de Craon, archbishop of Reims, was the representative of the clergy in 1356 and 1357, as well as a member of the dauphin's council, nominated by the October 1356 Estates. And Philippe de Vitry, bishop of Meaux, was one of the three bishops among the nine reformers-general named by the Estates of February-March 1357 (R. Cazelles 1982, 259–61), charged with investigating and punishing royal officers who had abused their power.[141]

1.12.1. MACHAUT THE REFORMER. (For a more general "catalogue of counsels" offered by Machaut, see Palmer 1992, lvii–lviii.) Several points of the reform platform find expression in Machaut's *Confort*:

a. *Confort* (ll. 3140–44, 3545–52, 3785–86). Machaut counseled Charles not to give his heritage away, something for which reformers had reproached kings of France since Philip the Fair. The thought was that if the king would just retain all his lands, he could govern with his own income, without the constant necessity of raising taxes.

b. *Confort* (ll. 3105–12; 3294–95). Machaut warned Charles of the danger of bad counselors.[142] The elimination of the group of counselors that had advised John II and that were still sitting in the dauphin's council was a major demand of the reformers. Machaut mentions in ll. 3759–60 that young counselors are not good; surely he was aware that the aged Philippe de Vitry was one of the reformers-general!

c. *Confort* (ll. 3825–36). Here Machaut emphasizes the importance of coining good money. The constant mutation of the currency practiced in the reigns of Philip VI and John II hit the clergy with benefices especially hard, since their income was fixed in the money of account, the *livre* of Tours, whose value in real money fluctuated constantly (R. Cazelles 1982, chap. 5). This is a reform that was actually carried out after John II returned from England in 1360, when the stable monetary program of Nicole Oresme—whose monetary treatise dates from December 1355—was adopted (R. Cazelles 1982, 510–12, 558–60; Henneman 1976, 117–18). For additional literary references to the mutation of the currency, see Cerquiglini 1985b, 161–62.

E. *The weakening popularity of Charles of Navarre.* Sympathy for the king of Navarre began to wane only slowly. Although a few had begun to keep their distance as early as 1355 (R. Cazelles 1982, 193, 222), it was only by the end of 1357, after he had sealed an alliance with the English, that many patriots turned against Charles of Navarre. For instance, by July 1357 the archbishop of Reims, Jean de Craon, had deserted the ruling council that had issued from the February-March Estates to become the most influential personal counselor of the dauphin.[143] Certain regions, such as Burgundy and notably Champagne, also left the Navarrese camp in 1357 (R. Cazelles 1982, 290, 296, 314, 318).

---

[139] Henneman 1976, 17–25; R. Cazelles 1982, 62–63; Gauvard 1982; Bessen 1985, 47–48, 55–57.

[140] Delachenal 1909–31, 1:257; Henneman 1976, 25–26; R. Cazelles 1982, 231.

[141] Delachenal 1909–31, 1:305–6; Machabey 1955b, 1:74 n. 212; Henneman 1976, 46, 54–55, 66.

[142] Cf. chap. 1.13.1 on Machaut's motet *Tu qui gregem / Plange* (M22). Gauvard (1982, 34 n. 50) further cites a passage in the *Voir Dit* (ll. 5100–5101; ed. P. Paris 1875, 219); see also the comments of Hoepffner (1908–21, 3:xv), Cerquiglini (1985b, 160–61), and Kelly (1987, 89).

[143] Delachenal 1909–31, 1:316; Henneman 1976, 54; R. Cazelles 1982, 279, 430. We do not know when Philippe de Vitry broke with Charles of Navarre.

The marshall of Champagne, Jean de Conflans, had been sympathetic to the Navarrese, but his assassination on 22 February 1358 by the Parisian mob under Etienne Marcel, in the very presence of the dauphin Charles, had the effect of ending Navarrese sympathies in Champagne.[144]

On the night of 8–9 November 1357, Charles of Navarre was aided in escaping from his prison at the château of Arleux (dépt. Nord). He fled first to sympathetic supporters at Amiens, entering Paris on 29 November. His speeches played on the popular conviction that he had been arrested without cause and detained arbitrarily (Delachenal 1909–31, 1:323–26; R. Cazelles 1982, 288–90).

Early in 1358 both the University of Paris and the clergy of the city, strongly in favor of reform, showed their continued support for Charles of Navarre, although by May they had rallied to the dauphin Charles (Delachenal 1909–31, 1:349, 393), by then known as the regent.[145] Many more former supporters were alienated from the Navarrese camp after Charles of Navarre's famous speech of 15 June 1358, in which he went as far as to assert his pretensions to the throne of France: as he himself put it, he was of the *fleur-de-lis* on all sides, and if his mother had been a man, she would have been king of France (Delachenal 1909–31, 1:77–78, 418; cf. Gauvard 1982, 25). Although amusing on the face of it, Charles' observation made the most of the fact that his grandfather was King Louis X (d. 1316).

During the anti-royalist revolt known as the Jacquerie (28 May–10 June 1358), many nobles supported the king of Navarre over the regent, while larger cities, notably Reims, supported Etienne Marcel (R. Cazelles 1982, 315–16, 331–33; Bessen 1985).[146] Thus, in Reims, there was for a time contention between the archbishop, Jean de Craon, a close advisor and counselor of the regent, and the bourgeoisie, supporters of Etienne Marcel and the king of Navarre (R. Cazelles 1982, 333). But the dauphin had become more politically savvy in the course of the crisis years of 1357–58,[147] and most of the reformers quit their association with Charles of Navarre during the year 1358. Etienne Marcel was assassinated on 31 July 1358, and the regent returned to Paris on 3 August, marking a decisive resolution to the period of unrest since Poitiers (Delachenal 1909–31, 1:457–61). Finally, the treaty of Pontoise, 21 August 1359, ended hostilities between Charles of Navarre and the dauphin, at least long enough so that Charles of Navarre was out of the picture when the English again invaded France later in 1359 (Henneman 1976, 100–101).

F. *Machaut's* Confort d'Ami. As for Machaut, the *Confort* was completed probably in October 1357, when Charles was still held at Arleux (Delachenal 1909–31, 1:164–65; see also chap. 5.10). It seems questionable that the king would have had the time to pay much attention to Machaut's admonitions during the extremely busy time between his escape from prison and the treaty of Pontoise. Hoepffner noted that there is no mention of Charles of Navarre in Machaut's works after 1357 (1908–21, 1:xxxiii, 3:xiv), but we now have documentation showing that Machaut still had some dealings with Charles perhaps as late as 1361, and the *complainte Sire, a vous* (Cp7) has recently

---

[144] Henneman 1976, 67. The marshall of Normandy was also murdered on this occasion, see Delachenal 1909–31, 1:355–61; R. Cazelles 1982, 305.

[145] The dauphin Charles called himself regent from 14 March 1358 on (Delachenal 1909–31, 1:370–71).

[146] The towns deserted the opposition during the course of 1358 (Henneman 1976, 23).

[147] See Guillaume de Machaut 1982, 63 (comments by Gauvard).

been associated with this time as well. Perhaps it was only in 1361 that Charles
acknowledged Machaut's composition of the *Confort*.[148]

1.12.2. CA. 1361: GIFT OF A HORSE FROM CHARLES OF NAVARRE. A document summarized
by Castro (1953; see Gómez 1987, 116 n. 29) records that on 16 October 1361, Charles of
Navarre, then at Gavray (dépt. Manche), ordered the treasurer of Navarre in Pamplona to pay
Charles's squire Jehan Testedor fifty *écus de Jehan* (the *écu* struck during the reign of King
John) for a "haguenee preuse" [trusty hackney] given to Machaut.[149]

Günther first reported the document (1964, 195 n. 160; 1966). Anglès (1970, 196–97)
published it independently, concluding incredibly that Machaut had been in the service of
Charles of Navarre at Pamplona. Chailley disproved this, published a better reading of the
document, and went on to associate the ballade *Donnez, signeurs* (B26) with the incident
(Chailley 1973, 253–56).[150] Finally, Günther (1982, 115) again took up the question, rightly
pointing out that the text of the ballade is too vague to be associated convincingly with this
incident, and suggested that instead the *complainte Sire, a vous* (Cp7) may have prompted the
gift from the king of Navarre. This interpretation was advanced independently by Cerquiglini
(1985b, 128–29 n. 36), who dated Cp7 at the beginning of the year 1361. Fourrier (1979, 73,
87–89) dissented from this view, placing Cp7 early in 1365, for King Charles V. Wathey
(1994, 15–16) warns that the date 1361 should be regarded only as a *terminus*, because
creditors sometimes waited as long as four or five years before such a warrant was issued for
settlement of dues. See below, chap. 6.5, for earlier interpretations of this *complainte*.

13. Machaut's works of the 1350s. The Siege of Reims

The decade of the 1350s was a turbulent one for Machaut. With the death of
Bonne of Luxembourg in 1349 of the plague, his long service to the House of
Luxembourg ended. In the aftermath of the plague, Machaut temporarily
abandoned his role as the poet of the idealized love posturing at court in order to
leave a personal account of the plague at the opening of the *Jugement Navarre*.
And in the aftermath of the disastrous Battle of Poitiers (1356) and the ensuing
political crisis of 1357–58, Machaut's works appear for a time to be more
topical and less concerned with *fin' amors*, just as the later poets Froissart,
Deschamps, and Christine de Pizan reached a point when their response to the
state of the world around them seemed to require a more matter-of-fact and
socially committed kind of literary activity.[151]

Of Machaut's narrative poems, only *Jugement Navarre* and *Confort*, neither
poem an amorous *dit*, can be placed in the 1350s. Although a continuing stream
of lyrical poems still exploited images of the *Roman de la Rose* and the idealized
conceits of Courtly Love, the ballade *Mes dames qu'onques ne vi* (Lo250),
which exhibits a personal tone rare in Machaut's lyrics, may stem from this

---

148 Gómez has signaled a document showing that Charles had a manuscript of the *Confort*
copied in 1384; see the commentary to MS [24] in chap. 3.

149 A hackney was a gentle sort of horse ridden by ladies and churchmen. Perhaps the gift
hackney was the one that Machaut repeatedly bragged about in the *Voir Dit* (ll. 1011–12;
ed. P. Paris 1875, 43), still in 1363 "grosse et grasse et bien reposee" [big and fat and
well-rested]. See also ll. 1507–8 (P. Paris 1875, 70), ll. 3366–68 (143) and l. 3921
(163). On the literary significance of Machaut's equestrian terminology, see Cerquiglini
1985b, 126–30, 135; Deschaux 1979, 8–9; Roques 1982, 173.

150 Machabey (1955b, 2:40) already suggested that *Donnez, signeurs* was somehow associated
with Charles of Navarre (see also Reaney 1958b, 42; Poirion 1965, 194; Anglès 1970,
196).

151 In this regard, it is interesting that *Confort*, along with *Fonteinne*, Machaut's next *dit*,
provided rich sources mined for themes and even individual lines for many lyrics in the
productive period of the early 1360s (cf. Hoepffner [1908–21, vol. 3], whose notes to
Confort and *Fonteinne* outline borrowings in the lyrics). Cerquiglini (1985b, 165–66)
compares Machaut's use of real events as the background to the love story of the *Voir Dit*
with Deschamps's more refracted vision, placed in a myriad of individual ballades.

period as well. The political ballade set to music, *Donnez, seigneurs* (B26), has recently been dated 1360, in connection with the treaty of Brétigny (Arlt 1993, 59, reporting research of Dominik Sackmann). More specific dates, ca. 1358–59, can be proposed for four further works. The three motets *Christe / Veni* (M21), *Tu qui gregem / Plange* (M22), and *Felix virgo / Inviolata* (M23) all exhibit a similar style and were probably written at about the same time.[152] Two of the motets have topical references in their texts that suggest a reasonable dating for the whole group. By the late 1350s Machaut did not write amorous motets; the function of the genre had become more clearly defined, and the topical and polemical function of the motet, brilliantly exploited by Philippe de Vitry, was now taken up by Machaut for the first time since his earliest years.

Tu qui gregem / Plange (M22), which admonishes the dauphin Charles, is probably datable to the spring of 1358 (chap. 1.13.1), while *Christe / Veni* (M21) can be associated with the Siege of Reims (winter of 1359–60).[153] When the conditions of the Second Treaty of London were rejected by the French in May 1359 (Delachenal 1909–31, 2:87), it was clear that King John would remain a captive and that the war would be resumed. The dauphin Charles wrote to the city officials of Reims on 10 July 1359, warning them that the English would attack. After much delay the English reached the newly completed city walls in mid-November or early December. The ramparts proved impenetrable, and the siege was lifted around 11 January 1360.[154] *Felix virgo / Inviolata* (M23), a prayer to the Virgin for peace, is less clearly topical, although it can be associated with M21–22 on stylistic grounds.

It seems further that the *complainte A toi, Hanri* (Cp3) was composed in response to the Siege of Reims. The *complainte* henceforth was a genre often used by Machaut for topical and personal works (Hoepffner 1908–21, 1:xxiii–xxiv n. 1). Although Machaut's friend Henry remains unidentified, references in the poem to Machaut's serving guard duty on the walls of the city, to wearing a coat of mail, to the various extra taxes (one specifically for the king's ransom), and a reference that Wimsatt has associated with the captivity of King John (chap. 1.10.2a), all point to the period of the siege.[155]

1.13.1. 1358: MOTET 22. The motet *Tu qui gregem / Plange* (M22) refers in its texts to a leader who is ineffective. A pun on *dux:duc* (leader:duke) seems likely, and the motet is

---

[152] See Leech-Wilkinson (1989, 105–7) for a study of the stylistic relationship of the three motets. He suggests the possibility of disassociating the chronological positioning of the motets but ends up grouping them on stylistic grounds. For references to editions and translations of the texts, see chap. 7.3, commentaries to *Christe / Veni* (M21), *Tu qui gregem / Plange* (M22), and *Felix virgo / Inviolata* (M23).

[153] Ludwig associated the prayer to the Virgin Mary for peace in the motet *Felix virgo / Inviolata* (M23) with the Siege of Reims, which he erroneously placed in 1356 (due to a typographical error? see Ludwig 1930, 1:268 [=1924 ed., 231]), an error with long-lasting ramifications for subsequent chronologies of Machaut's works (Leech-Wilkinson 1989, 105–7).

[154] On the Siege of Reims, see Delachenal 1909–31, 2:145–61; Henneman 1976, 102–5. The English were again near Reims in August 1373, but did not attack the city (Delachenal 1909–31, 4:494–95). Emerson (1912) provides a detailed account of the progress of the English army.

[155] For a full translation and analysis of Cp3, including its influence on Chaucer, who was taken prisoner during the campaign and ransomed by King Edward III, see Wimsatt 1991b, 78–82, and below, chap. 6.5. Wilkins (1972, 15, 175 n. 150; 1984, 157–58) tentatively relates the ballade *On ne doit pas croire en augure* (Lo264; Wilkins no. 150) to the Siege of Reims.

probably to be taken as an exhortation to the duke of Normandy (the dauphin Charles) to effective leadership. A likely date is the grim time before August 1358, when the dauphin was the dupe of Robert le Coq, bishop of Laon, Etienne Marcel, provost of the merchants of Paris, and King Charles of Navarre. The motetus text seems specifically to refer to those evil influences: "Sua virtus augmentatur / Nunc patenter. / Te rexerunt imprudenter / Lice forte innocenter / Tui cari" [Their own power is being increased / Now quite openly. / You have been unwisely directed, / Perhaps even innocently / Dear one (trans. from the sound recording Telefunken 6.41125AS; see chap. 8.8)].

It is also possible that the text refers to the old counselors of the dauphin: in an ordinance of February 1358, deputies of the Estates still held to the reform ideals of the previous two years, blaming the problems of the country on the counselors of the dauphin, and calling for effective leadership (Delachenal 1909–31, 1:354). The tide was beginning to turn in the dauphin's favor after he left Paris in March 1358. Even so, he did not regain control of Paris until after the assassination of Etienne Marcel on 31 July 1358, and re-entered the city on 3 August (Delachenal 1909–31, 1:461). It seems likely that the motet was composed for a special occasion, perhaps for the Estates of Compiègne in May 1358 (cf. Delachenal 1909–31, 1:389–92). Markstrom (1989, 27–29) proposes the Estates General of Champagne at Provins (10 April 1358) as the occasion for the motet, and this, too, is reasonable. It is notable that Machaut felt free to address Charles in a familiar tone (tui cari). He was already an intimate of the future Charles V, whom he had no doubt had known since the latter's birth in 1338.

14. Ca. 1360–77. Works written for John, duke of Berry

It was not until the early 1360s that Machaut was again writing larger works for the House of France. It had become clear to the reformers that Charles of Navarre was not their representative of change, and in any case the dauphin had begun to rule more effectively, now with Guillaume de Melun, archbishop of Sens, firmly in control (R. Cazelles 1982, 402–10). With the restoration of peace and the return of the king, Machaut again began to cultivate the amorous *dit* as a genre.

King John II returned to France in 1360, and the political events of the treaties of Brétigny and Calais provided a frame for a new amorous *dit*, the *Fonteinne*, dedicated to John, duke of Berry (1340–1416).[156] Machaut had probably come to know John in the 1340s at the court of Bonne of Luxembourg.[157] John married Jeanne d'Armagnac at Carcassone on 24 June 1360, at a time when he already knew he would have to serve as a hostage of the English under the terms negotiated at Brétigny (Lehoux 1966–68, 1:155–56). Doubtless Machaut found John's fate, a young newlywed faced with indefinite exile across the sea, suitable for treatment in a narrative poem designed to comfort the duke's distress.

The poet may even have accompanied John to Calais. The itinerary of the

---

[156] The hypothesis that relates the *Fonteinne* with the departure of John of Berry as a hostage under the conditions of the treaty can be traced to Paulin Paris (1875, xxx). See also Hoepffner 1908–21, 3:xxii–xxx; Chichmaref 1909, 1:li–liii (with a different solution to the anagram in ll. 40–41); Coville 1949, 331; and Lehoux 1966–68, 1:163. Ehrhart (1974, 155–56, 197–99, 210–13; 1980b, 120–23; 1987, 131–32) contests the dedication to John of Berry, but I think unconvincingly. She rightly emphasizes some problems with the anagram (cf. also Cerquiglini 1985b, 236 n. 28) but gives too little credence to the fact that the date of the work, which can be established within fairly close bounds, supports the old argument, and that the historical asides and references fit well with the France of 1360. On the other hand, Ehrhart's interpretation of passages in *Fonteinne* that emphasize the chaotic state of the kingdom and tend to indict its rulers (1980b, 124), is historically significant, and recalls the admonitions to the regent Charles in the motet *Tu qui gregem / Plange* (M22); see chap. 1.13.1.

[157] John of Berry is mentioned with the other sons of King John and Bonne of Luxembourg in the *Prise* (ll. 793–98).

duke of Berry established by Lehoux (1966–68, 3:423–513) does not document the presence of the duke at Reims at any time during his life, but the details of the route he took during the September 1363 journey from Languedoc to the north have not been determined, and perhaps the duke passed by Reims on this occasion. He left Languedoc to travel north on 5 September 1360 and arrived at Boulogne-sur-Mer before the end of the month.[158] Final conferences were held at Calais on 9–24 October 1360, after which John signed the treaty, for the first time as duke of Berry and Auvergne (Lehoux 1966–68, 1:160–61). Although the itinerary of Lehoux does not document John's presence at St-Omer (dépt. Pas-de-Calais), Froissart reported that the hostages were subsequently gathered there.[159] Alternatively, perhaps Machaut met the duke at St-Omer, and accompanied him to the seaport Boulogne-sur-Mer or to Calais as he describes at the end of the *Fonteinne*.[160] Perhaps the gift of jewels mentioned in ll. 2836–38 may be considered the patron's advance payment on the composition of the new *dit*. Further, Arlt (1993, 59) reports research linking the composition of the occasional ballade with music, *Donnez, signeurs* (B26), to this occasion.

The events of October 1360 may also have provided a moment when three great poets of the day—Machaut, Chaucer, and Froissart—could have met, as Wimsatt has recently speculated. Chaucer carried a message from Calais to London for Prince Lionel sometime in October, and Froissart may have set off for his first trip to England at this same time.[161]

The young duke of Berry may soon have obtained a copy of the *Fonteinne*. He enjoyed safe-conduct to France on various occasions in the following years, first in May 1361. He is again found in London in December 1362. In May 1363 the hostages were delivered to Calais, in the expectation that a treaty resolving their fate would be ratified. They were still waiting in September, when John's brother Louis, duke of Anjou, against his word refused to return to Calais after a pilgrimage to Notre-Dame de Boulogne, where he was reunited with his young wife Marie de Châtillon (Delachenal 1909–31, 2:346–47). The hostages were forced to return to England on 3 January 1364. This time the duke of Berry was accompanied by his father King John II, who went in place of his son Louis, still recusant.[162]

The king fell ill and died in London on 8 April 1364, and John of Berry returned to France probably at the end of the same year.[163] He returned to

---

[158] Lehoux 1966–68, 1:159–60, 3:429. The dates of the itinerary given by Machabey (1955b, 1:53 n. 146) do not make sense.

[159] Hoepffner 1908–21, 3:xxvii–xxviii. Money from all over France for the down payment on King John's ransom was collected at the abbey of St-Bertin at St-Omer (Henneman 1976, 113).

[160] On Machaut's unflattering description of the town Boulogne-sur-Mer, see Hoepffner 1908–21, 3:xxvi–xxviii, and the comments in Eichelberg 1935, 74–75; and Cerquiglini 1985b, 131.

[161] For the full development of these possibilities, see Emerson 1912, 357–61; Crow/Olson 1966, 19–21; and especially Wimsatt 1991b, 78, 82–83, 96, 180.

[162] R. Cazelles (1982, 447–52) provides a brilliant explanation of King John's rationale for returning to England. Wimsatt suggests that the *Lay de Confort* is a lament of Jeanne d'Armagnac, penned by Machaut in the early 1360s and sent to John of Berry in London; see chap. 7.3 on the date of *S'onques* (L17/12).

[163] The duke of Berry was back in France at least by 4 June 1365 (Delachenal 1909–31, 3:218).

London in January 1366 for the final resolution of the hostage issue and by February had definitively returned to France.[164]

An entry in an account of 1371 provides another point of contact between Machaut and John of Berry, although we do not know any of the details of this business affair (chap. 1.14.1b). John of Berry maintained an enthusiasm for the works of Machaut long after the poet's death, for in the 1390s he had a large Machaut manuscript copied, known today as MS E [7]. The readings in this manuscript, often corrupt in its text and transmitting non-authentic extra voices for some musical works, show nevertheless that many works of Machaut, poetry as well as music, continued in active circulation long after the author's death.

1.14.1. MACHAUT AND JOHN OF BERRY

a. References in the *Fonteinne Amoureuse*. The association of the duke of Berry with the young nobleman in the *Fonteinne* is based on the anagram at the beginning of the work, ll. 40–41, and the following three passages:

i. *Fonteinne* (ll. 41–42). "Avec mon cuer y a chier gage, / Car mes corps en est en ostage" [Along with my heart, he has a good pledge / For my body is hostage to this task (trans. Palmer 1993a, 93)]. Machaut is referring here to his own heart and body held in hostage for his patron—l. 32, "Celui pour qui je fais ce livre" [The man for whom I'm making this book (trans. Palmer 1993a, 91)]—but the terminology seems significant.

ii. *Fonteinne* (ll. 1157–60). "Brief, tant estoit de bel arroy / Qu'il sambloit estre fils a roy / Ou sires souverains naïs / De la terre et tout le païs" [In brief, he was of such noble bearing / That he seemed a king's son, / Or born the sovereign lord / Of the land and all the country (trans. Palmer 1993a, 153)].

iii. *Fonteinne* (ll. 1885–86). "Car tant estoit de bel arroy / Qu'estre sambloit bien fils a roy" [For his demeanor was so impressive / That he seemed very much a king's son (trans. Palmer 1993a, 189)].

iv. *Fonteinne* (ll. 2767–847). The lover explains to the narrator in this passage that he must depart on the morrow, and the narrator accompanies him to a town on the sea, where he sings a rondeau of farewell to his lady, and then departs.

b. 1371 Account. An account of 15 October 1371 indicates that John, duke of Berry paid 10 *livres* of Tours to one Person de Suygnon, cousin of "Mestre Guille de Machaut," in recompense for the intervention of Person in a business affair between John of Berry and Guillaume (Mas Latrie 1877a, 188 [as "Person de Fuygnon"]; 1877b, xvii n. 2; Machabey 1955b, 1:66–67 and nn. 182–83).[165] Chichmaref (1909, 1:li), followed by Poirion (1965, 195) attaches the document to the acquisition of MS E, a hypothesis that now can be disputed in view of the late date of that manuscript. Hoepffner (1908–21, 1:xxxix) is more cautious, and suggests that the document of 1371 may refer to late remuneration for *Fonteinne*; Hoepffner considers MS E itself too faulty to have been a manuscript offered by Machaut to a patron. He further suggests (3:xxviii) that this reference referred to a second Machaut manuscript that had been noted by Delisle (1868–81, 3:193) in the library of the duke of Berry. Ludwig (1926–54, 2:11a* n. 1), however, shows that Delisle had later changed his mind (Delisle 1907, 2:268* nos. 282–83), and that actually MS E was the only Machaut manuscript referred to in early fifteenth-century inventories of the duke of Berry's library.

15. Machaut and King Charles V. Other patrons of the 1360s

Another son of Bonne of Luxembourg and King John was even more important

---

[164] Besides the references given above, see the account of this entire episode in Lehoux 1966–68, 1:165–78. The information in Hoepffner (1908–21, 3:xxx) is incomplete.

[165] Machabey expresses some doubt as to the year (which may be 1372), and corrects the erroneous shelfmark given by Mas Latrie and reproduced by Chichmaref and Hoepffner, as well as by Wilkins (1983b, 279 n. 4), *recte* Archives nationales, KK 251, fol. 72r, art. 6. Lehoux (1966–68, 1:xiii) describes the source as "Chambre aux deniers du duc de Berri (1er juin 1370–31 décembre 1373)."

as a patron of Machaut, namely the dauphin Charles (b. 1338, r. 1364–1380).[166] Machaut must have been acquainted with Charles at the court of Bonne of Luxembourg virtually from birth. As mentioned above (chap. 1.12a), Machaut's rondeau *Cinc, un, trese* (R6) may have been written for the 8 April 1350 marriage of Charles and Jeanne de Bourbon.

We have already detailed Machaut's admonitions to the young and inexperienced regent of 1358 in the motet *Tu qui gregem / Plange* (M22; chap. 1.13.1). In 1361 a document from Reims indicates that Charles was a houseguest of Machaut during a visit to mediate a conflict between the archbishop, Jean de Craon, and the secular authorities of the city. In the course of the early 1360s, several passages in the *Voir Dit* (written 1363–65) further show that Machaut was a favorite of Charles.[167]

The *Voir Dit* [True Story] is a love story that waxes and then wanes, carried on largely in the exchange of lyrics and letters between Guillaume and a young admirer whom he dubbed "Toute Belle" [All Beautiful]. The question of the degree of "truth" of the *Voir Dit* has been debated by philologists for over one hundred years. Currently, the most widespread view is that Toute Belle and the love story are entirely fabricated. Yet even if this extreme position is taken, it is evident that Machaut took great pains to give the work at least the appearance of truth, and that the many historical events—some with verifiable dates supplied—and personal references recorded in it have nearly the force of documentary evidence (see the discussion of autobiography in chap. 5.13).

In several passages in the *Voir Dit*, Machaut touts his relationship with his patrons, even complaining of the (presumably welcome) difficulties of balancing their various demands. Besides his association with the dauphin Charles, who is almost a major character in the poem, he specifically mentions Robert, duke of Bar.[168] Both the 1361 document of a visit of the dauphin and the references in the *Voir Dit* suggest that Machaut's house—documented in the 1370s in a location outside the cloister (chap. 1.18.1a)—was a favorite hostel for cultivated aristocratic visitors to Reims.

Several other aristocrats who patronized Machaut in the 1360s are not specifically named in the *Voir Dit*. In the *complainte Sire, a vous* (Cp7; ca. 1361), Machaut mentions Jean de Melun, the count of Tancarville, in a tone too familiar for one not well acquainted with the count. Amadeus VI, the Green Count of Savoy (b. 1334, r. 1343–1383), purchased a *roman* from Machaut—most likely a Machaut manuscript—in the spring of 1368, during the magnificent festivities at Paris honoring Lionel, duke of Clarence, then on his way to Milan to marry Violante Visconti. We know that Froissart was in attendance, and this provides a likely occasion for a meeting of the two poets. Finally, Robert d'Alençon, count of Perche (r. 1361–1377), also obtained a Machaut manuscript—though apparently not one authorized by Machaut—around the same time, in the late 1360s or early 1370s (MS **J** [16]).

Machaut mentions the coronation of Charles V on 19 May 1364 in the *Prise* (ll. 805–7). Not surprisingly, the reference seems to be the recollection of an eyewitness (Chichmaref 1909, 1:lxiv).[169] The notion that Machaut composed his Mass specifically for the coronation ceremonies goes back at least as far as a

---

166 Machaut praised Charles in the *Prise*, ll. 799–804.

167 Hoepffner (1908–21, 1:xxxvii–xxxviii) provides a general discussion of Machaut and Charles V, based primarily on literary references in the *Voir Dit*.

168 Cerquiglini (1985b, 140–41) provides interesting commentary on the passages mentioning Charles of Normandy and the duke of Bar.

169 On duties of the canons at the coronation, see Machabey 1955b, 1:63.

library catalogue of 1769, which does at least qualify the claim: "Messe mise en musique à 4 parties, et que l'on prétend avoir été chanté au sacre de Charles V" [Mass set to music in four parts, which is claimed to have been sung at the coronation of Charles V].[170] Recently, Leech-Wilkinson (1990c) and A.W. Robertson (1992) have provided strong evidence that the Mass was actually composed for a foundation made by Guillaume and Jean de Machaut for the commemoration of their deaths. Several important leaders were present for the coronation of Charles V, many of them patrons of Machaut or at least mentioned by Machaut in his writings, including Philip the Bold, duke of Burgundy, Robert, duke of Bar, and Pierre de Lusignan, king of Cyprus (Delachenal 1909–31, 3:68–69, 101).

Finally, the Holy Roman Emperor Charles IV (b. 1316, r. 1346–1378), son of John of Luxembourg, should be mentioned. Although Machaut praises the emperor in the *Prise* (ll. 763–78, 987–1059; see Hoepffner 1908–21, 1:xviii–xix), there is no evidence of any particular service of Machaut to Charles IV; throughout most of the time of Machaut's earlier association with the House of Luxembourg, Charles had remained in Prague.[171]

1.15.1. MACHAUT AT REIMS IN THE 1360S

a. 1361: the dauphin lodges at Machaut's house in Reims. Excepting the references in the *Voir Dit*,[172] the only documentary proof of an association between the dauphin Charles and Machaut comes from commentary in the *Mémoires* of Jehan Rogier (*F:RS 1629*, fol. 155v, written 1617–19, published in Varin 1843–48, 3:206a n.) that refers to a visit of Charles to Machaut in Reims in December of 1361.[173] "Et se recongnoist par aucunes lettres missives que, au mois de décembre suyvant [1361], mondict seigneur duc de Normandye vint en ladicte ville de Reims, où il estant, il manda aux eschevins dudict Reims l'aller veoir en son logis chez maistre Guillyaume de Machault, où estans…"[174] [And let it be known by certain letters that in the month of December following, my aforementioned lord the duke of Normandy came to the aforementioned city of Reims where he was staying, and he commanded the aldermen[175] of Reims to come to see him at his lodging at master Guillaume de Machaut's, where he was staying].

The dauphin Charles was trying to mediate a dispute between the archbishop of Reims, Jean de Craon, and the town government. Encroachments had been made upon the archbishop's château in the late 1350s by the construction of fortifications against the English. The damage had been caused by orders of the captain of the city, Gaucher de Châtillon, whose vigilance in constructing the walls had saved the city during the 1359–60 siege. Jean de Craon wished to regain the control that archbishops of Reims had formerly had over the appointment of this important officer. In essence, the archbishop was fighting a fundamental change in the administrative structure of the town (R. Cazelles 1982, 103). The dispute was not resolved until 18 April 1364, with no one receiving absolute satisfaction.[176]

b. 1362: Machaut taxed for his benefice at St-Quentin. An article in an account of clerical tenths levied in 1362, for the diocese of Noyon, chapter of St-Quentin, lists a tax on 40

---

[170] Ludwig 1926–54, 2:8* n. 2; see also Ludwig 1925, 420–21 n. 2; 1926–54, 4:1; Leech-Wilkinson 1990c, 8–9; A.W. Robertson 1992, 102–3.

[171] The incredible claims of Vachulka (1982) should be dismissed. See also Nejedlý (1904; 1905–6) on Machaut's influence at the court of the emperor.

[172] The *complainte Sire, a vous* (Cp7), formerly attached to Charles V, has more recently been associated with King Charles of Navarre (chap. 1.12.2).

[173] More recently, Leech-Wilkinson (1990c, 5 n. 18) cites *F:RS 1628*, fol. 236r.

[174] Cited in Hoepffner 1908–21, xxv, xxxvii; Machabey 1955b, 1:56.

[175] Desportes (1979, 505) indicates that twelve aldermen served the city of Reims.

[176] R. Cazelles 1982, 430, 441–42, 455–56; for more on the proceedings, see Desportes 1979, 564–68, and the references therein to the documents published by Varin.

livres for *G. de Machau* (Machabey 1955b, 1:30, n. 60, 2:173, citing Longnon 1908). See also chap. 1.6.1e above.

c. Charles V and the *Voir Dit*. Several passages in the *Voir Dit* refer to the dauphin Charles (see Machabey 1955b, 1:56–62; Imbs 1991, 54).

i. ll. 1529–31 (ed. P. Paris 1875, 71; see also 389–90 nn. xviii–xix), early May 1363. Machaut indicates that he has been commanded to go to a *seigneur* who has no equal in France, except for one, doubtless referring to the dauphin Charles and his father the king. The visit was presumably to Crécy-en-Brie (today Crécy-la-Chapelle, south of Meaux, dépt. Seine-et-Marne).

ii. letter 13 (ed. P. Paris 1875, 118), late May 1363. In this letter Guillaume writes his young correspondent Toute Belle that "Monseigneur" (i.e., the dauphin Charles) had informed him by letter that he should come to him after he had finished his novena (a nine-day period of devotion).

iii. ll. 3104–20 (ed. P. Paris 1875, 131–32), late May 1363. After visiting Toute Belle in Paris, Guillaume returned to the dauphin, where he was indulged with sporting activities normally reserved for the nobility.[177]

iv. ll. 3151–56 (ed. P. Paris 1875, 136), early June 1363. Immediately after the insertion of letter 18 from Toute Belle, Machaut picks up the narrative: "Je reçus ceste lettre cy / Droit en la ville de Crecy. / Là fu le duc de Normandie, / Mon droit Signeur, quoy que nuls die. / Car fais suis de sa nourriture, / Et suis sa droite créature" [I received this letter in the town of Crécy. The duke of Normandy was there; he is my true lord, no matter what anyone says. For I have been made by his beneficence and I am his devoted servant].[178]

v. ll. 3253–59 (ed. P. Paris 1875, 139), early June 1363. Guillaume wished to leave Crécy in order to visit Toute Belle a second time but was kept waiting against his will for three or four days by "Monseigneur," i.e., the dauphin, in order to provide him with comfort and amusement.

vi. ll. 4934–5467 (ed. P. Paris 1875, 213–32), mid-August 1363. During Guillaume's first dream sequence in the second part of the *Voir Dit*, a courtly entourage is playing the popular game of "le Roi qui ne ment" [the king who does not lie]. In ll. 4990–5243, Guillaume questions the king, who responds in ll. 5254–461. The sort of advice Guillaume offers the king (ll. 4990–5117; ed. P. Paris 1875, 215–20; cf. 397 n. lvi) makes it likely that Machaut is referring here to the dauphin. By the time Machaut wrote this passage (early in 1364?), King John had doubtless departed once more for England and Charles was again serving as regent of France.

vii. Letter 35 (ed. P. Paris 1875, 266), dated 17 October [1363]. Guillaume planned a trip for 1 November to St-Quentin, and from there a visit to the duke of Normandy.

viii. Letter 36 (ed. P. Paris 1875, 268), dated 28 October [1363]. Toute Belle repeats the information of letter 35 given above, item vii.

ix. Letter 37 (ed. P. Paris 1875, 276), dated 3 November [1363]. Guillaume writes Toute Belle that he did not travel to St-Quentin because of enemy companies in the Beauvaisis.

x. ll. 7580–89 (ed. P. Paris 1875, 306–7), early February 1364?[179] Machaut went to see "un mien signeur, / Mille fois de l'autre gringneur" [one of my lords, a thousand times greater than the other], presumably the duke of Normandy, who in this passage causes further estrangement between Guillaume and Toute Belle.

xi. Letter 43 (ed. P. Paris 1875, 346), dated 10 October [1364]. Toute Belle seeks to defend herself from the charges that had been leveled by "uns bien grans sires et pluseurs

---

[177] Cerquiglini (1985b, 140) provides interesting commentary on this passage. In later years there was a royal ordinance forbidding non-nobles to hunt (De Winter 1985, 21).

[178] P. Paris (1875, 136 n. 3) suggests that with the words "de sa nourriture," Machaut wished to indicate that he was a member of the household of Charles. Yet the phrase could mean simply that Charles had given Machaut money, or that he had been raised in the same way that Charles had been, i.e., at the court of Bonne of Luxembourg. Cf. also chap. 2.1.1j. P. Paris (1875, 189–90 n. xix) indicates that King John II was also at Crécy-en-Brie in June 1363, but see Leech-Wilkinson 1993b, 115–16 n. 50.

[179] Dated in Leech-Wilkinson 1993b, 128. Machabey (1955b, 1:61), who notes that the chronology is not sure from this point on, suggests ca. 20 December 1363 as a date for this event.

autres" [a very great lord and many others], a reference to the accusations made presumably by the regent during the game of "le Roi qui ne ment" (item vi above).

d. 1364: Machaut pays property taxes. This new document was discovered independently by Leech-Wilkinson and A.W. Robertson. Taxes are assessed for a property owned by "Guillemete de Machaut" in the parish of the collegiate church of St-Timothée in Reims.[180] An exact date has not been established.

1.15.2. MACHAUT'S PATRONS OF THE 1360S

a. References in the *Voir Dit* to Robert, duke of Bar. Machaut refers three times in the *Voir Dit* to the duke of Bar.

    i. letter 33 (ed. P. Paris 1875, 259), dated 9 October [1363]. Cf. chap. 1.10.2d item iv.

    ii. letter 35 (ed. P. Paris 1875, 262), dated 17 October [1363]. "Car monseigneur le duc de Bar et pluseurs autres seigneurs ont esté en ma maison: si y avoit tant d'alans et de venans, et me couchoie si tart et me levoie si matin, que je ne l'ay peu amender" [for my lord the duke of Bar and many other lords were at my house, and there was so much coming and going, and I went to bed so late and got up so early, that I could not write].

    iii. a further indirect reference appears near the end of letter 35 (ed. P. Paris 1875, 265). "li estranges qui estoient à Reins" [the strangers who were at Reims]. Items ii and iii are discussed by Cerquiglini (1985b, 140–41).

b. 1361: Machaut and Jean de Melun, count of Tancarville. Jean II de Melun, count of Tancarville, was a very important royal officer during the reigns of John II and Charles V. Captured with King John at Poitiers in 1356, he accompanied the king to England, but returned to France several times as a messenger. Jean de Melun carried the second treaty of London to the dauphin, and after its rejection, was frequently in the dauphin's council during the invasion of Edward III, from December 1359 until February 1360. He assisted at the peace talks at Brétigny (1–8 May 1360), and served as a hostage under the terms of the treaty. In 1361, he was back in France (Chichmaref 1909, 1:lxv). With two other *seigneurs,* he brought the body of King John back to France in 1364 and continued to serve King Charles V.[181] Machaut mentions the count of Tancarville in the *complainte Sire, a vous fais ceste clamour* (Cp7). The most recent views of the date of this work place it early in 1361 (chap. 1.12.2).

c. 1368: Machaut and Amadeus VI of Savoy. A document of 5 May 1368 at Paris records payment of 300 gold francs, along with an additional favor of 10 francs, from Amadeus VI, the Green Count of Savoy (b. 1334, r. 1343–1383) to Machaut for a *roman* (document published in Edmunds 1971; Cordey 1911, 185 n. 3). Some previous discussions of this document give the date as 1371 (Hoepffner 1908–21, 1:xxvii; Machabey 1955b, 1:66). Machabey (1955b, 1:66) goes on to attach MS K [15], dated 1371, to this document, a suggestion that Poirion (1965, 195) repeats, and Earp (1983, 34–35 n. 75; 1989, 476 and n. 31) disputes. The discussions in Cordey (1911, 184–85) and Cox (1967, 248) verify the 1368 date. Festivities at Paris in honor of Lionel, duke of Clarence (1338–1368), en route to Milan for his short-lived marriage to the thirteen-year-old Violante Visconti, provided the occasion for the meeting of Machaut and the Green Count. Froissart was present on the same occasion. The Green Count had left Paris on 19 April, was soon joined by the duke of Clarence, and the company reached Chambéry on 11 or 12 May (Cox 1967, 249); thus presumably the document accounts for an earlier out-of-pocket payment.

d. Robert d'Alençon, count of Perche. Robert, fourth son of Charles II of Valois, count of Alençon and brother of King Philip VI, ruled as count of Perche 1361–1377.[182] For the inscription attaching MS J to Robert d'Alençon, see chap. 3 MS [16].

16. Machaut and Pierre de Lusignan, king of Cyprus

Machaut recounts the career of Pierre I de Lusignan, king of Cyprus (b. 1329, r. 1359–1316 January 1369), in the verse chronicle *La Prise d'Alexandre*, his

---

180 AMR 2G 191, pièce 1, fol. 141r (cited in Leech-Wilkinson 1990c, 5 n. 20; A.W. Robertson 1992, 135).

181 Delachenal 1909–31, 2:58, 83–84, 195, 205, 319–20; R. Cazelles 1982 passim.

182 Fourrier 1979, 76–77; cf. also Machabey 1955b, 1:55 n. 158.

last major work, possibly written on the command of Charles V.[183] When the abbé Lebeuf rediscovered Machaut's works in the 1740s, his first interest was the *Prise*. It was primarily Machaut the historian that engaged eighteenth-century amateurs of medieval French literature.

In 1362 Pierre announced that he would lead a crusade to the Holy Land, a project that King John II enthusiastically supported. Pope Urban V (r. 1362–1370) proclaimed the crusade on 31 March 1363 at Avignon, and gave the cross to John and Pierre.[184] Pierre then accompanied King John, named the leader of the new crusade, to Paris (Delachenal 1909–31, 2:345). On the death of King John in London in April 1364, the pope named Pierre as the head of the crusade.[185] After the king's body was returned to France, Pierre was a member of the funeral cortège in Paris on 5 May 1364 (Delachenal 1909–31, 3:18–19; R. Cazelles 1982, 452). On 9 May Pierre accompanied the dauphin Charles, Philip the Bold, and Louis d'Anjou on the journey from St-Denis to Reims, where the coronation of the new king took place on 19 May. Pierre also took part, with Robert, duke of Bar, in the tournament held in the court of the royal palace on the Ile de la Cité, 27–28 May 1364 (Delachenal 1909–31, 3:101).

Pierre's 1364 tour of Europe, undertaken to raise funds and to enlist help for his planned crusade, yielded much good will but little money.[186] Two works of Machaut are apparently connected to Pierre de Lusignan's tour, as "courtly compliments to a grand lady who might help Pierre gain support for his projects" (Wimsatt 1970, 50): (1) the *complainte Mon cuer, m'amour ma dame souvereinne* (Cp6), with the acrostic "MARGVERITE / PIERRE," which Wimsatt has dated after the coronation of Charles V on 19 May 1364 (1970, 47, 49; see below, chap. 6.5); and (2) the *Dit de la Marguerite*, written in 1366 or later for Pierre and his ally Marguerite of Flanders.[187]

Pierre left 27 June 1365 from Venice for the short-lived conquest of Alexandria. The city fell on 10 October 1365. After sacking the city, news that Moslem reinforcements were approaching forced the troops to withdraw to Cyprus on 16 October. Pierre's relationship with his vassals in Cyprus became strained late in the 1360s, and he was stabbed to death in his bed in the royal palace at Nicosia by his own nobles, with the complicity of his younger brothers.[188]

---

[183] See Tyson 1986. Perhaps Charles V knew something of the chronicles of Froissart, who served as secretary to Queen Philippa of England from 1361 to 1369, and wished to have a historical work on the illustrious career of Pierre de Lusignan from his court poet Machaut. Lanoue (1985) argues that Machaut intended the *Prise* as an epic poem celebrating a great crusading knight who vainly sought Christian unity against the enemies of Christendom. On the date of the assassination of Pierre (16 not 17 January), see Edbury 1980, 223–24; for other historical studies, see chap. 5.17. Calin (1974, 203–26) provides an excellent overview of the *Prise*. This might be the moment to mention a theory that Machaut authored an early version of the *Roman de Mélusine*, or *Histoire des Lusignan* of Jean d'Arras, ordered by John, duke of Berry in 1392 (R.J. Nolan 1974).

[184] For an historical overview with further references, see Housley 1986, 40–42.

[185] Delachenal 1909–31, 3:245; R. Cazelles 1982, 436; Housley 1986, 42–44.

[186] Delachenal 1909–31, 3:494–96. Machaut's description of the itinerary of Pierre de Lusignan in 1364 is in *Prise*, ll. 875–1623 (see Mas Latrie 1852, 237–45; Wimsatt 1970, 42–47). Machaut's detailed knowledge of central Europe displayed in the *Prise* doubtless derives from experiences at the side of John of Luxembourg in the 1320s and 1330s (chap. 1.5.3d).

[187] Machaut's *Marguerite* began a long tradition of "marguerite" poems in French and English; see chap. 5.14 and 5.18.

[188] A full account of the murder, with recent bibliography, is provided in Edbury 1980.

Hoepffner (1908–21, 1:xli–xliii) argues that Machaut did not seem to have had any personal relationship with Pierre, while Chichmaref (1909, 1:xvi–xviii) finds the description of Pierre's 1364 tour of Europe in the *Prise* exact enough to imply that Machaut did indeed know him. Machaut's account of Pierre is more detailed beginning with the coronation of Charles V in May 1364, indicating perhaps that Machaut had some personal knowledge of Pierre from that point on (Chichmaref 1909, 1:lxiv; Wimsatt 1970, 44; Calin 1974, 212–13). He was a popular prince, celebrated by both Froissart and Chaucer, and the memory of his noble exploits surely fired Machaut's imagination as he wrote the *Prise*.

17. Machaut and Philip the Bold, duke of Burgundy

When Philippe de Rouvre, the last Capetian duke of Burgundy, died of the plague at the age of fifteen on 21 November 1361, King John II took over and ruled the duchy through his lieutenant Jean de Melun, the count of Tancarville (Delachenal 1909–31, 2:287–91, 345; Henneman 1976, 215–16). John's son Philip, duke of Touraine (1342–1404), was formally, though secretly, named duke of Burgundy on 6 September 1363 (Delachenal 1909–31, 2:355), causing another crisis with Charles of Navarre (who also had pretensions to Burgundy). On 31 May 1364, the new king, Charles V, publicly confirmed the donation of Burgundy to his younger brother Philip (Delachenal 1909–31, 3:101–2; R. Cazelles 1982, 411).

Machaut must have known Philip—one of the children of Bonne of Luxembourg and King John—from birth. He was celebrated in France as the brave young son who did not desert his father's side at the Battle of Poitiers (hence the sobriquet *le Hardi*), and accompanied his father to England into exile in 1357. In the *Prise* Machaut characterizes him as "Phelippe, / Qui moult en armes se delite" (ll. 797–98) [Philip, who delights much in arms].

In letter 33 of the *Voir Dit* (ed. P. Paris 1875, 259), dated 9 October [1363], Machaut indicates that members of the king's entourage ["des gens du roi"] were lodging at his house (chap. 1.10.2d item iv); the presence of Philip the Bold at Reims is documented for October 1363, and surely Machaut renewed his acquaintance with the young duke on this occasion.

Wimsatt (1970, 54–58) has suggested that the *Fleur de Lis et Marguerite* can be connected to Philip the Bold, who married Marguerite of Flanders (1350–1405) at Ghent on 19 June 1369 (Delachenal 1909–31, 3:499–509). This is the latest work of Machaut to which a specific occasion and date can be attached. Surely Philip had a manuscript of Machaut's works in his library; one appears in the 1405 inventory of the library of his wife Marguerite of Flanders, possibly the manuscript described more fully in later Burgundian inventories, but now lost (chap. 3 MS [8]).

18. 1369–77. Last years

In the *Fonteinne* and *Voir Dit*, we see a portrait of the aging poet in the 1360s. A master of his craft, a master of the demands and conceits of his several patrons, his services were prized by the elite. He occupied much of his time with the various levels of transmission of his works, the everyday circulation of individual lyrics, both with and without music, the copying of individual narrative poems for various patrons, and finally, the copying of comprehensive manuscripts from his personal exemplar of all his works. In his last years, there was apparently a constant demand for manuscripts of his complete works.

With the death of his younger brother Jean probably in 1372, Machaut was reminded of his own mortality. His poetic production was mostly broken off, and now the arrangement of his oeuvre into a definitive collection seems to have been his main concern. He settled on a revised organization of the works, set down and copied as the index of MS A [5], before the redaction of the codex was begun (Earp 1983, 51–87; 1989, 482–87). As the need arose, he composed a few more works specifically to round off and articulate the new collection,[189] and finally he wrote the *Prologue* to introduce the book, perhaps after 1372. Machaut's active role in the production of codices, particularly MS A, has been studied by S.J. Williams (1969), Earp (1983, chap. 2; 1989), and Huot (1987).

The problem of the ordering of the works within the manuscripts continued to occupy the author, and even MS A, which shows signs of a struggle between the prescriptions of the index and the practical problems of the scribes entrusted with executing the instructions, cannot be regarded as definitive. The order of works in the posthumous MS F-G [6] may come closer to Machaut's definitive order, but even there one can find a few practical difficulties in the arrangement of the varied genres, suggesting that the problems of organization were never finally resolved (Earp 1983, 99–101). Finally, the late MS E [7], copied ca. 1390 for John, duke of Berry, provides an example of a complete-works manuscript collected and edited according to principles very different from the author's.

A. *Anniversary foundation of Guillaume and Jean de Machaut.* Machaut died in April 1377 and was buried in the cathedral of Reims, in the same tomb as his brother Jean. Although Machaut's will has not survived, a brass epitaph affixed to a pier at Reims cathedral at least as late as the seventeenth century provides us with some indication of its terms. We learn that a very generous anniversary foundation perpetuated the memory of the two brothers.[190]

Machabey (1955b, 1:69–70, 2:114–15) suggests that Machaut's *Messe de Nostre Dame* was composed for the foundation,[191] an idea that Leech-Wilkinson (1990c, 8–13) develops further. More recently, Anne W. Robertson (1992) has proved that Machaut's Mass is liturgically suitable for Reims cathedral, in that Machaut's *cantus firmi* are chants appropriate for Marian feasts there. Further, the work is musically proper to Reims, in that musical variants found in Reims sources are seen in Machaut's *cantus firmi* for the Kyrie and Sanctus. The Mass was sung as the Saturday Mass for the Virgin, perhaps thirty-five to forty times per year, at the altar of the Rouelle, an oratory dedicated to the Virgin on the right side of the rood screen near the center of the nave.[192] The Machaut brothers' endowment—300 florins, a significant sum—augmented the Saturday Mass of the Virgin that had already been established in 1341 at the altar of the Rouelle by Jean de Vienne, archbishop of Reims from 1334 until 1351. King Charles V also made two foundations at this important altar, one probably in 1364, after his coronation, and one in 1380, the year of his death. Haggh notes that such endowed Marian Masses "were thought to ensure the salvation of the soul after death and, in particular, to reduce the amount of time spent in purgatory" (1988, 1:503–26, esp. 508).

---

[189] For instance, Earp (1989, 487 n. 44) argues that the function of *Vezci les biens* is essentially codicological, composed specifically for a point of internal articulation in MS A.

[190] On anniversary foundations, see n. 124 above. Jean de Machaut served as the chapter's officer of the *anniversaria* in 1357 and 1358 (chap. 1.11.1i).

[191] This possibility is also cautiously reported in Hoppin 1978b, 419–20; see also Haggh 1988, 523.

[192] The Rouelle, a round stone in the floor of the cathedral, marked the site of the martyrdom of Bishop Nicasius of Reims in A.D. 406 or 407 (A.W. Robertson 1992, 126–31). On the frequency of performance of the Mass, see A.W. Robertson 1992, 133, 135.

It was probably in the early 1360s that Machaut composed his *Messe de Nostre Dame* for the foundation (Leech-Wilkinson 1990c, 8; A.W. Robertson 1992, 133; Leech-Wilkinson 1993a, 45, 48). During the remainder of the lives of the brothers, the Machaut Mass would have been performed as a Mass to the Virgin, hence its title, known from the rubric in MS **Vg** [3], a manuscript copied in the early 1370s. After the death of Jean de Machaut in 1372, the addition of a prayer recited for the dead effectively transformed Machaut's Mass into a Requiem Mass. A.W. Robertson (1992, 120, 125, 132 n. 96) suggests that this change of function may explain the lack of the specific association of the Mass with Our Lady in subsequent manuscripts that transmit the Mass, i.e., MSS **A**, **F-G**, and **E**.

The original endowment of the Machaut brothers was augmented subsequently, possibly on several occasions, and others may have had the Machaut Mass performed for their memory as well, even as late as 1411 (A.W. Robertson 1992, 125, 135). The last document to mention Machaut's Mass, from the year 1431, refers to its appearance in a manuscript now lost (chap. 3, MS [60]).

1.18.1. MACHAUT AT REIMS IN THE 1370S

a. 1372: Machaut's house. A document that includes a listing of the ten houses of canons situated outside the confines of the cloister mentions the house of Guillaume de Machaut: *"Item, domum in qua inhabitat Guillermus de Machaudio, sitam prope Pourcelettam, et retro domum dicti magistri Stephani"*[193] [Item, the house which Guillaume de Machaut inhabits, situated near the Pourcelette and behind the house of the aforementioned master Stephan]. Scholars have placed the current location of the house, with its courtyard and garden, at 4–10 rue d'Anjou and 25–37 rue des Fuseliers.[194] Documents of the eighteenth century establish the large size of the house, and we know that Machaut was able to lodge very important visitors and their retenues in it (chap. 1.10.2d item iv; 1.15.1a). We do not know how long Machaut had lived in the house before 1372.[195]

b. 1375: Machaut absent from Reims. Machaut was absent on 29 December 1375, when Richard Pique was sworn in as archbishop of Reims.[196]

18.2. 1377. MACHAUT'S DEATH. MS *F:RS 1773*, fol. 284r (MS Weyen), records the death of Guillaume de Machaut in April 1377: "obiit can. rem[ensis] ... april 1377."[197] The brothers Guillaume and Jean de Machaut were buried beside each other in the cathedral (Hoepffner 1908–21, 1:xliii; Machabey 1955b, 1:69–70; Goy 1982, 154). A further reference to Machaut's death around this time is the letter of Deschamps of 28 May (chap. 2.1.1h). Machaut's prebend, no. 40, was taken over by one Johannes Gibourty on 9 November 1377 (Machabey 1955b, 1:69).

---

193 AMR 2G 318, no. 5, cited in Chichmaref 1909, lxvii; Hoepffner 1908–21, 1:xxvi n. 2; Brejon de Lavergnée 1982, 149 n. 2; Leech-Wilkinson 1990c, 5 n. 23. The document is published in Varin 1843–48, 3:369–70 art. 10. Brejon de Lavergnée (1982) describes the substance of the document.

194 See Machabey 1955b, 1:38–40, 67 (floor plan facing p. 17); Desportes 1979, 298 nn. 26–27; Brejon de Lavergnée 1982, 149–52 and plates i–ii, facing p. 152.

195 There is no proof for the hypothesis of Douce (1948, 16), that Machaut himself had the house built in 1335 (Brejon de Lavergnée 1982, 149). Many of the fantastic speculations of Douce apparently derive from Kalas (1921, 117–25; cf. Machabey 1955b, 1:40 n. 107).

196 *F:RS 1780*, pp. 75–77, cited in Leech-Wilkinson 1990c, 5 n. 17. According to Goy (1982, 155), the speeches of both Louis Thésart in 1374 (archbishop of Reims from March 1374 until October 1375, see Desportes 1979, 318 n. 77) and Richard Pique in 1375 (archbishop from February 1376 until December 1389) are lacking in the archives.

197 Cited in Tarbé 1849, xxxiv; Chichmaref 1909, 1:lxviii; Hoepffner 1908–21, 1:xliii; Machabey 1930, 446; 1955b, 1:69, 1:71 n. 202, 2:185; 1955c, 249, 251.

1.18.3. FOUNDATION OF A MASS FOR THE VIRGIN ON SATURDAYS

a. Epitaph. According to the brass inscription, Jean and Guillaume de Machaut left money for the performance of a sung Mass to the Virgin: "oratio de defunctis . diebus sabbathi cunctis. / pro animabus eorum . amicorumque suorum. / dicetur a sacerdote . celebraturo devote. / ad roëllam in altari . missam quae debet cantari" [a prayer for the dead will be said every Saturday for their souls and for those of their loved ones by a priest who will devoutly celebrate the Mass which should be sung, by virtue of their prayer, with pious devotion to their memory at the altar near the *Rouelle* (ed. and trans. A.W. Robertson 1992, 100, 101)].[198]

There are two sources for the reading of the lost epitaph: (1) *F:RS 1941*, p. 94, an early eighteenth-century copy by Charles Drouin Regnault, curé of Bezannes, which includes an introductory paragraph: "Guillaume et Jean de Machaux, tous deux frères et chanoines de l'église de Notre-Dame de Reims. Ce sont eux qui ont fondé la messe de la Vierge qu'on chante les samedis dans la susdite église. C'est ainsi que s'en explique leur épitaphe que l'on voit sur du cuivre proche l'autel de la Roëlle, à la nef" (ed. A.W. Robertson 1992, 103 n. 11) [Guillaume and Jean de Machaut were both brothers and canons of the church of Notre-Dame of Reims. They are the ones who founded the Mass of the Virgin that is sung on Saturdays in the aforementioned church, as explained in their epitaph which can be seen on the brass plaque near the altar of the *Rouelle* in the nave (trans. adapted from A.W. Robertson 1992, 103)]; (2) *F:RS 1773* (MS Weyen), fol. 488v (cited in Leech-Wilkinson 1990c, 11 n. 39).

b. 1407 and 1411: money added to the foundation of Guillaume and Jean de Machaut. An ordinance of the cathedral chapter of 3 August 1411 records the sum of 300 French florins added to the foundation for the anniversary service of Guillaume and Jean de Machaut.[199] By then the endowment had reached at least forty *livres* per year, large enough for us to assume that a polyphonic Mass was being performed (A.W. Robertson 1992, 135–36).

---

[198] See also the edition and translation by Leech-Wilkinson (1990c, 10–11), improved in the 1992 paperback edition based on discussions with Roger Bowers. A less accurate reading of the inscription is given by Goy (1982, 154, with French translation); another translation is in Machabey 1955b, 1:69–70; also published in Tarbé 1849, 184–85; Hoepffner (1908–21, xliii) cites some other modern publications of the epitaph.

[199] AMR 2G 357 no. 20, cited in Chichmaref 1909, 1:lxviii n. 2; Machabey 1955b, 1:70; Goy 1982, 153; Leech-Wilkinson 1990c, 11 n. 40. For a full discussion, see A.W. Robertson 1992, 124–25, 135–36.

II

Machaut's Literary and Musical Legacy

1. Literary legacy in the fourteenth century[1]

Gilles Li Muisis (1272–1352), abbot at St-Martin of Tournai, mentioned Machaut along with Philippe de Vitry and Jean de le Mote in his *Méditations* of 1350.[2] From about this point on, Machaut's literary influence can be considered pervasive. The lyrical forms consolidated by Machaut—the lais, *chants royaux, complaintes*, ballades, rondeaux, and virelais—provided models for succeeding generations of poets. Similarities of story line or narrative structure or even close quotation and translation of Machaut's language are common among his literary heirs. Further, the cowardly and humorously inept narrator figure, characteristic of Machaut's amorous *dits*, is often met with in works of the following generation.[3] Indeed, Machaut's influence was so pervasive, his style so commonplace, that the novelty of his achievements was soon forgotten. If one considers the major poets who immediately followed Machaut, including Jean Froissart, Geoffrey Chaucer, Eustache Deschamps, Oton de Granson, and Christine de Pizan, only Deschamps and Oton mention Machaut by name.

A. *Jean Froissart* (1337?–after 1404). Froissart must have known Machaut's poetry intimately. His poetical forms, rhetorical techniques, and language derive from Machaut. He was particularly influenced by Machaut's *dits* with interpolated lyrics, the *Remede, Fonteinne*, and *Voir Dit*.[4]

Examples of Machaut's influence on Froissart's four long *dits* are discussed by Wimsatt (1991b, 189–90). The *Paradis d'Amour* (ca. 1365), written in England, was modeled on the *Remede* and the *Fonteinne* (Wimsatt 1968, 120–21); the *Espinette Amoureuse* (ca. 1370) is also modeled on *Fonteinne*[5]; the

---

[1] An excellent summary of Machaut's renown is given in Cerquiglini 1986b, 19–21; see also Hoepffner 1908–21, 1:i–x; Machabey 1931, 411–15; Eichelberg 1935, 125–29; Machabey 1955b, 2:163–70; Sonnemann 1969, 11–14; Calin 1974, 245–46; Brownlee 1989a, 113; Mühlethaler 1989, 405–9; Calin 1994, 227–28.

[2] Ed. Kervyn de Lettenhove 1882; cf. Hoepffner 1908–21, 1:iv; Gennrich 1926–27, 516; Machabey 1955b, 1:46; G. Olson 1979, 284–85; Wilkins 1979, 1 (with trans.); Palmer 1988, xv (with trans.); Earp 1989, 462; Mühlethaler 1989, 408; Wimsatt 1991b, 51 (with trans.), 275; Cerquiglini-Toulet 1993b, 9–10. For further bibliography on Gilles Li Muisis, see Badel 1980, 74 n. 52.

[3] See, for instance, Calin 1978, 177; 1979, 127, 137.

[4] There are relatively few studies of Machaut and Froissart. The only monograph on the subject is Geiselhardt 1914. Material can be gleaned from the introductions to the recent eds. of Fourrier (1963; 1974; 1975; 1979) and books by Poirion (1965, 205–18 et passim; 1971, 197–202), Wimsatt (1968; 1991b, chap. 6, esp. 181–90), Wilkins (1969a), Kelly (1978), Dembowski (1983), Cerquiglini (1985b), Huot (1987), and Figg (1994b). See also the articles by Whiting (1946), Cartier (1966; 1967), Wimsatt (1970–71; 1972a), Kibler (1978), Wolfzettel (1980), Wilkins (1983b), Nouvet (1986), R. Morris (1988), Bennett (1991), Calin (1993), and Figg (1994a). For brief overviews of Froissart's poetical works, see Dembowski 1978; Figg 1994b, 5–18. Dembowski (1987b, 99–100 and notes 1–7) considers Froissart's reception, with a bibliographical overview.

[5] Wimsatt (1968, 127) also mentions the *Remede* and *Voir Dit* as sources; see further Poirion 1965, 213–14.

Prison Amoureuse, written for the captivity of Wenceslas of Luxembourg in 1371–72, relates to the situation of the *Confort* but is most strongly modeled on Machaut's *Voir Dit* (Fourrier 1974, 15–16); finally, Froissart's *Joli Buisson de Jonece* (ca. 1373) is influenced by all three of Machaut's narratives with lyrical interpolations, the *Remede*, *Fonteinne*, and *Voir Dit*. One of Froissart's shorter narratives, the *Dittié de la Flour de la Marguerite*, makes it clear that he knew Machaut's *Marguerite* as well as his *Lis et Marguerite*. Wimsatt also sees a relation between Machaut's *complainte A toi, Hanri* (Cp3) and Froissart's *Dit dou Florin* and discusses in detail Froissart's imitation of Machaut's double ballade *Quant Theseüs / Ne quier* (B34) in a similar ballade, *Ne quier veoir Medée ne Jason*.[6]

Two occasions for a possible meeting of Machaut and Froissart have come to light, one in October 1360 at Calais (chap. 1.14), and another in April 1368 at Paris (chap. 1.15.2c). Although Froissart never mentioned Machaut by name, perhaps the closest he came to a direct reference is a moment in the *Joli Buisson de Jonece* of ca. 1373, in which the narrator sets off "En chantant un motet nouviel / Qu'on m'avoit envoiiet de Rains" (ll. 5075–76; ed. Fourrier 1975) [singing a new motet sent to me from Reims]. Machaut's last motet dates from ca. 1360, and it seems reasonable to suggest that Froissart did not mean a piece that we call a motet, but rather a new polyphonic ballade or rondeau, the sort of work that to a non-musician would surely have sounded as complicated and learned as a motet.[7]

Froissart also shows his debt to Machaut through his manuscripts. The complete poetical works of Froissart are preserved in two large manuscripts, dating from 1393 and 1394, that are carefully ordered by genre and chronology, in imitation of Machaut's complete-works manuscripts.[8]

B. *Geoffrey Chaucer* (ca. 1343–1400). Fascination with the genius of the English poet Chaucer has brought forth a great deal of scholarship, and the aspect of his literary sources has not been slighted. Much of his poetic work is modeled on French forms and the courtly themes of the *Roman de la Rose*. Among Chaucer's contemporaries, Machaut was the most important influence on his formation as a poet. Machaut's poetry is especially important for the *Book of the Duchess* and *Legend of Good Women*, but Chaucer also used Machaut for the *House of Fame*, *Troilus and Criseyde*, and for the Monk's Tale.[9] Several Chaucer scholars have provided English translations of

---

[6] See chap. 7.3, "textual legacy" of *Quant Theseüs / Ne quier*. Other lyrics of Froissart imitate Machaut's *De toutes* (B31) and *Je puis* (B28); see these titles in chap. 7.3.

[7] On the term "motet" in this context, see Frobenius 1985, 6–7. The word is possibly intended in the same sense in Christine de Pizan's *Dit de la Rose* of 1402 (l. 103; ed. M. Roy 1886–91, 2:32; see the quotations and discussion in Dömling 1970, 18–19), and in the *Dit de la Pastoure* (l. 643; ed. M. Roy 1886–91, 2:243).

[8] See the description of the two Froissart manuscripts in Fourrier 1963, 7–12, and the comments in Geiselhardt 1914, 12–16; Poirion 1965, 206; Huot 1987, 238–41 and chap. 10. Some arguments against the view that Froissart's manuscripts present his works in chronological order are given in Wimsatt 1972a, 393–96.

[9] For contexts, consult the notes to the editions of F.N. Robinson (1957) or Benson (1987), although the references there are far from complete. A wealth of material on Chaucer's borrowings from Machaut is found in the writings of Wimsatt (1967a; 1967b; 1968; 1970; 1970–71; 1972a; 1974; 1975; 1976; 1977; 1978; 1979; 1981; 1985; 1991a; 1991c; and especially 1991b; Wimsatt/Kibler 1988); see also Dillon 1974, 142–45. For a look at Machaut's importance for Chaucer's works from the point of view of a scholar of French poetry, see Calin 1987b; 1994, 273–370. L.K. Morris (1985, 285–89) provides a recent bibliography on Chaucer's sources, and Peck (1983; 1988) has prepared detailed

Machaut's narrative poetry, intended for students and scholars of Chaucer's works, but valuable for any English-speaking Machaut enthusiast as well.[10]

Judging from the wide range of Machaut's works—both narrative and lyrical—that Chaucer used, he may have read Machaut's poetry from a complete-works manuscript (Wimsatt 1968, 86–87). Perhaps Chaucer was able to consult the extant MS C during the captivity of King John II in London (Wimsatt/Kibler 1988, 53–54), or he may have been able to consult a Machaut manuscript that Froissart might have brought to London with him in the early 1360s, or perhaps there was a Machaut manuscript in the possession of one of the French hostages brought to England late in 1360 in fulfillment of the terms of the Treaty of Brétigny. Chaucer also could have read Machaut on his many travels and diplomatic missions to the continent, for instance in 1359–60, when he was captured by the French during the Siege of Reims (Emerson 1912, 352–55; Crow/Olson 1966), an occasion which may have provided him with an opportunity to meet Machaut himself. Machaut and Chaucer might also have met at Calais in 1360 (see chap. 1.14). A final occasion for a possible meeting between Machaut, Froissart, and Chaucer presented itself in April 1368 (chap. 1.15.2c), however, it seems more probable that Chaucer did not travel to Milan in the spring of 1368 in the entourage of Lionel, duke of Clarence, although he may have arrived there in time for the wedding. See also Wimsatt (1991b, 96) for speculations concerning John, duke of Berry as an intermediary for a meeting between Machaut and Chaucer.

C. *Eustache Deschamps* (ca. 1346–ca. 1406/7). The poet Eustache Deschamps was probably a student of Machaut at Reims, and there is even a reference that Deschamps was Machaut's "nephew," whom he raised from childhood (chap. 2.1.1c; 2.1.1j).[11] Although Deschamps's poetry is formally in the tradition of Machaut and he doubtless knew all of the works of the older master, he did not often write amorous poetry like Machaut's (see the analysis in Kendrick 1992). Poirion provides informative surveys (1965, 224–26; 1971, 282–83),[12] and Wimsatt has recently provided the most complete treatment of Machaut's

---

bibliographies of some selected works, but note that Chaucer bibliographies fast go out of date. Rather than listing dozens of books and articles, I refer the reader to these bibliographies for further information. For selected bibliography relating to individual Machaut works, see the discussions below, chaps. 5–7. Yearly updates of Chaucer bibliography are found in the *Chaucer Review, Neophilologus,* and *Yearbook of Chaucer Studies.* For references to music in Chaucer, see C. Olson 1941; Preston 1951; Wilkins 1979, chap. 4.

[10] There are complete translations of *Prologue* (Palmer 1993a), *Vergier* (Palmer 1993a), *Jugement Behaingne* (Windeatt 1982; Palmer 1984; Wimsatt/Kibler 1988), *Remede* (Wimsatt/Kibler 1988), *Jugement Navarre* (Palmer 1988), *Alerion* (Gaudet/Hieatt 1994), *Confort* (Palmer 1992), and *Fonteinne* (Palmer 1993a; Cerquiglini-Toulet 1993d in modern French). Forthcoming are translations of *Voir Dit* (Palmer/Leech-Wilkinson) and *Prise* (Palmer). Partial translations of material relating specifically to Chaucer's *Book of the Duchess* (from *Jugement Behaingne, Remede, Lyon,* and *Fonteinne*) are found in Windeatt 1982 and Phillips 1982; see also Windeatt 1982 for material relating to the *Legend of Good Women* (extracts from *Jugement Navarre* and *Lis et Marguerite,* as well as the complete *Marguerite*). Windeatt (1982) does not limit himself to Machaut's works, but provides translations of excerpts from various works of Nicole de Margival, Jean de Condé, Froissart, Deschamps, Granson, and others. Translations of a few of Machaut's lyrics are found in Wimsatt 1991b, and among recordings of the music (see chap. 8.3 and 8.8).

[11] In a review of Imbs 1991, Aloysia R. Berens suggests that Deschamps was the secretary Machaut referred to in the *Voir Dit.*

[12] See also Queux de Saint-Hilaire/Raynaud 1878–1903, 11:223–24.

influence on Deschamps.[13]

The Deschamps manuscript tradition shows some influence of the Machaut manuscripts in that all of Deschamps's works are collected into a single enormous manuscript (*F:Pn 840*, 582 fols.). This manuscript was copied posthumously, however, and displays a haphazard organization.[14]

A professional court poet *par excellence*, Deschamps was no musician, and the distinction drawn between poetry to be read (natural music) and poetry set to music (artificial music) in his treatise *L'Art de Dictier* (1392) has been widely studied (see chap. 2.1.1m). It provides official acknowledgement of the disassociation of lyrical poetry and music that by then had long been in force. Machaut stands as the last major poet of the time who was epoch-making in music as well.

Deschamps, alone among the poets influenced by Machaut, made many direct references to him, doubtless further evidence of the close personal relationship he enjoyed during Machaut's lifetime. The most important of Deschamps's works connected with Machaut include the double ballade on Machaut's death (2.1.1f–g), and several references relating to the *Voir Dit* (2.1.1e; 2.1.1i–k).

2.1.1. REFERENCES LINKING MACHAUT AND DESCHAMPS

a. A report of the Siege of Reims (1359–60) is in the *Miroir de Mariage* (ed. Queux de Saint-Hilaire/Raynaud 1878–1903, 9:375, 380). Machaut was of course present on this occasion. Unfortunately, Deschamps's report merely translates from the *Grandes Chroniques de France*, and this lends it less value as a potential eyewitness account.[15]

b. Ballade, *Veulz tu la congnoissance avoir / Des Champenoys et leur nature?* (ed. Queux de Saint-Hilaire/Raynaud 1878–1903, 8:177–78, no. 1474) [Would you like to know about the nature of the Champenois?]. In the third strophe, Deschamps cites the accomplishments of Philippe de Vitry and Guillaume de Machaut: "Vittry, Machault de haulte emprise, / Poetes que musique ot chier" (ll. 28–29) [Vitry and Machaut of great enterprise, poets whom Music held dear (trans. Wimsatt 1991b, 244)]. This reference was cited as long ago as Tarbé (1849, vi); cf. also Hoepffner 1908–21, 1:iv; Poirion 1965, 225; Cerquiglini 1985b, 83; and above, chap. 1.2.2.

c. An anonymous treatise of the second rhetoric datable between ca. 1404 and 1432, the *Regles de la Seconde Rettorique*, provides our only evidence of a blood relation of Deschamps to Machaut: "Aprèz vint Eustace Morel, nepveux de maistre Guillaume de Machault lequel fut bailli de Senliz et fut trés souffisant de diz et balades et d'aultres choses" (ed. Langlois 1902, 14) [afterwards came Eustache Morel (i.e., Eustache Deschamps), nephew of master Guillaume de Machaut, who was bailiff of Senlis and was very skilled at *dits*, ballades, and other poems].[16] Deschamps's most direct statement of his relationship with Machaut is that Machaut "nourished" him (below, item j).

d. *Lay Amoureux, Contre la saison nouvelle* (ed. Queux de Saint-Hilaire/Raynaud 1878–1903, 2:193–203 no. 306). The scene in ll. 296–99 (ed. 2:202), with Deschamps hidden behind a bush, recalls the scene near the opening of the *Jugement Behaingne*. A lover addresses the god of Love: "... Vez la Eustace / Qui doit bien estre en vostre grace. / Guillaume et lui noz faiz escriprent; / Venus et Juno les nourrirent" [See Eustache there, who well deserves to enjoy your grace; Guillaumé and he have written our (lovers') deeds;

---

[13] Wimsatt 1991b, 82, 244–48; see also Deschaux 1978b; J. Stevens 1984; Brownlee 1984, 209–11; and Walters 1992, 64–66, 72.

[14] Poirion 1965, 218–19; see the study of *F:Pn 840* in Tesnière 1986. In his ballade *Doulz Zephirus qui faiz naistre les flours* (ed. Queux de Saint-Hilaire/Raynaud 1878–1903, 5:229–30 no. 984), Deschamps laments the theft of a manuscript of his works (str. 2 is translated in Wimsatt 1991b, 252–53); see Queux de Saint-Hilaire/Raynaud 1878–1903, 1:203–4; and Geiselhardt 1914, 11.

[15] Queux de Saint-Hilaire/Raynaud 1878–1903, 11:198; Machabey 1955b, 1:50–51; Wimsatt 1991b, 245.

[16] Discussed in Queux de Saint-Hilaire/Raynaud 1878–1903, 11:11–12; Wimsatt 1991b, 244–45.

Venus and Juno nurtured them (trans. Wimsatt 1991b, 245)]. See also the discussion in Cerquiglini 1985b, 114. The *Lay de Franchise, Pour ce que grant chose est d'acoustumance* (ed. Queux de Saint-Hilaire/Raynaud 1878–1903, 2:203–14 no. 307) also has a scene in which the narrator hides in a bush: "En un busson me mis en tapinage / Pour regarder de celle gent la vie (ll. 99–100, ed. 2:207) [I stealthily hid myself in a bush to watch the life of these people (trans. Palmer 1984, xvi; 1988, xi; 1992, xi)], cited by Poirion 1965, 413; Windeatt 1982, xv.

e. 1369 or 1375. Ballade, *Treschiers sires, vueillez remercier* (ed. Tarbé 1849, xvi–xvii n. [excerpts]; Queux de Saint-Hilaire/Raynaud 1878–1903, 1:248–49 no. 127). The ballade, addressed to Guillaume de Machaut, documents an occasion when Deschamps read aloud an extended passage on Fortune from the *Voir Dit* before Louis de Male, count of Flanders and many knights. Significantly, MS K [15] (dated 1371) and the related MS J [16] contain only this passage excerpted from the *Voir Dit* (cf. Ludwig 1926–54, 2:14* and n. 3; Cerquiglini 1982, 257; 1985b, 63, 88). Deschamps also delivered a letter and a manuscript (presumably a copy of the *Voir Dit* itself) to Count Louis on this occasion.[17] Two dates have been proposed for the events described in the ballade; (1) the 19 June 1369 marriage at Ghent of Philippe the Bold and Marguerite of Flanders, proposed by the marquis de Queux de Saint-Hilaire (Queux de Saint-Hilaire/Raynaud 1878–1903, 1:377; see chap. 1.17); and (2) the March–May 1375 peace conference held at Bruges, with Philip the Bold in attendance, a date proposed by Raynaud (Queux de Saint-Hilaire/Raynaud 1878–1903, 11:22, 224).[18] Wimsatt (1991b, 245 and n. 18) leans towards the 1369 date, because the *Voir Dit* would have been more current then. Hoepffner (1908–21, 1:iv–v n. 4) also apparently thought 1375 too late a date. For further discussion of this episode, see Chichmaref 1909, 1:lxvii–lxviii; Hoepffner 1908–21, 1:xxvii; Sonnemann 1969, 140–41; Ruhe 1975, 284.

f and g. 1377. A *déploration* on the death of Machaut in the form of a double-ballade, (f) *Balade pour Machaut: Armes, Amours, Dames, Chevalerie*; and (g) *Autre Balade: O fleur des fleurs de toute melodie* (ed. Queux de Saint-Hilaire/Raynaud 1878–1903, 1:243–46 nos. 123–24; see also the notes on pp. 375–76), set to music by F. Andrieu. See chap. 7.4 and 8.5 for additional bibliography and a brief account of the textual and musical legacy of this important work.

h. 28 May [1377?]. Deschamps sent a letter to a nun of a convent at les Andelys (dept. Eure), which mentions Machaut (ed. Queux de Saint-Hilaire/Raynaud 1878–1903, 8:52–53 no. 1416; cf. also 11:24; Ruhe 1975, 278–79, 448 n. 13). "Vous envoi de maistre Guillaume / De Machaut ce que fait en ay / Avec un povre virelay" (ll. 44–46) [I send to you what I have made concerning master Guillaume de Machaut, along with a poor virelai]. Presumably Deschamps is referring here to the double ballade on Machaut's death, items f and g above. The virelai is apparently on another subject, since no such *déploration* on Machaut is known, and in any case, the virelai form seems inappropriate for such a work. On the other hand, there is nothing in the letter to suggest an exact year, and Deschamps may be referring to other poems on Machaut now lost. See the discussion in Cerquiglini 1985b, 46–47.

i. Rondeau, *Cilz qui onques encores ne vous vit* (ed. Queux de Saint-Hilaire/Raynaud 1878–1903, 4:94 no. 685, and cited in the *Art de Dictier*, 7:284; Patterson 1935, 121–22 [wrongly attributed to Machaut]). This work parodies the first lyrical interpolation of the *Voir Dit*, the rondeau *Celle qui unques ne vous vid* (l. 169, ed. P. Paris 1875, 7), ascribed in the *Voir Dit* to Toute Belle.

j. Ballade, *Apres Machaut qui tant vous a amé* (ed. Tarbé 1849, xxxiv [str. 1]; P. Paris 1875, xxvi [str. 1]; Queux de Saint-Hilaire/Raynaud 1878–1903, 3:259–60 no. 447; Wilkins 1969a, 68–69 no. 52). This ballade contains the oft-cited remark that Machaut "nurtured" Deschamps: "Qui m'a nourry et fait maintes douçours" (l. 5) [who nurtured me and did me many kindnesses (trans. Wimsatt 1991b, 248)].[19] The entire work is

---

17 Tarbé (1849, xvi–xvii n. 1) discusses passages from strophes 2–3.

18 On the conference, see Delachenal (1909–31, 4:568–70). After a further peace conference held a year later (31 March–1 April 1376), Louis de Male provided a large tournament (Delachenal 1909–31, 4:587).

19 Wimsatt (1991b, 245) also suggests "educated" as a translation for "nourry." See further

supposedly aimed at Peronne, Machaut's young admirer in the *Voir Dit*, who is directly addressed in the third strophe (l. 16, "Hé! Peronne..."). Deschamps proposes that he be her loyal lover now that Machaut is dead. Such an absurd conceit would have been savored by all at court with a knowledge of Machaut's *dit* (see Wimsatt 1993, 22–23). Brownlee (1978a, 219–20; 1984, 7–8) discusses Deschamps's application in this poem of the term *poète* to Machaut. It provides an earlier date for the use of this term for a vernacular poet than the date ca. 1400, proposed previously by Jung (1971, 55). See also discussion in Zumthor 1972, 274 (=Eng. ed., 220); Cerquiglini 1985b, 88–89; Zeeman 1988, 837; Lowinsky 1989, 1:368 (with trans. of str. 1 and 3); Mühlethaler 1989, 405; Imbs 1991, 252–53; Wimsatt 1991b, 247–48; Walters 1992, 65–66 (with trans. of str. 1).

k. Ballade, *A vous m'octroy de vray cuer et de bon* (ed. Queux de Saint-Hilaire/Raynaud 1878–1903, 3:318–19 no. 493). Peronne's evident refusal to the advance made in ballade 447 (above, item j) is recorded here. Addressed to a lady named Gauteronne, the refrain urges: "Recevez moy: j'ay failli a Perronne" [Take me, I failed with Peronne (trans. Wimsatt 1991b, 248)]. This ballade is further discussed in Poirion 1965, 226 n. 118; Thiry-Stassin 1970, 51; Cerquiglini 1985b, 228, 235 n. 27; Zeeman 1988, 837; Imbs 1991, 252–53; Wimsatt 1991b, 248; 1993, 23.

l. Ballade, *He! gentils rois, dus de Poligieras* (ed. Queux de Saint-Hilaire/Raynaud 1878–1903, 5:53–54 no. 872). As in ballade no. 1474 (above, item b), Deschamps mentions Machaut and Vitry together. "Puis que la mort fist Machaut departir / Et que Vitry paia de mort la debte" (ll. 5–6) [Since death made Machaut depart, and Vitry paid his debt to death]. The poem celebrates a great poet, and as Raynaud comments (Queux de Saint-Hilaire/Raynaud 1878–1903, 5:53 n. a), the work appears to be addressed to Deschamps by another poet (see also Poirion 1965, 228). Wilkins (1968, 47) suggests that Deschamps is indeed the author, addressing perhaps Froissart.

m. 1392. *Art de Dictier* (ed. Queux de Saint-Hilaire/Raynaud 1878–1903, 7:266–92; extract, with glossary in modern French in Poirion 1971, 246–47; ed. and trans. Sinnreich 1987). Deschamps cites two rondeaux of Machaut (ed. Queux de Saint-Hilaire/Raynaud 1878–1903, 7:286–87; Sinnreich 1987, 114–15; trans. pp. 139–40), without attribution, to illustrate aspects of rondeau form: *Vo dous regars* (R8), and *Certes, mon oueil* (R15=Lo234). On the important discussion of "natural" and "artificial" music, see Patterson 1935, 1:84–96 et passim; Lote 1949; Preston 1951, 618–19; S.J. Williams 1952, 23–26; Dragonetti 1961; Laurie 1964; Poirion 1965, 146–47, 167, 232, 316; Varty 1965; Sonnemann 1969, 26–27; G. Olson 1973; Silver 1975, 157–58; Page 1977; Kelly 1978, 10–11, 255; Lühmann 1978, 7, 33–39; Lubienski-Bodenham 1979, 33–35; Winn 1981, 121; Zink 1982; Cerquiglini 1983, 283–85; Lukitsch 1983, 264–66; Günther 1984a, 229–30; J. Stevens 1984, 121–29; Cerquiglini 1985b, 85; Brownlee 1989a, 112–13; Mühlethaler 1989, 402–3; Wilkins 1989, 348–52; L.W. Johnson 1990, 57; Brownlee 1991a, 25 n. 23, 232 n. 32; Wimsatt 1991a; 1991b, chaps. 1 and 9, esp. 12–16, 281–91; Welker 1992, 188–89; Zink 1992, 277–78; Magnan 1993, 51–64; Wimsatt 1994, esp. 28–40. De Winter (1985, 27) suggests that Deschamps wrote the *Art de Dictier* for the instruction of Duke Philip the Bold of Burgundy; cf. also Poirion 1965, 147–48.

n. *Lay de Plour, Lais je fui jadis contrains* (ed. Queux de Saint-Hilaire/Raynaud 1878–1903, 2:306–14 no. 310). This work is related to Machaut by virtue of its title, familiar from Machaut's two *Lays de Plour: Malgré Fortune* (L19/14), and *Qui bien aimme* (L22/16); in addition, it contains a eulogy of John of Luxembourg (ll. 177–204) and may thus have been inspired by the *Confort*, where Deschamps would have found several passages celebrating John (cited by Poirion 1965, 225, 419; for specific passages from the *Confort* that praise John of Luxembourg, see chap. 1.5.1c and 1.5.3).

D. *Oton de Granson* (ca. 1345–1397). A Savoyard knight renowned as a poet, Oton de Granson was also influenced by Machaut, although interestingly, much of Machaut's influence on Granson was distilled through the works of Chaucer, whom Oton knew well. Wimsatt (1991b, 219–27) provides the best recent

discussion in Poirion 1965, 225–26; Cerquiglini 1985b, 89 n. 77; Imbs 1991, 268 n. 70 (to p. 162), 252.

discussion of Machaut's influence on Oton, tracing some echoes of Machaut's *Lyon* and *Alerion* in Oton's *Songe Saint Valentin*. The *Livre de Messire Ode*, modelled on Machaut's *Voir Dit*, further demonstrates Oton's familiarity with the *Jugement Behaingne*, *Remede*, *Alerion*, and *Fonteinne* (Wimsatt 1991b, 227–34).

Oton directly mentions Machaut once, in his *Lay de Desir en Complainte*: *Belle, tournez vers moy voz yeux* (ed. Piaget 1941, 229–36). In strophe 10, he cites the authority of Guillaume de Machaut concerning Desire: "Maistre Guillaume de Machault / Dit bien que revengier n'y vault" (ll. 157–58, ed. Piaget 1941, 234; cited already in Sandras 1859, 289) [master Guillaume de Machaut well advises that it is not worth taking revenge over], before going on to mention Guillaume de Saint-Amour (l. 161) and Jean de Meun (ll. 179–80). Poirion (1965, 418–19) suggests that the *Lay de Plour* in Oton's *Livre Messire Ode* (ed. Piaget 1941, 409–14) was inspired both by Machaut's first *Lay de Plour*, *Malgré Fortune* (L19), and by the *complainte Amours, tu m'as tant* (Cp1). Finally, Cerquiglini-Toulet (1993d, 25) notes that the title of the *Complainte de l'an nouvel que Gransson fist pour un chevalier qu'il escoutoit complaindre* (ed. Piaget 1941, 199–201) [New Year's *complainte* that Granson wrote for a knight he heard complaining] recalls the opening situation of Machaut's *Fonteinne*.

Alain Chartier specifically associated Oton and Machaut (chap. 2.3.2b), and the two poets are further linked by the fact that the transmission of Oton's poetry is somewhat confused with works of Machaut (chap. 3.5 below, introduction).

E. *Anonymous authors.* Machaut also exerted influence on less gifted anonymous authors, for example, the author of the *Dit dou Cerf Blanc* (an *opus dubium* sometimes ascribed to Machaut; see chap. 5.19), the author of *Ou mois qui est peres de joie*, an imitation of *Jugement Behaingne* (see chap. 3, MS **Kr** [36]), and the author of the prose romance known as the *Roman de Cardenois* (see chap. 3, MS **Mn** [43]).

An additional citation of Machaut is found in a Latin letter of ca. 1395 by Jean Lebègue (1368–1457), then a secretary at the royal chancery, to Pierre Lorfèvre, chancellor of Louis d'Orléans, requesting the hand of his daughter Catherine (Ouy 1967). The single allusion in the letter to contemporary literature is to Machaut: "eximium condam rethoricum Guillelmum de Mascaudio" (Ouy 1967, 401; see also 379, 385, 389) [eminent erstwhile rhetorician Guillaume de Machaut].[20] He will depart, and in the wasteland, unconsoled, lament his misery, perhaps recalling Machaut's *complainte A toi, Hanri* (Cp3).

2. Literary legacy in Spain, 1380–1470

Machaut's works were also known on the Iberian peninsula, especially in the Francophile court of Aragon, where his works exerted an influence well into the fifteenth century.[21] John I, king of Aragon (b. 1349, r. 1387–1396), himself a poet and composer of French rondeaux, ballades, and virelais, is well known as a patron of French minstrels.[22] Several letters of his wife, Yolande of Bar

---

[20] Ouy (1967, 385 n. 59) points out that this phrase may refer to Deschamps's "La mort Machaut le noble rethorique," the refrain of the two ballades of *déploration* discussed above, chap. 2.1.1f–g.

[21] The standard work on French literary influence in Catalonia from the thirteenth to the fifteenth century is Pagès 1936.

[22] On John I as poet-musician, see Ludwig 1926–54, 2:32a* and the extensive bibliography cited there; Pagès 1936, 26–30; Günther 1964, 172–73; Gómez 1979; 1985a, 166–68;

(1365–1431; married 2 February 1380), record her intense interest in Machaut's works (chap. 2.2.1).[23] There is also a Catalan imitation of the *Voir Dit* (ed. Meyer 1891). Some fifteenth-century Catalan poets, such as Andreu Febrer (ca. 1375–ca. 1444) and Pere Torroella (fl. ca. 1438–ca. 1501), were greatly influenced by Machaut's poetry.[24] Knowledge of Machaut's musical works is attested in a backhanded way by the anonymous author of a fifteenth-century hunting book of King John I of Portugal (b. 1357, r. 1385–1433), who compares the harmonious effect of hunting dogs running together in coordination to the harmonies of Machaut's polyphony: "Guilherme de Machado nom fez tam fermosa concordança de melodia, nem que tam bem pareça como a fazem os caães quando bem correm" (cited by Ludwig 1926–54, 2:32*; quotation of larger context on p. 70*) [Guillaume de Machaut has not composed such a beautifully harmonious melody, or one that might even seem so beautiful, as that which the dogs make when they run well]. Finally, in a famous letter of 1449 to the constable of Portugal that provides a brief history of Romance poetry, Ignatius Lopez de Mendoza, Marqués de Santillana (1398–1458), a nobleman poet at the court of Aragon, speaks enthusiastically of Machaut's works in a manner that implies knowledge of one of the complete-works manuscripts, perhaps the manuscript that previously belonged to Yolande of Bar: "Michaute escriuio asy mismo vn grand libro de baladas, cançiones, rondeles, lays, virolays, & asono muchos dellos" [Machaut also wrote a large book of balades, chansons, rondeaux, lais, virelais, and set many of them to music].[25]

2.2.1. MACHAUT MANUSCRIPTS AT THE COURT OF ARAGON, 1380–1417 [26]

a. 20 October 1380. The infante John asked his mother-in-law, the duchess of Bar for "lo romanç de Mexaut" [the romance of Machaut], presumably the *Voir Dit* (published in Rubió y Lluch 1908–21, 2:225 no. 238).

b. 29 August 1386. Yolande of Bar wrote to Guillem de Perapertusa, castellan of Rebollet, requesting him to lend her his Machaut manuscript, in order that she might determine which works of Machaut were lacking in her own manuscript (published in Vielliard 1930, 33–34 no. 15).

c. 18 June 1389. Yolande of Bar thanked Gaston Fébus, count of Foix, for sending her his Machaut manuscript, and promised to return it after she had read it (published in Rubió y Lluch 1908–21, 1:360 no. 403).[27]

Scully 1990. It has even been suggested that as duke of Gerona, John patronized Machaut's brother Jean de Machaut (Johan de Mascó or Maschó), a jongleur and cornemuse player (Anglès 1970, 193; Holzbacher 1983–84, 186 n. 26). Of course Jean de Machaut was in a different social class altogether.

[23] Vielliard (1935) provides a general account of the life of Yolande of Bar. See chap. 1.11 on the House of Bar and Machaut.

[24] See Pagès 1936; Reaney 1958c, 97; Holzbacher 1983–84, 188–90. Machaut's lai *Loyauté, que* (L1) was the model for Febrer's lai *Amors, qui tost fer,* and Torroella quotes *Se quanque Diex* (L11) in his lai *Tant mon voler* (see chap. 7.3). Holzbacher (1983–84, 185–87) argues that Machaut wrote the *Roman de Cardenois* in Catalonia (see chap. 3, MS [43]).

[25] *Prohemio é carta* [Prologue and Letter] to Don Pedro of Portugal, ed. Sorrento 1922, 31 (many other eds. available). Cited also in Chichmaref 1909, 1:lxx and Hoepffner 1908–21, 1:viii. Seronde (1915) discusses the Marqués de Santillana's borrowings from Machaut, Oton de Granson, and Alain Chartier.

[26] Pagès (1936, 85–87) briefly discusses documents (a) through (f); see also Ludwig 1926–54, 2:32*.

[27] This is the document that Hoepffner (1908–21, 1:vii–viii) and Chichmaref (1909, 1:lxx) cited from Morel-Fatio (1893, 276). Ludwig (1926–54, 2:32b* n. 1) corrects the date.

d. 31 January 1390. Yolande asked madame Carroça de Vilargut to hand over the Machaut manuscript she had borrowed to Yolande's treasurer Antoni Nosar (published in Rubió y Lluch 1908–21, 1:361 no. 404).[28]

e. An additional document of the same day, related to the same incident, is published by Pagès (1936, 86 n. 6; cf. Ludwig 1926–54, 2:32b*).

f. 25 May 1390. Yolande directed a servant to lend her Machaut manuscript to a noble priest, Mossèn n'Uch de Çervelló (Vielliard 1930, 38 no. 21).

g. 4 April 1391. The infante Martin, duke of Montblanc, asked for the return of the Machaut manuscript that had been lent out to Hugo de Cervillione (Gómez 1985b, 6), i.e., the Uch de Çervelló of the previous document.

h. 15 July 1417. Item no. 17 in an inventory at Valencia (published in Alós-Moner 1924, 397) of the books of Alphonso V the Magnanimous, king of Aragon and Sicily (r. 1416–1458), relates, I believe, to the same manuscript, the manuscript previously owned by Yolande of Bar. Earp (1989, 478 n. 35) translates the relevant portion of the inventory, describing a Machaut manuscript that is very probably the manuscript we know today as **Vg** (see chap. 3, MSS [3] and [3a]).

3. Literary reputation in the fifteenth century[29]

In France, Machaut's reputation as an author lasted well into the fifteenth century, although it is difficult sometimes to know how far beyond mere name recognition knowledge of his works extended. It appears that the *Jugement Behaingne* exerted the most lasting influence of all his works, although it was usually transmitted without attribution. Of the some seven anthology manuscripts of the fifteenth century that transmit *Jugement Behaingne*, only MS **St** [46] provides an attribution to Machaut.

Following Deschamps's *Art de Dictier* of 1392, two treatises of the fifteenth-century "second rhetoric" demonstrate a knowledge of Machaut.[30] The anonymous *Regles de la Seconde Rettorique* (ca. 1404–32)[31] cites Machaut by name and provides some authoritative judgments on his importance. Baudet Herenc's *Doctrinal de la Secunde Retorique* (1432) quotes without attribution some excerpts from three of Machaut's lais, a difficult genre by then no longer cultivated. But most of Machaut's narrative and lyrical forms continued to be cultivated in fifteenth-century France, and poets at least knew something of his reputation. Four of them mention him by name: Alain Chartier (ca. 1385–ca. 1435), from 1418 to 1428 notary and secretary to the future King Charles VII; Michault Taillevent (ca. 1390/95–ca. 1458), from 1426 *valet de chambre* of Duke Philip the Good of Burgundy; the prince and poet René d'Anjou, king of Naples (1409–1480); and Martin Le Franc (b. ca. 1410, fl. ca. 1440), canon and later provost of Lausanne. In addition, Poirion (1965, 277) gives some very inconclusive links between Machaut and works of Charles d'Orléans (1394–1465). Finally, three works of Machaut—the *Jugement Behaingne*, the motet texts *Qui es / Ha! Fortune* (M8), and the rondeau text *Douce dame, tant* (R20)—appear with attributions a little before 1480 in the MS **St** [46], a miscellany especially important for Villon's works.

---

[28] On Na Carroça de Vilargut (or Vilaragut), see Pagès 1936, 33–34, 86–87.

[29] See the references given above, n. 1. L.W. Johnson's treatment of fifteenth-century French literature emphasizes the influence of Machaut (L.W. Johnson 1990). On links between the old tradition and the sixteenth century, see L.W. Johnson 1990, 289–301.

[30] The two rhetorics referred to in the title of the treatise are first prose and second poetry, or first Latin and second vernacular, depending on the treatise (Langlois 1902, i–ii). See also Lubienski-Bodenham 1979; Brownlee 1984, 208–10.

[31] The date given by Langlois (1902, xxvi–xxviii), ca. 1411–32, depends for its *terminus post quem* on the death of Froissart, which is now placed at ca. 1404. Mühlethaler (1989, 408) dates the treatise "1420/30?".

By the sixteenth century, Machaut's name was all but forgotten. The best Antoine Du Verdier could do in his *Bibliotheque françoise* of 1585 was the following: "GVILLAVME DE MACHANT. Cestui-cy fut un Trouverre qui vivoit environ l'an M.CCC. & composa un livre de ses amours en rime lequel i'ay escrit en main sur parchemin" (Du Verdier 1585; Rigoley de Juvigny 1773) [he was a trouvère who lived around 1300 and composed a book of his love life in rhyme, which I inscribed on parchment]. On the face of it, it would seem that Du Verdier copied all or part of a Machaut manuscript, but I think it more likely that the last phrase should be understood to say, "a description that I inscribed on a Machaut manuscript." Was it Du Verdier who penned the late sixteenth-century inscription "Les amours de Guillaume Machaut en vielles rithmes" found on the first flyleaf verso of MS **A**?

2.3.1. CA. 1404–32. CITATIONS IN SECOND RHETORIC TREATISES.[32]

a. Anon. *Regles de la Seconde Rettorique* (ca. 1404–32). "Après vint maistre Guillaumé de Machault, le grant retthorique de nouvelle fourme, qui commenca toutes tailles nouvelles, et les parfais lays d'amours" [Afterwards came master Guillaume de Machaut, the great versifier of the new school, who originated all manner of new strophic forms, and perfect amorous lais].[33]

b. Anon. *Regles de la Seconde Rettorique* (ca. 1404–32). See chap. 2.1.1c.

c. Anon. *Regles de la Seconde Rettorique* (ca. 1404–32). The form of the strophe of the *Jugement Behaingne* is cited as if everyone would be familiar with it: "Une autre taille avons qui est de 3 et 1, sy comme le Temps Pasquour..." (ed. Langlois 1902, 33) [we have another metrical form which is of three and one, as in *Le Temps Pascour*]. *Le Temps Pascour* is another title for the *Jugement Behaingne*, which begins "Au temps pascour que toute rien s'esgaie" [At Easter time when everything rejoices (ed. and trans. Wimsatt/Kibler 1988, 60–61; cf. Cerquiglini-Toulet 1993b, 94)]. This title is used as the *explicit* of *Jugement Behaingne* in MS **C**, and as the rubric introducing the poem in MSS **Vg** and **B**. In addition, a lost Burgundian manuscript is cited in fifteenth-century library inventories as "Le livre du Temps Pastour [*sic*] et plusieurs Balades et Laiz" (chap. 3, MS [12]).

d. Baudet Herenc, in *Le Doctrinal de la Secunde Retorique* (1432), cites the first strophe from three lais of Machaut as models of the form (ed. Langlois 1902, 166–68): *Par trois raisons* (L6/5), *Amours doucement* (L7/6, with many substantive variants in the text), and *Qui bien aimme* (L22/16). By 1432, the lai form, quite complex metrically, was all but extinct. See Ludwig 1926–54, 2:17b* and Patterson 1935, 1:121–28 for further commentary.

2.3.2. MACHAUT AND FIFTEENTH-CENTURY FRENCH POETS

a. Christine de Pizan (ca. 1364–ca. 1430). Growing up at the court of Charles V, Christine de Pizan must have been well acquainted with Machaut's poetry (Yenal 1989, 85–92). Christine's three debate poems, the *Dit de Poissy* (1400), the *Livre des Trois Jugemens*, and the *Debat de Deux Amans* (or *Livre des Vrais Amans*) are all related to Machaut's two debate poems, *Jugement Behaingne* and *Jugement Navarre*; the *Debat de Deux Amans* is also related to Machaut's *Voir Dit*.[34] *Fonteinne* influenced the *Epistre Othea* (P.G.C. Campbell 1924, 100, 131; Ehrhart 1987, 118; 1990, 128, 132, 135–39, 148–49) as well as an early ballade, *Se de Pallas me peüsse accointier* (Ehrhart 1990, 126–31, 146, 148). Machaut's debate poems and a passage from *Confort* also influenced Christine's *Livre du*

---

33 Ed. Langlois 1902, 12; already cited in Tarbé 1849, xxxii n. 3. Facsimile of the folio mentioning Philippe de Vitry and Machaut (*F:Pn 4237*, fol. 1v) in Wilkins 1989, 356. For further commentary, see Hoepffner 1911, 162–63; Patterson 1935, 1:119–21, 127; Brownlee 1984, 210; Wilkins 1989, 353–59; Earp 1991b, 119–24.

34 On the literary connections between Machaut and Christine, see Pugh 1894; Hoepffner 1908–21, 1:iii, v, vi, xxix; 3:xli; Schilperoort 1936; Poirion 1965, 266; Calin 1974; Deschaux 1978b; Cerquiglini 1982; Willard 1985; Altmann 1987; 1988; 1992. The annotated bibliographies by Yenal (1989, nos. 39–44) and Kennedy (1984) contain further references.

Chemin de Long Estude (Schilperoort 1936, 34 n. 2, 44 n. 2), as did his *Fonteinne* (Hoepffner 1908–21, 3:xli; de Boer 1914, 37–39; Schilperoort 1936, 62–63; Ehrhart 1990, 144).

As was the case with Froissart, the manuscript presentation of Machaut's works exerted an influence on Christine. A large manuscript of her works once owned by John, duke of Berry in 1413 is ordered in twenty-three sections.[35] The fascinating story of Christine as a copyist of her own works is told in Laidlaw 1987, with ample references to previous studies.

b. Alain Chartier (ca. 1385–ca. 1435). In the *Debat de Reveille Matin* (ca. 1420), Chartier mentions Guillaume de Machaut and Oton de Granson together: "Mais au fort, qui plus bee hault, / Il a plus fort a besoingnier; / Par Messire Ode et par Machaut / Se puet il assez tesmoingner" (str. 29, ll. 229–32; ed. Laidlaw 1974, 314) [But in fact, he who aspires to more has to work harder; he can find much testimony on this in *Messire* Oton and in Machaut]. See the interesting comments in Cerquiglini 1985b, 137–38.

The popular *Jugement Behaingne* provided the model for the framing story in Chartier's *Livre des Quatre Dames* (1415–16); see Hoepffner 1908–21, 1:vii. Poirion (1965, 262, 266 n. 78) cites some further works of Machaut possibly used by Chartier, including *Hareu! / Helas!* (M10), *Quant je vous voy crier "a l'arme"* (Lo122),[36] *Souvenirs fait meint amant resjoïr* (Lo23), and finally *Aucun gent / Qui plus* (M5).

As was the case for Oton de Granson, the manuscript traditions of the works of Chartier and Machaut are somewhat intertwined; see the introduction to chap. 3.5.

c. Michault Taillevent (1390/95–ca. 1458).[37] Since the fifteenth century, there has been some confusion over references to Michault and Machaut. This problem was cleared up by Piaget (1892). Michault himself once referred to Machaut at the end of his *Dialogue fait par Michault de son voiage de Saint Glaude* (ca. 1430), in order to take advantage of the rhyme provided by their names: "Et s'il n'est aussi bien dicté / Que de Mehun ou de Machaut, / On preigne en gré: c'est de Michaut" (str. 12, ll. 82–84; ed. Deschaux 1975, 57) [And if it's not as well written as de Meun or de Machaut, take it gladly: it's by Michault].

d. Martin le Franc (ca. 1410–1461). In his *Champion des Dames* (1440–42), Martin Le Franc reserves his highest praise for Christine de Pizan but also cites Machaut, Froissart, Alain Chartier, and others. We await Deschaux's projected complete edition; only one passage is available in Piaget's edition of part 1: "Et Jehan de Meün le villain, / Qui en parlant courtoisement / N'a pas ressemblé maistre Alain, / Failly et pecha grandement. / Mathiolet semblablement / Qui n'a pas ensuÿ Machault, / A mal dit du saint sacrement, / Mais de leur jengle ne me chault (pt. 1, ll. 6913–20, ed. Piaget 1968, 219 [And the evil Jean de Meun, who, in speaking in a courteous manner did not resemble master Alain (Chartier), erred and sinned greatly. Similarly Mathiolet (i.e., *Lamentations de Matheolus*, translated ca. 1370 by Jean Le Fevre), who did not follow Machault, said bad things about the holy sacrament (of marriage), but I don't care about their chatter].[38] A further mention of Machaut shows that Le Franc was also familiar with the *déploration* of Deschamps (chap. 2.1.1f–g), since he cites the refrain: "La mort Machaut, grant rethorique, / Les facteurs amoureux lamentent" [love poets lament the death of Machaut, the great versifier].[39] Even so, Le Franc could not agree with the final decision of the *Jugement Behaingne*: "Je ne m'accorde au jugement / Machaut..." [I do not agree with the judgment of Machaut].[40]

---

[35] It is now split into four manuscripts, *F:Pn 835, 606, 836*, and *605*.

[36] Elsewhere, Poirion emends this reading to *Quant je vous voy crier a larme* (1965, 435 n. 27), which would seem to eliminate the example he cited earlier (1965, 262).

[37] For the biography of Michault Taillevent, see Deschaux 1975, chap. 3.

[38] See also H.F. Williams 1987, 191.

[39] Ed. G. Paris 1887, 415; also cited in H.F. Williams 1987, 190; Mühlethaler 1989, 409 (discussed p. 401).

[40] Ed. G. Paris 1887, 409; Chichmaref 1909, 1:lxxi; Hoepffner 1908–21, 1:v, vii. H.F. Williams (1987, 190–91) cites some further passages related to *Jugement Behaingne*, although he erroneously associates them with the *Voir Dit*.

e. René d'Anjou (1409–1480). King René d'Anjou places Machaut second among the six
great poets in the cemetery of the *ospital d'Amours* in his *Livre du Cuer d'Amours Espris*
(1457):[41] *Icy parle l'acteur et dit* / Joignant de celle tombe haulte et auctentique a
merveilles, riche, belle et plaisant et faicte de grant estoffe, estoit celle de Machault,
poethe renommé, laquelle estoit sans tabernacle nul, mais touteffoiz n'estoit pource
moins qu'elle ne fust d'argent fin toute faicte, et a l'entour escripte d'esmail bleu, vert et
violet, et ensise a chanczons bien notees, a virelaiz aussi, a servantoys, a laiz et a motez
en diverses faczons faictes et composees; aussi en epitaphe en peu de vers escript avoit
pareillement: / *Telz estoient les vers escripz a la sepulture de Machault* / Guillaume de
Machault, ainsi avoye nom. / Né en Champagne fuz, et si euz grant renom / D'estre fort
embrazé du penser amoureux / Pour l'amour d'une, voir, dont pas ne fuz eureux / Ma vïe
seulement tant que la peusse voir, / Mais pource ne laissay, pour vous dire le voir, / Faire
ditz et chançons tant que dura la vie, / Tant avoye forment de lui complaire envye, / Et
tant que cuer et corps asprement luy donnay / Et fis mainte balade, complainte et virelay,
/ Et incontinent, voir, je rendi a Dieu l'ame / Dont le corps gist ycy en bas soubz ceste
lame (ed. Wharton 1980, 142–43) [*Here the author speaks and says*: adjoining this tomb,
marvelously grand and celebrated, rich, beautiful and enjoyable and made of rich material,
was the tomb of the renowned poet Machaut, without a tabernacle, but even so no less
sumptuous for it was all made of pure silver, and around it was writing in blue, green and
violet enamel, and it was inscribed with well notated chansons, virelais too, *serventois*,
lais, and motets, made and composed in diverse ways; also there was an epitaph written in
only a few lines as follows: *Such were the verses written on the tomb of Machault*:
Guillaume de Machault, thus was I named. I was born in Champagne, and enjoyed great
renown for being inflamed with amorous thoughts for the love of a lady, which, indeed,
only made my life happy when I could see her, but even so I did not cease, to tell you the
truth, from making *dits* and chansons as long as I lived, so much did I desire to please
her, and keenly I gave her my heart and body. And I made many a ballade, complainte and
virelai, and forthwith, in truth, did I give up my soul to God, while my body lies here
below this gravestone].
    This reference has been cited since Rigoley de Juvigny (1773), e.g., Rive 1780, 2,
Tarbé 1849, xxxiii; P. Paris 1875, xi–xii; Hoepffner 1908–21, 1:v–vi; Chichmaref 1909,
1:lxxi; Machabey 1955b, 1:15. In an important recent discussion, Cerquiglini (1985b,
173, 239–43), who gives the passage after a different manuscript, discounts the old notion
that René d'Anjou was referring to the title of Machaut's *Voir Dit*; see further the discussion in Mühlethaler 1989, 402, 405–6.

4. Musical reputation[42]

A. *Manuscript ascriptions of musical works.* Without the large complete-works
manuscripts of Machaut, we could guess little of his importance as a musician.
Indeed, Mühlethaler (1989, 401–2) remarks that after Gilles Li Muisis and
Eustache Deschamps, mentions of Machaut scarcely ever associate him with
music. The transmission of the works of Philippe de Vitry (1291–1361), by all
accounts an extremely influential figure, provides interesting material for
comparison. A few external attributions in theory treatises or literary works,
coupled with internal stylistic and textual evidence, have been used to delineate
the Vitry canon of some thirteen works, a list that nevertheless remains
tentative.[43] Even so, the pattern of transmission of musical works seen in the

---

[41] Attribution to Achille Caulier (as Hoepffner 1908–21, 1:v–vi) is no longer accepted (Cer-
    quiglini 1985b, 241 n. 38). The six poets are Ovid, Machaut, Boccaccio, Jean de Meun,
    Petrarch, and Alain Chartier (discussion in Poirion 1990). Rigoley de Juvigny (1773) was
    perhaps first to signal the mention of Machaut in the *Livre du Cuer d'Amours Espris*.

[42] An excellent summary of this aspect is given in Ziino 1982b and 1982c, based partly on
    an essential article of Günther (1972); see also Borren 1946, 116; Calin 1974, 246 n. 1;
    Fallows 1977a, 289; Jankowski 1983; Leech-Wilkinson 1990a, 231, 237–38.

[43] See Sanders 1980c; Earp 1983, 5 n. 9; Roesner/Avril/Regalado 1990, 38–42. Leech-
    Wilkinson (1982–83) is more liberal in ascribing motets to Vitry on stylistic grounds, as

motets of Vitry is actually rather good for the first half of the fourteenth century.[44]

By contrast, if the manuscripts exclusively transmitting works of Machaut did not exist, only four pieces of music could be attributed to him: (1) *De petit po* (B18) and (2) *Quant Theseüs / Ne quier* (B34) would be known through ascriptions in the Chantilly codex, **Ch** [59] (the popular *De Fortune* [B23] is unattributed in **Ch**), while (3) *Qui es / Ha! Fortune* (M8) and (4) *Douce dame, tant* (R20) would be known through ascriptions in the Stockholm Villon manuscript, **St** [46] (no music would be known for R20, however). Erroneous attributions to Machaut in two other manuscripts, the destroyed Strasbourg MS, **Str** [73] and the Fribourg MS, **Frib** [70], would add four works we know to be spurious, since they do not appear in the complete-works manuscripts.[45] Unlike the situation for Vitry, there are no external attributions in theory treatises or literary works for Machaut's music, except the 1431 borrowing slip for Marguerite of Burgundy (chap. 3 item [60]), which informs us that Machaut wrote a Mass.[46] But without the Machaut manuscripts, we could not identify it, and in any case, only the Ite, missa est appears in an anthology MS, **PadA** [62], of course unattributed there. We would be left only with the unspecific mention of Machaut's name in two "musician motets," *Musicalis scientia / Sciencie laudabili*[47] and *Apollinis eclipsatur / Zodiacum signis.*[48]

B. *Musical imitations.* This is not the place to undertake a thoroughgoing examination of the influence of Machaut's musical compositions on his contemporaries and followers.[49] Only the most striking and directly palpable

---

is Kügle (1993, 155–206, 293–96). On the question of composer individuality in the fourteenth century, see Finscher 1975.

[44] Leech-Wilkinson (1982–83, 20) suggests the possibility that Vitry's motets were transmitted as a corpus.

[45] The works include the following: (1) *Jour a jour* is ascribed to Machaut only in **Str** [73] (ed. Apel 1970–72, 3:102–5 no. 250; Greene 1981–89, 22:78–79 no. 47a). The same manuscript also ascribes both (2) *Par maintes foys* (ed. Apel 1970–72, 1:222–25 no. 115; Greene 1981–89, 19:170–74 no. 100, 21:158–64) and (3) *Che qui vol pense* [read *De ce que fol pense*] (ed. Apel 1970–72, 1:159–61 no. 84; Greene 1981–89, 19:123–29 nos. 87a–b) to Machaut, but there are conflicting ascriptions of these works in **Ch** [59], to Jo. Vaillant and to P. des Molins, respectively. Finally, (4) the motet *Li enseignement / De touz* (see chaps. 7.4 and 8.5), is ascribed to *Guillermus de Mascardio* in **Frib** [70]. It should be noted that **Str** and **Frib**, two musical sources unreliable in their attributions to Machaut, are also the only musical sources with attributions to Vitry, which however are accepted. On attributions to Machaut in **Str**, see the interesting speculations of Ludwig (1926–54, 2:39*), and the discussion of the phenomenon of false attributions by Finscher (1975, 34).

[46] The borrowing slip also names (cyclic?) Masses by Jean Vaillant and Philippe Royllart, works that may be partially extant, but which cannot be identified. See Earp's review of Leech-Wilkinson 1990c, p. 296.

[47] He is named in the triplum as "de Machau Guillelmo" in the unique source, *F:Pn 67* (ed. Harrison 1968, 5:181–84 no. 33 and supplement, text no. 46); on the names cited, see Guesnon 1912, 97–99; Ludwig 1926–54, 2:21*; Gómez 1985b, 18.

[48] He is variously named in the triplum as "Guilhermus de Mascaudio" (**Iv** [57]); "G. de Mascaudio" (*E:Bc 971*); "Wilhelmi de Mascaudo" (**Str**); or "Gulielmus de Mascadio" (*I:Pu 658*); see the ed. of Harrison (1968, 5:50–61, Nos. 9–9a and supplement, text no. 18; also the commentary in Ludwig 1926–54, 2:22a*). Additional sources have since been discovered; see Gómez (1985b, 9), and Bent (1990b, 231, under "Zodiacum").

[49] More general studies of Machaut's influence on later fourteenth-century musical style may be listed briefly: Apel 1946–47; Günther 1957, 205–22; Reaney 1958c; Schrade 1960, 868–69; Günther 1961–62, 165–74; Hirshberg 1971. Based on the evidence of manuscript

instances can be included here. Concerning the motets, Earp (1983, 328; 1989, 495) discusses the case of *Degentis vita / Cum vix artidici,* an anonymous motet related to Machaut's *Qui es / Ha! Fortune* (M8). Other motets that are structurally interrelated—although often it is Machaut doing the imitating in these cases—are discussed by Leech-Wilkinson (1982–83) and Kügle 1993.[50]

Several fourteenth-century ballades have been found to borrow directly from works of Machaut.[51] The anonymous *Ma dame m'a congié donné* is based on Machaut's *Se je me pleing* (B15) by reversing first line and refrain: the refrain of Machaut's ballade, text and music, forms the first line of the anonymous ballade, while Machaut's first line is made the refrain of the new work. The same relationship obtains for the anonymous *Dame qui fust si tres bien assenee,* related to Machaut's popular *De Fortune* (B23). In *Phiton, Phiton beste tres venimeuse* by Magister Franciscus, the first three breve measures, along with other melodic details, are borrowed from Machaut's *Phyton, le mervilleus serpent* (B38).

A different sort of imitation has been noted by Lucy Cross (reported in Günther 1980a): Matteo da Perugia (fl. 1402–1418) quotes the beginning text of Machaut's *Se je me pleing* (B15) in his ballade *Se je me plaing de Fortune.* On the words "de Fortune," Matteo quotes text and music—cantus and tenor— of Machaut's *De Fortune* (B23). Christopher Page (personal communication) has recently discovered that the refrain of an anonymous ballade, *S'espoir n'estoit*[52], quotes text and music of the cantus and tenor of the B-section of Machaut's popular rondeau *Se vous n'estes* (R7). Fallows (1990, 22–23) finds Machaut's late polyphonic virelais—*Se je souspir* (V36/30), *Moult sui* (V37/31), and *De tout sui* (V38/32)—influential on some anonymous late fourteenth-century virelais. Anthonello da Caserta's setting of Machaut's ballade *Biauté parfaite et bonté souvereinne* (Lo140) apparently does not cite any of Machaut's musical works.[53]

There are also textual connections to Machaut works in several ballades of Filippotto da Caserta.[54] His *De ma dolour ne puis trouver confort* (ed. Apel 1950, no. 60; 1970–72, 1:145–47 no. 78; Greene 1981–89, 18:117–19 no. 42)

---

concordances and Machaut's secondary position in the listings in the musician motets compared to de Vitry and de Muris, Besseler (1925, 198–99) noted Machaut's distance from influential French musical circles, suggesting that Machaut drew students only in his late years at Reims.

[50] See below, chap. 7.3, discussions of *Tous corps / De* (M2), *Aucune gent / Qui plus* (M5), *Qui es / Ha! Fortune* (M8), *Fons / O livoris* (M9), *Hareu! / Helas!* (M10), *Amours qui a / Faus Samblant* (M15), *Quant vraie amour / O series* (M17), *Bone pastor / Bone pastor* (M18), *Martyrum / Diligenter* (M19), *Christe / Veni* (M21), *Tu qui gregem / Plange* (M22), and *Felix virgo / Inviolata* (M23).

[51] Most of these examples are discussed in Günther 1972, 55–58. For sources and editions, see the discussion of the musical legacy of the relevant Machaut works in chap. 7.3 below. Besides the works specifically mentioned in this paragraph, namely *Se je me pleing* (B15), *De Fortune* (B23), and *Phyton* (B38), see the discussions of *Se quanque amours* (B21), *Je puis trop* (B28), *De toutes flours* (B31), *Ma fin* (R14), and *Puis qu'en oubli* (R18). See also Guillaume de Machaut 1982, 338 (Reaney's comments). Snizkova (1982, 73–74) discusses some supposed influence of Machaut on Czech music, but his argument is unconvincing. In addition, Handschin (1923, 7 n. 1) discusses the dependence of the text of an anonymous virelai *Fist on, dame,* on Machaut's *Lyon,* ll. 1523–36; the relationship remains speculative.

[52] Ed. Apel 1970–72, 2:97–99 no. 175; Greene 1981–89, 21:204–6 no. 62.

[53] For editions, see chap. 6.4, commentary to Lo140.

[54] For the following relationships, see Günther 1972, 62–68; Strohm 1989, 68–70; 1993, 57, 59–60.

quotes Machaut's *De ma dolour ne puis avoir confort* (Lo 210). His *En attendant souffrir m'estuet* (ed. Apel 1950, no. 56; 1970–72, 1:56–57 no. 28; Greene 1981–89, 18:125–27 no. 45; attributed in **Ch** [59] to Jo. Galiot) is related—through intermediate stages—to Machaut's *En amer* (RF4). His *En remirant vo douce pourtraiture* (ed. Apel 1950, no. 59; 1970–72, 1:148–50 no. 79; Greene 1981–89, 19:21–24 no. 57) cites Machaut's *En remirant vo gracieus viaire* (Lo110), and has references to the opening text of *De triste* (B29) and the refrain of *Plourez, dames* (Lo229=B32) (Reaney 1980b). Other members of the complex include the rondeau *En attendant d'amer la douce vie* attributed to J. Galiot, the anonymous rondeau *Esperance qui en mon cuer s'en bat / D'amour me fait sentir la douce vie*, Jacob de Senleches's ballade *En attendant esperance*, and Johannes Ciconia's virelai *Sus un fontayne* (ed. Apel 1970–72, 1:25–27 no. 14; Bent/Hallmark 1985, 170–74 no. 45), which cites the three ballades of Filippotto, *De ma dolour*, *En attendant*, and *En remirant*. Another work of music related to a Machaut text is the anonymous ballade *Pour che que je ne puis* (see chap. 6.4, commentary to Lo60).

C. *Music theory treatises*. Machaut is not well represented by citations of specific works in extant music theory treatises, perhaps due to the limited circulation of his motets, the only genre that music theorists cited by title until later in the fourteenth century. Only two theoretical works cite specific works by Machaut, both of course without attribution: (1) the St-Victor redaction of the Vitriacan *Ars nova* cites the motet *Qui es / Ha! Fortune* (M8)[55]; (2) an anonymous early fifteenth-century south or southwest German treatise cites three widely circulated chansons, the ballades *De petit po* (B18), and *De toutes* (B31), as well as the rondeau *Se vous n'estes* (R7).[56]

Another branch of the theoretical tradition does not cite specific titles of Machaut works but rather shows the theorists' acquaintance with certain of his notational practices. A treatise attributed to Johannes de Muris, the *Libellus cantus mensurabilis* (ca. 1340–50)[57] mentions "Guillelmus de Maschandio" in connection (1) with the imperfection of a perfect breve in minor prolation by a single minim; and (2) the imperfection of an imperfect breve in major prolation by two successive minims, both before or both after the breve. In modern terms, this amounts to changing between the meters 6/8 and 3/4 in the course of a single composition, with eighth-note equivalency (chap. 2.4.1a).[58] Examples of case (1) appear several times in Machaut's most widely known chanson, the ballade *De petit po* (B18), while examples of case (2) are most often met with in the rondeau *Rose, lis* (R10). Similar discussions appear in later treatises based on the *Libellus*. Machaut's usage of this aspect of the mensural system in

---

[55] *F:Pn 14741*; ed. Reaney/Gilles/Maillard 1964, 32 §10. See Roesner 1990, 31 n. 70. Fuller (1985–86) provides a fundamental reappraisal of the *Ars nova* complex of theory.

[56] Ed. Staehelin 1974; see Frobenius 1986, 12; *RISM* 1992. In addition, the treatise cites "*Se fortune*" as an example of a rondeau, perhaps intending Machaut's ballade *De Fortune* (B23).

[57] On the attribution to Johannes and the date, see Michels 1970, 27–40; Katz 1989, 23–34; Balensuela 1994, 70–72. Padre Martini (1706–1784) also noted this passage (Vecchi 1977). On the enormous importance and influence of the *Libellus*, see Gallo 1984; Balensuela 1994, 88–89.

[58] A clear discussion of the theoretical distinctions involved (imperfection *quo ad partes*) is given in Ellsworth 1969, 146–48; see also Michels 1970, 93; Berger 1992, 29–37; Balensuela 1994, 27–31. The imperfection of an imperfect breve in major prolation by two minims before or after the breve would of course soon be handled conveniently by means of coloration. The hemiola effect is often heard in early fifteenth-century chansons in *tempus imperfectum prolatio maior*.

practical examples is of some interest, because theoretical speculation about this feature of the new notational system seems to have significantly antedated any practical examples.[59]

The anonymous Italian author of the *Opusculum artis musice* also pairs Machaut and Johannes de Muris: "Measured music is that which was composed and devised by numerous masters, especially by Master Johannes de Muris and Master Guillaume de Machaut... (Page 1993, 113).

2.4.1. MACHAUT'S NOTATIONAL LICENSE

a. Johannes de Muris(?), *Libellus cantus mensurabilis.* "Et nota quod quidam cantores scilicet Guillelmus de maschandio, et nonnulli alii imperficiunt brevem perfectam minoris prolationis ab una sola minima, et brevem imperfectam majoris prolationis a duabus minimis simul sequentibus vel precedentibus ut hic: [musical example]. Et dicunt ibi mutari qualitatem" (ed. Katz 1989, 270 §119–24; cf. Coussemaker 1864–76, 3:50a; delete the first *punctus* on the second line of the musical example) [And note that some singers, namely Guillaume de Machaut and some others, imperfect the perfect breve of minor prolation by a single minim and the imperfect breve of major prolation by two minims, both preceding or following, as here [example]. And they say that the quality is changed there (trans. after Balensuela 1994, 235 n. 140)]. Machaut's use of this notational practice is discussed by Wolf (1904, 1:170–72; 1913, 1:342); see also Apel 1953, 345; Hoppin 1960, 13–14, 20–22; Berger 1992, 32–34. Wolf adduces examples from *S'amours ne fait* (B1), *De petit po* (B18), and *Rose, lis* (R10). Earp (1983, 20–21 n. 36) mentions several others.

Later treatises based on the *Libellus* also mention Machaut, up to the very end of the fifteenth century:[60]

b. 12 Jan. 1376.[60] A revision of the *Libellus* attributed to the Parisian Goscalcus, now at Berkeley (*US:BE 744*). "Et nota quod quidem cantores, puta Guillermus de Mascandio et plures alii, imperficiunt brevem perfectam minoris prolacionis ab una sola minima, et brevem imperfectam maioris prolacionis a duabus minimis simul, ambabus precedentibus vel sequentibus. Et debent ibi mutari qualitatem, capientes brevem perfectam minoris prolacionis, ac si esset imperfectam maioris prolacionis, et e converso" (ed. Ellsworth 1984, 160) [Note that some singers, such as Guillaume de Machaut and many others, imperfect the perfect brevis in minor prolation by a single minima and the imperfect brevis in major prolation by two minimae together, both either preceding or following. They ought to change the quality there, treating the perfect brevis in minor prolation as if it were imperfect in major prolation and conversely (trans. Ellsworth 1984, 161)].[61]

c. *Ars cantus mensurabilis mensurata per modos iuris.* An anonymous Italian treatise based on the *Libellus.*[62] "Hec quoque magister Iohannes de Muris videtur consentire cum dicit quod nonnulli cantores imperficiunt brevem imperfectam maioris prolationis ut esset brevis perfecta minoris prolationis, ut puta, Gulielmus de Mastodio dicit ibi mutare qualitatem, ut hic: [musical example] Et e contra, ut his: [musical example]" (ed. Balensuela 1994, 234; Anon. 5 of Coussemaker 1864–76, 3:395)[63] [Master Johannes de Muris seems to allow this when he says that some singers imperfect the imperfect brevis

---

59 See Johannes de Muris, *Notitia artis musicae* (1321; ed. Michels 1972; discussed in Michels 1970, 36, 88); students of Philippe de Vitry, *Ars nova* (ca. 1320; ed. Reaney/Gilles/Maillard 1964, 30 §5–6 and 31 §5); and the St-Victor redaction of the same treatise (ed. Reaney/Gilles/Maillard 1964, 32 §8–9). Long (1981, 54–56) adduces some early practical examples in Italy.

60 On the date, see Katz 1989, 13 n. 20.

61 Commentary in Ellsworth 1969, 2:153–55; on the date and provenance of the treatise, see Michels 1970, 29–30 and Sachs 1974, 184–85. Fétis (1860–65, 4:158) notes the mention of Machaut in this treatise. Katz (1989, chap. 2) argues that the source Fétis knew, owned by Roquefort-Flamméricourt, was not identical to the Berkeley manuscript.

62 On the relationship between the *Libellus* and the *Ars cantus mensurabilis*, see Balensuela 1994, 69–82.

63 On the musical examples in Anon. 5, see Ludwig 1926–54, 2:39b* n. Balensuela (1994) of course provides new editions of the examples.

of major prolation so that it becomes a perfect brevis of minor prolation. For instance, Guilielmus de Mastodio states that the quality is changed there, as here: (ex.) And the opposite, as here: (ex.) (trans. Balensuela 1994, 235)].

d. ca. 1404. Prosdocimus de Beldemandis (d. 1428), *Expositiones tractatus practice cantus mensurabilis magistri Johannis de Muris*. Prosdocimus quotes the above passage from Johannes de Muris (item a), and provides a very extensive gloss: "De prima ergo parte dicit: et nota quod, id est notare debes ex supradictis quod, quidam cantores, et illorum unum nominando ait: ut puta Guilielmus de Mascandio, et multi alii.... Supra quam partem notandum, quod iste Guilielmus de Mascandio quem nominat auctor in littera, fuit in arte musicali magister singularis, in qua arte multa composuit" (revised version of 1411, ed. Gallo 1966, 83–84) [Therefore, of the first part he says: and note that, that is, you ought to note from the aforesaid, that certain singers, and of them naming one he says: as for instance Guilielmus de Mascandio, and many others.... Beyond this, note that this Guilielmus de Mascandio, whom the author named by name, was a distinguished master in the art of music, in which art he composed many things]. See the discussion in Ziino 1982c, 508–9.

e. Anon. Seville, *E:Sco* 5.2.25, fol. 111r (cited by Ludwig 1926–54, 2:32b*). See the discussion, with further bibliography, in Gallo 1968, 59–73. This part of the treatise (Gallo's item xl, p. 71), is described as a "reelaboration" of the *Libellus* (Gallo 1968, 61).

f. 1410. The Spanish theorist Fernando Estevan mentions *Guillelmus de Mascadio* in his *Reglas de canto plano e de contrapunto*, a treatise written in 1410 (cited in Ludwig 1926–54, 2:32b*, with further references; Esteve Barba 1942; Faulhaber 1984, no. 3159).

g. ca. 1430–35. Ugolino of Orvieto (ca. 1380–1457), *Declaratio musicae disciplinae* (ed. Seay 1960, vol. 2). Ugolino's book 3 is a commentary on the *Libellus*. Machaut is mentioned in chap. 3, *Quomodo mensurarum notae perficiantur vel imperficiantur* [How notes of the different mensurations can be perfected or imperfected], part 18, *De opinione Gulielmi de Mascandio et aliorum* [On the opinion of *Gulielmus de Mascandio* and others], and part 19, *Ratio dicti Gulielmi et suorum sequacium* [the reasoning of the aforementioned *Gulielmus* and his followers]. Ugolino cites the above passage from Johannes de Muris (item a), and provides a very extensive gloss, partly depending on Prosdocimus: "Hic ponit auctor quorundam cantorum antiquorum opinionem, de quorum numero quidam Gulielmus de Mascandio nominatus per auctorem in littera fuit. Iste Gulielmus in musicis disciplinis fuit singularis et multa in ea arte optime composuit, cuius cantibus temporibus nostri usi sumus bene politeque compositis ac dulcissimis harmoniarum melodiis ornatis. Sed quamvis dulcissima fuerit iste cantus harmonia refertus, tamen duabus in mensuris errorem commisit, prout egregius auctor hic in suo textu ostendit...." [Here the author gives the opinion of certain ancient singers, of whose number a certain Gulielmus de Mascandio was specifically named by the author. This Gulielmus was distinguished in musical science and composed very well many things in that art; his songs, elegantly composed with the sweetest harmonies and melodies, are still in use today. But although this song is filled with the sweetest harmony, nevertheless he committed an error in two mensurations, as the excellent author shows here in his text]. See the discussion in Ziino 1982c, 508–9 (there are earlier discussions in La Fage 1864; Ambros 1891, 26; Kornmüller 1895; Ludwig 1926–54, 2:39b* n.).

h. 1496. Franchino Gafori (1451–1522), *Practica musice*, book 2. "Gulielmus de Mascandio brevem temporis perfecti et imperfectae prolationis a sola minima imperfectam posuit, quod absurdum est" (Gafori 1496, bb iiii) [Gulielmus de Mascandio has made a breve of *tempus perfectum* and *prolatio imperfecta* imperfect by a single minim. This is absurd... (trans. Miller 1968, 96; trans. and commentary in I. Young 1969, 98–99 n. 29, p. 78 n. 14)]. Cf. Lenneberg (1988, 20) for mention of this citation in Walther in 1732.

5. Modern musical works inspired by Machaut

The following provides at least the beginnings of a listing of modern musical compositions related to or inspired by Machaut. Some of these works are known to me only as references to recordings, while others are published scores. Newspaper references for some items are taken from Higgins 1993a, 122 notes 49–52 (to p. 117).

Adolphe, Bruce (b. 1955). *Machaut is My Beginning.*

Based on *Ma fin* (R14). Review: John Henken, "A Solid Program by Da Capo Players," *The Los Angeles Times*, 2 Dec. 1992, p. F3.

Bedford, David (b. 1937). *Hoquetus David* (2 pianos). 1987.

An arrangement for two pianos. Notice by Keith Potter, *Musical Times* 128 (1987): 639.

Beglarian, Eve (b. 1958). *Machaut in the Machine Age.*

Pop reworkings of motets and chansons. Review: John Henken, "Basso Bongo Duo Offers an Engaging Concert at Museum," *The Los Angeles Times*, 24 March 1993, p. F4.

Berio, Luciano (b. 1925). *A-Ronne.* Radio version for five actors, 1974. Version for eight singers, 1974–75. Recording. Decca Head 15. Swingle II. Recorded Feb. 1976.

Berio's work elaborates a poem of Edoardo Sanguineti; Machaut's *Ma fin* (R14) seems to provide one of the many textual borrowings in the poem.

Birtwistle, Harrison (b. 1934). *Hoquetus David. Instrumental Motet. Guillaume de Machaut / Harrison Birtwistle.* UE 15368. London: Universal, 1981.

Colorful modern arrangement of Machaut's *Hoquetus David.*

―――. *Machaut à ma manière* [for orchestra]. UE 19152. London: Universal, 1989. Duration 10'00".

Composition (finished August 1988) for symphony orchestra, with movements based on Machaut's *Fons / O livoris* (M9), *Hoquetus David*, and the Amen of the Credo. Notice of premiere in *Orchester* 38 (1990): 292. Reviews: Anthony Pople, *Music & Letters* 73 (1992): 169–70; Jerome Rosen, *Notes* 49 (1992–93): 810–12; John Warnaby, *Tempo* 173 (June 1990): 68, 70 (mentions two arrangements of *Hoquetus David* by Birtwistle, from 1969 and 1987). Notice of 1987 arrangement by Keith Potter, *Musical Times* 128 (1987): 639.

Bossert, Christoph. *Messe de Nostre Dame.*

Arrangement for three choral groups and instrumental ensemble (brass, strings, percussion). Review: Richard Lorber, *Musik und Kirche* 56 (1986): 206–7.

Bourcier, Thomas Murray. "Rose, Lily, Spring for Chamber Orchestra." Master's Thesis, Western Michigan University, 1991. Ann Arbor: University Microfilms. Order no. MA 1345232.

Composition for chamber orchestra based on Machaut's *Rose, lis* (R10). Abstract: *Master's Abstracts International* A 30/1 (1992): 8.

Cardy, Patrick (b. 1953). *Virelai.*

Variations on a Machaut tune. Review: William Littler, *The Toronto Star*, 23 Feb. 1991, p. H4.

Dinescu, Violeta (b. 1953). *Amont* (Guillaume de Machaut), pour mezzo-soprano et piano (1985). AV 0143. Berlin: Astoria, 1989.

A contemporary composition on the text of the rondeau *Tant com je seray vivant* (VD59, ed. P. Paris 1875, 278), attributed to Toute Belle in the *Voir Dit.*

Fišer, Luboš (b. 1935). *Písně pro slepého krále Jana Lucemburského na slova Guillaume de Machauta* (Songs for the Blind King John of Luxembourg on text by Guillaume de Machaut). 1975. Recording. *Dialogues.* Symposium Musicum, dir. Svatopluk Jányš. Panton 81 0771 (LP). Recorded 11 Sept. 1988. Released 1989. Duration 7'13".

This work, for chamber choir and orchestra , is framed by the tenor of the motet *Trop plus / Biauté / Je ne sui mie certains d'avoir amie* (M20). The music in between is newly composed to text incipits from various other Machaut motets.

Fortner, Wolfgang (1907–1987). *Machaut-Balladen für Gesang und Orchester.* Musik des 20. Jahrhunderts. Edition Schott 6620. Mainz, London, New York: Schott, 1975. Duration: ca. 25'00" (version for two tenors); ca. 21'00" (version for one tenor).

Composed in 1973. Settings of *S'Amours ne fait* (B1), *De Fortune* (B23), *Tres douce dame que* (B24), *Tu qui gregem / Plange* (M22) (instrumental), *Tant doucement me sens* (R9), *Puis qu'en oubli* (R18) (instrumental), *Armes, Amours / O fleur* (Deschamps's *déploration*). The voice(s) sing Machaut's music, while the orchestra elaborates more or less on the accompanying voices. Includes German translations of the texts by Arnold Rothe.

Gieseler, Walter (b. 1919). 1984. *Guillaume de Machault (ca. 1300–1377): La messe de nostre dame (1349/1363). (Kyrie—Sanctus—Agnus Dei).* EG 1540. Bad Schwalbach: Gravis.

Orchestral arrangement (1982) of three movements of the Mass.

Gilbert, Anthony (b. 1934). *String Quartet no. 3, "Super Hoqueto 'David'* (Machaut)." 1987.

Notice by Keith Potter, *Musical Times* 128 (1987): 639.

Gilbert, Yvette, and Edmond Rickett. *Chanteries du Moyen Age. Quarante chansons recueillies et adaptées par Yvette Gilbert et harmonisée par Edmond Rickett.* Vol. 1, *Vingt chansons.* Vol. 2, *Vingt chansons.* Paris: Heugel, 1926.

Arrangements, with piano accompaniment. Four works relate to Machaut: an arrangement of *Pour quoy me bat mes maris?* (M16, tenor), here attributed to Adam de la Halle (1:12–13 no. 6); a second arrangement of the same tenor (1:32–33 no. 11); an arrangement of *Loyauté vueil* (V2) (1:66–67 no. 27); and an arrangement of *Hé! dame de vaillance* (V1) (1:68–69 no. 28). Discussed in Ludwig 1926–54, 2:6a*, 3:61n.

Grunenwald, Jean-Jacques (1911–1982). *Variations sur un thème de Machaut pour clavecin.* Paris: Bornemann, 1957.

Modern composition. Not examined.

Hand, Frederic (b. 1947). *Rose liz.* Guillaume de Machaut and Frederic Hand. Recording. RCA Victor RCD1 7126 (CD; also Musical Heritage Society MHS 4887 [LP]; 11049K and 416887 [CD]; MusicMasters MM 60208T [CD]). *Frederic Hand's Jazzantiqua.* Frederic Hand. Recorded June 1983. Released 1984. CD released 1989. Duration 5'20".

Jazz arrangement of R10. Not heard.

Holt, Simon (b. 1958). *David Hoquetus.* 1987.

Arrangement for tuned percussion. Notice by Keith Potter, *Musical Times* 128 (1987): 639.

Keane, David (b. 1940). *Variations on a Theme of Guillaume de Machaut.*

Uses material from the Mass; see Lisa R. Dominick, *Perspectives of New Music* 21 (1982–83): 378–79.

Martin, Frank (1890–1974). *Ode à la musique.* Kassel: Bärenreiter, 1979. Duration 9'00".

Modern musical setting of part of the *Prologue* (Hoepffner 1908–21, 1:9–10 ll. 85–146), composed in 1961, for baritone, four-part mixed choir, trumpet, two horns, three trombones, piano, and string bass. Includes a German translation by Ellen Bosenius and Günther Massenkeil.

Matoušek, Lukáš (b. 1943). *Hoquet Guillauma de Machaut* (Guillaume de Machaut's Hocket) for flute, clarinet and viola (1972). Recording. Ars Camerialis, Prague, dir. Lukáš Matoušek. Panton 8111 0056 (LP). Released 1978. Duration 2'47".

Modern arrangement of the *Hoquetus David.* Record review: J.F. Weber 1982.

Muldowney, Dominic (b. 1952). *Paraphrase on Machaut's Hoquetus David.*

Modern recomposition of the *Hoquetus David* (1987). Review: Paul Griffiths, "Composers Ensemble Asbury," *The Times* (London), 14 January 1992.

Nelson, Ron (b. 1929). *Medieval Suite. Homage to Leonin; Homage to Perotin; Homage to Machaut.* n.p.: Boosey & Hawkes, 1981. Duration ca. 5'00"; 4'25"; 6'15"; total ca. 15'40". Recording. *The Compositions of Ron Nelson and John Corigliano.* Kent State University Wind Ensemble, dir.

John Boyd. Golden Crest ATH 5083 (LP). Released 1984. Duration 19'00".
Modern work for wind ensemble.

Rheinberger, Josef (1839–1901). *Sonate Nr. 19 in G-moll (Präludium, Provençalisch, Introduction und Finale)*, Op. 193. Leipzig: Forberg, 1899.
A harmonization of the beginning of *J' aim la flour* (L2) opens the second movement of this organ sonata.

Rubbra, (Charles) Edmund (1901–1986). *Fantasia on a Theme of Machault for Recorder, String Quartet and Harpsichord, Op. 86*. London: Lengnick, 1956.
Modern composition; not examined.

Sciarrino, Salvatore (b. 1947). *Guillaume de Machaut: Rose liz* (voices, flute, clarinet, bassoon, viola, cello).
Modern arrangement, composed in 1984. See Higgins 1993a, 122 n. 52 (to p. 117).

Spears, Gay Holmes. "Tapestries." D.M.A. diss., Memphis State University, 1993. Ann Arbor: University Microfilms. Order No. 9322853. Duration ca. 20'00".
Composition for chamber orchestra in four movements, based on the Unicorn tapestries in the Cloisters Museum, New York. The fourth movement incorporates Machaut's *Comment qu'a moy* (V5). Abstract: *DAI* A54/4 (Oct. 1993): 1146.

Štědroň, Miloš (b. 1942). *Mistr Machaut v Čechách* (Maitre Machaut in Bohemia) for mezzo-soprano, flute, clarinet, viola, piano (1975). Recording. Ars Camerialis, Prague, dir. Lukáš Matoušek. Panton 8111 0056 (LP). Released 1978. Zuzana Matoušková, mezzo-soprano. Duration 11'42".
Modern composition. Record review: J.F. Weber 1982.

Steel, Christopher C. (b. 1939). *Variations on a Theme of Machaut* for organ (1981).
Notice of premiere in *Composer* 73 (Summer 1981): 33.

Thiele, Siegfried (b. 1934). *Hommage à Machaut für Alt-Solo, Bariton-Solo und Orchester*. Edition Peters 9215. Leipzig: Peters, 1979. Duration ca. 25'00".
I. Ballade (based on Deschamps's *déploration, Armes, amours / O fleur*); II. Genèse et Motet (based on *Quant / O series* [M17]); III. Ballade (based on Deschamps's *déploration*); IV. Motet (based on *Christe / Veni* [M21]); V. Ballade (based on Deschamps's *déploration*).

Weckerlin, Jean-Baptiste Théodore (1821–1910), arr. *Echos du temps passé*. Paris: Durand, 1857.
Includes an arrangement for voice and piano of *Douce dame jolie* (V4) (p. 10 no. 5). See Ludwig 1926–54, 2:5b*.

Wagner-Régeny, Rudolf (1903–1969). *Acht Kommentare zu einer Weise des Guillaume de Machaut* [for orchestra]. Leipzig: Peters, [1967].
Modern composition (1967).

Wuorinen, Charles (b. 1938). *Machault mon chou* [for orchestra]. Edition Peters 67254. New York: Peters. Duration ca. 11'00".
Orchestral work based on the Mass (1988). Reviews: Richard Dyer, "Comet's BSO Debut: Grace Under Pressure," *The Boston Globe* (16 Nov. 1990), 77; Jerome Rosen, *Notes* 49 (1992–93): 810–12.

III

The Manuscripts

1. Introduction

From around 1350 to around 1420, several large manuscripts were copied that transmit works exclusively by Machaut, arranged according to the distinct genres of narrative poem, lyrical poem, motet, Mass, and secular song. This manner of presentation of a large and diverse oeuvre has some precedents in the chanson collections of the second half of the thirteenth century, culminating in the complete-works manuscript of Adam de la Halle, *F:Pn 25566*.[1] And yet the prior examples do not prepare us for the Machaut manuscripts. Here one can trace the evolution and refinement of a single author's conception of the presentation of his works as new manuscripts were copied. Indeed, in Machaut's last years, it was the organization and presentation of his life's works—rather than the composition of new works—that was his main preoccupation as an artist.

The complete-works manuscript can be considered the highest of the levels of transmission of Machaut's works. Yet Machaut was also subject to the more modest and traditional lower levels. Narrative poems circulated in anthologies. Lyrical poems were grouped anonymously and haphazardly into collections. On the lowest and most immediate level, individual narratives circulated separately, and a single lyric could be transmitted on a small swatch of parchment and enclosed in a letter, or sent with other swatches in a small box.[2] For instance, in letters 6 and 10 of Machaut's *Voir Dit* (ed. P. Paris 1875, 53, 69), there is discussion of a separate manuscript of the *Fonteinne*, at the time Machaut's most recently completed narrative poem; in letters 31 and 32 (ed. P. Paris 1875, 242, 250), there is mention of the small box, or *laiette*. S.J. Williams (1969, 437–38) discusses additional passages in the *Voir Dit* that mention individual copies of Machaut lyrics and musical chansons.

This chapter is divided into sections that organize the Machaut manuscript tradition, including the evidence we have of lost sources, according to these several levels of transmission. First come the complete-works manuscripts, followed by a group of manuscripts that were influenced by the idea of a complete-works manuscript but that also contain a few works not by Machaut. We then consider small anthologies that contain only works of Machaut and those manuscripts that transmit individual works. Finally, the largest group of manuscripts—and here we also include the two early prints that contain a few works of Machaut—is made up of anthologies, both text anthologies and music anthologies.

On the literary side, Machaut's concern for the manuscript presentation of his works in large deluxe manuscripts profoundly influenced his followers. Froissart had at least two complete-works manuscripts of his own narrative and lyric amorous poetry prepared.[3] The immense collection of Deschamps's poetry

---

[1] The study of the manuscript presentation of an author's works is a relatively recent direction in French literary studies. For our purposes, we need only mention Huot 1987 and now Switten 1995, introduction, which brings the bibliography on the subject up to date. For precedents to the Machaut manuscripts, see Huot 1987, 232–36. On *F:Pn 25566*, see Huot 1987, 64–74.

[2] On the image of enclosing poems in boxes in Froissart, see Cerquiglini-Toulet 1991a.

[3] On the Froissart manuscripts, see chap. 2 n. 8.

(*F:Pn 840*) was copied posthumously, apparently from a large collection of notes and scraps, but there is evidence that Deschamps owned a manuscript of his works.[4] Christine de Pizan contributed her part as a scribe for the several large manuscripts of her works copied for various patrons, and was clearly interested in the process of bookmaking and illustration.[5] For England, Burrow (1971, 61) has studied the example of John Gower.

The influence of Machaut's complete-works manuscripts on the accustomed patterns of transmission for musical works, however, would seem to be slight. Manuscripts transmitting musical works in fourteenth-century France never reached the high level of a Machaut manuscript, the unified and ordered retrospective collection of a single composer's works. Instead, the anthology remained the normal means of circulation.[6] Musical works also circulated separately, probably on individual bifolios or *rotuli*.[7] Most clerical composers of complex polyphony—motet, Mass, and chanson—remained anonymous, as had been true for most of the clerical composers of polyphony in the thirteenth century. Only in the late fourteenth century did this veil of anonymity begin to be lifted, in manuscripts such as the Chantilly codex [59].[8]

The task of identifying manuscripts that transmit works of Machaut was largely accomplished by the early twentieth-century editors of Machaut's texts and music. Hoepffner (1908–21, 1:xliv–li, 3:xix) listed seventeen manuscripts and provided a first attempt at a manuscript filiation, based on the items in the first volume of his edition of the narrative poems. Hoepffner's *sigla* are the basis for most subsequent citations of the core group of manuscripts.[9] Chichmaref (1909, 1:lxxii–cxvi), working independently at around the same time as Hoepffner, listed twenty-one manuscripts, along with fragments and citations in prints of Alain Chartier, and in the second rhetoric treatises of Eustache Deschamps and Baudet Herenc, bringing the total number of sources to twenty-four. Chichmaref also listed one lost manuscript.[10] In addition, he attempted a manuscript filiation based on the lyrical works. Subsequent scholars have made little use of Chichmaref's comments on the manuscripts, perhaps because he employed a series of manuscript *sigla* quite different from and less logical than those of Hoepffner. Finally, Ludwig (1926–54, 2:7a*) proclaimed that he had succeeded in raising the total number of sources to forty-one, along with citations to five untraced or lost manuscripts.

Several sources have come to light since Ludwig's listing of 1928. Most

---

[4] See chap. 2 n. 14.

[5] See Laidlaw 1987, and the many references in Bergeron 1992, 174–75. There are no comparable manuscripts for Alain Chartier's works, perhaps because the rich courts were so severely tried by the wars (Poirion 1965, 255).

[6] See Nádas 1985, chap. 1, "Introduction to the Trecento Sources and an Appraisal of Scholarly Studies." Despite the Italianate title, this chapter provides an excellent overview of the entire fourteenth-century tradition of musical manuscripts. For further general bibliography on musical sources, see the introductory remarks on the manuscript anthologies below, chap. 3.5. On the tantalizing possibility that the motets of Philippe de Vitry were transmitted as a corpus, see Leech-Wilkinson 1982–83, 20.

[7] Compare also references such as the following entry from an early fifteenth-century library inventory: "Item quatre feuillets ou [sont] plusieurs Chansons notées" (Champion 1910, xxviii no. 44) [*Item*, four leaves containing several notated chansons].

[8] On the question of composer attributions, see Finscher 1975.

[9] Ludwig (1926–54, 2:8a* n. 1) introduced one refinement in changing Hoepffner's *siglum* V to *Vg* for the Vogüé MS [3].

[10] Ludwig (1926–54, 2:11a*, 40b* no. 2) found this item actually to be an unrecognized reference to MS **E** [7].

important is a fragment of a complete-works manuscript, MS **W** [2], probably the second in chronological order after MS **C** [1], described by Earp (1989, 472–74), Wathey in *RISM* 1993, and in the catalogue below. Four further manuscripts of the *Jugement Behaingne* listed by Långfors (1917), had been overlooked until their incorporation into the discussion in Earp 1983.[11] These new sources were evaluated by Wimsatt and Kibler (1988) for their new critical edition of the *Jugement Behaingne*.

Six new sources for Machaut lyrics are now known, of which the most important is the Pennsylvania MS **Pa** [50], first described by Bertoni (1932) and utilized in the edition of the *Loange des dames* published by Wilkins (1972). Other lyrical anthologies include four important sources of the lyrics of Oton de Granson (*F:Pn 2201* [51], **Ta** [52], **La** [54], and **Bc** [55]), and a prose work with interlarded lyrics by Machaut (**Mn** [43]).

We have evidence for sixteen lost manuscripts. One of these, a manuscript owned by Alfonso the Magnanimous in the fifteenth century [3a], was probably the manuscript previously owned by Yolande of Bar, queen of Aragon, and almost certainly survives today as **Vg** [3]. I have speculated that manuscript [9], in the library of Turquam, a bourgeois of Paris, may be identified as MS **B** [4], and that the manuscript once owned by the Bastard of Orléans [14] may survive as the recently discovered fragment **W** [2].[12]

Ludwig knew of eleven musical anthologies containing Machaut's music. Two further sources (**Fa** [67] and **Frib** [70]) were discussed in Besseler's *Nachtrag* to the Ludwig edition (1928–54, vol. 4). Gilbert Reaney added **Utr** [69] and **Nur** [71] as a result of his researches for *RISM* (1969). More recently discovered sources for the music of Machaut include an early source for a lai described in Fallows 1977b (*F:La 134* [26]), a fragment of an Ars Nova chansonnier from the Low Countries described in Strohm 1984a (**Gr 3360** [68]), and a large new Italian anthology—unfortunately a palimpsest—described in d'Accone 1984 and Nádas 1987 (**SL** [65]).

This chapter provides information on the manuscripts that transmit Machaut works. Because the large complete-works manuscripts make up the most characteristic and important part of the Machaut manuscript tradition, I consider them in greater detail than the other manuscripts. On the other hand, since musicologists have carefully studied most musical anthologies in recent years, I have done little more than cite the relevant bibliographical resources for these manuscripts, along with a list of the Machaut works contained in them. For most Machaut sources, I employ the short one or two-letter manuscript sigla in common use; otherwise, I employ *sigla* in *RISM* format, familiar to musical scholars, but easily understood by others as well (country code, city and library code, shelfmark).

DESCRIPTION. Descriptions are based either on my own examination of the manuscript or from microfilms or information in the most recent catalogues or other descriptions. (I have examined MSS [1], [2], [4], [5], [5a], [6], [7], [10], [11], [15], [16], [17], [18], [20], [21], [28], [31], [33], [34], [35], [37], [38], [40], [41], [44], [45], [48], [50], [51], [53], [56], [57], [58], [59], [63], [64],

---

[11]MSS **Ys** [37], **Pc** [38], and **Ra** [44] (Earp 1983, 40–41). Earp (1983, 41 n. 98) traced the **Kr** [36] to the New York firm H.P. Kraus. Perhaps these are the four additional manuscripts that Gennrich (1930, 351) reported Ludwig had come across since the publication of his commentary volume.

[12] The sixteen lost manuscripts include six described by Ludwig, MSS [8], [12], [19], [23], [25], and [27]; I have identified nine additional references, MSS [3a], [9], [13], [14], [22], [29], [30], [39], and [60]. Gómez (1987, 115) identified MS [24].

and [69].) Descriptions in Ludwig's Machaut edition (1926–54, vol. 2), an essential starting point often ignored, may contain important older bibliography. When possible, I provide information on the material of the manuscript, the number of folios, systems of foliation, the overall dimensions, the dimensions of the writing block, scribes, and collation.[13] Information on the binding is usually limited to a simple description of material; when possible, reference is made to a volume of the new catalogue of Latin manuscripts at the Bibliothèque Nationale (*Bibliothèque Nationale* 1981), which includes descriptions and illustrations of arms and monograms found on the bindings of many of the manuscripts at the Bibliothèque Nationale. For the musical anthologies, thorough descriptions are found in the studies cited.

DECORATION. Here I provide information on initials and miniatures. For descriptions of styles of initials, my terminology is based on Muzerelle 1985, which includes plates: "floriated initial" = *lettre fleurie* (1985, §561.12); "initial with filigree" = *lettre filigranée* (1985, §561.10); "solid initial" = *initiale nue* (1985, §561.03); "highlighted capital" = *lettre rehaus ée* (1985, §561.07); "divided initial" = *lettre émanchée* (1985, §561.09 with fig. 270a). In addition, I have retained Muzerelle's term *lettre rechampie* (1985, §561.15; the letter may also be *échancrée*, §543.06), because it describes exactly certain styles of decoration seen in manuscripts of Machaut's works. For more complete information on the location and description of miniatures, refer to chapter 4.4 below. Border decorations, obviously important for dating and localization, are not yet well studied for the fourteenth century.

FACSIMILES. Here I list references to published reproductions of miniatures, pages of text, or musical works. Miniatures are identified by numbers keyed to the concordance of miniatures in chapter 4.4. For musical works, information is organized into categories by genre (lais, motets, Mass, *Hoquetus David*, ballades, rondeaux, virelais). In the case of the musical anthologies, I provide references to facsimiles only of works of Machaut or works directly related to Machaut; for other facsimiles of these manuscripts, I refer to standard published bibliographies. No integral facsimile of a complete Machaut manuscript has yet been published. The most extensive excerpt from a Machaut manuscript is the facsimile of the Mass from MS **B** [4] in Gennrich 1957. A sample of a late lyrical anthology is provided by the facsimile of the early sixteenth-century print **Jp** [49], containing a few Machaut lyrics. For a sample of a musical anthology manuscript, there is an excellent facsimile of **FP** [61] (Gallo 1981).

INSCRIPTIONS. Stray jottings on flyleaves or elsewhere that may be of interest for the provenance of the manuscript are mentioned here.

DATE AND PROVENANCE. Information on the provenance and the subsequent history of a manuscript may be found here, though original owners are known for only a few of the Machaut manuscripts. I also note the appearance of a manuscript in early library inventories, which provides clues to the manuscript's whereabouts since the fourteenth or fifteenth century. Often descriptions in early inventories are too incomplete to allow for the unequivocal identification of a manuscript, and thus it is possible that some of the lost manuscripts listed below survive but cannot be identified as an extant manuscript from the available information. When a library inventory is thorough, however, the information gained about early owners of manuscripts is interesting and

---

[13] In the account of collation, a colon between gatherings indicates that the end of a poem or group of works coincides with the end of a gathering. Earp (1983, 343–79) gives detailed diagrams of the gathering structure of (in this order) MSS **A** [5], **F-G** [6], **Vg** [3], **B** [4], **E** [7], **C** [1], **J** [16], and **K** [15].

significant. The most complete information on the early libraries that held Machaut manuscripts is available for the fifteenth-century Burgundian library. De Winter (1985, 115–20) provides an excellent summary of the many inventories of the Burgundian library, from the 1404 inventory prepared after the death of Philip the Bold, up to the 1842 catalogue of the Belgian Bibliothèque Royale (a shorter summary is in Meiss 1967, 352–53). Early shelfmarks are also listed here, when possible with reference to the catalogue to which they refer. The physical appearance of the shelfmarks used in old catalogues of the Parisian Bibliothèque du Roy are now described and illustrated in *Bibliothèque Nationale* 1981, 481 nos. 6–8 (plates xiii–xv); summary bibliographical information on the old catalogues themselves (published in Omont 1908–21) is provided in *Bibliothèque Nationale* 1975, 815.

CONTENTS. Here I provide a summary listing of the works of Machaut in the manuscript in question. Limitations of space have made complete inventories impractical, particularly for the large anthologies.

LITERATURE. Finally, additional bibliography—catalogues and inventories of a given manuscript—are listed here, as well as other studies. For the well-studied musical anthologies, I list only main sources of bibliographical information and recent studies.

2. Complete-works manuscripts

This is the most essential part of the Machaut manuscript tradition, the group of manuscripts containing only works of Machaut, in an ordered and complete collection: *dits*, lyrical poetry, and music. Some of these complete-works manuscripts were probably in some sense supervised by the author during their production (see Earp 1989 for a study of the current state of research on this issue). The manuscripts are listed here in two groups: (a) manuscripts containing both texts and music; and (b) manuscripts containing texts only. Each of these groups is arranged in an approximate chronological order. Lost or untraced manuscripts are included at the end of the relevant series. Earp (1989, 474 table I) proposes an overall chronology.

A. *Manuscripts containing both texts and music*

[1] **PARIS, Bibliothèque Nationale, fonds français 1586** (C; *F:Pn 1586*; Hoepffner: *C*; Chichmaref: *E*)

DESCRIPTION. Parchment, 225 + i fols., with two paper flyleaves in front and two in back; eighteenth-century Arabic foliation, 1–225, top right recto.[14] Dimensions: 29.9 × 22 cm, writing block ca. 21.2 × 14.2 cm, two cols. at 37–38 ll./col. Contains music. Formal bookhand; two scribes divided the copying; see Keitel 1976, 33, 42; 1982c, 79. Scribe A wrote fols. 1r–22v (*Behaingne*), 93r–120v (*Vergier, Lyon*), 137r–146v (middle part of *Loange*), and 165r–225v (lais, music section to end of the manuscript). Scribe B wrote fols. 23r–92v (*Remede, Alerion*), 121r–136v (first part of *Loange*), and 147r–165r (end of *Loange*, virelais and ballades of first music section). Collation 1–2⁸ 3⁶ : 4–7⁸ 8⁴ : 9–11⁸ 12¹⁰ : 13¹⁰ : 14⁸ 15¹⁰ : 16–17⁸ 18¹⁰ 19–25⁸ 26¹²⁻⁴ 27–28⁸; more on signatures and collation in Earp 1983, 133, 371–73. Red staves 1.3 cm. tall, drawn with a rastrum. Bound in brown leather with gilt tooling, crowns over letter "N" (Napoleon I).

DECORATION. Blue titles frequently used in the *Remede* only. Initials one to six lines tall, alternating blue with red filigree and gold with black filigree; the style of the filigree is different in the *Remede*. On the 107 miniatures in *grisaille*, divided between three artists, see the descriptions below, chap. 4.4. MS C is one of the most significant manuscripts for the history of illumination in fourteenth-century France; on the artists, see chap. 4.2 table 4.1. Huot (1987, chap. 8) discusses aspects of the iconography.

---

[14] Inscription on the last parchment flyleaf: "Les feuillets de ce manuscrit ont été cotés par 1.2.3 &c en l'annĕe 1740—le 18ᵉ may."

FACSIMILES.
Miniatures (refer to chaps. 4.3 and 4.4): C8, C10–44, C68, C73, C92–96, C106.
Ballades: see miniature C33 (fol. 47v, *Dame, de qui* [RF5]); Bofill Soliguer 1991, 22–23 (fols. 199v–201r, with end of *De petit peu* [B18], and *Je sui aussi* [B20], *De Fortune* [B23], *Se quanque* [B21] complete).
Virelai: miniature C36 (fol. 51r, *Dame, a vous* [RF6]).

DATE AND PROVENANCE. 1350–56 (closer to 1356); see Avril 1973, 112–14; 1978, 26–28, plates 19, 21–26; 1982a, 119–24.[15] The original owner is not known, although some evidence suggests that the manuscript was originally destined for Bonne of Luxembourg; after her death in 1349, the manuscript may have been finished for King John II (Earp 1989, 467–68, drawing together suggestions in Wimsatt/Kibler 1988, Günther 1982, and Avril 1982a; see also above, chap. 1.9 and 1.10.1, and the description of *Trop plus / Biauté* [M20] in chap. 7.3). Art historical studies indicate that the manuscript was decorated in Paris, at an atelier with connections to the royal court (Avril 1973, 1978, 1982a). R. Cazelles (1982, 43) notes that the illuminator Jean de Viarmes (Wirmes) illustrated a "book of motets" for King John II; this description may tentatively be associated with MS C, since it would seem odd in this period to illustrate a book of motets (see chap. 1.10.1).
Earlier shelfmarks of the Bibliothèque du Roy (all visible on fol. 1r): MDCCC (Nicolas Rigault catalogue of 1622, Omont 1908–21, 2:352); 151 (brothers Dupuy catalogue of 1645, Omont 1908–21, 3:11); Regius 7612 (Nicolas Clément catalogue of 1682, Omont 1908–21, 4:47). The early shelfmarks indicate that MS C was at the Bibliothèque du Roy at least since the seventeenth century, although until the late eighteenth century it was known as a manuscript of "les chansons de Thibault, comte de Champagne, roy de Navarre, mises en musique. Diverse chansons antiennes" (1645 catalogue, others are similar), and was even grouped with the MS Regius 7613 (Omont 1908–21, 4:205), now *F:Pn 1591*, trouvère MS *R*; thus, MS C may stand unrecognizable as a Machaut source in earlier inventories. See also below on MS A [5], which was similarly described.
Avril (1973, 99 n. 1, 100 n. 2) notes that a manuscript of Jacobus de Cessolis's *Jeu des Echecs Moralisés* in the translation of Jean de Vignay (*US:NYpm Glazier G.52*; see Plummer 1959; *International Style* 1962) is from the same atelier and date as MS C, and may have been intended for the same patron. *Glazier G.52* dates from near the time King John II commanded the translation. The many contemporary marks of ownership in *Glazier G.52* have not yet received much study beyond the identifications in the dossier at the Pierpont Morgan Library.

CONTENTS. On the division between CI and CII, see Ludwig 1926–54, 2:10b*; Günther 1963a, 96–100; Huot 1987, 265. Earp (1983, 138–42, 176–77) emphasizes that the motets form a division independent of the chansons; CII was inserted between the lais and a closed motet section.

---

[15] Until the work of Avril became widely known, MS C was misdated as a fifteenth-century source after the description in *Bibliothèque Impériale* 1868, 259. Guelliot (1914, 312) was the first to question the old date.

LITERATURE. *Bibliothèque Impériale* 1868, 259; Ludwig 1926–54, 2:10b*; Schrade 1956c, 27–28; *RISM* 1969, 179–82; Reaney 1980c, 661–62; Earp 1983, 131–42; Harden 1983, 122–37. On Machaut's personal supervision: Huot 1987, 246–49; Earp 1989, 463–72.

[2] ABERYSTWYTH, National Library of Wales, 5010 C (W; *GB:AB 5010 C*)

DESCRIPTION. Parchment, fragmentary, i + 74 + i fols.; modern Arabic pencil foliation, 1–74, top right recto. Dimensions: 27 × 19 cm, writing block ca. 19 × 14 cm, 2 cols. at 40 ll./col. Contains music. Formal bookhand; four text scribes may be distinguished. Scribe A, who utilized double hairline strokes in capital letters at the beginning of each verse of poetry, wrote fols. 1r–5v (*Loange*), 23r–23v (*Vergier*), 31r–41v (*Remede*), 64r–64v (*Alerion*), 71r (L9), 72r–73v (lais), 74v (M1). Scribe B did not employ the hairlines in capitals but made large apostrophe-shaped strokes in round letters (O, Q, C); he wrote fols. 6r–21v (*Loange, Jugement Behaingne*), 42r–46v and 48r–55v (*Alerion*). Scribe C, who ornamented round letters with double hairline strokes like scribe A, wrote fols. 24r–29v (*Vergier*) and 47r–47v (*Alerion*). Scribe D did not employ the hairlines in capitals, and similar to scribe B made large apostrophe-shaped strokes in round letters (O, Q, C, D). Characteristic is his use of the Tironian sign for "Et" at beginnings of lines. Scribe D wrote fols. 30r–30v (*Remede*), 56r–63v and 65r–70v (*Alerion*). The manner of copying the *Remede* indicates that different scribes were copying different parts of the text simultaneously. What is left of the *Remede* begins on fol. 30r with l. 69, and thus it began on the previous verso. Scribe D copied three columns and a catchword but left column d blank. Scribe A, who copied the rest of the surviving portions of the poem, continued the text without a break on fol. 31r. An infelicity such as this, probably due to haste, may indicate that the many irregularities in the collation of the manuscript, not all of which are due to vandalism, do not signal gross losses in the text section.

A few catchwords and signatures are visible, in ink. A chart of the gathering structure follows this description. Music remains only on fol. 74v, with ten lines of red staves in double columns, each 1.25 cm tall and drawn with a rastrum. The remainder of the music section is lost. Fol. 74v, with most of the triplum of *Quant en moy* (M1), was originally ruled for text (writing block 21.1 × 14.6 cm). This suggests that if lais immediately preceded the motets, the final lai was not set to music. The first five staves were originally drawn straight across in long lines, later erased at mid-column to allow for a double column format. This may suggest that music previously copied in the manuscript, presumably the lais, was written in long lines. It is worth remarking that of all the principal Machaut manuscripts transmitting motets, only the early MS C employs double columns like W.

MS W is tightly bound in white leather over boards, probably from the early twentieth century. Interior columns are water damaged to the point that some of the writing is practically illegible. Wathey (*RISM* 1993) notes physical characteristics indicating that W was originally in two volumes, a text volume and a music volume (cf. descriptions below of MS Vg [3] and a lost Burgundian manuscript [12]). In the following diagram, dotted lines indicate probable lost leaves; most of the stubs in the present manuscript also mark lost leaves. Gathering signatures are partially visible in gatherings eight and twelve.

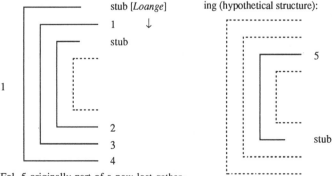

Fol. 5 originally part of a now-lost gather-

Present structure:

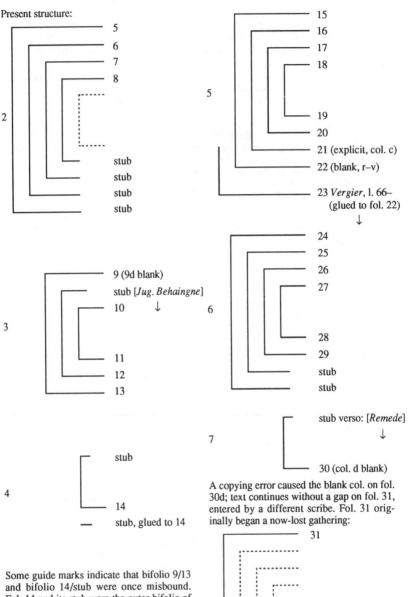

2

5
6
7
8
stub
stub
stub
stub

3

9 (9d blank)
stub [*Jug. Behaingne*]
10   ↓
11
12
13

4

stub
14
— stub, glued to 14

5

15
16
17
18
19
20
21 (explicit, col. c)
22 (blank, r–v)
23 *Vergier*, l. 66–
   (glued to fol. 22)
   ↓

6

24
25
26
27
28
29
stub
stub

7

stub verso: [*Remede*]
   ↓
30 (col. d blank)

A copying error caused the blank col. on fol. 30d; text continues without a gap on fol. 31, entered by a different scribe. Fol. 31 originally began a now-lost gathering:

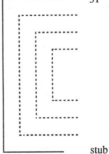

31
stub

Some guide marks indicate that bifolio 9/13 and bifolio 14/stub were once misbound. Fol. 14 and its stub were the outer bifolio of gathering 3: text between fols. 13v and 14r is continuous. *Vergier* probably began on a verso near the end of a now-lost gathering, which may have included the missing *Lyon*. The two or more gatherings in question may have fallen later in the original manuscript.

Present structure:

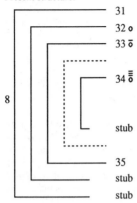

8

31
32 o
33 ō
34 ☰̄ō
stub
35
stub
stub

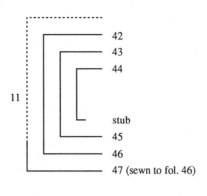

11

42
43
44
stub
45
46
47 (sewn to fol. 46)

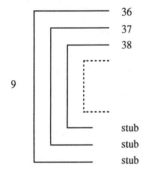

9

36
37
38
stub
stub
stub

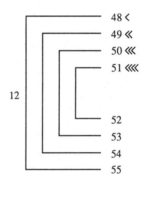

12

48 ‹
49 ‹‹
50 ‹‹‹
51 ‹‹‹‹
52
53
54
55

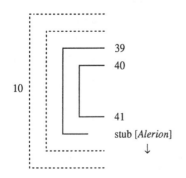

10

39
40
41
stub [*Alerion*]
↓

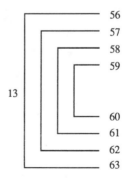

13

56
57
58
59
60
61
62
63

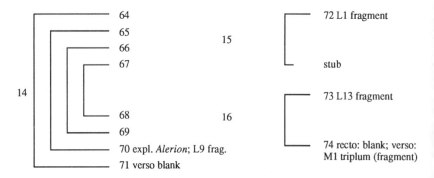

DECORATION. Rubrics. Gold initials on a cusped blue and purple background with white tracery (*lettres rechampies échancrées*), two lines tall.[16] Background colors alternate, so that if the interior background of one letter is blue, and the exterior is purple, the next letter has the opposite pattern. A few short stems extend from some initials but no flowers or fancier stems. All initials are of the same design throughout the volume; larger initials are now lost. The manuscript was doubtless originally fully illuminated, but all folios containing illuminations were removed in their entirety. The faint mirror image of one miniature (originally on fol. 6 bottom left verso) is visible on fol. 7, bottom right recto (a lady standing in a green field). The miniature was only seven lines tall and filled the space left for the missing third strophe of the ballade *Ne cuidés pas* (Lo129), a practice also seen in **Vg** (see miniatures Vg2–4, described in chap. 4.4p).[17] Capitals at the beginnings of lines are highlighted in yellow wash, except in parts of the manuscript that required music, namely throughout the *Remede* (fols. 30r–41v), and the lais and motet (fols. 72r–74v).

FACSIMILE. Motet: *RISM* 1993, 101 plate 1 (fol. 74v, fragment of *Quant en moy* [M1]).

INSCRIPTIONS. On fol. 71r (the end of the original first volume of the manuscript) there is a motto in a fifteenth- or sixteenth-century hand: "Joyeulz espoir a. &c."[18] Below this, in a messy fifteenth-century cursive bastard script, is a poem, perhaps a bergerette:

> Et ne seserés vous jamais[19]
> Faulx, jaloux, envieulx
> De voloir médire en tous lieulx
> sur celle ou tout biens sont parfais
> 5   Je croy que vous prenés [MS: predés] plaisanche
> a la voir vivre en desplaisir[20]
> ~~Et~~ n'avés vous point de soufissance
> Ci se elle a des maulx a souffrir

---

[16] The description in Barrois 1830, 198 no. 1354, a lost manuscript described below as MS [12], mentions "les grans lettres d'or et d'azur," which recalls MS **W**. MS [12], however, ended with the *Fonteinne,* and I have resisted the identification because the small number of poems in the *Loange* in **W** implies a much earlier manuscript.

[17] The third strophe of Lo129 is also missing in MS **C** but not in later manuscripts.

[18] "Joyeux Espoir" appears in a *rondel* of Charles d'Orléans (ed. Mühlethaler 1992, 400; cf. Poirion 1965, 301 n. 111).

[19] A *rondel* of Charles d'Orléans has the same first line: "Et ne cesserez vous jamais? / Tousjours est a recommancer; / C'est folie d'y plus penser, / Ne s'en soussier desormais..." (ed. Mühlethaler 1992, 426). Perhaps the poem in MS **W** was written by a member of the circle around Charles d'Orléans, a circle noted for writing chansons on a given incipit.

[20] Two lines that resemble ll. 5–6 appear in the rondeau *Me ferés vous tousjours languir* (printed in Piaget 1905, 602), added on a flyleaf of the Diesbach MS of works of Alain Chartier, a manuscript still untraced (Laidlaw 1974, 128, *siglum Qj*): "Je croy que vous prenés plaisir / A moy voir vivre en desplaisir."

Hellas che sont bien petits fais
10 Envieulx
Deportés vous en pour le mieulx
Et sentiés a icelle vivre en pais.

DATE AND PROVENANCE. Judging from the extent of the contents of the manuscript, in particular the identity in the size of the *Loange* section with that of MS C, the lack of any trace of poems after *Alerion* (a factor not alone convincing due to the fragmentary nature of the source), the manner in which the motet *Quant en moy* (M1) is copied, and the corruptions in the text of the *Jugement Behaingne* (see Earp 1989, 473n. item 2), it seems safe to place the time of the copying of MS W immediately after C, i.e., ca. 1356. The unidentified fifteenth-century bergerette discussed above perhaps connects W to the circle around Charles d'Orléans, and perhaps W is the manuscript that later belonged to the count of Dusnois [14]. According to the dossier on file at the Institut de Recherches et d'Histoire des Textes in Paris, assembled from information acquired on an excursion of a staff member of the I.R.H.T. to Wales in 1957, a letter inserted into the manuscript indicated that Sir Francis William Bourdillon (1852–1921) purchased MS W from Bernard Quaritch Ltd. in London on 30 June 1919 for £25. In the intervening years, the letter has unfortunately gone astray, and none of the account books that Bourdillon kept on his library, all of which are in the possession of the National Library of Wales, reaches as late as 1919.[21] The only mention of the manuscript is in MS 5078 C, "Catalogue of MSS at Buddington," which includes on the last written page, p. [50], a brief note listing the contents of the Machaut manuscript. Inquiries at the offices of Quaritch in London in the summer of 1989 proved fruitless; a manuscript in the mutilated condition of W would have received little attention. Thus, the history of the manuscript before Bourdillon acquired it has not been traced.

CONTENTS. Given the very damaged state of the manuscript, only the relative positions of the *Loange* and *Jugement Behaingne* are fixed: *Jugement Behaingne* must follow the *Loange*. The positions of *Vergier, Remede,* and *Alerion* are flexible, except that *Alerion* is locked in with the following section of lais.

Text:
Loange (probably originally 198 texts)

Lo7–14 (str. 1)	fols. 1r–v
Lo34–50	fols. 2r–4v
Lo70 (l. 4)–Lo78 (l. 3)	fols. 5r–5v
Lo121 (l. 3)–Lo147 (l. 2)	fols. 6r–8r
Lo196 (l. 2)–Lo200	fols. 9a–9c
blank	fol. 9d
Jugement Behaingne, ll. 145–2079 (expl.)	fols. 10r–21v
blank	fols. 22r–22v
Vergier, ll. 66–1186	fols. 23r–29v
Remede	
ll. 69–348	fols. 30r–31v
ll. 1161–1480	fols. 32r–33v
ll. 1631–1790	fols. 34r–34v
ll. 2062–2218	fols. 35r–35v
ll. 2367–2832	fols. 36r–38v
ll. 3629–4096	fols. 39r–41v
Alerion	
ll. 158–637	fols. 42r–44v
ll. 798–4814 (expl.)	fols. 45r–70
Lais	
Amours se plus (L9)	fols. 70r–71r
Fifteenth-century inscriptions	fol. 71r
blank	fol. 71v

---

[21] I examined the following Bourdillon manuscripts for information on MS W: 5071 C, 5072 B, 5073 B, 5074 B, 5075 B, 5077 B, 5078 C, 5079 D, 5101 A. MS 5148 C, "Letters to F. W. Bourdillon, &c," does contain two letters from Quaritch (dated 3 October 1917 and 8 October 1917), but they do not pertain to the Machaut manuscript.

[*Loyauté, que*] (L1, ll. 127–286)	fol. 72r
[*Maintes foys*] (L13, ll. 57–217)	fol. 73r–v
blank	fol. 74r
Music:	
[*Quant*] *en moy* (M1), ll. 1–33 of triplum	fol. 74v

LITERATURE. Description in *Handlist* 1951, 63. Machabey (1960, 1394) mentioned **W**, but only as a single page of music, ignoring the text. The contents of the manuscript are thoroughly described in a typewritten dossier on file at the Institut de Recherche et d'Histoire des Textes, Paris. See also Earp 1989, 472–73 n. 24, 474, 479–80; and the excellent description by Wathey in *RISM* 1993. My research on MS **W** was carried out in the summer of 1989 with the help of a grant from the American Philosophical Society.

[3] **NEW YORK, Wildenstein Collection, MS without shelfmark** (**Vg**; *US:NYw*; Hoepffner: *V*; Chichmaref: *N*; Ludwig: *Vg*)

DESCRIPTION. Parchment, 390 + ii fols. (fols. 321 and 383 are missing); old foliation i–cccxcii, top right recto. Dimensions: ca. 32 × 22 cm, writing block ca. 21.5 × 15.6 cm, 2 cols. at 40 ll./col. Contains music. Formal bookhand. Collation 1–10^8 11^{10} (irregular) 12–17^8 : 18–27^8 : 28–41^8 42^4 : 43–45^8 46^3 47–49^8 50^6; more on signatures and collation in Earp 1983, 355–67. The first folio of the music section appears dirty and worn, and probably **Vg** was once split into two volumes (cf. above, MS **W** [2], and below, MS [12]).

DECORATION. Rubrics. Initials eight lines tall with a basket-weave background; floriated initials with stems and ivy leaves, four to eight lines tall; letters on a cusped background (*lettres rechampies échancrées*) probably similar to those in MS **W**, two lines tall. Major divisions have bar borders with stems and ivy leaves, sometimes with a dragon. On the 118 miniatures, divided between four artists, see the descriptions in chap. 4.2 table 4.2 and chap. 4.4. Such a large number of collaborators may suggest that the book had to be produced quickly (see De Winter 1978, 180; 1985, 88). The miniature at the beginning of the *Loange* (chap. 4.4.p, miniature **Vg**1) and the miniature at the beginning of *Alerion* (chap. 4.4.g, miniature **Vg**44) each have a multi-lobed frame with tricolor border, a design often found in Parisian manuscripts during the reign of Charles V (compare Avril 1978, plates 32–33).

FACSIMILES.
Miniatures (refer to chaps. 4.3 and 4.4): **Vg**1, **Vg**45, **Vg**93.
Mass: Barksdale 1953a, fig. viii no. 57 (fol. 285v, beginning of Et in terra); 1953b, 564 (fols. 283v–284r, first opening of the Mass).

INSCRIPTIONS. According to Ludwig (1911, 407–8n.; 1926–54, 2:10a*), the recto of the second flyleaf has the following motto in a fifteenth-century hand, which breaks off with the first letter of the second line:
"J'ay belle dame assouvie
t..."
Ludwig notes the similarity to the motto of Jean de Grailli, count of Foix (r. 1412–1436): "J'ay belle dame." On this motto, see Lewis 1985.

DATE AND PROVENANCE. Decorated ca. 1370 (Avril 1982a, 124–25). It is possible that MS **Vg** made its way to Yolande of Bar, Queen of Aragon in the 1380s (chap. 1.11b and 2.2.1), a gift of Gaston Fébus, count of Foix (Earp 1989, 478–79). Perhaps it was the strong connection between Charles of Navarre and the south (cf. R. Cazelles 1982, 85–86) that brought a Machaut manuscript to Gaston Fébus, the brother-in-law of Charles of Navarre. Note that **Vg** has thirty-nine miniatures (**Vg**44–51; see chap. 4.4h), more than any other extant manuscript, for the *Confort*, a poem written for Charles of Navarre, and eight miniatures (**Vg**52–90; see chap. 4.4g), most of which feature hunting birds—a favorite subject of the count of Foix—for *Alerion*. Based on the detailed contemporary inventory description, a manuscript in the 1417 inventory of the books of Alfonso V the Magnanimous at Valencia can be identified as **Vg** (see MS [3a]). In the late nineteenth and early twentieth century, **Vg** was in the possession of the Marquis Melchior de Vogüé (d. 1916), Paris. It was purchased from the Vogüé family by Georges Wildenstein between 1928 and 1933 and exhibited at the Toledo Museum of Art in 1952 (Barksdale 1953a; 1953b; Levarie 1954, 107–8). MS **Vg** has been notoriously unavailable to scholars for examination, except for a brief viewing in 1977 attended by Bernard Bailly de Surcy, Margaret Bent, Harry Bober, and Elizabeth Keitel.

CONTENTS.
Text:

LITERATURE. Mas Latrie 1877b, xxviii–xxix; Ludwig 1926–54, 2:9b*–10a*; Barksdale 1953a, no. 57; Schrade 1956c, 25–26; *RISM* 1969, 342–68; Reaney 1980c, 662; Bent 1983.

[3a] VALENCIA, manuscript in the library of Alfonso V

PROVENANCE. A manuscript described in the 1417 inventory of the books of Alfonso V the Magnanimous at Valencia (Alós-Moner 1924, 397 no. 17) seems identical with MS **Vg** (Earp 1989, 478–79). See above on the provenance of **Vg**.

CONTENTS. This manuscript began with the *Loange* and ended with the *Prise*.

[4] PARIS, Bibliothèque Nationale, fonds français 1585 (B; *F:Pn 1585*; Hoepffner: *B*; Chichmaref: *D*)

DESCRIPTION. Paper, 395 fols. (old fols. 138 and 218, and the bifolio surrounding present fols. 330–331 are missing), with two paper flyleaves in front and three in back; nineteenth-century Arabic foliation, 1–395, top right recto; two late fifteenth- or sixteenth-century foliations include only the text section, fols. 1–217: xi–ii^{C}xvii (bottom middle recto, earlier); i–x (top right recto) and xi–ii^{C}xvii (top middle recto, slightly later). On the differences between foliations, and the current misbinding, see Earp 1983, 113–18. Watermarks are described in Keitel 1982b, 83–87. Bifolios 1/8, 9/16, 17/24 (old fols. 210 and 217), and fol. 33 (old fol. 177) are fifteenth-century replacement folios. Dimensions: ca. 29 × 21 cm, writing block ca. 23 × 17 cm (varies greatly), 2 cols. at 40 ll./col. Fols. 1r–33v and 389r–395v have been covered with gauze. Contains music. On the nine text scribes and two music scribes of the main corpus (omitting the *Prise*), see Earp 1983, 196–214 and the additional notes in Bent 1983, 59, 77. A scribal hand of correction, labeled *B^1* by Hoepffner (1908–21, 1:xlvi; Ludwig 1926–54, 2:10*), remains unstudied. Collation (following the current misbound state) 1–2^8 27^8 22^{8+1} (first fol. was originally last fol. of gathering 21)

$3-10^8$ 11^{8+2} $12-16^8$ 17^{8-1+1} (old fol. 138 lost between new fols. 154v–155r; first fol. of gathering 18 added) 18^{8-1} $19-20^8$ 21^{8-1} (last fol. added to gathering 22) $23-26^8$ 28^{8-1} $29-38^8$ 39^{8+1} $40-41^8$ 42^{4-2+1} (outer bifolio lost; first folio of gathering 43 added) 43^{12-1} 44^{10} 45^{12} 46^{14} 47^{10} 48^{12-5} (structure now altered to $8-1$); more on signatures and collation in Earp 1983, 109–113, 355–67. Red staves 1.25 cm tall (*Qui bien aimme* [L22/16], *Remede*, and fols. 297r–304v), or 1.35 cm tall (all other music), in red ink except for fol. 132r (residuum of *Dame, a vous* [RF6], which is black). Bound since the 1960s in light brown pigskin. For additional information on scribal practice, see Harden 1983, 110–21.

DECORATION. Rubrics. Initial six lines tall on fol. 1r (fifteenth-century replacement folio), with crude filigree in blue ink, possibly added much later. Red and blue divided letter on fol. 332r at the opening of the *Prise*, nine lines tall. Otherwise, there are only solid red initials, four to ten lines tall. As in the exemplar, MS **Vg**, room was left for illuminations. These were never executed, but of course they were never meant to be executed, since the manuscript is on paper.

FACSIMILES. Mass: Gennrich 1957 (fols. 281v–294r, complete Mass); Seay 1965, 146 (fols. 283v–284r, first opening of the Gloria).

INSCRIPTIONS. On fol. 1r, in the space reserved for a miniature, a seventeenth-century hand has written: "Compositions de Guillaume de Machaut de Loris Poete & Musicien qui florissoit sur la fin du XIVe siecle," an inscription which provides an interesting link to MS **D** [11] and the researches of Châtre de Cangé (d. 1746). The last folio of the *Prise* is signed "Guyon" (unidentified) in a fifteenth-century hand. Also unidentified is the motto on the same folio: "Cum bono bonus eris / Cum perverso perverteris" (a paraphrase of 2 Reg. xxii.27 and Ps. xvii.27: "Cum electo electus eris, et cum perverso perverteris"); cf. *Alerion*, ll. 4433–34: "Aïde toy; je t'aideray. / Honnis toy; je te honniray [help yourself, and I will help you: shame yourself, and I will shame you (trans. Gaudet/Hieatt 1994, 156)].

DATE AND PROVENANCE. On the basis of the watermarks, copied ca. 1370–72 (Keitel 1982c, 83–87); seven replacement folios were added in the early fifteenth century. MS **B** is a direct copy of **Vg** (Ludwig 1911, 409; 1926–54, 2:9b* n. 2, 10a* n. 3), except for the *Prise*, which in turn served as the exemplar for the *Prise* in **Vg**; objections to this relationship raised by Keitel (1976, 114–15; 1982c, 87–89) were refuted by Bent (1983, 53–60) and Earp (1983, 102–3).

B was copied from **Vg** in an unbound and unilluminated state (Bent 1983, 57, 79) and copied quickly, probably for use as an unauthorized exemplar (Earp 1989, 477), and it indeed served as an exemplar for portions of MS **E** (Bent 1983, 62–82). Perhaps the unidentified Turquam manuscript of 1519 [9] is identical with MS **B**. Machabey (1960, 1398) indicates that in 1635 Mersenne and Nicolas-Claude Fabri de Peiresc cited a manuscript of the *Prise* in the possession of Jean-Baptiste Hautin (ca. 1580–1640). Hautin, one of the scholars who helped Nicolas Rigault with the 1622 catalogue of the Bibliothèque du Roy, had a library of 10,000 volumes that was purchased by Jean-Baptiste Colbert (1619–1683) in 1674 (Balayé 1988, 59 n. 7). The interest of contemporary scholars in oriental matters, in this case, the history of Cyprus, explains why the volume would be identified by the *Prise*: it was the one item of interest in the manuscript. The enormous collection of over 8000 manuscripts of Colbert and his heirs was purchased by King Louis XV in 1732 for the Bibliothèque du Roy.

Earlier shelfmarks (all visible on fol 1): Codex Colbert 835 (listed in Montfaucon 1739, 2:937); Regius 7609[1].

CONTENTS (modern Arabic foliation, following the present misbound order).

Text:

Lyon	fols. 139r–154v
lost folio	(old fol. 138)
Alerion	fols. 155r–185r
blank	fol. 185v
Confort	fols. 25r–33v, 186r–203v
Fonteinne	fols. 204r–217v, 17r–22r
Harpe	fols. 22r–24v
Music:	
lost folio with beginning of *Loyauté, que* (L1)	(old fol. 218)
18 lais (5 without music)	fols. 218r–258r
23 motets	fols. 258v–281r
Mass	fols. 281v–294r
27 ballades	fols. 294v–308v
3 rondeaux (1 without music)	fols. 309r–309v
9 ballades	fols. 310r–315r
14 rondeaux	fols. 315v–320r
27 virelais (3 without music); *Mors sui* (V29/26) incomplete	fols. 320v–329v
lost folio (with 2 virelais)	
1 virelai and ballade text *Amis sans toy*	fol. 330r
3 virelais without music	fols. 330v–331r
Hoquetus David (incomplete)	fol. 331v
lost folio	
Text:	
Prise	fols. 332r–395v

LITERATURE. *Bibliothèque Impériale* 1868, 259; Ludwig 1926–54, 2:9b* n. 2, 10*; Schrade 1956c, 26–27; *RISM* 1969, 178–79; Reaney 1980c, 663.

[5] **PARIS, Bibliothèque Nationale, fonds français 1584** (A; *F:Pn 1584*; Hoepffner: *A*; Chichmaref: *C*)

DESCRIPTION. Parchment, ii + vii + 493 + 8 paper + 1 + iv fols., with one additional paper flyleaf in front and one in back; foliation A–G (modern, top right recto), i–iiii^{C}iiii^{XX}xiiii (red ink, top middle recto), 494–505 (eighteenth century, top right recto). A paper quaternion (ink Arabic foliation 494–501) was added between fols. 493v and 494r, containing a paper index (fols. 494r–498r) with concordances to MS Regius 7612, i.e., MS C. On fols. 498v–499r the same hand continues with studies of anagrams, then fols. 500r–501v are blank. In the new Arabic foliation, old fol. 494r is renumbered 502 (top right recto). Dimensions: 31 × 22 cm, writing block ca. 22/22.8 × 16/17.5 cm, 2 cols. at 40–41 ll./col. Contains music. Formal bookhand; two main scribes, one for the *Prologue* ballades, the other for the corpus; several correctors' hands. Collation A^4 : B$^{6-2}$ (irregular) : 1^8 2^6 3–16^8 : 17–27^8 28^6 : 29–39^8 : 40–45^8 46^{8+2} : 47–51^8 52$^{8-1}$: 53–57^8 : 58–62^8 [paper quaternion inserted] 63^{4+1}; signatures partly visible on bottom right recto, in red ink and Roman numerals; more on signatures and collation in Earp 1983, 85, 88–89, 344–49. Red staves 1.35 cm tall (*Remede*) and 1.2 cm tall (other music). Bound in red morocco with gilt tooling, French royal arms, seventeenth or eighteenth century (resembles *Bibliothèque Nationale* 1981, 482 plate xxiv, item 2). For additional information on scribal practice, see Earp 1983, 102–19; Harden 1983, 107–10.

An original index appears on two unfoliated leaves at the front of the manuscript with the heading "Vesci l'ordenance que G. de Machau wet qu'il ait en son livre" [Here is the order that G. de Machaut wants his book to have].[22] The order of the index was established before the copying of the manuscript itself, strengthening the possibility that this order was indeed prescribed by Machaut himself (Earp 1983, 52–83; 1989, 482–87. S.J. Williams (1978, 195–96) provides a more general description of the index.

DECORATION. Rubrics. Blue and gold divided initials three lines tall for the first ballade of each pair at the opening of the *Prologue,* with red and black filigree. On fols. Dv and Ev,

---

[22] For a literary interpretation of the heading, see Huot 1987, 274–75; de Looze 1988b, 538 and n. 3. On *ordenance,* see Cerquiglini 1985b, index s.v. "Ordener, Ordenance"; Huot 1987, 237–39, and the works cited there.

initials one to two lines tall alternating gold and blue with black and red filigree, and blue with red filigree. Beginning with the narrative portion of the *Prologue,* all initials are penned with *grisaille* shading, and most are unpainted. Most capital letters at beginnings of lines are highlighted with yellow wash. Many animals and drolleries in the margins. On the 154 miniatures in *grisaille,* see the descriptions below, chap. 4.4; only the first two, for the introductory ballades of the *Prologue,* are by a known artist, the Master of the Bible of Jean de Sy (see chap. 4.2 table 4.5).

FACSIMILES.
Original index: Earp 1989, 483–85, figs. 1–3 (fols. Av–Bv).
Miniatures (refer to chaps. 4.3 and 4.4): A1–2, A80–87, A117, A125, A147, A149, A152, A154. The reproductions of miniatures in Loomis 1965 (plates 45–47, 103) include entire folios (fols. 157v–158v, 309r).
Lai: Hoepffner 1908–21, vol. 2, appendix, 25 (fol. 52r, *Qui n'aroit* [RF1], beginning).
Mass: Douce 1948, facing p. 54 (fols. 444v–445r, Qui propter nos ... judicare vivos et mortuos).
Motets: Wolf 1923, plates 41–42 (fols. 429v–430r, *Lasse! comment / Se j'aim* [M16]); Gennrich 1948, plates 4a–4b (fols. 429v–430r, *Lasse! comment / Se j'aim* [M16]); Machabey 1966, 216 (fol. 415v, *Tous corps / De* [M2]); Wilson 1990b, 294 (fol. 414v, *Quant en moy / Amour* [M1]).
Hoquetus David: MGG 10 (1962), plate 50 (fols. 451v–452r).
Ballades: Apel 1953, facs. 69 (fol. 456v, *Dous amis, oy* [B6]), facs. 68 (fol. 459v, *Ne pensez pas* [B10]); Bofill Soliguer 1991, 24 (fols. 465v–466r, *De Fortune* [B23] and *Tres douce dame que* [B24]); Paulsmeier 1986, 81 (fol. 466r, *Tres douce dame que* [B24]); Besseler-Gülke 1973, 63 plate 21 (fol. 468r, *Donnez, signeurs* [B26]); Earp 1991c, 196 (fol. 468r, *Donnez, signeurs* [B26]); Wilkins 1979, 17 (fol. 472v, *Gais et jolis* [B35], beginning of *Se pour ce muir* [B36]).
Virelais: Hoepffner 1908–21, vol. 2, plate 27 (fol. 74r, *Dame, a vous* [RF6]); Aubry 1905, plate 21 (fol. 482r, *He! dame de vaillance* [V1] and *Loyauté vueil* [V2]); Reaney 1952a, 1045–46 (fol. 482r, *He! dame de vaillance* [V1]).

INSCRIPTIONS. "Les amours de Guillaume Machaut en vielles rithmes" (verso of first parchment flyleaf, corresponding to a late sixteenth century inventory entry for the Bibliothèque du Roy, Omont 1908–21, 1:385 no. 2519)[23]; "ne me metés en oblyance / car ye de vos sovena[n]ce" "of my me ensvryd may ye be / to love beste tyl that I dye" (fol. 505v, fifteenth-century cursive bastard script); "Item y have payd to Jhon; fayrest dolour doth ye saye; ...desyre doth me avance...& byddyth in a...love..." (fol. 506v, same script).

DATE AND PROVENANCE. On art historical grounds, early 1370s (Avril 1982a, 126–27). Owing to the artist of the miniatures in the body of the codex, Avril (1978, 36, commentary to plates 29–30; 1982a, 126, 131–32) suggests that the codex may have originated at Reims, under the supervision of Machaut himself; see also Earp 1983, 92–93. The two miniatures at the opening of the codex, however, were painted probably between 1370 and 1377 in Paris (Avril 1982a, 127), by the Master of the Bible of Jean de Sy (see chap. 4.2 table 4.5). The original owner of MS A is unknown; the manuscript does not appear in any of the inventories (1373–1424) of the libraries of Charles V and Charles VI published by Delisle (1907). MS A was still in France ca. 1430, when it served as the exemplar for MS **Pm** (Avril 1982a, 130). In the late fifteenth century, MS A belonged to Louis of Bruges, sire of Gruthuyse (1422–1492; see Delisle 1868–81, 1:144). The writing in English on the last guard leaves of the manuscript may indicate that MS A had the same history as many of the manuscripts formerly owned by Charles V and Charles VI, making its way to England after the death of the duke of Bedford in 1435, where it was purchased by Louis of Bruges and taken back to the continent (Delisle 1907, 1:138–41; Avril 1978, 36, commentary to plates 29 and 30). Owing to the presence of the English in northern France at this time, however, the English inscriptions cannot be taken as conclusive evidence that the manuscript was in England. On the death of Louis of Bruges, most of his manuscripts went to the library of Louis XII (r. 1498–1515) at Blois. The arms of Louis of Bruges, painted on fol. Dr, were then covered by those of France (Avril 1982a, 127 n. 31). MS A

---

[23] The inscription is also close enough to a statement of Du Verdier (1585, 498; see chap. 2.3) to make one wonder if perhaps Du Verdier himself wrote it.

appears in the 1518 inventory of the royal library at the château de Blois (Omont 1908–21, 1:15 no. 108), and MS **A** is probably the manuscript appearing in the 1544 inventory of manuscripts at Blois as "ung autre livre, en parchemyn, couvert de veloux bleu, figuré, intitulé: 'Guillaume Marchaut'" (Omont 1908–21, 1:227 no. 1404). It is curious that seventeenth-century inventories of the French royal library, unfamiliar with Machaut but still familiar with the trouvère Thibaut of Champagne, king of Navarre, and perhaps noticing Machaut's *Jugement Navarre*, describe MS **A** as "Les amours de Guillaume de Machaud, en rimes. Poésies de Thibaud, roy de Navarre. La Prise d'Alexandre et autres romans anciens."[24] As noted above, MS **C** [1] was long identified as a manuscript of Thibaut of Navarre before it was recognized as a manuscript of Machaut. Earlier shelfmarks: 333 (brothers Dupuy catalogue of 1645, Omont 1908–21, 3:20); Regius 7609 (Nicolas Clément catalogue of 1682, Omont 1908–21, 4:47).

CONTENTS.

Original index	fols. A^v–B^v
blank	fols. C–C^v
Text:	
Prologue ballades	fols. Dr–Ev
blank	fol. Fr
Narrative *Prologue*	fols. Fv–Gv
Vergier	fols. 1r–9r
Jugement Behaingne	fols. 9v–22r
Jugement Navarre	fols. 22v–49r
Remede (with music)	fols. 49v–80r
Lyon	fols. 80v–96r
Alerion	fols. 96v–126r
blank	fol. 126v
Confort	fols. 127r–153v
Fonteinne	fols. 154r–173v
Harpe	fols. 174r–177
Loange (268 texts)	fols. 177v–213r
Marguerite	fols. 213v–214v
Complaintes	fols. 214v–219v
blank	fols. 220r–220v
Voir Dit	fols. 221r–306r
blank	fols. 306v–308v
Prise	fols. 309r–365r
Rose	fols. 365v–366r
Vesci les biens	fols. 366r–366v
Music:	
22 lais (6 without music)	fols. 367r–412v
blank ruled	fols. 413r–414r
23 motets	fols. 414v–437v
Mass	fols. 438v–451r
Hoquetus David	fols. 451v–452r
blank ruled	fols. 452v–453v
37 ballades	fols. 454r–474v
19 rondeaux (one copied twice)	fols. 475r–481r
blank ruled	fol. 481v
38 virelais (6 without music)	fols. 482r–494v [502v]

LITERATURE. *Bibliothèque Impériale* 1868, 259; Ludwig 1926–54, 2:9*; Schrade 1956c, 24–25; *RISM* 1969, 174–78; Reaney 1980c, 662–63. On Machaut's supervision of the production of MS **A**, see Avril 1982a, 131–32; Huot 1987, 274–75; Earp 1989, 480–88.

---

[24] Catalogue of 1645 (Omont 1908–21, 3:20), similar in the 1682 catalogue (1908–21, 4:47), and retained in Montfaucon's *Bibliotheca bibliothecarum* (1739, 2:793).

[5a] **PARIS, Bibliothèque Nationale, nouvelles acquisitions françaises 11198**, fol. 26r (*F:Pn 11198*)

DESCRIPTION. Parchment fragment belonging to MS A, discovered by François Avril in a miscellaneous collection of fragments. Dimensions: 13.5 × ca. 13.2 cm (left margin irregular). A matching stub is visible between fols. 297v–298r in MS A, near the top of the binding area.

DECORATION. Two unpainted initials are penned with *grisaille* shading, exactly as in MS A.

CONTENTS. Rubric "Response au secont article" (fol. 26r), followed by 16 ll. of text; rubric "Respons au tiers article" (fol. 26v), followed by 16 ll. of text, then a final rubric, "Response." The fragment serves to correct a thirty-two-line eye skip in the *Voir Dit* of MS A (ll. 8315–46, ed. P. Paris 1875, 336–37); see chap. 4, n. 199.

LITERATURE. Omont 1918, 149 (the present fragment is not described).

[6] **PARIS, Bibliothèque Nationale, fonds français 22545–22546** (**F-G**; *F:Pn 22545–22546*; Hoepffner: *F* and *G*; Chichmaref: *K*)

DESCRIPTION. Parchment, 2 vols.; MS F: 200 fols., with three paper flyleaves in front and two in back; eighteenth-century Arabic ink foliation, 1–200; MS G: 164 fols., with three paper flyleaves in front and two in back; eighteenth-century Arabic ink foliation, 1–164, top right recto. Dimensions: 35.5 × 26 cm, writing block ca. 29 × 19 cm (MS F), ca. 28.5 × 18.5 cm (MS G), 2 cols. at 52 ll./col. Contains music. Formal bookhand, one scribe throughout. Collation (MS F:) $1-25^8$ (MS G:) $26-29^8$ 30^{10} 31^2 : $32-34^8$ 35^{6-1} : $36-46^8$ 47^4; more on signatures and collation in Earp 1983, 99–101, 350–54. Water damage to tops of folios was probably repaired in the late fifteenth century. Red staves 1.25 cm tall for *Remede* (MS F), ruled, it seems, without a rastrum; red staves 1.35 cm tall (MS G), ruled with a rastrum. Bound in red morocco, eighteenth (?) century. For additional information on scribal practice, see Earp 1983, 97–101; Harden 1983, 138–47.

DECORATION. Rubrics. MS F fol. 1r has a floriated initial three lines tall for the opening rubric of the *Prologue*, pink and blue with gold background, and an initial eight lines tall for the first ballade of the *Prologue*, with gold bar borders with ivy and dragon at top. New poems usually begin with a gold and blue divided initial four lines tall, with red and black filigree. Other initials are two lines tall, alternating solid red with black filigree and solid blue with red filigree. On the 148 miniatures, see the descriptions in chap. 4.4. Avril (1982a, 128–29), discusses the date of the miniatures and identifies the illuminator as Perrin Remiet (or Remy). For further on Remy, see chap. 4.2 tables 4.7 and 4.10.

Of the forty-six prose letters in the *Voir Dit*, all except the following thirteen are marked off to the left with the sign ".;.": no. 1, fol. 140r; no. 2, fol. 140r (ed. P. Paris 1875 as no. 4); no. 7, fol. 147r (ed. as no. 3); no. 9, fol. 148r; no. 14, fol. 156v; no. 23, fol. 167r; no. 25, fol. 167v; no. 34, fol. 179v; no. 36, fol. 180v; no. 38, fol. 182v; no. 39, fol. 183r; no. 41, fol. 189r; no. 44, fol. 195r. Four ballades are marked by the initials .y.p. near the flourish initial for the first line of the poem, some of which were apparently written before the flourish initial itself was painted (fol. 154r, *Le plus grant bien* [VD30]; fol. 162r, *Gent corps* [VD42]; fol. 170v, *Hui ha .i. mois* [VD48]; fol. 181v, *Quant Theseüs* [VD56=B34]). Finally, the monogram "R" appears twice, below col. 1 on fol. 172r, and near the bottom of fol. 181v.

FACSIMILES (musical works referenced are all in MS G).

Miniatures (refer to chaps. 4.3 and 4.4): F6, F7, F9, F22, F58, F73, F89, F112, F114, F116, F117–118, F123, F128, F130, F132, F134–135, F139, F140, G143.

Lais: *MGG* 8 (1960), plate 73 facing cols. 1409–10 (fol. 74a, *Loyauté, que* [L1]).

Motets: Wolf 1904, 2:16 no. xiii (fols. 102v–103r, *Quant en moy / Amour* [M1]; diplomatic facs.); 2:19, no. xiv (fols. 104v–105r, *He! Mors / Fine* [M3]; diplomatic facs.); 2:21 no. xv (fols. 105v–106r, *De Bon Espoir / Puis que* [M4]; diplomatic facs.); 2:24 no. xvi (fols. 124v–125r, *Felix virgo / Inviolata* [M23]); Parrish 1957, plates lii–liii (fols. 124v–125r, *Felix virgo / Inviolata* [M23]; diplomatic facs.).

Mass: Wolf 1904, 2:28 no. xvii (fols. 125v–126a, Kyrie I, Christe, Kyrie II; diplomatic facs.); 2:30 no. xviii (fols. 128v–131r, Credo; diplomatic facs.); Gastoué 1922, 65 (fol. 131v, Sanctus); Gérold 1936, facing p. 364 (fol. 131v, Sanctus); Parrish 1957, plates l–li (fols. 131v–132r, complete Sanctus); Reaney 1961, 123 (fol. 131v, Sanctus); Besseler/Gülke 1973, 61 plate 20 (fol. 125v, Kyrie I, Christe); Kügle 1991, 374 (fol.

125v, detail of Kyrie I only).

Ballades: Wolf 1904, 2:40 no. xxiii (fol. 134r, *S'Amours ne fait* [B1]; diplomatic facs.); 2:41 no. xxiv (fol. 140r, *De petit po* [B18]; diplomatic facs.); 2:43 no. xxv (fol. 145v, *Plourez, dames* [B32]; diplomatic facs.); Bofill Soliguer 1991, 25 (fols. 141v–142r, *Il m'est avis* [B22], *De Fortune* [B23]).

Rondeaux: Wolf 1904, 2:37 no. xix (fol. 150r, *Helas! pour quoy se demente* [R2]; diplomatic facs.); 2:38 no. xx (fol. 151v, *Rose, lis* [R10]; diplomatic facs.); 2:39 no. xxi (fol. 152r, *Comment puet* [R11]; diplomatic facs.); 2:40 no. xxii (fol. 153r, *Ma fin* [R14]; diplomatic facs.); Reaney 1980c, 664 (fol. 153r, *Ma fin* [R14], *Certes, mon oueil* [R15]); Newes 1990, 225 (fol. 153r, R14).

Virelais: Wolf 1904, 2:45 no. xxvi (fol. 162r, *Se je souspir* [V36/30]; diplomatic facs.).

INSCRIPTIONS. Vers françois / Tome Premier / Conventus Parisiensis / Carmilitarum Discalccatorum (MS **F**, fol. iii v at bottom). Vers francois / Tome Second / Conventus Parisiens. / Carmilit. Discalccat. (MS **G**, fol. iii v at bottom).

DATE AND PROVENANCE. A dating ca. 1390 was proposed in Rive 1780, (1). Most later studies, on the basis of the contents of the manuscript, have placed **F-G** within Machaut's lifetime as the last of the manuscripts prepared under the supervision of the author (Hoepffner 1908–21, 1:xlvi, li; Reaney 1952b, 34; 1967, 88). On art historical grounds, however, Avril (1982a, 129) has again placed it in the 1390s. Readings in the music section indicate that it is closely related to MS **A**, although not a direct copy; they probably shared the same exemplars (cf. Earp 1989, 488–89; Leech-Wilkinson 1990c, 96–98). The original owner is unknown, but the many representations of a coat of arms in several miniatures may identify the original owner, a member of the upper middle class and not a member of the aristocracy (Avril 1982a, 129). Keitel (1982c, 92) provides a description and diagram of the coat of arms; see also the various heraldic descriptions in Rive 1780, (1); Tarbé 1849, 182; and Guelliot 1914, 299 ("De sable, au sautoir d'or, cantonné de quatre mouchetures d'hermine d'argent"); Cerquiglini 1987a has color facsimiles of several miniatures that bear the coat of arms.

MS **F-G** was apparently first rediscovered by the abbé Lebeuf ca. 1735 in the library of the Carmes déchaussés (Discalced Carmelites), rue de Vaugirard, Paris. Inscriptions in the front of both manuscripts identify them as volumes of that library. Lebeuf, whose work marks the beginning of modern interest in Machaut, first mentioned the manuscript in print in his 1743 *mémoire* on Philippe de Mezières (Lebeuf 1751), followed by the *mémoire* of 1746 (Lebeuf 1753). MS **F-G** then appeared in the library of Louis-Jean Gaignat (1697–1768), which was catalogued after his death by De Bure (1769, 451–52 no. 1778). It was then purchased by the duke of La Vallière (1708–1780), and again catalogued by De Bure (1783, 262, 253–54 [*recte* 262–64] no. 2771). It came to the Bibliothèque du Roy after the death of the duke. Perhaps there are some further notes on the eighteenth-century state of MS **F-G** in an unpublished study by the abbé Rive, "Notice sur des poésies manuscrites de Guillaume de Machau qui sont dans la bibliothèque de M. de La Vallière," preserved in Carpentras, Bibliothèque Municipale, MS 1259 (Duhamel 1901). Earlier shelfmarks: La Vallière 25^1 and 25^2; 2771 (fol. ii r; De Bure catalogue of 1783).

CONTENTS.

MS **F**

Text:

Vesci les biens	fols. 200r–200v
MS G	
Prise	fols. 1r–44r
Loange (225 texts)	fols. 45r–67r
Complaintes (11 texts)	fols. 67v–71v
Lis et Marguerite	fols. 71v–73v
Music:	
21 lays (6 without music)	fols. 74r–102r
23 motets	fols. 102v–125r
Mass	fols. 125v–133v
39 balades	fols. 134r–149v
21 rondeaux (1 without music)	fols. 150r–154r
38 virelais (6 without music)	fols. 154v–163v
Hoquetus David	fols. 163v–164r
blank	fol. 164v

LITERATURE. Omont 1898, 520–21; Wolf 1904, 1:157–62; Ludwig 1904–5, 610–11; Ludwig 1926–54, 2:8*–9* et passim; Schrade 1956c, 24; *RISM* 1969, 192–97; Reaney 1980c, 663; Wilkins 1989, 298–99.

[7] **PARIS, Bibliothèque Nationale, fonds français 9221** (E; *F:Pn 9221*; Hoepffner: *E*; Chichmaref: *J*)

DESCRIPTION. Parchment, iv + 238 + iii fols., with four additional paper flyleaves in front and four in back; foliation A–F (second two parchment flyleaves, then old index); old foliation i–ccxxxviii, top right recto. Dimensions: 40.6 × 30 cm, writing block ca. 29.5 × 20.5 cm, 3 cols. at 60 ll./col. Contains music. Formal bookhand; two scribes divided the copying: scribe A wrote fols. 1r–58r (*Prologue, Loange, Vergier, Remede, Jugement Behaingne, Jugement Navarre, Lay de Plour*) and fols. 107r–129r (Lais). Scribe B wrote fols. 61r–106v (*Lyon, Alerion, Fonteinne, Confort, Harpe*), fols. 131r–238r (remainder of music section, *Voir Dit, Prise*), and the original index on fols. Cr–Er. Prose letters of *Voir Dit* are in a formal cursive script, written in a second pass in long lines with a lighter brown ink (see comments in Cerquiglini 1985b, 41–42; 1991b, 343, 346). Collation A^2 : B^4 : 1–5^8 6^4 : 7–8^8 : 9^8 : 10^8 11^6 : 12^8 13^2 : 14^8 15^6 : 16–18^8 : 19–20^8 : 21^8 22^4 : 23^8 24^4 : 25–29^8 30^2 : 31–33^8 34^2; more on signatures and collation in Earp 1983, 123–24, 368–70. Red staves 1.45 cm tall. Bound in brown leather over boards, with the arms of Napolcon I on the cover, and the monogram "N" on spine, different in only a few details from the design given by Guigard (1890, 1:32). For further discussion of scribal practice, see Earp 1983, 120–29, 146–47; Harden 1983, 148–68.

DECORATION. Rubrics. Solid initials one to five lines tall, alternating red with black filigree and blue with red filigree. Beginnings of many pieces of music have blue and red divided initials with red and black filigree. The gathering of lais is exceptional in that each first strophe begins with a blue and white or pink and white floriated letter with gold background, most with stems and ivy leaves. On the 38 miniatures, see the descriptions below, chap. 4.4. On the artists, see chap. 4.2 table 4.8.

FACSIMILES.
Ex-libris: Lanson 1923, 110 (fol. Br).
Miniatures (refer to chap. 4.4): E1a–b, 6, 17, 31.
Lais: Hoepffner 1908–21, vol. 2, appendix, 25 (fol. 23r, *Qui n'aroit* [RF1]); Reaney 1961, 124 (fol. 107r, *Loyauté, que* [L1] beginning).
Motets: Wolf 1913 and 1923, 23 (fol. 131r, *Trop plus / Biauté* [M20]); Parrish 1957, plate xlviii (fol. 141r, end of *Hareu! / Helas!* [M10]).
Mass: Wilkins 1979, 12 (fol. 164v, Kyrie).
Ballade: Apel 1953, 359 facs. 70 (fols. 152v–153r, *Biauté qui* [B4]).
Rondeaux: Parrish 1957, plate xlviii (fol. 141r, *Dame, se vous n'avez* [R13], *Quant ma dame les maus* [R19]); Gallo 1985, 43 (entire fol. 198v, *Dix et sept* [R17]).
Virelais: Hoepffner 1908–21, vol. 2, appendix, 27 (fol. 33r, *Dame, a vous* [RF6]); Parrish 1957, plate xlvii (fol. 161r, *Tuit mi penser* [V28/25], *Mors sui* [V29/26], *Liement* [V30/27]).

INSCRIPTIONS. The second parchment bifolio guard sheet at the front of the manuscript has an Ex-libris inscribed in a very ornate script (*Cadeaux* or *cadelure*, Muzerelle 1985, §561.11) by Nicolas Flamel, secretary of John, duke of Berry (Poirion 1965, 172): "Ce livre de Machaut est de Jehan, filz de roy de France Duc de Berry et d'Auvergne, Conte de Poitou, d'Estampes, de Bouloingne et d'Auvergne. FLAMEL" [This book of Machaut belongs to John, son of the king of France, duke of Berry and Auvergne, count of Poitou, Estampes, Boulogne and Auvergne], with the monogram "N" below (reproduced in Lanson 1923, 110). The last folio (fol. 238v) contains an inscription effaced but still legible: "Ce livre est au duc de Berry et d'Auvergne, conte de Poitou et d'Auvergne" [This book belongs to the duke of Berry and Auvergne, count of Poitou and Auvergne], with the duke's signature, *JEHAN*. The original binding called E the book of *maistre* Guillaume de Machaut; see chap. 1.2.8j.

DATE AND PROVENANCE. Some scholars had associated the copying of E with a pay document of 1371 from the duke of Berry to Machaut; see chap. 1.14.1b. On art historical grounds, dated ca. 1390 by Meiss (1967, 1:315) and Avril (1982a, 128). MS B served as the exemplar for about half of the music (Bent 1981, 301–2; 1983, 78 table 2). The musical notation shows signs of later fourteenth-century practice (Earp 1983, 125–26). The inclusion of voice parts not found in the central Machaut manuscripts also points to a later date, out of the purview of the author (Earp 1989, 489–92; for a different view, see Bent 1983, 72–74; 1990a, 139).[25] Arguing from the readings for the rondeau *Se vous n'estes* (R7) in the Flemish source **Gr 3360** [68], Strohm (1984a, 116 no. 7) suggests that E's exemplar for R7 may have come from a Machaut manuscript in Flanders; further, **Gr 3360** stands in an intermediate position between E's exemplar for R7 and the many Italian anthology manuscripts that transmit the rondeau. Thus, it would seem that the Italian sources received their Machaut through Flanders, and that the filial relationships often noted between E and the anthology manuscripts (e.g., Dömling 1969) point to a Flemish source for the music in E not copied from B.

MS E appears in the 1402 inventory of the library of the duke of Berry (Delisle 1907, 2:268* nos. 282–83). Ludwig (1926–54, 2:11a*) discusses references to inventories of 1404 (books promised to the Ste-Chapelle at Bourges), and 1413 (books lent on 22 December 1412 to Thomas, duke of Clarence, son of King Henry IV of England); see also Wathey 1988. Bowers (1975–76, 107) suggests that Lionel Power, a member of Thomas's chapel, could have become acquainted with Machaut's Mass through MS E. The manuscript appears in later inventories of the library of the dukes of Burgundy, beginning with the Bruges inventory of ca. 1467, and is catalogued at Brussels from 1487 until 1731. Ludwig was the first to identify the Burgundian manuscript as E (1926–54, 2:11a*, 40b* no. 2), but his assertion (1926–54, 2:11a*) that E entered the library of the dukes of Burgundy between 1420 and 1467 is not necessarily accurate (cf. De Winter 1985, 31, 282 n. 18).

Caylus (1753a, 399) used MS E in 1747 for his description of the works of Machaut, implying that E was already in Paris by that date and not among the Belgian manuscripts taken to Paris by the French in 1794–96, as Ludwig (1926–54, 2:11a*) had suggested (see also De Winter 1985, 115). As Ludwig states, however (1926–54, 2:11a*; see also De Winter 1985, 119), reference to the Gérard inventory of 1797 could resolve this question. Some Belgian manuscripts taken in 1746 were returned in 1770—perhaps E was among these. Earlier shelfmarks: 53 (fol. ii, top middle recto); Regius 7609² (fol. B, bottom middle recto); Supplément français 43 (fol. C, top right recto).

CONTENTS.

Ex-libris penned by Flamel	fol. Br
blank	fol. Bv
original index[26]	fols. Cr–Er
blank	fol. Ev

---

[25] Other studies that deal with the transmission of music in MS E include Hoppin 1960; S.J. Williams 1968; Dömling 1969; Hasselman/Walker 1970; and Strohm 1984a, 118–23. On the transmission of texts in MS E, see Hoepffner 1908–21, 1:xlvii; Bent 1983, 61–76; Kibler/Wimsatt 1987; Wimsatt/Kibler 1988. I consider Imbs's wise statement (Guillaume de Machaut 1982, 138) to summarize the issue fairly.

[26] Bent (1990b, 223) discusses the fact that motets are indexed by their triplum voices, not by their motetus voices, as had been true in earlier musical manuscripts.

Text:

Prologue (four ballades only)	fol. 1r
Loange (237 texts)	fols. 1v–13r
Complaintes	fols. 13r–15v
Rondeaux	fols. 16r–17r
blank	fol. 17v
Vergier	fols. 18r–21v
L'Ecu Bleu [*Remede*] (with music)	fols. 22r–36v
Jugement Behaingne	fols. 37r–42v
Jugement Navarre	fols. 45r–56v
Lay de Plour, Qui bien aimme (L22/16)	fols. 57r–58r
blank	fols. 58v–60v
Lyon	fols. 61r–67r
Dit des .iiii. Oysiaulx [*Alerion*]	fols. 69r–82v
Le Livre Morpheus [*Fonteinne*]	fols. 83r–91r
Confort	fols. 93r–104r
Harpe	fols. 105r–106r
blank	fol. 106v

Music:

19 lais (the last 2 are *opera dubia*; 5 are without music)	fols. 107r–129r
blank	fols. 129v–130v
22 motets, 19 rondeaux (1 rondeau without music)	fols. 131r–146r
blank	fol. 146v
35 ballades (1 copied twice)	fols. 147r–157r
blank	fols. 157v–158v
29 virelais (3 without music)	fols. 159r–164r
Mass (fol. 167 blank)	fols. 164v–170r
Voir Dit (with music)	fols. 171r–210r
Lay de Plour, Malgré Fortune (L19/14)	fols. 210r–211r
Doulz cuers gentilz (rondeau, *opus dubium*)[27]	fol. 211r
blank	fols. 211v–212v
Prise	fols. 213r–238r
blank	fol. 238v

LITERATURE. Delisle 1868–81, 1:58 nn. 1–2, 66; 3:193 nos. 282–83; Omont 1895, 326; Ludwig 1926–54, 10b*–12a*; S.J. Williams 1952, 344–51; Schrade 1956c, 28–30; Meiss 1967, 1:315; *RISM* 1969, 182–92; Reaney 1980c, 663. A partial copy of MS **E** made for La Curne de Sainte-Palaye (1697–1781) is in the MS *F:Pa 3297* (see Martin 1886–89, 3:312; Ludwig 1926–54, 2:12a*). La Curne de Sainte-Palaye annotated the margins with his lexicographical studies.

[8] BRUSSELS, lost manuscript in the Burgundian library

PROVENANCE. A lost manuscript with music, clearly described first in the 1420 inventory of the Burgundian library (Doutrepont 1906, 143 no. 212; see Ludwig 1926–54, 2:40* no. 1; C. Wright 1979, 146 no. 34). It may have been the Machaut manuscript listed in the 1405 inventory of the goods of Marguerite of Flanders, and thus may have once belonged to her father, Count Louis de Male of Flanders (De Winter 1985, 45, 52, 56 n. 12, 156–57 no. 135).[28] It reappeared in the inventories of 1467 (Barrois 1830, 191 no. 1307) and 1487 (Barrois 1830, 270 no. 1888) and can be traced as late as 1797 (Marchal 1842, 1:ccliv, Viglius no. 200). Compare MS [19].

CONTENTS. MS [8] began with *Vergier*, and ended with the *Hoquetus David* and *Sé je souspir* (V36), the hocket copied in the same manner as in **Vg** and **B**. Earp (1983, 35 n. 76, 82 n. 168; 1989, 475, 481) tentatively identifies this manuscript as the exemplar of MS **M** [10].

---

[27] L19 and this rondeau are copied together as item nos. 196 and 197 in MS **Pa** [50], solid evidence that many of the Machaut works in **Pa** derive from MS **E**.

[28] The listing of a "livre de Machaut" in both the 1405 and 1477 inventories is too vague to identify a specific manuscript; see Peignot 1841, 67 (1405 inventory), 97 (1477 inventory).

[9] PARIS, lost manuscript in the library of Jean Turquam

PROVENANCE. An untraced manuscript in the 1519 inventory of the library of Jean Turquam, a bourgeois, "La Prinse d'Alexandre avecques plusieurs aultres livres, ballades et chançons" (Schutz 1951, 29; 1955, 65, 86 no. 207; Jurgens 1982, 57 no. 83; Genevois 1987, 230 no. 1870). The manuscript doubtless contained music and is perhaps extant; unfortunately, the contemporary description is not exact enough to allow for an identification. Yet the fact that the *Prise* is singled out is significant, and perhaps this provides a clue for an association of this reference to MS **B**, which would possibly have had a loose or separate *Prise*, and which would have been a manuscript suitable for a bourgeois collection.

B. *Manuscripts containing texts only*

[10] PARIS, Bibliothèque Nationale, fonds français 843 (M; *F:Pn 843*; Hoepffner: *M*; Chichmaref: *A*)

DESCRIPTION. Parchment, ii + 255 + ii fols., with two additional paper flyleaves in front and two in back. Dimensions: 32.6 × 23 cm, 2 cols. at 40 ll./col. One scribe throughout. Collation 1–31⁸ 32⁸⁻¹; see also Earp 1983, 93–96. Bound in brown leather over boards, with the arms of Napoleon I on the cover, and the monogram "N" on the spine, different in only a few details from the design given by Guigard (1890, 1:32).

DECORATION. Rubrication is complete, but the initials and illuminations were not entered. Room was left for a miniature at the beginning of the thirteen major divisions, from *Vergier* to the lais.

DATE AND PROVENANCE. Late fourteenth or early fifteenth century, a copy of a manuscript probably of the late 1360s, representing a stage of the collection of the works between MSS **Vg** and **A** (see Earp 1983, 93–96; and below, chap. 6.2). Earlier shelfmarks of the Bibliothèque du Roy: 431 (Nicolas Rigault catalogue of 1622, Omont 1908–21, 2:283); 751 (brothers Dupuy catalogue of 1645, Omont 1908–21, 3:40); Regius 7221 (Nicolas Clément catalogue of 1682, Omont 1908–21, 4:27; P. Paris 1836–48, 6:447–50).

CONTENTS.

Vergier	fols. 1r–9r
Jugement Behaingne	fols. 9r–21v
Jugement Navarre	fols. 21v–48v
Lay de Plour, Qui bien aimme (L22/16)	fols. 48v–49v
Remede	fols. 50r–77r
Lyon	fols. 77r–91r
Alerion	fols. 91r–121r
Confort	fols. 121r–146r
Fonteinne	fols. 146r–164r
Harpe	fols. 164r–166v
Marguerite	fols. 166v–167v
Loange (271 texts)	fols. 168r–198r
Complaintes	fols. 198r–207r
20 lais	fols. 207v–237r
38 ballades	fols. 237r–243v
20 rondeaux	fols. 244r–245r
37 virelais	fols. 245v–255v

LITERATURE. *Bibliothèque Impériale* 1868, 98; Ludwig 1926–54, 2:12b*–13a*; Schrade 1956c, 35. Eighteenth-century inventory by La Curne de Sainte-Palaye in *F:Pn Moreau 1655* no. 581 (fols. 233r–234v).

[11] PARIS, Bibliothèque Nationale, fonds français 1587 (D; *F:Pn 1587*; Hoepffner: *D*; Chichmaref: *F*)

DESCRIPTION. Parchment, iii + 108 + i folios. Dimensions: 26 × 19 cm. Collation 1–10⁸ 11⁸ (irreg.) 12–13⁸ 14⁴; more details on collation in Earp 1983, 119–20. Bound in red morocco.

DECORATION. Rubrics. Solid initials one to two lines tall alternate red and blue. *Vergier* and *Jugement Behaingne* begin with divided initials five lines tall. Capital letters at beginning of lines are highlighted with yellow wash. On the twelve miniatures, see the descriptions below, chap. 4.4; on the artist, see chap. 4.2 table 4.9.

FACSIMILES. Miniatures (refer to chap. 4.4): **D1, D7**.

INSCRIPTIONS. "Ce livre est a maistre Jehan desertement channon de Renes" [This book belongs to master John, formerly canon of Rennes] (fol. 108r, end of col. b, effaced). There is much writing by Châtre de Cangé on the inside front and back cover, on all flyleaves, on fol. 108v, and elsewhere in the manuscript. His studies are mainly an effort to trace the author, whom he called "Guillaume de Machaut de Loris" (cf. above, inscriptions in MS **B** [4]).

DATE AND PROVENANCE. Decorated in Paris ca. 1430 (Avril 1982a, 130). It is clear from the mentions of "Mestre Guillaume de Loris" in the rubric of the first miniature of the *Loange* (**D1**; see chap. 4.4p) that the scribe was already confused about the identity of Guillaume de Machaut ("Loris" appears to be added over an erasure). Purchased by Châtre de Cangé in 1724 for 150 *livres* from the library of the princess of Anet, after her death in 1723.[29] Many of Cangé's manuscripts were purchased by Louis XV for the Bibliothèque du Roy in 1733. Earlier shelfmarks: Cangé 70; Regius 7612[2].

CONTENTS.

Loange (256 texts)[30]	fols. 1r–47v
Vergier	fols. 48r–58r
Jugement Behaingne	fols. 58v–74v
Jugement Navarre [31]	fols. 74v–108r
blank, except for notes by Cangé	fol. 108v

LITERATURE. *Bibliothèque Impériale* 1868, 259; Ludwig 1926–54, 2:14b*–15a*; Schrade 1956c, 35.

[12] BRUSSELS, lost manuscript in the Burgundian library

PROVENANCE. This manuscript appears in the ca. 1467 inventory of the Burgundian library of Duke Charles the Bold (Barrois 1830, 198 no. 1354), the Brussels inventory of 1487 (Barrois 1830, 257 no. 1793), and subsequent inventories; discussed by Ludwig (1926–54, 2:41a* as Burgundian MS no. 4; see also Earp 1989, 473–75).[32] The manuscript was apparently lost in the late seventeenth or early eighteenth century, since it appears in the 1643 inventory of the Brussels manuscripts but is lacking the 1731 inventory (Marchal 1842, 1:cclvi, Viglius no. 274); it may have been among the manuscripts lost in the palace fire of 1731 (cf. De Winter 1985, 115).

CONTENTS. A text manuscript beginning with the *Loange* and ending with *Fonteinne*. Although no extant manuscript matches this disposition, it is approximately the extent of the text portion of MS **Vg**, which itself appears at one time to have been divided into two volumes, perhaps to allow the text portion of the manuscript to remain in the house library, while the music was used by the chapel musicians (compare the descriptions above of MSS **W** [2] and **Vg** [3].[33]

    The identification of MS [12] in inventories as "Le Livre du Temps Pastour [*sic*] et plusieurs Balades et Laiz" provides a further connection to a **Vg**-style manuscript. In MSS **Vg** and **B**, as well as the *explicit* in MS **C**, the *Jugement Behaingne* is named *Le Livre du Temps Pascour*.[34]

---

[29] The library of Diane de Poitiers (1499–1566) formed the core of the library of Anet (P. Paris 1836–48, 6:210; Delisle 1868–81, 1:188–89). Anet was built for her by King Henry II.

[30] Title: *Ci commence le livre mestre Guill'e de Loris*. On the title, see Ludwig 1926–54, 2:7* and 14*–15*; and especially the discussion in Sonnemann 1969, 28–29.

[31] Although there is a new miniature at the beginning of *Jugement Navarre*, no *explicit* or identifying rubric sets off the end of *Jugement Behaingne* from the beginning of *Jugement Navarre*.

[32] Perhaps this manuscript is the one vaguely described in the inventory of 1477 (Peignot 1841, 97).

[33] Fol. 2 of MS [12] began with l. 8 of the ballade Lo7, "si n'en puis mais" (thus it is not identical with MS **Vg**).

[34] Compare also the reference to the metrical scheme of the *Jugement Behaingne* in the anonymous *Regles de la Seconde Rettorique* (chap. 2.3.1c).

[13] **CHAMBÉRY, lost manuscript in the Savoy library**
PROVENANCE. In the spring of 1368, Machaut was given a total of 310 gold francs for a *roman* presented to Amadeus VI, Count of Savoy. The manuscript is included here among the complete-works text manuscripts because this seems like too much money for a single *dit*. See chap. 1.15.2c.

[14] **CHATEAUDUN (Eure-et-Loir), lost manuscript in the library of the Bastard of Orléans**
PROVENANCE. An untraced manuscript owned by Jean, the Bastard of Orléans, count of Dunois (1403–1468), item no. 12 in the 1468 inventory at Châteaudun of the library of Dunois: "Ung autre livre appellé le livre de Machault" (Delisle 1868–81, 3:194; Champion 1910, 126; Ludwig 1926–54, 2:40a* n. 2, 41b*–42a*; Genevois 1987, 100 no. 795). The manuscript may have contained music and is perhaps extant; unfortunately, the contemporary description is not exact enough to allow for an identification. Some later inscriptions in MS W [2] provide evidence of a link to the circle around Charles d'Orléans, and thus it is possible that MS [14] partially survives as MS **W**. La Monte (1932, 53) theorizes that François Villon could have become acquainted with Machaut's *Prise* through this manuscript. For speculation on the possible influence of Machaut on Charles d'Orléans, again through this manuscript, see Poirion 1965, 277–78 (see also below, MS **Ra** [44]).

3. Partial complete-works manuscripts that include works by other authors

This category comprises manuscripts containing portions of a complete collection of Machaut's works, along with works by other authors. The order of the works of Machaut in these collections corresponds to the authoritative order of one or another of the complete-works manuscripts in chap. 3.2.[35] Some of the manuscripts described in this section are miscellanies, in which fragments of larger Machaut manuscripts were subsequently bound with unrelated works. Whether these new collections represent the desires of medieval collectors is unclear. MS H [17] and the lost Burgundian manuscript [19] are possibly such miscellanies. The remaining manuscripts, K [15], J [16], and **Pm** [18], are integral sources and open for inquiry as to the reasons for the juxtaposition of the different works.

The collection of non-Machaut works in MS **J** has occasioned some problems of attribution. Some of the lyrics from **J** have been edited as if they were works of Machaut, even though they are absent from the central group of complete-works manuscripts.[36] In addition, the narrative *Dit du Cerf Blanc* at the end of MS **J** has been edited by Fourrier (1979, 302–29) as an authentic work of Machaut (discussed in chap. 5.19 as an *opus dubium*).

[15] **BERN, Burgerbibliothek, 218** (**K**; *CH:BEb 218*; Hoepffner: *K*; Chichmaref: *R*)
DESCRIPTION. Parchment, 103 fols., with two paper flyleaves in back; modern pencil foliation, 1–103, top right recto; old foliation i–vi^XX xviii (i.e., 138), top middle recto (originally 140 fols.); old fols. 4, 5, 9–20, 29, 41, 48–49, 61–68, 71, 80, 83, 94, 107, 115, 124, 126, and 129 are missing.[37] Old fols. 86–93 are misnumbered as 87, 80, 80, 89,

---

[35] For a chronological overview of most of the manuscripts in chaps. 3.2–3, see Earp 1989, 474 table I.

[36] A rondeau that appears uniquely in the *Loange* of MS K is edited as Lo273 in Chichmaref 1909, 1:236; twenty lyrics that appear uniquely in the *Loange* of MS J are edited in the appendix of Chichmaref 1909, 2:637–53 (two of the lyrics have some outside concordances in anthologies; see chap. 6.1b and chap. 6.3). Chichmaref's views on the attribution of these works largely leaves the question of attribution open (1909, 1:cii n. 1).

[37] The account of Gröber (Hagen 1875, 263), repeated by Ludwig (1926–54, 2:13b* n. 2), is in error.

90, 91, 91, and 88 respectively, but there are no losses in the text; old fols. 127–128 are reversed in the modern binding. Dimensions: 29.5 × 20.7 cm, writing block 21 × 14.5 cm, 42 ll./col. Contains music. Fourteenth-century formal bookhand, one scribe throughout. Collation 1^{8-2} : 2^8 (irregular) : 3^{8-1} 4^{8-1} 5^{8-2} 6^8 : 7^{8-1} 8^{8-2} 9^8 10^{8-1} 11^{8-1} 12^{8-1} 13^{8-1} 14^{8-2} 15^4 (irregular) 16^2; more on signatures and collation in Earp 1983, 374–78. Bound in white vellum over cardboard, ca. 1700 (*RISM* 1969, 52). See the very thorough description with additional bibliography in Ludwig 1926–54, 2:13b*–14a*.

DECORATION. Rubrics. Major divisions begin with a pink and blue floriated initial three to four lines tall, with stems and ivy leaves, or a red and blue divided initial with filigree. Other initials one to two lines tall in alternating colors, with filigree. On the thirteen miniatures, see the descriptions below, chap. 4.4, and the discussion in Homburger 1953, 124–25. Little is known of the artist (see chap. 4.2 table 4.4).

FACSIMILES. Miniatures (refer to chap. 4.4). K4 (with entire fol. 46v [30v]), K12–13. See also Bertoni 1917.

INSCRIPTION. Colophon printed in Hagen 1875, 269; Chichmaref 1909, 1:lxxiii; Schrade 1956c, 33; and Fourrier 1979, 77–78.

DATE AND PROVENANCE. Dated Friday of the second week of April (11 April) 1371, copied by Guiot de Sens. On J as a copy of K, see Hoepffner 1908–21, 1:xlvii (cf. also Chichmaref 1909, 1:ci–ciii; Wimsatt 1976, 293 n. 21; Fourrier 1979, 77–79; Wimsatt/Kibler 1988, 17–18, 21–32, 40–46). MS K has been erroneously associated with a document of 1371 (see above on the lost Savoyard MS [13]). The manuscript probably belonged to the library of Jacques Bongars (1554–1612), whose library came to Bern in 1632 (Dr. Christian von Steiger, librarian of the Burgerbibliothek, reported in Fourrier 1979, 78). Earlier shelfmarks: m 28 (fol. 1r; sixteenth or seventeenth century, according to *RISM* 1969, 52).

CONTENTS (old foliation).

Loange (47 texts extant)	fols. 1r–3r; 6r–8r
Vergier (complete)	fols. 21r–28r
Jugement Behaingne (incomplete)	fols. 30r–40r
Lay de Plour, Qui bien aimme (L22/16) (incomplete)	fols. 42r–42v
Chanson desesperee (Lo55)	fol. 42v
Remede (inc.; music for RF4–5)	fols. 43r–47r; 50r–60r
[E]n amer (RF4, three-voice)	fol. 59v
[D]ame, de qui (RF5, two-voice)	fol. 60v
Lyon (incomplete)	fols. 69r–70r; 72r–79r; 81r–82r
Confort (incomplete)	fols. 84r–93r; 95r–106r
Fonteinne (incomplete)	fols. 108r–114r; 116r–123r
Harpe (incomplete)	fols. 125r–125v
Lais (*Un mortel lay*, L12/8 [inc.]; *S'onques*, L17/12 [inc.]; *Amours, se plus*, L9 [inc.]; *Amis, t'amour*, L10/7)	fols. 128r–131r
Chastel d'Amours (not Machaut)[38]	fols. 132r–132v
[10 short *Jeux*, not by Machaut][39]	fol. 132v–133
Anonymous, *Je Fortune*[40]	fol. 133r
Voir Dit (2 fragments)[41]	fols. 133r–135r
[*Jeux*, not Machaut][42]	fols. 136v–138r

[38] Ed. Hoepffner 1909, 702–10; Klein 1911, 153–56; see Bertoni 1917; Huizinga 1924, 108 (=1953, 126).

[39] Ed. Hoepffner 1906, 411–13, with solutions to several of the names they hide; see also Chichmaref 1909, 1:ciii n. 1. The solution to riddle no. 8 may be "Toute belle," a clear link to the *Voir Dit* and therefore possibly proof that these poems, although not by Machaut himself, may stem from Machaut's immediate circle (Hoepffner 1906, 412–13); Guesnon (1912, 93n.) gives the alternative solution "Isabeau."

[40] This anonymous ballade, also in this position in MS J [16], has further concordances in text manuscripts (Ludwig 1926–54, 2:14a* n. 3); it is also the text of a very popular musical setting, discussed in Strohm 1984a, 115 no. 5.

[41] On the extent of the *Voir Dit* excerpt, see Ludwig 1926–54, 14a* n. 3 and chap. 2.1.1e.

[42] On these works, see Bergeron 1992, 180, 183–85 (*siglum B*).

LITERATURE. Hagen 1875, 263–69; Handschin 1923; Ludwig 1926–54, 13b*–14*; Schrade 1956c, 32–33; *RISM* 1969, 52–53.

[16] **PARIS, Bibliothèque de l'Arsenal, 5203 (J;** *F:Pa 5203*; Hoepffner: *J*; Chichmaref: *M*)

DESCRIPTION. Parchment, 165 + ii fols., with two paper flyleaves in front and two in back; foliated 1–80, 80*bis*, 81–86, 86*bis*, 87–92, 92*bis*, 93–161, [162] (unnumbered, blank). Dimensions: 29 × 21 cm, writing block 20.5 × 16 cm, 2 cols. at 36 ll./col. Space left for music, but no music was entered. Fourteenth-century formal bookhand, one scribe throughout. Collation: $1-2^8\ 3^4 : 4-6^8 : 7^8\ 8^8$ (irregular) $9-10^8 : 11-12^8 : 13-15^8\ 16^{8-1}$ $17-18^8\ 19^{8-1}\ 20^8\ 21^4\ 22^{6+1}$; more on signatures and collation in Earp 1983, 374–78. Bound in red morocco with gilt tooling. See the very thorough description with additional bibliography in Ludwig 1926–54, 2:14a*.

DECORATION. Rubrics. Major divisions begin with a pink or blue floriated initial three to four lines tall, with a gold border and stem with ivy leaves. Other initials two lines tall, alternating gold with black filigree and blue with red filigree. Capitals are highlighted in yellow wash. On the thirty-five miniatures (twenty-four illustrate works of Machaut), see the descriptions below, chap. 4.4. Little is known of the artist (chap. 4.2 table 4.3). Given the spacing of the words for melismas, and blank areas for untexted lower voices, it seems that the two ballades of the *Remede* (RF4–5) were intended to be copied with their music, but the scribe handled this ineptly, leaving only two lines blank for the subsequent entry of staves for *En amer* (RF4); *Dame, de qui* (RF5) has three lines blank, which is adequate.

FACSIMILES. Samaran/Marichal 1959, plate clxxxvii (fol. 29r, part of *Vergier*). Miniatures (refer to chap. 4.4x): J28, J32.

INSCRIPTION. Martin (1886–89, 5:149) indicates that on fol. 161v, the following effaced note is found: "Cest livre est a mon trés redoubté seigneur monseigneur le conte du Perche, et fut escript a Bellesme" [This book belongs to my very redoubtable lord, monseigneur the count of Perche, and was written at Bellême (dept. Orne)].[43]

DATE AND PROVENANCE. MS J is related to MS K, dated 1371. On J as a copy of K, see Hoepffner 1908–21, 1:xlvii (cf. also Chichmaref 1909, 1:ci–ciii; Wimsatt 1976, 293 n. 21; Wimsatt/Kibler 1988, 17–18, 21–32, 40–46). Fourrier (1979, 76–77) identified the count of Perche in the inscription as Robert d'Alençon, count of Perche from 1361 until his death in 1377; his projected marriage in 1371 to Jeanne de Navarre, sister of King Charles of Navarre, was successfully opposed by Charles V. Perhaps this political circumstance explains the fact that Machaut's *Jugement Navarre* does not appear in the manuscript, although later *dits* do. In the eighteenth century, MS J belonged to the marquis de Paulmy (1722–1787), whose library forms the core of the Bibliothèque de l'Arsenal. Earlier shelfmarks: 18171 (fol. i verso); B.L.F. 97 (fols. ii recto and ii verso); Belles-Lettres, 1714A (fol. ii recto; library of the marquis de Paulmy).

CONTENTS.

---

[43] The note was apparently briefly rendered legible by means of a chemical; it is no longer visible. The text of the inscription is also given in Chichmaref 1909, 1:lxxiv; Samaran/Marichal 1959, 408 no. 130; Fourrier 1979, 76. A further now-illegible inscription on fol. [162], bottom left recto, also seems to have had a chemical poured on it.

[44] Twenty items are *unica*, see chap. 6.1b and 6.3.

Amours, se plus, L9; *Amis, t'amour*, L10/7)	fols. 139v–146v
Chastel d'Amours (not Machaut)[45]	fols. 146v–147r
[10 short *Jeux*, not by Machaut][46]	fols. 147r–147v
Anonymous, *Je Fortune*[47]	fol. 147v
Voir Dit (2 fragments)[48]	fols. 147v–151v
Coq-a-l'Ane (not Machaut)	fols. 151v–153r
Rose	fol. 153r–154r
blank	fol. 154v
Cerf Blanc (opus dubium)[49]	fols. 155r–161v
blank ruled	fol. [162r–162v]

LITERATURE. Martin 1886–89, 5:143–49; Ludwig 1926–54, 2:14b*; Schrade 1956a, 33–34; Samaran/Marichal 1959, 408 no. 130.

[17] PARIS, Bibliothèque Nationale, fonds français 881 (H; *F:Pn 881*; Hoepffner: *H*; Chichmaref: *B*; Roy: *C*)

DESCRIPTION. Parchment, iii + 112 + iii fols., with one paper flyleaf in front and one in back. Dimensions: 31 × 23.5 cm, 2 cols. at 32–36 ll./col. Cursive bookhand. G. Paris identified a scribal concordance with *F:Pn 840*, the manuscript of the complete works of Eustache Deschamps signed by Raoul Tainguy, a Breton copyist who worked at Paris in the late fourteenth century.[50] At least one gathering at the end is missing, more probably several. Bound in red morocco with gilt tooling, French royal arms, seventeenth or eighteenth century (cf. *Bibliothèque Nationale* 1981, 482, plate xxiv, item 2).

DECORATION. Rubrics. Gold floriated initials with bar borders and ivy leaves; smaller initials one to two lines tall, alternating red with black filigree and blue with red filigree. The first initials for the ballades of Machaut's *Prologue* are blue and red divided initials, with red and black filigree. One miniature (fol. 1r); there is space for a miniature at the beginning of Machaut's *Prologue* (fol. 97r), but it was never executed. The rubric reads: *Comment Nature, voulant orendroit plus que onques mais reveler et faire exaucier les biens et honeurs qui sont en Amours, vient a Guillaume de Machaut et lui ordonne et encharge a faire sur ce noveaus dis amoureux, et lui baille pour lui conseillier et adviser a ce faire trois de ses enfans, c'est assavoir Sens, Rethorique et Musique. Et lui dit par ceste maniere* (cf. below, chap. 4.4a, first miniature of the *Prologue* for a translation).

INSCRIPTION. "Ce livre est a Jehan Martel. Ovide de la vieille auquel sont contenuz / plusiers nobles ditz et enseignementz. / Ensemble le livre de l'art d'amour. / Davantage les Dicts amoureux de Guillaume de Machault" (verso of first parchment flyleaf) [This book belongs to Jehan Martel. Ovid's *De Vetula*, containing many noble poems and lessons; the entire *Ars Amatoria*; in addition the amorous *dits* of Guillaume de Machaut]. Other pen tries on last parchment flyleaf verso.

DATE AND PROVENANCE. Late fourteenth or early fifteenth century. Tesnière (1986, 323 n. 1 and 343 n. 2) indicates that Raoul Tainguy copied the Machaut works in H from E, but this is unlikely because H follows the authoritative order of *Loange* lyrics, not the unique arrangement of E. In the library of Arnaud de Corbie (ca. 1325–1414), first president of Parlement (1373) and Chancellor of France (1388–1413) (Tesnière 1986, 313). Nothing is known of the library of the Jehan Martel mentioned in the inscription (Delisle 1868–81, 2:382). The manuscript had entered the royal library by 1622. Earlier shelfmarks: MDCCCXLI (Nicolas Rigault catalogue of 1622, Omont 1908–21, 2:354); 159 (brothers Dupuy catalogue of 1645, Omont 1908–21, 3:12); Regius 7235 (Nicolas Clément catalogue of 1682, Omont 1908–21, 4:28; P. Paris 1836–48, 7:74–78).

---

[45] See n. 38.

[46] See n. 39.

[47] See n. 40.

[48] See n. 41.

[49] Ed. Fourrier (1979, 302–29), who attributes the *dit* to Machaut. See chap. 5.19.

[50] See Queux de Saint-Hilaire/Raynaud 1878–1903, 2:vi–xvi (notice by Siméon Luce); 11:103–5, 108–9; B. Roy 1974, 22–23; and especially Tesnière's impressive study (1986).

CONTENTS.

Ovid, *De Vetula* (French trans. by Jean Lefevre)[51]	fols. 1r–48r
Ovid, *Ars Amatoria* (French trans.)	fols. 48r–96r
Machaut *Prologue* (4 ballades only)[52]	fol. 97r
Loange (96 texts with many gaps)[53]	fols. 98r–112v

LITERATURE. *Bibliothèque Impériale* 1868, 147–48; Gennrich 1921–27, 2:211–19; Ludwig 1926–54, 2:15a*; Schrade 1956c, 35; B. Roy 1974, 21–23; Tesnière 1986, 342–45. Eighteenth-century inventory by La Curne de Sainte-Palaye, MS *F:Pn Moreau 1655* no. 596 (fols. 259r–259v). Further bibliography in Tesnière 1986, 288, 313.

[18] NEW YORK, Pierpont Morgan Library, M.396 (**Pm**; *US:NYpm 396*; Ludwig: *Morg*; Laidlaw: *Gf*)

DESCRIPTION. Parchment, 247 fols., with two paper flyleaves in front and two in back; nineteenth-century (?) Arabic foliation, 1–252, bottom middle recto, modern pencil foliation, 1–251, top right recto (the two foliations do not correspond). Many lacunae. Dimensions: 32.5 × 25 cm, writing block ca. 24.5 × 18 cm, 2 columns at 43–44 ll./col. Contains music. One scribe throughout, who employed a cursive bookhand with uniform ink ruling. Collation 1–10⁸ 11⁸ (irregular) 12⁸⁻¹ 13⁶ (lacuna) 14⁸⁻¹ 15⁸⁻¹ 16⁸⁻¹ 17–19⁸ 20⁷ (irregular) 21⁸ 22⁶⁻¹ (probably originally ⁸⁻³) 23–28⁸ : 29⁸⁻¹ 30⁸ 31⁸⁻¹ 32⁸⁻¹ 33⁶⁻¹. Formerly bound in eighteenth-century brown calf, rebound in 1933 in three-quarter brown morocco by Marguerite Lahey.

DECORATION. Rubrics. On the 126 colored wash drawings, see the descriptions below, chap. 4.4; on the artist, see chap. 4.2 table 4.6. The 1940 dossier at the Pierpont Morgan Library distinguishes three artists (dossier, p. 4). Written instructions to the illuminator are visible for miniatures **Pm**43–45, 63–67, 69–71. The iconography is dependent on MS **A**, see Avril (1982a, 130), the comparative table of miniatures (chap. 4.3), and compare the descriptions of miniatures in **A** and **Pm** in the concordance of miniatures (chap. 4.4).

FACSIMILES. Miniatures (refer to chap. 4.4): **Pm**1, **Pm**3, **Pm**110–111.

   Ballades: Hoppin 1978b, 423 (fol. 213v, *De Fortune* [B23]); Besseler 1949–51, 717 (fol. 213v, *De toutes flours* [B31]).

   Rondeau: Hoppin 1978b, 427 (fol. 214v, *Se vous n'estes* [R7])

INSCRIPTIONS. The signature of Garson de Boiaval (seventeenth century, from the region of Artois) appears on fol. 1r (the second parchment flyleaf).

DATE AND PROVENANCE. The date of Alan Chartier's *La Belle Dame sans Merci* (1424) provides a terminus after which the manuscript was copied (Laidlaw 1974, 7, 39). The miniatures date from ca. 1425–30 (Avril 1982a, 129–30). The text of Chartier's *La Belle Dame sans Merci* contains some Northeastern dialect forms (Laidlaw 1974, 73). "The spelling of such words as beauté, ioli, menchonge, auxi, oeul, cuers, viengne, chastiaux, ricesses, and the use of the article (ly tristes, ly ioieux), may indicate a South Burgundian scribe" (1940 Pierpont Morgan Library dossier, p. 3). Avril (1982a, 129–30) noted the dependence of the program of illuminations on MS **A**. Conjunctive variants with MS **A** in the few musical works in MS **Pm** support Avril's thesis of direct copy (Dömling 1969, 194). Purchased by J. Pierpont Morgan in 1910 through Th. Belin, from northern France.

CONTENTS (new foliation at top right recto).

Prologue (complete)	fols. 1r–3b
Vergier	fols. 3b–11a
Jugement Behaingne	fols. 11b–23a
Jugement Navarre	fols. 23b–47d

---

[51] Gennrich (1926–27, 515–16) publishes the description of musical instruments. See also Tesnière 1986, 316–17.

[52] The *Prologue* is somewhat truncated, since Guillaume's ballade in response to Lady Nature lacks its third strophe, evidently to keep the scene with Nature all on the recto. Thus shortened, the *Prologue* perfectly fills fols. 97r–97v.

[53] See chap. 6.3. Many corruptions are recorded in the notes to the edition of Chichmaref 1909 (*siglum B*); see also Wilkins 1972, 174 n. 121.

Remede (without music)	fols. 47d–73c
Lyon (lacunae)	fols. 73c–86d
Confort (lacunae)	fols. 87a–101d
Fonteinne (lacunae)	fols. 102a–117d
Harpe	fols. 118a–120c
Marguerite	fols. 120c–121d
Voir Dit (lacunae)	fols. 122a–182c
Rose	fols. 182c–183b
Vecy les biens	fols. 183b–183d
Alerion	fols. 183d–211c
3 *Complaintes* (*Amours, tu m'as* [Cp1], *Quant Ecuba* [Cp4],	
Mes dous amis [Cp5])	fols. 211c–213c
De toutes flours (B31) (ca, ten, ct)	fols. 213v–214r
De Fortune (B23) (ca, ten)	fol. 214r
Se vous n'estes (R7) (ca, ten)	fol. 214v
Tant doucement me sens (R9) (ca, ten)	fol. 214v

The function of the small number of musical works in **Pm** seems to be one of articulation in the manuscript, making the juncture between the Machaut works and the non-Machaut works easy to find. The end of the Machaut section provides the first real articulation in the through-copied structure of the manuscript (see the summary of the collation given above, gatherings 28–29).

LITERATURE. Guesnon 1912, 94–95; Ludwig 1926–54, 2:13*, 4:[82] (*Nachtrag*, description by Heinrich Besseler); Ricci/Wilson 1937; Reese 1940, 348 n. 47; 1940 typescript dossier by "MPH" at the Pierpont Morgan Library; Schrade 1956c, 31–32; *Pierpont Morgan Library* 1957; Faye/Bond 1962, 344; *RISM* 1969, 341–42; Laidlaw 1974, 73. The miscellaneous works in MS **Pm** not by Machaut (fols. 215r–247r) are described most recently by Cropp (1982–83, 263–68, 284–85). See also the comments of Cerquiglini (1985b, 75).

[19] BRUSSELS, lost manuscript in the Burgundian library

PROVENANCE. It is possible that MS [19] was the Machaut manuscript mentioned in the 1405 inventory of the books of Marguerite of Flanders, duchess of Burgundy (De Winter 1985, 156–57 no. 135), although the description there is not detailed enough to be certain. The description in the 1420 inventory of the books of duke Philip the Good (Doutrepont 1906, no. 243) is more thorough; the manuscript reappears in the inventory of 1467 (Barrois 1830, 192 no. 1309) and 1487 (Barrois 1830, 250 no. 1748).[54] Further discussed by Ludwig (1926–54, 2:40b*–41a*) as Burgundian MS no. 3; C. Wright 1979, 146 no. 35; De Winter 1985, 157 no. 135B; Earp 1989, 474, 475. This manuscript can be traced as late as 1797 (Marchal 1842, ccliv, Viglius no. 199). Compare MS [8]

CONTENTS. MS [19] retained the organizational plan of placing the *Loange* at the head of the manuscript, as in MSS **W**, **Vg(B)**, **K**, **J**, **E**, and **D**, as well as the lost MS [12] (Earp 1989, 481), although the *Loange* was possibly preceded by the short form of the *Prologue*, consisting of the four introductory ballades alone. The work at the end of the manuscript is unidentified; the last folio began "dont j'ay en ce rommant traictie," and the last line of the last poem was "se fables non et monsonges" (cf. *Roman de la Rose*, l. 2: "n'a se fables non et mensonges").

4. Manuscripts of individual works and small anthologies of a single genre

This category of manuscripts, transmitting individual works, or a small group of works of like genre (as MSS [28]–[30], perhaps also [26]), is in many respects the most important group of all. These are the potential representatives of the crucial lower level of transmission, the everyday circulation of works. A

---

54 De Winter (1985, 157 no. 135B) asserts that this manuscript does not correspond to the citation of 1487, but he is mistaken. The listing of a "livre de Machaut" in both the 1405 and 1477 inventories is too vague to identify a specific manuscript; see Peignot 1841, 67 (1405 inventory), 97 (1477 inventory).

few of the manuscripts in this group are presentation copies (**Bk** [21] and possibly **Pe** [20]), others are potentially early copies of individual works, perhaps quite close to the author, at least in a temporal sense (MS [27]). No doubt once the most numerous group, it is now represented largely by references to lost manuscripts.

A. *Manuscripts of individual narrative poems*

[20] **CAMBRIDGE, Magdalene College, Pepysian Library, 1594** (**Pe**; Pep; *GB:Cmc 1594*)

DESCRIPTION. Parchment, iii + 44 fols. + iii Dimensions: 20.6 × 14.9 cm, thoroughly described in Leech-Wilkinson 1982 and McKitterick/Beadle 1992. Contains music.

DECORATION. One miniature on fol. 12v to *Remede* l. 1481 (see below, chap. 4.4e; on the artist, see the brief note at the end of chap. 4.2).

FACSIMILES. Ballade: *The Consort* 33 (1977), cover (fols. 25v–26r, *Dame, de qui* [RF5] complete); Wilkins 1979, 22 (fol. 23v, part of *En amer* [RF4]); Leech-Wilkinson 1982, 102 (fols. 23v–24r, *En amer* [RF4] complete).

CONTENTS. Originally contained the *Remede* only. An unidentified prose treatise copied by a different scribe was later bound after the *Remede*.[55]

Remede ["*Remede d'Amour*"]	fols. 1r–36v
lai, *Qui n'aroit* (RF1)	fols. 4r–6r
complainte, Telz rit (RF2)	fol. 8r–12v
chant royal, Joie, plaisance (RF3)	fol. 17r
ballade, *En amer* (RF4)	fols. 23v–24r
ballade, *Dame, de cui* (RF5)	fol. 25v
virelai, *Dame, a vous* (RF6)	fols. 29r–29v
rondeau, *Tant doucement me sens* (R9)[56]	fol. 35r

LITERATURE. James 1923; Ludwig 1926–54, 2:12*; Schrade 1956c, 34; *RISM* 1969, 210–11; Leech-Wilkinson 1982, 100–103; J. Stevens et al. 1989; McKitterick/Beadle 1992.

[21] **BERLIN, Staatliche Museen Preussischer Kulturbesitz, Kupferstichkabinett, 78 C 2** (**Bk**; *D:Bkk 78 C 2*)

DESCRIPTION. Parchment, 16 fols., with three paper flyleaves in front and four in back; modern Arabic foliation, 1–16, top right recto. Dimensions: 30.2 × 19.6 cm, writing block 22.5 × 15.8 cm, two cols. at 40 ll./col. Formal bastard bookhand. Collation: $1^1\ 2^8\ 3^{8-1}$. Catchwords on fols. 1v and 9v, gathering signatures "m i" through "m iii" visible in first quartern. Tightly bound in red morocco with gilt tooling on spine: LE DIT DU LION M.^{SS} PRET. EN VERS S. VEL. DU 15. S. AV. MIN, identified as the work of Derome in *Sotheby and Co.* 1882.

DECORATION. Rubrics. The first initial is four lines tall, a blue "Q" with red leaves inside, all within a gold square; all the others are gold initials two lines tall on a cusped blue and pink background with white tracery (*lettres rechampies échancrées*) in gold squares. A few initials have blue and white or pink and white floriated letters with gold background, with stems and ivy leaves or connected to gold bar borders with ivy leaves and dragon. Ten of thirty planned miniatures are described in Wescher 1931 and chap. 4.4f. Many of the miniatures are rubbed and worn; the best preserved are on fols. 4r and 11v. Though mostly trimmed, written instructions to the illuminator are partially visible on fols. 1r, 4r, 10v, and 11v. On the artist, see chap. 4.2 tables 4.7 and 4.10.

FACSIMILE. Miniature (refer to chap. 4.3 and 4.4f): Bk5.

DATE AND PROVENANCE. ca. 1390 (François Avril, personal communication). The irregular collation and signature markings suggest that **Bk** was removed from a larger manuscript, perhaps one that began with *Vergier*, as the exemplar of MS **M**. An alternative hypothesis is that **Bk** is a surviving fragment from MS [12]. MS **Bk** cannot be identified as the manuscript of *Lyon* in the Visconti library (below, MS [39]). In the eighteenth century, **Bk**

---

[55] For a literary study of the relationship of this work to Machaut's *Remede*, see Huot 1993, 254–56.

[56] On the substitution of this rondeau for *Dame, mon cuer* (RF7), see chap. 7.3.

was in the library of the duke of La Vallière. Perhaps there are some further notes on the eighteenth-century state of MS **Bk** in an unpublished study by the abbé Rive, "Notice sur des poésies manuscrites de Guillaume de Machau qui sont dans la bibliothèque de M. de La Vallière," preserved in Carpentras, Bibliothèque Municipale, MS 1259 (Duhamel 1901). Alexander Douglas, duke of Hamilton (1767–1852) purchased the manuscript in the nineteenth century from the library of William Beckford (1759–1844). In 1882 the Prussian State Library purchased almost the entire collection of Hamilton manuscripts (a front paper flyleaf is inscribed "116—1884"). Earlier shelfmarks: La Vallière 2772 (De Bure 1783, 254–55 [*recte* 264–65]); Beckford 54; Hamilton 214.

CONTENTS. *Lyon*, complete.

LITERATURE. Rive 1780, 20–21 n. 66; *Sotheby and Co.* 1882; Lemm/Löpelmann 1918; Ludwig 1926–54, 2:7a* n. 2; Wescher 1931, 40; Olschki 1932, 39 and plate xlv.

[22] **Lost manuscript of the *Voir Dit* of the count of Flanders**
PROVENANCE. An individual manuscript copy of the *Voir Dit* was taken in 1375(?) by Eustache Deschamps to Louis de Male, count of Flanders (see chap. 2.1.1e).

[23] **Lost manuscript of the *Voir Dit* of the king of Aragon**
PROVENANCE. An individual manuscript of the *Voir Dit* was given by the duchess of Bar (sister of Charles V) to King John I of Aragon in 1380 (see chap. 2.2.1a).

[24] **PAMPLONA, lost Navarrese manuscript of *Confort***
PROVENANCE. An individual manuscript of *Confort* was ordered by King Charles of Navarre in 1384 (Gómez 1987, 115; document printed in Castro 1956, 19–20).

[25] **BRUGES, lost Burgundian manuscript of the *Prise***
PROVENANCE. An individual paper manuscript of the *Prise* in the library of Philip the Good (inventory of Bruges, ca. 1467, Barrois 1830, 186 no. 1265), described in Ludwig 1926–54, 2:41a*. Since the beginning line of fol. 2 of this manuscript is given in the inventory, we can verify that it was not the paper manuscript of the *Prise* now bound at the end of MS **B**.

B. *Manuscripts of individual lyrical poems, with or without music*

[26] **LILLE, Archives départementales du Nord, 134** (*F:La 134*)
DESCRIPTION. Contains music. Single parchment leaf, trimmed a little at the top. Dimensions: 16 × 13 cm, seven red staves.

DECORATION. Initials alternate blue with red filigree and red with blue filigree.

PROVENANCE. Perhaps *La 134* is a folio from a lost complete-works manuscript, but the format is very small, perhaps too small for polyphony (Fallows 1977b, 479–80). Alternatively, it may be a folio from a lost manuscript containing lais only, several of which are known from contemporary library inventories (MSS [29] and [30] are manuscripts known to have contained lais of Machaut).

CONTENTS. *Pour ce qu'on puist* (L3), fragment including the end of strophe 4 through most of strophe 7 (gaps are due to the double text underlay).

LITERATURE. Fallows 1977b.

[27] **Lost manuscript of the *Lay mortel* (Maggs)**
DESCRIPTION. Parchment *rotulus*, 64 lines of text, 19 and one-half lines of music. Dimensions: 59 × 27 cm. Crude cursive script, fourteenth century. In buckram case, taken from a binding.

DECORATION. None.

FACSIMILE. *Maggs Bros.* 1928, plate iii (partial).

DATE AND PROVENANCE. *Maggs* may provide a very early copy of the lai, ca. 1350. The *rotulus* was sold before 1931, since it is not included in the catalogue of that year. A visit to the offices of Maggs Brothers in London in the summer of 1989 produced no new information, except that the manuscript was probably transferred to the Paris store for sale (Earp 1989, 465 n. 8).

CONTENTS. *Un mortel lay* (L12/8, *Le Lay Mortel*)

LITERATURE. *Maggs Bros.* 1926; Droz 1927; Ludwig 1926–54, 2:14*; *Maggs Bros.* 1928; Schrade 1956c, 20–21, 46.

[28] **PARIS, Bibliothèque de l'Arsenal, 683** (Ars; *F:Pa 683*; Chichmaref: *L*; Ludwig: *Ars*)

DESCRIPTION. Parchment bifolio; original foliation "xii" and "xiii." No music. Dimensions: 32.5 × ca. 22.5 cm (orig. ca. 24.5 cm), writing block ca. 24.5 × 15.5 cm, 2 cols. at 42 ll./col. Late fourteenth-century cursive bookhand. Used as binding material (rear flyleaves, modern fols. 213–214) for a thirteenth-century juridical manuscript. Some glue is visible on fol. xiii v.

DECORATION. Rubrics not entered. At the beginning of each lai, space was left for initials five to six lines tall, and space was left for initials two lines tall at beginnings of lai strophes; no initials were executed, however. Enough room was left before *Un mortel lay* (L12/8) for a miniature, which was also not executed.

DATE AND PROVENANCE. A fragment from a fifteenth-century text anthology that began with Machaut lais, or contained Machaut lais exclusively. Formerly at the Collège de Navarre. Earlier shelfmarks: A. 191 (library of the Collège de Navarre); 12 J.L. Cf. also MSS [29] and [30], which may have contained lais exclusively.

CONTENTS.

Amis, t'amour (L10/7), ll. 228–38 (end)	fol. xii r
Se quanque Diex (L11), complete	fols. xii r–xiii v
Un mortel lay (L12/8), ll. 1–66	fol. xiii v

LITERATURE. Martin 1886–89, 2:36; Ludwig 1926–54, 2:15a*; Schrade 1956c, 36.

[29] **PARIS, Librairie du Louvre, lost manuscript of lais**

PROVENANCE. An untraced manuscript of lais with music that opened with *Amis, t'amour me contreint* (L10): "Laiz notez en ung cayer couvert de parchemin" (Delisle 1907, 2:199* no. 1233) [Notated lais in a gathering with a parchment wrapper]. It appeared in the first inventory of the library of the Louvre in 1373, where it was item no. 177 (no. 117 in the 1411 inventory, and no. 98 in the 1423 inventory, see Douët-d'Arcq 1867, 30). The line identified in the inventories, "Tant en amendoie" (l. 87 of L10) was apparently at the beginning of the second recto. The end of the manuscript, "doulce amour," is unidentified.

[30] **BRUGES, lost Burgundian manuscript of lais**

PROVENANCE. The Bruges inventory of the library of the dukes of Burgundy (ca. 1467) includes a manuscript that opened with *Aus amans pour exemplaire* (L4); see Barrois 1830, 201 no. 1379: "Ung livret en papier couvert de cuir rouge sans boiz, escript en rime; quemenchant, *Aux amans pour exemplaire*, et le second feuillet, *Les regarde tous longuement*, et le dernier, *dont sans votre honeur*" [a paper booklet covered in red leather without boards, written in rhyme, beginning *Aux amans pour exemplaire*, and the second folio *Les regarde tous longuement*, and the last, *dont sans votre honeur*]. The second folio began with l. 41 of L4 ("Las! resgarde com longuement"); the cue for the beginning of the last folio, "dont sans votre honeur," is unidentified. The 1577 Viglius inventory of manuscripts at Brussels identifies the manuscript with the indication "Ce sont ballades" (Marchal 1842, cclxii, Viglius no. 586).

5. Anthologies with isolated works by Machaut

Anthology manuscripts of various genres by various authors, usually anonymously transmitted, form a primary link in the transmission of narrative poetry, lyrical poetry, and music in late fourteenth-century France, and this manner of transmission continued through the fifteenth century.[57] For authors such as Oton de Granson (ca. 1345–97) and Alain Chartier (1385?–1433?), who did not insure that their works would remain intact by the preparation of large complete-works manuscripts, anthologies formed the primary channel by which their works circulated. Chartier's works remained so popular that a printed edition of his "complete works" was prepared posthumously in 1489 [47]. But since it was collected from anthology manuscripts, many spurious works, among them Machaut's lai *Amis t'amour* (L10), were included. Among the

---

[57] Cerquiglini (1987c) discusses of the typology of lyrical collections.

sources in chap. 3.5b (anthologies containing both narrative and lyrical poetry), the MSS **I** [40], *F:CF 249* [42], **Ra** [44], **R** [45], **St** [46] and the early print *Chartier* [47] place works of Machaut with works of Alain Chartier. Among the anthologies of lyrical poetry (chap. 3.5c), all of the manuscripts, [50] to [55], place Machaut among works of Oton de Granson, who in turn went unrecognized and was confused with the more popular Alain Chartier.[58]

Eighteen musical anthologies transmit works of Machaut.[59] Since the comparatively small number of sources for fourteenth-century music have been far more carefully researched than the enormous number of text manuscripts, we rely here on citations of detailed studies of the musical anthologies. Our aim is not to undertake a new study of these manuscripts but simply to place them in the larger context of the Machaut manuscript tradition.

The complexion of most musical anthologies is rather different from that of the sources for the texts.[60] Although rich and noble patrons of culture did pay for manuscripts of polyphonic music, those manuscripts often were not designed to grace the patron's house library but rather were destined for the library of the chapel. Thus, one difficulty with music manuscripts of this period is that they were usually not luxuriously produced and as a result were less treasured by succeeding generations. A beautifully decorated manuscript is a joy to behold, whether one is able to read the text or not. Indeed, it is probably by virtue of their beautiful illuminations that so many of the large Machaut manuscripts survive. Most manuscripts of fourteenth-century French polyphony were not beautifully decorated, and most have been lost. That Machaut was also a composer of music and included his musical works in his richly produced manuscripts is fortunate for us, but very much the exception for fourteenth-century musical collections.

Further, musical style and notation is even more ephemeral than the language and dialect of a written text. Surely early manuscripts of romances and lyrics were not easily read after fifty or sixty years. But musical style and notational practices went out of currency even more quickly. Doubtless a great deal of the music in Machaut's complete-works manuscripts was out of style and was no longer actively performed even by the end of his life.

A. *Anthologies containing narrative poems only*

[31] **PARIS, Bibliothèque Nationale, fonds français 2165–2166 (P;** *F:Pn 2165–2166*; Wimsatt/Kibler: *P*)

DESCRIPTION (*Pn 2166*). The MSS *Pn 2165–2166* are a pair (only *2166* contains Machaut; it is described here). Parchment, ii + 95 + ii fols. Dimensions: 22.3 × 16.5 cm, writing area ca. 17.5 × 10.4 cm, lead rule, 1 col. at 32 ll./col. Script is *littera cursiva textualis* (see note by Karen Gould in Wimsatt/Kibler 1988, 18–19). Quaternions throughout. Bound in red morocco, with arms and monogram of Count Philippe de Béthune (d. 1649), similar to the binding illustrated in *Bibliothèque Nationale* 1981, 283 no. 4 (plate xxv).

DECORATION. Initials two lines tall, alternating blue with red filigree and red with black filigree. Fol. 1r has a gilt floriated initial six lines tall, with bar border. *Jugement Behaingne* begins with a gilt floriated initial five lines tall. The two-line initials were not entered for

[58] For some further interconnections between Granson and MSS **Mn** [43], **Pa** [50], and **Bc** [55], see Badel 1986, 375–78.

[59] Schrade's term "repertory manuscripts" is often employed for this category of manuscript (see his discussion in 1956c, 19–23, 39, 52).

[60] A small sampling of studies that discuss the special problems related to musical transmission includes Besseler 1925, 1:169–76; 1949–51, 703–7; Schrade 1959, 43–48; Hamm 1962; Dömling 1969; Keitel 1977a; Boorman 1980; Bent 1981; Leech-Wilkinson 1982–83, esp. 18–21; Bent 1983; Earp 1983; Strohm 1984a; Nádas 1985, chap. 1; Huot 1987; Switten 1988a; Wathey 1989; Bent 1990a; Kügle 1993, 355–57 et passim.

Jugement Behaingne; only the guide letters are visible. Three miniatures (also three in *Pn 2165*). On the one miniature at the beginning of Machaut's *Jugement Behaingne* (fol. 64r), see the description in chap. 4.4c; on the artist, see the brief note at the end of chap. 4.2.

DATE AND PROVENANCE. Mid fourteenth century. François Avril (personal communication) dates the miniatures in the early 1360s, before the reign of Charles V. On the some 2000 manuscripts from the library of Count Philippe de Béthune that entered the Bibliothèque du Roy in 1662, see Delisle 1868–81, 1:266–69. Earlier shelfmarks: Béthune 35–36 (catalogue of 1662, Omont 1908–21, 4:242); Regius 7989–7990 (Nicolas Clément catalogue of 1682, Omont 1908–21, 4:65).

CONTENTS. P is the base manuscript for the edition of Wimsatt and Kibler (1988).

3. *Jugement Behaingne* (anonymous)   fols. 64r–95v
The last 18 ll. are lost with fol. 96r, which would have begun a new gathering; perhaps a single folio was tipped-in and subsequently lost.

LITERATURE. *Bibliothèque Impériale* 1868, 366.

[32] **ARRAS, Bibliothèque Municipale, 897** (Ar; *F:AS 897* [anc. 587]; Chichmaref: *U*; Wimsatt/Kibler: *Ar*)

DESCRIPTION. Parchment, 182 fols. Dimensions: 30 × 20 cm, 2 cols. at 38 ll./col. Script is *littera textualis* (see the note by Karen Gould in Wimsatt/Kibler 1988, 20).

DECORATION. Initials alternate red and blue. On the miniature to Machaut's *Jugement Behaingne* (fol. 152v); see chap. 4.4c; on the artist, see the note at the end of chap. 4.2.

DATE AND PROVENANCE. The *explicit* of the *Testament* of Jean de Meun (fol. 134a) indicates that the manuscript was copied by Jehanz Desirés, notary of the court of Arras, on 15 February 1369 (1370 new style) (the text of the *explicit* is given in Liborio 1973, 106). In the fifteenth century the manuscript belonged to a certain Ballet (inscription on fol. 182d), and by 1628 to the monastery of St-Vaast (Liborio 1973, 107). Earlier shelfmarks: Monastery of St-Vaast, K. 10 (fol. 1r); 587.

CONTENTS. Principally a manuscript of the *Roman de la Rose* with the *Testament* of Jean de Meun, but including several other *dits* and poems; see Langlois 1910 or Liborio 1973.

5. *Jugement Behaingne* (anonymous)   fols. 152v–166v

LITERATURE. Caron 1860; Quicherat 1872; Chichmaref 1909, lxxiv; Langlois 1910, 110–16; Liborio 1973, 105–7; Wimsatt/Kibler 1988, 19–20.

[33] **CHANTILLY, Bibliothèque du Musée Condé, 485 (570)** (*F:CH 485*)

DESCRIPTION. Parchment, i + 128 + ii fols. Dimensions: 32.7 × 27.3 cm, writing block ca. 24 × 19 cm, 2 cols. at 39–40 ll./col. Late fourteenth or early fifteenth century cursive bookhand. Signatures visible, bottom middle recto. Bound in green morocco, with the arms of Bourbon-Condé.

DECORATION. Rubrics not entered. Major divisions begin with blue or pink floriated letters three to six lines tall with white tracery and bar borders with ivy. Secondary initials one to two lines tall, alternating blue with red filigree and gold with black filigree. Capitals at beginnings of lines are highlighted in yellow wash.

DATE AND PROVENANCE. Late fourteenth or early fifteenth century. The manuscript was at the Hôtel de Condé for an inventory of 1654.

CONTENTS.

1. *Livre de Boece de consolation* (anonymous verse trans.)   fols. 1r–71r
2. *Confort* (anonymous, no rubric).   fols. 71d–96a
blank   fols. 96b–96v
3. *Le Codicille maistre Jehan de Meun*   fols. 97r–107r

LITERATURE. Delisle 1900, 2:71–75; Hoepffner 1908–21, 3:xix; *Catalogue général* 1928, 105.

[34] **BERN, Burgerbibliothek, A 95 (10)** (L; *CH:BEb A 95*; Hoepffner: *L*; Chichmaref: *Q*)

DESCRIPTION. Parchment fragment, 8 fols. Dimensions: 32.1 × 24.1 cm, 2 cols. at 44 ll./col. One quaternion.

DECORATION. Red initials with simple brown filigree for the *Confort*; the decoration for the Boethius is completely different, with alternating blue and red solid initials.

DATE AND PROVENANCE. Late fourteenth century. Some inscriptions on fol. 5v.

CONTENTS. On the juxtaposition of Boethius' *Consolation* with Machaut's *Confort*, see Cerquiglini 1985b, 75 n. 40.

1. *Livre de Boece de consolation*	fols. 1r–5r
2. *Je ne scay raison ne pourquoy* (anonymous)	fol. 5r
blank, with later inscriptions and pen tries	fol. 5v
3. *Confort* (frag., with attribution)[61]	fols. 6r–8v

LITERATURE. Hagen 1875, 145–46; Hoepffner 1908–21, 3:xix.

[35] **PARIS, Bibliothèque Nationale, fonds français 994** (*F:Pn 994*)

DESCRIPTION. Parchment, ii + 56 + ii fols. Dimensions: 29 × 21.5 cm, writing block 21.6 × 15.5 cm, 2 cols. at 42 ll./col. Fourteenth century book hand. Bound in brown leather with gilt tooling, eighteenth century, for the Bibliothèque du Roy.

DECORATION. Floriated initial on fol. 1r with bar border and ivy leaves (cf. Muzerelle 1985, fig. 223b). A divided letter heads Machaut's *Confort*, both segments in red. Secondary initials solid red, two lines tall. Capitals at line beginnings are highlighted with red strokes.

DATE AND PROVENANCE. Late fourteenth century. See further notes on the provenance of the manuscript in Hasenohr-Esnos 1969, lxxx. Earlier shelfmarks: 266 (first flyleaf verso); Regius 7310[3] (fol. 1r); Supplément français 98[5] (second flyleaf recto).

CONTENTS.

3. *Confort* (anonymous, no rubric)[62]	fols. 33r–44r (pp. 65–87)

LITERATURE. *Bibliothèque Impériale* 1868, 171–72; Delisle 1868–81, 1:479 item 1849; Hoepffner 1908–21, 3:xix; Hasenohr-Esnos 1969, lxxx–lxxxiii.

[36] **NEW YORK, H.P. Kraus, MS without shelfmark** (**Kr**; Wimsatt/Kibler: *Kr*)

DESCRIPTION. Parchment, 41 fols., foliated 1–49 (fols. 33–40 are missing). Dimensions: 18.5 × 13.5 cm. One scribe. Late fourteenth- or early fifteenth-century bookhand. Collation 1–5[8] 6[1].

DECORATION. "Initials in gold with penwork ornament on ff. 1 and 18, a few small initials in red elsewhere" (*Sotheby and Co.* 1966, 53).

FACSIMILE. Eleven lines of *Ou mois qui est peres de joie* in *Sotheby and Co.* 1966, 53.

INSCRIPTION. Last page: *l'an de grace ... cccc ...* (*Sotheby and Co.* 1966, 53).

DATE AND PROVENANCE. Late fourteenth or early fifteenth century. Bought by Sir Thomas Phillipps (1792–1872) from the booksellers Payne (*Sotheby and Co.* 1966, 53). Formerly Cheltenham, Phillipps Library MS 6740, sold at Sotheby's, 29 November 1966 (*Sotheby and Co.* 1966, 53–57). Recent history traced in Earp 1983, 41.

CONTENTS.

1. *Ou mois qui est peres de joie* [imitation of *Jugement Behaingne*]	fols. 1r–17r
2. *Jugement Behaingne* (frag., anonymous)	fols. 18r–41r

LITERATURE. Långfors 1917, 30; Phillipps 1968; Kraus 1968, 97–98 no. 30; Wimsatt/Kibler 1988, 20.

[37] **PARIS, Bibliothèque Nationale, fonds français 1595** (**Ys**; *F:Pn 1595*; Hervieux: *B*; Wimsatt/Kibler: *Ys*)

DESCRIPTION. Parchment, i + 38 + i fols. Dimensions: 23.7 × 14.4 cm, writing block 19.5 × 9.9 cm, lead rule, 1 col. at 30 ll./col. Quaternions, catchwords. Cursive bookhands, similar to those seen in MS B [4]. Machaut's *Jugement Behaingne* was copied by a hand different from the *Ysopet*, in order to fill out the last gathering, but was left incomplete. Bound in brown calf, restored in 1980.

---

[61] Rubric, fol. 6r: *Cy comence Confort d'ami qui traita et fist maistre Guillaume de Machaut. Confort* ends with l. 1712; ll. 427–1624 are lacking.

[62] Extracts of the *Confort* in this manuscript include ll. 1–426, 1625, 1856, 2645–82, 2763–3978; it also lacks the last 26 ll., supposedly by King Charles of Navarre.

DECORATION. Initials four lines tall in gold, pink, and blue, with white tracery as background, historiated in black ink (*lettres rechampies*) illustrate each fable. No decoration or large capitals for *Jugement Behaingne*, just guide letters (room for a capital four lines tall at the beginning). One miniature (fol. 1r), mediocre, late fourteenth or early fifteenth century.

INSCRIPTIONS. Signed by Châtre de Cangé on the inside front cover.

DATE AND PROVENANCE. Last quarter of the fourteenth century (Wimsatt/Kibler 1988, 21). Many of Cangé's manuscripts were purchased by Louis XV for the Bibliothèque du Roy in 1733. Earlier shelfmarks: Cangé 106; Regius 7616[3].

CONTENTS. On the juxtaposition of a particular fable with *Jugement Behaingne*, see Cerquiglini 1985b, 120 n. 19.

1. *Ysopet* (fables)	fols. 1r–36r
2. *Jugement Behaingne* (frag., anonymous)[63]	fols. 36v–37v

LITERATURE. *Bibliothèque Impériale* 1868, 270; Hervieux 1893, 528–30; Långfors 1917, 30; Wimsatt/Kibler 1988, 21.

[38] PARIS, Bibliothèque Nationale, fonds français 1149 (Pc; *F:Pn 1149*; Wimsatt/Kibler: *Pc*)

DESCRIPTION. Parchment, i + 182 fols., with three paper flyleaves in front and three in back. Dimensions: 27.7 × 20.8 cm, writing block ca. 21.5 × 16 cm, fols. 1r–85v in long lines; fols. 86r–182r in 2 cols. at 34 ll./col. Fifteenth-century French bastard bookhand. Quaternions, with catchwords visible. Bound in red morocco, with arms and monogram of Jean-Baptiste Colbert, similar to the binding illustrated in *Bibliothèque Nationale* 1981, 483 no. 7 (plate xxviii).

DECORATION. Solid red capitals. Capitals at line beginnings are highlighted with red strokes. Spaces were left for larger initials or miniatures at the head of major divisions, but these were not executed.

INSCRIPTIONS. Pen tries and crude designs in several places. Claude Fauchet (1530–1601) wrote a Latin description of the *Vision de Jean Dupin* on the verso of the front flyleaf.

DATE AND PROVENANCE. Probably fifteenth century. The manuscripts of Jean-Baptiste Colbert and his heirs were purchased by King Louis XV in 1732 for the Bibliothèque du Roy. Earlier shelfmarks: Colbert 613 (Montfaucon 1739, 2:927); Regius 7379[5].

CONTENTS.

1. *Vision de Jean Dupin* (1340)	fols. 1r–123v
2. *Anticlaudianus* (Alain de Lille in French trans.)	fols. 124r–166r
3. *Jugement Behaigne* (anonymous, no rubric)[64]	fols. 167r–182r
blank except for pen tries	fol. 182v

LITERATURE. *Bibliothèque Impériale* 1868, 193–94; Långfors 1917, 30; Schrade 1956c, 38; Wimsatt/Kibler 1988, 20.

[39] PAVIA, lost Visconti manuscript of *Lyon*

PROVENANCE. Michael P. Long has drawn my attention to Pellegrin 1955, 271 item A. 889 (inventory of 1426): "Liber unus in gallico in versibus parvi et grossi voluminis qui incipit: *Quant la ceson diver decline* et finitur: *mon bien ma pars ma souffisance* et est cum assidibus et copertura corii nigri" [a French book in short and long verses that begins *Quant la ceson diver decline* and ends: *mon bien ma pars ma souffisance* and has clasps and bound in black leather]. This inventory largely describes the collection under Giangaleazzo Visconti (1351–1402), duke of Milan, before his death (Vaughan 1962, 192 n. 1). Giangaleazzo married Isabelle (d. 1372), daughter of King John II, in 1360 at Milan. Most of the ninety books in French were probably inherited from Giangaleazzo's mother, Blanche of Savoy (Vaughan 1962, 193). The manuscript does not correspond to **Bk** [21].

CONTENTS. *Lyon* followed by an unknown work or works. The *explicit* has not been identified; it is apparently not a work of Machaut.

---

[63] The text breaks off at the top of fol. 37v, after two words of l. 66 (fol. 38r is blank ruled).

[64] Two-thirds of the right-hand column of fol. 179r is cut out.

B. *Anthologies of both narrative and lyrical poetry*

[40] **PARIS, Bibliothèque Nationale, nouvelles aquisitions françaises 6221** (I; *F:Pn 6221*; Chichmaref: *I*; Laidlaw: *Ne*)

DESCRIPTION. Paper, 35 fols. Watermarks are described in Laidlaw 1974, 77. Dimensions: 28.4 × 22.5 cm, writing block ca. 24.7 × 16 cm (very variable), 2 cols. at ca. 60 ll./col. The cursive script is very irregular; the manuscript has the look of a personal book, added to over a period of years. Queux de Saint-Hilaire (1878–1903, 2:xxi) suggests that the book is made up of rough drafts or notes to be recopied more neatly at a later time. Bound in cardboard and white leather.

DECORATION. A single solid red letter on fol. 1r, and the heading *Vn lay* highlighted with red. No other decoration.

FACSIMILE. Wilkins 1989, 335 (fol. 19r

DATE AND PROVENANCE. Fifteenth century. The five MSS *Pn 6220–6224* were originally once a single manuscript of 252 fols., which had belonged to the library of St-Victor at least since the beginning of the sixteenth century (Delisle 1888, 255). The manuscript came to the Bibliothèque du Roy in the early nineteenth century, was stolen in the 1840s by Barrois, and divided into five manuscripts. These were later purchased by the Bibliothèque Nationale from the Ashburnham Library (fonds Barrois 373, 523, 498, 494, 492). Delisle (1888) recounts the entire sordid story. Earlier shelfmarks: Saint-Victor TT 23 and 275 (see Ouy et al., 1983); Barrois 523 (see Delisle 1888, 254–61).

CONTENTS. Over 155 lyric texts, all anonymous Problems of attribution are discussed by Ludwig 1926–54, 2:15b*, with further bibliography. At least fourteen works are by Machaut. The manuscript also contains the first of the two ballades by Deschamps on Machaut's death (chap. 2.1.1f), and Deschamps's ballade to Peronne (chap. 2.1.1j), and one of the ballades that Chichmaref (1909) placed in his appendix (see chap. 6.1b and 6.3):

1. *Un mortel lay* (L12), six strophes[65]	fol. 1r
1a. *J'aim la flour* (L2), complete	fol. 1r
74. [Deschamps], *Armes amours*	fol. 16v
81. [Deschamps], *Apres Machaut qui tant vous a amé*	fol. 17r
93. *Ne quier veoir* (B34 text 2=VD57)	fol. 18v
94. *Plourez dames* (Lo229=VD5=B32)	fols. 18v–19r
96. *Mes esperiz se combat* (Lo258=B39)	fol. 19r
96a. 7 ll. of *Quant vraiz amans* (B29 text 2) crossed out	fol. 19r
97. *De triste cuer* (B29 text 1)	fol. 19r
100. *De petit peu* (B18)	fol. 19v
103. *Jugiés amans* (=MS J no. 117, *opus dubium*)	fol. 20r
104. *Honte paour* (Lo201, B25)	fol. 20r
105. *Quant Theseus* (B34 text 1=VD56)	fol. 20r
106. *Dame de qui* (RF5)	fol. 20r
108. *Doulce dame* (Lo65)	fol. 20v

In addition, two rondeaux of Machaut are cited by Deschamps in his *Art de Dictier*, which appears in MS I on fols. 28d–32d:

Vo doulz regard (R8)	fol. 32r
Certes mon oeil (R15)	fol. 32r

LITERATURE. Delisle 1866, 236–42; 1888, 254–61; Omont 1900b, 420; Queux de Saint-Hilaire/Raynaud 1878–1903, 2:xvii–xliv; 10:i–v, with edition, pp. v–xciv; 11:106–7; Ludwig 1926–54, 2:15*; Schrade 1956c, 37; Laidlaw 1974, 77; Wilkins 1989, 334–35.

[41] **LONDON, Westminster Abbey Library, 21** (**Wm**; *GB:Lwa 21*; Ludwig: *Westm*)

DESCRIPTION. Paper, 80 surviving fols. (many folios fragmentary). Dimensions: 28 × 20 cm, writing block in ballade section 16 × 12 cm, 1 col. at 31 ll./col. (elsewhere, occa-

---

65 Laidlaw (1974, 77 n. 1) notes that previous inventories have wrongly attributed no. 1 to Alain Chartier. Actually, what is labeled as no. 1 in the inventories is made up of two works of Guillaume de Machaut, namely, the first half of L12 and the entire L2, written together without a break.

sionally 2 cols.). Cursive bastard script. Collation in Robinson/James 1909, 77. Individual folios have since been glued to stubs, restored, and rebound.

DATE AND PROVENANCE. Early fifteenth century? Most of the repertory dates from the fourteenth century, including works by Machaut, Christine de Pizan, and Oton de Granson, but none by Alain Chartier. Nothing is known of the manuscript's provenance, but the name Robert Acland appears on a flyleaf. Pen tries in English, Greek, and Latin.

CONTENTS. 68 ballades survive among the miscellaneous works (all anonymous), including fifteen by Machaut:

8. *Gais et jolis* (Lo39=B35)	fol. 16r
17. *Se quantqu'amours* (B21)	fol. 20r
20. *J'aims mieulx* (B7)	fol. 21v
22. *Honte paour* (Lo201=B25)	fol. 22v
23. *Une vipere* (Lo204=B27)	fol. 23r
26. *De dueil espris* [*sic*] (Lo2)	fol. 24r
27. *Gent* (Lo5=VD42)	fol. 24r
28. *Se je ne say* (Lo6)	fol. 24v
29. *Se vo regard* (Lo9)	fol. 25r
30. *Dame, comment que vous* (Lo13)	fol. 25v
31. *On dit souvent* (Lo14)	fol. 26r
32. *Langue poignant* (Lo190)	fol. 26r
33. *Bonté qui toutes* [=*Biauté qui toutes*] (B4)	fol. 26r
45. *He! gentil corps* [=*He! gentils cuers*] (Lo37)	fol. 30r
46. *Helas! pourquoy* (Lo53)	fol. 30r

Further, there is a concordance between MSS **K** [15], **J** [16], and **Wm** of the anonymous *Chastel d'Amours*, ed. Klein 1911, 158–61 after **Wm**.

LITERATURE. Meyer 1875; Robinson/James 1909, 77; Ludwig 1926–54, 2:15b*–16a*; Schrade 1956c, 37.

[42] CLERMONT-FERRAND, Bibliothèque Municipale, 249 (*F:CF 249*; Constans: *C*; Laidlaw: *Nh*)

DESCRIPTION. Paper, 89 fols. (fragment). Incomplete information on watermarks is given in Couderc 1889, 99; Laidlaw (1974, 80–81) gives more complete information. Dimensions: 29 × 21 cm, writing block and number of cols. varies. Script is illegible in some parts. Collation and missing folios described in Couderc 1889, 98–99. Bound in parchment.

DATE AND PROVENANCE. Early fifteenth century, written in an area where the *langue d'oc* was spoken (Couderc 1889, 99; Constans 1904, 493). Acquired by the library at Clermont-Ferrand between 1847 and 1857 (Couderc 1889, 98).

CONTENTS. 64 works, including works by Deschamps and Alain Chartier, among many anonymous works.

64. *Harpe* (anonymous, fragment)	fols. 85v–89r

LITERATURE. Queux de Saint-Hilaire/Raynaud 1878–1903, 11:107–8; Couderc 1889, 98–114; Couderc et al. 1890; Constans 1904, 491–94; Laidlaw 1974, 80–81.

[43] MADRID, Biblioteca Nacional, 10264 (*Mn*; *E:Mn 10264*)

DESCRIPTION. Paper, 100 fols., modern foliation.[66] Dimensions: 30 × 21 cm. Script *littera cursiva textualis*.

FACSIMILES. Speroni (1977, 113 n. 5) makes reference to a facs. of fol. 92v, but it is not the same scribe as that of the *Roman de Cardenois*.

DATE AND PROVENANCE. Fifteenth century. The main contents of the manuscript consists of the *Roman de Cardenois*, a prose romance with lyric insertions. Cocco (1975, 13–18) considers the manuscript readings to suggest an origin in East Picardy; Speroni (1977, 114–15) suggests rather an origin in the south part of the region of *langue d'oïl*, around Burgundy. Speroni (1977, 119–20) further adduces an interesting, although possibly fortuitous, link between the *Roman de Cardenois* and the Catalan contents of the rest of the manuscript (see n. 68 below). Holzbacher (1983–84) found contemporary allusions to

---

[66] Speroni (1977, 111 n. 3) discusses a discrepancy between the foliation visible to Speroni (100 fols.) and the foliation recorded by Schiff (106 fols.).

Catalonia in the *roman* itself. Formerly in the library of the Marquís de Santillana (1398–1458); see chap. 2.2. Badel (1986, 377) suggests that the author could have been a French companion of Oton de Granson, prisoner in Spain 1372–74.

CONTENTS. On the collection of Catalan texts that make up the rest of the manuscript, see Speroni 1977, 111–13; Domínguez Bordona 1931.

1. *Roman de Cardenois* (modern title)   fols. 1r–74r

A prose work with interpolated prose letters and lyrics. The unique source is incomplete at the beginning due to a loss of folios and incomplete at the end because the scribe broke off work. Holzbacher (1983–84, 178, 186–87) presents weak arguments for attributing the work to Machaut. Machaut's *Jugement Behaingne* is an important source (Cocco 1975, 35); indeed, the portrait of Lady Passebeauté is a prose recasting of ll. 302–407 of *Jugement Behaingne* (Cocco 1975, 29–34). Cocco (1975, 28–29 n. 3) and Speroni (1977, 118–19) enumerate further links to Machaut within the prose section of the *Roman de Cardenois*:

a. *en un point il ot mis tout son cuer et sa pancee* (fol. 5r §1) reminiscent of *Amis, mon cuer* (Lo220 l. 1), which appears as lyric insertion no. 10.

b. *bien seroyt de boune heure nez qui de celle dame seroit améz* (fol. 14v §8) reminiscent of *Moult sui* (V37) ll. 1–2; Lo56 ll. 1–2; and letter 25 of the *Voir Dit* (ed. P. Paris 1875, 189).

c. *On ne doit si hault monter qui puis ait honte du d'avaller* (fol. 27v §23) directly quotes *Remede* ll. 3785–86/3787–88.

d. *...qu'elle puet fere d'un sage foul* (fol. 28r §18) reminiscent of *Vergier* l. 305.

e. *Or soit ainsi com Dieux ha ordonné...* (fol. 42v §1) quotes in the context of a letter the last six verses of *Mes dous amis* (Cp5=VD15). See below, MS **Bc** [55], item 15c.

f. *Qui bien aimme a tart oublie* (fol. 64r §6 and fol. 73v §12) a refrain employed by Machaut as l. 1 of L22/16, and many other places (see chap. 7.3).

In addition, nine lyrics of Machaut are interpolated in the *Roman de Cardenois*:

1. *He gentilz cuers, me convient il mourir* (Lo37)	fols. 5v–6r
2. *Et pour ce sans nul descour* (lai *Qui n'aroit* [RF1]; begins immediately after Lo37 with str. 12 of the lai [lacking last 12 ll.], followed by str. 1–11)	fols. 6r–8r
3. *Je ne me puis saouller* (V33=VD11)	fol. 14r
4. *Dieux, Beauté, Douceur, Nature* (V19; introduced as *Un Lay d'Esperance*)	fol. 18v
6. *Mon cuer, m'amour, ma dame souveraine* (Cp6; l. 1 only, introduced as a *Balade*)	fol. 27r
7. *Riche d'amour et mendiant d'amie* (B5)	fols. 29r–29v
8. *Doulce dame, vous ouciéz a tort* (Lo73; ll. 1–2 only, but blank space was left on fol. 30v)	fol. 30r
10. *Amis, mon cuer et toute ma penssee* (Lo220). See below, MS **Bc** [55], item 15.	fols. 61r–61v
11. *Quant vrais amans de sa dame se depart* (Lo216 l. 1 only, but blank space was left on fol. 64v)	fol. 64r

Two further lyrics have not been identified:

5. *De la plus au plus bel regart / que onques fu en ce monde nee...*[67]	fol. 21r
9. *Amis, se par ma foulie...*[68]	fol. 37v

---

[67] Cocco (ed. 1975, 88 §19) and Speroni (1977, 119) give the complete citation.

[68] Cocco (ed. 1975, 126 §11–14) and Speroni (1977, 119) give the complete citation. This lyric has a concordance in the Catalan MS **Bc** [55], which also contains two of the Machaut lyrics quoted in *Cardenois*, Lo220 and Cp5 (=VD15). All this is of interest because following *Cardenois*, MS **Mn** continues with a collection of Catalan poetry, tending to strengthen the otherwise seemingly fortuitous link between *Cardenois* and the rest of the manuscript (Speroni 1977, 119–20). Holzbacher (1983–84) finds *Cardenois* historically and geographically related to Catalonia.

Finally, Speroni (1977, 119) has identified eight further passages that may be citations of lyrics, one with a concordance in MS **Bc** [55] and elsewhere (see Badel 1986, 375–77, who also comments on the appearance of the above items [e] and [10] in both manuscripts). LITERATURE. Schiff 1905, 380–82; Domínguez Bordona 1931; Cocco 1971; 1975; Speroni 1977; Holzbacher 1983–84.

[44] **PARIS, Bibliothèque Nationale, fonds français 20026** (**Ra**; *F:Pn 20026*; Laidlaw: *Pj*; Wimsatt/Kibler: *Ra*)

DESCRIPTION. Parchment, iii + 176 + iii fols. Dimensions: 22 × 15 cm, writing block 13.5 × 7.3 cm. Cursive bookhand, scribal concordance with MS **R**. Detailed description in Laidlaw 1974, 111–12. Bound in blue velour (recent restoration).

DECORATION. Gilt floriated initials and elaborate floral and ivy borders in margins of folios that begin major works. Most of the borders incorporate the motto of Marie de Clèves, "Rien ne m'est plus," or simply "R.N.M.P." No miniatures.

FACSIMILES. Champion 1910.

INSCRIPTIONS. The several signatures and mottos on the flyleaves are discussed by Champion (1910, 320–36); see also Poirion 1965, 186; Higgins 1991, 170.

DATE AND PROVENANCE. After 1440 (Laidlaw 1974, 111). Arms of Marie de Clèves, duchess of Orléans, third wife of Charles d'Orléans (married 1440). **Ra** must have been known to Charles d'Orléans (cf. Poirion 1965, 278 n. 33); it later went to the library of the abbey of St-Germain-des-Prez, Paris. MS **Ra** is closely related to MS **R**, which belonged to Marie's sister, Marguerite de Rohan. Based on a collation of Machaut's *Jugement Behaingne*, Wimsatt and Kibler (1988, 22) indicate that **Ra** is the source of **R**. Earlier shelfmarks: St-Germain 2045 (fol. 1r); 2217 (fol. 1, bottom right recto); 344 (first flyleaf verso).

CONTENTS. *Jugement Behaingne* (fols. 81v–115r, entitled *Jugement d'Amours* in the *explicit*) appears anonymously among works of Alain Chartier and others. The quality of the Machaut text is poor (Wimsatt/Kibler 1988, 21–25), as are the texts of the relatively contemporary works of Alain Chartier (Laidlaw 1974, 56, 109).

LITERATURE. Delisle 1868–81, 3:345; Omont 1900a, 463–64; Laidlaw 1974, 111–12; Cerquiglini 1987c, 324; Wimsatt/Kibler 1988, 20.

[45] **PARIS, Bibliothèque Nationale, fonds français 2230** (**R**; *F:Pn 2230*; Wimsatt/Kibler: *R*; Laidlaw: *Pf*)

DESCRIPTION. Parchment, i + 248 + i fols., with three paper flyleaves in front and three in back. Dimensions: 21 × 15 cm, writing block 13.6 × 7.6 cm. Cursive bookhand, scribal concordance with MS **Ra**. Detailed description in Laidlaw 1974, 108–9. Bound in red morocco, similar to the bindings illustrated in *Bibliothèque Nationale* 1981, 483 nos. 3a–b (plate xxiv).

DECORATION. Gilt floriated initials and elaborate floral and ivy borders in margins of folios that begin major works. A few other less elaborate gilt floriated initials begin new works, while less important divisions are marked by solid initials one line tall, alternating red and blue. Capitals at beginnings of lines are highlighted with yellow wash. One miniature, fol. 211v.

INSCRIPTIONS. The several signatures and mottos on the front flyleaf are discussed by Laidlaw (1974, 108, 111 n. 2); see also Poirion 1965, 186.

DATE AND PROVENANCE. After 1445 (Laidlaw 1974, 108). Arms of Marguerite de Rohan, wife of Jean d'Angoulême (married 1445); see Delisle 1868–81, 1:148. MS **R** is closely related to MS **Ra**, which belonged to Marguerite's sister Marie de Clèves, duchess of Orléans. Based on a collation of Machaut's *Jugement Behaingne*, Wimsatt and Kibler (1988, 22) indicate that **R** is a copy of **Ra**. Earlier shelfmarks (all on fol. 1r): MMCCCX (Nicolas Rigault catalogue of 1622, Omont 1908–21, 2:377); 1205 (brothers Dupuy catalogue of 1645, Omont 1908–21, 3:64); Regius 8009 (Nicolas Clément catalogue of 1682, Omont 1908–21, 4:66).

CONTENTS. *Jugement Behaingne* (fols. 27v–61r, entitled *Jugement d'Amours* in the *explicit*) appears anonymously among works of Alain Chartier and others. The quality of the Machaut text is poor (Wimsatt/Kibler 1988, 21–25), as are the texts of the relatively contemporary works of Alain Chartier (Laidlaw 1974, 56, 109).

LITERATURE. *Bibliothèque Impériale* 1868, 388; Laidlaw 1974, 108–9; Cerquiglini 1987c, 324; Wimsatt/Kibler 1988, 19.

[46] STOCKHOLM, Kungliga Biblioteket, V.u.22 (St; *S:Sk Vu 22*; editors of Villon: *F*; Chichmaref: *T*; Ludwig: *Stockh*; Laidlaw: *Om*; Wimsatt/Kibler: *St*)

DESCRIPTION. Paper, iv + 272 fols., with two parchment flyleaves in back; fols. 63–66 lacking; fols. 114, 123, 145, 152, 153, 157, 214 counted twice. Dimensions: 20.5 × 15 cm, writing block ca. 16.5 × 9 cm, 1 col. at 33–44 ll./col. (description based on the dossier at the I.R.H.T.). Script *littera cursiva currens* (see note by Karen Gould in Wimsatt/Kibler 1988, 21). Bound in parchment.

FACSIMILES. Schwob 1905 (2 unnumbered fols. + fols. 1r–75v, with the *Petit* and *Grand Testament* of Villon).

DATE AND PROVENANCE. Shortly before 1480 (Piaget/Droz 1932, 239). Late fifteenth century, after 1477 (Laidlaw 1974, 96–97, 117). From the area of Compiègne; once in the possession of Claude Fauchet, president of the *Cour des Monnaies*, who wrote a short index on a flyleaf and annotated the manuscript in various places; then to the book collector Paul Petau (d. 1614); finally, Queen Christine of Sweden acquired St in 1650 from his son Alexandre Petau. Details of the inscriptions on the guard sheets and the early history of the manuscript are given in Schwob 1905, 7–13. Earlier shelfmark: Fr. LIII.

CONTENTS. 114 texts, with 4 by Machaut.
[*Qui es / Ha! Fortune* (M8)]:
84. *Tresble Guillaume de Marchant. Qui es promesses*
84bis. *Hay Fortune*   fol. 138v
89. *Rondel de Machault. Doulce dame, tant* (Lo235=R20)   fol. 141v
111. *Guillaume de Machault. Jugement Behaigne*[69]   fols. 160r–183r

LITERATURE. Stephens 1847, 155–80 (prints considerable excerpts); Piaget/Droz 1932; Schrade 1956c, 38; Laidlaw 1974, 96–97, 117; Wimsatt/Kibler 1988, 20–21.

[47] *Les faits maistre Alain Chartier* (Paris: Pierre Le Caron, 1489) (Laidlaw: *Xa*)

DESCRIPTION. Printed editions of works of Alain Chartier from 1489 to 1617 (the edition of André du Chesne, published in Paris by Thiboust) contained the text of Machaut's lai *Amis t'amour* (L10), erroneously attributed to Chartier as a "*Complainte.*" (On other attribution problems in the 1489 print, see Laidlaw 1968, 569–70.) The MS *Pn 833* [48] is a copy of the second (undated) edition of the 1489 Le Caron print.

CONTENTS.
Amis t'amour (L10)

LITERATURE. Ludwig 1926–54, 2: 17a*; Laidlaw 1968, 569–70; Walravens 1971, 223–30; Laidlaw 1974, 142–44.

[48] PARIS, Bibliothèque Nationale, fonds français 833 (*F:Pn 833*; Laidlaw: *Pa*)

DESCRIPTION. Copied from the undated second edition of the 1489 Le Caron print of Alain Chartier's works (cf. [47] above); see the thorough description in Laidlaw 1974, 99–101.

CONTENTS.
19. *Amis t'amour* (L10)   fols. 176v–178r

LITERATURE: P. Paris 1836–48, 6:386–87; *Bibliothèque Impériale* 1868, 92–93; Laidlaw 1974, 99–101. Earlier shelfmarks: Colbert 2258 (listed in Montfaucon 1739, 2:955–56); Regius 7215$^{2.2}$.

[49] *Le Jardin de Plaisance et Fleur de Rethoricque* (Paris: Ant. Vérard, [1501]) (Jp)

FACSIMILES. *Jardin* 1910–25, vol. 1 (complete); Wilkins 1989, 337 (fol. 65v).

PROVENANCE. Compiled by "L'infortuné," perhaps Regnaud Le Queux (*Jardin* 1910–25, 2:36–40).

---

[69] Lacks ll. 1–152.

CONTENTS. 672 texts. Seven chansons of Machaut are included, interestingly all works that he had set to music. Later editions, ca. 1504 to 1527, have contents that are more or less reduced (*Jardin* 1910–25, 2:12–26; Ludwig 1926–54, 2:16b*–17a*).

In addition, there are two concordances with *opera dubia* in MS **J** (see chap. 6.1b and 6.3):

LITERATURE. *Jardin* 1910–25, vol. 2; Ludwig 1926–54, 2:16*–17a*; Cerquiglini 1987c, 325–26; Wilkins 1989, 336–37.

C. Anthologies of lyrical poetry

[50] PHILADELPHIA, University of Pennsylvania Libraries, Fr. 15 (Pa; *US:PHu 15*; Wimsatt: *Penn*)

DESCRIPTION. Parchment, i + 101 + i fols.; modern foliation 1–68, 68–100. Dimensions: 30.1 × 24 cm, writing block ca. 19.5 × 16.5 cm (varies by as much as a centimeter in height and width), 2 cols. at 36 ll./col. Fols. 93r–95r and 96v–100v originally blank ruled, but a later Italian hand has written on fols. 93a and 100v. Fol. 96r contains a partial index of works in a fifteenth–century Italian hand (on the Italian scribe, see Mudge 1972, 2–3). Different pens and different shades of ink are evident, but probably written by a single scribe throughout (capital letter shapes may vary greatly even on the same page). Mudge (1972, 1) believes that several similar hands were involved; see also Wimsatt 1982, 131 n. 1 (to chap. 2). Collation $1-12^8$ 13^{1+4}. Faint red or brown signatures a, b, d, e, f, g, h in gatherings 1–2 and 4–8. Bound in red morocco. Mudge (1972, 1) believes binding is English.

FACSIMILES. Wimsatt 1982, 48 (fol. 1r); viii (fol. 74v); 6 (fol. 75v).

INSCRIPTIONS. Fol. 1r: "Droit et ferme" (Isabeau of Bavaria?); see Mudge 1972, 10–16; Wimsatt 1982, 132 n. 2.

DATE AND PROVENANCE. Around 1400, perhaps owned by Isabeau of Bavaria, queen of France (b. 1370, r. 1389–1435) (Wimsatt 1982, 50–51, 66–67). Mudge (1972, 15–16) seems to connect MS **Pa** to a 1401 payment made by Isabeau of Bavaria to a goldsmith for gold clasps for "le livre des *Balades*, Messire Othes de Grantson" (Vallet de Viriville 1858). Wimsatt (1982, 66–68; 1991b, 238–39) suggests that Oton de Granson was the anthologist of **Pa** (see further Badel 1986, 378). MS **Pa** was formerly in the possession of Leo S. Olschki and purchased by the University of Pennsylvania Library in 1954 from Laurence Witten (Schrade 1956c, 36; Mudge 1972, 1 n. 1).

Wimsatt (1982, 49) notes that the order of the Machaut lyrics in **Pa** is not random, but that the scribe "went back and forth within the sections in which the Machaut manuscripts were always divided." He further suggests that of the extant complete-works manuscripts, only MS **E** exhibits an order of works that conforms to the order of **Pa**'s exemplar. Earp (1989, 492 n. 56) takes Wimsatt's suggestion a step further and posits that "107 of the 109 texts of Machaut in *PHu 15*, a full third of the 310 items in the manuscript, derive directly from *E*." The scribe first mixed the genres of selected lyrics of the *Loange* by flipping back and forth between *E*'s ballade/*chant royal* section and rondeau section. Then the scribe explored some lyrics in a later portion of *E*. Next, the section of musical ballades was mined. Finally, the scribe flipped all the way to the end of the *Voir Dit* in MS *E*. The copying from the *Voir Dit* proceeded in reverse order, starting at the very end of the manuscript (fols. 210v–211r) with the two lyrics that appear after the *Voir Dit* in *E* (**Pa** nos. 196–97), and then flipping back to works on fols. 207r, 200r, 196r, 187r, etc. In order to provide a suitable mix of lyrical genres, the scribe again alternated his copying, this time between lyrics of the *Voir Dit* and the virelais. Especially suggestive is the inclusion of two

items that appear after the *Voir Dit* only in MS **E**, *Malgré Fortune* (L19/14) and the unique
rondeau *Doulz cuers.*[70]

CONTENTS. 310 *complaintes, pastourelles, chants royaux,* ballades, virelais, and rondeaux, all
anonymous (the best list of the complete contents is Wimsatt 1982). The 109 lyrics of
Machaut in **Pa** are listed in table 3.1; in addition, *opera dubia* in MS **J** (see chap. 6.1b and
6.3) are listed with their incipits in brackets. **Pa** is also a source for Oton de Granson's *Lay
de Desir en Complainte,* which mentions Machaut by name (see chap. 2.1d).

Table 3.1
Concordance Table of Machaut Works in MS **Pa**

No.[71]form[72]		Text[73]	Lo[74]	VD[75]	other MSS[76]
36	B	[*Ce qu' ay pensé, voulez que je vous die?*]	LoA13		**J**
37	B	[*En un vert jardin joly*]	LoA14		**J**
72	B	*Qui des couleurs sauroit a droit jugier*	272		
81	R	*Doulce dame, quant vers vous fausseray* (=119)	64		
82	B	*Dame plaisant, nette et pure*	26		
83	R	*Mon cuer, qui mis en vous son desir a*	67		
84	B	*Il n' est doulour, desconfort ne tristece*	194	47	
85	R	*Cuer, corps, desir, povoir, vie et usage*	80		
86	B	*Trop est crueulz le mal de jalousie*	51		**J**
87	R	*Blanche com lis, plus que rose vermeille*	82		
88	B	*Doulce dame, vo maniere jolie*	65		**I**
89	R	*Dame, je muir pour vous, com pris*	97		
90	B	*Nulz homs ne puet en amours prouffiter*	108		
91	R	*Partuez moy a l' ouvrir de voz yeulx*	118		
92	B	*Je ne sui pas de tel valour*	11		**K, J**[77]
93	CR	*Onques mais nul n' ama si folement*	19		
94	R	*Par souhaidier est mes corps avec vous*	123		
95	R	*Trop est mauvais mes cuers qu' en .ii. ne part*	126		
96	CR	*Amour me fait desirer loyaument*	45		
97	R4	*San cuer, dolans de vous departiray*	148	31	
98	CR	*Cuers ou merci faut et cruautez y dure*	46		
99	R	*Quant ma dame ne m' a recongneü*	151		
100	CR	*Je croy que nulz fors moy n' a tel nature*	47		
101	R	*De plus en plus ma grief doulour empire*	157		
102	CR	*Se trestuit cil qui sont et ont esté*	48		

[70] Manuscript readings support the proposed relationship. For instance, **Pa** no. 90, *Nulz
homs ne puet en amours prouffiter* follows the reading in **E** fol. 7c, *Nulz homs ne puet en
amours p(ro)ufiter,* a corruption of Machaut's *Nuls homs ne puet plus loyaument amer*
(Lo108). **Pa** no. 151, *Une vipere ouy cuer ma dame maint* follows the reading of **E** fol.
148r, from the collection of ballades in the music section, not the reading of *En cuer ma
dame une vipere maint* (Lo204), which had been edited out of **E**'s *Loange* section. MS **Pa**
no. 220, *Tres belle et bonne mi oeil* does not follow **E**'s correct text, *Tres bonne et bele
mi oueil,* and yet the transposed word order may be a new error, since in **Pa** the three short
cues to repeat the refrain after each strophe all read *Tres bonne &c.* Some other corruptions
introduced in **Pa** include no. 85, *Cuer corps desir povoir*] *Cuer corps povoir desir* **E**; and
no. 185, *Combien*] *Comment* **E**.

[71] Numbers follow the sequential numbers in Wimsatt 1982.

[72] Works set to music by Machaut are listed with Ludwig's numbers.

[73] *Opera dubia* are given in square brackets.

[74] Location in Chichmaref 1909 (abbreviations, all referring to the number in Chichmaref
vol. 2): LoA = Appendix; Cp = *Complainte;* L = Lais; Rn = *rondeaux notés;* Bn = *ballades
notées;* Vn = *chansons baladées notées).* For nos. 149–50, RF = insertion in *Remede.*

[75] Lyrical insertions in the *Voir Dit,* see chap. 5.13 table 5.3.

[76] For concordances in the main Machaut manuscripts (**C, W, Vg(B), M, A, F-G,** and **E**),
see chap. 6.3 under the appropriate "Lo" number.

[77] Also in **La** [54].

No.	form	Text	Lo	VD	other MSS
103	R	*Pour dieu, frans cuers, soiez mes advocas*	183		
104	CR	*Se loyautez et vertus ne puissance*	117		
105	R15	*Certes, mon oeil richement visa bel*	234		**I, Jp**
106	B	*Deux choses sont qui me font a martire*	Cp2		
107	R20	*Doulce dame, tant com vivray*	235		**S t**
108	B	*Je prens congie aus dames, a amours*	223		
109	R	*Se tenir veulz le droit chemin d'onneur*	241		
110	Cp	*Amours, tu m'as tant esté dure*	Cp1		
111	R	*Se vo courroux me dure longuement*	247		
112	Cp	*Mon cuer, m'amour, ma dame souveraine*	Cp6		
113	R	*Je ne pourroye en servant desservir*	251		
114	R3	*Mercy vous pri, ma doulce dame chiere*	Rn3		
115	B19	*Amours me fait desirer*	177		
116	R5	*Quant j'ay l'espart*	Rn5		
117	R11	*Comment puet on mieulx ses maulz dire*	Rn11		
118	B	*Trop me seroit grief chose a soustenir*	50		
119	R	*=81*	64		
120	L3	*Pour ce qu'en puist mieulx retraire*	L3		
137	L9	*Amours, se plus demandoie*	L9		
142	B	*Amis, mon cuer et toute ma pensée*	220		
145	R18	*Puis qu'en oubli sui de vous, doulz amis*	Rn18		
146	B	*En l'onneur de ma doulce amour*	230		
147	B25	*Honte, paour, doubtance de meffaire*	201		**I, Wm**[78]
148	R2	*Helas! pourquoy se demente et complaint*	Rn2		
149	CR	*Joie, plaisance, et doulce nourreture*	RF3		
150	V	*Dame, a vous sans retollir*	RF6		
151	B27	*Une vipere ou cuer ma dame maint*	204		**Wm**
152	B11	*N'en fait n'en dit n'en pensée*	Bn14		
153	B28	*Je puis trop bien ma dame comparer*	203		
154	B5	*Riches d'amour et mendians d'amie*	Bn5		
155	B6	*Douls amis, oy mon complaint*	Bn6		
156	B8	*Le desconfort, de martire amoureux*	Bn8		
157	B	*[Ceulz dient qui ont amé]*	A2		**J**
158	B15	*Se je me plain, je n'en puis mais*	Bn18		
160	B38	*Phiton, le merveilleux serpent*	Bn43		
161	R13	*Dame, se vous n'avez aperceü*	Rn13	14	
162	B13	*Esperance qui m'asseüre*	Bn16		
163	R19	*Quant ma dame les mauls d'amer m'aprent*	R19		
164	B23	*De Fortune me doy plaindre et loer*	195		(⁷⁹)
166	B21	*Se quanqu'amours puet donner a ami*	Bn23		**Wm**
167	L14	*Ne sçay comment commencier*	L14		
168	B4	*Beauté qui toutes autres pere*	Bn4		**J**
169	B17	*Sans cuer m'en vois, doulent et esplourez*	Bn9		**J**
170	B17	*Amis, dolens, mas et desconfortez*	Bn10		**J**
171	B17	*Dame, par vous me sens reconfortez*	Bn11		**J**
172	B40	*Ma chiere dame, a vous mon cuer envoy*	Bn45		
173	B35	*Gais et jolis, liés, chantans et joyeux*	39		**Wm**[80]
174	B29	*De triste cuer faire joyeusement*	Bn32		**I**
175	B29	*Quant vrais amans aime amoureusement*	Bn33		
176	B29	*Certes, je dy et s'en quier jugement*	Bn34		
177	R9	*Tant doulcement me sens emprisonnez*	Rn9		(⁸¹)

---

[78] Also in **Trém** [58]; **FP** [61]; **SL** [65].
[79] Also in **Trém** [58]; **Ch** [59]; **PR** [63]; **Str** [73].
[80] Also in **PR** [63]; **Mod** [66].
[81] Also in **Pe** [20]; **Trém** [58].

No.	form	Text	Lo	VD	other MSS
178	B34	Quant Theseüs, Hercules et Jason	Bn39	56	I[82]
179	B34	Ne quier veoir la beauté d'Absalon	Bn38	57	I[82]
181	R7	Se vous n'estes pour mon guerredon née	Rn7		([83])
182	L17	S'onques doloureusement	L17		
185	V5	Combien qu'a moy lointeine	Vn5		
186	V7	Puis que ma doulour agrée	Vn7		
188	B	[Jugiez, amans, et ouez ma dolour]	LoA20		J, I, Jp
192	V15	Se mesdisans en accort	Vn15		
193	V16	C'est force, faire le vueil	Vn16		
196	L19	Malgré Fortune et son tour	L19		
197	R	[Doulz cuers gentilz plain de toute franchise]			E fol. 211r
198	V	Cent mil fois esbaye		61	
199	R	Tant com je seray vivant		58	
200	B	Se par Fortune, la lasse et la desvee		59	
201	V17	Dame, vostre doulz viaire	Vn17		
203	B	Ne soyés en nul esmay		53	
204	V	Onques si bonne journee		44	
206	V18	Helas! et comment aroye	Vn18		
207	R	Autre de vous jamais ne quier amer		43	
208	B	Le plus grant bien qui me viengne d'amer	180	30	
209	R	Tresdouls amis, quant je vous voy		28	
210	V19	Dieux, Beauté, Doulceur, Nature	Vn19		
211	B	Le bien de vous qui en beauté florist	179	29	
212	V20	Se d'amer me repentoye	Vn20		
213	V27	En mon cuer a un descort	Vn27		
215	V29	Mors sui, se je ne vous voy	Vn29		
217	V31	Plus dure que un dyament	Vn31		
219	V32	Dame, mon cuer emportez	Vn32		
220	V26	Tres belle et bonne mi oeil	205		
221	V	Doulce, plaisant et debonnaire		25	
222	V24	Cilz a bien fole pensee	Vn24		
223	B33	Nes qu'on pourroit les estoilles nombrer	232	16	
225	V34	L'oeil qui est le droit archier	Vn35	9	
226	V35	Plus belle que le beau jour	Vn36	10	
227	V33	Je ne me puis saouler	Vn34	11	Mn
269	B	Pluseur se sont repenti	109		
270	B	Langue poignant, aspre, amere et agüe	190		Wm
271	B	Amis, si parfaitement	199	49	

LITERATURE. Bertoni 1932; Piaget 1941, 115–16; Schrade 1956c, 36–37; Faye/Bond 1962, 480–81; Zacour/Hirsch 1965; Mudge 1972; Wimsatt 1982; Kibler/Wimsatt 1983, 22–23 n. 3; Wimsatt 1984; Earp 1989, 492 n. 56.

[51] **PARIS, Bibliothèque Nationale, fonds français 2201** (*F:Pn 2201*)

DESCRIPTION. Parchment, 131 fols. Dimensions: 20.4 × 13.5 cm, writing block 14.5 × 8.9 cm, 1 col. at 26–27 ll./col. Fifteenth-century script. Collation: $1-5^{12}$ 6^{12-2} $7-8^{12}$ 9^{12-1} 10^{6-1} : 11^{12} 12^8. Bound in red morocco, with the initial "L" for "Louis," seventeenth or eighteenth century, similar to the binding illustrated in *Bibliothèque Nationale* 1981, 483 nos. 3a–b (plate xxiv).

DECORATION. Machaut's lai begins with a gold initial with rose, blue, and white tracery (*lettre rechampie*, Muzerelle 1985, §561.15 [fig. 275c], with *antenne*, §532.03 [fig. 223b]), and a bar border. Other strophes alternate solid blue and solid red initials. Room was left for eight miniatures, although only the first was completed.

---

[82] Also in **Ch** [59]; **PR** [63].

[83] Also in **CaB** [56]; **FP** [61]; **Mod** [66]; **Gr** 3360 [68]; **Pg** [72].

DATE AND PROVENANCE. Early fifteenth century. Piaget (1941, 110–12) and Mudge (1972, 13–15) rejected the possibility that this manuscript is the Oton de Granson manuscript of Isabeau of Bavaria, mentioned in accounts of 1399 and 1401.[84] The manuscript entered the Bibliothèque du Roy in 1668 from the library of Cardinal Mazarin (1602–1661); see Delisle 1868–81, 1:279–83. Earlier shelfmarks: Mazarin 770 (catalogue of 1668, Omont 1908–21, 4:311); Regius 7999 (Nicolas Clément catalogue of 1682, Omont 1908–21, 4:65).

CONTENTS.

1. *Livre des Cent Ballades* (incomplete at end)	fols. 1r–70v
2. Works of Oton de Granson (incomplete at beg.)	fols. 71r–104v
3. (no rubric) *Amis t'amour me contraint* (L10)[85]	fols. 105r–109r
4. *L'Istoire de Grisilides, Marquise de Saluces*	fols. 111r–130v

LITERATURE. *Bibliothèque Impériale* 1868, 374–75; Piaget 1941, 109–12.

[52] TURIN, Archivio di Stato, J.b.IX.10 (Ta; *I:Ta J.b.IX.10*)

DESCRIPTION. Paper, ii + 91 fols. Dimensions: 29.5 × 10.5 cm. Three watermarks are distinguished in Vitale-Brovarone 1980, xiii. Five cursive hands (1980, xv–xvi). Several later hands entered various inscriptions and pen tries. Collation (Vitale-Brovarone 1980, xi–xii, xiv): 1–2²⁰ (fols. 1–40) 3¹⁸ ⁽⁺¹⁾ (fols. 42–60; fol. 41 belongs at the beginning of gathering 4, although it is unclear how this affects the conjugate of fol. 60; one bifolio lost between fols. 44–45 and 56–57) 4¹⁶ (fols. 41, 61–75; one leaf lost between fols. 62–63, although it is unclear how this affects the conjugate; one bifolio lost between fols. 66–67 and 68–69, removed because a leaf was presumably spoiled by ink spots from fol. 67) 5¹⁶ ⁽⁺¹⁾ (fols. 76–86, 86*bis*–91; fol. 86 is a fragment of a late fifteenth-century letter; fol. 86*bis* is the conjugate of fol. 81). Signs of use at the beginning and ending of fascicles 4 and 5, suggesting that they were each independent of fascicles 1–3 (1980, xii). Vitale-Brovarone (1980, xiv, xvi) believes that the fascicles were assembled before they were written on. Binding in cardboard and parchment, second half of the eighteenth century (1980, xx).

INSCRIPTIONS. Later hands have entered several inscriptions and pen tries. On fol. 64r, there are two mentions of *Amé de Savoye* and *Ludovicus dux Sabaudie, Chablasii et Auguste,* referring to Amadeus VIII, first duke of Savoy (1416–1434) or else Amadeus IX (1465–1472), and to Lodovico I (1440–1465), providing a date at or a little later than the middle of the fifteenth century (Vitale-Brovarone 1980, xvi). Vitale-Brovarone (1980, xvii) discusses some other inscriptions: *Jehen Achier qui a ecrit ces balades l'an mil CCCC et ung* (fol. 59v); *Guillaume Dyn*; *Ugo di Fausonay*; *Johannes de Domes*; *Petrus Espoulaz*. On the first guard sheet is the name Jerôme d'Arblay, with the date 1792.

DATE AND PROVENANCE. On the basis of the watermarks and contents, Vitale-Brovarone (1980, xiii) dates the manuscript between the last years of the fourteenth century and the first two decades of the fifteenth. The manuscript was added to gradually, and seems like a portable manuscript, the work of a circle of dilettantes who alternated their professional duties at the chancery with literary pursuits. Two lyrics are datable, one late 1395, the other May 1398 (1980, xvi). Considerations of dialect in some inscriptions of the days of the week suggest the region of Savoy, Geneva, and French Jura (1980, xviii).

CONTENTS. The *Cent Ballades* and the *Responses* (twenty-one texts, twelve of which appear in no other source) form the main corpus of 229 texts. Vitale-Brovarone (1980) ascribes six works to Machaut, but only three are certainly works of Machaut. Ta also contains three other texts of interest to music historians:

15. Hasprois, *Ma doulce amour, je me doy bien* (ballade, ed. Apel 1970–72, 1:41; Greene 1981–89, 18:46)	fol. 5v
19. *Mercy ou mort ay longtamps desiré* (ballade, ed. Apel 1970–72, 2:81–83; Greene 1981–89, 20:184–90)	fol. 7r
171. *Par maintes fois ay ouy recorder* (an obscene ballade unrelated after l. 1 to Jean Vaillant's famous virelai)	fol. 69r–69v

Works of Machaut, or works related to Machaut, include the following:

---

[84] Vallet de Viriville 1858, 666, 684; De Winter 1978, 192 (s.v. "Pierre [le] Portier, 1399").

[85] Gathering 10 (fols. 106–110) serves to complete *Amis t'amour*; fols. 109v and 110r are blank, followed by a stub.

10. *Il ne m'est pas tant du mal que j'endure* (Lo265)[86]   fol. 4r
11. *Machaut. Avec raison l'Escripture (opus dubium)*[87]   fol. 4v
14. *Helas! pour quoy* (Lo53)   fols. 5r–5v
16. *Machaut. De petit peu* (B18)   fol. 6r
18. *Honte, paour, doubtance de mesfaire* (Lo201= B25)   fol. 6v
20. *Se pour ce muyr* (Lo248=VD60=B36)   fols. 7r–7v
166. *En con estrange (opus dubium,* LoA9)   fol. 67v
169. *J'é mon bejaune (opus dubium,* LoA7)   fol. 68v
211. *Doulce dame, tant vous aim sans meffaire* (Lo58)   fol. 84r
220. *Balade de Naudin Alis. Honte, paour de doubte de*
meffaire (first line only related to Machaut Lo201=B25)   fol. 87v

LITERATURE. Vitale-Brovarone 1980.

[53] **PARIS, Bibliothèque Nationale, fonds français 24440** (*F:Pn 24440*; Laidlaw: *Pk*)

DESCRIPTION. Parchment, 2 + 270 fols. Dimensions: 29.5 × 20.5 cm. See the detailed description in Laidlaw 1974, 112–14.

DATE AND PROVENANCE. Fifteenth century. Acquired by the abbey of St-Victor in 1683 (Delisle 1868–81, 2:233 and n. 5; Omont 1902, 379–80). Earlier shelfmark: Saint-Victor 394 (Laidlaw 1974, 112).

CONTENTS. Machaut's lai anonymous among works of Alain Chartier and others.
Lay de Complainte. Amis t'amour (L10)   fols. 226r–228v

LITERATURE. Omont 1902, 379–80; Laidlaw 1974, 112–14.

[54] **LAUSANNE, Bibliothèque Cantonale et Universitaire, 350** (**La**; *CH:LAcu 350*; Wilkins: *Neuchâtel*; Laidlaw: *Np*)

DESCRIPTION. Paper, 180 fols., modern foliation. Has original binding.

INSCRIPTIONS. The red initials A.P. occur in several places, accompanied by two unidentified coats of arms and the unidentified motto "Tant me dure." The initials on the front flyleaf have a fifteenth-century inscription: *Je Jehan Devillers. Sine macula.*

DATE AND PROVENANCE. Ca. 1430 (Piaget 1941, 112). Contains a *Complainte* that mourns the death of Bonne d'Artois, duchess of Burgundy (d. 15 September 1425). Formerly in the possession of Arthur Piaget, who purchased it in 1939 from the sale of the library of Henri Baudot (Piaget 1941, 113). Laidlaw's examination of Chartier works in this manuscript reveals poor texts (1974, 87).

CONTENTS.
4. *Balades, rondeaux, lais, virelais et autrez dis compilez par*
noble homme messire Ode de Granson, chevalier   fols. 84r–151v
Of the 77 works in this collection (ed. Piaget 1941, 283–380), ten are by Machaut:
5. *Fueille, ne flour* (Lo18)
6. *Gentil cuer, me convient* (Lo37)
7. *Gent corps, faitiz* (Lo5)
8. *Je ne suis pas de tel valour* (Lo11)
9. *Je ne fine, nuit et jour* (Lo40)
11. *Las! Amours* (Lo52)
12. *Loing de vous souvant* (Lo30)
35. *Riens ne me puet* (Lo29)
36. *Se je ne sçay que c'est* (Lo6)
37. *Se faire sçay chançon* (Lo55)

LITERATURE. Piaget 1941, 112–14; Wilkins 1972, 30–31; Laidlaw 1974, 86–87.

[55] **BARCELONA, Biblioteca de Catalunya, 8** (**Bc**; *E:Bbc 8*; Torrents: *H^b*; Jeanroy: *v*; Pillet/Carstens: *Ve.Ag.*)

DESCRIPTION. Continuation of *Bc* 7 (*H^a*). Paper, 376 fols. Dimensions: 27.5 × 20.8 cm.

---

[86] Perhaps the ascription to Machaut on fol. 4v, which Vitale-Brovarone applies to no. 11, belongs instead to this work.

[87] Cerquiglini (1985b, 164 n. 19) accepts the attribution to Machaut. (Cf. n. 86 above.)

DATE AND PROVENANCE. Catalonia, second half of fifteenth century (Piaget 1941, 117).
CONTENTS.
  15. *Amis, mon cuer* (Lo220)   fol. 408r (p. 643)
  15c. *Or soyt eynsi* (Cp5; last six verses)[88]   fol. 408r (p. 643)
LITERATURE. Torrents 1913–14, 72–76; Pagès 1936, 173–244; Piaget 1941, 116–19; Badel
  1986.

D. *Musical anthologies: French sources*

Note: one could well argue that **Iv** [57] and **Ch** [59] are not French sources; but
they can be viewed as close to central French manuscripts and thus are included
in this category.

[56] CAMBRAI, Bibliothèque Municipale, B.1328 (CaB; *Ca(n)*; *F:CA 1328*)

DESCRIPTION. Parchment fragments removed from bindings of incunabula, deriving from
perhaps as many as six original manuscripts. The fourteenth-century polyphonic fragments
derive mostly from two manuscripts, a motet manuscript and a chansonnier, which may
have been bound with the motet book (Lerch 1987, 1:22–23). The fragments are no longer
in the order described by *RISM*, or in the order of the restoration described by Hasselman
(1970, 17). Lerch (1987) provides the details of the latest restoration of 1983, which
includes new leaves described in Fallows 1976.

FACSIMILES. Motet: Lerch 1987, 1:202 (fol. 16v, M8). A complete facsimile of the motet
manuscript is in Lerch 1987, 1:171–202; facsimiles of works not related to Machaut are
listed in *RISM*.

DATE AND PROVENANCE. ca. 1370. Northern France, probably Cambrai (Fallows 1976); for
further details, see Lerch 1987, 1:153–58. Earlier shelfmark: 1176.

CONTENTS. Machaut works include *RISM* nos. 49, 29, and 35; cited here after the order of
  Lerch (1987, 1:159, 167).
  Motet and Mass manuscript:
  Qui es / Ha! Fortune (M8)   fol. 16v (previously 12v or 2v)[89]
  Chansonnier:
  Se vous n'estes (R7) (tr, ca, ten, ct)   fol. 6v (previously 13v)
  De petit po (B18) (tr, ca, ten, ct)   fol. 8v (previously 15v or 15r)[90]
LITERATURE. Ludwig 1923, 283–87; Besseler 1925, 197–99; Ludwig 1926–54, 2:20b*–
  21a*, 22a*; Schrade 1956c, 42–43; *RISM* 1969, 119–28; Hasselman 1970, 15–35; Fallows
  1976; Ludwig 1978, 698–99; Leech-Wilkinson 1982–83, 19; Lerch 1987; Kügle 1991,
  362, 364; 1993, 101–2.

[57] IVREA, Biblioteca Capitolare, 115 (CXV) (Iv; *I:IVc 115*)

DESCRIPTION. Parchment, 64 fols. survive. Dimensions: 32×22.5 cm, writing block varies,
ca. 26.5×18.2 cm. Modern foliation. Two main scribes, with later additions by others.
Collation 1–2[10] 3[12] 4[8] 5–6[12]. Unbound when discovered in 1921, it was restored and bound
in the 1960s. Kügle (1993, 4–79) provides the most detailed description.

FACSIMILES. Professione 1967, plate 5 (fol. 21r, *Amours qui a / Faus Samblant* [M15] mot
and ten); facsimiles of works not related to Machaut are listed in *RISM*.

DATE AND PROVENANCE. References to Pope Clement VI may indicate an origin at Avignon
after ca. 1365, with additions in the 1370s, brought to Ivrea in the late fourteenth century

---

88 Torrents (1913–14, 74) gives only the incipit for Lo220, omitting the poems numbered 2
  and 3 by Pagès (1936, 174–75). I have numbered this work no. 15c because it is the third
  work given in Pagès 1936, 175. **Mn** [43] also contains items (e) and (10), along with an
  anonymous virelai with concordances in **Pa** [50] and elsewhere (see Badel 1986, 375–77).
89 Removed from Cambrai, Bibliothèque Municipal, Inc. B 144. The music is legible,
  because this side was not glued to a board of the book's cover.
90 Mirror image in Cambrai, Bibliothèque Municipale, Inc. B 447. Fallows (1976, 279),
  reports that there is also a fifth voice. The music is almost illegible, because this side was
  glued to a board.

(*RISM* 1969, 282); from the court of Gaston Fébus (Günther); Savoyard area, probably copied at Ivrea in the 1380s and 1390s—though the repertory mostly falls before 1360—by Jacometus de ecclesia and Jehan Pellicier (Kügle 1990; 1993, 130–34).

CONTENTS. 87 works, including 37 motets, 26 Mass movements, 6 rondeaux and 5 virelais, 4 *chaces*, etc. Contains 3 motets and 1 rondeau of Machaut. Tomasello (1988, 83) proposes that the three Machaut motets circulated together, despite their separation in the manuscript (but see Kügle 1993, 40 n. 31). Cited here after the order of Kügle (1993, 358–82).

6. *Dix et sept* (R17)	fol. 3v
19. *Martirum / Diligenter* (M19)	fols. 10v–11r
35. *Amors qui a / Faus Samblant* (M15)	fols. 20v–21r
41. *Qui es / Hay! Fortune* (M8)	fols. 24v–25r
44. *[L]i enseignement / De tous* (*opus dubium*, see chap. 7.4)	fols. 26v–27r

LITERATURE. Borghezio 1921; Ludwig 1923, 281–82; Besseler 1925, 185–94; Ludwig 1926–54, 2:17b*–18a*; Schrade 1956c, 42; Professione 1967, 86; *RISM* 1969, 282–304; Hasselman 1970, 35, 38–50; Günther 1975, 291–93; 1980b, 663; Tomasello 1988; Leech-Wilkinson 1989, 1:142–45; Kügle 1991, 362, 363; 1993.

[58] PARIS, Bibliothèque Nationale, nouvelles aquisitions françaises 23190 (Trém; *F:Pn 23190*; *RISM*: F-SERRANT)

DESCRIPTION. Parchment, originally 48 fols.; 1 bifolio survives, fols. 1 (with the original index) and 8 (with music for four motets, two complete and two fragmentary). Dimensions: originally ca. 49 × 32.5 cm, now 42.5 × 31.7 cm, writing block ca. 40 × 24 cm.

INSCRIPTIONS. The Bibliothèque Nationale provides an ultraviolet photograph of the inscription at the top of the index: "Iste liber motetorum pertinet capelle illustrissimi principis <Philippi ducis Burgondie et comitis Flandrie>" (the segment in angle brackets was written by a different hand over an erasure; the erased inscription continues on a second line, which has been partially deciphered:) "quem scripsit Michael... de ...ia ejusdem principis capellanus millesimo trecentesimo septuagesimo sexto" [this book of motets belongs to the chapel of the illustrious prince Philip duke of Burgundy and count of Flanders, which Michael... de ...ia, chaplain of the same prince, wrote in the year 1376].

FACSIMILES. Droz/Thibault 1926 (complete); C. Wright 1979, 138 (index, fol. 1r); De Winter 1985, fig. 142 (index, fol. 1r); Bent 1990b, 220 (index, fol. 1r, detail), 228 (fol. 1r).

DATE AND PROVENANCE. Original index dated 1376. Perhaps copied for the French Royal Court under Charles V (the "Michael... de ...ia" of the inscription has been identified with Michel de Fontaine, first chaplain of Charles V from 1370, but this is now in doubt; see Bent 1990b). The inscription may likelier be understood as indicating an origin at the court of Philip the Bold, duke of Burgundy, and De Winter (1985, 63 and 181) suggests that **Trém** belonged to Philip the Bold, not to Charles V, from the beginning. By 1384, when Philip the Bold became count of Flanders on the death of Louis de Male, **Trém** had entered the Burgundian library. See also Strohm (1984a, 124–25 n. 21) for Craig Wright's more recent view and Strohm's further speculations. The manuscript is listed in inventories of the Burgundian library from 1404 (De Winter 1985, 63, 124 no. 8). When Burgundy came to France in 1477, Louis XI ceded all of the goods of the ducal palace at Dijon to Georges de La Trémoïlle, the new governor of the province. By the early sixteenth century, the codex had been disbound. Only the single bifolio is known to survive, used as a cover for accounts of 1512, and rediscovered ca. 1920 by Charles Samaran in the archives of the Trémoïlle family at the château Serrant in Anjou (dept. Maine-et-Loire). The duchess of la Trémoïlle gave the fragment to the Bibliothèque Nationale in the 1920s. Chronological stages of the copying of the manuscript, based on the various stages of work on the index, are discussed by Ludwig, Hasselman, and most thoroughly by Bent. Bent emphasizes the caution with which the 1376 date of the index must be treated, a date that has long been a central pillar in the chronology of fourteenth-century music, especially important in the work of Günther.

CONTENTS. 114 works, including 7 motets, 5 Mass movements, 1 hymn, 31 chansons. Seventeen or 18 works are by Machaut:

7. *[Hareu!] / Helas! ou sera pris* (M10)	fol. iiii
8. *[Maugré mon cuer] / De ma dolour* (M14)	fol. iiii
9. *[Lasse! comment] / Se j'aim mon loyal* (M16)	fol. v
13. *[Qui es] / Ha! Fortune* (M8) (tr and ten extant)	fol. viii

14. [*Amours qui a*] / *Faux semblans* (M15) (mot and ten extant)   fol. viii
23. [*Trop plus*] / *Biauté paree* (M20)   fol. xii
27. *De toutes flours* (B31)   fol. xiii
33. *En amer* (RF4)   fol. xvi
40. *Phiton le merveilleux* (B38)   fol. xix
45. *De petit peu* (B18)   fol. xxi
46. *De Fortune* (B23)   fol. xxi
51. [*Martyrum*] / *Diligenter* (M19)   fol. xxiiii
62. *Dame de qui* (RF5)   fol. xxvii
63. [*Li enseignement*] / *De tous les biens* (motet, *opus dubium*)   fol. xxviii
67a. *Phiton le merveilleux* (B38)[91]   fol. xxix
70. *Honte paour* (B25)   fol. xxx
75. [*Felix*] / *Inviolant* (M23) (disputed by Schrade [1956a, 40–41])   fol. xxxii
76. *Tant doucement* (R9)   fol. xxxii
80. [*Fons*] / *O livoris* (M9)   fol. xxxiiii
90. *Ma dame m'a congé* (not Machaut, but based on B15)   fol. xxxvii
97. *Biauté qui toutes* (B4)   fol. xli

LITERATURE. Droz/Thibault 1926; Ludwig 1926–54, 2:18*–20*; Besseler 1927, 235–41; Schrade 1956c, 39–42; Günther 1957, 165–68; 1963b, 113; *RISM* 1969, 205–6; Hasselman 1970, 51–69; C. Wright 1979, 147–58; Leech-Wilkinson 1982–83, 19–20; De Winter 1985, 124 no. 8, 180–82; Bent 1990b; Kügle 1990, 534–35; 1991, 362; 1993, 100–101.

[59] **CHANTILLY, Bibliothèque du Musée Condé, 564 (Ch; *F:CH 564*; CCMS: ChantMC 564)**

DESCRIPTION. Parchment, 4 (numbered 9–12 in nineteenth-century pencil foliation) + 64 (old foliation, numbered 13–72) fols., with a paper quaternion numbered 1–8 added at the front. Fifteenth-century index, fols. 9v–10r. Dimensions: 38.5 × 28 cm, writing block 29 × 22.2 cm. Two scribes, one for the main corpus and one for the fifteenth-century additions. For a detailed description, see *CCMS*.

FACSIMILES. *MGG* 4 (1955), plate 28 and Gennrich 1948, plate 10 (fol. 20v, Magister Franciscus, *Phiton, Phiton*); Gennrich 1948, plate 16 (fol. 52r, Deschamps/Andrieu *Armes, amours* / *O flour des flours*); facsimiles of works not related to Machaut are listed in *CCMS*.

DATE AND PROVENANCE. Main corpus completed ca. 1395, in southern France; or, an early fifteenth century northern Italian copy of a French original (Günther 1980b; 1984b); or, copied in Catalonia for the court of John I of Aragon (Scully 1990). After 1428 (Kügle 1991, 368). See the summary of the various arguments in Brown 1987, 75–76. Earlier shelfmark: 1047.

CONTENTS. 112 works, including 70 ballades, 17 rondeaux, 12 virelais, and 13 motets; 34 composers named. Three works are by Machaut; three others directly relate to him.

6. Anonymous, *Ma dama m'a congié donné* (cf. *Se je* [B15])   fol. 14v
14. *G de Machaut. De petit peu* (B18)   fol. 18v
18. *Magister Franciscus. Phiton, Phiton, beste* (cf. *Phyton* [B38])   fol. 20v
78. *Guillaume de Machaut. De Fortune me doi* (B23)   fol. 49r
84. *F. Andrieu. Armes, amours* / *O flour des flours* (double ballade *déploration* on the death of Machaut, with texts by Eustache Deschamps; see chap. 2.1.1f–g, and chap. 7.4)   fol. 52r
88. *Machaut. Quant Theseüs* / *Ne quier veoir* (B34)   fol. 54r

LITERATURE. Delisle 1900, 2:277–303 no. 564; Ludwig 1926–54, 2:22b*–24a*; *Catalogue générale* 1928, 122; Reaney 1954b; Schrade 1956c, 43–44; Günther 1960a; *RISM* 1969, 128–60 (extensive bibliography); *CCMS* 1 (1979): 147–48; Günther 1980b, 663 (extensive bibliography); *CCMS* 4 (1988): 329 (extensive bibliography); Günther 1984b; Greene 1981–89, 18:x–xi; Wilkins 1989, 302–3.

---

91 Bent (1990b, 240 n. 22) notes that the duplication of *Phyton* may be an error; note that no. 40 is fol. "xix," while no. 67a is fol. "xxix."

[60] **Quesnoy, lost Burgundian manuscript of the Mass**

DATE AND PROVENANCE. A document recording books borrowed on 16 February 1431 from the château of Quesnoy (dept. Nord) by Marguerite of Burgundy, duchess of Bavaria, countess of Hainaut, Holland and Zeeland[92] mentions a manuscript containing the Machaut Mass: "et ung grant livre de chant, couvert de cuir vert à ii clowans de laiton, commenchant par une table: *la Messe de Machault, la Messe Vaillant, la Messe Rouillart*, et fine: *le Firmament qui long tamps a esté*, tout notté" [and a large music book, covered in green leather with two brass clasps, beginning with a table of contents: "the Mass of Machaut, the Mass of Vaillant, the Mass of Rouillart," and ends: "the firmament which has long endured," all notated]. The document is published in Devillers 1896; see Earp 1983, 16 n. (f). I am grateful to Lawrence Gushee for bringing this document to my attention.

E. *Musical anthologies: Italian sources*

[61] **FLORENCE, Biblioteca Nazionale Centrale, Panciatichiano 26** (**FP**; *I:Fn 26*; Ludwig: *Fl*; Besseler: *FP*; *CCMS*: FlorBN Panc. 26)

DESCRIPTION. Paper, ii + 115 + ii fols. Original index, fols. 2r–4v (inc.). Dimensions: 29.5 × 22 cm. See Nádas 1985 for the most detailed description.

FACSIMILES. Pirrotta 1955, 405–6 (fol. 60r, *Se vous n'estes* [R7]); Gallo 1981 (complete).

DATE AND PROVENANCE. Main corpus ca. 1380–90, with later additions up to ca. 1450; Florence (*RISM*). Main corpus 1397–1406 (Nádas 1989, 60 n. 28).

CONTENTS. 185 works. Among the Italian Trecento works are 15 ballades, 9 rondeaux, and 2 virelais. Five works are by Machaut:

110. *Se vous n'estes* (R7) (ca, ten, ct)	fol. 60r
139. *Honte paour* (B25) (ca, ten, ct)	fols. 76r–75v
171. *En amer* (RF4) (ca, ten, ct)	fol. 97r
175. *De toutes flours* (B31) (ca, ten, ct)	fol. 99v
176. *De petit* (B18) (ca, ten, ct)	fol. 100r

LITERATURE. Ludwig 1926–54, 2:28b*–30a*; Pirrotta 1955; Schrade 1956c, 50–51; *RISM* 1972, B IV³:835–96; Günther 1980b, 667; *CCMS* 1 (1979): 231–32; 4 (1988): 375; Nádas 1981; 1985, 56–117.

[62] **OXFORD, Bodleian Library, Canonici Pat. lat. 229** (**PadA**; *GB:Ob 229*; *CCMS*: OxfBC 229). **PADUA, Biblioteca Universitaria, 1475** (**PadA**; *I:Pu 1475*; *CCMS*: PadU 1475)

DESCRIPTION. The fragments *GB:Ob 229* (2 bifolios), *I:Pu 1475* (3 bifolios), and another fragment, *I:Pu 684* (3 leaves), belonged to the same original manuscript. Only *Ob 229* and *Pu 1475* contain works of Machaut. For a detailed description, see *CCMS*; Fischer 1990.

DATE AND PROVENANCE. Late fourteenth or early fifteenth century, St. Giustina Benedictine Abbey, Padua (*RISM*; *CCMS*). The original music anthology was disbound for use as binding material. See also Hallmark 1983, 196–97.

CONTENTS.

Ob 229 no. 10 *Ma fin. mo començament* (R14)	fol. 38r [new 56r]
Pu 1475 no. 6 *Ite mis[sa est]*[93]	fol. [44r] [new 4r]

LITERATURE. Ludwig 1926–54, 2:25b*–27a*. *GB:Ob 229*: *RISM* 1972, B IV⁴:668–71; Fischer 1980, 667; *CCMS* 2 (1987): 277; 4 (1988): 454. *I:Pu 1475*: *RISM* 1972, B IV⁴: 998–1002; *CCMS* 3 (1987): 10–11; 4 (1988): 461.

[63] **PARIS, Bibliothèque Nationale, nouvelles aquisitions françaises 6771** (**PR**; *F:Pn 6771*; *CCMS*: ParisBNN 6771; Ludwig: *R*; Codex Reina)

DESCRIPTION. Paper, 122 + iv fols. (very complex structure; see catalogue descriptions). Dimensions: 27 × 21 cm, writing block varies. Composed of three sections, a fourteenth-

---

[92] Marguerite of Burgundy (1374–1441), daughter of Duke Philip the Bold and Marguerite of Flanders, married William IV, count of Hainaut, also known as William VI, count of Holland and Zeeland (r. 1404–1417), in 1385.

[93] Right margin trimmed; incomplete.

century Italian part (I); a fourteenth-century French part (II); and a much later fifteenth-century French part (III). A highly nuanced breakdown of the sections is part of the exhaustive description in Nádas 1985.

FACSIMILES. See *CCMS* (none of the published facsimiles include works of Machaut).

DATE AND PROVENANCE. ca. 1400–10 for the main corpus (parts I and II), ca. 1430–40 (part III). From Padua-Venice area (Fischer 1980, 667; Nádas 1985, 187–88).

CONTENTS. Parts I–II contain 183 secular works of the fourteenth century, 80 of which are French: 43 ballades, 29 virelais, 8 rondeaux; Part III contains 34 French and one Italian secular work of the fifteenth century, mostly rondeaux. Seven works are by Machaut (all but one in part II), three others are related to him.

91. [A. da Caserta], *Biauté porfaite* (setting of Lo140) (ca, ten, ct)	fol. 46v
109. *Quant Theseüs / Ne quier* (B34) (ca^1, ca^2, ten, ct)	fols. 54v–55r
112. [Magr Franciscus], *Phiton phiton* (cf. *Phyton* [B38]) (ca, ten, ct)	fol. 56r
113. *Dame qui fust* (cf. *De Fortune* [B23]) (ca, ten, ct)	fol. 56v
124. *S'espoir n'estoit* (cf. *Se vous n'estes* [R7])	fol. 60v
130. *En amer* (RF4) (tr, ca, ten, ct)	fol. 63r
134. *De Fortune me doy* (B23) (tr, ca, ten, ct)	fol. 64v
135. *Gais et iolis* (B35) (ca, ten, ct)	fol. 65r
143. *Dame de qui* (RF5) (tr, ca, ten, ct)	fol. 68v
145. *Il m'est avis* (B22) (tr, ca, ten, ct)	fol. 69v
150. *De toutes flours* (B31) (tr, ca, ten, ct)	fol. 72r

LITERATURE. Ludwig 1926–54, 2:24b*–25*; Schrade 1956c, 48; Fischer 1957; Günther 1960a; *RISM* 1972, B IV^3:485–549; Fischer 1980, 667; *CCMS* 3 (1984): 33–34; 4 (1988): 464; Nádas 1985, 118–215; Wilkins 1989, 300–301; Strohm 1993, 75.

[64] **PARIS, Bibliothèque Nationale, fonds italien 568** (Pit; *F:Pn 568*; Ludwig and Besseler: *P*; *CCMS*: ParisBNI 568)

DESCRIPTION. Parchment, i + 150 fols. Dimensions: 25.7 × 17.5 cm. For a detailed description, see Nádas 1985; 1989.

FACSIMILES. See *CCMS* (none of the published facsimiles include works of Machaut).

DATE AND PROVENANCE. 1405/6–8 (Günther, cited in Nádas 1989, 50). Florence, or Lucca and Pisa. Strohm (1984a, 118; 1993, 75) argues for Lucca, ca. 1407. Earlier shelfmark: Supplément français 535.

CONTENTS. 199 works, including 10 ballades, 13 rondeaux, and 8 virelais among Italian Trecento secular works and Mass movements. Three works are by Machaut:

175. *De toutes flours* (B31) (textless ca, ten, ct)	fol. 120v
177. Anonymous, *Je Fortune*^{94} (textless ca, ten)	fol. 121v
180. *En amer la douce vie* (RF4) (textless ca, ten, ct)	fol. 122r
183. *De petit peu* (B18) (textless ca, ten, ct)	fol. 124v

LITERATURE. Ludwig 1926–54, 2:27*–28*; Reaney 1960c; *RISM* 1972, B IV^4:436–85; *CCMS* 3 (1984): 25–26; 4 (1988): 463; Fischer 1980, 667; Nádas 1985, 216–90; 1989; Wilkins 1989, 309–11.

[65] **FLORENCE, Biblioteca Medicea-Laurenziana, Archivio capitolare di San Lorenzo, 2211** (SL; *I:Fl 2211*)

DESCRIPTION. Parchment palimpsest, 111 leaves; at least 79 leaves lost (Nádas 1985, 459–60). Gathering structure and contents in Nádas 1985, 463–77. On a scribal concordance between SL and *GB:Lbl 29987*, see Nádas 1985, 425n.

FACSIMILE. Complete facs. ed. by Nádas is forthcoming.

DATE AND PROVENANCE. Florence, ca. 1420 (Nádas 1985, 478, 482).

CONTENTS (new foliation). At least five works are by Machaut; more may well be identified:

Quant Theseüs / Ne quier (B34) (ca1 only)	fol. 51r
De Fortune (B23) (ca, ten, ct)	fol. 74r

De petit peu (B18) (ca, ten, ct)   fol. 90r
Se vous n'estes (R7) (ca, ten, ct)   fol. 77r
Honte, paour (B25) (ca, ten, ct)   fol. 77v
LITERATURE. D'Accone 1984; Nádas 1985, 459–86; 1992.

[66] **MODENA, Biblioteca Estense, α.M.5.24** (Mod; *ModA*; *I:MOe 5.24*; *CCMS*: ModE M.5.24)
DESCRIPTION. Parchment, 52 fols. Dimensions: 28 × 19.8 cm. For a detailed description, see Günther 1970.
FACSIMILES. Apel 1953, 411 facs. 82 (fol. 34r, *Se vous n'estes* [R7]); other facsimiles listed in *CCMS*.
DATE AND PROVENANCE. Bologna and Milan, ca. 1410–18 (*New Grove*); see also comments in Nádas 1985, 514; Strohm 1993, 60–61. Earlier shelfmarks: IV D 5; lat. 568.
CONTENTS. 103 works, including 12 Mass movements, 3 motets, 36 ballades, 17 rondeaux, 19 virelais, etc. Four works are by Machaut; there is also a new contratenor by Matteo da Perugia for Machaut's popular rondeau *Se vous n'estes* (R7), and a setting by Anthonello da Caserta of *Biauté parfaite* (Lo140).
7a. *Se vous n'estes* (R7, new ct only)   fol. 5v
18. *Beauté parfaite* (setting of Lo140 by A. da Caserta)   fol. 13
43. *De toutes flours* (B31)   fol. 25r
46. *De petit* (B18)   fol. 26r
55. *Gais et jolis* (B35)   fol. 29v
66. *Se vous n'estes* (R7)   fol. 34r
LITERATURE. Wolf 1904, 1:335–39; Ludwig 1926–54, 2:30*–31*; Schrade 1956c, 49–50; *RISM* 1972, B IV⁴:950–81; Günther 1970; 1980b, 663; *CCMS* 2 (1982): 168–69; 4 (1988): 441; Wilkins 1989, 304–5.

[67] **FAENZA, Biblioteca Comunale, 117** (Fa; *I:FZc 117*; *CCMS*: FaenBC 117)
DESCRIPTION. Parchment, i + 95 + i fols. Dimensions: 24.8 × 17.5 cm.
FACSIMILES. Carapetyan 1961 (musical portion of the manuscript, complete). Kugler (1972) provides an edition in diplomatic facsimile of most of the repertory, with vertically-aligned diplomatic facsimiles of the model compositions.
DATE AND PROVENANCE. Intabulations made ca. 1410–20 at the Carmelite convent in Ferrara, with additions from the later fifteenth century.
CONTENTS. 48 instrumental intabulations of Mass music and secular works, including arrangements of two Machaut works:
15. *Hont paur* (B25)   fols. 37r–37v
16. *De tout flors* (B31)   fols. 37v–38v
LITERATURE. Ludwig 1926–54, vol. 4 (*Nachtrag*); Kugler 1972; *RISM* 1972, B IV⁴:898–920, *CCMS* 1 (1979): 215–16; Caldwell 1980, 718; *CCMS* 4 (1988): 369. Additional bibliography in Nádas 1985, 199–200 n. 218. On performance, see Bukofzer 1960; Reaney 1966, 708; Kugler 1975; McGee 1986; 1987; Eberlin 1992, McGee 1992.

F. *Musical anthologies: Imperial sources*

[68] **GHENT, Rijksarchief, Varia D.3360** (Gr 3360; *B:Gr 3360*)
DESCRIPTION. Parchment fragments, one bifolio and one single folio. Dimensions: orig. ca. 31 × 23 cm, writing block ca. 22.5 × 18.9 cm. Detailed description in Strohm 1984a.
DATE AND PROVENANCE. Flanders, ca. 1385. Used as binding material on different occasions in the late fifteenth and sixteenth century for rent registers at the Abbey Ter Haeghen at Ghent (Cistercian nuns). Concerning the relation of MS **Gr 3360** to Machaut MS **E**, see above on "date and provenance" of MS [7].
CONTENTS.
5. Anonymous, *Je Fortune* (see n. 94 above) (ca, ten, ct)   fol. 2v
7. *Se vous n'estes* (R7) (frag. ten, ct)   fol. 3r
8. *De petit peu* (B18) (frag. ca, ten)   fol. 3r

LITERATURE. Known by F.-J. Fétis (Ludwig 1926–54, 2:44a*); rediscovered and thoroughly described by Strohm (1984a).

[69] UTRECHT, Universiteitsbibliotheek, 6 E 37 II (Utr; NL:Uu 37 II)

DESCRIPTION. Parchment fragments. Original dimensions: ca. 22 × 16.5 cm, writing block ca. 18.6 × 13 cm. Thoroughly described in Biezen/Gumbert 1985.

FACSIMILES. See Biezen/Gumbert 1985, 24–25 (none of the facsimiles include works of Machaut).

DATE AND PROVENANCE. Netherlands or Brabant, late fourteenth or early fifteenth century; see the remarks in Strohm 1985, 106; Haggh 1988, 1:491.

CONTENTS. Works related to Machaut include *RISM* nos. 14, 8, and 10; cited here after the order utilized in Biezen/Gumbert 1985.

   8. *Pleurez dames* (B32), end of ten and most of ct only. The entire cantus voice is lost with the lost previous verso (Biezen/Gumbert 1985, 130). fol. 27r

  13. *Biauté qui* (B4), most of three voices, ca ten ct (the right side of the page is cut vertically; see Biezen/Gumbert 1985, 132). **Utr** provides a concordance for the late addition of a contratenor, otherwise transmitted only in MS E. fol. 29r

  14. Anonymous *S'espoir n'estoit* (related to *Se vous n'estes* [R7], see chap. 7.3) fol. 29v

LITERATURE. *RISM* 1969, 317–25; Hasselman 1970, 91, 94–96; Biezen/Gumbert 1985, 7, 11, 13–14; 17–19; Haggh 1988, 1:491.

[70] FRIBOURG, Bibliothèque Cantonale et Universitaire, Z 260 (Frib; CH:Fcu 260; Frib)

DESCRIPTION. Parchment fragment, original folio number xx$_{iiii}$ vi (i.e., 86), top right recto. A single bifolio was cut in half to form binding material for an incunabulum. Dimensions: 37 × 26.7 cm.

FACSIMILE. Zwick 1948.

DATE AND PROVENANCE. Latter half of the fourteenth century, Switzerland?

CONTENTS. Despite the ascription to Machaut, this motet considered to be unauthentic, since it does not appear in any of the main Machaut manuscripts (see chap. 7.4).

   1. Guillermus de Mascandio, *Li enseignement / De touz / Ecce* fol. 86r

LITERATURE. Zwick 1948; Ludwig 1926–54, vol. 4 (*Nachtrag*); Schrade 1956c, 44–46; *RISM* 1969, 60–61.

[71] NUREMBERG, Stadtbibliothek, Fragm. lat. 9 and 9a (Nur; D:Nst 9/9a (previously Nst III, 25); CCMS: NurS 9; NurS 9a)

DESCRIPTION. Parchment fragments. Dimensions: 29.1 × 28.5 cm, originally ca. 35.5 × 27.5 cm (*CCMS*). Flyleaves detached from Nuremberg MSS Centurio V, 61 (fragm. lat. 9) and Centurio III, 25 (fragm. lat. 9a). The MS Melk, Stiftsbibliothek, 749 (*CCMS:* MelkS 749) provides more fragments from the same manuscript; see Strohm 1984a, 126 n. 33; 1984b, 215–17; 1985, 104–5, 168 n. 9; and *CCMS* 2 (1982): 140; 4 (1988): 437.

FACSIMILE. Strohm 1985, plate 4.

DATE AND PROVENANCE. St. Stephen's cathedral, Vienna, ca. 1400 or slightly later (Strohm, *CCMS*; Strohm 1984b, 215–16).

CONTENTS. Machaut is in *Nst 9a* only:

   2. *De petit peu* (B18), ca and ct (text incipit only; fol. cut away on right side) fol. [1r]

LITERATURE. *RISM* 1969, 82–84; *CCMS* 2 (1982): 258–59; 4 (1988): 451.

[72] PRAGUE, Národní knihovna (formerly Universitní knihovna), XI.E.9 (Pg; CZ:Pu XI E 9; CCMS: PragU XI E 9)

DESCRIPTION. Paper miscellany, bound together in the early fifteenth century; music on fols. 247r–251v, 257v–261r.

DATE AND PROVENANCE. Strasbourg, ca. 1400 (Strohm 1985, 107); ca. 1415–20? (Strohm 1984a, 118); from the Collegiate church of St. Thomas in Strasbourg and linked to the monastery of the Clarisses (Strohm 1984a, 121).

CONTENTS. 37 works, including 15 French secular works.

14. Anonymous, *Je Fortune* (see n. 94 above) (ca, ten; text incipit only)   fol. 249r
25. *Se vous n'estes* (R7) (ca, ten; text incipit only)   fol. 257v
32. *De petit peu* (B18) (ca, ten; text incipit only)   fols. 259v–260r

LITERATURE. Ludwig 1926–54, 2:36*–37a*; Schrade 1956c, 53–54; *RISM* 1972, B IV³:255–62; *CCMS* 3 (1984): 63–64; 4 (1988): 469; Staehelin 1989, 17–18.

[73] **STRASBOURG, Bibliothèque Municipale, M. 222 C. 22** (destroyed in 1870) (**Str**; *F:Sm 222*; *CCMS*: StrasBM 222)

DESCRIPTION. Paper, 155 fols. Dimensions: ca. 29 × 21 cm. See the thorough descriptions in *RISM* and *CCMS*.

FACSIMILES. Vander Linden 1972 (Coussemaker's incipit catalogue and selected individual copies).

DATE AND PROVENANCE. 1411 (fol. 142r), later additions up to ca. 1450. From choir school of Strasbourg cathedral, ca. 1420–ca. 1445 (Strohm 1984a, 121–23); or, most probably, from Zofingen (SE of Basel), then perhaps Basel, then to Strasbourg (Staehelin 1989, 17–19).

CONTENTS. 212 works, including 35 Mass movements, 25 motets, 88 French secular works. Three unascribed works are by Machaut; three other very popular works are not by Machaut, but were ascribed to him in **Str**.

52. Wilhelmi de Maschaudio (*recte*, Pierre des Molins), [*De*]
    Che qui vol pense (also supplied with contrafact text,
    Surge anima, or *Surge amica mea speciosa*)   fol. 36v
69. Anonymous, *Je Fortune* (not Machaut; see n. 94 above)   fol. 47v
72. Wilhelmi de Maschaudio (*recte*, anonymous), *Jour au jor la*
    vie (also has contrafact text *Ave virgo mater pia*)   fol. 48r
101. Wilhelmi de Maschaudio (*recte*, Jean Vaillant), *Par*
    maintes foys (also has contrafact text *Ave virgo gloriosa*)   fol. 65v
102. *De fortune* (B23) (also supplied with a contrafact text,
    Rubus ardens)   fol. 66v
119. *Se vous n'etes* (R7)   fol. 73v [73r?]
168. *De toutes flours* (B31)   fol. 95r [94r, 95v?]

LITERATURE. Borren 1923–27; Besseler 1925, 218–19; Ludwig 1926–54, 2:37*–40a*; *RISM* 1972, B IV²:550–92; Vander Linden 1972; Günther 1980b, 665; Strohm 1984a, 118–23; *CCMS* 3 (1984): 163–64; Staehelin 1989 (with additional bibliography).

IV

The Miniatures

1. Introduction

Study of the art-historical aspects of the Machaut manuscripts is the youngest field of inquiry in Machaut studies, and yet already significant results have been achieved. Most important is the work of François Avril, for it has allowed a much more detailed chronological placement of the manuscripts than had been possible before. Avril (1982a) provides a detailed exposition of the miniature painters involved in the manuscripts, and establishes a chronology of the manuscripts based on the miniatures: C [1], **K** [15], **Vg** [3], **A** [5], **E** [7], **F-G** [6], **Pm** [18], and **D** [11] (Avril does not discuss MSS **J** [16], or **Pe** [20]). Other studies that bear on the artists and the chronology of their work include Avril/Lafaurie 1968 (**E** and **F-G**), Avril 1969 (**F-G** and **Bk** [21]), Avril 1973 (**C**), Avril 1978 (**C**, **A** and **E** with color plates of folios in MSS **C** and **A**), Baron/Avril 1981 (**C** and **A**), and Avril 1982b (**C**), as well as some important recent studies of the same artists and ateliers by De Winter (1982 and 1985).[1]

The most extensive study of the iconography of the illuminated manuscripts of Machaut is the dissertation of Kumiko Maekawa (1985), which includes a list of miniatures in the manuscripts, studies of selected themes, and a description of each manuscript, including a catalogue of the miniatures, the size of each miniature in centimeters, and a detailed description of the miniature and associated border decorations. It is much more thorough than the descriptions given in the concordance of miniatures in chap. 4.4. Studies excerpted and revised from the 1985 dissertation include Maekawa 1988 and 1989b, although these two articles unfortunately give a poor and incomplete impression of the work in the dissertation.

Wallen (1980) provides a most interesting and thorough literary analysis of Machaut's *Confort*, based on an analysis of miniatures that illustrate it. Huot (1987) uses the program of miniatures in MSS **C** and **A** illustrating the *Remede* in her characterization of the changing attitude of our author towards the presentation of his works and also offers analyses of the series of miniatures illustrating the lais in **C** and *Harpe* in **A**.

In order to facilitate further study of the miniatures in the Machaut manuscripts, this chapter consists mainly of three indices, an index of miniatures and artists by manuscript (chap. 4.2), a comparative table of miniatures (chap. 4.3), and a concordance of miniatures (chap. 4.4).

Chap. 4.2, the index of miniatures and artists by manuscript, is organized according to the order of manuscripts used throughout this chapter: **C**, **Vg**,[2] **J**, **K**, **A**, **Pm**, **F-G**, **E**, and **D** (in approximate chronological order, except that

---

[1] For a general overview of the art of miniature painting in fourteenth-century France, see Avril 1978 or 1982a, Baron/Avril 1981, M. Thomas 1978, De Winter 1985 chap. 9, or Sterling 1987. Questions concerning the book trade in Paris and the organization of the craftsmen who made and illuminated books are studied in two important articles by De Winter (1978; 1982).

[2] I thank Mr. Bernard Bailly de Surcy of New York for generously supplying me with a film of the inaccessible MS **Vg**, upon which my descriptions are based. All films I have seen of MS **Vg** are faint, and caution is in order when consulting my descriptions in the concordance of miniatures.

MSS **A** and **Pm** have been placed side-by-side to show their close relationship). The miniatures of each manuscript are through-numbered in the sequential order in which they appear in each respective manuscript, a numbering system retained for all references to specific miniatures in this book.[3] Since the comparative table of miniatures and the concordance of miniatures are both arranged according to the nearly definitive order of poems in MS **F-G**, however, the index of miniatures and artists by manuscript is useful for verifying the order of miniatures in the other manuscripts. In addition, this index provides an overview of the artists involved in the decoration of the Machaut manuscripts, based mainly on the work of Avril. Following the tabulation of each manuscript is a bibliography providing some sources of information on each artist.

The comparative table of miniatures provides a quick overview of the disposition of the miniatures in each of Machaut's works, allowing a comparison between the MSS **C**, **Vg**, **J**, **K**, **A**, **Pm**, **F-G**, **E**, and **D**, **Bk**, and **Pe**.[4] For each work, the first column gives the line number or individual lyrical poem *before which* each miniature is placed. The remaining columns identify the manuscript and each miniature in the manuscript by a number I have assigned, following the sequential order of miniatures within each manuscript. The order of Machaut's works in the table follows the order of MS **F-G**, the latest and most inclusive of the manuscripts, and one whose contents are arranged authoritatively. The sequential order of the miniatures in the other manuscripts can be determined by following their miniature numbers (for a specific poem, the reader should refer to chap. 4.2, the index of miniatures and artists by manuscript, for orientation).

By using the comparative table of miniatures, one can readily note, for instance, not only the remarkable similarity in the locations of miniatures in MSS **A** and **F-G**, but also the independence of the illustration programs in MSS **C** and **Vg**. Nevertheless, one can occasionally see internal divisions in a poem that are unanimously chosen as important points of articulation in the poem, and marked by an illumination.

For the *Remede* in **Vg**, I have indicated by means of an asterisk the location of some very large initials filled with a basket-weave background pattern. Since spaces of a similar size were illuminated in **Vg**'s *Alerion* and *Fonteinne*, these spaces in the *Remede* were possibly initially intended for illumination and for some reason were eventually left without illustrations. Either the patron of the manuscript was not so interested in the *Remede*, or else the *Remede* was one of the last *dits* to be decorated (perhaps withheld in order to copy the music?) and the miniatures were left out because the illuminator(s) were no longer easily available. It is also possible that their omission may reflect an effort to save money or time.

The concordance of miniatures is arranged in the same order as the foregoing comparative table of miniatures, first indicating the line or individual lyric *before which* a miniature appears, then the sequential number of the miniature in the manuscript, any rubric present immediately above or below the miniature and its translation, a brief identification of the scene, and finally the folio number of the miniature in the manuscript.[5] I have supplied running summaries

---

[3] MSS **F** and **G** are through-numbered as a single source; miniature G142 (to the *Prise*) is the first miniature in MS **G**.

[4] This table is expanded and corrected from the version in Earp 1983, Appendix B.

[5] When more than a single miniature appears on a folio, the column (a-d) is also indicated. This concordance expands and thoroughly revises the version in Earp 1983, Appendix C.

of the narrative content and context for two brief works, *Vergier* and *Jugement Behaingne*. For other works, limitations of space have led me to omit all but identification of the sources of Biblical and mythological *exempla*. Bibliographical references relevant to individual miniatures, including information on published reproductions, are also included in the concordance of miniatures.

The iconographical representation of Guillaume in the *Prologue* of MSS **A**, **F-G**, and **Pm** is retained for the narrator-protagonist throughout each of these manuscripts (Maekawa 1985, 52–58; 1988, 148–50). I have labeled the narrator-protagonist "Guillaume" in these manuscripts, but simply "narrator" or "lover" in the other, iconographically less consistent codices (and also in the few places in MSS **A**, **F-G**, and **Pm** where the "Guillaume" iconography seems to break down).[6] Author portraits in the Machaut manuscripts are discussed by Avril (1982a, 123), Maekawa (1985, 51–54, 58, 128–31), and De Winter (1985, 89, fig. 112); further details on the Machaut iconography (consistent in MSS **A**, **F-G**, **Pm**, and **D**; inconsistent in MSS **C**, **Vg**, **K**, **J**, and **E**) are discussed in Maekawa 1985, 132–34.[7]

Several of the miniatures in MS **A** have a Roman-numeral through-numbering still visible in the manuscript. Probably the numerals, which ought to have been erased, were keyed to a list of directions indicating the subject matter of the miniature for a given location, indeed probably one prepared by the author himself.[8] The number "xi" for miniature **A**14 on fol. 54v (before l. 771 of the *Remede*) is the first one visible, and the numbers continue to be visible occasionally through "xl" on fol. 91v. The next visible number, "liii" (fol. 128v, miniature **A**57, before l. 253 of the *Confort*) is one less than seems to be required (perhaps the single miniature at the opening of *Alerion* was left off). The last number visible before the beginning of the *Voir Dit* (fol. 221) is "lviii" (fol. 130v, miniature **A**62, before l. 513 of the *Confort*). The numbers are three less than the total number of miniatures up to that point: the two Parisian miniatures of the *Prologue* ballades, and the provincial miniature at the beginning of the narrative portion of the *Prologue,* were not included. This further attests to the fact that the *Prologue* was added to MS **A** at a late stage in its production. For the *Voir Dit*, there is an independent numbering system, first visible with "viii" on fol. 259v (actually the thirteenth miniature of the *Voir Dit*). Perhaps this indicates that the program of miniatures for the *Voir Dit* was more recently thought out. The only other instance of what may be a similar type of numbering that I have noticed in any of the Machaut manuscripts is the numeral "iii" visible above the frame of miniature **C**70 (fol. 104v), the third miniature in *Lyon*.

One also encounters hairline written instructions given directly at the location of the desired illustration. Most of these directions were erased, but there are two examples in MS **F-G**, to miniatures **F**121 and 125 in the *Voir Dit*. Traces of many such directions remain in MSS **Bk** (especially miniature **Bk**9), and **Pm** (miniatures **Pm**45, 63, 65, and 69). Avril (1982a, 129–30) notes that MS

---

[6] That this iconography specifically identifies the narrator with the author—Guillaume de Machaut—is brought home by a surviving marginal instruction to the artist in MS **F**, fol. 173r (miniature **F**125, in the *Voir Dit*): "Ung roy assis et Machaut a genoulx devant li" [a king seated and Machaut kneeling before him].

[7] See also the general discussion in Salter/Pearsall 1980. Machabey's discussion of the Machaut iconography is absurdly based on MS **D**, now known to date from ca. 1430 (Machabey 1955b, 1:45–46).

[8] An example of the kind of program I am thinking of is that published by Delisle (1907, 1:244–46). Avril (1982a, 131–32) and Huot (1987, chaps. 8–9) study Machaut's possible role in the illustration of his manuscripts.

Pm was copied from MS **A**; my descriptions in chap. 4.4 confirm that the coordinator of the program of illustrations in **Pm** based his descriptions on the miniatures in MS **A**.

The most thorough study of the aspect of a medieval French author's role in manuscript illustration known to me is Hindman 1986, a study of Christine de Pizan's *Epistre Othea*. Hindman makes the point that the program of illustrations in a given manuscript was already determined before the manuscript reached the artists' atelier, since the location of the miniatures had to be planned from an early stage of work (1986, 64). Most miniaturists were artisans, craftsmen who exercised little initiative; they simply carried out the work that was appointed for them (1986, 65–66). She concludes that "Christine seems to have been involved to a considerable degree in the make-up of the pictorial cycle [of the *Epistre Othea*]. The degree of her involvement fully justifies claims that the illuminators worked under Christine's direction, following her verbal instructions. It is clear, moreover, that she gave explicit instructions in the form of the purple rubrics to the illuminators. She certainly supervised the illustration" (1986, 98). On written programs for the illuminator, see Hindman 1986, 64–66 and the references given there.[9]

Hindman's work also suggests a new avenue for research on Machaut's iconography. Several miniatures that illustrate mythological scenes in Christine's *Epistre Othea* are modeled on illustrations in manuscripts of the *Ovide Moralisé*.[10] It is known that Machaut mined the *Ovide Moralisé* for many of his mythological allusions (A. Thomas 1912; De Boer 1913; 1914), but his possible use of the iconography of the *Ovide Moralisé* for the programs of illustration in the manuscripts that he supervised has gone unstudied, except for Wallen's study of *Confort* (1980, 197–99).[11]

2. Index of miniatures and artists by manuscript

For further discussion of aspects of decoration in individual manuscripts, with additional bibliography, see above, chap. 3. The association of specific artists with specific miniatures in tables 4.1–10 below is based almost entirely on the work of François Avril. For the location of the miniatures, descriptions, and bibliography on individual miniatures, see the comparative table of miniatures (chap. 4.3) and the concordance of miniatures (chap. 4.4).

Table 4.1
Artists in MS **C** [1]

MIN.	WORK	ARTIST
1–9	*Jug. Behaingne*	2. First assistant to the Master of the *Remede de Fortune*
10–43	*Remede*	1. Master of the *Remede de Fortune*
44–61	*Alerion*	3. Master of the Coronation Book of Charles V
62–67	*Vergier*	3. Master of the Coronation Book of Charles V
68–91	*Lyon*	2. First assistant to the Master of the *Remede de Fortune*
92	*Loange*	3. Master of the Coronation Book of Charles V
93–107	Lais	3. Master of the Coronation Book of Charles V

[9] De Winter (1978, 181) discusses manuscripts commissioned by authors for presentation to patrons.

[10] Hindman 1986, esp. 82–85 and the Appendix, "A Concordance of the Subjects of Miniatures in the *Epistre Othéa* and their Antecedents" (1986, 189–203).

[11] At least one manuscript of the *Ovide Moralisé* (*F:Pn 871*) was illuminated by the Master of the Coronation of Charles VI, one of the artists who contributed to MS **Vg** (see below, table 4.2). Lord (1975) provides a concordance of miniatures for three manuscripts of the *Ovide Moralisé*. Machaut utilized many of the same stories.

Bibliography on artists in MS **C**:

1. Master of the *Remede de Fortune* (fl. ca. 1349–56). Avril 1973, 112–14; Schmidt 1975, 57–58; 1977–78, 192–93, fig. 101; Avril 1978, 26–28, plates 19, 21–22, 23–25; Baron/Avril 1981, 278, 280–81, nos. 271–73; Avril 1982a, 119–23; 1982b; De Winter 1982, 805–6 (on a later and lesser student of this master); 1985, 84, 92; Sterling 1987, 150–65 (with additional bibliography).

Byrne (1984) links a parchment strip containing court scenes preserved at Berlin (Staatliche Museen Preussischer Kulturbesitz, Kupferstichkabinett) to the Master of the *Remede de Fortune* (the scene is reproduced in Avril 1978, 23 plate X; Baron/Avril 1981, 322–23 no. 275; Byrne 1984, 70, 71, 75; Sterling 1987, fig. 88). Byrne considers the fragment to be a *bas-de-page* from a lost *rotulus* of ca. 1365 illustrating a single excerpt of the *Voir Dit* that circulated individually, namely, Machaut's comparison of Toute Belle to the ancient queen Semiramis (ed. P. Paris 1875, 196–201, ll. 4567–726). Both Avril (Baron/Avril 1981, 322) and Sterling (1987, 169–70) point out a relationship to the style of the Master of the *Remede de Fortune,* but they do not think that the fragment is by the same artist. Sterling suggests that the court scenes are a sketch for a painting. (Note also that any illustration by the Master of the *Remede de Fortune* for the *Voir Dit* would have to be dated a good ten years later than his known period of activity.)

2. First assistant to the Master of the *Remede de Fortune* (fl. ca. 1350–1356). Baron/Avril 1981, no. 272; Avril 1982a, 121 n. 13, 123; 1982b, 27.

3. Second assistant to the Master of the *Remede de Fortune* (= Master of the Coronation Book of Charles V, at the beginning of his career; fl. ca. 1350–1380). The Coronation Book of Charles V (dated 1365) is *GB:Lbl Cotton Tiberius B.VIII.* This artist was prominent throughout the reign of Charles V; see Delisle 1907, 1:218–19; J. White 1957, 221; Avril/Lafaurie 1968, 89, nos. 167, 170, 177, 196, 200, 203, 205, plate VI; Avril 1973, 114 n. 1, 123 n. 4; 1978, 28–29, plates 27–28, with bibliography, p. 32; De Winter 1978, 187 (s.v. Henri du Trévou); Baron/Avril 1981, nos. 276–79, 281, 284, and 319 (with additional bibliography on each manuscript); De Winter 1985, 90. On this artist's contribution to MS **C**, see Avril 1982a, 123–24. See also below, MS **Vg** (table 4.2).

Table 4.2
Artists in MS **Vg** [3]

MIN.	WORK	ARTIST
1	*Loange*	2. Master of the Bible of Jean de Sy
2–4	"	5. Master of Jean de Mandeville
5–6	*Complaintes*	2. Master of the Bible of Jean de Sy
7	*Vergier*	2. Master of the Bible of Jean de Sy
8	*Jug. Behaingne*	3. Master of the Coronation of Charles VI (or assistant)
9	*Jug. Navarre*	3. Master of the Coronation of Charles VI (or assistant)
10–12	*Remede*	3. Master of the Coronation of Charles VI (or assistant)
13–30	*Lyon*	4. Minor Master of the *Grandes Chroniques* of Charles V
31–33	"	2. Master of the Bible of Jean de Sy
34–38	"	1. Master of the Coronation Book of Charles V
39–41	"	2. Master of the Bible of Jean de Sy
42–43	"	1. Master of the Coronation Book of Charles V
44–51	*Alerion*	2. Master of the Bible of Jean de Sy
52–55	*Confort*	3. Master of the Coronation of Charles VI (or assistant)
56–81	"	3. Master of the Coronation of Charles VI (?)
82–90	"	2. Master of the Bible of Jean de Sy
91–101	*Fonteinne*	3. Master of the Coronation of Charles VI
102–10	"	4. Minor Master of the *Grandes Chroniques* of Charles V
111–16	"	1. Master of the Coronation Book of Charles V
117	*Harpe*	1. Master of the Coronation Book of Charles V
118	*Prise*	2. Master of the Bible of Jean de Sy

Bibliography on artists in MS **Vg**:

Note: It is not particularly unusual that so many artists should have collaborated in the production of a single manuscript during the period of the reign of Charles V, nor is it unusual that their individual contributions should be disposed so chaotically throughout the manuscript; it may indicate, however, that the book had to be produced quickly (see De Winter 1978, 180; 1985, 88).

1. Master of the Coronation Book of Charles V (fl. ca. 1350–1380). On this artist's contribution to MS **Vg**, see Avril 1982a, 124 n. 20, n. 25; for additional bibliography; see above, MS C (table 4.1).

2. Master of the Bible of Jean de Sy, also known as the *Maître aux boqueteaux* (fl. ca. 1355–80). The Bible that King John II had translated into French by Jean de Sy is *F:Pn 15397* (dated 1356; left unfinished after the defeat at Poitiers).[12] Had the enormous project been completed, it would have "represented the most extraordinary literary and editorial enterprise of the fourteenth century" (Avril 1982b, 26); see further Delisle 1907, 1:135, 146, 404–10; J. White 1957, 220–21; Avril 1978, 28–29, fig. xi, plates 29–32, and bibliography, pp. 32 and 33; Baron/Avril 1981, nos. 280–84, 286–87 (with additional bibliography for each manuscript); Avril 1982a, 120 n. 9, 125 n. 21; Sterling 1987, 162, 174–86 (with additional bibliography).

   Avril sets himself against the view, formerly very widespread, of identifying miniatures of this artist with the painter Jean Bondol (John of Bruges) and his followers. The style, found in many books that belonged to Charles V, was first isolated and described by Martin (1923, chap. 4; 1928, 48–51), who coined the appellation *Maître aux boqueteaux*. Since then, a few more manuscripts have been associated with this artist, but the Bible of Jean de Sy has always been considered the earliest example. In 1953, Erwin Panofsky suggested that Bondol, painter of a full-page illustration of Charles V for the 1371 Bible of Jean de Vaudetar (*NL:DHmw 10 B. 23*; reproduced in Avril 1978, plate 36), was the *chef d'atelier* for the miniatures seen elsewhere in the Bible, which are in the style of the *Maître aux boqueteaux* (Panofsky 1953, 1:35–38). This view was accepted and further developed by Meiss (1956; 1967, 1:20–23), and by Harry Bober, whose study of the Gotha Missal (*US:CLm 62.287*) is published in Wixom 1963 and 1964. Avril's opposing view attaches to the review of Panofsky 1953 by L.M.J. Delaissé (1957; see also Delaissé's review of Meiss 1967). In his discussion of the Bible of Jean de Vaudetar, Delaissé emphasized that Bondol was a painter, not a manuscript illuminator (1957, 110–11). This view is affirmed by Avril (1978, 110, cf. also 28, 30; further exposition of Avril's position is in Avril/Lafaurie 1968, 89–90, nos. 136, 166, 168, 169, 173, 177, 187, 189, 193, 195, 196, 198, 199, 202, 203, 208). Beyond the stylistic evidence for a rejection of the identification of the *Maître aux boqueteaux* with Bondol lies Avril's path breaking discovery of the importance of the Master of the *Remede de Fortune* (Avril 1973, 116; see the very readable discussion in Avril 1982b). In effect, the northerner Bondol is no longer necessary as a source for the new naturalist-empirical direction in Parisian miniatures evident by 1356 in the Bible of Jean de Sy, since these currents were already anticipated by the Master of the *Remede de Fortune* in the Moralized Bible of John the Good, *F:Pn 167*. Sterling (1987, 176–79), however, maintained that the Master of the Bible of Jean de Sy was not French, but a Netherlander who came to Paris from the court of Wenceslas, duke of Brabant (r. 1355–1383) at Brussels. De Winter (1982, 793–96 et passim; 1985, 7–8, 10, 87–93) has analyzed work of the Boqueteaux Master (De Winter's preferred name) in terms of an atelier made up of a Master and two assistants. See also below on MS A (table 4.5).

3. Master of the Coronation of Charles VI (fl. ca. 1372–80). This illuminator is named after a miniature in a copy of the *Grandes Chroniques* made for Charles V, *F:Pn 2813*, a manuscript produced between ca. 1375–80; see Delisle 1907, 1:312–14, 412; Avril 1973, 97–98 (with much additional bibliography); 1978, 29, plate 35, with bibliography, p. 32; De Winter 1978, 187 (s.v. Henri du Trévou), 193 (s.v. Pierre [le] Portier); Baron/Avril

---

12 De Winter (1982, 794 n. 31) suggested that the Bible of Jean de Sy was decorated 1360–64, after the return of King John II from captivity, and that work was broken off on his death in 1364. More recently, he has again dated the beginning of the style to 1356 (De Winter 1985, 87).

1981, nos. 272, 281, 284, 286 (with additional bibliography for each manuscript); De Winter 1982, 796–97 et passim; 1985, 90–91; Sterling 1987, 248–49. On this artist's contribution to MS **Vg**, as well as the possible contributions of an assistant, see Avril 1982a, 125 n. 22.

4. Minor Master of the *Grandes Chroniques* of Charles V (fl. ca. 1372–79). On the *Grandes Chroniques (F:Pn 2813)* see above, artist 3. This artist also contributed to the decoration of *F:B 434*, a miscellany copied in 1372 for Charles V; see Delisle 1907, 258–60; Avril/ Lafaurie 1968, no. 184; De Winter 1978, 187 (s.v. Henri du Trévou); Baron/Avril 1981, 329–31 no. 284 (with additional bibliography); Sterling 1987, 245–48 (with additional bibliography). On this artist's contribution to MS **Vg**, see Avril 1982a, 125 n. 23.

5. Master of Jean de Mandeville (fl. early 1370s). The *Voyages* of Jean de Mandeville, *F:Pn 4515–4516* (dated 1371), were illuminated for Charles V by this artist in 1372; see Delisle 1907, 1:275–76, 411–12; Avril/Lafaurie 1968, no. 178; De Winter 1978, 193. On this artist's contribution to MS **Vg**, see Avril 1982a, 125 n. 24.

Table 4.3
Artist in MS **J** [16]

MIN.	WORK	ARTIST
1	*Loange*	same artist throughout (Parisian atelier)
2	*Vergier*	
3	*Jug. Behaingne*	
4	*Qui bien aimme* (L22/16)	
5–9	*Remede*	
10–15	*Lyon*	
16–17	*Confort*	
18–20	*Fonteinne*	
21–22	*Un mortel lay* (L12/8) and *Amours, se plus* (L9)	
23	*Chastel d'Amours* (not by Machaut)	
24–25	*Voir Dit*	
26–35	*Cerf Blanc* (*opus dubium*; see chap. 5.19)	

Bibliography on the artist in MS **J**:

The artist of the miniatures in MS **J** also painted the miniatures in MS **K** (Maekawa 1985, 46).

Table 4.4
Artist in MS **K** [15]

MIN.	WORK	ARTIST
1	*Loange*	same artist throughout (Parisian atelier)
2	*Vergier*	
3–5	*Remede*	
6–9	*Lyon*	
10	*Fonteinne*	
11	*Chastel d'Amours* (not by Machaut)	
12–13	*Voir Dit*	

Bibliography on the artist in MS **K**:

The miniatures stem from a Parisian atelier of secondary importance (Avril 1982a, 124 n. 18). See above, MS **J** (table 4.3).

Table 4.5
Artists in MS **A** [5]

MIN.	WORK	ARTIST
1–2	*Prologue*	1. Master of the Bible of Jean de Sy
3	"	2. Provincial master, perhaps at Reims
4–7	*Vergier*	(the same artist for the rest of the manuscript)
8–11	*Jug. Behaingne*	
12	*Jug. Navarre*	
13–24	*Remede*	
25–50	*Lyon*	
51	*Alerion*	
52–77	*Confort*	
78–102	*Fonteinne*	
103–16	*Harpe*	
117	*Loange*	
118	*Marguerite*	
119–48	*Voir Dit*	
149	*Prise*	
150	*Rose*	
151	*Les biens*	
152	Lais	
153	Motets	
154	Ballades	

Bibliography on artists in MS **A**:

1. Master of the Bible of Jean de Sy (fl. ca. 1355–80). See above, MS **Vg** (table 4.2). Studies of the two *Prologue* miniatures, this artist's masterpiece, include Martin 1923, 45–46, 94–95, fig. lxv–lxvi; Ludwig 1926–43, 2:9a* n. 1; Martin 1928, 50–51, 105, fig. lxiii; Porcher 1959, 56 and plate lvi; Avril 1978, plates 29–30; Baron/Avril 1981, no. 283 (with additional bibliography); Avril 1982a, 126–27; De Winter 1982, 801 n. 50; Ferrand 1987; Sterling 1987, 180–83 (with additional bibliography).

2. Provincial master, perhaps at Reims. Baron/Avril 1981, 307 no. 256; on this artist's contribution to MS **A**, see Avril 1982a, 126–27.

Table 4.6
Artist in MS **Pm** [18]

MIN.	WORK	ARTIST
1–3	*Prologue*	Related to style of the Medalion Master
4–7	*Vergier*	(the same artist for the entire manuscript)
8–11	*Jug. Behaingne*	
12	*Jug. Navarre*	
13–24	*Remede*	
25–45	*Lyon*	
46–50	*Confort*	
51–72	*Fonteinne*	
73–85	*Harpe*	
86	*Marguerite*	
87–111	*Voir Dit*	
112	*Rose*	
113	*Les biens*	
114	*Alerion*	

Bibliography on the artist in MS **Pm**:

Related to style of Medalion Master (fl. ca. 1425–30). Avril (1982a, 130 n. 40) cited the style of the Medalion Master as close, though not identical, to the work of the artist of **Pm**. On this artist's contribution to MS **Pm**, see Avril 1982a, 129–30. The 1940 dossier at the Pierpont Morgan Library distinguishes three artists (dossier, p. 4).

Table 4.7
Artist in MS **F-G** [6]

MIN.	WORK	ARTIST
1–5	*Prologue*	Remiet (or Perrin Remy)
6–9	*Vergier*	(the same artist for the entire manuscript)
10–12	*Jug. Behaingne*	
13	*Jug. Navarre*	
14–15	*Remede*	
16–33	*Lyon*	
34	*Alerion*	
35–61	*Confort*	
62–88	*Fonteinne*	
89–103	*Harpe*	
104–40	*Voir Dit*	
141	*Marguerite*	
142	*Prise*	
143	*Loange*	
144	*Complaintes*	
145	Lais	
146	Ballades	
147	Rondeaux	
148	Virelais	

Bibliography on the artist in MS **F-G**:

Remiet (or Perrin Remy; fl. ca. 1368–ca. 1401, Parisian). See Delisle 1868–81, 1:37 and n. 6, 3:310–11; Avril/Lafaurie 1968, 90, nos. 195 and 203; Avril 1969, 303 n. 3, 307–8; De Winter 1978, 176 n. 12, 190–91 (s.v. Oudin de Carvancy), 194 (s.v. Regnault du Montet), 196–97 (s.v. Thévenin l'Angevin; see De Winter 1980, 291 and 1985, 91); Baron/Avril 1981, no. 294 (with additional bibliography); Avril 1982a, 128–29; De Winter 1985, 88, 91–93, 96. On this artist's contribution to MS **F-G**, see Avril 1982, 128–29.

Table 4.8
Artists in MS **E** [7]

MIN.	WORK	ARTIST
1	*Prologue*	1. Master of the *Policraticus* of John of Salisbury
2–5	*Complaintes*	1. Master of the *Policraticus* of John of Salisbury
6	Rondeaux of *Loange*	1. Master of the *Policraticus* of John of Salisbury
7	*Vergier*	2. Master of a *Grandes Chroniques de France*
8–9	*Remede*	(the same artist for the rest of the manuscript)
10	*Jug. Behaingne*	
11–12	*Jug. Navarre*	
13–16	*Lyon*	
17–21	*Alerion*	
22–25	*Fonteinne*	
26–29	*Confort*	
30	*Harpe*	
31	Lais	
32–35	*Voir Dit*	
36–38	*Prise*	

Bibliography on artists in MS **E**:

1. Master of the *Policraticus* of John of Salisbury (fl. ca. 1372–1390s, Parisian). The *Policraticus* of John of Salisbury refers to the French translation by Denis Foullechat for Charles V in *F:Pn* 24287, dated 1372; see Delisle 1907, 1:85–88, 263–64; J. White 1957, 221–22; Avril/Lafaurie 1968, no. 206, color plate on cover (the first artist of the *Policraticus* is the same as the first artist of MS **E**); De Winter 1978, 187 (s.v. Henri du Trévou), 193 (s.v. Pierre [le] Portier); De Winter 1985, 91. On this artist's contribution to MS **E**, see Avril 1982a, 128.

2. Master of a *Grandes Chroniques de France* (fl. ca. 1390). The manuscript of the *Grandes Chroniques* in question is *F:Pn 20350*. On this artist's contribution to MS E, see Avril 1982a, 128 n. 36.

Table 4.9
Artist in MS **D** [11]

MIN.	WORK	ARTIST
1	*Loange*	Parisian emulator of the Master of the duke of Bedford
2–3	*Complaintes*	(the same artist for the entire manuscript)
4	*Vergier*	
5–8	*Jug. Behaingne*	
9–12	*Jug. Navarre*	

Bibliography on the artist in MS **D**:

Parisian emulator of the Master of the Duke of Bedford (fl. ca. 1430). See Panofsky 1953, 1:384–85 n. 3; Porcher 1959, 67–68 and plate lxxii; De Winter 1985, 99 (with additional bibliography). On this artist's contribution to MS **D**, see Avril 1982a, 130.

Table 4.10
Artist in MS **Bk** [21]

MIN.	WORK	ARTIST
1–10	*Lyon*	Assistant to Remiet (or Perrin Remy)

Bibliography on the artist in MS **Bk**:

Assistant to Remiet (or Perrin Remy; fl. ca. 1375–95). For Remiet, see the bibliography for MS **F-G** (table 4.7). The assistant collaborated with Remiet in a copy of the *Pèlerinages* of Guillaume de Digulleville, now *F:Pn 823*, copied in 1393; see Delisle 1868–81, 1:37, n. 6, 3:310–11; Avril/Lafaurie 1968, 90, nos. 195, 203; Avril 1969, 303 n. 3, 307–8; Baron/Avril 1981, no. 294 (with additional bibliography). He was one of the five artists that decorated the *Grandes Chroniques* of Charles V, *F:Pn 2813* (Baron/Avril 1981, no. 284). Wescher (1931, 40) describes each miniature in **Bk**.

To finish this index of artists, let us briefly consider three manuscripts containing illuminations of individual narrative poems.

Pe [20] was probably originally a manuscript transmitting only the *Remede*. It contains a single miniature on fol. 12v, of mediocre quality. It is unusual that the opening of the poem is not illustrated. See the description by Leech-Wilkinson (1982, 100–103).

P [31], an anthology of narrative poems, contains Machaut's *Jugement Behaingne,* with a single miniature at the beginning. François Avril (personal communication) places this artist in the early 1360s, before the reign of Charles V. A similar artist is seen in the Moralized Bible of John the Good (*F:Pn 167*), discussed in Avril 1973, 104 (artist E), with several other manuscripts cited.

Ar [32] also contains Machaut's *Jugement Behaingne,* with a single miniature at the beginning, described by Wimsatt/Kibler (1988, 20) and Liborio (1973, 127).

3. Comparative table of miniatures

Note that the miniatures appear *before* the cited line number or poem.

Work	Poem or line					Manuscripts				
		C	Vg	J	K	A	Pm	F-G	E	D
a. *Prologue*	1Bal					2	1	1	1a	
	2Bal							2		
	3Bal					1	2	3	1b	
	4Bal							4		
	1					3	3	5		
b. *Vergier*	1	62	7	2	2	4	4	6	7	4
	109					5	5	7		
	159	63								
	207					6	6	8		
	245	64								
	247					7	7	9		
	377	65								
	1039	66								
	1195	67								
c. *Jugement Behaingne* †	1	1	8	3		8	8	10	10	5
	41					9	9	[10]		
	81	2								
	257	3								
	881	4								
	973	5								
	1185	6				10	10	11		6
	1381									7
	1465	7								8
	1509					11	11	12		
	1609	8								
	1941	9								
d. *Jugement Navarre*	1		9			12	12	13	11	9
	465									10
	541								12	
	549									11
	1475									12
	[L22]	102		4						
e. *Remede*	1	10	10	5	3	13	13	14	8	
	135	11								
	431	12								
	693	13								
	771		11	6	4	14	14	15		
	921	14a–b								
	1001	15		7		15	15			
	1193	16								
	1273	17								
	1401	18								
	1481	19	*						9	1

† In addition, MSS **P** [31] and **Ar** [32] each have a miniature at the beginning.
* Location of large initials in MS **Vg**.

Work	line	Manuscripts								
		C	Vg	J	K	A	Pm	F-G	E	Pe
Remede, cont'd.	1671	20								
	1821	21								
	1863		*	8	5	16	16			
	1881	22								
	1977	23								
	2039	24								
	2097		*			17	17			
	2148	25								
	2287	26								
	2289		*			18	18			
	2353	27								
	2403	28								
	2522	29								
	2685	30								
	2857	31								
	2893	32				19	19			
	3013	33	12							
	3077	34	*			20	20			
	3181	35								
	3205		*	9		21	21			
	3349		*			22	22			
	3451	36								
	3573	37								
	3729	38								
	3847	39								
	3947	40								
	4077	41								
	4107	42								
	4115		*			23	23			
	4217	43								
	4275		*			24	24			
		C	Vg	J	K	A	Pm	F-G	E	Bk
f. *Lyon*	1	68	13	10	6	25	25	16	13	1
	107		14							†
	151	69	15			26	26	17		2
	175	70	16			27	27	18		3
	279	71	17			28	28	19	14	†
	325	72	18							4
	433	73	19			29	29	20	15	†
	442			11						
	453		20			30	30	21		5
	515	74	21			31	31	22		6
	535			12	7					
	591		22			32	32	23		†
	625	75	23			33	33	24		†
	709		24			34	34	25		†
	747	76	25							†
	767		26			35	35	26	16	
	923	77	27			36	36	27		7
	989	78	28			37	37	28		†
	1119	79	29	13	8	38	38	29		†
	1213	80	30			39	39	30		†
	1345	81	31			40	40			8

* Location of large initials in MS **Vg**.
† Space left for a miniature in MS **Bk**.

Work	line	C	Vg	J	K	A	Pm	F-G	E	Bk
Lyon, cont'd.	1505	82	32			41	41	31		9
	1523	83	33					32		†
	1545			14	9					
	1587	84	34			42	42			†
	1607		,35			43		33		†
	1621	85	36			44				10
	1635	86	37			45				†
	1657	87	38			46				†
	1667	88	39			47				†
	1773	89								
	1801		40			48	43			†
	1810				15					
	1845	90	41			49	44			†
	1975		42			50	45			†
	2077		43							†
	2129	91								
		C	Vg			A	Pm	F-G	E	
g. *Alerion*	1	44	44			51	114	34	17	
	477	45							18	
	775	46								
	863		45							
	945	47	46							
	1015		47							
	1111	48	48							
	1151		49							
	1307	49								
	1495	50								
	1511		50							
	1819	51								
	2091	52								
	2181	53								
	2401	54								
	2471		51						19	
	2761	55								
	3029	56							20	
	3401	57								
	3803	58								
	3987								21	
	4209	59								
	4341	60								
	4569	61								
			Vg	J	K	A	Pm	F-G	E	
h. *Confort*	1		52	16		52		35	26	
	57		53			53		36		
	73		54							
	83		55			54		37		
	135		56							
	161		57			55		38		
	181		58			56		39		
	199		59							
	221		60							
	253		61			57		40		
	273		62			58		41		
	329		63						42	

† Space left for a miniature in MS **Bk**.

Work	line	Manuscripts							
		Vg	**J**	**K**	**A**	**Pm**	**F-G**	**E**	
Confort,	330				59				
cont'd.	351	64							
	357				60		43		
	393	65							
	481	66			61		44		
	513	67			62		45		
	545	68							
	565	69			63		46		
	583	70					47		
	619				64		48		
	624	71							
	633							27	
	671	72							
	719							28	
	753	73			65	46	49		
	943	74							
	955	75							
	1045	76							
	1057	77			66		50		
	1089	78			67		51		
	1131	79			68		52		
	1155	80							
	1157				69				
	1193	81			70	47	53	29	
	1225	82					54		
	1245	83					55		
	1257				71	48			
	1421	84			72		56		
	1979		17						
	2277	85			73	49	57		
	2517	86			74		58		
	2535	87			75		59		
	2645	88			76		60		
	2683	89			77	50	61		
	3979	90							
		Vg	**J**	**K**	**A**	**Pm**	**F-G**	**E**	
i. *Fonteinne*	1	91	18		78	51	62	22	
	55	92			79	52	63		
	235	93			80		64		
	539	94			81	53	65		
	555	95					66		
	571	96			82	54	67		
	587	97	19	10	83	55	68		
	603	98			84	56	69		
	619	99			85	57	70		
	651	100			86	58	71		
	667	101			87	59	72		
	811				88	60	73		
	1075	102			89	61	74		
	1135	103			90	62	75		
	1205	104							
	1313		20		91	63	76		
	1333	105			92	64	77		
	1371	106			93	65	78	23	
	1511	107			94	66	79		
	1609	108			95	67	80		

Work	line	*Manuscripts*							
		Vg	**J**	**K**	**A**	**Pm**	**F-G**	**E**	
Fonteinne, cont'd.	1715	109			96	68	81		
	1851	110			97		82		
	2125	111			98	69	83		
	2145	112			99	70	84		
	2207	113			100	71	85	24	
	2527	114					86		
	2745	115			101	72	87	25	
	2789	116			102		88		
		Vg			**A**	**Pm**	**F-G**	**E**	
j. *Harpe*	1	117			103		89	30	
	31				104		90		
	83					73*	91		
	111				105	74	92		
	129				106	75	93		
	143				107	76	94		
	157				108	77	95		
	165				109	78	96		
	175				110	79	97		
	187				111	80	98		
	197				112	81	99		
	207				113	82	100		
	221				114	83	101		
	233				115	84	102		
	285				116	85	103		
			J	**K**	**A**	**Pm**	**F-G**	**E**	
k. *Voir Dit*	1				119	87	104	32	
	169						105		
	315				120	88	106		
	571						107		
	637				121	89	108		
	1003				122	90	109		
	1228				123	91	110		
	1250				124	92	111		
	1384				125	93	112		
	1503				126	94	113		
	2245				127	95	114		
	2623				128	96	115		
	2891				129	97	116		
	3712						117		
	3760				130		118		
	3947						119		
	4362				131		120		
	4563				132	98	121		
	4814				133	99	122		
	4910						123		
	4990				134	100	124		
	5124						125		
	5244						126		
	5462								
	5468				135	101	127		
	5536				136	102	128		
	5907				137		129		
	6063				138		130		
	7070				139		131		

---

* Miniature **Pm**73 is between the columns of text.

Work	line		Manuscripts							
		C	V g	J	K	A	Pm	F-G	E	D
Voir Dit, cont'd.	7292					140	103	132	33	
	7616					141	104	133		
	7719					142	105	134		
	7773					143	106	135		
	7863					144	107	136		
	8111					145	108			
	8147							137		
	8179					146	109	138		
	8239			24	12	147	110	139	34	
	8652			25	13	148	111	140	35	
l. *Marg.*	1					118	86	141	E	
m. *Rose*	1					150	112	F-G	E	
n. *Les biens*	1					151	113	F-G	E	
o. *Prise*	1		118			149	Pm	142	36	
	5004								37	
	7896								38	
p. *Loange*	poem / Lo1	92	1	1	1	117		143	E	1
	[Lo27								6]†	
	Lo67		2							
	Lo94		3							
	Lo109		4							
q. *Compl.*	Cp1		5			A		144	2	2
	Cp3		6						3	3
	Cp4								4	
	Cp6								5	
r. Lo Rond.	Lo27								6	
s. Lais	L1	93	V g	J	K	152		145	31	
	L2	94								
	L3	95								
	*L4	96								
	L5	97								
	L6	98								
	L7	99								
	L10	100								
	L12	101								
	L22	102		4						
	L14	103								
	*L11	104								
	*L13	105								
	*L8	106								
	*L9	107								
t. Motets	M1	C	V g			153		F-G	E	

---

† In MS **E**, Lo27 is placed in a separate section of rondeaux; see below, section r.
* Asterisk indicates a lai without music.

Work	poem	Manuscripts								
u. Ballades	B1	C	Vg			A 154		F-G 146	E	
v. Rondeaux	R1	C	Vg			A		F-G 147	E	
w. Virelais	V1	C	Vg			A		F-G 148	E	
x. Chastel *	line 1			J 23	K 11					
Cerf Blanc †	1			J 26						
	125			27						
	189			28						
	228			29						
	421			30						
	472			31						
	509			32						
	576			33						
	601			34						
	697			35						

* *Chastel d'Amours* is not by Machaut.
† *Cerf Blanc* is an *opus dubium*; see chap. 5.19.

4. Concordance of miniatures

Note: miniatures appear *before* the line number or poem cited in the table.

a. *Prologue* [13]

Ballade 1: *Je, Nature, par qui tout est fourmé*

A2[14] *Comment Nature, voulant orendroit plus que onques mes reveler et faire essaucier les biens et honneurs qui sont en Amours, vient a Guillaume de Machaut et li ordene et encharge a faire sur ce nouveaux dis amoureux, et li baille pour li conseillier et aidier a ce faire trois de ses enfans, c'est a savoir Sens, Retorique et Musique. Et li dit par ceste maniere* [How Nature, wishing more than ever before to make known and exalted the goods and honors pertaining to Love, comes to Guillaume de Machaut, ordering and charging him herein to compose new poems about love, entrusting to him, for counsel and aid in this enterprise, three of her children, to be specific Meaning, Rhetoric, and Music. And she speaks to him thus: (trans. Palmer 1993, 3)]. Nature, dressed as a queen, presents her son Sense and her daughters Rhetoric and Music to Guillaume de Machaut, who stands before a building; a fountain, shepherd, and peasant farmer are visible in the background (fol. Er).[15]

Pm1 *Comme Nature, voullant orendroit plus que onques mais reveller et faire essaucier les biens et honneurs qui sont en Amours, vient a Guillaume de Machaut et ly ordonne et encharge a faire sur ce nouviaux dis amoureux, et luy baille pour luy aidier et conseillier a ce faire trois de ses enfans, c'est assavoir Sens, Rhetorique et Musique. Et luy dit par ceste maniere* [see trans. of miniature A2]. Nature, dressed as a queen,

---

[13] For a discussion of author portraits in the *Prologue* and elsewhere in the Machaut manuscripts, see Maekawa 1985, 51–54, 128–31; 1988, 148–50.

[14] Iconography described in Mulder 1978, 44–49, 56–64; Ferrand 1987, 14–16; Sterling 1987, 182; Mulder 1990, 203–9. Cerquiglini (1984, 479–80n.; 1985b, 112–13; cf. also 1985a) discusses the depiction of Guillaume's eyes, his *borgne oeil*.

[15] Color reproductions in Porcher 1959, plate lvi; Chailley 1972, 78; *Early Music* 5/4 (October 1977), front cover; Avril 1978, plate 29; Mulder 1990, 206; black-and-white reproductions in Chichmaref 1909, vol. 1, facing p. 2; Martin 1923, fig. lxvi; Gérold 1936, facing p. 364; Borren 1946, 115; Reaney 1961, 123; Meiss 1969, 385 (plate vol.); Poirion 1971, plate 4 (detail); Heitmann 1978, 355; Mulder 1978, 42; Reaney 1980a, 429; Avril 1982a, fig. 11; Ferrand 1987, 204; Sterling 1987, fig. 105; Wimsatt 1991b, plate 1.

presents her son Sense and her daughters Rhetoric and Music to Guillaume de Machaut, who stands before a building holding a book (fol. 1r).[16]

F1   *Comment Nature, voulant orendroit plus que onques mais reveler et faire essaucier les biens et honneurs qui sont en Amours, vient a Guillaume de Machau et li ordene et encharge a faire seur ce nouviaus dis amoureus, et li baille pour lui consillier et aidier ad ce faire trois de ses enfans, c'est assavoir Sens, Retorique et Musique. Et li dit par ceste maniere* [see trans. of miniature A2]. Nature, dressed as a queen, presents her daughters Sense, Rhetoric, and Music to Guillaume de Machaut, who kneels before them (fol. 1r).[17]

E1a   [left-hand scene of two-column-wide miniature] *Comment Nature, voulant orendroit plus que onques mais reveler et faire exaucier les biens et honneurs qui sont en Amours, vient a Guillaume de Machaut. Et lui ordenne et encharge a faire sur ce nouveaux dis amoureux, et lui baille pour lui conseiller et adviser a ce faire .iii. de ces enffans, c'est a savoir Sens, Rhetorique, Musique. Et lui dist par ceste maniere* [see trans. of miniature A2]. Nature presents her daughters Sense, Rhetoric, and Music to Guillaume de Machaut, who kneels before them (fol. 1r).[18]

Ballade 2: *Riens ne me doit excuser ne deffendre*
F2   *Comment Guillaume de Machau respont a Nature* [How Guillaume de Machaut answers Nature]. Guillaume kneels before Nature (fol. 1c).

Ballade 3: *Je sui Amours qui maint cuer esbaudi*
A1[19]   *Comment Amours qui a ouy Nature vient a Guillaume de Machaut et li ameine trois de ses enfans, c'est a savoir Doux Penser, Plaisance et Esperance, pour li donner matere a faire ce que Nature li a enchargié. Et li dit par ceste maniere* [How Love, hearing Nature, comes to Guillaume de Machaut leading three of his children, and these are Sweet Thought, Pleasure, and Hope, in order to provide him the material to carry out what Nature has charged him with. And he speaks to him in this way: (trans. Palmer 1993, 5)]. The god of Love presents his son Sweet Thought, and his daughters Pleasure and Hope to Guillaume, who is seated in his chamber with an open book on his desk (fol. Dr).[20]

Pm2   [large two-column format] *Comment Amours qui a ouy Nature vient a Guillaume de Machaut et ly amaine trois de ses enfans, c'est assavoir Doulx Penser, Plaisance et Esperance, pour luy donner matere a faire ce que Nature ly a enchargié. Et ly dit par ceste maniere* [see trans. of miniature A1]. The god of Love presents his son Sweet Thought, and his daughters Pleasure and Hope to Guillaume, who is reading a book at his desk, which has three closed books scattered upon it (fol. 1v).

F3   *Comment Amours qui a oy nature vient a Guillaume de Machau et li amaine trois de ses enfans, c'est assavoir Dous Penser, Plaisance et Esperance, pour lui donner voie a faire ce que Nature li a enchargié. Et li dit par cest maniere* [see trans. of miniature A1]. The god of Love presents his three daughters Sweet Thought, Pleasure, and

---

[16] Color reproduction in Cosman 1978, frontispiece; black-and-white reproduction in Hoppin 1978b, 404. For MS **Pm**, the new foliation at top right recto is always given.

[17] Reproductions in Maekawa 1988, plate 3; 1989b, 90 plate 7a.

[18] See also n. 21. Reproductions in Machabey 1960, 1393–94; Wilkins 1972, facing p. 96, Mulder 1978, 49 (detail); Avril 1982a, fig. 13. Cerquiglini (1985b, 111) discusses the *Prologue* miniature in MS E.

[19] Iconography described in Ferrand 1987, 16–18; Sterling 1987, 182 (resembles Annunciation).

[20] Color reproduction in Avril 1978, plate 30; B. and J. Cerquiglini 1984, 29; Sterling 1987, fig. 104; Mulder 1990, 207; Eggebrecht 1991, plate 7 after p. 416; black-and-white reproductions in Suchier/Birch-Hirschfeld 1900, 236 (=1913 ed., 243); Chichmaref 1909, vol. 1, between pp. 4 and 5; Couderc 1910; Foulet 1923, 87 (=1948 ed., 115); Martin 1923, fig. lxv; 1928, fig. lxiii; Besseler 1931, 138; Douce 1948, facing p. 56 (detail); de Van 1943, facing p. 24; J. White 1957, plate 52d, facing p. 221; Komma 1961, 51 no. 121; Loomis 1965, plate 9; Machabey 1966, 217; Keitel 1977a, 469; Mulder 1978, 55; M. Thomas 1978, 160 fig. 9; Reaney 1980a, 429; Avril 1982a, fig. 12; Ferrand 1987, 203; Leech-Wilkinson 1990a, 230 fig. 68; Wimsatt 1991b, plate 2.

Hope to Guillaume, who kneels before them (fol. 1c).

E1b [right-hand scene of two-column-wide miniature] *Comment Amours qui a oy Nature vient a Guillaume de Machaut. Et lui amaine .iii. de ses enfans, c'est assavoir Doulz Penser, Plaisance et Esperance, pour lui donner matere a faire ce que Nature lui a enchargié* [see trans. of miniature A1]. The god of Love presents his three daughters Sweet Thought, Pleasure, and Hope to Guillaume, who kneels before them (fol. 1r).[21]

Ballade 4: *Graces ne say, loange ne merci*

F4 *Comment Guillaumes de Machau respont a Amours.* Guillaume kneels, paying homage to the god of Love (fol. 1d).

line 1 [Narrative portion of *Prologue:*]
A3 Guillaume seated at his desk, writing in a book (fol. Fv).[22]
Pm3 Guillaume seated at his desk, writing in a book (fol. 2r).[23]
F5 Guillaume seated at his desk, writing in a book (fol. 2r).[24]

line 184 End

Total number of miniatures for the *Prologue:*   **A** 3   **F** 5
                                                         Pm 3   **E** 1

b. *Le Dit dou Vergier* [25]

line 1 [ll. 1–154: Evocation of Spring, entry into the garden]
C62 [two-column format] The young narrator stands in a garden looking at a flowering bower (fol. 93r).[26]
Vg7 *Ci commence le Dit dou Vergier* [Here begins the Poem of the Garden]. Guillaume stands before a grove of trees filled with birds (fol. 39r).
D4 [two-column format] *Comment le Dieu d'Amours est assis sur .i. abre et ne voit goute et tient en sa main .i. dart et en l'autre .i. brandon de feu et .vi. demoiselles et .vi. escuriers qui dancent et l'acteur se dort sos un abre. Ci commence le Dit du Vergier.* [How the god of Love is seated on a tree and is blind and holds an arrow in his hand and a torch in the other; and six ladies and six squires dance, and the author is asleep under a tree. Here begins the Poem of the Garden]. Guillaume asleep on a hill; the god of Love seated on a tree, holding a torch and an arrow; his entourage dances in a circle below (fol. 48r).
J2 *Ci commence le Dit du Vergier.* The god of Love, holding a torch and an arrow sits in a tree; the narrator sits below the tree (fol. 21r).[27]
K2 *Ci commence le Dit du Verger.* The god of Love, holding a torch and an arrow sits in a tree; the narrator sits below the tree (fol. 21r [new 7r]).
A4 [fol. Gv:] *Ci apres commence le Dit dou Vergier.* The narrator at the gate of the walled garden; within, birds sing in the trees (fol. 1r).
Pm4 The narrator at the gate of the walled garden (fol. 3r).
F6 *Ci commence le Dit dou Vergier.* Guillaume within the wall of the garden; birds sing in the trees. Elements of an unidentified coat of arms form the decorative background (fol. 3r).[28]

---

21 See also n. 18. Reproductions in Wilkins 1972, facing p. 96; Avril 1982a, fig. 13.
22 Discussion in Huot 1987, 284 n. 7, 294–96. Cf. miniature A78, to *Fonteinne* (chap. 4.4i).
23 Reproduction in Hoppin 1978b, 399.
24 Reproduction in Lanson 1923, 108.
25 On the depiction of the god of Love, see Panofsky 1939; Davis 1991, 25–31.
26 Iconography discussed in Huot 1987, 244.
27 Reproduction in Bossuat 1931, plate xxi no. 4, facing p. 368.
28 Color reproduction in Cerquiglini 1987a, 5; whole page reproduced in Maekawa 1988, plate 12.

E7   *Cy commence le Dit du Vergier.* The narrator kneels before the god of Love, who sits
        in a tree holding an arrow and a torch; six people from his entourage dance in a circle
        on the left (fol. 18r).[29]

        line 109
A5   The god of Love sits in a tree holding an arrow and a torch; maidens on his left and
        youths on his right render homage (fol. 1v).
Pm5   The god of Love sits in a tree holding an arrow and a torch; maidens standing below
        on his left and youths standing below on his right render homage (fol. 4r).
F7   Guillaume sits pensively in the garden, near a fountain; birds sing in the trees (fol.
        3v).[30]

        line 159 [ll. 155–246: description of the god of Love and his entourage]
C63   The god of Love, winged, with his eyes closed, holding an arrow in his left hand and
        a torch in his right, and wearing a chaplet of pink flowers, sits in a tree; four maidens
        seated on the left and five youths on the right render him homage (fol. 94r).

        line 207 [The narrator approaches and salutes the god of Love; he asks the
        significance of his accoutrements]
A6   The god of Love sits on a tree; the narrator stands speaking to him (fol. 2r).
Pm6   The god of Love sits on a tree with his accoutrements; Guillaume stands before him
        (=Pm7) (fol. 4v).
F8   The god of Love in a tree, holding an arrow and a torch; his entourage standing below
        looks up to him, while the narrator kneels in supplication (fol. 4a).

        line 245
C64   Four people look on as the narrator kneels before the god of Love, seated in a tree
        (fol. 95r).

        line 247 [ll. 247–376: first speech of the god of Love]
A7   The god of Love on a tree talks as the narrator kneels before him (fol. 2v).
Pm7   The god of Love sits on a tree with his accoutrements; Guillaume stands before him
        (=Pm6) (fol. 5r).
F9   The god of Love on a tree talks as the narrator kneels before him (fol. 4b).[31]

        line 377 [l. 376: the god of Love names himself; ll. 377–400: the narrator kneels and
        prays to him]
C65   Five people look on as the narrator kneels before the god of Love, who is seated on a
        stone bench (fol. 96r).

        line 1039 [ll. 401–1070: the second speech of the god of Love, in which he describes
        his accoutrements and allegorical entourage; ll. 1037–38: the Friend is brought before
        the god of Love by the six maidens and six youths in Love's entourage]
C66   Six people look on as the Friend kneels before the god of Love, who is seated on a
        stone bench (fol. 100v).

        line 1195 [ll. 1151–94: third speech of the god of Love; ll. 1195–1210: departure of
        the god of Love as the narrator awakens from his trance]
C67   The torso of the god of Love is visible above the trees; the narrator sits on the
        ground looking over his right shoulder at him (fol. 102r).

        line 1293   End

        Total number of miniatures for *Vergier*:

C	6	A	4
Vg	1	Pm	4
D	1	F	4
J	1	E	1
K	1		

---

[29] Reproduction in Droz/Thibault 1924, facing p. 13.

[30] Color reproduction in Cerquiglini 1987a, 116.

[31] Color reproduction in Cerquiglini 1987a, 71.

c. *Le Jugement dou Roy de Behaingne*

line 1 [ll. 1–40: in a springtime landscape, the narrator hides himself to hear the song of a bird]

C1   [two-column format] The narrator, wearing a pink hat, listens from behind a grove of trees as the Knight talks to the lady (fol. 1r).[32]

P3   The Knight and lady plead their cases before the king, who is seated on a throne with four courtiers behind him (fol. 64r).

Ar   Two scenes. The Knight and the lady, the latter accompanied by a maidservant and a dog, amongst some trees; the narrator seated beneath a tree, hidden (fol. 152v).[33]

Vg8   *Ci commence le Temps Pascour* [Here begins Easter Time]. The narrator sits looking up at birds in a tree (fol. 47v).

D5   [two-column format] *Ci commence le Jugement du Roy de Behanie comme l'acteur est en .i. jardin et d'une autre part .i. chevalier et d'autre une dame. et une pucelle et .i. petit chien* [Here begins the Judgment of the king of Bohemia, how the author is in a garden and at one side a knight and at the other side a lady, a maidservant, and a little dog]. Guillaume observes the meeting between the Knight and the lady, the latter accompanied by her maidservant and dog, all within an enclosed garden (fol. 58v).

J3   *Le Jugement du Roy de Behaine.* The king of Bohemia gestures to the kneeling Knight, and to the lady, maidservant, and dog; behind them, with only his face visible, the narrator is seen observing from within a bush (fol. 30v).[34]

[K   lacuna]

A8   [fol. 9r:] *Ci apres commence le Jugement dou Roy de Behaingne.* The narrator stands next to a stream within a walled garden with tower, looking at a bird in a tree (fol. 9c).

Pm8   A landscape scene: a stream flows through a walled garden to a tower on the left (fol. 11r).

F10   [two-column format] *Ci commence le Jugement du bon Roy de Behaingne.* Kneeling behind some trees, Guillaume observes the meeting between the Knight and the lady, the latter accompanied by her maidservant and dog; many birds sing in the trees (fol. 9v).

E10   *Cy commence le Jugement du Roy de Behangne.* The narrator reclines behind some trees, observing the meeting between the Knight and the lady, the latter accompanied by her maidservant and dog; behind, a tower of Durbuy Castle is visible (fol. 37r).

line 41 [ll. 41–80: the Knight and the lady meet by chance]

A9   The Knight and the lady, the latter accompanied by her maidservant and dog, discover the narrator, who is hiding behind a bush (fol. 9d).

Pm9   The narrator, hiding behind some trees, observes the meeting of the Knight and the lady, the latter accompanied by her maidservant and dog (fol. 11v).

[F10   is two-columns wide, and serves here also] (fol. 9v)

line 81 [ll. 81–205: the lady tells her story, after which she faints]

C2   The Knight talks to the lady; nearby, the maidservant plays with the dog (fol. 1v).

line 257 [ll. 206–57: the Knight revives the lady and agrees to tell his story; ll. 258–880: the Knight tells his story]

C3   The Knight holds the lady's arm to support her as she faints; nearby, the maidservant plays with the dog (fol. 3r).

line 881 [ll. 881–1184: the debate between the lady and the Knight]

C4   The lady talks to the Knight (fol. 9r).

line 973 [the detailed rebuttal by the Knight begins]

C5   The Knight talks to the lady (fol. 10r).

---

[32] Color reproduction in Maekawa 1989b, 87 plate 4a. Iconography discussed in Huot 1987, 244.

[33] See the descriptions in Liborio 1973, 107; Wimsatt/Kibler 1988, 20.

[34] Reproduction in Bossuat 1931, plate xxi no. 1, facing p. 368.

line 1185 [ll. 1160–1184: the Knight and lady call for a judge; ll. 1185–1378: the narrator approaches, and proposes John of Luxembourg as a judge]

C6   The narrator, with the dog barking at him, approaches the Knight and lady, who have not yet noticed him (fol. 12v).

D6   *Comment l'acteur parle au chevalier et a la dame dedens le jardin* [How the author speaks to the knight and lady in the garden]. Guillaume talks to the Knight and the lady (fol. 67v).

A10   The king of Bohemia sits on his throne, with the Knight and the lady standing on either side of him (fol. 16v).[35]

Pm10   The king of Bohemia sits on his throne, with the narrator (*sic*) and the lady standing on either side of him (=**Pm**11) (fol. 17v).

F11   Guillaume, holding the dog, approaches the Knight and the lady (fol. 15r).

line 1381 [ll. 1379–1422: description of Durbuy castle]

D7   *Comme le chevalier et la dame et l'acteur regardent Durbui le chastel* [How the knight, lady, and the author look at Durbuy Castle]. Guillaume shows Durbuy Castle to the Knight and lady (fol. 69r).[36]

line 1465 [ll. 1445–67: The Knight and lady are taken to the King by Honor and Courtesy]

C7   The Knight and lady before the steps of Durbuy Castle are greeted by Honor and Courtesy (fol. 16r).

D8   [two-column format] *Comme il sont assis a .ii. costes du bon roy et sont et les compaignent plusieurs dames* [How they are seated on either side of the good king and are accompanied by several ladies]. The King and his entourage welcome the Knight and lady to Durbuy Castle (fol. 70r).

line 1509 [ll. 1509–1608: the Knight recounts the whole story to the King and asks for a judgment]

A11   The Knight and lady before the king of Bohemia (fol. 18v).

Pm11   The king of Bohemia sits on his throne, with the narrator (*sic*) and the lady standing on either side of him (=**Pm**10) (fol. 19v).

F12   The Knight and lady kneel before the king of Bohemia; some courtiers stand behind the king. Elements of an unidentified coat of arms form the decorative background (fol. 16v).[37]

line 1609 [ll. 1609–1922: the King restates the facts of the case and hears counsel of Reason, Love, Loyalty, and Youth]

C8   The narrator stands behind the lady and the Knight as they kneel before the king of Bohemia, who is speaking; several courtiers stand behind the king; complex towers, roofs, and gables provide the upper frame of the miniature (fol. 17v).[38]

line 1941 [ll. 1923–56: the judgment in favor of the Knight]

C9   Scene as in miniature C8; the King holds the hands of the kneeling lady and Knight as he pronounces his judgment (fol. 21r).[39]

line 2079   End

Total number of miniatures for *Jugement Behaingne*:

C	9	A	4
Vg	1	Pm	4
D	4	F	3
J	1	E	1

---

[35] Reproduction in R. Cazelles 1947, facing p. 287.

[36] Reproductions in Machabey 1930, 424; 1955b, vol. 1, facing p. 16; E. Pulido 1978a, 19; 1978b, 10.

[37] Whole page reproduced in Maekawa 1988, plate 10.

[38] Reproduction in Avril 1982a, fig. 7.

[39] Reproduction in R. Cazelles 1947, facing p. 17.

d. *Le Jugement dou Roy de Navarre*

line 1

Vg9   *Ci commence le Jugement dou Roy de Navarre* [Here begins the Judgment of the King of Navarre]. The narrator standing (nothing else is visible) (fol. 60v).

D9   *Comment l'acteur se meict a merencolier pour le temps qui se change* [How the author begins to lament about the changing times]. Guillaume stands in his chamber; a book is on the table (fol. 74v).[40]

A12   [fol. 22r:] *Ci apres commence le Jugement dou Roy de Navarre, contre le Jugement dou Roy de Behaingne* [After this begins the Judgment of the King of Navarre, against the Judgment of the King of Bohemia]. Guillaume looks sadly out of the window of a tower (fol. 22v).

Pm12   Guillaume looks sadly out of the window of his house (fol. 23r).

F13   *Le Jugement du Roy de Navarre contre le Jugement du bon Roy de Behangne.* Guillaume in his bed chamber (fol. 19v).

E11   *Cy commence le Jugement du Roy de Navarre. Machaut.* Guillaume sits at his writing desk with a book; outside, flowering trees are visible (fol. 45r).

line 465

D10   *Comment l'atteur regarde les noce qui se font apres la grant morie* [How the author observes the marriages that take place after the great mortality]. Guillaume stands watching a wedding feast (fol. 78r).

line 541

E12   Three men on horseback (one of them the narrator) and three dogs hunting, as Lady Good Fortune approaches on horseback (fol. 46v).

line 549

D11   [two-column format] *Comment Guillaume chevauche Grisart et court apres le lievre et la dame chevauche a grant compaignie et fait venir Guillaume de Loris et argue a lui* [How Guillaume rides on Grisart and runs after the rabbit and the lady rides with a great entourage and has Guillaume de Loris come to her and argues with him]. Guillaume on horseback, leading the rabbit hunt (fol. 79r).[41]

line 1475

D12   [two-column format] *Comme le Roy de Navarre se siet et la royne et les .xii. demoisselles en estant devant le roy desputantes a l'encontre de Guillaume de Loris* [How the king of Navarre is seated and the queen and the twelve ladies are before the king arguing against Guillaume de Lorris]. The King and Queen (Good Fortune) seated; nine allegorical ladies are on the right, Guillaume in the middle (fol. 86v).

line 4212   End

Total number of miniatures for *Jugement Navarre*:

Vg	1		**Pm**	1
D	4		**F**	1
A	1		**E**	2

---

[40] This miniature provides the only separation (there are no rubrics or extra space) between the two *jugement* poems in MS **D**. Reproduction in Douce 1948, facing p. 56 (no. 1).

[41] Color reproduction in Machabey 1970, plate 117; black-and-white reproductions in Machabey 1930, 424; 1954, 36–37 (large format); 1955b, vol. 1, facing p. 32. In miniatures **D**11 and **D**12, "Loris" appears over an erasure. Cerquiglini (1985b, 127) discusses the rubric.

e. *Remede de Fortune* [42]

line 1

C10   [two-column format] The lover, accompanied by a young manservant, observes the
        lady of a magnificent castle; three ladies also look up to her, as she gestures towards
        the lover. She is identified by a pink hat (fol. 23r).[43]

Vg10   *Ci commence Remede de Fortune* [Here begins the Remedy of Fortune]. A lady,
        holding a child's hand, stands before a clerk, who is instructing the child (fol. 90r).[44]

J5   *Ci commence Remede de Fortune*. The lady gives a ring to the narrator, who holds
        out his hand; Hope (?) stands behind him (fol. 47r).[45]

K3   *Ci commence Remede de Fortune*. The lady gives a ring to the narrator, who holds
        out his hand; Hope (?) stands behind him (fol. 43r [27r]).

A13   *Ci commence Remede de Fortune*. An old man with a beard sits instructing a child
        (fol. 49v).

Pm13   *Cy commence Remede de Fortune* [hairline within the frame of the miniature]. An
        old man holding a rod for discipline sits instructing a young man (identifiable as the
        lover of miniatures Pm17 and following) (fol. 47v).

F14   *Ci commence Remede de Fortune*. Guillaume sits at a rostrum, reading from a book
        to a group of students (cf. miniature F34, chap. 4.4g) (fol. 40r).[46]

E8   *Ci commence L'Ecu Bleu* [Here begins the Blue Shield]. The narrator walks in a
        grove of trees holding a flower (fol. 22r).

line 135

C11   *Comment Amours chastie l'amant*. The goddess of Love talks to the lover (fol.
        24r).[47]

line 431 [before the lai *Qui n'aroit* (RF1)]

C12   [two-column format] *Comment l'amant fait un lay de son sentement*. The lover sits
        on the grass in a grove of trees, writing his lai on a long scroll (fol. 26r).[48]

line 693 [after the lai RF1]

C13   *Comment la dame fait lire a l'amant le lay qu'il a fait*. The lady, holding a small dog,
        directs the lover to read from the long scroll he is holding; off to the side, a king sits
        on a hill talking to courtiers (the game of "le Roi qui ne ment") (fol. 28v).[49]

line 771

Vg11   A king and some courtiers sit on a bench (the game of "le Roi qui ne ment") (fol.
        95v).

J6   *Comment l'amant se depart de sa dame* [How the lover takes leave of his lady]. The

---

[42] Huot (1987, 249–59) discusses the iconography of the *Remede* in MS C; she also
compares MSS C and A (1987, 275–80), and includes a Table of Miniatures (appendix B)
with descriptions of the miniatures in the *Remede* in MSS C and A (1987, 343–45). Huot
(1987, 250) links the technique of rubrication in MS C to the *Roman de la Rose*.

[43] Color reproduction in Avril 1978, plate 23; black-and-white reproductions in Avril 1982a,
fig. 2; 1982b, 27; Byrne 1984, 76; Sterling 1987, fig. 84; Wimsatt/Kibler 1988 miniature
1; Wimsatt 1991b, plate 17; discussed in Schmidt 1977–78, 192–93, plate 101; Huot
1987, 244, 250.

[44] The whole page is reproduced in Maekawa 1988, plate 7; 1989b, 88 plate 5b.

[45] Reproduction in Bossuat 1931, plate xxi no. 2, facing p. 368.

[46] Reproductions in Douce 1948, facing p. 56 (no. 4); Salter/Pearsall 1980, 122 (discussed p.
116); Wimsatt 1991b, plate 10.

[47] Reproduction and trans. of rubric in Wimsatt/Kibler 1988 miniature 2.

[48] Reproductions in Huot 1987, 251 fig. 19 (discussed pp. 250–51); Wimsatt 1991b, plate
18; Kibler/Earp 1995, 574; reproduction and trans. of rubric in Wimsatt/Kibler 1988
miniature 3.

[49] Color reproduction in Avril 1982b, 27; black-and-white reproductions in Avril 1973, fig.
23; Fallows 1980, 364; Wimsatt/Kibler 1988 miniature 4 (with trans. of rubric). On the
game of "le Roi qui ne ment," see Green 1990; the game is also depicted in the *Voir Dit*,
miniatures A134 and Pm100 (chap. 4.4k).

narrator and the lady, standing (fol. 51v).

K4   *Comment l'ament se depart de sa dame.* The narrator and the lady, standing (fol. 46v [30v]).[50]

A14   Guillaume takes leave of his lady and enters the Park of Hesdin (fol. 54v).[51]

Pm14 Guillaume takes leave of his lady (fol. 52r).

F15   The narrator washes his hands at a fountain (fol. 44r).

line 841

[Vg   very large initial] (fol. 96r)[52]

line 921 [after music for first strophe of the *complainte Tels rit* (RF2)]

C14a–b [two-column format, two large miniatures] *Comment l'amant fait une complainte de Fortune et de sa roe.* At the top (a), the lover sits in a walled garden (the Park of Hesdin), writing his *complainte*; at the bottom (b), Fortune, blindfolded, turns a wheel with three people on it: at the top a king, on the right side a man falling off, and on the left side another man climbing up (fol. 30v).[53]

line 1001 [Nebuchadnezzar's dream[54]: Daniel ii.31–35]

C15   [fol. 31r:] *Comment Nabugodonosor songa qu'il veoit une figure qui se claimme statua.* King Nebuchadnezzar asleep in bed; a black statue with gold head and brown feet stands beside the bed (fol. 31v).[55]

J7   *Le songe du Roy Nabugodonosor* [King Nebuchadnezzar's dream]. King Nebuchadnezzar asleep in bed; the statue stands on the bed (fol. 53r).

[K   lacuna]

A15   A black statue with gold hair and savage appearance (fol. 56v).[56]

Pm15 A statue with a gold head, dark copper torso, bronze legs, grey feet, and savage appearance (fol. 53v).

line 1193

C16   *Commant l'amant se plaint de Fortune.* The lover sits on the ground with his head in his hand, pointing to a blindfolded Lady Fortune (fol. 32v).[57]

---

[50] Reproduction of entire folio in Homburger 1953, plate 30 (description pp. 124–25).

[51] The number "xi" is visible beside the miniature.

[52] A similar amount of space is supplied with a miniature elsewhere in **Vg** (cf. *Alerion* and *Confort*).

[53] Color reproductions in Wimsatt/Kibler 1988, frontispiece; Cerquiglini-Toulet 1993b, xiii; detail of the Wheel of Fortune on the sound recording New Albion NA068CD (chap. 8.8); black-and-white reproductions in Patch 1927, plate 9, facing p. 158 (miniature **C**14b); Loomis 1965, plate 58; Kurose 1977, 315 plate 137; A.H. Nelson 1980, plate 23a; Avril 1982a, fig. 1; cover of Cerquiglini 1985b; Wimsatt/Kibler 1988 miniature 5 (with trans. of rubric); Leech-Wilkinson 1990a, 226 fig. 66. Discussion in Huot 1987, 252; on the Park of Hesdin, see Van Buren 1986a, esp. 123. A.H. Nelson (1980, 227) makes the following observation about the depiction of Lady Fortune in this miniature: "the rim of Fortune's wheel is supplied with cogs which are engaged by corresponding cogs on a second, adjacent wheel. Both wheels are supported on double bearings. Fortune turns her wheel not directly, but by turning a crank on the secondary wheel. A count of the cogs on the two wheels reveals that Fortune has gained a mechanical advantage of approximately 4:3. The secondary wheel has no apparent symbolic function, but rather betrays the artist's fascination with the marvels of technology."

[54] The iconography of this scene is comparable to an image that heads many manuscripts of the *Roman de la Rose*, with *Dangier* standing beside the dreamer asleep in bed; see Huot 1987, 258–59.

[55] Reproductions in Huot 1987, 253 fig. 20 (discussed pp. 252–54); Wimsatt/Kibler 1988 miniature 6 (with trans. of rubric).

[56] Reproduction in Huot 1987, 276 fig. 27 (discussed pp. 275–77).

[57] Reproduction and trans. of rubric in Wimsatt/Kibler 1988 miniature 7; whole page reproduced in Maekawa 1988, plate 6. Discussion in Huot 1987, 254.

line 1273
C17   *Comment l'amant entrevit sa dame.* The lover sees his lady entering the castle; a maidservant holds the train of her dress (fol. 33v).[58]

line 1401
C18   [fol. 34r:] *Comment l'amant se complaint a lui meismes.* The lover sits dejected on a hill (fol. 34v).[59]

line 1481 [after the text of the *complainte* RF2]
C19   *Comment Esperance vint conforter l'amant.* Hope, with a transparent scarf in her hair, holds the lover's hand as he begins to doze off (fol. 35r).[60]
Pe1   Hope sitting on grassy slope next to castle, talking to the narrator, who is reclining on one elbow (fol. 12v).
[Vg   very large initial (fol. 100v)]
E9   [room for rubric, but none entered] The narrator and Hope recline next to a spring in a walled garden (fol. 27r).

line 1671
C20   [fol. 36r:] *Comment Esperance ensaigne et aprent l'amant.* The lover listens to Hope (fol. 36v).[61]

line 1821
C21   *Comment Esperance chastie l'amant.* Hope stands scolding the lover (fol. 37v).[62]

line 1863
[Vg   very large initial] (fol. 103r)
J8   *Les droites armes des amans: l'escu bleu* [The true lover's arms: the blue shield]. A blue escutcheon with white teardrops (cf. miniature A16) (fol. 59r).
K5   *Les droites armes des amens: el escu bleu.* A blue escutcheon with white teardrops (cf. miniature A16) (fol. 53r [35r]).
A16   A blue escutcheon with a red heart pierced by an arrow (fol. 62r).[63]
Pm16   A blue escutcheon with white teardrops and a red heart pierced by an arrow (fol. 58v).

line 1881
C22   *Comment Esperance moustre les droites armes d'Amours a l'amant.* The lover and Hope sit on either side of an escutcheon (a red heart pierced by an arrow), which is hanging from a tree (fol. 38r).[64]

line 1977
C23   *Comment l'amant s'en dort en ooiant chanter Esperance.* Hope sits singing from long scroll while the lover sleeps (fol. 38v).[65]

line 2039
C24   *Comment Esperance demande a l'amant s'elle a bien chanté.* Hope, with her hand on the lover's head, places a ring on his finger (fol. 39v).[66]

---

[58] Reproductions in Wimsatt/Kibler 1988 miniature 8 (with trans. of rubric); Maekawa 1989b, 86 plate 2. Discussion in Huot 1987, 254.

[59] Reproduction and trans. of rubric in Wimsatt/Kibler 1988 miniature 9. Discussion in Huot 1987, 254.

[60] Reproduction and trans. of rubric in Wimsatt/Kibler 1988 miniature 10. Discussion in Huot 1987, 252.

[61] Reproduction and trans. of rubric in Wimsatt/Kibler 1988 miniature 11.

[62] Reproduction and trans. of rubric in Wimsatt/Kibler 1988 miniature 12.

[63] The number "xiii" is visible beside the miniature. Reproduction in Huot 1987, 278 fig. 28 (discussed pp. 275–77).

[64] Reproductions in Huot 1987, 255 fig. 21 (discussed pp. 254–56); Wimsatt/Kibler 1988 miniature 13 (with trans. of rubric).

[65] Reproductions in Wimsatt/Kibler 1988 miniature 14 (with trans. of rubric); Wimsatt 1991b, plate 20. Discussion in Huot 1987, 256.

[66] Reproduction and trans. of rubric in Wimsatt/Kibler 1988 miniature 15. Discussion in Huot 1987, 256.

line 2097
[**Vg**   very large initial] (fol. 104v)
A17   Hope places a ring on Guillaume's finger as he sleeps on a hillside (fol. 63v).[67]
Pm17   Hope places a ring on the lover's finger as he sleeps beneath a tree on a hillside (fol. 60r).

line 2148
C25   [fol. 40r:] *Comment Esperance dit a l'amant quel pouer elle a.* Hope talks to the lover (fol. 40v).[68]

line 2287
C26   *Comment l'amant parle a Esperance.* The lover talks to Hope, who has her back turned to him (fol. 41v).[69]
[**Vg**   very large initial] (fol. 105v)
A18   Guillaume talks to Hope (fol. 65r).
Pm18   The lover and Hope (fol. 61r).

line 2353
C27   *Commant l'amant mercie Esperance.* The lover, cape in hand, bows to thank Hope (fol. 42r).[70]

line 2403
C28   *Comment Esperance parle a l'amant de Fortune.* Hope talks to the lover (fol. 42v).[71]

line 2522
C29   *Comment l'amant parle a Esperance.* The lover talks to Hope (fol. 43r).[72]

line 2685
C30   *Comment Esperance parle a l'amant.* Hope and the lover converse (fol. 44v).[73]

line 2857 [before the ballade *En amer* (RF4)]
C31   *Comment Esperance baille a l'amant une chancon et la chante devant li.* Hope offers a scroll to the lover (fol. 45v).[74]

line 2893 [after the ballade RF4]
C32   *Comment Esperance se depart de l'amant.* Hope's torso is visible above the trees; below, the lover holds a scroll (fol. 46v).[75]
A19   Guillaume listens as Hope sings the ballade (no scroll present) (fol. 69v).
Pm19   The lover and Hope (fol. 65r).

line 3013 [before the ballade *Dame, de qui* (RF5)]
C33   *Comment l'amant fait une balade.* The lover sits on the ground with his legs crossed, writing on a scroll draped across his knee (fol. 47v).[76]
Vg12   The narrator kneels with an open book before Hope, who holds a dog (fol. 47v).

line 3077
C34   *Comment Esperance tient l'amant par la main et le mainne veoir le manoir sa dame.*

---

[67] The number "xiiii" is visible beside the miniature.

[68] Reproduction and trans. of rubric in Wimsatt/Kibler 1988 miniature 16.

[69] Reproduction and trans. of rubric in Wimsatt/Kibler 1988 miniature 17.

[70] Reproduction and trans. of rubric in Wimsatt/Kibler 1988 miniature 18.

[71] Reproduction and trans. of rubric in Wimsatt/Kibler 1988 miniature 19.

[72] Reproduction and trans. of rubric in Wimsatt/Kibler 1988 miniature 20.

[73] Reproduction and trans. of rubric in Wimsatt/Kibler 1988 miniature 21.

[74] Reproduction and trans. of rubric in Wimsatt/Kibler 1988 miniature 22. Discussion in Huot 1987, 256.

[75] Reproduction and trans. of rubric in Wimsatt/Kibler 1988 miniature 23. Discussion in Huot 1987, 256.

[76] Reproductions of the whole page, with the music of the ballade *Dame, de qui* in Parrish 1957, plate xlix; Reaney 1980a, 433; Wimsatt/Kibler 1988 miniature 24 (with trans. of rubric); reproduction of miniature in B. and J. Cerquiglini 1984, 34. Discussion in Huot 1987, 256.

Hope holds the hand of the lover in front of the castle (fol. 48r).[77]

[**Vg**]   very large initial] (fol. 112v)

A20   [fol. 71r:] *L'amant*. Guillaume and Hope speak (fol. 71v).

Pm20   *L'amant* [hairline]. The lover and Hope (fol. 66r).

line 3181

C35   *Commant l'amant s'agenoille en la saute devant le manoir sa dame.* Hope's head is visible above the trees; the lover, seated before his lady's castle, writes on a scroll draped across his knee (fol. 49r).[78]

line 3205 [before the *priere*]

[**Vg**]   very large initial] (fol. 113r)

J9   *Les graces et mercis que l'amant rent a Amours* [The thanks the lover renders to Love]. The narrator thanks the god of Love (fol. 69r).

[**K**   lacuna]

A21   *L'amant*. Guillaume kneels before his lady's castle, his hands clasped in prayer (fol. 72r).[79]

Pm21   The lover kneels before his lady's castle, his hands clasped in prayer (fol. 67r).

line 3349 [after the *priere*]

[**Vg**]   very large initial] (fol. 114r)

A22   Guillaume is welcomed by the lady and courtiers onto the grounds of the castle (fol. 73r).[80]

Pm22   The lover is welcomed by the lady and courtiers onto the grounds of the castle (fol. 67v).

line 3451 [before the virelai *Dame, a vous* (RF6)]

C36   [two-column format] *Comment l'amant chante empres sa dame.* Five ladies and five men in a round dance near the castle; the lady with the pink hat directs her gaze at the lover, who approaches from the right with two other men (fol. 51r).[81]

line 3573

C37   *Commant l'amant parle a sa dame.* Three couples converse as they return to the castle; the last couple is the lady and the lover (fol. 52r).[82]

line 3729/3731

C38   *Comment la dame parle a l'amant.* The lady and the lover talk face to face; a maidservant holds the lady's train (fol. 53v).[83]

line 3847/3849

C39   [fol. 54v:] *Comment l'amant mercie sa dame.* The lover kneels before his lady as three other ladies look on (fol. 54r).[84]

line 3947/3949

C40   [two-column format] *Comment l'amant fu au disner sa dame.* The lady and the lover

---

[77] Reproduction and trans. of rubric in Wimsatt/Kibler 1988 miniature 25.

[78] Reproduction and trans. of rubric in Wimsatt/Kibler 1988 miniature 26. Discussion in Huot 1987, 256.

[79] The number "xviii" is visible beside the miniature.

[80] The number "xix" is visible beside the miniature.

[81] Color reproductions on the cover of the sound recording Reflexe 1C 063–30 106 (chap. 8.8); Avril 1978, plate 24; 1982b, 26; black-and white reproductions in Besseler 1931, 141; Reaney 1952a, 1043–44; Komma 1961, 51 no. 122; Machabey 1966, 218; Roussel 1967, 55; Chailley 1972, 77; Sterling 1987, fig. 86; Wimsatt/Kibler 1988 miniature 27 (with trans. of the rubric); Wimsatt 1991b, plate 19; Boulton 1993, frontispiece. Huot (1987, 344) indicates that the Lover is already taking part in the dance beside his Lady, a possible alternative interpretation (see also Wimsatt 1991b, commentary to plate 19). Further discussion of the *carole* in Huot 1987, 256, 272.

[82] Reproduction and trans. of rubric in Wimsatt/Kibler 1988 miniature 28.

[83] Reproduction and trans. of rubric in Wimsatt/Kibler 1988 miniature 29.

[84] Reproduction and trans. of rubric in Wimsatt/Kibler 1988 miniature 30.

(here wearing a pink hat like the lady's) stand at opposite ends of a large banquet hall in the castle; on the right are two musicians with straight trumpets; on the left are two bagpipers; a complex of chapel roofs, towers, and gables form the upper frame of the miniature (fol. 55r).[85]

line 4077/4079
C41   *Comment la dame et l'amant changent d'aniaus.* The lady and the lover exchange rings as Hope stands in between, with a hand on the back of each of the two (fol. 56r).[86]

line 4107/4109 [before the rondeau *Dame, mon cuer en vous* (RF7)]
C42   [two-column format] *Comment l'amant s'en va chantant.* A tournament, with knights in armor jousting; the lover departs on horseback, singing from a scroll; in the back five ladies observe from a spectator's box (none wears a pink hat) (fol. 56v).[87]

line 4115/4117 [after the rondeau RF7]
[Vg   very large initial] (fol. 119v)
A23   The lover on horseback takes leave of his lady (fol. 78v).[88]
Pm23   The lover on horseback takes leave of his lady (fol. 72r).

line 4217/4219
C43   *Comment l'amant parle a sa dame.* The lover and the lady talk (fol. 58r).[89]

line 4275/4277
[Vg   very large initial] (fol. 120v)
A24   Guillaume on one knee renders hommage to the god of Love, who is sitting on a tree (cf. miniature **A7**, chap. 4.4b) (fol. 80r).[90]
Pm24   The lover on his knees renders hommage to the god of Love, who is sitting on a tree with his accoutrements (cf. miniature **Pm7**, chap. 4.4b) (fol. 73r).

line 4298/4300 End

Total number of miniatures for *Remede*:

C	34	**A**	12
Pe	1	**Pm**	12
Vg	3	**F**	2
J	5	**E**	2
K	3		

f. *Le Dit dou Lyon* [91]

line 1
C68   The enchanted island: a springtime landscape with birds and animals in the woods, the encircling stream in the foreground, and a castle behind (fol. 103r).[92]
Vg13   *Ci commence le Dit dou Lyon* [Here begins the Poem of the Lion]. The narrator sits before the lion (fol. 122r).

---

85 Color reproduction in Avril 1978, plate 25; black-and-white reproductions in Besseler 1931, 143; Borren 1946, 116; Komma 1961, 58 no. 136; Machabey 1966, 220; Avril 1982a, fig. 3; 1982b, 27; Sterling 1987, fig. 85; Wimsatt/Kibler 1988 miniature 31 (with trans. of the rubric). Ehrhart (1990, 152 n. 14) notes that men and women occupy separate tables (see note to *Fonteinne* l. 1715, chap. 4.4i); further discussion in Huot 1987, 257.

86 Color reproduction in Coen Pirani 1966, 131; black-and-white reproduction and trans. of rubric in Wimsatt/Kibler 1988 miniature 32.

87 See comment in Huot 1987, 257–58. Reproductions in Baron/Avril 1981, 319; Wimsatt/Kibler 1988 miniature 33 (with trans. of rubric).

88 The number "xx" is visible beside the miniature.

89 Reproduction and trans. of rubric in Wimsatt/Kibler 1988 miniature 34.

90 The number "xxi" is visible beside the miniature. Discussion in Huot 1987, 279.

91 Aspects of the iconography of *Lyon* are discussed in Sasaki 1982, 29–30, 34–37.

92 Color reproductions in Avril 1978, plate 26; 1982b, 27; Sterling 1987, fig. 83; Cerquiglini-Toulet 1993b, xii. Discussion in Huot 1987, 244.

J10   *Ci commence le livre du Dit du Lyon*. The narrator encounters the lion, who enters from behind some trees (fol. 77r).

K6   *Ci commence le Dit du Lion*. The narrator encounters the lion, who enters from behind some trees (fol. 69r [43r]).

A25   *Ci commence le Dit dou Lyon*. Guillaume stands within a walled garden surrounded by a stream (fol. 80v).

Pm25   The lover stands in a grove of trees encircled by a stream (fol. 73v).

F16   [double scene] *Ci commence le Dit dou Lyon*. Guillaume washes his hands in his bed chamber; outside, the stream encircling the enchanted island, and a grove of trees with birds are visible (fol. 63v).[93]

E13   *Ci commance le Dit du Lyon*. The narrator in bed looks out on a garden (fol. 61r).

Bk1   *Ci commence le Dit du Lion*. The narrator stands in a grove of trees beside a building with a stream in the foreground. A lion and other animals are visible among the trees (fol. 1a).

line 107

Vg14   The narrator stands before the stream encircling the island (fol. 122v).

[Bk   blank space for miniature] (fol. 1d)

line 151

C69   The narrator rows a boat across the stream (fol. 104r).

Vg15   The narrator in a boat at the edge of a forest (fol. 123a).

A26   Guillaume in a boat (fol. 81c).

Pm26   The lover in a boat in the stream of miniature **Pm25** (fol. 74r).

F17   Guillaume boards a boat at the forest's edge. Unidentified coat of arms (fol. 64c).

Bk2   The narrator rowing a boat in the stream (fol. 2a).

line 175

C70   The narrator stands on the shore, with the boat in the stream; birds and animals are all around (fol. 104v).[94]

Vg16   The narrator in the forest next to the stream (fol. 123b).

A27   Guillaume ties the boat to a tree (fol. 81d).

Pm27   The lover ties the boat to a tree in the grove (fol. 74v).

F18   Guillaume ties the boat to a tree. Unidentified coat of arms (fol. 64c).

Bk3   The narrator stands on the shore, with the boat in the stream, tied to a tree (fol. 2b).

line 279

C71   The narrator stands as a lion emerges from the bush (fol. 105v).

Vg17   The narrator stands in the forest (fol. 124a).

A28   The lion holds part of Guillaume's robe in his jaws (fol. 82v).

Pm28   The lion holds part of the lover's robe in his jaws; the encircling stream is still visible (fol. 75r).

F19   The lion holds part of Guillaume's robe in his claws as savage beasts threaten. Elements of an unidentified coat of arms form the decorative background (fol. 65r).

E14   *Comment le lyon prist l'amant par le giron* [How the lion took the lover by the robe]. The lion holds part of the narrator's robe in his jaws as several savage beasts threaten from the side; the stream is visible in the background (fol. 61v).

[Bk   blank space for miniature] (fol. 3a)

line 325

C72   The lion holds part of the narrator's robe in his jaws as several savage beasts threaten from the side (fol. 106r).

Vg18   The narrator stands in the forest, with the lion visible behind a tree (fol. 124b).

Bk4   The narrator, in the forest, pets the lion on the head (fol. 3b).

line 433

C73   The narrator and the lion drink from the encircling stream (fol. 106v).[95]

---

[93] The whole page is reproduced in Maekawa 1988, plate 9; 1989b, 90 plate 7b.

[94] The number "iii" is visible above the miniature.

[95] Reproduction in Avril 1982a, fig. 8.

Vg19   The narrator watches as the lion drinks from the stream (fol. 125a).
A29   The lion leads Guillaume to a fountain, holding part of Guillaume's robe in his jaws (fol. 83c).
Pm29   The lion leads the lover to a spring, holding part of his robe in his jaws (fol. 76b).
F20   The narrator and the lion drink from a fountain (fol. 66a).
E15   *Comment le lyon mena l'amant devant la dame* [How the lion led the lover before the lady]. The narrator kneels before the lady, who is seated in front of a canopy; the lion looks up at her as savage beasts threaten from the side (fol. 62r).
[Bk   space for a miniature] (fol. 4a[96])

line 442
J11   The lion drinks from a fountain, with the narrator beside him (fol. 80r).
[K   lacuna]

line 453
Vg20   The narrator stands before the lady (queen), who is seated (fol. 125b).
A30   Guillaume at the spring; two ladies and two men have appeared (fol. 83d).
Pm30   The lover at the spring; two ladies and two men have appeared (fol. 76b).
F21   Guillaume and the lion beside a fountain; the lion holds part of Guillaume's robe in his claw; the lady (a queen) appears with her entourage (fol. 66a).
Bk5   Two couples sit on either side of the lady (a queen), who is seated with her hand on the head of the lion, lying at her feet (fol. 4b).[97]

line 515
C74   The narrator stands before the lady, who is seated on a throne under a canopy; the lion sits beside her, and her followers stand behind as several savage beasts threaten from the side, behind the narrator (fol. 107v).
Vg21   The lady pets her lion (fol. 125v).
A31   The lady and her lion (fol. 84r).
Pm31   The lion kneels before his lady (fol. 76v).
F22   The lady pets the lion's head; several savage beasts threaten from the side (fol. 66v).[98]
Bk6   Five women seated; in the middle, the lady pets the lion (fol. 4d).

line 535
J12   The lady pets the lion's head (fol. 80v).
K7   The lady pets the lion's head (fol. 72r [45r]).

line 591
Vg22   The lady standing (fol. 126r).
A32   The lion kneels before his lady as several savage beasts threaten (fol. 84v).[99]
Pm32   The lion kneels before his lady as several savage beasts threaten from behind the lady (fol. 77r).
F23   Guillaume, the lady, and her lion; several savage beasts threaten. Elements of an unidentified coat of arms form the decorative background (fol. 67a).[100]
[Bk   blank space for miniature] (fol. 5b)

line 625
C75   The narrator stands before the lady, who is seated on a throne under a canopy; the lion sits beside her, with two ladies on either side of her; savage beasts threaten the lion from the right (fol. 108r).
Vg23   The lady stands before the lion (fol. 126v).
A33   The lady proffers her hand to the lion (fol. 85r).[101]
Pm33   The lady pets the lion's head (fol. 77v).

---

[96] This folio reproduced in Olschki 1932, plate xlv.
[97] Reproductions in Wescher 1931, plate 31; Olschki 1932, plate xlv.
[98] Color reproduction in Cerquiglini 1987a, 95.
[99] The number "xxix" is visible beside the miniature.
[100] Reproduction in Avril 1982a, fig. 15.
[101] The number "xxx" is visible beside the miniature.

F24   The lady speaks to the lion; several savage beasts are visible behind him (fol. 67a).
[Bk   blank space for miniature] (fol. 5c)

line 709
Vg24   The narrator stands before the lion (fol. 127a).
A34   Guillaume kneels before the lady (fol. 85v).
Pm34   The lover kneels before the lady (fol. 78r).
F25   Guillaume kneels before the lady; the lion is between them (fol. 67v).
[Bk   blank space for miniature] (fol. 6a)

line 747
C76   An old knight talks to the narrator as the lady sits in a bower; three other ladies stand
       to the side (fol. 109r).
Vg25   The narrator kneels before the lady (fol. 127b).
[Bk   blank space for miniature] (fol. 6b)

line 767
Vg26   The narrator and the lady sit next to each other (fol. 127v).
A35   A knight speaks to Guillaume (fol. 86r).[102]
Pm35   The old knight speaks to the lover (fol. 78v).
F26   The old knight (bearded, with the robe of a clerk) speaks to the lover in the lady's
       presence (fol. 68r).
E16   *Comment la dame araisona l'amant.* The narrator kneels before the lady, who is
       standing before her tent; the old knight stands by the narrator; the stream is visible
       on the side (fol. 63r).

line 923 [ll. 853–1800: speech of the old knight[103]; ll. 923–1586 on various types
       of men, ll. 939–88 on false men]
C77   The old knight talks to the narrator; to the right a king is surrounded by nobles and
       other men, including one with a bishop's mitre (fol. 110v).[104]
Vg27   The narrator and the lady stand conversing (fol. 128v).
A36   Three ladies and three gentlemen face each other (fol. 87r).
Pm36   Three ladies and three gentlemen face each other (fol. 79v).
F27   Three ladies sit on the left before a group of men; various estates are represented (fol.
       68v).
Bk7   Three groups of people outdoors: three kings on left, three clerics in middle, and five
       noble persons in a round dance on the right (fol. 7c).

line 989 [ll. 989–1118: faithful men]
C78   Three noble couples talk (fol. 111r).
Vg28   Two men kneel before two ladies (fol. 129r).
A37   Three ladies and three gentlemen face each other (fol. 87v).
Pm37   Three ladies and three gentlemen face each other (fol. 80r).
F28   Three ladies sit on the left before three kneeling gentlemen (fol. 69r).
[Bk   blank space for miniature] (fol. 8a)

line 1119 [ll. 1119–212: deceitful men]
C79   Two men bow before two ladies (fol. 112r).
Vg29   A man stands before a monk (fol. 130r).[105]
J13   A couple converse standing beside three trees (fol. 83v).
K8   *Des faus amens* [false lovers]. A couple converse standing beside three trees (fol. 75v
       [48v]).
A38   Three ladies and three gentlemen face each other (fol. 88v).
Pm38   Three ladies and three gentlemen face each other (fol. 80v).

---

[102] Reproduction of a detail of the narrator in Maekawa 1988, plate 16; the whole page is
reproduced in 1989b, 89 plate 6b.

[103] Here and below, I have borrowed several summary descriptions from Kelly (1978, 105).

[104] Reproduction of a detail of the narrator in Maekawa 1988, plate 15.

[105] Maekawa (1985, 105 n. 284), notes that all of the types of lovers condemned in the
following passage are represented in **Vg** by priests (see the miniatures **Vg**29, 32, 35).

F29   Three ladies sit on the left before two kneeling gentlemen (fol. 69v).
[Bk   blank space for miniature] (fol. 9a)

       line 1213 [ll. 1213–344: recreants]
C80   A tournament: two knights in armor charge each other with lances, while three ladies
       observe from a spectator's box (fol. 113r).
Vg30   Two knights in armor charge each other with lances (fol. 130v).
A39   A knight, fully armed, mounted on a charging horse (fol. 89r).
Pm39   A knight, fully armed, mounted on a charging horse (fol. 81r).
F30   Two knights in armor, each with a shield, ride towards three ladies (fol. 70r).
[Bk   blank space for miniature] (fol. 9c)

       line 1345 [ll. 1345–504: chivalrous knights]
C81   Five knights on horses bid farewell to two ladies who observe from behind the walls
       of a castle (fol. 114r).
Vg31   Four men sit on the left; one points towards three ladies, who stand off to the right
       (fol. 131v).
A40   Several knights mounted on horses (fol. 90r).[106]
Pm40   Several knights in armor, mounted on horses (fol. 82r).
Bk8   Three ladies stand at the door of a castle; one man holds both hands of the first lady;
       another man stands behind him (fol. 10c).

       line 1505 [ll. 1505–22: braggarts]
C82   The philanderer sits holding the hand of each of two ladies beside him; another lady
       stands to the right (fol. 115r).
Vg32   Three monks and three nuns stand before each other (fol. 132c).
A41   The philanderer speaks to two ladies (fol. 91r).
Pm41   The philanderer speaks to two ladies (fol. 83r).
F31   Three ladies sit before two kneeling gentlemen (fol. 71v).
Bk9   Three men and two ladies seated on a grassy hill (fol. 11c).[107]

       line 1523 [ll. 1523–86: peasants]
C83   Six peasant couples dance in a circle; on the left, a peasant couple (Robin and Marote
       of l. 1545) and dog (fol. 115v).
Vg33   Two peasant couples seated (fol. 132d).
F32   A peasant couple eat with three other peasants (fol. 72a).
[Bk   blank space for miniature] (fol. 11d)

       line 1545
J14   *De Robin et de Marote en sothas* [?] [On the peasants Robin and Marote (?)]. Robin
       hands Marote a purse (fol. 86*bis* r).
K9   *De Robin et de Mariom en sothas* [?]. Robin hands Marion a purse (fol. 78r [51r]).

       line 1587 [ll. 1587–698: on types of women; ll. 1593–606 on deceitful ladies]
C84   A bearded gentleman gestures to a group of five ladies and gentlemen (fol. 116a).
Vg34   A lady kneels before a man (fol. 133b).
A42   The beguiling woman begins to embrace a gentleman (fol. 91d).
Pm42   The beguiling woman begins to embrace a gentleman (fol. 83v).
[Bk   blank space for miniature] (fol. 12b)

       line 1607 [ll. 1607–20: perspicacious ladies]
Vg35   Two ladies stand before two kneeling monks (fol. 133b).
A43   Two lovers; the lady dismisses a third man (fol. 91d).[108]
[Pm   lacuna]
F33   A lady places a chaplet on a kneeling gentleman (fol. 72b).

---

[106] The number "xxxvii" is visible beside the miniature.

[107] Written instructions to the illuminator are partially visible in the bottom margin: "i
jardin ou il ara damez hommez asis ensemble et requiroient les damez d'amer et dariere eux
ar/..." (trimmed) [a garden with ladies and men seated together and the men beseech the
ladies to love them and behind them trees(?)].

[108] The number "xl" is visible beside the miniature.

[Bk   blank space for miniature] (fol. 12b)

          line 1621 [ll. 1621–34: women who pursue pleasure and amusements]
C85   Three men and two ladies dance in a circle, accompanied by a fourth man playing
          bagpipes (fol. 116b).
Vg36   Three men and two ladies dance in a row (fol. 116b).
A44   Four couples dance in a circle (fol. 92a).[109]
[Pm   lacuna]
Bk10   Three couples in a round dance before a grove of trees (fol. 12c).

          line 1635 [ll. 1635–56: ladies devoted to chivalrous knights]
C86   Two pairs of knights on horseback in hand-to-hand combat; three ladies observe from
          the tower of a castle (fol. 116c).
Vg37   A lady stands looking on as several knights on horseback do battle (fol. 133d).
A45   A lady standing alone between two trees (fol. 92b).
[Pm   lacuna]
[Bk   blank space for miniature] (fol. 12d)

          line 1657 [ll. 1657–66: seductresses]
C87   A gentleman bows before a lady, who holds his hand as she places a chaplet of
          flowers on his head (fol. 116d).
Vg38   A lady kneels holding a chaplet to a man standing before her (fol. 133d).
A46   A lady gives a chaplet of flowers to Guillaume (fol. 92c).
[Pm   lacuna]
[Bk   blank space for miniature] (fol. 12d)

          line 1667 [ll. 1667–98: ladies haughty because they fear deception]
C88   A gentleman and a lady stand holding hands (fol. 117r).
Vg39   A man and a lady sit in a forest, conversing (fol. 134r).
A47   A man and a lady converse (fol. 92c).
[Pm   lacuna]
[Bk   blank space for miniature] (fol. 13a)

          line 1773
C89   A bearded gentleman, standing next to the stream with the boat, appears to bless the
          island (fol. 117v).[110]

          line 1801
Vg40   The narrator and the lady talk, her hand on the head of the lion beside her (fol. 134v).
A48   Seated on a cushion beside a spring, the lady pets the head of the lion lying beside
          her as she talks with Guillaume (fol. 93c).
Pm43   Seated on a cushion beside a spring, the lady pets the head of the lion lying beside
          her as she talks with the lover (fol. 84c).[111]
[Bk   blank space for miniature] (fol. 13d)

          line 1810
J15   The narrator and the lady sit on the grass beneath a tree as the lady pets the lion (fol.
          87v).
[K   lacuna]

          line 1845
C90   The lady pets the head of the lion lying beside her as she talks to the narrator, who is
          seated beside her; savage beasts threaten from the left, and two other men look on
          (fol. 118r).
Vg41   The narrator and the lady stand and talk (fol. 135r).
A49   Nearly the mirror image of miniature A48 (fol. 93d).

---

[109] Reproduction in *MGG* 8 (1960), plate 73, facing cols. 1409–10.

[110] Maekawa (1989b, 72–73) indicates that the iconography recalls that of God creating the
      world (reproduction in 1989b, 85 plate 1a).

[111] Long written instructions for the illuminator (effaced), to the right of the frame of the
      miniature.

Pm44   = **Pm**43, with the lover standing (fol. 84d).[112]
[**Bk**   blank space for miniature] (fol. 14b)

line 1975
Vg42   The narrator kneels before the lady; the lion lies beside her (fol. 136r).
A50   The lady feeds the lion a leg of lamb or deer (fol. 94v).
Pm45   The lady feeds the lion a leg of lamb (fol. 85v).[113]
[**Bk**   blank space for miniature] (fol. 15a)

line 2077
Vg43   The narrator and the lion stand next to the stream; the boat is visible (fol. 136v).
[**Bk**   blank space for miniature] (fol. 15d)

line 2129
C91   The narrator rows the boat as the lion looks on from the bank of the stream (fol. 120r).

line 2204   End

Total number of miniatures for *Lyon*:

C	24	**Pm**	20
Vg	31	**F**	18
J	6	**Bk**	10 (20 others left blank)
K	4	**E**	4
A	26		

g. *Le Dit de l'Alerion*

line 1
C44   [two-column format] Springtime scene with four children playing: in the foreground, two catch butterflies with a net; to the right, another holds a bird in his hand; in the background, another sits beside a nest of birds with a bird perched on his finger, keeping another bird at bay with his outstretched hand (fol. 59r).[114]

Vg44   *Ci commence le Dit de l'Alerion* [Here begins the Poem of the Alerion]. A clerk stands holding a crying child by the hand; a nobleman appears to instruct them (cf. miniature **Vg**10, chap. 4.4e) (fol. 139r).[115]

A51   *Ci commence le Dit de l'Alerion.* A nobleman riding on horseback, with a hunting bird perched on his hand (fol. 96v).

Pm114   A nobleman on horseback with a hunting bird perched on his hand (fol. 183v).

F34   *Ci commence le Dit de l'Alerion.* Guillaume sits at a rostrum reading from a book to a group of students (cf. miniature **F**14, chap. 4.4e) (fol. 75v).

E17   *Cy commance le Dit des .iiii. Oysiaulx* [Here begins the Poem of the Four Birds]. A Knight, with a bird perched on his hand, stands before a forest full of birds (fol. 69r).[116]

line 477
C45   The narrator walks pensively beside a grove of trees (fol. 62r).

E18   *Comment l'amant s'en amoura de l'espervier* [How the lover fell in love with the sparrow hawk]. The narrator watches the sparrow hawk perched in a tree, holding a small bird in its claws; four other birds are in flight (fol. 70r).

---

[112] Short written instructions for the illuminator (effaced), to the right of the frame of the miniature.

[113] Written instructions for the illuminator to the right of the frame of the miniature: "Une dame tenant en sa main i. quantité de mothon dont elle repaist i. lion . . . la buce" (deciphered in the dossier at the Pierpont Morgan Library) [A lady holding in her hand a quantity of mutton, which she feeds to a lion].

[114] Reproductions in Avril 1982a, fig. 9; Maekawa 1988, 146–47, plate 11. Discussion in Huot 1987, 244.

[115] This miniature has a multi-lobed frame with tricolor border, similar to those in the miniatures reproduced in Avril 1978, plate 32–33 (cf. the miniature **Vg**1, at the beginning of the *Loange*).

[116] Reproduction in Avril 1982a, fig. 14.

line 775
C46   The narrator, holding a stick in his gloved hand, looks up at four birds in a tree (fol. 64v).

line 863
Vg45   [fills only two-thirds of the column width[117]] The narrator looks up at a sparrow hawk in a tree (fol. 144r).

line 945
C47   The sparrow hawk is perched in one tree as the narrator climbs another (fol. 65v).
Vg46   [fills only two-thirds of the column] The narrator looks up at a sparrow hawk in a tree (fol. 145a).

line 1015
Vg47   [fills only two-thirds of the column] The narrator stands with the sparrow hawk perched on his hand (fol. 145b).

line 1111
Vg48   [fills only two-thirds of the column] Two men stand by a forest and talk (fol. 146a).
C48   The narrator stands with the sparrow hawk perched on his hand (fol. 66v).

line 1151
Vg49   [fills only two-thirds of the column] The god of Love talks to a lady and a man (fol. 146b).

line 1307
C49   A large sparrow hawk, perched on a pole extending between two trees, holds a smaller blue bird in its claws; a falconer's glove is draped over the pole (fol. 68r).

line 1495
C50   The goddess of Love talks to the narrator (fol. 69v).

line 1511
Vg50   [fills only two-thirds of the column] Two men, each with a bird perched on his arm, face the seated narrator (fol. 148v).

line 1819
C51   Venus accepts the golden apple from Paris as two other ladies look on (fol. 71v).

line 2091 [Expedition of Guillaume Longue-Epée[118]]
C52   St. Louis and knights on horseback (fol. 73v).

line 2181
C53   St. Louis sits on a throne before his tent as three knights stand on the right; one is in armor (Guillaume Longue-Epée); a walled city or castle is visible in the background (fol. 74r).

line 2401
C54   The goddess of Love, with the alerion perched on her gloved hand, offers the bird to the narrator, who kneels to accept it; three ladies, two with red apples, look on (fol. 76r).

line 2471
Vg51   [fills only two-thirds of the column] The goddess of Love, with the alerion perched on her arm, offers the bird to the narrator (fol. 154v).
E19   *Commant Amours envoia l'alerion a l'amant* [How Love sent the alerion to the lover]. The god of Love, with the alerion perched on his gloved hand, offers the alerion to the narrator (fol. 75v).

line 2761
C55   A man on horseback with a lure; six birds, with the alerion among them, are flying in the air (fol. 78v).

---

[117] The amount of space filled here with a miniature (the same practice is seen in *Confort*) is equal to the space that was filled with large initials in the *Remede* in MS **Vg**.

[118] Hoepffner 1908–21, 2:lxv and n. 2, lxix; Calin 1974, 96–97; Brownlee 1984, 74.

line 3029
C56   The goddess of Love talks to the narrator (fol. 80r).
E20   *Comment l'amant s'enamoura de l'aigle* [How the lover fell in love with the eagle].
A man shows an enormous eagle to the narrator, whose finger is held in the bird's beak (fol. 77v).

line 3401
C57   A king and others (among whom two lovers embrace), all on horseback, watch as a large blue falcon attacks a brown eagle, which sits on a bush with its wings outstretched (fol. 82v).[119]

line 3803
C58   Reason, holding an apple, appears to hit the narrator with a stick as two other ladies (Courtesy and Love) look on (fol. 85v).

line 3987
E21   *Comment l'amant demanda le gerfaut* [How the lover asked for the gyrfalcon]. Inside a building, the narrator looks at the gyrfalcon, which is perched on the hand of a man dressed in blue; a man dressed in green holds the first man's arm (fol. 80r).

line 4209
C59   The narrator, holding a lure, has the gyrfalcon perched on his hand; on a hill are four birds, one holding a smaller bird in its claws (fol. 88r).

line 4341
C60   Lady Reason talks to the narrator (fol. 89r).

line 4569
C61   The narrator stands with two birds perched on each hand, one large (the alerion) and one small (fol. 91r).

line 4814   End

Total number of miniatures for *Alerion*:

C	18	Pm	1
Vg	8	F	1
A	1	E	5

h. *Le Confort d'Ami* [120]

line 1
Vg52   *Ci commence Confort d'Amy* [Here begins Friend's Comfort]. Guillaume kneels presenting his book to King Charles of Navarre, seated on a throne; two retainers stand behind the king (fol. 170a).
J16   *Ci commence le livre de Confort d'Ami.* Guillaume (clerk) talks to King Charles of Navarre, who is in a tower (fol. 91r).
[K   lacuna]
A52   *Ci apres commence Confort d'Amy.* Guillaume talks to King Charles of Navarre, who is leaning out the window of a tower (fol. 127a).
[Pm   lacuna]
F35   *Ci commence Confort d'Ami.* Guillaume stands on the opposite side of a stream, observing as King Charles of Navarre accepts a book from a valet; two courtiers stand behind him (fol. 98v).
E26   *Cy commance le Confort d'Amy.* Within a walled garden, the two elders stand on either side of Susanna, who is bathing nude in a stream (fol. 93r).

line 57
Vg53   [fills only three-quarters of the column[121]] Guillaume, in front of the king and his

---

[119] Discussion in Maekawa 1989b, 73–74, 86 plate 3.

[120] Sources for the various interpolated *exempla* are derived from Hoepffner 1908–21, 3:i–xx. Aspects of the iconography of *Confort* are discussed in Wallen 1980, with a Table of Illuminations in MSS **A** and **F** (p. 204); she finds illustrations for the *Ovide Moralisé* important sources for the five mythological miniatures in MS **F** (F57–61).

[121] The amount of space filled here with a miniature (the same practice is seen in *Alerion*) is

retainers, kneels praying to God, who looks down from behind the king, outside the
upper-left frame of the miniature (fol. 170b).

A53   Christ in Majesty (fol. 127b).

[Pm   lacuna]

F36   Susanna and Joachim kneel in prayer, as God looks down from the upper right-hand
      corner (fol. 99a).

      line 73 [ll. 73–410: the story of Susanna. Daniel xiii (Apocrypha)]

Vg54 [fills only three-quarters of the column] Susanna sits between two men (?) (fol.
      170c).

      line 83

Vg55 Susanna, Joachim and three others in the garden (?) (fol. 170c).

A54   Two ladies watch as two maidens bathe in a stream; a fourth lady (Susanna) is
      undressing (fol. 127v).

[Pm   lacuna]

F37   The two elders hide and watch Susanna talking to a maid, as another maid enters the
      castle (fol. 99b).

      line 135

Vg56 Susanna speaks to the two maids (fol. 171a).

      line 161

Vg57 [fills only three-quarters of the column] The two elders threaten Susanna (fol. 171b).

A55   The two elders and Susanna (fol. 128b).

[Pm   lacuna]

F38   One of the elders talks to Susanna as the other enters the castle. Unidentified coat of
      arms (fol. 99c).

      line 181

Vg58 Palace domestics arrive on the scene with Susanna and the elders (fol. 171b).

A56   The two elders watch as Susanna prays to God, who is visible in the upper right-hand
      corner of the miniature (fol. 128b).

[Pm   lacuna]

F39   Susanna, in the custody of a manservant, and a group of people hear the accusations
      of the two elders, who are sitting on a bench (fol. 99d).

      line 199

Vg59 Susanna kneels as four men stand over her, pulling her hair (fol. 171c).

      line 221

Vg60 The two elders and Susanna before the judges on the bench (fol. 171d).

      line 253

Vg61 [fills only three-quarters of the column] Susanna kneels in prayer as God looks down
      from above, blessing her (fol. 172a).

A57   The two elders and Susanna stand before two seated judges (fol. 128v).[122]

[Pm   lacuna]

F40   Susanna, barefooted and dressed in white, kneels in prayer; behind her are several
      people, including the two elders (fol. 100b).

      line 273

Vg62 On one side, the baby Daniel in his mother's arms begins to speak; in the middle,
      Susanna, barefooted, with her hands tied, is held by two men; on the other side,
      people look on (fol. 172a).

A58   The elders look on as two men are about to toss Susanna into a fire (fol. 129r).[123]

[Pm   lacuna]

F41   From within a group of people, the baby Daniel speaks from his mother's arms;
      Susanna, barefooted and dressed in white with her hands tied, is being led off by a

---

equal to the space that was filled with large initials in the *Remede* in MS **Vg**.

[122] The number "liii" is visible beside the miniature.

[123] The number "liiii" is visible beside the miniature.

manservant (fol. 100b).

line 329
Vg63   Daniel questions one of the elders (fol. 172c).
F42   The young Daniel questions one of the elders; a group of people off to the side look
       on (fol. 100d).

line 330
A59   The baby Daniel, held by his mother, questions the elders; a group of people to the
       left look on (fol. 129c).
[Pm   lacuna]

line 351
Vg64   Daniel questions the other elder; an angel behind brandishes a sword and is about to
       strike (fol. 172d).

line 357
A60   The group of people approach Daniel and his mother as he questions the two elders
       (fol. 129d).
[Pm   lacuna]
F43   On the right, Daniel with a group of people question one elder; an angel hovering
       above the elder brandishes a sword and is about to strike; the other elder stands off to
       the left (fol. 100d).

line 393
Vg65   A group of people worship God (fol. 173r).

line 481 [ll. 451–646: The fiery furnace. Daniel iii]
Vg66   King Nebuchadnezzar and his court stand before the golden statue (?) (fol. 173c).
A61   King Nebuchadnezzar and a bearded Daniel converse (fol. 130c).
[Pm   lacuna]
F44   King Nebuchadnezzar and others stand before the golden statue. Unidentified coat of
       arms (fol. 101c).

line 513
Vg67   Nebuchadnezzar and others worship the statue on their knees (fol. 173d).
A62   A group of people worship the statue on their knees as a group of musicians play
       two harps and two trumpets before it (fol. 130d).[124]
F45   King Nebuchadnezzar and others stand looking at the golden statue as a group of
       musicians play a fiddle, a harp, and a trumpet before it (fol. 101d).[125]

line 545
Vg68   Nebuchadnezzar questions the three Jews; the statue is visible in the background (fol.
       174a).

line 565
Vg69   Nebuchadnezzar gestures as the three Jews are led away to the furnace (fol. 174b).
A63   The three Jews stand in the furnace; two men outside fan the flames with bellows
       (fol. 131r).
[Pm   lacuna]
F46   Nebuchadnezzar has three men toss the three Jews into the fiery pit (fol. 102a).

line 583
Vg70   The three Jews stand in the furnace (fol. 174c).
F47   On the left, the three Chaldeans burn; on the right, the three Jews and an angel, all
       inside the furnace, remain unhurt. Unidentified coat of arms (fol. 102b).

line 619
A64   An angel joins the three Jews in the furnace (fol. 131v).

---

[124] The number "lviii" is visible beside the miniature. Machaut's text (l. 503) calls for a
    trumpet, flute, and harp.
[125] Color reproduction on the cover of the sound recording Reflexe 1C 063–30 109 (see chap.
    8.8); black-and-white reproduction in Machabey 1960, 1397–98.

[Pm   lacuna]
F48   Nebuchadnezzar and two others find the three Jews and the angel safe in the furnace;
         the fire has been extinguished (fol. 102v).

         line 624
Vg71   Nebuchadnezzar and the three Jews worship Christ in Majesty (fol. 174d).

         line 633
E27   *Comment Nabugudonosor fist mettre les .iii. juis en la fornaise ardant* [How
         Nebuchadnezzar had the three Jews put in the fiery furnace]. King Nebuchadnezzar and
         two men watch the three Jews (one with a crown) in the fire; an angel hovers above
         them (fol. 94v).

         line 671 [ll. 661–954: Belshazzar's feast. Daniel v]
Vg72   King Belshazzar and several men at a banquet table; behind them on the right, a man
         stands writing on the wall (?) (fol. 175r).

         line 719
E28   *Comment le roy Balthasar vit la main qui escrisoit* [How King Belshazzar saw the
         hand that was writing]. King Belshazzar at a banquet table with his queen and another
         man; a hand is writing on the wall with a pen (fol. 95r).

         line 753
Vg73   Belshazzar turns toward the wall in a gesture of surprise; behind him Daniel explains
         the vision, as four people look on from the right (fol. 175v).
A65   King Belshazzar and Daniel converse (fol. 132v).
Pm46   King Belshazzar and Daniel converse (fol. 87r).
F49   King Belshazzar and Daniel converse (fol. 103r).

         line 943
Vg74   Men wielding swords (mostly illegible; apparently represents the death of Belshazzar)
         (fol. 177a).

         line 955 [ll. 955–1287: Daniel in the lion's den. Daniel vi, plus the last portion of
         the Story of Bel and the Dragon from the Apocrypha]
Vg75   The princes look on as Daniel talks to King Darius (fol. 177a).

         line 1045
Vg76   Three men kneel before King Darius, accusing Daniel (fol. 177d).

         line 1057
Vg77   On the left, Daniel prays to God above; on the right, two men inform King Darius
         (fol. 177d).
A66   Three bearded men accuse Daniel (not present) before King Darius (fol. 134c).
[Pm   lacuna]
F50   Three bearded men kneel before King Darius and point towards Daniel, who is held
         by another man. Unidentified coat of arms (fol. 104c).

         line 1089
Vg78   Daniel in a crenelated tower (the lion's den) (fol. 178a).
A67   Daniel sits in the lion's den, unharmed by the six lions (fol. 134d).
[Pm   lacuna]
F51   Darius and two others look on as a man drops Daniel naked into the lion's den (fol.
         104d).

         line 1131
Vg79   An angel carries Habakkuk by the hair (fol. 178b).
A68   King Darius and another man cover the opening of the lion's den with a stone;
         Daniel's head is visible underneath (fol. 135r).
[Pm   lacuna]
F52   An angel carries Habakkuk by his hair; he is carrying his stew pot to Daniel, who
         appears happy in the pit with the lions (fol. 105c).

         line 1155
Vg80   Habakkuk offers his stew pot to Daniel, who is in a tower with the lions (fol. 178c).

line 1157
A69   An angel carries Habakkuk by his hair; he is carrying his stew pot (fol. 135c).
[Pm   lacuna]

line 1193
Vg81 Darius sees Daniel in the tower with a lion (fol. 178d).
A70   The angel lets Habakkuk with his stew pot down by the den that holds Daniel, whose head is visible (fol. 135d).
Pm47 The angel lets Habakkuk with his stew pot down into the den that holds Daniel, whose head is visible (fol. 89r).
F53   King Darius comes to the lion's den and finds Daniel safe with the lions (fol. 105c).
E29   *Comment li roys Daries vit Daniel en la fosse au lyons* [How King Darius saw Daniel in the lion's den]. King Darius and another man come up to the lion's den and find Daniel safe with the lions (fol. 96r).

line 1225
Vg82 Darius speaks to Daniel; the lions stand behind (fol. 179a).
F54   Darius directs as a man with a rope and pulley frees Daniel from the lion's den (fol. 105d).[126]

line 1245
Vg83 Darius points as Daniel's accusers are eaten by the lions (fol. 179b).
F55   Darius directs another man to throw one of Daniel's accusers to the lions; the others are already being eaten (fol. 105d).

line 1257
A71   King Darius and others watch as the lions eat Daniel's accusers (fol. 136r).
Pm48 King Darius and others watch as the lions eat Daniel's accusers (fol. 89v).

line 1421 [ll. 1361–548: Manasseh. 2 Paralipomenon xxxiii.10–13 and the Prayer of Manasseh from the Apocrypha]
Vg84 King Manasseh looking out of a tower (fol. 180v).
A72   King Manasseh sits head in hand in a tower, with irons on his ankles (fol. 137r).
[Pm   lacuna]
F56   King Manasseh in a tower, praying (fol. 106v).

line 1979
J17   *Comment le Roy Salemon requeroit a Dieu qu'il le gardast de grant richesse et de grant povreté* [How King Solomon asked God to protect him from great wealth and from great poverty]. King Solomon prays as God looks down from the corner, smiling (fol. 103v).
[K   lacuna]

line 2277 [ll. 2277–352: Orpheus and Eurydice]
Vg85 Orpheus (tonsured) kneels playing his harp before three ladies, Pride, Envy, and Trickery, who comb their hair (fol. 185v).
A73   Guillaume bends down to console King Charles of Navarre, whose head is visible at the window of the tower (fol. 142v).
Pm49 The narrator stands outside a tower, talking to King Charles of Navarre, who is visible at the window (fol. 94v).
F57   Orpheus plays his harp for Eurydice, who is held by two devils coming from the gates of hell (cf. miniature A75) (fol. 111r).

line 2517 [ll. 2353–516: Pluto and Proserpina[127]; ll. 2517–640: continuation of Orpheus myth]
Vg86 Tantalus kneels by a stream; he and another man listen to Orpheus playing his harp (fol. 187r).

---

[126] Reproduction in Wallen 1980, 203.
[127] Machaut's treatment of the myth and aspects of the iconography are discussed in Anton 1967, 28–32.

A74   Pluto, dressed as a king devil and holding Proserpina, gallops away on horseback (fol. 144r).[128]
[Pm   lacuna]
F58   Orpheus plays his harp for Tantalus, who is tied to a tree within a body of water (fol. 112b).[129]

        line 2535
Vg87   Orpheus looks back at Eurydice with a mirror; three ladies (the Danaides), one with a crown, look on (fol. 187v).
A75   Orpheus plays his harp for Eurydice, who is held by a devil coming from the gates of hell (cf. miniature F57) (fol. 144v).[130]
[Pm   lacuna]
F59   The three Danaides draw water from a river with buckets (fol. 112b).

        line 2645 [ll. 2645–82: Paris and Helen]
Vg88   Paris holds the hand of Helen, who kneels before him; her castle is behind (fol. 188r).
A76   Orpheus is cudgeled and stoned by the five Maenads (fol. 145r).
[Pm   lacuna]
F60   Paris holds the arm of Helen as she leaves a church (fol. 112v).

        line 2683 [ll. 2683–716: Hercules and Deianira]
Vg89   Ladies watch as a bearded Hercules strikes Achelous with his sword (fol. 188v).
A77   Paris, with several other armored knights in a boat, helps Helen, who has come from a castle, on board (fol. 145v).
Pm50   Paris, with several other knights in a boat, helps Helen on board (fol. 96r).
F61   Hercules (a knight in armor) strikes Achelous on the head. Elements of an unidentified coat of arms form the decorative background (fol. 113r).

        line 3979
Vg90   [Only six text-lines in height] King Charles of Navarre raises up in bed (fol. 196v).[131]

        line 4004   End

        Total number of miniatures for *Confort*:

Vg 39		Pm 5	(21 missing)
J 2		F 27	
K 0	(1 missing)	E 4	
A 26			

i. Le Dit de la Fonteinne Amoureuse [132]

        line 1
Vg91   *Ci commence le Dit de la Fonteinne Amoureuse* [Here begins the Poem of the Fountain of Love]. The narrator sits before the Fountain of Love (fol. 197a).
J18   *Ci commence le Livre de la Fontainne Amoureuse.* Beside the fountain, Paris kneels and gives an apple to one of three ladies (Venus); a man with bird perched on his hand looks on (fol. 118r).
[K   lacuna]
A78   *Le Livre de la Fonteinne Amoureuse.* Guillaume sits at his desk writing in a book (cf. miniature A3, chap. 4.4a) (fol. 154a).[133]
Pm51   The narrator sits at his desk, writing in a book (fol. 102a).

---

[128] Reproduction in Anton 1967, plate 5 fig. 8.
[129] Color reproduction in Cerquiglini 1987a, 28.
[130] Reproduction in Anton 1967, plate 5 fig. 9.
[131] This miniature is placed directly before the twenty-six-line coda supposedly composed by the king of Navarre.
[132] Huot (1987, 293–301) discusses aspects of the iconography of *Fonteinne* in MS A.
[133] Huot (1987, 284 n. 7) notes Guillaume's portrayal as a professional writer.

F62   *Ci commence le Dit de la Fonteinne Amoureuse.* Guillaume looking at the Fountain of Love (fol. 119v).

E22   *Cy commance le Livre Morpheus* [Here begins the Book of Morpheus]. The narrator sits writing at a long desk; a pen case and ink well are visible on the desk (fol. 83r).

line 55

Vg92   The lover lying in bed, dreaming; his lady stands at the foot of the bed (fol. 197b).
A79   Guillaume asleep in his bed chamber (fol. 154b).
Pm52   The narrator in his bed, trying to sleep (fol. 102b).
F63   Guillaume on his bed (fol. 120r).

line 235 [before *Complainte d'amant*]

Vg93   *Vecy la Compleinte de l'Amant* [Here is the *complainte* of the lover]. The lover laments, as his lady stands behind him on the right (fol. 198v).[134]
A80   *La Complainte de l'Amant.* Guillaume sitting in his chamber taking dictation of the *complainte* from the lover, who stands outside (fol. 155v).[135]
[Pm   lacuna]
F64   Guillaume walking in a forest with his arms crossed. Coat of arms used as a decorative background (fol. 121r).

line 539 [ll. 543–698: Ceyx and Alcyone]

Vg94   Ceyx drowned in the sea (fol. 200c).
A81   The lover despondent (fol. 157c).[136]
Pm53   The lover despondent (fol. 104r).
F65   Queen Alcyone stands yawning beside her bed. Coat of arms used as a decorative background (fol. 122c).

line 555

Vg95   Alcyone kneels in prayer before Queen Juno (fol. 200d).
F66   Alcyone kneels in prayer before Queen Juno (fol. 122c).

line 571

Vg96   Iris (an angel) kneels before the god of Sleep (a king) (fol. 200d).
A82   King Ceyx drowned in the sea; Queen Alcyone kneels in prayer before Juno (fol. 157d).[137]
Pm54   King Ceyx drowned in the sea; Queen Alcyone kneels in prayer before Queen Juno (fol. 104c).
F67   Iris (an angel) kneels before Juno and Alcyone (fol. 122d).

line 587

Vg97   Iris flies over the house of the god of Sleep (fol. 201a).
J19   *Le massage Venus fait au Dieu de Sommeil* [The message Venus delivers to the god of Sleep]. The god of Sleep asleep on the grass (fol. 122r).
K10   *Du Dieu de someil et de sa couche* [On the god of Sleep and his bed]. The god of Sleep asleep on the grass (fol. 110v [79v]).
A83   Iris (an angel) hovers over Queen Alcyone, asleep on her bed (fol. 158a).[138]
Pm55   Iris (an angel) hovers over Queen Alcyone, asleep on her bed (fol. 104d).
F68   Iris (an angel) flies over a lake (fol. 122d).

line 603

Vg98   Iris kneels before a dozing god of Sleep as his children look on (fol. 201a).
A84   Iris flies over the god of Sleep, who is sleeping in a castle next to a stream (fol. 158b).[139]

---

[134] Page reproduced in Maekawa 1988, plate 8.

[135] Reproductions in Huot 1987, 295 fig. 31 (discussed pp. 284 n. 7, 294, 296); Wimsatt 1991b, plate 16.

[136] Reproduction in Loomis 1965, plate 45.

[137] Reproduction in Loomis 1965, plate 45.

[138] Reproductions in Loomis 1965, plate 46; Poirion 1971, plate 23; S.J. Williams 1977, 463.

[139] Reproductions in Loomis 1965, plate 46; Poirion 1971, plate 23; S.J. Williams 1977,

Pm56   =Pm55, a closer view (fol. 104d).
F69   Iris in the bedroom of the god of Sleep (a king), who lies asleep (fol. 123a).

        line 619
Vg99   The god of Sleep asleep in his bed as his children fly overhead (fol. 201b).
A85   The god of Sleep sits on his bed, half asleep (fol. 158b).[140]
Pm57   The god of Sleep sits on his bed, half asleep (fol. 105a).
F70   The god of Sleep awakens to see Iris; his children are under the bed (fol. 123a).

        line 651
Vg100   Morpheus kneels before his father, the god of Sleep (fol. 201c).
A86   Morpheus comes to the sleeping Alcyone as the ghost of King Ceyx (fol. 158d).[141]
Pm58   Morpheus comes to the sleeping Alcyone as the ghost of King Ceyx (fol. 105b).
F71   The god of Sleep sits on his bed talking to Morpheus (fol. 123b).

        line 667
Vg101   Morpheus, as the ghost of Ceyx, kneels before Queen Alcyone, who is in bed (fol. 201d).
A87   Ceyx and Alcyone stand by the sea and watch two sea birds flying above the water (fol. 158d).[142]
Pm59   Ceyx and Alcyone stand by the sea and watch two sea birds flying above the water (fol. 105v).
F72   Morpheus, as the ghost of Ceyx in a boat, floats next to Queen Alcyone, who is in bed (fol. 123v).

        line 881
A88   The lover places an opium poppy nightcap on the head of the god of Sleep, who sits dozing on his soft feather bed [ll. 807–9] (fol. 159v).
Pm60   The lover places an opium poppy nightcap on the head of the god of Sleep, who sits dozing on his bed (fol. 106r).
F73   The lover kneels paying homage to the god of Love (fol. 124r).[143]

        line 1075
Vg102   A man with a hunting bird speaks to narrator (fol. 204r).
A89   A man with a hunting bird shows Guillaume the entry to the lover's chamber (fol. 161v).
Pm61   The lover with a hunting bird shows Guillaume the entry to the lover's chamber (fol. 108a).
F74   A man with a hunting bird perched on his arm presents Guillaume to the lover in his bed chamber (fol. 125c).

        line 1135
Vg103   A friend kneeling before the lover presents him with a horse, a sparrow hawk, and a dog (fol. 204v).
A90   A friend aided by a young page presents a horse, a sparrow hawk, and a dog to the lover; Guillaume is behind, with the castle and two courtiers off to the side (fol. 162r).
Pm62   A friend aided by a young page presents a horse, a sparrow hawk, and a dog to the lover (fol. 108b).
F75   A friend kneeling before the lover presents him with a horse, a sparrow hawk, and a dog (fol. 125d).

        line 1205
Vg104   The narrator takes the kneeling lover by the hand (fol. 205r).

---

[140] Reproductions in Loomis 1965, plate 46; Poirion 1971, plate 23; S.J. Williams 1977, 465. 466.

[141] Reproduction in Loomis 1965, plate 47.

[142] Reproduction in Loomis 1965, plate 47.

[143] Color reproduction in Cerquiglini 1987a, 41.

line 1313

J20 *La maniere et les contenances de la fontaine* [The appearance and the countenances of the fountain]. Helen and Paris aboard a boat (cf. *Confort*, chap. 4.4h, miniatures to l. 2683) (fol. 127r).

[K lacuna]

A91 Guillaume and the lover stand beside the Fountain of Love (fol. 163r).

Pm63 Guillaume and the lover stand beside the Fountain of Love (fol. 109c).[144]

F76 Guillaume and the lover stand before the Fountain of Love (fol. 126v).

line 1333

Vg105 Knights on horseback, fighting with swords (the combat between Achilles and Hector) (fol. 206a).

A92 A detail of the Fountain shows the mythological figures carved on it (fol. 163c).

Pm64 A detail of the Fountain shows the mythological figures carved on it (fol. 109d).[144]

F77 Guillaume and the lover stand before the Fountain of Love; a twelve-headed serpent is visible on the fountain (fol. 127a).

line 1371

Vg106 The lover and the narrator sit beside the Fountain of Love (fol. 206b).

A93 The Fountain Love with its mythological figures, surrounded by trees (fol. 163d).

Pm65 The Fountain Love with its mythological figures, surrounded by trees (fol. 110r).[144]

F78 The lover and Guillaume sit by the Fountain of Love, which is again depicted with the serpent (fol. 127b).

E23 *Comment l'amant et l'amy regardent la fontaine* [How the lover and the Friend look at the fountain]. The lover and the narrator stand beside the Fountain of Love (fol. 86v).

line 1511

Vg107 The narrator hands a scroll (with the *Complainte d'amant*) to the lover (fol. 207r).

A94 The lover talks to Guillaume (fol. 164v).

Pm66 The lover talks to Guillaume (fol. 110v).[144]

F79 The lover receives the *Complainte d'amant* from Guillaume (fol. 128r).

line 1609

Vg108 The lover and the narrator asleep next to the fountain; in their dream, Venus looks on (fol. 208r).

A95 Guillaume and the lover (lying against Guillaume and covered by Guillaume's robe) asleep beside the Fountain of Love (fol. 165v).

Pm67 Guillaume kneeling beside the fountain; the lover is asleep, leaning against him (fol. 111v).[144]

F80 Guillaume and the lover (lying against Guillaume and covered by Guillaume's robe) asleep beside the Fountain of Love; in their dream, Venus (queen), holding the golden apple, is accompanied by the Beloved (fol. 128v).

line 1715 [ll. 1633–2144: Wedding of Peleus and Thetis, Judgement of Paris][145]

Vg109 Discord stands before three seated goddesses (Minerva, Juno, and Venus) (fol. 208v).

A96 Four queens (Minerva, Juno, Venus, and a sibyl) sit at a table; Discord displays the golden apple, labeled *"a la plus bele"* [to the most beautiful] (fol. 166r).

Pm68 Three queens (Minerva, Juno, and Venus) sit at a table; Discord displays the golden apple, labeled *"a la plus belle."* (fol. 112r).

F81 Three queens (Minerva, Juno, and Venus) sit at a table; Discord holds the golden apple as a courtier looks on (fol. 129r).

line 1851

Vg110 The three goddesses stand before Paris, a shepherd with his sheep (fol. 209v).

A97 Vergil hung from a tower in a basket by the daughter of the emperor; two men stand behind her with torches, one of whom is setting fire to her dress (fol. 167r).

---

[144] Written instructions for the illuminator to the left of the frame of the miniature.

[145] Ehrhart (1990, 136) discusses this scene; in n. 14 (p. 152), she compares the banquet to a similar scene in *Remede* (miniature C40, chap. 4.4e).

[**Pm** lacuna]

F82 Mercury offers the golden apple to Paris, who is holding a bow and surrounded by cows and sheep; the three queens, Minerva, Juno, and Venus, stand behind Mercury (fol. 129v).[146]

line 2125

Vg111 Paris speaks to the three goddesses (fol. 211r).

A98 Paris, with a dog on a leash, gives an apple labeled "*pulchriori dei*" [to the more beautiful god] to Venus, as Minerva and Juno look on (all three are dressed as queens) (fol. 169a).

Pm69 Paris, with a club in his hand and a dog on a leash, gives the apple to Venus, as Minerva and Juno look on (fol. 113v).[147]

F83 Paris gives the apple labeled "*belle*" to Venus as the other two goddesses watch (fol. 131a).

line 2145

Vg112 The lover asleep on the right as Venus talks to the narrator (fol. 211v).

A99 Guillaume and the lover asleep beside the Fountain of Love (fol. 169a).

Pm70 Guillaume and the lover asleep beside a spring (fol. 114a).[148]

F84 Venus, holding the hand of the Beloved, approaches the sleeping lover (fol. 131b).

line 2207 [before the *Confort de l'Amant et de la Dame*]

Vg113 [fol. 211v:] *Le Confort de Venus et de la dame* [Poem of Comfort of Venus and the lady]. Venus and the Beloved talk to the seated lover (fol. 212r).

A100 *Le Confort de l'Amant et de la Dame* [The Poem of Comfort of the lover and the lady]. The Beloved, accompanied by Venus, speaks to the lover by the Fountain of Love (fol. 169v).

Pm71 The Beloved, accompanied by Venus, speaks to the lover by the spring (fol. 114b).[148]

F85 *Le Confort de Venus. Et de la Dame.* The Beloved, seated before the lover, holds his hand; Venus stands behind her (fol. 131v).

E24 *Comment Venus et la dame reconfortent l'amant* [How Venus and the lady comfort the lover]. Venus (queen), with an apple in her hand, stands holding the hand of the Beloved beside the Fountain of Love; they observe the lover asleep across the lap of the narrator (fol. 89r).[149]

line 2527 [after the *Confort de l'Amant et de la Dame*]

Vg114 The narrator and the lover at the fountain; the lover washes his hands (fol. 214r).

F86 Guillaume and the lover wash their hands at the fountain (fol. 133r).

line 2745

Vg115 A Knight kneels before the narrator and the lover (fol. 215c).

A101 Guillaume and the lover seated on either side of the Fountain of Love (fol. 173a).

Pm72 Guillaume and the lover seated next to the Fountain of Love (fol. 117v).

F87 A knight kneels before Guillaume and the lover (fol. 134r).

E25 *Commant l'amy conforte l'amant* [How the Friend comforts the lover]. The narrator and the lover sit next to the Fountain of Love (fol. 90v).

line 2789

Vg116 The narrator watches as the lover gives money to the poor (fol. 215d).

A102 The lover, with two other men in a boat, bids farewell to Guillaume, who remains on the shore on horseback (fol. 173b).

[**Pm** lacuna]

F88 Guillaume and the lover arrive on horseback by the sea (fol. 134v).

---

[146] Reproduction in Ehrhart 1987, 217 fig. 6 (discussed p. 224).

[147] Written instructions for the illuminator to the left of the frame of the miniature. Brief mention of the iconography in Ehrhart 1987, 224.

[148] Written instructions for the illuminator to the left of the frame of the miniature.

[149] Color reproduction on cover of Cerquiglini-Toulet 1993d.

line 2848   End

Total number of miniatures for *Fonteinne*:   **V g** 26   **P m** 22
                                                      J   3   **F**   27
                                                      K   1   **E**   4
                                                      A   25

j. *Le Dit de la Harpe* [150]

line 1

Vg117 *Ci commence le Dit de la Harpe* [Here begins the Poem of the Harp]. The narrator
           sits playing a harp (fol. 216r).
A103   [fol. 173v:] *Ci apres commence le Dit de la Harpe*. King David plays a harp before a
           lady (fol. 174a).
[Pm   lacuna]
F89   *Ci commence le Dit de la Harpe*. A lover plays a harp for his lady (fol. 135a).[151]
E30   *Cy commence le Dit de la Herpe*. A young lady plays a harp outdoors next to a
           spring; birds are in the trees behind her (fol. 105r).[152]

line 31

A104   Orpheus plays his harp for Eurydice, who is held by three devils coming from the
           gates of hell (cf. miniature A75, chap. 4.4h) (fol. 174b).
[Pm   lacuna]
F90   Orpheus plays his harp for Eurydice, who is held by two devils coming from the
           gates of hell (cf. miniature F57, chap. 4.4h) (fol. 135a).

line 83

F91   King David plays a harp (fol. 135c).
Pm73   [in the middle of the page, between the columns of text[153]] King David plays a harp
           as God looks down from heaven (fol. 118r).

line 111

A105   King David plays a harp for God, who is seated with a halo and a ball-shaped scepter
           (fol. 74v).[154]
Pm74   Three men stand accusingly before a lady (fol. 118b).
F92   A crowned lady being accused by two courtiers (fol. 135c).

line 129

A106   A lady avoided by three gentlemen (fol. 175a).
Pm75   A knight on horseback (fol. 118c).
F93   A man with a whip riding a horse with ornamental trappings (fol. 135d).

line 143

A107   A knight on a horse with ornamental trappings (fol. 175a).
Pm76   Meekness (*Debonnaireté*) and her sister Humility (*Humilité*) (fol. 118c).
F94   Meekness plays a harp for her sister Humility (fol. 135d).

line 157

A108   Meekness and her sister Humility (fol. 175b).
Pm77   Honesty (*Honesté*) and her sister Truth (*Verité*) (fol. 118d).
F95   Honesty and her sister Truth shake hands (fol. 136a).

---

[150] Huot (1987, 286–93) discusses the iconography of *Harpe* in MS A. For MS **F-G**, see
     Huot 1987, 292 n. 10.
[151] Color reproduction in Cerquiglini 1987a, 18.
[152] Reproductions in Droz/Thibault 1924, facing p. 13; Besseler 1931, 139.
[153] Miniature **Pm73** is catalogued in Ford 1988, 22 as item 640[52]. Note that the miniatures
     in MS A have become out of sequence, an error corrected in this unusual manner in MS
     Pm (on the location of this miniature in **Pm**, and the omission of a comparable
     miniature in **A**, see Maekawa 1985, 42 n. 104).
[154] Erasure of an earlier sketch is apparent.

line 165

A109   Honesty and her sister Truth (fol. 175b).

Pm78   Charity (*Charité*) and her sister Sweet Pity (*Douce Pité*) hand out alms to the poor (fol. 118d).

F96   Charity and her sister Sweet Pity hand out bread from a basket to beggars. Elements of an unidentified coat of arms form the decorative background (fol. 136a).

line 175

A110   Charity and her sister Sweet Pity hand out bread to the poor and infirm (fol. 175c).[155]

Pm79   Youth (*Jeunesse*) holds Diversion (*Deduit*) and Joy (*Leësse*) by the hands (fol. 119a).

F97   Youth holds Diversion and Joy by the hands (fol. 136b).

line 187

A111   Youth holds Diversion and Joy by the hands (fol. 175c).[155]

Pm80   Peace (*Pais*), Health (*Santé*), Wealth (*Richesse*), and Youth hold hands (all look the same) (fol. 119a).

F98   An old man walking with a crutch (fol. 136b).

line 197

A112   Peace, Health, and Wealth admire Youth (fol. 175d).[155]

Pm81   Nobility (*Noblesse*), with a hunting bird perched on his hand, stands next to his siblings Sincerity (*Franchise*) and Gentility (*Gentillesse*) (one male, the other female) (fol. 119b).

F99   Nobility, Sincerity and Gentility; one plays a harp (fol. 136c).

line 207

A113   Nobility, with a hunting bird perched on his hand, stands next to his sisters Sincerity and Gentility (fol. 175d).[155]

Pm82   Wealth and her sister Generosity (*Largesse*); one offers a piece of money to the other (fol. 119b).

F100   Wealth and her sister Generosity hold hands (fol. 136c).

line 221

A114   Wealth and her sister Generosity (fol. 176a).

Pm83   Simplicity (*Simplesse*), Fear of Wrongdoing (*Doubtance de meffaire*), Shame (*Honte*), and Love (*Amour*) hold hands (fol. 119c).

F101   Love kneels before Simplicity, Fear of Wrongdoing, Shame, and Trust (fol. 136c).

line 233

A115   Simplicity, Fear of Wrongdoing, Shame, and Love (fol. 176b).

Pm84   Prudence (*Avis*), Knowledge (*Congnoissance*), Grace (*Grace*), Behavior (*Maintieng*), and Decency (*Maniere*) hold hands (fol. 119d).

F102   A man plays a harp before Prudence, Knowledge, Grace, Behavior, and Decency (fol. 136d).

line 285

A116   The narrator's beloved seated on a throne (fol. 176v).

Pm85   The narrator's beloved seated on a throne (fol. 120r).

F103   Guillaume kneels before his lady (fol. 137r).[156]

line 354   End

Total number of miniatures for *Harpe*:   A   14   V g   1
                                             Pm 13   E   1
                                             F   15

---

[155] Reproduction in Huot 1987, 289 fig. 30.
[156] Huot (1987, 292 n. 10) discusses Marian associations.

k. Le Livre dou Voir Dit [157]

line 1 (all line numbers refer to the edition P. Paris 1875)

A119   Ci commence le Livre dou Voir Dit [Here begins the Book of the True Story]. The messenger kneels and doffs his hat as he hands Guillaume a letter marked "a Guillem" [to Guillaume], who sits outdoors on a cushion (fol. 221r).

Pm87   [fol. 121v:] Ci commence le Livre dou Voir Dit. The messenger kneels as he hands a letter to Guillaume, who sits outdoors on a cushion (fol. 122r).

F104   Ci commence le Livre du Voir Dit. Guillaume and the messenger converse out of doors. Elements of an unidentified coat of arms form the decorative background (fol. 137v).

E32   Cy commance le Livre du Voir Dit. The messenger hands a letter to the narrator (here dressed in blue with a skullcap), who reclines in an enclosed garden (fol. 171r).

line 169 [before the rondeau Celle qui unques ne vous vid (VD1)]

F105   Rondel. la dame. The messenger kneels as he hands a letter to Guillaume (fol. 138v).

line 315 [after the rondeau Tres-belle, riens ne m'abelist (VD2)]

A120   L'amant. The messenger bids farewell to Guillaume (fol. 223v).

Pm88   The messenger, holding a spear, bids farewell to Guillaume (fol. 124r).

F106   [fol. 139r:] L'amant. The messenger bids farewell to Guillaume, who holds an open letter (fol. 139v).

line 571 [before the ballade Pleurez, dames (VD5=Lo229=B32)]

F107   L'amant. Balade et y a chant. Guillaume lies on his bed, handing his testament (the ballade) to the messenger (fol. 141r).

line 637 [after the rondeau Celle qui nuit et jour desire (VD7)]

A121   L'amant. Guillaume on his bed receives a letter marked "a Guillaum" from the messenger (fol. 227r).

Pm89   Guillaume in his bed receives a letter from the messenger (fol. 126v).

F108   Guillaume reads a letter in bed as the messenger stands beside it (fol. 142r).

line 1003 [after Letter 4[158]]

A122   Guillaume and two other men on horseback (fol. 230v).

Pm90   Guillaume and two other men on horseback (fol. 129r).

F109   L'amant. Guillaume on horseback (fol. 144v).

line 1228 [after Letter 6[159]]

A123   L'amant. The messenger hands a letter marked "a ma dame" [to my lady] to Toute Belle (fol. 233r).

Pm91   The messenger hands a letter to Toute Belle (fol. 131a).

F110   Toute Belle beside her bed, reading a letter; a maidservant stands behind her (fol. 146c).

line 1250 [before complainte Mes dous amis a vous (VD15)]

A124   La dame. Complainte. Toute Belle seated on her bed lamenting (fol. 233v).

Pm92   Complainte. Toute Belle seated on her bed lamenting (fol. 131b).

F111   La dame. Complainte. Toute Belle stands beside her bed lamenting; a maidservant stands in the doorway (fol. 146d).

line 1384 [Guillaume takes the portrait of Toute Belle and places it above his bed][160]

A125   The messenger hands Guillaume a portrait of Toute Belle (fol. 235v).[161]

---

[157] Huot (1987, 280–86) discusses aspects of the iconography of the Voir Dit.

[158] Printed out of order as Letter 6 in P. Paris 1875.

[159] Printed out of order as Letter 2 in P. Paris 1875.

[160] On the iconography of the image (portrait or statue?), see Cerquiglini 1985b, 204–5 and 273 s.v. "Ymage."

[161] Reproduction in Van Buren 1986b, 100 (incorrectly identified as fol. 291r); she comments: "consequently, the miniatures, illustrating a text that specifically says the

Pm93 The messenger hands Guillaume a portrait of Toute Belle (fol. 132v).

F112   Guillaume kneels beside his bed, hands clasped in supplication before the statue of
        Toute Belle, standing at the head of the bed (fol. 148r).[162]

        line 1503 [after Letter 10]

A126   Guillaume and his companions on horseback approach the gate of a walled city (fol.
        237r).

Pm94 Three men on horseback approach a castle (cf. miniature A122) (fol. 133v).

F113   L'amant. Guillaume on horseback approaches a church (fol. 149r).

        line 2245

A127   Guillaume sits before Toute Belle writing a ballade with music, labeled "balade" (fol.
        242r).[163]

Pm95 Guillaume sits before Toute Belle writing a ballade (fol. 138r).

F114   Guillaume's secretary holds a leaf out towards Guillaume, who is seated under a tree
        with Toute Belle asleep across his lap (fol. 153r).[164]

        line 2623 [after the rondeau Sans cuer, de moi (VD32)]

A128   L'amant. Guillaume looking out of a church as Toute Belle and two female com-
        panions approach on horseback (fol. 245r).[165]

Pm96 Guillaume stands at the door of a church holding a book as Toute Belle and two
        female companions approach on horseback (fol. 140v).

F115   L'amant. Guillaume's secretary informs Guillaume, who stands surprised by an altar
        in the church, of the arrival of Toute Belle and another lady on horseback (fol.
        155r).[166]

        line 2891 [after the rondeau Trembler, fremir et muer me couvient (VD41)]

A129   L'amant. Guillaume, his secretary, and Toute Belle sit next to each other outdoors
        (fol. 248r).

Pm97 Guillaume and Toute Belle seated outdoors holding hands, with the secretary behind
        in the middle (fol. 143r).

F116   The messenger peeks at Toute Belle and Guillaume, who are sitting far apart on a
        bench (fol. 157v).[167]

        line 3712 [before the priere Venus, je t'ay tousjours servi]

F117   Guillaume kneels at the end of a bed and begins to pray; Toute Belle lies nude in the
        bed, while her cousin Guillemette stands to the side. Elements of an unidentified coat
        of arms form the decorative background (fol. 162c).[168]

        line 3760 [Directly after the prière, Venus envelopes the lovers in a fragrant fog]

A130   Venus, dressed as a queen, envelops Guillaume and Toute Belle, who are lying next
        to each other on a bed, in a blue cloud (fol. 255r).[169]

[Pm   lacuna]

F118   L'amant. Guillaume embraces Toute Belle under a tree; Venus, dressed as queen,

---

portrait was a likeness, may cause us to revise the prevailing view that the first painted
portraits in France were limited to profile heads or busts."

[162] Color reproduction in Cerquiglini 1987a, 117.

[163] Reproduction and discussion in Kügle 1991, 353. This scene is also discussed in
Cerquiglini 1985b, 216 and Huot 1987, 284. There is a diplomatic facsimile of the
miniature in P. Paris 1875, 94, misplaced twenty lines too late in the text.

[164] Color reproduction in Cerquiglini 1987a, 70.

[165] Reproduction and discussion in Kügle 1991, 378.

[166] Color reproduction on cover of the sound recording Erato STU 71303 (see chap. 8.8).

[167] Color reproduction in Cerquiglini 1987a, 19.

[168] Color reproduction in Cerquiglini 1987a, 94.

[169] On the iconography of this important scene, see the comments of Cerquiglini in
Guillaume de Machaut 1982, 137 and Huot 1987, 285–86. There is a diplomatic facsimile of the miniature in P. Paris 1875, 158, misplaced to a slightly later position in
the text.

looks down from the heavens (fol. 162d).[170]

line 3947 [after the rondeau *Merveille fu quant mon cuer ne parti* (VD46)]

F119   *L'amant.* Machaut meets Hope with her entourage—Measure, Temperance, Good Advice and Friend's Comfort—all on horseback (fol. 164r).

line 4362 [after the lai *Longuement me sui tenus* (VD47=L18)]

A131   *L'amant.* Guillaume and two men meet Hope and her entourage, all on horseback; Hope and Guillaume touch hands (fol. 259v).

[Pm   lacuna]

F120   *L'amant.* Guillaume hands a letter to the messenger. Unidentified coat of arms (fol. 166r).

line 4563 [after Letter 26, before the story of Queen Semiramis[171]]

A132   *Vostre loyal amie* (added in grey ink, by a different scribe). A messenger speaks to Queen Semiramis on her throne (fol. 264r).[172]

Pm98   A messenger holding a spear speaks to Queen Semiramis on her throne (fol. 154r).

F121   *L'amant.* A messenger with a spear kneels before Queen Semiramis, who stands behind her bed; three courtiers look on (fol. 169r).[173]

line 4814 [after the ballade *Puis que tant a languir hai* (VD51)]

A133   A messenger hands Guillaume a letter marked "*a Guil*" (fol. 267v).

Pm99   A messenger hands Guillaume a letter (fol. 156r).

F122   *L'amant.* Guillaume stands with an open box. Unidentified coat of arms. (fol. 171r).

line 4910 [before the dream in which the portrait of Toute Belle has turned its head away and has dressed in green]

F123   Guillaume sleeping; in his dream, the statue of Toute Belle standing by the foot of the bed has its back turned to him (fol. 172a).[174]

line 4990 [after the scene with the game of "le Roi qui ne ment" is described; Guillaume is about to question the king][175]

A134   *Le roy qui ne ment* [the king who does not lie]. A king talks to five people (fol. 268v).

Pm100 *Le roy qui ne ment.* A king talks to a group of eight people (fol. 157r).

F124   Guillaume kneels before a king and his entourage. Unidentified coat of arms (fol. 172b).

line 5124

F125   Guillaume kneels before a king (fol. 173r).[176]

line 5244

F126   *Le roy respont* [The king replies]. The king speaks to Guillaume, who kneels before him. Unidentified coat of arms (fol. 173v).

line 5468 [after the dream; Guillaume awakens to find that the portrait has not turned its head away]

A135   *L'amant.* The king talks to Guillaume (fol. 271v).

---

[170] Color reproduction in Cerquiglini 1987a, 80.

[171] On Semiramis, see Cerquiglini 1985b, 149 n. 24. Byrne (1984) associates a court scene in the Berlin Kupferstichkabinett with this moment in the *Voir Dit*, and identifies the artist as the Master of the *Remede de Fortune*. The Berlin fragment includes two scenes: on the left an older man and a young lady; on the right a messenger and a woman combing her hair. See the discussion above, chap. 4.2, commentary to table 4.1.

[172] The number "ix" is visible beside the miniature. Reproduction in Byrne 1984, 80.

[173] Written instructions to the artist below col. a (Maekawa 1985, 281). Cf. below, miniature F125.

[174] Color reproduction in Cerquiglini 1987a, 40.

[175] On the game of "le Roi qui ne ment," see Green 1990; the game is also depicted in the *Remede,* miniatures C13 and Vg11.

[176] Hairline writing below col. a: "Ung roy assis et Machaut [!] a genoulx devant li" [a king seated and Machaut kneeling before him]. Cf. Maekawa 1985, 42 n. 104.

Pm101   The king talks to Guillaume (fol. 160r).
F127   [fol. 175r:] *L'amant*. Guillaume kneels beside his bed, hands clasped in supplication before the statue of Toute Belle, standing at the head of the bed; the messenger stands at the door (cf. miniature F112) (fol. 174v).

line 5536 [after Letter 31, before the *complainte Dous amis* (VD53)]
A136   *L'amant*. Toute Belle sits on her bed lamenting (fol. 274v).
Pm102   Toute Belle sits on her bed lamenting, her right hand on her heart (fol. 161r).
F128   *L'amant*. Toute Belle sits on her bed lamenting. Unidentified coat of arms (fol. 176v).[177]

line 5907 [Assassination of Julius Caesar[178]; after the *complainte Dame en qui j'ay mis toute m'esperance* (VD55)]
A137   Three men with knives attack and kill Caesar as another man looks on (fol. 278r).[179]
[Pm   lacuna]
F129   *L'amant*. Guillaume gives a letter to the messenger kneeling before him (fol. 179r).

line 6063 [ll. 6063–66: Hero and Leander]
A138   Leander, swimming nude in the Dardanelles, approaches Hero, who observes from a tower (fol. 281v).[179]
[Pm   lacuna]
F130   Guillaume dictates to his secretary, who is writing. Unidentified coat of arms (fol. 181r).[180]

line 7070 [ll. 7070–221: Acis and Galatea][181]
A139   From the shore, Polyphemus sinks a ship sailing on the sea (fol. 285v).[182]
[Pm   lacuna]
F131   From the shore, Polyphemus uses a hook to tip a boat with Acis and Galatea aboard (fol. 184r).

line 7292 [Illustration of the speech of the first *losengier*]
A140   *L'ymage de vraie Amour* [The portrait of True Love]. A barefooted Amour, dressed in green, points to his heart. Banderoles label the head: *hiens et estas* [*sic*; winter and summer], heart: *longe et prope* [far and near], and feet: *mors et vita* [death and life] (fol. 289r).[183]
Pm103   Amour, dressed in green. Banderoles label his head: *hiens et esta,* abdomen: *longe et prope,* and the hem of his cassock: *mors et vita* (fol. 168v).
F132   *L'ymage de vraie Amour*. Amour dressed in green points to his heart, which is visible through an opening in his cassock. Elements of an unidentified coat of arms form the decorative background (fol. 186v).[184]
E33   *Comment li ancien paignoient l'ymage du Dieu d'Amours* [How the ancients painted the portrait of the god of Love]. The god of Love stands pointing to his heart; he wears a cassock with gold writing on it: *a mort et a vie* [in death and in life] (fol. 202v).

line 7616
A141   *Comment l'amant emprisonna l'image de Toute Bele* [How the lover imprisoned the portrait of Toute Belle].[185] Guillaume places the portrait of Toute Belle in a trunk

---

[177] Color reproduction in Cerquiglini 1987a, 58.
[178] On this scene, see Cerquiglini 1985b, 230 and 272 s.v. "Jules Cesar."
[179] Erasure of an earlier sketch is visible.
[180] Color reproduction in Cerquiglini 1987a, 8.
[181] This is a segment particularly poorly represented in the P. Paris 1875 edition; A. Thomas (1912) publishes a long omission.
[182] The number "xv" is visible beside the miniature. An erasure of an earlier sketch is visible; perhaps some figures were left out in the final version.
[183] Discussion in Huot 1987, 280–81.
[184] Color reproduction in Cerquiglini 1987a, 59.
[185] On the moment when Guillaume locks the portrait of Toute Belle in the trunk, see Cerquiglini 1985b, 231.

(fol. 291r).[186]

Pm104 [fol. 170r:] *Comme l'amant emprisonna l'ymage de Toute Belle*. Guillaume places the portrait of Toute Belle in a trunk (fol. 170v).

F133 *Comment l'amant emprisonna L'ymage de Toute Bele*. Guillaume locks a trunk. Elements of an unidentified coat of arms form the decorative background (fol. 188r).

line 7719 [Before the dream in which Toute Belle's portrait reproaches Guillaume for his suspicions]

A142 *Comment l'image de Toute Belle se complainte a l'amant* [How the portrait of Toute Belle complains to the lover]. The portrait of Toute Belle (fol. 293r).

Pm105 The portrait of Toute Belle weeping (fol. 171v).

F134 *Comment l'ymage de Toute Bele se complaint a l'amant*. Guillaume asleep in bed; the statue of Toute Belle standing at the foot of the bed wrings its hands (fol. 189c).[187]

line 7773 [ll. 7773–8110: The story of Apollo and Coronis[188]]

A143 *Comment li corbiaus blans fu muez en plume noire* [How the white raven was changed to black feathers]. A crow and a (white) raven face each other (fol. 293v).[189]

Pm106 *Comme li corbiaux blans fu mués en plume noire* [hairline]. A crow and a (white) raven face each other (fol. 172r).

F135 *Comment li corbiaus blans fu mues en plume noire*. Coronis and the page embrace as two black birds fly overhead (fol. 189d).[190]

line 7863 [intercalated story of how Pallas banished the crow[191]]

A144 [fol. 294a, before l. 7827:] *Comment la corneille reprist et chastia le corbel* [How the crow reproved and chastised the raven]. The crow spreads his wings before the raven (fol. 294v).

Pm107 =Pm106 (fol. 172v).

F136 A crow is perched in a tree; below, Aglauros opens a trunk, finding the two-faced child Erichthonius inside (fol. 190r).

line 8111

A145 A bearded Apollo shakes his finger reprovingly at the raven, which flies off (fol. 296r).

Pm108 Apollo claps his hands at the raven, which flies off (fol. 174r).

line 8147 [After the dream, Guillaume takes the portrait of Toute Belle out of the trunk]

F137 Guillaume asleep on his bed; the statue of Toute Belle stands at the foot of the bed (fol. 191v).

line 8179

A146 *Comment l'amant desprisonna l'image de Toute Belle* [How the lover freed the portrait of Toute Belle]. With the trunk opened, Guillaume holds the statue of Toute Belle (fol. 296v).

Pm109 With the trunk opened, Guillaume holds the portrait of Toute Belle (fol. 174v).

F138 *Comment l'amant desprisonna l'ymage de Toute Belle*. Guillaume opens the trunk; the statue of Toute Belle is seen lying inside (fol. 192r).

line 8239 [Guillaume compares Toute Belle to Lady Fortune][192]

J24 *Comment Titus Livius figure l'ymage de Fortune* [How Titus Livius describes the portrait of Fortune]. Lady Fortune stands in a large wheel, surrounded by three small wheels (fol. 147v).

K12 *Comment Titus Livius figure l'ymage de Fortune*. Lady Fortune stands in a large

[186] Diplomatic facsimile in P. Paris 1875, facing p. 309.

[187] Color reproduction in Cerquiglini 1987a, 29.

[188] On this example, see Calin 1974, 200; Cerquiglini 1985b, 152–55, 232–33.

[189] The number "xix" is visible beside the miniature.

[190] Color reproduction in Cerquiglini 1987a, 81.

[191] See the discussion in Cerquiglini 1985b, 152–54; Leupin 1986, 141–42.

[192] Cerquiglini (1985b, 62–63) comments on the size of the two miniatures of Fortune.

wheel, surrounded by three smaller wheels (fol. 133r [98r]).[193]

A147   [two-column, large format] *Comment Titus Livius descript l'ymage de Fortune*. Lady Fortune stands behind a large wheel that has four smaller wheels inside it; each wheel bears a Latin couplet, translating in verse what appears in French in the body of the *dit*. Large wheel: *Affluo, discedo, talis ludus cui me do* [I am abundant, I vanish; such is the trick I play on one]; smaller wheel, top left: *Vivens sum cara; dum mors accedit amara* [living I am dear; when death comes, bitter]; smaller wheel, bottom left: *Exceco mentem, ne diligat omnipotentem* [I blind the mind so that it should not love God]; smaller wheel, top right: *Ludo, compsallo, deludens carmine fallo* [I play and sing; deceiving with song I lead astray]; smaller wheel, bottom right: *Quid sum discerne, cum sciveris me fuge, sperne* [Recognize what I am; when you know, you will flee and spurn me] (fol. 297r).[194]

Pm110   [two-column, large format] *Comment Titus Livius descript l'ymage de Fortune* [hairline at top of miniature]. Lady Fortune (queen) stands behind a large wheel that has four smaller wheels inside it; her arms are laced through the four wheels, two in each arm. Each wheel bears a Latin inscription (fol. 175r).[195]

F139   [fol. 192r:] *Comment Tytus Livius descript L'ymage de Fortune*. Lady Fortune stands behind a large wheel that has four smaller wheels inside it; people at the side look on (fol. 192v).[196]

E34   [fol. 206r:] *Comment Tytus Lyvius descript l'ymage de Fortune*. Lady Fortune stands in a large wheel that has four smaller wheels inside it; each wheel bears a French inscription, taken from Machaut's text (fol. 206v).

line 8652 [The messenger describes Fortune and compares Guillaume to Fortune]

J25   *Comment les paiens contrefirent l'ymage de Fortune a .ii. visages* [How the pagans made the portrait of Fortune with two faces]. A two-faced Lady Fortune stands inside a large wheel (fol. 150r).[197]

K13   *Coment les paiens figurent l'ymage de Fortune*. A Lady Fortune with two faces stands inside a large wheel, holding it (fol. 135r [100r]).[198]

A148   [two-column, large format] *Comment li paien figuroient l'ymage de Fortune*. A two-faced Lady Fortune holds a large wheel; to the right, five maidens stand above five springs. A different hand has added Latin inscriptions to the bottom margin, translating what is given in French in the text: *Primum signum erat si aqua foncium inciperet movere* [the first sign was if the water of the springs began to move]; *Secundum si inciperet affluere* [the second if it began to flow]; *Tertium si inciperet tumestere* [the third if it began to swell]; *Quartum si inciperet clarescere* [the fourth if it began to clear]; *Quintum si inciperet totalo evanescere* [the fifth if it began totally to disappear] (fol. 301v).[199]

---

[193] Reproduction in Kurose 1977, 318 plate 140.

[194] The number "xxiii"(?) is visible beside the miniature. Reproductions in Patch 1927, facing p. 158, plate 8 (large wheel only; commentary p. 170 n. 2); Kurose 1977, 316 plate 138; Avril 1982a, fig. 10; Huot 1987, 282 fig. 29 (discussed pp. 280–81). The Latin couplets, given in P. Paris 1875, 334–35nn., must derive from Machaut (Avril 1982a, 131 nn. 44–45). Heinrichs (1994, 9 nn. 12–13) translates the French versions.

[195] Reproductions in Kurose 1977, 317 plate 139; Hoppin 1978b, 401; S.J. Williams 1987, 5; Avril 1982a, fig. 16. The Latin inscriptions are identical to those in MS A.

[196] Color reproduction in Cerquiglini 1987a, 98.

[197] Reproduction in Bossuat 1931, plate xxi no. 3, facing p. 368.

[198] Reproduction in Kurose 1977, 289 plate 112.

[199] The number "xviii"(?) appears beside the miniature. Avril (1982a, 131–32) indicated that the Latin inscriptions for miniatures A147 and A148 could not have been furnished by the illuminator, and that the exact indications must have been supplied by the author. Earp (1989, 486 n. 43) called attention to an error in the copying of the poem, a 32-line eye skip, that would seem to lessen the authority of MS A, but Avril has since found the missing text on a small swatch of parchment copied and decorated like MS A and presently bound in a volume of miscellaneous fragments (*F:Pn 11198*, fol. 26r; see chap. 3, MS [5a]).

Pm111 [two-column, large format] A two-headed Lady Fortune holds a large wheel; five maidens, each with a flower, stand beside five springs (fol. 178v).[200]

F140 *Comment li paien figuroient l'ymage de Toute Bele.*[201] A two-faced Lady Fortune holds a large wheel; five maidens, each holding a flower, stand beside five springs (fol. 195v).[202]

E35 [fol. 208r:] *Comment li paien figuroient l'ymage de Fortune.* Lady Fortune with two heads (male and female), stands behind a large wheel; five streams issue from the ground in front of the wheel (fol. 208v).

line 9037   End (according to the edition of P. Paris 1875)

Total number of miniatures for the *Voir Dit*:

J	2	**Pm**	22
K	2	**F**	37
A	30	**E**	4

l. *Le Dit de la Marguerite*

line 1

A118 [fol. 213r:] *Ci commence le Dit de la Marguerite* [Here begins the Poem of the Daisy]. A King (Pierre I de Lusignan, king of Cyprus) kneels before a lady seated on a hill; flowers are painted on her dress (fol. 213v).

Pm86 *Ci commence le Dit de la Marguerite* [hairline]. A King (Pierre I de Lusignan, king of Cyprus) kneels before a lady seated on a chair covered by a cloth painted with flowers; flowers are also painted on her dress and his robe (fol. 120v).

F141 *Ci commence le Dit de la Marguerite.* A noble lover offers a rose to a lady (fol. 198v).

Total number of miniatures for *Marguerite:*

A	1	**F**	1
Pm	1		

m. *Le Dit de la Rose*

line 1

A150 Guillaume finds a rose in the middle of a thorny bush (fol. 365v).[203]

Pm112 *Explicit le Livre du Voir Dit et commence le Dit de la Rose* [Here ends the Book of the True Story and begins the Poem of the Rose]. Guillaume finds a rose in the middle of a bush (fol. 182v).

Total number of miniatures for *Rose:*   **A**   1   **Pm**   1

n. *Vezci les biens que ma dame me fait*

line 1

A151 *Vezci les biens que ma dame me fait / pour amender moy m'onneur et mon fait* [Here are the good things my lady does for me to ameliorate my honor and condition]. A gentleman talks to a lady (fol. 366r).

Pm113 *Vecy les biens que ma dame m'a fait / Pour amender moy m'onneur et mon fait.* A lady seated on a cushion (fol. 183r).

Total number of miniatures for *Vezci les biens*:   **A**   1   **Pm**   1

o. *La Prise d'Alexandre*

line 1

Vg118 Christian knights descend from ships and attack a Saracen fortress (fol. 336r).

A149 [two-column format] *Ci commence li Livre de la Prise d'Alexandre* [Here begins the

---

[200] Reproduction in Kurose 1977, 326 plate 148.

[201] Cerquiglini (1985b, 151) discusses the rubricator's slip, substituting the name of Toute Belle for that of Fortune.

[202] Color reproduction in Cerquiglini 1987a, 99.

[203] Reproduction in Poirion 1971, plate 24; S.J. Williams 1977, 467.

Book of the Capture of Alexandria]. Christian knights descend from ships and attack a Saracen fortress (fol. 309r).[204]

G142 [two-column format] The goddess of Love and other allegorical characters (all represented as angels) in the presence of Pierre I de Lusignan (fol. 1r).

E36 *Cy commance la Prise d'Alexandre.* The birth of the king of Cyprus; the mother lies in bed and watches as two midwives bathe the baby in a wooden tub; a third lady speaks to the mother (fol. 213r).

line 5004

E37 *Comment les crestiens desploierent une baniere de Notre Dame* [How the Christians unfurled a banner of Our Lady]. A battle between Christian knights and Saracens; the knights hold a banner with the image of a queen (Notre Dame) and child (fol. 226v).

line 7896

E38 *Comment l'acort fu du roy de Chipre et de Lesparre* [How the king of Cyprus and Lesparre were reconciled]. Florimont, sire de Lesparre, kneels before the king of Cyprus and the Pope, who are seated beside each other; three other nobles stand off to the side (fol. 235v).

line 8886   End (according to the ed. of Mas Latrie 1877)

Total number of miniatures for the *Prise*:   V g   1   G   1
                                                A   1   E   3

p. *La Loange des Dames*

En haut penser (Lo1)

C92 Guillaume sits under a tree writing on a narrow scroll; four other scrolls are scattered on the ground[205] (fol. 121r).

Vg1 *Ci commencent les balades ou il n'a point de chant* [Here begin the ballades without music]. Guillaume (a tonsured clerk) sits at his writing desk, his hand on a book, looking out at the reader (cf. miniature G143) (fol. 1r).[206]

D1 *Ci commence le livre de mestre Guillaume de Loris* [Here begins the book of magister Guillaume de Lorris]. Guillaume sits reading a book from a lectern (fol. 1r).[207]

J1 *Ci commencent les Balades.* Guillaume, with his arms crossed, walks beside three trees (fol. 1r).

K1 *Ci commencent les balades. L'amant.* Guillaume, with his arms crossed, walks beside three trees (fol. 1r).

A117 *Les Balades ou il n'a point de chant.* Guillaume kneels with his hands joined in supplication before a lady seated on a hill. (cf. miniature A118, chap. 4.4l) (fol. 177v).[208]

G143 *Ci commence la Loange des Dames* [Here begins the Praise of Ladies]. Guillaume at his writing desk points to an open book (cf. miniature Vg1). Unidentified coat of

---

[204] Reproduction in Loomis 1965, plate 103.

[205] Reproductions in Wilkins 1972, facing p. 64; *Early Music* 5 (1977): 460; Huot 1987, 245 fig. 18 (discussed pp. 244–246).

[206] Reproductions in Maekawa 1988, plate 1; 1989b, 88 plate 5a. This miniature has a multi-lobed frame with tricolor border, similar to those in the miniatures reproduced in Avril 1978, plates 32–33 (cf. the miniature Vg44, at the beginning of *Alerion*). An entry in the 1417 inventory of the library of Aragon (Alós-Moner 1924, 397 no. 17, trans. Earp 1989, 478 n. 35) corresponds to this miniature.

[207] Color reproduction in Chailley 1972, 79; black-and-white reproductions in R. Cazelles 1947, facing p. 161; Douce 1948, facing p. 56 (no. 3); Wilkins 1972, frontispiece; Boorman 1977a, 496; Wilkins 1979, 10; Wimsatt 1991b, plate 3. It is significant that the name "Loris" appears added over an erasure.

[208] Reproduction in Wilkins 1972, facing p. 48; Boorman 1977a, 459. Maekawa (1985, 69–70) and L.W. Johnson (1990, 66) discuss the iconographic significance: this miniature in effect is a representation of the rubric *Loange des Dames*, first found in MS G.

arms (fol. 45r).[209]

[E   large initial only]

Mon cuer, qui mis en vous (Lo67)

Vg2   A nobleman talks to a lady (fol. 11r).[210]

D'un dous ueil vairs (Lo94)

Vg3   A nobleman with a bird perched on his hand stands before a lady (fol. 14r).[210]

Pluseurs se sont repenti (Lo109)

Vg4   A nobleman bows before a lady holding a dog (fol. 16r).[210]

Total number of miniatures for the *Loange*:

C	1	K	1
Vg	4	A	1
D	1	G	1
J	1		

q. *Complaintes*

Amours, tu m'as tant (Cp1)

Vg5   Guillaume, kneeling, offers a scroll to the god of Love, who holds his hand out to receive it (fol. 31r).

D2   [fol. 38r:] *Comme l'acteur se complaint au Dieu d'Amours et est a genouz devant lui* [How the author laments to the god of Love and is on his knees before him]. Guillaume kneels before the god of Love, who holds three arrows (fol. 38v).[211]

G144   *Ci commencent les complaintes* [Here begin the *complaintes*]. Guillaume kneels before the goddess of Love. Unidentified coat of arms (fol. 67r).

E2   *Complainte d'amant* [*Complainte* of the lover]. A man kneels before the god of Love (fol. 13r).

A toi, Hanri (Cp3)

Vg6   Guillaume and Henry stand before a castle (fol. 32v).

D3   *Comment l'acteur se complaint du temps qu'il voit* [How the author complains of the times he sees]. Guillaume gestures as he talks to a nobleman (Henry) (fol. 40v).

E3   *Complainte de Guillaume Machaut*. Guillaume kneels before Henry (fol. 13v).

Quant Ecuba vit (Cp4)

E4   *Complainte de dame* [*Complainte* of the lady]. A lady sits outside next to a fountain watching a white dog with a bone (fol. 14a).[212]

Mon cuer, m'amour (Cp6)

E5   *Complainte d'amant*. A lover kneels, hat doffed, before his lady (fol. 14b).[213]

Total number of miniatures for the *Complaintes*:

Vg	2	G	1
D	2	E	4

---

[209] Color reproduction in Cerquiglini 1987a, 9; black-and-white reproduction in Keitel 1977a, 471; *Early Music* 5 (1977): 461 (detail).

[210] Miniatures Vg2–4 fill in small blanks left by the lacking third strophes of some ballades. Two similar blanks later in the *Loange*, after Lo136 and Lo164, were left unfilled. Other Machaut manuscripts with the *Loange* leave the space for missing strophes blank. MS **W** [2] had a miniature filling a missing third strophe to Lo129, a ballade also defective in **C**.

[211] Reproduction in Wilkins 1977, 213.

[212] Color reproduction in B. and J. Cerquiglini 1984, 28.

[213] Color reproduction in B. and J. Cerquiglini 1984, 28.

r. Rondeaux in the *Loange des Dames*[214]

Gentils cuers, souveingne vous (Lo27)

E6   [fol. 15v:] *Cy apres commencent les rondeaux* [After this begin the rondeaux]. [fol. 16r:] *Rondiau.* A group of six people stand around a barrel, singing from a music scroll (cf. miniatures E31, chap. 4.4s, and A154, chap. 4.4t) (fol. 16r).[215]

Dit de la Fleur de lis et de la Marguerite

G only   Not illustrated (fol. 71v).

s. Lais[216]

Loyauté, que (L1)

C93   Loyalty, wearing a transparent scarf, stands dictating the lai to a man seated on the ground, who is writing on a scroll (fol. 165r).[217]

A152   A nobleman with his hands clasped together in a supplicating pose before his lady (cf. miniature A117, chap. 4.4p). The "L" of the word "Loyauté" provides the frame for the miniature (fol. 367r).[218]

G145   *Ci commence les lays* [Here begin the lais]. Guillaume sits at his writing desk writing the lai, whose text is visible in the book: "*Loyaute que point ne delay wet sans delay que fa* [*ce*]" (fol. 74r).[219]

E31   *Cy commencent les lays Guillaume de Machaut.* A group of five men standing in a garden, singing from a music book (fol. 107r).[220]

J'aim la flour (L2)

C94   A man walks between two flowery bushes (fol. 168v).[221]

Pour ce qu'on puist (L3)

C95   A man sits on the ground writing on a long scroll (fol. 170r).[222]

Aus amans (L4)

C96   A bearded man stands holding a long scroll before an audience of noblemen and ladies, one of whom gestures to the man holding the scroll (fol. 173r).[223]

Nuls ne doit (L5/4)

C97   A man stands next to a grove of trees (fol. 174r).

Par trois raisons (L6/5)

C98   A man stands pointing a finger at the beginning of the lai (fol. 176v).

Amours doucement (L7/6)

C99   A man stands next to a tree (fol. 179r).

Amis, t'amour (L10/7)

C100   A lady stands among flowers (fol. 181v).

---

[214] The rondeaux form a separate section in MS E only.

[215] Color reproduction on cover of *Early Music* 5/4 (Oct. 1977); black-and-white reproductions in Droz/Thibault 1924, facing p. 13; Besseler 1931, 126; Reese 1940, plate 8; Reaney 1952a, 1040; Komma 1961, 50; Wilkins 1972, facing p. 112; Keitel 1977a, 472; *New Grove* 1980, 14:376; Leech-Wilkinson 1990a, 229; Kügle 1991, 361 (with discussion); Wimsatt 1991b, plate 12; also discussed in Hoffmann-Axthelm 1991, 343.

[216] The iconography of the lais in MS C is discussed in Huot 1987, 260–72.

[217] Reproduction in Huot 1987, 261 fig. 22 (discussion of the scarf, p. 272).

[218] Reproduction in Wimsatt 1991b, plate 15.

[219] Reproduction in *MGG* 8 (1960), plate 73 (facing cols. 1409–10); Roussel 1967, 41 (caption in error). Discussion in Huot 1987, 301.

[220] Reproductions in Droz/Thibault 1924, facing p. 13; Besseler 1931, 129; Reaney 1952a, 1037; 1961, 124; Wimsatt 1991b, plate 14. Discussion in Huot 1987, 301.

[221] Reproduction in Huot 1987, 262 fig. 23 (discussed pp. 262–64).

[222] Reproduction in Huot 1987, 264 fig. 24 (discussed pp. 262–64).

[223] Reproduction in Huot 1987, 267 fig. 25 (discussed pp. 262–64).

Un mortel lay (L12/8)

C101   A bearded man looks with reproach towards a bush; the face of another man is visible in the bush (fol. 184r).[224]

J21   *Ci commence le Lay Mortel* [Here begins the Mortal Lai]. Orpheus plays the harp before the gates of hell (fol. 139v).

[K   lacuna]

Qui bien aimme (L22/16)

C102   A man and a lady converse (fol. 187r).[225]

J4   *Le Lay de Plour* [The Lai of Tears]. A lady dressed all in black, with a black hood, sits next to a black-draped coffin (fol. 45r).

[K   lacuna]

Ne say comment (L14/9)

C103   A lady stands among flowers; outside the frame of the miniature, to the right of the text residuum of the previous lai, a man holding a blue flower points to her (fol. 189r).

Se quanque Diex (L11)

C104   The inverse of miniature C103: a man stands among flowers holding a blue flower; outside the frame of the miniature, to the right of the right column of text, a lady points to him (fol. 191r).

Maintes fois (L13)

C105   A man stands before an audience of four ladies and a gentleman (fol. 192v).

On parle (L8)

C106   A man sits on the ground, writing on a long scroll; a lady observes from the tower of a castle (fol. 194v).[226]

Amours, se plus (L9)

C107   A lady stands before three other ladies, gesturing to them (fol. 196r).

J22   *Ci commence le Paradis d'Amours* [Here begins the Paradise of Love]. The god of Love talks to a lady (fol. 143r).

[K   lacuna]

Total number of miniatures for the lais: C   15   A   1
                                                             J   3   G   1

t. Motets

Quant en moy / Amour (M1)

A153   A group of men—clerics and nobles—stand around a wine barrel, drinking and singing from a music scroll (cf. miniature E6, chap. 4.4r) (fol. 414v).[227]

[G   Room was left for miniature, two staves entered instead] (fol. 102v).

Total number of miniatures for the motets: A   1

u. Ballades

S'Amours ne fait (B1)

A154   A couple embraces inside the "S" (a winged dragon) of the opening word of the first ballade, "S'Amours" (fol. 454r).[228]

G146   [fol. 133v:] *Ci commencent les balades notees* [Here begin the ballades with music]. A gentleman speaks to a lady (fol. 134r).

Total number of miniatures for the ballades: A   1   G   1

---

[224] Huot (1987, 265) identifies the man in the bush with the character *Mesdis* (Slander), who appears in the lai in strophe 1, l. 9.

[225] Huot (1987, 266) recalls the debate of the *Jugement Behaingne* in this connection.

[226] Reproduction in Huot 1987, 270 fig. 26 (discussed pp. 269–71).

[227] Reproductions in Wilson 1990b, 294; Kügle 1991, 361 (with important discussion); Wimsatt 1991b, plate 13. Discussion in Huot 1987, 300–301.

[228] Reproductions in Machabey 1960, 1391–92; S.J. Williams 1977, 462; Poirion 1971, plate 22.

v. Rondeaux

Dous viaire (R1)

G147 [fol. 149v:] *Ci commencent li Rondeaulz* [Here begin the rondeaux]. A knight speaks
to a lady seated outdoors (fol. 150r).

Total number of miniatures for the rondeaux: **G**   1

w. Virelais

Hé! dame de vaillance (V1)

G148 [fol. 154r:] *Ci commencent les chansons baladees* [Here begin the virelais]. A
gentleman speaks to a lady. Unidentified coat of arms (fol. 154v).

Total number of miniatures for the virelais: **G**   1

x. Appendix: Miniatures for *opera dubia* in MSS **K** and **J**

1. *Le Chastel d'Amours* (not by Machaut)

line 1

J23   *Ci commence le Chastel d'Amours* [Here begins the Castle of Love]. A lady next to
a castle waves to a man holding a club, who waves back (fol. 146v).

K11   *Ci commence le Chastel d'Amours*. A lady at the door of a castle waves to a man
holding a club on his shoulder, who waves back (fol. 132r [97r]).

2. *Le Dit du Cerf Blanc* (*opus dubium*; see chap. 5.19)

line 1

J26   *Le Dit du Cerf Blanc* [The Poem of the White Stag]. The narrator walking in a grove
of trees (fol. 155r).

line 125

J27   The narrator kneels in obeisance to the queen of lovers, who is dressed in white and
seated on a white horse (fol. 156r).

line 189

J28   The narrator and the queen are seated, watching the white stag within a walled park
(fol. 156c).[229]

line 228

J29   The narrator holds the stag with a chain (fol. 156d).

line 421

J30   The narrator with the stag. The stag looks up at a rose on a tall stem (fol. 158r).

line 472

J31   The narrator sits as the stag continues to look at the rose. The stag is tormented by
flies (fol. 158v).

line 509

J32   The narrator and the stag walk by the rose. The stag is tormented by flies (fol.
159r).[230]

line 576

J33   The narrator and the stag by the rosebush. The stag looks up at the rose (fol. 159c).

line 601

J34   The narrator ties the stag to the rose by means of the chain (fol. 159d).

line 697

J35   The narrator kneels before the queen. Her white horse looks on (fol. 160v).

---

[229] Reproduction in Thiébaux 1974, 162.

[230] Reproduction in Thiébaux 1974, 165.

V

The Narrative Dits

1. The chronology of the *dits*

The possibility of determining a chronology of the works of Machaut has been recognized as an ideal since the very first publication of the narrative poems. Ernest Hoepffner found a situation in which many codices of the complete works of Machaut were extant, arranged by genre, each with a different number of items. Larger manuscripts often had works in the same order as the less complete ones, with additional works for each genre added after the end of the series found in the smaller manuscripts. A natural hypothesis to explain this state of affairs is one that calls on chronology. In a passage that has since been oft-quoted, Hoepffner stated (1908–21, 1:xlix):

> Thus, even during the lifetime of the poet manuscripts existed that contained only a part of his works, a part more or less extensive according to the time in which they were written, following the more or less advanced state of Guillaume's original. These copies present the works of Machaut in different phases of their development, and the manuscripts which we possess even today reproduce in some manner at least a few of these stages in the progress of the works of the poet. The first of these stages is represented by manuscript *C*. . . .[1]

By combining this theory of the gradual growth in the Machaut corpus observable from the extant manuscripts with a few more-or-less solid dates for individual poems, Hoepffner brilliantly arrived at an overall chronology of the large narrative poems of Machaut.[2] In addition, his study laid the foundation for a chronology of the musical works.

For the following discussion of the chronology of the *dits*, reference should be made to table 5.1, which gives the complete contents of the text section of those Machaut manuscripts that are crucial to a study of chronology. Further details on the dating of individual *dits* may be found below in the separate discussion of each work. On the chronology of the musical works, see chapter 7.1.

The fixed dates for the longer narrative poems are the following:

1. *Lyon* is dated 2 April 1342 near its beginning (ll. 32–33), and this has been taken as a date near the period of the composition of the poem since Lebeuf

---

[1] Il existait donc du vivant même du poète des manuscrits qui ne contenaient qu'une partie de ses œuvres, partie plus ou moins considérable selon l'époque où ils furent écrits, d'après l'état plus ou moins avancé de l'original de Guillaume. Ces copies présentaient les œuvres de Machaut dans les différentes phases de leur développement, et les manuscrits que nous possédons encore aujourd'hui reproduisent en quelque sorte quelques-unes au moins de ces étapes dans le progrès de l'œuvre du poète. La première de ces étapes est représentée par le manuscrit *C*. . . .

[2] Hoepffner's chronology of Machaut led him to propose a chronology of the works of Froissart, since it seemed that Froissart was influenced in the ordering of his works by the model of his predecessor (Hoepffner 1913); see also Whiting 1946, 210–12; Poirion 1965, 206; Wimsatt 1972a, 393–96; Dembowski 1978; Fourrier 1979, 7–12; Wimsatt 1991b, 320–21 n. 50, 323–24 n. 22, 327 n. 27, 328 n. 40.

Table 5.1
Chronological Growth of the Main Machaut MSS[3]

	Date of work	C ca.1353	W ca.1356	Vg late '60s*	M late '60s*	index A ca.1370	codex A ca.1375	F-G late '70s*
Prologue	ca.1372						1	1
Vergier	1330s	4	3?	2	1	1	2	2
Jug. Behaingne	before 8/1346	1	2	3	2	2	3	3
Jug. Navarre	"1349"			4	3	3	4	4
Lay de Plour †	1349?	in 7		5	4+in 13	in 16	in 18	
Remede	before 1357	2	4?	6	5	4	5	5
Lyon	"1342"	5		7	6	5	6	6
Alerion	1340s	3	5	8	7	6	7	7
Confort	1357			9	8	7	8	8
Fonteinne	11/1360–61			10	9	8	9	9
Harpe	1360s?			11	10	9	10	10
Voir Dit	1362–65					13	14	11
Marguerite	after 1366				11	12	12	12
Rose	ca.1372?					15	16	13
Vezci les biens	ca.1372?						17	14
Prise	after 1369			13		14	15	15
Lis et Marguerite	1369							18
Loange des Dames		6	1	1	12	10	11	16
(No. of texts)		(198)	(198)††	(256)	(271)		(268)	(225)
Complaintes				in 1	in 12	11	13	17
(No. of texts)				(7)°	(8)°		(8)	(11)
Music section		7		12	13	16	18	19

* The dates for MSS **Vg**, **M**, and **F-G** are the dates of the corpus of works, not the dates of the copy of the respective manuscripts.

† The *Lay de Plour, Qui bien aimme* (L22/16) is placed in the lai section in MSS **C** and **A**; it is placed after *Navarre* in **Vg**, included in both places in **M**, and is missing entirely from **F-G**.

†† The *Loange* in MS **W** has only 67 surviving texts and fragments of texts, but since the very end of the collection survives, it is clear that the original extent of the section was either 198 or 200 works. The last text is Lo200 as in MS **C**, but as in that manuscript, Lo51 and Lo108 may have been lacking in **W**.

° In MSS **Vg** and **M**, the *complaintes* are incorporated into the *Loange* section; they are placed in a separate section in the later manuscripts; see chap. 6.3 and 6.5.

(1753, 379).[4] Because *Remede* appears before *Lyon* in the manuscripts, this early date has had the effect of fixing the date of the *Remede* before 1342 (Hoepffner 1908–21, 1:lxiv–lxvi, 2:xv n. 1), an early date that has not always met with acceptance.

2. *Jugement Behaingne* was surely written before John of Luxembourg fell on the field of Crécy, 26 August 1346, since John is a living character in the story line of the *dit* (Hoepffner 1908–21, 1:lix).

3. *Jugement Navarre* specifically refers to the *Jugement Behaingne,* reversing the decision taken in the earlier *dit.* I agree with those scholars who believe that Bonne of Luxembourg, who died on 11 September 1349, urged the composition of *Jugement Navarre.* Much of the poem therefore predates her death (see chap. 1.8–9, 1.12). A passage near the beginning, relating to the great plague of 1348–49, includes the date 9 November 1349 (ll. 24–25). Scholars have disputed the connection of this prologue to the rest of the poem. I have argued that if the passage was added, it was added to a nearly complete poem and thus is very close to the period of the composition of the poem (Earp 1989, 468 n. 16).

---

[3] I have left the non-authoritative order in MS **E** out of consideration here, but I have distinguished between the order of works reflected in the index of MS **A** and the order of works actually carried out in the manuscript.

[4] See Beer's interesting literary analysis of the date (1980, 28; 1981, 74).

4. *Confort* was written to console and instruct Charles II, king of Navarre, during the period of his imprisonment, from April 1356 until November 1357 (see chap. 1.12d and 1.12f), and was probably finished in the second half of 1357 (Hoepffner 1908–21, 3:i).
5. *Remede* must pre-date the *Confort* of 1357, since the *Remede* is cited in *Confort* (ll. 2248–49; see Hoepffner 1908–21, 2:ii).
6. *Fonteinne* was written for John, duke of Berry, son of King John II, some time after his departure for England, 31 October 1360, and probably during the first half of 1361 (Hoepffner 1908–21, 3:xxvi–xxx).
7. During the course of the long composition of the *Voir Dit*, Machaut chronicled events from 1362 to 1364, while the period of composition seems to range from 1363 to 1365 (see chap. 5.13). This chronology is further corroborated by the fact that on four occasions in the *Voir Dit* Machaut refers to *Fonteinne* as his then most recent long poem.
8. The *Prise* chronicles the life and death of Pierre I de Lusignan, king of Cyprus. Since he was assassinated 16 January 1369, the poem—a long one of nearly 9000 lines—is to be dated after this event (see chap. 1.16 and chap. 5.17).

To summarize these points, the following relatively fixed and approximate dates obtain for the longer narratives (table 5.2).

Table 5.2
Dates for the Longer Narrative Poems

Fixed	Approximate
Lyon (1342?)	*Jugement Behaingne* (before 1346; before or
Jugement Navarre (after 1349)	after *Lyon* and *Remede?*)
Confort (1357)	*Remede* (before 1357; before or after
Fonteinne (ca. 1360–61)	*Jugement Navarre, Jugement Behaingne,*
Voir Dit (ca. 1363–65)	and *Lyon?*)
Prise (ca. 1370–72)	

At this point, Hoepffner's observation of the gradual manuscript-to-manuscript growth of the Machaut corpus can be brought into play for further refinement of the picture. In addition, it allows a relative chronology of those works lacking external clues to their date. Table 5.1 shows that all manuscripts except **C** and **W** give narrative poems from *Vergier* to *Harpe* in the same order. The manuscript with the fewest works, **C**, has these works in an order very different from what appears as a canonical order in the remaining manuscripts, and it was the seemingly random order in **C** that led Hoepffner to discount this manuscript to an extent and to cast doubt on its authority.[5] The logical inconsistency between this evaluation and the view Hoepffner expressed in the quotation given above ("the first of these stages is represented by manuscript *C*...") was emphasized by S.J. Williams (1969, 448–54), and further explored by Keitel (1976). Williams's objections, logical given the state of knowledge in 1969, turned out to be superfluous once Avril had redated MS **C** to the 1350s.[6]

Except in the case of the *Jugement Navarre*, the manuscript order upholds the order of the fixed dates, and it appears in general to suggest solutions to the remaining questions:
1. *Vergier* is not dated but appears first in the series in all of the central complete-works manuscripts except **C**, and possibly **W**. Seeking support for

---

[5] Hoepffner 1908–21, 1:xlvii–xlviii. Until Avril 1973, C was considered to be a fifteenth-century codex, following the dating in *Bibliothèque Impériale* 1868, 259.

[6] Avril 1973; 1978; 1982a; the current state of knowledge on the dates of the manuscripts is summarized in Earp 1989, table 1.

the chronological primacy of *Vergier*, Hoepffner noted that the rhymes are less rich than for any other narrative poem of Machaut. Further, the narrative structure of the work is less developed than in other long poems, and for the most part it lacks the lively personal note that the poet usually takes on as a character in his own poems. In addition, of Machaut's longer narratives, only *Vergier* lacks an anagram giving the name of the author, a situation that makes sense for the earlier period, before his fame as a poet was established. Finally, the work is heavily derivative of the *Roman de la Rose*. Taken together, these facts argue for considering *Vergier* Machaut's first narrative poem, an order constant in all manuscripts from **Vg** on.[7]

2. The earliest of the poems with an internal date is *Lyon* (1342). In the canonically-ordered manuscripts, this *dit* occurs fifth in the series: (1) *Vergier*, (2) *Jugement Behaingne*, (3) *Jugement Navarre*, (4) *Remede*, (5) *Lyon* (cf. table 5.1). Hoepffner again calls on the rhymes to justify its position in the series as a chronological one. *Jugement Navarre*, dated 1349, remains the only real disruption in Hoepffner's chronology, and his explanation of this anomaly is central to his thesis. *Jugement Navarre* is normally dated 1349 because of the chronicle of the great plague found near the beginning of the poem. According to Hoepffner, the complementary nature of the two judgment poems led Machaut to relocate *Jugement Navarre* to a position following *Jugement Behaingne*—out of its chronological position—in order to group it with the earlier judgment poem.[8] The fact that *Jugement Navarre* is lacking in **C**, a manuscript now dated to the early 1350s, gives the point an interesting twist.

At the end of *Jugement Navarre*, the judge metes out a punishment that amounts to a demand for further poetical works, namely, a lai, a virelai, and a ballade (ll. 4177–89). Of these, it is only the first and most difficult of the demands, the lai, that appears in some manuscripts immediately following *Navarre,* the so-called *Lay de Plour, Qui bien aimme* (L22/16). This lai is included in MS **C**, even though it lacks the long *Jugement Navarre*. Further, *Alerion* (not dated) is present in MS **C**, suggesting that *Alerion* was written before 1349, and that it predates *Jugement Navarre*.

The most controversial aspect of Hoepffner's chronology, to judge from recent literary studies, is his date for the *Remede*. Based on manuscript order, the relative richness of the rhymes, and on a passage describing the characteristics of the true lover that is less developed in the *Remede* than in *Lyon* (Hoepffner 1908–21, 2:ii, xv n. 1), Hoepffner proposes a date before 1342 (i.e., before *Lyon)*. This view is not accepted by Poirion (1965, 201 and

---

[7] Hoepffner (1908–21, 1:lvi n.) uses a comparison of the relative richness of rhymes between several *dits*, some of known date, to confirm that *Vergier* was Machaut's first narrative work, a view that he regarded as certain based on its position in the best manuscripts: "it is notably by the poverty of the rhymes that the *Dit dou Vergier* distinguishes itself from the other poems of Machaut. The proportion of leonine rhymes in the *Dit dou Vergier* is 19 percent, in the *Roy de Navarre* 35 percent, in the *Remede de Fortune* 31 percent, in the *Dit dou Lion* 34 percent. If one adds the feminine rhymes, considered as leonine by the poets of the Middle Ages, their number reaches only 50 percent in the *Dit dou Vergier*, against an average of 71 percent to 84 percent elsewhere. The *rimes suffisantes* in the *Dit dou Vergier* are 14 percent, in the *Remede de Fortune* 3 percent, in the *Roy de Navarre* 0.4 percent, and in the *Dit dou Lion* 0.6 percent." Guthrie (1987, 65–66) compares the rhythmic structure of *Vergier* with that of *Navarre*, finding a clear chronological dimension that supports a very early date for *Vergier*. Kelly's thesis of the development of Machaut's treatment of *fin' amors* also supports Hoepffner's chronology (Kelly 1978, 137–48).

[8] Hoepffner 1908–21, 1:lxiv–lxvi; cf. Cerquiglini 1985b, 16.

n. 28), who dates the *Remede* several years later, namely ca. 1350.[9] Poirion
further proposes that Machaut dedicated the work to Bonne of Luxembourg
(daughter of the king of Bohemia, mother of the future Charles V, John of
Berry, Louis of Anjou and Philip of Burgundy). This suggestion is fleshed out
remarkably and convincingly in Wimsatt/Kibler 1988, but these scholars retain
Hoepffner's earlier date (see the detailed discussion in chap. 5.7).

Thus, the question of the date of the *Remede* remains unresolved.[10] From the
standpoint of the musicologist, a dating of 1342 or earlier would seem
extraordinarily early for the most advanced of the musical interpolations, the
ballades *En amer* (RF4) and *Dame, de qui* (RF5), and the rondeau *Dame, mon
cuer en vous* (RF7). Although the activity of revision appears out of character
for Machaut (we do not have several versions of works, unlike the situation for
some other medieval poets),[11] perhaps Machaut did rework the music of the
Remede in the late 1340s for inclusion in his first complete-works manuscript,
destined for Bonne of Luxembourg.

3. The next datable work is the *Confort* (ca. 1357), although, as we have seen,
apparently *Alerion* is earlier, since it appears in MSS C and **W**. Thus, *Alerion*
may be placed before 1349 (Hoepffner 1908–21, 1:lxv n.).

4. The later, larger narrative poems (*Fonteinne, Voir Dit, Prise*) have dates that
can be determined independently of their position in the manuscripts, and they
uphold the chronological ordering of the works in the manuscripts (see the fixed
dates in table 5.2).

One other problem with the manuscript ordering should also be noted. MS
Vg lacks the *Voir Dit* of ca. 1363–65 (although the music section of the manuscript includes the *Voir Dit* musical compositions). This manuscript does, however, include the *Prise* of ca. 1370–72 as an appendix. Perhaps the recipient of
the manuscript already had a copy of the *Voir Dit* (Earp 1989, 478–79).

The dating of the later, smaller dits remains to be considered:

1. *Harpe* apparently lacks any internal clues to dating. Because it appears last in
the *dit* section of MS **Vg**, it presumably dates from the late 1360s. Its position
after the *Fonteinne* in manuscripts from **Vg** on is fixed.

2. *Marguerite* is dated "1366 or later" by Wimsatt (1970, 49), and apparently
ca. 1364 by Fourrier (1979, 73).[12] It is lacking in **Vg**, though present in **M**. Its
position is variable in manuscripts that include the lengthy *Voir Dit*. This may
indicate that the *Voir Dit* was never through-copied into Machaut's exemplar,
leaving its position relative to the surrounding works somewhat fluid.

3. *Rose* lacks internal clues to dating, and appears to be a new work at the time
of the compilation of MS **A** (ca. 1372–77). It does appear in **A**'s old index,
established prior to the copying of the manuscript. *Rose* was copied as the
penultimate work in the *dit* section of **A** (cf. Brownlee 1978a, 230).

4. *Vezci les biens* is a short work that appears to be closely connected to the
compilation of MS **A**, since it provides an important articulating function in that
manuscript (see chap. 5.16). It does not appear in **A**'s index, and was copied at

---

[9] Poirion does not mention Hoepffner's argument; cf. Earp 1983, 135 n. 259; 1989, 470–71
n. 20.

[10] Except for Guthrie's work (see n. 7 above), literary critics have not pursued Hoepffner's
use of the relative sophistication of rhymes as a kind of dispassionate index for dating.
Poirion's discussion of rhyme, for instance, is more general (1965, 433–38).

[11] The different versions of the *Jugement Behaingne* and *Remede* discussed by Wimsatt/Kibler
(1988, 11–32, 40–54; summarized in Earp 1989, 479–80) are the result of corruptions
introduced in the process of transmission, not authorial revision.

[12] The date 1364 makes more sense on grounds of manuscript order, but Wimsatt has good
grounds for the 1366 date.

the very end of the *dit* section in **A**. If *Vezci les biens* has a function linked specifically to the copying of MS **A**, this purpose was lost when the work was displaced in the later MS **F-G**, although there it serves to articulate a different unit, namely, the end of MS **F**.

5. *Lis et Marguerite* was probably composed for the wedding of Marguerite of Flanders and Philip of Burgundy in 1369 (see chap. 1.17), and is an *unicum* in MS **F-G**. Perhaps it was retained as the personal property of the patrons for a time, explaining its absence from MS **A**.

The order of the works listed in the leftmost column of table 5.1 is close to the final desired order of Machaut's text section, although this order cannot be determined conclusively. Machaut was extraordinarily active as a poet at the very end of his life, and left many shorter narrative works without fixing a definitive place for them in relation to the bulky segments represented by the *Voir Dit*, the *Prise*, the *Loange*, and the beginning of the music section. Machaut probably controlled the order of earlier narrative poems by means of a through-copied exemplar (S.J. Williams 1969, 442–45, 454; Cerquiglini 1985b, 217–18; Earp 1989, 471–72). But at the end of his life, the condition of the last portion of his exemplar was doubtless chaotic. Two of the later works are of a length unprecedented in Machaut (*Voir Dit* and *Prise*), while the others, *Marguerite*, *Rose*, *Vezci les biens*, and *Lis et Marguerite*, are very short occasional works of various kinds, and scribes were apt to tack them on wherever the gathering structure of a new manuscript allowed them most conveniently. The condition of the exemplar was probably further confused by Machaut's decision to change the location of the collection of lyrics not set to music—the *Loange*—from the beginning of the manuscript (the preferred order in those manuscripts related to **Vg**'s order) to the end of the text section, before the musical works (an order that hearkens back to the order of the earliest manuscript, MS **C**; see Earp 1989, 474, 481–82). The new order, which first appeared late in the 1360s in the now-lost manuscript from which MS **M** was copied, is seen in MSS **A** and **F-G**.

To conclude, we can confirm that the order of the Machaut manuscripts is generally chronological. A few questions remain, most crucially the date of the *Remede*, but I believe that Hoepffner's overall chronological ordering is sound. Further, one need not insist that the later items in the text section necessarily appear in chronological order, for here, technical problems of manuscript production, literary concerns, and Machaut's conception of *ordenance* conflict. Machaut was tinkering with his unwieldy collection of works up to the end of his life, and there is no conclusive proof that he arrived at a final ordering for his manuscript. Thus, table 5.1 shows some confusion at the end of the series.

MS **F-G**, whatever its actual date of production, appears to come closest to a definitive order, and yet even this manuscript shows physical evidence of a change of order of the last series of *dits* (Earp 1983, 99–101). Further, the final order was not necessarily strictly chronological because of the dramatic differences in length among the late works. It would doubtless neither have been aesthetically pleasing nor sound judgement from the point of view of manuscript production for these works to follow each other in strict chronological order. A better plan is to group the smaller works in some manner. In MS **F-G**, such a plan suffers the single exception of the short *Lis et Marguerite*, added before the opening of the lais to the end of the *Loange* section. Ideally, *Lis et Marguerite* in MS **F-G** perhaps ought to have joined the other shorter *dits* before the *Prise*, leaving the *Loange* to form a lyrical bridge to the music section of the codex.

2. A brief historiography of literary studies

The narrative *dits* form the largest bulk of material in the main Machaut manuscripts. Long neglected, they have increasingly come under the scrutiny of literary critics in the last thirty years.[13] In the eighteenth century, when scholars rediscovered Machaut after three hundred years of almost total eclipse, it was Machaut the historian that first attracted them. Accounts of actual events—the depiction of the plague in the opening segment of the *Jugement Navarre*, the vivid picture of Jean de Luxembourg as the ideal prince in the *Confort*, and above all, the verse chronicle of the crusade to Alexandria of Pierre de Lusignan, king of the French outpost in Cyprus, in the *Prise*—were read and excerpted for their value as documents of French history.[14]

By the middle of the nineteenth century, growing interest in the medieval past allowed a further step. Prosper Tarbé, an indefatigable and devoted champion of the achievements of the region of Champagne, published in 1849 the first modern edition devoted entirely to works of Machaut—mostly in the form of excerpts—along with a biography that marked a serious advance over the previous state of knowledge of the poet's life. Tarbé presented a cross-section of works, although the emphasis remained on works of historical or biographical value, and especially on works that mirrored the morals and customs of the French Middle Ages. Significantly, Tarbé published many letters ("Correspondance de Guillaume de Machaut et de sa dame par amour") and a few lyrics from the *Voir Dit*, which Tarbé considered the memoirs of Machaut's love affair, reluctantly written by the aged poet at the insistence of his beloved Agnès of Navarre, sister of King Charles of Navarre, and later wife of Gaston Fébus, count of Foix.[15] Seven years later Tarbé published an entire volume of poetry he ascribed to Agnès of Navarre (Tarbé 1856). Half of her works he extracted from the *Voir Dit*; the remainder are lyrics with a feminine voice scattered throughout Machaut's collection of works.

In 1875 Paulin Paris published the *Voir Dit* in a "complete" edition.[16] Again, it was primarily the historical and "autobiographical" references in the work, which Paris brilliantly succeeded in narrowing down to the years from 1362 to 1364, that were of interest. As for the love affair depicted, Paris—who proposed a new solution to the question of the identity of the lady—took it at face value, the reaction until recently of all ages since the fifteenth century to medieval courtly poetry. (Sixteenth-century library inventories matter-of-factly

---

13 Calin (1987b, 21–22; 1994, 123–25) discusses the lack of interest until recently in the literary fourteenth century, even among native French scholars. See also de Looze 1988b, 537; L.W. Johnson 1990, 10–14; and especially Sturges 1992. Reference to more general works on the historiography of French literature would lead too far afield here; see the essays by Wolfzettel, Grimm, and others in the GRLMA Begleitreihe, vols. 1 (reference as for Cerquiglini 1980a) and 2 (reference as for Cerquiglini-Toulet 1991b). Sonnemann (1969, 15–22) provides a good summary of this aspect. See also below, chap. 6.4, focusing on the lyrics. The excellent recent survey and bibliography by Switten (1995, introduction) came too late for full consideration here.

14 The count of Caylus put it this way: "j'avoue que le Poëte m'a semblé plus intéressant du moment que j'ai pû le regarder comme un historien" (1753b, 416) [I confess that the poet seemed more interesting to me from the moment I could regard him as a historian]. See also Lebeuf 1743; 1751; 1753; Caylus 1753a; 1753b; Rive 1780.

15 The lady's identity is masked in the poem; it was the count of Caylus (1753a, 413–14) who had identified "Machaut's mistress" as Agnès of Navarre. P. Paris (1875, xviii–xx) proved that Agnès was not a possible candidate.

16 On Paris's shortcomings as an editor of *Voir Dit*, see A. Thomas 1912; Calin 1974, 167n.; and especially Cerquiglini-Toulet 1991b.

labeled Machaut's works "les amours de Guillaume de Machaut.") For Paulin Paris, "elle lui accorde des faveurs qui pourront sembler assez grandes, avant qu'il ait eu la hardiesse de les demander. O mes amis! c'étoit là le bon temps" (P. Paris 1875, xxxiii) [she accords him (Machaut) favors which could seem rather generous, before he had the fortitude to ask for them. O my friends! Those were the good days]. Our knowledge of patronage and the function of the *dit* in Machaut's day, along with our appreciation of the subtlety and sophistication of the narrative techniques involved, has long put absurd interpretations of this sort by the wayside.

The last major contribution of the nineteenth century to our knowledge of Machaut's narrative poems was the 1877 edition of Machaut's verse chronicle, the *Prise d'Alexandrie*, by the historian Louis de Mas Latrie, an active member of the *Société de l'Orient latin*. Perhaps it was another member of the society, the Marquis Melchior de Vogüé, himself an owner of an important manuscript of Machaut's works, who piqued Mas Latrie's interest in Machaut. The goal of this research was again historical, a document of the French presence on Cyprus in the Middle Ages.

Thus, at the turn of the nineteenth century, as Gustav Gröber assembled the monumental *Grundriss der romanischen Philologie* (vol. 2/1, 1902), the only works of Machaut available in print were Tarbé's two volumes of lyric, narrative, and prose excerpts (1849; 1856), the defective Paris edition of the *Voir Dit,* and Mas Latrie's edition of the *Prise.* In addition, excerpts from *Lyon* and *Harpe* were available in Bartsch's *Chrestomatie,* first published in 1866. Dictionaries and surveys from this period are valuable today mainly for historiographical reasons,[17] although Gröber's characterization of the court poet of the fourteenth century is notably advanced, and his view of the *Voir Dit* remains interesting.

The foundation for modern work on Machaut was laid in the first few years of the twentieth century with the publication of a scientifically precise edition of most of Machaut's remaining narrative poems by the Alsacian philologist Ernest Hoepffner (three volumes, 1908, 1911, and 1921), the publication of a less impressive edition of the lyrical poems by the Russian philologist Vladimir Chichmaref (1909), and the copies of Machaut's music made by the German music historian Friedrich Ludwig in the period 1900–1903, published in four volumes (1926, 1928, 1929, and posthumously in 1954). By 1979, a few smaller *dits* that Hoepffner omitted had been re-edited or edited for the first time (*Harpe* in Young 1943; *Lis et Marguerite* in Wimsatt 1970; *Marguerite, Rose,* and again *Lis et Marguerite* in Fourrier 1979). Nevertheless, much remains to be done for Machaut's narrative *dits.* A thorough study of Machaut's language and the filiation of the major manuscripts based on his complete poetical works was left undone by Hoepffner, who was perhaps discouraged by Chichmaref's publication of the lyrics.[18] We have new critical editions and translations of two works, *Jugement Behaingne* and *Remede,* published in 1988 by James I. Wimsatt and William W. Kibler. Paul Imbs's critical edition of the *Voir Dit,* promised since 1952, was broken off on his death in 1987; Jacqueline Cerquiglini-Toulet will soon complete the edition for the *Société des Anciens Textes Français.* In addition, Barton Palmer and Daniel Leech-Wilkinson are at work on a new edition with translation. A modern critical edition of the *Prise*

---

[17] Petit de Julleville 1892–93; Lanson 1894; G. Paris 1895; Petit de Julleville 1896; Suchier/Birch-Hirschfeld 1900; G. Paris 1907; Guelliot 1914.

[18] The study of vocalism in Aust 1890 is based on selected passages from Tarbé 1849, the *Voir Dit* (P. Paris 1875), and *Prise* (Mas Latrie 1877b). In his review of Wimsatt/Kibler 1988, Gilles Roques reports on Hoepffner's unpublished study of Machaut's language.

d'Alexandre (restoring Machaut's spelling) by Angela Dzelzainis awaits publication. Because of these delays, modern editions of Machaut's poetry are on the whole not as solid philologically as the material now available for, say, Froissart. This situation has not, however, greatly hindered important literary studies, particularly in recent years.

Hoepffner's introductions to each of the *dits* he edited are the most important contribution to Machaut literary studies of the period up to around 1965 and remain the best starting points for students as well as seasoned scholars.[19] Of the dictionaries and surveys from this middle period of criticism, Stefan Hofer's revision of the Gröber *Grundriss* (Gröber/Hofer 1933) stands out as a dispassionate overview of all of Machaut's works, still valuable especially for the discussion of themes treated in the lyrical poems.[20] Other surveys from this period tend to view the French fourteenth and fifteenth centuries as a dreary two centuries of transition between the magnificent achievements of the thirteenth century and the French Renaissance.[21] The only ongoing scholarship directed at Machaut's works in this part of the twentieth century is found in the work of Chaucer scholars, especially John Livingston Lowes and George Lyman Kittredge, who proceeded to map out in scientific detail the extent of the younger English poet's use of Machaut's poetry.[22] Even so, the view of Chaucerians until fairly recently has been largely unsympathetic to Machaut.[23]

By the mid 1960s, literary scholars began to see the French fourteenth and fifteenth centuries as a fertile ground for investigation.[24] Critical appreciation and serious evaluation of Machaut's literary works began with Daniel Poirion's 1965 study of the conditions of courtly patronage, which includes a critical evaluation of Machaut's lyrics. James I. Wimsatt's book on French sources for Chaucer's *Book of the Duchess* (1968) includes a serious examination of the literary tradition of the fourteenth-century *dit*. William Calin's 1974 volume is the first book-length study devoted entirely to Machaut's narrative *dits*.[25]

---

[19] An essential complement to the first two volumes of Hoepffner's edition is De Boer's study of Machaut and the *Ovide Moralisé* (1914; edition of the *Ovide Moralisé* 1915–38).

[20] Although, as Sonnemann (1969, 15) notes, Hofer omitted Gröber's comparison of Machaut with Dante and Petrarch (Gröber 1902, 1043; Gröber/Hofer 1933, 14–29).

[21] See Jeanroy 1921 (the nadir of Machaut criticism); Foulet 1923; Lanson 1923; Bossuat 1931; Frank 1961; and Flutre/Reaney 1967. Frank's survey is often cited as an early rehabilitation of the fourteenth century; this applies only to the survey of her own area of specialty, drama, an area peripheral to the work of the court poets. It would seem that Chichmaref (1911) anticipated many of the concerns of recent critics. Unfortunately, he published his work in Russian and it therefore remained without influence.

[22] Lowes 1904; Kittredge 1909–10; 1910; Lowes 1910; Kittredge 1915a; 1915b; 1915c; Lowes 1918; Fabin 1919; Kitchel 1923; Shannon 1929; Meech 1931; Estrich 1939; R.K. Root 1941; Work 1941; Schaar 1954, 175–77; 253–56; 1955, 125–28, 432–37. Other studies of sources include Geiselhardt 1914 (Machaut and Froissart); Pugh 1894 and Schilperoort 1936 (Machaut and Christine de Pizan). A few other literary studies from these years draw upon a wide cross-section of Machaut's works as part of a broader literary inquiry: Patch 1923 and 1927 (theme of Fortune); Knowlton 1922–23 (theme of Nature); Siciliano 1934 (sources of Villon's poetry).

[23] See, for instance, Muscatine (1957, 99–101). Palmer 1987a provides an interesting historiographical survey of Chaucer scholarship involving Machaut; see also Davis 1991, 1–17.

[24] See the little book of Le Gentil (1963, 158–63). Guiette 1960 (with material dating back to the mid 1940s) was also enormously influential.

[25] Sonnemann's excellent 1969 thesis has remained little known. Although Zumthor (1972) does not address Machaut as directly as other studies cited in this paragraph, his formulation of new questions has been path breaking.

Machaut's works also figure prominently in Douglas Kelly's 1978 monograph on medieval imagination, a study of late medieval poetry of Courtly Love. More recent works include Kevin Brownlee's 1984 monograph on the narrator persona in Machaut, covering most of the narrative *dits*; Jacqueline Cerquiglini's 1985 monograph on the *Voir Dit*, an extremely rich study that goes far beyond a consideration of this single work; Paul Imbs's posthumous 1991 monograph on the same work; and finally, two superb treatments of the Machaut literary tradition and Machaut's poetic colleagues in France and England, Wimsatt 1991b and Calin 1994. As far as the more recent general introductions and dictionaries are concerned, only Becker (1964) provides a true survey of all of Machaut's literary works, although there are plenty of surveys that reflect more current critical concerns.[26]

A concise statement of the revolution in literary criticism of the French fourteenth and fifteenth centuries is seen in the heading for the relevant section in Poirion's *Précis de littérature française du moyen âge* (1983): "Le renouvellement de la littérature aux XIVe et XVe siècles" (the renewal of literature in the fourteenth and fifteenth centuries). The rehabilitation has proceeded on several fronts. Since I treat each of Machaut's narrative works separately in the body of this chapter , I provide here an overview of recent literary criticism of Machaut to pull together in a general way some of the main currents.

At the end of the fourteenth century Deschamps's *Art de Dictier* (1392) formalized the split between poetry and music as a distinction between "artificial music" (lyrical poetry set to music, the old norm) and "natural music" (lyrical poetry intended solely for reading) (see chap. 2.1.1m). Poets compensated for the loss of the musical component in an increased "textuality," a heightened concern for all aspects of writing (Cerquiglini[-Toulet] 1983; 1985b; 1991a, 233; 1993b). Attention to the play of rhyme and form is attested most dramatically in the rhetorical acrobatics and innovative forms seen in Christine de Pizan and the *Rhétoriquers* of the fifteenth century, and in the proliferation of versification manuals beginning with Deschamps's *Art de Dictier* itself. But it was Machaut who established the fixed forms as the preferred vehicles for lyrical expression, defining lyrical activity for the remainder of the fourteenth century, and throughout most of the fifteenth century. In addition, we can view his *Prologue,* and before that the *Remede*, in part as artfully didactic forerunners to Deschamps's more practically oriented treatise (Calin 1974, 70; Brownlee 1984, 232 n. 32).

Although scholars often cite Machaut as the last of the great poets to set his verses to music, it is worth emphasizing that the vast majority of his lyrical poetry was in fact not destined for musical setting. Indeed, even the lyrics he did set to music do not continue the lyrical/musical tradition of the twelfth and

---

26 See Le Gentil 1963; Roussel 1967; Poirion 1971; Wimsatt 1972b; Fox 1974; Phillips 1982, 19–27; Heitmann 1978; Cerquiglini 1983; B. and J. Cerquiglini 1984; Cerquiglini 1987a, 123–44; 1987b; Baumgartner 1988, 165–74; Poirion 1988a; Brownlee 1989a; Wild 1990; Zink 1990 and 1992; Kibler/Earp 1995; and others. Orientation into the various schools of literary criticism of the period between ca. 1965 and 1985 is provided in Palmer 1987b, 23–26; Sturges 1991a, 100–101; and especially Zink/Badel 1991 and Sturges 1992. For a useful brief bibliographical overview, see Knight 1982. More recent studies that draw on a wide cross-section of Machaut's literary works include: R. Morris 1988 (Arthurian antecedents); Gorcy 1961; Roques/Musso 1978; and Roques 1982 (vocabulary); Poirion 1978, Planche 1982 and 1993 (poetic language and images); Deschaux 1979, Poirion 1978, 202–3 and Planche 1980 (Machaut's bestiary); Pearsall/Salter 1973 (garden landscapes). Calin (1974) touches on most of these issues.

thirteenth centuries, universal lyrical outpourings accessible (and performable) by anyone in the upper class, but rather are complex works utilizing advanced musical notation and intricate polyphony, and so are performable only by specialists. A subtle "musicality" thus goes hand in hand with textuality, reaching a peak of complexity in the generation after Machaut.[27]

Lyrical poetry in the fourteenth century took on a less universal, more narrative, and more personal aspect. This is expressed in a number of ways, and Machaut effectively created all of them. His separate collection of lyrics not set to music, called the *Loange des Dames* in one manuscript (see chap. 6), is organized to the extent that small groups of poems with similar themes can be isolated. Poirion (1965, 204, 543 n. 127 et passim) and Wilkins (1972, 14–17) note such nests of poems treating similar proto-narrative themes. Machaut's collection was the model for similar collections in Froissart's poetry manuscripts, and the idea developed into the *Cent Ballades* by Jean le Seneschal and friends, the *Cent Ballades d'Amant et de Dame* of Christine de Pizan, the *Cinkante Ballades* of John Gower, and the organization of Charles d'Orléans autograph of his lyrics, *F:Pn 25458*.[28]

The *dit* with lyrical insertions most clearly demonstrates the new concern for the narrative aspects of the lyrics. The *Roman de la Rose* of Jean Renart (second quarter of the thirteenth century) counts as the first example of this typically French genre, which was transformed in the fourteenth century most dramatically in Machaut's *Remede, Fonteinne*, and *Voir Dit*. Earlier, the citation of fragments of performance pieces from the living repertory gave spice to the narrative; in Machaut, lyrics of his own composition form the kernel of the narrative, its point of departure.[29] The *recueil* (collection), an aspect of textuality, is seen here in microcosm, and there are broad ramifications. Machaut's self-conscious concern for his complete-works manuscript collections (pointedly evoked by the rubric heading the original index of MS A, "Here is the *ordenance* that G. de Machaut wants his book to have") influenced a generation of poets.[30] In addition, the same manuscript—MS A—includes the first, and most elaborate, presentation of the *Prologue*, serving to endow every single item in the enormous 500-folio codex with a place in the artistic oeuvre (Brownlee 1984, chap. 1; Huot 1987, 232–38). Machaut supervised the production of several of his complete-works manuscripts by establishing the order in which the works were copied and likely also by establishing the program of illustrations for the narrative poems.[31] Machaut's professional activities as a writer are even thematized in his narrative poetry, especially in the

---

[27] Baumgartner (1988, 168) views Adam de la Halle as one of the last poets to compose *chansons courtoises* in the old style, while at the same time presaging the fourteenth century in his polyphonic motets and rondeaux.

[28] See Cerquiglini 1980b; 1985b, 34–37; 1986a; 1987c; Baumgartner 1988, 170–71; Burrow 1988, 234–35; Zink 1990, 123; 1992, 270–72. Poirion (1965, 173) makes the point that the function of the secretary lies behind this desire for organization.

[29] Cerquiglini contrasts the thirteenth-century narrative with lyrical insertions as an anthology, exhibiting the quality of *collage* (juxtaposition of lyrics), with the fourteenth-century *art poétique* exhibiting the quality of *montage* (in which the lyrics are the source of the narrative); see 1977a; 1977b; 1980a; 1982; 1983, 290–92; 1985b, part 1 chap. 1. See further Huot 1987, chaps. 8–9; and many literary studies of the *Voir Dit* by a variety of scholars (chap. 5.13).

[30] The translation of the heading is that of Peggy McCracken (Leupin 1986, 137). On the term "ordenance," see Leupin 1986, 137–38; Huot 1987, 237–39 and the works cited there.

[31] Avril 1982a, 131–32; Brownlee 1984, 15–16; Huot 1987, chaps. 8–9. The supervision did not extend to careful proofreading (Kibler/Wimsatt 1987; Earp 1989, 493–97).

Voir Dit, and Machaut's self-conscious emphasis on his *metier* as a professional writer influenced Froissart, Chaucer, Deschamps, and Christine de Pizan. Textuality also finds expression in Machaut's penchant for citing *exempla*. Myths from Ovid, usually filtered through the anonymous moralized French translation of the early fourteenth century, the *Ovide Moralisé*, were a favorite source of material, but Machaut also drew upon the Old Testament.[32] Earlier critics found the poet's use of these *exempla*, beginning with *Alerion* and particularly prominent in *Jugement Navarre*, *Confort*, *Fonteinne*, and *Voir Dit*, to be at best valuable reflections of the sort of story-telling that went on at court, and at worst tedious and pointless digressions serving only to pad a jejune narrative. Recent critics, however, see the *exempla* as central, serving as intertextual commentaries to the unfolding narrative.[33] For instance, the lengthy recounting of the myth of Apollo and Coronis in the *Voir Dit* comments directly on the jealousy felt by the narrator at that point in the larger narrative: he should not "kill" his love of Toute Belle by reacting too hastily to stories of indiscretion. At the same time, Coronis was, in fact, guilty of adultery, and this lends a tinge of ambiguity to Toute Belle's professed innocence. Finally, the episode comments on the ongoing composition of the poem itself: in the myth, love dies with Coronis, but a son is born. The love between Guillaume and Toute Belle dies, but a book—the *Voir Dit* itself—is born (Calin 1974, 194, 200; Brownlee 1984, 147; Cerquiglini 1985b, 152–55; Leupin 1986, 141–43; Calin 1994, 356–66).

Other *exempla*, such as the long recounting of the marriage of Peleus and Thetis and the Judgment of Paris in the *Fonteinne*, allowed the clerk-poet a safe way to admonish the prince-patron to better conduct. By this means, the poet sought to influence a high-born patron, without being forward in an unseemly fashion (Ehrhart 1980b; 1987, 130–41; 1990; 1992, 14–19).

The problem just alluded to, the tension produced by the requirement of the clerk to give voice to the loves of a high patron, even though forbidden to experience such love himself, is well emphasized in modern criticism.[34] Again, the *Voir Dit* provides the extreme case, in which the clerkly poet-narrator plays the role of lover.

The paradoxical relation to the patron is also an aspect of recent studies of the first-person narrator. All recent literary critics emphasize the separation of a poem's first-person narrator from the author. Indeed, the concern for strategies of narration among recent literary critics has been a primary reason for the renewed interest in Machaut's narratives, which provide extraordinarily rich materials unappreciated before the development of new critical tools.[35]

---

[32] Some recent studies of this aspect of Machaut's work include Kelly 1978, 49–56, 125, 150–51; Badel 1980, 90–91; Burke 1980; Ehrhart 1980a; 1980b; 1980c; Kelly 1981; Ehrhart 1990; Heinrichs 1990; Wimsatt 1991b, 69–76. On Machaut's literary sources, see the general overview in chap. 1.2.6 and the details for each work in chap. 5.3–18.

[33] Some critics employ the terminology of narratology: *mise en abyme*. See F. and W. Calin 1974, 243–46; Calin 1983a, 84–87; de Looze 1984; Calin 1987b; 1988–89; 1994. Kelly (1989) emphasizes that the use of such *exempla* was valued in medieval rhetoric.

[34] See Poirion 1965, 192–205; Cerquiglini 1978b; Cerquiglini 1984; 1985a; 1985b, part 2 chap. 1; Leupin 1986; Nouvet 1986; Kelly 1987; Zeeman 1988; Cerquiglini-Toulet 1991a, 226–27, 230–32; Davis 1991; Huot 1991; Palmer 1993b; and Ehrhart's interpretation of the Judgment of Paris tradition, cited in the previous paragraph.

[35] Calin (1974, 241 et passim) is the first to demonstrate this strongly in Machaut studies. Brownlee (1978b; 1984) studies the *dits* according to the kind of first-person poet-narrator, who serves either as "lover-protagonist" (*Vergier*, *Remede*, *Alerion*, *Voir Dit*), or as "witness-participant" (*Jugement Behaingne*, *Lyon*, *Fonteinne*). On Machaut's first-person

The personality of Machaut's narrator figure, "prone to cowardice, sloth, snobbery, misogyny, and pedantry" (Calin 1974, 241) influenced the next generation of poets, Froissart, Chaucer, Christine de Pizan, and others.[36] Occasionally Machaut himself undermined the convention, for instance in *Jugement Navarre*, in which the narrator is specifically identified as "Guillaume de Machaut." Contemporaries too misunderstood, as in the *Voir Dit* in MS **F**, where unerased directions to an illuminator ask for the depiction of "Machaut kneeling before a king."[37] It appears that Machaut himself was well aware of the pseudo-autobiographical illusion he was promoting, and that he enjoyed leading his own contemporaries astray in this aspect. He does not, of course, deceive modern critics.[38]

Machaut's preoccupation with *sentement* (sincere feeling) reflects the new emphasis on personal expression. Faced with the paradoxical requirements of the patron, Machaut's *sentement* serves to authenticate his poetry.[39] Douglas Kelly's thesis of Machaut's poetics of love poetry is that Machaut—beginning with *Remede*—no longer requires *merci* (fulfillment), and thus he promotes *Esperance* (Hope) as sufficient reward.[40] This view can also be related to the question of the patron. Since authentic *sentement* is not allowed, Hope is sufficient to generate the *sentement* necessary to write authentic love poetry: the relationship of poet and patron is central.

In another view, the ultimate verification of Machaut's *sentement* came in textuality. Machaut's failure as a lover—a necessary condition of his class— was balanced by his success as a love poet, an aspect that he never ceased to boast of.[41] The poet's love can thus exist without association with the lady; the sublimation of desire lies in writing (Cerquiglini 1985b, 154, 223).

In sum, Machaut is a central player in many of the critical discussions of the last thirty years: "natural" vs. "artificial" music; textuality expressed in lyrics as proto-narratives, in manuscript collections, and in new kinds of lyrical insertions; authorial self-awareness; intertextuality and the use of *exempla*; levels and strategies of narration; and the role of the patron.

The remainder of this chapter provides information on all of the works in the narrative section of the manuscripts. Various categories of information are given, although rarely are all categories included for any single work.

FORM. The metrical scheme and total number of lines. For *dits* with lyrical insertions, the form of each lyric is listed separately. More general studies of form include Hieatt (1979–80), who provides an excellent account of narrative

---

narrator as a development of the narrator of the *Roman de la Rose*, see Calin 1978; Uitti 1978; Brownlee 1984; Guthrie 1985, 236–38; Calin 1987a, 17–18, 153; Huot 1993, 239–72; Palmer 1993b, 289–91, 296–97. De Looze (1988a; 1988b; 1991) has studied the identity of the narrator as revealed by authorial naming in anagrams.

[36] Wimsatt 1968, 96–102; Calin 1974, 116–19, 196–99, 241, 246 et passim; 1978; 1983b; 158–64; 1987a, 17–18, 133, 153; 1987b, 10–17; 1994, 227–28; Cerquiglini 1978b; 1984; 1985a; 1985b; and many others; Heinrichs (1990, 1–7) discusses scholarship on this question.

[37] See chap. 4.4k, miniature F125; recall the consistent program of iconography for the narrator figure in the miniatures seen in the late MSS **A** and **F** (chap. 4.1).

[38] For example, Palmer (1987a, 4) refers to "his fictional persona (a poet named Guillaume de Machaut)."

[39] On "sentement," see chap. 5.7 (*Remede*), under the rubric "related Machaut works."

[40] Kelly 1978, chap. 6; 1985, 300; 1992, 138, 146–48. See also Imbs 1991, esp. 197–212; Huot 1994, 227.

[41] Calin 1974, 199–200; Boulton 1993, 276–77; see also the writings of Cerquiglini-Toulet, Brownlee, de Looze, Palmer, etc.

form in Machaut; see also works on the definition of the term *dit* (Hoepffner 1920, 228–30; Sonnemann 1969, 4–6, 185–93; Zumthor 1972, 406–20 (=Eng. ed., 336–48); Fourrier 1979, 12–22; Cerquiglini 1980a; Poirion 1980; Zink 1982, 231–32; Cerquiglini 1988a; Ribémont 1990; Imbs 1991, 213–15; Boulton 1993, 181–83; Butterfield 1994, 9–13), and the medieval conceptions of form discussed in Kelly 1985, who deals with concepts such as *montage, forma tractatus*, and *ordonnance*. For an interesting discussion of what is common among French, Italian, and English narratives of this period, see Heinrichs (1990, 161, 213–14).

MANUSCRIPTS. Sources are labeled with a number in square brackets, keyed to the numerical listing in chapter 3. I supply a rubric of *incipit* or *explicit* only in particularly interesting or significant cases; other rubrics are not given. Lost manuscripts are listed only when it is certain that they contained a given work.

FACSIMILES. For the *dits*, references to facsimiles are usually given as a miniature number, which the reader must locate in chapter 4.4 for a bibliographical reference.

EDITIONS. Modern editions.

ASCRIPTION. I treat this question only in chapter 5.19, with regard to the *Dit du Cerf Blanc*.

TRANSLATIONS. Extensive excerpts or complete translations into English, unless otherwise labeled. Plot summaries of the *dits* in modern French may be found in the prefaces to the editions of Hoepffner (1908–21), and in English at the beginning of each chapter of Calin 1974. The discussion in Brownlee 1984 proceeds in order from the beginning to the end of a given work, providing a foothold for readers in the process of familiarizing themselves with the originals. Chapter 2 n. 10 provides an overview of available complete translations of the *dits*.

ANAGRAM. Studies that propose solutions to an anagram, or that provide discussions of anagrams. Since such studies usually discuss several works of Machaut, it may be of use to list the most important ones here: Tarbé 1849, 167–73 s.v. "énigme"; Suchier 1897; Hoepffner 1906; de Looze 1984, 153; Leupin 1986, 133; Cerquiglini 1988a, 94; de Looze 1988a; 1988b. Schilperoort (1936, 80–83) and de Looze (1991, 171–76) compare anagrams in Christine de Pizan with those in Machaut. A related issue is Machaut's frequent use of phrases that give his name, such as "ne m'en chaut" (I don't care); see Cerquiglini 1985b, 100 n. 27.

PATRON. Studies that propose a patron for a given poem. It is of course unnecessary to repeat each time that the "patron" of a given work may be a literary construct rather than a faithful account of the patron's personality. Important studies of this aspect include Poirion 1965 (a classic study); Kibler 1978; Gauvard 1982; Leupin 1986; Nouvet 1986; Kelly 1987 (an important study; on women patrons, see esp. p. 94).

DATE. Internal mention of a date in a given poem, or other criteria that have been brought to bear on dating.

BIOGRAPHY. The uses made of a given poem for biographical studies. In recent years, literary critics have become very cautious with this aspect. Most deny any direct connection between the narrator and real life conditions, treating the works as aesthetic documents only. For Chaucer studies, the *locus classicus* is the narrator's reference near the beginning of the *Book of the Duchess* to eight years' sickness, considered a biographical fact in need of interpretation until scholars found an analogous passage in Machaut's *Jugement Behaingne*, an important source for Chaucer.[42] Calin (1974, 38 et passim; 1987a, chap. 2) has constantly emphasized that realistic elements in Machaut's poetry are not necessarily autobiographical. For example, Machaut's frequent mention of his weak eyes—along with other denigrative physical characteristics—may be an example of a conventional clerkly literary attribute, not an item of biography (Cerquiglini 1984; 1985a; 1985b, part 2, esp. 112–13, 144–45, 150–51, 167).

DISCUSSION (historical, literary, art historical, codicological, or musical). These categories provide little more than chronological listings of relevant bibliographical references.

LITERARY ANTECEDENTS. Studies that discuss Machaut's literary sources for a given work. Hoepffner (1908–21) and De Boer (1914) provide the most important spadework on this aspect. For a general overview of Machaut's sources, see chap. 1.2.6.

RELATED MACHAUT WORKS. Relationships between works that have been noted by scholars. The sorts of relationships range from the complementary nature of the two judgment poems, to the specific citation of *Remede* in *Confort* and of *Fonteinne* in *Voir Dit*, to the controversial links between the narrative and the lyric that Hoepffner noted for *Confort* and *Fonteinne*.

TEXTUAL LEGACY (France, England, or Spain). Studies of the influence of a particular work on later authors. This is a particularly daunting undertaking given the bulk of Chaucer scholarship on the subject of sources and analogues in Machaut. Although new Chaucer bibliographies are fast appearing, I have nevertheless undertaken to provide references to some important studies, in order that the student may have some solid leads for a more detailed pursuit of this aspect of Machaut's literary legacy. Seasoned Chaucer scholars will know to look to the specialized bibliographies (see chap. 2 n. 9).

PROVERBS. Since Hassell (1982) does not index his table of proverbs by work, I have provided a listing for each work here.

3. Le Prologue

FORM. The *Prologue* (so called from the index of MS E, fol. Cr; the name may not be authorial, since the more reliable manuscripts do not name the work in a rubric) is divided into two sections. The first comprises four ballades, the first pair with three strophes of nine lines each, the second pair with three strophes of ten lines each (a total of 114 lines), followed by 184 lines in octosyllabic rhyming couplets. The ballades are highly elegant, displaying complex metrical forms unique among Machaut's many ballades. In the first group of two ballades, *Nature* offers her three children *Scens*, *Rhetorique*, and *Musique*, whose help the author gratefully accepts.[43] In the second group of two ballades, *Amours* in turn offers his children, *Dous Penser* [Sweet Thought], *Plaisance* [Pleasure], and *Esperance* [Hope] to the poet, who again gladly accepts.[44] The elaborate rubrics that introduce each pair of ballades, surely Machaut's own prose, are given with the descriptions of the miniatures in chap. 4.4a.

---

[42] On this question, see Loomis 1944; Heinrichs 1990, 214; B. Nolan 1981, 211n. (with many additional references).

[43] Kelly (1978, 3) offers a gloss for the character *Nature*, or *natura:* "natural talent, inborn inclination"; for *Scens*, Calin (1974, 235) suggests several possible interpretations: "inspiration? the faculty of reason which plans and controls artistic creation? the art of composition?" See also Kelly 1978, 11; Cerquiglini 1985b, 18–19; Newels 1989, 194 n. 2 ("Kunstsinn"); L.W. Johnson 1990, 33 and n. 46, 36; Lukitsch 1983, 259–62; Kelly 1992, 137–39. *Rhetorique* personifies the technical aspects of versification.

[44] For *Dous Penser*, Newels (1989, 194 n. 5) gives "Gedanken ohne Falsch" [Guileless Thought]; for *Plaisance*, "glückliches Begehren" [Propitious Desire]. Many of the literary studies listed below provide further discussion of the personification figures.

1. Ballade, *Je, Nature, par qui tout est fourmé*
   Refrain: [*Nommé sont*] *Scens, Retorique et Musique* (first three syllables vary)
   3 strophes: $\frac{a\ b\ \ a\ b\ c\ c\ d\ c\ D}{1010\ 1010\ 8107'1010'}$ a: *-mé*, b: *-mer*, c: *-ans*, d: *-ique*

2. Ballade, *Riens ne me doit excuser ne deffendre*
   Refrain: *Tant qu'en ce mont vous plaira que je vive*
   3 strophes: $\frac{a\ b\ \ a\ b\ c\ c\ d\ c\ D}{10'10\ 10'10\ 8108'1010'}$ a: *-endre*, b: *-ement*, c: *-ez*, d: *-ive*

3. Ballade, *Je sui Amours qui maint cuer esbaudi*
   Refrain: [*C'est*] *Dous Penser, Plaisance et Esperance* (first syllable varies)
   3 strophes: $\frac{a\ b\ \ a\ b\ \ c\ \ d\ c\ d\ D}{1010'\ 1010'\ 8'10'10'10'10'10'}$ a: *-di*, b: *-ie*, c: *-aire*, d: *-ance*

4. Ballade, *Graces ne say, loange ne merci*
   Refrain: *A mon pooir, tant comme je vivray*
   3 strophes: $\frac{a\ b\ \ a\ b\ c\ c\ d\ c\ d\ D}{1010\ 1010\ 81010101010}$ a: *-ci*, b: *-er*, c: *-is*, d: *-ray*

5. Narrative. Having mentioned the *dit* genre in the four lyrical ballades, Machaut enumerates several other genres in the following narrative section: *chansonnettes, doubles hoqués, lais, motés, rondiaus, virelais* or *chansons baladees, complaintes*, and *balades entees* (pt. V, ll. 13–16).[45] The longest portion of the narrative *Prologue* is the section devoted to music, juxtaposing sacred music—David and his harp (pt. V, ll. 126–34)—with secular music—Orpheus and his harp (pt. V, ll. 135–43).[46] In the section devoted to *Retorique*, Machaut lists several technical categories of rhymes—*rime serpentine, equivoque, leonine, croisie, retrograde, sonant*, and *consonant* (pt. V, ll. 147–58)—a catalogue predating the tabular enumerations in treatises of the Second Rhetoric by twenty years (on the rhymes listed, see Wimsatt 1991b, 299 n. 62).

MANUSCRIPTS.
   Complete *Prologue:*
   [5] **A**   fols. Dr–Ev (ballades); Fv–Gv (narrative portion)
   [6] **F**   fols. 1r–3r
   [18] **Pm**   fols. 1r–3b

   Only the four ballades:
   [7] **E**   fol. 1r
   [17] **H**   fol. 97r–97v (ballade no. 4 lacks str. 3)

FACSIMILES (refer to chap. 4.4a). Miniatures A1–2; Pm1 and 3; F1; E1a–b.

EDITIONS. Tarbé 1849, 3–10 (incomplete, corrupt); Chichmaref 1909, 1:3–13 (omits three lines, see Cerquiglini 1985b, 16 n. 6); Hoepffner 1908–21, 1:1–12; Patterson 1935, 2:72–74 (ballades 1 and 3); Poirion 1971, 243–45 (pt. V, ll. 1–180, with glossary in modern French); Palmer 1993a, 2–18. The edition of Hoepffner is the one cited here.

TRANSLATIONS. Complete translation in Palmer 1993a, 3–19. Excerpts in Kelly 1978, 4, 11–12; Mulder 1978, 46–50 (Dutch); Huot 1987, 237; Newels 1989, 193–95 (German); Steinle 1989, 75–78; Wilkins 1989, 343, 345; L.W. Johnson 1990, 29–33; and Cerquiglini-Toulet 1991a, 228.

PATRON. Strikingly, the *Prologue* is a work not associated with a patron, but rather with Machaut's own desire to preface the collection of his life's works—we know it as MS A—with an all-encompassing statement of his artistic aims. This is carried into the iconography of the *Prologue* miniatures, where the author, not the patron, is depicted (Ferrand 1987).

---

[45] For possible interpretations of the term *balade entée*, see Reaney 1954a, 635; 1959b, 25–27; Sonnemann 1969, 29 n. 13; Wilkins 1969a, 130 n. 39; Günther 1972, 53–59; Wilkins 1972, 177 n. 188; Arlt 1982, 206, 239–40; Frobenius 1986, 11. Perhaps it refers to the phenomenon of crosswise borrowing between lyrics, documented in Roques 1982.

[46] The segment on music (pt. V, ll. 85–146) has been set to music by the Swiss composer Frank Martin (1890–1974); see chap. 2.5.

DATE. ca. 1372. The formal division of the *Prologue* into a lyrical section (the four ballades) and a narrative section (the 184 ll. in rhyming couplets) may explain the curious source situation. The "shorter" form of the *Prologue* serves to introduce manuscripts that place the lyrical works, the *Loange*, at their head (**E** and **H**), while the complete *Prologue* introduces manuscripts that place the narrative poems at their head (**A**, **F**, **Pm**). It appears that Machaut's final choice was to begin with the narrative poems, yet it does not necessarily follow that there are two chronological stages to the composition of the *Prologue*. Later collections that began with the lyrical poems (MSS **E** and **H**) simply took the four *Prologue* ballades as introductory works, and placed them at the head of the collection. The gatherings that include the *Prologue* in MS **A** are very irregular with regard to manuscript structure (Earp 1983, 85, 344), and this, taken with the fact that the *Prologue* does not appear in the index of **A**, implies that this work was new at the time of the redaction of **A**, and that the problems of incorporating it into a large manuscript had not yet been solved.[47] It appears that the author, grappling with the efforts of executing a definitive manuscript of his oeuvre, wrote the *Prologue* expressly for this occasion, and sent the text of the opening ballades to Paris, a commission by the author, to be copied and illustrated in the most luxurious fashion by the most distinguished illuminator of the capital (see chap. 4.2 table 4.5). The long rubrics that accompany the ballades served as Machaut's detailed instructions to the illuminator.

DISCUSSION (literary). Hoepffner 1908–21, 1:lii–lv; Patterson 1935, 1:80–83, 95–96, 2:72–73nn.; S.J. Williams 1952, 6–31; Laurie 1964, 561–62, 568; Poirion 1965, 90–91, 96–97 n. 78, 97, 103, 193, 194, 196, 200–201, 204–5, 369, 428, 487, 514, 516, 535 n. 106, 582 n. 6; Brewer 1966, 21–22; Heger 1967, 88; Sonnemann 1969, 26–36; Jung 1971; Poirion 1971, 50–51; Oliver 1972; G. Olson 1973, 718–19; Calin 1974, 234–37; Connery 1974, 98–100 (links *Prologue* with *Remede*); Jonen 1974, 91–92; Brownlee 1978a, 221–22, 227–30; 1978b, 5–8; Kelly 1978, 4, 11–12 et passim; Mulder 1978, 17, 35, 44–64, 80; S.J. Williams 1978, 189–93; Lubiensky-Bodenham 1979, 37; Badel 1980, 87; Little 1980, 48–49; Ferrand 1982; Kelly 1983, 105, 117, 120; Lukitsch 1983 (also deals with musical discussions); Brownlee 1984, 16–20; Palmer 1984, xix–xxii; J. Stevens 1984, 119–21; Cerquiglini 1985b, 15–21, 111, 119, 154, 212, 225; Tavani 1985, 248–54 (also deals with musical discussions); Nouvet 1986, 355–56 n. 10; Cerquiglini 1987c, 316; Huot 1987, 236–38, 303–4; Kelly 1987, 96; Palmer 1987b, 31–33; Baumgartner 1988, 171; Frobenius 1988, 6–7 (hocket); R. Morris 1988, 552; Palmer 1988, xix–xxix, xxxiii, xxxviii; Zeeman 1988, 832–35; Edwards 1989, 55, 71–72; Kelly 1989, 96; Mühlethaler 1989, 404 (musical discussion); Newels 1989, 193–95, 196; Steinle 1989, 75–79; Wilkins 1989, 342–45; L.W. Johnson 1990, 28–35; Cerquiglini-Toulet 1991a, 227–28; Wimsatt 1991a, 134–35; 1991b, 3–5, 15; Kelly 1992, 137–39, 148–49 et passim; Arlt 1993, 42–43; Cerquiglini-Toulet 1993b, 73–74; 1993c, 40; Page 1993, 13–14; Palmer 1993b, 286–88, 290–91, 299, 304.

DISCUSSION (codicological, art historical). See chap. 4.2 table 4.5; Mulder 1978, 44–49, 56–64; Earp 1983, 83–87; Ferrand 1987; Sterling 1987, 182.

LITERARY ANTECEDENTS. Alain de Lille, *De Planctu Naturae* (Huot 1993, 270, 272). *Roman de la Rose* (Brownlee 1984, 17, 19–20; Huot 1993, 242, 267–72). Wimsatt (1991b, 56) considers the first 96 ll. of Jean de le Mote's *Regret Guillaume* (1339) as the most important antecedent of Machaut's *Prologue*.

TEXTUAL LEGACY (France). Froissart, *Paradis d'Amour* (Huot 1987, 303–4)[48]; *Joli Buisson de Jonece* (Zeeman 1988, 838). Deschamps, ballade *Armes, Amours, dames, chevalerie* (Mühlethaler 1989, 395, 401).

---

[47] Some details of the ruling of the parchment in MS **A** further reflect on the chronology of the collection of that manuscript (see Earp 1983, 173 n. 330).

[48] Note, however, that Froissart's *Paradis* was written too early for Machaut's *Prologue* to have exerted influence (on the date, see below, n. 105).

4. *Le Dit dou Vergier*

FORM. Octosyllabic rhyming couplets, 1293 lines.

MANUSCRIPTS.

[1] **C**	fols. 93r–102v		[7] **E**	fols. 18r–21v		
[2] **W**	fols. 23r–29v		[10] **M**	fols. 1r–9r		
[3] **Vg**	fols. 39r–47r		[11] **D**	fols. 48r–58r		
[4] **B**	fols. 56r–64r		[15] **K**	fols. 21r–28r		
[5] **A**	fols. 1r–9r		[16] **J**	fols. 21r–30r		
[6] **F**	fols. 3r–9v		[18] **Pm**	fols. 3r–11r		

FACSIMILES (refer to chap. 4.4b). Miniatures **J**2; F6, 7, and 9; E7. Samaran/Marichal 1959, plate clxxxvii (MS **J**, fol. 29r).

EDITIONS. Tarbé 1849, 11–39 (incomplete, corrupt); Hoepffner 1908–21, 1:13–56; Palmer 1993a, 22–86.

TRANSLATIONS. Excerpts in Kelly 1978, passim; complete in Palmer 1993a, 23–87.

ANAGRAM. None (Hoepffner 1908–21, 1:lv and n. 3; de Looze 1988b, 552, 556; 1991, 169).

PATRON. John of Luxembourg, king of Bohemia (Poirion 1965, 194). Davis (1991, 27–28, 30–31) relates aspects of the description of the god of Love to John.

DATE. *Vergier* is undated and contains no historical references that could aid an attempt to date it. Tarbé (1849, xi) does not consider *Vergier* an early work, but Hoepffner (1908–21, 1:lv–lvi) adduces four criteria that argue for an earlier date: (1) position in the manuscripts; (2) lack of an anagram; (3) technical inferiority (see above, n. 7); and (4) the content largely lacks the personal note present in Machaut's other *dits*. Subsequent studies of the poem have not questioned Hoepffner's dating. The earliest date associated with a Machaut *dit* is 1342 (*Lyon*), which might place *Vergier* in the early-to-mid 1330s (cf. Calin 1974, 41), written for John of Luxembourg (cf. chap. 1.5).

DISCUSSION (literary). Chichmaref 1909, 1:xl–xli; Hoepffner 1908–21, 1:lv–lix; Patch 1950, 204; Poirion 1965, 488; Wimsatt 1968, 74–76; Sonnemann 1969, 36–43; Calin 1974, 23–38; Connery 1974, 30–43; Spearing 1976, 41–43, 45; Calin 1978, 181–82; Kelly 1978, 122, 137–38 et passim; Badel 1980, 85–86; Brownlee 1984, 24–37; Cerquiglini 1985b, 178 n. 43; 1986a, 110–11; Davenport 1988, 61; Davis 1991, 24–36, 111–13, 115–18; Imbs 1991, 104–10.

LITERARY ANTECEDENTS. *Roman de la Rose* (Hoepffner 1908–21, 1:lvi–lix; Sonnemann 1969, 39–42, 164; Calin 1974, 23–24, 29–33; 1978, 181–82; Brownlee 1984, 27–32, 36, 227–28 nn. 3–4, 6).

TEXTUAL LEGACY (France). Froissart, *Paradis d'Amours* (Geiselhardt 1914, 38–46). Alain Chartier, *Excusacion aux Dames* (Jonen 1974, 189).

TEXTUAL LEGACY (England). Chaucer, *Book of the Duchess* (Schaar 1955, 274, 380–81; F.N. Robinson 1957, 776 n. to l. 805; Severs 1963; Davis 1991, 45–46); *Complaint unto Pity* (Flügel 1901; Clemen 1963, 181 n. 3; Wimsatt 1978, 79); "Prologue" to the *Legend of Good Women* (Fansler 1914); "Franklin's Tale" (Schofield 1901, 446).

PROVERBS (references to Hassell 1982). A117; A120 (twice).

5. *Le Jugement dou Roy de Behaingne*

FORM. 2079 lines in quatrains concatenated in the following pattern:

a a a b b b c c
1010104 1010104 10 ···, etc. (masculine or feminine rhymes).

Machaut never again utilized the stanzaic form of *Jugement Behaingne* for a narrative work,[49] but similar forms appear especially in some of the *complaintes*: *Tels rit au main* (RF2); *Amours, tu m'as tant* (Cp1); *Mon cuer, m'amour* (Cp6); *Douce dame, vueilliez oïr* (*Complainte de l'Amant* in *Fonteinne*); *Amis, je te vieng* (*Confort de l'Amant et de la Dame* in *Fonteinne*); *Ma chiere dame* (B40); *Marguerite*; *Venus, je t'ay tousjours servi* (VD44); and *Dous amis, que t'ay-je meffait?* (VD53). In these examples, however, the

---

[49] Fourrier (1979) attributes *Cerf Blanc*, which has the same form as *Behaingne*, to Machaut

strophes are not concatenated by rhymes as in *Jugement Behaingne* (see Hoepffner 1908–21, 2:xxxix n. 1). For more on this stanzaic form, see Gröber 1902, 706; Kastner 1905; Hoepffner 1908–21, 1:lix n. 3; Chichmaref 1909, 1:lxix n. 4; Lote 1949–51, 1/2:88–90; Poirion 1965, 407–8; Sonnemann 1969, 68–69, 115–119, 164; Jonen 1974, 82–83; Badel 1980, 156; Dembowski 1987a, 100 n. 18; Ziino 1990, 21–27. For later imitations of this form, see below concerning textual legacy.

MANUSCRIPTS.[50]

[1]	C	fols. 1r–22v	[16]	J	fols. 30v–44v
[2]	W	fols. 10r–21v	[18]	Pm	fols. 11b–23a
[3]	Vg	fols. 47v–60r	[31]	P	fols. 64r–95v
[4]	B	fols. 64v–77r	[32]	Ar	fols. 152v–166v
[5]	A	fols. 9v–22r	[36]	Kr	fols. 18r–41r
[6]	F	fols. 9v–19r	[37]	Ys	fols. 36v–37v
[7]	E	fols. 37r–42v	[38]	Pc	fols. 167r–182v
[10]	M	fols. 9r–21v	[44]	Ra	fols. 81v–115r
[11]	D	fols. 58v–74v	[45]	R	fols. 27v–61r
[15]	K	fols. 30r–40r	[46]	St	fols. 160r–183r (lacks ll. 1–152)

Lost manuscript:
[12] Brussels, lost manuscript in the library of the Burgundian dukes

FACSIMILES (refer to chap. 4.4c). Miniatures C1, 8, and 9; J3; A10; F12 (with fol. 17v); D7.

EDITIONS. Caron 1861; Hoepffner 1908–21, 1:57–135; Palmer 1984; Wimsatt/Kibler 1988, 59–165.

TRANSLATIONS. Windeatt 1982, 3–25; Palmer 1984; Wimsatt/Kibler 1988, 60–164.

ANAGRAM. *Guillemin de Machaut*; see Hoepffner 1906, 405; Frese 1981–82; de Looze 1988a, 207–9; 1988b, 541–43, 546.

PATRON. John of Luxembourg, king of Bohemia. For a literary discussion of the role of the patron in *Jugement Behaingne*, see Kelly 1987, 84–85.

DATE. The rubric in MS M, *Le Jugement dou bon Roy de Behaigne dont dieus ait l'ame*, implies that the patron had died by the time this manuscript was copied, and this led Tarbé (1849, xxiii) to date the work 1347–49, probably 1348, since *Jugement Navarre*, which responds to *Jugement Behaingne*, is dated 1349. It is clear from the narrative, however, that the king of Bohemia was still alive at the time of the composition, and Tarbé's thesis was rejected by Hoepffner (1908–21, 1:lix n. 1). Most scholars have accepted Hoepffner's date of before 1346 (the year of the death of the king of Bohemia). If the basically chronological arrangement of large poems in the manuscripts is sound, and it does seem to be for all larger works after ca. 1350 except *Jugement Navarre*, the work dates from before 1342. Most likely, Machaut composed *Jugement Behaingne* in the mid 1330s, during the heyday of the king of Bohemia, the glitter of whose court is celebrated in this, Machaut's most popular narrative work.

BIOGRAPHY. It appears that Machaut was still in the service of John of Luxembourg, king of Bohemia, at the time of the writing of *Jugement Behaingne*. Indirect reference to Machaut's duties as clerk in the service of John of Luxembourg appear in ll. 1474–75 (see chap. 1.2.7). Machaut's demand as a court poet is evoked at the end of the work, ll. 2052–54. Most scholars agree that Machaut left John's immediate entourage to take up residence in Reims around 1340. For a study of what is known of John's court, see Wilkins 1983b and the references above, chap. 1.5 and 1.5.1.

DISCUSSION (literary). Hoepffner 1908–21, 1:lix–lxiv; Chichmaref 1909, 1:xxx, xli–xlii; Patch 1923, 23 n. 91; 1927, 92 n. 1, 96n.; 1950, 204; Luttrell 1965; Poirion 1965, 115, 194, 418, 488; Wimsatt 1968, 88–93, 96–98, 102; Sonnemann 1969, 44–54; Calin 1974, 39–54; Connery 1974, 44–61; Pelen 1976–77, 128–30; Spearing 1976, 64 n. 22 (citation of *Jugement Navarre* is an error); Brownlee 1978b, 13–14; Calin 1978, 182–84; Kelly

---

(see chap. 5.19).

[50] On the filiation of these many sources, see Kibler/Wimsatt 1987; Wimsatt/Kibler 1988, 11–32.

1978, 137–44 et passim; Luttrell 1978, 276; Planche 1980; Lanoue 1981b, 37–45; Brownlee 1984, 158–171; Palmer 1984, xxiii–xli; 1987b; Guthrie 1985, 210–14, 226–29; Badel 1988, 103–4, 105 et passim; de Looze 1988a; Guthrie 1988–89, 40–47; Heinrichs 1989b, 104–9 et passim; Calin 1990, 76–78; Heinrichs 1990, 185–89; Imbs 1991, 110–16; Wimsatt 1991b, 126–27; Kelly 1992, 146–48; Cerquiglini-Toulet 1993b, 94; Palmer 1993b, 289–90, 297–98 et passim; Butterfield 1994, 10–11.

RELATED MACHAUT WORKS. *Jugement Behaingne* was obviously the inspiration for *Jugement Navarre*; the most nuanced discussion of the series (with the *Lay de Plour, Qui bien aimme* [L22/16]) is Palmer 1993b. Imbs (1991, 110–16) seeks points of contact with the later *Voir Dit*. Huot (1994, 229–32) relates *Jugement Behaingne* and *Jugement Navarre* to the two motets *Tous corps / De* (M2) and *He! Mors / Fine* (M3).

LITERARY ANTECEDENTS. Boethius, *Consolation of Philosophy* (Palmer 1980, 392; Heinrichs 1989b, 104–9 et passim). *Jeux partis* (Hoepffner 1908–21, 1:lx; Sonnemann 1969, 52–53; Calin 1974, 39–40, 43; Feil 1985, 62–68). *Chastelaine de Vergi* (Frappier 1946, 106–7; Calin 1974, 49; Brownlee 1984, 161). *Altercatio Phyllidis et Florae* and love debate tradition (Hoepffner 1908–21, 1:lxi; Scully 1966; Wimsatt 1968, 88–89; Calin 1974, 39–40, esp. n. 2; Jonen 1974, 76–80; Schlumbohm 1974; Pelen 1976–77, 128–33; 1979, 286–97; Wimsatt/Kibler 1988, 9; Wimsatt 1991b, 127 esp. n. 42). *Roman de la Rose* (Calin 1974, 39, 45–46; Kelly 1978, 139–41; Brownlee 1984, 158–59; Palmer 1984, xxix–xxxvii; 1987a, 28–29, 31; 1993b, 289–90, 297). Giles of Rome (Poirion 1965, 605 n. 105). More French works are cited by Hoepffner (1908–21, 1:lxi) and Badel (1988, 108).

TEXTUAL LEGACY (France). Hoepffner (1908–21, 1:iii) notes that Machaut created the genre *jugement d'amour*. *Jugement Behaingne* was doubtless the work that established Guillaume de Machaut's fame as a poet (Hoepffner 1908–21, 1:xxviii). It was the most widely copied, and perhaps most influential, of all of Machaut's larger poems (the twenty extant manuscripts include three from the late fifteenth century). Further, *Jugement Behaingne* is cited by its stanzaic form in the anonymous *Regles de la Seconde Rettorique*; see chap. 2.3.1d. Froissart, *Paradis d'Amour* (Bennett 1991, 286); *Joli Buisson de Jonece* (Bennett 1991, 287). Eustache Deschamps recalled the opening scene of *Jugement Behaingne*, in which the author is hiding in a bush, in two lais (chap. 2.1.1d).[51] Alain Chartier, in his *Belle Dame sans Mercy*, also borrowed the hidden narrator motive from *Jugement Behaingne* (Jonen 1974, 85 n. 37). Martin Le Franc stated in his *Champion des Dames* (ca. 1442) that he did not agree with Machaut's judgment (chap. 2.3.2c).

The following works, which employ the stanzaic form of *Behaingne*, are mentioned in Kastner 1905, 291–92 and Poirion 1965, 401 n. 8, along with some other examples: Jean Froissart, *Dit dou Bleu Chevalier* (Geiselhardt 1914, 47–50; Whiting 1946, 201; Wimsatt 1968, 129–33; 1972a). Oton de Granson, *Livre de Messire Ode* (Wimsatt 1991b, 227–28 nn. 33–34). Christine de Pizan, *Debat de Deux Amans, Livre des Trois Jugemens,* and *Dit de Poissy* (Pugh 1894; Hoepffner 1908–21, 1:vi, lxiv; Schilperoort 1936, 17, 32–38, 46–47, 90; Scully 1966, 159–61; Palmer 1984, xxxii–xxxiii; Willard 1985; Altmann 1987; 1988; 1992, esp. 140–45, 150–52). Alain Chartier, *Debat des Deux Fortunés d'Amours* (Jonen 1974, 82); *Debat de Reveille Matin* (Laidlaw 1974, 39 n. 1); *Livre des Quatre Dames* (a related form, see Jonen 1974, 75, 82–83, 101). Anon., *Cerf Blanc* (see chap. 5.19).

TEXTUAL LEGACY (England). Chaucer, *Book of the Duchess* (for the context, see F.N. Robinson 1957 or Benson 1987, explanatory notes, passim; Kittredge 1909–10, 465–71; 1915a, 60–66; 1915c, passim; B. Harrison 1934, 436–41 et passim; Loomis 1944; Schaar 1955, 22–23, 173–75, 269, 274, 381; Lawlor 1956; Clemen 1963, 47–48, 51–56; Moreton 1963; Brewer 1966, 22–24; Wimsatt 1967a; 1968 appendix, with a line-by-line list of parallelisms, et passim; Brosnahan 1974; Calin 1974, 50, 53–54; Wimsatt 1974, 119–21; Pelen 1976–77, 128–33, 139–47; Wimsatt 1976; 1977; Calin 1978, 177, 186; Palmer 1980; Pearcy 1980; Kaiser 1981; Wimsatt 1981, 120–21; Frese 1981–82; Phillips 1982, 170–76 [excerpts with translations], explanatory notes, passim; Windeatt 1982, ix–xiii [trans. with parallel passages in notes]; Palmer 1984, xxxiii–xxxvii; Cerquiglini 1985b, 144; Kooper 1985, 104–8, 172, 179, 185; S.A. Wright 1986, chap. 3 passim; Calin

---

[51] Cerquiglini (1985a, 25–27) discusses the literary theme of the clerk listening from a concealed position.

1987b, 10; Donnelly 1987, 428; Guthrie 1988–89; Wimsatt/Kibler 1988, 26–32, 473–90; Edwards 1989, 85–88; Stevenson 1989–90, 16–17; Heinrichs 1990, 214; Butterfield 1991, 36–37; Davis 1991, 153–55; Wimsatt 1991b, 126–29; J.J. Anderson 1992; David 1992; Calin 1994, 276–89); *Complaynt d'Amours* (Wimsatt 1978, 72–73); *Complaint of Mars* (Wimsatt 1978, 72–74); *Anelida and Arcite* (Wimsatt 1970–71, 4–5); *Troilus* (Wimsatt 1976; 1977, 216 n. 22; Kelly 1978, 197–98; Guthrie 1985, 210–14, 226–29, 235–41; Wimsatt 1985, 26, 29, 31; 1991b, 150–57; Heinrichs 1989b, esp. 109–15; J.J. Anderson 1991; Windeatt 1992, 118–20); "Prologue" to the *Legend of Good Women* (Calin 1994, 290–91). For Scotland, cf. Wm. Dunbar, *Tretis of the Tua Mariit Wemen and the Wedo* (Pearcy 1980).

PROVERBS (references to Hassell 1982). A10; A75; A89; B199; C24; C209; E26; E62; F4; F25; F75; F123; F125; G10; G36; H22; L92; L101; M37; M210; N12 (twice); N35; O3; O70; O71; P7; P232; P290; R74; R77; S105.

6. Le Jugement dou Roy de Navarre

FORM. Octosyllabic rhyming couplets, 4212 lines. In some manuscripts, Machaut intended the *Lay de Plour, Qui bien aimme* (L22/16; 210 lines) to follow *Jugement Navarre*, although his final decision was to place it with the other lais; see the discussion in chap. 7.3 under *Qui bien aimme*.

MANUSCRIPTS.

[3]	**Vg**	fols. 60v–87r	[7]	**E**	fols. 45r–56v
[4]	**B**	fols. 77v–104r	[10]	**M**	fols. 21v–48v
[5]	**A**	fols. 22v–49r	[11]	**D**	fols. 74v–108r
[6]	**F**	fols. 19v–40r	[18]	**Pm**	fols. 23r–47v

FACSIMILES (refer to chap. 4.4d). Miniatures D9 and 11.

EDITIONS. Hoepffner 1908–21, 1:137–282; Palmer 1988.

RECORDINGS (refer to chap. 8.8). 1750 Arch Records S-1773 (LP) (recitation of some passages from the historical prologue in English trans.); Harmonic Records H/CD 8825 (CD) (recitation of ll. 4199–212).

TRANSLATIONS. Windeatt 1982, 139–44 (partial); Palmer 1988.

ANAGRAM. None needed, since the narrator names himself several times as Guillaume de Machaut (cf. Cerquiglini 1985b, 119–20; de Looze 1988a, 205–6).

PATRON. King Charles of Navarre (based on the title). The characterization of the allegorical figure *Beneürté* [Good Fortune] is so realistic that commentators have sought a historical person behind the description.[52] Paulin Paris (1875, xv n. 1) suggested Béatrix de Bourbon, the widow of John of Luxembourg, while Poirion (1965, 194; but see 604) suggested Bonne of Luxembourg, daughter of John of Luxembourg, king of Bohemia, and wife of John, duke of Normandy (crowned John II on 22 August 1350). In my opinion, this latter identification may hit the mark (cf. chap. 1.9 and 1.12). Machaut apparently served her after the death of her father at Crécy, 26 August 1346 until her death on 11 September 1349 (chap. 1.8).

It is not known under what circumstances Machaut entered the service of the king of Navarre. Hoepffner (1908–21, 3:xxix) asserts that it was Charles's accession to the throne of Navarre in 1349 that occasioned the *Jugement Navarre*, which was surely completed after this date (see chap. 1.12). Lanoue (1981a, 12 n. 14) agrees that *Beneürté* may have been inspired by Bonne of Luxembourg but further notes the death of the queen of France around the same time, and the quick marriage of King Philip VI to Blanche of Navarre, sister of Charles of Navarre, proposing that Machaut's poem served perhaps to celebrate this political marriage. Against this view, see Heinrichs 1990, 189–90 n. 41, 191 n. 43. For a literary discussion of the role of the patron in *Jugement Navarre*, see Kelly 1987, 84–86. Palmer (1993b, 294–95) argues against an extratextual source for the work.

DATE. 9 November 1349 (ll. 24–25), noted since Lebeuf 1753. At the beginning of the poem (ll. 309–458), Machaut chronicled events of the years 1348–49 that were connected with the Black Death. The chronology of the poem is further linked with the copying of MS C, now placed in the early 1350s. Günther (1982, 103) suggested that C was begun for Bonne of

---

[52] On the literary tradition of "Bonneürté," see Patch 1927, 40–42; Planche 1990b.

Luxembourg, and that work was interrupted at her death. The later completion of the manuscript for some other royal patron would explain the breaks in the order of works in the music collection of the manuscript. *Jugement Navarre* does not appear in C, and Machaut may not have completed the narrative until as late as ca. 1355.

BIOGRAPHY. Because the narrator is named "Guillaume de Machaut," early scholars often utilized the *Jugement Navarre* for biographical information concerning the author. Indeed, l. 573 ("C'est la Guillaumes de Machaut" [that's Guillaume de Machaut there]) provided the first modern evidence of Machaut's name (Lebeuf 1753, 378). Mas Latrie (1877b, xii) quoted a passage near the end of *Jugement Navarre* to prove that Machaut was of non-noble birth: "Je, Guillaumes dessus nommez / Qui de Machau sui seurnommez" (ll. 4199–200; see chap. 1.2.3b). P. Paris (1875, xv) quoted the speech of *Souffisance*: "Car vous estes trop jeunes homs / Pour dire si faites raisons" (ll. 3139–40) [For you are too young a man / To support such an opinion (trans. Palmer 1988, 141)] to affirm Machaut's youth, thinking he would have to have been less than fifty years old (see the comment in Imbs 1991, 154 n. 59). Calin (1974, 117), on the other hand, noted that the traits Machaut ascribes to the narrator in *Jugement Navarre* (timidity, cowardice, misogyny) were stereotypical literary traits of a clerk. See further Cerquiglini 1985b, part 2; Palmer 1987a, 31–39.

DISCUSSION (historical). Petit de Julleville 1892–93, 290–92; Coville 1938, 328–29; 1949; Machabey 1955b, 1:43–45; Grimm 1965; Desportes 1979, 544–49; S. Taylor 1980; Lanoue 1981a; Cerquiglini 1985b, 163; Palmer 1988, xxxi–xxxii; Zink 1991. Historical discussions have focused on the chronicle of the plague of 1348–49 in the introductory 430 lines, in which Machaut mentions an eclipse, the charge that the Jews had poisoned the wells, and the flagellants.[53] Desportes (1979, 544–49) gives a detailed account of the chronology of the plague as it affected the area of Reims based on documentary evidence, demonstrating that Machaut's chronicle is generally accurate, although it compresses events lasting eighteen months into a single winter. The plague hit Reims in the autumn of 1348 but was much slowed by the winter. In the spring of 1349, beginning around April, it became more serious, and was at its worst from August to October 1349. Machaut's response to the plague, closing himself up at the beginning of the summer of 1349, not to emerge until the spring of 1350, was a typical precaution. Desportes (1979, 549) estimates that one-fourth to one-third of the population of the town of Reims was wiped out.

On the connection of the historical prologue to the rest of the poem, see Hoepffner 1908–21, 1:lxvii; Lawlor 1956; Muscatine 1957, 100–101; D.W. Robertson 1962, 236n.; Clemen 1963, 136 n. 1; Poirion 1965, 488; Calin 1971, 296–97; 1974, 123–28; Kelly 1978, 147; Mulder 1978, 16–17; Poirion 1978, 203–4; Hieatt 1979–80, 109–10; Ehrhart 1980c; Lanoue 1981a; 1981b, 45–66; Calin 1983b, 147–50; Cerquiglini 1985b, 122; Guthrie 1985, 237 n. 4; Palmer 1987b, 34–35; de Looze 1988a, 206; Palmer 1988, xxix–xxx; Earp 1989, 468 n. 16; Heinrichs 1990, 196 nn. 47–48; Imbs 1991, 264 n. 47; Zink 1991; Kelly 1992, 147; Butterfield 1994, 13–18; Calin 1994, 210–12; Huot 1994, 230–31.

DISCUSSION (literary). Chichmaref 1909, 1:xliv–xlvi; Hoepffner 1908–21, 1:lxiv–lxxxvii; Patch 1923, 23 n. 91; 1927, 64 n. 2; 76 n. 1; Schaar 1954, 93–94; D.W. Robertson 1962, 235–36; Poirion 1965, 80 n. 45, 565 n. 81, 582 n. 6; Heger 1967, 81–91 (prologue); Wimsatt 1968, 93–102; Sonnemann 1969, 91–99, 101–3, 165; Calin 1971; 1974, 110–29; F. and W. Calin 1974, 243; Connery 1974, 62–78; Fox 1974, 294–95; Ehrhart 1974, 96–152; Pelen 1976–77, 133–34; Spearing 1976, 43–46, 69 n. 30; Brownlee 1978b, 10–11; Kelly 1978, 137–44 et passim; Burke 1980; Ehrhart 1980b; S. Taylor 1980; Lanoue 1981a; 1981b, 45–66; Rychner 1981, 66–68; G. Olson 1982; Picherit 1982; Calin 1983b, 141–50; Cerquiglini 1985b, 121–22, 127, 135–36, 174, 181–82, 184, 185, 186 n. 13; Huot 1987, 247–48; Palmer 1987b; Davenport 1988, 62–63; de Looze 1988a; Palmer 1988, intro.; Calin 1990, 76–78; Heinrichs 1990, 185, 189–96; J. Root 1990, 179–91; Davis 1991, 109; Imbs 1991, 146–55; Zink 1991; Ehrhart 1992, 9–14; Kelly 1992, 138–39, 146–48; Cerquiglini-Toulet 1993b, 93–94; Palmer 1993b, 291–93 et passim; Butterfield 1994; Calin 1994, 205–12.

Badel (1988, 108) mentions several further examples of literary controversies in the fourteenth and fifteenth centuries.

---

[53] On Machaut's account of the persecution of the Jews, see Girard 1986 and remarks in Margolis 1992, 56, 58, 66.

RELATED MACHAUT WORKS. *Jugement Navarre* ll. 1272–74=*Confort* ll. 2930–33; see chap.
1.6.2a, and chap. 7.3, literary discussion of *Donnez, signeurs* (B26). *Doubtance de meffaire,
Honte,* and *Paour* (*Jugement Navarre* ll. 1179–86) are again linked in the ballade *Honte,
paour* (Lo201=B25); see chap. 7.3, literary discussion. On the *Lai de Plour, Qui bien
aimme* (L22/16), see chap. 7.3. The complementary relationship of *Jugement Navarre* to
Machaut's own *Jugement Behaingne* is obvious; see, for example, Calin 1974, 110–11;
Cerquiglini 1985b, 61; de Looze 1988a; 1988b, 541; Palmer 1993b. Several scholars
contest the view (explicitly noted in l. 811) that *Jugement Navarre* is a reversal of the
judgement rendered in *Jugement Behaingne*; on the controversy, see Pelen 1976–77, 133–
34; Lanoue 1981a; Palmer 1987b, 32–36; 1988, xxiv–xxix, xxxii–xxxiv, xxxviii–xxxix,
xl–xli; Heinrichs 1990, 189–90 n. 41). On *Jugement Navarre* and the *Remede,* see Kelly
1978, 138–39. See Imbs (1991, 146–55) on links to the later *Voir Dit.* Huot (1994, 229–
32) relates *Jugement Behaingne* and *Jugement Navarre* to the two motets *Tous corps / De*
(M2) and *He! Mors / Fine* (M3).
LITERARY ANTECEDENTS. Boethius, *Consolation of Philosophy* (Lanoue 1981a, 9; Kelly
1987, 86; Palmer 1987b, 37; Kelly 1992, 138, 147–48). Marie de France, *Lanval* (Palmer
1987b, 34). *Lancelot, Tristan,* or *Chastelaine de Vergi* (Hoepffner 1908–21, 1:lxxxiii,
lxxxvii; Frappier 1946, 107–8; Calin 1974, 111; 1983b, 145). Bestiaries (Hoepffner 1908–
21, 1:lxxxiii–lxxxv). Personified virtues, derived from four cardinal virtues and seven gifts
of the Holy Spirit (Ehrhart 1979; 1992, 10–11); or, derived from the zodiac (Lanoue 1981a,
8). Duties of rulers tradition (Ehrhart 1992, 9, 13–14). *Roman de la Rose* (Pelen 1976–77,
133; Palmer 1987b, 32; 1988, xxxix–xli; 1993b, 296–97). On the tradition of the love
debate, see Scully 1966; Pelen 1976–77, esp. 133–34; 1979. An important element in
Jugement Navarre is the extensive use of *exempla* drawn from the Bible (cf. esp. Imbs
1991, 153–54) and from Greek and Roman mythology. The most important are borrowed
from the *Ovide Moralisé*: (1) the abandonment and death of Dido; (2) the myth of Theseus
and Ariadne; (3) the myth of Jason and Medea; (4) the myth of Pyramus and Thisbe; (5) the
myth of Hero and Leander, etc. (Hoepffner 1908–21, 1:lxxii–lxxxii [summarized in Palmer
1988, xlii–xliii]; De Boer 1913, 89–90; 1914, 342–46; Geiselhardt 1914, 34–37; Poirion
1965, 588; Leube 1969; Sonnemann 1969, 93–95; Kelly 1978, 157; Burke 1980; Kelly
1981, 87; Picherit 1982; Davis 1991, 59–69, 157–58). Jean de le Mote, *Regret Guillaume*
(Hoepffner 1911, 165; Wimsatt 1991b, 70, 163).
TEXTUAL LEGACY (France). Froissart, *Prison Amoureuse* (Heinrichs 1990, 196–97); *Joli
Buisson de Jonece* (Geiselhardt 1914, 34–36; Bennett 1991, 287 n. 8). Deschamps, *Lay de
Plour* and *Lay du Roy* (Gröber/Hofer 1933, 19). Christine de Pizan, *Epistre au Dieu
d'Amours* (Leube 1969, 55–56); *Debat de Deux Amans* and *Livre des Trois Jugemens*
(Schilperoort 1936, 32–33, 61–65; Willard 1985; Poirion 1965, 249 n. 33); *Epistre Othea*
(P.G.C. Campbell 1924, 116–17); *Dit de Poissy* (Altmann 1987; 1988); *Livre du Chemin
de Long Estude* (Willard 1985, 389); *Livre du Duc des Vrais Amans* (Cerquiglini 1985b,
122). Alain Chartier, *Excusation aux Dames* also calls for an *amende* from the author, as at
the end of Machaut's *Jugement Navarre* (Jonen 1974, 195–96; ed. Laidlaw 1974, 366 ll.
111–12). For other examples of juridical debate works, see Badel 1988, 109–10.
TEXTUAL LEGACY (England). Chaucer, *Book of the Duchess* (Kittredge 1915c, 3–4; Schaar
1955, 274–75; Lawlor 1956; Wimsatt 1968, 156, 159; Longo 1982, 238–39, 246–47;
Benson 1987, 969 note to l. 346; Palmer 1988, xliii–xlv; Butterfield 1994, 18–27; Calin
1994, 278, 283); *Complaint unto Pity* (Clemen 1963, 181 n. 3); *House of Fame* (Lowes
1918, 324–25; Shannon 1929, 67–68; Meech 1931); "Prologue" to the *Legend of Good
Women,* or *Legend of Ariadne,* etc. (Kittredge 1909–10, 471–74; Lowes 1918, 320–24;
Shannon 1929, 229–49; Meech 1931; Estrich 1939; Schaar 1955, 294–95; Wimsatt 1968,
93–94, 96; 1974, 121–22; 1976, 278; Hieatt 1979–80, 109; Longo 1982, 212–13;
Windeatt 1982, 139; Calin 1987b, 13–14; Palmer 1987b, 38; 1988, xlv–xlvi; Heinrichs
1990, 250–51, 253–56; Wimsatt 1991b, 70, 75, 162–65; Calin 1994, 290–301). Gower,
Confessio Amantis (Calin 1994, 388). Hoccleve, *Regement of Princes* (Calin 1994, 408–
11); *The Series* (Calin 1994, 415, 417).
PROVERBS (references to Hassell 1982). A59; A200; B68; B79; C74; C99; C228; C292;
D67; F4; F44; F63; F109; F147; G46; H38; H60; L7; L68; M66; M192; M242; P232;
R43; S57; T70.

7. Remede de Fortune

FORM. Octosyllabic rhyming couplets, 4298 lines (ed. Hoepffner 1908–21); 4300 lines (ed. Wimsatt/Kibler 1988). There are nine lyrical insertions, with music supplied for seven of them (for the metrical forms of the lyrics, with further bibliography, see chap. 7.3):

1. *Qui n'aroit autre deport* (RF1), a lai with music (twelve strophes, 250 ll.).[54]
2. *Tels rit au main qui au soir pleure* (RF2), a *complainte* with music (thirty-six sixteen-line strophes, 576 ll.), with a total of sixty-one different rhyming syllables.
3. *Joie, plaisance, douce norriture* (RF3), a *chant royal* with music (five ten-line strophes plus an envoy of three lines, 53 ll.).
4. *En amer a douce vie* (RF4), *balade* (or *baladelle*) with music (duplex ballade, three 12-line strophes, 36 ll.).
5. *Dame, de qui toute ma joie vient* (RF5), *balade* with music (three 8-line strophes, 24 ll.).
6. *Amours, je te lo et graci*, a *priere* without music (twelve 12-line strophes, 144 ll.) with the metrical pattern $\frac{aaaaab\ a\ aaaab\ ccccb\ c\ ccccb}{888884\ 888884\ 888884\ 888884}$ etc.[55]

7. *Dame, a vous sans retollir* (RF6), a *chanson baladée* (virelai) with music (three 13-line strophes plus a seven-line refrain, 67 ll.).
8. *Dieus, quant venra le temps et l'eure / Que je voie ce que j'aim si?* (ll. 3502–3), a two-line refrain to a dance song, perhaps a virelai, without music.
9. *Dame, mon cuer en vous remaint* (RF7), a rondeau with music (8 ll.). MS **Pe** [20] substitutes the rondeau *Tant doucement* (R9), see n. 60 below.

MANUSCRIPTS.[56]

[1]	**C**	fols. 23r–58v (with music)	[7]	**E**	fols. 22r–36v[57] (music)
[2]	**W**	fols. 30r–41v (frag.; music lost)	[10]	**M**	fols. 50r–77r (text only)
[3]	**Vg**	fols. 90r–121r (music)	[15]	**K**	fols. 43r–47r; 50r–60r (music)[58]
[4]	**B**	fols. 107r–138r (music)	[16]	**J**	fols. 47r–76r (text only)[59]
[5]	**A**	fols. 49v–80r (music)	[18]	**Pm**	fols. 47v–73v (text only)
[6]	**F**	fols. 40r–63v (music)	[20]	**Pe**	fols. 1r–36v (music)[60]

FURTHER SOURCES FOR INDIVIDUAL LYRICAL INSERTIONS.

[40]	**I**	fol. 20r	*Dame, de qui* (RF5; text only)
[49]	**Jp**	fol. 68r	*Dame, de qui* (RF5; text only)
[50]	**Pa**	fol. 49r	*Joie, plaisance* (RF3; text only)
[50]	**Pa**	fol. 49r	*Dame, a vous* (RF6; text only)
[58]	**Trém**	fol. xvi	*En amer* (RF4; index only; text and music lost)
[61]	**F P**	fol. 97r	*En amer* (RF4; text and music)
[63]	**P R**	fol. 63r	*En amer* (RF4; text and music)
[63]	**P R**	fol. 68v	*Dame, de qui* (RF5; text and music)
[64]	**P it**	fol. 180r	*En amer* (RF4; text and music)

FACSIMILES (refer to chap. 4.4e). Miniatures C10–43 (i.e., all of the miniatures in C for the *Remede*; the reproduction of C33 includes the music of *Dame, de qui* [RF5]; one of the reproductions of C36 includes part of the music of *Dame, a vous* [RF6]); K4 (with fol. 46v [new 30v]); J5; A15–16; Vg10 (with fol. 90r); F14.

---

[54] The lai is entitled *Lay de Bon Espoir* in MSS **K** and **J**. In *Confort*, Machaut refers to a lai by that title (see chap. 5.10, "related Machaut works," item h).

[55] For a discussion, see Poirion 1965, 417.

[56] On the filiation of these many sources, see Kibler/Wimsatt 1987; Wimsatt/Kibler 1988, 40–54.

[57] *Ci commence L'Escu Bleu*. For the symbolism of the color blue, see Fourrier 1979, 57–59. On the coat of arms, see Kelly 1978, 136, 150; Huot 1987, 254–56. Sonnemann (1969, 59–61) considers the title *L'Escu Bleu* more apt than *Remede de Fortune*.

[58] Music for *En amer* (RF4) and *Dame, de qui* (RF5) only.

[59] Blank space for music for *En amer* (RF4) and *Dame, de qui* (RF5) only.

[60] In MS **Pe** [20], the musically more modern rondeau *Tant doucement* (R9) was substituted for *Dame, mon cuer en vous* (RF7).

EDITIONS (text). Tarbé 1849, 83–88 (ll. 1863–922, 1935–40, 3891–4018); Hoepffner 1908–21, 2:1–157; Wimsatt/Kibler 1988, 167–409.

EDITIONS (text and music of the lyrical insertions). See chap. 7.3.

RECORDINGS (refer to chap. 8.8). Harmonic Records H/CD 8825 (CD) (ll. 3960–86/3962–88). For recordings of the music of the lyric insertions, see chap. 8.6.

TRANSLATIONS. Kelly 1978 (many excerpts, passim); Windeatt 1982, 58–64 (excerpts); Gallo 1985, 132–33 (excerpts concerning music); Switten 1988b and 1988c (all seven lyrics, with excerpts from the narrative); Wimsatt/Kibler 1988, 168–408 (complete). For other translations of the lyrical insertions, see the discography (chap. 8.3 and 8.8). Heinrichs (1990, 222–23) provides a summary of the speech of Hope (ll. 1608–3180).

ANAGRAM. *Guillemins de Machaut*; see Hoepffner 1906, 405; de Looze 1988b, 546n., 547; Davis 1991, 93; de Looze 1993b, 83.

PATRON. Bonne of Luxembourg, a possibility suggested by Poirion (1965, 201 n. 28, but see p. 604), and bolstered by Wimsatt/Kibler (1988, 33–36, 53; see also Wimsatt 1991b, 32–34).[61] Some literary historians argue that it would have been a serious breach of decorum for anyone in Machaut's social position to dare to call the wife of the future king of France *"amie"* (see, for instance, Margaret J. Ehrhart's review of Wimsatt/Kibler 1988). And yet a link to Bonne of Luxembourg serves to tie together some loose ends, allowing a broader understanding of the transformed treatment of love seen in *Remede*. Hope, instead of *merci* (fulfillment), becomes sufficient as a response to Desire (Kelly 1978, chap. 6; 1992, 138, 146–49). Since this view is first palpable in the *Remede*, it serves as further corroboration for Hoepffner's chronology, and Kelly (1978, 144) agrees with Hoepffner in placing *Lyon* after *Remede*.[62] Machaut's approach to this problem is remarkably fitting, since he was serving a high-born female patroness at a time when—as Machaut himself constantly reminds us—the position of the clerk-poet, serving to celebrate but not participate in the loves of the aristocracy, was severely tried. Indeed, the most oft-quoted passage in the *Remede*—even by Machaut himself in the *Voir Dit*—is "Car qui de sentement ne fait, / son oeuvre et son chant contrefait" (ll. 407–8) (see below, "related Machaut works"). Machaut, in effect, informs us of the importance of inspiration for the artistic fulfillment of his patron's command, while at the same time, by adjusting his treatment of sufficiency in love, he comes to terms with the new requirements of serving his patroness Bonne of Luxembourg. R. Morris (1988, 554) has thus missed the point: "how can a man live forever on the long straw of Hope?" Heinrichs (1990, 195 n. 46) brings objections to Kelly's arguments; her interpretations are wholly divorced from a consideration of factors of patronage. See further chap. 1.9.

DATE. a. before 1342. Hoepffner (1908–21, 1:lxiv–lxvi) based this date first on the order of works in the manuscripts. Second, he noted (2:ii) that *Confort*, datable 1357, refers back to *Remede*.[63] Third (2:xv, n. 1), Machaut composed *Remede* before *Lyon* of 1342, because *Lyon* adds new examples to the enumeration of the characteristics of the true lover in the *Remede*. Finally (2:xxxi–xxxii), Machaut did not utilize a translation of Boethius's *Consolation of Philosophy* that was completed 31 May 1336.[64] Wimsatt and Kibler (1988, 33) also argue for the earlier date.

b. before 1357. Machabey 1955b, 1:50; Poirion 1965, 201 and n. 28; Poirion 1971, 195 ("1356"); Earp 1989, 470–71 n. 20. See chap. 5.1.

---

[61] In a different context, Poirion (1965, 194 and 211) proposed that literary invocations of the god of Love refer to the patron. It would then seem logical that an invocation of "Bonne Amour" should serve as a cover for a female patron. Bonne of Luxembourg is the obvious candidate.

[62] For additional passages that concern chronology, see Kelly 1978, 131 and 137–39. Sonnemann (1969, 61) considers the motto of l. 1888, "Qui sueffre, il vaint" ["He who endures, conquers!" (trans. Wimsatt/Kibler 1988, 270)] to characterize Machaut's conception of love, and mentions frequent occurrences of the noun "souffisance" in Machaut's works.

[63] See chap. 5.10, "related Machaut works." Rive (1780, 20 n. 65) was the first to notice this.

[64] Hoepffner did not know of Jean de Meun's prose translation of Boethius; see Brownlee 1984, 50 n. 22.

DISCUSSION (literary). Hoepffner 1908–21, 2:i–liv; 3:256 n. to l. 905 of *Fonteinne* (color); Patch 1923, 21–23; 1927, passim; Siciliano 1934, 298–99, 302, 427 n. 4; Moore 1951, 39–40; Huizinga 1953, 126–27; Poirion 1965, 84–85, 469 n. 53, 535; Wimsatt 1968, 106–11; Sonnemann 1969, 54–77 (pp. 65–76 on lyrics), 164; Oliver 1972; J. Stevens 1973, 201–3; Calin 1974, 55–74 (pp. 70–72 on lyrics); Connery 1974, 80–108; Jonen 1974, 101–2; B. and J. Cerquiglini 1976; Pelen 1976–77, 134–36; Cerquiglini 1977a; Kelly 1978, 3–4, 100–104, 121–23, 130–37 149–50 et passim; Hieatt 1979–80, 110–11 (numerology); Beer 1980, 30–31; Lanoue 1981b, 66–83; Kelly 1983, 111; Brownlee 1984, 37–63, 231 n. 26; Lanoue 1984; Malizia 1984; Cerquiglini 1985b, 61–62, 101, 178 n. 43, 182, 200; Wimsatt 1985, 26–29, 32; Huot 1987, 249–59, 275–80 (lyrics, iconography); Switten 1988a (manuscript presentation); Calin 1988–89; Brownlee 1989a, 109–11; Newels 1989, 201–3; Steinle 1989 (lyrics); Switten 1989 (lyrics); Heinrichs 1990, 221–24; Brownlee 1991a (lyrics); Butterfield 1991, 42–48; Davis 1991, 82–94 (lyrics); Imbs 1991, 116–25; Wimsatt 1991b, 30–36, 127–28; 1991c; Zeeman 1991, 224–25; Enders 1992 (lyrics); Boulton 1993, 188–92, 291 (lyrics); de Looze 1993b; Butterfield 1994, 11; Calin 1994, 198–205 (lyrics); Gaudet/Hieatt 1994, 185 (numerology of lyrics). For further references to the lyrics, see chap. 7.3 under the individual titles. On the game of "le Roi qui ne ment" (ll. 767–70), see Calin 1974, 67; Cerquiglini 1985b, 133 n. 46; Green 1990.

DISCUSSION (musical). Ludwig 1911; Günther 1957, 115–20; Fowler 1979, 120–22, 288; Lanoue 1984; Malizia 1984; J. Stevens 1984, 109–19; Gallo 1985, 41–42; Wimsatt/Kibler 1988, 413–15 (discussion by Baltzer); Switten 1988c; 1989; Hoffmann-Axthelm 1991, 351. For further references to musical works, see chap. 7.3 under the individual titles.

Machaut refers to the Ars Antiqua and Ars Nova (cf. Cerquiglini 1985b, 212, 246): Et s'i ot des musicïens / Milleurs assez et plus scïens / En la vieus et nouvelle forge / Que Musique qui les chans forge (ll. 3999–4002/4001–4) [And there were musicians more skilled and knowledgeable in both the new and old styles, and who could sing better than Music, who writes the songs (ed. and trans. Wimsatt/Kibler 1988, 392–93)].

Concerning the list of instruments (ll. 3961–86/3963–88), see Lebeuf 1753, 379; Roquefort-Flaméricourt 1815; Duval 1824; Bottée de Toulmon 1838; Travers 1881; Abert 1904–5, 354–55 (with a similar list); Ludwig 1926–54, 1:102, 2:53a* n. 1 (with additional bibliography); Gennrich 1926–27 (with other lists); Pirro 1930, 71; Machabey 1931, 409–11; Pirro 1940, 10–12; Reese 1940, 383–84; Machabey 1955b, 2:135–57 (with additional bibliography); Reaney 1956, 10–17; Calin 1974, 63 n. 5; Connery 1974, 97–98; Godwin 1977; L. Wright 1977; Gómez 1979; Wilkins 1983b, 259–60; Lanoue 1981b, 127–31; 1984, 368; Vellekoop 1984; L. Wright 1986; Bec 1992, 128, 223; 1993.

DISCUSSION (art historical). Avril 1973; 1978; 1982a; Pearsall/Salter 1973, 224 n. 62 (park of Hesdin); Van Buren 1986, esp. 123 (park of Hesdin, with additional bibliography); Huot 1987, 249–59 (iconography of MS C); Wimsatt/Kibler 1988, 35–36.

RELATED MACHAUT WORKS. Cited in *Confort* (l. 2248); *Remede* was influential for *Fonteinne* (Wimsatt/Kibler 1988, 39). *Confort* (l. 2249) may cite the lai *Qui n'aroit* (RF1); see n. 54 above). Lines 407–8, "Car qui de sentement ne fait, / Son oeuvre et son chant contrefait" [because he who does not compose according to his feelings falsifies his work and his song (ed. and trans. Wimsatt/Kibler 1988, 188–89)], are cited twice in the *Voir Dit*; see letter 8 (ed. P. Paris 1875, 61), and the mention of "sentement" in letter 35 (ed. P. Paris 1875, 263 and 264); see also Ludwig 1926–54, 2:55b* n. 2; Sonnemann 1969, 141–44; Burrow 1971, 52–53 and n. 18 (mention of "sentement" in Boccaccio, Froissart, and Chaucer); Cerquiglini 1977a, 25; Kelly 1978, 12, 245–53; Lühmann 1978, 50; Little 1980, 45–48; Winn 1981, 119–20; Cerquiglini 1983, 285; Brownlee 1984, 41, 104–5; de Looze 1984, 147; J. Stevens 1984, 112–13; Cerquiglini 1985b, 273 s.v. "sentement," esp. 196; Zeeman 1988, 821–22, 832–42 (also considers Froissart, Christine, and Chaucer); Butterfield 1991, 42–48; Imbs 1991, 118; Cerquiglini-Toulet 1991a, 226–27 (Froissart). The proverb "Qu'assés rueve qui se complaint" (l. 3764/3766) [he who laments has much to request (ed. and trans. Wimsatt/Kibler 1988, 378–79)] reappears in the *Voir Dit* and in the *complainte Sire, a vous* (Cp7); see below, n. 85. Additional passages of the *Remede* are compared to the *Voir Dit* in Eichelberg 1935, 80–86 (including instances of direct borrowing); see also Cerquiglini 1983, 288; Huot 1987, 280; Imbs 1991, 116–25, 245–46, 253; Boulton 1993, 198; Huot 1993, 271.

LITERARY ANTECEDENTS. Bible (Brownlee 1991a, 5). Boethius, *Consolation of Philosophy*, cited specifically in the *complainte Tels rit* (RF2), l. 982 (Hoepffner 1908–21, 2:xix–xxxii; Patch 1935, 96; Poirion 1965, 604; Calin 1974, 57, 60–61, 64, 70; Connery 1974, 8–9, 83–84, 106–8; Pelen 1976–77, 134–36; Kelly 1978, 130, 132–36, 146, 150; Mulder 1978, 40–41; Brownlee 1984, 45–46, 50–52, 230 n. 22; Butterfield 1988, 142–43; Wimsatt/Kibler 1988, 37–39; Heinrichs 1989b, 98–103 et passim; 1990, 222–24, with further references to other scholars; Wimsatt 1991c, 201–4; Kelly 1992, 138, 147–49; Huot 1993, 253–54; Calin 1994, 199). *Roman de la Rose* (Calin 1974, 56–58, 61, 64, 66; Kelly 1978, 121–23; Mulder 1978, 38–39; Badel 1980, 88–89, 90; Brownlee 1984, 39–42, 45, 48–49, 53, 55; Wimsatt/Kibler 1988, 37–39; Huot 1993, 249–56). Giles of Rome (Poirion 1965, 605 n. 105). Nicole de Margival, *Dit de la Panthere* (Hoepffner 1920a, 227; Brownlee 1984, 229 n. 15, 231–32 n. 31; Wimsatt/Kibler 1988, 39; Boulton 1993, 188; de Looze 1993b, 82–83). Jehan de le Mote, *Regret Guillaume* (Hoepffner 1911; Wimsatt/Kibler 1988, 39; Wimsatt 1991b, 55–58).

TEXTUAL LEGACY (France). Froissart, *Dit dou Bleu Chevalier* (Wimsatt 1972a); *Espinette Amoureuse* (Geiselhardt 1914, 50–52; Boulton 1993, 209); *Prison Amoureuse* (Kibler 1978, 34, 46; Boulton 1993, 214); *Paradis d'Amour* (Boulton 1993, 203, 204, 207); *Paradis d'Amour* and *Joli Buisson de Jonece* (Wimsatt 1972a, 392–93; 1975, 15; Dembowski 1987b, 106; Wimsatt/Kibler 1988, 39; Wimsatt 1991b, 178, 189–90). Anon. *Songe Vert* (Wimsatt/Kibler 1988, 39). Deschamps, *Art de Dictier* (Lote 1949; Machabey 1955b, 1:50–51). Oton de Granson, *Livre Messire Ode* (Wimsatt 1991b, 227; Boulton 1993, 224, 225); *Complainte de l'An Nouvel* (Wimsatt/Kibler 1988, 39). Anon. prose treatise bound with *Remede* in MS Pe [20] (Huot 1993, 254–56).

TEXTUAL LEGACY (England). Chaucer, *Book of the Duchess* (for the context, see the eds. F.N. Robinson 1957 and Benson 1987 explanatory notes, passim; Sandras 1859, 90–95, 289–94; Kittredge 1915c, 9–13, 16–23; Schaar 1955, 171–73, 274–75, 381; Wimsatt 1967a; 1968 appendix; 1974, 123–24; 1975, 13–14; Pelen 1976–77, 134–36, 139–47; Longo 1982, 232–35, 245–46; Phillips 1982, 176–80 [excerpts with translations], explanatory notes, passim; Windeatt 1982, 58–64 [trans. with parallel passages in notes]; Dean 1985; Kooper 1985, 108–13, 187; Burnley 1986, 16–19; Donnelly 1987, 425, 227; Wimsatt/Kibler 1988, 39–40; Edwards 1989, 86–88; Heinrichs 1990, 224–27; Butterfield 1991, 35–36; Wimsatt 1991b, 126–29; J.J. Anderson 1992, 420, 425 n. 11; Calin 1994, 284–85); *Anelida and Arcite* (Braddy 1968, 129; Wimsatt 1970–71, 5; Wimsatt/Kibler 1988, 39–40); *Troilus* (Kittredge 1915b; Wimsatt 1974, 123–24; 1976; 1977, 207–9; 1985, 26–32; Wimsatt/Kibler 1988, 39–40; Heinrichs 1989b, esp. 103, 109–15; J.J. Anderson 1991; Wimsatt 1991b, 150–57; 1991c, 201–4; Windeatt 1992, 118–20); "Franklin's Tale" (Wimsatt 1991b, 171; 1991c, 204–10). Gower, *Confessio Amantis* (Zeeman 1991, 227; Olsson 1992, 46–48, 137–38, 178, 227).

PROVERBS (references to Hassell 1982). A53 (*priere*); A58; A63; A76; A82 (*complainte*); A100; B54; B93; B105; B141; C62; C153; C244 (*priere*); C286; C288; C289; C292; D21; D22; D24; D67; D119; D123; E15 (*complainte*); E29; E56; F13; F51; F72; F88 (twice); F109 (*complainte*); F127; F172; G46; H22; M151 (*complainte*); M176 (twice); M242; N36; O59; O67 (*complainte*); P39; P51 (twice); P76; P135; P208; P209; P226; P290; P290 (*complainte*); P296; R16; R46; R55 (*complainte*); R85 (*complainte*); S25; S48 (*complainte*); S100; S108 (twice); V68. Note the large number of proverbs in the *complainte Tels rit* (RF2).

8. *Le Dit dou Lyon*

FORM. Octosyllabic rhyming couplets, 2204 lines.

MANUSCRIPTS.

[1]	C	fols. 103v–120v	[10]	M	fols. 77r–91r
[3]	Vg	fols. 122r–137v	[15]	K	fols. 69r–70r; 72r–79r; 81r–82r
[4]	B	fols. 139r–154v	[16]	J	fols. 77r–90v
[5]	A	fols. 80v–96r	[18]	Pm	fols. 73v–86v
[6]	F	fols. 63v–75r	[21]	Bk	fols. 1r–16v
[7]	E	fols. 61r–67r			

Lost manuscript:
[39] Pavia, lost Visconti MS

FACSIMILES (refer to chap. 4.4f). Miniatures C68, 73, 77 (detail), and 89; A35 (and fol. 86r); F16 (and fol. 63v), F22–23; Bk5.

EDITIONS. Tarbé 1849, 40–44 (fragments); Bartsch 1880 (ll. 1589–698); Patterson 1935, 2:199–200 (ll. 1587–698); Hoepffner 1908–21, 2:159–237.

TRANSLATION. Excerpts in Woledge 1961, 226–29.

ANAGRAM. Solution unsuccessful; see Hoepffner 1906, 406; de Looze 1988b, 547, 548–49; 1991, 169.

PATRON. None has been proposed. John of Bohemia was still alive at this point, but perhaps Bonne of Luxembourg should also be considered.

DATE. 2 April 1342 (ll. 32–33), reported since the earliest modern work on Machaut (Lebeuf 1753, 379). Machaut expended much effort to exploit the verisimilitude of an exact date. In l. 140, the narrator indicates that he finds the boat that leads him to the island on 3 April; in l. 2088, the narrator indicates that he was in the *vergier* for nearly a day and a half of summer; in l. 2143, the narrator reports that he was lost to his friends in the real world for a day and a half. Tarbé (1849, xi) named *Lyon* Machaut's earliest poem, but was not convinced of the absolute veracity of the date. Most later scholars have accepted the date without question. It provides one of the main pillars of Hoepffner's chronology of the narrative poems (1908–21, 1:xxviii, lix; 2:lvi–lvii n. 2). Beer (1980, 28; 1981, 74) provides an interesting literary analysis of the date; Sonnemann (1969, 80, 82–84) notes inconsistencies and considers *Lyon* possibly earlier than *Remede*, even possibly earlier than *Jugement Behaingne*.

BIOGRAPHY. The list of countries where knights have been bold (ll. 1416–57) may include countries that Machaut visited with John of Bohemia (Hoepffner 1908–21, 2:lxi); see chap. 1.5.1b, 1.5.3a, 1.5.3j.

DISCUSSION (literary). Tarbé 1849, xi; Hoepffner 1908–21, 2:liv–lxiii; Siciliano 1934, 165 n. 3, 321 n. 2; Patch 1950, 204–5; Poirion 1965, 488; Wimsatt 1968, 76–80; Sonnemann 1969, 77–84, 164; Vesce 1969–70; Calin 1974, 75–91; Ehrhart 1974, 16–46; Brownlee 1978b, 14–15; Kelly 1978, 105, 144–45 et passim; Deschaux 1979, 14–15; Beer 1980, 28–29; 1981, 74–75; Brownlee 1984, 171–88; Kelly 1985, 295; Davenport 1988, 62; Davis 1991, 54–56, 112–13, 116, 118–19; Imbs 1991, 125–32; Butterfield 1994, 11.

DISCUSSION (art historical). Sasaki 1982.

RELATED MACHAUT WORKS. Mulder (1978, 121=1979, 61) links a list of the attributes of *Amours* in the *Lay de l'Ymage, Ne say comment* (L14/9) to *Lyon*. See Imbs (1991, 131–32) on links to the later *Voir Dit*.

LITERARY ANTECEDENTS. Boethius, *Consolation of Philosophy* and anon. *Ovide Moralisé* (Ehrhart 1980). Chrétien de Troyes, *Erec* and *Yvain* (Hoepffner 1908–21, 2:lix; 1917–19; Calin 1974, 77, 81, 88; Brownlee 1984, 176, 181; R. Morris 1988, 550–51; Imbs 1991, 125); *Conte du Graal* (Brownlee 1984, 180). Bestiaries (Hoepffner 1908–21, 2:lxii; Calin 1974, 82 and n. 8; Brownlee 1984, 248 n. 10). *Roman de la Rose* (Brownlee 1984, 173). The Nine Worthies (ll. 1315–20) derive from the *Voeux du Paon* by Jacques de Longuyon (Hoepffner 1908–21, 2:lxi n. 1; Poirion 1965, 587 n. 31; Tyson 1981; Wimsatt 1991b, 53; Cerquiglini-Toulet 1993c, 35–36). Nicole de Margival, *Dit de la Panthere* (Calin 1974, 78–79; Brownlee 1984, 176–77, 183). Baudoin de Condé, *Prison d'Amours* and *Voie de Paradis* (Pelen 1976–77, 153–54 n. 17). *Roman de Perceforest* (Huot 1987, 298).

TEXTUAL LEGACY (France). Oton de Granson, *Songe Saint Valentin* (Wimsatt 1991b, 334 n. 25). Handschin (1923, 7 n. 1) noted the dependance of the text of an anonymous musical virelai, *Fist on, dame* (ed. Apel 1970–72, 3:18–19 no. 196; Greene 1981–89, 21:82–83 no. 33), to *Lyon* ll. 1523–36.

TEXTUAL LEGACY (England). Chaucer, *Book of the Duchess* (Kittredge 1915c, 4–5, 7, 21–22; Langhans 1928, 117–18; B. Harrison 1934, 432–33; Schaar 1954, 112–15; 1955, 270, 274–75, 382; F.N. Robinson 1957, 777 n. to ll. 1024ff; Wimsatt 1968, 156, 158, 161; Pelen 1976–77, 143; Phillips 1982, 180–81 [summary], explanatory notes, passim; Windeatt 1982, xii–xiii, and parallel passages in notes; Davis 1991, 54); "Franklin's Tale" (F.N. Robinson 1957, 722 n. to ll. 771ff). Machaut's *Lyon* was a possible model for

Chaucer's lost *Book of the Leoun* (Langhans 1928; Dear 1938; Wimsatt 1968, 76; 1991b, 268–69). Anon., Alliterative *Morte Arthure* (Finlayson 1963–64).

PROVERBS (references to Hassell 1982). A58; C58; D25; F26; F75; G46; H25; J40; L57; M54; M180; N35; P39; P201; R96; S81; S108; V79 (twice).

9. *Le Dit de l'Alerion*[65]

FORM: octosyllabic rhyming couplets, 4814 lines.

MANUSCRIPTS.

[1] **C**	fols. 59r–92v	[6] **F**	fols. 75v–98v
[2] **W**	fols. 42r–72r	[7] **E**	fols. 69r–82v[66]
[3] **Vg**	fols. 139r–169r	[10] **M**	fols. 91r–121r
[4] **B**	fols. 155r–185r	[18] **Pm**	fols. 183r–211v
[5] **A**	fols. 96v–126r		

FACSIMILES (refer to chap. 4.4g). Miniatures C44; E17.

EDITION. Hoepffner 1908–21, 2:239–403.

TRANSLATION. Windeatt 1982, 65–70 (excerpts); Gaudet/Hieatt 1994 (complete).

ANAGRAM (not technically an anagram, rather a numerical signature). *Guillemins de Machaut*; see Tarbé 1849, 170–71 s.v. "énigme"; Hoepffner 1906, 405–6 (corrects error of Tarbé); de Looze 1988b, 546–47n. (against de Looze, it seems that the verse in question does specifically call for the doubling of the required letters); Gaudet/Hieatt 1994, 11–12.

PATRON. Perhaps *Alerion* was written when vain attempts were made to teach the dauphin Charles (the future King Charles V) to hunt with birds (cf. R. Cazelles 1982, 233), perhaps at the court of Bonne of Luxembourg. John, duke of Normandy (the future King John II), made several payments in the late 1340s for hunting, especially for birds (Lehoux 1966–68, 1:38). Later, when King John and his young son Philip, the future Philip the Bold, were in captivity in England, John's chaplain Gace de la Buigne wrote a long poem on the pleasures of birding and hunting, the *Roman des Deduis* (begun 1359, finished in Paris, 1377).[67] Sonnemann (1969, 188–90) notes many passages that show contacts between the poet and his audience (e.g., ll 1633–37, 3049–50, 3369–71, 4179–84, 4785–800), perhaps indicating that it was composed and read for a special social occasion. Beer (1980, 29) mentions an intriguing possibility, no longer verifiable to us today, that "Guillaume's elaborate use of the didactic *exempla* transparently and titillatingly conveyed actual personalities at court."

DATE. Hoepffner (1908–21, 1:lxv n.; 2:lxix) placed *Alerion* between *Lyon* (1342) and *Confort* (1357), further narrowing the date to probably before 1349 (1342–49 in Van den Abeele 1990, 229). The appearance of *Alerion* in MS C narrows the date of composition to a time before ca. 1350, before *Jugement Navarre*, which is lacking in MS C.

BIOGRAPHY. Rive (1780, 5) was the first to cite the last lines of *Alerion* as evidence of Machaut's non-noble extraction (see chap. 1.2.3a). More likely, this passage does not indicate that Machaut was a *damoiseau* [gentleman], rather it points up the essential position of the author in relation to this *dit*: Machaut, the *clerc*, was writing a poem celebrating the noble pastime of hunting with birds, but with himself as the protagonist, thus the poem explores the possibility of a *clerc-chevalier*, and in fact says nothing about the social position of Guillaume (Cerquiglini 1985b, 122–24).

DISCUSSION (literary). Hoepffner 1908–21, 2:lxiii–lxx; Patch 1923, 23 n. 91; 1927, 63 n. 2, 75 n. 3, 76 n. 1, 91 n. 1, 100 n. 2, 104 n. 2; Luttrell 1965; Poirion 1965, 529 n. 82; Wimsatt 1968, 81–82; Sonnemann 1969, 85–90, 165, 188–90; Calin 1974, 92–109; Ehrhart 1974, 47–95; Cerquiglini 1978b, 119–20; Kelly 1978, 141, 143, 145–46, 151–54 et passim; Luttrell 1978, 280, 286; Poirion 1978, 202–3; Sasaki 1978; Deschaux 1979, 13–14; Beer 1980, 29; Planche 1980; Hieatt 1979–80; Beer 1981, 75–76; Brownlee 1984,

---

65 On the alternative title *Le Dit des .iiii. Oiseaus*, see Hoepffner 1908–21, 2:lxiii–lxiv; 3:xxii n.; Cerquiglini 1980a, 153 n. 5.

66 *Deo gracias. Explicit le Dit des .iiii. Oisiaux.* The explicit in MS **E** is redundant, since the last line of the poem (l. 4814) provides the explicit.

67 Gaston Fébus's *Livre de la Chasse* (1387–91) was also dedicated to Philip the Bold (De Winter 1985, 20–21, 137–38 no. 53).

63–93; Cerquiglini 1985b, 62, 122–24, 181; Leupin 1986, 128–32; Cerquiglini 1988a, 88; Davenport 1988, 62; Van den Abeele 1990; Imbs 1991, 132–46; Gaudet/Hieatt 1994.

RELATED MACHAUT WORKS. The basic theme of *Alerion* ("do not grieve over lost love, do not remain faithful to dead love. Live and love again" [Calin 1974, 107]) seems to recall the situation in *Jugement Behaingne*. Perhaps this new and very different treatment of the same theme was a further catalyst to the composition of Machaut's next work, the *Jugement Navarre*. Cerquiglini (1985b, 62) points out a reference to raising hunting birds in the *Voir Dit* (ed. P. Paris 1875, 339–41) that recalls *Alerion*. See Imbs (1991, 145–46) on links to the later *Voir Dit*.

LITERARY ANTECEDENTS. Vincent of Beauvais and Thomas de Cantimpré (Hoepffner 1908–21, 2:lxviii; see esp. Gaudet/Hieatt 1994, 180–83). Bestiaries and falconry manuals (Hoepffner 1908–21, 2:lxviii n. 3; Calin 1974, 98; Van den Abeele 1990, 233–35). On falconry, see esp. Calin 1974, 94 n. 4; Van den Abeele 1990; Gaudet/Hieatt 1994, esp. 12–19; on other French poems featuring birds, see Calin 1974, 104–5.

TEXTUAL LEGACY (France). Froissart, *Orloge Amoureus* (Geiselhardt 1914, 46–47); *Espinette Amoureuse* (Gaudet/Hieatt 1994, 20). Oton de Granson, *Songe Saint Valentin* and *Livre Messire Ode* (Wimsatt 1991b, 334 n. 25, 226–27, 229; Gaudet/Hieatt 1994, 20).

TEXTUAL LEGACY (England). Chaucer, *Book of the Duchess* (Schaar 1955, 270, 274); *House of Fame* (Schaar 1955, 387–88); *Parliament of Fowls* (Wimsatt 1968, 85–86; 1991b, 138; Gaudet/Hieatt 1994, 20–21). "Squire's Tale" and "Nun's Priest's Tale" (Hieatt 1979–80, 111; on the "Squire's Tale," see also Wimsatt 1991b, 170–71; Gaudet/Hieatt 1994, 20–21).

PROVERBS (references to Hassell 1982). C101; C198; D37; O28; O68; P51; P136; P200; R5 (twice); R15; T24.

10. Le Confort d'Ami

FORM. Octosyllabic rhyming couplets, 4004 lines (3978 lines plus a codetta of twenty-six lines all rhyming in *-mi*, constituting a reply from *Ami*, i.e., King Charles of Navarre). Hoepffner (1908–21, 3:xvii–xviii) contends that the final twenty-six lines are actually the work of Machaut, due to their technical mastery and the musical reference in ll. 3493–94 to the solmization system (see chap. 1.2.5e); Calin (1974, 130), however, does not attribute these lines to Machaut; cf. also Palmer (1992, xxxi–xxxii).

MANUSCRIPTS.[68]

[3]	**Vg**	fols. 170r–196v	[15]	**K**	fols. 84r–93r; 95r–106r
[4]	**B**	fols. 25r–33v; 186r–203v	[16]	**J**	fols. 91r–117v
[5]	**A**	fols. 127r–153v	[18]	**Pm**	fols. 87r–101v
[6]	**F**	fols. 98v–119v	[33]	*F:CH 485*	
[7]	**E**	fols. 93r–104r	[34]	*L*	fols. 6r–8r (frag.)[69]
[10]	**M**	fols. 121r–146r	[35]	*F:Pn 994*	fols. 33r–44r (frag.)

Lost manuscript:
[24] Pamplona, lost manuscript of King Charles II of Navarre.

FACSIMILES (refer to chap. 4.4h). Miniatures C44; A74–75; F45, 54, and 58; E17.

EDITIONS. Hoepffner 1908–21, 3:1–142 (notes, pp. 245–53); Palmer 1992.

TRANSLATION. Palmer 1992.

ANAGRAM. *Guillaume de Machaut*; *Charles roi de Navarre*; see Suchier 1897, 542–43; Hoepffner 1906, 404; 1908–21, 3:xvii; Cerquiglini 1985b, 236; de Looze 1988b, 544; 1991, 172.

PATRON. King Charles of Navarre; see commentary in Kelly 1987, 88–89; Nouvet 1986, 356 n. 12. Gómez (1987, 115) discovered a reference to a manuscript of *Confort*, copied in 1384, in the possession of Charles of Navarre.

DATE. The historical circumstances that generated the poem allow a very exact dating. Since Caylus (1753a, 410; Rive 1780, 21–25 n. 68), it has been known that *Confort* dates from shortly before the escape of Charles II, king of Navarre, from his prison in the Château d'Arleux. Charles was arrested 5 April 1356 at Rouen by King John II and remained in

---

[68] On the manuscript transmission, see Hoepffner 1908–21, 3:xviii–xix.

[69] *Cy comence Confort d'Ami qui traita et fist maistre Guillaume de Machaut*

captivity just over eighteen months, until the night of 8–9 November 1357. Further, since Machaut makes mention of King John's capture by the English at the Battle of Poitiers (19 September 1356), composition of the poem must have fallen after this date. In a twenty-six-line segment supposedly composed by Charles for the very end of the poem (see the comments above on form), he states that he had been imprisoned "plus d'an et demi" (l. 3988) [more than a year and a half], indicating that the poem was finished probably in the second half of 1357 (Chichmaref 1909, 1:xlvii; Hoepffner 1908–21, 3:i). Machabey (1955b, 1:48) suggests more specifically the date of October 1357. See chap. 1.12d and 1.12f. Palmer (1992, xxviii–xxix) argues that *Confort* was written for Charles's impending release.

BIOGRAPHY. Several scholars have speculated on the question of Machaut's relation to King Charles II of Navarre in the period after 1357 (see chap. 1.12.2).

DISCUSSION (historical). Chichmaref 1909, 1:xlvi–xlviii; Gauvard 1982; Voisé 1982, 52–54; Palmer 1992, xvi–xxv; see also chap. 1.12–1.12.1. It was the extended account in *Confort* of the campaigns of John of Luxembourg, king of Bohemia (chap. 1.5.1c and 1.5.3), that provided the material for the first extended excerpts of Machaut's poetry in the eighteenth century (Lebeuf 1753, 382–93; Caylus 1753a, 409–12; Rive 1780).

DISCUSSION (literary). Rive 1780 (extensive discussion, with complete plot summary); Petit de Julleville 1892–93, 292–96; Hoepffner 1908–21, 3:i–xx; Françon 1947; Schaar 1954, 94–95; Joukovsky-Micha 1968; Sonnemann 1969, 104–10; Frappier 1973; Calin 1974, 130–45; Connery 1974, 108–21; Wimsatt 1975, 14; Deschaux 1978a; Kelly 1978, 123–30 et passim; Wallen 1980; Kelly 1983, 112 n. 33; Cerquiglini 1985b, 147, 205–7; Leupin 1986, 134–37; Nouvet 1986, 356 n. 12; Ehrhart 1987, 192–93; Cerquiglini 1988a, 89; Mühlethaler 1989, 404; Davis 1991, 119–25; Imbs 1991, 156–64; Palmer 1992, introduction.

DISCUSSION (art historical). Anton 1967, 28, 29; Wallen 1980.

RELATED MACHAUT WORKS.

    a. *Remede*. Machaut playfully referred to the *complainte Tels rit* (RF2) in ll. 438–50 (Hoepffner 1908–21, 3:246–47), saying that he would not recount the dream of Nebuchadnezzar, because it would require too long a time to set it to verse, something he had already done in the *Remede*. Gauvard (1982, 39 n. 64) discusses the possible evolution of Machaut's view of Fortune since *Remede*.

    b. *Lyon*. A partial list of the Nine Worthies is found in both poems, and *Confort* l. 2803= *Lyon* l. 1321 (Hoepffner 1908–21, 3:vii). *Confort* further amplifies *Lyon* in its discussion of campaigns of John of Luxembourg.

    c. *Alerion* (ll. 13–14). See Hoepffner 1908–21, 3:253, note to ll. 3934–35.

    d. *Jugement Navarre* (ll. 1273–74). See chap. 1.6.2a.

    e. *Remede* (*Confort*, l. 2248). See next item.

    f. *Lay de Bon Espoir* (*Confort*, l. 2249). Hoepffner (1908–21, 3:249–50) related this reference to the *Lay de Confort*, *S'onques* (L17/12), an identification accepted by Poirion (1965, 409). It appears more likely that this refers to the lai of the *Remede*, *Qui n'aroit* (RF1), which is given this title in MSS **K** and **J** (see chap. 7.3, commentary on the date of *S'onques*).

    g. *Nes qu'on* (Lo232=B33=VD16). See chap. 7.3 on the date of *N'es qu'on*.

    h. ballade *Phyton* (B38). Similar images appear in *Confort*, ll. 2623, 2691–92.

    i. rondeau *Se tenir vues le droit chemin d'onneur* (Lo241). See Hoepffner 1908–21, 3:251, note to ll. 3129–34. Compare also the language describing the character *Largesse* in *Jugement Navarre*, ll. 1266–78, and the description of John of Luxembourg's generosity in *Confort*, ll. 2930–33 (see chap. 1.6.2a), and the ballade *Donnez, seigneurs* (B26). Hoepffner's notes relating *Confort* to various lyrical poems are treated cautiously by more recent scholars (see Reaney 1952b, 37; Sonnemann 1969, 120–21, 165).

    j. *Voir Dit*. See Imbs 1991, 156–59.

LITERARY ANTECEDENTS. Old Testament (Hoepffner 1908–21, 3:ii–vi; B. Harrison 1934, 434–35 n. 28; Calin 1974, 131–45; Wallen 1980, 191–94; Imbs 1991, 159–62; Palmer 1992, xxxiii–xlv, lix–lxx). Boethius, *Consolation of Philosophy* (Patch 1935, 104; Anton 1967, 29–30; Calin 1974, 130–31; Kelly 1978, 124, 127, 146; Kelly review of Brownlee 1984; Cerquiglini 1985b, 64; Kelly 1987, 79; Palmer 1992, xxxiv, xlvi–xlviii; Kelly

1992, 138). Duties of rulers tradition (Hoepffner 1908–21, 1:ix–xii; Calin 1974, 131, 141; Ehrhart 1992, 6–8; Palmer 1992, lviii–lix). *Roman de la Rose* (Badel 1980, 88–89, 90 n. 76; Roques 1982, 161–62). Gilles of Rome (Poirion 1965, 605 n. 105). *Ovide Moralisé* (De Boer 1914, 348–50; Anton 1967, 28–32; Frappier 1973; Kelly 1978, 157; Wallen 1980, 197–201; Kelly 1981, 87–88, 90; Mühlethaler 1989, 396; Heinrichs 1990, 87–89; Long 1992, 259–60; Palmer 1992, l–liv, lxx–lxxviii). In l. 3818, there may be reference to the rondeau *Porchier mieus estre amoeroie*, a lyrical insertion in the *Roman de Fauvel* of the MS *F:Pn 146* (ed. Rosenberg/Tischler 1991, 44 no. 16; cited in Hoepffner 1908–21, 3:253). On the Nine Worthies, see the discussion of the literary antecedents of *Lyon*, chap. 5.8; Connery 1974, 115–16.

TEXTUAL LEGACY (France). Froissart, *Prison Amoureuse* (Whiting 1946, 199; Nouvet 1986, 356 n. 12); Cerquiglini-Toulet 1991a, 232; Wimsatt 1991b, 190); *Joli Buisson de Jonece* (Fourrier 1975, 24). Deschamps (Hoepffner 1908–21, 3:xi n. 3), especially lais 7 and 8 (ed. Queux de Saint-Hilaire/Raynaud 1878–1903, 2:306–14; 314–23; see Hoepffner 1908–21, 3:xix–xx; Palmer 1992, lxxviii). Christine de Pizan, *Livre du Chemin de Long Estude* (Schilperoort 1936, 44 n. 2).

TEXTUAL LEGACY (Italy). Boccaccio, *Amorosa visione* (Anton 1967, 31).

TEXTUAL LEGACY (England). Chaucer, *Book of the Duchess* (Schaar 1955, 270, 274–75); *Legend of Good Women* (Schaar 1955, 295). Gower, *Confessio Amantis* (Anton 1967, 31). Hoccleve, *Regement of Princes* (Calin 1994, 407–11); *The Series* (Calin 1994, 415).

PROVERBS (references to Hassell 1982). A38; A73; A102; B102; C101; C220; E4; E15; E90; F46; F50; F59; F142; G33; G46; H25; M4; M160; M225; M246; N12; P175; P232; R26 (twice); S28; V22; V79.

11. *Le Dit de la Fonteinne Amoureuse*[70]

FORM. Octosyllabic rhyming couplets, 2848 lines. Three lyrics are inserted (see Sonnemann 1969, 115–19 on the metrics of the insertions):

1. *La Complainte de l'Amant*, composed of fifty sixteen-line strophes (800 lines) with the following metrical pattern:

$$\underset{1010104}{a\ a\ ab}\Big|\ \underset{1010104}{a\ a\ ab}\Big\|\ \underset{1010104}{b\ b\ ba}\Big|\ \underset{1010104}{b\ b\ ba}\Big\|\ \text{(masculine or feminine rhymes).}[71]$$

Since each succeeding large strophe has different rhymes, there are a total of one hundred different rhyming syllables; on verse structures of this sort, see Dembowski (1987a, 100 n. 18).

2. *Le Confort de l'Amant et de la Dame*, composed of twenty sixteen-line strophes (320 lines) on the same metrical pattern as the *complainte*.[71]

3. *Rondel*, 8 lines, in isometric eight-syllable lines: 8AAaAaaAA a: -maint.

MANUSCRIPTS.

[3] **Vg**	fols. 197r–216r	[10] **M**	fols. 146r–164r[72]
[4] **B**	fols. 204r–217v	[15] **K**	fols. 108r–114r; 116r–123r
[5] **A**	fols. 154r–173v	[16] **J**	fols. 118r–137v
[6] **F**	fols. 119v–134v	[18] **Pm**	fols. 102r–117v (incomplete at end)
[7] **E**	fols. 83r–91r[73]		

Lost manuscripts:
Machaut refers to individual copies of *Fonteinne* in the *Voir Dit*, letter 4 (ed. P. Paris 1875, 53, letter no. 6), and letter 10 (ed. 1875, 69).

FACSIMILES (refer to chap. 4.4i). Miniatures Vg93 (with fol. 198v); A80–87; F73; E24. The facsimiles in Loomis 1965 (plates 45–47) include entire folios from MS A (fols. 157v–158v).

---

[70] On the title *Morpheus* in MSS E and M, see Hoepffner 1908–21, 3:xxi–xxii; Cerquiglini 1980a, 153 n. 5; de Looze 1984, 156 n. 21; Cerquiglini-Toulet 1993d, 10–11; on the meaning of *Morpheus* to the poem, see especially Kelly 1985, 294.

[71] On the form, see chap. 5.4, introduction to *Jugement Behaingne*.

[72] *Ci commence le Dit de la Fonteinne Amoureuse que l'en appelle Morpheus.*

[73] *Cy commance le Livre Morpheus / Explicit le Dit de la Fontainne Amoureuse.*

EDITIONS. Hoepffner 1908–21, 3:143–244 (notes pp. 253–63); Palmer 1993a, 90–238; Cerquiglini-Toulet 1993d.

TRANSLATIONS. Windeatt 1982, 26–40 (extensive excerpts); complete in Palmer 1993a, 91–239; Boulton 1993, 193–97 (excerpts); Cerquiglini-Toulet 1993d (in modern French).

ANAGRAM. *Guillaume de Machaut; Je[h]ans duc [de] Berry et [d']Overgne*; see P. Paris 1875, xxx; Hoepffner 1906, 407; 1908–21, 3:xxvi, n. 2 (xxii–xxx on further clues to the identity of the lover); Chichmaref 1909, 1:li–liii (with a slightly different solution to the anagram); Eichelberg 1935, 29–30 n. 44; de Looze 1988b, 545; 1991, 172; Cerquiglini-Toulet 1993d, 22–23. Ehrhart (1975, 155–56, 197–99, 210–13; 1980b, 120–23; 1987, 131–32) argues against Hoepffner's solution; Cerquiglini (1985b, 236 n. 28) also notes problems with it. Brownlee (1989b, 155 n. 4) disagrees with Ehrhart; Heinrichs (1990, 217–18 n. 15) has taken a middle position.

PATRON. John, duke of Berry (first identified in P. Paris 1875, xxx); see commentary in Kelly 1987, 79–80. Ehrhart has rejected the identification (see above concerning the anagram, and chap. 1 n. 156). The connection of the story frame to the duke of Berry seems clear, but Ehrhart's analysis of Machaut's admonitory posture—skillfully masked, as was appropriate to his position—is very appropriate for the period around 1360. Perhaps the moral is directed at the Regent Charles, recent recipient of far more direct and artless criticism in the motet *Tu qui gregem / Plange* (M22). See chap. 1.13.1.

DATE. 1360–61 on the basis of historical references and an anagram; see P. Paris 1875, xxx, 53 n. 3, 69 n. 1; Chichmaref 1909, 1:li–liii; Hoepffner 1908–21, 1:xxxviii, xxxix; Machabey 1955b, 1:52–58 (esp. 57–58 on a terminus of 1362, before letter 6 of the *Voir Dit*). For a dissenting view, see Ehrhart 1974, discussed in chap. 1.14.1.

BIOGRAPHY. See chap. 1.5.3c (accounts of campaigns of John of Luxembourg), and chap. 1 n. 156 (departure of Jean de Berry from Calais) and 1.14.1a.

DISCUSSION (literary). Hoepffner 1908–21, 3:xx–xlii; Patch 1950, 203–4; D.W. Robertson 1962, 234; Cartier 1966, 295–97; Wimsatt 1968, 112–17; Sonnemann 1969, 111–21, 165; Calin 1974, 146–66; F. and W. Calin 1974, 245, 248; Connery 1974, 122–51; Ehrhart 1974, 153–204; B. and J. Cerquiglini 1976; Pelen 1976–77, 136–39; Brownlee 1978b, 15–17; Cerquiglini 1978b, 120–21; Deschaux 1978a; Kelly 1978, 53–54 et passim; Ehrhart 1980b; Palmer 1980; 1981; Rychner 1981, 58–66; Calin 1983a; Brownlee 1984, 188–207; de Looze 1984; Cerquiglini 1985b, 113–14, 116–17, 124–25, 175–76, 177–78 n. 42, 205–6; Kelly 1985, 292–94; Leupin 1986, 134; Ehrhart 1987, 130–41; Huot 1987, 293–301; Baumgartner 1988, 172–73; Brownlee 1989b; Ehrhart 1990, 142 et passim; Heinrichs 1990, 214–21; Planche 1990c; Cerquiglini-Toulet 1991a, 230–32 (=1993b, 64–65); Davis 1991, 125–45; Imbs 1991, 164–72; Wimsatt 1991b, 83–84; Ehrhart 1992, 14–19; Palmer 1992, xxvi–xxvii; Boulton 1993, 192–97; Cerquiglini-Toulet 1993b, 74–76, 95, 97–98, 149; 1993d, 9–32; Butterfield 1994, 11–13; Calin 1994, 212–19; Medeiros 1994.

RELATED MACHAUT WORKS.

a. *Jugement Behaingne*. See Hoepffner 1908–21, 3:xxxii.

b. *Remede*. See Hoepffner 1908–21, 3:xxxiv n. 1; Wimsatt 1968, 106, 115; Calin 1994, 212, 214, 217, 219.

c. *Alerion*. See Hoepffner 1908–21, 3:xxxiv.

d. *Jugement Navarre* (ll. 493–94). See Hoepffner 1908–21, 3:253 (to ll. 1–2).

e. *Confort*. See Hoepffner 1908–21, 3:xxxiii–xxxv.

f. *Voir Dit*. Machaut cites *Fonteinne* (called *Morpheus*) in four places: letter 6 (ed. P. Paris 1875, 53); letter 10 (ed. 1875, 69; see also 389 n. xvii); letter 31 (ed. 1875, 241–42); l. 8177 (ed. 1875, 331 n. 1; for the context, see de Looze 1984, 145; Cerquiglini 1985b, 176, 218; Kelly 1985, 294 n. 16; Imbs 1991, 164–72). On a structural relationship, see Boulton 1993, 198.

g. lyrics. See Hoepffner 1908–21, vol. 3, notes to the lines cited: *Se trestuit cil* (Lo48, l. 905); *Sans cuer, dolens* (Lo148=R4, ll. 203–4); *Je puis trop* (Lo203=B28, l. 963); *Amis, je t'aporte* (Lo212, l. 2207); *De Fortune* (Lo195=B23, l. 443); *Amis, si* (Lo199, l. 2319); *Je pers mon temps* (Lo209, l. 1487); *Onques mes cuers* (Lo218, ll. 2508–10); *Loial amour* (Lo219, l. 2335); *Quant Ecuba* (Cp4, l. 1644); *J'ay tant / Lasse!* (M7, l. 1309); *Quant j'ay l'espart* (R5, l. 276); *Cinc, un* (R6, l. 2207; Hoepffner's date is erroneous); *Vo dous regars* (R8, l. 340); *De tout sui* (V38/32, l. 1013).

Hoepffner's notes relating *Fonteinne* to various lyrical poems have been treated more cautiously by more recent scholars (see Reaney 1952b, 37; Sonnemann 1969, 120–21). LITERARY ANTECEDENTS. Boethius, *Consolation of Philosophy* (Wimsatt 1968, 106; Palmer 1980; 1981; Kelly 1987, 79; Heinrichs 1990, 184, 217–18). *Altercatio Phyllidis et Florae* (Pelen 1976–77, 139). Duties of rulers tradition (Ehrhart 1980b, 131–36; 1992, 14–15, 18–19). *Roman de la Rose* (Hoepffner 1908–21, 3:xxxii–xxxiii; Poirion 1965, 494–95 and n. 22; Thiry-Stassin 1970, 49; Calin 1974, 154, 162–63; Rychner 1981, 58–66; Brownlee 1984, 189, 194–95, 197–98, 200–201, 202, 205, 208, 249 n. 23; Huot 1987, 296–97; 1993, 242–49; Medeiros 1994). *Ovide Moralisé* (De Boer 1914, 346–48; D.W. Robertson 1962, 234; Pelen 1976–77, 136–39, esp. 152 n. 14; Ehrhart 1980a; Brownlee 1984, 250 n. 26; Cerquiglini 1985b, 171 n. 35; Kelly 1985, 292–94, 296; Ehrhart 1987, 133–41; 1990, 135–39, 142; Planche 1990c, 29–31; Huot 1993, 246–48; Calin 1994, 215–19). Watriquet de Couvin, *Dis de la Fontaine d'Amours* (Wimsatt 1968, 64; Huot 1987, 299–300). *Roman de Perceforest* (Huot 1987, 297–98 and app. C).

TEXTUAL LEGACY (France). Froissart, *Paradis d'Amour* (Whiting 1946, 191; Calin 1974, 158; Dembowski 1986, 13, 26; 1987b; Huot 1987, 304–7; Wimsatt 1991b, 178, 189); *Dit dou Bleu Chevalier* (Geiselhardt 1914, 47–50; Whiting 1946, 201; Cartier 1966, 297–306; 1967, 237–38, 243, 250–51; Wimsatt 1968, 129–33; Wimsatt 1972a; Calin 1974, 158; Fourrier 1979, 53); *Espinette Amoureuse* (Geiselhardt 1914, 19, 50–52; Whiting 1946, 195–97; Fourrier 1963, 34–37; Calin 1974, 158; Dembowski 1987b; Huot 1987, 305–7); *Espinette Amoureuse* and *Joli Buisson de Jonece* (Fourrier 1975, 26; Wimsatt 1991b, 189–90); *Prison Amoureuse* (Calin 1974, 158; Kelly 1985, 296; Boulton 1993, 214, 215); *Joli Buisson de Jonece* (Huot 1987, 317–18). Oton de Granson, *Lay de Desir en Complainte* (Cerquiglini-Toulet 1993d, 25); *Livre Messire Ode* (Wimsatt 1991b, 227). Christine de Pizan, *Epistre Othea* (P.G.C. Campbell 1924, 100, 131; Ehrhart 1987, 118; 1990, 128, 132, 135–39, 148–49); *Livre du Chemin de Longue Estude* (De Boer 1914, 347n. [=De Boer 1915–38, 1:38–39 n. 1]; Hoepffner 1908–21, 3:xli; Schilperoort 1936, 62–63; Ehrhart 1990, 144); ballade *Se de Pallas me peüsse accointier* (ed. M. Roy 1886–91, 1:214–15; cited in Ehrhart 1990, 126–31, 146, 148). Anon. ballade *Plus a destroit* (MS **Pa** fol. 77v; ed. and trans. Wimsatt 1982, 24–25; cited in Davis 1991, 143 n. 55). Anon. *Dit de l'Orthie* (Langlois 1902, 34 n. 3; Cerquiglini-Toulet 1993d, 19).

TEXTUAL LEGACY (England). Chaucer, *Book of the Duchess* (for the context, see the eds. F.N. Robinson 1957 and Benson 1987, explanatory notes, passim; ten Brink 1870; Kittredge 1915a, 54–58; 1915c, 1, 5; Kitchel 1923; Shannon 1929, 3–12; Schaar 1954, 18–19 [with further references, n. 2], 108–11; 1955, 20–23, 270, 274–75, 377; Clemen 1963, 29–37; Wimsatt 1967b; 1968, 115–17, 156–57; Finlayson 1973; Calin 1974, 158; Wimsatt 1974, 124; 1975, 14–16; Pelen 1976–77, 136–42; 1979; Palmer 1980; Pearcy 1980; B. Nolan 1981; Wimsatt 1981, 116; Edwards 1982; Longo 1982, 250, 256–75; Phillips 1982, 28–32, 181–84 [detailed summary], explanatory notes, passim; Windeatt 1982, xiii; de Looze 1984, 159 n. 10; Kooper 1985, 113–15, 194–97; Hanning 1986; S.A. Wright 1986, chap. 3 passim; Calin 1987b, 10–13; A. Taylor 1987; Davenport 1988, 61; Edwards 1989, 74–82; Stevenson 1989–90, 4–5, 11–16; Heinrichs 1990, 214–15, 219–21; Butterfield 1991, 43–44, 46; Davis 1991, 69–79, 146–49; Wimsatt 1991b, 83–84; Knopp 1992; Calin 1994, 276–89); *Anelida and Arcite* (Wimsatt 1970–71, 7); *Parliament of Fowls* (Moore 1951, 41); "Prologue" to the *Legend of Good Women* (Schaar 1955, 194); "Merchant's Tale" (Kitchel 1923, 229; Calin 1987b, 18–20; 1994, 322–23). Gower, *Confessio Amantis* (Kelly 1978, 201–2; Olsson 1992, 136).

PROVERBS (references to Hassell 1982). A53; A75; A89; A119; A120; B54; B102; C60; C130; C221; C320; D122 (l. 63); E71; F39; G46; J35; L5; L48; M40; O72; P3; P200; P232; P290; R26; S28; S87; S107; V66 (cf. ll. 1203–4). Cerquiglini-Toulet (1993d, 209–10) gives additional items; two of these also appear in *Voir Dit*.

12. *Le Dit de la Harpe*

FORM. Decasyllabic rhyming couplets, 354 lines.

MANUSCRIPTS.

[3]	**Vg**	fols. 216r–218v	[10]	**M**	fols. 164r–166v
[4]	**B**	fols. 22r–24v	[15]	**K**	fols. 125r–125v
[5]	**A**	fols. 174r–177r	[16]	**J**	fols. 138r–139v (beginning lost)
[6]	**F**	fols. 135r–137r	[18]	**Pm**	fols. 118r–120v
[7]	**E**	fols. 105r–106r	[42]	*F:CF 249*	fols. 85v–89r

FACSIMILES (refer to chap. 4.4j). Miniatures A110–13; F89; E30.

EDITIONS. Bartsch 1880 (ll. 1–92); Patterson 1935, 2:197–99 (ll. 1–92); Young 1943 (complete).

ANAGRAM. Solution unsuccessful; see Suchier 1897, 545 n. 2; Hoepffner 1906, 407–8; Young 1943, 13–14; Huot 1987, 288, 290; de Looze 1988b, 547–48 n. 15, 548.

PATRON. Unknown. Caylus (1753a, 413) wrote that "ce morceau très-ennuyeux est adressé à Agnès de Navarre, femme de Phébus Comte duc de Foix" [this very boring piece is addressed to Agnes of Navarre, wife of Fébus, count of Foix]; both Rive (1780, 26 n. 70) and Tarbé (1849, xxi–xxii) repeated the incorrect ascription. Suchier (1897) and Gröber (1902, 1047) indicated that *Harpe* was written for Peronne after the completion of the *Voir Dit*, thus adopting her new identity to Caylus's old view. Hoepffner (1906, 408) rejected this.

DATE. On the basis of manuscript transmission, late 1360s.

DISCUSSION (literary). Calin 1974, 227–29; Lukitsch 1983, 266; Cerquiglini 1985b, 19, 110 n. 5, 259 n. 11; Huot 1987, 286–93; Bec 1992, 169–70.

DISCUSSION (art historical). Langner 1982; Huot 1987, 286–93.

LITERARY ANTECEDENT. Chrétien de Troyes, *Le Chevalier de la Charrette* (Huot 1987, 292).

RELATED MACHAUT WORKS. The first line is also l. 1 of the ballade *Je puis trop bien* (B28).

TEXTUAL LEGACY (France). Christine de Pizan, *Epistre Othea* (P.G.C. Campbell 1924, 120–21).

TEXTUAL LEGACY (Italy). Vannozzo, *Contrasto dell'Arpa e del Liuto* (Levi 1908).

13. *Le Livre dou Voir Dit* [74]

FORM. Octosyllabic rhyming couplets and lyrical interpolations, 9009 lines (Cerquiglini 1985b, 53); not included in the line count are forty-six inserted prose letters (on lines misnumbered in P. Paris 1875, see Calin 1974, 167n.). Table 5.3 provides a complete listing of the lyrical and prose insertions.

MANUSCRIPTS.

[5]	**A**	fols. 221r–306r	[15] **K**	fols. 133r–135r (cf. chap. 2.1.1e)
[5a]	*F:Pn 11198*	fol. 26r [75]	[16] **J**	fols. 147r–151v (cf. chap. 2.1.1e)
[6]	**F**	fols. 137v–198v	[18] **Pm**	fols. 122r–182v
[7]	**E**	fols. 171r–210r		

In addition, a few of the individual lyrics from the *Loange,* and a few of the musical works inserted in the *Voir Dit* are transmitted in MSS C, **Vg, B,** and **M.**

Lost Manuscripts. See chap. 2.1.1e for the individual manuscript of the *Voir Dit* that Eustache Deschamps took to Louis de Male, Count of Flanders, in 1369 or 1375. King John I of Aragon may have owned another individual manuscript of the *Voir Dit*; see chap. 2.2.1a.

FACSIMILES (refer to chap. 4.4k). K12–13; J25; A125, 127, 128, 130, 132, and 147; F112, 114, 116, 117, 118, 123, 128, 130, 132, 134, 135, 139, and 140; Pm110 and 111. Gallo 1985, 43 (MS E fol. 198v, with *Dix et sept* [R17], letter 36 and narrative beginning with l. 6005 [ed. P. Paris 1875, 266–69]).

---

[74] On the title "*Le Livre dou Voir Dit,*" given in the rubrics of MSS **A, F,** and **E,** see Cerquiglini 1980a, 154–55.

[75] Parchment fragment correcting a 32-line eye skip in MS **A** [5]; see chap. 3 [5a] and chap. 4 n. 199.

Table 5.3
Prose and Lyrical Insertions in the *Voir Dit*[76]

lyr.	genre	d/a	Title	PP	Lo	Wilk	other sources
1	R	d	*Celle qui unques ne vous vid* [77]	7			
2	R	a	*Tres-belle, riens ne m'abelist* [78]	12			
3	R	d	*Pour vivre en joieuse vie*	15			
	1 Let.	d		16			
4	R	a	*Belle, bonne et envoisie*	18			
	2 Let.	a	[No. IV in P. Paris 1875]	41			
5	B32	a	*Plourez, dames, plourez vostre servant*	25	229	162	I Utr
6	B	a	*Amours, ma dame et Fortune et mi oueil*	26	227	13	
	3 Let.	d	[No. V in P. Paris 1875][78]	47			
7	R	d	*Celle qui nuit et jour desire*	29			
8	B	a	*Veoir n'oïr ne puis riens qui destourne*	36	238	212	
9	[V34]	a	*L'ueil, qui est le droit archier*	37		278	Pa
10	[V35]	a	*Plus belle que le biau jour*	38		279	Pa
11	[V33]	a	*Je ne me puis saouler*	39		277	Pa Mn
	4 Let.	a	[No. VI in P. Paris 1875][78]	52			
	5 Let.	d	[No. VII in P. Paris 1875]	57			
12	V	d	*Ne vous estuet guermenter* (1 str.)	49			
13	B	a	*Quant ma dame est noble et de grant vaillance*	51	239	174	
14	R13	a	*Dame, se vous n'avez aperceü*	52			Pa
	6 Let.	a	[No. II in P. Paris 1875]	18			
	[R]	a	*Quant vous m'apellez ami* [79]	18			
	[B]	a	*Que on porroit espuisier la grant mer* (1 str.)[79]	20			
15	Cp	d	*Mes dous amis a vous me veuil-je plaindre*	56	Cp5		
	7 Let.	d	[No. III in P. Paris 1875]	27			
	8 Let.	a	([80])	60			
	9 Let.	d	([81])	62			

[76] Column one assigns numbers to the lyrical insertions; column two gives the genre of each item (B = balade; Cp = *complainte*; L = lai; Let. = letter [the order given here follows the manuscript order, not the transposed order of P. Paris (cf. 1875, 387 n. vii)]; Pr = *prière*; R = rondeau; Rfr. = refrain; V = virelai); works given a number, e.g., B32 *Plourez, dames,* are set to music, except the three virelais V33–35, which were not set to music, but which were taken into the music section of the manuscripts (the numbering follows Ludwig 1926–54; for further sources of the musical works, see chap. 7.3); column three indicates whether the *dame* (d) or *amant* (a) is given as the author of a work (for item 57, "T" indicates Machaut's ascription to Thomas Paien); column four ("PP") gives the page number of a given item in the edition of P. Paris 1875; column six ("Lo") gives the number in Chichmaref 1909 of those lyrics duplicated in the *Loange*; column seven ("Wilk.") gives the page number of a given item in the edition of Wilkins 1972 (see also his notes to individual poems); finally, column eight lists concordances of *Voir Dit* lyrics in text MSS I [40] and Pa [50]. Fowler (1979, 289–93) indexes the lyrical insertions alone. On pairings of lyrics, see S.J. Williams 1977; Cerquiglini 1985b, 34–37, 96–99.

[77] Translated in Boulton 1993, 163. Imitated in Deschamps's rondeau 685; see chap. 2.1.1i. On this rondeau as the point of departure for the *Voir Dit*, see Cerquiglini 1987b, 54; S.J. Williams 1993, 7–8

[78] Partial translation in Boulton 1993, 164.

[79] Letter 6 incorporates three lyrical passages not distinguished from the surrounding prose. The first is a rondeau, *Quant vous m'apellez ami*; the second an eight-line strophe, possibly the first strophe of a ballade, *Que on porroit espuisier la grant mer*; while the third, *Car je vous ameray / et obieray*, is composed of ten lines, all rhyming on *-ay*.

[80] Partial translation in Boulton 1993, 198.

[81] Partial translation in Boulton 1993, 199.

lyr.	genre	d/a	Title	PP	Lo	Wilk.	other sources
16	B33	a	*Nes qu'on porroit les estoilles nombrer* [82]	67	232	143	**Pa**
	10 Let.	a		67			
17	B	a	*De mon vrai cuer jamais ne partira*	71			
18	V24	d	*Cilz ha bien fole pensee*	72		275	
19	R	a	*Belle, vostre doulz ymage*	73			
20	R	d	*Amis, pour ce l'envoiai je*	73			
21	R	a	*Se mes cuers art et li vostres estaint*	74			
22	R	d	*L'amour de vous, qui en mon cuer remaint*	74			
23	R	a	*Vos pensees me sont commandement*	76			
24	R	d	*Amis, venés vers moy seürement*	76			
25	V	a	*Douce, plaisant et debonnaire*	77			**Pa**
26	V	d	*Des que premiers oÿ retraire* (1 str.)	78			
	Rfr.	d	*Amis amés de cuer d'amie...* [83]	92			
27	R	a	*Douce dame quant je vous voi* [84]	92			
28	R	d	*Tresdoulz amis quant je vous voi* [84]	93			**Pa**
29	B	a	*Le bien de vous qui en biauté florist*	93	179	124	**Pa**
30	B	a	*Le plus grant bien qui me viengne d'amer* [85]	100	180	127	**Pa**
31	R4	a	*Sans cuer, dolens de vous departirai*	108	148	264	**Pa**
32	R	d	*Sans cuer, de moi pas ne vous partirés* [86]	108			
33	R	a	*Toute Belle, vous m'avez visité*	112			
	11 Let.	a		112			
34	R	d	*Tresdoulz amis, j'ay bonne volenté*	114			
	12 Let.	d		114			
35	R	a	*Long sont mi jour et longues sont mes nuis* [87]	116			
36	R	d	*Amis, bien voy que tu pers tous deduis*	116			
37	R	a	*Belle, quant vous m'arés mort*	117			
38	R	d	*Amis, se Dieus me confort* [88]	117			
39	R	a	*Puis que languir sera ma destinee* [89]	117			
	13 Let.	a		118			
40	R	d	*Vostre langueur sera par moy sanee* [89]	119			
	14 Let.	d		119			
	15 Let.	a		122			
41	R	a	*Trembler, fremir et muer me couvient*	123			
	16 Let.	a		130			
	17 Let.	a		133			
	18 Let.	d		135			
42	B	a	*Gent corps, faitis, cointe, apert et joli* [90]	152	5	77	

---

[82] Text recited on the compact disc Harmonic Records H/CD 8825 (see chap. 8.8); see also chap. 7.3 on *Nes qu'on* (B33).

[83] On this refrain, sung by Toute Belle, see Cerquiglini 1985b, 96 n. 18; translation in Boulton 1993, 178.

[84] Beginning translated in Boulton 1993, 178.

[85] The refrain, "Qu'assez rueve qui se va complaignant" [He who complains asks much, i.e., he who complains in this manner need not importune the lady further] is cited four more times in the *Voir Dit* (ed. P. Paris 1875, 105 [l. 2530 and l. 2548]; 134 [letter 17]; 277 [letter 37]); in addition, it is the last line of the *complainte Sire, a vous* (Cp7), and l. 3764/3766 of *Remede* (see chap. 5.7, "related Machaut works"). See Hassel 1982, proverb no. D21; and commentary in Eichelberg 1935, 85; Cerquiglini 1985b, 37, 118 n. 18; Imbs 1991, 122. Beginning translated in Boulton 1993, 199.

[86] Translation by Jacques LeClercq in Flores 1962, 158–59.

[87] Text recited on the compact disc Harmonic Records H/CD 8825 (see chap. 8.8).

[88] Translation by Jacques LeClercq in Flores 1962, 158.

[89] Partial translation in Boulton 1993, 200.

[90] Poirion (1965, 200) indicates that this text must be one of Machaut's early ballades. The

lyr.	genre	d/a	Title	PP	Lo	Wilk.	other sources
43	R	d	*Autre de vous jamais ne quier amer*	153			**Pa**
44	Pr	a	*Venus, je t' ay tousjours servi* [91]	155			
45	V	a	*Onques si bonne journee*	159			**Pa**
	19 Let.	a		163			
	20 Let.	d		165			
46	R	d	*Merveille fu quant mon cuer ne parti*	166			
47	L18	a	*Longuement me sui tenus*	172			
	21 Let.	a		180			
	22 Let.	d		182			
	23 Let.	a	*Mon cuer, ma suer, ma douce amour* (Cp)[92]	184			
	24 Let.	d		186			
48	B	d	*Il n' est dolour, desconfort ne tristesse*	187	194	100	**Pa**
	25 Let.	a		189			
	26 Let.	d		193			
	27 Let.	a	([93])	201			
49	B	a	*Hui ha .i. mois que je me departi* [94]	204	161	95	
50	B	d	*Amis si parfaitement* [95]	205	199	11	**Pa**
	28 Let.	d	([96])	206			
51	B	d	*Puis que tant a languir hai* [97]	208			
	29 Let.	d		233			
52	B	d	*Nuit et jour en tel traveil* (2 str.)	236			
	30 Let.	a	*"Longue demouree fait changier ami"* [98]	238			
	31 Let.	a		239			
53	Cp	d	*Dous amis, que t' ay-je meffait?* [99]	242			
	32 Let.	d		248			
54	B	d	*Ne soiez en nul esmay*	251			**Pa**
55	Cp	a	*Dame en qui j' ay mis toute m' esperance*	252			
	33 Let.	a		257			
	34 Let.	d		260			
	35 Let.	d		262			
	Rfr.	a	*Trop font de peine et de haire*	264			
56	R17	a	*Dix et sept, .v., .xiii., .xiiii. et quinse* [100]	266			**I v**
	36 Let.	d		267			

---

text is related to strophe 2 of *Pas de tor* (B30); see chap. 7.3.

[91] Three 16-line strophes in a pattern similar to *Marguerite*, but with long lines in eight instead of ten syllables, as in *Dous amis, que t' ay-je meffait?* (VD53). On the form, see chap. 5.4, introduction to *Jugement Behaingne*.

[92] Partial translation in Fox 1974, 296; discussed in Cerquiglini-Toulet 1991b, 345. Cohen (1952, 99) comments: "Ici trois fois *ou* répété en sourdine pour conclure cette pièce en *ou* mineur, dans laquelle le poète a oublié les règles des formes fixes, ballades ou rondeaux et le musicien s'est contenté de l'harmonisation de nos adorables voyelles françaises si nettes et si pures" [here a muted threefold repetition of *ou* to conclude this piece in *ou* minor, in which the poet forgot the rules of the fixed forms, ballades or rondeaux, and the musician is content with the harmonization of our adorable French vowels, so clear and pure].

[93] Partial translation in Boulton 1993, 164.

[94] See Poirion 1965, 138; Cerquiglini 1985b, 39.

[95] See Poirion 1965, 138.

[96] Text recited on the compact disc Harmonic Records H/CD 8825 (see chap. 8.8).

[97] Discussed in Cerquiglini 1985b, 38–39.

[98] See Hassell 1982, proverb no. D25.

[99] Twelve 16-line strophes in a pattern similar to *Marguerite*, but with long lines in eight instead of ten syllables, as in *Venus, je t' ay tousjours servi* (VD44). On the form, see chap. 5.4, introduction to *Jugement Behaingne*.

[100] On the number riddle, see P. Paris 1875, xx; Hoepffner 1906, 409.

lyr.	genre	d/a	Title	PP	Lo	Wilk.	other sources
57	B34	T	*Quant Theseüs, Hercules et Jason*	274			Pa I Ch PR SL
58	B34	a	*Ne quier veoir la biauté d'Absalon*	275			Pa I Ch PR SL
	37 Let.	a		276			
59	R	d	*Tant com je seray vivant*	278			Pa
60	B	d	*Se par Fortune, la lasse et la dervee*	278			Pa
	38 Let.	d		279			
	39 Let.	d		281			
61	B36	a	*Se pour ce muir qu'Amours ai bien servi*	309	248	193	Ta
	40 Let.	d		310			
	41 Let.	a		313			
	42 Let.	a		341			
	Rfr.	a	*"S'il est voirs ce qu'on m'en a dit / Autrement, ne di-je en mon dit"* (5 circles)[101]	336			
62	V	d	*Cent mille fois esbahie* (2 str.)	343			Pa198
	43 Let.	d		344			
	44 Let.	d		350			
	Rfr.		*Et tout par legierement croire* (5 virgins)[102]	356			
	45 Let.	a		360			
	46 Let.	d		367			
63	R	d	*Cinc, .vii., .xii., .i., .ix., .xi. et .xx.* [103]	369			

EDITIONS. Tarbé 1849, 45–50, 135–154 and 1856 (partial); P. Paris 1875. Paris's edition is incomplete; the editor has omitted passages ranging from a line or two to long sections, with no editorial indication of their omission (according to Cerquiglini-Toulet 1991b, 363, 595 lines were cut in 111 different places). A. Thomas (1912) published the longest missing segment; ll. 7200–7218 (ed. P. Paris 1875, 294) are replaced by 265 ll., including the 230-line song of Polyphemus to Galatea, quoted directly by Machaut from the *Ovide Moralisé* (Paris's excision is discussed in Cerquiglini 1985b, 166 n. 23). Calin (1974, chap. 9) quotes a few other lines lacking in P. Paris 1875 (using MS A), and Brownlee (1984, 155) quotes a few more from the same manuscript. A new, unpublished edition by the late Paul Imbs, based on MS F-G, is utilized in the work of Cerquiglini-Toulet, who often cites lines lacking in the P. Paris edition. At present, then, the *Voir Dit* is the only work of Machaut lacking a critical edition. Cerquiglini-Toulet's reworking of the unpublished Imbs edition is forthcoming from the Société des Anciens Textes Français. A complete edition and translation by Palmer and Leech-Wilkinson is forthcoming from Garland.

TRANSLATIONS. Suchier/Birch-Hirschfeld 1900, 238 (rondeau VD1 only, German); Weiss 1967 (letter 10); Weiss/Taruskin 1984 (letter 10). Excerpts in Kelly 1978, passim; Brownlee 1984; Leupin 1986; Sturges 1991a; S.J. Williams 1993. A complete edition and translation by Palmer and Leech-Wilkinson is forthcoming from Garland.

RECORDINGS (refer to chap. 8.6).

ANAGRAM. *Guillaume de Machaut; Peronelle d'Armentiere*; see P. Paris 1875, xix–xxiii. Imbs (1991, 253–55) agrees, but with the emendation *Armantiere. Guillaume de Machaut amera fille Perronne*; see Suchier 1897; Hanf 1898, 147–48; G. Paris 1898; Hoepffner 1906, 408–9; 1908–21, 1:xl–xli; Guesnon 1912, 93n.; Eichelberg 1935, 27–31; Brownlee 1984, 239 n. 25. *Guillaume de Machaut; Perronne fille a amer*; see Cerquiglini 1985b, 233–39; and comments in Badel 1985, 558–59; de Looze 1988a, 208–9; 1988b, 548n., 548, 550–56; Higgins 1991, 174–75; Sturges 1991b). In addition, Mulder (1979, 62) has signaled a possible anagram near the end of the *Lay de l'Ymage, Ne say comment* (L14/9) that resembles the anagram of the *Voir Dit*.

---

[101] The five responses to the five circles surrounding Fortune (ed. P. Paris 1875, 336–39) all have this refrain, which was introduced earlier in ll. 8229–30 (ed. P. Paris 1875, 333).

[102] Five ten-line strophes in rhyming couplets, each of which end with this refrain.

[103] On the number riddle, see P. Paris 1875, 369–70 n. 2; Hoepffner 1906, 409.

PATRON. Peronne d'Armentières (P. Paris 1875, xviii–xxvii). Peronne, but not d'Armentières (Guelliot 1914, 304; Cerquiglini 1985b, 223–43). See also Hanf 1898, 153–55; Cerquiglini 1985b, 116; Kelly 1987, 83. See above concerning the anagram. Cerquiglini-Toulet has eliminated Peronne d'Armentières from consideration, but perhaps too soon: R. Cazelles (1982, 90) makes some interesting circumstantial historical references that are strengthened by Machaut's acquaintance with Raoul de Vienne, sire de Louppy, and the newly-discovered ties of his brother Jean de Machaut with Bar (see chap. 1.11c).

Charles, duke of Normandy (Gauvard 1982, 23; Kendrick 1992, 39–40 n. 7). The accepted date of the work does not admit the earlier view (Caylus 1753a, 413; Rive 1780; Tarbé 1849, xiii–xxi), attaching the work to Agnès of Navarre, wife of Gaston Fébus.

Toute Belle's heraldic motto in the *Voir Dit* is given as "Gardés moy bien" (ed. P. Paris 1875, 83 l. 1905).

On the feminine voice of Toute Belle, see Calin 1974, 193; Guillaume de Machaut 1982, 263 (comments of Poirion); Musso 1982; Cerquiglini 1985b, 100–103, esp. p. 102 n. 28; Higgins 1991, 166 n. 69 (see esp. pp. 158–72 for an important discussion of the woman's voice in late medieval poetry); 1993b, 177–78, 183. S.J. Williams (1977, 463–64) notes technical problems in some of the lyrics attributed to Toute Belle and concludes that they may well be the work of an amateur.

For Deschamps's references to the "Peronne" of the *Voir Dit*, see chap. 2.1.1j–k.

DATE. The events of the narrative cover the years July 1362 until 1364, while the work itself was written between 1363 and 1365 (P. Paris 1875, xxviii–xxxi, 387 n. ix, 389 n. xvi, 390 n. xxiv, 401 n. lxxiii; Hoepffner 1908–21, 1:xl–xli; Chichmaref 1909, 1:lv–lxiv; Machabey 1955b, 1:56–64; Brownlee 1984, 235 n. 8; Cerquiglini 1985b, 54, 72–74, 223–24; Leech-Wilkinson 1993b, esp. 106 nn. 12–13, 116 n. 51, 119 n. 63.

AUTOBIOGRAPHY. The question of the "truth" of the *Voir Dit* has been debated for over one hundred years. Opinions range from literal interpretation to the view that the work is a "monumental hoax" (Beer 1981, 11). See Tarbé 1856, xiv; P. Paris 1875; Mas Latrie 1877b; G. Paris 1877; Petit de Julleville 1892–93, 330–37; 1896, 340–43; Suchier 1897; Hanf 1898 (a point-by-point analysis); Gröber 1902, 1046; G. Paris 1907, 223; Hoepffner 1908–21, 1:xl–xli, 3:xxxix; Chichmaref 1909, 1:liv; Eichelberg 1935 (also very methodical); Huizinga 1953, 122–24; Becker 1964, 356–57; Schrade 1967; Sonnemann 1969, 122, 132–34, 148–51; Burrow 1971, 48–49; Poirion 1971, 193–94; Zumthor 1972, 66, 173–74, 310–11 (=Eng. ed., 42, 130–31, 255–56); Gybbon-Monypenny 1973, 134–35; Zumthor 1973; Calin 1974, 167–78, 192–93; F. and W. Calin 1974, 247–48; Connery 1974, 10–11; S.J. Williams 1977, 462–64; Beer 1980, 27; Little 1980, 45–47; Beer 1981, chap. 6; Calin 1982, 248–50; 1983b, 150–53; Brownlee 1984, 234 n. 4, 235–36 n. 8, 236 n. 9; de Looze 1984, 146; Cerquiglini 1985b, part 3, esp. 101–2, and index, s.v. "vérité"; Sturges 1986; Huot 1987, 283, 286; Heinrichs 1990, 162 n. 6; Butterfield 1991, 45; Davis 1991, 104–5; Imbs 1991, 225–57; Sturges 1991a; Wimsatt 1991b, 105; Sturges 1992, 140–42; de Looze 1993b, 73–79; Higgins 1993b, 183; Leech-Wilkinson 1993a, 63; 1993b, 103–6 et passim; J.H.M. Taylor 1993; Wimsatt 1993; Calin 1994, 219–20, 222–24; Suard 1994.

The poem refers to several verifiable historical personages or events, such as the following (see Calin 1974, 173–74; Cerquiglini 1985b, 165–66; Leech-Wilkinson 1993b):
(a) Arnaud de Cervole, the "Archpriest" (d. 1366), the most notorious of the French brigands (P. Paris 1875, xxix–xxx, 167, 171, 181, 222, 285, 289, 345; see also Cerquiglini 1985b, 160; Leech-Wilkinson 1993b, 117–18 n. 56, 127–28 n. 105, 129 n. 115, 131 n. 123).
(b) 1363 Paris plague (P. Paris 1875, xxix, 265, 314; see also Cerquiglini 1985b, 165 n. 21; Leech-Wilkinson 1993b, 120 n. 67).
(c) unusual weather (P. Paris 1875, 283, 285, 289, 295, 401 n. 73; see Chichmaref 1909, 1:lxii; Delachenal 1909–31, 2:356–58; Leech-Wilkinson 1993b, 128 n. 106).

DISCUSSION (literary). Tarbé 1849, xiii–xxi; Magnin 1851 (with additional excerpts not printed in Tarbé); P. Paris 1875; Petit de Julleville 1892–93, 330–37; 1896, 340–43; Gröber 1902, 1046–47; Lowes 1904, 618n.; Chichmaref 1909, 1:liii–lxiii; Chichmaref 1911; Gourmont 1913; Foulet 1923, 88; Patch 1923, 23 n. 91; Huizinga 1924, 109–11 (=1953, 127–30); Patch 1927, 83 n. 4, 91 n. 1, 92 n. 1, 96n., 96 n. 2, 98 n. 1, 115 n. 2; Siciliano 1934, 294–95, 297–98; Eichelberg 1935; Levy 1935; Patterson 1935, 1:77–78; Cohen 1947; 1949; 1951; Moore 1951, 38–39; Cohen 1952; S.J. Williams 1952, 62–83; Huizinga 1953, 349, 351; Gybbon-Monypenny 1957, 70–74; Poirion 1965, 138, 199–200,

201–3, 205, 529–30; Wimsatt 1968, 82–85; Sonnemann 1969, 121–63; S.J. Williams 1969; Poirion 1971, 92–93; Zumthor 1972, 66, 173–74, 310–11 (=Eng. ed., 42, 130–31, 255–56); Gybbon-Monypenny 1973, 133–35; Zumthor 1973; Calin 1974, 167–202; F. and W. Calin 1974, 239–40, 247–48; Connery 1974, 152–74; Amon 1976; B. and J. Cerquiglini 1976; Jordan 1976; Cerquiglini 1977a; S.J. Williams 1977; Brownlee 1978a, 223–27; 1978b, 11–12; Calin 1978, 184–86; Cerquiglini 1978a; 1978b, 122–27; Kelly 1978, 54–56, 147–49, 243–55 et passim; S.J. Williams 1978, 193–95; Beer 1980, 27; Cerquiglini 1980a; 1980b; Beer 1981; Boulton 1981; Cerquiglini 1981; 1982; Musso 1982; Zink 1982; Calin 1983b, 150–62; Cerquiglini 1983, 290–92; Brownlee 1984, 94–156; Cerquiglini 1984; de Looze 1984, 145–48, 154–57; Steinle 1984; Cerquiglini 1985a, 21–22; 1985b, passim; Kelly 1985, 290; Cerquiglini 1986a, 1986b; Leupin 1986, 134, 137–47; Nouvet 1986, 342; Sturges 1986; Huot 1987, 280–86; Löfstedt 1987, 231; Burrow 1988; Cerquiglini 1988b, 54; Davenport 1988, 62; R. Morris 1988, 551–52, 554; Zeeman 1988, 835–37; Boulton 1989; Heinrichs 1989a, 595; Boulton 1990; Planche 1990a; J. Root 1990, 12, 177–79, 189–23; J.H.M. Taylor 1990, 548 n. 26; Butterfield 1991, 44–46; Cerquiglini-Toulet 1991a, 233–34, 237–38; 1991b; Higgins 1991, 147–48, 166, 174–75, 189 n. 127, 191–92; Huot 1991, 240, 244; Imbs 1991; Sturges 1991a; Wimsatt 1991b, 104–5; Sturges 1992; Zink 1992, 280–81; Boulton 1993, 162–67, 177–80, 197–202, 241, 242, 276; Cerquiglini-Toulet 1993b; 1993b, 74, 76, 97, 110–12, 149; de Looze 1993a; Leech-Wilkinson 1993b; J.H.M. Taylor 1993; S.J. Williams 1993; Wimsatt 1993; Calin 1994, 219–27, 359–61; Heinrichs 1994; Suard 1994.

Musso (1982) undertakes a statistical comparison of the vocabulary of the letters of the narrator compared with the letters of Toute Belle, finding those of Toute Belle more restrained lexically, while the narrator employed a richer and more variegated vocabulary, and thus implying that Toute Belle's letters were genuine. See the interesting discussion of this study in Guillaume de Machaut 1982, 215–16 (Calin), 216–21 (Imbs, Calin, and B. Cerquiglini); Calin 1982, 248–49; Guillaume de Machaut 1982, 264–67 (Imbs, J. Cerquiglini, Poirion, Calin, and Zumthor). Imbs (1991, 226) seems to accept that the letters are genuine.

The order of the letters is discussed in P. Paris 1875, 387 n. vii; Hanf 1898, 177–94; Eichelberg 1935, 15–16, 24 n. 31, 35–69; Brownlee 1984, 235–36 n. 8, 237–38 n. 12; Cerquiglini 1985b, 9 n. 10; Huot 1987, 283. Leech-Wilkinson 1993b, 104 n. 9) supports Eichelberg in exchanging the order of Paris's letters 6–7 (=letters 4–5 in the manuscripts), 2–3 (=letters 6–7 in manuscripts), and 40–41. Ruhe (1975) and Cerquiglini (1985b, 39–49, 102 n. 28, 193–94, 219–20 esp. nn. 11–12; 1991, 342–62) analyze aspects of the letters.

Holzbacher (1973–74) satisfactorily explains two passages that editors have misinterpreted (see also Eichelberg 1935, 106–7; Calin 1974, 190–92; Cerquiglini 1985b, 135), namely, the "clavette," (P. Paris 1875, 161 l. 3887), and the jewel to Toute Belle's treasure (P. Paris 1875, 361–62, letter 45), this latter in light of a passage in the *Roman de Cardenois*. Tarbé had considered the "key to Toute Belle's treasury" to refer to the key of a chastity belt (1849, 161 s.v. "clavette"); all this might best be left to obscurity, but that Tuchman uses the absurd notion in her *A Distant Mirror*. Paulin Paris (1875, 162 n. 1, 405 n. lxxxix) already dismisses Tarbé's fancy.

On the game of "le Roi qui ne ment" (P. Paris 1875, 215, 218), see Calin 1974, 67; Cerquiglini 1985b, 133 n. 46, 171 n. 34; Green 1990; Cerquiglini-Toulet 1993a; 1993c, 37–38.

See also literary discussions in chap. 7.3 of the twelve lyrical insertions transmitted in the music section of the manuscripts (*Longuement* [L18/13], *Plourez, dames* [B32], *Nes qu'on* [B33], *Quant Theseüs / Ne quier* [B34], *Se pour ce muir* [B36], *Sans cuer, dolens* [R4], *Dame, se vous n'avez* [R13], *Dix et sept* [R17], *Cilz ha bien* [V24], *Je ne me puis* [V33], *L'ueil, qui est* [V34], *Plus bele* [V35]).

DISCUSSION (codicological). Cerquiglini 1987c, 314–21; S.J. Williams 1969.

DISCUSSION (art historical). Cerquiglini 1985b, 168–71 (iconography of the *image*); Van Buren 1986b; Huot 1987, 280–86. On color symbolism in the *Voir Dit*, see P. Paris 1875, 82–83, 213–214, 221, 225, 240, 299–300, 309, 313, 347, 351; comments on *Se pour ce muir* (B36) in chap. 7.3; Huizinga 1924, 107 (=1953, 125); Amon 1976; Jordan 1976, 32–40; van Uytven 1984, 447 n. 7, 448–49. See also Steinle's discussion of the description of the *écu bleu* in *Remede* (1989, 68–69); *Remede* ll. 1888–914 (Wilkins 1972, 176 n. 176).

DISCUSSION (musical). Quittard 1917–19, 96–105, 123–27; Ludwig 1926–54, 2:53b*–58b*; S.J. Williams 1969; 1977, 466–68; Fowler 1979, 122–24, 289–93; Little 1980; Gallo 1985; Tavani 1985, 251–52, 254–55; Leech-Wilkinson 1993a. See also chap. 7.3 on the eight musical works inserted into the *Voir Dit* (*Longuement* [L18/13], *Plourez, dames* [B32], *Nes qu'on* [B33], *Quant Theseüs / Ne quier* [B34], *Se pour ce muir* [B36], *Sans cuer, dolens* [R4], *Dame, se vous n'avez* [R13], *Dix et sept* [R17]). RELATED MACHAUT WORKS. *Remede* (see chap. 5.7); *Fonteinne* (see chap. 5.11); *Trop ne me puis de bonne Amour loer* (Lo225; see chap. 6.4) *A toi, Hanri* (Cp3; see chap. 6.5); and the following motets: *Lasse! comment / Se j'aim* (M16), *Christe / Veni* (M21), *Tu qui gregem / Plange* (M22) (see chap. 7.3). Imbs 1991 discusses the relation of all of Machaut's earlier *dits* to *Voir Dit*.
LITERARY ANTECEDENTS. Bible (Cerquiglini 1985b, 213). Boethius, *Consolation of Philosophy* (Patch 1935, 91, 105–6; Kelly 1978, 285 n. 15; Cerquiglini 1982, 256; 1985b, 39). Arthurian romance (Calin 1983b, 153–55; Huot 1993, 258). Guillaume le Clerc de Normandie (Cerquiglini 1985b, 210 n. 10). Andreas Capellanus (Calin 1974, 201; Cerquiglini-Toulet 1991b, 354–55). *Prose Tristan* (L.K. Morris 1985, 551; Huot 1993, 258). *Jeux partis* (Cerquiglini 1985b, 91–95). *Roman de la Rose* (Burrow 1971, 151 n. 6; Brownlee 1978a; 1978b; Uitti 1978; Badel 1980, 90 n. 76, 91; Diekstra 1983, 136–37; Brownlee 1984, 96–98, 134, 138, 241 n. 45; Cerquiglini 1985b, passim; Huot 1993, 256–67, 271–72). *Chastelaine de Vergi* (Frappier 1946, 108 n. 2). Jakamés, *Roman du Castelain de Couci* (Gybbon-Monypenny 1973, 149–51). Nicole de Margival, *Dit de la Panthere* (Gybbon-Monypenny 1973, 150–51). *Ovide Moralisé* (A. Thomas 1912; De Boer 1913, 88–89; 1914, 336–42; B. and J. Cerquiglini 1976, 372–74; Cerquiglini 1985b, 152–55, 166–68, 178–79, 208 n. 9, 224, 229–33, 269 s.v. *Ovide Moralisé;* Mühlethaler 1989, 398; Heinrichs 1990, 12–14, 161–74). *Romans de la Dame a la Lycorne* (Geiselhardt 1914, 54; Boulton 1993, 162–63).
TEXTUAL LEGACY (France). Hoepffner 1906, 411–13 (a riddle found in MSS **K** and **J** may relate to the *Voir Dit*). Froissart, *Espinette Amoureuse* (Geiselhardt 1914, 50–52; Eichelberg 1935, 128–29; Whiting 1946, 197; Fourrier 1963, 34–35; Poirion 1965, 213–14; Wimsatt 1968, 127; Zumthor 1972, 311 (=Eng. ed., 256); Gybbon-Monypenny 1973, 133, 136; Huot 1987, 308); *Prison Amoureuse* (Geiselhardt 1914, 28, 54–57; Eichelberg 1935, 128; Whiting 1946, 199; Wimsatt 1968, 129; Fourrier 1974, 15–16; Ruhe 1975, 283, 284; Kibler 1978, 34, 46; Kelly 1983, 118; Bennett 1991, 291; Cerquiglini-Toulet 1991a, 225; Wimsatt 1991b, 189–90; Boulton 1993, 214–15, 217); *Joli Buisson de Jonece* (Whiting 1946, 203; Fourrier 1975, 32–33; Cerquiglini 1985b, 217 n. 6; Huot 1987, 317; Zeeman 1988, 838; Wimsatt 1991b, 190; Zeeman 1991, 225–26). Deschamps (see chap. 2.1.1i). Oton de Granson, *Livre de Messire Ode* (Wimsatt 1991b, 227, 232; Boulton 1993, 224, 225). Christine de Pizan, *Epistres sur le Roman de la Rose* (Brownlee 1988, 215); *Livre du Duc des Vrais Amans* (Pugh 1894, 585–86; Gröber 1902, 1095; Schilperoort 1936, 123–25; Poirion 1965, 249 n. 36; Ruhe 1975, 283, 284; Cerquiglini 1983, 290; 1985b, 217 n. 6; Boulton 1993, 234). Baudet Harenc, *Le Parlement d'Amours* (Cerquiglini 1985b, 217 n. 6). Poirion (1965, 277 n. 29) dismissed the possibility that Charles d'Orléans referred to the *Voir Dit* virelai *Douce, plaisant et debonnaire* (VD25; ed. P. Paris 1875, 77, l. 1697) in his ballade *Ieune, gente, plaisant et debonnaire* (ed. Mühlethaler 1992, 100, 102). René d'Anjou, *Livre dou Cuer d'Amours Espris* (Hoepffner 1908–21, 1:v [attrib. Achille Caulier]; Cerquiglini 1985b, 173, 239–43 [proves the old view false]); see chap. 2.3.2d.
The *Voir Dit* may have inspired two further lyrics, the rondeau *Toute belle bonne cointe et jolie* (MS **Pa** [50], fol. 70b no. 224), and a lyric that opened a lost book of "plusieurs balades et rondeaux," beginning *Toute Belle, que veulz-tu, mon amy;* cited in the inventory of the Burgundian library made at Bruges, ca. 1467 (Barrois 1830, 201 no. 1383).
TEXTUAL LEGACY (England). Chaucer, *Book of the Duchess* (Wimsatt 1968, 84–85, 156; Calin 1994, 285); *Troilus* (F.N. Robinson 1957, 833 n. to Bk. 5 l. 460); "Franklin's Tale" (Schofield 1901, 445); "Manciple's Tale" (Stillwell 1940; Work 1941; Severs 1952; Wimsatt 1968, 84; Westervelt 1981; Diekstra 1983, 135–38, 141; Calin 1987b, 18; 1994, 356–66). Gower, *Confessio Amantis* (Burrow 1971, 50; 1983, 6, 19, 21; Diekstra 1983, 147 n. 13; Zeeman 1991, 225–26; Olsson 1992, 39, 209n.; Calin 1994, 388, 394–96).

TEXTUAL LEGACY (Spain). Anon. Catalan *Storia de l' amant Frondino de Brisona* (ed. Meyer 1891; French lyrics only in Pagès 1936, 126–27, 136–40). See Ruhe 1975, 451 n. 34; the last of the five inserted rondeaux (*Le grand desir que j' ay puise veoÿr*; ed. Pagès 1936, 140) is related to the refrain of *Nes qu' on* (B33=VD16=Lo232).

PROVERBS (references to Hassell 1982). A11; A63 (three times); A64; A94; A126: A134: A135 (three times): A144: A193: A203; A229 (twice); B31; B59; B60; B112; B140; B151; B166; B199; C25; C72; C86 (twice); C99; C101; C140; C189; C190; C198; C228; C233; C235 (three times); C247; C286; C319 (twice); C323; C348; C349; C363; C364; D21 (three times); D22; D25 (four times); D39; D120; E67; E74; F19; F44; F61; F72; F74; F75; F76; F88; F96; F120; F127; H15; H23; J33; L4 (twice); L7; L30; L65; L73; M6; M42; M59; M106; M145; M190; N12 (twice); N40 (twice); O9; O10; O12; O68; P51; P175; P193; P218; P234; P295; R16; R72 (twice); R85; S25; S31; S34; S72; S100; S104; S106; S107; T70 (twice); U1; V43; V66 (twice); V75 (seven times, with the ballade *Se pour ce muir*); V79; Y5 (twice). Cerquiglini-Toulet (1993d, 209–10) notes two additional proverbs that also appear in *Fonteinne*.

14. *Le Dit de la Marguerite*

FORM. 208 lines, composed of thirteen sixteen-line strophes with the pattern:

a a a b a a a b b b b a b b b a (masculine or feminine rhymes).[104]
1010104 1010104 1010104 1010104

Since each of the thirteen large strophes has different rhymes, there are a total of twenty-six different rhyming syllables.

MANUSCRIPTS.

| [5] | **A** | fols. 213v–214v | [10] | **M** | fols. 166v–167v |
| [6] | **F** | fols. 198v–199v | [18] | **Pm** | fols. 120v–212v |

EDITIONS. Tarbé 1849, 123–29; Fourrier 1979, 277–84.

TRANSLATIONS. Windeatt 1982, 145–47; Wimsatt 1991b, 166 (ll. 1–5).

PATRON. Tarbé (1849, xxviii–xxix) and Lowes (1904, 595–96) linked *Marguerite* to Pierre de Lusignan, an association Hoepffner rejected (1908–21, 1:xlii–xliii). Wimsatt (1970, 40–42, 47–50; 1991b, 100) and Fourrier (1979, 74–75) connect *Marguerite* to the *complainte Mon cuer, m'amour* (Cp6), which has the acrostic MARGVERITE / PIERRE (see chap. 6.5). Since *Marguerite* has the same metrical scheme and strophic form, the connection to Pierre de Lusignan seems assured (who moreover had a tower on Cyprus called "Marguerite" [*Prise*, l. 8365]; see the discussion in Lowes 1904, 596–97n.; Wimsatt 1970, 60–62). On *Marguerite* and Marguerite of Flanders, see Wimsatt 1970, 48–59; Akehurst review of Wimsatt 1970; De Winter 1985, 13.

DATE. Between 1364 and 1369 (Lowes 1904, 595–96; see Wimsatt 1970, 49 n. 25). Around the time of the 19 May 1364 coronation of Charles V at Reims (Fourrier 1979, 73, following Chichmaref 1909, 1:lxiv). 1366 or later (Wimsatt 1970, 48–49; Calin 1974, 231).

DISCUSSION (literary). Hoepffner 1908–21, xlii–xliii; Chichmaref 1909, 1:lxiv; Wimsatt 1970, 47–48 et passim; Calin 1974, 229–31; Fourrier 1979, 72–75; Wimsatt 1991b, 99–101.

TEXTUAL LEGACY (France). Froissart,[105] *Paradis d' Amour* (ll. 1627–53) ballade *Sus toutes flours tient on la rose a belle*, with the refrain "Sus toutes flours j'aime la margherite" (ed. Patterson 1935, 2:65; Wilkins 1969a, 51 no. 37; Dembowski 1986, 79–80; str. 1 trans. Wimsatt 1991b, 179; ed. and trans. Figg 1994b, 153–54, 158); the same ballade also appears in the separate section of ballades, with a different third strophe (ed. McGregor 1975, 211 no. 8; Baudouin 1978, 13–15 no. 8; ed. and trans. Figg 1994b, 153–54); see the

---

104 On the form, see chap. 5.4, introduction to *Jugement Behaingne*.

105 The dependence of Froissart on Machaut depends on a later date for Froissart's *Paradis d'Amour* than 1361–62, proposed by Dembowski (1986, 12–13); see Wimsatt 1972a, 393–96; 1991b, 320–21 n. 50, 328 n. 40; Butterfield 1991, 55–56 n. 7. Wimsatt (1991b, 181, 189) dates *Paradis d' Amour* ca. 1365.

discussion in Lowes 1904, 599; Poirion 1965, 213; Dembowski 1986, 28; Figg 1994a, 135–37; 1994b, 153–59. Froissart, *Dittié de la Flour de la Margherite* (Lowes 1904, 597–99; Whiting 1946, 206; Wimsatt 1970, 30–34, 41–50, 58–59; Fourrier 1979, 46, 49–51; Calin 1987b, 13; Wimsatt 1991b, 185–87); *Plaidoire de la Rose et de la Violette* (Lowes 1904, 600). Deschamps, ballade *Tresdoulce fleur toute blanche et vermeille* (ed. St-Hilaire/Raynaud 1878–1903, 3:379–80 no. 539; see Lowes 1904, 601–2, 608; Wimsatt 1970, 30, 32 n. 6); *Lai de Franchise* (ed. St-Hilaire/Raynaud 1878–1903, 2:203–14 no. 307, lai no. 4; see Lowes 1904, 601–11; Wimsatt 1970, 30–35, 57–58).

For additional works of Froissart and Deschamps belonging to the complex of *Marguerite* poems, see Lowes 1904, 600–603 and the discussion of Froissart in Huot 1991, 246–51; Figg 1994b, 11–12. Wilkins (1987, 81–82; see also Wilkins's review of Wimsatt 1970) mentions two ballades set to music, *Roses et lis* by Egidius, and *Passerose de beauté* by Trebor; see also Kibler/Wimsatt 1983, *pastourelles* 17 and 19. See also chap. 5.18. On the flower motif in general, see Calin 1974, 231.

TEXTUAL LEGACY (England). Chaucer, "Prologue" to the *Legend of Good Women* (Lowes 1904, 593, 611–30; F.N. Robinson 1957, explanatory notes, passim; Wimsatt 1970, 30–33, 41–50, 63–64; 1991b, 165–66). For further influence on English poetry, see Falke 1986.

15. Le Dit de la Rose

FORM. Octosyllabic rhyming couplets, 108 lines.

MANUSCRIPTS.

| [5] **A** | fols. 365v–366r | [16] **J** | fol. 153r–154r |
| [6] **F** | fols. 199v–200r | [18] **Pm** | fols. 182v–183r |

FACSIMILES (refer to chap. 4.4m). Miniatures A150; Pm112.

EDITIONS. Tarbé 1849, 65–67 (omits 3 ll.); Fourrier 1979, 285–88.

DATE. Possibly connected to copying of **A** (Brownlee 1978a, 230) in the early 1370s.

DISCUSSION (literary). Lowes 1904, 629; Calin 1974, 231–34; Fourrier 1979, 75, 83; Brownlee 1978a, 230.

TEXTUAL LEGACY (France). Christine de Pizan, *Dit de la Rose* (Brownlee 1988, 208 n. 11).

16. Vezci les biens que ma dame me fait

FORM. Hexasyllabic lines (only l. 64 is decasyllablic), all rhyming in *-our*, 64 lines.

MANUSCRIPTS.

| [5] **A** | fols. 366r–366v | [18] **Pm** | fols. 183r–183v |
| [6] **F** | fols. 200r–200v | | |

EDITION. Chichmaref 1909, 1:273–75.

DATE. MS **A**'s old index, a prescriptive listing of all works that were at hand before the copying of the codex, does not list *Vezci les biens*. The function of the work may be linked closely to the copying of **A**. It was copied directly after *Rose* onto a bifolio tipped-in at the end of the *Prise*. Thus, Machaut may have composed *Vezci les biens* quite soon before its inclusion at the very end of the text portion of MS **A**, directly before the beginning of the lai section. With *Rose*, it rounds off the text section of the manuscript, and makes a lyrical transition between the *Prise* and the beginning of the music section. In MS **F-G**, it lost this transitional function, and was relocated near, but not at, the end of the text section. Nevertheless, it does serve to articulate the end of MS **F**, which may have been planned as a separate volume from the beginning; after *Vezci les biens*, there appears a decorative "A..M..E..N..".

DISCUSSION (literary). Brownlee 1978a, 230.

DISCUSSION (codicological). Earp 1983, 92–93, 347 (see diagram of gathering XLVI in MS **A**); 1989, 486–88, especially 487 n. 44.

PROVERB (reference to Hassell 1982). F96.

17. *La Prise d'Alexandre*

FORM. Octosyllabic rhyming couplets, 8886 lines (on an error in the line count in Mas Latrie 1877b, see Calin 1974, 203n.); the three interpolated prose letters are not counted.

MANUSCRIPTS.

[3]	**Vg**	fols. 336r–392v	[6]	**G**	fols. 1r–44r
[4]	**B**	fols. 332r–395v	[7]	**E**	fols. 213r–238r
[5]	**A**	fols. 309r–365r			

LOST MANUSCRIPTS.

[3a] A complete-works manuscript containing the *Prise* was in the library of Alfonso V at Valencia in 1417. I identify this manuscript with **Vg** [3] (see chap. 3).

[9] Paris, untraced manuscript (see chap. 3, MS **B** [4], "provenance").

[25] Bruges, lost paper manuscript.

FACSIMILE (refer to chap. 4.4o). Miniature A149. The facsimile in Loomis 1965 (plate 103) includes all of the opening folio in MS **A** (fol. 309r).

EDITIONS. Mas Latrie 1877b; Dzelzainis 1985 (publication forthcoming).

TRANSLATION. Palmer (forthcoming).

ANAGRAM. *Pierre de Lusigna, roi de Chypre, & Guillaume de Machaut*; see Mas Latrie 1877b, 277 n. 2. *Guillaume de Machaut*; *Pierre roi de Chipre e de Iherusalem*; see Cerquiglini 1985b, 119, 236 and n. 29; 1993c, 39; see also Tarbé 1849, 167–68 s.v. "énigme"; Suchier 1897, 543; Hoepffner 1906, 404–5; Leupin 1986, 133; de Looze 1988b, 543–44, 556. Machaut names himself in ll. 8876–77 (cf. Cerquiglini 1985b, 182).

PATRON. Tyson (1986) notes the possibility that the *Prise* was composed on the command of Charles V; see above, chap. 1.16. Emperor Charles IV (Palmer 1988, xiv). Imbs (1991, 256) notes a possible link to the Peronne of the *Voir Dit*.

DATE. After the 16 January 1369 assassination of Pierre de Lusignan, king of Cyprus; see chap. 1.16. The length of the work argues an extended period of composition, ca. 1370–72.

BIOGRAPHY. See Voisé 1982, 49–52. On Pierre de Lusignan and Guillaume de Machaut, see Wimsatt (1991b, 96–100), and above, chap. 1.16. On material in the *Prise* concerning Machaut and John of Luxembourg, see chap. 1.2.7f, 1.5.1e, 1.5.2, 1.5.3d, and 1.6.3b. On Machaut and John II, see chap. 1.10.2e; on Machaut and Charles V, as well as the Emperor Charles IV, see chap. 1.15.

DISCUSSION (historical). Because of its value as a chronicle of Pierre I de Lusignan's crusade, the *Prise* was the first poem of Machaut to be studied in modern times; interest in this work, known at first only from MS **F-G**, brought about the reawakening of interest in Machaut's works in the eighteenth century, first in 1743 (Lebeuf 1751, 497–500; Caylus 1753b). Other studies of historical issues include Mas Latrie 1844–45; 1852; 1876; 1877b; Lowes 1904; 594–97; Chichmaref 1909, 1:lxvi–lxvii; Hoepffner 1908–21, 1:xli–xliii; Delachenal 1909–31, 3:93–94; La Monte 1932; Hoppin 1957, 82–83, 90; Wimsatt 1970, 42–47, 60–65; Calin 1974, 203n., 203–26; Tyson 1975, 1, 20, 24–26; Edbury 1980; Voisé 1982, 49–52; Lanoue 1985; Levine 1985; Housley 1986.

DISCUSSION (literary). Petit de Julleville 1892–93, 429–34; La Monte 1932; Calin 1974, 203–26; Kelly 1978, 53; Beer 1980, 29–30; Lanoue 1985; Leupin 1986, 132–33, 148–49; Roques 1986. The thesis of Dzelzainis (1985) was unavailable to me.

DISCUSSION (list of musical instruments, ll. 1140–68). Bottée de Toulmon 1838; Travers 1881; Abert 1904–5, 354–55 (with a similar list); Ludwig 1926–54, 2:53a* (with additional bibliography); Gennrich 1926–27 (with other lists); Machabey 1931, 409–11; Pirro 1940, 10–12; Reese 1940, 383–84; Machabey 1955b, 2:135–57 (with additional bibliography); Reaney 1956, 10–17; Hoppin 1957, 90; Voisé 1982, 54–55; Ripin 1975; Godwin 1977; L. Wright 1977; Gómez 1979; L. Wright 1986; Bec 1992, 128–29, 223, 248; 1993. Komma (1961, 56), Snizkova (1982, 71 and n. 11) and Vachulka (1982, 324) speculate that Machaut was describing instruments in use at the Prague court; Wilkins (1983b, 259–60) speculates that Machaut was describing instruments at the court of John of Luxembourg in his lists of instruments in both the *Remede* and *Prise*. Gastoué (1921, 56) may have been the first of many to indicate that Machaut (*Prise*, ll. 1146–48) originated the expression that the organ is the "king of instruments"; Bec (1993) proves this interpretation false.

LITERARY ANTECEDENTS. *Roman de la Rose* (Roques 1982, 162–63). On the Nine Worthies, see chap. 5.8, literary antecedents, and Cerquiglini-Toulet 1993c, 37.

TEXTUAL LEGACY (France). Chandos Herald (a native Frenchman writing in England or Gascony), *La Vie du Prince Noir* (Tyson 1975, 25–26, 29). Villon, *Ballade des Seigneurs de Temps Jadis* (La Monte 1932, 53; Calin 1974, 226; Brownlee 1984, 253 n. 23).

TEXTUAL LEGACY (England). Chaucer, "Monk's Tale" (La Monte 1932; Braddy 1935; R.K. Root 1941; Braddy 1947; Calin 1974, 226).

PROVERBS (references to Hassell 1982). A74; A82: A196; B121; C99 (twice); C144 (twice); C234; C248; C263; C277; C284; D36 (twice); D80; D122; D125; E90 (three times); F15; F88 (twice); F123 (twice); F139; F157; G18; G55 (twice); G58; H15; I4; J46; L70 (twice); M228; M242; N12 (twice); N13; N27; O68 (twice); P232 (twice); P248; P257; S82; T60; T69; T71; V68; V126.

18. *Le Dit de la Fleur de Lis et de la Marguerite*

FORM. Octosyllabic rhyming couplets, 416 lines.

MANUSCRIPT.

    [6] **G**   fols. 71v–73v

EDITIONS. Wimsatt 1970, 15–26; Fourrier 1979, 289–301.

TRANSLATIONS. Windeatt 1982, 147–48 (excerpts); Wimsatt 1991b, 135–36, 186 (excerpts).

PATRONS, DATE. For the 1369 wedding of Philip the Bold and Marguerite of Flanders (Wimsatt 1970, 15, 54–58; 1991b, 100–101). See also chap. 1.17.

DISCUSSION (literary). Hoepffner 1908–21, 1:xlii–xliii; Wimsatt 1970, 26–29, 56–57 et passim; Calin 1974, 229–31; Fourrier 1979, 75–76; Wimsatt 1991b, 100–101.

TEXTUAL LEGACY (France). Froissart, *Dittié de la Flour de la Marguerite* (Wimsatt 1970, 30–34; 1991b, 185–87); *Espinette Amoureuse* (Huot 1987, 324–25 n. 27); *Joli Buisson de Jonece* (Huot 1987, 322); *La Plaidoire de la Rose et de la Violette* (Fourrier 1979, 67–68). Deschamps, *Lai de Franchise* (ed. St-Hilaire/Raynaud 1878–1903, 2:203–14 no. 307, lai no. 4; see Wimsatt 1970, 30–35, 57–58); ballade *Tresdoulce fleur toute blanche et vermeille* (ed. St-Hilaire/Raynaud 1878–1903, 3:379–80 no. 539; see Wimsatt 1970, 30, 32 n. 6). For additional works in the *Marguerite* complex, see chap. 5.14, textual legacy.

TEXTUAL LEGACY (England). Chaucer, *House of Fame* (Wimsatt 1970, 37–38; 1974, 127–29; 1991b, 135–36); "Prologue" to the *Legend of Good Women* (Wimsatt 1970, 31–39, 63–64; 1974, 127; Falke 1986, 147; Wimsatt 1991b, 165–67). Anon. *Pearl* and Usk, *Testament of Love* (Wimsatt 1970, 38–39, 64–65). For further influence on English poetry, see Falke 1986.

19. *Le Dit du Cerf Blanc* [*opus dubium*]

FORM. Four-line stanzas (concatenated in the same pattern as Machaut's popular *Jugement Behaingne*), 863 lines.

MANUSCRIPT.

    [16] **J**   fols. 155r–161v

FACSIMILES (refer to chap. 4.4x). Miniatures **J**28 and 32.

EDITION. Fourrier 1979, 302–29.

ASCRIPTION. Hoepffner (1906, 403; 1908–21, 1:lx n. 1, 2:xxxiv n. 2) denied Machaut's authorship; see also Brownlee 1984, 220 n. 9. Fourrier (1979, 79–85) agreed with Gröber's ascription to Machaut (Gröber 1902, 1045), and tried to support the case in his introduction to the poem. Three reviewers of Fourrier 1979 (Andrieux, Roques, and Wilkins) accept Fourrier's ascription of *Cerf Blanc* to Machaut, as does Kelly (1987, 87) and R. Morris (1988, 555). Yet the work is an *unicum* in MS **J**, which contains many poems not by Machaut; how could we accept that a large work of Machaut was omitted in the collecting efforts of the 1370s? It would seem more likely that *Cerf Blanc* is merely an early imitation of the strophic structure of the popular *Jugement Behaingne*.

PATRON. Wenceslas, duke of Brabant (Fourrier 1979, 81–86). Fourrier argues that the connection of Wenceslas to *Cerf Blanc* is based on the similarity of the form of the poem to Machaut's *Behaingne*, dedicated of course to Wenceslas's father, John of Luxembourg, king of Bohemia. In addition, there is mention near the end of the work to "Rose," the code-name for Wenceslas in Froissart's *Prison Amoureuse.* Thus, Machaut returned to the form of the older poem in playful hommage to father and son, which also explains the many lines in *Cerf Blanc* that recall lines of *Behaingne.* All this seems inconclusive to me, since a great many poems imitate Machaut's *Behaingne* (see chap. 5.5).

DATE. Fourrier (1979, 83) links both *Cerf Blanc* and Machaut's *Rose* to the festivities surrounding the coronation of Charles V at Reims on 19 May 1364, where both the owner of MS **J**, Robert d'Alençon, count of Perche, and the patron—according to Fourrier—of *Cerf Blanc*, Wenceslas of Luxembourg, duke of Brabant, were present. The count of Perche received a copy of both *Cerf Blanc* and *Rose,* which were subsequently copied at Bellême into MS **J**. Against this, *Rose* appears closely attached to the copying of MS **A** (see chap. 5.15), and probably dates from 1371 or later.

DISCUSSION (literary). Thiébaux 1974; Fourrier 1979, 76–86; Calin 1983b, 144 (on the "chase of love" theme); R. Morris 1988, 555.

LITERARY ANTECEDENTS. Machaut, *Jugement Behaingne* (Fourrier 1979, 81–83).

Lyrical Poetry: The Loange des Dames

The collection of fixed-form lyrics in Machaut's *Loange des Dames* is too large to allow for a discussion of each individual work. Instead, this chapter provides the following: (1) Some introductory remarks and a count of the total number of Machaut's lyrics; (2) a discussion of some questions of order in the *Loange* lyric collection that bear on the filiation and chronology of the manuscripts; (3) a table of concordances for the *Loange* lyrics, giving the sequential order of works in each of the principal manuscripts; outwardly similar to the listing of Chichmaref (1909, 1:lxxx–c), this table incorporates Ludwig's corrections (1926–54, 2:7a* n. 3) and supplies concordances for manuscripts unknown to both Chichmaref and Ludwig[1]; (4) a bibliographical overview of studies that deal with Machaut's lyrics, followed by selective bibliographical references to specific lyrics of the *Loange*, drawn especially from the notes in Chichmaref 1909 and Wilkins 1972, but also from Poirion 1965, and several studies by Wimsatt (1976, 1978, 1979, and 1991b); and finally, (5) a table of concordances for the eleven *complaintes* and a brief discussion of each *complainte*. Since a few of the *complaintes* seem to contain autobiographical references, especially *A toi, Hanri* (Cp3), and *Sire, a vous* (Cp7), I have provided more complete discussions, in a format similar to that employed in chapter 5 for the narrative *dits*.

1. Introduction

La Loange des Dames is the name usually applied in modern writings to the section in the complete-works manuscripts that contains lyrical poetry not set to music, following the rubric in the latest collection of lyrics, MS **G** (fol. 45r: *Ci commence la Loange des Dames*) [Here begins the *Praise of Ladies*].[2] Most of the lyric collections in earlier Machaut manuscripts have introductory rubrics that emphasize the lack of music for the lyrics, while others have very simple rubrics or lack rubrics altogether:

Les balades ou il n'a point de chant / Les chansons roiaus et les complaintes
[the ballades without music; the chants royaux and the complaintes] (MS **A**, index, fol. Ac).

Ci commencent les balades ou il n'a point de chant [here begin the ballades without music] (MS **Vg**, fol. 1r; MS **A**, fol. 177v).

Ci comencent les balades et les rondiaus ou il n'a point de chant [here begin the ballades and rondeaux without music] (MS **M**, fol. 167v).

Les balades (MS **J**, fol. 1r).

Cy est le livre de maistre Guillaume de Machaut la ou sont les balades et chansons royaux et complaintes et rondiaux non mises en chant et plusieurs

---

[1] For a table providing folio number locations of the lyrics in the various manuscripts, see the alphabetical listing in Wilkins 1972, 26–41.

[2] Modern scholars most often follow the modernized spelling of Chichmaref (1909): *La Louange des Dames*. Although MS **F-G** was surely copied from Machaut's exemplar, it is a posthumous copy, and thus the title may not be authorial. Maekawa (1985, 69–70) remarks that the miniature at the head of the collection in MS **A**, with a clerk (Guillaume) kneeling before a lady, with his hands raised in supplication, provides a visual analogue to the title "*Loange des Dames*" (see chap. 4.4p, miniature A117).

livres qui sensuivent et apres ce sensuivent lays et motés rondyaux et balades et virelays baladez fais par le dit maistre Guillaume de Machaut et mis en chant [here is the book of master Guillaume de Machaut where there are ballades, chants royaux, *complaintes,* and rondeaux not set to music and several books follow and after this follow lais and motets, rondeaux, ballades, and *virelais baladés* composed by the said master Guillaume de Machaut and set to music]. After an announcement of the *Prologue,* with incipits of the *Prologue* ballades, the rubric continues: *Cy commencent les balades* (MS **E** index, fol. Cr; the collection itself begins without a title on fol. 1v, after the *Prologue*).

Les balades et les rondeaulx (MS **H**, fol. 98r).

No rubric: MSS **C** and **K**.

Ci commence le livre de mestre Guillaume de Loris [here begins the book of master Guillaume de Lorris] (MS **D**, fol. 1r).[3]

The *Loange* text collection gathers together especially ballades, the most prestigious lyrical genre, along with a group of rondeaux, a group of *chants royaux,* and a group of *complaintes* (in later manuscripts, the *complaintes* form a separate section). Only one virelai, a purely musical form for Machaut until his later years, was taken into the *Loange.*[4] Machaut's self-contained lyrical collection, with internal runs of poems exhibiting proto-narrative continuity, was a model that influenced later poets, for example, Jean le Seneschal's *Cent Ballades,* Christine de Pizan's *Cent Ballades d'Amant et de Dame,* and John Gower's *Cinkante Balades* (see chap. 5.2, esp. n. 28).

A. *Machaut lyrics inside and outside the* Loange *section.* We have already had occasion to deal with some of Machaut's lyrical poems. Two of the *complaintes* provide material of potential biographical value and were introduced in chapter 1. Other lyrics are taken into the narrative portion of the codex, and were introduced in chapter 5. The *Remede* includes nine lyrical insertions, a lai, a *complainte,* a *chant royal,* two forms of ballade, a *prière,* a virelai, a refrain quotation, and a rondeau. Seven of these were set to music by Machaut and are discussed further in chapter 7.3. *Remede* lyrics and music were always copied with the narrative and were never duplicated in the lyrical sections of Machaut's complete-works manuscript. In the index to the late MS **A**, written at a time when Machaut was intensely interested in the presentation of his oeuvre, the seven musical lyrics of the *Remede* are listed separately at the end of the index, in a sense giving the lyrics in this self-contained narrative a place in the larger collection of Machaut's oeuvre (Earp 1989, 485 gives a facsimile of the index).

The *Lay de Plour, Qui bien aimme* (L22/16) is a lyrical pendant to the *Jugement Navarre.* Indeed, the fact that the lai appears in MS **C**, while the *Jugement Navarre* does not, suggests that the lai predates the completion of the *Jugement.* It casts the "retraction," the judgment *contre le Jugement dou Roy de Behaingne,* in a beautiful lyrical light, combining the image of a lady lamenting over her husband's coffin, the image of an uprooted tree, and the image of a river of tears (cf. Calin 1983a). The mutual influence between the lyric and narrative styles characteristic of Machaut's poetry, and seen especially in the *Remede* and *Voir Dit,* is met with here. Later in Machaut's career, as more and more collected manuscripts of his works had been copied, the *Lay de Plour* had to cede its position of close association with *Jugement Navarre* and find a place in the separate collection of lais.

---

[3] On the ascription, see the discussion of the date and provenance of MS **D** [11] in chap. 3.

[4] Arlt (1982, 263–64) suggests that the clear dance function of the virelais is a possible reason for the virtual exclusion of this genre from the *Loange.*

Fonteinne incorporates three lyrical insertions, the *Complainte d'Amant*, the *Confort d'Amant*, and a single rondeau. None of these lyrics was set to music. The narrative with the most extensive collection of lyrics outside the *Loange* is of course the *Voir Dit*. An overview of the *Voir Dit* lyrics was provided in the previous chapter (table 5.3). Among the thirty-one rondeaux, nineteen ballades, nine virelais, three *complaintes*, one lai, and one *prière*—let us overlook here possible questions of attribution—are works that have various relationships to Machaut's overall collection. Some of the *Voir Dit* lyrical insertions include works that had appeared in the *Loange* since the time of MS C, some are duplicated in the music section (sometimes with, sometimes without music), and of course some of the lyrics appear uniquely within the *Voir Dit*.

After the completion of the *Voir Dit* in the mid 1360s, Machaut incorporated lyrics in one further work, the *Prologue*, originally composed in the early 1370s as an introduction to MS A. Lyrics head this definitive introduction to the oeuvre in the form of four exquisitely refined ballades.

A final work included in the narrative section of the manuscripts that resembles a lyric is a tour de force on the rhyme *-our*, *Vezci les biens*. Rather than adhering to one of the standard lyrical forms, it resembles more closely the sort of highly-charged moment that one occasionally meets with in the narrative poems, in which a concentration of similar rhymes forms a kind of lyrical transition segment.[5] Machaut may have composed *Vezci les biens* to serve as a bridge between the narrative and musical portions of MS A (see chap. 5.16).

Thus, at the end of Machaut's career, the total number of lyrics appearing among the narrative poems includes two lais (here not counting the *Lay de Plour*), five *complaintes*, twenty-five ballades, thirty-three rondeaux, ten virelais, and two *prières*, with one example each of *chant royal* and *confort*.

Returning now to the *Loange* collection itself, little can be said about its development before the stage represented by MS C, which already contains 198 items. It is curious that two works, the ballades *Trop est crueus* (Lo51), and *Nulz homs ne puet* (Lo108) are lacking in C.[6] Earp (1983, 133 table 2.11, 137) noted an irregularity in the gathering structure in MS C near the end of the *Loange* section but was unable to determine the exact extent of what originally may have been a slightly smaller collection.

Due to the editing the collection underwent in successive manuscripts throughout Machaut's career, it is difficult to state conclusively exactly how many works the *Loange* contains, even in its latest version. The *complaintes* are first met with in MS Vg, and although they are set off with a decorative border and miniature, the *complaintes* themselves are not all contiguous, and the *Loange* collection of ballades and rondeaux continues after them without a break. Signs of more deliberate editing are first seen in the prescriptive index to MS A, which indicates that both the *chants royaux* and the *complaintes* were to form a section unto themselves. This would provide a more rational layout, avoiding the mixture of genres characteristic of the earlier *Loange*. In the body of MS A, however, only the *complaintes* were removed to a separate section.

In the posthumous MS F-G, the *Loange* has undergone further editing. The *complaintes* retain their separate section, which now includes a ballade that had earlier appeared in A's *Loange*, along with two new *complaintes* that have been added at the end of the series (see the concordance table for the *complaintes*,

---

[5] See Earp (1989, 487 n. 44), with reference to Cerquiglini's discussion of this phenomenon in Guillaume de Machaut 1982, 217.

[6] See the further discussion of these two ballades in chap. 6.4. Both ballades were no doubt also lacking in the original state of MS W, whose lyrical collection seems to have exactly duplicated MS C's.

chap. 6.5 table 6.9). In addition, some duplications—texts that had appeared both in the *Loange* and later in the music section with their music—were eliminated from **G**'s *Loange*. We cannot know whether this bit of editing is authorial; in any case, it was incompletely carried out, because four duplications between the *Loange* and the music section remain in **G**.[7] Further, even though **G** contains new works at the end of the series, its *Loange* collection is corrupt: a gap of thirty-four consecutive works (Lo187–220) appears in the middle of the collection.[8] Due to the uncertainty of the collection in MS **G**, our statistics on the final state of the collection are given on the basis of MS **A**, with the *unica* from MS **G** simply added in. At this latest stage, we can say that the *Loange* comprises 283 texts, distributed among the following genres[9]:

Table 6.1
The Size of the *Loange* Collection at the End of Machaut's Life

Ballades not set to music	189	(of these, 9 are also taken into the *Voir Dit*)
Ballades elsewhere set to music	16	(of these, 3 are also taken into the *Voir Dit*)
Double ballade (Lo26)	1	
Chants royaux	7	
Rondeaux not set to music	54	
Rondeaux elsewhere set to music	4	(of these, 1 is also taken into the *Voir Dit*)
"*Dit notable*" (Lo233)	1	
Virelai elsewhere set to music (V26)	1	
Total:	273	
Complaintes in separate section	10	(of these, 1 is also taken into the *Voir Dit*)
Grand Total:	283	(14 *Loange* texts reappear in the *Voir Dit*)

B. Opera dubia *in the* Loange. I regard all twenty items edited in the appendix of Chichmaref 1909 as *opera dubia*. This collection, largely made up of *sottes chansons*, is for the most part unique to MS **J**.[10] Some scholars have cited

---

[7] The late editing was sometimes destructive: Lo13–15 are related works, but Lo15 was eliminated from the *Loange* in MS **G** because it appears in the music section as *Dame, se vous m'estes* (B37). A further piece of editing, though carried out in no manuscript, would have been the elimination from the *Loange* of those lyrics that were taken into the *Voir Dit*.

[8] This section had no doubt gone missing in the exemplar. A nested group of four folios would be sufficient to hold the thirty-four lyrics. The changes in the order of the *Loange* discussed below demonstrate that the end of the lacuna in MS **G** corresponds to the beginning of the section of *complaintes* in the group of manuscripts related to **Vg**. Thus, the "editing" of this section (the separation of the *complaintes* as a group unto themselves for MS **A**) may have caused a disturbance in the gathering structure in the exemplar that eventually led to the loss of two bifolios.

[9] In this tabulation, I have not counted *De regarder et d'estre regardez* (Lo273), a rondeau that appears uniquely as no. 6 in the *Loange* collection in **K**, a less reliable manuscript; nor have I counted the rondeau *Quant ma dame les maulx d'amer m'aprent*, found at the end of the *Loange* in MS **M** as no. 271, but in other manuscripts only in the music fascicles as R19. Although the ballade *En l'onneur de ma douce amour* (Lo230) is counted among the *complaintes* in the late MSS **A** and **G**, I have counted it as a ballade here (following MSS **VgBDME**); for the manuscript-to-manuscript growth of the separate *complainte* section, see chap. 6.5 table 6.9. Note that even though the majority of the *Loange* text collection was never set to music, twenty of the texts (still less than 1 percent) do appear set to music in the late and reliably authorial MS **A**. The tabulation offered here is slightly different from Wilkins's tabulation (1972, 13–14), since he counts lyrics without music that were copied in the music sections as part of the *Loange*.

[10] Item no. 1 in Chichmaref's appendix (I have adopted the shorthand "LoA1," etc. to designate these works) is unique to the *Loange* in MS **J**, where it appears in the midst of secure works of Machaut as item no. 63 (see the item after Lo178 in chap. 6.3 table 6.7). The rest of the twenty works in Chichmaref's appendix (LoA2–20) appear at the end of the

passages from among these works to bolster observations on Machaut's lyrical art.[11] And yet these *sottes chansons* belie the supremely elevated tone of the rest of Machaut's lyrical works.[12] Poirion (1965, 364) leaves them out of consideration, and Wilkins omits them from his edition, finding them "mostly untypical of Machaut" (1972, 14).[13] They may fit into the fourteenth-century tradition of realistic poetry discussed by Wimsatt (1984; see also Kibler/Wimsatt 1983). For a recent study of bawdy poetry, particularly of the fifteenth century, see L.W. Johnson 1990, chap. 5.

C. *Machaut's lyrical output: the number of works at the end of his career.* To arrive at a final total number of works for each of the lyric genres that Machaut cultivated is not easy, since works may be duplicated as many as three times in a single manuscript. There are 205 ballade texts in the *Loange*, plus a double ballade (Lo26).[14] Sixteen ballades are duplicated in the music section, and twelve are duplicated in the *Voir Dit* (three works appear in all three sections). There is a total of forty-four ballade texts among the thirty-nine ballades set to music in the music section (two of the musical works are triple ballades, setting a total of six texts, along with one double ballade, setting two texts). If we subtract the sixteen ballade texts duplicated in the *Loange*, twenty-eight ballade texts (in twenty-three musical works) remain in the music fascicle. I do not count *Ma chiere dame* (B40), which in form and versification, and in its lack of a refrain, is closer to a *complainte*. There are nineteen ballades in the *Voir Dit*. Twelve are duplicated in the *Loange*, three are duplicated both in the *Loange* and in the music fascicles, and two more texts are duplicated in the music section as the double ballade *Quant Theseüs / Ne quier* (B34). Only five ballades remain that are unique to the *Voir Dit*.

One ballade without music, *Amis, sans toy tout m'anoie*, was copied into the virelai section in MSS **Vg** and **B** (ed. Chichmaref 1909, 2:632–33; Wilkins 1972, 52 no. 10). Two ballades appear in the *Remede*, and four in the *Prologue*. Thus, if we add the 205 ballades in the *Loange*, the twenty-eight musical ballades not duplicated in the *Loange*, the five ballades that appear uniquely in the *Voir Dit*, the two in the *Remede*, the four in the *Prologue*, and the single extra ballade in **VgB**, plus the double ballade (Lo26), we arrive at a lifetime total of 246 ballades.[15]

Loange in MS **J** as items 94–117, broken up by five secure works of Machaut (see chap. 6.3 table 6.8).

[11] See, for example, Gröber 1902, 1045; Siciliano 1934, 358 n. 1, 398 n. 4, 369 n. 3; Schilperoort 1936, 26–27, 38; Kelly 1978, 282 n. 22; Cerquiglini 1985b, 146; Heinrichs 1990, 209; Cerquiglini-Toulet 1993d, 16 n. 1.

[12] Wilkins (1972, 15) lists six non-courtly love lyrics whose attribution is not in question, the *dit notable Dire scens et folie faire* (Lo233), the rondeau *Se tenir vues* (Lo241), and the ballades *Mes dames qu'onques* (Lo250), *Dou memoire des hommes* (Lo253), *On ne doit pas* (Lo264), and *Douceur, charité* (Lo271). One could also add the ballade with music *Donnez, seigneurs* (B26), and four *complaintes*: *A toi, Hanri* (Cp3), *Sire, a vous* (Cp7), *Tu qui vues* (Cp8), and *Je me plein de celui* (Cp9).

[13] Sonnemann (1969, 28 n. 7, 97) argues that the twenty works are not Machaut's, since they all treat thematic material that is elsewhere quite unusual in Machaut, and since they are in part "brutally erotic" ["brutal-erotisch"].

[14] Again, *En l'onneur de ma douce amour* (Lo230) is counted here as a ballade, although late manuscripts range it among the *complaintes*.

[15] Six of the ballades are attributed to Toute Belle in the *Voir Dit* (two of these also appear in the *Loange*, Lo194 and 199). There is a possible additional ballade strophe written out as prose in letter 6 of the *Voir Dit*, *Que on porroit espuisier la grant mer*. The ballade *Amis, sans toy tout m'anoie* that appears near the end of the virelai music section in MSS **Vg**

There are fifty-eight rondeaux in the *Loange*. Of these, four are duplicated in the music section (I have not counted the duplication of *Quant ma dame les maus* [R19], added to the end of the *Loange* in MS **M**). One of these four also appears in a third location, the *Voir Dit*. A total of twenty-one rondeaux appear in the music fascicle, one of which is not set to music. If we subtract the four works duplicated in the *Loange*, seventeen rondeaux remain unique to the music fascicle. There are thirty-one rondeaux in the *Voir Dit*, two of which are duplicated in the music section and one of which is duplicated both in the *Loange* and in the music section. Twenty-eight rondeaux remain that are unique to the *Voir Dit*. An additional single rondeau is inserted into the *Remede*, and another in the *Fonteinne*. Thus, if we add the fifty-eight rondeaux of the *Loange*, the seventeen rondeaux musical not duplicated in the *Loange*, the twenty-eight rondeaux that appear uniquely in the *Voir Dit*, the single rondeau in the *Remede*, and the single rondeau in the *Fonteinne*, we arrive at a lifetime total of 105 rondeaux.[16]

There are thirty-eight virelais in the music section, one of which is duplicated in the *Loange*, which includes only this single virelai. Two of the thirty-eight virelais are hybrid works with ballade-like end refrains (*Quant je sui* [V13] and *J'aim sans* [V14]), and will not be counted here. Nine virelais appear in the *Voir Dit*, four of which are duplicated in the music section. Five virelais remain that are unique to the *Voir Dit*. An additional single virelai is inserted into the *Remede*. Thus, if we add the thirty-six true virelais of the music section, the five virelais that appear uniquely in the *Voir Dit*, and the single virelai in the *Remede*, we arrive at a lifetime total of forty-two virelais.[17]

Chants royaux are more easily counted. There are seven in the *Loange* and one in the *Remede*, for a lifetime total of eight *chants royaux*.

There are a total of eleven *complaintes* in a separate section at the end of Machaut's career. One of these (Lo230) is a ballade in form, and so has been counted among works of that genre; another is also found in the *Voir Dit*. One *complainte* appears in the *Remede*, one in the *Fonteinne*, and three in the *Voir Dit*, one of which is duplicated in the separate *complainte* section. The final total is fourteen *complaintes*.[18]

A complete count of the lyrics should include a few other unusual works. Similar to the *complainte* form is the *prière*, of which there are two examples, one in the *Remede*, and one in the *Voir Dit*, and the single *confort* in the *Fonteinne*. The *Loange* contains the *dit notable* (Lo233), composed of twelve lines of octosyllabic rhyming couplets; the musical fascicles contain three unusual works already mentioned above, namely, the *complainte*-like work set to music in the ballade section (B40), and two hybrid works, each unique in form, in the virelai section (V13–14).

(fol. 333r), duplicated of course in the copy, MS **B** (fol. 330r), is possibly of questionable attribution, though related to Lo270. One might also wish to delete *Quant Theseüs* (VD57 in table 5.3), attributed in the *Voir Dit* to one Thomas Paien, which Machaut set to music with his ballade *Ne quier veoir* as the double ballade *Quant Theseüs / Ne quier* (B34).

[16] Fifteen of the rondeaux are attributed to Toute Belle in the *Voir Dit*. I have not counted the rondeau *Doulz cuers*, an *opus dubium* that appears at the end of MS **E** (fol. 211r), and which was copied from this manuscript into **Pa** [50].

[17] Four of the virelais are attributed to Toute Belle in the *Voir Dit*; however, one of those four, *Cils a bien* (V24), already appeared in the music section of the early MS **C**, though Machaut never composed music for it.

[18] Two of the *complaintes* are attributed to Toute Belle in the *Voir Dit*, but one of these is in the separate *complainte* section, and was already part of the *Loange* in MSS **Vg** and **M** (*Mes dous amis* [Cp5]).

Finally, we should count the lais, although they never form a part of the *Loange*. By the end of his career, Machaut intended the lais to form a separate section at the head of the music fascicles in the manuscript, including not only works that earlier had had a different position in the manuscript (see the discussion of the *Lay de Plour* (L22/16) above, chap. 6.1a), but also works that figured as lyrical insertions in narrative *dits*—a situation well known in the case of the *Lay de Bonne Esperance, Longuement* (L18/13), associated with the *Voir Dit*—but also true of *Qui n'aroit* (RF1), the lai of the *Remede*.[19] The final count of lais includes twenty-three works, plus two additional works that appear only in MS E, the *Lay de Consolation, Pour ce que plus* (L23/17) and *En demantant* (L24/18). See the discussion in chapter 7.3 on the authenticity of these works.

2. Questions of order in the *Loange des Dames*

Table 6.2 provides an overview of the chronological growth of the contents of the *Loange* collection in the main manuscripts, as well as a tabulation of the extent of the *Loange* collections in the less central manuscripts K, J, and H. For the central manuscripts (C, Vg family, M, A, G, and E), the order across the top of table 6.2 is chronological, and one may follow the gradual growth of the collection of lyrics.[20] On the generally chronological order of the lyrics within the manuscripts, see Hoepffner (1911, 164).

Table 6.2
Chronological Growth of the *Loange*, by Manuscript

	C	VgBD	M	A	G	E	K	J	H
Ballades	145	177	180	185	163	175	40	88	67
Ball. elsewhere set to music	9	15	16	16	2	5	–	7	4
Double ballade (Lo26)	1	1	1	1	1	1	1	1	1
Chants royaux	6	6	7	7	7	6	–	2	6
Rondeaux	36	46	54	54	49	45	5	–	17
Rond. elsewhere set to music	1	3	4	3	2	1	–	–	1
Compl. within the *Loange*	–	6	7	–	–	6	–	–	–
Dit notable (Lo233)	–	1	1	1	1	1	–	–	–
Vir. elsewhere set to music	–	1	1	1	–	–	–	–	–
Total:	198	256	271	268	225	240	46	98	96
Compl. as separate section				8	11		–	–	
Opera dubia (MSS K and J)				–	–		1	19	
Grand Total:	198	256	271	276	236	240	47	117	96

Lo230 is counted as a ballade in MSS VgBDME; it is counted as part of the separate *complainte* section in MSS AG (see tables 6.5 and 6.9).
VgBD: one ballade (Lo216) is copied twice (=176), making a total of 255 works.
M: one ballade (Lo216) is copied twice (=179), and one rondeau (Lo240) is copied twice (=53), making a total of 269 works.
A: one rondeau (Lo240) is copied twice (=53), making a total of 275 works.
J: three of the ballades comprise *Sans cuer / Amis, dolens / Dame, par vous* (B17), which appears in no other *Loange* section.

[19] The index of MS A reserves a place for *Qui n'aroit* in the lai section between *Par trois raisons* (L6/5) and *Amours doucement* (L7/6); see the transcription of the index in Earp 1983, 54 (discussion p. 62), or the facsimile in Earp 1989, 483 fig. 1. The scribe of MS A left it out, doubtless because he could not find it in the exemplar material.

[20] For MSS D and M I am of course speaking of the chronological placement of their respective exemplars, not the extant fifteenth-century manuscripts; MS E may also relate to the Vg family (see below). J. Cerquiglini's comment (1985b, 34–35 n. 27) that the *Loange* in MS C belongs to the second chronological layer of that manuscript (CII) is in error; CII involves only musical works. The missing items in MS G's *Loange* are discussed above, chap. 6.1a.

The order of works in the *Loange* is remarkably consistent from manuscript to manuscript (see chap. 6.3 table 6.7). Nevertheless, there are four locations in the *Loange* series that exhibit some minor changes in the ordering of works. In addition, problems arose when the *complaintes* were separated from the other genres in order to be placed in their own separate section. The slight differences in order can serve as a guide to a familial grouping of manuscripts, and can also provide some further evidence for chronology. In the four tables given below, the left-hand column, headed "Lo," gives the reference numbers assigned to the individual works in Chichmaref's 1909 edition of the *Loange*.[21] The numbers in the other columns show the sequential number of a given lyric in a given manuscript (as in table 6.7). As an example (table 6.3), the ballade *Tres douce dame debonnaire* (Lo136) is no. 133 in the *Loange* series of MSS **Vg**, **B**, and **D**, no. 107 in **E**, no. 90 in **H**, lacking in **J**, no. 136 in **M** and **A**, etc. For the purposes of this demonstration, I have listed the works according to the sequential order in MSS **VgBD** (thus, the numbers in the "Lo" column are out of sequence).

Table 6.3
The Order of the Lyrics Lo132–39

Lo		VgBD	E	H	J	MA	C	G
132	*Douce dame, plaisant*	132	106	–	54	132	130	128
136	*Tres douce dame debonnaire*	133	107	90	–	136	134	132
137	*Amis, vostre demouree*	134	108	91	55	137	135	133
133	*Gentil dame de tres noble*	135	109	–	–	133	131	129
134	*Dame, lonteins de vostre*	136	220	–	–	134	132	130
135	*Selonc ce qu j'aim chierement*	137	110	92	56	135	133	131
138	*Dame, de tous biens assevie*	138	111	93	–	138	136	134
139	*Douce dame, je vous requier*	139	112	–	57	139	137	135

Table 6.4
The Order of the Lyrics Lo190–96

Lo		VgBD	E	H	J	MA	C	G
190	*Langue poignant, aspre, amere*	190	150	–	67	190	188	–
191	*La grant douçour de vostre*	191	151	–	–	191	189	–
192	*On ne puet riens savoir si*	192	152	–	68	192	190	–
194	*Il n'est doulour, desconfort*	193	153	–	69	194	192	–
193	*Il ne m'est pas tant dou mal*	194	154	–	–	193	191	–
195	*De Fortune me doy pleindre*	195	–	–	–	195	193	–
196	*Tout ensement que le monde*	196	155	–	–	196	194	–

Tables 6.3–4 show the first two places in the *Loange* series that exhibit irregularities of order. The two different placements of Lo136–37 seen in table 6.3 suggest two families of manuscripts, **VgBDEHJ** : **MACG** (there is just enough of a *Loange* collection in MSS **HJ** to establish family ties). This grouping is corroborated for MSS **VgBDEJ** : **MAC** by table 6.4, due to the two different placements of Lo193. The most curious result of this grouping of manuscripts is its non-chronological nature: if one were awaiting a linear development, the earliest manuscript, **C**, would not be expected to appear with one of the latest, **A**. Could this suggest that the **Vg** group lies a bit outside the Machaut circle? In the **Vg** group, the *Loange* collections appear at the head of each manuscript, while in **CMAG** the narrative poems begin each manuscript and the *Loange* is placed close to the music section (see Earp 1989, 481–82).

---

[21] The "Lo" numbers correspond to the numbers of the poems in the body of Chichmaref's edition and not necessarily to the numbers in his concordance table (1909, 1:lxxx–c), which is replete with errors.

The third and fourth locations in the *Loange* series that exhibit irregularities of order both have to do with to the separation of the group of *complaintes* from the other works within the *Loange* (tables 6.5–6). Again, the "Lo" numbers are keyed to Chichmaref's edition. Roman numerals are used for the separate *complainte* section of Chichmaref's edition, as well as for the works in the *complainte* sections of MSS **A** and **G**.[22]

Table 6.5
The Order of the Lyrics Lo216–31 and *Complaintes* I–V

Lo		VgBD	M	E	J	A	G
216	*Quant vrais amans de sa dame*	216	216	168	79	216	–
217	*Aucuns dient qu' on ne puet dame*	217	217	169	80	217	–
218	*Onques mes cuers ne senti*	218	218	170	–	218	–
219	*Loial amour est de si grant*	219	219	171	–	219	–
220	*Amis, mon cuer et toute ma*	220	220	172	–	220	–
I	*Amours, tu m' as tant esté dure*	221	221	173	–	I	I
230	*En l' onneur de ma douce amour*	222	222	178	–	II	II
III	*A toi, Hanri, dous amis*	223	223	174	–	III	IV
221	*Onques dame ne fu si belle*	224	224	179	–	221	182
222	*Ma dame a tout ce qu'il faut*	225	225	180	81	222	183
IV	*Quant Ecuba vit la destruction*	226	226	176	–	IV	V
V	*Mes dous amis, a vous me vueil*	227	227	175	–	V	VI
223	*Je preing congié a dames*	–	228	40	–	223	184
224	*Amis, comment que m' aiés*	–	229	–	–	224	185
225	*Trop ne me puis de bonne Amour*	–	230	–	–	225	186
226	*Douce dame, cointe, apperte*	–	231	–	–	226	187
216	*Quant vrais amans de sa dame*	228	232	–	–	–	–
227	*Amours, ma dame et Fortune*	229	233	181	–	227	188
228	*Ce qui contreint mon cuer a*	230	234	182	92	228	–
229	*Plourez, dames, plourez vostre*	231	235	–	–	229	–
II	*Deus choses sont qui me font*	232	236	183	–	230	III
231	*Se je vous aim de fin loyal corage*	233	237	184	93	231	189

In table 6.5, the horizontal line after Lo220 indicates where the *complaintes* begin in MSS **VgBDM**. In **VgBD**, the *complaintes* are set off from the preceding lyrics by a miniature and decorated initial, marking the beginning of a new series in the *Loange,* including ballades and rondeaux, not just a separate section of *complaintes.* It is no doubt significant that the end of the large lacuna in the *Loange* of MS **G** (Lo187–220 are lacking in **G**) corresponds to the point where the *complaintes* begin in the earlier manuscripts (see above, n. 8).

Unlike the situation seen in tables 6.3–4, MS **M** is now closer to the **Vg** group than to the **A** group. *Quant vrais amans* (Lo216, no. 216 in **VgBD**), was recopied later as no. 228 in **VgBD**, and the same error occurs in **M**: Lo216 (no. 216 in **M**) is recopied later as no. 232. Perhaps it is significant that the point where Lo216 was recopied marks the point before which a group of lyrics was added in **M**, nos. 228–31 (Lo223–26). In any case, note that both **A** and **G** avoid the duplication of Lo216.

Finally, in table 6.6, MS **M** is again seen to be closer to MS **A**, as in tables 6.3–4. *Biauté, douceur* (Lo240) was copied twice in MSS **M** and **A** (Lo240 = nos. 246 and 258 in **M**, and nos. 240 and 251 in **A**), though it had been correctly copied into **VgBD**. The editor of the later MS **F-G** weeded out this inconsistency.

22 The table shows one of the inconsistencies in Chichmaref 1909: he kept the ballade *En l'onneur de ma douce amour* in the *Loange* as Lo230, even though both **A** and **G** place it in second position in their separate sections of *complaintes* (see chap. 6.3 table 6.9).

Table 6.6
The Order of the Lyrics Lo238–54 and *Complaintes* VI–VII

Lo		VgBD	M	E	J	A	G
238	*Veoir n' oïr ne puis riens qui*	240	244	–	–	238	193
239	*Quant ma dame est noble et de*	241	245	185	–	239	194
240	*Biauté, douceur et maniere jolie*	–	246	–	–	240	195
VI	*Mon cuer, m'amour, ma dame*	242	247	177	–	VI	VII
241	*Se tenir vues le droit chemin*	243	248	237	–	241	196
242	*Je di qu'il n'a en amour vraie*	244	249	186	82	242	197
243	*Amours qui m'a nouvellement*	245	250	187	–	243	198
244	*Sans departir est en mon cuer*	246	251	188	–	244	199
245	*Ma dame a qui sui donné ligement*	247	252	238	–	245	200
246	*Quant je commensay l'amer*	248	253	189	83	246	201
247	*Se vos courrous me dure*	249	254	–	–	247	202
248	*Se pour ce muir qu'Amours ai*	250	255	–	84	248	–
249	*En desespoir, dame, de vous me*	251	256	190	85	249	203
250	*Mes dames qu'onques ne vi*	252	257	191	–	250	204
240	*Biauté, douceur et maniere jolie*	253	258	239	–	251	–
251	*Je ne pourroie en servant desservir*	254	–	240	–	252	205
252	*Puis qu'Amours faut et Loyauté*	255	259	192	86	253	206
253	*Dou memoire des hommes*	256	260	193	–	254	207
VII	*Sire, a vous fais ceste clamour*	–	261	–	–	VII	VIII
254	*Amis, je t'ay tant amé et cheri*	–	262	–	–	255	208

All of this supports the thesis that **M** derives from a stage of the collection
after **Vg** and before **A** (with respect to the order of the contents, not with
respect to the date of the manuscript: **M** remains a fifteenth-century copy of the
manuscript in question). One further point. Table 6.6 takes us to the very end of
the *Loange* in the **Vg** group of manuscripts—there are 256 items in the *Loange*
in **VgBD**—and shows that MS **E** ends at the same point as the **Vg** group, with
item no. 193, suggesting that the *Loange* in **E** derives from an exemplar of the
Vg family.[23]

---

[23] The total count is smaller for **E** because the rondeaux were extracted and put into a separate
collection. A collation of manuscript readings would determine if the exemplar was in fact
our MS **B**; we know from Bent 1983 that **B** served as the exemplar for a large part of the
music collection in MS **E**.

3. Concordances: ballades, rondeaux, chants royaux

Table 6.7 La Loange des Dames. Concordances[1]

form	Wilk	Lo	Text	G	A	M	VgB/D	W	C	H	E	J	K	Pa	other text MSS
B	71	1	En haut penser, plein d'amoureus desir	2	1	1	1		1	1	1	1	1		Wm
B	44	2	D'ardeur espris et d'esperence nus	3	2	2	2		2	2	2	2	2		
B	195	3	Seur tous amans me doy pleindre et loer	4	3	3	3		3	3	3				
B	52	4	Douce dame, que j'aim tant et desir	5	4	4	4		4	4	4	3	3		Wm La
B	77	5	Gent corps, faitis, cointe, apert et joli (VD)	6	5	5	5		5	5	5	4	4		Wm La
B	186	6	Se je ne scay que c'est joie d'ami	7	6	6	6		6	6	6				
B	151	7	On ne porroit penser ne souhaidier (B3)	*	7	7	7	1	7	7	7				
B	205	8	Tout ensement que la rose a l'espine	8	8	8	8	2	8	8	8	5	5		
B	197	9	Se vos regars, douce dame, n'estoit	9	9	9	9	3	9	9	9		6		
R		273	De regarder et d'estre regardez (opus dubium)	10				4						92	Wm
B	37	10	Dame, ne regardez pas (B9)	*	10	10	10	5	10	10	10	6	7		
B	112	11	Je ne sui pas de tel valour	11	11	11	11	6	11	11	11	7	8		La
B	156	12	Or voy je bien, ma dolour renouvelle	12	12	12	12	7	12	12	12	8	9		
B	32	13	Dame, comment que vous soie longtains	13	13	13	13	8	13	13	13	9	10		Wm
B	149	14	On dist souvent que longue demouree	14	14	14	14		14	14	14				Wm
B	42	15	Dame, se vous m'estes lonteinne (B37)	*	15	15	15		15	15	15	10	11		
B	194	16	Se pour longue demouree	15	16	16	16		16	16	16				
B	157	17	Ou païs ou ma dame maint	16	17	17	17		17	17	17				
B	75	18	Fueille ne flour ne verdure	17	18	18	18		18	18	18				La
CR	5	19	Onques mais nulz m'ama si folement	18	19	19	19		19	19	55			93	
B	103	20	J'aim tant ma dame et son bien et s'onnour	19	20	20	20		20	20	19	11	12		
B	80	21	Gentilz dame, douce, plaisant et sage	20	21	21	21		21	21	20	12	13		
B	125	22	Le grant desir que j'ay de repairier	21	22	22	22		22	22	21	13	14		
B	199	23	Souvenirs fait meint amant resjoïr	22	23	23	23		23	23	22	14	15		
B	184	24	Se je me fusse envers Amours meffais	23	24	24	24		24	24	23				
B	118	25	La loyauté, ou mes cuers se norrist	24	25	25	25		25	25	24	15	16		
dB	214	26	Dame plaisant, nette et pure		26	26	26		26	26	25			82	

1 Column one gives the genre of each item (B = ballade; Cp = complainte; CR = chant royal; dB = double ballade; R = rondeau; V = virelai); column two ("Wilk.") gives the page number of a given item in Wilkins 1972 (see his notes to individual poems); column three ("Lo") gives the number in Chichmaref 1909; sometimes additional information is appended to the text incipit in column four: "VD" indicates works that also appear in the Voir Dit; works given a number, e.g., B3 for Lo7 On ne porroit, are also set to music (the numbering follows Ludwig 1926–54; for further sources of the musical works, see chap. 7.3); the remaining columns give the sequential order of works in the respective Loange sections. For manuscripts that transmit individual lyrics, see the relevant contents listings in chap. 3 for the location of a given poem (Bc [55]; I [40]; Jp [49]; La [54]; Mn [43]; St [46]; Ta [52]; Wm [41]).

* In music section.

form	Wilk	Lo	Text	G	A	M	VgBD	W	C	H	E	J	K	Pa	other text MSS
R	236	27	Gentils cuers, souveingne vous	24	27	27	27		27	27	194				
B	105	28	Jamais ne quier joie avoir	25	28	28	28		28	28	26	16	17		La
B	177	29	Riens ne me puet anuier ne desplaire	26	29	29	29		29	29	27	17	18		La
B	129	30	Loing de vous souvent souspir	27	30	30	30		30	30	28	18	19		
B	43	31	D'amour loial et de m'amour	28	31	31	31		31	31	29	19	20		
B	200	32	Souvent me fait souspirer	29	32	32	32		32	32	30	20	21		
B	116	33	La dolour ne puet remeindre	30	33	33	33		33	33	31		22		
B	166	34	Pour Dieu vous pri que de moy vous souveingne	31	34	34	34	9	34	34	32				
B	185	35	Se je n'avoie plaisence	32	35	35	35	10	35	35	33				
B	203	36	Tenus me sui longuement de chanter	33	36	36	36	11	36	36	34				
B	83	37	Hé! gentils cuers, me convient il morir	34	37	37	37	12	37	37	35				Wm La Mn
B	155	38	On verroit meint amant desesperer	35	38	38	38	13	38	38	36				
B	76	39	Gais et jolis, liés, chantans et joieus (B35)	*	39	39	39	14	39	39	*	21		173	
B	111	40	Je ne fine nuit ne jour de penser	36	40	40	40	15	40	40	37				Wm
B	55	41	Douce dame, soiés toute seüre	37	41	41	41	16	41	41	38	22			La
B	22	42	Bien me devroit d'aucuns dous mos refaire	38	42	42	42	17	42	42	39				
R	266	43	Se je vous ay riens meffait	39	43	43	43	18	43	43	195				
B	81	44	Grant merveille ont de ce que plus ne chant	40	44	44	44	19	44	44	41	23			
CR	2	45	Amours me fait desirer loyaument	41	45	45	45	20	45	45	56	24		96	
CR	3	46	Cuers ou merci faut et cruautés dure	42	46	46	46	21	46	46	57	25		98	
CR	4	47	Je croy que nulz fors moy n'a tel nature	43	47	47	47	22	47	47	58			100	
CR	7	48	Se trestuit cil qui sont et ont esté	44	48	48	48	23	48	48	59			102	
B	54	49	Douce dame, si loyaument conquis	45	49	49	49	24	49	49	42				
B	208	50	Trop me seroit grief chose a soustenir	46	50	50	50	25	50	50	43				
B	207	51	Trop est crueus li maus de jalousie	47	51	51	51			51	44	105			
B	120	52	Las! amours me soloit estre	48	52	52	52		51	52	45	33	25	118	La
B	92	53	Helas! pour quoy virent onques mi oueil	49	53	53	53		52	53	46	34	26	86	Wm Ta
R	247	54	Ou loyauté ne repaire	50	54	54	54		53	54	196		27		
B	182	55	Se faire sçay chançon desesperee	51	55	55	55		54	55	47	f.46v	f.42v		La
B	89	56	Helas! je sui de si male heure nez	52	56	56	56		55	56	48	35	28		
B	84	57	Helas! Amours, que vous ay je meffait	53	57	57	57		56	57	49	36	29		
B	57	58	Douce dame, tant vous aim sans meffaire	54	58	58	58		57	58	50				Ta
R	242	59	Loiaus pensers et desirs deliieus	55	59	59	59		58	59	197				
R	216	60	Au departir de vous mon cuer vous lais	56	60	60	60		59	60	198				
B	148	61	Nulz ne me doit d'ore en avant reprendre	57	61	61	61		60	61	51		30		
B	41	62	Dame que j'aim, ne vous veingne a merveille	58	62	62	62		61	62	52	37			
B	123	63	Las! tant desir l'eure que je vous voie	59	63	63	63		62	63	53				
R	232	64	Douce dame, quant vers vous fausseray	60	64	64	64		63	64	199			81=119	

* In music section.

form	Wilk	Lo	Text	G	A	M	VgB D	W	C	H	E	J	K	Pa	other text MSS
B	58	65	*Douce dame, vo maniere jolie*	61	65	65	65		64	65	54	38		88	I
B	36	66	*Dame, mercy vous requier humblement*	62	66	66	66		65	66	61		31	83	
R	246	67	*Mon cuer, qui mis en vous son desir a*	63	67	67	67		66	67	200				
R	270	68	*Se vos courrous me dure longuement*	64	68	68	68		67	68	201				
R	40	69	*Dame, pour vous ma joie se define*	65	69	69	69		68	69	62	39	32		
B	121	70	*Las! j'ay failli a mon tres dous desir*	66	70	70	70	26	69	70	63				
B	169	71	*Puis que Desirs ne me laisse durer*	67	71	71	71	27	70		64				
R	252	72	*Puis que Desirs me veut dou tout grever*	68	72	72	72	28	71		202	40	33		Mn
B	59	73	*Douce dame, vous ociés a tort*	69	73	73	73	29	72		65				
B	99	74	*Il n'est confors qui me peüst venir*	70	74	74	74	30	73		66				
B	18	75	*Aucunes gens me demandent souvent*	71	75	75	75	31	74		67				
B	51	76	*Douce dame, prendés temps et loisir*	72	76	76	76	32	75		68	41	34		
B	170	77	*Puis que j'empris l'amer premierement*	73	77	77	77	33	76		69		35		
R	229	78	*De vous servir loyaument et amer*	74	78	78	78	34	77		203				
B	183	79	*Se j'ay esté de maniere volage*	75	79	79	79		78		70				
R	220	80	*Cuer, corps, pouoir, desir, vie et usage*	76	80	80	80		79		204	89		85	
B	189	81	*Se ma dame me mescroit, c'est a tort*	77	81	81	81		80		71	42	36		
R	218	82	*Blanche com lis, plus que rose vermeille*	78	82	82	82		81		205			87	
R	144	83	*N'est pas doleur qui me tient, eins est rage*	79	83	83	83		82		72				
B	136	84	*Mes cuers ne puet a nulle riens penser*	80	84	84	84		83		73				
R	230	85	*De vraie amour, loyal et affinee*	81	85	85	85		84		206				
B	128	86	*Loing de mon cuer et de ma douce amour*	82	86	86	86		85		74	43	37		
R	134	87	*Maugré mon cuer me convient eslongier*	83	87	87	87		86		75				
R	106	88	*J'ay par lonc temp amé et ameray*	84	88	88	88		87		76	44	38		
B	135	89	*Mercy, merci de ma dure dolour*	85	89	89	89		88		77				
B	26	90	*Certes mes dous amis fu nez*	86	90	90	90		89		78				
B	15	91	*Amours ne veut et ma dame ne deingne*	87	91	91	91		90		79				
B	213	92	*Vo dous gracieus samblant*	88	92	92	92		91		80				
B	167	93	*Pres durer ne loing garir*	89	93	93	93		92		81				
B	66	94	*D'uns dous ueil vairs, rians, fendus*	90	94	94	94		93		82	87			
B	211	95	*Un dous regart par desir savouré*	91	95	95	95		94		83				
B	146	96	*Nulz homs ne puet en amours pourfiter*	92	96	96	96		95		84	45	39		
R	222	97	*Dame, je muir pour vous, com pris*	93	97	97	97		96		207				
B	35	98	*Dame d'onnour, plaisant et gracieuse*	94	98	98	98		97		85			89	
R	240	99	*La grant ardeur de mon plaisant desir*	95	99	99	99		98		208				
B	33	100	*Dame, de moy tres loyaument amee*	96	100	100	100		99		86	46	40		
B	172	101	*Quant de vous departirai*	97	101	101	101		100		87				
B	101	102	*Dame, pour moy desconfire*	98	102	102	102		101		209				
R	224	103	*Las! je voy bien que ma dame de pris*	99	103	103	103		102		88	47	41		
R	241	104	*Li cuers me tramble et la char me tressue*	100	104	104	104		103		210		42		

form	Wilk	Lo	Text	G	A	M	VgB D	W	C	H	E	J	K	Pa	other text MSS
B	202	105	Tant sui chetis, las et maleüreus	101	105	105	105		104		89	48	43		
B	132	106	Ma dame, n'aiés nul espoir	102	106	106	106		105		90				
B	161	107	Plaisant dame, je recueil plaisenment	103	107	107	107		106		91			90	
B	147	108	Nulz homs ne puet plus loyaument amer	104	108	108	108				92	49	44	269	
B	163	109	Pliseurs se sont repenti	105	109	109	109		107	*	93	50	45		
B	74	110	En remirant vo gracieus viaire	106	110	110	110		108	71	94				
B	90	111	Helas! mon cuer, bien le doy pleindre	107	111	111	111		109	72	95	51	46		
R	237	112	Helas! dolens, or vueil je bien morir	108	112	112	112		110	73	211		47		
B	171	113	Puis qu'Eürs est contraire a mon desir	109	113	113	113		111	74	96				
B	159	114	Plaisant accueil et gracieus attrait	110	114	114	114		112	75	97				
B	82	115	Hé! gentils cuers, loyaus, dous, debonnaire	111	115	115	115		113	76	98				
B	274	116	Vueillés avoir de moy le souvenir	112	116	116	116		114	77	212	88			
CR	6	117	Se loyaulés a vertus ne puissance	113	117	117	117		115	78	60			104	
R	249	118	Partués moy a l'ouvrir de vos yex	114	118	118	118		116	79	213			91	
B	145	119	Nulle dolour ne se puet comparer	115	119	119	119		117	80	99				
R	234	120	En souspirant vueil a Dieu commander	116	120	120	120		118	81	214				
B	86	121	Helas! dolens, que porray devenir	117	121	121	121	35	119	82	100				
R	260	122	Quant je vous voy crier: "a l'arme"	118	122	122	122	36	120	83	215				
R	248	123	Par souhaidier est mes corps aveuc vous	119	123	123	123	37	121	84	216			94	
R	255	124	Quant j'aproche vo dous viaire cler	120	124	124	124	38	122	85	217				
R	235	125	Faites mon cuer tout a .i. cop morir	121	125	125	125	39	123	86	218				
R	273	126	Trop est mauvais mes cuers qu'en .ii. ne part	122	126	126	126	40	124	87	219			95	
B	93	127	Hé! mesdisans, com je vous doy hair	123	127	127	127	41	125	88	101	90			
B	23	128	Ce que je fais de bonne chiere	124	128	128	128	42	126	89	102				
B	141	129	Ne cuidiez pas que d'amer me repente	125	129	129	129	43	127		103				
B	31	130	Dame, comment que souvent ne vous voie	126	130	130	130	44	128		104	52			
B	20	131	Biaus dous amis, parfaitement amés	127	131	131	131	45	129		105	53			
B	50	132	Douce dame, plaisant et gracieuse	128	132	132	132	46	130		106	54			
B	79	133	Gentil dame de tres noble figure	129	133	133	133	47	131		109				
R	223	134	Dame, lonteins de vostre noble atour	130	134	134	134	48	132		220	56			
B	188	135	Selonc ce que j'aim chierement	131	135	135	135	49	133	92	110				
B	206	136	Tres douce dame debonnaire	132	136	136	136	50	134	90	107	55			
B	12	137	Amis, vostre demouree	133	137	137	137	51	135	91	108				
B	34	138	Dame, de tous biens assevie	134	138	138	138	52	136	93	111				
B	49	139	Douce dame, je vous requier mercy	135	139	139	139	53	137		112	57			
B	21	140	Biauté parfaite et bonté souvereinne	136	140	140	140	54	138		113				
B	87	141	Helas! dolens, que porray devenir	137	141	141	141	55	139	94	114				da Caserta†

* See Wilkins note to no. 121 (1972, 174): a few lines of the end of Lo109 are copied for the missing strophes 2–3 of Lo70.

† Text set to music by Anthonello da Caserta, in MSS Mod [66] and PR [63].

form	Wilk	Lo	Text	G	A	M	VgB D	W	C	H	E	J	K	Pa	other text MSS
B	48	142	*Douce dame, de joie diseteus*	138	142	142	142	56	140		115				
B	28	143	*Comment me puet mes cuers en corps durer*	139	143	143	143	57	141		116	26			
B	39	144	*Dame, pour Dieu ne metez en oubli*	140	144	144	144	58	142		117	27			
B	192	145	*Se pleins fusse de matiere joieuse*	141	145	145	145	59	143		118				
B	91	146	*Helas! pour quoy m'est bonne Amour si dure*	142	146	146	146	60	144	95	119	28			
B	158	147	*Peinnes, doleurs, larmes, soupirs et pleins*	143	147	147	147	61	145		120				
R	264	148	*Sans cuer, dolens, de vous departirai* (R4/VD)	144	148	148	148		146		121	29		97	
B	68	149	*Eimmi! dolens, chetis, las, que feray*	145	149	149	149		147		122	30			
B	67	150	*Eimmi! dame, coment puet endurer*	146	150	150	150		148		221			99	
R	262	151	*Quant ma dame ne m'a recongneü*	147	151	151	151		149		123				
B	126	152	*Li doulz parler, plein de toute douçour*	148	152	152	152		150		124				
B	165	153	*Pour Dieu, dame, n'amés autre que my*	149	153	153	153		151	96	222				
R	227	154	*De moy ferés toute joie eslongier*	150	154	154	154		152		222				
B	72	155	*Ou lieu de ce que je puis deservir*	151	155	155	155		153		125	31			
B	133	156	*Martyrés sui de l'amoureus martyre*	152	156	156	156		154		126		23		
R	228	157	*De plus en plus ma grief dolour empire*	153	157	157	157		155		223			101	
B	108	158	*Je m'aim trop miex tous a paressilier*	154	158	158	158		156		127				
R	272	159	*S'il me convient morir par desirer*	155	159	159	159		157		224				
B	60	160	*Douce dame, vous savez que je n'ay*	156	160	160	160		158		128	32	24		
B	95	161	*Hui ha .i. mois que je me departi* (VD)	157	161	161	161		159		129				
B	181	162	*Se Diex me doint de ma dame joir*	158	162	162	162		160		130				
R	226	163	*De morir sui pour vous en grant paour*	159	163	163	163		161		225				
B	210	164	*Trop se peinne de mi mettre a la mort*	160	164	164	164		162		131				
B	160	165	*Plaisant dame de noble accueil*	161	165	165	165		163		132				
B	65	166	*D'une si vraie volenté*	162	166	166	166		164		133				
B	101	167	*Ja Diex pouoir ne me doint ne loisir*	163	167	167	167		165		226				
R	221	168	*Dame, de moy tres loyaument amee*	164	168	168	168		166		134				
B	27	169	*Certes, moult me doi doloir*	165	169	169	169		167		135				
B	198	170	*Si com je sueil ne puis joie mener*	166	170	170	170		168		136	58			
B	104	171	*J'aim trop mon cuer de ce qu'il m'a guerpi*	167	171	171	171		169		137				
B	64	172	*D'un cuer si fin et d'une amour si pure*	168	172	172	172		170		138				
B	78	173	*Gente de corps et tres bele de vis*	169	173	173	173		171		139				
B	142	174	*Ne pensés pas que je retraie*	170	174	174	174		172		140	59			
B	110	175	*Je ne croy pas c'onques a creature* (B14)	171	175	175	175		173		141	60			
B	140	176	*Ne cuidiés pas que li cuers ne me dueille*	172	176	176	176		174		*	61			
B	14	177	*Amours me fait desirer* (B19)	173	177	177	177		175		142	62		115	
B	85	178	*Helas! Desirs, que me demandes tu*	174	178	178	178		176			63			
B		A1	*J'amay entan environ .xv. jours* (opus dubium)									64			
B		Bn43	*Fauston* [sic] *li merveilleus serpens* (B38)												
B	124	179	*Le bien de vous qui en biauté flourist* (VD)	175	179	179	179		177		143	65		211	

form	Wilk	Lo	Text	G	A	M	VgBD	W	C	H	E	J	K	Pa	other text MSS
B	127	180	Le plus grans biens qui me veingne d'amer (VD)	176	180	180	180		178		144	66		208	
B	190	181	Se mes dous amis demeure	177	181	181	181		179		145				
B	29	182	Dame, comment qu'amez de vous ne soie (B16)	*	182	182	182		180		146				
R	251	183	Pour Dieu, frans cuers, soies mes advocas	178	183	183	183		181		227			103	
B	25	184	Certes, je croy que ma fin est venue	179	184	184	184		182		147				
R	265	185	Se j'avoie corage de fausser	180	185	185	185		183		228				
B	191	186	Se par amour ou par fiance	181	186	186	186		184		148				
B	53	187	Douce dame, savoir ne puis n'oïr		187	187	187		185		149				
B	96	188	Il m'est avis qu'il n'est dons de Nature (B22)	*	188	188	188		186		*				
R	238	189	Helas! pour ce que Fortune m'est dure		189	189	189		187		229				
B	119	190	Langue poignant, aspre, amere et aiguë		190	190	190		188		150	67		270	Wm
B	117	191	La grant douçour de vostre biauté fine		191	191	191		189		151				
B	152	192	On ne puet riens savoir si proprement		192	192	192		190		152				
B	97	193	Il ne m'est pas tant dou mal que j'endure		193	193	193		191		154	68			
B	100	194	Il n'est dolour, desconfort ne tristece (VD)		194	194	194		192		153	69			
B	45	195	De Fortune me doy pleindre et loer (B23)	*	195	195	195		193		*			84	Jp
B	204	196	Tout ensement que le monde enlumine		196	196	196	62	194		155	70		164	
B	38	197	Dame parfaite dou tout entierement		197	197	197	63	195		156	71			
B	180	198	Se bons et biaus, pleins de toute valour		198	198	198	64	196		157	72			
B	11	199	Amis si parfaitement (VD)		199	199	199	65	197		160				
B	19	200	Aucuns parlent de .x. plaies d'Egipte	*	200	200	200	66	198		158			271	
B	94	201	Honte, paour, doubtance de meffaire (B25)	*	201	201	201				159	73		147	Wm ITa
B	201	202	Tant ay perdu confort et esperence	*	202	202	202				*	91			
B	115	203	Je puis trop bien ma dame comparer (B28)	*	203	203	203				*			153	Jp
B	69	204	En cuer ma dame une vipere maint (B27)	*	204	204	204							151	Wm
V	281	205	Tres bonne et belle, mi oueil (V26)	*	205	205	205							220	
R	259	206	Quant je vous voy autre que my amer		206	206	206				230				
R	268	207	Se par amours n'amiés autrui ne moy		207	207	207				231				
R	250	208	Pour Dieu, dame, n'amez autre que my		208	208	208				232				
B	113	209	Je pers mon temps et ma peine est perie		209	209	209				161	74			
B	46	210	De ma dolour ne puis avoir confort		210	210	210				162				
B	61	211	Douce, plaisant, simple et sage		211	211	211				163	75			
B	8	212	Amis, je t'aporte nouvelle		212	212	212				164	76			
B	109	213	Je maudi l'eure et le temps et le jour		213	213	213				165	77			
B	139	214	Morray je dont sans avoir vostre amour		214	214	214				166	78			
B	88	215	Helas! dolens, ma rose est mise en mue		215	215	215				167				
B	175	216	Quant vrais amans de sa dame se part		216	216	216				168	79			
B	17	217	Aucuns dient qu'on ne puet dame amer		217	217	217				169	80			Mn

* In music section.

form	Wilk	Lo	Text	G	A	M	Vg B D	W	C	H	E	J	K	Pa	other text MSS
B	154	218	Onques mes cuers ne senti		218	218	218				170				
B	130	219	Loial amour est de si grant noblese		219	219	219				171			142	Mn Bc
B	9	220	Amis, mon cuer et toute ma pensee		220	220	220				172			110	
Cp		Cp1	Amours, tu m'as tant esté dure	I†	I	221	221				173			146	
Cp	73	230	En l'onneur de ma douce amour	II	II	222	222				178				
Cp		Cp3	A toi, Hanri, dous amis, me complain	IV	III	223	223				174				
B	153	221	Onques dame ne fu si belle	182	221	224	224				179				
B	131	222	Ma dame a tout ce qu'il faut	183	222	225	225				180	81			
Cp		Cp4	Quant Ecuba vit la destruction	V	IV	226	226				176				
Cp		Cp5	Mes dous amis, a vous me vueil compleindre (VD)	VI	V	227	227				175				
B	114	223	Je preing congié a dames, a amours	184	223	228	228				40			108	Mn Bc
R	215	224	Amis, comment que m'aiés en oubli	185	224	229									
R	209	225	Trop ne me puis de bonne Amour loer	186	225	230									
R	231	226	Douce dame, cointe, apperte et jolie	187	226	231									
B			Lo216, Quant vrais amans recopied here	188	227	232	229				181				
B	13	227	Amours, ma dame et Fortune et mi oueil (VD)	189	228	233	230				182	92		106	
B	24	228	Ce qui contreint mon cuer a toy amer	*	229	234	231								
B	162	229	Plourez, dames, plourez vostre servant (B32/VD)	*	230	235	232					93			
Cp		Cp2	Deus choses sont qui me font a martire	III	VI	236	233				183				
B	187	231	Se je vous aim de fin loyal corage	190	231	237	234				184				
B	143	232	Nes qu'on porroit les estoilles nombrer (B33/VD)	*	232	238	235							223	I
Dit	282	233	Dire scens et folie faire	191	233	239	236				233				
R	219	234	Certes, mon oueil richement visa bel (R15)	192	234	240	237				234			105	Jp
R	233	235	Douce dame, tant com vivray (R20)	*	235	241	238				235			107	St
R	256	236	Quant je me depart dou manoir	193	236	242	239				236				
R	254	237	Quant Colette Colet colie	194	237	243	240								
B	212	238	Veoir n'oïr ne puis riens qui destourne (VD)	*	238	244	241				185				
B	174	239	Quant ma dame est noble et de grant vaillance (VD)	*	239	245	253				239				
R	217	240	Biauté, douceur et maniere jolie	195	240	246	242				177				
Cp		Cp6	Mon cuer, m'amour, ma dame souvereinne	VII	VII	247	243								Mn
R	269	241	Se tenir vues le droit chemin d'onneur	196	241	248	244				237	82		112	
B	107	242	Je di qu'il n'a en amour vraie et pure	197	242	249	245				186			109	
B	16	243	Amours qui m'a nouvellement espris	198	243	250	246				187				
B	179	244	Sans departir est en mon cuer entree	199	244	251	247				188				
B	243	245	Ma dame a qui sui donné ligement	200	245	252	248				238				
B	173	246	Quant je commensay l'amer	201	246	253	249								
R	271	247	Se vos courrous me dure longuement	202	247	254					189	83		111	

† Roman numerals denote complaintes in separate complainte sections.
* In music section.

form	Wilk	Lo	Text	G	A	M	VgBD	W	C	H	E	J	K	Pa	other text MSS
B	193	248	Se pour ce muir qu'Amours ai bien servi (B36/VD)	*	248	255	250					84			Ta
B	70	249	En desespoir, dame, de vous me part	203	249	256	251				190	85			
B	137	250	Mes dames qu'onques ne vi	204	250	257	252				191			113	
			Lo240, Biaué, douceur recopied here		251	258									
R	239	251	Je ne pourroie en servant desservir	205	252	259	254				240				
B	168	252	Puis qu'Amours faut et Loyauté chancelle	206	253	260	255				192	86			
B	63	253	Dou memoire des hommes degradés	207	254	261	256				193				
Cp		Cp7	Sire, a vous fais ceste clamour	VIII	VII										
CR	1	254	Amis, je t'ay tant amé et cheri	208	255	262									
R	245	255	Mon cuer, m'amour, ma deesse, m'amie	209	256	263									
R	253	256	Puis qu'en douceur vo gentilz cuers se mue	210	257	264									
R	267	257	Se li espoirs qui maint en moy ne ment	211	258	265									IJp
B	138	258	Mes esperis se combat a Nature (B39)	*	259	266									
R	244	259	Mi mal seront dous, plaisant et legier	212	260	267									
R	257	260	Quant je ne voy ma dame n'oy	213	261	268									
R	263	261	De vray desir, d'amoureuse pensee	214	262	269									
R	47	262	Qui sert se faire vuet a point	*	263	270									
R	261	Rn19	Quant ma dame les maus d'amer m'aprent (R19)	215	*	271								163	Ta
B	196	263	Se vo grandeur vers moy ne s'umilie	216	264										
B	150	264	On ne doit pas croire en augure	217	265										
B	98	265	Il ne m'est pas tant du mal que j'endure	218	266										
B	102	266	J'aim mieux languir en estrange contree	219	267										
B	56	267	Douce dame, tant vous aim et desir	220	268										
B	178	268	Riens ne me puet annuier ne desplaire	221											
R	258	269	Quant je ne voy ma dame n'cy (R21)	222											
B	164	270	Plus qu'onques mais vous desir a veoir	223											
B	62	271	Douceur, charité ne confort	224										72	
B	176	272	Qui de couleurs saroit a droit jugier												
		273	= MS K item No. 6, see above												
B	30	274	Dame, comment que n'aie pas veü	225											
B	10	Vn39	Amis, sans toy tout m'anoie (opus dubium?)				†				f.211			197	
R			Douli cuers gentilz (opus dubium)												

* In music section.
† MS **Vg**, fol. 333r; **B**, fol. 330r.

Table 6.8: Items in Chichmaref (1909) Appendix (mostly opera dubia)

form	Wilk	Lo	Text	J	K	Pa	other text MSS
B		A1	J'amay entan environ .xv. jours [1]	64			
B		A2	Ceulx dient qui ont amé [2]	94		157	
B		A3	Cuer qui se sent jeune, jolis et gais	95			
B		A4	Amours me point si tres forment et mort	96			
B		A5	S'il n'est d'argent ou de joyaux garni [3]	97			Jp Pn 1130 [4]
B		A6	Puis que je voy que j'ay le temps perdu [5]	98			
B		A7	J'ay mon bec jaune poié trop folement	99			Ta
B		A8	Estrange femme est d'omme appetit [6]	100			
B		A9	En oil estrange ne se doit nulz fier	101			Ta
B		A10	Folle largesse pour croire faulx semblant [7]	102			
B		A11	Doleur de chief et mal de trenchoisons	103			
B		A12	C'est grant doleur que d'estre en maladie	104			
B		51	Trop est crueus li maus de jalousie	105			
B		A13	Ce qu'ay pensé, voulez que je le die?	106		36	
B		A14	En un vert jardin joli [8]	107		37	
B		A15	Je fui yer en tel frenesie	108			
V		A16	Un mien voisin se complaignoit l'aurier	109			
B		A17	Par trois resons c'on peut prouver	110			
B		Bn9	Sans cuer m'en vois, dolens et esplourez (B17)	111		169	
B		Bn10	Amis, dolens, maz et desconfortez (B17)	112		170	
B		Bn11	Dame, par vous me sens reconfortez (B17)	113		171	
B		A18	S'Amours vousist que chascuns fust peüz	114			
B		Bn4	Biauté qui toutes autres pere (B4)	115		168	Wm
B		A19	Dous amis, pour toy conforter	116			
B		A20	Jugez, amans, et voiez ma dolour!	117		188	Jp I
B			[Avec raison l'Escripture est d'acord]				
B			Je Fortune (anon.)	(?)	(?)	(?)	

1 Hassell (1982, no. T9) indexes a proverb.   2 Hassell (1982, no. S62) indexes a proverb.
3 Hassell (1982, no. H52) indexes a proverb.   4 F:Pn 1130, fol. 150v (works of Alain Chartier).
5 Hassell (1982, no. F41) indexes a proverb.   6 Hassell (1982, no. P9) indexes a proverb.
7 Hassell (1982, no. P16) indexes a proverb.   8 Mentioned in Cerquiglini-Toulet 1993b, 16 n. 1.
9 J fol. 147v; K fol. 133r; for further text concordances, see Ludwig 1926–54, 2:14a* n. 3; also the text of a popular musical work, see Strohm 1984a, 115 no. 5.

4. Bibliographical references to *Loange* lyrics

A. *Introduction.* Appreciation of Machaut's lyrical poetry has been slower to develop than appreciation—or at least tolerance—of his narrative poetry. The narratives provide occasional historical or pseudo-biographical references. In contrast, Machaut's lyrics provide only the abstract essence of the courtly love aesthetic, usually without the slightest hint of a specific occasion with which a poem may have been associated.[24] It is not difficult to collect quotations from early twentieth-century studies amusing to our sensibilities, as in Jeanroy's assessment: "Jamais la banalité, la prolixité, la platitude n'ont sévi plus cruellement qu'alors. Ces défauts s'étalent dans les deux énormes volumes où s'alignent à perte de vue les innombrables ballades, rondeaux, lais, chansons royales et motets de Guillaume de Machaut, dont on aurait peine à extraire vingt vers valant d'être cités" (Jeanroy 1921, 465) [never have banality, prolixity, and platitude raged more cruelly than back then. These flaws extend through the two enormous volumes (i.e., MS **F-G**) where, as far as the eye can see, are arrayed innumerable ballades, rondeaux, lais, *chants royaux*, and motets of Guillaume de Machaut, from which one would have trouble extracting twenty verses worth citing].[25] Bartlett J. Whiting's view, expressed twenty-five years later, shows no advance in sympathy: "the ballade, like the sonnet, is a poetical type which requires great skill if the reader is not soon to feel a satiety bordering on nausea. This skill, and that despite consummate metrical ability, Machaut did not have and the artificial puling melancholy and histrionic love-sick whining, the tiresome adulation and namby-pamby praise of his ballades produce a genuine sense of oppression before many pages have been read" (Whiting 1946, 209–10). Exceptional understanding of Machaut's lyrics for this period of literary history is seen in the systematic and dispassionate survey of the themes of the lyrics in Gröber/Hofer (1933, 21–25), and in the non-derogatory study of conventional themes in the poetry in Schilperoort (1936, 19–47).[26]

A major advance in the appreciation of French medieval lyric came in 1949 with Robert Guiette's publication of a 1946 lecture that emphasizes formal structure in the aesthetic of the *chanson courtoise*. This article was reprinted in 1960 along with the first publication of another 1946 lecture that enumerates important characteristics of fourteenth- and fifteenth-century lyrics, including their use of *exempla*, their emphasis on personal experience and reality, and their extremes of formal play. Unlike more recent scholars, Guiette did not connect these developments to the fourteenth-century break between lyrics and music, but rather to the thirteenth-century bourgeois and professional jongleurs who tended to focus on the consolidation of forms.

Roger Dragonetti's book (1960), on all aspects of style, language, versification and metrics of thirteenth-century trouvère poetry, is useful for the study of Machaut's lyrics, although it does not cover Machaut directly. The most important work for the appreciation of lyrics in the fourteenth and fifteenth centuries remains Daniel Poirion's classic *Le poète et le prince* of 1965, which undertook a reevaluation of courtly poetry from Guillaume de Machaut to Charles d'Orléans. Poirion studies the changing circumstances under which the great poets wrote their poetry, and provides a sympathetic analysis of the evolution of style, language, and form in late medieval France.[27]

---

[24] This is perhaps one reason for the scholarly interest in narrative poems with lyrical insertions: the narrative provides contexts for otherwise abstract lyrics (cf. Poirion 1965, 138).

[25] See also Siciliano 1934, 325–26.

[26] Later surveys of themes include Wilkins 1969a, 5–12 and Cerquiglini 1987a, 132–38.

[27] See also Zumthor's approach (1972, 265–79 [=Eng. ed., 212–25]).

Jacqueline Cerquiglini (1983) provides a succinct exposition of what recent scholars find new in lyrics of the fourteenth and fifteenth centuries.[28] There is a tendency towards narrative continuity, dealing with the real world; there is a change from the universal poetic "I" of the thirteenth-century courtly lyric to a character in a dialogue, often in debates, judgments, or personal testaments. The break between lyrical poetry and music leads to an exaltation of poetic techniques and tricks of versification to replace the music. Poetry is composed for one's personal expression of feeling; the concomitant problems of the poet composing on command and the verification of feeling (*sentement*) are solved in textuality, i.e., self-conscious attention to bookmaking and the business of the professional writer, who utilizes *exempla* and mythological images.

The question of Machaut's role in the early development and consolidation of the fixed forms in the fourteenth century—principally the ballade, rondeau, and virelai—is a subject most thoroughly treated by Hoepffner (1910; 1911, 162–66; 1920a; 1920b), whose work is the basis of the summary in Reaney 1962.[29] More recently, Earp (1991a; 1991b) attempts to answer the question of why fixed-form poetry supplanted the preferred forms of the trouvères early in the fourteenth century and considers anew the question of Machaut's role in the establishment of the fixed forms.

Finally with regard to Machaut's lyrics, a few further surveys and specialized studies should be mentioned. Wilkins provides good surveys of the fixed forms in the fourteenth century (1969a; 1969b; 1972, introduction). Chapters in Poirion (1965), devoted to specific forms, the rondeau, virelai, *chant royal*, ballade, lai, and *complainte*, include valuable comparative tables of formal structures.[30] In addition, see the following works: for the ballade, Wilkins 1980a; Kooijman 1982; Frobenius 1986; Heger 1988; Ziino 1990; Zink 1992, 275–76. For the rondeau, Reckow 1972; Wilkins 1980c; Calvez 1981–82; Kehler 1984; Cerquiglini 1988b; Zink 1992, 272–74. For the virelai, Wilkins 1980d; Frobenius 1985; Mullally 1986 and 1990; Earp 1991a; Zink 1992, 274–75.[31] For the *chant royal*, Stewart 1973; Van der Werf/Frobenius 1983; Heger 1988; L.W. Johnson 1990, 35; Zink 1992, 275–76; and the works cited in Arlt 1982, 274. For the lais, see Deschaux 1988, esp. 72–77; Zink 1992, 276–77; and the additional bibliography given below, chapter 7.2. For the *complainte*, see the introduction to chapter 6.5.

Works to consult for questions of French versification include Lote 1949–51 and Elwert 1965. A succinct description of the different rhyme types is given in Wimsatt 1991b, 299 n. 62. Guthrie (1987 and 1991) has discovered differences between the metrics of the ballades that appear exclusively in the music section of Machaut's manuscripts, and the metrics of ballades that appear in the *Loange*

---

[28] Another modern introduction, with points similar to Cerquiglini's, is by Zink (1990, 122–27); see also Heitmann (1978), Wolfzettel (1980), and Wimsàtt (1991b, 5–12), with references to other literary studies, and the excellent recent book by Switten (1995).

[29] Reaney (1952c) reviews theories for the earliest development of the rondeau, virelai, and ballade. See also Machabey 1955b, 1:138–51.

[30] See also Gröber 1902, 88–96, still worth reading; Ritter 1914 (on ballades only); Lote 1949–51, vol. 1/2 chap. 4; Reaney 1959b, 25–38; Poirion 1971, 60–63; Wilkins 1972, 18–23; Ferrand 1994; and the brief comments in Zink 1990, 124–25.

[31] On Machaut's insistent use of the term *chanson baladée* instead of virelai, see *Remede* (ll. 3448–50); *Jugement Navarre* (ll. 4184–88); *Voir Dit* (ed. P. Paris 1875, 151 ll. 3574–75); *Prologue* (l. 14–15); and the commentary in Hoepffner 1909–21, 2:xlix–lii; Poirion 1965, 327; Lühmann 1978, 18–20; Arlt 1982, 262–63; Frobenius 1985, 3–4 (with quotations of the passages from the narrative poems); 1986, 9b; Cerquiglini-Toulet 1991b, 353–54; Weber-Bockholdt 1992, 275–76 n. 20.

text collection. Many sympathetic analyses of several of the lyrics are found in scholarly works of Wimsatt (esp. 1975, 1978, 1979; 1991b). Huot (1987, 260–72) has studied lais in MS **C** through the iconography of their miniatures. For the many ballades that mention Fortune, see Patch 1923, 23 n. 91 (the specific poems he cites are itemized in the bibliography below), and the excellent study of selected ballades on Fortune by L.W. Johnson (1979; 1990, 41–58). A few articles treat individual lyrics, for instance, Audbourg-Popin's 1986 study of *Riches d'amours* (B5). As for vocabulary, Lowes (1910) treats the phrase "simple et coie" in Machaut and in other contemporary poets; Heger (1967) treats "merencolie"; Luttrell (1978) treats "dous dangier" and "amoureus dangier"; Scully (1980) treats "douce dame"; while Planche (1982; 1990b; 1993) treats a variety of terms and locutions; see also Roques/Musso 1978.

Music historians of course deal almost exclusively with lyrical poetry. Gilbert Reaney is the first musicologist to consider the nuances expressed in the lyrics in some detail, and in an early article (1958b), he sets out a typology of twelve themes treated in the lyrics, based primarily on those works set to music.[32] Recently, musicologists have begun to develop the literary analysis of individual works to a greater extent than ever before (Arlt 1983; 1984; 1993; Fuller 1987a; 1992a).

B. *Bibliographical references.* In the bibliographical listing given below, "Lo" numbers indicate the number of a work in the edition of the *Loange* by Chichmaref (1909), which is arranged for the most part according to manuscript order. "Wilk." numbers are keyed to the edition of Wilkins (1972), which is arranged in alphabetical order by incipit. Modern critics have often found small nests of lyrics within the *Loange* that share a common theme, and these groupings are reflected in the listing below, followed by any notes on individual lyrics within the group.[33] Only more significant references are taken into the listing below (there are many more minor citations of *Loange* poems in Poirion [1965; 1978; 1982] and Schilperoort [1936], for instance). Proverbs indexed in Hassell 1982 are noted. For mention of interesting manuscript rubrics, see the commentary notes to the editions of Chichmaref and Wilkins. I have omitted reference here to most older editions. For an enumeration of lyrics in the nineteenth-century editions of Tarbé (1849 and 1856), works with concordances in MS **I** (see chap. 6.3 table 6.7) and edited by Queux de Saint-Hillaire/ Raynaud (1878–1903, vol. 10), works with concordances in MS **La** (see table 6.7) edited by Piaget (1941), works with concordances in MS **Ta** (see table 6.7) edited by Vitale-Brovarone (1980), and works edited by Patterson (1935), see the main bibliography under these editor's names. For specific titles to the following works, consult table 6.7 above.

Lo1–3 (Wilk. 71, 44, 195). A group of three ballades on the theme of timidity (Poirion 1965, 543 n. 127). Davis (1991, 84) notes a parallel between the "lady's ignorance of the lover's suffering" in Lo1 and the situation of the *Remede*.

Lo4–5 (Wilk. 52, 77=VD42). A group of two ballades on the theme of avowal (Poirion 1965, 543 n. 127). Compare the refrain for Lo4 with first line of R.1591, *Amours qui a son oes m'a pris* (Roques 1982, 158 n. 5). Lo5 is called "new" in the *Voir Dit* (VD42), but this ballade must have been composed much earlier (Poirion 1965, 200). Further, it is related to a ballade in a Turin manuscript of Granson (Piaget 1941, 291). The refrains of Lo5, Lo225, and *De toutes flours* (B31) are related (Wilkins 1972, 173 n. 77).

Lo7 (Wilk. 151=B3). Closely related to the first ballade in Jean de le Mote's *Regret Guillaume*. See comments on *On ne porroit* (B3) in chap. 7.3.

[32] Apel (1978), another musicologist, also provides a brief overview of themes.

[33] For groupings of lyrics in the *Loange,* I have drawn upon Poirion (1965, 204, 543 n. 127); Wilkins (1972, 14–16); Cerquiglini (1980b; 1985b, 34–37, 96–99), and others.

Lo9–11 (Wilk. 197, 37=B9, 112). Three ballades related by refrain or incipit (Poirion 1965, 204). Lo9 is a ballade that influenced Chaucer's *Troilus* (Wimsatt 1976, 293 n. 19). Concerning Lo10, see the comments on *Dame, ne regardez* (B9) in chap. 7.3. Poirion (1965, 449 n. 70) notes technical faults in Lo11; Cerquiglini (1985b, 109 n. 4) notes that its refrain is related to Lo263 l. 19 and to letter 10 of the *Voir Dit*.

Lo12–17 (Wilk. 156, 32, 149, 42=B37, 194, 157). A group of six ballades on the theme of separation (Poirion 1965, 543 n. 127). Lo12, 119, and 169 all have the same refrain, which is the same as the first line of R.1441, *Puis qu'il m'estuet de ma dame partir* (Roques 1982, 158–61, supplying corrected editions of the ballades). The three ballades Lo13–15 are further related by refrain or incipit (Poirion 1965, 204, 278 n. 34, 369). The first line of Lo13 is the refrain of Lo14 and the refrain of Lo129 (Wilkins 1972, 15, 16). See Luttrell (1978, 276) on "amoureus dangier" in Lo14. Hassell (1982, no. D25) indexes a proverb in Lo14. The first line of Lo16—identical to the first line of the two-line refrain of Lo28—has borrowings from Gautier d'Epinal (Roques 1982, 158 n. 5). Concerning Lo15, see the commentary to *Dame, se vous m'estes* (B37) in chap. 7.3.

Lo19 (Wilk. 5). Also ed. Wilkins 1969a, 31–32 no. 20 (notes, pp. 125–26). Poirion (1965, 371 n. 44) mentions the logical strophe-by-strophe development of the argument.

Lo23 (Wilk. 199). The refrain is related to Froissart's rondeau *Joie me fuit* (ed. McGregor 1975, 289–90 no. 106; Baudouin 1978, 99 no. 106; cited in Poirion 1965, 215). Cf. also Alain Chartier, rondeau *Joie me fuit* (ed. Laidlaw 1974, 382–83 no. 17; cited in Poirion 1965, 262).

Lo24–27 (Wilk. 184, 118, 214, 236). A group of four ballades on the theme of harsh pain (Poirion 1965, 204). Lo26 is a double ballade, with strophes alternating masculine and feminine voice; also ed. Wilkins 1969a, 29–30 no. 19 (notes, p. 125). Poirion (1965, 368 n. 35) mentions the aspect of dialogue in Lo26.

Lo28 (Wilk. 105). The first line of the two-line refrain of Lo28 is the same as the first line of Lo16, and has borrowings from Gautier d'Epinal (Roques 1982, 158 n. 5).

Lo32 (Wilk. 200). Poirion (1965, 378) briefly discusses the manner of introducing the two-line refrain.

Lo37 (Wilk. 83). Lyrical insertion no. 1 in the *Roman de Cardenois* (ed. Cocco 1975, 52).

Lo38 (Wilk. 155). The refrains of Lo38 and Lo61 are the same. Planche (1990b, 357) studies the use of the term "ëur."

Lo41–48 (Wilk. 55, 22, 266, 81, 2, 3, 4, 7). A group of eight ballades on the theme of the unfeeling woman (Poirion 1965, 204). Poirion (1965, 523) briefly mentions Lo41, and has further comments on the theme of Lo46–48 (1965, 554 n. 32). Lo45 l. 46 is related to the refrain of Lo42 (Wilkins 1972, 171 n. 2). Lo48 is related to Lo53 (Wilkins 1972, 171 n. 7), and to a line in *Fonteinne* (Hoepffner 1908–21, 3:256, note to l. 905). Wilkins (1989, 18) and Wimsatt (1991b, 276 and n. 10) suggest that Lo48 may be connected to a *puy*.

Lo49–57 (Wilk. 54, 208, 207, 120, 92, 247, 182, 89, 84). A group of nine ballades on the theme of the unfaithful woman (Poirion 1965, 204). Wimsatt (1978, 87 n. 40) comments on the influence of Lo49 on Chaucer's *Merciles Beaute*. Although Lo51 (see also Lo108) is lacking in MS C, Wilkins (1972, 13) presumes it had been written by 1349. Strophe 3 is headed *Guillaume* in MSS **VgBDEH**, thus perhaps the first two strophes are not by Machaut and this may be a reason for its exclusion from MS C. Lo53 also has a theme of desire in common with Lo69–72 (Poirion 1965, 204), and its first line is identical with the first line of *Helas! pour quoy virent* (M12, triplum) (Dömling 1970, 15). Lo53 is further related to Lo48, to a ballade of Oton de Granson, and to a similar ballade in MS **Pa** [50], no. 279 (Wilkins 1972, 173 n. 92). Lo54 is also ed. Wilkins 1969a, 33 no. 22 (notes, p. 126). Wilkins (1972, 16) indicates that the three ballades Lo55–57 are grouped by a theme of despair. Lo55 is entitled *chanson desesperee* in MSS **K** and **J**; Poirion (1965, 198n.) relates the theme of Lo55 to *Aucune gent / Qui plus aimme* (M5) and *Pour ce que tous* (B12); Estrich (1939, 37–38) conjectures that Lo55 provided the ballade portion of the *amende* at the end of *Navarre*. Wimsatt (1978, 79–81) comments on the influence of Lo56 on Chaucer's *Complaint unto Pity* and provides a complete translation (1991b, 88–89, 118). Poirion (1965, 375) briefly discusses Lo57.

Lo58 (Wilk. 57). Briefly discussed by Poirion (1965, 375–76).

Lo60 (Wilk. 216). Translated in Huizinga 1924, 274 (=1953, 324). The incipit provides the refrain of an anonymous ballade with music, *Pour che que je ne puis* (ed. Apel 1970–72, 2:86–88; G. Greene 1981–89, 20:194–96 no. 59; cited in Arlt 1982, 206). Possible influence on a ballade by the Catalan poet Andreu Febrer (Holzbacher 1983–84, 188).

Lo61 (Wilk. 148). The refrains of Lo38 and Lo61 are the same.

Lo63–72 (Wilk. 123, 232, 58, 36, 246, 270, 40, 121, 169, 252). A group of six ballades and four rondeaux on the theme of desire (Poirion 1965, 543 n. 127). Planche (1982, 198) discusses the technical aspect of *rime annexée* in Lo65 (called *rimes reprises* in Poirion, 1965, 379; *rimes enchaînées* in Dömling 1970, 12; and *rimes équivoques et retrogrades* in Wimsatt 1991b, 16). Wimsatt (1991b, 16–19) provides a translation and discussion of Lo65 (partial translation in L.W. Johnson 1990, 251); Schilperoort (1936, 7–8) compares Machaut's use of the technique to a ballade of Christine de Pizan. The refrain of Lo68 is the same as the refrain of the rondeau Lo247. See Luttrell (1978, 276) on "amoureus dangier" in Lo69. The four ballades and one rondeau on desire, Lo69–72, are also grouped by Poirion (1965, 204), while Wilkins (1972, 16) singles out the ballade and rondeau Lo71–72. Lo70 has a line in common with Lo129 (Wilkins 1972, 175 n. 141); on the characterization of Fortune in Lo70, see Patch 1927, 96n.

Lo73–76 (Wilk. 59, 99, 18, 51). A group of four ballades on the theme of healing (Poirion 1965, 543 n. 127). Lo73 is lyrical insertion no. 8 in the *Roman de Cardenois* (only ll. 1–2 appear in the manuscript, but space was left for the rest; ed. Cocco 1975, 110). Lo74 has the acrostic ISABELLE in ll. 1–4 (see discussion of *Certes, mon oueil* (R15) and *Dame, qui vuet* (R16) in chap. 7.3; Poirion 1965, 197 n. 19). Wimsatt (1978, 70) notes the influence of Lo76 on Chaucer's *Anelida and Arcite*.

Lo82 (Wilk. 218). Translation by Dwight Durling in Flores 1962, 152; German translation in Suchier/Birch-Hirschfeld 1900, 237 (=1913 ed., 1:244); modern French translation in Cerquiglini/Berthelot 1987, 120. Hassell (1982, nos. F96, R77, R92) indexes proverbs.

Lo90 (Wilk. 26). Translation in Kelly 1978, 6 (strophe 1 only). Feminine voice.

Lo91 (Wilk. 15). The first line of Lo91 is the same as the refrain of Lo152 (Roques 1982, 158 n. 5). Poirion (1965, 389) discusses the construction of the final strophe of Lo91, with correction of text and punctuation.

Lo92 (Wilk. 213). On the rhyme scheme, see Wimsatt 1991b, 318 n. 20.

Lo94 (Wilk. 66). Wimsatt (1976, 292–93 n. 11) notes the influence of Lo94 on Chaucer's *Troilus*. Partial translation in L.W. Johnson 1990, 251.

Lo100 (Wilk. 33). Same incipit as Lo168.

Lo105 (Wilk. 202). *Balade de desconfort* (rubric in MS J).

Lo108 (Wilk. 147). Although Lo108 (see also Lo51) is lacking in MS C, Wilkins (1972, 13) presumes it had been written by 1349.

Lo109 (Wilk. 163). The two-line refrain quotes Adam de la Halle (Roques 1982, 158 n. 5).

Lo110 (Wilk. 74). Wilkins (1972, 173 n. 74) notes that many late fourteenth-century ballades set to music have similar opening phrases. See also note to Lo210, and above, chap. 2.4b.

Lo115 (Wilk. 82). See Roques (1982, 161 n. 6) for some relationships among individual lines of Lo115 and 149.

Lo118 (Wilk. 249). Translation by Norman R. Shapiro in Flores 1962, 155–56.

Lo119 (Wilk. 145). Lo12, 119, and 169 all have the same refrain, which is the same as the first line of R.1441, *Puis qu'il m'estuet de ma dame partir* (Roques 1982, 158–60, supplying corrected editions of the ballades). See Roques (1982, 161 n. 6) for some relationships among individual lines of Lo119, 121, 149, 169.

Lo121 (Wilk. 86). Lo121 and 141 begin alike. Strophe 3 of Lo121 and 127 are almost equivalent (Wilkins 1972, 173 nn. 86 and 93). See Roques (1982, 161 n. 6) for some relationships among individual lines of Lo119, 121, 149.

Lo122 (Wilk. 260). Poirion (1965, 435 n. 27) emends Chichmaref's reading of the refrain to "crier a larme," although he earlier quotes the old reading (1965, 262 n. 66).

Lo125 (Wilk. 235). Translation by Norman R. Shapiro in Flores 1962, 154–55.

Lo127 (Wilk. 93). Strophe 3 of Lo121 and 127 are almost equivalent (Wilkins 1972, 173 nn. 86 and 93). Poirion (1965, 434) indicates that Machaut had to rewrite the third strophe of Lo127 and notes a fault in the rhymes, unaware of the relationship to Lo121; see Chichmaref (1909, 123) for the variant third strophe in MS **E**.

Lo129–30 (Wilk. 141, 31). A group of two ballades òn the theme of distance between lover and lady (Wilkins 1972, 16). The first line of Lo13 provides the refrain of Lo14 and the refrain of Lo129 (Wilkins 1972, 15, 16). There is also a line in common between Lo129 and Lo70 (Wilkins 1972, 175 n. 141).

Lo131 (Wilk. 20). Feminine voice. Guthrie (1991, 87) discusses poetic stress.

Lo132 (Wilk. 50). Only MS **C** gives the same refrain as Lo129, *Dame, comment que vous soie lonteins.* Wimsatt (1978, 81–82) notes the influence of Lo132 on Chaucer's *Merciles Beaute,* and provides an emendation based on an earlier text tradition. Partial translation in L.W. Johnson 1990, 251.

Lo135–39 (Wilk. 188, 206, 12, 34, 49). Five ballades form a group: Lo136–38 use as their refrain the first line of strophes 1, 2, and 3 of Lo135 respectively, while the refrain of Lo139 uses the penultimate line of strophe 3 of Lo135. In addition, all five works play on the word "chiere" in their first lines. Wilkins (1972, 177 n. 188; 1984, 162–63) suggests that this procedure, similar to the *motet enté,* inspired the formal experiments in the rondeau-ballades inserted into the *Tresor Amoureux.* One also wonders if this technique is related to Machaut's term *balade entée,* mentioned in the *Prologue* (see chap. 5 n. 45). Lo139 is a *Balade de merci* (rubric in MS **J**). Lo139 l. 8 is the same as Lo144 l. 17, see Wilkins 1972, 172 n. 49.

Lo140 (Wilk. 21). Guthrie (1991, 87) discusses poetic stress. Set to music by Anthonello da Caserta (ed. Apel 1950, 31*–32* no. 23; 1970–72, 1:5–6 no. 4; Wilkins 1972, 167–70; G. Greene 1981–89, 20:7–10 no. 3; facs. of MS *Pn 6771* [63] in Apel 1953, 421 no. 86).

Lo141 (Wilk. 87). Lo141 and 121 begin alike.

Lo142 (Wilk. 48). See Roques (1982, 161 n. 6) for relationships among individual lines of Lo142, 144, 147, 163.

Lo144 (Wilk. 39). See Roques (1982, 161 n. 6) for relationships among individual lines of Lo142, 144, 147, 163; see also Lo139 (Wilkins 1972, 172 n. 39).

Lo146–47 (Wilk. 91, 158). A group of two ballades on the theme of a lover dying of grief (Wilkins 1972, 16). See Roques (1982, 161 n. 6) for relationships among individual lines of Lo142, 144, 147, and 163, and between Lo147 and 149.

Lo148 (Wilk. 264=R4=VD31). The lyric following this one in the *Voir Dit* (VD32) is a rondeau in direct imitation of Lo148, supposedly composed by Peronne. See the comments on *Sans cuer, dolens* (R4) in chap. 7.3.

Lo149 (Wilk. 68). See Roques (1982, 161 n. 6) for relationships among individual lines of Lo119, 121, and 149; between Lo149 and 147; and between Lo149 and 115.

Lo152 (Wilk. 126). The refrain of Lo152 is the same as the first line of Lo91 (Roques 1982, 158 n. 5).

Lo153, 155, 158 (Wilk. 165, 72, 108). A group of three ballades on the theme of loyalty (Poirion 1965, 204). The ballade Lo153 begins the same as the rondeau Lo208.

Lo156 (Wilk. 133). The first line was taken up in several ballades of Deschamps (Poirion 1965, 559 and n. 60).

Lo158 (Wilk. 108). See comments on Lo153.

Lo161 (Wilk. 95=VD49). Sonnemann (1969, 153–56) discusses some interesting problems concerning the reuse of this ballade in the *Voir Dit.* Brief mention in Cerquiglini 1985b, 39.

Lo162 (Wilk. 181). A ballade with a similar incipit is in MS **Pa** [50], no. 71 (Wimsatt 1982, 94).

Lo163 (Wilk. 226). Translation by Norman R. Shapiro in Flores 1962, 156. See Roques (1982, 161 n. 6) for relationships among individual lines of Lo142, 144, 147, and 163.

Lo164 (Wilk. 210). Planche (1990b, 357) studies the use of the term "ĕur."

Lo165–77 (Wilk. 160, 65, 101, 221, 27, 198, 104, 64, 78, 142, 110=B14, 140, 14=B19).
Poirion (1965, 521 n. 45) notes that the motive of "coeur" (heart) is important in this
group of twelve ballades and one rondeau. See the following comments on some individual
works in this series.

Lo165–66 (Wilk. 160, 65). The two ballades Lo165–66 are grouped by a theme of "adieu"
(Poirion 1965, 550 n. 13). A number riddle in Lo165 yields the name "Jehanne" (Hoepffner
1906, 409; the solution of Monod (1903)—Marie—is erroneous); cf. also Lo212 and the
comments on *Cinc, un* (R6) in chap. 7.3. See the comments above on the series Lo165–77.

Lo167 (Wilk. 101). See the comments above on the series Lo165–77.

Lo168 (Wilk. 221). Same incipit as Lo100. See the comments above on the series Lo165–77.

Lo169 (Wilk. 27). Feminine voice. Lo12, 119, and 169 all have the same refrain, which is
the same as the first line of R.1441, *Puis qu'il m'estuet de ma dame partir* (Roques 1982,
158–61, supplying corrected editions of the ballades). See the comments above on the series
Lo165–77.

Lo170–72 (Wilk. 198, 104, 64). See the comments above on the series Lo165–77.

Lo173 (Wilk. 78). Poirion (1965, 495) briefly discusses the image of the fountain; translation
of strophe 1 in Kelly 1978, 47–48. See the comments above on the series Lo165–77.

Lo174 (Wilk. 142). Compare the opening of *Ne pensez pas* (B10). See the comments above
on the series Lo165–77.

Lo175 (Wilk. 110=B14 with slightly different incipit). Feminine voice. Wimsatt (1976, 289–
90) notes influence on Chaucer's *Troilus*. See the comments above on the series Lo165–77
and the comments on *Je ne cuit* (B14) in chap. 7.3.

Lo176 (Wilk. 140). See the comments above on the series Lo165–77. Hassell (1982, no.
O67) indexes a proverb. Read on Club National du Disque CND9 (chap. 8.8).

Lo177 (Wilk. 14=B19). On the metrics, see Wilkins 1972, 172 n. 14. See the comments
above on the series Lo165–77 and the comments on *Amours me fait* (B19) in chap. 7.3.

Lo179–80 (Wilk. 124=VD29, 127=VD30). Two ballades discussed by Cerquiglini (1985b,
34–37). Both were supposedly improvised in the context of the *Voir Dit* (cf. Poirion 1965,
201; Wilkins 1972, 174–75 nn. 124 and 127). Lo180 is further mentioned by Poirion
(1965, 524); see also chap. 5 n. 85.

Lo181 (Wilk. 190). Feminine voice.

Lo186 (Wilk. 191). There are interesting textual problems in this ballade; see Wilkins 1972,
177 n. 191.

Lo187 (Wilk. 53). See Luttrell (1978, 290 n. 9) on the phrase "dous dangier."

Lo188–89 (Wilk. 96=B22, 238). A ballade and a rondeau on Fortune (Patch 1927, 75 n. 3,
96n.; Wilkins 1972, 16; Calin 1974, 244; Wimsatt 1979, 131 n. 28). See comments on *Il
m'est avis* (B22) in chap. 7.3.

Lo190 (Wilk. 119). Lo190 influenced Chaucer's *Merchant's Tale* (Wimsatt 1979, 124, with
partial translation). Brief mention in Wimsatt 1991b, 93.

Lo192 (Wilk. 152). A ballade discussed by Cerquiglini (1985b, 79 n. 52). Hassell (1982, no.
C347) indexes a proverb that appears in strophe 1 and in the refrain.

Lo193 (Wilk. 97). Wilkins (1972, 174 n. 97) notes the unusually bitter mood of this ballade.

Lo194 (Wilk. 100=VD48). Poirion (1965, 215) notes a resemblance to Froissart's rondeau *Il
n'est deduis, esbatemens, ne joie* (ed. Mc Gregor 1975, 262 no. 32; Baudouin 1978, 68–69
no. 32). Sonnemann (1969, 153–56) discusses some interesting problems concerning the
reuse of this ballade in the *Voir Dit*.

Lo195 (Wilk. 45=B23). See comments on *De Fortune* (B23) in chap. 7.3. Hassell (1982, no.
R85) indexes a proverb.

Lo196 (Wilk. 204). Wimsatt (1991a, 136–40) provides complete translation and analysis; he
also notes influence on Chaucer's *Complaint of Mars* (1978, 75) and *To Rosemounde*
(1978, 76–77; 1991a, 143–44; 1991b, 22–25 [with translation of strophe 1]).

Lo198 (Wilk. 180). Feminine voice.

Lo199 (Wilk. 11=VD50). Feminine voice. Related to a passage in *Fonteinne* (Hoepffner 1908–21, 3:262, note to l. 2319).

Lo202 (Wilk. 201). On the characterization of Fortune, see Patch 1927, 96n.

Lo203 (Wilk. 115=B28). See comments on *Je puis trop* (B28) in chap. 7.3.

Lo204 (Wilk. 69=B27, with different word order in the first line). Poirion (1965, 497) notes the strong image of the viper and scorpion. See the comments on *Une vipere* (B27) in chap. 7.3.

Lo206–8 (Wilk 259, 268, 250). A group of three rondeaux on the theme of the lady's infidelity (Wilkins 1972, 16). The rondeau Lo208 begins the same as the ballade Lo153.

Lo209 (Wilk. 113). Refrain related to a passage in *Fonteinne* (Hoepffner 1908–21, 3:258, note to ll. 1487–88).

Lo210 (Wilk. 46). Wilkins (1972, 172 n. 46) notes a textual relationship to a ballade of Filippotto da Caserta, *De ma dolour ne puis trouver confort* (see chap. 2.4). See also note to Lo110.

Lo212 (Wilk. 8). *Balade de Bon Espoir* (rubric in MS **J**). A number riddle in strophe 3 gives NEEAHJ (i.e., Jehane; see P. Paris 1875, xx; Hoepffner 1906, 409; 1908–21, 1:xli n. 2, 3:261, note to l. 2207; Chichmaref 1909, 191 n. 16); compare Lo165 and the discussion of *Cinc, un* (R6) in chap. 7.3. Composed for the marriage of John of Berry and Jehanne d'Armagnac in 1360 (Machabey 1955b, 1:89; Poirion 1965, 195).

Lo213 (Wilk. 109). Translation by Jacques LeClercq in Flores 1962, 154. Briefly discussed by Poirion (1965, 381). Similar to Pierre des Molins's popular ballade *De ce que folz pense* (Reaney 1958b, 41; ed. Apel 1970–72, 1:159–61 no. 84; G. Greene 1981–89, 19:127–29 no. 87a). The first line of strophe 3 of Lo213 is the same as the fifth line of strophe 3 of *Se pour ce muir* (B36) (Dömling 1970, 15) but is not found in Lo248, otherwise identical to B36. Wilkins (1972, 174 n. 109) remarks on the bitter tone, recalling Lo253. See the literary analysis in Marks (1984, 109–11), and L.W. Johnson (1979, 22–23; 1990, 50–51 with translation of strophe 3), especially on the theme of Fortune. Hassell (1982, no. F125) indexes a proverb.

Lo215 (Wilk. 88). Wilkins (1972, 173 n. 88) notes a relationship to *De toutes flours* (B31).

Lo216 (Wilk. 175). A motif in Charles d'Orléans may derive from this ballade (Poirion 1965, 278 n. 35). Lyrical insertion no. 11 in the *Roman de Cardenois* (only l. 1 cited, but room left for the rest; ed. Cocco 1975, 186–87). Possible influence on a ballade by the Catalan poet Andreu Febrer (Holzbacher 1983–84, 188–89; ed. Riquer 1951, 53).

Lo218 (Wilk. 154). German translation in Suchier/Birch Hirschfeld 1900, 238 (=1913 ed., 245). Related to a passage in *Fonteinne* (Hoepffner 1908–21, 3:262, note to ll. 2508–10).

Lo219 (Wilk. 130). Related to a line in *Fonteinne* (Hoepffner 1908–21, 3:262, note to l. 2335). Brief mention in Wimsatt 1991b, 93.

Lo220 (Wilk. 9). Feminine voice. Lyrical insertion no. 10 in the *Roman de Cardenois* (ed. Cocco 1975, 179).

Lo223–26 (Wilk. 114, 215, 209, 231). These two ballades and two rondeaux are lacking in **VgBD**, but they may already have been composed by period of the redaction of **Vg** (Wilkins 1972, 13). Lo223 is on the widespread theme of *congié d'amour*, see Poirion 1965, 567 n. 91. Deschamps recalled Lo223 in his ballade of *déploration, Armes, Amour.* Wimsatt notes its influence on Chaucer's *Troilus* (1976, 293 n. 12) and *Complaint unto Pity* (1978, 81) see also brief mention in Wimsatt 1991b, 93. Feminine voice in Lo224. Wilkins (1972, 177 n. 209) notes that the refrains of Lo5, Lo225, and *De toutes flours* (B31) are similar, and that the beginning of Lo225 l. 23 is the same as *Ne quier* (B34), l. 13. There is a partial translation of Lo225 in Kelly 1978, 104; Zeeman (1991, 226) relates Lo225 to the *Voir Dit*; Wimsatt (1976, 289) notes influence on Chaucer's *Troilus*; see also the brief mention in Poirion 1965, 551 n. 22. Lo226 translation by Norman R. Shapiro in Flores 1962, 155.

Lo227 (Wilk. 13=VD6). On the theme of Fortune, see Patch (1927, 92 n. 1) and especially L.W. Johnson (1979, 19–22; 1990, 47–50, with complete translation).

Lo228 (Wilk. 24) Wimsatt notes the influence of Lo228 on Chaucer's *Anelida and Arcite*
(1978, 70) and *Troilus* (1976, 286; 1991b, 157–58). Hassell (1982, no. M246) indexes a
proverb.

Lo229 (Wilk. 162=B32=VD5). Related to Deschamps's *déploration* for Machaut (Wilkins
1972, 175–76 n. 162). See the comments on *Plourez, dames* (B32) and Deschamps's
déploration in chap. 7.3 and 7.4.

Lo230 (Wilk. 73). Wilkins (1972, 173 n. 73) considers MSS **AG** to be in error in grouping
this ballade among the *complaintes*. See chap. 6.5.

Lo231 (Wilk. 187). Also ed. Woledge (1961, 224–25). P. Paris (1875, 407–8) places the
composition of this ballade after the marriage of Peronne, the "Toute Belle" of the *Voir Dit*;
cf. also Wilkins 1972, 176–77 n. 187; Imbs 1991, 93. Partial translation with commentary
in Kelly 1978, 128.

Lo232 (Wilk. 143=B33=VD16). See the comments on *Nes qu'on* (B33) in chap. 7.3.

Lo233 (Wilk. 282). Octosyllabic rhyming couplets, 12 lines; labeled *Aucun dit notable* in
MS **M**; *Rondel* in MS **G**. This short non-lyric work is on the virtues of saying and doing
the wise thing. See Cerquiglini 1988b, 47.

Lo234 (Wilk. 219=R15). Discussed in Wilkins 1983b, 262; quoted in Deschamps' *Art de
Dictier* (see chap. 2.1.1m). See the comments on *Certes, mon oueil* (R15) in chap. 7.3.
Hassell (1982, no. A10) indexes a proverb.

Lo235 (Wilk. 233=R20). Briefly mentioned by Poirion (1965, 69). See the comments on
Douce dame, tant (R20) in chap. 7.3.

Lo237 (Wilk. 254). Modern French translation in Cerquiglini/Berthelot 1987, 120–21.
Poirion (1965, 325 n. 21) notes similar rondeau in a Wolfenbüttel manuscript. Briefly
mentioned by Guiette (1960, 29) and Cerquiglini (1988b, 51, 53).

Lo241 (Wilk. 269). See the comments in chap. 5.10 ("related Machaut works," item i) on the
relation of this work to *Confort*.

Lo243 (Wilk. 16). On the characterization of Fortune, see Patch 1927, 91 n. 1.

Lo247 (Wilk. 271). The refrain of the rondeau Lo247 is the same as the refrain of the rondeau
Lo68. Translation by Norman R. Shapiro in Flores 1962, 152–53; German translation in
Suchier/Birch-Hirschfeld 1900, 237 (=1913 ed., 244).

Lo248 (Wilk. 193=B36=VD61). On color, see the comments on Lo272 below. The fifth line
of strophe 3 of *Se pour ce muir* (B36) is the same as the first line of strophe 3 of Lo213
(Dömling 1970, 15) but is not found in Lo248, otherwise identical to B36. Wilkins (1989,
334–35) notes a related ballade in MS **I** [40], fol. 19r, *En lieu de bleu qui porte la figure*.
See further the comments on *Se pour ce muir* (B36) in chap. 7.3.

Lo249 (Wilk. 70) Wimsatt notes influence on Chaucer's *Complaynt d'Amours* (1978, 71) and
Merciles Beaute (1978, 81–82; 1991b, 313 n. 14).

Lo250 (Wilk. 137). Discussed by Wilkins (1972, 13, 15), and by Cerquiglini (1985b, 196 n.
30). Lo250 specifically mentions "monseigneur de Loupy" (cf. Hoepffner 1908–21, 1:xl).
See the discussion above, chap. 1.11c.

Lo252 (Wilk. 168). Wimsatt (1978, 82–83) notes the influence of Lo252 on Chaucer's
Merciles Beaute and on his *Envoy to Scogan*. A complete translation is provided in
Wimsatt 1991b, 93–95, with discussion of the influence of Lo252 on Chaucer's *Against
Women Unconstant*. Hassell (1982, no. L55) indexes a proverb.

Lo253 (Wilk. 63). A curse on the month of March, the cause of gout in Machaut's foot.
Wilkins (1972, 173 n. 63) remarks that this work may have inspired Deschamps's
humorous treatments of his own maladies and compares the bitter tone of Lo213 and Lo253
(1972, 174 n. 109). Discussion in J.A. Nelson 1982–83 (Lo253 based on Job 3:1–10);
mentioned in Huot 1994, 224. Also ed. Wilkins 1969a, 23 no. 13 (notes, p. 124); German
translation of strophe 1 in Suchier/Birch-Hirschfeld 1900, 237 (=1913 ed., 244); modern
French translation in Cerquiglini/Berthelot 1987, 119–20.

Lo254 (Wilk. 1). Feminine voice (cf. L.W. Johnson 1979, 18; 1990, 45–46, with translation of strophe 4). Complete translation in Wimsatt 1991b, 90–92 (partial translation in Kelly 1978, 6). Wilkins (1972, 171 n. 1) notes a relationship between Lo254 l. 52 and the opening of *Plus dure* (V31/28). Wimsatt (1978, 67–70; 1991b, 90–93, 124–25) notes influence on Chaucer's *A Complaint to His Lady* and *Anelida and Arcite*. This *chant royal* has a two-line refrain that recalls the first line of ballade no. 14 in Jean de le Mote's *Regret Guillaume* (Hoepffner 1911, 163, 164; Wilkins 1983a, 194; Wimsatt 1991b, 61–63, with ed. and translation). On the use of a refrain in this *chant royal*, see Poirion 1965, 372; Wimsatt 1991b, 92. Wimsatt (1991b, 347 n. 10) suggests that Lo254 could have been destined for a *puy* at Valenciennes, or at some other town in Jean de le Mote's home province. Hassell (1982, no. D67) indexes a proverb.

Lo258 (Wilk. 138=B39). See the comments on *Mes esperis* (B39) in chap. 7.3

Lo260 (Wilk. 257). Similar to Lo269 (Ludwig 1926–54, 1:69, note to R21). Discussed in Sonnemann 1969, 119. Hassell (1982, no. N14) indexes a proverb.

Lo262 (Wilk. 263). Hassell (1982, nos. S87, V35) indexes proverbs.

Lo263 (Wilk. 196). Also ed. Woledge (1961, 225–26). Feminine voice. Cerquiglini (1985b, 109 n. 4) notes that l. 19 is related to the refrain of Lo11 and letter 10 of the *Voir Dit*. On the characterization of Fortune, see Patch 1927, 91 n. 1. Hassell (1982, no. A126) indexes a proverb.

Lo264 (Wilk. 150). Wilkins (1972, 15, 175 n. 150; 1984, 157–58) tentatively relates this ballade to the Siege of Reims. Strophe 3 quoted in Patch 1923, 23 n. 91.

Lo266 (Wilk. 102). Also ed. and translation by Woledge (1961, 222–23).

Lo267 (Wilk. 56). Partial translation in Wimsatt 1991b, 138–39.

Lo269 (Wilk. 258=R21). Similar to Lo260 (Ludwig 1926–54, 1:69, note to R21). See the comments on *Quant je ne voy* (R21) in chap. 7.3.

Lo270 (Wilk. 164). A related rondeau attributed to Wenceslas of Brabant is in Froissart's *Meliador* (ll. 2148–57). Lo270 is related to the ballade inserted into the virelai section in MSS **Vg** and **B**, *Amis, sans toy tout m'anoie* (ed. Chichmaref 1909, 2:632–33; Wilkins 1972, 52 no. 10).

Lo271 (Wilk. 62). Discussed by Poirion (1965, 594) and Wilkins (1972, 15, 172–73 n. 62).

Lo272 (Wilk. 176). Feminine voice. Also ed. Wilkins 1969a, 24 no. 14 (notes, p. 124). Translation of strophe 1 in Wimsatt 1991b, 103–4. On the color symbolism in this work, see Hoepffner 1908–21, 3:256 n. to l. 905 of *Fonteinne;* Schilperoort 1936, 74–75; Wimsatt 1970, 15; Zumthor 1972, 273–74 (=Eng. ed., 219–20); Kelly 1978, 287 n. 39; Fourrier 1979, 57–59; Cerquiglini 1985b, 169. Wimsatt notes the influence of this ballade on the color symbolism in Chaucer's *Anelida and Arcite* (1978, 70), as well as in *Against Women Unconstant* and the *Squire's Tale* (1991b, 315 n. 40). Hassell (1982, nos. B112, J8, V75) indexes proverbs. For more on color, see chap. 5.13, art historical discussion.

5. The *complaintes*

For a discussion of the *complainte*, including themes and formal aspects of the genre, see Gröber/Hofer 1933, 26; Lote 1949–51, 1/2:305–7; Poirion 1965, 406–9, 415–18; Ruhe 1975; Lühmann 1978, 40–41; Cerquiglini 1985b, 100 n. 27 (on feminine voice); Dembowski 1987, 100 n. 18; Deschaux 1988, esp. 77–85; and Ferrand 1988. Maekawa (1985, 70–71) discusses the question of the degree of separation of this section in the manuscripts. On the influence of Machaut's *complaintes* on Chaucer, see Davenport 1988, 6–7, 29; and Wimsatt 1991b, 29, 110–11.

Table 6.9 *Complaintes:* Concordances[34]

Wilk	Lo	poem	G	A	M	VgB D	E	Pa	Pm
	I	*Amours, tu m' as tant esté dure*	I	I	221	221	173	110	I
73	230	*En l' onneur de ma douce amour* (ballade)	II	II	222	222	178	146	
	II	*Deus choses sont qui me font a martire*	III	230	236	232	183	106	
	III	*A toi, Hanri, dous amis, me complain*	IV	III	223	223	174		
	IV	*Quant Ecuba vit la destruction*	V	IV	226	226	176		II
	V	*Mes dous amis, a vous me vueil* (VD15)	VI	V	227	227	175		III
	VI	*Mon cuer, m' amour, ma dame souvereinne*	VII	VI	247	242	177	112	
	VII	*Sire, a vous fais ceste clamour*	VIII	VII	261				
	VIII	*Tu qui vues avoir mon cheval*	IX	VIII					
	IX	*Je me plein de celui qui en celier converse*	X						
	X	*J' ay, passét a plus de .x. ans*	XI						
Remede		*Tels rit au main qui au soir pleure*	RF2 (see chap. 7.3)						
Fonteinne		*Douce dame, vueilliez oïr la vois*	chap. 5.11						
Voir Dit		*Mes dous amis a vous me veuil-je plaindre*	VD15 (see chap. 5.13 table 5.3)						
"		*Dous amis, que t' ay-je meffait?*	VD53 (see chap. 5.13 table 5.3)						
"		*Dame en qui j' ay mis toute m' esperance*	VD55 (see chap. 5.13 table 5.3)						

Note: *Mes dous amis* (Cp5) also appears in the MSS **Mn** [43] and **Bc** [55];
l. 1 of *Mon cuer, m' amour* (Cp6) also appears in MS **Mn** [43].

A toi, Hanri, dous amis, me complain (*complainte* Cp3)

FORM. Decasyllabic rhyming couplets, 58 lines.

MANUSCRIPTS.

    [3] **V g** fols. 32v–33r   [7] **E** fols. 13v[35]
    [4] **B** fols. 32v (49v)–33r (50r)   [10] **M** fols. 199v–200r
    [5] **A** fols. 216v–217r   [11] **D** fols. 40v–41r
    [6] **G** fol. 69r

EDITIONS. Tarbé 1849, 89–90 (incomplete); P. Paris 1875, 384–85 (incomplete); Chichmaref 1909, 1:251–53.

TRANSLATION. Cerquiglini/Berthelot 1987, 113–15; Wimsatt 1991b, 79–82.

DATE. (1) ca. 1340 (P. Paris 1875, 383 n. iii; Chichmaref 1909, 1:xxxiv–xxxix; Markstrom 1989, 33–34). The thirtieths (a kind of tax) mentioned in ll. 19–20 were first levied in 1351 (Samaran/Mollat 1905, 17), making the 1340 date impossible.
(2) ca. 1358 (Tarbé 1849, vii, xxviii, 89).
(3) 1359 (Hoepffner 1908–21, 1:xxiii n. 1; Machabey 1955b, 1:44, 51–52; Wimsatt 1991b, 312 n. 3). Machabey's argument concerning Machaut's horse is absurd; see chap. 1.7.1a.
(4) ca. 1360 (R. Cazelles 1982, 445, since ll. 19–20 indicate he has paid thirtieths for eight years). With the return of King John in 1360, the currency in France remained stable for the next twenty-five years (Henneman 1976, 117–18; R. Cazelles 1982, 418).
    The manuscript transmission confirms a date in the late 1350s or early 1360s. The reference in ll. 27–28 concerning the king of England (see below) would suggest that the Siege of Reims (winter 1359–60) had not yet occurred (cf. chap. 1.13).

BIOGRAPHY. Cp3 is one of Machaut's most-discussed works, owing to the many apparent historical references in its fifty-eight lines (see the analysis in Wimsatt 1991b, 78–82). Below, the work will be considered line-by-line in order to treat speculations concerning each reference separately. Several of the references seem to refer to Machaut's central complaint, that even though he is an important official of the church, his rights in the

---

34 Roman numerals in the "Lo" column give the number in the section of *complaintes* in Chichmaref 1909, 1:241–69; the ballade Lo230 is edited with the poems of the *Loange* (Chichmaref 1909, 1:207). Numerals in the manuscript columns give the serial order of works; Roman numerals indicate a separate section of *complaintes*; Arabic numerals indicate the serial order within a given manuscript's *Loange* section (as in table 6.7).

35 *Complainte de Guillaume Machaut.*

present circumstances are worth little. Desportes (1979, 301) discusses the participation of churchmen in payments for the fortification of Reims and their service as watchmen.

l. 1: address to "Hanri." Perhaps Henry served as the messenger of the *Voir Dit* (Chichmaref 1909, 1:lvii n. 1; see P. Paris 1875, iv, 195, 268, 282, 314, 383 n. iii, and 401 n. lxxii; Hanf 1898, 155–56; Eichelberg 1935, 115–16; see also Badel 1985, 552). P. Paris (1875, 383–86) incorrectly linked Cp3 with a pair of documents from Reims that mention Machaut in connection with "H. li Large" (see chap. 1.7.1a).

ll. 2–6: Machaut is without his horse, and without Esmeraude, Belle and Lancelot. The names have been interpreted as names of hunting dogs. Hunting is not a suitable pastime for a cleric (Cerquiglini 1985b, 271 s.v. "chasse"), though Machaut as narrator hunts in the *Jugement Navarre* and in the *Voir Dit*.

l. 8: Machaut brought to his knees by his enemies.

ll. 9–12: Machaut made a slave; he has to be on the walls of the city and wear a coat of mail. The clergy had been forced to give money for building fortifications in 1339; work was broken off in 1340 and not taken up again until 1346 (Desportes 1979, 541).

l. 13: otherwise he would have to leave Reims.

ll. 14–17: also unpleasant are the *maletoste*, the subsides, the *gabelle*, and the weak currency. *Maletoste* is a pejorative term for taxes, used in the mid-fourteenth century in northern France (Henneman 1971, 4). The *gabelle*, or salt tax, had been introduced in 1341, collected until 1346–47, and reintroduced in 1358. It became permanent in 1360 (Henneman 1976, 15, 91, 119). For the collection at Reims in early 1359, see Henneman 1976, 97. Revaluations of the currency hit the clergy hard in the 1350s. Since the income of the clergy was set in the money of account, it lost value against the money in circulation (R. Cazelles 1982, 18–22, esp. p. 19, with documents from Reims). The devaluation closest to the apparent time of Cp3 was 14 January 1358 (R. Cazelles 1982, 301). For further literary mentions of the revaluations of the currency, see Cerquiglini 1985b, 161–62. Note that the narrator had counselled Charles of Navarre in the *Confort* (ll. 3789–818) to keep tabs on tax collectors and to punish their excesses.

l. 18: the visitation by the pope.

ll. 19–20: Machaut has had to pay *trentismes* [thirtieths] for eight years, and without delay three tenths for the king. Machaut's specific mention of money "for the king" must refer to the ransom of King John. Money had to be raised quickly and both nobles and clergy had to contribute (Delachenal 1909–31, 2:220–23). Pope Innocent VI had authorized two tenths on the French clergy, first payable on 1 November 1358 (Henneman 1976, 86). After several letters from King John II in London, Reims raised 20,000 *écus*, thanks to large loans made by the secular clergy and religious orders (Delachenal 1909–31, 2:229–31; Henneman 1976, 113–14, 228 n. 141). Perhaps the third tenth mentioned by Machaut was that ordered by the Estates General in April/May 1358 (Henneman 1976, 71–73). On 27 February 1363, the thirtieths were revoked in Reims (Samaran/Mollat 1905, 18), and the tenths reduced by half (1905, 21).

ll. 23–24: Machaut would rather be a swineherd than to see himself skinned alive. The rhyme *porchier:escorchier* recalls a rondeau in the *Roman de Fauvel* (*F:Pn 146, Porchier mieus estre ameroie*; ed. Rosenberg/Tischler 1991, 44 no. 16). Cf. also Gauvard (1982, 28), on *Confort* ll. 3817–18.

ll. 25–26: the church has been destroyed to the point that its *franchise* [tax exemption?] is worthless. As a secretary of John of Luxembourg, Machaut may have expected a tax exemption; cf. chap. 1.6.3.

ll. 27–28: and the king of England is coming to get the rest of his goods. A reference to the Siege of Reims, which seemingly has not yet happened.

ll. 28–29: he is ill and has little money, nor do his brothers, perhaps a reference to his fellow canons (Wimsatt 1991b, 81).

ll. 31–33: further, he is forgotten by his patron ("earthy god"). Perhaps a reference to Charles of Navarre, who would be dunned for payment for the *Confort* in the *complainte Sire, a vous* (Cp7), according to the most recent interpretations of that work (see chap. 1.10.2b and chap. 1.12.2; for another view, see chap. 1.10.2a).

ll. 34–38: with his one eye, he can see that at a king's court everyone must fend for himself, for nobody cares about his problems. On the "borgne oeil" theme, cf. Cerquiglini 1984, 486–87; 1985a, 28; 1985b, 112.

ll. 39–40: he loves the flower of all creation, but fears she doesn't love him, perhaps a reference to a patroness (Wimsatt 1991b, 82).

ll. 41–42: Fortune is hard on him.

ll. 43–50: therefore he will go live in exile in the Empire, since priest or lay, all are in the hands of the common people. He would rather have freedom (*franchise*) and little means than be very rich and in servitude. Again, this appears to be a reference to the severe exactions that the city required of the clergy (cf. Gauvard 1982, 29 n. 28; Imbs 1991, 191, 196).

ll. 51–58: adieu to Henry; Machaut will go into exile and never make another song or lai.

LINKS TO OTHER MACHAUT WORKS. Chichmaref (1909, 1:lx–lxi) links the complaints in Cp3 with the narrator's complaint to the "Roi qui ne ment" in the *Voir Dit* (ll. 5176–233, ed. P. Paris 1875, 222–24), with references also to *Christe / Veni* (M21) and *Tu qui gregem / Plange* (M22).

TEXTUAL LEGACY (France). Froissart, *Dit dou Florin* (Wimsatt 1991b, 206–9; Calin 1994, 404–5). Perhaps the reference to Machaut in the Latin letter of Jean Lebègue of ca. 1395 recalls Cp3 (see chap. 2.1e).

TEXTUAL LEGACY (England). Chaucer, *Complaint to His Purse* (Wimsatt 1991b, 79, 82, 113, 206–9; Calin 1994, 404–5).

Amours, tu m'as tant esté dure (*complainte* Cp1)

FORM. Thirty-two eight-line strophes (256 ll.), concatenated in the pattern:

$$\frac{\text{a a a b}}{\text{8 8 8 4}} \frac{\text{a a a b}}{\text{8 8 8 4}} \Big| \frac{\text{b b b c}}{\text{8 8 8 4}} \frac{\text{b b b c}}{\text{8 8 8 4}} \Big| \frac{\text{c}}{\text{8}} \dots, \text{ etc. (masculine or feminine rhymes).}[36] \text{ Each succeeding}$$

strophe introduces a new rhyme, for a total of thirty-three different rhyming syllables.

MANUSCRIPTS.

[3]	**V g**	fols. 31r–32v	[7]	**E**	fols. 13r–13v *Complainte d'amant*
[4]	**B**	fols. 31r (new 48r)–32v	[10]	**M**	fols. 198r–199v
[5]	**A**	fols. 214v–216v	[11]	**D**	fols. 38v–40v
[6]	**G**	fols. 67v–68v	[18]	**P m**	fols. 211v–213r
[50]	**Pa**	fols. 35r–37r			

FACSIMILE (refer to chap. 4.4q). Miniature D2.

EDITION. Chichmaref 1909, 1:241–49 no. 1.

TRANSLATION. Phillips 1982, 185 (beginning); Wimsatt 1991b, 111–12 (strophes 1–2).

DATE. Based on the manuscript transmission, probably late 1350s or early 1360s.

TEXTUAL LEGACY (France). Oton de Granson, *Lay de Plour* in the *Livre Messire Ode* (Poirion 1965, 419; ed. Piaget 1941, 409–14).

TEXTUAL LEGACY (England). Chaucer, *Book of the Duchess* (Kittredge 1915c, 2–3; Phillips 1982, 142 n. to ll. 16–21, 185; Wimsatt 1968, 156; 1991b, 111–13); *Complaint to His Lady* (Wimsatt 1991b, 111–13).

Deus choses sont qui me font a martire (*complainte* Cp2)

FORM. Decasyllabic rhyming couplets, 37 lines (last three lines are on the same rhyme).

MANUSCRIPTS.

[3]	**V g**	fol. 34v *Balade*	[7]	**E**	fol. 15r *Balade*
[4]	**B**	fol. 34v (51v)	[10]	**M**	fol. 202r *Chanson*
[5]	**A**	fols. 208v–209r *Balade*	[11]	**D**	fols. 42v–43r *L'envoy*[37]
[6]	**G**	fol. 68v	[50]	**Pa**	fols. 34r–34v *Balade*

EDITIONS. Tarbé 1856, 36; P. Paris 1875, 406–7 n. xciv; Chichmaref 1909, 1:249–50 no. 2; Wilkins 1972, 176–77 n. 187.

DATE. Based on the manuscript transmission, probably late 1350s or early 1360s.

DISCUSSION. Ascribed to Peronne in P. Paris 1875, 406–7 n. xciv (see also Wilkins 1972, 176–77 n. 187; Imbs 1991, 93). Feminine voice (cf. Poirion 1965, 416; Cerquiglini 1985b, 100 n. 27).

---

[36] On the form, see chap. 5.4, introduction to *Jugement Behaingne*.

[37] Attached to the ballade *Plorez, dames* (B32), which has only two strophes.

En l'onneur de ma douce amour (*complainte* [ballade] Lo230)
Refrain. Mais s'il leur plaist, il me plaist bien aussi

FORM. Ballade; 3 strophes: $\begin{smallmatrix} a\,b\,a\,b\,c & c & d\,D \\ 88\ 88 & 7101010 \end{smallmatrix}$ a:*-our,* b:*-ent,* c:*-er,* d:*-i*

MANUSCRIPTS.

[3]	**V g**	fol. 32v *Balade*		[7]	**E**	fol. 14v *Balade*
[4]	**B**	fol. 32v (new 49v) *Balade*		[10]	**M**	fol. 199v
[5]	**A**	fol. 216v		[11]	**D**	fol. 40v *Balade*
[6]	**G**	fol. 68v		[50]	**Pa**	fol. 48v *Balade*

EDITIONS. Chichmaref 1909, 1:207 (printed as Lo230, although both MSS **A** and **F-G** place it in the separate section of *complaintes*); Wilkins 1972, 68 no. 73.

DATE. Based on the manuscript transmission, probably late 1350s or early 1360s.

J'ay, passét a plus de .x. ans (*complainte* Cp10)
FORM. Octosyllabic rhyming couplets, 269 lines.

MANUSCRIPT.
[6] **G** fols. 71r–71v

EDITION. Chichmaref 1909, 1:267–69, as the *Dit des Mesdisans.*

DISCUSSION. Schilperoort 1936, 29; Cerquiglini 1985b, 100 n. 27. Feminine voice.

Je me plein de celui qui en celier converse (*complainte* Cp9)
FORM. Duodecasyllabic lines, all on the rhyme *-erse* (30 lines), with the following three-line explicit: "Je n'ay pas fait les .iiii. premiers vers, / Mais j'ay fait le seurplus. / G. de Machau" [I didn't write the first four verses, but I wrote the rest. G. de Machaut].

MANUSCRIPT.
[6] **G** fol. 71r

EDITION. Chichmaref 1909, 1:266.

DATE. Judging from the manuscript transmission, this is one of Machaut's last works.

DISCUSSION. Cerquiglini 1985b, 119.

PROVERB (see Hassell 1982). Q6.

Mes dous amis, a vous me vueil compleindre (*complainte* Cp5)
FORM. Decasyllabic rhyming couplets, 38 lines.

MANUSCRIPTS.

[3]	**V g**	fols. 33v–34r		[10]	**M**	fols. 200v–201r
[4]	**B**	fol. 33v–34r (new 50v–51r)		[11]	**D**	fols. 41v–42r *Envoy*
[5]	**A**	fols. 217r–217v		[18]	**Pm**	fols. 213r–213v
[6]	**G**	fols. 69r–69v		[43]	**Mn**	fol. 27r (last 6 ll. only)
[7]	**E**	fols. 13v–14r *Complainte de dame*		[55]	**Bc**	fol. 408r (last 6 ll. only)

VD15 **AFEPm** (chap. 5.13 table 5.3)

EDITIONS. Tarbé 1856, 9; P. Paris 1875, 56–57 (VD15, attributed to Toute Belle); Chichmaref 1909, 1:254–55.

DATE. Early 1360s, based on the manuscript transmission and appearance in the *Voir Dit.*

DISCUSSION (literary). Feminine voice (cf. Cerquiglini 1985b, 100 n. 27). Poirion 1965, 416 (motive of complaint repeats like a leitmotif).

TEXTUAL LEGACY (England). Chaucer, *Anelida and Arcite* (Shannon 1929, 32–33).

Mon cuer, m'amour, ma dame souvereinne (*complainte* Cp6)
FORM. 192 lines, composed of twelve 16-line strophes with the pattern:

$$\begin{smallmatrix} a\ \ a\ ab\ \ a\ \ a\ ab & b\ \ b\ \ ba\ \ b\ \ b\ \ ba \\ 1010104\ \ 1010104 & 1010104\ \ 1010104 \end{smallmatrix}\text{(masculine or feminine rhymes).}$$

Each succeeding strophe introduces a new rhyme, giving a total of twenty-four different rhyming syllables. This is the same strophic form as in *Marguerite*; it also appears in Froissart, Granson, Christine de Pizan, and Chartier; see chap. 5.4, introduction to *Jugement Behaingne.*

MANUSCRIPTS.

[3]	**V g**	fol. 35v–36v	[10]	**M**	fols. 203r–204r *Rime amoureuse*[39]
[4]	**B**	fol. 35v (52v) *Rondeau*[38]	[11]	**D**	fols. 44r–45v *Balade*
[5]	**A**	fols. 217r–218v	[50]	**Pa**	fols. 37r–38v
[6]	**G**	fols. 69v–70v	[43]	**Mn**	fol. 27r (l. 1 only)
[7]	**E**	fols. 14r–14v *Complainte d'amant*[39]			

FACSIMILE (refer to chap. 4.4q). Miniature E5.

EDITION. Chichmaref 1909, 1:256–61.

TRANSLATION. Wimsatt 1991b, 98 (strophe 1).

ACROSTIC AND PATRON. MARGVERITE / PIERRE (strophe 1); see Poirion 1965, 195 n. 17; Wimsatt 1970, 40–41; Fourrier 1979, 74–75. Written for Pierre de Lusignan and addressed to Marguerite of Flanders (Wimsatt 1970, 48–54; 1991b, 33–34, 99). See chap. 1.16.

DATE. Based on the manuscript transmission, probably early 1360s. Late spring 1364 (Wimsatt 1970, 48–49); ca. 1366 (Wilkins 1987, 82).

TEXTUAL LEGACY (France). An anonymous *Complainte amoureuse* in the MS **Pa** [50] (no. 243), *Ma doulce amour ma dame souverainne*, is related to Machaut's Cp6 (Wimsatt 1982, 120, note to no. 243).

TEXTUAL LEGACY (England). Chaucer, *Complaint of Mars* (Wimsatt 1978, 75–76).

DISCUSSION. Wimsatt 1970, passim; Cerquiglini 1985b, 81 (Marian image).

PROVERBS (see Hassell 1982). G46; V46.

Quant Ecuba vit la destruction (*complainte* Cp4)

FORM. Decasyllabic rhyming couplets, 37 lines.

MANUSCRIPTS.

[3]	**V g**	fol. 33v	[7]	**E**	fol. 14r *Complainte de dame*
[4]	**B**	fol. 33v (50v)	[10]	**M**	fol. 200v
[5]	**A**	fol. 217r	[11]	**D**	fol. 42v *L'envoy*[40]
[6]	**G**	fol. 69r	[18]	**Pm**	fol. 213r

FACSIMILE (refer to chap. 4.4q). Miniature E4.

EDITIONS. Tarbé 1856, 10; Chichmaref 1909, 1:253–54.

DATE. Based on the manuscript transmission, probably late 1350s or early 1360s. Poirion (1965, 415) states that this is a *complainte* for the captivity of John of Berry. The mention in ll. 19–23 of an "amis" [friend] traversing the sea, into a distant country full of enemies, suggests the occasion of the departure of the hostages in fulfillment of the treaty of Brétigny in October 1360. Perhaps Cp4 is a prelude to the *Fonteinne amoureuse,* written for John, duke of Berry.

DISCUSSION (literary). Patch 1927, 83 n. 3 (on Fortune). Feminine voice (cf. Poirion 1965, 416).

LINKS TO OTHER MACHAUT WORKS. Related to *Fonteinne* l. 1644 (Hoepffner 1908–21, 3:259).

PROVERBS (see Hassell 1982). B55; F125.

Sire, a vous fais ceste clamour (*complainte* Cp7)

FORM. Octosyllabic rhyming couplets, 44 lines.

MANUSCRIPTS.

[5]	**A**	fols. 218v–219r	[10]	**M**	fol. 206r
[6]	**G**	fol. 70v			

EDITIONS. Tarbé 1849, 78–79; Chichmaref 1909, 1:262–63; Fourrier 1979, 330–31.

DATE. Cp7 is addressed to a king (ll. 1 and 34); several candidates have been proposed (cf. chap. 1.10.2b and chap. 1.12.2):

a. John of Luxembourg, king of Bohemia (Wilkins 1983b, 258).

---

[38] Added in a fifteenth-century hand, above the rubric: "*a nostre dame.*"

[39] On the rubrics in MSS **E** and **M**, see Cerquiglini 1985b, 81.

[40] Attached to the ballade *Madame a tout* (Lo222).

b. Pierre de Lusignan, king of Cyprus (La Monte 1932, 52 n. 14).
c. John II, king of France (Lebeuf 1753, 381; Tarbé 1849, xxvi, 78, and 197 s.v. "Tancarville, le comte de"; Mas Latrie 1877b, xvi n. 2).
d. John II or Charles V, king of France (Chichmaref 1909, 1:xliii, lxv–lxvi).
e. Charles V, king of France (Hoepffner 1908–21, 1:xxxv–xxxvii), Machabey (1955b, 1:64–65) also opted for Charles V, followed by Poirion (1965, 415), and also Fourrier (1979, 88–89), who dated Cp7 to the first months of 1365.
f. Charles, king of Navarre (Chichmaref [1909, 1:lxvi] had rejected Charles because he believed that he was in the Midi from 1361–71; nevertheless, documents place him in the Cotentin in 1361, and recent views associate Cp7 with him; see chap. 1.12.2).
Chichmaref (1909, 1:lxv) puts the date of composition between 1364–66, which Machabey (1930, 445; 1955b, 2:64–65, 173) repeats. After 4 February 1352, when Jean II de Melun received the title of the count of Tancarville (Fourrier 1979, 87; R. Cazelles 1982, 161). Fourrier (1979, 89) places composition after the coronation of Charles V at Reims (19 May 1364), and, due to historical situation of the absence of the *grands companies* from the area around Reims, in the early months of 1365; Cerquiglini (1985b, 128–29 n. 36) thoroughly discusses this argument. The manuscript transmission separates Cp7 from the earlier group Cp1–6, and for this reason Cp7 is readily placed in the early 1360s.

BIOGRAPHY. As with Cp3, the many references are best treated separately:
ll. 1–10: addressed to a sire who used to love and treat Machaut well. When the king made him his secretary, he promised to help Machaut if he needed it. On the duties of a secretary to a king, see chap. 1.6.3.
ll. 11–17: the count of Tancarville sent Machaut a hackney in miserable condition, and so he is without a horse (on the count of Tancarville, see chap. 1.15.2b).
ll. 18–31: Machaut would gladly travel to France [Ile-de-France?] to see him, but the way is blocked by pillagers, wind, rain, winter that disturbs his gout, besides, he might fall into a ditch, if he doesn't die of the plague (Cerquiglini [1985b, 128 n. 36] notes that the plague of 1360–61 is meant here).
ll. 32–44: Machaut will never be able to come to the good king unless he has a hackney or a mule, the traditional mounts of the cleric (see chap. 1 n. 149).
On the last line of the complaint, "Qu'assez rueve qui se complaint," see chap. 5 n. 85.

DISCUSSION. See chap. 1.12.2 and chap. 1.15.2b. P. Paris (1875, 404 n. lxxxvii) notes that the *Livres du Roy Modus et de la Royne Ratio* includes mention of a judgment rendered by the count of Tancarville on the advantages of falconry. Jacques Monfrin (Guillaume de Machaut 1982, 141) warns against trusting any such poem for biographical material. The "gift of a horse" theme is too common; see also Cerquiglini 1985a, 25 and n. 14; 1985b, 129.

PROVERBS (see Hassell 1982). D21; E90.

Tu qui vues avoir mon cheval (*complainte* Cp8)
FORM. Octosyllabic rhyming couplets, 80 lines.
MANUSCRIPTS.
[5] A   fols. 219r–219v   [6] G   fols. 70v–71r

EDITIONS. Tarbé 1849, 80–82 as *Le Dit du Cheval;* Chichmaref 1909, 1:263–65; Fourrier 1979, 332–34 (notes, pp. 335–37) as *[Le Dit du Cheval]*.

DATE. Based on the manuscript transmission, probably late 1360s or early 1370s.

DISCUSSION. Machabey 1955b, 1:65 (same horse as Cp7). Fourrier (1979, 89–90) gives bibliography on a related anonymous work; see also Ribémont 1992.

TEXTUAL LEGACY (France). Froissart, *Debat dou Cheval et dou Levrier* (Fourrier 1979, 90). G. Raynaud (1903) edited a work he related to Machaut's Cp8, without indicating chronological priority; see also Meyer's review of Raynaud and Ribémont 1992.

PROVERBS (see Hassell 1982). L108; O40.

VII

The Music

1. The chronology of the music

The characteristics of the Machaut manuscript tradition that allowed development of a chronology of the large narrative poems also hold for the musical works. Again, there is a gradual growth of the corpus of works from manuscript to manuscript, and again there are a few tentative dates that may be attached to particular works along the way. Unlike the narrative poems, however, there is a much larger number of works to consider, and even in the early MS C, some genres already comprise a significant corpus of works (for instance, C contains 19 of the 23 motets). Characteristics of musical style that develop and evolve within a genre, and to some extent between genres, provide some indices for relative dating, although characteristics of style may not be conclusive, and many unresolved inconsistencies remain. The problem of reconciling the chronologies of the individual genres in order to construct one single overall chronology is a central problem for a chronology of Machaut's music, although recently Daniel Leech-Wilkinson (1993a) has made some important advances. The rewards with regard to our understanding of the development of musical style and notational practices in the fourteenth century are great and guarantee continued interest in the chronology of Machaut's music.

It was Friedrich Ludwig who first suggested that Hoepffner's methodology for obtaining a chronology of the narrative works could be applied to the musical works:

> In the large Machaut manuscripts, lais, motets, ballades, rondeaux, and virelais form closed groups.... The size of the groups varies a little, so that for all genres, a large corpus of works can be recognized, already complete at the time of the writing of the oldest manuscript. This corpus subsequently underwent expansion to a greater or lesser extent.[1]

General aspects of the growth of the corpus from manuscript to manuscript are utilized in the early chronologies of Reaney (1952b) and S.J. Williams (1952, 118–19). But it is Ursula Günther who provides the first detailed chronology of the musical works, based on Ludwig's valuable concordance tables of the various genres of musical works, combined with some specific dates derived from the scholarship of Hoepffner, Ludwig, Reaney, and Machabey (Günther 1957, 17–22, 45–163; 1963a). She utilizes the results to isolate several style characteristics that exhibit chronological development. In its overall outline, Günther's chronology of works, as well as the broad discussion of Machaut's musical style, is unsurpassed. Reaney (1967) presents a related chronology that emphasizes some of the specific dates of works found in Machabey (1955b), and yet also unfortunately misrepresents some of Günther's conclusions. Keitel (1976) challenges Günther's chronology, on the grounds that the methodology underpinning the whole structure, the thesis of the gradual growth of the corpus from manuscript to manuscript, is faulty. But art historical

---

[1] "In den grossen Machaut-Hss. bilden Lais, Motetten, Balladen, Rondeaux und Virelais geschlossene Gruppen.... Der Umfang der Gruppen variiert ein wenig, so dass für alle Gattungen ein grosses, zur Zeit der Niederschrift der ältesten Handschrift bereits abgeschlossenes Korpus zu erkennen ist, das in der Folgezeit dann noch grössere oder geringere Erweiterungen erfuhr" (Ludwig 1926–54, 2:7*).

work by François Avril—first published in 1973—allows a more precise dating of the manuscripts and upholds the basic structure of Ludwig's, and thus Günther's, conclusions.[2]

Günther divides the musical works into four groups, most clearly seen in her table (1957, 46; 1963a, 99; summarized again in 1982, 98). The main structure of the table is distilled here for discussion:

Table 7.1
Growth of the Corpus of Musical Works in Günther's Chronology

	Vir.	Bal.	Rond.	Lais	Mot.	other
1. CI (before 1349)	20	16	—	8	—	7 (*Remede* pieces)
2. CII (before 1356)	5	8	9	2	19	—
3. Vg (before 1365)	5	12	7	4	4	Mass, Hocket
4. M, A, F-G, E	2	4	4	4	—	—

The thesis that the manuscripts represent gradual chronological stages is unassailable, and thus the progression of earlier to later manuscripts, with its growing corpus of works, stands. New with Günther is the breakdown of earlier stages of the chronology, again based on Ludwig's observation that there are really two music sections in MS C:

> a second, as yet unordered series of lais, ballades, rondeaux, and virelais begins on fol. 186v, a series that offers a valuable clue to the time of origin of these works.[3]

The dates Günther attaches to the four groups in table 7.1 need to be reconsidered in light of recent art historical research, which provides some firmer dates for individual manuscripts, and also in light of the makeup and construction of the manuscripts themselves. Günther dates group CI "before 1349" because, she argues, the *Lay de Plour, Qui bien aimme* (L22/16) of 1349 appears as the second composition of the unordered series of works in CII, and thus all works in CI must have been written before this date (Günther 1963a, 100). We cannot however be certain that the *Lay de Plour* dates from 1349, even though it often appears associated with the *Jugement Navarre*, dated 9 November 1349 in ll. 24–25. The lai could well have been written before *Jugement Navarre*. It foreshadows, in lyrical form, the essence of the narrative content of the *Jugement Navarre*, namely, the new judgment in favor of the Lady. But we now know that MS C was being written ca. 1350 (Avril 1973; 1982a). Indeed, Günther (1982, 101–2) suggests that it may have been planned for Bonne of Luxembourg, and that work on the codex was broken off upon her death on 11 September 1349 (see chap. 1.10.1). The unordered section CII would then reflect a new stint of collecting hastily undertaken as the codex was completed for a new patron, perhaps for King John II. In any case, Günther's date originally attached to CI can for all practical purposes stand, though for slightly different reasons from those she originally envisaged.

Group two, the additions in CII, is placed "before 1356" on the grounds that the three motets *Christe / Veni* (M21), *Tu qui gregem / Plange* (M22) and *Felix virgo / Inviolata* (M23), composed ca. 1356, are lacking. The date "1356" is not secure, however. It is based apparently on Ludwig's incorrect date for the Siege

---

[2] Neither Swartz (1974) nor Keitel (1976) meets acceptable scholarly standards; Günther (1982) provides only the beginnings of a critique of these works.

[3] "f. 186' beginnt eine 2. noch ungeordenete Serie von Kompositionen von Lais, Balladen, Rondeaux und Virelais, die für die Entstehungszeit dieser Werke einen wertvollen Anhalt bietet" (Ludwig 1926–54, 2:10b*). In fact, the motets form a separate, third part of the music section in MS C (Earp 1983, 140–42).

of Reims, which actually occurred 4 December 1359–11 January 1360 (see chap. 7.3, commentary on the date of *Felix virgo / Inviolata*). Nevertheless, C must have been finished by the mid 1350s (Günther proposes attaching a pay document of 1353 to its manufacture; see chap. 1.10.1), and so again for all practical purposes her date for the CII group of works can stand.

Günther places group three, the additions in MS **Vg**, before 1365, reasoning that the *Voir Dit*, completed about 1365, is not present in the manuscript, yet the musical works inserted into the *Voir Dit* are found in the music section, ranged with works of similar genre. Recent art historical work on **Vg** places its decoration in the early 1370s (Avril 1982a, 124–25). The process of copying may have begun late in the 1360s, to be completed early in the 1370s; thus, the date for Günther's group three might be adjusted to include an extra five years or so.

Group four includes the additions in manuscripts more inclusive (and thus presumably later) than **Vg**, which I list in table 7.1 in their approximate chronological order. Günther does not attach a date to this group, but it can easily be placed ca. 1370–77. Günther further breaks this group down in the commentary that accompanies her table (summarized in table 7.2); Reaney (1952b; 1967) emphasizes the resulting small stages of chronological development.

Table 7.2
Growth of the Corpus of Musical Works in Later Manuscripts

	Vir.	Ball.	Rond.	Lais
New works in **A**:	V37–38	B37–38	R18–20	L19–21
New works in **G**:		B39–40	R21	
New works in **E**:				L23–24

With very few modifications, then, the outline of Günther's chronology of the works of Machaut can stand. Günther 1963a remains the single most important study of the overall chronology of Machaut's music.

The chronology of the individual genres. Details on the dating of a few individual works are found below in the body of this chapter. A few words on the division between motets and chansons may be of use as an introduction.

Motets. Manuscript transmission is of less help with the motets than with most other genres; at least it affirms that almost all of the motets are early works. The collection in MS **C** implies that at least nineteen of the twenty-three motets date from before ca. 1350–56, the date of the completion of the manuscript.[4] The large group of motets, nos. 1–20, is complete as a unit in its definitive order in MS **C**, though lacking *De Bon Espoir / Puis que* (M4), which I believe was nevertheless a part of the corpus at the time of the production of MS **C**, and only left off by accident due to mechanical problems in the copying of the manuscript (see chap. 7.3, comments on the date of *De Bon Espoir / Puis que*).

The rhythmic uniformity of the majority of the motets discourages the determination even of a rough chronological order for the early group. We have a few dates for individual works: 1324 or early 1325 for *Bone pastor / Bone pastor* (M18), and a very tentative 1335 for *Martyrum / Diligenter* (M19). The last group of motets, *Christe / Veni* (M21), *Tu qui gregem / Plange* (M22), and *Felix virgo / Inviolata* (M23), may be placed in the late 1350s or early 1360s, based on the evidence of manuscript transmission as well as suggestions in the texts (see chap. 1.13.1, and the remarks on individual works in chap. 7.3).

---

[4] Reaney (1967, 92, 95), Clarkson (1971, 178), Keitel (1976, 19), and Hirshberg (1980, 22) seem to have misunderstood Günther's dating of the motets; she did not intend to imply that they were all written between 1349 and 1363, only that the dates 1356 and 1365 are *termini ante quem* (see table 7.1, items 2 and 3).

At the time of the production of **C**, ca. 1350–56, two of the smaller genres of Machaut's works had been grouped in miniature collections, whose order was set for the rest of Machaut's career: the *Loange des Dames*, a collection mostly of ballades not set to music, 70 percent complete in MS **C**, and nineteen or twenty works of the final collection of twenty-three motets. It would appear likely that at this early stage, Machaut had not thought of organizing these sub-collections chronologically; the early date suggested by the texts of *Bone pastor / Bone pastor* (M18), mentioned above, surely indicates that this large motet corpus, no doubt the earliest of the lyrical-musical genres cultivated by Machaut, is not chronologically ordered.[5]

What order is there? The position of *Quant en moy / Amour* (M1) was probably fixed on the basis of the opening of the triplum text, *Quant in moy vint premierement Amours* [When Love *first* came to me], and it is followed by several French motets. The Latin motet *Fons / O livoris* (M9) marks a break in the series, before an unordered series of motets. *Maugré mon cuer / De ma dolour* (M14) and *Amours qui a / Faus Samblant* (M15), both employing iambic rhythms, are more advanced than other motets in imperfect time and major prolation; these and *Lasse! comment / Se j'aim* (M16) are readily comparable with developments in the fixed-form genres that must be contemporary with these motets and might for this reason be placed later than 1340, when I believe Machaut's composition of fixed-form poetry and music began (Earp 1991b). Perhaps these three motets, along with the rhythmically advanced *Trop plus / Biauté* (M20), are Machaut's most recent motets in **C**. The Latin motets round out the closed corpus of motets in **C**, with *Bone pastor / Bone pastor* (M18) and *Martyrum / Diligenter* (M19) preceded by the macaronic *Quant vraie amour / O series* (M17). A few other internal groupings, in the form of some paired motets, are obvious: *J'ay tant / Lasse!* (M7) and *Qui es / Ha! Fortune* (M8) are both in *tempus imperfectum prolatio minor*; as mentioned above, *Maugré mon cuer / De ma dolour* (M14) and *Amours qui a / Faus Samblant* (M15) are grouped on rhythmic grounds; and *Bone pastor / Bone pastor* (M18) and *Martyrum / Diligenter* (M19) are the two dedicatory Latin motets. Sylvia Huot (1994) demonstrates that *Tous corps / De souspirant* (M2) and *He! Mors / Fine* (M3) are complementary literary works. *Trop plus / Biauté* (M20) was doubt-less the latest addition to the motet corpus of MS **C**, composed specifically, I believe, as a memorial to Bonne of Luxembourg (see chap. 1.9). Boogaard (1993b, 28–30) has some interesting further proposals concerning the overall ordering of the motet collection, based on numerical musical relationships and the thematic nature of the texts.

It seems that Machaut's early motets were intended as strophic settings of French love poetry, in a form that Machaut had learned as a student, perhaps, as Leech-Wilkinson (1989, 1:89, 104) argues, from Philippe de Vitry himself.[6] The isorhythmic motet was a primary vehicle for the projection of courtly love poetry at the court of John of Luxembourg in the 1330s. Machaut's cultivation of fixed-form lyrics and music beginning in the 1340s marked a definitive break with the isorhythmic motet as a lyric genre, and his last works in this medium,

---

[5] Besseler (1927, 216–17; table pp. 222–24) treats the issue of range as a factor for motet development: the older, lower range is seen in *He! Mors / Fine* (M3), *Aucune gent / Qui plus* (M5), *J'ay tant / Lasse!* (M7), *Qui es / Ha! Fortune* (M8), *Helas! pour quoy virent / Corde* (M12), *Lasse! comment / Se J'aim* (M16), *Trop plus / Biauté* (M20), and *Felix virgo / Inviolata* (M23), while the other motets have at least one of the upper voices in a higher range, towards the more "modern" discant duet. There are also a number of comments relevant to a chronology of the motets in Günther 1958.

[6] On other models for Machaut, see Sanders 1973, 560–61; Leech-Wilkinson 1989.

composed in the late 1350s or early 1360s, exhibit the dedicatory or polemical function more typical of de Vitry's motets.

Chansons and lais. The most difficult problem for a chronology of the chansons, now worked out in varying detail for each genre, is to cut across genres to provide an overall chronology. The most promising steps along this line have been taken recently by Daniel Leech-Wilkinson in his study of the Mass and *Voir Dit* music (1990c; 1993a). Through an analysis of interpolated chansons new to the *Voir Dit*, composed as work on the narrative proceeded, and thus presumably products of the early 1360s, Leech-Wilkinson has isolated some musical ideas that inform several works of diverse types and genres. The parallels in musical ideas can be extended to the Mass, which can now be placed in the early 1360s with reasonable assurance. Leech-Wilkinson's view of abstract "musical ideas" that reappear in several contexts parallels one of Machaut's primary compositional procedures for the *Voir Dit* text itself: a single textual idea appears in several guises, in the prose of a letter, in the rhyming couplets of the narrative, or in the more abstract verse structure of a lyric. Just so, a single musical idea can appear in several genres.

The lais, like the motets, already formed a large corpus by the time of the copying of MS C. Unlike the motets, however, their order in C is different in many points from the later, canonically ordered manuscripts. Huot (1987, 260–72) provides some interesting groupings on literary grounds.

2. A brief historiography of musical studies

Machaut reception in the nineteenth century. Most eighteenth- and early nineteenth-century scholars believed that no music of the fourteenth, or even fifteenth century, had survived. In his important history of 1801, J.N. Forkel asserted: "Of the earliest practitioners of all, namely of Wilhelm Dufay and Binchois, who according to Tinctoris's account were the first to have exercised counterpoint in France, by all probability not a single note is extant."[7] Just a year later, in 1802, Christian Kalkbrenner supplied a diplomatic facsimile of the opening of Machaut's Gloria that would be reprinted many times. By the end of the nineteenth century, only a few fragments of Machaut were known, for the most part repeated printings of the following works: the *chant royal Joie, plaisence* (RF3), the virelai *Dame, a vous* (RF6), the lai *J'aim la flour* (L2), the rondeau *Dous viaire* (R1), and the opening of the Gloria.[8] Opinions concerning such oddities were even more severe than those voiced against the poetry. The poetry was considered boring and colorless for the most part, but at least a few works were redeemed by historical references, such as the *Prise*, or by titillating biographical confessions, such as the *Voir Dit*. The music, on the other hand, was considered unspeakably inept, the pitifully crude attempts of an amateur.

An enormous advance of the early nineteenth century was unfortunately denied us. A complete transcription of the Machaut Mass made in 1814 is preserved among the papers of François Louis Perne (1772–1832).[9] It was to

---

[7] J.N. Forkel, *Allgemeine Geschichte der Musik* (cited in Bockholdt 1971, 149).

[8] Concerning the gradual reawakening of interest in Machaut's music, it is difficult to go much beyond Ludwig's list of compositions published between 1802 and 1927 (1926–54, 2:5*–6*). Bockholdt (1971, 149–50) discusses Burney and Gerbert, and Wozna (1982, 57) mentions some nineteenth- and early twentieth-century publications and concerts of Machaut's music in Poland. A fascinating brief historiography of the study of medieval music is given in Ludwig 1922–23, 434–36; see also Gérold 1933; Maillard 1954, 4–5, 8; Lenneberg 1988, esp. 31 n. 24; Vellekoop 1990; Owens 1990–91; Switten 1995.

[9] Perne's transcription of the Mass, with related materials, is preserved in MSS *F:Pi 930–31*. See the inventory in Bouteron/Tremblot 1928, 218.

be included with Francisque Michel's two-volume edition of Machaut's poetry, planned for 1831 but never carried out (Ludwig 1926–54, 6b*).[10] Concerning Machaut's Mass, Perne wrote the following:

> There is no denying that the harmony of this Mass offers no charm to a practiced ear. Its effect is hard and savage; at every turn the sound is betrayed by false relations, by parallel fifths and octaves and by passing tones that proceed by skips. The foundation of this harmony is composed of nothing but fourths, fifths, and octaves. Rarely a third or a sixth appears to soften the harshness—if I dare to call it thus—that results from such a bizarre assemblage. Let us add that the rhythm of this composition is worth no more than the harmony. Thus must moderns judge such monstrosities; but if we look back to the time when this composition was made, should we not be astonished by the amazing degree of genius required to succeed in composing on plainchant an entire Mass in four parts without employing anything but fifths, fourths, and octaves, and in forming in each voice a melody analogous to the principal chant?[11]

The degree of understanding displayed here—such as it is—is far ahead of Perne's most learned contemporaries. Most scholars knew only a representative sample of treatises of music theory, works that were too rational for a time that valued the antirational in the medieval world; speculative music theory was not welcome to those who sought medieval naiveté. For this age of Herder, with its confidence in the innate genius of the *Volk*, it was the troubadours who represented the natural and naive simplicity that was prized. Raphael Georg Kiesewetter wrote in 1841 that "the troubadours, Provençal as well as French, following natural feeling in their songs, and not confused by scholastic rubbish, invented melodies and rhythms that surely would never have occurred to the learned musicians of that time."[12]

Machaut occupied an ambiguous position in such a history. On the one hand, scholars praised the style of his monophonic works, suitably *volksmäßig* [popular]. The two examples published by Auguste Bottée de Toulmon in 1836—part of the opening stanza of *J'aim la fleur* (L2) and the refrain of *Dame,*

---

[10] Fallows (1977a, 289) reports that Perne performed the "singularly useless" task of transcribing Gluck's *Iphigénie en Tauride* into ancient Greek notation. MS *F:Pi 929* contains Perne's transcription of Act 1, and the first and fourth scenes of Act 3, not the whole opera. Beautifully copied full scores in modern notation and Greek notation—always with the French text underlaid—appear on opposite pages.

[11] "On ne saurait disconvenir que l'Harmonie de cette Messe n'offre aucun charme à une oreille exercée, L'Effet en est dur et sauvage, à chaque instant le ton s'y trouve trahi par les fausses relations, par les quintes et les Octaves de Suite, et par les notes de passage qui marchent par saut. Le fond de cette Harmonie n'est composé que de quinte, quarte et octave. Rarement une tierce ou une sixte viennent adoucir l'asperité, si j'ose le dire ainsi, qui resulte d'un assemblage aussi bizarre. Ajoutons que le Rhtme de cette Composition ne vaut pas mieux que l'Harmonie. C'est ainsi que les modernes doivent juger de pareilles monstruosités; mais si nous nous reportons aux temps où cette composition a été faite, ne devons nous pas être étonnés des efforts prodigieux de combinaisons qu'il a fallu pour parvenir a composer sur le Plainchant une messe entière à Quatre Parties, en n'employant que des quintes, des quartes et des octaves, et former dans chacune d'elles un chant qui ait de l'analogie avec le chant principal" (MS *F:Pi 931*, p. 97).

[12] "Die Troubadours, Provenzalen sowohl als Franzosen, in ihren Gesängen dem natürlichen Gefühl folgend, und unverwirrt durch scholastischen Plunder, erfanden Melodien und Rhythmen, auf welche damals die gelehrten Musiker gewiss nie verfallen wären" (Kiesewetter, *Die Verdienste der Niederländer um die Tonkunst*, quoted in Kneif 1964, 132).

a vous (RF6)—were reproduced in many subsequent studies. Kiesewetter, for instance, noted that later "Contrapunctisten von *métier*"—such as Machaut—did not scorn the writing of simple songs for one voice without accompaniment (Kiesewetter 1841, 9). On the other hand, the style of Machaut's polyphony was damned as unnatural, crude, and crabbed, in short, learned. Kiesewetter aimed at the polyphony of Landini and Machaut when he wrote, again in 1841: "It seems completely impossible that such compositions were ever heard by those who had a taste only for simple song and were accustomed to take delight in it: they were probably only written for a closed society of school pedants, or for those who were determined enough and had enough self-denial, to be considered connoisseurs of the 'new art' even at the cost of their ears."[13] Having marked the parallel fifths and sevenths in his transcription of *Dous viaire* (R1), Kiesewetter, in a state of apparent disgust, could do no more than quote Cicero's "O tempora! O mores!" The example with its annotation was taken over unchanged by August Wilhelm Ambros—Kiesewetter's nephew— for volume 2 of his *Geschichte der Musik* of 1864, a work path breaking for the historiography of music from 1400–1650, but which offered no advances for the earlier period (Ambros 1891, 374–75).

Kiesewetter had demonstrated that Italy was not the land of origin of all music, as many had thought, and that the Netherlanders of the fifteenth and early sixteenth century had made important contributions (Kneif 1964, 131 and n. 20). But that was as far back as he dared go. The perceived harmonic and contrapuntal roughness of earlier music only served to prove the point that polyphonic music did not really begin until the fifteenth century, with the compositions of Guillaume Dufay, exhibiting smooth dissonance treatment, predilection for consonant thirds and sixths, and cadence structures that were more recognizably tonal.[14] Kiesewetter illustrated his view of music history with his "Gallery of Contrapuntists" (1847). The exhibition proper began with Dufay and the Netherlanders, Josquin and Isaac, while he relegated the polyphony of Adam de la Halle and Machaut to the "Vorsaal," the vestibule. Even late in the nineteenth century, in spite of impressive knowledge of medieval art, architecture and literature, medieval music was still considered to exhibit a primitive state.[15]

Twentieth-century editions. Work on Machaut's music began in earnest at the very beginning of the twentieth century, first in 1904 with Johannes Wolf's *Geschichte der Mensuralnotation*, which included the Kyrie I, Christe, Kyrie II and Credo (lacking the Amen) in diplomatic facsimile and transcription. Wolf's editions served scholars (e.g., Riemann 1905; M. Schneider 1931) for a number of years. The earliest performances of his music followed.[16]

---

[13] "Es scheint ganz unmöglich, dass solche Compositionen dort, wo man nur für das einfache Lied Sinn hatte und daran sich zu ergötzen gewöhnt war, jemals zum Anhören gebracht worden seien: sie waren wohl nur für eine geschlossene Gesellschaft von Schul-Pedanten geschrieben, oder für solche, die entschlossen waren, und Selbstverläugnung genug hatten, auf Kosten ihrer Ohren für Kenner der *'neuen Kunst'* gelten zu wollen" (Kiesewetter 1841, 10; partially quoted in Pelinski 1975, 62). Cf. also Kiesewetter 1843.

[14] As Bockholdt (1971, 150) notes, until F.X. Haberl's researches, Dufay was thought to have been active in Rome in 1380 and to have died there in 1432.

[15] See Ficker 1929, 483. In 1875, Paulin Paris eloquently apologized for Machaut's music (1875, xxxv).

[16] Guelliot (1914, 306–7) reports on a 29 December 1917 concert of "motets, chansons baladées" by the Société Française de Musicologie and a 9 January 1918 lecture by Henry Quittard, after which a soloist performed fourteen pieces, sometimes accompanied by one or two instruments. On a 1918 performance of parts of the Mass, see chap. 8.4 n. 15.

In the meantime, the travels of the German music historian Friedrich Ludwig had laid the foundation for the publication of the complete works of Machaut. In the quarter-century from 1899 to 1925, Ludwig visited libraries throughout Europe, carefully copying sources of medieval polyphony by hand, later to transcribe them in his study at home in Strasbourg, and after World War I in Göttingen. This exercise laid the foundation for an unparalleled knowledge of the music of the twelfth through the fourteenth century in France, Italy, and Germany.[17] The essential part of Ludwig's work on Machaut, including studies of the manuscript sources, incipit catalogues of the music in the principal manuscripts, a copy of the original notation from MS F-G, the collation of the music with MS A, and transcription of the music into modern notation was finished between 1900 and 1903. The most important later addition to this work was the collation of the copies of the music from MS F-G with the manuscript of the marquis de Vogüé (Vg), a source he saw for a total of about thirty hours on eight occasions between 15 and 28 April 1910. As he explained, this was enough time to collate all of the music, and most of the texts set to music (Ludwig 1926–54, 9b*).

The first publication of Ludwig's musical transcriptions of Machaut began in 1911 with the seven lyrical-musical insertions to the *Remede* in an appendix to Hoepffner's volume 2 of the narrative poems. Ludwig's edition of the complete musical works of Machaut began to appear in 1926, with the ballades, rondeaux, and virelais. Volume 2, the introduction to the edition (1928), with studies of the manuscripts, remains essential for scholars of French and Italian music of the fourteenth century. Volume 3, the motets, followed in 1929. After Ludwig's death in 1930, his student Heinrich Besseler completed the editorial work on the lais and the Mass. We learn from Besseler's afterword to volume 4 that the plates for the volume were destroyed in an allied bombing raid on Leipzig in 1943; the volume was reset from a single set of proof sheets that had been run off previously and the volume finally appeared in 1954, more than fifty years after Ludwig's original transcription of the Mass, a manuscript dated 16 November 1903.[18] By 1954, several scholars, impatient for the completion of Ludwig's edition, had already published their own editions of the Mass (Chailley 1948; Machabey 1948; de Van 1949; Hübsch 1953).

Ludwig's Machaut edition aspires to a level of philological detail rarely seen in editions of music (cf. Bockholdt 1971). It is not absolutely complete in its listings of variants—for instance, except for some individual copies of unique works in MSS C and E, Ludwig only had an incipit catalogue copied from these manuscripts available for the comparison of readings. Ludwig's utilization of the musically excellent MS Vg—inaccessible to scholars today except on film—makes his edition a particularly important witness.

---

[17] With characteristic attention to detail, Ludwig charted his travels in a handwritten document of 1913 entitled "Meine Studienreisen," subsequently brought up to date through 1925 (Göttingen, Niedersächsische Staats- und Landesbibliothek, Nachlass Ludwig, Kasten xxxiii). By 4 May 1913, 149 of the 435 manuscripts he had studied up until then were in French libraries, including 120 at the Bibliothèque Nationale alone.

[18] I am not certain how much of the editorial work for the final volume was completed by Besseler. He states in his afterword to vol. 4 that for the Mass and lais, "die eigentliche Redaktionsarbeit war noch zu tun." This may mean merely that the critical notes needed to be written in proper form. Ludwig did a great deal of work on the Mass that is still found in the Nachlass Ludwig at Göttingen, but there are no transcriptions into modern notation of his copies of the original notation of the lais; perhaps Besseler retained them.

In 1956, Leo Schrade published another edition of Machaut's complete musical works for the series Polyphonic Music of the Fourteenth Century. It is totally dependent upon Ludwig. In fact, except for the use of modern clefs and barring by *tempus* in the chansons, making the music vastly easier to read, it is usually inferior to Ludwig's edition. Schrade's text underlay is not trustworthy (Earp 1983, 222–27), and his edition provides far less information on accidentals. Its shortcomings soon became known to scholars—though unfortunately not to performers—largely through the work of Richard Hoppin and Ursula Günther. Today, it is clear that there are errors in both Ludwig's and Schrade's transcriptions of the *Lay de Confort, S'onques* (L17/12), the *Lay de Consolation, Pour ce que plus* (L23/17), *En demantant* (L24/18), *Trop plus / Biauté* (M20), *Dous amis, oy* (B6), *Ne pensez pas* (B10), *Esperance* (B13), *Sanz cuer m'en / Amis / Dame* (B17), *Donnez, signeurs* (B26), *Une vipere* (B27), *Je puis trop* (B28), and *Rose, lis* (R10); minor adjustments need to be made to many other works.[19]

Machaut reception in the twentieth century. After the perfection of contrapuntal voice leading principles brought about in the course of the sixteenth century, and the perfection of the system of tonality brought about in the course of the seventeenth century, there was little room for the appreciation of other systems of musical organization. The dissolution of tonality and tonal counterpoint in serious music was necessary before scholars could seriously study and appreciate music written before the consolidation of that system. This thought is stated eloquently by the composer George Perle (1948, 176):

> The enlargement of our musical understanding to include these wonderful works of many centuries ago is one of the ways that history has of compensating us for bringing us into a world at a time of ferment and strife, of negation and revolution, when fundamental principles, whose immutable government of musical structure had been considered forever assured, are being overthrown.[20]

Arnold Schoenberg, in his well-known essay "Brahms the Progressive," characterized his own music, attacked as radical and decadent, as a logical development of the great tradition of German music history reaching back through Brahms to Beethoven, Haydn and Mozart. Schoenberg provided himself with a respectable historical pedigree, tempering the truly radical aspects of his musical innovations by prefiguring them in Brahms. By the mid twentieth century, composers had to seek elsewhere for historical authority. Following the lead of Schoenberg's pupil Anton Webern, the most progressive serial composers of the late 1940s and early 1950s sought ever-more complex manipulations of structural parameters in their music. Some sought historical precedents, and found them in Machaut's Mass and isorhythmic motets. Indeed, the Mass was published complete for the first time in 1948 (the same year as Perle's analytical article) by both Machabey and Chailley, and in 1949

---

[19] Schrade's printing of the residual text of the virelais implies a double repeat of the refrain between stanzas, an error which has spoiled many a recorded performance (see chap. 8.2). Further comments on editorial procedure in the editions of Ludwig and Schrade may be found in Hoppin 1958; 1960; Günther 1962–63, 24–25; Bockholdt 1971; Boorman 1977a.

[20] Even earlier, Ludwig exhibited a very modern view of the music; see, for example, 1902–3, 39–40, 69; 1904–5, 620, 633 n. 1; and subsequently Besseler (1924–25, 46) and Ficker (1929, 486). A reactionary view is also seen. In the middle part of the century, Armand Machabey (1928; 1955a) sought to extend the legitimacy of Machaut's music by tracing the genesis of tonal cadences to a particular cadence in Machaut's ballade *Il m'est avis* (B22). The third in the final cadence, which positively delighted Machabey, is found in one manuscript and rests on an error.

by de Van, followed in 1950 by Otto Gombosi's important analysis in *The Musical Quarterly*. The unspeakable crudeness of the harmonic aspects of the work by nineteenth-century conceptions of tonality were now seen as a positive virtue. Even more important, *color* and *talea* in isorhythm—the independent structuring of pitch and rhythm not even discovered in medieval music until the early twentieth century—provided a clear analogy to the expanded parameters of serial manipulation in the music of Ernst Krenek, Wolfgang Fortner, Olivier Messiaen, Milton Babbitt, Karel Goeyvaerts, Pierre Boulez, Karlheinz Stockhausen, and others.[21] The idea that pitch and rhythm could be manipulated separately and laid out in advance—one aspect of medieval "successive composition"—was a particularly apt parallel to the compositional procedures of the avant garde of the early 1950s. Pierre Boulez speaks to this:

> For the most rational attitude to rhythm in our western music one must turn to Philippe de Vitry, Guillaume de Machaut, and Guillaume Dufay. Their isorhythmic motets are decisive testimony to the architectural value of rhythmic structures in relation to the strictly different sequences implied by the cadences.... We can see from this—something unthinkable to many listeners and even many composers of our day— that the rhythmic structure of these motets preceded the actual writing. Not only is there a phenomenon of dissociation, but an actual procedure directly contrary to that which we observe in the history of western music from the seventeenth century on" (Boulez 1991, 109).

A concert series organized by the young Boulez in 1954 included three levels of activity, the reference level, the educational level, and the level of research or discovery. The reference level was "to include works which, either in their stylistic leanings or as concepts, have a particular relevance for our own time; hence the isorhythmic motets of Machaut and Dufay, the chromaticism of Gesualdo and the formal inspiration of *The Musical Offering* by Johann Sebastian Bach" (quoted in Jameux 1991, 61). Zenck (1990, 337), in his recent study of the serial composers of the early 1950s, even suggests "that the principles of construction of the isorhythmic motet were just as fundamental for the constitution and formation of early serial music as the compositional appropriation of Webern's row technique." Thus, part of the twentieth century's stake in Machaut—particularly in the Mass and motets—is the realization that it comes closer to the most progressive music of our own time than any music of the common practice period.[22]

The last forty years have seen the publication of a vast amount of detailed critical material on Machaut's music. Since the body of this chapter treats each of Machaut's musical works separately, I provide here an overview of scholarly works on his music as an introduction to the more narrowly focused discussions of individual pieces.

---

[21] Boulez and Goeyvaerts learned of Machaut through the analysis courses taught by their teacher Messiaen in the late 1940s (Zenck 1990, 340 n. 22). Boulez considers Machaut "one of the greatest composers of all time.... The music of Machaut displays a quite remarkable complexity, subtlety, and refinement; he was a complete master, as much of melodic as of rhythmic counterpoint, his work is a landmark in the evolution of European music" (Boulez 1991, 229). On isorhythmic technique in Wolfgang Fortner's cantata *The Creation*, see Kühn 1973, 110–12. On Machaut and Stockhausen, see Angiolini 1987. On Machaut and Stravinsky, see Briner 1960 and H. Weber 1987.

[22] Although it is often said that Stravinsky's Mass of 1943–47 was influenced by Machaut's Mass, Stravinsky himself denied it (Stravinsky/Craft 1962). Stravinsky apparently ordered a copy of Ludwig's edition of Machaut in 1954 (Stravinsky 1985); cf. Chailley 1960, 779.

General surveys. For a recent brief overview of music in fourteenth-century France, see Leech-Wilkinson 1990a, or the excellent older surveys by Reaney (1960a; 1960b). The best brief introduction to Machaut's musical works is the chapter in Hoppin's survey of medieval music (1978b, chap. 17). Reaney's book (1971) also provides an introduction to each of the musical genres cultivated by Machaut. The only detailed book-length treatment of Machaut's entire musical corpus is Machabey's monograph (1955b).[23]

With the exception of the many pioneering studies of Gilbert Reaney, especially of Machaut's secular works, Germans have led the way until recently with critical studies of the music. The work of Ursula Günther is particularly important in this regard, along with individual studies by Reichert (1956) and Eggebrecht (1962–63; 1968). More recently, studies completed in the 1960s and 1970s by Martinez, Dömling, and Kühn have laid the foundation for the excellent critical stylistic studies of Arlt, Leech-Wilkinson, and Fuller. Three broad areas have seen the most attention in recent years: harmonic analysis, compositional procedure, and text-music relationships.

Harmonic analysis. Many earlier analyses of Machaut's harmonic and dissonance technique either drew upon traditional terminology or were hampered by anachronistic tonal or modal expectations (Machabey 1928; Reaney 1953; Machabey 1955a; 1955b; Harman 1958; Oana-Pop 1966; Junger 1967; Reaney 1968; Heinz 1976; Covington 1978; exceptional in this regard is Reichert 1962). Dahlhaus (1982) questioned such undertakings, and more recently, concepts of prolongation—inspired by the work of the German music theorist Heinrich Schenker (1868–1935) on music of the common-practice period—have been found useful for the analysis of fourteenth-century melody and harmony. Elaboration of a background structural framework is implied not only in the typical motet texture—fast moving diminutions in the upper voices over a slow harmonic rhythm in the lower voice or voices—but also in the "displacement technique" employed in Machaut's later chansons, and first discussed by Reaney (1953, 132, 141–44; 1971, 44–45; see also Crocker 1966, 129). More recently, Leech-Wilkinson and Fuller ground their use of voice-leading reduction analysis in the fourteenth-century music theory of Petrus *palma ociosa* (dated 1336) and Johannes Boen (dated 1357).[24]

Questions of harmony, or more generally of "sonority," have been a major subject of investigation in recent years for the motet, balancing out the earlier

---

23 Other recent surveys include Gallo 1985, Yudkin 1989, and Wilson 1990b. The first comprehensive overview of fourteenth-century music was Ludwig 1902–3; some later surveys and dictionary articles include Wooldridge 1905 (rev. 1929); Gastoué 1922; Ludwig 1930; Besseler 1931; Machabey 1931; Gérold 1932; Wooldridge 1932; Gérold 1936; Reese 1940; Borren 1946; Handschin 1948; Besseler 1949–15, 707–17; Chailley 1950; Reaney 1952a; S.J. Williams 1952, 35–62; Machabey 1954; 1957; Maillard 1957; Harman 1958; Machabey 1958; Schrade 1959; Chailley 1960; Machabey 1960; Reaney 1960a; 1960b; 1960d; Gagnepain 1961; Reaney 1961; Morgan 1963; Machabey 1964; Seay 1965; Crocker 1966, 121–29; Machabey 1966; Pirrotta 1966; Flutre/Reaney 1967; Ballif 1969; Machabey 1970; Chailley 1972; Bridgman 1973; Boorman 1977b; Obniska 1977; Pryer 1977; Wilkins 1977; Caldwell 1978; E. Pulido 1978a; 1978b; Wilkins 1979, 9–23; Reaney 1980a; Obniska 1983; Pirrotta 1983; Pryer 1983; Earp 1986; Machabey/Capriolo 1986; S.J. Williams 1987; Hughes 1989; Eggebrecht 1991. There is a good list of older surveys, with additional references, in Günther 1957, 3 n. 12. For Machaut's own view of the role of music in his art, see Lukitsch 1983, 263–69; Lanoue 1984. Winn (1981) provides a general account of the aesthetics of motets and chansons.

24 See Leech-Wilkinson 1984; 1990c; 1993a; Fuller 1986; 1987a; 1991; 1992a; 1992b, 229–30; Hughes 1989, 241–46; Eggebrecht 1991, 238–40. Sachs (1974, 140–54) treats the fourteenth-century doctrine of *contrapunctus diminutus*.

emphasis on rhythmic aspects. Two ideas have been especially influential: Crocker's study (1966, esp. p. 126) of the use of dissonance to produce a sense of harmonic progression or direction in medieval counterpoint— applicable to both chanson and motet—and Eggebrecht's analysis (1968) of an "isoharmonic" plan in *Fons / O livoris* (M9). These studies have laid the foundations for the analyses of Kühn (1973),[25] Pelinski (1975), and Leech-Wilkinson (1989, 1:116, 127, 134–37; 1990c; 1993a, 45), recently systematized in Fuller's studies of sonority in Machaut (1986; 1990; 1992b). Most recently, Arlt (1993) has written of the "neue Klanglichkeit" (new sonority) in Machaut that distinguishes him from his contemporaries. The new conception also expresses itself in recent trends in performance practice, notably in the homogeneous sonorities of the Gothic Voices, directed by Christopher Page (Page 1993, 40–42; see below, chap. 8.2).

Many older analyses have assumed that the church modes were inherent in fourteenth-century music (Reaney 1959a; 1963; 1982; Hoppin 1966; Hirshberg 1980), but more recent analyses of fifteenth- and sixteenth-century polyphony have taught us to be cautious on this point. Although Grocheio around 1300 specifically noted that modes do not concern polyphony, about seventy-five years later the Berkeley anonymous asserts that the modes are indeed applicable to chansons (see citations in Fuller 1990, 210–12). Scholars have not reached a consensus: Fuller (1990) demonstrates that the variety of musical developmental strategies exhibited in the motets she has studied are quite different from the musical concerns of the modal treatises, while Berger's approach (1992) is frankly modal.[26]

Studies of *musica ficta* in Machaut emphasize to varying degrees factors such as mode, counterpoint, hexachords and solmization, and to the abundant accidentals in the many musical sources.[27] Some recent studies have argued for a literal interpretation of the source accidentals, even when they may subvert expectations: not surprisingly, Machaut seems to call for sonorities and progressions not allowed in fifteenth- and sixteenth-century terms.

Compositional procedure (motets). The priority of the tenor is a basic tenet of motet composition, and in this sense such works are successively composed (Eggebrecht 1968, 194–95).[28] But a more sophisticated view goes beyond imagining the mechanical addition of a motetus and then a triplum. Kühn (1973, 81) proposes a compositional model in which the main sonorities were planned, with the individual measures subsequently filled with melodic formulas that are largely interchangeable, a view also supported by Leech-Wilkinson (1989, 1:140–41). Leech-Wilkinson's analyses often approach the music by considering the choices available to the composer given the preexisting material

---

[25] Dobrzańska (1979b) applies Kühn's terminology for harmonic classification in voice-leading diagrams for a group of motets.

[26] I do not know the views of Lebedev (1988) concerning mode. Although Brown (1987) accepts a less current view of the term "modality" than Fuller, his study provides some ideas for further work in this area. Some other studies of aspects of Machaut's harmony may be briefly listed here. For some further aspects of motet composition, see Apfel 1961, 37; 1964–65, 1:39–41; 1974, 162–65 (dissonances with lower voices; support of fourths). Cadence types in the chansons are catalogued in Margraf 1966; Baumann 1979, 108–9; Hirshberg 1971, 98–104; 1980, 41–42. Apfel (1974, 181–82) provides a dense list of cadence-forming voices.

[27] See Reaney 1955; Allaire 1972; Bent 1972; Hughes 1972; Harden 1977; Hirshberg 1980; Harden 1983; Brown 1987; Cross 1990; Leech-Wilkinson 1990c; Berger 1992.

[28] Ludwig (1926–54, 2:58b*, 60*; vol. 3, notes) and G.A. Anderson (1976) identify most of the tenors.

(e.g., stanzas and syllables of text, number of notes in *color* and *talea*), considering alternative solutions to compositional problems, and explaining the path chosen by the composer (1989; 1990c). Fuller (1990, 213–14; 243–45) provides a most developed discussion of tonal planning, with consideration of the initial importance of the tenor to the self-conscious planning of sonorities in the motet.

Compositional procedure (chansons). Studies of compositional procedure in the chansons have also raised the question of successive versus simultaneous composition.[29] The *Ars discantus* (Coussemaker 1864–76, 3:125) teaches us that chansons were composed successively, by adding a tenor to a cantus voice, while the *Ars discantus secundum Johannem de Muris* (Coussemaker 1864–76, 3:93–94) indicates that in the chanson the tenor was composed first (quoted in Fischer 1961, 49 n. 15). The first scenario—that a text was set to music in the cantus voice, and then an accompaniment was devised, one voice at a time—is supported by the testimony near the end of letter 31 of the *Voir Dit,* in which Machaut speaks of adding tenor and contratenor to a cantus voice composed long before.[30]

More recently, the view of musical composition as always successive has been challenged. One of the earliest scholars to argue for simultaneous conception was S.J. Williams (1952), with further comments by Fischer (1961, 44) and Martinez (1963, 112–13), and developed systematically as a thesis in Dömling 1970. These leads have been followed in important studies by Arlt, Leech-Wilkinson, and Fuller.[31] Close analyses of the music shows that in many cases, a degree of simultaneous conception of the music is the only way to explain the sophistication and complexity of the interaction of the voices.

Text-music relationships (motets). Egidius de Murino (ed. and trans. Leech-Wilkinson 1989, 1:18–24) teaches us that the texts of isorhythmic motets were haphazardly added to the finished musical structure. Detailed analysis of fourteenth-century motets, however, often shows a sophisticated interaction of texts and musical structure (Reichert 1956 is the path-breaking study).[32]

Recently, literary scholars have become interested in fourteenth-century motet poetry, providing close analyses of the "verbal counterpoint" of the texts of

---

[29] For a historiography of the question of successive *versus* simultaneous composition, see Arlt 1982, 200–202, 228; Fuller 1987a, 44 and 56 n. 10; Karp 1988, 66–67. The view of the chanson as a two-voice framework, expanded to three- or four-voice textures in some cases, goes back at least as far as Ludwig 1902–3, 35–38. This conception is central to the work of Apfel (1960, 92–93; 1974, 169–82), who sets great store on alternative, fewer-voiced versions of some of the chansons; see also Reaney 1953, 135–37; Karp 1988, 66. Page (1993, 36–42) dubs this model "architectonic."

[30] See chap. 7.3, literary discussion to *Dix et sept* (R17), item d.

[31] Arlt 1982, 200–202, 231–34, 253–58, 279; 1993; Leech-Wilkinson 1984, 9–11; 1990c; 1993a, 49–50, 55–58; and Fuller 1986; 1987a, 44, 56 n. 10; 1991; 1992a; 1992b; see also Treitler's comments in Gushee 1980, 157 and Gushee 1982, 166–67. Karp (1988) adheres to the earlier viewpoint, though arguing that sometimes the cantus was composed first, at other times the tenor. Despite the title, Leguy (1982) is not helpful for this aspect. Danckwardt (1993, 374–77, 381–83) distinguishes two varieties of 3-voice structure, one more homogeneous than the other.

[32] See also Eggebrecht 1962–63; Kühn 1973, 97–98; Clarkson 1971, 200–281; Ziino 1978; Angiolini 1987; Leech-Wilkinson 1989; Koehler 1990, 1:105–7, 2:25, 28; Bent 1991. Günther (1961) supplements and completes Reichert's study for later fourteenth-century motets. Lühmann (1978, 141–72) studies text declamation in motets compared to chansons.

tenor, motetus, and triplum.[33] Purely literary studies include Brownlee 1991b and Huot 1994.[34] Bent provides a sample of forthcoming work in her 1991 essay, which combines investigation of symbolic and literary aspects of the texts with musical aspects; see also studies by Boogaard (1990; 1993a; 1993b).

Text-music relationships (chansons). Several recent studies have turned to a question that would have been considered unthinkable a few years ago, namely, that Machaut in his own way was as careful as a Renaissance composer with text setting, even to the point of "word painting." Dömling (1972, 301–7) led the way, but seems to have inspired few followers until Arlt raised the issue anew.[35] Now one can also consult Fuller, some occasional remarks of Leech-Wilkinson, and a variety of other scholars.[36] Further, many of Fuller's sophisticated analyses of directed progressions discussed above are relevant to text expression.[37] The opposing view, that Machaut's music operates largely independently of the subtleties of the text, is represented in studies by Audbourg-Popin (1986), and Leech-Wilkinson (1984, 13).[38] The two views are not mutually exclusive; Machaut took text as his point of departure sometimes merely in a general but at other times in a specific way. M.L. Göllner (1989) emphasizes the complexities and varieties of relationships between text and music: Machaut used different procedures in different works. Angiolini (1987) also demonstrates the possibility of a middle ground.

The following paragraphs provide some references to musical discussions that survey specific genres, the lais, motets, ballades, rondeaux, and virelais. For literary surveys, see chap. 6.4a. Studies of the Mass and hocket are given in chap. 7.3 under *Messe de Nostre Dame* and *Hoquetus David.*

Lais (surveys). On the history of the lai before Machaut, including the history of the important lais in the *Roman de Fauvel* of *F:Pn 146* (ed. Rosenberg/ Tischler 1991, nos. 21, 23, 48, 64), see Machabey 1931, 329–32; 1955b, 1:98–110; Reaney 1955–56; 1958a; 1960d; Maillard 1963; 1973; Fallows 1980; Cyrus 1991–92; Tischler 1988. Reaney (1952a, 1039) attributes the *Fauvel* lais to Philippe de Vitry. Schrade (1958–61) relates aspects of Machaut's lais to the *Fauvel* lais and proposes further that Machaut derived the titles of his lais from the *Roman de Perceforest.* Kügle (1993, 313–18; ed. 403–12) finds a fourteenth-century Latin rhymed sequence to St. John the Baptist, *Basis prebens,* comparable in style to the lais of Machaut. For a very late example of a lai with music (early fifteenth century), see C. Wright 1974.

Surveys of Machaut's lais include Gröber/Hofer 1933, 25–26; S.J. Williams 1952, 272–91; Reaney 1955–56; Günther 1957, 120–31, 160–61; 1963a, 111–12; Poirion 1965, 396–406, 409–14; Fallows 1977b, 480–83 (with strategies for analysis); Hoppin 1978b, 403–9; Wilkins 1979, 21–23; Fallows 1980 and table, 374; Huot 1987, 260–73 (iconographical study of lais in MS **C**); Deschaux 1988, esp. pp. 72–77. On the element of *chace,* see Feininger 1937;

---

[33] L. Wright coined the term "verbal counterpoint" in his pioneering literary study of *Trop plus / Biauté* (M20) (L. Wright 1985–86).

[34] See Page (1993, 89–93) for some caveats.

[35] See Arlt 1982, 234–36, 239–52, 258–61; 1983; 1984; 1993, 47–48, 57. Günther's early analysis of text-determined motives and isomelism seems relevant here (1957, 131–49).

[36] See Mulder 1978, esp. 30–35 (this work, in Dutch, has not received the attention it deserves); 1979; Little 1980, 58–59; Dahlhaus 1982, 281–82; 300–305; Günther 1984a; Fuller 1987a, 50, 57 n. 18; Leech-Wilkinson 1989, 1:58, 78, 100, 113; 1993a, 60.

[37] See Fuller 1992b, 254 n. 17 (*De Bon Espoir / Puis que* [M4]), 245 (Credo; *Honte, paour* [B25]), and 248 (*Mes esperis* [B39]).

[38] See also the tension expressed in Wimsatt/Cable 1991, 8–10.

Newes 1987; Kügle 1991, 381–82; Newes 1991b; Kügle 1993, 258–82. Earp (1983, 283–88, 309–26) discusses aspects of manuscript presentation of the Machaut lais.

Motets (surveys). After a brief study of four motets by Ficker (1924–25, 210–13), surveys of Machaut's motets start with the important work of Besseler (1927, 217–229; 1949–51, 707–14). Interest in isorhythmic technique after World War II is seen in Perle (1948, 174–76) and Gombosi (1950, 220–24). Günther (1957, 131–49, 161–62; 1958, 28–35; 1963a, 112–13) focuses on statistical comparisons of stylistic characteristics, and, with Besseler's earlier study, her work provides a foundation for further research. More recent studies that focus on rhythmic aspects include Kurtzman 1967; Dömling 1971, 28–29; Prisor 1971, 97–110, 143–47; Sanders 1973, 562–65; Della Seta 1975; Hoppin 1978b, 410–14; Dobrzańska 1978; Saponov 1978, 31–35; Dobrzańska 1979a; 1979b; Sanders 1980a; 1980b; Zipay 1983; Koehler 1990, 1:93–95, 2:21, 26, 27. See Leech-Wilkinson (1989, 1:9–15) for a fine chronological survey of the most important scholarly literature on the isorhythmic motet.

Refined recent surveys of the stages of development of the motet in the fourteenth century include those by Leech-Wilkinson (1982–83; 1989) and Kügle (1991, 355–74; 1993, 139–258, 282–96). Leech-Wilkinson (1989, vol. 1, chapters 2–3) provides thorough and multi-faceted analyses of Machaut's four-voice motets. The last three motets, *Christe / Veni* (M21), *Tu qui gregem / Plange* (M22), and *Felix virgo / Inviolata* (M23), are also treated together in Machabey 1955b, 2:111; Clarkson 1971, 254; Prisor 1971, 197–210; Ziino 1978, 441.

Chansons (surveys). For literary studies of the various genres of chansons, see chap. 6.4a. Poirion's 1965 book, so important for Machaut's lyrical poetry, includes a section on music, rhythm and poetic accent (1965, 439–47), as well as the large chapter on each of the fixed forms. Poetical features of ballades set to music are treated in Gieber 1982, including caesura, metrical structure, and enjambment, with many examples. Guthrie (1987, 68–69) emphasizes that the poetry of the *ballades notées* is different from the ballades not intended for a musical setting, and Tavani (1985) asserts that Machaut treats the poetry more seriously than other Ars Nova composers.

Although primarily addressed to the question of chronology, Günther (1963a) provides an excellent discussion of many of the stylistic traits of the music of Machaut's chansons. The best brief survey of the music of Machaut's chansons in English is by Hoppin (1978b, 421–32); some other surveys of the musical development of the chanson in the fourteenth century include Ludwig 1925, 418; 1930, 268–72; Apel 1950; Reaney 1952a; S.J. Williams 1952, 180–210; Reaney 1955; Günther 1957; Reaney 1960a; 1960b; 1960d; 1962; Crocker 1966; Hasselman 1970; Apel 1973; Dolidze 1975; Lühmann 1978, 57–61; Gushee 1980, 147–48; Greckel 1981; Arlt 1982; Gushee 1982, 165–69; 173–74; Frobenius 1985; 1986; Plumley 1990; Earp 1991a; 1991b; Hoffmann-Axthelm 1991, 343; Kügle 1991, 375–84; Berger 1992.

For approaches to the melodic and motivic analysis of the chansons, see Reaney 1955 (melodic and rhythmic motives); Günther 1957, 131–49 (text-determined melodic designs; use of isomelism); Damerini 1960 (Italian influence); Hirshberg 1971; 1973–74, 61 (location of melismas); Salop 1971 (melodic design); Fässler 1973 (cadences); Mulder 1978, 79–91; 1979, 61–62; Arlt 1980 (phrasing and mensuration). Fuller (1987a; 1992a) provides some model exhaustive analyses of *J'aim miex* (B7) and *De toutes flours* (B31). On vocal scoring and added voices in Machaut's chansons, see chap. 8 n. 4.

On the subsequent influence of the style of Machaut's chansons, see Apel 1946–47; Hoppin 1957, 117–18; Schrade 1960; Günther 1961–62, 165–74; Hirshberg 1971; Böker-Heil 1989; see also above, chap. 2.4.

Ballades. Musical studies that focus specifically on Machaut's ballades include Machabey 1931, 340–44; S.J. Williams 1952, 211–56; Machabey 1955b, 2:9–57; Günther 1957, 67–97, 155–57; 1963a, 103–7; Salop 1971, 48–49; Hirshberg 1971; 1973–74; Fuller 1987a; Hughes 1989, 431–32; Ziino 1990; Fuller 1992a.

Rondeaux. Machaut's rondeaux are the focus in Machabey 1931, 337–40; S.J. Williams 1952, 256–62; Machabey 1955b, 1:151–72; Günther 1957, 97–115, 157–59; 1963a, 107–9; Salop 1971, 74. See also the interesting analysis in Page 1993, 163–69.

Virelais. Stylistic studies of the virelais include Machabey 1931, 334–36; S.J. Williams 1952, 262–68; Machabey 1955b, 172–97; Günther 1957, 53–67, 159–60; 1963a, 109–10; Salop 1971, 72–74; Arlt 1982, 257, 262–71; Leech-Wilkinson 1991 and a forthcoming study; Weber-Bockholdt 1992. The virelais of Machaut's contemporaries often show very different stylistic characteristics; see Hasselman 1970.

The remainder of this chapter provides information on each of Machaut's musical works. The general layout is familiar from chapters 5 and 6. The categories of information provided for musical works include the following:

MANUSCRIPTS WITH TEXT AND MUSIC. In each case, a source is associated with a number in square brackets, giving the location of the discussion of that source in chapter 3. I have included information on the number of voices in abbreviated form (cantus "ca"; triplum "tr"; motetus "mot"; tenor "ten"; contratenor "ct").

TEXT MANUSCRIPTS. This category also includes information on duplication of a given work in the *Loange des Dames*, or in the *Voir Dit*.

TREATISES. Citation of a specific work in literary or music theory treatises.

FACSIMILES. Facsimiles or diplomatic facsimiles—modern printed approximations of the old notation—of musical works.

EDITIONS OF TEXT. Usually a reference to the edition of Chichmaref (1909).

TRANSLATIONS. Complete or partial translations or summaries. Many recordings of Machaut's music include translations of musical works. I give reference to the discography, chapter 8, in these instances. First consult chap. 8.3 to determine the individual recordings I have reviewed; the list of recordings by record label (chap. 8.8) notes which recordings include translations.

ASCRIPTION. Grounds for ascription in doubtful works.

TEXT STRUCTURE. I have included metrical analyses of all of the musical works, with a list of rhyming syllables.[39] When a strophe is isometric and consistent in its use of all masculine or all feminine rhymes, I have conserved space by using only a single number, e.g., *Merci vous pri* (R3) is in isometric decasyllabic lines with feminine rhymes: 10'AB aA ab AB (capital letters denote refrain lines). In order to convey the relative richness of rhymes in a given work, I give all vowels and consonants that are consistently rhymed. (For *rimes équivoquées*, I provide a single spelling; for instance, the a-rhyme in *Se vous n'estes pour mon guerredon nee* (R7) is listed as "a:-*guerredon née*," although later it is rhymed with *guerredonnee* and *guerre donnee*.) Individual text lines in a motet or in a lai not set to music may exhibit epic caesura, that is, an uncounted feminine syllable after the fourth, accented, syllable of the line, a

---

[39] Reaney (1959b, 39–41) provides metrical analyses for the ballades, rondeaux, and virelais, but he does not distinguish feminine from masculine rhymes.

characteristic normally avoided in lyric poetry, but acceptable in the through-composed motet (Elwert 1965, §87; cf. also Lühmann 1978, 166–67). In lyric caesura, the feminine syllable counts as the fourth syllable of the line (Elwert 1965, §88). Poirion (1965, 442) and Dembowski (1987a) discuss the aspect of epic and lyric caesura. For the metrics of Latin motets, I simply indicate the number of syllables without further comment. Machaut rhymed Latin like French, without distinguishing proparoxytonic rhymes from paroxytonic rhymes; for example, it was perfectly acceptable for Machaut to rhyme *"erat"* and *"venerat"* (*Martyrum / Diligenter* [M19], motetus, ll. 9 and 11).

TEXT STRUCTURE AND RELATIONSHIP TO ISORHYTHM. An important category for motet analysis since the work of Reichert (1956).

DATE, OCCASION. Specific datings of works.

DISCUSSION (literary). Comments and analyses by literary scholars. For works appearing in the *Voir Dit*, I have summarized mentions of a given work in the letters and narrative.

LITERARY ANTECEDENTS. Studies that discuss Machaut's literary sources for a given work. Little has been done on this aspect, a difficult undertaking for lyrical works.

TEXTUAL LEGACY (England or France). Studies of the influence of a particular work on the poetry of later authors.

TENOR SOURCE. An important aspect of motet analysis, inasmuch as the themes of the upper voices often play off the theme of the tenor.

EDITIONS OF MUSIC. Usually a reference to the critical editions of Ludwig and Schrade. Occasionally, references to emendations or editorial problems are given here. For general studies of editorial practices, see Günther 1957, 26–35; Bockholdt 1971; Lühmann 1978, 66–68.

DISCUSSION (musical). Comments and analyses by music historians, comments and bibliography of potential importance to performers, and mentions of related works of Machaut.

MUSICAL ANTECEDENTS. Studies that propose specific musical models for a given work.

MUSICAL LEGACY. Studies of the influence of a particular work on the music of a later composer.

3. Works in the music fascicles in alphabetical series by title

A Christo honoratus. See *Martyrum / Diligenter* (M19).

Ad te suspiramus. See *Felix virgo / Inviolata* (M23).

Agnus Dei. See *Messe de Nostre Dame.*

Amara valde. See *Quant en moy / Amour* (M1).

Amis, dolens. See *Sans cuer / Amis / Dame* (B17).

Amis, t'amour me contreint. [*Le Lay des Dames*] (lai L10; Schrade lai 7)
MANUSCRIPTS WITH TEXT AND MUSIC (all monophonic).

[1]	C	fols. 181v–184r	no. 8	[5]	A	fols. 384r–386r	no. 10
[3]	V g	fols. 237r–239r	no. 10	[6]	G	fols. 85r–86v	no. 10
[4]	B	fols. 235r–237r	no. 10	[7]	E	fols. 115v–117r	no. 9

TEXT MANUSCRIPTS.

[10]	M	fols. 222v–224r	no. 12	[47]	*Chartier*		
[15]	K	fols. 130v–132r	no. 4 (has title)	[48]	*F:Pn 833*	fols. 176v–178r	
[16]	J	fols. 144v–146v	no. 4 (has title)	[51]	*F:Pn 2201*	fols. 105r–109r	
[28]	Ars	fol. 12r	no. 1	[53]	*F:Pn 24440*	fols. 226r–228v	

LOST MANUSCRIPT.
   [29] lost Paris MS of lais
EDITION OF TEXT. Chichmaref 1909, 2:352–61 no. 10.

TEXT STRUCTURE. 12 strophes, 238 lines:

1a. $\frac{a\,b\,b\,b\,a}{77'3'3'7}\,\big|\,\frac{a\,b\,b\,b\,a}{77'3'3'7}\,\|$ 1b. same ‖

2a. $\frac{c\,c\,c\,d}{3'3'7'7}\,\big|\,\frac{c\,c\,c\,d}{3'3'7'7}\,\|$ 2b. same ‖

3a. $\frac{e\,e\,e\,e\,f}{75437}\,\big|\,\frac{e\,e\,e\,e\,f}{75437}\,\|$ 3b. same ‖

4a. $\frac{g\,h\,g\,h}{7'37'3}\,\big|\,\frac{h\,g}{77'}\,\|\,\frac{h\,h\,g\,h}{737'3}\,\|$ 4b. same ‖

5a. $\frac{i\;i\;i\;i\;i\;i\;i}{5'5'5'5'5'5'7'}\,\big|\,\frac{i\;i\;i\;i\;i\;i\;i}{5'5'5'5'5'5'7'}\,\|$ 5b. same ‖

6a. $\frac{j\,j\,j\,k}{4446'}\,\big|\,\frac{j\,j\,j\,k}{4446'}\,\|$ 6b. same ‖

7a. $\frac{1\;1\;1\;1\;m}{7'7'7'7'5}\,\big|\,\frac{1\;1\;1\;1\;m}{7'7'7'7'5}\,\|$ 7b. same ‖

8a. $\frac{n\,n\,n\,n\,o}{555557}\,\big|\,\frac{n\,n\,n\,n\,o}{555557}\,\|$ 8b. same ‖

9a. $\frac{p\,p\,q}{888'}\,\big|\,\frac{p\,p\,q}{888'}\,\|$ 9b. same ‖

10a. $\frac{r\,r\,s\;\;r\,r\,s\;\;s\,s\,r\;\;s\,s\,r}{343\;\;343\;\;433\;\;433}\,\|$ 10b. same ‖

11a. $\frac{t\,t\,u\,u\,t\,t\,u\,u\,t}{774747474}\,\|$ 11b. same ‖

12a–b. = 1a–b.

a:-*eint*, b:-*ire*, c:-*eure*, d:-*our*, e:-*ent*, f:-*uis*, g:-*ente*, h:-*oy*, i:-*oie*, j:-*is*,
k:-*ière*, l:-*ée*, m:-*i*, n:-*er*, o:-*ray*, p:-*os*, q:-*einne*, r:-*ort*, s:-*as*, t:-*ir*, u:-*aut*

DISCUSSION (literary). Patch 1927, 94 n. 1, 96 n. 2 and Calin 1974, 244 (theme of Fortune); Huot 1987, 265 (feminine voice; pairing of L10/7 and *Amours doucement* [L7/6] in MS C). Hassell (1982, nos. C212, M246) indexes proverbs.

TEXTUAL LEGACY (England). Chaucer, *Troilus* (Wimsatt 1976, 287; 1991b, 148–49, 158).

EDITIONS OF MUSIC. Ludwig 1926–54, 4:35–37 (ed. Besseler); Schrade 1956b, 2:22–25 (critical notes 1956c, 60–61). The music of strophes 1 and 12 is the same, except that strophe 12 is a perfect fifth higher.

DISCUSSION (musical). Machabey 1955b, 1:117 and Reaney 1955–56, 26 ("isorhythmic" construction of strophe 10).

Amour et biauté. See *Quant en moy / Amour* (M1).

Amours doucement me tente (lai L7; Schrade lai 6)
MANUSCRIPTS WITH TEXT AND MUSIC (all monophonic).
[1] **C** fols. 179r–181v no. 7   [5] **A** fols. 379r–381v no. 7
[3] **V g** fols. 232r–234v no. 7   [6] **G** fols. 82r–83r no. 7
[4] **B** fols. 230r–232v no. 7   [7] **E** fols. 112v–113v no. 7
TEXT MANUSCRIPT.
[10] **M** fols. 216r–217v no. 7
TREATISE. Baudet Herenc, *Doctrinal de la Secunde Retorique* (1432); see chap. 2.3.1d.
EDITION OF TEXT. Chichmaref 1909, 2:330–37 no. 7.
TEXT STRUCTURE. 12 strophes, 216 lines:

1a. $\frac{a\,a\,a\,b}{7'3'7'5}\,\big|\,\frac{a\,a\,a\,b}{7'3'7'5}\,\|$ 1b. same ‖

2a. $\frac{c\,c\,c\,d}{75575}\,\big|\,\frac{c\,c\,c\,d}{75575}\,\|$ 2b. same ‖

3a. $\frac{e\;e\;e\;e\;e}{5'5'5'5'7'}\,\big|\,\frac{e\;e\;e\;e\;e}{5'5'5'5'7'}\,\|$ 3b. same ‖

4a. 7*fffg* | *fffg* ‖ 4b. same ‖

5a. $\frac{h\,h\,h\,i}{7'3'7'7}\,\big|\,\frac{h\,h\,h\,i}{7'3'7'7}\,\|$ 5b. same ‖

6a. $\frac{j\;\;k}{1010'}\,\big|\,\frac{j\;\;k}{1010'}\,\|$ 6b. same ‖

7a. $\frac{1\;1\;1\;m}{8'4'8'8'}\,\big|\,\frac{1\;1\;1\;m}{8'4'8'8'}\,\|$ 7b. same ‖

8a. $\frac{n\,n\,n\,n\;\;o}{43343310'}\,\big|\,\frac{n\,n\,n\,n\;\;o}{43343310'}\,\|$ 8b. same ‖

9a. $\frac{p\;p\;p\;p\;q}{7'3'7'5}\,\big|\,\frac{p\;p\;p\;p\;q}{7'3'7'5}\,\|$ 9b. same ‖

10a. $\frac{r\,r\,r\,r\,s}{737375}\,\big|\,\frac{r\,r\,r\,r\,s}{737375}\,\|$ 10b. same ‖

11a. $\frac{t\,t\,t\,u}{3375'}\,\big|\,\frac{t\,t\,t\,u}{3375'}\,\|$ 11b. same ‖

12a–b. = 1a–b.

a:-*ente*, b:-*ir*, c:-*ment*, d:-*ay*, e:-*oie*, f:-*is*, g:-*on*, h:-*ure*, i:-*oir*, j:-er, k:-*einne*,
l:-*üe*, m:-*ance*, n:-*our*, o:-*ourne*, p:-*aire*, q:-*ail*, r:-*é*, s:-*oit*, t:-*ier*, u:-*ière*
DISCUSSION (literary). Huot 1987, 265 (pairing of L7/6 and *Amis, t' amour* [L10/7] in C).

EDITIONS OF MUSIC. Ludwig 1926–54, 4:33–34 (ed. Besseler); Schrade 1956b, 2:19–21 (critical notes 1956c, 60). The music of strophes 1 and 12 is the same, except that strophe 12 is a perfect fourth higher.

DISCUSSION (musical). Machabey 1955b, 1:117 ("isorhythmic" structure of strophe 10); Günther 1957, 128–29 (rhythmic analysis).

Amours me fait desirer (ballade B19)
Refrain: *Que je l'aie sans rouver*
MANUSCRIPTS WITH TEXT AND MUSIC.

[1]	C	fol. 186v	no. 17	3v (tr, ca, ten)	[6]	G	fol. 140v	no. 19	3v (tr, ca, ten)
[3]	V g	fol. 306r	no. 19	3v (tr, ca, ten)	[7]	E	fol. 152r	no. 18	2v (ca, ten)
[4]	B	fol. 304r	no. 19	3v (tr, ca, ten)	[7]	E	fol. 155r	no. 29	3v (tr, ca, ten)
[5]	A	fol. 463v	no. 19	3v (tr, ca, ten)					

TEXT MANUSCRIPTS.

[10]	M	fol. 240r	no. 19		Lo177	CVgBAGMD (chap. 6.4)
[50]	Pa	fol. 38v	no. 115			

EDITIONS OF TEXT. Monod 1903, no. 5; Chichmaref 1909, 1:160 no. 177; Wilkins 1969a, 25–26 no. 15; 1972, 53–54 no. 14.

TRANSLATIONS. Wilson 1990a, 244; see also discography (chap. 8.3 and 8.8).

TEXT STRUCTURE. 3 strophes, duplex ballade. See Gieber (1982, 10) on the short text lines and the rare use of enjambment. Text form is a *sixain* followed by its retrograde (Clarkson 1971, 266 n. 93), as in *En amer* (RF4) and *Fons / O livoris* (M9), motetus. Further brief discussion of text in Ziino 1990, 19–20. $\frac{\text{a ab a ab bba bbA}}{737\ \ 737\ \ 737\ \ 737}$ a:-er, b:-ent

EDITIONS OF MUSIC. Ludwig 1926–54, 1:20; Schrade 1956b, 3:92–93 (critical notes 1956c, 109); Wilson 1990a, 242–43 no. 72.

DISCUSSION (musical). Machabey 1955b, 2:33; Wykes 1956, 58–62 (analysis); Salop 1971, 68–69 (weight of cadences); Kühn 1973, 219–20 (harmony); Lühmann 1978, 175–81 (declamation); Arlt 1982, 258–60 and 1983, 500 (rhetorical reason to allow augmented second in cantus at the text "c'est si folettement"); Karp 1988, 72 (compositional priority of the tenor); Cross 1990, 52–53, 99–100, 231, 259–61, 264 (solmization, tritone, augmented seconds).

Amours qui a / Faus Samblant / Vidi Dominum (motet M15)
MANUSCRIPTS WITH TEXT AND MUSIC.

[1]	C	fols. 219v–220r	no. 14	3v (tr, mot, ten)
[3]	V g	fols. 274v–275r	no. 15	3v (tr, mot, ten)
[4]	B	fols. 272v–273r	no. 15	3v (tr, mot, ten)
[5]	A	fols. 428v–429r	no. 15	3v (tr, mot, ten)
[6]	G	fols. 116v–117r	no. 15	3v (tr, mot, ten)
[7]	E	fol. 143v	no. 18	3v (tr, mot, ten)
[57]	I v	fols. 20v–21r	no. 35	3v (tr, mot, ten)
[58]	Trém	fol. viii	no. 14	frag. (mot, ten)

FACSIMILE. Droz/Thibault 1926 (MS **Trém**); Professione 1967, plate 5 (mot and ten).

EDITION OF TEXT. Chichmaref 1909, 2:511–12 no. 15.

TRANSLATION. Brownlee 1991b, 2–3.

DATE. Use of iambic rhythm rare in motets, probably a late trait (yet still before 1350); cf. *Maugré mon cuer / De ma dolour* (M14).

TEXT STRUCTURE AND RELATIONSHIP TO ISORHYTHM. Both triplum and motetus exhibit regular correlation between text and *talea* structure (Besseler 1927, 223; Reichert 1956, 202). The strophic structure of the triplum helps define a larger *talea*, or "Grosstalea," combining Ludwig's *taleae* I–II and III–IV (Reichert 1956, 202; Sanders 1973, 558 n. 257; Pelinski 1975, 69; Ziino 1978, 450; Bent 1991, 20, 22; Kügle 1991, 370). See also Reichert 1956, ex. 8 (after p. 212), discussed p. 213 (motivic correspondences); Clarkson 1971, 267, 271 (strophic structure of triplum); Lühmann 1978, 163–65 (text structure of motetus); Clarkson 1971, 286–87, 291 and Bent 1991, 20–23 (declamation rate of triplum and motetus); Ziino 1978, 444–45 (text structure of triplum and motetus).

Triplum: aab aab cccb ccbcb cccb ddbddb eeeb eebeb eeeb
$\frac{775'775'}{}$ $\frac{7775'}{}$ $\frac{775'75'}{}$ $\frac{7775'}{}$ $\frac{775'775'}{}$ $\frac{7775'}{}$ $\frac{775'75'}{}$ $\frac{7775'}{}$

a:-*oir*, b:-*ure*, c:-*ment*, d:-*iés*, e:-*é*

Motetus: $\frac{abc\ abc\ abc\ abc}{77'7\ 77'7\ 77'7\ 77'7}$ a:-*eü*, b:-*ance*, c:-*oir*

DISCUSSION (literary). Badel 1980, 210; Bent 1991; Brownlee 1991b.

TENOR SOURCE. *Vidi Dominum* [*facie ad faciem*; (*et*) *salva facta est*] (Gen. 32:30) is the beginning of the mode 6 Responsory for the second Sunday in Lent (Ludwig 1926–54, 2:60a*, 3:57).

EDITIONS OF MUSIC. Ludwig 1926–54, 3:55–57 (criticism of Ludwig's analytical layout in Sanders 1973, 558 n. 257); Schrade 1956b, 2:157–59 (critical notes 1956c, 84–85); Bent 1991, 16–19 (with suggested emendation of the ending).

DISCUSSION (musical). Unipartite, pan-isorhythmic. Machabey 1955b, 2:92–94; Günther 1957, 135–36 (melodic design is text-determined); Pelinski 1975, 69 (harmonic structure articulated by sonorities of repose, or "Ruheklänge"; further developed in Fuller 1986, 57–59); Bent 1991 (aspect of number symbolism in text and music); Kügle 1991, 370 (pan-isorhythm). Concerning melodic analogies between *taleae*, see Reichert 1956, 213 and ex. 8; Günther 1958, 32; Ziino 1978, 449; Bent 1991, 23.

Musical characteristics make M15 a pair with *Maugré mon cuer / De ma dolour* (M14). Compare the beginning of the motetus with the anonymous rondeau *Faus Samblant* (ed. Greene 1981–89, 22:64 no. 35; cited in Machabey 1955b, 2:93, n. 535). The three-breve to one-chant note ratio may demonstrate imitation of Vitry's usual procedure, cf. also *Bone pastor / Bone pastor* [M18] and *Christe / Veni* [M21] (Leech-Wilkinson 1982–83, 4, 14). Musical antecedent in Philippe de Vitry, *Vos / Gratissima* (Leech-Wilkinson 1989, 1:110 n. 15; ed. Schrade 1956a, 76–81 no. 7). Stylistically similar to *Petre / Lugentium* and *Apta / Flos* (Kügle 1993, 250–51).

Amours, se plus demandoie. Le Paradis d'Amours (lai L9)
TEXT MANUSCRIPTS.[40]
[1] C   fols. 196r–197v   no. 15
[2] W   fols. 70r–71r
[3] Vg   fols. 235v–236v   no. 9 (has title)
[4] B   fols. 233v–234v   no. 9 (has title)
[5] A   fols. 382v–383v   no. 9 (has title)
[6] G   fols. 84r–85r   no. 9 (has title)
[7] E   fols. 108v–109r   no. 3
[10] M   fols. 218v–220r   no. 9 (has title)
[15] K   fols. 130r–130v   no. 3 (has title; frag.)
[16] J   fols. 143r–144v   no. 3 (has title)
[50] Pa   fols. 44v–46r   no. 137 (has title)

EDITION OF TEXT. Chichmaref 1909, 2:345–51 no. 9.

TEXT STRUCTURE. 12 strophes, 198 lines:

1a. $\frac{a\ a\ ab}{7'3'7'7}$ | $\frac{a\ a\ ab}{7'3'7'7}$ || 1b. same ||

5a. $\frac{i\ i\ i\ i\ j}{7'3'3'7'5}$ | $\frac{i\ i\ i\ i\ j}{7'3'3'7'5}$ || 5b. same ||

2a. $\frac{cdcd}{7575}$ | $\frac{dcdc}{7575}$ || 2b. same ||

6a. $\frac{k\ k\ k\ l}{5'5'7'5}$ | $\frac{k\ k\ k\ l}{5'5'7'5}$ || 6b. same ||

3a. $\frac{eeffeefef}{774747474}$ || 3b. same ||

7a. $\frac{mmn}{7'7'3}$ | $\frac{mmn}{7'7'3}$ || 7b. same ||

4a. $\frac{g\ g\ g\ h}{7'7'7'5}$ | $\frac{g\ g\ g\ h}{7'7'7'5}$ || 4b. same ||

8a. $\frac{o\ p\ o\ p}{1010'1010'}$ || 8b. same ||

---

40 There is no concordance in the MS *F:Pn 7220* (listed in Mudge 1972, 289 and Wimsatt 1982, 104).

9a. $\frac{q\,qqq\,r}{7\,7775}$, | $\frac{q\,qqq\,r}{7\,7775}$, || 9b. same ||
         11a. $\frac{v\ v\ v\ v\ w}{7'7'7'7'7}$ | $\frac{v\ v\ v\ v\ w}{7'7'7'7'7}$ || 11b. same ||

10a. $\frac{s\ s\ t\ t\ u}{7'7'344}$ | $\frac{s\ s\ t\ t\ u}{7'7'344}$ || 10b. same ||
        12a–b. = 1a–b.

a:-*oie*, b:-*ient*, c:-*oy*, d:-*is*, e:-*ent*, f:-*ir*, g:-*ée*, h:-*ay*, i:-*ie*, j:-*our*, k:-*einne*, l:-*i*,
m:-*ire*, n:-*eur*, o:-*er*, p:-*ance*, q:-*oit*, r:-*age*, s:-*ise*, t:-*oir*, u:-*ueil*, v:-*ure*, w:-*ours*
DISCUSSION (literary). Huot 1987, 268. Feminine voice.
TEXTUAL LEGACY (France). Froissart, *Paradis d'Amour* (Whiting 1946, 191; Poirion 1965, 409).
TEXTUAL LEGACY (England). Chaucer, Antigone's song in *Troilus* (Kittredge 1910; corrections in Wimsatt 1976, 288; 1982, 104; 1991b, 159; Windeatt 1992, 120–21).

Apprehende arma. See *Tu qui gregem / Plange* (M22).

Armes, Amours (by Eustache Deschamps and F. Andrieu). See chap. 7.4.

Aucune gent / Qui plus aimme / Fiat voluntas tua (motet M5)
MANUSCRIPTS WITH TEXT AND MUSIC (all 4v: tr, mot, ten, ct).

[1] **C** fols. 209v–210r no. 4   [5] **A** fols. 418v–419r no. 5
[3] **Vg** fols. 264v–265r no. 5   [6] **G** fols. 106v–107r no. 5
[4] **B** fols. 262v–263r no. 5   [7] **E** fols. 135v–136r no. 7
EDITION OF TEXT. Chichmaref 1909, 2:491–92 no. 5.
TRANSLATION. See discography (chap. 8.3 and 8.8).
DATE. Leech-Wilkinson's analysis of the compositional difficulties Machaut encountered in this work indicate that M5 is a very early work: "Machaut might have been forced into this position by being required to base his composition on material supplied from external sources: the requirements of a patron, an occasion, or perhaps even a fellow musician" (1989, 1:89; see especially p. 104, where he suggests that the tenor text, *Fiat voluntas tua* [thy will be done] could be understood as an ironic comment on Machaut's presumed master, Philippe de Vitry; see also 1982–83, 5; above, chap. 1.4; below, "literary antecedents").
TEXT STRUCTURE AND RELATIONSHIP TO ISORHYTHM. No correlation between strophe and *talea* (Reichert 1956, 198–99, 201). Leech-Wilkinson (1989, 96–98, 102–3) notes no correlation in the triplum, but the fifteen lines of the motetus are distributed in the pattern of 10 + 5. See also Clarkson 1971, 262–63 (strophic structure of motetus); Lühmann 1978, 142–56 (declamation compared with ballades); Ziino 1978, 440 n. 6, 444–45, 451 (strophic structure of triplum).

Triplum: $\frac{ab\,ab\,cd\ \ eb\,eb\,cd\ \ fg\ \ fg\ \ hd\ \ ig\ \ ig\ \ hd\ \ jk\ \ jk\ \ ld\ \ mk\ \ mk\ \ ld\ \ no\ \ no\ \ pd}{46\ \ 46\ \ 46'\ \ 46\ \ 46\ \ 46'\ \ 46'\ \ 46'\ \ 46'\ \ 46'\ \ 46'\ \ 46'\ \ 46'\ \ 46'\ \ 46'\ \ 4\ \ 6'\ \ 4\ \ 6'\ \ 46'\ \ 46'\ \ 46'}$

$\frac{qo\ \ qo\ \ pd\ \ rs\ \ rs\ \ d\ \ d}{46'\ \ 46'\ \ 46'\ \ 46\ \ 46\ \ 10'10'}$ a:-*ent*, b:-*ay*, c:-*ueil*, d:-*age*, e:-*i*, f:-*our*, g:-*ée*, h:-*uer*,

i:-*ien*, j:-*oy*, k:-*aire*, l:-*uet*, m:-*is*, n:-*us*, o:-*oie*, p:-*oit*, q:-*il*, r:-*er*, s:-*on*

An analysis combining the short lines into longer lines with internal rhyme reveals a regular isometric decasyllabic scheme, and this is the way the triplum is printed by Chichmaref (cf. Lühmann 1978, 168):

$\frac{aab\ \ aab\ \ ccb\ \ ccb\ \ ddb\ \ ddb\ \ eeb\ \ eeb}{101010'\ \ 101010'\ \ 101010'\ \ 10'10'10'\ \ 101010'\ \ 101010'\ \ 10'10'10'\ \ 10'10'10'}$

$\frac{f\,f\ \ b\,b}{1010\ \ 10'10'}$, a:-*ay*, b:-*age*, c:-*ée*, d:-*aire*, e:-*oie*, f:-*on*

Motetus: $\frac{ab\,ab\ aabb\ aab\ aab\ \ b}{7'7'7'7'\ \ 7'7'7'7'\ \ 7'7'7'\ \ 7'7'10'\ \ 10'}$ a:-*ure*, b:-*ie*

DISCUSSION (literary). Poirion 1965, 198n. (theme of M5, *Pour ce que tous* [B12], and *Se faire sçay* [Lo55] are related), 611 (tenor theme); Cerquiglini 1985b, 60 n. 13 (retrograde relationship of tenor and contratenor as the image of a circle); Huot 1994, 223.
LITERARY ANTECEDENTS. Chrétien de Troyes, *Yvain* (Hoepffner 1908–21, 2:lix n. 2) "Et c'est tout cler que monsignour Yvon / Par bien servir, non pas par vasselage, / Conquist

l'amour dou grant lion sauvage" (triplum, ll. 26–28) [And it's quite clear that Monsieur Yvain / —By serving well, not vassel-like— / Won the love of a great savage lion (trans. Davis 1991, 55)]. In light of an explicit link to Vitry's motets *Douce playsense / Garison* and *Tuba / In arboris* (see below), and the theme of the tenor text, the reference to Chrétien de Troyes's *Yvain* may provide a hint of a master-pupil relationship between Machaut and Vitry (Leech-Wilkinson 1982–83, 5, 20; 1989, 1:30, 97–98). The beginning of the motetus, "Qui plus aimme plus endure" [Who loves most endures most] quotes the beginning of a chanson of Thibaut de Navarre, R.2095 (Ludwig [1926–54, 2:23] noted that it seemed a proverb). The last two lines of motetus, "Tels est amés qui ne le seroit mie / Et tels haïs qui tost aroit amie" [This one is loved, who is unwilling, and that one is hated, who soon will have a lady], may be a proverb (Machabey 1955b, 2:76).

TEXTUAL LEGACY (France). Poirion (1965, 266 n. 78) notes similar themes in Alain Chartier and Christine de Pizan.

TENOR SOURCE. *Fiat voluntatis tua* is related in phrases one and three to part of a *Pater noster* chant (Sanders 1973, 563–64 n. 287), and in phrases two and four to the tenor of *Douce playsense / Garison* by Philippe de Vitry (ed. Schrade 1956a, 72–75 no. 6), discussed in Leech-Wilkinson 1989, 1:91–93 and vol. 2 ex. 19. Anderson (1976, 124 n. 18) sought unsuccessfully for a source among Responsories. See also Wolf 1904, 1:174 (diplomatic facs. of tenor notation).

EDITIONS OF MUSIC. Ludwig 1926–54, 3:18–23; Schrade 1956b, 2:123–26 (critical notes 1956c, 77–78); Leech-Wilkinson 1989, 2:64–66 (critical notes 1989, 1:239–41).

MUSICAL ANTECEDENTS. Philippe de Vitry, *Douce playsense / Garison* (ed. Schrade 1956a, 72–75 no. 6), discussed in Leech-Wilkinson 1989, 1:89–98; a second motet that possibly influenced Machaut was *In virtute nominum / Decens carmen* (ed. F.Ll. Harrison 1968, 95–99 no. 18), discussed in Leech-Wilkinson 1982–83, 5–8; 1989, 1:193, 196 and vol. 2, ex. 66 (ascribed to Philippe de Vitry).

DISCUSSION (musical). Bipartite, with diminution by one-half. The rhythm of the contratenor is derived from the tenor by retrograde. M. Schneider 1931, 41, ex. 5 (isorhythm); Gombosi 1950, 223 (symmetrical rhythmic layout in tenor and contratenor, the "crowning of all symmetrical arrangements"; see also Reaney 1971, 56–57); Machabey 1955b, 2:75–77 (melodic correspondences); Günther 1958, 34 (diminution produces conflicts of tempus; use of red notation based on the model of Vitry); Apfel 1961, 37 (=1964–65, 1:40–41) (sonority problems in tenor-contratenor pair); Prisor 1971, 203 (chart of tenor-contratenor structure); Kühn 1973, 244 n. 252 (rhythmic crab in tenor-contratenor pair is not audible); Hoppin 1978b, 413–14 and Newes 1990, 226 (diagram of symmetrical tenor and contratenor *taleae*); Leech-Wilkinson 1989, 1:43, 46, 88–104 (thorough analysis of the motet); Koehler 1990, 1:102–4 (rhythmic proportions).

Newes 1987, 205–10 (comparison of complementary tenor-contratenor pair in M5, *Christe / Veni* [M21], *Tu qui gregem / Plange* [M22], and *Felix virgo / Inviolata* [M23]); Leech-Wilkinson 1989, 1:131–34, 2:24 ex. 38 (explores the connections between two motets of de Vitry—*Douce playsense / Garison*, and *Tuba / In arboris*—and several works of Machaut—M5, *Hareu! / Helas!* [M10], *Felix virgo / Inviolata* [M23], and the Amen of the Credo); 1989, 1:165 n. 45 (rate of harmonic change compared to several other motets).

Aus amans pour exemplaire (lai L4)

TEXT MANUSCRIPTS.

[1] C	fols. 173r–174r	no. 4	[6] G	fols. 78v–79r	no. 4
[3] V g	fols. 226v–227r	no. 4	[7] E	fol. 108v	no. 2
[4] B	fols. 224v–225r	no. 4	[10] M	fols. 212v–213v	no. 4
[5] A	fols. 374r–374v	no. 4			

LOST MANUSCRIPT.

[30] lost Burgundian MS of lais

FACSIMILE (refer to chap. 4.4s). Miniature C96.

EDITION OF TEXT. Chichmaref 1909, 2:309–13 no. 4.

TEXT STRUCTURE. 12 strophes, 144 lines:

1a. $\frac{a\ a\ a\ a\ a\ b}{7'5'5'5'7'7}$ ‖ 1b. same ‖   2a. $\frac{c\ c\ c\ c}{5\ 5\ 5\ 7\ 5}$ ‖ 2b. same ‖

3a. $\dfrac{ddddd}{55575}$ ‖ 3b. same ‖   8a. $\dfrac{1b\ 1b\ 1b\ 1b}{3'3\ 3'3\ 3'3\ 3'7}$ ‖ 8b. same ‖

4a. 8eeef ‖ 4b. same ‖   9a. $\dfrac{mmmmn}{8\ 8\ 8\ 8\ 8'}$ ‖ 9b. same ‖

5a. 8gggf ‖ 5b. same ‖   10a. $\dfrac{ooooop}{88888'}$ ‖ 10b. same ‖

6a. $\dfrac{h\,h\,h\,i}{5'5'5'7}\mid\dfrac{h\,h\,h\,i}{5'5'5'7}$ ‖ 6b. same ‖   11a. $\dfrac{qqqq\ r\ q}{72237'7}$ ‖ 11b. same ‖

7a. $\dfrac{j\,k\ j\,k\ j\,k\ j\,k}{3'3\ 3'3\ 3'3\ 3'7}$ ‖ 7b. same ‖   12a. $\dfrac{s\ s\ s\ s\ s\,t\ s\,t}{7'7'7'7'7'57'7}$ ‖ 12b. same ‖

a:-*aire*, b:-*mort* (strophe 8 b:-*ort*), c:-*tret*, d:-*our*, e:-*cours*, f:-*té*, g:-*ment*, h:-*ine*, i:-*iner*, j:-*oie*, k:-*art*, l:-*eure*, m:-*tourné*, n:-*tourne*, o:-*tiray*, p:-*partie**, q:-*ueil*, r:-*lie**, s:-*elle*, t:-*lay*
*: Note the distinction between -*ie* rhymes p and r (perhaps the two b rhymes [strophes 1 and 8] should be distinguished as well).
DISCUSSION (literary). Patch 1927, 156 n. 1 (theme of Fortune); Poirion 1965, 412 (theme); Cerquiglini 1985b, 211 (term "soustil," l. 5); Huot 1987, 262–63 (iconography; pairing of L4 and *Pour ce qu'on puist* [L3]). Hassell (1982, nos. F129, R74, T68, T69) indexes proverbs. In this lai, the last strophe is not equivalent to the first in metrical structure or rhyme scheme, perhaps one reason why Machaut never composed music for the work.
TEXTUAL LEGACY (England). Chaucer, *Anelida and Arcite* (Wimsatt 1978, 86 n. 10); *Complaynt d'Amours* (Wimsatt 1978, 72; 1991b, 313 n. 14).

Aymi! dame de valour (virelai V3)
MANUSCRIPTS WITH TEXT AND MUSIC (all monophonic).

[1]	C	fol. 149v	no. 3	[5]	A	fol. 482v	no. 3
[3]	V g	fol. 323r	no. 3	[6]	G	fol. 155r	no. 3
[4]	B	fol. 321r	no. 3	[7]	E	fol. 161v	no. 16

TEXT MANUSCRIPT.
[10] M   fol. 246r   no. 3
EDITION OF TEXT. Chichmaref 1909, 2:583–84 no. 3.
TRANSLATIONS. Little 1983, 217 (strophe 1); see also discography (chap. 8.3 and 8.8).

TEXT STRUCTURE. 3 strophes: $\dfrac{ABAB}{7575}\ \|\ \dfrac{ca\ ca}{6'8\ 6'8}\mid\dfrac{abab}{7575}\ \|\ \dfrac{ABAB}{7575}$ a:-*our*, b:-*ir*, c:-*ure*

EDITIONS OF MUSIC. Ludwig 1926–54, 1:71; Schrade 1956b, 3:168 (critical notes 1956c, 136–37); Arlt 1982, 266 (after Schrade).
DISCUSSION (musical). Machabey 1955b, 1:177–78; Arlt 1982, 266–67; Little 1983; Weber-Bockholdt 1992, 265–67; M.L. Göllner 1989, 64–65 (text/music relationship).

Biauté paree. See *Trop plus / Biauté* (M20).

Biauté qui toutes autres pere (ballade B4)
Refrain: *M'ont ad ce mis que pour amer morray*
MANUSCRIPTS WITH TEXT AND MUSIC.

[1]	C	fols. 159r–159v	no. 4	2v (ca, ten)
[3]	V g	fol. 298r	no. 4	2v (ca, ten)
[4]	B	fol. 296r	no. 4	2v (ca, ten)
[5]	A	fol. 455v	no. 4	2v (ca, ten)
[6]	G	fol. 135r	no. 4	2v (ca, ten)
[7]	E	fols. 152v–153r	no. 20	3v (ca, ten, ct)
[58]	Trém	fol. xli	no. 97	(index only)
[69]	Utr	fol. 29r	no. 13	3v (ca, ten, ct)

TEXT MANUSCRIPTS.

[10]	M	fol. 237v	no. 4		[41]	Wm	fol. 26r	no. 33
[16]	J	fol. 26r	no. 115[41]		[50]	Pa	fol. 54v	no. 168

---
[41] *Balade. De triste cuer. l'amant.*

FACSIMILES. Apel 1953, 359 facs. 70 (MS E); Bank 1972, 38 ex. 12 (diplomatic facs. in score of refrain); Saponov 1978, 18 (MS E); Yudkin 1989, 517 (MS E).

EDITION OF TEXT. Chichmaref 1909, 2:539 no. 4.

TRANSLATIONS. See discography (chap. 8.3 and 8.8)

TEXT STRUCTURE. 3 strophes: $\frac{a\,b\ \ a\,b\ cc\,d\,D}{8'8'\ \ 8'8'\ 881010}$ a:-ere, b:-ange, c:-ant, d:-ay

EDITIONS OF MUSIC. Ludwig 1926–54, 1:4 ; Schrade 1956b, 3:74–75 (critical notes 1956c, 100–101); Harman 1958, 145–47); Kohn 1981, 47 (differently barred and beamed; discussed pp. 46–48). The contratenor, which appears only in MS E, is surely not authentic.

DISCUSSION (musical). The only secular work of Machaut that uses coloration to indicate a change of *tempus*, except in MS E, which uses mensuration signs. Machabey 1955b, 2:21–22 (brief overview); Günther 1957, 96 (syncopation passage); Harman 1958, 144–48 (brief analysis); Martinez 1963, 102–3 (text setting in an unusual metrical structure); Reaney 1968, 63–65 (counterpoint); Salop 1971, 60 (melodic direction in the cantus); Bank 1972, 39, 43 (tempo); Dömling 1972, 304 (text setting in refrain); Lühmann 1978, 222 (declamation); Arlt 1982, 260–61 (rhetorical basis for syncopation); Dahlhaus 1982 (discussion in broad terms of the same passage); Karp 1988, 75 (compositional priority of the cantus); Cross 1990, 265 (chromatic intervals); Koehler 1990, 1:102–3, 110–13 (rhythmic proportions).

Bone pastor Guillerme / Bone pastor qui pastores / Bone pastor (motet M18)

MANUSCRIPTS WITH TEXT AND MUSIC (all 3v: tr, mot, ten).

[1] **C**	fols. 222v–223r	no. 17	[5] **A**	fols. 431v–432r	no. 18
[3] **V g**	fols. 277v–278r	no. 18	[6] **G**	fols. 119v–120r	no. 18
[4] **B**	fols. 275v–276r	no. 18	[7] **E**	fol. 144v	no. 20

FACSIMILE. Bank 1972, 38 ex. 11 (diplomatic facs. in score of beginning).

EDITION OF TEXT. Chichmaref 1909, 2:518–20 no. 18.

TRANSLATIONS. Wennerstrom 1983, 17–18; Fuller 1987b, 108; see also discography (chap. 8.3 and 8.8).

DATE AND OCCASION. 1323 or 1324 (Machabey 1955b, 2:62 and 100–101; he further notes [1955b, 99, 101] that musical resemblances between M18 and *Quant vraie amour / O* series [M17] place them in the same chronological layer). 1325 (Fuller 1986, 68 n. 38; 1990, 202). 1334 (Kügle 1993, 147 n. 15). Probably composed in 1324 for the appointment of Guillaume de Trie as Archbishop of Reims; see the discussion above, chap. 1.4.

TEXT STRUCTURE AND RELATIONSHIP TO ISORHYTHM. Both triplum and motetus exhibit regular correlation between text and *talea* structure (Besseler 1927, 222; Reichert 1956, 201). Both triplum and motetus change strophic forms for the diminution section, a situation unique to M18 and *Quant en moy / Amour* (M1) (Reichert 1956, 205–6, 209; Clarkson 1971, 255). See also Reichert 1956, exx. 5 and 6 (following p. 212), discussed pp. 207–8, 211–12 (irregular strophic structure at end of triplum; diminution section); Ziino 1978, 442, 444, 446, 451 (sequence-like structure of both triplum and motetus); Bent 1984 (compositional planning; comments on Ziino).

Triplum: $\frac{aabccbddeffe\,gghi\,ih\ jjkllk\,mmimi\ nnini\ oopop\,qqpqp}{776776\ \ 776776\ \ 776776\ 776776\ \ 7\ 7\ 6\ 7\ 4\ 77674\ \ 77674\ 77674}$ a:-erme,

b:-atum, c:-erva, d:-ostes, e:-entur, f:-aro, g:-ingit, h:-amenta, i:-ere, j:-utus,

k:-atis, l:-igna, m:-uli, n:-ia, o:-amine, p:-ili, q:-ium

Motetus: $\frac{aabccbddeffe\,ghgh\ ijij}{884884\ \ 884884\ \ 8484\ 8484}$ a:-ores, b:-enus, c:-iorum, d:-enter, e:-it, f:-orum,

g:-estum, h:-igne, i:-ale, j:-egi

TENOR SOURCE. Unidentified. Chichmaref (1909, 2:520n.) notes a resemblance to the sequence *Lauda Sion,* but this includes only eight notes; Ludwig (1926–54, 3:67) rejects the suggestion.

EDITIONS OF MUSIC. Ludwig 1926–54, 3:65–67 (criticism of Ludwig's analytical layout in Sanders 1973, 563 n. 286); Schrade 1956b, 3:4–7 (critical notes 1956c, 86–87);

Wennerstrom 1983, 13–17 (after Schrade); Fuller 1987b, 104–7 no. 17 (based on Schrade with emendations, but tenor rebarred in the diminution section like the Ludwig edition, as suggested in Hoppin 1960, 26). Harmonic augmented second in m. 56 (Ludwig 1926–54, 3:67, Machabey 1955b, 2:100).

DISCUSSION (musical). Bipartite, with diminution by one-half (diminution section is panisorhythmic). Machabey 1955b, 2:98–101; Günther 1958, 34 (diminution produces conflicts in *tempus* groups); Dömling 1970, 68–69 (different sonorities built on recurring tenor pitches); Bank 1972, 39, 43 (tempo); Kühn 1973, 131–37 (harmonic analysis of the first *color*, criticized in Fuller 1986, nn. 25, 37, 39, 46; Machaut staggers the three elements of *color*, sonority, and text, which can take on an "imperfecting" function to attenuate a cadence); Pelinski 1975, 69–70 and table 3 (the pitch *f* appears isoharmonically at the end of each *talea*); Wernli 1977, 19–21 (musical techniques that render the structure perceptible to the listener); Ziino 1978, 449 (instances of complete isorhythmic agreement); Leech-Wilkinson 1982–83, 15 n. 24 (number symbolism); Fuller 1986, 47–55, 61–62 (prolongations and progressions; weights of the cadences at *talea* ends; see summary in 1990, 202–3); 1987b, 109 (brief introduction).

MUSICAL ANTECEDENTS. Leech-Wilkinson 1982–83, 4, 14 (three-breve to one-chant note ratio may demonstrate imitation of Vitry's usual procedure, cf. also *Amours qui a / Faus Samblant* [M15] and *Christe / Veni* [M21]). Related to *Se paour / Diex* (ed. F.Ll. Harrison 1968, 84–87 no. 16); see Leech-Wilkinson 1982–83, 7, 14–15; less related to *L'amoureuse / En l'estat* (ed. F.Ll. Harrison 1968, 108–12 no. 21); see Leech-Wilkinson 1982–83, 15.

C'est force, faire le vueil (virelai V16)

MANUSCRIPTS WITH TEXT AND MUSIC (all monophonic).

[1]	C	fols. 203v–204r	no. 26	[5]	A	fol. 486v	no. 16
[3]	V g	fol. 327v	no. 16	[6]	G	fol. 158r	no. 16
[4]	B	fol. 325v	no. 16	[7]	E	fol. 160r	no. 7

TEXT MANUSCRIPTS.

| [10] | M | fol. 249r | no. 16 | [50] | Pa | fol. 62r | no. 193 |

FACSIMILE. Ultan 1977b, 91 (diplomatic facs.).

EDITION OF TEXT. Chichmaref 1909, 2:599–600 no. 16.

TRANSLATION. See discography (chap. 8.3 and 8.8).

TEXT STRUCTURE. 3 strophes: $\frac{ABBABA}{747474} \parallel \frac{bbc\ bbc}{747\ 747} \mid \frac{a\,bba\,ba}{747474} \parallel \frac{ABBABA}{747474}$ a:-*ueil*, b:-*ir*

EDITIONS OF MUSIC. Ludwig 1926–54, 1:77; Schrade 1956b, 3:175 (critical notes 1956c, 141).

DISCUSSION (musical). Machabey 1955b, 1:184.

Ce qui soustient moy, m'onneur et ma vie (rondeau R12)

MANUSCRIPTS WITH TEXT AND MUSIC (all 2v: ca, ten).

[3]	V g	fol. 320r	no. 12	[6]	G	fol. 152r	no. 12
[4]	B	fol. 319r	no. 12	[7]	E	fol. 132r	no. 2
[5]	A	fols. 478v–479r	no. 13				

TEXT MANUSCRIPT.

| [10] | M | fol. 244v | no. 12 |

EDITIONS OF TEXT. Tarbé 1849, 51; Chichmaref 1909, 2:573 no. 12; Lucas 1957.

TEXT STRUCTURE. 10'AB aA ab AB a:-*ie*, b:-*ame*

EDITIONS OF MUSIC. Ludwig 1926–54, 1:62; Schrade 1956b, 3:155 (critical notes 1956c, 130).

DISCUSSION (musical). Machabey 1955b, 1:162–63 (melodic aspects); Dömling 1970, 69–70 (sonority, simultaneous conception); Salop 1971, 76 (melodic planning).

Certes, je di. See *De triste / Quant / Certes* (ballade B29).

Certes, mon oueil richement visa bel (rondeau R15)

MANUSCRIPTS WITH TEXT AND MUSIC (all 3v: ca, ten, ct).

| [4] | B | fol. 309v | no. 15 | [6] | G | fol. 153r | no. 16 |
| [5] | A | fols. 480r–480v | no. 17 | [7] | E | fol. 135r | no. 5 |

TEXT MANUSCRIPTS.
[10] **M**   fol. 245r   no. 16   [50] **Pa** fol. 34r   no. 105
[49] **Jp** fol. 69r   no. 77   Lo234 **VgBMAD** (see chap. 6.4)
TREATISE. Deschamps, *Art de Dictier* (*F:Pn 840*, fol. 399r; **I** [40], fol. 32r) (chap. 2.1.1m).
FACSIMILE. *Jardin* 1910–25, vol. 1, fol. 69r (**Jp**); *New Grove* 17:664 (MS **G**, fol. 153r).
EDITIONS OF TEXT. Queux de Saint-Hilaire/Raynaud 1878–1903, 7:287; Chichmaref 1909, 1:210 no. 234; Wilkins 1972, 106 no. 219; Sinnreich 1987, 114–15.
TRANSLATION. Sinnreich 1987, 140.
DATE, OCCASION. See the discussion of *Dame, qui vuet* (R16).
TEXT STRUCTURE. $\begin{array}{cccc} A & B & aA & a b & A B \\ 1010 & 1010 & 1010' & 1010' \end{array}$ a:-[*sab*]*el*, b:-*elle*

EDITIONS OF MUSIC. Ludwig 1926–54, 1:64–65; Schrade 1956b, 3:158–59 (critical notes 1956c, 132).
DISCUSSION (musical). Machabey 1955b, 1:167 (melodic rhyme); Günther 1957, 108 (motivic analysis); 1958, 35 n. 27 (*tempus* changes).

Christe qui lux es / Veni Creator Spiritus / Tribulatio proxima est et non est qui adjuvet (motet M21)

MANUSCRIPTS WITH TEXT AND MUSIC (all 4v: tr, mot, ten, ct).
[3] **V g** fols. 280v–281r no. 21   [6] **G** fols. 122v–123r no. 21
[4] **B**   fols. 278v–279r no. 21   [7] **E** fols. 145v–146r no. 21
[5] **A**   fols. 434v–435r no. 21

EDITION OF TEXT. Chichmaref 1909, 2:526–28 no. 21 (the last line of the motetus should read: "Et da nobis tuam pacem").
TRANSLATIONS. See discography (chap. 8.3 and 8.8).
DATE AND OCCASION. Siege of Reims (Leech-Wilkinson 1989, 1:105–7; Markstrom 1989, 29–34; Yudkin 1989, 476); see chap. 1.13. Note that the last word of the triplum is "pace"; the last word of the motetus is "pacem."
TEXT STRUCTURE AND RELATIONSHIP TO ISORHYTHM. Only in the triplum exhibits regular correlation between text and *talea* structure (Reichert 1956, 201, 206; Günther 1958, 33). The distribution of syllables in section A of the motetus defines a "Grosstalea" (Reichert 1956, 203). Leech-Wilkinson (1989, 1:108–13) gives reasons for irregular text placement in the motetus, perhaps due to emphasis placed on the word *Veni*, the principal theme. See also Reichert 1956, ex. 7 (following p. 212), discussed p. 203 (four *integer valor* triplum periods); Machabey 1955b, 2:106 (first words of motetus borrowed from the hymn); Ziino 1978, 440, 443 (sequence-like structure of triplum), 444 (hymn-like structure of motetus).

Triplum: $\begin{array}{l} \text{aabaab bbcbbc ccdccd d dedde e e fee f f fg f fg} \\ \text{884884 884884 884884 884884 884884 884888} \end{array}$ a:-*ies*, b:-*ita*, c:-*erant*, d:-*ortis*,

e:-*egas*, f:-*ator*, g:-*ace*

Motetus: 8aabb ccdd eeff gghh iijj kjk a:-*itus*, b:-*era*, c:-*ficit*, d:-*ia*, e:-*itas*, f:-*amus*, g:-*ici*, h:-*ones*, i:-*ile*, j:-*uli*, k:-*acem*

DISCUSSION (literary). Chichmaref 1909, 1:lxi (the lament on current conditions seen in triplum l. 17 recalls the tirade of the *complainte A toi, Hanri* [Cp3], as well as the complaint of the narrator to the "Roi qui ne ment" in the *Voir Dit*, and the motetus of *Tu qui gregem / Plange* [M22]); Leech-Wilkinson 1989, 138 (Machaut possibly not the author of the texts); Yudkin 1989, 481–82 (text allusions).
TENOR SOURCE. *Tribulatio proxima est et non est qui adjuvet* (Psalm 21 [22]:12) ["trouble is near; for there is none to help"] is from the final melisma of the verse *Quoniam tribulatio* of the mode 2 Responsory for Passion Sunday, *Circumdederunt me mendaces viri* (Ludwig 1926–54, 2:60a*, 3:32, 78; Leech-Wilkinson 1989, 1:108 n. 12; the same tenor is used in *Qui es / Ha! Fortune* [M8]). See also Machabey 1955b, 2:105 (sees a liturgical borrowing in the opening of the contratenor); Leech-Wilkinson 1989, 1:107 (connection of tenor text to the Siege of Reims).
EDITIONS OF MUSIC. Ludwig 1926–54, 3:73–78; Schrade 1956b, 3:13–21 (critical notes 1956c, 88–89); Leech-Wilkinson 1989, 2:67–70 (critical notes, 1:242–44).

DISCUSSION (musical). *Introitus*, then bipartite, with diminution by one-half. Besseler 1924–25, 48 and Haas 1931, 95–96 (early performance at Hamburg); Machabey 1955b, 2:104–7; Günther 1958, 34 (conflicts in *tempus* groups); Kühn 1973, 93–97 (harmonic organization in the first *color*; rhythmic motives are handled like building blocks); Sanders 1973, 565 (pan-isorhythm); Wernli 1977, 23–24 (structure too complex to be easily perceived by the listener); Ziino 1978, 440 (near isomelism of the last two sections of the diminution section perhaps inspired by the sequence-like nature of the triplum text, although the regular structure of the sequence is masked in Machaut's other motets), 448 (melodic correspondences in triplum); Leech-Wilkinson 1989, 1:114–18 (lower-voice *taleae*, harmony, *introitus*), 124–26 (phrase lengths of M21–22 related).

Leech-Wilkinson 1982–83, 3–4 (summary of related features among M21, *Tu qui gregem / Plange* [M22], and *Felix virgo / Inviolata* [M23]); Newes 1987, 205–10 (comparison of complementary tenor-contratenor pair in *Aucune gent / Qui plus* [M5], M21–23); Leech-Wilkinson 1989, 1:105–7, 135–36, 138–41 (summary comparison of M21–23), 1:165 n. 45 (rate of harmonic change compared to several other motets).

MUSICAL ANTECEDENT. Philippe de Vitry, *Impudenter / Virtutibus* (ed. Schrade 1956a, 91–96 no. 11; Leech-Wilkinson 1989, 2:55–60; discussed in Leech-Wilkinson 1982–83, 3–4; 1989, 114). Use of imperfect and perfect *modus* in tenor and contratenor borrowed from Vitry (Leech-Wilkinson 1989, 1:41 n. 50, chap. 3 [esp. p. 114], 117 and 2:21 ex. 31). Leech-Wilkinson 1982–83, 4, 14 (three-breve to one-chant note ratio may demonstrate imitation of Vitry's usual procedure, cf. also *Amours qui a / Faus Samblant* [M15] and *Bone pastor / Bone pastor* [M18]).

MUSICAL LEGACY. Cypriot-French motet *Amour trestout / La douce art* (ed. Hoppin 1960–63, 177–81 no. 40; cited in Hoppin 1957, 109–10). For a twentieth-century composition inspired by M21, see chap. 2.5 (Thiele).

Cilz ha bien fole pensee (virelai V24)
TEXT MANUSCRIPTS.

[1]	C	fol. 157v	no. 23	[6]	G	fol. 159v	no. 24
[3]	V g	fol. 329v	no. 24	[7]	E	fols. 162v–163r	no. 22 [42]
[4]	B	fol. 327v	no. 24	[10]	M	fols. 251r–251v	no. 24
[5]	A	fol. 489r	no. 24	[50]	Pa	fols. 69v–70r	no. 222

VD18 AFEPm (chap. 5.13 table 5.3; attributed to *La dame*)

EDITIONS OF TEXT. Tarbé 1856, 26; P. Paris 1875, 72–73; Chichmaref 1909, 2:610–11 no. 24.

TEXT STRUCTURE. 3 strophes: $\frac{ABAB}{7'77'7} \| \frac{ccd\,ccd}{737\,737} \mid \frac{abab}{7'77'7} \| \frac{ABAB}{7'77'7}$ a:-*ée*, b:-*er*, c:-*ir*, d:-*ent*

DATE. Machabey (1955b, 1:187) places V24 in 1362 because of its position in the *Voir Dit*, but it must date from before 1350, since it is present in the old corpus of MS C.

DISCUSSION (literary). V24 is not singled out for special mention in the *Voir Dit*. In ll. 1516–18 (ed. P. Paris 1875, 70), Guillaume vowed to write something new every day. Shortly thereafter, there is a group of six interpolated lyrics in three pairs (VD17–22), whereby a lyric by Guillaume is answered in turn with a lyric by Toute Belle. According to the rubrics, V24, the second lyric of the series, was composed by Toute Belle, but it was an older virelai, composed by Machaut before 1350 (see above on the date). Strophe 3 of V24 picks up on the image of the refrain ("Ne qu'on tarir la haute mer") of the preceding ballade, *De mon vrai cuer jamais ne partira* (VD17).

Cinc, un, trese, huit, nuef d'amour fine (rondeau R6)
MANUSCRIPTS WITH TEXT AND MUSIC (all 2v: ca, ten).

[1]	C	fols. 203r–203v	no. 6	[5]	A	fol. 477r	no. 8
[3]	V g	fol. 317v	no. 6	[6]	G	fols. 150v–151r	no. 6
[4]	B	fol. 316v	no. 6	[7]	E	fol. 142r	no. 18

TEXT MANUSCRIPT.

[10]	M	fol. 244r	no. 6

---

[42] A staff was drawn above first line of text; see Earp 1983, 186 n. 347.

EDITIONS OF TEXT. Tarbé 1849, 171; Chichmaref 1909, 2:571 no. 6.

TRANSLATION. See discography (chap. 8.3 and 8.8).

DATE, OCCASION. P. Paris (1875, xx) solved the cryptogram (e a n h j) as Jehan or Jehanne (see also Hoepffner 1906, 409).[43] Hoepffner (1908–21, 3:xxix and 3:261, note to l. 2207 of *Fonteinne*; repeated in Ludwig 1926–54, 1:55) was the first to connect R6 to the 24 June 1360 marriage of Duke John of Berry and Jeanne d'Armagnac, and further linked the ballade *Amis, je t'apporte nouvelle* (Lo212) to the same occasion (see chap. 6.4, commentary to Lo165 and Lo212). See chap. 1.12a for some other possible occasions ca. 1352 for the composition of the rondeau. Machabey (1955b, 1:156) took over Hoepffner's date of the work as 1360–61, linking it to a small cycle of lyrical pieces connected to the *Fonteinne*. Machabey also compared the number riddle of R6 with that of a rondeau near the end of the *Voir Dit* that contains the name "Guillem," that is, Guillaume (ed. P. Paris 1875, 369); see also Cerquiglini 1985b, 228 n. 13, 229 n. 15. Günther (1963a, 99) placed the rondeau in the group of works found in the unordered part of the music section of MS C, a group of works which she dated "before 1356"; S.J. Williams (1969, 452) also questioned the 1360 date. The new dating of MS C supports an earlier date for the work.

TEXT STRUCTURE. 8'AB aA ab AB a:-*ine*, b:-*ent*

EDITIONS OF MUSIC. Ludwig 1926–54, 1:55; Schrade 1956b, 3:146 (critical notes 1956c, 126); Ultan 1977b, 96; Earp 1991a, 133. See Boorman (1977a, 497) and Earp (1991a, 135 n. 22) on variants in the opening measures.

DISCUSSION (musical). Machabey 1955b, 1:156 (beginning patterns are later split up); Günther 1957, 105 (motivic analysis); Mulder 1978, 87 (motivic analysis, symbolism); Cross 1990, 259, 284–85 (chromatic intervals); Earp 1991a, 132–35 (motivic analysis). The pervasive use of certain melodic formulas in *tempus imperfectum, prolatio major* links *Donnez, signeurs* (B26), *Une vipere* (B27), and *Je puis trop* (B28) as one group, and *Plourez, dames* (B32), *Nes qu'on* (B33), and *Se pour ce muir* (B36) as another; the same formulas are seen to a lesser extent in *En amer* (RF4), *Cinc, un* (R6), and *Douce dame, tant* (R20) (cf. Reaney 1955, 47; Hirshberg 1971, 120–33; Little 1980, 49). Hirshberg 1980, 30–31 (R6 has the pitch structure of *Se quanque amours* [B21] and the melodic material of *Plourez, dames* [B32]).

Comment puet on miex ses maus dire (rondeau R11)

MANUSCRIPTS WITH TEXT AND MUSIC (all 3v: ca, ten, ct).

[3] **V g**	fol. 319v	no. 11	[6] **G**	fol. 152r	no. 11
[4] **B**	fol. 318v	no. 11	[7] **E**	fol. 142r	no. 17
[5] **A**	fol. 478v	no. 12			

TEXT MANUSCRIPTS.

[10] **M**	fol. 244v	no. 11	[50] **Pa**	fol. 39r	no. 117

FACSIMILE. Wolf 1904, 2:39 no. 21 (diplomatic facs., MS **G**).

EDITION OF TEXT. Chichmaref 1909, 2:573 no. 11.

TRANSLATION. Yudkin 1989, 502–3.

TEXT STRUCTURE. 3 strophes: $\frac{\text{ABB abAB abb ABB}}{8'88 \; 8'88'8 \; 8'88 \; 8'88}$ a:-*ire*, b:-*our*

EDITIONS OF MUSIC. Wolf 1904, 3:62–63 no. 21; Schering 1911–12, 199 (errors); Ludwig 1926–54, 1:61; Schrade 1956b, 3:154 (critical notes 1956c, 130); Allaire 1972, 112–14; Yudkin 1989, 500–502.

DISCUSSION (musical). Schering 1911–12, 199 (removes diminutions to obtain skeletal melody); Ludwig 1926–54, 1:61 (criticism of Schering 1911–12); Machabey 1955b, 1:161–62; Günther 1957, 107 (motivic analysis); Dömling 1970, 31–32 (parallel passage in A- and B-section); Allaire 1972, 111–14 (solmization); Fuller 1986, 36–37 (criticism of Dömling 1970); Yudkin 1989, 500–503 (analysis).

---

[43] P. Paris (1875, 383 n. ii) amusingly identifies this Jehanne as Machaut's mistress prior to his association with Peronne d'Armentières: "La mort, ou l'inconstance de celle qu'il amoit & chantoit, avoit fortement ébranlé sa santé" [Death, or the inconstancy of her whom he loved and of whom he sang, had strongly shaken his health].

Comment qu'a moy lonteinne (virelai V5)
MANUSCRIPTS WITH TEXT AND MUSIC (all monophonic).
   [1] **C**   fols. 150r–150v no. 5   [5] **A**   fol. 483r   no. 5
   [3] **V g** fols. 323v–324r no. 5   [6] **G**   fol. 155v   no. 5
   [4] **B**   fols. 321v–322r no. 5   [7] **E**   fol. 159r   no. 3
TEXT MANUSCRIPTS.
   [10] **M** fol. 246v   no. 5   [50] **Pa** fols. 59v–60r   no. 185
EDITION OF TEXT. Chichmaref 1909, 2:585–86 no. 5.
TRANSLATIONS. Davison/Apel 1949, 245 no. 46a (strophe 1); see also discography (chap. 8.3 and 8.8).
TEXT STRUCTURE. 3 strophes: $\frac{\text{ABAB}}{6'66'6} \parallel \frac{\text{ab ab}}{6'6\ 6'6} \mid \frac{\text{abab}}{6'66'6} \parallel \frac{\text{ABAB}}{6'66'6}$ a:-*einne*, b:-*our*

EDITIONS OF MUSIC. Ludwig 1926–54, 1:72; Davison/Apel 1949, 49 no. 46a; Schrade 1956b, 3:169 (critical notes 1956c, 137); Hamburg 1976, 19–20 no. 24.
DISCUSSION (musical). Machabey 1955b, 1:178.
MUSICAL ANTECEDENT. The refrain is a reworked contrafact of a *chanson de toile*, *Belle Doette aus fenestres se siet* (R.1352), discussed by Arlt (1982, 268–71).
MUSICAL LEGACY. For a twentieth-century composition inspired by V5, see chap. 2.5 (Spears).

Contre ce dous mois de may. [*Le Lay de Nostre Dame*] (lai L15; Schrade lai 10)
MANUSCRIPTS WITH TEXT AND MUSIC (all monophonic).
   [3] **V g** fols. 247v–250v no. 15   [6] **G**   fols. 91v–93r   no. 15
   [4] **B**   fols. 245v–248v no. 15   [7] **E**   fols. 119v–121r no. 12 (has title)
   [5] **A**   fols. 393v–396r no. 15
TEXT MANUSCRIPT.
   [10] **M** fols. 232r–233v no. 18
EDITION OF TEXT. Chichmaref 1909, 2:397–405 no. 15.
TEXT STRUCTURE. 12 strophes, 260 lines.

1a. $\frac{\text{aa bb aa bba}}{77\ 47\ 47\ 474} \parallel$ 1b. same $\parallel$ 7a. $\frac{\text{nnnnnnno}}{88888886'} \mid \frac{\text{nnnnnnno}}{88888886'} \parallel$ 7b. same $\parallel$

2a. $\frac{\text{c c c d}}{8'8'8'6} \mid \frac{\text{c c c d}}{8'8'8'6} \parallel$ 2b. same $\parallel$ 8a. $\frac{\text{pppq}}{7775} \mid \frac{\text{pppq}}{7775} \parallel$ 8b. same $\parallel$

3a. $\frac{\text{e e e e ffg}}{5'5'5'7'347} \mid \frac{\text{e e e e ffg}}{5'5'5'7'347} \parallel$ 3b. same $\parallel$ 9a. $\frac{\text{rrr s}}{7345'} \mid \frac{\text{rrr s}}{7345'} \parallel$ 9b. same $\parallel$

4a. $\frac{\text{h h h h i}}{7'5'5'7'7} \mid \frac{\text{h h h h i}}{7'5'5'7'7} \parallel$ 4b. same $\parallel$ 10a. $\frac{\text{t u t u t u t u t u t u t u t u}}{5'5\ 5'5\ 5'5\ 5'5\ 5'5\ 5'5\ 5'5\ 5'5} \parallel$ 10b. same $\parallel$

5a. $\frac{\text{j k j k k j k j}}{74747477} \mid \frac{\text{j k j k k j k j}}{74747477} \parallel$ 5b. same $\parallel$ 11a. $\frac{\text{v w w x x v v v w w x x x v}}{73\ 45\ 75345\ 75345} \parallel$ 11b. same $\parallel$

6a. $\frac{\text{1 1 1 1 m}}{44486'} \mid \frac{\text{1 1 1 1 m}}{44486'} \parallel$ 6b. same $\parallel$ 12a–b. = 1a–b.

a:-*ay*, b:-*i*, c:-*ée*, d:-*ente*, e:-*ele*, f:-*uit*, g:-*iel*, h:-*ure*, i:-*ité*, j:-*ort*, k:-*is*, l:-*it*, m:-*oire*, n:-*ion*, o:-*ite*, p:-*our*, q:-*oit*, r:-*in*, s:-*ange*, t:-*ine*, u:-*er*, v:-*uis*, w:-*ier*, x:-*ent*
DISCUSSION (literary). Poirion 1965, 113 n. 33, 421 (Marian image); Maillard 1984, 332–33, 333–34, 336–37 (literary models and successors for Marian lais; analysis); Cerquiglini 1985b, 81 (Marian image).
EDITIONS OF MUSIC. Ludwig 1926–54, 4:42–45 (ed. Besseler); Schrade 1956b, 2:34–38 (critical notes 1956c, 63–64). The music of strophes 1 and 12 is the same, except that strophe 12 is a perfect fifth higher.
LITERARY AND MUSICAL ANTECEDENT. Schrade (1956c, 21; 1958–61, 846–47) indicates that L15/10 is a reworking of a lai in the *Roman de Fauvel, En ce dous temps d'esté* (ed. Rosenberg/Tischler 1991, 131–42 no. 64). Schrade maintained that Philippe de Vitry could

have composed only those *Fauvel* lais in *tempus* notation (1958–61, 846); both the *Fauvel* lai and L15/10 are notated on the level of *modus*.

DISCUSSION (musical). Machabey 1955b, 1:118 (isorhythmic structure of strophes 2, 7, 11); Ballif 1969, 269 (motive common to L15/10 and the Mass); Lühmann 1978, 193–95 (declamation); Mulder 1978, 115–16 (Marian motives and numbers).

MUSICAL LEGACY. Cypriot-French motet *Toustans que mon esprit / Qui porroit amer* (ed. Hoppin 1960–63, 2:156–60 no. 35; cited in Hoppin 1957, 96; Wilkins 1987, 172).

Corde mesto. See *Helas! pour quoy virent / Corde* (M12).

Credo. See *Messe de Nostre Dame*.

Dame, a qui (virelai V12)

MANUSCRIPTS WITH TEXT AND MUSIC (all monophonic).

[1]	C	fols. 153r–153v	no. 12[44]	[5]	A	fol. 485v	no. 12
[3]	V g	fol. 326r	no. 12	[6]	G	fol. 157r	no. 12
[4]	B	fol. 324r	no. 12	[7]	E	fol. 163v	no. 25

TEXT MANUSCRIPT.
[10] M   fols. 248r–248v no. 12

EDITIONS OF TEXT. Chichmaref 1909, 2:594–96 no. 12; Wilkins 1969a, 36–38 no. 25 (notes 127).

TRANSLATION. See discography (chap. 8.3 and 8.8).

TEXT STRUCTURE. 3 strophes:
$$\underset{3\ 2\ 7'7\ \ 3\ 2\ 7'7}{AABA\ AABA}\ \|\ \underset{727\ 727}{cca\,cca}\ |\ \underset{327'7\ 327'7}{aab\,a\,aab\,a}\ \|\ \underset{3\ 2\ 7'7\ \ 3\ 2\ 7'7}{AABA\ AABA}\ \ a\text{:-}i,\ b\text{:-}ure,\ c\text{:-}our$$

DISCUSSION (literary). Poirion 1965, 328 (short lines suggest sobs).

EDITIONS OF MUSIC. Ludwig 1926–54, 1:75; Schrade 1956b, 3:173 (critical notes 1956c, 139–40).

DISCUSSION (musical). Machabey 1955b, 1:181–82 (duplex virelai); Leech-Wilkinson 1991 (voice-leading reduction reveals circular nature).

Dame, a vous sans retollir (virelai RF6; Schrade virelai 33)

MANUSCRIPTS WITH TEXT AND MUSIC (all monophonic).

[1]	C	fols. 51r–51v		[6]	F	fol. 59r
[3]	V g	fols. 114v–115r		[7]	E	fol. 33v
[4]	B	fols. 114v–115r (new 131v–132r)		[20]	P e	fols. 29r–29v
[5]	A	fols. 74r–74v				

TEXT MANUSCRIPTS.

[10]	M	fols. 71v–72r	[18]	P m	fol. 68v
[15]	J	fol. 71r (strophes 2–3 only)	[50]	P a	fols. 49r–49v no. 150

FACSIMILES (refer to chap. 4.4e). Miniature C36. Bottée de Toulmon 1836, appendix 2, p. 4 (diplomatic facs. of refrain, MS A); Kiesewetter 1838, no. 13 (diplomatic facs.); Ludwig 1911, 27 (appendix; MSS A and E).

EDITIONS OF TEXT (*Remede*, ll. 3451–96). Hoepffner 1908–21, 2:126–28; Wimsatt/Kibler 1988, 361–63.

TRANSLATIONS. Fuller 1987b, 114–15; Switten 1988c, 67–68; Gallo 1985, 132–33 (translation of the context in the *Remede*); Wimsatt/Kibler 1988, 360–62; Boulton 1993, 192 (refrain only); see also discography (chap. 8.3 and 8.8).

TEXT STRUCTURE. 3 strophes[45]: $\underset{7\,7\,4\,7\,4\,7\,4}{AABBAAB}\ \|\ \underset{774\ 774}{bba\ bba}\ |\ \underset{7747474}{aabba\,ab}\ \|\ \underset{7\,7\,4\,7\,4\,7\,4}{AABBAAB}\ \ a\text{:-}ir,\ b\text{:-}our$

DISCUSSION (literary). Poirion 1965, 327; Marks 1984, 105–8; Huot 1987, 256. For some literary studies that deal with all of the inserted lyrics, see chap. 5.7.

---

[44] Some text and music of the refrain is missing.

[45] Cf. the text structure of *En mon cuer* (V27), *Plus dure* (V31), *Dame, mon cuer* (V32), *Je ne me puis* (V33=VD11), *L'ueil* (V34=VD9), *Plus belle* (V35=VD10).

EDITIONS OF MUSIC. Bottée de Toulmon 1836, musical supplement, 5 ex. 3 (refrain only); Kiesewetter 1838, no. 13; 1841, *Beilagen*, 3 no. 9 (after Bottée de Toulmon 1836); Ambros 1891, 251 (=1864 ed., 230) (after Bottée de Toulmon 1836); Ludwig 1911, 20 (appendix); 1926–54, 1:101–2; Schrade 1956b, 3:192 (critical notes 1956c, 147–48); Fuller 1987b, 113; Switten 1988c, 67 (after Schrade); Wimsatt/Kibler 1988, 430, critical notes 444–45 (ed. Baltzer).

DISCUSSION (musical). Bottée de Toulmon 1836, 217; Ludwig 1911, 412–13; Günther 1957, 118 (analysis); Arlt 1982, 263 (context in *Remede*); Malizia 1984, 37–40 (general); Fuller 1987b, 115; Earp 1991a, 127–32 (rhythmic analysis); Hoffmann-Axthelm 1991, 351 (context in *Remede*); Leech-Wilkinson 1991, 27–30 (rhythmic and voice-leading reduction emphasizes circular nature). For some musical studies that deal with all of the inserted lyrics, see chap. 5.7.

Dame, comment qu'amez de vous ne soie (ballade B16)
Refrain: *S'il avenoit, fors seulement morir*

MANUSCRIPTS WITH TEXT AND MUSIC (all 2v: ca, ten).

[1] **C**	fols. 164v–165r	no. 16		[5] **A**	fol. 462v	no. 17
[3] **V g**	fol. 304r	no. 16		[6] **G**	fols. 139v–140r	no. 17
[4] **B**	fol. 302r	no. 16		[7] **E**	fol. 154r	no. 25

TEXT MANUSCRIPTS.

[10] **M** fols. 239r–239v no. 16 Lo182 **C V g B A E M D**

FACSIMILE. Ultan 1977a, 123 (diplomatic facs.).

EDITIONS OF TEXT. Chichmaref 1909, 1:165 no. 182; Wilkins 1972, 57 no. 29.

TRANSLATION. See discography (chap. 8.3 and 8.8).

TEXT STRUCTURE. 3 strophes: $\begin{smallmatrix} a & b & a & b & b & c & C \\ 10 & 10 & 10 & 10 & 5 & 10 & 10 \end{smallmatrix}$ a:-*oie*, b:-*er*, c:-*ir*

EDITIONS OF MUSIC. Ludwig 1926–54, 1:15; Schrade 1956b, 3:87 (critical notes 1956c, 107); Wilkins 1972, 125–26.

DISCUSSION (musical). Lowinsky 1945, 238 (partial signature); Machabey 1955b, 2:30; Günther 1960b, 296 and 1982, 112 (rhythmic augmentation); Salop 1971, 69 (gradual assertion of *B*-flat final); Dömling 1972, 302, 303–4, 306 (text setting, refrain); Lühmann 1978, 122–25 (declamation).

Dame, de qui toute ma joie vient (ballade RF5; Schrade ballade 42)
Refrain: *Qu'en cent mil ans desservir ne porroie*

MANUSCRIPTS WITH TEXT AND MUSIC.

[1] **C**	fols. 47v–48r		2v (ca, ten)
[3] **V g**	fols. 111v–112r		4v (tr, ca, ten, ct)
[4] **B**	fols. 111v–112r (new 128v–129r)		4v (tr, ca, ten, ct)
[5] **A**	fols. 70v–71r		4v (tr, ca, ten, ct)
[6] **F**	fol. 56v		4v (tr, ca, ten, ct)
[7] **E**	fol. 32r		4v (tr, ca, ten, ct)
[15] **K**	fol. 60v (text of strophe 3 lost)		2v (ca, ten)
[20] **P e**	fol. 25v		4v (tr, ca, ten, ct)
[58] **Trém**	fol. xxvii	no. 62	(index only)
[63] **P R**	fol. 68v	no. 143	4v (tr, ca, ten, ct)

TEXT MANUSCRIPTS.

[10] **M**	fols. 68v–69r		[40] **I**	fol. 20r	no. 106
[16] **J**	fols. 67r–68r (space for staves)		[49] **Jp**	fols. 68r–68v	no. 72
[18] **Pm**	fol. 65v				

FACSIMILES (refer to chap. 4.4e). Miniature C33. *The Consort* 33 (1977), cover (fols. 25v–26r); *Jardin* 1910–25, vol. 1, fols. 68r–68v (**Jp**).

EDITIONS OF TEXT (*Remede*, ll. 3013–36). Queux de Saint-Hilaire/Raynaud 1878–1903, 10:lxvii–lxviii no. 61; Hoepffner 1908–21, 2:110–11; Wilkins 1987, 34; Wimsatt/Kibler 1988, 337–39.

TRANSLATIONS. Wilkins 1987, 34; Switten 1988b; 1988c, 60–61; Wimsatt/Kibler 1988, 336–38; Boulton 1993, 191 (strophe 1); see also discography (chap. 8.3 and 8.8).

TEXT STRUCTURE. 3 strophes: $\frac{a\ b\quad a\ b\ c\ c\quad d\ D}{1010\ \ 1010\ \ 71010'10'}$ a:-*ient*, b:-*ir*, c:-*oir*, d:-*oie*

DISCUSSION (literary). Poirion 1965, 383; Huot 1987, 256. For some literary studies that deal with all of the inserted lyrics, see chap. 5.7.

EDITIONS OF MUSIC. Ludwig 1911, 15–19 (appendix); 1926–54, 1:99–101; Schrade 1956b, 3:140–41 (critical notes 1956c, 123); Wilkins 1987, 32–35 no. 7; Switten 1988c, 59–60 (after Schrade); Wimsatt/Kibler 1988, 428–29, critical notes pp. 442–44 (ed. Baltzer).

DISCUSSION (musical). Günther 1957, 117–18 (motivic analysis); Hirshberg 1980, 38 (*ficta*); Reaney 1980a, 430, 435 (four voices not to be performed together, but as alternative 3v versions with triplum or with contratenor); Malizia 1984, 34–37; Wilkins 1987, 35 (general). For some musical studies that deal with all of the inserted lyrics, see chap. 5.7.

Dame, je sui cilz / Fins cuers doulz / Fins cuers doulz (motet M11)
MANUSCRIPTS WITH TEXT AND MUSIC (all 3v: tr, mot, ten).

[1]	**C**	fols. 215v–216r	no. 10	[5]	**A**	fols. 424v–425r	no. 11
[3]	**V g**	fols. 270v–271r	no. 11	[6]	**G**	fols. 112v–113r	no. 11
[4]	**B**	fols. 268v–269r	no. 11	[7]	**E**	fol. 140r	no. 13

EDITION OF TEXT. Chichmaref 1909, 2:503–4 no. 11.

TRANSLATIONS. See discography, chap. 8.3 and 8.8.

TEXT STRUCTURE AND RELATIONSHIP TO MUSICAL STRUCTURE. The work is not isorhythmic, and so is not analyzed in this respect in Reichert 1956. Nevertheless, there are parallelisms in the strophic disposition between triplum and motetus. Each has three hocket sections, which provide upper-voice isorhythm (cf. Günther 1958, 29; Sanders 1973, 564; 1980a, 352). Further, the longer lines of text in the triplum result in the faster text declamation typical of motet tripla.

Triplum: $\frac{a\ a\ b\quad b\quad c\ c\ d d^{\dagger}\ e\ e\quad f\quad f\quad g\ g\ f\ g\ f}{101010'10'\ \ 10'10'1010\ \ 10'10'10'10'\ \ 101010'1010'}$ a:-*durer*, b:-*dure*, c:-*aie*,

d:-*our*, e:-*aire*, f:-*voie*, g:-*ent* (†: lyric caesura)

Motetus: $\frac{a b a b\ c c b\ d d b\ e e b\ f f b}{77'77'\ \ 777'\ \ 777'\ \ 777'\ \ 777'}$ a:-*ent*, b:-*oie*, c:-*ay*, d:-*ir*, e:-*é*, f:-*oir*

TENOR SOURCE. *Fins cuers doulz* is an unidentified irregular virelai. Ludwig (1926–54, 3:43) notes that the tenor label may simply cite the beginning of the motetus voice, and thus we may not have the text of the *cantus firmus*.

EDITIONS OF MUSIC. Ludwig 1926–54, 3:41–43; Schrade 1956b, 2:144–46 (critical notes 1956c, 81–82). Transcription problems discussed in Hoppin 1960, 19–20; Machabey 1955b, 2:86 n. 530; Keitel 1976, 97–102.

DISCUSSION (musical). Tenor is structured as an irregular virelai, making a *talea* structure supported by the tenor impossible. Reese 1940, 355 (example of masked imitation between triplum and motetus); Machabey 1955b, 2:85–87; Günther 1960b, 296 (rhythmic augmentation); Kühn 1973, 144–51 (harmonic analysis); Fuller 1992b, 243–44 (treatment of opening imperfect sonority); Boogaard 1993b, 28, 29 n. 47 (relationship to *Trop plus / Biauté* [M20]; hocket sections); Danckwardt 1993 (compositional procedure).

Dame, je vueil endurer (virelai V9)
MANUSCRIPTS WITH TEXT AND MUSIC (all monophonic).

[1]	**C**	fol. 152r	no. 9	[5]	**A**	fol. 484v	no. 9
[3]	**V g**	fol. 325r	no. 9	[6]	**G**	fol. 156v	no. 9
[4]	**B**	fol. 323r	no. 9	[7]	**E**	fol. 163v	no. 27

TEXT MANUSCRIPT.

[10]	**M**	fol. 247v	no. 9

EDITION OF TEXT. Chichmaref 1909, 2:590–91 no. 9.

TRANSLATION. See discography (chap. 8.3 and 8.8).

TEXT STRUCTURE. 3 strophes: $\frac{AABB}{7\ 7\ 5'2'}\ \|\ \frac{c\ a\ c\ a}{87\ 77}\ |\ \frac{a a b\ b}{775'2'}\ \|\ \frac{AABB}{7\ 7\ 5'2'}$ a:-*er*, b:-*ure*, c:-*ant*

The last line of the refrain proper (the single word *m'ardure*) also appears as a refrain in each of the three strophes (cf. Hoepffner 1920b, 26–27; Poirion 1965, 329 and n. 28). Compare *Se ma dame m'a* (V6).

EDITIONS OF MUSIC. Ludwig 1926–54, 1:74; Schrade 1956b, 3:171 (critical notes 1956c, 138–39). Arlt (1982, 264–65) proposes different barring.

DISCUSSION (musical). Machabey 1955b, 1:180; Saponov 1978, 23 (rhythmic motives vertically aligned).

Dame, le doulz souvenir (virelai V21)

TEXT MANUSCRIPTS.

[1]	C	fols. 156v–157r	no. 20		[6]	G	fol. 159r	no. 21
[3]	V g	fol. 329r	no. 21		[7]	E	fols. 163v–164r	no. 28[46]
[4]	B	fol. 327r	no. 21		[10]	M	fol. 250v	no. 21
[5]	A	fols. 488r–488v	no. 21					

EDITION OF TEXT. Chichmaref 1909, 2:607–8 no. 21.

TRANSLATION. Wimsatt 1991b, 27–28, 85–86 (partial).

TEXT STRUCTURE. 3 strophes. Note the irregularity in the second half of the strophe: the refrain rhymes ABBAAB, but the second half of the strophe rhymes abbaba.

$$\underset{7\,4\,7\,4\,7\,4}{ABBAAB} \parallel \underset{774\;\;774}{cca\,cca} \mid \underset{747474}{abbaba} \parallel \underset{7\,4\,7\,4\,7\,4}{ABBAAB} \quad a:\text{-}ir,\ b:\text{-}our,\ c:\text{-}er$$

DISCUSSION (literary). Hassell (1982, no. E14) indexes a proverb.

TEXTUAL LEGACY (England). Chaucer, *Womanly Noblesse* (Wimsatt 1978, 77–78; Wimsatt 1991b, 27–28, 85–86).

Dame, mon cuer emportez (virelai V32; Schrade virelai 29)

MANUSCRIPTS WITH TEXT AND MUSIC (all 2v: ca, ten).

[3]	V g	fol. 333r	no. 32		[6]	G	fol. 162r	no. 32
[4]	B	fol. 330r	no. 32		[7]	E	fol. 162v	no. 20
[5]	A	fol. 492v	no. 33					

TEXT MANUSCRIPTS.

[10]	M	fols. 253v–254r	no. 32		[50]	Pa	fols. 68*bis* v–69r	no. 219

EDITION OF TEXT. Chichmaref 1909, 2:622–23 no. 32.

TEXT STRUCTURE. 3 strophes: $\underset{7\,7\,4\,7\,4\,7\,4}{AABBAAB} \parallel \underset{774\;\;774}{bba\,bba} \mid \underset{7747474}{aabbaab} \parallel \underset{7\,7\,4\,7\,4\,7\,4}{AABBAAB}$ a:-*ez*, b:-*ent*

EDITIONS OF MUSIC. Ludwig 1926–54, 1:88; Gleason 1945, 80; Schrade 1956b, 3:188 (critical notes 1956c, 146); Salop 1971, 42 (textless).

DISCUSSION (musical). Salzer 1952, 1:275, 2:328 ex. 529 (voice-leading reduction of opening, showing "tonic" and "dominant" chords); Machabey 1955b, 1:193; Salop 1971, 41–43 (melodic style).

Dame, mon cuer en vous remaint (rondeau RF7; Schrade rondeau 22)

MANUSCRIPTS WITH TEXT AND MUSIC (all 3v: tr, ca, ten).

[1]	C	fol. 57r		[5]	A	fol. 78v
[3]	V g	fol. 119v		[6]	F	fol. 62v
[4]	B	fol. 119v (new 136v)		[7]	E	fol. 35v

TEXT MANUSCRIPTS.

[10]	M	fol. 76r		[18]	P m	fol. 72r
[15]	J	fol. 75r				

FACSIMILES (refer to chap. 4.4e). Miniature C42.

EDITIONS OF TEXT (*Remede*, ll. 4107–14/4109–16). Hoepffner 1908–21, 2:151; Wimsatt/Kibler 1988, 399–401.

TRANSLATIONS. Switten 1988c, 75; Wimsatt/Kibler 1988, 398–400; Calin 1994, 203 (after Wimsatt/Kibler); see also discography (chap. 8.3 and 8.8).

TEXT STRUCTURE. $\underset{8\,8}{AB}\ \underset{8\,8}{aA}\ \underset{8\,8}{ab}\ \underset{8\,8}{AB}$ a:-*maint*, b:-*parte*

---

[46] A staff was drawn above first line of text; see Earp 1983, 186 n. 347.

DISCUSSION (literary). Poirion 1965, 318; Huot 1987, 257–58; Cerquiglini 1988b, 53; Calin 1994, 203. For some literary studies that deal with all of the inserted lyrics, see chap. 5.7.

EDITIONS OF MUSIC. Ludwig 1911, 21–23 (appendix); 1926–54, 1:103; Schrade 1956b, 3:166 (critical notes 1956c, 135); Switten 1988c, 67 (after Schrade); Wimsatt/Kibler 1988, 431–33, critical notes pp. 445–47 (ed. Baltzer).

DISCUSSION (musical). Machabey 1955b, 1:151–53; Apel 1957 (instances of imitation between cantus and tenor); Günther 1957, 118–19 (melodic analysis); Newes 1977, 42–43 (exchange of motives not true imitation); Ziino 1982b, 330 (imitation); Malizia 1984, 40–42 (general); Page 1990, 104 n. 65 (all three voices should be texted). For some musical studies that deal with all of the inserted lyrics, see chap. 5.7.

Dame, ne regardez pas (ballade B9)
Refrain: *Par vostre dous plaisant regart*
MANUSCRIPTS WITH TEXT AND MUSIC (all 2v: ca, ten).

[1]	**C**	fol. 161v	no. 9	[5]	**A**	fol. 459r	no. 10
[3]	**V g**	fol. 300v	no. 9	[6]	**G**	fol. 137v	no. 10
[4]	**B**	fol. 298v	no. 9	[7]	**E**	fols. 154v–155r	no. 28

TEXT MANUSCRIPTS.

[10] **M**   fol. 238v   no. 9   Lo10 **CWVgBAEHMD** (chap. 6.4)

EDITIONS OF TEXT. Chichmaref 1909, 1:25 no. 10; Wilkins 1972, 59 no. 37.

TEXT STRUCTURE. 3 strophes (see Poirion [1965, 452] and Gieber [1982, 10] on the unusual metric structure): $\frac{ab\,ab\,bc\,C}{75\,75\,78\,8}$ a:-*ez*, b:-*ie*, c:-*eure*

EDITIONS OF MUSIC. Ludwig 1926–54, 1:8 ; Schrade 1956b, 3:80 (critical notes 1956c, 103); Wilkins 1972, 126–28. Bent (1983, 64–66) gives variants in MSS **VgBE**.

DISCUSSION (musical). Machabey 1955b, 2:24–25; Salop 1971, 71–72 (unsuccessful melodic design); Lühmann 1978, 199 (declamation); Hirshberg 1980, 28 (*ficta*); Fuller 1987a, 54 (tonal structure).

Dame, par vous. See Sans cuer / Amis / Dame (ballade B17)

Dame, qui vuet vostre droit nom savoir (rondeau R16)
TEXT MANUSCRIPTS.

[4]	**B**	fol. 309v	no. 16	[7]	**E**	fol. 135r	no. 6
[6]	**G**	fol. 153v	no. 17	[10]	**M**	fol. 245r	no. 17

EDITIONS OF TEXT. Tarbé 1849, 173; Hoepffner 1906, 410 (anagram unsolved); Chichmaref 1909, 2:575 no. 17; Ludwig 1926–54, 1:65; Schrade 1956b, 3:159.

DATE, OCCASION. The solution to the riddle of the lady's name eluded scholars until Poirion (1965, 197 n. 19) saw the key in the preceding rondeau, *Certes, mon oueil* (R15), which yields the name "Isabel" ("Isabelle" also appears in *Il n'est confors* [Lo74] as an acrostic). Wilkins (1972, 178 n. 225; 1983b, 262) solves the riddle of R16 as "Bonne grise," and refers both works to Bonne of Luxembourg. This seems incorrect, since both rondeaux postdate Bonne (d. 1349) on grounds of manuscript dating.

TEXT STRUCTURE. $\frac{A\ B}{1010}, \frac{a\,A}{1010}\ \frac{a\ b}{1010}, \frac{A\ B}{1010}$ a:-*oir*, b:-*eingne*

Dame, se vous m'estes lointeinne (ballade B37)
Refrain: *Comment que soie long de vous*
MANUSCRIPTS WITH TEXT AND MUSIC (all monophonic).

[5] **A**   fol. 473v   no. 36   [6] **G**   fol. 147r   no. 34

TEXT MANUSCRIPT.

[10] **M**   fols. 243r–243v   no. 37   Lo15 **CVgBAEHMD** (chap. 6.4)

EDITIONS OF TEXT. Chichmaref 1909, 1:30 no. 15; Wilkins 1972, 61 no. 42. Some comments on the text in Reaney 1958b, 50.

DATE. Reaney (1952b, 36 n. 7; 1956, 9; cf. Günther 1957, 69; 1963a, 102) suggests that B37 falls outside the generally chronological order of the ballades, and is actually an earlier work, on the basis of its rhythm, lack of accompanying voices, and early position in the *Loange* section; Earp (1991a, 140) argues that B37 is not necessarily early.

TEXT STRUCTURE. 3 strophes: $\dfrac{ab\ ab\ bcC}{8'8\ 8'8\ 888}$ a:-*einne*, b:-*eins*, c:-*ous*

EDITIONS OF MUSIC. Ludwig 1926–54, 1:45; Machabey 1931, 343 (1 strophe); Schrade 1956b, 3:132 (critical notes 1956c, 119–20).

DISCUSSION (musical). Machabey 1955b, 2:51–52 and Reaney 1956, 9 (possibly the work is a dance song); Reaney 1955, 52 (refrain may be borrowed); Escot 1991.

Dame, se vous n'avez aperceü (rondeau R13)

MANUSCRIPTS WITH TEXT AND MUSIC (all 3v: ca, ten, ct).

[3]	**V g**	fol. 320v	no. 13	[6]	**G**	fol. 152v	no. 13
[4]	**B**	fol. 319v	no. 13	[7]	**E**	fol. 141r	no. 15
[5]	**A**	fol. 479r	no. 14	[7]	**E**	fol. 176r	in *Voir Dit*

TEXT MANUSCRIPTS.

[10]	**M**	fol. 244v	no. 13	VD14 **AFEPm** (chap. 5.13 table 5.3)
[50]	**Pa**	fol. 52r	no. 161	

FACSIMILE. Parrish 1957, plate xlviii (MS E), discussed pp. 153–54.

EDITIONS OF TEXT. P. Paris 1875, 52; Chichmaref 1909, 2:574 no. 13.

TRANSLATION. See discography (chap. 8.3 and 8.8).

DATE. Machabey (1955b, 1:164) places the rondeau between letters 5 and 6 of the *Voir Dit*, thus probably after Christmas 1361, because of mention in those letters of a recent copy of the *Fonteinne*, Machaut's latest *dit* at the time. At another point, Machabey dated letter 6 to the end of December 1362 or January 1363 (1955b, 1:57). Following the two dates in Machabey, Reaney (1967, 89) and Gagnepain (1982, 274) placed the composition of the cantus after Christmas 1361, and the composition of the tenor and contratenor in April 1363. Leech-Wilkinson (1993a, 48) places R13 early in 1363. According to Leech-Wilkinson (1993a, 49–50), a compositional process whereby the cantus predates the lower voices by a substantial time-lag cannot apply to this work; thus, the confusion of the two dates does not concern R13, but may refer to *Puis qu'en oubli* [R18], a work that does not appear in the *Voir Dit* (see below, discussions of R18 and *Dix et sept* [R17]).

TEXT STRUCTURE. 10AB aA ab AB a:-*eü*, b:-*oir*

DISCUSSION (literary). The following *Voir Dit* passages concern R13: (a) Guillaume sends the rondeau in letter 6 (ed. P. Paris 1875, 21 as letter 2); (b) Toute Belle writes in letter 7 that she has learned the rondeau (ed. 1875, 28 as letter 3); (c) the text of R13 is inserted into the narrative (ll. 1215–27, ed. 1875, 52). For excerpts from or commentary on these passages, see Ludwig 1926–54, 2:56b*; Leech-Wilkinson 1993a, 48–49; 1993b, 109–10, 134.

EDITIONS OF MUSIC. P. Paris 1875, facing p. 52 (ed. Marie Colas, errors; see also p. xxxv); Ludwig 1926–54, 1:62–63; Schrade 1956b, (critical notes 1956c, 131); Wilkins 1980b, 29 (Chaucer, *Now welcom somer* underlaid).

DISCUSSION (musical). Machabey 1955b, 1:164–65; Salzer 1952, 1:276, 2:229–31 ex. 531 (voice-leading reductions that emphasize certain pitches to obtain a more traditional tonal plan; see criticism in Kühn 1973, 33); Apfel 1974, 173 (unusual compositional structure; cf. Leech-Wilkinson 1993a, 49–50); Leguy 1982, 311–13 (successive composition); Leech-Wilkinson 1993a, 62 (relation between R13 and *Ma fin* [R14]).

Dame, vostre dous viaire (virelai V17)

MANUSCRIPTS WITH TEXT AND MUSIC (all monophonic).

[1]	**C**	fols. 154v–155r	no. 16	[5]	**A**	fols. 486v–487r	no. 17
[3]	**V g**	fols. 327v–328r	no. 17	[6]	**G**	fol. 158r	no. 17
[4]	**B**	fols. 325v–326r	no. 17	[7]	**E**	fols. 160r–160v	no. 8

TEXT MANUSCRIPTS.

[10]	**M**	fols. 249r–249v	no. 17	[50]	**Pa**	fols. 65r–65v	no. 201

EDITION OF TEXT. Chichmaref 1909, 2:600–602 no. 17.

TRANSLATIONS. Wilson 1990a, 233–34; see also discography (chap. 8.3 and 8.8).

TEXT STRUCTURE. 3 strophes:

$$\dfrac{AAB\ AAB}{7'3'7\ 7'3'7}\ \|\ \dfrac{bb\ a\ bb\ a}{737'\ 737'}\ |\ \dfrac{a\ ab\ a\ ab}{7'3'7\ 7'3'7}\ \|\ \dfrac{AAB\ AAB}{7'3'7\ 7'3'7}$$ a:-*aire*, b:-*oy*

EDITIONS OF MUSIC. Ludwig 1926–54, 1:78; Schrade 1956b, 3:176 (critical notes 1956c, 141); Wilson 1990a, 232 no. 68.

DISCUSSION (musical). Machabey 1955b, 1:184–85 (duplex virelai); Wilson 1990b, 337–38 (melodic analysis).

David Hoquetus. See *Hoquetus David.*

De Bon Espoir / Puis que la douce / Speravi (motet M4)

MANUSCRIPTS WITH TEXT AND MUSIC (all 3v: tr, mot, ten).

[3] **V g** fols. 263v–264r no. 4	[6] **G** fols. 105v–106r no. 4
[4] **B** fols. 261v–262r no. 4	[7] **E** fols. 134v–135r no. 6
[5] **A** fols. 417v–418r no. 4	

FACSIMILE. Wolf 1904, 2:21–23 no. 15 (diplomatic facs., MS **G**).

EDITION OF TEXT. Chichmaref 1909, 2:489–90 no. 4.

TRANSLATIONS. Wilson 1990a, 216; see also discography (chap. 8.3 and 8.8).

DATE. Because M4 is missing in MS C, it is often considered a late work (Günther 1958, 28, 30, etc.; Reaney, 1967, 92). Earp (1983, 140–42), however, noted an irregularity in the gathering structure in MS C, which may indicate that M4 was left off inadvertently, and thus that it too can be placed before ca. 1350, like motets 1–3 and 5–20.

TEXT STRUCTURE AND RELATIONSHIP TO ISORHYTHM. Both triplum and motetus exhibit regular correlation between text and *talea* structure (Reichert 1956, 201 and n. 2; ex. 2 facing p. 204). See also Clarkson 1971, 262 (strophic structure of motetus); Ziino 1978, 444 n. 13 (strophic structure of triplum).

Triplum: 10aabb ccdd eeff ggee ddhh iijj k⁺kk a:-*ir*, b:-*ouru*, c:-*oit*, d:-*té*, e:-*er*, f:-*uet*,
g:-*ort*, h:-*i*, i:-*us*, j:-*uer*, k:-*ent* (†: lyric caesura)

Motetus: $\begin{smallmatrix} \text{abab a abab a ababb} \\ 7'77'7\ 7'\ 7'77'7\ 7'\ 7'77'7\ 7 \end{smallmatrix}$ a:-*ée*, b:-*ir*

DISCUSSION (literary). Poirion 1965, 536; 1978, 199; Sonnemann 1969, 63; and Brownlee 1991b, 13–14 (thematic relationship of voices); Boogaart 1993b, 32 (*desmesure*).

LITERARY ANTECEDENT. The end of the motetus may be a refrain, "je weil humblement souffrir / leur voloir jusqu'au morir" [I want to suffer their will humbly until I die] (Ludwig 1926–54, 3:12).

TENOR SOURCE. *Speravi* (Psalm 12:6) is from the fifth-mode Introit *Domine, in tua misericordia speravi* for the first Sunday after Pentecost (Ludwig 1926–54, 2:60a*, 3:17).

EDITIONS OF MUSIC. Wolf 1904, 3:36–41 no. 15; Ludwig 1926–54, 3:13–17; Gleason 1945, 88–96; Schrade 1956b, 2:119–22 (critical notes 1956c, 76–77); Harman 1958, 132–37; Burkhart 1979; Wilson 1990a, 212–15 no. 65. Barring discussed in Hoppin 1960, 26.

DISCUSSION (musical). Bipartite, with diminution by one-half (diminution section is pan-isorhythmic). *Modus* is broken at the end of the diminution *talea* (Günther 1958, 34). Ficker 1924–25, 211 (brief analysis); Apel 1938, 9–10 (accidentals); Gombosi 1950, 221 (symmetrical analysis of tenor rhythms); Machabey 1955b, 2:73–75; Günther 1958, 31 n. 17 (deviations from pan-isorhythmic structure); Harman 1958, 130–31, 138–39 (isorhythm; partial signature); Pelinski 1975, 70–71 (tonal plan of the *integer valor* section); Dobrzańska 1979b, 64 (harmonic reduction of mm. 1–102); Wilson 1990b, 306, 316–17 (isorhythmic analysis); Fuller 1992b, 234–41 (directed progressions; tonal orientation; text painting). On melodic correspondences between *taleae*, see Machabey 1955b, 2:74; Reichert 1956, 212; Günther 1958, 32; Ziino 1978, 448–49.

De bonté, de valour (virelai V10)

MANUSCRIPTS WITH TEXT AND MUSIC (all monophonic).

[1] **C** fols. 152r–152v no. 10	[5] **A** fols. 484v–485r no. 10
[3] **V g** fol. 325v no. 10	[6] **G** fol. 156v no. 10
[4] **B** fol. 323v no. 10	[7] **E** fol. 163r no. 23

TEXT MANUSCRIPT.

[10] **M** fols. 247v–248r no. 10

EDITION OF TEXT. Chichmaref 1909, 2:591–93 no. 10.

TRANSLATIONS. Hoppin 1978a, 146–47; see also discography (chap. 8.3 and 8.8).

TEXT STRUCTURE. 3 strophes: $\dfrac{AABAB}{6\,65'6\,8'}$ ‖ $\dfrac{b\,ba\,b\,ba}{5'6'3\,5'6'3}$ | $\dfrac{aabab}{665'68'}$ ‖ $\dfrac{AABAB}{6\,65'6\,8'}$ a:-*our*, b:-*ée*

EDITIONS OF MUSIC. Ludwig 1926–54, 1:74; Schrade 1956b, 3:172 (critical notes 1956c, 139); Hoppin 1978a, 146–47 no. 64. On the different music for the B-section in MSS **B** and **E**, see Bent 1983, 57–58, 69.

DISCUSSION (musical). Machabey 1955b, 1:188–81 (duplex virelai).

De desconfort, de martyre amoureus (ballade B8)
Refrain: *En desirant vostre douce merci*

MANUSCRIPTS WITH TEXT AND MUSIC (all 2v: ca, ten).

[1]	**C**	fols. 161r–161v	no. 8		[5]	**A**	fol. 457v	no. 8
[3]	**V g**	fol. 300r	no. 8		[6]	**G**	fol. 136v	no. 8
[4]	**B**	fol. 298r	no. 8		[7]	**E**	fol. 154v	no. 27

TEXT MANUSCRIPTS.

[10]	**M**	fol. 238r	no. 8		[50]	**Pa**	fols. 50v–51r	no. 156

EDITION OF TEXT. Chichmaref 1909, 2:542–43 no. 8.

TEXT STRUCTURE. 3 strophes: $\dfrac{a\ \ b}{1010'}$, $\dfrac{a\ \ b}{1010'}$, $\dfrac{b\ cC}{10'1010}$ a:-*eus*, b:-*ure*, c:-*i*

TEXTUAL LEGACY (England). Chaucer, *Complaynt d'Amours* (Wimsatt 1978, 72; 1991b, 313 n. 14).

EDITIONS OF MUSIC. Ludwig 1926–54, 1:7; Schrade 1956b, 3:79 (critical notes 1956c, 103); Wilkins 1980b, 25–26 (Chaucer, *O love, to whom* underlaid).

DISCUSSION (musical). The unusual tonality may be text-determined. Lowinsky 1945, 241; 1954, 186 (partial signature); Machabey 1955b, 2:24; Hoppin 1956, 109–10 (partial signature); Reaney 1963, 141–42 (partial signature); Salop 1971, 61–62 (melodic direction in cantus); Dömling 1972, 302 (text setting); Hirshberg 1980, 38–39 (*ficta*); Reaney 1982, 238–39 (mode, text painting); Fuller 1987a, 54 (tonal structure); Karp 1988, 71 (compositional priority of the tenor); Hoppin 1989 (partial signature).

De Fortune me doy pleindre et loer (ballade B23)
Refrain: *Dame qui fust si tres bien assenee* [47]

MANUSCRIPTS WITH TEXT AND MUSIC.[48]

[1]	**C**	fols. 200r–200v	no. 21	3v (tr, ca, ten)
[3]	**V g**	fol. 308v	no. 23	3v (tr, ca, ten)
[4]	**B**	fol. 306v	no. 23	3v (tr, ca, ten)
[5]	**A**	fol. 465v	no. 22	3v (tr, ca, ten)
[6]	**G**	fol. 142r	no. 23	3v (tr, ca, ten)
[7]	**E**	fols. 150v–151r	no. 14	4v (tr, ca, ten, ct)
[18]	**P m**	fol. 214r	no. 2	2v (ca, ten)
[58]	**Trém**	fol. xxi	no. 46	(index only)
[59]	**C h**	fol. 49r	no. 78	4v (tr, ca, ten, ct)
[63]	**P R**	fol. 64v	no. 134	4v (tr, ca, ten, different ct)
[65]	**S L**	fol. 74r		
[73]	**Str**	fol. 66v	no. 102	3v (tr, ca, ten)[49]

TEXT MANUSCRIPTS.

[10]	**M**	fols. 240v–241r	no. 23		[50]	**Pa** fol. 52v	no. 164
[49]	**Jp**	fol. 65v	no. 45			Lo195 **CVgBAMD** (chap. 6.4)	

TREATISE. Anonymous Pennsylvania/Schloss Harburg treatise cites "Se fortune" as a rondeau, either an error or a reference to another work (Staehelin 1974, 239).

FACSIMILES. *Jardin* 1910–25, vol. 1, fol. 65v (**Jp**); Bofill Soliguer 1991, 22–23 (MS C), 24 (MS A), 25 (MS G).

EDITIONS OF TEXT. Chichmaref 1909, 1:176 no. 195; Wilkins 1972, 61–62, no. 45.

---

[47] Cf. the *Lay du Mirouer, Se quanque Diex* (L11), ll. 57–59.

[48] Four-voice versions include unauthentic contratenors.

[49] With added contrafact text *Rubus ardens*.

TRANSLATIONS. L.W. Johnson 1990, 43–45 (strophe 1 and end of strophe 3); see also discography (chap. 8.3 and 8.8).

TEXT STRUCTURE. 3 strophes: $\frac{a\ b}{1010}, \frac{a\ b\ c\ c\ d\ D}{1010}, \frac{D}{71010'10}$ a:-*er*, b:-*ure*, c:-*ir*, d:-*ée*

DISCUSSION (literary). Hoepffner 1908–21, 3:256 n. to l. 443 of *Fonteinne*; Patch 1927, 96n. (theme of Fortune); Mulder 1978, 76 (image of Fortune in the music); L.W. Johnson 1979, 16–19; 1990, 43–47 (theme of Fortune). Feminine voice.

EDITIONS OF MUSIC. Ludwig 1926–54, 1:25–27 (omits more correct contratenor in MS E); Schrade 1956b, 3:101–3 (critical notes 1956c, 111–12); Wilkins 1972, 130–32. On barring, see Günther 1957, 92 n. 54.

DISCUSSION (musical). Ficker 1929, 501–2 (many errors in the musical example); Machabey 1955b, 2:36–37; Günther 1957, 79–80 (motivic analysis); Kämper 1971, 362–63 (musical image of Fortune's Wheel); Salop 1971, 71 (melodic planning); Hirshberg 1973–74, 61–62 (declamation); Lühmann 1978, 77–85, 113–17, 119–20 (rhythm and declamation); Berger 1987, 203–5 (modality, declamation); Bofill Soliguer 1991. Four-voice versions present a choice of dispositions, cantus and tenor plus either triplum or contratenor (Reaney 1955, 48; Günther 1957, 76 n. 41; Apfel 1960; 1961; Dömling 1970, 79, 80). The contratenor has often been cited as an example of an instrumental part suitable for a string instrument, because of the prominent melodic fifths (e.g., Machabey 1955b, 2:36). Reaney (1953, 141) prefers the substitute contratenor, apparently considering the contratenor in MS E authentic.

MUSICAL LEGACY. (a) Related to *Dame qui fust si tres bien assenee*, an anonymous 3v ballade (ed. Apel 1970–72, 2:21–23 no. 131; Wilkins 1966, 6–8 no. 4 and facs. p. xxi (MS PR); Greene 1981–89, 20:99–101 no. 30). The first line of this ballade quotes the text and music of the refrain of Machaut's B23, while the refrain of the Reina ballade quotes the text and music of Machaut's first line. Günther (1972, 55–56) discusses the anonymous ballade as a *balade entée*; Reaney (1982, 297–98) and Berger (1987) provide a "modal" analysis. (b) A ballade by Matteo da Perugia, *Se je me plaing de Fortune* (ed. Apel 1970–72, 1:104–6 no. 53; Greene 1981–89, 20:72–75 no. 21) begins by quoting the opening text of Machaut's *Se je me pleing* (B15). On the words "de Fortune," the text and music of B23 (cantus and tenor) are quoted (Lucy Cross, reported in Günther 1980a).

De ma dolour. See *Maugré mon cuer / De ma dolour* (M14).

De petit po, de niant volenté (ballade B18)
Refrain: *Onques n' ama qui pour si po haÿ*
MANUSCRIPTS WITH TEXT AND MUSIC.

[1] **C**	fols. 199r–199v	no. 19	3v (tr, ca, ten)	
[3] **V g**	fol. 305v	no. 18	3v (tr, ca, ten)	
[4] **B**	fol. 303v	no. 18	3v (tr, ca, ten)	
[5] **A**	fol. 463r	no. 18	3v (tr, ca, ten)	
[6] **G**	fol. 140r	no. 18	3v (tr, ca, ten)	
[7] **E**	fol. 147r	no. 2	3v (tr, ca, ten)	
[56] **CaB**	fol. 8v		5v (tr1, tr2, ca, ten, ct)[50]	
[58] **Trém**	fol. xxi	no. 45	(index only)	
[59] **C h**	fol. 18v	no. 14	3v (ca, ten, ct) "G de Machaut"	
[61] **F P**	fol. 100r	no. 176	3v (ca, ten, ct)	
[64] **Pit**	fol. 124v	no. 183	3v (untexted ca, ten, ct)	
[65] **S L**	fol. 90r	no. 100		
[66] **Mod**	fol. 26r	no. 46	4v	
[68] **Gr 3360**	fol. 3r	no. 8		
[71] **Nur**	fol. [1r]	no. 2		
[72] **P g**	fols. 259v–260r	no. 32	2v (untexted ca, ten)	

TEXT MANUSCRIPTS.

[10] **M**	fol. 240r	no. 18		[49] **Jp**	fol. 66r	no. 48
[40] **I**	fol. 19v	no. 100		[52] **Ta**	fol. 6r	no. 16

---

[50] On the fifth voice, see Fallows 1976, 279.

TREATISE. Anonymous Pennsylvania/Schloss Harburg (Staehelin 1974, 239). In addition, the very widely circulated B18 may be the work that occasioned discussion in Johannes de Muris, *Libellus cantus mensurabilis*, and in derivative treatises (see chap. 2.4.1).

TRANSLATIONS. Dömling 1972, 304 (refrain only, German); see also discography (chap. 8.3 and 8.8).

FACSIMILES. Wolf 1904, 2:41–43 no. 24 (diplomatic facs., MS G); *Jardin* 1910–25, vol. 1 fol. 66r (Jp); Apel 1953, 349 (MS A fragment); Bofill Soliguer 1991, 22 (MS C ending).

EDITIONS OF TEXT. Queux de Saint-Hilaire/Raynaud 1878–1903, 10:lxii no. 55 (MS I); Chichmaref 1909, 2:550–51 no. 20; Vitale-Brovarone 1980, 18 no. 16 (MS Ta). Feminine voice.

TEXT STRUCTURE. 3 strophes: $\begin{matrix} \text{a} & \text{b} & & \text{a} & \text{b} & \text{c} & \text{c} & \text{d} & \text{D} \\ 1010 & & & 1010 & & & 7101010 \end{matrix}$ a:-é, b:-is, c:-oir, c:-i

DISCUSSION (literary). Hassell (1982, nos. A57, P139) indexes the opening line and the refrain as proverbs.

EDITIONS OF MUSIC. Wolf 1904, 3:67–68 no. 24; Ludwig 1926–54, 1:18; Kammerer 1931, 164–65 no. 32; Schrade 1956b, 3:90–91 (critical notes 1956c, 108–9). The unauthentic contratenor has been much discussed (see below).

DISCUSSION (musical). Wolf 1904, 171 (Machaut's "notational license," with two examples from B18); Apel 1953, 345 (same two examples); Machabey 1955b, 2:32–33; Hirshberg 1971, 136–38 (motivic analysis); Salop 1971, 56 (melodic direction of cantus); Dömling 1972, 302, 306 (text setting, refrain). On the unauthentic contratenor, see Apfel 1960, 92 (dissonances between triplum and contratenor prevent 4v performance; also 1964–65, 1:54; 1974, 170–71); Martinez 1963, 112–13 (contratenor inessential); Reaney 1968, 65–66 (voice-leading gives a 2v framework, with added parts; alternative performance possible as a 3v work, either with triplum or contratenor); S.J. Williams 1968, 252 (alternative versions); Dömling 1970, 79 (quotes Apfel 1960); Berger 1992, 32–34 (*mutatio qualitatis*; readings in MSS C and E).

De souspirant cuer. See *Tous / De* (M2).

De tout sui si confortee (virelai V38; Schrade virelai 32)

MANUSCRIPTS WITH TEXT AND MUSIC (all 2v: ca, ten).

[5] A   fol. 494v   no. 38   [6] G   fol. 163v   no. 38

EDITION OF TEXT. Chichmaref 1909, 2:631–32 no. 38.

TRANSLATIONS. Allorto 1983, 157 (strophe 1; Italian).

DATE. Hoepffner (1908–21, 3:257, n. to *Fonteinne*, l. 1013) links the date of this work to that of *Sans cuer, dolens* (R4); see the commentary in Reaney 1952b, 37.

TEXT STRUCTURE. 3 strophes: $\begin{matrix}\text{AABBAB} \\ 7'7'577'5\end{matrix}$ ‖ $\begin{matrix}\text{bba bba} \\ 775' 775'\end{matrix}$ ∣ $\begin{matrix}\text{a abbab} \\ 7'7'577'5\end{matrix}$ ‖ $\begin{matrix}\text{AABBAB} \\ 7'7'577'5\end{matrix}$ a:-ée, b:-ay

EDITIONS OF MUSIC. Wooldridge 1905, 36–38=1929, 250–52; Quittard 1917–19, facing p. 138; Ludwig 1926–54, 1:92; Schrade 1956b, 3:191 (critical notes 1956c, 147); Gushee 1980, 156 (after Schrade); Allorto 1983, 44 no. 49.

DISCUSSION (musical). Salzer 1952, 1:275, 2:328 ex. 528 (voice-leading reduction of opening, showing "tonic" and "dominant" chords); Machabey 1955b, 1:195–96; Gushee 1980, 155–57 (analysis by Arlt).

MUSICAL LEGACY. On a group of late fourteenth-century virelais in similar style to Machaut's *Se je souspir* (V36/30), *Moult sui* (V37/31), and V38, see Fallows 1990, 22–23.

De toutes flours n'avoit et de tous fruis (ballade B31)
    Refrain: *Autre apres li ja mais avoir ne quier*
MANUSCRIPTS WITH TEXT AND MUSIC.

[3]	V g	fol. 313r	no. 31	3v (ca, ten, ct)
[4]	B	fol. 312r	no. 31	3v (ca, ten, ct)
[5]	A	fol. 470r	no. 30	3v (ca, ten, ct)
[6]	G	fols. 144r–144v	no. 29	3v (ca, ten, ct)
[7]	E	fol. 150v	no. 13	4v (tr, ca, ten, ct)
[18]	P m	fols. 213v–214r	no. 1	3v (ca, ten, ct)

[58] **Trém**	fol. xiii	no. 27	(index only)
[61] **FP**	fol. 99v	no. 175	3v (ca, ten, ct)
[63] **PR**	fol. 72r	no. 150	4v (tr, ca, ten, ct)
[64] **Pit**	fol. 120v	no. 175	3v (textless ca, ten, ct)
[66] **Mod**	fol. 25r	no. 43	3v (ca, ten, ct)
[67] **Fa**	fols. 37v–38v	no. 5	2v (anonymous instr. arr.)
[73] **Str**	fol. 95r [94r? 95v?]	no. 168	4v (tr, ca, ten, ct)

TEXT MANUSCRIPT.

[10] **M**   fols. 242r–242v   no. 31

TREATISE. Anonymous Pennsylvania/Schloss Harburg treatise (Staehelin 1974, 239).

FACSIMILES. Plamenac 1951, 189–90, facs. i b, Illus. 1 (MS **Fa**); Carapetyan 1961; Gallo 1981, fol. 99v (MS **FP**).

EDITIONS OF TEXT. Chichmaref 1909, 2:556 no. 31; Woledge 1961, 220–21 (strophes 2 and 3 inverted); Wilkins 1969a, 21–22 no. 11, notes pp. 123–24.

TRANSLATIONS. Riemann 1906, no. 3 (strophe 1); Woledge 1961, 220–21; Kelly 1978, 149 (from strophe 2); Wilkins 1989, 153–54 (strophe 1); L.W. Johnson 1990, 51–52; Wilson 1990a, 250; Fuller 1992a, 42; see also discography (chap. 8.3 and 8.8).

TEXT STRUCTURE. 3 strophes: $\frac{a\ b}{1010}$, $\frac{a\ b\ c\ c\ d\ D}{1010\ 7101010}$ a:-*uis*, b:-*ose*, c:-*our*, d:-*ier*

DISCUSSION (literary). Patch 1927, 64 n. 2 (theme of Fortune); Kuhn 1967 (analysis after Woledge edition, with strophes 2 and 3 inverted; see L.W. Johnson 1979, 28 n. 16; 1990, 312 n. 67); Zumthor 1972, 274 (=Eng. ed., 220); Calin 1974, 244 (theme of Fortune); L.W. Johnson 1979, 23–26; 1990, 51–56 (very sympathetic analysis, especially on the theme of Fortune); Fuller 1992a, 42–44 (musical setting of poetry). See chap. 6.4, commentaries to Lo5, Lo215, and Lo225.

TEXTUAL LEGACY (France). Froissart, ballade *Sur toutes flours tient on la rose a belle* from *Paradis d'Amour* (ll. 1627–53; ed. Patterson 1935, 2:65; Wilkins 1969a, 51 no. 37; Dembowski 1986, 79–80; strophe 1 trans. Wimsatt 1991b, 179; ed. and trans. Figg 1994b, 153–54, 158); the same ballade also appears in the separate section of ballades, with a different third strophe (ed. McGregor 1975, 211 no. 8; Baudouin 1978, 13–15 no. 8; ed. and trans. Figg 1994b, 153–54). For an analysis, see Figg 1994a, 135–37; 1994b, 153–59.

EDITIONS OF MUSIC. Wooldridge 1905, 2:33–36=1929, 247–50 (errors); Riemann 1906, no. 3 (errors); Ludwig 1926–54, 1:35–36; Einstein 1927; 1947; Plamenac 1951, 189–90 (notes, 194; MS **Fa**); Preston 1952; Schrade 1956b, 3:118–19 (critical notes 1956c, 115–16); Wilkins 1969a, 147–50 no. 4 (after Schrade); 1979, 39 (beginning of **Fa** intabulation); Kugler 1972 (Notenteil), x (critical notes, 11–17 (diplomatic facs. of **Fa** vertically aligned with diplomatic facs. of B31); Plamenac 1972, 16–19 no. 5 (ed. of **Fa** vertically aligned with B31); Wilson 1990a, 248–50 no. 74; Fuller 1992a (commentary and critical notes, pp. 41–42, 65).

DISCUSSION (musical). Besseler 1927, 226–27 (stylistic comparison of B31 with motet style and with Vitry); Preston 1951, 616 (romanticized text setting); Machabey 1955b, 2:44–46 (melodic motives); Günther 1957, 72 (internal rhymes clarified by music), 86 (motivic analysis); Bukofzer 1960, 858–59 (example from **Fa** intabulation); Reaney 1966, 708 (performance of **Fa** intabulation); Dömling 1970, 79, 80 (likes it as 4v work; essential contratenor); Hirshberg 1971, 141–42 (motivic analysis), 399–404 (harmonic analysis); Dömling 1972, 302, 304 (text painting, text setting of refrain); Kugler 1972, 112–18 (detailed study of techniques of intabulation in **Fa**); Kühn 1973, 213 (melodic design); Kugler 1975, 44–45 (syncopation in **Fa** intabulation); DeLone 1978 (4v reduction of A-section); Lühmann 1978, 87–92 (rhythm and declamation); Mulder 1978, 77 (image of Fortune in music); Hirshberg 1980, 35–37 (*ficta*); Wilkins 1980a, 77; Berger 1992, 67–68 (text underlay and corruption in MS **PR**); Fuller 1992a (exhaustive analysis); 1992b, 233–35 (directed progressions).

MUSICAL LEGACY. Musical imitation in Suzoy's ballade *A l'arbre sec* (ed. Apel 1970–72, 1:201–2 no. 104; Greene 1981–89, 19:117–19 no. 85).

***De triste cuer faire joyeusement / Quant vrais amans aimme amou-
reusement / Certes, je di et s'en quier jugement*** (ballade B29)
Refrain: *Triste, dolent, qui larmes de sanc pleure*
MANUSCRIPTS WITH TEXT AND MUSIC (all 3v: ca1, ca2, ca3).

[3]	**V g**	fols. 311v–312r	no. 29		[6]	**G**	fols. 144v–145r	no. 30
[4]	**B**	fols. 310v–311r	no. 29		[7]	**E**	fol. 150r	no. 12
[5]	**A**	fols. 468v–469r	no. 28					

TEXT MANUSCRIPTS.

[10]	**M**	fols. 241v–242r	no. 29a–c
[40]	**I**	fol. 19r	no. 97 (*De triste* only)
[40]	**I**	fol. 19r	no. 96a (7 ll. of *Quant* crossed out)
[50]	**Pa**	fols. 56r–56v	nos. 174–76

EDITIONS OF TEXT. Queux de Saint-Hilaire/Raynaud 1878–1903, 10:lviii no. 51 (*De triste*
only, after MS I); Chichmaref 1909, 2:557–59 nos. 32, 33, 34.

TRANSLATION. See discography (chap. 8.3 and 8.8).

TEXT STRUCTURE. 3 x 3 strophes, triple ballade: $\frac{a}{10}\frac{b}{10}$, $\frac{a}{10}\frac{b}{10}$, $\frac{b}{10}\frac{c}{10}\frac{C}{10}$ a:-*ent*, b:-*aire*, c:-*eure*

DISCUSSION (literary). Patch 1927, 96n. (*De triste*); Poirion 1965, 611 (simultaneous presentation of texts); Kelly 1978, 104 n. 22 (religious sentiment in *Quant*); Zeeman 1988, 834–
35 (sad subject matter); Newes 1991a, 75–76 (the three poems consist of the poet and two
speakers). Note the textual reminiscence, particularly of the refrain, to *Voir Dit* letter 8 (ed.
P. Paris 1875, 61). Hassell (1982, no. M246) indexes a proverb in *De triste*.

TEXTUAL LEGACY (England). Chaucer, *Complaint of Mars* (Wimsatt 1978, 74–75; 1991b,
294 n. 3, concerning *De triste* only).

EDITIONS OF MUSIC. Ludwig 1926–54, 1:32–33; Schrade 1956b, 3:114–15 (critical notes
1956c, 114–15).

DISCUSSION (musical). S.J. Williams 1952, 250; Machabey 1955b, 2:42–43; Günther 1957,
84–85 (motivic analysis); Dömling 1972, 301, 303 (text painting, text setting of l. 5);
Kühn 1973, 213 (melodic design); Newes 1987, 160–64; 1991a, 76–77 (texture).

MUSICAL LEGACY. Anonymous ballade, *Dame vailans / Amis de tant / Certainement puet on
bien* (ed. Apel 1970–72, 2:26–28 no. 134; Greene 1981–89, 20:105–7 no. 32); see Berger
1992, 227.

Diex, Biauté, Douceur, Nature (virelai V19)
MANUSCRIPTS WITH TEXT AND MUSIC (all monophonic).

[1]	**C**	fols. 155v–156r	no. 18		[5]	**A**	fol. 487v	no. 19
[3]	**V g**	fol. 328v	no. 19		[6]	**G**	fol. 158v	no. 19
[4]	**B**	fol. 326v	no. 19		[7]	**E**	fol. 160v	no. 10

TEXT MANUSCRIPTS.

[10]	**M**	fol. 250r	no. 19		[50]	**Pa**	fols. 67r–67v	no. 210
[43]	**Mn**	fol. 18v	no. 4	*Un Lay d'Esperance*				

EDITION OF TEXT. Chichmaref 1909, 2:603–5 no. 19.

TRANSLATION. Reaney 1959b, 30 (summary only).

TEXT STRUCTURE. 3 strophes:
$$\underset{7'7'7'5'}{AAAB\ AAAB} \parallel \underset{7'7'5'\ 7'7'5'}{bbc\ bbc} \mid \underset{7'7'7'5'\ 7'7'7'5'}{aaab\ aaab} \parallel \underset{7'7'7'5'\ 7'7'5'}{AAAB\ AAAB}$$ a:-*ure*, b:-*ée*, c:-*ance*

EDITIONS OF MUSIC. Ludwig 1926–54, 1:79; Schrade 1956b, 3:178 (critical notes 1956c,
142).

DISCUSSION (musical). Machabey 1955b, 1:186 (duplex virelai); Mulder 1978, 80–81
(motivic analysis); M.L. Göllner 1989, 66–67 (text/music relationship).

Diligenter inquiramus. See *Martyrum / Diligenter* (M19).

Dix et sept, .v., .xiii., .xiiii. et quinse (rondeau R17)
MANUSCRIPTS WITH TEXT AND MUSIC.

[3]	**V g**	fol. 322r	no. 17	3v (ca, ten, ct)
[4]	**B**	fol. 320r	no. 17	3v (ca, ten, ct)

[5] **A**	fol. 475v	no. 2 (added later)	3v (ca, ten, ct)
[6] **G**	fol. 152v	no. 14	3v (ca, ten, ct)
[7] **E**	fol. 198v	in *Voir Dit*	2v (ca, ten)
[57] **I v**	fol. 3v	no. 6	3v (ca, ten, ct)

TEXT MANUSCRIPTS.

    [10] **M**   fol. 244v   no. 14   VD56 **AFEPm** (chap. 5.13 table 5.3)

FACSIMILE. Gallo 1985, 43 (MS **E**).

EDITIONS OF TEXT. Tarbé 1849, 171; P. Paris 1875, 266; Chichmaref 1909, 2:574 no. 14; Wilkins 1969a, 32 no. 21, notes p. 126.

TRANSLATION. See also discography (chap. 8.3 and 8.8).

DATE. (a) 27 October 1363 (Machabey 1955b, 1:168); (b) composed by 28 September 1363, sent by 17 October 1363 (Leech-Wilkinson 1993a, 53–54, 58).

TEXT STRUCTURE. $\begin{smallmatrix} A & B & a & A & a & b & A & B \\ 10 & 10 & 10 & 10 & 10 & 10 & 10 & 10 \end{smallmatrix}$ a:-*ise*,* b:-*is* (*: *quinse* rhymes with *emprise*)

DISCUSSION (literary). P. Paris (1875, xx–xxi and 266) solved the cryptogram (r e n o p) as Peronne, an important element of his identification of Toute Belle as one Peronne d'Armentières. The following *Voir Dit* passages concern R17: (a) Guillaume indicates in letter 25 that he has composed the text (P. Paris 1875, 190); (b) Toute Belle replies in letter 26 that she has seen the rondeau and has found her name in it (1875, 194); (c) Guillaume indicates in letter 31 that he has composed the music (1875, 241); (d) at the end of the same letter, he says he will send a rondeau to which he has newly added a tenor and contratenor (1875, 242); formerly thought to refer to R17 or *Dame, se vous n'avez* (R13), Leech-Wilkinson (1993a, 49–50) proposes that this refers to *Puis qu'en oubli* (R18), which better corresponds musically to such a compositional process; (e) in letter 33, Guillaume again indicates that he has composed music for R17, but since he has not yet heard the work performed, he will delay sending it (P. Paris 1875, 258); (f) near the end of the same letter, he promises to send the rondeau soon, along with the unfinished *Voir Dit* (1875, 259); (g) a narrative passage tells of sending the incomplete *Voir Dit* along with R17 (1875, 261, ll. 5976–86); (h) Guillaume sends R17 in letter 35, apologizing that others have seen the music before Toute Belle (1875, 265); (i) R17 finally appears in the narrative, inserted as ll. 5993–6000 (1875, 266–67); (j) in the last letter, no. 46, Toute Belle indicates that she is sending a rondeau which contains a cryptogram yielding Guillaume's name, and that she learned how to write it from him, i.e., from R17 (1875, 369). For excerpts from or commentary on these passages, see Besseler 1924–25, 48; Ludwig 1926–54, 2:56b*–57*; Martinez 1963, 115; Poirion 1965, 324; Zumthor 1972, 275 (=Eng. ed., 221–22); Cerquiglini 1985b, 227–29, 235 n. 27; Leech-Wilkinson 1990a, 230; 1993a, 53–55; 1993b, 122–24, 137–39.

EDITIONS OF MUSIC. Wooldridge 1905, 31–33 (errors); Ludwig 1926–54, 1:66; Schrade 1956b, 3:160–61 (critical notes 1956c, 133); Wilkins 1969a, 156–57 no. 7 (after Schrade). Barring discussed in Hoppin 1960, 23–24.

DISCUSSION (musical). Machabey 1955b, 1:167–68 (melodic recurrences); Günther 1957, 108–9 and 1963a, 108–9 n. 102 (motivic development); Salop 1971, 75–76 (melodic planning); Kühn 1973, 214–18 (melodic correspondences, sonority); Winn 1981, 120 (number symbolism); Leech-Wilkinson 1993a, 55, 58, 60–61 (simultaneous conception of parts; relationship to *Plourez, dames* [B32], *Nes qu'on* [B33], *Quant Theseüs / Ne quier* [B34], and *Se pour ce muir* [B36]; questions of genre; names possibly concealed in opening music).

Donnez, signeurs, donnez a toutes mains (ballade B26)

Refrain: *Et terre aussi qu'est despendue / vaut trop miex que terre perdue*

MANUSCRIPTS WITH TEXT AND MUSIC (all 3v: ca, ten, ct).

[3] **V g**	fol. 310r	no. 26	[6] **G**	fol. 143r	no. 26
[4] **B**	fol. 308r	no. 26	[7] **E**	fol. 155v	no. 30
[5] **A**	fol. 467r	no. 26			

TEXT MANUSCRIPT.

    [10] **M**   fol. 241r   no. 26

FACSIMILE. Besseler/Gülke 1973, 63 plate 21 (MS **A**); Earp 1991c, 196.

EDITIONS OF TEXT. Tarbé 1849, 131; Chichmaref 1909, 2:554–55 no. 28.

TRANSLATIONS. Suchier/Birch-Hirschfeld 1900, 237 (=1913 ed., 244) (in German, strophe 1 only); see also discography (chap. 8.3 and 8.8).

DATE. (a) between 1359 and October 1361 (Chailley 1973, 256–58; but see chap. 1.12.2); (b) between 1356 and 1362 (Arlt 1993, 58, based on manuscript transmission); (c) 1360, in connection with the treaty of Brétigny, specifically, at St-Omer in October 1360 (Dominik Sackmann, reported in Arlt 1993, 59).

TEXT STRUCTURE. 3 strophes: $\frac{a\ b\ \ \ a\ b\ \ \ b\ CC}{1010\ \ 1010\ \ 108\text{'}8}$, a:-ains, b:-eur, c:-ue

DISCUSSION (literary). A similar call for largesse is seen in the rondeau Se tenir vues le droit chemin (Lo241), linked to Confort by Hoepffner (1908–21, 3:251, note to ll. 3129–34), who considered the lyric to date from ca. 1357. Compare also the language describing the character Largesse in Jugement Navarre, ll. 1266–78, and the description of John of Luxembourg's generosity in Confort, ll. 2930–33, quoted above, chap. 1.6.2a.

EDITIONS OF MUSIC. Ludwig 1926–54, 1:29 (syncopation errors), version of MSS **VgBE**; Schrade 1956b, 3:108–9 (critical notes 1956c, 113–114), version of MSS **AG**. Transcription errors discussed in Hoppin 1960, 16 n. 15; Günther 1962–63, 21. The two distinct lines of musical transmission (MSS **VgBE**: **AG**) were signaled in Machabey 1955b, 2:39, n. 486bis, and discussed further in Bent 1981, 308; 1983, 66–69; Arlt 1993. Arlt (1993, 46–47, see also 60–61) provides a convincing emendation of the earlier version.

DISCUSSION (musical). Salzer 1952, 1:278, 2:332–36 ex. 533 (edition, with voice-leading reductions that emphasize certain pitches to obtain a more traditional tonal plan); Machabey 1955b, 2:39–40; Günther 1958, 35, n. 27 (tempus changes); Martinez 1963, 107–8 (articulative function of ouvert and clos phrases); Hirshberg 1971, 111–12 (based on Günther 1957; tempus changes respond to expansion or contraction of motivic work); Dömling 1972, 303, 305 (musical aspects of refrain, text setting, repeats of similar musical material); Besseler/Gülke 1973, 62 (motivic work); Fuller 1991, 8–13 (tonal and rhythmic analysis); Arlt 1993, 44–64 (thorough analysis of the two versions; directed progressions; text painting; compositional process); Leech-Wilkinson 1993a, 45 n. 4 (directed progressions). The pervasive use of certain melodic formulas in tempus imperfectum, prolatio major links Donnez, signeurs (B26), Une vipere (B27), and Je puis trop (B28) as one group, and Plourez, dames (B32), Nes qu'on (B33), and Se pour ce muir (B36) as another; the same formulas are seen to a lesser extent in En amer (RF4), Cinc, un (R6), and Douce dame, tant (R20) (cf. Reaney 1955, 47; Günther 1957, 80–84; Hirshberg 1971, 120–33; Little 1980, 49; Arlt 1993, 63).

Dou mal qui m'a longuement (virelai V8)

MANUSCRIPTS WITH TEXT AND MUSIC (all monophonic).

[1] **C**	fols. 151v–152r	no. 8		[5] **A**	fol. 484r	no. 8
[3] **Vg**	fols. 324v–325r	no. 8		[6] **G**	fol. 156r	no. 8
[4] **B**	fols. 322v–323r	no. 8		[7] **E**	fol. 163v	no. 26

TEXT MANUSCRIPT.
  [10] **M**   fols. 247r–247v   no. 8

EDITION OF TEXT. Chichmaref 1909, 2:589–90 no. 8.

TRANSLATION. See discography (chap. 8.3 and 8.8).

TEXT STRUCTURE. 3 strophes: $\frac{AAAB}{7\,6\,5\,5}$ ‖ $\frac{a\,b\ \ a\,b}{7\,6\text{'}\ \ 7\,6\text{'}}$ | $\frac{aaab}{7655}$ ‖ $\frac{AAAB}{7\,6\,5\,5}$, a:-ent, b:-ie

EDITIONS OF MUSIC. Ludwig 1926–54, 1:73; Schrade 1956b, 3:171 (critical notes 1956c, 138).

DISCUSSION (musical). Machabey 1955b, 1:180; Göllner 1989, 65–66 (last two phrases of A-section exchanged to form the B-section); Weber-Bockholdt 1992, 269–70 (melody clarifies verse structure).

Douce dame jolie (virelai V4)

MANUSCRIPTS WITH TEXT AND MUSIC (all monophonic).

[1] **C**	fols. 149v–150r	no. 4		[5] **A**	fols. 482v–483r	no. 4
[3] **Vg**	fol. 323v	no. 4		[6] **G**	fol. 155r	no. 4
[4] **B**	fol. 321v	no. 4		[7] **E**	fol. 159r	no. 2

TEXT MANUSCRIPT.
[10] **M** fols. 246r–246v no. 4

EDITION OF TEXT. Chichmaref 1909, 2:584–85 no. 4.

TRANSLATIONS. Reese 1940, 350; Reaney 1959b, 30 (summary only); see also discography (chap. 8.3 and 8.8).

LITERARY ANTECEDENT. Reaney (1959b, 37) indicates that l. 33, "A jointes mains deprie," resembles l. 1 of a rondeau by Adam de la Halle, *A jointes mains vous proi* (ed. Gennrich 1921–27, 1:65 no. 75 [commentary 2:82–83]; Wilkins 1967, 56 no. 10)

TEXT STRUCTURE. 3 strophes: $\frac{AAAB}{6'6'6'7} \parallel \frac{a\,ab\,a\,ab}{6'2'6\;6'2'6} \mid \frac{a\,a\,ab}{6'6'6'7} \parallel \frac{AAAB}{6'6'6'7}$ a:-*ie*, b:-*ent*

EDITIONS OF MUSIC. Ludwig 1926–54, 1:71; Reese 1940, 349–50 no. 105; Schrade 1956b, 3:168 (critical notes 1956c, 137); Brandt 1980, 70; Arlt 1982, 267 (after Schrade); Lincoln/Bonta 1986, 51–52 no. 19; Wilkins 1989, 164 (after Schrade).

DISCUSSION (musical). Machabey 1955b, 1:178; Hatten 1978, 10 (modal influence); Arlt 1982, 267 (text/music relationship); Weber-Bockholdt 1992, 267–68 (text accent and music); Leech-Wilkinson 1991 (voice-leading reduction; link to *Merci vous pri* [R3]).

MUSICAL LEGACY. For a nineteenth-century arrangement inspired by V4, see chap. 2.5 (Weckerlin).

Douce dame, tant com vivray (rondeau R20)

MANUSCRIPTS WITH TEXT AND MUSIC (all 2v: ca, ten).

[5] **A** fol. 481r no. 21   [6] **G** fol. 154r no. 20

TEXT MANUSCRIPTS.

[10] **M** fol. 245r no. 19   [50] **Pa** fol. 34v no. 107
[46] **St** fol. 141v no. 89   Lo235 **VgBAEMD**

EDITIONS OF TEXT. Tarbé 1849, 54; 1856, 56; Chichmaref 1909, 1:210 no. 235; Wilkins 1972, 108 no. 233.

TRANSLATION. See discography (chap. 8.3 and 8.8).

TEXT STRUCTURE. 8AB aA ab AB a:-*vivray*, b:-*vis*

EDITIONS OF MUSIC. Ludwig 1926–54, 1:68; Schrade 1956b, 3:163 (critical notes 1956c, 134).

DISCUSSION (musical). Machabey 1955b, 1:170; Wykes 1956, 19–23 (analysis); Günther 1957, 98, 104, 110, 112 (early date). The pervasive use of certain melodic formulas in *tempus imperfectum, prolatio major* links *Donnez, signeurs* (B26), *Une vipere* (B27), and *Je puis trop* (B28) as one group, and *Plourez, dames* (B32), *Nes qu'on* (B33), and *Se pour ce muir* (B36) as another; the same formulas are seen to a lesser extent in *En amer* (RF4), *Cinc, un* (R6), and *Douce dame, tant* (R20) (cf. Reaney 1955, 47; Hirshberg 1971, 120–33; Little 1980, 49).

Dous amis, oy mon complaint (ballade B6)
Refrain: *Quant tes cuers en moy ne maint*

MANUSCRIPTS WITH TEXT AND MUSIC (all 2v: ca, ten).

[1] **C** fols. 160r–160v no. 6   [5] **A** fol. 456v no. 6
[3] **Vg** fol. 299r no. 6   [6] **G** fols. 135v–136r no. 6
[4] **B** fol. 297r no. 6   [7] **E** fol. 154r no. 24

TEXT MANUSCRIPTS.

[10] **M** fol. 237v–238r no. 6   [50] **Pa** fol. 50v no. 155

FACSIMILE. Apel 1953, 357 facs. 69 (MS A) (discussed pp. 355–56).

EDITIONS OF TEXT. Tarbé 1856, 22; Chichmaref 1909, 2:540–41 no. 6; Wilkins 1969a, 26–27 no. 16.

TRANSLATION. Hoppin 1978a, 141–42.

TEXT STRUCTURE. 3 strophes, duplex ballade: $\frac{aaab\,aaab\,bba\,bbA}{7437\;7437\;437\;437}$ a:-*aint*, b:-*ours*

The short verses may be combined into isometric heptasyllabic verses with internal rhyme: 7aab aab ba bA (brief discussion in Ziino 1990, 18–19).

EDITIONS OF MUSIC. Ludwig 1926–54, 1:5 (errors); Schrade 1956b, 3:77 (errors; critical notes 1956c, 101–2); Wilkins 1969a, 150–51 no. 5 (after Schrade); Hoppin 1978a, 140–42 no. 62 (errors corrected, but text underlay better in Ludwig); Arlt 1982, 249–50 (by Karin Smith-Paulsmeier). Discussion of transcription problems in Günther 1957, 92 n. 54; Hoppin 1960, 19, n. 25, 24; Arlt 1982, 250.

DISCUSSION (musical). Machabey 1955b, 2:22–23; Salop 1971, 53–54 (melodic direction in cantus); Dömling 1972, 302 (text painting); Lühmann 1978, 118–19 (declamation); Baumann 1979, 31 (textless transition passage); Wilkins 1980a, 77; Arlt 1982, 249–52; 1983, 499 and 1984, 274–75 (text painting); Günther 1984a, 231 n. 5 (text painting); Karp 1988, 69–70 (compositional priority of the tenor); Kügle 1991, 376 (compares Lescurel).

Dous viaire gracieus (rondeau R1)
MANUSCRIPTS WITH TEXT AND MUSIC.

[1] C	fol. 203r	no. 5	3v (tr, ca, ten)	[5] A	fol. 476r	no. 3	2v (ca, ten)[51]
[3] V g	fol. 316v	no. 1	3v (tr, ca, ten)	[6] G	fol. 150r	no. 1	3v (tr, ca, ten)
[4] B	fol. 315v	no. 1	3v (tr, ca, ten)	[7] E	fol. 139r	no. 12	3v (tr, ca, ten)

TEXT MANUSCRIPT.

[10] M   fol. 244r   no. 1

EDITION OF TEXT. Chichmaref 1909, 2:569 no. 1.

TRANSLATIONS. Caldwell 1978, 176; Yudkin 1989, 499; Eggebrecht 1991, 238 (German); see also discography (chap. 8.3 and 8.8).

TEXT STRUCTURE. 7AB aA ab AB a:-*eus*, b:-*i*

EDITIONS OF MUSIC. Kiesewetter 1841, *Beilagen*, 7 no. 14 (disapproving of the counterpoint, Kiesewetter comments "O tempora! o mores!"), 1841, 10 (commentary); Ambros 1891, 374–75 (=1864 ed., 341–42) (after Kiesewetter); Ludwig 1926–54, 1:52; Schrade 1956b, 3:142 (critical notes 1956c, 124); Caldwell 1978, 175–76; Yudkin 1989, 498–99 (after Schrade); Eggebrecht 1991, 237. See Fuller (1992b, 255 n. 27) on the *F*-sharp in m. 3.

DISCUSSION (musical). Combarieu 1913, 399 (dissonant cadential progression); Machabey 1955b, 1:153–54; Günther 1957, 105 (motivic analysis); Eggebrecht 1968, 190 n. 21 (text painting of the word "dous"); Salop 1971, 77–78 (melodically unsuccessful due to imitative passage); Hatten 1978, 5–7, 10–11 (consonance and dissonance; melody); Yudkin 1989, 498–99 (analysis); Cross 1990, 269–70 (chromatic gestures); Eggebrecht 1991, 238–40 (sonority and text setting); Fuller 1992b, 244 (opening sonority, directed progressions).

Ego moriar pro te. See *J'ay tant / Lasse!* (M7).

Eins que ma dame. See *Tant doucement m'ont / Eins* (M13).

En amer a douce vie (ballade RF4; Schrade ballade 41)
Refrain: *Fait cuer d'ami et d'amie*
MANUSCRIPTS WITH TEXT AND MUSIC.

[1] C	fols. 46r–46v		4v (tr, ca, ten, ct)
[3] V g	fols. 109v–110v		4v (tr, ca, ten, ct)
[4] B	fols. 109v–110v (new 126v–127v)		4v (tr, ca, ten, ct)
[5] A	fols. 68v–69v		4v (tr, ca, ten, ct)
[6] F	fols. 54v–55v		4v (tr, ca, ten, ct)
[7] E	fols. 31r–31v		4v (tr, ca, ten, ct)
[15] K	fol. 59v		3v (ca, ten, ct)
[20] P e	fols. 23v–24v		4v (tr, ca, ten, ct)
[58] Trém	fol. xvi	no. 33	(index only)
[61] F P	fol. 97r	no. 171	3v (ca, ten, ct)
[63] P R	fol. 63r	no. 130	4v (tr, ca, ten, ct)
[64] Pit	fol. 122r	no. 180	3v (ca, ten, ct)

TEXT MANUSCRIPTS.

[10] M	fol. 68r	
[16] J	fols. 66r–66v	empty space for staves
[18] P m	fols. 64v–65r	

---

51 On the missing triplum, see Dömling 1970, 78 n. 18 (criticized in Earp 1983, 69 n. 152).

FACSIMILES (refer to chap. 4.4e). Miniatures C31–32. Wilkins 1979, 22 (MS **Pe**, fol. 23v); Leech-Wilkinson 1982, 102 (MS **Pe**, fols. 23v–24r).

EDITIONS OF TEXT (*Remede*, ll. 2857–92). Hoepffner 1908–21, 2:105–6; Wimsatt/Kibler 1988, 327–29.

TRANSLATIONS. Switten 1988c, 55–56; Wimsatt/Kibler 1988, 326–28; see also discography (chap. 8.3 and 8.8).

TEXT STRUCTURE. 3 strophes, duplex ballade[52]: $\dfrac{a\,a\,b}{7'3'7}\,\dfrac{a\,ab\,bb\,a}{7'3'7}\,\dfrac{bb\,a}{737'}\,\dfrac{}{737'}$ a:-*ie*, b:-*ir*

DISCUSSION (literary). Poirion 1965, 387–88, 529; Huot 1987, 256. For some literary studies that deal with all of the inserted lyrics, see chap. 5.7.

TEXTUAL LEGACY (France). On the complex of poetic and musical quotations linking RF4 to Jacob de Senleches's ballade *En attendant esperance*, Galiot's isorhythmic rondeau *En attendant d' amer la douce vie*, and the rondeau *Esperance qui en mon cuer s'en bat*, see chap. 2.4, "musical imitations."

EDITIONS OF MUSIC. Ludwig 1911, 11–15 (appendix); 1926–54, 1:98–99; Schrade 1956b, 3:138–39 (critical notes 1956c, 121–23); Switten 1988c, 54–55 (after Schrade); Wimsatt/Kibler 1988, 425–27, critical notes pp. 440–42 (ed. Baltzer).

DISCUSSION (musical). Ludwig 1911, 408 n. 1 (syncopation in cantus); Günther 1957, 116–17 (motivic analysis); Reaney 1980a, 430, 435 (four voices not to be performed together, but as alternative 3v versions with triplum or with contratenor); Malizia 1984, 30–34. The pervasive use of certain melodic formulas in *tempus imperfectum, prolatio major* links *Donnez, signeurs* (B26), *Une vipere* (B27), and *Je puis trop* (B28) as one group, and *Plourez, dames* (B32), *Nes qu' on* (B33), and *Se pour ce muir* (B36) as another; the same formulas are seen to a lesser extent in *En amer* (RF4), *Cinc, un* (R6), and *Douce dame, tant* (R20) (cf. Reaney 1955, 47; Hirshberg 1971, 120–33; Little 1980, 49). For some musical studies that deal with all of the inserted lyrics, see chap. 5.7.

En demantant (lai L24; Schrade lai 18)

MANUSCRIPT WITH TEXT AND MUSIC (monophonic; strophes 1–3, 4–6, 7–9, and 10–12 combine as 3v polyphony).[53]

[7] **E**   fols. 128r–129r   no. 19

EDITION OF TEXT. Chichmaref 1909, 2:474–80 no. 24.

ASCRIPTION. *Explicit. Cy fine un autre lay de Guille' Machaut. Deo gracias.* See *Pour ce que plus* (L23/17); see also chap. 1.10.2c.

DATE. (a) 1356, on the basis of a relation to the battle of Poitiers (Chichmaref 1909, 1:xliii; Hoepffner 1908–21, 3:xiii n. 2; Machabey 1955b, 1:50); see chap. 1.10.2c; (b) ca. 1367–77 for both L24 and *Pour ce que plus* (L23/17) (Reaney 1967, 89–90, 95).

TEXT STRUCTURE. 12 strophes, 210 lines:

1. $\dfrac{aab}{446}\,\Big|\,\dfrac{aab}{446}\,\|\,\dfrac{bba}{446}\,\Big|\,\dfrac{bba}{446}\,\|$

6. $\dfrac{k\,k\,k\,k\,l}{7'3'7'3'7'}\,\Big|\,\dfrac{k\,k\,k\,k\,l}{7'3'7'3'7'}\,\|\,\dfrac{l\,l\,l\,l\,k}{7'3'7'3'7'}\,\Big|\,\dfrac{l\,l\,l\,l\,k}{7'3'7'3'7'}\,\|$

2. 6cccd I cccd II 6dddc I dddc II

7. $\dfrac{m\,m\,m\,n}{5\,5\,7\,5}\,\Big|\,\dfrac{m\,m\,m\,n}{5\,5\,7\,5}\,\|\,\dfrac{n\,n\,n\,m}{5575}\,\Big|\,\dfrac{n\,n\,n\,m}{5575}\,\|$

3. $\dfrac{e\,f\,f\,f\,fee}{7733334}\,\Big|\,\dfrac{e\,f\,f\,f\,fe}{773337}\,\|\,\dfrac{feee\,e\,f\,f}{7733334}\,\Big|\,\dfrac{feee\,e\,f}{773337}\,\|$

8. $\dfrac{o\,o\,p}{886'}\,\Big|\,\dfrac{o\,o\,p}{886'}\,\|\,\dfrac{p\,p\,o}{8'8'6}\,\Big|\,\dfrac{p\,p\,o}{8'8'6}\,\|$

4. $\dfrac{ggggh}{75557}\,\Big|\,\dfrac{ggggh}{75557}\,\|\,\dfrac{hhhhg}{75557}\,\Big|\,\dfrac{hhhhg}{75557}\,\|$

9. $\dfrac{q\,qqq\,r}{33337'}\,\Big|\,\dfrac{q\,qqq\,r}{33337'}\,\|\,\dfrac{r\,r\,r\,r\,q}{3'3'3'3'7}\,\Big|\,\dfrac{r\,r\,r\,r\,q}{3'3'3'3'7}\,\|$

5. $\dfrac{i\;i\;i\;i\;j}{4'4'4'4'8}\,\Big|\,\dfrac{i\;i\;i\;i\;j}{4'4'4'4'8}\,\|\,\dfrac{j\,j\,j\,j\,i}{44448'}\,\Big|\,\dfrac{j\,j\,j[\;][\;]}{444[\;][4]}\,\|$[54]

10. $\dfrac{ssssh}{44448}\,\Big|\,\dfrac{ssssh}{44448}\,\|\,\dfrac{hhhhs}{44448}\,\Big|\,\dfrac{hhhhs}{44448}\,\|$

---

[52] A *sixain* followed by its retrograde, cf. *Fons / O livoris* (M9, motetus) and *Amours me fait* (B19) (Clarkson 1971, 266 n. 93). Brief discussion of text form in Ziino 1990, 16–18.

[53] Could the indication "primus" in the right margin (fol. 128r) refer to the polyphony?

[54] The explanation of the text corruption given by Hasselman/Walker (1970, 10 n. to m. 42), that only four syllables of what would be the last 8-syllable line are given in the source,

11. $\frac{t\,t\,t\,u}{5333}\mid\frac{t\,t\,t\,u}{5333}\parallel\frac{u\,u\,u\,t}{5333}\mid\frac{u\,u\,u\,t}{5333}\parallel$ 12. = 1.

a:-*ant*, b:-*ay*, c:-*oy*, d:-*é*, e:-*i*, f:-*u*, g:-*té*, h:-*er*, i:-*une*, j:-*eulz* [-*eus*, -*ues*], k:-*une*, l:-*ie*, m:-*as*, n:-*a*, o:-[*i*]*er*, p:-*ance*, q:-*ains*, r:-*aindre*, s:-*ours*, t:-*is*, u:-*ort*

DISCUSSION (literary). Patch 1927, 64 n. 1, 68 n. 3, 80 n. 2, 119 n. 1; Calin 1974, 244 (theme of Fortune). Hassell (1982, nos. A95, L114) indexes proverbs.

EDITIONS OF MUSIC. Ludwig 1926–54, 4:80–81 (ed. Besseler; errors); Schrade 1956b, 2:99–101 (critical notes 1956c, 71–72; errors); Hasselman/Walker 1970 (polyphonic, combining strophes 1–3, 4–6, 7–9, 10–12); see also Fuller 1971, 188–90. Odd notation in strophe 11, with one instance of triple subdivision of a breve in prevailing duple time (Hoppin 1960, 18–19; Hasselman/Walker 1972, 11 [note to strophe 11, m. 84]). Note that the edition of Hasselman/Walker does not solve musical problems of mixing masculine and feminine rhyming syllables in strophes 5, 8, and 9. The music of strophes 1 and 12 is the same, except that strophe 12 is a perfect fourth lower. The polyphonic presentation of strophe 1, in combination with strophes 2–3, is of course completely different from the presentation of strophe 12, which appears in combination with strophes 10–11.

DISCUSSION (musical). Machabey 1955b, 1:121–22 (the slow values of strophe 1 recall the lai *Qui n'aroit* [RF1]); Günther 1957, 130–31 (rhythm and chronology); Newes 1987, 149–50 (polyphony leads to constant conflict of phrase length and rhymes).

En mon cuer ha un descort (virelai V27; Schrade virelai 24)
MANUSCRIPTS WITH TEXT AND MUSIC (all 2v).

[3]	**V g**	fols. 330v–331r	no. 27 (ca, ten; empty space for tr)
[4]	**B**	fols. 328v–329r	no. 27 (ca, ten; empty space for tr)
[5]	**A**	fol. 490v	no. 28 (ca, ten)
[6]	**G**	fol. 160v	no. 27 (ca, ten)
[7]	**E**	fol. 162r	no. 18 (ca, ten)

TEXT MANUSCRIPTS.

[10]	**M**	fol. 252r	no. 27		[50]	**Pa**	fols. 68r–68v	no. 213

FACSIMILE. Ultan 1977a, 122 (diplomatic facs.).

EDITION OF TEXT. Chichmaref 1909, 2:613–15 no. 27.

TEXT STRUCTURE. 3 strophes: $\frac{\text{AABBAAB}}{7\,7\,4\,7\,4\,7\,4}\parallel\frac{\text{bba bba}}{774\ 774}\mid\frac{\text{aabbaab}}{7747474}\parallel\frac{\text{AABBAAB}}{7\,7\,4\,7\,4\,7\,4}$ a:-*ort*, b:-*ir*

EDITIONS OF MUSIC. Ludwig 1926–54, 1:83; Schrade 1956b, 3:183 (critical notes 1956c, 144); Burkhart 1972, 7–9.

DISCUSSION (musical). Machabey 1955b, 1:189–90; Günther 1957, 63 (melodic correspondences); Reaney 1958b, 42 (the discord expressed in the text is not mirrored in the music).

Esperance qui m'asseüre (ballade B13)
Refrain: *Que j'aim dame, s'aten merci*
MANUSCRIPTS WITH TEXT AND MUSIC (all 2v: ca, ten).

[1]	**C**	fol. 163v	no. 13		[5]	**A**	fol. 461r	no. 14
[3]	**V g**	fol. 302v	no. 13		[6]	**G**	fols. 138v–139r	no. 14
[4]	**B**	fol. 300v	no. 13		[7]	**E**	fol. 147v	no. 3

TEXT MANUSCRIPTS.

[10]	**M**	fol. 239r	no. 13		[50]	**Pa**	fol. 52r	no. 162

EDITION OF TEXT. Chichmaref 1909, 2:548–49 no. 16.

TRANSLATION. Wimsatt 1991a, 150.

TEXT STRUCTURE. 3 strophes: 8ab ab bcC a:-*ure*, b:-*ueil*, c:-*i*

DISCUSSION (literary). Planche 1990b, 358 (use of the term "ĕur").

EDITIONS OF MUSIC. Ludwig 1926–54, 1:12; Schrade 1956b, 3:84 (critical notes 1956c, 106); Arlt 1982, 242; Baltzer 1991b, 149–50 (comments pp. 154–55). Arlt (1982, 246–48) offers some convincing emendations (cf. Earp 1989, 493–94 n. 57).

makes more sense than Chichmaref's emendation (1909, 2:477).

DISCUSSION (musical). Machabey 1955b, 2:28 (cantus consists of variations on a "generative cell"); Salop 1971, 51–52 (directed motion in cantus); Dömling 1972, 303 (refrain); Lühmann 1978, 217–18 (declamation); Mulder 1978, 92–93 (motivic analysis and symbolism); Arlt 1982, 239–48 (analysis of several literary and musical aspects), 252 (suggestion for adjustment of text underlay).

ANTECEDENTS (textual and musical). Ludwig (1926–54, 1:12) suggested that text and music of the refrain were pre-existing; Spanke (1929, 187) identified its text as the last line of the refrain *Por mon tans useir liéement, / amors m'ont de toz biens garni, / car j'ai dame, s'atant merci* (ed. Gennrich 1921–27, 1:96–97 no. 137; Van den Boogaard 1969, 226 no. 1511).

Et gaudebit. See *S'il estoit / S'Amours* (M6).

Et in terra pax. See *Messe de Nostre Dame.*

Et non est qui adjuvet. See *Qui es / Ha! Fortune* (M8).

Faus Samblant. See *Amours qui a / Faus Samblant* (M15).

Felix virgo mater / Inviolata genitrix / Ad te suspiramus gementes et flentes etc. (motet M23)

MANUSCRIPTS WITH TEXT AND MUSIC.

[3]	**V g**	fols. 282v–283r	no. 23	4v (tr, mot, ten, ct)
[4]	**B**	fols. 280v–281r	no. 23	4v (tr, mot, ten, ct)
[5]	**A**	fols. 436v–437v	no. 23	4v (tr, mot, ten, ct)
[6]	**G**	fols. 124v–125r	no. 23	4v (tr, mot, ten, ct)
[58]	**Trém**	fol. xxxii	no. 75	(index only)[55]

FACSIMILES. Wolf 1904, 2:24–27 no. 16 (diplomatic facs., MS **G**); Parrish 1957, plates lii–liii (MS **G**), discussed pp. 159–60; Apel 1953, 360 (MS **G**, tenor and contratenor only); Bank 1972, 42 ex. 14 (diplomatic facs. in score of beginning of *talea* I).

EDITIONS OF TEXT. Lebeuf 1743, 432–33 (triplum); Chichmaref 1909, 2:531–33 no. 23.

TRANSLATION. See discography, chap. 8.3 and 8.8.

DATE. "1356," Siege of Reims (Ludwig 1930, 268=1924 ed., 231). Leech-Wilkinson (1989, 1:105–7) notes that the Siege of Reims took place from 4 December 1359 to 11 January 1360 and follows the ramifications of what may have been a printing error in Ludwig through the chronologies of Günther (1958, 28 and 1963a, 100) and Reaney (1967). Leech-Wilkinson's suggestion (1989, 1:134) of the possibility of an earlier date is difficult to reconcile with the manuscript evidence; M23 is "a radical departure from conventional isorhythmic practice" (137). On the Siege of Reims, see also Markstrom (1989, 29–34), and above, chap. 1.13.

TEXT STRUCTURE AND RELATIONSHIP TO ISORHYTHM. Only the triplum exhibits regular correlation between text and *talea* structure (Reichert 1956, 201), but the correlation breaks off at the diminution section (1956, 206; Ziino 1978, 451; Leech-Wilkinson 1989, 1:131–32). Uniquely for this motet, Leech-Wilkinson entertains the possibility that texts were fitted to pre-conceived music (1989, 1:134; cf. Günther 1958, 33). See also Clarkson 1971, 214–15 (unique lack of distinction between the strophic form of the triplum and the motetus); Ziino 1978, 441, 451 (sequence-like nature of both triplum and motetus texts); 1978, 443 (strophic structure of motetus); Leech-Wilkinson 1989, 1:131–33, 2:24 ex. 38 (correspondences between the texting of M23 and *Hareu! / Helas!* [M10]).

Triplum: aaabaaab bbbcbbbc c ccdcccd d ddeddde
          88848884 88848884 88848884 88848888   a:-*isti*, b:-*ima*, c:-*imur*, d:-*utis*, e:-*io*

Motetus: aabaab bbcbbc ccdccd d dedde
          884884 884884 884884 884888   a:-*trix*, b:-*aris*, c:-*iter*, d:-*imus*, e:-*erte*

DISCUSSION (literary). Cerquiglini 1985b, 81 (thematic connection to the Marian hymn *Ave maris stella*); Leech-Wilkinson 1989, 138 (Machaut possibly not the author of the texts); Brownlee 1991b, 14 (thematic relationship of tenor to upper voices).

TENOR SOURCE. *Ad te suspiramus gementes et flentes* [*in hac lacrimarum valle. Eia ergo, advocata nostra*] is from the Marian antiphon *Salve Regina* (Ludwig 1926–54, 2:60a*,

---

[55] Schrade (1956c, 40–41) disputes identification of this index item with Machaut's M23.

3:86). See also Machabey 1955b, 2:109–10 (end of motetus quotes "Eya ergo").

EDITIONS OF MUSIC. Wolf 1904, 3:41–49 no. 16; Ludwig 1926–54, 3:82–86; Schrade 1956b, 3:26–33 (critical notes 1956c, 90–91); Leech-Wilkinson 1989, 2:74–76 (critical notes 1989, 1:246–47). Barring discussed in Hoppin 1960, 25.

DISCUSSION (musical). *Introitus*, then bipartite with diminution by one-half (diminution section is pan-isorhythmic). Rhythm of contratenor derived from tenor by voice exchange. Ficker 1924–25, 211–12 (isorhythmic analysis); Machabey 1955b, 2:108–11; Günther 1958, 34 (diminution produces conflicts in *tempus* groups; change of mode in the tenor and contratenor indicated by red notes, on the model of Vitry); Prisor 1971, 204 (chart of tenor-contratenor structure); Bank 1972, 41, 43 (tempo); Hoppin 1978b, 413–14 (diagram of symmetrical tenor and contratenor *taleae*); Leech-Wilkinson 1989, 1:129–37 (texts, *color*, isoperiodic structure, lower-voice *taleae*, phrase structure, harmony), Cross 1990, 230–31, 266, 267, 271 (chromatic intervals); Koehler 1990, 1:102–5 (rhythmic proportions).

Gombosi 1950, 222 (voice exchange between tenor and contratenor recalls the Amen of the Credo); Leech-Wilkinson 1982–83, 3–4 (summary of related features among *Christe / Veni* [M21], *Tu qui gregem / Plange* [M22], and M23); Newes 1987, 205–10 (comparison of complementary tenor-contratenor pair in *Aucune gent / Qui plus* [M5], M21–23); Leech-Wilkinson 1989, 1:105–7, 135–36, 138–41 (summary comparison of M21–23); 1:131–34, 2:24 ex. 38 (explores the connections between two motets of de Vitry—*Douce plaisance / Garison*, and *Tuba / In arboris*—and several works of Machaut—*Aucune gent / Qui plus* [M5], *Hareu! / Helas!* [M10], M23, and the Amen of the Credo); 1:165 n. 45 (rate of harmonic change compared to several other motets).

Fera pessima. See *Fons / O livoris* (M9).

Fiat voluntas tua. See *Aucune / Qui plus* (M5).

Fine Amour qui. See *He! Mors / Fine* (M3).

Fins cuers. See *Dame, je sui / Fins cuers* (M11).

Fons tocius superbie / O livoris feritas / Fera pessima (motet M9)
MANUSCRIPTS WITH TEXT AND MUSIC.

[1] **C**	fols. 213v–214r	no. 8	3v (tr, mot, ten)
[3] **V g**	fols. 268v–269r	no. 9	3v (tr, mot, ten)
[4] **B**	fols. 266v–267r	no. 9	3v (tr, mot, ten)
[5] **A**	fols. 422v–423r	no. 9	3v (tr, mot, ten)
[6] **G**	fols. 110v–111r	no. 9	3v (tr, mot, ten)
[7] **E**	fol. 139v	no. 9	3v (tr, mot, ten)
[58] **Trém**	fol. xxxiiii	no. 80	(index only)

EDITION OF TEXT. Chichmaref 1909, 2:499–500 no. 9.

TRANSLATIONS. Eggebrecht 1962–63, 288 (German); Markstrom 1989, 36–37 (trans. by Anna Kirkwood); see also discography (chap. 8.3 and 8.8).

DATE. Possibly an early work, since style and texts are based on Fauvel motets (Reaney 1967, 92, without further amplification). Fall 1347 or Spring 1348 (Markstrom 1989, 17–26, 34).

TEXT STRUCTURE AND RELATIONSHIP TO ISORHYTHM. Both triplum and motetus exhibit regular correlation between text and *talea* structure (Besseler 1927, 222; Reichert 1956, 201); according to Günther (1958, 33), only the beginning is regular. See also Reichert 1956, ex. 4 after p. 204, discussed p. 211 (beginnings of all nine *taleae* of the triplum); Clarkson 1971, 266 n. 93 (motetus *sixain* pattern followed by its retrograde is also found in *En amer* [RF4] and *Amours me fait* [B19]); Ziino 1978, 440, 442–43 (motetus structure resembles the sequence *Veni Sancte Spiritus*), 443 (strophic structure of triplum).

Triplum: $\frac{\text{aaab bbbc cccd d dde e ee f fff g gggh hhh i i i j i i i j}}{\text{8884 8884 8884 8884 8884 8884 8884 8884 8884 8884}}$ a:-*ie*, b:-*atus*, c:-*ere*,

d:-*imo*, e:-*atum*, f:-*ernis*, g:-*ibus*, h:-*eris*, i:-*ia*, j:-*avit*

Motetus: 7aab aab bba bba a:-*itas*, b:-*ius*

DISCUSSION (literary). Eggebrecht 1962–63, 286–93 (thematic relation of tenor to upper voices).

322 THE MUSIC

TEXTUAL LEGACY (England). Chaucer, *Book of the Duchess* (Kittredge 1915c, 11; Wimsatt 1968, 159; 1979, 130 n. 11; 1981, 232 n. 31; 1991b, 131).

TENOR SOURCE. *Fera pessima* (Genesis 37:33–34) is the beginning of *repetenda* of the mode 6 Responsory *Videns Jacob* for the third Sunday of Lent (Ludwig 1926–54, 2:60a*, 3:76; Eggebrecht 1962–63, 293). The tenor of Vitry's *Tribum / Quoniam* is from the same feast (Leech-Wilkinson 1982–83, 15 n. 25).

EDITIONS OF MUSIC. Ludwig 1926–54, 3:33–36 (criticism of Ludwig's analytical layout in Sanders 1973, 563 n. 286); Schrade 1956b, 2:137–40 (critical notes 1956c, 80–81). Harmonic augmented second in m. 68 (Ludwig 1926–54, 3:8). Machabey (1955b, 2:83–84) would adjust the text underlay near beginning of the motetus to correspond to mm. 15–16 of the first period. Earp (1983, 224 n. 390) criticizes Eggebrecht's comments on text underlay (1968, 181–82).

DISCUSSION (musical). Unipartite with *introitus*, described in Eggebrecht 1962–63, 282 (alternative analysis in Sanders 1973, 563 n. 286). Machabey 1955b, 2:82–84; Eggebrecht 1962–63; 1968 (thorough analysis; comments on compositional process, pp. 194–95); Kühn 1973, 104–10 and Fuller 1986, 36–37; 1990, 204 (criticism of Eggebrecht's "isoharmonic" analysis); Fuller 1990, 204–9 (influence of tenor pitches and rhythm on sonority and stability; includes discant reduction of main progressions, strategies of withholding tonal weight from the *G* tonal center).

MUSICAL LEGACY. For twentieth-century compositions inspired by M9, see chap. 2.5 (Birtwistle).

Foy porter (virelai V25; Schrade virelai 22)

MANUSCRIPTS WITH TEXT AND MUSIC.

[1]	C	fol. 197v	no. 24	1v (ca)
[3]	V g	fol. 330r	no. 25	1v (ca)
[4]	B	fol. 328r	no. 25	1v (ca)
[5]	A	fol. 489v	no. 25	1v (ca)
[6]	G	fol. 160r	no. 25	1v (ca)
[7]	E	fols. 162r–162v	no. 19	(ca; empty staves for ten)

TEXT MANUSCRIPT.

[10]	M	fol. 251v	no. 25

EDITION OF TEXT. Chichmaref 1909, 2:611–13 no. 25.

TRANSLATIONS. Wennerstrom 1983, 13 (strophe 1); see also discography (chap. 8.3 and 8.8).

TEXT STRUCTURE. 3 strophes: $\frac{AABBBABA}{3\,4\,4\,3\,4\,4\,7\,4} \parallel \frac{bba\ bba}{774\ 774} \mid \frac{a\,abbba\,ba}{34434474} \parallel \frac{AABBBABA}{3\,4\,4\,3\,4\,4\,7\,4}$ a:-*er*, b:-*ir*

TEXTUAL LEGACY (England). Chaucer, *To Rosemounde* (Wimsatt 1978, 77); *Womanly Noblesse* (Wimsatt 1978, 77–78).

EDITIONS OF MUSIC. Ludwig 1926–54, 1:81; Schrade 1956b, 3:181 (critical notes 1956c, 143); Wennerstrom 1983, 12–13 (after Schrade).

DISCUSSION (musical). Machabey 1955b, 1:187–88.

Gais et jolis, liés, chantans et joieus (ballade B35)
Refrain: *Tout pour l'espoir que j'ay de li veoir*

MANUSCRIPTS WITH TEXT AND MUSIC (all 3v: ca, ten, ct).

[3]	V g	fol. 315v	no. 35		[7]	E	fol. 153v	no. 22
[4]	B	fol. 314v	no. 35		[63]	P R	fol. 65r	no. 135
[5]	A	fol. 472v	no. 34		[66]	Mod	fol. 29v	no. 55
[6]	G	fol. 147v	no. 35					

TEXT MANUSCRIPTS.

[10]	M	fol. 243r	no. 35		[50]	Pa	fol. 56r	no. 173
[41]	Wm	fol. 16r	no. 8		Lo39	CWVgBAHMD		

FACSIMILE. Wilkins 1979, 17 (MS A).

EDITIONS OF TEXT. Chichmaref 1909, 1:52 no. 39; Wilkins 1972, 69 no. 76.

TRANSLATION. See discography (chap. 8.3 and 8.8).

TEXT STRUCTURE. 3 strophes[56]: 10ab ab bcC a:-*eus*, b:-*our*, c:-*oir*

EDITIONS OF MUSIC. Ludwig 1926–54, 1:42–43; Schrade 1956b, 3:128–29 (critical notes 1956c, 118–19); Wilkins 1980b, 9–10 (Chaucer, *Som tyme this world* underlaid). Aspects of barring discussed in Hoppin 1960, 23.

DISCUSSION (musical). Machabey 1955b, 2:49–50; Günther 1957, 88 (motivic analysis); Reichert 1962 (harmony); Dömling 1970, 76 (examples of similar progressions of sonorities in which tenor and contratenor exchange places, demonstrating simultaneous conception); Salop 1971, 54 (melodic direction in cantus); Kühn 1973, 218–19 (harmony); Saponov 1978, 30 (rhythmic structure; palindromic rhythmic motives).

Gloria. See *Messe de Nostre Dame*.

Ha! Fortune. See *Qui es / Ha! Fortune* (M8).

Hareu! hareu! le feu / Helas! ou sera / Obediens usque ad mortem (motet M10)

MANUSCRIPTS WITH TEXT AND MUSIC.

[1] C	fols. 214v–215r	no. 9	3v (tr, mot, ten)
[3] Vg	fols. 269v–270r	no. 10	3v (tr, mot, ten)
[4] B	fols. 267v–268r	no. 10	3v (tr, mot, ten)
[5] A	fols. 423v–424r	no. 10	3v (tr, mot, ten)
[6] G	fols. 111v–112r	no. 10	3v (tr, mot, ten)
[7] E	fols. 140v–141r	no. 14	3v (tr, mot, ten)
[58] Trém	fol. iiii	no. 7	(index only)

FACSIMILE. Parrish 1957, plate xlviii (MS E, with end of motetus and tenor only).

EDITIONS OF TEXT. Chichmaref 1909, 2:501–2 no. 10; Wilkins 1987, 24.

TRANSLATIONS. Wilkins 1987, 24–25; see also discography (chap. 8.3 and 8.8).

TEXT STRUCTURE AND RELATIONSHIP TO ISORHYTHM. Both triplum and motetus exhibit regular correlation between text and *talea* structure (Reichert 1956, 201), but triplum correspondence breaks down at end (1956, 206; Günther 1957, 139; 1958, 33). See also Ziino 1978, 444–45 (strophic structure of triplum); Leech-Wilkinson 1989, 1:131–33, 2:24 ex. 38 (correspondences between the texting of M10 and *Felix virgo / Inviolata* [M23]).

Triplum: $\begin{array}{l} \text{a a a a b b c c c c b b d d d d b b e}^\bullet\text{e e e b b} \\ \overline{1010101010}\,\text{'10'}\ \overline{1010101010}\,\text{'10'}\ \overline{1010101010}\,\text{'10'}\ \overline{1010101010}\,\text{'10'} \end{array}$

a:-*u*, b:-*ure*, c:-*ains*, d:-*aint*, e:-*iés* (*: lyric caesura)

Motetus: 8aabb ccdd eeff ggf a:-*ors*, b:-*uet*, c:-*us*, d:-*ir*, e:-*té*, f:-*oir*, g:-*ement*

DISCUSSION (literary). Poirion 1965, 527–28 (theme of the fire of love's desire); Sonnemann 1969, 63 (love and death in triplum and motetus; crucifixion in tenor); Boogaart 1993b, (conflict in texts also expressed in the music).

TEXTUAL LEGACY (France). Alain Chartier, rondeau *Au feu!* (ed. Laidlaw 1974, 383–84 no. 19); Chartier's rondeau was in turn imitated by a rondeau in the Bayeux manuscript and by Charles d'Orléans (cited in Poirion 1965, 262, 528).

TENOR SOURCE. *Obediens usque ad mortem* (Philippians 2:8) is from the mode 5 Gradual for the Solemn evening Mass on Maundy Thursday, *Christus factus est* (Ludwig 1926–54, 2:60a*, 3:40).

EDITIONS OF MUSIC. Ludwig 1926–54, 3:37–40; Schrade 1956b, 2:141–43 (critical notes 1956c, 81); Kamien 1984, 4–7 no. 3; Wilkins 1987, 20–25 no. 5. Barring discussed in Hoppin 1960, 25, 26; Günther 1990, 77.

DISCUSSION (musical). Bipartite, with diminution by one-half. Machabey 1955b, 2:84–85; Günther 1958, 30 (isorhythm of the text strophes defines a larger *talea*, or "Grosstalea," comprising two tenor *taleae*; Sanders [1973, 558 n. 257] finds this is true for the first section only); Günther 1958, 32, 34 (melodic rhyme at *talea* ends, conflicts of mensuration); Dobrzańska 1979b, 66–67 (comparisons in harmonic reduction of *integer valor* and diminution sections for the whole motet); Wilkins 1987, 25 (general discussion); Boogaard 1993b (conflicts of mensuration reflect texts; relationship to *Quant en moy / Amour* [M1]).

---

[56] Reaney (1958b, 50) comments on vowel sonorities.

Leech-Wilkinson 1982–83, 12 ex. 8; 1989, 1:131–34, 2:24 ex. 38 (explores the connections between two motets of Vitry—*Douce plaisance / Garison*, and *Tuba / In arboris*—and several works of Machaut—*Aucune gent / Qui plus* [M5], M10, *Felix virgo / Inviolata* [M23], and the Amen of the Credo).

Hé! dame de vaillance (virelai V1)

MANUSCRIPTS WITH TEXT AND MUSIC (all monophonic).

[1]	**C**	fols. 148v–149r	no. 1	[5]	**A**	fol. 482r	no. 1
[3]	**V g**	fol. 322v	no. 1	[6]	**G**	fol. 154v	no. 1
[4]	**B**	fol. 320v	no. 1	[7]	**E**	fol. 159r	no. 1

TEXT MANUSCRIPT.

[10] **M**   fol. 245v   no. 1

FACSIMILES. Aubry 1905, plate 21 (MS A); Reaney 1952a, 1045–46 (MS A); Ultan 1977b, 85 (diplomatic facs., MS C).

EDITIONS OF TEXT. Chichmaref 1909, 2:581–82 no. 1.

TEXT STRUCTURE. 3 strophes:

$$\underset{6'6'6'6'6}{AAAAB} \parallel \underset{86'\ 86'}{c\ d\ c\ d} \mid \underset{6'6'6'6'6}{a\ a\ a\ ab} \parallel \underset{6'6'6'6'6}{AAAAB}\quad a\text{:-}ance,\ b\text{:-}ent,\ c\text{:-}ueil,\ d\text{:-}iere$$

EDITIONS OF MUSIC. Ludwig 1926–54, 1:70; Wooldridge 1932, 308 (ed. Westrup); Schrade 1956b, 3:167 (critical notes 1956c, 136); Arlt 1982, 266 (after Schrade).

DISCUSSION (musical). Machabey 1955b, 1:176–77; Arlt 1982, 265–66 (text syntax and music), 267–68 (mode); Kügle 1991, 377 (elements of monophonic style); Weber-Bockholdt 1992, 270–71 (rhyme and musical structure).

MUSICAL LEGACY. For a twentieth-century composition inspired by V1, see chap. 2.5 (Gilbert and Rickett).

Hé! dame de valour (virelai V11)

MANUSCRIPTS WITH TEXT AND MUSIC (all monophonic).

[1]	**C**	fols. 152v–153r	no. 11	[5]	**A**	fol. 485r	no. 11
[3]	**V g**	fols. 325v–326r	no. 11	[6]	**G**	fols. 156v–157r	no. 11
[4]	**B**	fols. 323v–324r	no. 11	[7]	**E**	fol. 163r	no. 24

TEXT MANUSCRIPT.

[10] **M**   fol. 248r   no. 11

EDITION OF TEXT. Chichmaref 1909, 2:593–94 no. 11.

TEXT STRUCTURE. 3 strophes: $\underset{6\ 7\ 7\ 6\ 7}{AAAAB} \parallel \underset{87\ 77}{c\ a\ c\ a} \mid \underset{67767}{a\ aaab} \parallel \underset{6\ 7\ 7\ 6\ 7}{AAAAB}\quad a\text{:-}our,\ b\text{:-}ent,\ c\text{:-}té$

EDITIONS OF MUSIC. Ludwig 1926–54, 1:75; Schrade 1956b, 3:172 (critical notes 1956c, 139).

DISCUSSION (musical). Machabey 1955b, 1:181; Lühmann 1978, 207–8 (declamation); Cogan/Escot 1981, 11–13 (approaches to an analysis); Reaney 1982, 300 (mode).

Hé! Mors com tu / Fine Amour / Quare non sum mortuus (motet M3)

MANUSCRIPTS WITH TEXT AND MUSIC (all 3v: tr, mot, ten).

[1]	**C**	fols. 208v–209r	no. 3	[5]	**A**	fols. 416v–417r	no. 3
[3]	**V g**	fols. 262v–263r	no. 3	[6]	**G**	fols. 104v–105r	no. 3
[4]	**B**	fols. 260v–261r	no. 3	[7]	**E**	fols. 133v–134r	no. 5

FACSIMILE. Wolf 1904, 2:19–21 no. 14 (diplomatic facs., MS G).

EDITION OF TEXT. Chichmaref 1909, 2:487–88 no. 3.

TRANSLATION. Wimsatt 1991b, 129–30 (triplum, ll. 1–8).

TEXT STRUCTURE AND RELATIONSHIP TO ISORHYTHM. No correlation between strophe and *talea* (Reichert 1956, 200–201; Koehler 1990, 1:106–7); nevertheless, the nine lines of the motetus in the *integer valor* section add up to 154 syllables, while the five lines of the diminution section add up to 77 syllables, exactly half. See also Reichert 1956, 209 table (irregular strophic structure at end of triplum); Clarkson 1971, 244–45 and Ziino 1978, 443 n. 11 (on the structure of the quatrains); Clarkson 1971, 264 (strophic structure of motetus).

Triplum: a a ab bbbc cccd ddde eee f fffg gggh hhhi i i i a a a j jjj a a a a
7'7'7'3 7773 7773 7773 7773 7773 7773 7773 7773' 7'7'7'3 7773' 7'7'7'

a:-*ie*, b:-*as*, c:-*ir*, d:-*oit*, e:-*ours*, f:-*our*, g:-*ay*, h:-*ueil*, i:-*i*, j:-*oy*

Motetus: 8abab baab baab ab a:-*er*, b:-*on*

DISCUSSION (literary). Patch 1927, 108 n. 4 (theme of Fortune); Poirion 1965, 551 n. 22 (theme of death); Huot 1994, 227–32 (lament of a man whose lady has died; paired with *Tous corps* / *De* [M2], analogue to the pair *Jugement Behaingne* and *Jugement Navarre*; analogue to Boethius's *Consolation of Philosophy*). "Qui bien aimme a tart oublie" (triplum l. 39) is a proverb (Hassell 1982, no. A63); see also commentary to *Qui bien aimme* (L22/16), below.

LITERARY ANTECEDENTS. The last lines of the triplum, "Nulle si grief departie / com c'est d'ami et d'amie" [No parting is so painful as between lovers], may be a refrain ("d'ami et d'amie" is a refrain in Lescurel; see Gennrich 1921–27, 1:349; Ludwig 1926–54, 3:12; Van den Boogaard 1969, 457 no. 450).

TEXTUAL LEGACY (England). Chaucer, *Book of the Duchess* (Kittredge 1915c, 8; Ludwig 1926–54, 2:39*; Wimsatt 1968, 158; Butterfield 1991, 56 n. 10, 58 n. 26; Wimsatt 1991b, 129–30; Huot 1994, 237 n. 18).

TENOR SOURCE. *Quare non sum mortuus* is the end of the *repetenda* of the Responsory *Inclinans faciem* (cf. Job 9:28–29, 3:11, 6:11); see Anderson 1976, 122, 126; Huot 1994, 228–29.

EDITIONS OF MUSIC. Wolf 1904, 3:33–36 no. 14; Wooldridge 1905, 28–30 (partial); Ludwig 1926–54, 3:9–12; Schrade 1956b, 2:115–18 (critical notes 1956c, 76).

DISCUSSION (musical). Bipartite, with diminution by one-half. Ficker 1924–25, 211 (brief analysis); Machabey 1955b, 2:71–73; Fuller 1992b, 232–34 (directed progressions).

Helas! et comment aroie (virelai V18).

MANUSCRIPTS WITH TEXT AND MUSIC (all monophonic).

[1]	C	fols. 155r–155v	no. 17		[5]	A	fols. 487r–487v	no. 18
[3]	V g	fol. 328r	no. 18		[6]	G	fol. 158v	no. 18
[4]	B	fol. 326r	no. 18					

TEXT MANUSCRIPTS.

[7]	E	fol. 160v	no. 9 (empty staves)		[50]	Pa	fol. 66v	no. 206
[10]	M	fols. 249v–250r	no. 18					

EDITION OF TEXT. Chichmaref 1909, 2:602–3 no. 18.

TEXT STRUCTURE. 3 strophes:
AAB AAB ‖ ccb ccb | a ab a ab ‖ AAB AAB a:-*oie*, b:-*our*, c:-*ay*
7'3'7 7'3'7 ‖ 737 737 | 7'3'7 7'3'7 ‖ 7'3'7 7'3'7

EDITIONS OF MUSIC. Ludwig 1926–54, 1:78–79; Schrade 1956b, 3:177 (critical notes 1956c, 141–42).

DISCUSSION (musical). Machabey 1955b, 1:185; Weber-Bockholdt 1992, 280–81 (melodic connection between *clos* and beginning of strophe).

Helas! ou sera. See *Hareu!* / *Helas!* (M10).

Helas! pour quoy se demente et complaint (rondeau R2)

MANUSCRIPTS WITH TEXT AND MUSIC (all 2v: ca, ten).

[1]	C	fol. 201v	no. 1		[5]	A	fol. 476r	no. 4
[3]	V g	fol. 316v	no. 2		[6]	G	fol. 150r	no. 2
[4]	B	fol. 315v	no. 2		[7]	E	fol. 139r	no. 13

TEXT MANUSCRIPTS.

[10]	M	fol. 244r	no. 2		[50]	Pa	fol. 48v	no. 148

FACSIMILE. Wolf 1904, 2:37 no. 19 (diplomatic facs., MS G).

EDITION OF TEXT. Chichmaref 1909, 2:569 no. 2.

TEXT STRUCTURE. 10AB aA ab AB a:-*aint*, b:-*our*

EDITIONS OF MUSIC. Wolf 1904, 3:60 no. 19; Ludwig 1926–54, 1:52; Schrade 1956b, 3:142–43 (critical notes 1956c, 124). Boorman (1977a, 497) urges emendation of the cantus in the penultimate bar, presumably transposition up a second of the three notes before the final.

DISCUSSION (musical). Machabey 1955b, 1:154.

Helas! pour quoy virent / Corde mesto cantando / Libera me (motet M12)

MANUSCRIPTS WITH TEXT AND MUSIC (all 3v: tr, mot, ten).

[1]	**C**	fols. 216v–217r	no. 11		[5]	**A**	fols. 425v–426r	no. 12
[3]	**V g**	fols. 271v–272r	no. 12		[6]	**G**	fols. 113v–114r	no. 12
[4]	**B**	fols. 269v–270r	no. 12		[7]	**E**	fols. 141v–142r	no. 15

EDITION OF TEXT. Chichmaref 1909, 2:505–6 no. 12.

TEXT STRUCTURE AND RELATIONSHIP TO ISORHYTHM. Both French triplum and Latin motetus show regular correlation between text and *talea* structure (Besseler 1927, 223; Reichert 1956, 201), although the motetus is clearer than the triplum. Three large phrases of the motetus (each extended by textless passages) define a larger *talea*, or "Grosstalea," and belie the nine shorter periods in the tenor (Reichert 1956, 202; Sanders 1973, 558 n. 257; 1980a, 352). Machabey (1955b, 2:87) suspects that there is a mystical significance to this disposition of 3 x 3. See also Ziino 1978, 440 (sequence-like structure of motetus).

Triplum: a a b b   c c d d   e e f f   g   g h h   i i   j j   kk d d   l l m m
10 10 8'8'   10 10 10 10   8'8'10 10   10'10'10 10   10 10 10 10   88 10 10   10 10 10'10'

n n o o   p p
10'10'10 10 10'10', a:-*ueil*, b:-*ire*, c:-*ir*, d:-*er*, e:-*usse*, f:-*ust*, g:-*euse*, h:-*i*, i:-*té*,

j:-*our*, k:-*ent*, l:-*ier*, m:-*oie*, n:-*uer*, o:-*és*, p:-*ure*

Motetus: a b a b a b a b c d c d c d c d e f e f e f e f
46 46 46 46 46' 46' 46' 46' 46' 46' 46' 46'

a:-*esto*, b:-*eror*,[57] c:-*isum*, d:-*onis*, e:-*ece*, f:-*ia* If the internal rhymes at the caesuras are removed, a more readily grasped isometric scheme in monorhyming quatrains emerges (Clarkson 1971, 211–12): 10aaaa bbbb cccc a:-*or*, b:-*is*, c:-*ia*

DISCUSSION (literary). Patch 1927, 81 n. 2 (theme of Fortune in motetus); Dömling 1970, 15 (first line of the triplum is the same as the first line of *Helas! pour quoy* [Lo53]); Huot 1994, 233–35 (Latin motetus and tenor subvert the theme of the courtly triplum).

TENOR SOURCE. *Libera me* is from the beginning of the *repetenda* of the mode 4 Responsory for the second Sunday in Lent, *Minor sum cunctis* (cf. Genesis 32:10–11); see Anderson 1976, 122, 126; Huot 1994, 237–38 n. 22.

EDITIONS OF MUSIC. Ludwig 1926–54, 3:44–48 (criticism of Ludwig's analytical layout in Sanders 1973, 558 n. 257); Schrade 1956b, 2:147–50 (critical notes 1956c, 82–83).

DISCUSSION (musical). Unipartite. Machabey 1955b, 2:87–89. Related to Philippe de Vitry, *Vos / Gratissima* (Leech-Wilkinson 1989, 1:110 n. 15).

Helas! tant ay doleur et peinne (ballade B2)

Refrain: ... *que trop cruel seroit / Li cuers qui pitie n' en aroit*

MANUSCRIPTS WITH TEXT AND MUSIC (all 2v: ca, ten).

[1]	**C**	fols. 158r–158v	no. 2		[5]	**A**	fol. 454v	no. 2
[3]	**V g**	fol. 297r	no. 2		[6]	**G**	fol. 134v	no. 2
[4]	**B**	fol. 295r	no. 2		[7]	**E**	fols. 151r–151v	no. 15

TEXT MANUSCRIPT.

[10]   **M**   fols. 257r–257v   no. 2

EDITION OF TEXT. Chichmaref 1909, 2:538 no. 2.

TEXT STRUCTURE. 3 strophes with a 2-line refrain, which begins with the third syllable of the penultimate line: a b a b b c C
8'8 8'8 888 a:-*einne*, b:-*art*, c:-*oit*

EDITIONS OF MUSIC. Ludwig 1926–54, 1:2; Schrade 1956b, 3:70–71 (critical notes 1956c, 99). On barring, see Günther 1957, 92 n. 54.

DISCUSSION (musical). Machabey 1955b, 1:19–20 (repeating rhythmic motif relates to the concept of *talea*); Dömling 1970, 70–71 (a short 2v passage recurs like a building block); 1972, 305 (music emphasizes internal text rhymes); Lühmann 1978, 223–32 (declamation); Apfel 1982, 89 (harmonic reduction); Arlt 1982, 229–30 (summary of Dömling 1970).

Honte, paour, doubtance de meffaire (ballade B25)
Refrain: *Qui de s' onneur vuet faire bonne garde*
MANUSCRIPTS WITH TEXT AND MUSIC.

[3]	**V g**	fol. 309v	no. 25	3v (ca, ten, ct)
[4]	**B**	fol. 307v	no. 25	3v (ca, ten, ct)
[5]	**A**	fol. 466v	no. 24	3v (ca, ten, ct)
[6]	**G**	fols. 142v–143r	no. 25	3v (ca, ten, ct)
[7]	**E**	fols. 151v–152r	no. 17	3v (ca, ten, ct)
[58]	**Trém**	fol. xxx	no. 70	(index only)
[61]	**F P**	fols. 76r–75v	no. 139	3v (ca, ten, ct)
[65]	**S L**	fol. 77v		
[67]	**Fa**	fols. 37r–37v	no. 4	2v (anonymous instr. arr., "Hont Paur")

TEXT MANUSCRIPTS.

[10]	**M**	fol. 241r	no. 25	[50]	**Pa**	fol. 48v	no. 147
[40]	**I**	fol. 20r	no. 104	[52]	**Ta**	fol. 6v	no. 18
[41]	**Wm**	fol. 22v	no. 22	Lo201	**VgBJAMD** (chap. 6.4)		

FACSIMILE. Gallo 1981, fols. 75v–76r (MS **FP**).

EDITIONS OF TEXT. Queux de Saint-Hilaire/Raynaud 1878–1903, 10:lxvi no. 59; Chichmaref 1909, 1:181 no. 201; Wilkins 1972, 74 no. 94; Vitale-Brovarone 1980, 20 no. 18 (**Ta**).

TRANSLATIONS. Yudkin 1989, 506–7; see also discography (chap. 8.3 and 8.8).

TEXT STRUCTURE. 3 strophes: $\begin{array}{cccccc} a & b & a & b & c & c & d & D \\ 10 & 10 & 10 & 10 & 7 & 10 & 10 & 10 \end{array}$ a:-*aire*, b:-*é*, c:-*er*, d:-*arde*

DISCUSSION (literary). In the *Jugement Navarre* (ll. 1279–86), the eleventh maidservant of Lady Beneürté is *Doubtance de Meffaire*, who is guarded by *Honte* and *Paour*.

TEXTUAL LEGACY (France). Only the first line of the *balade de Naudin Alis*: *Honte, paour de doubte de meffaire* is related to Machaut's B25; see MS **Ta** [52], fol. 87v (ed. Vitale-Brovarone 1980, no. 220).

EDITIONS OF MUSIC. Ludwig 1926–54, 1:28; Schrade 1956b, 3:106–7 (critical notes 1956c, 113); Kugler 1972 (Notenteil), x (critical notes), 5–11 (diplomatic facs. of **Fa** vertically aligned with diplomatic facs. of B25); Plamenac 1972, 12–15 no. 4 (ed. of **Fa** vertically aligned with B25, transposed up a fifth); Brandt 1980, 67–69; Yudkin 1989, 504–6 (after Schrade). Questions of barring discussed in Hoppin 1960, 23; Dömling 1970, 39n.

DISCUSSION (musical). Machabey 1955b, 2:38–39 (the melody imposes an arbitrary verse disposition); Günther 1957, 80 (motivic analysis); Reaney 1966, 708 (performance of **Fa** intabulation); Salop 1971, 62–63 (melodic direction of cantus); Dömling 1972, 301–2 (text painting, refrain); Kugler 1972, 110–11 (techniques of arrangement in **Fa**); Kühn 1973, 219 (use of imperfect sonorities); Kugler 1975, 44–45 (treatment of syncopation in **Fa** intabulation); Mulder 1978, 83–85 (motivic analysis); Karp 1988, 68–69 (compositional precedence of the tenor); M.L. Göllner 1989, 71–73 (motivic analysis, text/music relations); Yudkin 1989, 504–7 (analysis); Cross 1990, 53, 274 (solmization, chromatic intervals); Berger 1992, 130–31, 133–34 (accidentals and mode); Fuller 1992b, 240–43, 245–46 (directed progressions serve text painting: the work is full of thwarted expectations).

Hoquetus David
MANUSCRIPTS WITH TEXT AND MUSIC (all 3v: tr, hoquetus, ten).

| [3] | **V g** | fol. 334v–335r | [5] | **A** | fol. 451v–452r |
| [4] | **B** | fol. 331v (triplum only) | [6] | **G** | fol. 163v–164r |

LOST MANUSCRIPT.
[8] lost Burgundian manuscript

FACSIMILES. *MGG* 10 (1962), plate 50; Allaire 1980, plate 4 (MS **A**).

TENOR SOURCE. Tenor is the melisma on "David" at the end of the Alleluia verse *Nativitas gloriose Virginis*, for the feast of the Nativity of the B.V.M. (8 September), which exactly recapitulates the jubilus (*Liber usualis*, Alleluia *Solemnitas gloriosae*, p. 1676A) (Ludwig 1926–54, 2:63*, 4:23). Leech-Wilkinson (1980, 100 n. 3) lists some chant sources in Reims manuscripts. Machabey (1931, 408–9) and Reaney (1960a, 288; 1977, 9; 1980a, 431; Flutre/Reaney 1967) agree with Gastoué (1922, 62–63) that Machaut's hocket formed a conclusion to the Alleluia *Nativitas* of Perotin, and thus was performed vocally; see the commentary in Leech-Wilkinson 1980, 100.

EDITIONS OF MUSIC. Gastoué 1921, 57 (beginning); Ludwig (1926–54), 4:21–23; de Van 1938; Schrade 1956b, 3:65–67 (critical notes 1956c, 98); Allaire 1980, 49–54.

DISCUSSION (musical). Gastoué 1921, 56; Günther 1957, 149–50; Reaney 1971, 67–68; Hoppin 1978b, 420–21; Allaire 1980, 43–56 (hexachordal interpretation of sharp signs in MS A as guides to solmization for the performers; see Berger 1992, 233–34); Leech-Wilkinson 1980 (step-by-step compositional procedure); Frobenius 1988 (terminology); Hughes 1989, 359 (unusual features); Eggebrecht 1991, 235 (hocket perhaps composed as a final work for Machaut manuscripts).

MUSICAL LEGACY. For a number of twentieth-century compositions inspired by Machaut's hocket, see chap. 2.5 (Bedford, Birtwistle, Gilbert, Holt, Matoušek, and Muldowney).

Il m'est avis qu'il n'est dons de Nature (ballade B22)
Refrain: *Se Fortune ne le tient a amy*
MANUSCRIPTS WITH TEXT AND MUSIC.

[1]	C	fols. 204r–204v	no. 24	1v (ca; empty staves for ten and ct)
[3]	V g	fols. 307v–308r	no. 22	4v (tr, ca, ten, ct)
[4]	B	fols. 305v–306r	no. 22	4v (tr, ca, ten, ct)
[5]	A	fols. 464v–465r	no. 21	4v (tr, ca, ten, ct)
[6]	G	fols. 141v–142r	no. 22	4v (tr, ca, ten, ct)
[7]	E	fol. 149r	no. 9	4v (tr, ca, ten, ct)
[63]	P R	fol. 69v	no. 145	4v (tr, ca, ten, different ct)

TEXT MANUSCRIPTS.

[10]	M	fol. 240v	no. 22	Lo188 **CVgBAMD** (see chap. 6.4)

FACSIMILE. Bofill Soliguer 1991, 25 (MS G).

EDITIONS OF TEXT. Chichmaref 1909, 1:170 no. 188; Wilkins 1972, 74 no. 96.

TRANSLATION. Wimsatt 1979, 120; 1991b, 102.

TEXT STRUCTURE. 3 strophes: $\begin{smallmatrix} a & b & a & b & c & c & d & D \\ 10 & 10 & 10 & 10 & 7 & 10 & 10 & 10 \end{smallmatrix}$ a:-*ure*, b:-*our*, c:-*é*, d:-*i*

DISCUSSION (literary). Patch 1927, 84 n. 1; L.W. Johnson 1979, 15–16; and 1990, 42–43 (theme of Fortune); Mulder 1978, 39 (Lady Reason), 77–78 (image of Fortune in music).

LITERARY ANTECEDENT. Boethius, *Consolation of Philosophy* (Wimsatt 1979, 120).

TEXTUAL LEGACY (France). Deschamps, ballade *Tant com j'ay eu Richesce avecques mi* (ed. Queux de Saint-Hilaire 1878–1903, 1:289–90 no. 160; cited in Wimsatt 1979, 126–27).

TEXTUAL LEGACY (England). Chaucer, *Book of the Duchess*, Boethius translation, "Merchant's Tale," triple ballade *Fortune*, and the late ballade *Lak of Stedfastnesse* (Wimsatt 1979; 1991b, 101–3, 131; on the triple ballade, see also Preston 1951, 616).

EDITIONS OF MUSIC. Ludwig 1926–54, 1:23–24; Schrade 1956b, 3:98–100 (critical notes 1956c, 110–11).

DISCUSSION (musical). Hindemith 1968 (melodic and harmonic analysis of beginning); Machabey 1955b, 2:35–36; Hirshberg 1971, 138–41 (motivic analysis of *Se quanque amours* [B21] and B22). Reaney (1953, 141) prefers the substitute contratenor over the authentic one. Machabey (1928, 213–14=1955a, 226–27) believed that the pitch *E*, providing the third over *C* in the final cadence in MS *G*, was significant for the development of tonal cadences (cited in Reaney 1953, 141 n. 21 and Machabey 1955b, 2:35). It is of course simply an error in the manuscript (see above, n. 20).

Inviolata genetrix. See *Felix virgo / Inviolata* (M23).

Ite, missa est. See *Messe de Nostre Dame.*

J'ai tant mon / Lasse! je sui / Ego moriar pro te (motet M7)

MANUSCRIPTS WITH TEXT AND MUSIC (all 3v: tr, mot, ten).

[1] C	fols. 211v–212r	no. 6	[5] A	fols. 420v–421r	no. 7
[3] V g	fols. 266v–267r	no. 7	[6] G	fols. 108v–109r	no. 7
[4] B	fols. 264v–265r	no. 7	[7] E	fols. 138v–139r	no. 7

EDITION OF TEXT. Chichmaref 1909, 2:495–96 no. 7.

TEXT STRUCTURE AND RELATIONSHIP TO ISORHYTHM. Both triplum and motetus exhibit regular correlation between text and *talea* structure (Besseler 1927, 223; Reichert 1956, 201). The beginning and ending of strophe and *talea* exactly correspond, virtually without staggered phrasing, a situation unique to M7 and *Quant en moy / Amour* (M1) (Reichert 1956, 205). See also Reichert 1956, 206, 209, ex. 9 facing p. 209, discussed p. 210 (irregular strophic structure at end of triplum; note that the final two lines of the triplum, "Qu'amours, besoins et desirs d'achever / Font trespasser mesure et scens outrer" [that love, need, and desire to be finished cause measure and reason to be exceeded] can be understood as a playful reference to the irregularity of the end of the strophe); Günther 1957, 140–42 (declamation and texting); Clarkson 1971, 266–67 (strophic form of triplum resembles the "*complainte* form" of *Tels rit* [RF2] and *Ma chiere* [B40], except that the triplum text concludes with a terzet); Sanders 1973, 559 n. 259 (overall musical phrase structure and triplum texting); Ziino 1978, 440 (sequence-like form of triplum).

Triplum: a a ab a a ab b b ba b b ba c c cd c c cd d d dc d d dc cᵗ c c
1010104 1010104 1010104 1010104 1010104 1010104 1010104 1010104 101010

a:-eü, b:-i, c:-er, d:-our (†: lyric caesura)

Motetus: a abb a abb a abb ab b a b a a:-ure, b:-i
8'8'88 8'8'88 8'8'88 8'8 88' 88'

DISCUSSION (literary). Hoepffner 1908–21, 3:258 n. to l. 1309 of *Fonteinne*, and Thiry-Stassin 1970, 49 (allusions to Narcissus); Boogaart 1993b, 32 (*desmesure*). Feminine voice.

TEXTUAL LEGACY (England). Chaucer, *Book of the Duchess* (Kittredge 1915c, 15–16; Wimsatt 1968, 159).

TENOR SOURCE. *Ego moriar pro te* is adapted from the antiphon *Rex autem David* (2 Samuel 18:32–33) (Sanders 1973, 563 n. 287; Fuller 1990, 223); this identification supercedes the speculation in Anderson 1976, 124 n. 18.

EDITIONS OF MUSIC. Ludwig 1926–54, 3:27–29; Schrade 1956b, 2:130–33 (critical notes 1956c, 78–79); Turek 1984. Harmonic problem in tenor, m. 52 (Ludwig 1926–54, 3:8); barring discussed in Hoppin 1960, 26.

DISCUSSION (musical). Bipartite, with diminution by one-half. Gombosi 1950, 221–22 (symmetrical rhythmic structure of the tenor); Machabey 1955b, 2:79–80; Günther 1958, 33–34 and 1990, 83–84 (changes of *tempus*, unique to this motet; conflicts of *modus*); Kühn 1973, 185–88 (sonorities); Sanders 1973, 559 n. 259 (numerical aspect); Dobrzańska 1979b, 65 (harmonic reduction of mm. 1–132); Fuller 1990, 223–31 (effect of the tenor on tonal structure; includes partial discant reduction of *taleae* I–III). On the melodic rhyme of four measures at end of each of the three *taleae* of the first *color*, see Reichert 1956, 212; Günther 1958, 32; Ziino 1978, 447); on some additional melodic correspondences, see Reichert 1956, 213, ex. 9; Ziino 1978, 449.

J'aim la flour (lai L2)

MANUSCRIPTS WITH TEXT AND MUSIC (all monophonic).

[1] C	fols. 168v–170r	no. 2	[5] A	fols. 370r–371r	no. 2
[3] V g	fols. 222r–223v	no. 2	[6] G	fols. 76r–77r	no. 2
[4] B	fols. 220r–221v	no. 2			

TEXT MANUSCRIPTS.

[10] M	fol. 210r	no. 2	
[40] I	fol. 1r	no. 1a (follows first six strophes of *Un mortel lay* [L12/8])	

FACSIMILES (refer to chap. 4.4s). Miniature C94. Bottée de Toulmon 1836, appendix, no. 2, p. 4 (diplomatic facs. of beginning, MS A); Kiesewetter 1838, no. 12 (diplomatic facs.).

EDITION OF TEXT. Chichmaref 1909, 2:294–99 no. 2.

TRANSLATION. Marrocco/Sandon 1977, 157.

330 THE MUSIC

TEXT STRUCTURE. 7 strophes, 164 lines[58]:

1. $\dfrac{aaaaaaaaaaaaaa}{33333333333377}\Big\|\ \dfrac{bbbbbbbbbbbbbb}{33333333333377}\ \|$

2. $\dfrac{ccccc}{844448}\Big|\dfrac{c\,ccccc}{844448}\Big\|\dfrac{dddddd}{844448}\Big|\dfrac{d\,ddddd}{844448}\ \|$

3. $\dfrac{e\,e\,ea}{7'7'7'3}\Big|\dfrac{e\,e\,ea}{7'7'7'3}\Big\|\dfrac{f\,f\,fa}{7'7'7'3}\Big|\dfrac{f\,f\,fa}{7'7'7'3}\ \|$

4. $\dfrac{gggggh}{8444448}\Big|\dfrac{gggggh}{8444448}\Big\|\dfrac{i\,i\,i\,i\,i\,h}{8444448}\Big|\dfrac{i\,i\,i\,i\,i\,h}{8444448}\ \|$

5. $\dfrac{j\,j\,j\,j\,j}{84448}\Big|\dfrac{j\,j\,j\,j\,j}{84448}\Big\|\dfrac{kkkkk}{84448}\Big|\dfrac{kkkkk}{84448}\ \|$

6. $\dfrac{1111m}{77777'}\Big|\dfrac{1111m}{77777'}\Big\|\dfrac{nnnnm}{77777'}\Big|\dfrac{nnnnm}{77777'}\ \|$

7. $\dfrac{aaaaaaaaaaaaaa}{33333333333377}\Big\|\ \dfrac{ooooooooooooo}{33333333333377}\ \|$

a:-*our*, b:-*art*, c:-*uit*, d:-*ours*, e:-*ire*, f:-*ame*,
g:-*ay*, h:-*ment*, i:-*oir*, j:-*iens*, k:-*oy*, l:-*ir*, m:-*ée*, n:-*eüst*, o:-*i*

DISCUSSION (literary). Huot 1987, 262–63 (iconography).

EDITIONS OF MUSIC. Bottée de Toulmon 1836, app. no. 2, p. 5 (strophe 1a only); ; Kiesewetter 1838, no. 12; 1841, *Beilagen*, 3 no. 8 (after Bottée de Toulmon 1836); Bottée de Toulmon [1846]b; Ambros 1891, 251 (=1864 ed., 230) (after Bottée de Toulmon 1836); Machabey 1931, 332 (strophe 2); Gérold 1936, 369 (strophe 1); Ludwig 1926–54, 4:25–26 (ed. Besseler); Schrade 1956b, 2:2–4 (critical notes 1956c, 56–57); Marrocco/Sandon 1977, 155–56 no. 69. The music of strophes 1 and 7 is the same.

DISCUSSION (musical). Bottée de Toulmon 1836, 216–17; Machabey 1955b, 1:115 (esp. n. 319 on a possible refrain at the beginning of strophe 2), 1:126 (text setting). Ludwig (1930, 268) noted that the tune was used in the second movement of J. Rheinberger's Organ Sonata no. 19, op. 193 (see chap. 2.5).

J'aim miex languir en ma dure dolour (ballade B7)
Refrain: *Et me fussiés .c. mille fois plus dure*

MANUSCRIPTS WITH TEXT AND MUSIC.

[1] C	fols. 160v–161r	no. 7	2v (ca, ten; empty staves for tr)
[3] V g	fol. 299v	no. 7	2v (ca, ten; empty staves for tr)
[4] B	fol. 297v	no. 7	2v (ca, ten; empty staves for tr)
[5] A	fol. 457r	no. 7	2v (ca, ten; empty staves for tr)
[6] G	fol. 136r	no. 7	2v (ca, ten)
[7] E	fol. 154v	no. 26	2v (ca, ten)

TEXT MANUSCRIPTS.

[10] M	fol. 238r	no. 7		[40] Wm	fol. 21v	no. 20

EDITION OF TEXT. Chichmaref 1909, 2:542 no. 7; Woledge 1961, 222–23.

TRANSLATIONS. Woledge 1961, 222–23; Fuller 1987a, 38 (strophe 1).

TEXT STRUCTURE. 3 strophes: $\begin{smallmatrix} a & b & a & b & b & c & C \\ 1010 & 1010 & 1010\text{'}10\text{'} \end{smallmatrix}$ a:-*our*, b:-*é*, c:-*ure*

EDITIONS OF MUSIC. Ludwig 1926–54, 1:6; Schrade 1956b, 3:78 (critical notes 1956c, 102); Wilkins 1980, 24 (Chaucer, *If no love is* underlaid); Fuller 1987a, 40 (from MSS C and A; text underlay is superior to any previous edition, except m. 28, where Ludwig is correct: a text-orientation line in MS A assures that the syllable -*re* should fall on the ligature).

DISCUSSION (musical). Machabey 1955b, 2:23–24; Lühmann 1978, 92–94 (declamation); Fuller 1987a (detailed analysis); M.L. Göllner 1989, 68–71 (text/music relationship; setting of word "dure").

J'aim sans penser laidure (virelai V14)

MANUSCRIPTS WITH TEXT AND MUSIC (all monophonic).

[1] C	fols. 153v–154r	no. 14		[5] A	fols. 485v–486r	no. 14
[3] V g	fol. 326v	no. 14		[6] G	fol. 157v	no. 14
[4] B	fol. 324v	no. 14				

TEXT MANUSCRIPT.

[10] M	fol. 248v	no. 14

---

[58] The pattern of rhymes can be understood to define more than seven strophes; cf. *Aus amans* (L4) and *On parle* (L8).

EDITION OF TEXT. Chichmaref 1909, 2:597 no. 14.

TEXTUAL LEGACY (England). The "God and Nature" theme makes V14 a possible source for Chaucer's *Complaynt d'Amours* (Wimsatt 1978, 72–73, 86 n. 18).

TEXT STRUCTURE. 3 strophes: $\frac{ababab}{6'66'66'6} \parallel \frac{AABAAB}{3'3'5\ 3'3'5}$ a:-*ure*, b:-*é*

EDITIONS OF MUSIC. Ludwig 1926–54, 1:76; Schrade 1956b, 3:174 (critical notes 1956c, 140).

DISCUSSION (musical). Machabey 1955b, 1:183.

Je ne cesse de prier. Le Lay de la Fonteinne (lai L16; Schrade lai 11)

MANUSCRIPTS WITH TEXT AND MUSIC (all monophonic; alternate strophes realized as 3v canons).

[3]	**V g**	fols. 250v–253v	no. 16	[5]	**A**	fols. 396r–399r	no. 16
[4]	**B**	fols. 248v–251v	no. 16	[6]	**G**	fols. 93r–94v	no. 16 (has title)
[7]	**E**	fols. 122v–124r	no. 14 *Item un Lay de Nostre Dame*				

TEXT MANUSCRIPT.

[10] **M** fols. 229r–230r no. 16

EDITION OF TEXT. Chichmaref 1909, 2:406–14 no. 16.

TRANSLATIONS. See discography (chap. 8.3 and 8.8).

TEXT STRUCTURE. 12 strophes, 234 lines:

1a. $\frac{ababbaba}{75'75'7'57'5} \parallel$ 1b. same $\parallel$ 7a. $\frac{mnmnmnmn}{7'77'77'77'7} \Big| \frac{mnmnmnmn}{7'77'77'77'7} \parallel$ 7b. same $\parallel$

2a. $\frac{ccddccddc}{775757575} \parallel$ 2b. same $\parallel$ 8a. $\frac{oop\ oop\ ppo\ ppo}{737\ 737\ 737\ 737} \parallel$ 8b. same $\parallel$

3a. 8'eeeef | eeeef $\parallel$ 3b. same $\parallel$ 9a. $\frac{qqqqr}{45335} \Big| \frac{qqqqr}{45335} \parallel$ 9b. same $\parallel$

4a. $\frac{ghghhghhgh}{7'57'577'757'5} \parallel$ 4b. same $\parallel$ 10a. $\frac{sssst}{55575} \Big| \frac{sssst}{55575} \parallel$ 10b. same $\parallel$

5a. $\frac{iiiiiij}{8448446} \Big| \frac{iiiiiij}{8448446} \parallel$ 5b. same $\parallel$ 11a. $\frac{uu\ uvv}{7'7'7'74} \Big| \frac{uu\ uvv}{7'7'7'74} \parallel$ 11b. same $\parallel$

6a. $\frac{kkkl\ kkkl}{6666'\ 6666'} \Big| \frac{kkkl\ kkkl}{6666'\ 6666'} \parallel$ 6b. same $\parallel$ 12a–b. = 1a–b.

a:-*ier*, b:-*ière*, c:-*ir*, d:-*er*, e:-*ance*, f:-*ère*, g:-*einne*, h:-*uis*, i:-*oit*, j:-*age*, k:-*é*, l:-*ose*, m:-*omme*, n:-*il*, o:-*oy*, p:-*ent*, q:-*i*, r:-*iés*, s:-*ort*, t:-*ire*, u:-*orde*, v:-*our*

DISCUSSION (literary). Poirion 1965, 421–22, 536–37 (Marian image); Mulder 1978, 69–71 (Marian image); Maillard 1984, 332–33 (possible literary models and literary successors for Marian lai); 335–37 (literary analysis with musical considerations); Cerquiglini[-Toulet] 1985b, 81 and 1993b, 98 (Marian image). Hassell (1982, no. P232) indexes a proverb.

EDITIONS OF MUSIC. Ludwig 1926–54, 4:45–53 (ed. Besseler); Schrade 1956b, 2:39–51 (critical notes 1956c, 64–65); Leguy 1977, 4:32–49. The music of strophes 1 and 12 is the same, except that strophe 12 is a perfect fifth higher, and is presented as a 3v *chace*. For the performance of the *chace*, MSS **Vg**, **B**, **A**, and **G** supply the rubric *iterum sine pausa* after each of the six even-numbered strophes.

DISCUSSION (musical). Feininger 1937 (canonic sections); S.J. Williams 1952, 291; Machabey 1955b, 1:122 (only recognizes 2v polyphony), 126; Günther 1957, 126–27 (text/music relationship); 1983, 264 (performance suggestions); 1984a, 263–64 (relationship between canonic structure and text); Newes 1987, 115–34 (awkward text setting in canonic strophes); Yudkin 1989, 488–91 (analysis); Newes 1991b, 103–15 (analysis).

MUSICAL LEGACY. Cypriot-French motet *Coume le serf / Lunne plainne d'umilité* (ed. Hoppin 1960–63, 2:161–65 no. 36); cited in Hoppin 1957, 97.

Je ne cuit pas qu'onques a creature (ballade B14)

Refrain: *Mon cuer, m'amour et quanque je desir*

MANUSCRIPTS WITH TEXT AND MUSIC (all 2v: ca, ten).

[1] **C**	fols. 163v–164r	no. 14	[5] **A**	fol. 461v	no. 15
[3] **Vg**	fol. 303r	no. 14	[6] **G**	fol. 139r	no. 15
[4] **B**	fol. 301r	no. 14	[7] **E**	fol. 147v	no. 4

TEXT MANUSCRIPTS.

[10] **M**   fol. 239r   no.14   Lo175 **CVgBJAGEMD** (chap. 6.4)

EDITIONS OF TEXT. Chichmaref 1909, 1:159 no. 175; Wilkins 1972, 78 no. 110. Feminine voice.

TEXT STRUCTURE. 3 strophes[59]: $\begin{smallmatrix} a & b & a & b & c & c & d\,D \\ 10{}'10 & 10{}'10 & 7101010 \end{smallmatrix}$ a:-*ure*, b:-*ent*, c:-*ir*

TEXTUAL LEGACY (England). Chaucer, *Troilus* (Wimsatt 1976, 289–90).

EDITIONS OF MUSIC. Ludwig 1926–54, 1:12 ; Schrade 1956b, 3:85 (critical notes 1956c, 106); Arlt 1982, 232 (after Schrade).

DISCUSSION (musical). Machabey 1955b, 2:28–29; Günther 1957, 79 and Martinez 1963, 108–9 (recurrence of musical segments); Arlt 1982, 231–39 (detailed analysis); Cross 1990, 267–68 (chromatic intervals).

Je ne me puis saouler (virelai V33)

TEXT MANUSCRIPTS.

[3] **Vg**	fol. 333v	no. 33	[10] **M**	fol. 254r	no. 33
[4] **B**	fol. 330v	no. 33	[43] **Mn**	fol. 14r	no. 3
[5] **A**	fol. 493r	no. 34	[50] **Pa**	fol. 71r	no. 227
[6] **G**	fol. 162v	no. 34		VD11 **AFEPm** (chap. 5.13 table 5.3)	

EDITIONS OF TEXT. P. Paris 1875, 39; Chichmaref 1909, 2:625–26 no. 34.

TEXT STRUCTURE. 3 strophes: $\begin{smallmatrix} AABBAAB \\ 7\,7\,4\,7\,4\,7\,4 \end{smallmatrix}$ ‖ $\begin{smallmatrix} bba\ bba \\ 774\ 774 \end{smallmatrix}$ | $\begin{smallmatrix} a\,abba\,ab \\ 7747474 \end{smallmatrix}$ ‖ $\begin{smallmatrix} AABBAAB \\ 7\,7\,4\,7\,4\,7\,4 \end{smallmatrix}$ a:-*er*, b:-*ay*

DISCUSSION (literary). The following *Voir Dit* passages concern V33: (a) in the introductory narrative, Guillaume presents the three virelais V33, *L'ueil, qui est* (V34), and *Plus belle* (V35) as having been dictated from his sickbed (ll. 821–22, ed. P. Paris 1875, 35); (b) the text of V33 is inserted in the narrative after V34–35 (ll. 954–1002, ed. 1875, 39–41); (c) Toute Belle wrote a paired virelai, *Ne vous estuet guermenter* (ll. 1135–56, ed. 1875, 49–50), with the same metrical scheme and rhymes, and expressed the hope in letter 5 (ed. 1875, 58 as letter 7) that Guillaume would set it to music with V33 as a double virelai. As S.J. Williams (1977, 466) remarks, this is not a genre cultivated by Machaut, although other composers did write double virelais. The theme of "saouler" [to satisfy] is anticipated in prose in *Voir Dit* letter 6 (ed. P. Paris 1875, 20–21 as letter 2); see also letter 2 (ed. 1875, 41 as letter 4). For excerpts from or commentary on these passages, see Wilkins 1972, 178–79 notes to nos. 277–79; Leech-Wilkinson 1993b, 110, 112. Hassell (1982, no. R72) indexes a proverb.

Je ne me say conforter. Le Lay de la Souscie (lai L20)

TEXT MANUSCRIPTS.

[5] **A**   fols. 407r–408r   no. 20 (title)   [6] **G**   fols. 99v–100v   no. 20 (title)

EDITION OF TEXT. Chichmaref 1909, 2:443–50 no. 20.

TEXT STRUCTURE. 12 strophes, 240 lines:

1a. $\frac{a\,abba\,abba}{774747474}$ ‖ 1b. same ‖   4a. $\frac{gh\ gh\ gh\ gh\ gh\ gh\ gh\ gh}{5{}'5\ 5{}'5\ 5{}'5\ 5{}'5\ 5{}'5\ 5{}'5\ 5{}'5\ 5{}'5}$ ‖ 4b. same ‖

2a. $\frac{c\,d\,d\,d\,dc\ c\,d\,d\,d\,dc}{77{}'3{}'3{}'7{}'7\ 77{}'3{}'3{}'7{}'7}$ ‖ 2b. same ‖   5a. $\frac{i\ i\ j\,j\,i\ i\ i\,j\,j\,i}{7{}'7{}'577{}'7{}'7{}'577{}'}$ ‖ 5b. same ‖

3a. $\frac{e\,eee\,f\,e\,eee\,f}{45335\ 45335}$ ‖ 3b. same ‖   6a. $\frac{k\,k\,k\,l\ k\,k\,k\,l}{3{}'3{}'7{}'3\ 3{}'3{}'7{}'3}$ ‖ 6b. same ‖

---

[59] See Gieber (1982, 3, 11 n. 23) on caesura and enjambment.

7a. $\frac{\text{mmmn}}{7\,7\,7\,5'}\,\frac{\text{mmmn}}{7\,7\,7\,5'}$ ‖ 7b. same ‖

10a. $\frac{\text{s t t u u s s}}{7434744}\,\frac{\text{s t t u u s s}}{7434744}$ ‖ 10b. same ‖

8a. $\frac{\text{o o o p}}{7'3'7'7}\,\frac{\text{o o o p}}{7'3'7'7}$ ‖ 8b. same ‖

11a. $\frac{\text{v v w v v w}}{8'8'8}\,\frac{\text{v v w v v w}}{8'8'8}$ ‖ 11b. same ‖

9a. $\frac{\text{q q q q q r}}{555577}\,\frac{\text{q q q q q r}}{555577}$ ‖ 9b. same ‖

12a–b. = 1a–b.

a:-*er*, b:-*oy*, c:-*oint*, d:-*ure*, e:-*ir*, f:-*oir*, g:-*ie*, h:-*our*, i:-*ée*, j:-*is*, k:-*ire*, l:-*uit*, m:-*ort*, n:-*ence*, o:-*orte*, p:-*in*, q:-*ay*, r:-*aint*, s:-*oint*, t:-*ement*, u:-*i*, v:-*einne*, w:-*eins*

DISCUSSION (literary). Fabin 1919, 267–68 (detailed description); Patch 1927, 96 n. 2 (theme of Fortune); Poirion 1965, 409 (L20 l. 176 refers to the opening line of *Amis, t'amour* [L10/7]); Calin 1974, 244 (theme of Fortune). Feminine voice.

TEXTUAL LEGACY (England). Chaucer, *Anelida and Arcite* (Fabin 1919; Benson 1987, 991a).

Je ne sui mie. See *Trop plus / Biauté* (M20).

Je puis trop bien ma dame comparer (ballade B28)
Refrain: *Qu'ades la pri et riens ne me respont*
MANUSCRIPTS WITH TEXT AND MUSIC.

[3] **V g**	fol. 311r	no. 28	3v (ca, ten, ct)
[4] **B**	fol. 310r	no. 28	3v (ca, ten, ct)
[5] **A**	fol. 468r	no. 27	3v (ca, ten, ct)
[6] **G**	fols. 143v–144r	no. 28	3v (ca, ten, ct)
[7] **E**	fol. 148v	no. 8	3v (ca, ten, ct)

TEXT MANUSCRIPTS.

[10] **M**	fol. 241v	no. 28	Lo203 **VgBAMD** (chap. 6.4)
[49] **Jp**	fol. 65v	no. 46 *Je doy tresbien*	
[50] **Pa**	fol. 50r	no. 153	

FACSIMILE. *Jardin* 1910–25, vol. 1 fol. 65v (**Jp**).

EDITIONS OF TEXT. Tarbé 1849, 60; 1856, xxxi (strophe 1); Chichmaref 1909, 1:183 no. 203; Wilkins 1972, 79 no. 115.

TRANSLATIONS. Davison/Apel 1949, 245 no. 45 (strophe 1); Reaney 1959b, 26 (summary only); Apel 1978, 40 (strophe 1); Allorto 1983, 157 (strophe 1; Italian); Cerquiglini/Berthelot 1987, 115–16 (modern French); Campbell 1989–90, 288–89 n. 6.

TEXT STRUCTURE. 3 strophes: $\frac{\text{a b \quad a b c c d D}}{\text{1010 \quad 1010 \quad 7101010}}$ a:-*er*, b:-*on*, c:-*oit*, d:-*ont*

DISCUSSION (literary). Hoepffner 1908–21, 3:257 n. to l. 963 of *Fonteinne*; Marks 1984, 108–9; Campbell 1989–90, 279–84 (thorough analysis). On Pygmalion, see, for instance, Reaney 1959b, 26; Kelly 1978, 48, 129–30, 234, 272 n. 71, 285 n. 19; Badel 1980, 91 n. 78; Cerquiglini 1980b, 85 n. 31; 1985b, 207–8, 272 s.v. "Pygmalion"; Huot 1987, 285 n. 8; Heinrichs 1990, 135 n. 32; Calin 1994, 217–18. The first line of B28 also opens Machaut's *Harpe* (see chap. 5.12).

TEXTUAL LEGACY (France). Froissart, ballade *Je puis moult bien ma dame comparer* (ed. McGregor 1975, 232–33 no. 35; Baudouin 1978, 44–45 no. 35; cited in Ludwig 1926–54, 1:31; Poirion 1965, 215); see discussion in Günther 1972, 57–58; cf. the ballade *Je puis moult bien comparer mon desir* (ed. McGregor 1975, 218–19 no. 17; Baudouin 1978, 24–25 no. 17; ed. and trans. Figg 1994b, 241–42). Cf. also two Cypriot-French ballades, *Je vous puis bien comparer* (ed. Hoppin 1960–63, 3:148–49 no. 83); and *Pymalion qui moult subtilz estoit* (ed. Hoppin 1960–63, 3:67–68 no. 39).

EDITIONS OF MUSIC. Ludwig 1926–54, 1:31 (errors); Davison/Apel 1949, 48, no. 45 (errors); Schrade 1956b, 3:112–13 (errors; critical notes 1956c, 114); Hamburg 1976, 19 no. 23; Allorto 1983, 44 no. 48 (errors); Campbell 1989–90, 280–81 (ed. Earp). Syncopation errors in the older editions discussed in Hoppin 1960, 16–17 n. 16.

DISCUSSION (musical). Machabey 1955b, 2:41–42; Martinez 1963, 104–5 (text setting); Junger 1967, 176–77 (aspects of *ouvert* cadence); Salop 1971, 64–65 (melodic direction in cantus); Dömling 1972, 305, 306–7 (musical rhyme and text rhyme; text setting and musical structure); Kühn 1973, 155–58, 213 (motivic analysis; sonorities); Saponov 1978,

36 (motivic analysis); Hirshberg 1980, 29 *(ficta)*; Karp 1988, 74–75 (compositional priority of the cantus); M.L. Göllner 1989, 73–75 (text/music relationship; text painting); Danckwardt 1993, 374–77, 381–82 (compositional procedure). The pervasive use of certain melodic formulas in *tempus imperfectum, prolatio major* links *Donnez, signeurs* (B26), *Une vipere* (B27), and *Je puis trop* (B28) as one group, and *Plourez, dames* (B32), *Nes qu' on* (B33), and *Se pour ce muir* (B36) as another; the same formulas are seen to a lesser extent in *En amer* (RF4), *Cinc, un* (R6), and *Douce dame, tant* (R20) (cf. Reaney 1955, 47; Günther 1957, 80–84; Hirshberg 1971, 120–33; Little 1980, 49; Arlt 1993, 63; Arlt, forthcoming study).

MUSICAL LEGACY. Compare the ballade in *US:BE 744, En la maison Dedalus* (cited in Crocker 1967, 166; ed. Crocker 1967, 169–70 (by Thomas Walker); Apel 1970–72, 2:37–38 no. 140; Greene 1981–89, 20:117–19 no. 36).

Je suis aussi com cils qui est ravis (ballade B20)
Refrain: *Fors li qu' aim miex cent mille fois que mi*

MANUSCRIPTS WITH TEXT AND MUSIC.

[1]	**C**	fols. 199v–200r	no. 20	2v (ca, ten)
[3]	**V g**	fol. 306v	no. 20	2v (ca, ten)
[4]	**B**	fol. 304v	no. 20	2v (ca, ten)
[5]	**A**	fol. 464r	no. 20	2v (ca, ten)
[6]	**G**	fols. 140v–141r	no. 20	2v (ca, ten)
[7]	**E**	fol. 152v	no. 19	3v (ca, ten, ct)

TEXT MANUSCRIPT.

[10]	**M**	fols. 240r–240v	no. 20

FACSIMILES. Bofill Soliguer 1991, 22 (MS **C**).

EDITION OF TEXT. Chichmaref 1909, 2:551–52 no. 22.

TRANSLATIONS. Baltzer 1991a, 100; see also discography (chap. 8.3 and 8.8).

TEXT STRUCTURE. 3 strophes: $\frac{a\ b}{1010}\ \frac{a\ b\ c\ c}{1010}\ \frac{d\ D}{7101010}$ a:-*is*, b:-*ent*, c:-*our*, d:-*i*

DISCUSSION (literary). Guthrie 1991, 86–87 (poetic stress).

TEXTUAL LEGACY (England). Chaucer, *A Complaint to his Lady* and *Anelida and Arcite* (Wimsatt 1978, 67–68).

EDITIONS OF MUSIC. Ludwig 1926–54, 1:21 ; Schrade 1956b, 3:94–95 (critical notes 1956c, 109–10); Baltzer 1991b, 98–99 (comments p. 154). The unauthentic contratenor is corrupt at the end. Both Ludwig and Schrade leave the ending blank, although one could be supplied from the end of the *clos* (Hirshberg 1971, 86 n. 73, 87–88 musical example).

DISCUSSION (musical). Machabey 1955b, 2:33–34; Dömling 1972, 305 (text setting); Hirshberg 1973–74, 63 (text lines/musical phrases); Berger 1992, 153 *(ficta)*.

Je vivroie liement (virelai V23; Schrade virelai 21)
MANUSCRIPTS WITH TEXT AND MUSIC (all monophonic).

[1]	**C**	fol. 156v	no. 20[60]		[5]	**A**	fol. 489r	no. 23
[3]	**V g**	fol. 329v	no. 23		[6]	**G**	fol. 159v	no. 23
[4]	**B**	fol. 327v	no. 23		[7]	**E**	fol. 162v	no. 21

TEXT MANUSCRIPT.

[10]	**M**	fol. 251r	no. 23

EDITION OF TEXT. Chichmaref 1909, 2:609–10 no. 23.

TRANSLATION. See discography (chap. 8.3 and 8.8).

TEXT STRUCTURE. 2 strophes: $\frac{ABAAB}{75'772}\ \|\ \frac{c\ b\ c\ b}{75'\ 75'}\ |\ \frac{a\ b\ a\ a\ b}{75'772}\ \|\ \frac{ABAAB}{75'772}$, a:-*ent*, b:-*ure*, c:-*i*

EDITIONS OF MUSIC. Ludwig 1926–54, 1:80–81; Schrade 1956b, 3:180 (critical notes 1956c, 142–43).

DISCUSSION (musical). Machabey 1955b, 1:187; Weber-Bockholdt 1992, 271–73 (text/music relationship); Leech-Wilkinson 1991 (voice-leading reduction reveals circular nature).

---

[60] Two strophes only.

Joie, plaisence et douce norriture (*chant royal* RF3)
MANUSCRIPTS WITH TEXT AND MUSIC (all monophonic).

[1] **C**	fols. 39r–39v			[6] **F**	fols. 50r–50v	
[3] **V g**	fols. 103v–104r			[7] **E**	fol. 28v	
[4] **B**	fols. 103v–104r (new 120v–121r)			[20] **P e**	fol. 17r	
[5] **A**	fols. 63v–64r					

TEXT MANUSCRIPTS.

[10] **M**	fols. 62r–62v	[18] **P m**	fol. 59v
[15] **K**	fol. 54r (strophe 1 is incomplete)	[50] **Pa**	fol. 49r no. 149
[16] **J**	fol. 60r (strophe 1 is incomplete)		

FACSIMILES (refer to chap. 4.4e). Miniatures C23–24. Kalkbrenner 1802, table 4 fig. 4 (diplomatic facs.; errors).

EDITIONS OF TEXT (*Remede*, ll. 1985–2032). Hoepffner 1908–21, 3:71–73; Wimsatt/ Kibler 1988, 277–79.

TRANSLATIONS. Switten 1988c, 47–48; Wimsatt/Kibler 1988, 276–78; Boulton 1993, 190 (strophe 2, excerpt); see also discography (chap. 8.3 and 8.8).

TEXT STRUCTURE. 5 strophes: $\begin{smallmatrix} a & b & a & b & b\,c\,c\,dd \\ 10 & 10 & 10 & 10 & 77\,7\,75 \end{smallmatrix}$ envoy: $\begin{smallmatrix} c\,dd \\ 7\,75 \end{smallmatrix}$ a:-*ure*, b:-*er*, c:-*ance*, d:-*i*

DISCUSSION (literary). Poirion 1965, 371 (on the narrator's falling asleep), 383; Lanoue 1984 (importance of RF3 to the spiritual recovery of the narrator); Cerquiglini 1985b, 200 (on the narrator's falling asleep); Heger 1988, 66 (RF3 is Machaut's oldest *chant royal*; he established the rules followed by later poets); van der Werf/Frobenius 1983, 2–3, 6; Imbs 1991, 120. For some literary studies that deal with all of the inserted lyrics, see chap. 5.7.

EDITIONS OF MUSIC. Kalkbrenner 1802, table 4 fig. 5 (errors); Ludwig 1911, 10 (appendix); 1926–54, 1:97; Schrade 1956b, 2:107 (critical notes 1956c, 74); Arlt 1982, 274–75 (after Schrade); Switten 1988c, 47 (after Schrade); Wimsatt/Kibler 1988, 424, critical notes p. 439 (ed. Baltzer).

DISCUSSION (musical). Ludwig 1911, 410–11; Machabey 1931, 334; 1955b, 1:133–37; Mulder 1978, 96–98 (rhythmic materials of *Qui n'aroit* (RF1), *Tels rit* (RF2) and *Joie, plaisence* (RF3) are similar); Arlt 1982, 273–76; Malizia 1984, 28–30 (general). For some musical studies that deal with all of the inserted lyrics, see chap. 5.7.

Kyrie eleyson. See *Messe de Nostre Dame.*

L'ueil, qui est le droit archier (virelai V34)
TEXT MANUSCRIPTS.

[3] **V g**	fols. 333v–334r no. 34		[10] **M**	fols. 254r–254v no. 34	
[4] **B**	fols. 330v–331r no. 34		[50] **Pa**	fol. 70v no. 225	
[5] **A**	fols. 493r–493v no. 35		VD9 **AFEPm** (chap. 5.13 table 5.3)		
[6] **G**	fols. 162v–163r no. 35				

EDITIONS OF TEXT. P. Paris 1875, 38; Chichmaref 1909, 2:626–28 no. 35.

TEXT STRUCTURE. 3 strophes: $\begin{smallmatrix} AABBAAB \\ 7\,7\,47\,4\,74 \end{smallmatrix}$ ∥ $\begin{smallmatrix} bba\ bba \\ 774\ 774 \end{smallmatrix}$ ∣ $\begin{smallmatrix} a\,abba\,ab \\ 7747474 \end{smallmatrix}$∥ $\begin{smallmatrix} AABBAAB \\ 7\,7\,47\,4\,74 \end{smallmatrix}$ a:-*ier*, b:-*ent*

DISCUSSION (literary). The following *Voir Dit* passages concern V34: (a) in the introductory narrative, Guillaume presents the three virelais *Je ne me puis* (V33), V34, and *Plus belle* (V35) as having been dictated from his sickbed (ll. 821–22, ed. 1875, 35); (b) the text of V34 is inserted in the narrative (ll. 856–904, ed. 1875, 37–38); Toute Belle asked repeatedly for Machaut to set V34 to music, see (c) letter 28 (ed. 1875, 207), and (d) letter 32 (ed. 1875, 250); (e) in letter 33, Guillaume made excuses for not setting V34 (ed. 1875, 259); indeed, as Machaut had already remarked when the works were first introduced, "Ce sont .iii. chansons baladees / Qui ne furent onques chantees" (ll. 829–30, ed. 1875, 36) [these are three *chansons baladées* that were never sung, i.e., never set to music]. Ludwig (1926–54, 2:53b*) suggested that perhaps it was due to Toute Belle's request for a musical setting that the virelais, though without music, were copied into the virelai music section of the manuscripts. We learn from letter 3 (ed. 1875, 49 as letter 5) that Toute Belle did obtain a virelai set to music by Machaut from her brother and Machaut's secretary, but the actual work cannot be identified. For excerpts from or commentary on these passages, see Ludwig

1926–54, 2:55*; Wilkins 1972, 178–79 notes to nos. 277–79; Cerquiglini 1985b, 141, 211; Leech-Wilkinson 1993b, 110, 112, 120, 123, 137 nos. 19 and 23.

Lasse! comment oublieray / Se j'aim / Pour quoy me bat mes maris? (motet M16)

MANUSCRIPTS WITH TEXT AND MUSIC.

[1] C	fols. 220v–221r	no. 15	3v (tr, mot, ten)
[3] V g	fols. 275v–276r	no. 16	3v (tr, mot, ten)
[4] B	fols. 273v–274r	no. 16	3v (tr, mot, ten)
[5] A	fols. 429v–430r	no. 16	3v (tr, mot, ten)
[6] G	fols. 117v–118r	no. 16	3v (tr, mot, ten)
[7] E	fols. 137v–138r	no. 10	3v (tr, mot, ten)
[58] Trém	fol. v	no. 9	(index only)

FACSIMILES. Wolf 1923, plates 41–42 (MS A); Gennrich 1948, plates 4a–4b (MS A).

EDITION OF TEXT. Chichmaref 1909, 2:513–15 no. 16.

TRANSLATIONS. See discography, chap. 8.3 and 8.8.

TEXT STRUCTURE AND RELATIONSHIP TO MUSICAL STRUCTURE. The work is not isorhythmic and so is not analyzed in this respect in Reichert 1956. Nevertheless, the phrase structures of both triplum and motetus are periodic: 6 triplum phrases, each 25 breves long, = 150; 10 motetus phrases, each 15 breves long, = 150 (Machabey 1955b, 2:95; Sanders 1973, 564; Clarkson 1971, 266, 317 n. 106). Clarkson (1971, 315–18) employs the term "phasic motet" for this; the two voices fall into phase in m. 75, the exact midpoint, but do not coincide with the tenor. Since these long patterns need the full length of the motet to come back into phase, Sanders considers the tenor "one long talea" (1973, 564; 1980, 352). See also Clarkson 1971, 212, 266, 317 n. 106 (text structure of motetus), 268 (virelai structure of tenor); Ziino 1978, 443 n. 11 (text structure).

Triplum: $\dfrac{\text{aaab bbbc cccd ddde eeef fffg gggh hhhi iiij jjjk kkkl lll}}{\text{8884 8884 8884 8884 8884 8884 8884 8884 8884 8884 8884 888}}$

a:-*ay*, b:-*i*, c:-*ent*, d:-*uet*, e:-*oy*, f:-*uis*, g:-*ien*, h:-*is*, i:-*ui*, j:-*ort*, k:-*our*, l:-*eins*

Motetus: $\dfrac{\text{aab aab bba bba aab aab bba bba aab aab}}{\text{734 734 734 734 734 734 734 734 734 734}}$ a:-*i*, b:-*ent*

Tenor (irreg. virelai): $\dfrac{\text{ABCAB dd ebceb ABCAB}}{\text{72372 77 72372 72'3'72}}$, a:-*is*, b:-*ette*, c:*Aymi, Diex!*, d:-*ait*, e:-*ay*

DISCUSSION (literary). Imbs 1991, 94 (relationship to *Voir Dit*). Feminine voice in all three texts. Hassell (1982, no. M54) indexes a proverb in the motetus.

TENOR SOURCE. *Pourquoy me bat mes maris* is an irregular virelai, a *chanson de malmariée* (Van den Boogaard 1969, 227 no. 1515). Machaut's motet provides the only source for the music. See Gennrich 1921–27, 1:102–3 no. 151 (commentary 2:104–9); Aubry 1907; and Ludwig 1926–54, 3:61 for text sources and a reconstruction of the original song.

EDITIONS OF MUSIC. Aubry 1907, 35–38; Ludwig 1926–54, 3:58–61; Gennrich 1921–27, 2:104–8; Schrade 1956b, 2:160–63 (critical notes 1956c, 16).

DISCUSSION (musical). Machabey 1955b, 2:94–96.

MUSICAL LEGACY. For twentieth-century compositions inspired by the tenor of M16, see chap. 2.5 (Gilbert and Rickett).

Lasse! je sui. See *J'ay tant / Lasse!* (M7).

Lay de Bon Espoir, Le. See *Qui n'aroit autre deport* (RF1/L19).

Lay de Bonne Esperance, Le. See *Longuement me sui tenus* (L18/13).

Lay de Confort, Le. See *S'onques dolereusement* (L17/12).

Lay de Consolation, Un. See *Pour ce que plus proprement* (L23/17).

Lay de l'Ymage, Le. See *Ne say comment commencier* (L14/9).

Lay de la Fonteinne, Le. See *Je ne cesse de prier* (L16/11).

Lay de la Rose, Le. See *Pour vivre joliement* (L21/15).

Lay de la Souscie, Le. See *Je ne me say conforter* (L20).

Lay de Nostre Dame, Le. See *Contre ce dous mois de may* (L15/10).

Lay de Plour, Le. See *Malgré Fortune et son tour* (L19/14); *Qui bien aimme a tart oublie* (L22/16).

Lay des Dames, Le. See *Amis, t'amour me contreint* (L10/7).

Lay du Mirouer Amoureux, Le. See *Se quanque Diex* (L11).

Lay Mortel, Le. See *Un mortel lay vueil commencier* (L12/8).

Le Paradis d'Amour. See *Amours, se plus demandoie* (L9).

Libera me. See *Helas! pour quoy virent / Corde* (M12).

Liement me deport (virelai V30; Schrade virelai 27)

MANUSCRIPTS WITH TEXT AND MUSIC (all monophonic).

[1]	**C**	fol. 205r	no. 27	[6]	**G**	fols. 161r–161v	no. 30
[3]	**V g**	fol. 332r	no. 30	[7]	**E**	fol. 161r	no. 146[61]
[5]	**A**	fol. 491v	no. 30				

TEXT MANUSCRIPT.

[10] **M** fol. 253r no. 30

FACSIMILE. Parrish 1957, plate xlvii (MS E), discussed pp. 149–51.

EDITION OF TEXT. Chichmaref 1909, 2:618–20 no. 30.

TRANSLATION. See discography (chap. 8.3 and 8.8).

TEXT STRUCTURE. $\frac{AAAB\ AAAB}{6\,6\,6\,6'\ 6\,6\,6\,6'}$ ‖ $\frac{b\ ba\ b\ ba}{6'6'6\ 6'6'6}$ ⏐ $\frac{aaab\ aaab}{6666'\ 6666'}$ ‖ $\frac{AAAB\ AAAB}{6\,6\,6\,6'\ 6\,6\,6\,6'}$ a:-*ort*, b:-*ure*

EDITIONS OF MUSIC. Ludwig 1926–54, 1:85–86; Schrade 1956b, 3:186 (critical notes 1956c, 145).

DISCUSSION (musical). Machabey 1955b, 1:191–92 (duplex virelai); Weber-Bockholdt 1992, 274 (frequency of -*ort* rhyme not underscored in the music).

Longuement me sui tenus. Le Lay de Bonne Esperance (lai L18; Schrade lai 13)

MANUSCRIPTS WITH TEXT AND MUSIC (all monophonic).

[3]	**V g**	fols. 256v–259v	no. 18
[4]	**B**	fols. 254v–257v	no. 18
[5]	**A**	fols. 401v–404r	no. 18 (has title)
[6]	**G**	fols. 96r–97v	no. 18 (has title)
[7]	**E**	fols. 188r–189v	in *Voir Dit* (*Le Lay d'Esperance*)

TEXT MANUSCRIPT.

[10] **M** fols. 233v–239r no. 19   VD47 **AFEPm** (chap. 5.13 table 5.3)

EDITION OF TEXT. P. Paris 1875, 172–80, 183; Chichmaref 1909, 2:425–33 no. 18.

TRANSLATION. See discography (chap. 8.3 and 8.8).

DATE. In the *Voir Dit*, the completed lai is sent with letter 21, dated to late June or early July 1363. Since there are no musical connections between the lai and the music composed specifically for the *Voir Dit*, Leech-Wilkinson (1993a, 62–63) believes that the lai is possibly an earlier work.

TEXT STRUCTURE. 12 strophes, 256 lines:

1a. $\frac{ab\,ab\,ba\,ab}{74747474}$ ‖ 1b. same ‖

2a. $\frac{ccc\,d\,ccc\,d}{7775'\ 7775'}$ ‖ 2b. same ‖

3a. $\frac{e\,f\,e\,f\,f\,e\,f\,f\,e\,f}{7'37'377'737'3}$ ‖ 3b. same ‖

4a. $\frac{g\,hg\,hg\,hg\,hg\,hg\,hg\,hh}{3'33'33'33'33'33'33'33'37}$ ‖ 4b. same ‖

5a. $\frac{i\,j\,i\,j\,i\,j\,i\,j}{75757577}$ ‖ 5b. same ‖

6a. $\frac{kkkkk\,l}{8444486'}$ ⏐ $\frac{kkkkk\,l}{8444486'}$ ‖ 6b. same ‖

---

[61] Short empty staff for tenor.

7a. $\frac{mmmmmn}{777777}$, $\frac{mmmmmn}{777777}$, ‖ 7b. same ‖   10a. $\frac{t\ t\ t\ u}{3'3'3'7}$ | $\frac{t\ t\ t\ u}{3'3'3'7}$ ‖ 10b. same ‖

8a. $\frac{ooppooppo}{774747474}$ ‖ 8b. same ‖   11a. $\frac{vw}{86}$, $\frac{vw}{86}$, $\frac{vw}{86}$, $\frac{vw}{86}$, $\frac{vw}{86}$, ‖ 11b. same ‖

9a. $\frac{q\ r\ rssqqqrrsssq}{73447434474344}$ ‖ 9b. same ‖   12a–b. = 1a–b.

a:-*us*, b:-*ais*, c:-*art*, d:-*ance*, e:-*aie*, f:-*ay*, g:-*oie*, h:-*is*, i:-*eil*, j:-*ueil*, k:-*er*, l:-*ée*, m:-*ort*,[62] n:-*ure*, o:-*i*, p:-*our*, q:-*ir*, r:-*oy*, s:-*ent*, t:-*ie*, u:-*oir*, v:-*ors*, w:-*ire*

DISCUSSION (literary). The following *Voir Dit* passages concern L18: (a) Lady *Esperance* [Hope] demands that Guillaume write a lai entitled *Lay d'Esperance*, ll. 4060–61 (ed. P. Paris 1875, 170); (b) the lai is inserted as ll. 4106–361 (ed. 1875, 172–80), and enclosed with letter 31 (ed. 1875, 180); (c) Toute Belle replies at the end of letter 32 that she received the lai, and will learn it as fast as she can (ed. 1875, 183). For excerpts from or commentary on these passages, see Ludwig 1926–54, 2:56*; Brownlee 1984, 124–27; Cerquiglini 1985b, 135; Imbs 1991, 44–45, 82; Leech-Wilkinson 1993a, 62–63; 1993b, 118, 135–36.

EDITIONS OF MUSIC. Ludwig 1926–54, 4:67–69 (ed. Besseler); Schrade 1956b, 2:75–80 (critical notes 1956c, 67–68). The music of strophes 1 and 12 is the same, except that strophe 12 is a perfect fifth higher.

DISCUSSION (musical). Besseler 1931, 137 ex. 91 (melodic language related to Vitry motets); Machabey 1955b, 1:119 ("isorhythmic" structure of strophe 7).

Loyauté, que point ne delay (lai L1)

MANUSCRIPTS WITH TEXT AND MUSIC (all monophonic).

[3] **V g** fols. 219r–221v no. 1   [6] **G** fols. 74r–76r   no. 1
[4] **B**   fols. 218r–219v no. 1[63]   [7] **E** fols. 107r–108v no. 1[64]
[5] **A**   fols. 367r–369v no. 1

TEXT MANUSCRIPTS.

[1]   **C** fols. 165r–168v no. 1 (empty staves)
[2]   **W** fols. 72r–72v   (ll. 127–286; music lost)
[10] **M** fols. 207v–210r no. 1

FACSIMILES (refer to chap. 4.4s). Miniatures C93, A152, G145, E31 (fol. 107r, with the beginning of the music).

EDITION OF TEXT. Chichmaref 1909, 2:279–93 no. 1.

TRANSLATION. See discography (chap. 8.3 and 8.8).

TEXT STRUCTURE. 12 strophes, 432 lines.

1a. $\frac{a\ a\ a\ a\ b}{8\ 4\ 4\ 4\ 8}$, $\frac{a\ a\ a\ b}{8\ 4\ 4\ 8}$, $\frac{b\ b\ b\ ba}{8'4'4'8}$, $\frac{b\ b\ ba}{4'4'4'8}$ ‖ 1b. $\frac{c\ c\ c\ cd}{8'4'4'8}$, $\frac{c\ c\ cd}{8'4'4'8}$, $\frac{d\ d\ d\ c}{8\ 4\ 4\ 4\ 8}$, $\frac{d\ d\ d\ c}{4\ 4\ 4\ 8}$, ‖

a:-*ay*, b:-*ie*, c:-*aire*, d:-*ait*

The remaining strophes have the same metrical structure with different rhymes. This work is unusual in that the metrical structure and music are the same for all twelve strophes; only the rhymes and the pattern of masculine and feminine endings change. On problems of adapting the text to the music supplied, see Earp 1983, 310–14.

Rhymes for the remaining strophes (patterns of masculine and feminine rhymes change):

2. -*ient*, -*nir*, -*ente*, -*ent*   6. -*age*, -*vis*, -*mi*, -*iere*   10. -*oint*, -*ointe*, -*oing*, -*eure*
3. -*pris*, -*ure*, -*ure*, -*mer*   7. -*ée*, -*art*, -*as*, -*asse*   11. -*it*, -*ert*, -*oie*, -*euse*
4. -*eint*, -*eindre*, -*our*, -*és*   8. -*aut*, -*té*, -*ier*, -*ance*   12. -*eü*, -*üe*, -*ine*, -*in*
5. -*ueil*, -*ire*, -*ort*, -*oir*   9. -*roit*, -*endre*, -*einne*, -*eins*

DISCUSSION (literary). Poirion 1965, 403 (strophic structure); 554 n. 32 (theme); Luttrell 1978, 290 n. 9 (phrase "dous dangier"); Huot 1987, 260–62 (position as first lai in the manuscripts). Hassell (1982, no. H23) indexes a proverb.

---

[62] On the choice of rhymes in strophe 7, see Poirion 1965, 437.
[63] First folio lost in MS B; begins with l. 125.
[64] *Explicit le premier lay de Machaut.*

TEXTUAL LEGACY (France). Froissart, *Espinette Amoureuse* (Fourrier 1963, 178 n. to ll. 1860–62).

TEXTUAL LEGACY (Catalonia). Andreu Febrer, lai *Amors, qui tost fér, quant li play* (ed. Pagès 1936, 274–83; Riquer 1951, 108–20).

EDITIONS OF MUSIC. Ludwig 1926–54, 4:24–25 (ed. Besseler); Schrade 1956b, 2:1 (critical notes 1956c, 56); Binkley 1977, 27 (performing ed. of strophe 1 with lute accompaniment).

DISCUSSION (musical). Machabey 1955b, 1:113; Hatton 1978, 10 (melodic analysis).

Loyauté vueil tous jours maintenir (virelai V2)

MANUSCRIPTS WITH TEXT AND MUSIC (all monophonic).

[1]	C	fols. 149r–149v	no. 2		[5]	A	fols. 482r–482v	no. 2
[3]	V g	fols. 322v–323r	no. 2		[6]	G	fols. 154v–155r	no. 2
[4]	B	fols. 320v–321r	no. 2		[7]	E	fol. 161v	no. 15

TEXT MANUSCRIPT.

[10] **M** fol. 246r no. 2

FACSIMILE. Aubry 1905, plate 21 (MS **A**, refrain and strophe 1 only).

EDITION OF TEXT. Chichmaref 1909, 2:582–83 no. 2.

TEXT STRUCTURE. 3 strophes: $\dfrac{AAB}{9\ 5\ 6}\ \|\ \dfrac{a\ b}{85},\ \dfrac{a\ b}{85},\ \left|\ \dfrac{a\ a\ b}{956}\ \right\|\ \dfrac{AAB}{9\ 5\ 6},$ a:-*ir*, b:-*aire*

EDITIONS OF MUSIC. Aubry 1905, 20–21 (errors); Ludwig 1926–54, 1:70–71; Schrade 1956b, 3:167 (critical notes 1956c, 136). Surely the *C*-sharp seen in the transcriptions in m. 1 is to be understood as *B*-natural, explicitly notated because the *F* tonality would normally require a *B*-flat.

DISCUSSION (musical). Machabey 1955b, 1:177.

MUSICAL LEGACY. For a twentieth-century composition inspired by V2, see chap. 2.5 (Gilbert and Rickett).

Ma chiere dame, a vous mon cuer envoy (B40)
No Refrain.

MANUSCRIPTS WITH TEXT AND MUSIC (all 3v: ca, ten, ct).

[6]	G	fol. 149v	no. 39		[7]	E	fol. 153r	no. 21

TEXT MANUSCRIPT.

[50] **Pa** fol. 55v no. 172 *Demi lay*

EDITION OF TEXT. Chichmaref 1909, 2:564–65 no. 45.

TRANSLATION. See discography (chap. 8.3 and 8.8).

TEXT STRUCTURE. 3 strophes; rhymes change for each strophe[65]:

a a a b a a a b b b b a b b b a c c c d c c c d d d d c d d d c
1010104 1010104 1010104 1010104

e e e f e e e f f f f e f f f e a:-*oy*, b:-*ent*, c:-*art*, d:-*our*, e:-*ort*, f:-*ir*

EDITIONS OF MUSIC. Ludwig 1926–54, 1:48–49; Schering 1931b, 17 no. 26a; Schrade 1956b, 3:136–37 (critical notes 1956c, 121).

DISCUSSION (musical). The form is similar to a duplex ballade, but B40 lacks a refrain, and lacks musical rhyme (although Karp 1988, 77 notes rhythmic recurrence, breve mm. 11–15 = 28–32). Machabey 1955b, 2:54–55; Günther 1957, 90–91; Dömling 1970, 32 (musical structure made up of several corresponding members); Covington 1978; Lühmann 1978, 205–6 (declamation).

Ma fin est mon commencement (rondeau R14)

MANUSCRIPTS WITH TEXT AND MUSIC (all 2v: ca, ten; canon gives ct).

[4]	B	fol. 309r	no. 14		[7]	E	fol. 136r	no. 8
[5]	A	fols. 479v–480r	no. 16		[62]	PadA	fol. 44r [4r]	no. 6
[6]	G	fol. 153r	no. 15					

---

65 The strophic form resembles the triplum of *J'ay tant* / *Lasse!* (M7) and *Tels rit* (RF2) (Clarkson 1971, 266–67); see also Spanke 1929, 185; Reaney 1952b, 35; 1959b, 33; 1971, 12; Ziino 1990, 21–24, and chap. 5.4, introduction to *Jugement Behaingne*.

TEXT MANUSCRIPT.
[10] **M**   fols. 244v–245r   no. 15

FACSIMILES. Wolf 1904, 2:40 no. 22 (diplomatic facs., MS **G**), Ultan 1977b, 99–100 (diplomatic facs., MS **A**); *New Grove* 17:664 (MS **G**); Wilkins 1980c, 167 (MS **G**); Cerquiglini 1987a (MS **G**); Newes 1990, 225 (MS **G**).

EDITIONS OF TEXT. Tarbé 1849, 173; Chichmaref 1909, 2:575 no. 15; Wilkins 1987, 42.

TRANSLATIONS. Reese 1940, 352; Günther 1962–63, 14–15 (critical comments); Wilkins 1979, 19; Cerquiglini/Berthelot 1987, 121 (modern French); Wilkins 1987, 42; Newes 1990, 226; see also discography (chap. 8.3 and 8.8).

TEXT STRUCTURE. 8AB aA ab AB   a:-*ement*, b:-*fin*

DISCUSSIONS (literary). Poirion 1965, 322 (image of circle, possibly as a metaphysical symbol; see also Cerquiglini 1985b, 60; 1988b, 50–51). The text may be taken as a metaphor for God, suggested by Ludwig (1926–54, 1:64; cf. also Günther 1962–63, 15–16; 1984a, 256; Newes 1990, 233–34), and confirmed by references in *Remede*, ll. 2793–96 (cited in Cerquiglini 1982, 257–58; cf. comment of Chailley, Guillaume de Machaut 1982, 216), and *Confort*, ll. 873–74. Sonnemann (1969, 64 n. 67) rejects the religious interpretation. Ludwig (1926–54, 1:64) notes that Mary, Queen of Scots had the motto "Et ma fin est mon commencement."

EDITIONS OF MUSIC. Wolf 1904, 3:64–65 no. 22; Riemann 1905, 341; Ludwig 1926–54, 1:63–64 (1926–54, 2:26b* n. 1 gives critical notes for **Pad A**); Reese 1940, 351–52 no. 107; Gleason 1945, 81–84; Schrade 1956b, 3:156–57 (critical notes 1956c, 131–32); Leuchter 1964, 26–27 no. 33; Starr/Devine 1964, 23–24=1974, 26–27; Wilkins 1987, 40–42 no. 9; Newes 1990, 228–29 (after Schrade); Stolba 1991, 70–71 no. 47. Cf. Günther 1962–63, 14–15 (incorrect voice names in editions of Ludwig and Schrade); Earp 1983, 182–86 (problems of copying text and music).

DISCUSSION (musical). Riemann 1905, 340; Combarieu 1913, 398–99 ("worthy of appearing in the *Art of the Fugue* of Bach"); M. Schneider 1931, 68 and ex. 6 (harmony); Machabey 1955b, 1:165–67; Reaney 1955, 51–52 (interpretation of text; notation); Günther 1957, 102–3, 108 and 1962–63, 13–16; 1984a, 256 (interpretation of text; notation); Harman 1958, 144 (chart illustrates form); Reaney 1966, 710 and 1984, 189–90 (R14 is instrumental); 1971, 48–49 (intended for intellectual audience); Salop 1971, 76–77 (melodic planning: cantus voice makes dramatic sense); Kühn 1973, 205–6 (sonority); Wilkins 1980c, 169 (form illustrates circular motion); Newes 1987, 280–91; Wilkins 1987, 42 (general discussion); Newes 1990; Leech-Wilkinson 1993a, 62 (relation between R14 and *Dame, se vous n'avez* [R13]).

MUSICAL LEGACY. On similar "retrograde" rondeaux, see Günther (1972, 60 n. 47; 1983, esp. pp. 260–61; 1984a, 256–62; 1990, 84), and Newes (1987, 280–84, 292–307; 1990, 225–33). Hallmark (1983, 215) notes possible influence of R14 on the retrograde tenor structure of the isorhythmic motet *Gratiosus fervidus / Magnanimus opere*, also transmitted in **Pad A**. On the retrograde ballata *O dolce conpagno*, see Feininger 1937, 21; Newes 1987, 292–98. For a twentieth-century composition inspired by R14, see chap. 2.5 (Adolphe).

Maintes fois oy recorder (lai L13)
TEXT MANUSCRIPTS.

[1]	**C**	fols. 192v–194v	no. 13	[5] **A**	fols. 390r–391v	no. 13
[2]	**W**	fols. 73r–73v	(ll. 57–217)	[6] **G**	fols. 89r–90r	no. 13
[3]	**V g**	fols. 243v–245r	no. 13	[7] **E**	fols. 127v–128r	no. 18
[4]	**B**	fols. 241v–243r	no. 13	[10] **M**	fols. 225v–227v	no. 14

EDITION OF TEXT. Chichmaref 1909, 2:380–88 no. 13.

TEXT STRUCTURE. 12 strophes, 270 lines:

1a. $\frac{aabbaabba}{775757575}$ ‖ 1b. same ‖

2a. $\frac{ccccccd}{555557} \mid \frac{ccccccd}{555557}$ ‖ 2b. same ‖

3a. 8'eeef I eeef ‖ 3b. same ‖

4a. $\frac{g\,g\,g\,g\,h}{5'5'5'7'7} \mid \frac{g\,g\,g\,g\,h}{5'5'5'7'7}$ ‖ 4b. same ‖

5a. $\frac{i\,i\,i\,i\,j}{84448}\,\frac{i\,i\,i\,j}{8448} \mid \frac{j\,j\,j\,j\,i}{84448}\,\frac{j\,j\,j\,i}{8448}$ ‖ 5b. same ‖

6a. $\frac{kk\,l\,l\,m}{45335} \mid \frac{kk\,l\,l\,m}{45335}$ ‖ 6b. same ‖

7a. $\frac{n\ n\ oop}{7'7'435}$ | $\frac{n\ n\ oop}{7'7'435}$ ‖ 7b. same ‖   10a. $\frac{w\ w\ w\ x}{7'7'7'5}$, $\frac{w\ w\ w\ w\ x}{7'7'7'7'5}$, ‖ 10b. same ‖

8a. $\frac{q\ r\ s\ q\ r\ s\ s\ r\ r\ s\ r\ s}{77'5\ \ 77'5\ \ 77'7'77'7}$ ‖ 8b. same ‖   11a. $\frac{yyyyy\ zz\Omega}{57223\ \ 257'}$ | $\frac{yyyyy\ zz\Omega}{57223\ \ 257'}$ ‖ 11b. same ‖

9a. $\frac{t\ t\ t\ uuv}{3'3'7'347}$ | $\frac{t\ t\ t\ uuv}{3'3'7'347}$ ‖ 9b. same ‖   12a–b. = 1a–b.

a:-*er*, b:-*ent*, c:-*oint*, d:-*on*, e:-*endre*, f:-*uire*, g:-*ne*, h:-*i*, i:-*ay*, j:-*our*, k:-*us*, l:-*ay*, m:-*oint*, n:-*ise*, o:-*ien*, p:-*é*, q:-*art*, r:-*age*, s:-*is*, t:-*ire*, u:-*ort*, v:-*oir*, w:-*aire*, x:-*ance*, y:-*ir*, z:-*ours*, Ω:-*ure*

DISCUSSION (literary). Huot 1987, 268–69. Feminine voice. Hassell (1982, nos. C62, F148, S47, T2, V143) indexes proverbs.

Malgré Fortune et son tour. *Le Lay de Plour* (lai L19; Schrade lai 14)

MANUSCRIPTS WITH TEXT AND MUSIC (all monophonic).

   [5] **A**   fols. 404r–406v   no. 19 (has title)
   [6] **G**   fols. 97v–99v   no. 19 (has title)
   [7] **E**   fols. 210r–211r   after *Voir Dit* (has title)

TEXT MANUSCRIPTS.

   [10] **M**   fols. 235v–237r   no. 20   [50] **Pa**   fols. 62v–64v   no. 196 (has title)

EDITION OF TEXT. Chichmaref 1909, 2:434–42 no. 19.

DATE. Schrade (1958–61, 848–49) dates L19 "1349 or shortly after," but Schrade has confused references to the two *Lays de Plour*, L19 and *Qui bien aimme* (L22/16); his remarks on the association of L19 with the *Jugement Navarre*, and on the date of L19, are thus incorrect (1958–61, 848, 849).

TEXT STRUCTURE. 12 strophes, 272 lines:

1a. $\frac{aa\ bb\ aa\ bba}{77\ 47\ 47\ 474}$ ‖ 1b. same ‖   7a. $\frac{mmmmmm}{5'5'5'5'7'}$ | $\frac{mmmmmm}{5'5'5'5'7'}$ ‖ 7b. same ‖

2a. $\frac{c\ c\ c\ cddd\ c}{8'8'8'8'4488}$ | $\frac{c\ c\ c\ cddd\ c}{8'8'8'8'4488}$ ‖ 2b. same ‖   8a. $\frac{n\ n\ n\ o}{3'3'7'7}$ | $\frac{n\ n\ n\ o}{3'3'7'7}$ ‖ 8b. same ‖

3a. $\frac{eee\ ffe}{777474}$ | $\frac{eee\ ffe}{777474}$ ‖ 3b. same ‖   9a. $\frac{pppppq}{555577}$ | $\frac{pppppq}{555577}$ ‖ 9b. same ‖

4a. $\frac{g\ g\ hhh}{8'8'433}$ | $\frac{g\ g\ hhh}{8'8'433}$ ‖ 4b. same ‖   10a. $\frac{rss\ t\ trrrss\ t\ ttr}{73447434474344}$ ‖ 10b. same ‖

5a. $\frac{i\ i\ i\ i\ i\ j}{7'7'3'3'7'7}$ | $\frac{i\ i\ i\ i\ i\ j}{7'7'3'3'7'7}$ ‖ 5b. same ‖   11a. $\frac{u\ u\ u\ u\ u\ v}{7'7'7'7'7'7}$ | $\frac{u\ u\ u\ u\ u\ v}{7'7'7'7'7'7}$ ‖ 11b. same ‖

6a. $\frac{kkkk\ l}{45577}$ | $\frac{kkkk\ l}{45577}$ ‖ 6b. same ‖   12a–b. = 1a–b.

a:-*our*, b:-*ay*, c:-*ie*, d:-*art*, e:-*ueil*, f:-*is*, g:-*stre*, h:-*ir*, i:-*ure*, j:-*iés*, k:-*i*, l:-*oir*, m:-*aire*, n:-*eindre*, o:-*aint*, p:-*ort*, q:-*ant*, r:-*ent*, s:-*er*, t:-*ire*, u:-*esse*, v:-*ais*

DISCUSSION (literary). Patch 1927, 92 n. 1 (theme of Fortune); Poirion 1965, 418–19 (comparison with *Qui bien aimme* [L22/16], the other *Lay de Plour*).

TEXTUAL LEGACY (France). On Deschamps's *Lay de Plour*, see chap. 2.1.1n. Oton de Granson, *Lay de Plour* in the *Livre Messire Ode* (ed. Piaget 1941, 409–14; cited in Poirion 1965, 419).

EDITIONS OF MUSIC. Ludwig 1926–54, 4:69–71 (ed. Besseler); Schrade 1956b, 2:81–84 (critical notes 1956c, 68). The music of strophes 1 and 12 is the same, except that strophe 12 is a perfect fifth higher.

DISCUSSION (musical). Machabey 1955b, 1:119–20. Schrade (1958–61, 848) indicates that L19 is modeled on Machaut's *Lay Mortel*, *Un mortel lay* (L12/8).

Martyrum gemma latria / Diligenter inquiramus / A Christo honoratus (motet M19)

MANUSCRIPTS WITH TEXT AND MUSIC.

[1]	C	fols. 223v–224r	no. 18	3v (tr, mot, ten)
[3]	**V g**	fols. 278v–279r	no. 19	3v (tr, mot, ten)
[4]	**B**	fols. 276v–277r	no. 19	3v (tr, mot, ten)
[5]	**A**	fols. 432v–433r	no. 19	3v (tr, mot, ten)
[6]	**G**	fols. 120v–121r	no. 19	3v (tr, mot, ten)
[7]	**E**	fol. 144r	no. 19	3v (tr, mot, ten)
[57]	**I v**	fols. 10v–11r	no. 19	3v (tr, mot, ten)
[58]	**Trém**	fol. xxiiii	no. 51	(index only)

FACSIMILE. Ultan 1977b, 106–7 (diplomatic facs.).

EDITION OF TEXT. Chichmaref 1909, 2:521–23 no. 19. Text appears corrupt in several places.

TRANSLATION. See discography (chap. 8.3 and 8.8).

DATE AND OCCASION. Texts celebrate St. Quentin. By 1337, perhaps as early as 1325, Machaut had obtained a canonicate at St-Quentin (see chap. 1.6.1e–f). Günther (1963a, 100) tentatively proposed a date ca. 1335 for this motet. Composition related to scenes from the life of St. Quentin carved around the choir of the collegiate church of St-Quentin in the 1340s (Kügle 1993, 149, reporting forthcoming work of A.W. Robertson).

TEXT STRUCTURE AND RELATIONSHIP TO ISORHYTHM. Both triplum and motetus exhibit regular correlation between text and *talea* structure (Reichert 1956, 201). Günther (1957, 139–40; 1958, 33) indicates that only motetus is clear. See also Ziino 1978, 444 n. 13 (triplum stylistically and poetically similar to Marian litany); 1978, 440 (sequence-like structure of motetus); Günther 1984a, 267 (pun on *Quintinus*: there are five isorhythmic periods).

Triplum: 8aaaa aaaaaaa aaaaaa aaaaaaa aaaaaa aaaaaa a:-*ia*

Motetus: $\dfrac{\text{abab c bc b dcdc e fe f}}{\text{8787 8787 8787 8787}}$ a:-*amus*, b:-*ia*, c:-*abilis*, d:-*erat*, [66] e:-*issime*, f:-*iter*

TENOR SOURCE. *A Christo honoratus* is the last phrase of the *repetenda* of the first Responsory at Matins for the feast of St. Quentin, *Sanctus namque Quintinus* (Fuller 1990, 231 n. 43; A.W. Robertson, forthcoming); this identification supercedes the speculation in Anderson 1976, 124 n. 18.

EDITIONS OF MUSIC. Ludwig 1926–54, 3:68–70; Schrade 1956b, 3:8–10 (critical notes 1956c, 87).

DISCUSSION (musical). Unipartite with *introitus*. *Color* and *talea* do not coincide (Sanders 1973, 563). M. Schneider 1931, ex. 3 (isorhythm in tenor); Machabey 1955b, 2:101–3; Fuller 1990, 231–43 (effect of tenor and rhythm on tonal structure; includes discant reduction and summary of deep-structure tonal "cycles"; A.W. Robertson (forthcoming analysis of text, tenor source, and the feast of St. Quentin). Related to *Impudenter / Virtutibus* and *Flos / Celsa*, both possibly works of Philippe de Vitry (Kügle 1993, 208–14, 240–41).

Maugré mon cuer / De ma dolour / Quia amore langueo (motet M14)

MANUSCRIPTS WITH TEXT AND MUSIC.

[1]	C	fols. 218v–219r	no. 13	3v (tr, mot, ten)
[3]	**V g**	fols. 273v–274r	no. 14	3v (tr, mot, ten)
[4]	**B**	fols. 271v–272r	no. 14	3v (tr, mot, ten)
[5]	**A**	fols. 427v–428r	no. 14	3v (tr, mot, ten)
[6]	**G**	fols. 115v–116r	no. 14	3v (tr, mot, ten)
[7]	**E**	fol. 143r	no. 17	3v (tr, mot, ten)
[58]	**Trém**	fol. iiii	no. 8	(index only)

EDITION OF TEXT. Chichmaref 1909, 2:509–510 no. 14.

TRANSLATION. See discography, chap. 8.5.

---

[66] Note the mixture of proparoxytonic and paroxytonic stress in the two words of the d-rhyme "-*erat*" rhymes with "*vénerat*."

DATE. Use of iambic rhythm rare in motets, probably a late trait (yet still before 1350); cf. *Amours qui a / Faus Samblant* (M15).

TEXT STRUCTURE AND RELATIONSHIP TO ISORHYTHM. Triplum and motetus exhibit regular correlation between text and *talea* structure (Besseler 1927, 224; Reichert 1956, 201). See also Reichert 1956, 208 and Clarkson 1971, 256 (text truncation at end of *talea* IV).

Triplum: a aba a ab b bcb b bc c cdc c cd a abd d d
101041010104 101041010104 101041010104 10104101010

a:-*ement*, b:-*our*, c:-*oy*, d:-*i*

Motetus: ababacac d defef a a gg† a:-*our*, b: -*ement*, c:-*is*, d:-*é*, e:-*eus*, f:-*us*, g:-*ans*
46464646 10104646 10101010

(†: lyric caesura) If the internal rhymes at the caesuras are removed, a more readily grasped isometric scheme in rhyming couplets emerges (cf. Lühmann 1978, 168): 10aabb ccdd aaee (each *talea* is set to three lines of text; see Lühmann 1978, 161–62).

DISCUSSION (literary). Patch 1927, 94 n. 1 (theme of Fortune); Huot 1994, 223. Hassell (1982, no. D37) indexes a proverb in the motetus.

TENOR SOURCE. *Quia amore langueo* (Song of Songs 5:8; cf. Burstyn 1976, 71) is the final phrase of the mode 7 antiphon for the Assumption of the B.V.M. *Anima mea liquefacta est* (Sanders 1973, 563 n. 287; Anderson 1976, 122).

EDITIONS OF MUSIC. Ludwig 1926–54, 3:52–54 (criticism of Ludwig's analytical layout in Sanders 1973, 563 n. 286); Schrade 1956b, 2:154–56 (critical notes 1956c, 83–84). Barring discussed in Hoppin 1960, 25.

DISCUSSION (musical). Unipartite. Rhythmic characteristics pair M14 and *Amours qui a / Faus Samblant* (M15). Machabey 1955b, 2:90–92.

Merci vous pri, ma douce dame chiere (rondeau R3)

MANUSCRIPTS WITH TEXT AND MUSIC (all 2v: ca, ten).

[1] **C**	fol. 204v	no. 7		[5] **A**	fol. 476v	no. 5
[3] **V g**	fol. 317r	no. 3		[6] **G**	fols. 150r–150v	no. 3
[4] **B**	fol. 316r	no. 3		[7] **E**	fol. 135r	no. 7

TEXT MANUSCRIPTS.

[10] **M**	fol. 244r	no. 3	[50] **Pa**	fol. 38v	no. 114

EDITION OF TEXT. Chichmaref 1909, 2:569–70 no. 3.

TEXT STRUCTURE. 10'AB aA ab AB a:-*iere*, b:-*ierie*

EDITIONS OF MUSIC. Ludwig 1926–54, 1:53; Schrade 1956b, 3:143 (critical notes 1956c, 124–25).

DISCUSSION (musical). Machabey 1955b, 1:154–55.

Mes esperis se combat a Nature (ballade B39)
Refrain: *Se ma dame n'en fait briefment l'accort*

MANUSCRIPTS WITH TEXT AND MUSIC (all 3v: ca, ten, ct).

[6] **G**	fol. 149r	no. 38	[7] **E**	fols. 149v–150r	no. 11

TEXT MANUSCRIPTS.

[40] **I**	fol. 19r	no. 96	Lo258	**M A**
[49] **Jp**	fol. 65r	no. 42 *Mon esperit se combat*		

FACSIMILE. *Jardin* 1910–25, vol. 1, fol. 65r (**Jp**).

EDITIONS OF TEXT. Queux de Saint-Hilaire/Raynaud 1878–1903, 10:lvii no. 50 (after MS **I**); Chichmaref 1909, 1:226 no. 258; Wilkins 1972, 85 no. 138.

TRANSLATION. Crocker 1966, 129 (strophe 1); see also discography (chap. 8.3 and 8.8).

TEXT STRUCTURE. 3 strophes: a b a b b c C a:-*ure*, b:-*is*, c:-*ort*
10'10 10'10 101010

DISCUSSION (literary). Hassell (1982, no. M82) indexes a proverb.

EDITIONS OF MUSIC. Ludwig 1926–54, 1:47–48 (after MS **G**); Gleason 1945, 85–87; Schrade 1956b, 3:134–35 (after MS **E**; critical notes 1956c, 120–21); Crocker 1966, 127–29; Wilkins 1980b, 7–8 (Chaucer, *The firste stok* underlaid); Lincoln/Bonta 1986, 54–56 no. 21. Hirshberg (1971, 143–47) demonstrates that the version of MS **G** is preferable.

DISCUSSION (musical). Besseler 1931, 138–40 (primacy of cantus); Machabey 1955b, 2:53 and Günther 1957, 90 (melodic and rhythmic recurrences); Günther 1958, 35 n. 27 (*tempus* changes); Crocker 1966, 126–29 (contrapuntal and harmonic aspects, with discant reduction of breve mm. 1–10); Dömling 1970, 21–25, 76–77 (analysis; comment in Fuller 1986, 69 n. 50); Hirshberg 1971, 66–68 (text/music relations), 143–47 (motivic analysis); Salop 1971, 43–45, 65–66 (melodic direction in cantus); Dömling 1972, 303 (refrain); Hirshberg 1973–74, 62–64 (text lines/musical phrases); Heinz 1976 (harmony); Lühmann 1978, 86 (rhythm and declamation); Hirshberg 1980, 31 (*ficta*); Karp 1988, 76 (compositional priority of the cantus); Fuller 1992b, 246–48 (directed progressions serve text expression).

Messe de Nostre Dame

MANUSCRIPTS WITH TEXT AND MUSIC (all 4v: tr, mot, ten, ct).[67]

[3]	**V g**	fol. 283v–296r *Ci commence la Messe de Nostre Dame*
[4]	**B**	fol. 281v–294r
[5]	**A**	fol. 438v–451r *La Messe* (original index)
[6]	**G**	fol. 125v–133v
[7]	**E**	fol. 164v–170r
[62]	**PadA**	fol. "44" (Ite, missa est only)

LOST MANUSCRIPT.
  [60] lost Quesnoy MS of Mass

FACSIMILES. Gennrich 1957 (complete Mass from MS **B**; Gennrich's description errs in labeling it MS **A**). Barksdale 1953b, 564 (MS **Vg**, fols. 283v–284r, Kyrie complete); Wolf 1904, 2:28–29 no. 17 (diplomatic facs., MS **G**, Kyrie I and Christe); Bank 1972, 45 ex. 17a (diplomatic facs. in score, beginning of Christe); Besseler/Gülke 1973, 61 plate 20 (MS **G**, fol. 125v, Kyrie I and Christe); Kügle 1991, 374 (MS **G**, fol. 125v, Kyrie I). Kalkbrenner 1802, table 5 fig. 1 (diplomatic facs., opening of Gloria); Kiesewetter 1846, *Beilagen*, 3 no. 2 (diplomatic facs., opening of Gloria); Ambros 1891, 370 (after Kiesewetter); Barksdale 1953a, plate 8 no. 57 (MS **Vg**, fol. 285v, beginning of Gloria); Seay 1965, 146 (MS **B**, fols. 283v–284r, first opening of Gloria); Bank 1972, 46 ex. 17b (diplomatic facs. in score, beginning of Gloria). Wolf 1904, 2:30–37 no. 18 (diplomatic facs., MS **G**, Credo); Douce 1948, facing p. 54 (MS **A**, from Credo). Gastoué 1922, 65 (MS **G**, fol. 131v, Sanctus tr and mot); Gérold 1936, facing p. 364 (MS **G**, fol. 131v, Sanctus tr and mot); Parrish 1957, plates l–li (MS **G**, fols. 131v–132r, Sanctus), discussed pp. 156–59; Reaney 1961, 123 (MS **G**, fol. 131v, Sanctus tr and mot).

DATE AND OCCASION. On the connection of the Mass to the coronation of Charles V, see De Bure 1769, 452; Rive 1780, 11; Burney 1776–89, 2:304n. (=rev. ed. 1:615); De Bure 1783; Castil-Blaze 1832; Bottée de Toulmon, [1846]a; Kiesewetter 1846, 41; Tarbé 1849, xxxii; Magnin 1851, 406; Fétis 1860–65, 4:158; Mas Latrie 1877b, xvi; Hoepffner 1908–21, 1:xxxvii–xxxviii; Delachenal 1909–31, 3:93–94; Ludwig 1925, 420–21 n. 2; 1926–54, 2:8* n. 2, 4:1; Leech-Wilkinson 1990c, 8–9; esp. A.W. Robertson 1992, 102–3.

Dömling (1971, 30 n. 21) and Keitel (1982a, 289=1982b, 308–10) summarize the different views on dating of Machabey, S.J. Williams, Apel, Günther, Reaney, and Stäblein-Harder. (a) Early work, perhaps late 1340 (Apel review of Chailley, Machabey and de Van eds.; Apel 1953, 345 n. 1; 1955, 71; Machabey 1960, 1397; see objections in Günther 1963a, 113); (b) ca. 1350, as Machaut worked for Bonne of Luxembourg, and given to Rouen Cathedral (Maillard 1954, 5); (c) Winter 1359–60 during Siege of Reims (Kügle 1991, 374; cf. Hughes 1989, 397); (d) early 1360s, as votive offering to Virgin, commemoration of the delivery of the city of Reims from the Siege (Markstrom 1989, 36); (e) Mass possibly for a courtly chapel (Gallo 1985, 42; Hoffmann-Axthelm 1991, 351); (f) early 1360s, because clearly linked to the late motets in style; possibly connected to his poetic "testament," *Plourez, dames* (B32) (Leech-Wilkinson 1993a, 45, 48; see also commentary below to *Plourez, dames*); (g) on the most likely destination of the Mass, for the anniversary foundation of Guillaume and Jean de Machaut in the early 1360s, see chap. 1.18a and 1.18.3.

TENOR SOURCES. See the discussion in A.W. Robertson 1992, 104–16. Kyrie: cf. Kyrie IV; T. Göllner 1981 (history of the tenor). Gloria: cf. Gloria IV (Leech-Wilkinson 1990c, 31–

---

[67] On the titles, see A.W. Robertson 1992, 101–2, 132 n. 96, 134.

35, 37–38, 66–67). Credo: cf. Credo I (Handschin 1927–28, 542–43; Machabey 1953–54, 40; Leech-Wilkinson 1990c, 39, 139). Sanctus: cf. Sanctus XVII. Agnus: cf. Agnus XVII (A.W. Robertson 1992, 104 n. 15). Ite: cf. Benedicamus Domino XVII, mode 6; cf. Sanctus VIII (Schalz 1980, 109 n. 52); see references in A.W. Robertson 1992, 108–9, esp. n. 28.

EDITIONS OF MUSIC.[68] *Complete editions*: Chailley 1948; Machabey 1948; de Van 1949; Hübsch 1953; Ludwig 1926–54, 4:1–20 (ed. Heinrich Besseler); Schrade 1956b, 3:37–64 (critical notes 1956c, 93–97); D. Stevens 1973; Wilheim 1974; Leech-Wilkinson 1982, 3:50–69; Leech-Wilkinson 1990b; 1990c. *Partial editions*: Kalkbrenner 1802 (extracts); Kiesewetter 1831; Bottée de Toulmon [1846]a (Gloria, fragment); La Fage 1864, 539; Ambros 1891, 370 (=1864 ed., 337–38) (Gloria, fragment); Wolf 1904, 3:50–53 no. 17 (Kyrie I, Christe, Kyrie II), 3:53–59 no. 18 (Credo, lacks Amen); Wooldridge 1905, 26–28=1929, 245–47 (Agnus II only); Guelliot 1914, 306; Ludwig 1922–23, 457–58 (Kyrie III); Besseler 1931, 149–50 (Agnus I, fragment); Gleason 1945, 97–98 (Agnus I); Parrish/Ohl 1951 (Agnus I); Leuchter 1964, 23–26 no. 32b (Agnus I); Maillard 1954, 4–5; Starr/Devine 1964, 20–23=1974, 22–25 (Kyrie); Schmidt-Görg 1968 (Kyrie); Kamien 1970 (Agnus I); 1972 (Kyrie); Godwin 1975, 45–49 no. 6b (Agnus, Ite); Ultan 1977b, 122–24 (Agnus); R. Robinson 1978 (Kyrie); Wilkins 1979, 14–15 (Kyrie I, with brief analysis); Palisca 1980, 82–86 no. 21 (=1988 ed., 87–91 no. 25) (Agnus); Allorto 1983, 35–43 (Kyrie, Gloria); Lincoln/Bonta 1986, 45–51 no. 18a (Kyrie); Yudkin 1989, 485–86 (Kyrie I); Stolba 1991, 68–70 no. 46 (Agnus).

On old editions and fragments, see Ludwig 1926–54, 2:5*–6*; Reese 1940, 356 n. 67. Editorial problems are reviewed in Cape 1959–60; Fallows 1977a; Parrott 1977; R. Robinson 1978, Leech-Wilkinson 1990c, 96–170. There are some suggested emendations in Gombosi 1950, 207 n. 6; Hoppin 1960, 24; Dömling 1971, 25 n. 6, 26 nn. 11–12; Fallows 1977a, 290 n. 7.

DISCUSSION (musical). Wagner 1913; Gastoué 1922, 63–67 (overview with first use of term "motif conducteur" or "generating cell"); Machabey 1931, 406–8 (overview; use of "generating cell"); Gérold 1932, 336–39 and 1936, 372–75 (survey); Reese 1940, 356–57 (translates passage from Machabey 1931 on "generating cell"); Chailley 1950, 246–49 (overview); Gombosi 1950; S.J. Williams 1952, 292–309; Machabey 1953–54, 38–42 (two motives guarantee unity); Barraque 1954 (rhythmic analysis); Blanchard 1956; Günther 1957, 150–54, 162–63 (overview; comments on "generating cell"); Hoppin 1957, 117 (comments on "generating cell"); Harman 1958, 148–53 (overview); Junger 1967, 173–74 (chromatic passage); Kuckertz 1968 (with analytical tables); Ballif 1969, 269 ("generating cell" common to Mass and *Lay de Nostre Dame, Contre ce dous* [L15/10]); Reaney 1971, 60–67 (overview); Bank 1972, 41, 43 (tempo); Apfel 1974, 235–37 (musical structure); Ultan 1977a, 109–19 (basic motives, isorhythm, cadences); Hoppin 1978b, 414–20 (overview); Frémiot 1981; Dricot 1982, 146; Petersen 1987; Hughes 1989, 396–97 (general style); Yudkin 1989, 482–87 (overview); Leech-Wilkinson 1990c (complete analysis); Kügle 1993, 345–48 (Machaut Mass an anomaly when compared to other fourteenth-century Mass movements); Leech-Wilkinson 1993a, 45, 56–57 (directed progressions, simultaneous conception of parts).

Kyrie. Ludwig 1922–23, 440–41 (style, transcription); Gombosi 1950, 215–17 (see criticism in Dömling 1971, 26 n. 9); Apfel 1964–65, 1:80=1974, 236 (harmonic reduction of Kyrie I); Kuckertz 1968, ex. 8 (discussed p. 49); Dömling 1971, 24–26; Besseler/Gülke 1973, 60 (isorhythm); Sabbé 1980–81 (isorhythmic construction of tenor-contratenor pair); Apfel 1982, 126–28 (harmonic reduction and analysis of beginning); Chailley 1982, 283–88 (hypothetical compositional process of Kyrie); Zillhardt 1986 (Pythagorean tonal system); Cross 1990, 232, 256 (chromatic intervals). See also above, "tenor sources."

Gloria. Gombosi 1950, 209–11 (strophic structure), 217 (Amen) (see criticism in Günther 1957, 152 n. 121); Kuckertz 1968, exx. 5, 6, 6a (discussed pp. 47–48); Kühn 1973, 189–92 (sonority, contrapuntal structure); Schalz 1980, 109–13 (text declamation; Gombosi's analysis; text expression); Karp 1988, 72–73 (compositional priority of the

---

[68] The bibliography in the de Van ed. (1949, iii) lists some additional partial editions and concert programs with partial editions. The complete transcription of Perne prepared in 1814 (*F:Pi 930–31*) and announced for publication in 1830 (Fétis 1860–65; Ludwig 1926–54, 2:6b*) never appeared.

tenor); Cross 1990, 231–33, 279–80 (chromatic intervals). *Related works.* Reaney 1960b, 21; 1971, 60–61; and Gómez 1985a (the Tournai Mass Gloria and Credo were written either in imitation of Machaut or were the model for Machaut's Gloria and Credo); Schalz 1980, 108, 109 (relationship to Tournai Mass Gloria). See also above, "tenor sources."

Credo. Ficker 1920 (brief paraphrase of plainsong Credo I in motetus); Handschin 1927–28 (paraphrase of plainsong Credo I throughout; simultaneous conception); Perle 1948, 173–74 (structural significance of certain sonorities); Gombosi 1950, 211–14 (strophic structure), 217–18 (Amen); Kuckertz 1968, ex. 7, discussed pp. 48–49; Dömling 1971, 27–28 (Amen); Cogan/Escot 1976, 228–39 (rhythmic analysis); Cross 1990, 220, 221, 223, 227 (chromatic intervals); Fuller 1992b, 244–52 (directed progressions, word painting, text setting). *Related works*: Apfel 1961, 43=1964–65, 1:77; 1974, 236–37 (compares Machaut Gloria and Credo to Credo in *F:APT 16bis* (ed. Stäblein-Harder 1962, 110–13 no. 55); Chailley 1950, 200, 248; Machabey 1953–54, 40–41; Leech-Wilkinson 1990c, 38–40; and Fuller 1992b, 256 n. 41 (relationship to Tournai Mass Credo); Reaney 1960b, 21; 1971, 60–61; and Gómez 1985a (the Tournai Mass Gloria and Credo were written either in imitation of Machaut or were the model for Machaut's Gloria and Credo); Leech-Wilkinson 1989, 1:131–34, 2:24 ex. 38 (explores the connections between Vitry's *Douce plaisance / Garison, Tuba / In arboris*, and Machaut's *Aucune gent / Qui plus* [M5], *Hareu! / Helas!* [M10], *Felix virgo / Inviolata* [M23], and the Amen of the Credo). See also above, "tenor sources."

Sanctus. Gombosi 1950, 218; Leech-Wilkinson 1989, 1:180 (possible influence of harmony of the motet *Portio / Ida*); Cross 1990, 265–66 (augmented seconds). See also above, "tenor sources."

Agnus. Besseler 1931, 148–50 (application of motet style is in part literal and in part free); Gombosi 1950, 219; Dömling 1971, 26–27; Cross 1990, 280–81 (*ficta*). See also above, "tenor sources."

Ite. A work in *F:AUT 152* has the same *cantus firmus* as Machaut's Ite (*RISM* 1969, 118 no. 2). See also above, "tenor sources."

MUSICAL LEGACY. Leech-Wilkinson (1982–83, 8 n. 10; 1990c, 17) notes that a Sanctus-Agnus pair of Lionel Power (ed. Hughes/Bent 1969, nos. 118 and 141) is stylistically similar to the Machaut Sanctus. Bowers 1975–76, 107 (MS E [7] was in the possession of the duke of Clarence from December 1412 probably until his death in 1421; thus, Lionel Power, a member of his chapel, could have studied Machaut's Mass from this manuscript).

Planche's mention (1980, 359) of a performance of the Mass in 1938 by Stravinsky is surely an error. See also Israel-Meyer in Guillaume de Machaut 1982, 339. Many have noted similarities between Stravinsky's Mass of 1943–47 and the Machaut Mass. Stravinsky denied a connection, stating that he did not hear the Mass until after his own Mass had been composed (Stravinsky 1962). On this question, see also Chailley 1960, 779 and especially H. Weber 1987, 317–19. On twentieth-century compositions inspired by the Mass, see chap. 2.5 (Birtwistle, Gieseler, and Wuorinen).

Mors sui, se je ne vous voy (virelai V29; Schrade virelai 26)

MANUSCRIPTS WITH TEXT AND MUSIC.

[1]	C	fol. 205v	no. 28	1v (ca)
[3]	V g	fols. 331v–332r	no. 29	2v (ca, ten)
[4]	B	fol. 329v	no. 29	2v (ca, ten) (continuation of ten lost)
[5]	A	fol. 491r	no. 29	2v (ca, ten)
[6]	G	fol. 161r	no. 29	2v (ca, ten)
[7]	E	fol. 161r	no. 13	2v (ca, ten)

TEXT MANUSCRIPTS.

[10] M fols. 252v–253r no. 29   [50] Pa fols. 68v–68*bis* r no. 215

FACSIMILE. Parrish 1957, plate xlvii (MS E), discussed pp. 149–53.

EDITIONS OF TEXT. Chichmaref 1909, 2:617–18 no. 29; Wilkins 1987, 37–38.

TRANSLATION. Wilkins 1987, 38.

TEXT STRUCTURE. 3 strophes: $\frac{ABBBAAB}{7434474} \parallel \frac{aab\,aab}{774\,774} \mid \frac{abbbaab}{7434474} \parallel \frac{ABBBAAB}{7434474}$ a:-*oy*, b:-*our*

EDITIONS OF MUSIC. Ludwig 1926–54, 1:84–85; Schrade 1956b, 3:185 (critical notes 1956c, 145); Wilkins 1980d, 2; 1987, 36–39 no. 8.

DISCUSSION (musical). Ludwig 1926–54, 1:85 (manuscript relations); Machabey 1955b, 1:191; Wykes 1956, 23–26 (analysis); Wilkins 1987, 38–39 (general discussion); Fuller 1991, 3–8 (contrasting analyses of the monophonic version of MS C and the 2v version of the later manuscripts).

Moult sui de bonne heure nee (virelai V37; Schrade virelai 31)

MANUSCRIPTS WITH TEXT AND MUSIC (all 2v: ca, ten).

| [5] A | fol. 494r | no. 37 | [6] G | fols. 163r–163v | no. 37 |

TEXT MANUSCRIPT.

[10] **M** fols. 255r–255v no. 37

EDITIONS OF TEXT. Tarbé 1856, 28; Chichmaref 1909, 2:630–31 no. 37.

TRANSLATION. Yudkin 1989, 495–96.

TEXT STRUCTURE. 3 strophes: $\frac{\text{A A B B A B}}{7\text{'}7\text{'}5\,7\,7\text{'}5}$ ∥ $\frac{\text{bb a bb a}}{757\text{'}\;\;757\text{'}}$ ∣ $\frac{\text{a abb ab}}{7\text{'}7\text{'}577\text{'}5}$ ∥ $\frac{\text{A A B B A B}}{7\text{'}7\text{'}577\text{'}5}$ a:-*ée*, b:-*i*

DISCUSSION (literary). Cerquiglini 1985b, 185 (on *souffisance*). Feminine voice.

TEXTUAL LEGACY (France). Christine de Pizan, *De bonne heure fus je nee*, no. 30 of the *Cent Ballades d'Amant et de Dame*.

TEXTUAL LEGACY (England). Chaucer, *Troilus* (Wimsatt 1976, 290–91).

EDITIONS OF MUSIC. Ludwig 1926–54, 1:90–91; Schrade 1956b, 3:190 (critical notes 1956c, 147); Yudkin 1989, 493–95 (after Schrade).

DISCUSSION (musical). Machabey 1955b, 1:194–95; Yudkin 1989, 493–97.

MUSICAL LEGACY. On a group of late fourteenth-century virelais in similar style to Machaut's *Se je souspir* (V36/30), V37, and *De tout sui* (V38/32), see Fallows 1990, 22–23.

N'en fait n'en dit n'en pensee (ballade B11)
Refrain: *Tant com je vivray*

MANUSCRIPTS WITH TEXT AND MUSIC.

[1] C	fol. 162v	no. 11	2v (ca, ten; empty staves for tr)
[3] **V g**	fol. 301v	no. 11	2v (ca, ten; empty staves for tr)
[4] B	fol. 299v	no. 11	2v (ca, ten; empty staves for tr)
[5] A	fol. 460r	no. 12	2v (ca, ten; empty staves for tr)
[6] G	fol. 138r	no. 12	2v (ca, ten)
[7] E	fol. 148r	no. 6	2v (ca, ten)

TEXT MANUSCRIPTS.

| [10] **M** | fol. 238v | no. 11 | [50] **Pa** fols. 49v–50r | no. 152 |

EDITION OF TEXT. Chichmaref 1909, 2:546–47 no. 14.

TEXT STRUCTURE. 3 strophes: $\frac{\text{ab ab b aB}}{7\text{'}5\;\;7\text{'}5\;57\text{'}5}$ a:-*ée*, b:-*ay*

DISCUSSION (literary). Hassell (1982, no. R71) indexes a proverb.

EDITIONS OF MUSIC. Ludwig 1926–54, 1:10; Schrade 1956b, 3:82 (critical notes 1956c, 104–5); Ultan 1977b, 97.

DISCUSSION (musical). Machabey 1955b, 2:26; Salop 1971, 50, 57–58 (melodic direction in cantus); Lühmann 1978, 118–19, 187–92 (declamation); Karp 1988, 70–71 (compositional priority of tenor).

ANTECEDENT (textual and musical). Ludwig (1926–54, 1:10; cf. Günther 1972, 54) noted that the refrain (compare *Tres douce dame que* [B24] and *De tout sui* [V38]) cites the first line of a rondeau by Adam de la Halle, *Tant con je vivrai* (ed. Gennrich 1921–27, 1:68 no. 80; Wilkins 1967, 58 no.15; text ed. Van den Boogaard 1969, 56 no. 83, 249 no. 1759); Frobenius (1986, 11 col. a) considers this uncertain because of the brevity of the citation.

Ne pensez pas, dame, que je recroie (ballade B10)
Refrain: *Ne riens qui soit ne me destourne /*
   Qu'a vous ne pense, ou que je tourne.[69]

MANUSCRIPTS WITH TEXT AND MUSIC.

[1]	**C**	fol. 162r	no. 10	2v (ca, ten; empty staves for ct)[70]
[3]	**Vg**	fol. 301r	no. 10	2v (ca, ten)
[4]	**B**	fol. 299r	no. 10	2v (ca, ten)
[5]	**A**	fol. 459v	no. 11	2v (ca, ten)
[6]	**G**	fols. 137v–138r	no. 11	2v (ca, ten)
[7]	**E**	fol. 156v	no. 35	2v (ca, ten)

TEXT MANUSCRIPT.

[10]	**M**	fol. 238v	no. 10

FACSIMILE. Apel 1953, 353 facs. 68 (MS **A**).

EDITION OF TEXT. Chichmaref 1909, 2:546 no. 13.

TEXT STRUCTURE. 1 strophe: $\frac{\text{a b a b bCC}}{10\,'10\ 10\,'10\ 108\,'8}$, a:-*oie*, b:-*oy*, c:-*ourne*

DISCUSSION (literary). See chap. 6.4, note to Lo174.

EDITIONS OF MUSIC. Ludwig 1926–54, 1:9 (Apel 1953, 354 provides an emendation of *clos* ending); Schrade 1956b, 3:81 (critical notes 1956c, 103–4). Bent (1983, 69) discusses variants in MSS **VgBE**. On barring, see Günther 1957, 92 n. 54; Koehler 1990, 1:110–11 n. 61.

DISCUSSION (musical). Apel 1953, 352–54 (notation); Machabey 1955b, 2:25; Wykes 1956, 10–18 and diagrams in appendix A (analysis); Dömling 1970, 57–58 (study of tenor), 67–68 (successions of similar sonorities); Salop 1971, 52 (directed motion in cantus).

Ne quier veoir. See *Quant Theseüs / Ne quier* (ballade B34)

Ne say comment commencier. Le Lay de l'Ymage (lai L14; Schrade lai 9)
MANUSCRIPTS WITH TEXT AND MUSIC (all monophonic).

[1]	**C**	fols. 189r–191r	no. 11 (has title)		[5]	**A**	fols. 391v–393v	no. 14 (has title)
[3]	**Vg**	fols. 245r–247v	no. 14		[6]	**G**	fols. 90r–91v	no. 14
[4]	**B**	fols. 243r–245v	no. 14		[7]	**E**	fols. 118v–119v	no. 11 (has title)

TEXT MANUSCRIPTS.

[10]	**M**	fols. 227v–228v	no. 15		[50]	**Pa**	fols. 53r–54v	no. 167 (has title)

EDITION OF TEXT. Chichmaref 1909, 2:389–96 no. 14.

TRANSLATION. Kelly 1978, 47 (a few lines of strophe 6).

TEXT STRUCTURE. 12 strophes, 224 lines:

1a. $\frac{\text{ab ab ba ba}}{74\ 74\ 74\ 77}$ ‖ 1b. same ‖

2a. $\frac{\text{c cdd}}{5'5'34} \mid \frac{\text{c cdd}}{5'5'34}$ ‖ 2b. same ‖

3a. $\frac{\text{eeef}}{7777} \mid \frac{\text{eeef}}{7777}$ ‖ 3b. same ‖

4a. $\frac{\text{g g g gh}}{5'5'5'7'7} \mid \frac{\text{g g g gh}}{5'5'5'7'7}$ ‖ 4b. same ‖

5a. $\frac{\text{iiij}}{8884} \mid \frac{\text{iiij}}{8884}$ ‖ 5b. same ‖

6a. $\frac{\text{kkkkllm}}{5557345'} \mid \frac{\text{kkkkllm}}{5557345'}$ ‖ 6b. same ‖

7a. $\frac{\text{n n n no}}{7'3'3'7'7} \mid \frac{\text{n n n no}}{7'3'3'7'7}$ ‖ 7b. same ‖

8a. $\frac{\text{p p p p q}}{8'5'5'8'8} \mid \frac{\text{p p p p q}}{8'5'5'8'8}$ ‖ 8b. same ‖

9a. $\frac{\text{rrss rrss r}}{774747474}$ ‖ 9b. same ‖

10a. $\frac{\text{t t tu}}{3'3'7'3} \mid \frac{\text{t t tu}}{3'3'7'3}$ ‖ 10b. same ‖

11a. $\frac{\text{vvvvu}}{45335} \mid \frac{\text{vvvvu}}{45335}$ ‖ 11b. same ‖

12a–b. = 1a–b.

---

[69] Reaney (1959b, 32, 39) argues for a two-line refrain in this ballade for which only the first strophe is transmitted.

[70] The empty space was probably intended for the text residuum and later filled with staves.

a:-*[i]er*, b:-*ay*, c:-*oie*, d:-*oir*, e:-*ueil*, f:-*is*, g:-*ance*, h:-*art*, i:-*é*, j:-*ient*, k:-*our*, l:-*i*, m:-*age*, n:-*ière*, o:-*or*, p:-*aire*, q:-*ans*, r:-*er*, s:-*ort*, t:-*ure*, u:-*ent*, v:-*ir*, u:-*uit*

DISCUSSION (literary). Luttrell 1978, 290 n. 9 (phrase "dous dangier"); Huot 1987, 266–68, 272–73 (pairing of L14/9 and the *Lay du Mirouer*, *Se quanque Diex* [L11] in MS C). Hassell (1982, no. O67) indexes a proverb.

EDITIONS OF MUSIC. Ludwig 1926–54, 4:40–42 (ed. Besseler); Schrade 1956b, 2:30–33 (critical notes 1956c, 62–63). The music of strophes 1 and 12 is the same, except that strophe 12 is a perfect fifth higher.

DISCUSSION (musical). Machabey 1955b, 1:118 ("isorhythm" in strophes 3 and 5); Mulder 1978, 81–82, 118–22; 1979 (Marian symbolism realized in the music).

Nes qu'on porroit les estoilles nombrer (ballade B33)
Refrain: *Le grant desir que j'ai de vous veoir*

MANUSCRIPTS WITH TEXT AND MUSIC (all 3v: ca, ten, ct).

[3]	**V g**	fol. 314r	no. 33		[6]	**G**	fols. 145v–146r	no. 32
[4]	**B**	fol. 313r	no. 33		[7]	**E**	fols. 178r–178v[71] in *Voir Dit*
[5]	**A**	fol. 471r	no. 32					

TEXT MANUSCRIPTS.

| [10] | **M** | fol. 242v | no. 33 | | Lo232 | **VgBAMD** (chap. 6.4) |
| [50] | **Pa** | fol. 70r | no. 223 | | VD16 | **AFEPm** (chap. 5.13 table 5.3) |

EDITIONS OF TEXT. P. Paris 1875, 67; Monod 1903, no. 10; Chichmaref 1909, 1:209 no. 232; Woledge 1961, 221–22; Wilkins 1972, 86 no. 143.

TRANSLATIONS. Reaney 1959b, 27–28 (summary only); Woledge 1961, 221–22; Weiss 1967 and Weiss/Taruskin 1984 (letter 10 of the *Voir Dit* [ed. P. Paris 1875, 67–70], with important passages that bear on B33); Little 1980, 50–51 (excerpt from letter 10, and 4 ll. of narrative from the *Voir Dit* that introduce the ballade); Fuller 1987b, 111; Wilkins 1989, 66 (strophe 1); Boulton 1993, 201 (strophe 3); Wimsatt 1994, 33 (strophe 1); see also discography (chap. 8.3 and 8.8).

DATE. Mentioned in letter 10 of the *Voir Dit*, which can be placed near the return of King John II from captivity in England (late 1363). Hoepffner (1908–21, 3:247–48, note to ll. 1325–28 of *Confort*) noted a relationship between B33 and *Confort*; later (3:255, note to l. 276 of the *Fonteinne*; see commentary to *Quant j'ay l'espart* [R5]), he asserted that such correspondences have relevance for dating the lyric in question, and specifically referred back to B33. Machabey (1955b, 2:57, 51) notes that this ballade appears in the *Voir Dit* between letters 9 and 10 and thus dates at least from 1362, five years after *Confort*, though he concurs however that the ballade may have existed prior to its inclusion in the *Voir Dit*. Leech-Wilkinson (1993a, 50; 199b, 110–11), based on the date of letter 4 in the *Voir Dit* (ed. 1875, 52–55 as no. 6), indicates that B33 was probably complete in March 1363.

TEXT STRUCTURE. 3 strophes: 10ab ab bcC a:-*er*, b:-*ent*, c:-*oir*

DISCUSSION (literary). Patch 1927, 96 n. 2 (theme of Fortune); Reaney 1959b, 27–28 (general discussion of content). The following *Voir Dit* passages concern B33: (a) Guillaume's letter 4 mentions composition of the ballade in the manner of a "rés d'Alemaingne" (ed. 1875, 55 as letter 6); (b) the text of B33 is inserted in the narrative (ll. 1482–1502, ed. 1875, 67); (c) Guillaume sends B33 and the *Fonteinne* with letter 10, again indicating that the ballade is "a la guise d'un rés d'Alemangne," and provides some directions for performance of the work (ed. 1875, 69). For excerpts from or commentary on these passages, see Quittard 1917–19, 125–26; Ludwig 1926–54, 2:54b*–55a*; Eichelberg 1935, 67–68; Little 1980, 49–52; Roques 1982, 168; Gallo 1985, 44 (with translation); Cerquiglini 1986a, 106; Leech-Wilkinson 1990a, 229–30; M.L. Göllner 1993, 147–48, 154; Leech-Wilkinson 1993a, 50–51, 53 n. 30; 1993b, 110, 113, 134–35. Cerquiglini (1985b, 219–21) rectifies an important omission in P. Paris's edition of the letter. See also below, musical discussion.

In the *Voir Dit*, the narrative verse, the lyrical verse, and the prose of the letters often relate to each other. To take B33 as an example, many lines are elsewhere presaged or recalled: (a) mention of "le tour dou firmament" near the beginning of the *Voir Dit* (l. 17,

---

[71] *Tenor G de Mascandio* (discussed in Earp 1983, 125–26).

ed. 1875, 1) is an image found in l. 5 of B33; (b) the phrase "le plus grant desir que j'ay, ce est de vous veoir," found near the beginning of letter 7 (ed. 1875, 27 as letter 3; cf. Leech-Wilkinson 1993b, 110 n. 32) anticipates the ballade's refrain; (c) *De mon vrai cuer jamais ne partira* (VD17), the ballade that is inserted next after B33, recalls the opening line of B33 by its refrain, *Ne qu'on porroit tarir la haute mer*; this theme in turn recurs in strophe 3 of the following virelai, *Cils a bien fole pensee* (V24=VD18), which is a much older work that appears in MS C; (d) mention of the "guise d'Alemaingne," though in a completely different context (l. 2490, ed. 1875, 103); (e) "Et faite estoile en firmament / Des Dieus, pour luire clerement" recalls images in strophe 1 of the ballade (l. 5959, ed. 1875, 261). Such textual reminiscences can also occur across works, e.g., a similar theme is treated in *Confort* (ll. 1325–28); see discussion above on the date of B33. Hassell (1982, no. E85) indexes a proverb.

TEXTUAL LEGACY (France). Christine de Pizan, *C. ballades* no. 28 (ed. M. Roy 1886–91, 1:29; cited in Poirion 1965, 249 n. 35).

TEXTUAL LEGACY (Catalonia). The last of the five inserted rondeaux (*Le grand desir que jay puise veoÿr*; ed. Pagès 1936, 140) in the Catalan *Storia de l'amant Frondino de Brisona* is related to B33; see chap. 5.13, textual legacy.

EDITIONS OF MUSIC. Quittard 1917–19, after p. 138; Ludwig 1926–54, 1:38–39; Schrade 1956b, 3:122–23 (critical notes 1956c, 116–17); Wilkins 1980b, 1–2 (Chaucer, *Hyd, Absolon* underlaid); Fuller 1987b, 109–11 no. 18a.

DISCUSSION (musical). Machabey 1955b, 2:47–48; Martinez 1963, 109–11 (melodic motives, rhythmic and harmonic uniformity), 113–16 (contrast between French and Italian style); Fuller 1987b, 115 (brief introduction); Günther 1990, 76 (unusual final cadence); M.L. Göllner 1993, 150 (simultaneous conception).

In letter 10 of the *Voir Dit*, Machaut says that the music of B33 is "a la guise d'un rés d'Alemaigne," a tantalizing piece of information that is unfortunately difficult to interpret. See Quittard 1917–19, 125; Handschin 1929–30; Pirro 1930, 71–72; Handschin 1931; 1949; Bukofzer 1960, 848; Kelly 1978, 253–54, 259 n. 15; Fallows 1983; Arlt 1993, 41 n. 7 (citing L. Welker); M.L. Göllner 1993; the term is also employed in the *Echecs Amoureux*, in the excerpt printed in Abert 1904–5, 354 l. 17 (cited in Pirro 1930, 71–72; new ed. Kraft 1977, 108 l. 633). Leech-Wilkinson (1993a, 50–52) provides the most plausible and thorough explanation, rather close to Handschin's: B33 is unusual in the frequent "dominant" to "tonic" motion in the lowest sounding voice, imitating the dance music of the German wind band presumably referred to by the name (i.e., *rés = Reihe*); despite their surface similarities, the harmonic backgrounds of *Plourez, dames* (B32) and B33 are very different. On a "danse d'Alemagne" cited by Froissart, see Mullally 1990, 250; Leech-Wilkinson 1993a, 51–52.

Letter 10 also provides information on performance practice, including instrumental performance; see Reaney 1954c, 246–47; 1956, 5–6, 7, 10; 1966, 709, 719; 1971, 16; 1977, 7; S.J. Williams 1977, 467–68; Leech-Wilkinson 1993a, 52–53 (the most reasonable solution). Specifically concerning the phrase "sans rien oster ne mettre" [without adding or taking anything away], see Haas 1931, 104; Handschin 1931, 38; Reaney 1954c, 246–47; 1960b, 24; 1971, 41–42; S.J. Williams 1977, 467; Cerquiglini 1985b, 47–48, 220–21; Leech-Wilkinson 1993a, 55–56.

The pervasive use of certain melodic formulas in *tempus imperfectum, prolatio major* links *Donnez, signeurs* (B26), *Une vipere* (B27), and *Je puis trop* (B28) as one group, and *Plourez, dames* (B32), *Nes qu'on* (B33), and *Se pour ce muir* (B36) as another; the same formulas are seen to a lesser extent in *En amer* (RF4), *Cinc, un* (R6), and *Douce dame, tant* (R20) (cf. Reaney 1955, 47; Günther 1957, 80–84; Hirshberg 1971, 120–33; Little 1980, 49; Arlt 1993, 63). On melodic formulae in B32–33 and B36, see also Reaney 1971, 42; Salop 1971, 54–55 (melodic direction, motives in cantus); Mulder 1978, 99–114 (the theme of despair common to the three ballades is mirrored in their similar musical material); Mulder 1978, 99–114; Little 1980, 57–59; M.L. Göllner 1993 (text/music relationship); Leech-Wilkinson 1993a, 50, 52–53 (differences between *Plourez, dames* [B32] and B33).

Nuls ne doit avoir merveille (lai L5; Schrade lai 4)
MANUSCRIPTS WITH TEXT AND MUSIC (all monophonic).

[1]	C	fols. 174r–176v	no. 5	[5]	A	fols. 374v–376v	no. 5
[3]	V g	fols. 227r–229v	no. 5	[6]	G	fols. 79r–80v	no. 5
[4]	B	fols. 225r–227v	no. 5	[7]	E	fols. 111r–112v	no. 6

TEXT MANUSCRIPT.
[10] **M** fols. 213v–214v no. 5
EDITION OF TEXT. Chichmaref 1909, 2:314–21 no. 5.
TRANSLATION. See discography (chap. 8.3 and 8.8).
TEXT STRUCTURE. 12 strophes, 194 lines:

1a. $\frac{a\,a\,ab}{7'7'7'7} \mid \frac{a\,a\,ab}{7'7'7'7}$ ‖ 1b. same ‖

7a. $\frac{bbmmn}{331'5'5} \mid \frac{bbmmn}{331'5'5}$ ‖ 7b. same ‖

2a. $\frac{c\,cd}{7'3'7} \mid \frac{c\,cd}{7'3'7}$ ‖ 2b. same ‖

8a. $\frac{o\,o\,o\,o\,o\,pp}{7'7'7'7'7'57}$ ‖ 8b. same ‖

3a. $\frac{e\,f\,g}{77'5} \mid \frac{e\,f\,g}{77'5} \mid \frac{g\,f\,f\,g\,f\,g}{77'7'77'7}$ ‖ 3b. same ‖

9a. 7qqqqq ‖ 9b. same ‖

4a. $\frac{h\,h\,h\,i}{3'3'7'3} \mid \frac{h\,h\,h\,i}{3'3'7'3}$ ‖ 4b. same ‖

10a. $\frac{r\,r\,r\,r\,r\,r\,r}{4343437}$ ‖ 10b. same ‖

5a. $\frac{j\,j\,j\,j\,j}{7'5'5'5'5'7'} , \mid \frac{j\,j\,j\,j\,j}{7'5'5'5'5'7'} ,$ ‖ 5b. same ‖

11a. $\frac{s\quad s\quad s\quad t\quad s\quad t}{10'10'10'4'10'4'}$ ‖ 11b. same ‖

6a. $\frac{k\,lk\,l}{7575} \mid \frac{k\,lk\,l}{7575}$ ‖ 6b. same ‖

12a. $\frac{u\,u\,u\,v}{7'7'7'7} \mid \frac{u\,u\,u\,v}{7'7'7'7}$ ‖ 12b. same ‖

a:-[u]eille*, b:-ueil, c:-einne, d:-our, e:-in, f:-ine, g:-oy, h:-eingne, i:-ui, j:-ire, k:-aut, l:-uis, m:-aire, n:-ort, o:-aie, p:-ir, q:-il, r:-ais, s:-eindre, t:-ame, u:-endre, v:-oir
*: This irregularity is acceptable (Hoepffner 1908–21, 3:252, note to *Confort*, ll. 3605–17; cf. *Pour ce qu' on puist* [L3]).
DISCUSSION (literary). Huot 1987, 264–65 (pairing of L5/4 and *Par trois raisons* [L6/5]).
EDITIONS OF MUSIC. Ludwig 1926–54, 4:29–30 (ed. Besseler); Schrade 1956b, 2:10–14 (critical notes 1956c, 58). The music of strophes 1 and 12 is the same, except that strophe 12 is a perfect fifth higher.
LITERARY AND MUSICAL ANTECEDENT. Schrade (1956c, 58; 1958–61, 847–48) indicates that L5/4 is metrically, rhythmically, and melodically closely related to the *Roman de Fauvel* lai *Talant que i' ai d' obeir* (ed. Rosenberg/Tischler 1991, 59–70 no. 21).
DISCUSSION (musical). Reaney 1955–56, 28–29 (analysis of strophes 1 and 5).

O fleur des fleurs. See *Armes, Amours* (by Eustache Deschamps and F. Andrieu), chap. 7.4.

O livoris. See *Fons / O livoris* (M9).

O series summe. See *Quant vraie amour / O series* (M17).

Obediens usque ad mortem. See *Hareu! / Helas!* (M10).

On ne porroit penser ne souhaidier (ballade B3)
Refrain: *Quant j' aim la flour de toute creature*
MANUSCRIPTS WITH TEXT AND MUSIC.

[1]	C	fols. 158v–159r	no. 3	2v (ca, ten; empty staves for tr)
[3]	V g	fol. 297v	no. 3	2v (ca, ten; empty staves for tr)
[4]	B	fol. 295v	no. 3	2v (ca, ten; empty staves for tr)
[5]	A	fol. 455r	no. 3	2v (ca, ten; empty staves for tr)
[6]	G	fols. 134v–135r	no. 3	2v (ca, ten)
[7]	E	fol. 148v	no. 7	3v (ca, ten, ct [corrupt at beginning])

TEXT MANUSCRIPTS.
[10] **M** fol. 237v   no. 3   Lo7 **CWVgBAEHMD**
EDITIONS OF TEXT. Chichmaref 1909, 1:23 no. 7; Wilkins 1972, 88 no. 151.

DATE. After 1339 (see below on "literary antecedent").

TEXT STRUCTURE. 3 strophes: $\dfrac{a\ b}{1010}\ \dfrac{a\ b}{1010}\ \dfrac{b\ c}{1010}\dfrac{C}{'10}$, a:-*ier*, b:-*our*, c:-*ure*

DISCUSSION (literary). Deschaux 1978b; Luttrell 1978, 290 n. 9 (phrase "plaisant dangier").

LITERARY ANTECEDENT. Text modeled on a ballade by Jean de le Mote, the first lyric insertion in his *Li Regret Guillaume* (dated 1339; ed. Scheler 1882, 20–21). Discussed in Hoepffner 1911, 163; Reaney 1959b, 26; Günther 1972, 53–54 (employs the term *balade entée* for B3; see Frobenius 1986, 11 col. b); Wilkins 1983a, 194; Frobenius 1986, 11 col. a (Machaut's lyric production must have started well before 1339 and thus B3 is prior to Jean de le Mote's ballade); Earp 1991b, 110–13.

EDITIONS OF MUSIC. Ludwig 1926–54, 1:3; Schrade 1956b, 3:72–73 (critical notes 1956c, 99–100); Wilkins 1980b, 11–12 (Chaucer, *Flee fro the prees* underlaid). The corrupt contratenor appears only in MS E; it is surely not authentic.

DISCUSSION (musical). Salzer 1952, 1:275, 2:329 ex. 530 (two levels of reduction of the refrain, considered as a 3v work); Machabey 1955b, 2:20–21; Wykes 1956, 43–49 (analyzed as a 3v work); Salop 1971, 55–56 (role of register in the melodic direction of the cantus); Dömling 1972, 304–5 (music emphasizes internal rhymes in the text); Lühmann 1978, 120–21 (declamation); Mulder 1978, 82–83, 94–95 (motivic analysis).

On parle de richesses et de grant signorie (lai L8)
TEXT MANUSCRIPTS.

[1] C   fols. 194v–196r no. 14   [6] G   fols. 83v–84r   no. 8
[3] V g fols. 234v–235v no. 8   [7] E   fols. 127r–127v   no. 17
[4] B   fols. 232v–233v no. 8   [10] M   fols. 217v–218v   no. 8
[5] A   fols. 381v–382v no. 8

FACSIMILE (refer to chap. 4.4s). Miniature C106.

EDITION OF TEXT. Chichmaref 1909, 2:338–44 no. 8.

TEXT STRUCTURE. 13 strophes, 178 lines[72]:

1. 12'a†a*a*a I a†a†a*a* II   8a. 7lmlmnnmnm II 8b. same II
2. 12'bbbb I bbbb II   9a. 5'oooooo II 9b. same II
3a. 12cccccccc II 3b. same II   10a. 5ppppppq I ppppppq II 10b. same II
4a. 10'deed II 4b. same II   11a. 4rrrrrrrr II 10b. same II
5a. 10fgfggffg II 5b. samc II   12a. $\dfrac{sst\ sst}{332\ 332}$ II 12b. same II

6a. 8'hhhi hhhi II 6b. same II   13. 12'a*a*a*a* I a* a†a†a* II
7a. 8jkkjjkkj II 7b. same II

a:-*ie*, b:-*ance*, c:-*ir*, d:-*ose*, e:-*ire*, f:-*er*, g:-*i*, h:-*esse*, i:-*ée*, j:-*ien*, k:-*té*,
l:-*ours*, m:-*is*, n:-*ort*, o:-*ure*, p:-*ay*, q:-*ment*, r:-*it*, s:-*our*, t:-*oy*
†: lyric caesura *: epic caesura

DISCUSSION (literary). Poirion 1965, 529 n. 82; Wimsatt 1968, 174 n. 9; Huot 1987, 269–71; Wimsatt 1991b, 323 n. 16. Feminine voice. Hassell (1982, nos. R60, S121, S122) indexes proverbs.

Par trois raisons me vueil deffendre (lai L6; Schrade lai 5)
MANUSCRIPTS WITH TEXT AND MUSIC (all monophonic).

[1] C   fols. 176v–179r no. 6   [5] A   fols. 377r–379r   no. 6
[3] V g fols. 229v–232r no. 6   [6] G   fols. 80v–82r   no. 6
[4] B   fols. 227v–230r no. 6   [7] E   fols. 124r–125r   no. 15

TEXT MANUSCRIPT.
[10] M   fols. 214v–216r no. 6

TREATISE. Baudet Herenc, *Doctrinal de la Secunde Retorique* (1432) (chap. 2.3.1d).

EDITION OF TEXT. Chichmaref 1909, 2:322–29 no. 6.

---

72 Strophes 1, 2, and 13 provide rare examples of the alexandrine in Machaut. Maillard (1984, 328) counts thirteen strophes, while Poirion (1965, 403) counts twelve, combining strophes 1 and 2.

TEXT STRUCTURE. 12 strophes, 218 lines:

1a. $\frac{a\ ab}{8'8'8} \mid \frac{a\ ab}{8'8'8}$ ‖ 1b. same ‖   7a. $\frac{m\ m}{7\ 5} \mid \frac{mmmmmmm}{5\ 5\ 5\ 5\ 5\ 7\ 5}$ ‖ $\frac{mmmmmmm}{5\ 5\ 5\ 5\ 5\ 7\ 5}$ ‖ 7b. same ‖

2a. $\frac{c\ c\ c\ cd}{5'5'2'2'7} \mid \frac{c\ c\ c\ cd}{5'5'2'2'7}$ ‖ 2b. same ‖ 8a. $\frac{nnnno}{45335} \mid \frac{nnnno}{45335}$ ‖ 8b. same ‖

3a. $\frac{e\ e\ e\ f}{7'5'5'7'} \mid \frac{e\ e\ e\ f}{7'5'5'7'}$ ‖ 3b. same ‖   9a. $\frac{p\ p\ p\ p\ p}{7'5'3'3'7'} \mid \frac{p\ p\ p\ p\ p}{7'5'3'3'7'}$ ‖ 9b. same ‖

4a. $\frac{gh\ hg}{46'4'6} \mid \frac{gh\ hg}{46'4'6}$ ‖ 4b. same ‖   10a. $\frac{qq\ rr\ qq\ rrq}{77\ 47\ 47\ 474}$ ‖ 10b. same ‖

5a. 10'ij ∣ ji ‖ 5b. same ‖   11a. $\frac{s\ s\ t\ s\ s\ t}{7'3'37'3'3} \mid \frac{s\ s\ t\ s\ s\ t}{7'3'37'3'3}$ ‖ 11b. same ‖

6a. $\frac{kkkk\ l}{77777'} \mid \frac{kkkk\ l}{77777'}$ ‖ 6b. same ‖   12a–b. = 1a–b.

a:-*endre*, b:-*tion* (b rhyme in strophe 12: -*on*), c:-*oie*, d:-*eus*, e:-*ace*, f:-*iere*, g:-*ait*, h:-*aire*, i:-*ine*, j:-*ère*, k:-*is*, l:-*ure*, m:-*our*, n:-*ay*, o:-*ir*, p:-*eingne*, q:-*ort*, r:-*ment*, s:-*ance*, t:-*art*

DISCUSSION (literary). Calin 1974, 232; Huot 1987, 264–65 (pairing of *Nuls ne doit* [L5/4] and L6/5). Hassell (1982, no. C62) indexes a proverb.

EDITIONS OF MUSIC. Ludwig 1926–54, 4:31–33 (ed. Besseler); Schrade 1956b, 2:15–18 (critical notes 1956c, 58–59). The music of strophes 1 and 12 is the same, except that strophe 12 is a perfect fifth higher.

DISCUSSION (musical). Machabey 1955b, 1:116–17 (melodic study of strophe 7).

Paradis d'Amour. See *Amours, se plus demandoie* (lai L9).

Pas de tor en thies païs (ballade B30)
Refrain: *Seur toute creature humeinne* [73]

MANUSCRIPTS WITH TEXT AND MUSIC (all 3v: ca, ten, ct; ten corrupt in all sources).

| [3] **V g** | fol. 312v | no. 30 | [5] **A** | fol. 469v | no. 29 |
| [4] **B** | fol. 311v | no. 30 | [7] **E** | fol. 156r | no. 32 |

TEXT MANUSCRIPT.
[10] **M** fol. 242r   no. 30

EDITIONS OF TEXT. Chichmaref 1909, 2:559–60 no. 35.

TRANSLATION. Keitel 1977b, 5; see also discography (chap. 8.3 and 8.8).

DATE. Reaney (1958b, 48) considers the poem early because of the apparent subject (a lady whom Machaut met while travelling in Germany), and the octosyllabic lines.

TEXT STRUCTURE. 3 strophes: $\frac{ab\ ab\ b\ cC}{88\ 88\ 88'8'}$, a:-*is*, b:-*té*, c:-*einne*

DISCUSSION (literary). Keitel 1977b, 6 (reports Sarah Jane Williams's observation that strophe 2 is related to *Gent corps, faitis, cointe, apert et joly* [VD42]); Guthrie 1991, 80 (poetic rhythmic stress in the octosyllabic lines). On the meaning of the text, see Raynaud 1909, 462; Reaney 1958b, 48. Hassell (1982, nos. F96, R70, R77) indexes proverbs.

EDITIONS OF MUSIC. Ludwig 1926–54, 1:33–34; Schrade 1956b, 3:116–17 (critical notes 1956c, 115); Keitel 1977b. See Günther (1957, 75 n. 40) on corruption in tenor and *ouvert* ending.

DISCUSSION (musical). Machabey 1955b, 2:43–44; Wykes 1956, 52–58 (analysis); Günther 1957, 85–86 (motivic analysis); Salop 1971, 69–70 (melodic direction); Kühn 1973, 213 (melodic design); Keitel 1977b, 6; Lühmann 1978, 220, 222 (declamation).

Patrem omnipotentem. See *Messe de Nostre Dame.*

---

[73] The line also appears in *Vergier*, l. 99, and *J'ay tant / Lasse!* (M7) motetus.

Phyton, le mervilleus serpent (ballade B38)
Refrain: *Quant a ma dame merci quier*
MANUSCRIPTS WITH TEXT AND MUSIC.

[5] **A**	fols. 473v–474r	no. 37	3v (ca, ten, ct)
[6] **G**	fol. 148v	no. 37	3v (ca, ten, ct)
[7] **E**	fol. 157r	no. 36	3v (ca, ten, ct)[74]
[58] **Trém**	fol. xix	no. 40	(index only)
[58] **Trém**	fol. xxix	no. 67a	(index only)

TEXT MANUSCRIPTS.

[10] **M**	fol. 243v	no. 38	[50] **Pa**	fols. 51v–52r	no. 160
[16] **J**	fol. 11v *Fauston li merveilleus serpens*				

EDITIONS OF TEXT. Chichmaref 1909, 2:563–64 no. 43; Wilkins 1969a, 22–23 no. 12, notes p. 124.

TRANSLATION. Pryer 1977, 29 (strophe 1); see also discography (chap. 8.3 and 8.8).

TEXT STRUCTURE. 3 strophes, duplex ballade[75]: 8ab ab bc bC a:-*ent*, b:-*it*, c:-*ier*

DISCUSSION (literary). Poirion 1965, 589 n. 39 (problems with the use of ancient mythology in this work); Lefferts/Huot 1989, ii; Guthrie 1991, 79–80 (stress patterns in the octosyllabic lines). Note the use of similar images in *Confort*, ll. 2623, 2691–92.

TEXTUAL LEGACY (France). Froissart, *Espinette Amoureuse* (Fourrier 1963, 177 note to ll. 1617–18).

TEXTUAL LEGACY (England). Chaucer, *Complaynt d'Amours* (Wimsatt 1978, 71; 1991b, 313 n. 14).

EDITIONS OF MUSIC. Ludwig 1926–54, 1:46; Schrade 1956b, 3:132–33 (critical notes 1956c, 120).

DISCUSSION (musical). Machabey 1955b, 2:52; Günther 1957, 88–90 (internal rhythmic and motivic correspondences); 1958, 35 n. 27 (changes of prolation); Fischer 1961, 44 (essential role of contratenor; criticism in Apfel 1974, 174); Günther 1963a, 106 (internal rhythmic and motivic correspondences); Hirshberg 1971, 147–61 (extended analysis); Salop 1971, 63–64 (melodic direction in cantus); Dömling 1972, 302 (text painting), 303 (text setting of l. 5); Karp 1988, 73–74 (compositional priority of the cantus).

MUSICAL LEGACY. The same music and text are cited at the beginning of *Phiton, Phiton, beste tres venimeuse*, a ballade for Gaston Fébus by Magister Franciscus.[76] Hirshberg (1971, 166–70; 1973–74, 65 n. 11) argues—in my opinion, unconvincingly—for the priority of Franciscus's ballade. See also Berger 1990.

Plange, regni respublica! See *Tu qui gregem / Plange* (M22).

Plourez, dames, plourez vostre servant (ballade B32)
Refrain: *Se Dieus et vous ne me prenez en cure*
MANUSCRIPTS WITH TEXT AND MUSIC.

[3] **V g**	fol. 313v	no. 32	3v (ca, ten, ct)
[4] **B**	fol. 312v	no. 32	3v (ca, ten, ct)
[5] **A**	fol. 470v	no. 31	3v (ca, ten, ct)
[6] **G**	fol. 145v	no. 31	3v (ca, ten, ct)
[7] **E**	fols. 173r–173v	in *Voir Dit*	3v (ca, ten, ct)
[69] **Utr**	fol. 27r	no. 8	frag. (ten, ct)[77]

TEXT MANUSCRIPTS.

[10] **M**	fol. 242v	no. 32	Lo229 **VgBAMD** (chap. 6.4)
[40] **I**	fols. 18v–19r	no. 94	VD5 **AFEPm** (chap. 5.13 table 5.3)

---

[74] *Tenor G de Mascandio* (discussed in Earp 1983, 125–26).

[75] Brief discussion of text form in Ziino 1990, 20.

[76] Facs. *MGG* 4 (1954), plate 28 facing col. 545; ed. Reaney 1954b, 98–100; Wilkins 1969a, 41 no. 27 (text only); Apel 1970–72, 2:54–55 no. 27; Greene 1981–89, 18:47–49 no. 18; Lefferts/Huot 1989, 1–3 no. 1 (literary note on the text, p. ii; translation, p. v). Analyzed in Reaney 1954a, 635–36; Günther 1972, 56; Berger 1990 (new emendations).

[77] Most of the tenor and the complete contratenor are extant; the cantus is lost.

FACSIMILE. Wolf 1904, 2:43–45 no. 25 (diplomatic facs., MS **G**); Bank 1972, 44 ex. 15 (diplomatic facs. in score of beginning).
EDITIONS OF TEXT. Tarbé 1849, 57–58; P. Paris 1875, 25; Queux de Saint-Hilaire/Raynaud 1878–1903, 10:lv no. 48 (after MS **I**); Chichmaref 1909, 1:206 no. 229; Wilkins 1972, 91 no. 162.
TRANSLATIONS. Little 1980, 52–55 (relevant passages from *Voir Dit* letter 2 [ed. P. Paris 1875 as letter 4], and verses that introduce the ballade, ll. 542–70); Cerquiglini/Berthelot 1987, 117–18 (modern French); Wimsatt 1991b, 37 (strophe 1); see also discography (chap. 8.3 and 8.8).
DATE. Machabey (1955b, 2:46) tentatively placed B32, as the "testament" of Machaut, in late 1360, though he later placed it in 1362 (2:51), and other dates can be extrapolated from his earlier discussion (1:57–58). Poirion (1965, 200) asserted that B32 had been composed before the *Voir Dit*, on an occasion when Machaut was truly ill. Leech-Wilkinson (1993a, 46–48; 1993b, 108 n. 21) places composition of the text, according to internal evidence in the *Voir Dit*, in the first half of 1362, and the composition of the music later in 1362.
TEXT STRUCTURE. 3 strophes: $\frac{a\ b\ \ a\ b\ c\ c\ d\ \ D}{1010\ \ 1010\ \ 71010'10}$, a:-*ant*, b:-*ente*, c:-*i*, d:-*ure*

DISCUSSION (literary). Amon 1976, 5 (color black); B. Cazelles 1984 (on devotional poetry); Wimsatt 1991b, 37–39 (analysis). The following *Voir Dit* passages concern B32: (a) the text and music are sent with Guillaume's letter 2 (ed. P. Paris 1875, 41–42 as letter no. 4); (b) the text of B32 is inserted in the narrative (ll. 571–94, ed. 1875, 25–26); (c) Toute Belle acknowledged receipt in her letter 3, and she indicated that she would sing it with Guillaume (ed. 1875, 47–48 as letter no. 5). For excerpts from or commentary on these passages, see Quittard 1917–19, 126–27; Ludwig 1926–54, 2:54*; Wilkins 1972, 175–76 n. 162; Little 1980, 52–55; Imbs 1991, 34; Leech-Wilkinson 1993a, 46–48; 1993b, 107–8, 133.
TEXTUAL LEGACY (France). Deschamps's ballade no. 123, *Armes, Amours, Dames, Chevalerie* (cited in Wilkins 1972, 176; see chap. 7.4 and chap. 8.5); Deschamps's ballade no. 206, on the death of DuGuesclin, *Estoc d'oneur et arbres de vaillance*, with the refrain *Plourez, plourez flour de chevalerie* (cited in Wimsatt 1991b, 301 n. 86). Several later poems recall l. 1 of B32 (Poirion 1965, 464–65).
TEXTUAL LEGACY (England). Chaucer, *Complaint of Mars* (Wimsatt 1978, 74; 1991b, 39, 122–23); *Troilus* (Wimsatt 1991b, 39–42).
EDITIONS OF MUSIC. Wolf 1904, 3:69–70 no. 25 (errors); Riemann 1912, 4–5 no. 4 (arr. after Wolf); Ludwig 1926–54, 1:37–38; Schrade 1956b, 3:120–21 (critical notes 1956c, 116).
DISCUSSION (musical). Machabey 1955b, 2:46–47; Günther 1962–63, 12–13 (notation); Apfel 1964–65 1:56, 2:10 (essential role of contratenor; see Dömling 1970, 75 n. 10); Fischer 1961, 44 (essential role of contratenor; criticized in Hirshberg 1971, 80–90); Martinez 1963, 106–7 (texting at refrain, musical rhyme), 111–12 (complementary nature of tenor and contratenor); Salop 1971, 66–68 (melodic tension and resolution); Bank 1972, 41, 43 (tempo); Dömling 1972, 301, 305 (text painting, text setting); Hirshberg 1973–74, 60 (text distribution in B-section); Kühn 1973, 213 (melodic design); Apfel 1974, 172–74 (tenor and contratenor both perform tenor role); Lühmann 1978, 181–83 (declamation); Leech-Wilkinson 1993a, 57 (part crossing in tenor and contratenor, simultaneous conception of voices).
    The pervasive use of certain melodic formulas in *tempus imperfectum, prolatio major* links *Donnez, signeurs* (B26), *Une vipere* (B27), and *Je puis trop* (B28) as one group, and *Plourez, dames* (B32), *Nes qu'on* (B33), and *Se pour ce muir* (B36) as another; the same formulas are seen to a lesser extent in *En amer* (RF4), *Cinc, un* (R6), and *Douce dame, tant* (R20) (cf. Reaney 1955, 47; Günther 1957, 80–84; Hirshberg 1971, 120–33; Little 1980, 49; Arlt 1993, 63). On melodic formulae in B32–33 and B36, see also Reaney 1971, 42; Mulder 1978, 99–114 (the theme of despair common to the three ballades is mirrored in their similar musical material; Little 1980, 57–59; Fuller 1992b, 248 (delayed resolutions serve text expression); Leech-Wilkinson 1993a, 50, 52–53, 57 (differences between B32 and B33; simultaneous conception of voices).

Plus belle que le biau jour (virelai V35)

TEXT MANUSCRIPTS.

[3] **V g**	fol. 334r	no. 35	[10] **M**	fol. 254v	no. 35
[4] **B**	fol. 331r	no. 35	[50] **Pa**	fols. 70v–71r	no. 226
[5] **A**	fol. 493v	no. 36	VD10 **AFEPm** (chap. 5.13 table 5.3)		
[6] **G**	fol. 163r	no. 36			

EDITIONS OF TEXT. P. Paris 1875, 38; Chichmaref 1909, 2:628–29 no. 36.

TEXT STRUCTURE. 3 strophes: $\dfrac{AABBAAB}{7\,7\,4\,7\,4\,7\,4}$ ‖ $\dfrac{bba\ bba}{774\ 774}$ ∣ $\dfrac{a\,abba\,ab}{7747474}$‖ $\dfrac{AABBAAB}{7\,7\,4\,7\,4\,7\,4}$ a:-*our*, b:-*i*

DISCUSSION (literary). The following *Voir Dit* passages concern V35: (a) in the introductory narrative, Guillaume presents the three virelais *Je ne me puis* (V33), *L'ueil, qui est* (V34), and V35 as having been dictated from his sickbed (ll. 821–22, ed. P. Paris 1875, 35); (b) the text of V35 is inserted in the narrative (ll. 905–53, ed. 1875, 38–39); (c) in letter 28, Toute Belle requested that this virelai be set to music (ed. 1875, 207). For excerpts from or commentary on these passages, see Ludwig 1926–54, 2:55*; Wilkins 1972, 178–79 notes to nos. 277–79; Leech-Wilkinson 1993b, 110, 120, 137 no. 19.

Plus dure qu'un dyamant (virelai V31; Schrade virelai 28)

MANUSCRIPTS WITH TEXT AND MUSIC (all 2v: ca, ten).

[3] **V g**	fol. 332v	no. 31	[6] **G**	fol. 161v	no. 31
[5] **A**	fols. 491v–492r	no. 31			

TEXT MANUSCRIPTS.

[10] **M**	fols. 253r–253v	no. 31	[50] **Pa**	fols. 68*bis* r–68*bis* v	no. 217

EDITIONS OF TEXT. Chichmaref 1909, 2:620–21 no. 31; Wilkins 1969a, 34–35 no. 24, notes p. 126.

TRANSLATIONS. Davison/Apel 1949, 246 no. 46b (strophe 1); Cogan/Escot 1976, 116 (strophe 1); Alton/Jeffery 1976, 65; see also discography (chap. 8.3 and 8.8).

TEXT STRUCTURE. 3 strophes: $\dfrac{AABBAAB}{7\,7\,4\,7\,4\,7\,4}$ ‖ $\dfrac{bba\ bba}{774\ 774}$ ∣ $\dfrac{a\,abba\,ab}{7747474}$‖ $\dfrac{AABBAAB}{7\,7\,4\,7\,4\,7\,4}$a:-*ant*[-*ent*], b:-*é*

DISCUSSION (literary). See chap. 6.4, commentary to Lo254. Alton/Jeffery 1976, 63–66 (guide to medieval pronunciation). Hassell (1982, nos. A59, D67) indexes proverbs.

EDITIONS OF MUSIC. Ludwig 1926–54, 1:86–87; Davison/Apel 1949, 49 no. 46b; Schrade 1956b, 3:187 (critical notes 1956c, 145–46); Wilkins 1969a, 158–59 no. 8 (after Schrade); Cogan/Escot 1976, 114–15.

DISCUSSION (musical). Salzer 1952, 1:277–78, 2:330–33 ex. 532 (edition, with voice-leading reductions that emphasize certain pitches to obtain a more traditional tonal plan); Machabey 1955b, 1:192–93; Reaney 1955, 52, 53 and Günther 1957, 62 (melodic-rhythmic motives); Cogan/Escot 1976, 114–24, 221–28, 238–39 (analysis); Covington 1978.

Pour ce qu'on puist miex retraire (lai L3)

MANUSCRIPTS WITH TEXT AND MUSIC (all monophonic).

[1] **C**	fols. 170r–173r	no. 3	[6] **G**	fols. 77r–78v	no. 3
[3] **V g**	fols. 223v–226r	no. 3	[7] **E**	fols. 113v–115v	no. 8
[4] **B**	fols. 221r–224r	no. 3	[26] *F:La 134* frag.		
[5] **A**	fols. 371r–373v	no. 3			

TEXT MANUSCRIPTS.

[10] **M**	fols. 211r–212v	no. 3	[50] **Pa**	fols. 39r–40v	no. 120

FACSIMILES (refer to chap. 4.4s). Miniature C95. Fallows 1977b, 478 (MS **La**).

EDITION OF TEXT. Chichmaref 1909, 2:300–308 no. 3.

TEXT STRUCTURE. 12 strophes, 240 lines:

1a. $\dfrac{a\,bbbb\,a}{7'77777'}$ ‖ 1b. same ‖   3. $\dfrac{fffg}{6666'}$ ∣ $\dfrac{fffg}{6666'}$ ‖ $\dfrac{hhhg}{6666'}$ ∣ $\dfrac{hhhg}{6666'}$ ‖

2. $\dfrac{ccccd}{55575}$ ∣ $\dfrac{ccccd}{55575}$ ‖ $\dfrac{eeeed}{55575}$ ∣ $\dfrac{eeeed}{55575}$ ‖   4a. $\dfrac{i\,j\,k}{77'5}$ ∣ $\dfrac{i\,j\,k\,k\,j}{77'5\,77'}$ ‖ $\dfrac{j\,k}{7'7}$ ∣ $\dfrac{j\,k}{7'7}$ ‖ 4b. same ‖

5a. $\dfrac{1\,1\,1\,1\,1\,1\,m}{7'5'5'5'5'7'7} \mid \dfrac{1\,1\,1\,1\,1\,1\,m}{7'5'5'5'5'7'7}$ ‖

5b. $\dfrac{n\,n\,n\,n\,n\,n\,m}{7'5'5'5'5'7'7} \mid \dfrac{n\,n\,n\,n\,n\,n\,m}{7'5'5'5'5'7'7}$ ‖

6a. $\dfrac{o\;\;p\;\;p\;\;o\;\;o\;\;p\;\;p\;\;o}{10\,10'10'10\,10\,10'10'10}$ ‖ 6b. same ‖

7a. $\dfrac{q\,q\,q\,q\,r}{88888}, \mid \dfrac{q\,q\,q\,q\,r}{88888},$ ‖ 7b. same ‖

8. $\dfrac{s\,s\,s\,s\,s\,s\,s\,s\,s}{4444844448} \mid\mid \dfrac{t\,t\,t\,t\,t\,t\,t\,t\,t}{4444844448}$ ‖

9. 10uub | uub ‖ 10vvb | vvb ‖

10a. $\dfrac{w\,w\,w\,w\,w\,w\,x}{4'2'4'2'4'2'7} \mid \dfrac{w\,w\,w\,w\,w\,w\,x}{4'2'4'2'4'2'7}$ ‖ 10b. same ‖

11a. $\dfrac{y\,y\,y\,y\,y\,y\,z}{43343346}, \mid \dfrac{y\,y\,y\,y\,y\,y\,z}{43343346},$ ‖

11b. $\dfrac{\Omega\Omega\Omega\Omega\Omega\Omega\,z}{4\,3\,3\,4\,3\,3\,4\,6}, \mid \dfrac{\Omega\Omega\Omega\Omega\Omega\Omega\,z}{4\,3\,3\,4\,3\,3\,4\,6},$ ‖

12a–b. = 1a–b.

a:-*aire*, b:-*ort*, c:-*oint*, d:-*art*, e:-*amer*, f:-*tieus*, g:-*ente*, h:-*uet*, i*:-[*u*]*eil*,
j:-[*u*]*eille*, k:-*our*, l:-*ie*, m:-*droit*, n:-*üe*, o:-*as*, p:-*ire*, q:-*ait*, r:-*aire*,
s:-*ueil*, t:-*aint*, u:-*té*, v:-*espoir*, w:-*ure*, x:-*ur*, y:-*oy*, z:-*endre*, Ω:-*is*
*: The irregularity in the i and j rhymes is acceptable (Hoepffner 1908–21, 3:252, note to *Confort*, ll. 3605–17; cf. *Nuls ne doit* [L5/4]).
DISCUSSION (literary). Huot 1987, 262–63 (iconography; pairing of L3 and *Aus amans* [L4]). Hassell (1982, no. B54) indexes a proverb.
EDITIONS OF MUSIC. Gérold 1932, 326–27 (strophe 1); Ludwig 1926–54, 4:26–28 (ed. Besseler); Schrade 1956b, 2:5–9 (critical notes 1956c, 57–58). The music of strophes 1 and 12 is the same.
DISCUSSION (musical). Machabey 1955b, 1:115–16 (melodic formulas in strophes 4, 10, 11); Fallows 1977b, 480–83 (musical analysis); Lühmann 1978, 132–34, 227–28 (declamation).

Pour ce que plus proprement. Un Lay de Consolation (lai L23; Schrade lai 17)
MANUSCRIPT WITH TEXT AND MUSIC (monophonic; halves of each strophe combine as 2v polyphony).
[7] E fols. 125v–126v no. 16 *Item un lay de consolation. Guille' Machaut* (fol. 125r)
EDITION OF TEXT. Chichmaref 1909, 2:467–73 no. 23.
TRANSLATION. See discography (chap. 8.3 and 8.8).
ASCRIPTION. Reaney 1955–56, 30 (the work is tonally unique); Hasselman/Walker 1970, 8 (against ascription to Machaut); Bent 1983, 72–73 (for ascription to Machaut); Earp 1983, 310–26 (against).
DATE. ca. 1367–77 for L23 and *En demantant* (L24/18) (Reaney 1967, 89–90, 95).
TEXT STRUCTURE. 12 strophes, 188 lines:

1a. $\dfrac{a\,a\,b}{777}, \mid \dfrac{a\,a\,b}{777},$ ‖ 1b. same ‖

2a. $\dfrac{c\,c\,c\;d}{7377}, \mid \dfrac{c\,c\,c\;d}{7377},$ ‖ 2b. same ‖

3a. 10ef | ef ‖ 3b. same ‖

4a. $\dfrac{b\,b\,b\,b\,c}{7'7'7'7'5} \mid \dfrac{b\,b\,b\,b\,c}{7'7'7'7'5}$ ‖ 4b. same ‖

5a. $\dfrac{g\,g\,g\,g\,h}{55555}, \mid \dfrac{g\,g\,g\,g\,h}{55555},$ ‖ 5b. same ‖

6a. 7'iiii | iiii ‖ 6b. same ‖

7a. $\dfrac{j\,j\,j\,j\,k}{7'3'3'7'5} \mid \dfrac{j\,j\,j\,j\,k}{7'3'3'7'5}$ ‖ 7b. same ‖

8a. 10lllm | lllm ‖ 8b. same ‖

9a. $\dfrac{n\,n\,n\,o}{7777}, \mid \dfrac{n\,n\,n\,o}{7777},$ ‖ 9b. same ‖

10a. $\dfrac{p\,p\,p\,p\;q}{33355}, \mid \dfrac{p\,p\,p\,p\;q}{33355},$ ‖ 10b. same ‖

11a. $\dfrac{r\;r\;s}{8'8'8} \mid \dfrac{r\;r\;s}{8'8'8}$ ‖ 11b. same ‖

12a–b. = 1a–b.

a:-*ent*, b:-*ée*, c:-*is*, d:-*ière*, e:-*é*, f:-*aint*, g:-*ant*, h:-*aire*, i:-*oie*, j:-*ie*,
k:-*ort*, l:-*ir*, m:-*ier*, n:-*oir*, o:-*ue*, p:-*ay*, q:-*aille*, r:-*ente*, s:-*our*
DISCUSSION (literary). Poirion 1965, 548 n. 2 (on *malebouche*). Hassell (1982, no. G46) indexes a proverb.

EDITIONS OF MUSIC. Ludwig 1926–54, 4:77–79 (ed. Besseler; errors); Schrade 1956b, 2:94–98 (critical notes 1956c, 70–71; errors discussed in Hoppin 1958, 93–94; 1960, 18, n. 22); Hoppin 1958, 96–101. The music of strophes 1 and 12 is the same.

DISCUSSION (musical). Machabey 1955b, 1:121. Hoppin (1958) was the first to recognize the polyphonic nature of the work, with a notation similar to the "hidden polyphony" seen in some twelfth-century manuscripts (Fuller 1971, 188–90).

Pour ce que tous mes chans fais (ballade B12)
Refrain: *Se je chant mains que ne sueil*
MANUSCRIPTS WITH TEXT AND MUSIC.

[1]	**C**	fols. 162v–163v	no. 12	2v (ca, ten; empty staves for tr)
[3]	**V g**	fol. 302r	no. 12	2v (ca, ten; empty staves for tr)
[4]	**B**	fol. 300r	no. 12	2v (ca, ten; empty staves for tr)
[5]	**A**	fol. 460v	no. 13	2v (ca, ten)
[6]	**G**	fol. 138v	no. 13	2v (ca, ten)
[7]	**E**	fol. 155v	no. 31	2v (ca, ten)

TEXT MANUSCRIPT.
[10] **M** fol. 238v no. 12

EDITION OF TEXT. Chichmaref 1909, 2:547–48 no. 15.

TRANSLATION. Wilkins 1989, 149 (strophe 1).

DATE. Machabey (1955b, 2:27) notes the similarity of the beginning of the tenor and cantus of l. 8 and the opening of the *Lay de Confort, S'onques* (L17/12) and suggests that both the ballade and the lai date from the same period. He is more precise later (2:57), citing Hoepffner's note to l. 2249 of the *Confort* (1908–21, 3:249), which indicates that the lai must date from the same period as the *dit* and is indeed the same lai referred to in *Confort* as the *Lay de Bon Espoir*. Nevertheless, after citing a counter example (see below, note on the date of *Nes qu'on* [B33]), Machabey admits that conjectures connecting lyrics with specific narrative poems are fragile. See commentary below on date of *S'onques*.

TEXT STRUCTURE. 3 strophes: 7ab ab ccdcD a:-*ais*, b:-*ent*, c:-*ueil*

DISCUSSION (literary). Poirion 1965, 198n. (themes of B12, *Aucune gent / Qui plus aimme* [M5], and *Se faire sçay* [Lo55] are related).

EDITIONS OF MUSIC. Ludwig 1926–54, 1:10–11; Schrade 1956b, 3:83 (critical notes 1956c, 105–6).

DISCUSSION (musical). Machabey 1955b, 2:26–29, 57; Dömling 1970, 30–31 (text setting and musical structure); Reaney 1971, 40–42 (brief analysis); Dömling 1972, 302, 303, 305 (text setting, refrain); Lühmann 1978, 201 (declamation); Hirshberg 1980, 38 (*ficta*); Welker 1992, 184 (text underlay).

ANTECEDENTS (textual and musical). The refrain quotes (a) the first line of the *ballete Se je chant mains que ne suel* (R.1000; ed. Gennrich 1921–27, 1:123–24 no. 171 [commentary 2:113); (b) the text of the motetus of a 3v motet in *F:MO 196*, *Coument se poet / Se je chante / Qui prendroit a son cuer*; and (c) text and music of the 3v *chace, Se je chant mains que ne suel* (ed. Apel 1970–72, 3:162–68 no. 290; Hoppin 1978b, 127–133 no. 60 [with text translation]; Greene 1981–89, 20:209–17 no. 64). Note that text and music of the first and last line of the *chace* appear to belong together: *Se je chant mains que ne suel / C'est pour ce que ne puis mie* [If I sing less than usual, it is because I cannot]. Discussed in Ludwig 1926–54, 1:11; Reaney 1955, 52; Günther 1972, 54–55; Frobenius 1986, 11 col. b; Newes 1987, 87–89, 99–101 and 1991b, 99–100 (Machaut may not have known the Ivrea *chace*); Kügle 1990, 534 n. 32 (ascribes Ivrea *chace* to Denis le Grant, first chaplain to King Philip VI in 1349); 1993, 274–80 (more on citations and ascription). For more on the development of the *chace*, see Kügle 1991, 379–84; 1993, 258–82.

Pour quoy me bat. See *Lasse! / Se j'aim* (M16).

Pour vivre joliement. Le Lay de la Rose (lai L21; Schrade lai 15)
MANUSCRIPTS WITH TEXT AND MUSIC (all monophonic).
[5] **A** fols. 408v–410v no. 21 (has title) [6] **G** fols. 100v–102r no. 21 (has title)
EDITION OF TEXT. Chichmaref 1909, 2:451–58 no. 21.

TRANSLATION. Kelly 1978, 48 (a few lines of strophe 3).

TEXT STRUCTURE. 12 strophes, 236 lines:

1a. $\dfrac{\text{a a b b a a b b a}}{774747474}$ || 1b. same ||

2a. $\dfrac{\text{c c c d c c c d}}{7775' \ 7775'}$ || 2b. same ||

3a. $\dfrac{\text{e f e f f e f f e f}}{7'37'377'737'3}$ || 3b. same ||

4a. $\dfrac{\text{g g g g h}}{75337}$ | $\dfrac{\text{g g g g h}}{75337}$ || 4b. same ||

5a. $\dfrac{\text{i i i i j}}{7'5'5'5'7}$ | $\dfrac{\text{i i i i j}}{7'5'5'5'7}$ || 5b. same ||

6a. $\dfrac{\text{k k k l}}{3'3'7'7}$ | $\dfrac{\text{k k k l}}{3'3'7'7}$ || 6b. same ||

7a. $\dfrac{\text{m m m m n}}{8\ 8\ 8\ 8\ 6'}$ | $\dfrac{\text{m m m m n}}{8\ 8\ 8\ 8\ 6'}$ || 7b. same ||

8a. $\dfrac{\text{o o o o p}}{7'7'7'7'5}$ | $\dfrac{\text{o o o o p}}{7'7'7'7'5}$ || 8b. same ||

9a. $\dfrac{\text{q r r r \ r q q q}}{10433\ 10433}$ $\dfrac{\text{q r r r \ r q q q}}{10433\ 10433}$ || 9b. same ||

10a. $\dfrac{\text{s s s s t}}{55575'}$ | $\dfrac{\text{s s s s t}}{55575'}$ || 10b. same ||

11a. $\dfrac{\text{u u u v}}{7'3'7'7}$ | $\dfrac{\text{u u u v}}{7'3'7'7}$ || 11b. same ||

12a–b. = 1a–b.

a:-*ent*, b:-*i*, c:-*oir*, d:-*ance*, e:-*aire*, f:-*oy*, g:-*ir*, h:-*oing*, i:-*ure*, j:-*a*, k:-*ée*, l:-*ait*, m:-*is*, n:-*age*, o:-*iere*, p:-*our*, q:-*ay*, r:-*er*, s:-*ier*, t:-*ie*, u:-*ire*, v:-*ort*

EDITIONS OF MUSIC. Ludwig 1926–54, 4:72–74 (ed. Besseler); Schrade 1956b, 2:85–89 (critical notes 1956c, 68–69). The music of strophes 1 and 12 is the same, except that strophe 12 is a perfect fifth higher.

DISCUSSION (musical). Machabey 1955b, 1:120; Günther 1957, 130–31 (rhythm and chronology).

Puis qu'en oubli sui de vous, dous amis (rondeau R18)
MANUSCRIPTS WITH TEXT AND MUSIC (all 3v: ca, ten, ct).

[5]	**A**	fol. 480v	no. 19	[7]	**E**	fol. 139r	no. 14
[6]	**G**	fol. 153v	no. 18				

TEXT MANUSCRIPT.

[10]	**M**	fol. 245r	no. 20	[50]	**Pa**	fols. 48r–48v	no. 145

EDITIONS OF TEXT. Tarbé 1856, 8; Chichmaref 1909, 2:576 no. 18. Feminine voice.

TRANSLATION. Wilson 1990a, 238.

TEXT STRUCTURE. 10AB aA ab AB a:-*is*, b:-*ant*

EDITIONS OF MUSIC. Ludwig 1926–54, 1:67; Machabey 1931, 339; Schrade 1956b, 3:161 (critical notes 1956c, 133); Wilson 1990a, 238 no. 70.

DISCUSSION (musical). Machabey 1955b, 1:168–69 (the poem was written by Peronne, and set to music by Guillaume; perhaps Machabey got this idea from the publication of R18 in Tarbé 1856, an edition of Toute Belle's "complete works"); Wykes 1956, 49–51 (analysis); Günther 1957, 109 (motivic analysis); Kühn 1973, 152–54 (sonority; manuscript tradition; the simpler version in MS E is by a musician who misunderstood the model and changed it along more traditional lines, thereby arriving at better voice-leading; the case is thus ambivalent, but similar ambivalent double versions are found from the Machaut period to the Dufay period; see comments in Stenzl 1975); Bent 1982, 308 (the version in MS E is in some ways better); Gagnepain discussion in Guillaume de Machaut 1982, 137, 274 (prefers the version in MS E); Cerquiglini 1985b, 150 (low tessitura for a poem spoken by a woman); Fuller 1986, 39 (both the first and second phrases close on unstable sonorities in need of resolution); Wilson 1990b, 340, 343 (harmonic framework); Leech-Wilkinson 1993a, 49, 61 n. 45 (lower voices provide a chordal accompaniment to a pre-existing cantus, which Machaut mentioned in letter 31 of the *Voir Dit*; see above, literary discussion of *Dix et sept* [R17], item d).

MUSICAL LEGACY. Günther (1972, 62 and 1975, 295, citing Suzanne Clercx) discusses a textual and musical link to Ciconia's virelai *Aler m'en veus* (ed. Apel 1970–72, 1:23–24 no. 13; Bent/Hallmark 1985, 167–69 no. 44); see also Hallmark 1983, 208–9).

Puis que la douce. See *De Bon Espoir / Puis que* (M4).

Puis que ma dolour agree (virelai V7)

MANUSCRIPTS WITH TEXT AND MUSIC (all monophonic).

[1] **C**	fols. 151r–151v	no. 7		[5] **A**	fols. 483v–484r	no. 7
[3] **Vg**	fol. 324v	no. 7		[6] **G**	fols. 155v–156r	no. 7
[4] **B**	fol. 322v	no. 7		[7] **E**	fol. 159v	no. 5

TEXT MANUSCRIPTS.

[10] **M**	fol. 247r	no. 7		[50] **Pa**	fols. 60r–60v	no. 186

EDITION OF TEXT. Chichmaref 1909, 2:587–89 no. 7.

TEXT STRUCTURE. 3 strophes:

$$\underset{7'7'7'5 \ 7'7'7'5}{AAAB\,AAAB} \parallel \underset{775' \ 775'}{bba\,bba} \mid \underset{7'7'7'5 \ 7'7'7'5}{a\,a\,ab\,a\,a\,ab} \parallel \underset{7'7'7'5 \ 7'7'7'5}{AAAB\,AAAB} \quad a\text{:-}ée,\ b\text{:-}our$$

EDITIONS OF MUSIC. Ludwig 1926–54, 1:72–73; Schrade 1956b, 3:170 (critical notes 1956c, 138).

DISCUSSION (musical). Machabey 1955b, 1:179–80 (duplex virelai).

Quant en moy / Amour et biauté / Amara valde (motet M1)

MANUSCRIPTS WITH TEXT AND MUSIC.

[1] **C**	fols. 206v–207r	no. 1		3v (tr, mot, ten)
[2] **W**	fol. 74v	no. 1		(frag.; incomplete tr)
[3] **Vg**	fols. 260v–261r	no. 1		3v (tr, mot, ten)
[4] **B**	fols. 258v–259r	no. 1		3v (tr, mot, ten)
[5] **A**	fols. 414v–415r	no. 1		3v (tr, mot, ten)
[6] **G**	fols. 102v–103r	no. 1		3v (tr, mot, ten)
[7] **E**	fols. 131v–132r	no. 2		3v (tr, mot, ten)

FACSIMILES (refer to chap. 4.4t). Miniature A153. Wolf 1904, 2:16–18 no. 13 (diplomatic facs., MS **G**); Wilson 1990b, 294 (MS **A**, fol. 414v, with beginning of triplum and complete motetus).

EDITION OF TEXT. Chichmaref 1909, 2:483–84 no. 1; Wilson 1990b, 311–12

TRANSLATION. Wilson 1990a, 210–11. See also discography, chap. 8.5.

TEXT STRUCTURE AND RELATIONSHIP TO ISORHYTHM. Both triplum and motetus exhibit regular correlation between text and *talea* structure (Besseler 1927, 224; Reichert 1956, 201). The beginning and ending of strophe and *talea* exactly correspond, without staggered phrasing, a situation unique to M1 and *J'ay tant / Lasse!* (M7) (Machabey 1955b, 2:65–66; Reichert 1956, 205–6). Reichert's figure of the first *color* (1956, ex. 1, discussed pp. 203, 209) shows that the upper-voice *talea* defines a "Grosstalea" that includes two internal repetitions of the tenor rhythm (see also Günther 1958, 30; Sanders 1973, 558 n. 257). Both triplum and motetus change strophic forms for the diminution section, a situation unique to M1 and *Bone pastor / Bone pastor* (M18) (Reichert 1956, 205–6). See also Clarkson 1971, 212, 263, 267, 271 (structure of the triplum text); 292–93 (rate of declamation in triplum and motetus); Newes 1984; Leech-Wilkinson 1989, 49 n. 65 (text declamation in the hocket sections); Wilson 1990b, 310–13 (analysis).

Triplum: $\underset{888 \ 888 \ 22688 \ 888 \ 888 \ 22688 \ 888 \ 888 \ 22688 \ 888 \ 888 \ 888}{aab\,aab\,c\,cbab\,aab\,aab\,ddbab\,aab\,aab\,e\,ebab\,aab\,aab\,aab}$

a:-*ment*, b:-*er*, c:-*oir*, d:-*ours*, e:-*ai*

Motetus: $\underset{7' \ 226 \ 7' \ 226 \ 7 \ 226' \ 77 \ 7'7' \ 77}{a\,bbc\ a\,ddc\,c\,ee\,a\ ff\ g\,g\ fg}$ a:-*aite*, b:-*er*, c:-*ement*, d:-*ous*, e:-*i*, f:-*ir*, g:-*ée*

An analysis combining the short lines into longer lines with internal rhyme yields the following structure: $\underset{7'107'10'10' \ 77 \ 7'7' \ 77}{a\,b\ a\,b\,b\,a\ cc\ d\,d\,c\,d}$ a:-*aite*, b:-*ement*, c:-*ir*, d:-*ée*

DISCUSSION (literary). The placement of the motet first in the series is doubtless a playful realization of the opening triplum text, "Quant en moy *vint premierement Amours*" [When Love first came to me] (Earp 1983, 66–67; Markstrom 1989, 17). The end of the triplum— "Grant folie est de tant amer / que de son doulz face on amer" [It is great folly to love so much that one should make something bitter from something sweet]—may be a refrain (Ludwig 1926–54, 3:12). See also Boogaard 1993b, 31–32 (number symbolism in texts).

TENOR SOURCE. *Amara valde* (Joel 1:8 and Soph. 1:14) is the end of the final melisma of the *repetenda* of *Plange quasi virgo*, third Responsory for Holy Saturday (Ludwig 1926–54, 2:58b*, 60a*, 3:5). The indication of the tenor source in Chichmaref (1909, 484n.) is incorrect. See also Wolf 1904, 1:175 (diplomatic facs. of tenor notation); Machabey 1955b, 2:63 (comparison of tenor with the modern version of the liturgical melody).

EDITIONS OF MUSIC. Wolf 1904, 3:28–32 no. 13; Ludwig 1926–54, 3:2–5; Schrade 1956b, 2:108–11 (critical notes 1956c, 75); Wilson 1990a, 206–9 no. 64.

DISCUSSION (musical). Bipartite, with diminution by one-third. Wolf 1904, 1:173, 175 (syncopation; diminution); Ficker 1924–25, 212 (isorhythmic analysis); Gombosi 1950, 220 (symmetrical rhythmic scheme); Machabey 1955b, 2:63–68; Eggebrecht 1961 (harmony); Pelinski 1975, 70, table 5 (tonal plan); Newes 1977, 47–48 (hockets emphasize internal rhymes); Mulder 1978, 88–90 (motivic analysis and text symbolism); Newes 1984 (declamation); Hughes 1989, 357–58 (hocket); Wilson 1990b, 296–306, 309 (isorhythmic analysis; harmony); Boogaard 1993b, 28–32 (related to *Hareu!* / *Helas!* [M10]; principles of ordering).

Quant j'ay l'espart (rondeau R5)

MANUSCRIPTS WITH TEXT AND MUSIC (all 2v: ca, ten).

[1]	C	fols. 202r–202v	no. 3		[5]	A	fol. 477r	no. 7
[3]	Vg	fol. 317v	no. 5		[6]	G	fol. 150v	no. 5
[4]	B	fol. 316v	no. 5		[7]	E	fol. 136r	no. 9

TEXT MANUSCRIPTS.

| [10] | M | fol. 244r | no. 5 | | [50] | Pa | fols. 38v–39r | no. 116 |

EDITIONS OF TEXT. Chichmaref 1909, 2:570 no. 5; Fuller 1987b, 113.

TRANSLATION. Fuller 1987b, 113; see also discography (chap. 8.3 and 8.8).

TEXT STRUCTURE. 4AABAAB aabAAB aabaab AABAAB a:-*art*, b:-*our*

DISCUSSION (literary). Hoepffner 1908–21, 3:254 n. to l. 276 of *Fonteinne* (relation to R5).

EDITIONS OF MUSIC. Ludwig 1926–54, 1:54–55; Schrade 1956b, 3:145 (critical notes 1956c, 125–26); Fuller 1987b, 112 no. 18b.

DISCUSSION (musical). Machabey 1955b, 1:155–56; Fuller 1987b, 115 (brief introduction).

Quant je ne voy ma dame n'oy (rondeau R21)

MANUSCRIPTS WITH TEXT AND MUSIC.

   [6] **G** fol. 154r no. 21 3v (ca, ten, ct)   [7] **E** fol. 141r no. 16 2v (ca, ten)

TEXT MANUSCRIPT.

Lo269 **G** only (closely related to Lo260; see chap. 6.4).

FACSIMILE. Parrish 1957, plate xlviii (MS E), discussed pp. 153–54.

EDITIONS OF TEXT. Chichmaref 1909, 1:233, 2:576 no. 21; Wilkins 1972, 111 no. 258.

TRANSLATION. Wilson 1990a, 241.

TEXT STRUCTURE. $\frac{AB\ aAab\ AB}{88'\ 88\ 88'\ 88'}$ a:-*noy[e]*,* b:-*noy*

*: Only l. 6 has the final "-*e*"; it is present in Lo269 as well as in the related Lo260.

DISCUSSION (literary). The first line is anticipated in the *Voir Dit*, l. 5233 (ed. P. Paris 1875, 224). Hassell (1982, no. N14) indexes a proverb.

EDITIONS OF MUSIC. Ludwig 1926–54, 1:69; Schrade 1956b, 3:164–65 (critical notes 1956c, 134–35); Wilson 1990a, 239–41 no. 71.

DISCUSSION (musical). Machabey 1955b, 1:170–71; Wykes 1956, 34–43, and appendix B diagrams (analysis); Günther 1957, 110–11 (motivic analysis); Reaney 1982, 296–97 (mode); Wilson 1990b, 339 (motivic analysis).

Quant je sui mis au retour (virelai V13)

MANUSCRIPTS WITH TEXT AND MUSIC (all monophonic).

[1]	C	fol. 153v	no. 13		[5]	A	fol. 485v	no. 13
[3]	Vg	fol. 326v	no. 13		[6]	G	fols. 157r–157v	no. 13
[4]	B	fol. 324v	no. 13					

TEXT MANUSCRIPT.

| [10] | M | fol. 248v | | | no. 13 *Balade* |

FACSIMILE. Ultan 1977b, 86 (diplomatic facs., MS C).

EDITION OF TEXT. Chichmaref 1909, 2:596 no. 13.

TRANSLATION. Reaney 1960b, 26–27; see also discography (chap. 8.3 and 8.8).

TEXT STRUCTURE. 3 strophes: $\frac{a\,b\,a\,b}{75\,'75\,'}$ ‖ $\frac{BA}{8\,'5}$ a:-*our*, b:-*ame*

EDITIONS OF MUSIC. Ludwig 1926–54, 1:76; Schrade 1956b, 3:173 (critical notes 1956c, 140); Reaney 1960b, 26.

DISCUSSION (musical). Machabey 1955b, 1:182.

Quant ma dame les maus d'amer m'aprent (rondeau R19)

MANUSCRIPTS WITH TEXT AND MUSIC (all 3v: ca, ten, ct).

[5] **A**	fols. 480v–481r	no. 20		[7] **E**	fol. 137r	no. 10
[6] **G**	fol. 153v	no. 19				

TEXT MANUSCRIPTS.

[10] **M**	fol. 207r[78]	no. 271		[50] **Pa**	fol. 52r	no. 163
[10] **M**	fol. 245r	no. 18				

FACSIMILE. Bank 1972, 44 ex. 16 (diplomatic facs. of A-section in score).

EDITIONS OF TEXT. Chichmaref 1909, 2:576 no. 19; Wilkins 1972, 112 no. 261.

TRANSLATION. See discography (chap. 8.3 and 8.8).

TEXT STRUCTURE. $\frac{AB}{1010}$, $\frac{aA}{1010}$ $\frac{a\,b}{1010}$, $\frac{AB}{1010}$, a:-*prent*, b:-*prendre*

EDITIONS OF MUSIC. Ludwig 1926–54, 1:67–68; Schrade 1956b, 3:162 (critical notes 1956c, 134); Günther 1962–63, 19; 1990, 78.

DISCUSSION (musical). Machabey 1955b, 1:169–70; Günther 1957, 103 (isorhythm); 1958, 35 n. 27 (mensuration); 1962–63, 18–21 (mensuration, isorhythmic structure); Bank 1972, 41, 43 (tempo); Saponov 1978, 25–27 (isorhythm); Arlt 1980, 126 and 1982, 234 (mensuration); Günther 1990, 77–80, 82 (use of three meters).

MUSICAL LEGACY. Günther (1990) discusses polymetric works possibly modeled on R19, including: (a) Jean Vaillant, rondeau *Pour ce que je ne say* (ed. Apel 1970–72, 1:227–28 no. 117; Greene 1981–89, 18:85–86 no. 30); (b) Vaillant, *Dame doucement / Doulz amis* (dated 1369; ed. Apel 1970–72, 1:225–26 no. 116; Greene 1981–89, 18:87–88 no. 31); (c) Vaillant, triple rondeau *Tres doulz / Ma dame / Cent mille* (ed. Apel 1970–72, 1:229–30 no. 118; Greene 1981–89, 18:31–32 no. 12); (d) anonymous, rondeau *Quiconques vuet* (tentatively ascribed to Vaillant by Günther; ed. Apel 1970–72, 3:126–27 no. 270; Greene 1981–89 22:116–18 no. 65); (e) anonymous, rondeau *Jour a jour la vie* (ed. Apel 1970–72, 3:102–5 no. 256; Greene 1981–89 22:78–79 no. 47a); (f) Solage, rondeau *Fumeux fume* (ed. Apel 1970–72, 1:200 no. 103; Greene 1981–89, 19:105–6 no. 98); (g) Garinus, rondeau *Loyauté me tient* (ed. Apel 1970–72, 1:62 no. 31; Greene 1981–89, 19:1–2 no. 51); (h) Johannes Galiot, rondeau *En atendant d'amer* (ed. Apel 1970–72, 1:60–61, no. 30; Greene 1981–89, 19:28–30 no. 59); (i) Matheus de Sancto Johanne, rondeau *Je chante ung chant* (ed. Apel 1970–72, 1:140–41 no. 75; Greene 1981–89, 18:22–24 no. 9); (j) Matheus de Sancto Johanne, rondeau *Fortune, faulce* (ed. Apel 1970–72, 1:138–39 no. 74; Greene 1981–89, 19:167–69 no. 99); (k) anonymous, ballade *Inclite flos* (ed. Apel 1970–72, 3:200–201 no. 296; Greene 1981–89, 19:37–39 no. 62); (l) Anthonello da Caserta, rondeau *Dame d'onour c'on* (ed. Apel 1970–72, 1:14–15 no. 9; Greene 1981–89, 22:1–3 no. 1). The priority of Machaut's rondeau is not always certain.

Quant Theseüs, Hercules et Jason / Ne quier veoir la biauté d'Absalon (ballade B34)

Refrain: *Je voy assez, puis que je voy ma dame*

MANUSCRIPTS WITH TEXT AND MUSIC.

[3] **V g**	fols. 314v–315r	no. 34	4v (ca1, ca2, ten, ct)
[4] **B**	fols. 313v–314r	no. 34	4v (ca1, ca2, ten, ct)

---

[78] R19 appeared as the last work in the *Loange* in the exemplar of MS **M**, but the work was edited out of the *Loange* by the time of MS **A**.

[5]	**A**	fols. 471v–472r	no. 33	4v (ca1, ca2, ten, ct)
[6]	**G**	fols. 146v–147r	no. 34	4v (ca1, ca2, ten, ct)
[7]	**E**	fols. 199v–200r	in *Voir Dit*	4v (ca1, ca2, ten, ct)
[59]	**C h**	fol. 54r	no. 88	4v (ca1, ca2, ten, ct)
[63]	**P R**	fols. 54v–55r	no. 109	4v (ca1, ca2, ten, ct)
[65]	**S L**	fol. 51r		frag. (ca1 only)

TEXT MANUSCRIPTS.

[10]	**M**	fols. 242v–243r	nos. 34a–b
[40]	**I**	fol. 18v	no. 93 (*Ne quier*)
[40]	**I**	fol. 20r	no. 105 (*Quant Theseüs*)
[50]	**Pa**	fols. 56v–57r	nos. 178–79

VD57–58 **AFEPm** (chap. 5.13 table 5.3; rubrics identify respective works of "Thomas" and "G de Machau").

EDITIONS OF TEXT. Tarbé 1849, 132–33; P. Paris 1875, 274; Queux de Saint-Hilaire/ Raynaud 1878–1903, 10:lxvi–lxvii no. 60, liv no. 47 (MS I); Chichmaref 1909, 2:560–62 nos. 38–39; Patterson 1935, 2:74 (*Ne quier*); Wilkins 1969a, 28–29 nos. 17–18, notes p. 125.

TRANSLATIONS. Palisca 1980, 81 (strophe 1) (=1988 ed., 86; strophes 1–3); Wimsatt 1991b, 181–82 (strophe 1 of each ballade); see also discography (chap. 8.3 and 8.8).

DATE. Sent 3 November 1363 with *Voir Dit* letter 32 (Leech-Wilkinson 1993a, 57, 58; 1993b, 126).

TEXT STRUCTURE. Double ballade: $\frac{a}{10} \frac{b}{10}$, $\frac{a}{10} \frac{b}{10}$, $\frac{c}{7} \frac{c}{10} \frac{d}{10}$, $\frac{D}{10}$ a:-*on*, b:-*onde*, c:-*our*, d:-*ame*

DISCUSSION (literary). Hoepffner 1908–21, 3:xxxviii (use of mythology); Poirion 1965, 611 (on simultaneous presentation of texts); Wolfzettel 1980 (*Ne quier*); Kooijman 1982, 43–44 (double ballade tradition); see also chap. 6.4, commentary to Lo225. Machaut tells of the genesis of B34 in the following *Voir Dit* passages: (a) Toute Belle writes in letter 32 that she found a ballade that someone sent to Guillaume (a possible reference to *Quant Theseüs*), mistakenly enclosed with his letter 31 to her (P. Paris 1875, 250); (b) Guillaume encloses the text of the two ballades in letter 35, with information on their origin, attributing *Quant Theseüs* to "T. Paien" (1875, 266); (c) Toute Belle's mention in letter 36 of "Thommas" may refer to T. Paien (1875, 268; but see Badel 1985, 552); (d) the narrative introduction to the ballades puts T. Paien's ballade in a more favorable light (ll. 6735–52; 1875, 273–74); (e) the texts of the two ballades are inserted in the narrative (ll. 6753–800; 1875, 274–76); (f) Guillaume expresses impatience in letter 37 (1875, 276–77) that Toute Belle has said nothing about the ballades, whose texts were already sent; the music is enclosed with the letter; (g) Toute Belle reviews the two ballades in letter 38, favoring Guillaume's effort (1875, 279). At least two other moments in the *Voir Dit* evoke B34: (a) the enumeration of some of the names that will appear in the ballade, e.g., Absalon (ll. 2000–2001; P. Paris 1875, 87); (b) mention of Medea and Jason in letter 40 (1875, 312). For excerpts from or commentary on these passages, see Ludwig 1926–54, 2:57b*–58a*; 1930, 270; Reaney 1958b, 46; S.J. Williams 1969, 438; 1977, 466 (with some translations); Cerquiglini 1978a, 72; Brownlee 1984, 140; Cerquiglini 1985b, 98–99, 167 n. 25; Newes 1991a, 69–70; Wimsatt 1991b, 181–82 (emphasizes that *Ne quier* is by Thomas Paien; there are palpable stylistic differences between the two ballades); Cerquiglini-Toulet 1993b, 62–63; Leech-Wilkinson 1993a, 57–58; 1993b, 125–26, 139. Concerning Thomas Paien, the author of the text of the ballade *Quant Theseüs*, see P. Paris 1875, 257, 274–76, 395 n. xlix, 400 n. lxix, 401 n. lxxii; Hanf 1898, 156; Chichmaref 1909, 1:lv; Ludwig 1926–54, 2:69*, note to p. 57*; Cerquiglini 1983b, 288 (Thomas Paien may be Eustache Deschamps); Leech-Wilkinson 1993b, 125 n. 96 (Paien died 30 December 1363). The opening line of *Ne quier* is a proverb (Hassell 1982, no. A11).

TEXTUAL LEGACY (France). Froissart, ballade *Ne quier veoir Medee ne Jason*, borrows the structure and refrain of B34 (ed. Patterson 1935, 2:64; Wilkins 1969a, 50–51 no. 36; McGregor 1975, 209–10 no. 6; Baudouin 1978, 11–12 no. 6 [see 105–7n.]; trans. Cerquiglini/ Berthelot 1987, 132–33 [modern French]; Wimsatt 1991b, 183; ed. and trans. Figg 1994b, 234–36; cited in Reaney 1958b, 47; Poirion 1965, 215–16; Günther 1972, 57). All three strophes begin "Ne quier veoir," and some of the same words and images in the Paien/Machaut ballades are borrowed, including "l'image que fist Pymalion" (cf. *Je puis trop* [B28]). Figg (1994b, 10) also notes a relationship to Froissart's ballade *J'ai tout veü quant j'ai veü ma dame* (ed. McGregor 1974, 234–35 no. 38; Baudouin 1978, 46–47 no. 38; ed. and trans. Figg 1994b, 250–51).

TEXTUAL LEGACY (England). Chaucer, *Book of the Duchess* (Wimsatt 1968, 161); ballade *Hyd, Absolon, thy gilte tresses clere* in the "Prologue" to the *Legend of Good Women* (Preston 1951, 623 n. 11; Wimsatt 1991b, 181–84 on the relation of both B34 and Froissart's ballade *Ne quier veoir* to Chaucer; see also Figg 1994b, 9–10).

EDITIONS OF MUSIC. Ludwig 1930, 270–72 (=1924 ed., 232–34); 1926–54, 1:40–42; Schrade 1956b, 3:124–27 (critical notes 1956c, 117–18); Wilkins 1969a, 152–55 no. 6 (after Schrade); Palisca 1980, 78–80 no. 20 (=1988 ed., 83–85 no. 24).

DISCUSSION (musical). Besseler 1927, 228 (stylistic comments); Ludwig 1930, 270; Perle 1948, 170–72 (free imitation of motives within and between the voices); Machabey 1955b, 2:48–49; Reaney 1955, 54–56 and 1960b, 27 (analysis of interlocking melodic motives in various voices); Günther 1957, 86–88 (motivic analysis); 1958, 35 n. 27 (*tempus* changes); 1960a (versions in **Ch** and **R**); Reaney 1968, 66–67 (close discussion of mm. 1 and 12: removing ornamental motives and syncopations reveals a clear contrapuntal progression); Dömling 1972, 303 (refrain); Kühn 1973, 159–63 (importance of underlying harmonic framework; the beginning of the refrain sums up the procedures of the entire chanson); Hirshberg 1973–74, 56 (refrain); Wilkins 1980a, 77; Angiolini 1987, 43–46 (polytextuality); Brown 1987, 83 n. 19 (manner of setting-off the refrain); Karp 1988, 75–76 (compositional priority of cantus 2); Berger 1992, 217–18 (solmization and text painting); Leech-Wilkinson 1993a, 57–59, 60–61 (simultaneous conception of parts; relationship to *Dix et sept* [R17], *Nes qu'on* [B33] and to Gloria and Credo of the Mass).

MUSICAL LEGACY. F. Andrieu, setting of Deschamps's double ballade *Armes, Amours / O fleur des fleurs* (Newes 1991a, 70); see chap. 7.4.

Quant vraie amour / O series / Super omnes speciosa (motet M17)

MANUSCRIPTS WITH TEXT AND MUSIC (all 3v: tr, mot, ten).

[1] **C** fols. 221v–222r no. 16	[5] **A** fols. 430v–431r no. 17
[3] **V g** fols. 276v–277r no. 17	[6] **G** fols. 118v–119r no. 17
[4] **B** fols. 274v–275r no. 17	[7] **E** fols. 136v–137r no. 9

EDITION OF TEXT. Chichmaref 1909, 2:516–17 no. 17.

TEXT STRUCTURE AND RELATIONSHIP TO ISORHYTHM. Both French triplum and Latin motetus exhibit regular correlation between text and *talea* structure (Besseler 1927, 224; Reichert 1956, 201; Reaney 1980a, 431–32). Günther (1957, 139; 1958, 33) considers only the triplum clear in this regard. See also Reichert 1956, 212, and ex. 11 (following p. 212) (entire motet); Clarkson 1971, 240 (quality of rhymes between triplum and motetus); Ziino 1978, 444, 446 (strophic structure of triplum).

Triplum: a a b a b   a a b a b   a a b a b   a a b a b   a a b a b   a a b a b   a:-*ée*, b:-*ie*
7'7'6'7'6'   7'7'6'7'6'   7'7'6'7'6'   7'7'6'7'6'   7'7'6'7'6'   7'7'6'7'6'

Motetus: a b a b a b a b a b a b a b   a:-*áta*, b:-*úram*
8686 8686 8686 8686

DISCUSSION (literary). Boogaard 1993b, 32, 33 and n. 58 (*Nature* and *Amour*).

LITERARY ANTECEDENTS. Boethius and *Roman de la Rose* (Boogaard 1993b, 33 n. 58).

TENOR SOURCE. *Super omnes speciosa* is from the mode 6 Marian antiphon *Ave regina caelorum* (Chichmaref 1909, 2:517n.; Ludwig 1926–54, 2:60a*, 3:64). The tenor of Vitry's *Vos / Gratissima* is from the same feast (Leech-Wilkinson 1982–83, 15 n. 25).

EDITIONS OF MUSIC. Ludwig 1926–54, 3:62–64 (criticism of Ludwig's analytical layout in Sanders 1973, 563 n. 286); Schrade 1956b, 3:1–3 (critical notes 1956c, 86). Barring discussed in Hoppin 1960, 25.

DISCUSSION (musical). Unipartite. Machabey 1955b, 2:96–98; Günther 1958, 34 (changes of *modus*); Pelinski 1975, 69 (harmonic structure articulated by sonorities of repose, or "Ruheklänge"); Fuller 1986, 45–46; Fuller 1990, 215–23 (tenor and tonal structure; discant reduction). On isomelism signaling each new *talea*, see Machabey 1955b, 2:97; Reichert 1956, 212; Günther 1958, 32; Reaney 1971, 53; Wernli 1977, 18–19; Ziino 1978, 447.

MUSICAL LEGACY. For a twentieth-century composition inspired by M17, see chap. 2.5 (Thiele).

Quant vrais amans. See *De triste* / *Quant* / *Certes* (ballade B29).

Quare non sum. See *He! Mors* / *Fine* (M3).

Qui bien aimme a tart oublie. *Le Lay de Plour* (lai L22; Schrade lai 16)

MANUSCRIPTS WITH TEXT AND MUSIC (all monophonic).[79]

[1]	**C**	fols. 187r–189r	no. 10	(has title, in lai section)
[3]	**V g**	fols. 87v–89v		(has title, after *Jugement Navarre*)
[4]	**B**	fols. 87v–89v (new 104v–106v)		(has title, after *Jugement Navarre*)
[5]	**A**	fols. 410v–412v	no. 22	(has title, in lai section as later addition)
[7]	**E**	fols. 57r–58r		(has title, after *Jugement Navarre*)

TEXT MANUSCRIPTS.

[10]	**M**	fols. 48v–49v		(has title, after *Jugement Navarre*)
[10]	**M**	fols. 221v–222v	no. 11	(has title, in lai section)
[15]	**K**	fols. 42r–42v		(has title; end of strophe 5–strophe 12)
[16]	**J**	fols. 45r–46r		

TREATISE. Baudet Herenc, *Doctrinal de la Secunde Retorique* (1432) (chap. 2.3.1d).

EDITIONS OF TEXT. Hoepffner 1908–21, 1:283–91; Chichmaref 1909, 2:459–66 no. 22.

DATE. ca. 1349 (see chap. 5.6 on date of *Jugement Navarre*; Günther 1963a, 100; Huot 1987, 265–66). The *Lay de Plour* appears in MSS **Vg**, **B**, **M**, and **E** immediately after *Jugement Navarre*, promised in the last four lines (ll. 4209–12) as partial fulfillment of the *amende*, and thus apparently written after *Jugement Navarre* was completed; the lai nevertheless appears in MS **C**, which lacks *Jugement Navarre*. (On the later manuscript tradition removing L22 from proximity to *Jugement Navarre*, see Palmer 1993b, 303–4.) Written for a lady grieving over her lover's coffin, precisely the character "wronged" by the unfavorable judgment in *Jugement Behaingne*, the *Lay de Plour* perfectly atones for Machaut's earlier judgment against the lady (Hoepffner 1908–21, 1:lxxxviii). Although the lai may antedate the composition of *Jugement Navarre*, surely its composition is connected to the artistic decision to reverse the judgment of the earlier *dit*. The lai also appears in MSS **K** and **J**, this time following the *Jugement Behaingne*. A miniature in MS **J** (see chap. 4.4s, miniature J4) effectively illustrates the lai: a figure in a black robe with black hood—the lady mourning her dead lover—sits on a small wooden bench next to a black-draped coffin. Wimsatt and Kibler (1988, 33) consider the lai a reference to the death of Bonne of Luxembourg (see also Butterfield 1994, 16).

On the curious musical notation of the last strophe of the *Lay de Plour*, which argues for a date very close to the time of the copying of MS **C**, see below, musical discussion.

TEXT STRUCTURE. 12 strophes, 210 lines:

1a. $\frac{abba}{7'777}$ ǀ $\frac{abba}{7'777}$ ‖ 1b. same ‖

2a. $\frac{ccd}{884}$ ǀ $\frac{ccd}{884}$ ‖ 2b. same ‖

3a. $\frac{eefg}{7'7'74}$ ǀ $\frac{eefg}{7'7'74}$ ‖ 3b. same ‖

4a. $\frac{hhi}{5'5'5}$ ǀ $\frac{hhi}{5'5'5}$ ‖ 4b. same ‖

5a. $\frac{jjkkjjkkj}{774747474}$ ‖ 5b. same ‖

6a. $\frac{1\ 1\ mmn}{10'10'4\ 3\ 3}$ ǀ $\frac{1\ 1\ mmn}{10'10'4\ 3\ 3}$ ‖ 6b. same ‖

7a. $\frac{ooooр}{55575}$ ǀ $\frac{ooooр}{55575}$ ‖ 7b. same ‖

8a. $\frac{q\ rrssqqqrrsssq}{73447434474344}$ ‖ 8b. same ‖

9a. $\frac{tttu}{3'3'7'5}$ ǀ $\frac{tttu}{3'3'7'5}$ ‖ 9b. same ‖

10a. $\frac{vvvw}{7'5'7'7}$ ǀ $\frac{vvvw}{7'5'7'7}$ ‖ 10b. same ‖

11a. $\frac{xxxxy}{45335}$ ǀ $\frac{xxxxy}{45335}$ ‖ 11b. same ‖

12a–b. = 1a–b.

---

[79] Ehrhart's comments on manuscript order (1974, 207–9) are not borne out by the chronology of the manuscripts; see also Huot 1987, 266.

a:-*ie*, b:-*art*, c:-*er*, d:-*ine*, e:-*eure*, f:-*ir*, g:-*uit*, h:-*ure*, i:-*oir*, j:-*ent*, k:-*our*, l:-*ointe*, m:-*ier*, n:-*oit*, o:-*ort*, p:-*i*, q:-*ueil*, r:-*aint*, s:-*oy*, t:-*ire*, u:-*einne*, v:-*ance*, w:-*ay*, x:-*is*, y:-*ient*

DISCUSSION (literary). The incipit is a proverb (see Spanke 1929, 183–84; Van den Boogaard 1969, refrain no. 1585; Speroni 1977, 119; Hassell 1982, no. A63; it also appears in the *Roman de Cardenois* [chap. 3, MS [43], item f]. Among Machaut's works, it also appears in *He! Mors / Fine* (M3), triplum l. 39 (Ludwig 1926–54, 2:34*, 3:12, 4:74); in the *Remede*, l. 4256/4258 (cf. Poirion 1965, 201 n. 28, whose assertion on the dating of the *Remede* seems unsupportable, since the text is a proverb; B. and J. Cerquiglini 1976, 367); in the *Voir Dit*, letter 10 (ed. P. Paris 1875, 67), letter 30 (ed. 1875, 238), and in l. 7357 (ed. 1875, 299); see the discussion in B. and J. Cerquiglini 1976, 363, 370; Imbs 1991, 124. On the grouping of the *Lay Mortel, Un mortel lay* (L12/8) with L22, see Poirion 1965, 418–19; Huot 1987, 266 n. 22. Further literary discussion in Hoepffner 1908–21, 1:lxxxvii–lxxxix; Luttrell 1965, 173; Sonnemann 1969, 99–101; Calin 1974, 126; de Looze 1988, 206; Palmer 1988, xxxvii–xxxviii, xliii; 1993b, 293–94, 296, 300–304; Calin 1994, 298, 299–300. Feminine voice.

TEXTUAL LEGACY (France). On Deschamps's *Lay de Plour*, see chap. 2.1.1n. Christine de Pizan, *C. ballades*, no. 55 (ed. M. Roy 1886–91, 1:56; cited in Poirion 1965, 249, n. 35). For other citations of the proverb in French poets, see Hassell 1982, no. A63.

TEXTUAL LEGACY (England). Chaucer, *Anelida and Arcite* (Braddy 1968, 129; Benson 1987, 991b). Several manuscripts of Chaucer's *Parliament of Fowls* have a rubric indicating that the music for the final *roundel, Now welcome, somer, with thy sonne softe*, set according to l. 677 to French music ("The note, I trowe, imaked was in Fraunce"), was *Qui bien aime a tard oublie* (see F.N. Robinson 1957, 796 n. to l. 677; Wilkins 1979, 121; Wimsatt 1978, 66; Benson 1987, 1002 n. to l. 677). The most important commentary on the passage is in Ludwig 1926–54, 2:33b*–34a*, with a complete bibliography of musical material—besides the lai of Machaut—that has been found to accompany these words. None of the settings fits the metrics of Chaucer's *roundel*, however. For other citations of the proverb in English poets, see Hassell 1982, no. A63.

EDITIONS OF MUSIC. Ludwig 1926–54, 4:74–76 (ed. Besseler); Schrade 1956b, 2:90–93 (critical notes 1956c, 69–70). The music of strophes 1 and 12 is the same, except that strophe 12 is a perfect fifth higher.

LITERARY AND MUSICAL ANTECEDENT. The remarks of Schrade (1958–61, 848–49) do not apply to L22, but rather to *Malgré Fortune* (L19/14), the other *Lay de Plour*. Cf. R.1188 (Moniot d'Arras), *Qui bien aime a tart oublie / Por ce ne puis oublier / La douce virge Marie*, in four sources with three melodies.

DISCUSSION (musical). Machabey 1955b, 1:120–21 (beginning of strophe 4). An irregularity in the musical text of L22 in MS C may indicate that it was a recent composition at the time it was copied into the manuscript. Most of the music for the last strophe is lacking, because the text scribe had entered only the first few words in a manner that allowed room above for the staff. The rest of the final strophe was entered as a text residuum, without music. No other lai in any Machaut manuscript is notated in this manner, which on the face of it would seem to be a sensible notational shorthand, since the music of the last strophe is identical to that for the first, except for the transposition of the music up a fifth. All this implies a clear knowledge of the lai form, and one could speculate that this is evidence of a copy from a very early redaction of the lai, perhaps even from the composer's "autograph." This irregularity argues against the idea of S.J. Williams (1969, 452; see also Keitel 1977a, 471) that L22 was an early work, attached to *Jugement Navarre* as an afterthought.

Qui es promesses / Ha! Fortune / Et non est qui adjuvet (motet M8)

MANUSCRIPTS WITH TEXT AND MUSIC.

[1]	C	fols. 212v–213r	no. 7	3v (tr, mot, ten)
[3]	V g	fols. 267v–268r	no. 8	3v (tr, mot, ten)
[4]	B	fols. 265v–266r	no. 8	3v (tr, mot, ten)
[5]	A	fols. 421v–422r	no. 8	3v (tr, mot, ten)
[6]	G	fols. 109v–110r	no. 8	3v (tr, mot, ten)
[7]	E	fol. 133r	no. 4	3v (tr, mot, ten)

[56] **CaB**	fol. 16v	no. 26	3v (tr, mot, ten)[80]
[57] **Iv**	fols. 24v–25r	no. 41	3v (tr, mot, ten)
[58] **Trém**	fol. viii	no. 13	(tr, ten)[81]

TEXT MANUSCRIPT.

[46] **St**	fol. 138v	nos. 84–84*bis* [82]

TREATISE. *Ars nova* in the version of *F:Pn 14741* (ed. Reaney/ Gilles/Maillard 1964, 32 §10), as an example of *tempus imperfectum prolatio minor*. This manuscript belonged formerly to the library of the Abbey of St-Victor in Paris. See discussion in Earp 1983, 328; 1989, 495.

FACSIMILES. Droz/Thibault 1926 (MS **Trém**); Lerch 1987, 1:202 (MS **CaB**).

EDITIONS OF TEXT. Chichmaref 1909, 2:497–98 no. 8.

TRANSLATIONS. Lerner 1968, 45–46; Hoppin 1978b, 138–39 (complete); Wimsatt 1979, 123 (triplum, ll. 7–8); Allorto 1983, 157 (Italian); Wimsatt 1991b, 130 (triplum, ll. 7–10); see also discography (chap. 8.3 and 8.8).

DATE. Günther (1958, 30) considers the short *talea* a characteristic of early motets.

TEXT STRUCTURE AND RELATIONSHIP TO ISORHYTHM. Both triplum and motetus exhibit regular correlation between text and *talea* structure (Reichert 1956, 201; Ziino 1978, 447). The text strophes define a "Grosstalea," comprising three tenor *taleae* (Sanders 1973, 558 n. 257; Hoppin 1978b, 413; Sanders 1980, 352). See also Clarkson 1971, 239 ("dissonant rhyme structure" of both texts); 1971, 248 (strophic structure of motetus).

Triplum[83]:
$$\begin{array}{cccccccccccccccccccc} \text{a} & \text{b} & \text{a} & \text{c} & \text{d} & \text{b} & \text{d} & \text{c} & \text{c} & \text{c} & \text{c} & \text{c} & \text{c} & \text{c} & \text{c} & \text{c} & \text{c} & \text{c} & \text{c} & \text{c} \\ 4'6' & 4'6' & 46' & 46' & 10' & 10'10'10'10' & & & & & 10'10'10'10'10' & & & & & 10'10'10'10'10' & & & & \end{array}$$

a:-*esses*, b:-*ie*, c:-[e]*ure*, d:-*oit*

If the internal rhymes at the caesuras in ll. 1–8 are removed, isometric decasyllabic lines emerge: 10'a†b†abb bbbbb bbbbb bbbbb a:-*ie*, b:-*ure*
Motetus: 10a†bab abab abab a:-*ort*, b:-*on* (†: epic caesura)

DISCUSSION (literary). Patch 1923, 23 n. 91; 1927, 50 n. 2, 56 n. 2, 65n., 101 n. 4, 119 n. 1; and Calin 1974, 244 (theme of Fortune); Kelly 1978, 284 n. 50 (interpretation of triplum, ll. 9–13); Mathews 1982 (musical setting renders poetry unintelligible); Markstrom 1989, 32 n. 96 (isorhythmic structure symbolically represents the Wheel of Fortune); Brownlee 1991b, 14 (thematic relationship of tenor to upper voices). Hassell (1982, no. F132) indexes a proverb in the triplum.

TEXTUAL LEGACY (England). Chaucer, *Book of the Duchess* (Kittredge 1915c, 10–12; Wimsatt 1968, 159–60; 1979, 123; 1991b, 130–31).

TENOR SOURCE. *Et non est qui adjuvet* (Psalm 21 [22]:12) is from the end of the verse *Quoniam tribulatio* of the mode 2 Responsory for Passion Sunday, *Circumdederunt me mendaces viri* (Ludwig 1926–54, 2:60a*, 3:32, 78); Machaut used the same tenor in *Christe / Veni* (M21).

EDITIONS OF MUSIC. Ludwig 1926–54, 3:30–32; Schrade 1956b, 2:134–36 (critical notes 1956c, 79–80); Lerner 1968, 45–48 no. 27; Hoppin 1978a, 134–39 no. 61; Lerch 1987, 2:216–19 (critical notes pp. 220–21) (CaB); Brandt 1980, 62–66; Allorto 1983, 33–34 no. 45. Further discussion of variants in Earp 1983, 327–41; 1989, 493–97.

DISCUSSION (musical). Unipartite. Machabey 1955b, 2:80–82; Crocker 1966, 122 and Lerch 1987, 1:118 (text painting in tenor); Lerner 1968, 45–46 (analysis); Dobrzańska 1979b, 52–54 (figure vertically aligning *taleae* 1–2); Lerch 1987, 1:115–18 (analysis); Hughes 1989, 355–57 (analysis); Danckwardt 1993, 372–74, 381–82 (compositional procedure). On isomelism at *talea*-ends, see Machabey 1955b, 2:81; Reichert 1956, 212; Günther 1957,

---

[80] Foliation and number after Lerch 1987, 1:167.

[81] Triplum and tenor survive on fol. 8r; the motetus is lost.

[82] *Tresble Guillaume de Machaut* (reading of Piaget/Droz 1932, 251); *Tresble Guillaume de Marchant* (reading of Stephens 1847, 171).

[83] Such irregularities in the rhyme scheme of the triplum are also seen in *Trop ay dure destinee / Par sauvage* (ed. F.Ll. Harrison 1968, 104–7 no. 20); see Leech-Wilkinson 1989, 1:199.

138–39; 1958, 32; Ziino 1978, 447 (cf. *De Bon Espoir / Puis que* [M4] and *Quant vraie amour / O series* [M17]). Sections of syncopation serve the same articulative purpose as hocket sections in many other motets. The first syncopation section begins with l. 5, "Que pour li soit en riens ferme ou seüre" [that for him (Lady Fortune) will be at all firm or steadfast], suggesting that the recurrent syncopated musical structure may have been set up as a musical response to this first "strophe" only, providing a rare analogue among the motets to a common occurrence in the secular songs, in which the music best fits the first strophe of text.

MUSICAL LEGACY. Relationship to *Zolomina / Nazarea* (ed. F.Ll. Harrison 1968, 62–65 no. 10) discussed in Leech-Wilkinson 1982–83, 12, 17; relationship to *Trop ay dure destinee / Par sauvage* (ed. F.Ll. Harrison 1968, 104–7 no. 20; Leech-Wilkinson 1989, 2:94–95) discussed in Leech-Wilkinson 1982–83, 17; 1989, 1:199–200; relationship to *Degentis vita / Cum vix artidici* (ed. Günther 1965, 4–7 no. 2; F.Ll. Harrison 1968, 116–27 nos. 23–23a) discussed in Earp 1983, 328; 1989, 495.

Qui n'aroit autre deport. [*Lay de Bon Espoir*] (lai RF1; Schrade lai 19)
MANUSCRIPTS WITH TEXT AND MUSIC (all monophonic).

[1]	**C**	fols. 26r–28r	[6]	**F**	fols. 42r–43v
[3]	**V g**	fols. 92v–95r	[7]	**E**	fols. 23r–24v
[4]	**B**	fols. 92v–95r (new 109v–112r)	[20]	**Pe**	fol. 4r–6r
[5]	**A**	fols. 52r–54r			

TEXT MANUSCRIPTS.

[10]	**M**	fols. 52v–54r		[18]	**Pm**	fols. 50r–51v	
[15]	**K**	fols. 45r–45v	(has title) (str. 1–6)	[43]	**Mn**	fols. 6r–8r	no. 2[84]
[16]	**J**	fols. 49v–50r	(has title) (str. 1–6)				

FACSIMILES (refer to chap. 4.4e). Miniature C12. Ludwig 1911, 25 (appendix; beginning in MSS A and E).

EDITIONS OF TEXT (*Remede*, ll. 431–680). Hoepffner 1908–21, 3:16–25; Wimsatt/Kibler 1988, 191–207.

TRANSLATIONS. Kelly 1978, 52–53 (passage from strophe 1); Switten 1988c, 23–29; Wimsatt/Kibler 1988, 190–206; see also discography (chap. 8.3 and 8.8).

TEXT STRUCTURE. 12 strophes, 250 lines[85]:

1a. $\dfrac{\text{a bbc c aaab bccca}}{7344\ 74344\ 74344}$ ‖ 1b. same ‖

2a. $\dfrac{\text{d ddd e}}{84488},\dfrac{\text{d ddd e}}{84488}$ ‖ 2b. same ‖

3a. $\dfrac{\text{f f f g}}{5'5'7'5},\dfrac{\text{f f f g}}{5'5'7'5}$ ‖ 3b. same ‖

4a. $\dfrac{\text{h hhh i}}{45335},\dfrac{\text{h hhh i}}{45335}$ ‖ 4b. same ‖

5a. $\dfrac{\text{j j j k}}{7774},\dfrac{\text{j j j k}}{7774}$ ‖ 5b. same ‖

6a. $\dfrac{\text{1 1 1 1 1 1 m}}{8'4'8'4'8'4'8},\dfrac{\text{1 1 1 1 1 1 m}}{8'4'8'4'8'4'8}$ ‖ 6b. same ‖

7a. $\dfrac{\text{n n n oo}}{3'3'7'34},\dfrac{\text{n n n oo}}{3'3'7'34}$ ‖ 7b. same ‖

8a. $\dfrac{\text{p p qp}}{5'5'55},\dfrac{\text{p p qp}}{5'5'55}$ ‖ 8b. same ‖

9a. $\dfrac{\text{r rrr s}}{55575},\dfrac{\text{r rrr s}}{55575}$ ‖ 9b. same ‖

10a. $\dfrac{\text{t t t t t u}}{444486},\dfrac{\text{t t t t t u}}{444486}$ ‖ 10b. same ‖

11a. $\dfrac{\text{v v w}}{8'8'8},\dfrac{\text{v v v w}}{8'8'8'8}$ ‖ 11b. same ‖

12a–b. = 1a–b.

a:-*ort*, b:-*er*, c:-*ir*, d:-*ier*, e:-*ance*, f:-*ée*, g:-*ient*, h:-*oy*, i:-*ai*, j:-*ueil*, k:-*ist*, l:-*iere*, m:-*ien*, n:-*oie*, o:-*our*, p:-*elle*, q:-*oir*, r:-*ri*, s:-*ire*, t:-*ment*, u:-*ie*, v:-*aille*, w:-*art*

DISCUSSION (literary). Poirion 1965, 400–401; 1971, 194–95; Kelly 1978, 102–3, 132–35; Huot 1987, 250–51; Davis 1991, 85–90; Imbs 1991, 119; Calin 1994, 200–201. A passage in *Confort* possibly refers to RF1 as the *Lay de Bon Espoir* (see commentary below

---

[84] Begins with *Et pour ce sans nul descour*, strophe 12 of the lai (lacking the last 12 lines), followed by strophes 1–11; ed. Cocco 1975, 52–59.

[85] See also Poirion 1965, 396–97.

to *S'onques* [L17/12]). For some literary studies that deal with all of the inserted lyrics, see chap. 5.7, literary and musical discussions.

EDITIONS OF MUSIC. Ludwig 1911, 1–8 (appendix); 1926–54, 1:93–95 (criticism in Machabey 1955b, 1:114–15, n. 318); Wooldridge 1932, 309 (ed. Westrup; strophe 1 only); Schrade 1956b, 2:102–5 (critical notes 1956c, 72–73); Switten 1988c, 19–23 (after Schrade); Wimsatt/Kibler 1988, 416–22, critical notes pp. 434–37 (ed. Baltzer).

DISCUSSION (musical). Ludwig 1911, 411–12; Machabey 1955b, 1:113–15 (rhythmic correspondences), 1:125–26 (text setting); Poirion 1965, 400; Mulder 1978, 96–98 (motivic analysis; rhythmic materials of *Qui n'aroit* (RF1), *Tels rit* (RF2) and *Joie, plaisence* (RF3) are similar), 122–23 (number symbolism, Marian image); Malizia 1984, 21–25 (general); J. Stevens 1984, 117–18 (opening figure rarely repeats a rhythm literally; changes of mode; tessitura). For some musical studies that deal with all of the inserted lyrics, see chap. 5.7.

Qui plus aimme. See *Aucune / Qui plus* (M5).

Quia amore langueo. See *Maugré mon cuer / De ma dolour* (M14).

Remede de Fortune. See *Dame, a vous* (virelai RF6); *Dame, de qui* (ballade RF5); *Dame, mon cuer en vous* (rondeau RF7); *En amer* (ballade RF4); *Joie, plaisance* (*chant royal* RF3); *Qui n'aroit* (lai RF1); *Tels rit* (*complainte* RF2).

Riches d'amour et mendians d'amie (ballade B5)
Refrain: *Quant ma dame me het et je l'aour*
MANUSCRIPTS WITH TEXT AND MUSIC.

[1] C	fols. 159v–160r	no. 5	2v (ca, ten; empty staves for tr)
[3] V g	fol. 298v	no. 5	2v (ca, ten; empty staves for tr)
[4] B	fol. 296v	no. 5	2v (ca, ten; empty staves for tr)
[5] A	fol. 456r	no. 5	2v (ca, ten)
[6] G	fol. 135v	no. 5	2v (ca, ten)
[7] E	fol. 153v	no. 2	2v (ca, ten)

TEXT MANUSCRIPTS.

| [10] M | fol. 237v | no. 5 | [50] Pa | fols. 50r–50v | no. 154 |
| [42] Mn | fols. 29r–29v | no. 7 | | | |

EDITIONS OF TEXT. Tarbé 1849, 59–60; Chichmaref 1909, 2:539–40 no. 5.

TRANSLATIONS. Flores 1962, 153 (by William M. Davis); Greckel 1981, 93 (from Flores 1962); see also discography (chap. 8.3 and 8.8).

TEXT STRUCTURE. 3 strophes: $\begin{smallmatrix} a & b & a & b & b & c & C \\ 10'10 & 10'10 & 101010 \end{smallmatrix}$ a:-*ie*, b:-*ir*, c:-*our*

DISCUSSION (literary). Audbourg-Popin 1986, especially for ll. 1–4.

TEXTUAL LEGACY (France). Froissart, *Rices d'espoir, vuis de toute ignorance* (ballade refrain, ed. McGregor 1975, 214–15 no. 12; Baudouin 1978, 19–20 no. 12; cited in Poirion 1965, 215). Alain Chartier, rondeau *Riche d'espoir et pouvre d'autre bien* (ed. Laidlaw 1974, 377 no. 7; cited in Audbourg-Popin 1986, 97 n.1).

EDITIONS OF MUSIC. Ludwig (1926–54), 1:5 ; Schrade 1956b, 3:76 (critical notes 1956c, 101); Wilkins 1980b, 27–28 (Chaucer, *I, which that am* underlaid).

DISCUSSION (musical). Machabey 1955b, 2:22 (rhythmic correspondence); Salop 1971, 66 (word painting), 70 (melodic planning); Audbourg-Popin 1986 (detailed discussion of text and music); Wilson 1990b, 351–54 (compositional procedure).

Rose, lis, printemps, verdure (rondeau R10)
MANUSCRIPTS WITH TEXT AND MUSIC.

[1] C	fols. 205v–206r	no. 9	3v (ca, ten, ct; room for tr; 2nd ct added below)[86]
[3] V g	fol. 319r	no. 10	4v (tr, ca, ten, ct)
[4] B	fol. 318r	no. 10	4v (tr, ca, ten, ct)
[5] A	fol. 478r	no. 11	4v (tr, ca, ten, ct)
[6] G	fol. 151v	no. 9	4v (tr, ca, ten, ct)
[7] E	fol. 132r	no. 1	4v (tr, ca, ten, ct)

---

[86] The added contratenor is not authentic. Discussed in Harden 1983, chap. 7.

TEXT MANUSCRIPT.
[10] **M**   fol. 244v   no. 10
FACSIMILES. Wolf 1904, 2:38 no. 20 (diplomatic facs., MS **G**).
EDITIONS OF TEXT. Chichmaref 1909, 2:572 no. 9; Wilkins 1969a, 33 no. 23, notes p. 126.
TRANSLATIONS. Leech-Wilkinson 1984, 12–13; see also discography (chap. 8.3 and 8.8).
TEXT STRUCTURE. $\dfrac{\text{ABB}}{7'77} \dfrac{\text{abAB}}{7'77'7} \dfrac{\text{abb}}{7'77} \dfrac{\text{ABB}}{7'77}$ a:-*ure*, b:-*our*

DISCUSSION (literary). Reaney 1958a, 51 (number symbolism at the beginning, where seven beauties of Spring are listed); Poirion 1965, 319, 323 (effect of thirteen-line form; possible religious image in music).
EDITIONS OF MUSIC. Wolf 1904, 3:61–62 no. 20 (errors); Combarieu 1913, 395–96 (errors); Ludwig 1926–54, 1:60–61 (errors); Schrade 1956b, 3:152–53 (errors; critical notes 1956c, 129–30); Brandt 1980, 71–73; Kamien 1984, 10–11 no. 5; Leech-Wilkinson 1984, 14–17 (correct); Lincoln/Bonta 1986, 53–54 no. 20. Wolf (1904, 1:168–70) and Ludwig (1904–5, 621) discuss transcription problems; Hoppin (1960, 20–23) discusses errors in earlier editions and notational variants in the triplum.
DISCUSSION (musical). Combarieu 1913, 393–98 (style, performance practice); Besseler 1931, 139–40 (aesthetic effect is one of enchantment); Machabey 1955b, 1:160–61; Wykes 1956, 68–76 (analysis); Günther 1957, 106 (motivic analysis); Dömling 1970, 78–79 (triplum essential); Mulder 1978, 85–87 (motivic analysis and symbolism); Leech-Wilkinson 1984 (thorough analysis); Page 1990, 82 (Pythagorean intonation); 1993, 163, 165, 167, 169 (rondeau form).
MUSICAL LEGACY. For twentieth-century compositions inspired by R10, see chap. 2.5 (Bourcier, Hand, and Sciarrino).

Ruina. See *Tant doucement m' ont / Eins* (M13).

S'Amours ne fait par sa grace adoucir (ballade B1)
Refrain: *Qu' en ma dolour languir jusqu' a la mort*
MANUSCRIPTS WITH TEXT AND MUSIC (all 2v: ca, ten).

[1] **C** fols. 157v–158r	no. 1	[5] **A** fol. 454r	no. 1
[3] **V g** fol. 296v	no. 1	[6] **G** fol. 134r	no. 1
[4] **B** fol. 294v	no. 1	[7] **E** fol. 147r	no. 1

TEXT MANUSCRIPT.
[10] **M**   fol. 237r   no. 1
FACSIMILES (refer to chap. 4.4u). Miniature A154. For the music, see Wolf 1904, 2:40–41 no. 23 (diplomatic facs., MS **G**); Machabey 1960, 1391–92 (MS **A**, miniature A154, including the first two lines of music); Poirion 1971, pl. 22 (MS **A**, miniature A154, including most of the music).
EDITION OF TEXT. Chichmaref 1909, 2:537 no. 1.
TEXT STRUCTURE. 3 strophes: 10ab ab bcC a:-*ir*, b:-*és*, c:-*ort*
EDITIONS OF MUSIC. Bottée de Toulmon [1846]b, 1; Wolf 1904, 3:66–67 no. 23; Riemann 1905, 338–40 (after Wolf, but all melismas are considered instrumental, a practice rejected in Machabey 1955b, 2:46 n. 488); Ludwig 1926–54, 1:1; Schrade 1956b, 3:68–69 (critical notes 1956c, 99); Wilkins 1980b, 5–6 (Chaucer, *To you, my purse* underlaid).
DISCUSSION (musical). Wolf 1904, 1:172 (on Machaut's "notational license"); Riemann 1905, 337, 340 ("one seeks in vain among Machaut's 3- and 4v works for anything similarly enjoyable"); Schering 1911–12, 180 (simplified harmonic reduction); Machabey 1955b, 2:18–19; Salop 1971, 52–53 (melodic direction in cantus); 58–59 (melodic strategies that contribute to word painting); Kühn 1973, 74–75 (melodic construction, not contrapuntal construction, is the basis for consonance and dissonance in this work); Lühmann 1978, 121–22 (declamation); Saponov 1978, 25 (*talea* structure); Apfel 1982, 88–89 (harmonic reduction); Arlt 1982, 229 and Günther 1982, 112 (on the location of B1 first in the series of ballades); Dahlhaus 1982 (dissonance treatment compared to a passage in *Biauté qui* [B4]).

S'Amours tous amans. See *S'il estoit / S'Amours* (M6).

S'il estoit nulz / S'Amours / Et gaudebit cor vestrum (motet M6)

MANUSCRIPTS WITH TEXT AND MUSIC (all 3v: tr, mot, ten).

[1] **C**	fols. 210v–211r	no. 5	[5] **A**	fols. 419v–420r	no. 6
[3] **V g**	fols. 265v–266r	no. 6	[6] **G**	fols. 107v–108r	no. 6
[4] **B**	fols. 263v–264r	no. 6	[7] **E**	fol. 136v	no. 8

EDITION OF TEXT. Chichmaref 1909, 2:493–94 no. 6.

TRANSLATION. Davison/Apel 1949, 245 no. 44; Boogaart 1993a, 6; see also discography (chap. 8.3 and 8.8).

TEXT STRUCTURE AND RELATIONSHIP TO ISORHYTHM. Both triplum and motetus exhibit regular correlation between text and *talea* structure (Besseler 1927, 224; Reichert 1956, 201). The triplum text is shifted three breve measures in relation to the isorhythm, and this staggered phrasing is compensated by a *talea* fragment of three breve measures at the end of the *integer valor* section and at the end of the diminution section. Reichert (1956, 208, ex. 10 facing p. 209) analyzes the phrase overlap in terms of the text; Wernli (1977, 18) notes that the extra measures allow full recurrence of upper-voice isorhythmic passages at the end of the motet, needed since the tenor's rhythmic patterns differ in the second half. See also Clarkson 1971, 264 (strophic structure of motetus); Ziino 1978, 443, 444–45 (strophic structure of triplum).

Triplum:
a a b* c c b d d b e e b f f b g g b
101010' 101010' 101010' 101010' 10'10'10' 101010'

a:-*eüst*, b:-*aire*, c:-*er*, d:-*ir*, e:-*on*, f:-*eüsse*, g:-*pité* (*: epic caesura)

Motetus: 7abab baab baab a a:-*ir*, b:-*oit*

DISCUSSION (literary). Poirion 1965, 611 (theme of tenor); Boogaart 1993a (full analysis).

TENOR SOURCE. *Et gaudebit cor vestrum* is not from the Alleluia *Non vos relinquam*, but from the final melisma of the *repetenda* of the mode 8 Responsory *Sicut mater consolatur* (Isaia 66:13–14) for the second Sunday of Advent (Anderson 1976, 122, 126). The indication of the tenor source in Chichmaref (1909, 494n.) is incorrect.

EDITIONS OF MUSIC. Ludwig 1926–54, 3:24–26; Davison/Apel 1949, 46–48 no. 44; Schrade 1956b, 2:127–29 (critical notes 1956c, 78); Hamburg 1976, 17–19 no. 22; Boogaart 1993a, 14–17 (analytical edition).

MUSICAL ANTECEDENTS. Philippe de Vitry, *Tuba / In arboris* (Crocker 1966, 121–22).

DISCUSSION (musical). Bipartite without diminution. Contrast results from beginning the tenor repeat on a different "beat," resulting in changes of rhythm due to differences in imperfection and alteration. Gombosi 1950, 220–21 (symmetrical construction of the tenor rhythm, criticized in Günther 1957, 133 n. 97; 1958, 30 n. 16; cf. also Dömling 1971, 26 n. 9); Machabey 1955b, 2:77–79; Günther 1958, 30 (unipartite analysis); Apel 1959 (brief analysis); Sanders 1973, 562–63 n. 279 (phrase structure; not unipartite as Günther argues); Powell 1979, 242–52 (Gombosi's suggestions carried to an extreme); Wernli 1977, 16–19 (strophic nature of the motet is perceptible; six instead of eight *taleae*); Boogaart 1993a (full analysis of text and music relationships).

S'onques dolereusement. Le Lay de Confort (lai L17; Schrade lai 12)

MANUSCRIPTS WITH TEXT AND MUSIC (all monophonic; presumably 3v canons intended for all strophes).

[3] **V g**	fols. 253v–256v	no. 17	[6] **G**	fols. 94v–96r	no. 17 (has title)
[4] **B**	fols. 251v–254v	no. 17	[7] **E**	fols. 121r–122v	no. 13 (has title)
[5] **A**	fols. 399r–401r	no. 17			

TEXT MANUSCRIPTS.

[10] **M**	fols. 230v–232r	no. 17	[16] **J**	fols. 141v–143r	no. 2
[15] **K**	fols. 127r–127v	no. 2 (frag.)	[50] **Pa**	fols. 57v–59r	no. 182

EDITION OF TEXT. Chichmaref 1909, 2:415–24 no. 17.

TRANSLATIONS. Wimsatt (1975, 18–23) gives a summary of the entire lai, and complete translations of strophes 1, 3, 5, 7, and 12; a few of these segments are also in Wimsatt 1991b, 113–14; see also discography (chap. 8.3 and 8.8).

DATE. Machaut's *Confort* refers the reader to the *Remede* (l. 2248) or to a "*Lay de Bon Espoir*" (l. 2249), a title close to the "*Lay de Bonne Esperance*," *Longuement* (L18/13=

372   THE MUSIC

VD47) in the *Voir Dit* (cf. Kelly 1978, 288 n. 59). But since the lover in L17 is referred to as being in prison (l. 262), Hoepffner (1908–21, 3:249–50, note to *Confort* l. 2249) linked L17, not *Longuement* (L18/13), to the *Confort*, written for King Charles II of Navarre during his incarceration (1356–57). According to Hoepffner, Machaut then would have changed the title of L17 to one that makes its connection to the *Confort* explicit, while neglecting to change the title in the *Confort* citation. L17 has on these grounds been dated ca. 1356–57 (accepted in Poirion 1965, 409; Wimsatt 1975, 14, 18; Reaney 1967, 90, 95; and Kügle 1991, 381–82). Literary scholars have not commented on Ludwig's note (1926–54, 2:14a* n. 1) that the lai of the *Remede* is entitled *Lay de Bon Espoir* in MSS **K** and **J**. Contrary to Ludwig's view, it seems to me quite possible that Machaut was referring to the lai of the *Remede* in the *Confort* citation, making in effect a double reference to the *Remede* at that point. Wimsatt (1991b, 129) suggests that Machaut sent the lai to the duke of Berry in London in the early 1360s, as a lament of the duke's new wife Jeanne d'Armagnac.

TEXT STRUCTURE. 12 strophes, 272 lines:

1a. $\frac{\text{a a b b a a b b a}}{774747474}$ ‖ 1b. same ‖

7a. $\frac{\text{n n o n n o n n o n n o}}{7'7'3\ 7'7'3\ 7'7'3\ 7'7'3}$ ‖ 7b. same ‖

2a. $\frac{\text{c d d e e c c c d d e e e c}}{73447434474344}$ ‖ 2b. same ‖

8a. $\frac{\text{p p p p q p p p p q}}{75335'\ 75335'}$ ‖ 8b. same ‖

3a. $\frac{\text{f f f f f g f f f f f g}}{8444486'\ 8444486'}$ ‖ 3b. same ‖

9a. $\frac{\text{r r s r r s r r s r r s}}{7'7'5'\ 7'7'5'\ 7'7'5'\ 7'7'5'}$ ‖ 9b. same ‖

4a. $\frac{\text{h i h i i h i i h i}}{7'57'577'757'5}$ ‖ 4b. same ‖

10a. $\frac{\text{t t t t t t t t t t}}{44448\ 44448}$ ‖ 10b. same ‖

5a. $\frac{\text{j k j k j k j k}}{77'\ 77'\ 77'\ 77'}$ ‖ 5b. same ‖

11a. $\frac{\text{u u v u u v v v u v v u}}{433\ 433\ 433\ 433}$ ‖ 11b. same ‖

6a. $\frac{\text{l l l m l l l m m m m l m m m l}}{5'5'5'5\ 5'5'5'5\ 5'5'5'5\ 5'5'5'5}$ ‖ 6b. same ‖

12a–b. = 1a–b.

a:-*ent*, b:-*on*, c:-*ueil*, d:-*é*, e:-*art*, f:-*ist*, g:-*ie*, h:-*ie*, i:-*ust*, j:-*ort*, k:-*orte*, l:-*ire*, m:-*our*, n:-*ence* [-*ance*], o:-*oir*, p:-*er*, q:-*arde*, r:-*ée*, s:-*aille*, t:-*uis*, u:-*ay*, v:-*aint*

DISCUSSION (literary). Patch 1927, 77 n. 1, 96 n., 119 n. 1, 134 n. 2 and Calin 1974, 244 (theme of Fortune); Wimsatt 1975, 13–15 (the earlier *Remede* and the later *Fonteinne* share the literary plan of the work, in which an opening complaint is answered by comfort); Günther 1984a, 264–65 and Newes 1991b, 115–16 (symbolic connection between the turning of the Wheel of Fortune and the musical realization as a 3v canon). See also the literary analysis by Kees Boeke in the notes accompanying the recording Channel Classics CCS 0390 (see chap. 8.8). Feminine voice. Hassell (1982, no. M160) indexes a proverb.

LITERARY ANTECEDENTS. Boethius, *Consolation of Philosophy*; *Roman de la Rose* (Wimsatt 1975, 18–19; Kelly 1978, 288 n. 59).

TEXTUAL LEGACY (England). Chaucer, *Book of the Duchess* (Kittredge 1915c, 13–14, 18; Wimsatt 1968, 159–60; 1975; 1991b, 113–14, 129).

EDITIONS OF MUSIC. Ludwig 1926–54, 4:54–66 (ed. Besseler); Schrade 1956b, 2:52–74 (critical notes 1956c, 65–67). On transcription problems, see Reaney 1955–56, 30–31; errors in the editions of strophes 3, 4, 9, and 10–11 are discussed in Hoppin 1960, 17 and n. 18; Günther 1957, 128; 1962–63, 21–22. Hoppin (1978b, 408) questions the realization of the work as a 3v canon, due to unusual dissonances.

For the performance of the canon, MS **A** gives only "*statim, etc.*"; MS **G** gives what must be the full direction from the exemplar: *statim et sine pausa dicitur secundus versus scilicet: Qu'en terre n'a element. Et sic de omnibus aliis* [immediately and without a rest sing the second verse, namely: *Qu'en terre n'a element*. And thus with all the others]. The music of strophes 1 and 12 is the same.

DISCUSSION (musical). Ludwig 1926–54, 2:14*a n. 1; Feininger 1937 (canon); Machabey 1955b, 1:119 ("isorhythmic" beginning of strophes 3 and 9); 1:123, 124, 126–27; Reaney 1955–56, 30–31 (polyphony); Günther 1957, 127–28 (text/music relationship); Newes 1987, 115–17, 134–50 (text/music relationship, "isorhythm" in strophe 10, semibreve syncopation); Cross 1990, 291 (canon has confusing *ficta*); Newes 1991b, 103, 115–21.

Sanctus. See *Messe de Nostre Dame.*

Sans cuer, dolens, de vous departirai (rondeau R4)

MANUSCRIPTS WITH TEXT AND MUSIC (all 2v: ca, ten).

[1] **C**	fol. 204v	no. 8		[6] **G**	fol. 150v	no. 4
[3] **V g**	fol. 317r	no. 4		[7] **E**	fol. 146r	no. 19
[4] **B**	fol. 316r	no. 4		[7] **E**	fol. 182r	in *Voir Dit*
[5] **A**	fol. 476v	no. 6				

TEXT MANUSCRIPTS.

[10] **M**	fol. 244r	no. 4		Lo148 **CVgBAGHMD**
[50] **Pa**	fol. 32r	no. 97		VD31 **AFEPm** (chap. 5.13 table 5.3)

EDITIONS OF TEXT. Tarbé 1849, 53; 1856, 55; P. Paris 1875, 108; Chichmaref 1909, 1:139 no. 148; Wilkins 1972, 112 no. 264.

DATE. Hoepffner (1908–21, 3:257 note to l. 1013 of *Fonteinne*) links the date of R4 and *De tout sui* (V38/32); see the commentary in Reaney 1952b, 37; Leech-Wilkinson 1993b, 114 n. 47.

TRANSLATIONS. L.W. Johnson 1990, 56–57; see also discography (chap. 8.3 and 8.8).

DISCUSSION (literary). Hoepffner 1908–21, 3:254 note to ll. 203–4 of *Fonteinne* (relationship to ll. 1 and 6 of Lo148=R4). Only one *Voir Dit* passage relates to R4. The work is inserted in the narrative after two introductory lines that treat it as if it had been improvised on the spot (ll. 2605–6, ed. P. Paris 1875, 108); but since it appears in MS C, it was composed before ca. 1355. Immediately following R4 is a paired rondeau by Toute Belle, *Sans cuer, de moi pas ne vous partirés* (VD32). For excerpts from or commentary on these passages, see Ludwig 1926–54, 2:56a*; Wilkins 1972, 178 n. 264; S.J. Williams 1977, 464; Brownlee 1984, 240 n. 36; Cerquiglini 1985b, 98 n. 21; L.W. Johnson 1990, 56–57; Leech-Wilkinson 1993a, 61–62; 1993b, 114, 135.

TEXT STRUCTURE. 10AB aA ab AB a:*-partiray*, b:*-our*

EDITIONS OF MUSIC. Ludwig 1926–54, 1:54; Schrade 1956b, 3:144 (critical notes 1956c, 125).

DISCUSSION (musical). Machabey 1955b, 1:155; Dömling 1972, 302 (text painting).

Sans cuer m'en vois, dolens et esplourez (ballade B17)
  Refrain: *En lieu dou cuer, dame, qui vous demeure*
  Amis, dolens, maz et desconfortez
  Refrain: *En lieu dou cuer, amis, qui me demeure*
  Dame, par vous me sens reconfortez
  Refrain: *En lieu dou cuer, dame, qui vous demeure*

MANUSCRIPTS WITH TEXT AND MUSIC (all 3v: ca1, ca2, ca3).

[1] **C**	fols. 198r–199r	no. 18		[5] **A**	fols. 458r–458v	no. 9
[3] **V g**	fols. 304v–305r	no. 17		[6] **G**	fols. 136v–137r	no. 9
[4] **B**	fols. 302v–303r	no. 17		[7] **E**	fols. 149r–149v	no. 10

TEXT MANUSCRIPTS.

[10] **M**	fols. 239v–240r	nos. 17a, b, c	
[16] **J**	fols. 19v–20r	nos. 111–13[87]	

FACSIMILE. Ultan 1977b, 127–28 (diplomatic facs.; error in interval between canonic voices)

EDITIONS OF TEXT. Chichmaref 1909, 2:543–45 nos. 9–11; Wilkins 1987, 28–29.

TRANSLATIONS. Marrocco/Sandon 1977, 159 (strophe 1 of all three ballades); Wilkins 1987, 29–30; see also discography (chap. 8.3 and 8.8).

TEXT STRUCTURE. 3 x 3 strophes (triple ballade). See Gieber (1982, 11) on the rare use of

enjambment. $\dfrac{a\ b\ \ a\ b\ c\ c\ d\ D}{1010\ 1010\ 71010'10'}$, a:*-és*, b:*-oie*, c:*-er*, d:*-eure*

DISCUSSION (literary). Poirion 1965, 611 (on simultaneous presentation of texts); J.R. White 1969, 88 and Newes 1977, 55 (literary reason for the order of entry of the voices); Mulder

---

[87] [*Sans cuer*]: *Chanson de ioie et esplourez.* [*Amis, dolens*]: *Response. la dame.* [*Dame, par vous*]: *Renvoy. l'amant.*

1978, 70–71 (three voices are male love, female love, and heavenly or Marian love); Newes 1987, 159–60 and 1991, 71–73 (literary reason for the order of entry of the voices; also reported in Günther 1983, 263–64; 1984a, 265).

EDITIONS OF MUSIC. Ludwig 1926–54, 1:16 (error in interval between canonic voices); Schrade 1956b, 3:88–89 (critical notes 1956c, 107–8; follows error of Ludwig); Reaney 1955, 57–58 (ed. after Feininger 1937; discussion p. 51); Marrocco/Sandon 1977, 157–59 no. 70 (after Reaney); Wilkins 1987 26–31 no. 6.

DISCUSSION (musical). Feininger 1937 (new interpretation of canon); Machabey 1955b, 2:31–32; Kühn 1973, 206–10 (analysis in support of Feininger transcription); Newes 1987, 150–69; Wilkins 1987, 30–31 (general discussion); Newes 1991a, 73–75 (analysis).

Se d'amer me repentoie (virelai V20)

MANUSCRIPTS WITH TEXT AND MUSIC (all monophonic).

[1] C	fol. 156r	no. 19		[5] A	fol. 488r	no. 20
[3] Vg	fols. 328v–329r	no. 20		[6] G	fols. 158v–159r	no. 20
[4] B	fols. 326v–327r	no. 20		[7] E	fols. 160v–161r	no. 11

TEXT MANUSCRIPTS.

[10] M   fols. 250r–250v   no. 20   [50] Pa   fols. 67v–68r   no. 212

EDITIONS OF TEXT. Tarbé 1856, 25; Chichmaref 1909, 2:605–6 no. 20.

TEXT STRUCTURE. 3 strophes: $\dfrac{AAB\,AAB}{7'3'7\ \ 7'3'7} \parallel \dfrac{b\,a\,b\,a}{77'\ \ 77'} \mid \dfrac{a\,ab\,a\,ab}{7'3'7\ 7'3'7} \parallel \dfrac{AAB\,AAB}{7'3'7\ \ 7'3'7}$ a:-oie, b:-i

EDITIONS OF MUSIC. Ludwig 1926–54, 1:80; Schrade 1956b, 3:179 (critical notes 1956c, 142).

DISCUSSION (musical). Machabey 1955b, 1:186–87; Weber-Bockholdt 1992, 276 (tonally clear).

Se j'aim mon loyal ami. See Lasse! / Se j'aim (M16).

Se je me pleing, je n'en puis mais (ballade B15)
Refrain: Ma dame m'a congié donné

MANUSCRIPTS WITH TEXT AND MUSIC (all 2v: ca, ten).

[1] C	fols. 164r–164v	no. 15		[5] A	fol. 462r	no. 16
[3] Vg	fol. 303v	no. 15		[6] G	fol. 139v	no. 16
[4] B	fol. 301v	no. 15		[7] E	fol. 156r	no. 33

TEXT MANUSCRIPTS.

[10] M   fol. 239r   no. 15   [50] Pa   fol. 51r   no. 158

EDITION OF TEXT. Chichmaref 1909, 2:549–50 no. 18.

TEXT STRUCTURE. 3 strophes: 8ab ab ccdD   a:-ais, b:-eus, c:-ours, d:-é

TEXTUAL LEGACY (France). Froissart, rondeau Se je me plains, dame, j'ai bien de quoi (ed. McGregor 1975, 274 no. 65; Baudouin 1978, 82 no. 65; cited in Poirion 1965, 215).

EDITIONS OF MUSIC. Ludwig 1926–54, 1:13; Schrade 1956b, 3:86 (critical notes 1956c, 106–7).

DISCUSSIONS (musical). Machabey 1955b, 2:29–30; Dömling 1970, 72–74 (recurring musical segments argue for simultaneous conception of voices); Salop 1971, 70–71 (melodic planning); Dömling 1972, 302 (text painting); Hirshberg 1980, 32–33 (ficta).

MUSICAL LEGACY. (a) Related to the anonymous ballade Ma dame m'a congié donné (ed. Ludwig 1926–54, 1:14; Günther 1957, no. 5; 1959, 10–11 no. 4; Apel 1970–72, 2:75–76 no. 163; Greene 1981–89, 20:99–101 no. 30; discussed in Günther 1957, 167, 196–98). The first line of this ballade quotes the text and music of the refrain of Machaut's B15, while the refrain of the anonymous ballade quotes the text and music of Machaut's first line (the remainder of the text is unrelated). Discussion in Günther 1972, 55 (as a balade entée). There is a similar pattern of borrowing in a ballade ascribed to Magister Franciscus, related to De Fortune (B23). (b) The beginning of text only is cited at the beginning of a ballade by Matteo da Perugia, Se je me pleing de Fortune (ed. Apel 1970–72, 1:104–6 no. 53; Greene 1981–89, 20:72–75 no. 21), which goes on to cite text and music of the cantus and tenor of Machaut's De Fortune (B23) (Lucy Cross, reported in Günther 1980a).

Se je souspir parfondement (virelai V36; Schrade virelai 30)

MANUSCRIPTS WITH TEXT AND MUSIC (all 2v: ca, ten).

[3] **V g** fol. 335v	no. 36		[6] **G** fols. 162r–162v	no. 33	
[5] **A** fols. 492r–492v	no. 32				

TEXT MANUSCRIPT.

[10] **M** fol. 255r   no. 36

LOST MANUSCRIPT.

[8] lost Burgundian manuscript

FACSIMILE. Wolf 1904, 2:45–46 no. 26 (diplomatic facs., MS G).

EDITION OF TEXT. Chichmaref 1909, 2:623–24 no. 33.

TRANSLATIONS. Marrocco/Sandon 1977, 154 (strophe 1); Wilson 1990a, 236–37; see also discography (chap. 8.3 and 8.8).

TEXT STRUCTURE. 3 strophes: $\dfrac{\text{AABBAB}}{8\,4\,4\,4\,8\,4}$ ‖ $\dfrac{\text{bba bba}}{844\ \ 844}$ | $\dfrac{\text{aabbab}}{844484}$‖ $\dfrac{\text{AABBAB}}{8\,4\,4\,4\,8\,4}$ a:-*ent*, b:-*oy*

DISCUSSION (literary). Hassell (1982, no. R59) indexes a proverb.

EDITIONS OF MUSIC. Wolf 1904, 3:71 no. 26; Ludwig 1926–54, 1:89–90; Schering 1931b, 18 no. 26b; Gérold 1932, 329–31; Schrade 1956b, 3:189 (critical notes 1956c, 146); Starr/Devine 1974, 25–26; Godwin 1975, 143–44 no. 19; Marrocco/Sandon 1977, 154 no. 68; Arlt 1982, 256 (after Schrade); Wilson 1990a, 235–36 no. 69.

DISCUSSION (musical). Machabey 1955b, 1:194; Covington 1978; Arlt 1982, 256–57 (successive composition); Wilson 1990b, 339, 342 (harmonic framework, displacement technique).

MUSICAL LEGACY. On a group of late fourteenth-century virelais in similar style to Machaut's V36, *Moult sui* (V37/31), and *De tout sui* (V38/32), see Fallows 1990, 22–23.

Se Loyauté m'est amie (virelai V22)

TEXT MANUSCRIPTS.

[1] **C** fols. 157r–157v	no. 22		[6] **G** fols. 159r–159v	no. 22	
[3] **V g** fol. 329r	no. 22		[7] **E** fol. 164r	no. 29	
[4] **B** fol. 327r	no. 22		[10] **M** fols. 250v–251r	no. 22	
[5] **A** fol. 488v	no. 22				

EDITION OF TEXT. Chichmaref 1909, 2:608–9 no. 22.

TEXT STRUCTURE. 3 str.: $\dfrac{\text{AABAAAB}}{7\,3\,77\,3\,7\,3}$ ‖ $\dfrac{\text{bba bba}}{737\ \ 737}$ | $\dfrac{\text{a aba a ab}}{7\,3\,77\,3\,7\,3}$ ‖ $\dfrac{\text{AABAAAB}}{7\,3\,77\,3\,7\,3}$ a:-*ie*, b:-*our*

Se ma dame m'a guerpi (virelai V6)

MANUSCRIPTS WITH TEXT AND MUSIC (all monophonic).

[1] **C** fols. 150v–151r	no. 6		[5] **A** fol. 483v	no. 6	
[3] **V g** fol. 324r	no. 6		[6] **G** fol. 155v	no. 4	
[4] **B** fol. 322r	no. 6				

TEXT MANUSCRIPTS.

[7] **E** fol. 159v   no. 4 (empty staves)   [10] **M** fols. 246v–247r no. 6

EDITION OF TEXT. Chichmaref 1909, 2:586–87 no. 6.

TEXT STRUCTURE. 3 strophes: $\dfrac{\text{AABB}}{7\,7\,5\,'8\,'}$ ‖ $\dfrac{\text{cca cca}}{837\ \ 837}$ | $\dfrac{\text{aab B}}{775'8'}$ ‖ $\dfrac{\text{AABB}}{7\,7\,5\,'8\,'}$ a:-*i*, b:-*ée*, c:-*ent*.

The last line of the refrain proper also serves as the last line of each of the three strophes (cf. Hoepffner 1920b, 26–27; Poirion 1965, 329 and n. 28). Compare *Dame, je vueil* (V9).

EDITIONS OF MUSIC. Ludwig 1926–54, 1:72; Schrade 1956b, 3:169 (critical notes 1956c, 137–38).

DISCUSSION (musical). Machabey 1955b, 1:179; Weber-Bockholdt 1992, 268–69.

Se mesdisans en acort (virelai V15)

MANUSCRIPTS WITH TEXT AND MUSIC (all monophonic).

[1] **C** fols. 154r–154v	no. 15		[5] **A** fols. 486r–486v	no. 15	
[3] **V g** fols. 326v–327r	no. 15		[6] **G** fol. 157v	no. 15	
[4] **B** fols. 324v–325r	no. 15		[7] **E** fols. 159v–160r	no. 6	

TEXT MANUSCRIPTS.
[10] **M**   fols. 248v–249r no. 15   [50] **Pa** fols. 61v–62r   no. 192
EDITIONS OF TEXT. Tarbé 1856, 29; Chichmaref 1909, 2:598–99 no. 15.
TRANSLATION. See discography (chap. 8.3 and 8.8).
TEXT STRUCTURE. 3 strophes:

AABBBA $\parallel$ ccb ccb $\mid$ aab b ba $\parallel$ AABBBA   a:-*ort*, b:-*ie*, c:-*ay*
7 7 5'7'7'5   775' 775'   775'7'7'5   7 7 5'7'7'5

EDITIONS OF MUSIC. Ludwig 1926–54, 1:76–77; Schrade 1956b, 3:174 (critical notes 1956c, 140–41).
DISCUSSION (musical). Machabey 1955b, 1:183.

Se pour ce muir qu'Amours ai bien servi (ballade B36)

Refrain: *Qu'en lieu de bleu, dame, vous vestez vert*
MANUSCRIPTS WITH TEXT AND MUSIC (all 3v: ca, ten, ct).

[3] **V g** fol. 316r   no. 36   [6] **G** fols. 147v–148v no. 36
[4] **B**   fol. 315r   no. 36   [7] **E** fols. 203v–204r in *Voir Dit*
[5] **A**   fols. 472v–473r   no. 35
TEXT MANUSCRIPTS.
[10] **M**   fol. 243r   no. 36   Lo248 **VgBJAMD** (chap. 6.4)
[52] **Ta** fols. 7r–7v   no. 20   VD61 **AFEPm** (chap. 5.13 table 5.3)

FACSIMILE. Wilkins 1979, 17 (MS A, beginning of cantus only).

EDITIONS OF TEXT. Tarbé 1849, 55–56; 1856, xxix (strophe 1); P. Paris 1875, 309; Chichmaref 1909, 1:218 no. 248; Wilkins 1972, 99 no. 193; Vitale-Brovarone 1980, 22 no. 20 (**Ta**).

TRANSLATIONS. Little 1980, 55–57 (includes verses from the *Voir Dit* that introduce the ballade, ll. 7638–44); Cerquiglini/Berthelot 1987, 116–17 (modern French); Wimsatt 1991b, 144–45; see also discography (chap. 8.3 and 8.8).

DATE. (a) Perhaps end of 1363 (after *Voir Dit* letter 39; see Machabey 1955b, 2:51); (b) after early February 1364 (Leech-Wilkinson 1993a, 59–60).

TEXT STRUCTURE. 3 strophes: 10ab ab bcC a:-*i*, b:-*our*, c:-*ert*

DISCUSSION (literary). The following *Voir Dit* passages concern B36: (a) the narrative immediately preceding the dream of the transformed *image* of Toute Belle, l. 4929 (ed. P. Paris 1875, 213) presages the refrain of B36; (b) there is further mention of colors later in the same dream, ll. 5162–67 (ed. 1875, 221); (c) the king replies, recalling the transformation of blue into green (ed. 1875, 225); (d) Guillaume mentions the dream with the color change in letter 31 (ed. 1875, 240); (e) the text of B36 is inserted in the narrative (ll. 7644–64, ed. 1875, 309); (f) another recollection of the color symbolism of B36, l. 7694 (ed. 1875, 313); (g) Toute Belle writes in letter 43 that she has seen B36, obtained from a source other than Guillaume (ed. 1875, 347); (h) the messenger reports the bad effect of B36 on Toute Belle, ll. 8623–35 (ed. 1875, 351–52). For excerpts from or commentary on these passages, see Huizinga 1924, 107 (=1953, 125); Ludwig 1926–54, 2:58*; Little 1980, 55–57; Brownlee 1984, 145, 347, 351–52; Cerquiglini 1985b, 169, 220; Leech-Wilkinson 1993a, 59–60; 1993b, 128–30, 139–40. Hassell (1982, no. B112) indexes a proverb. See also chap. 6.4, note to Lo213. For further on color symbolism in Machaut, see chap. 6.4, notes to Lo248 and Lo272.

TEXTUAL LEGACY (England). Chaucer, *Anelida and Arcite* (Wimsatt 1978, 70); *Against Women Unconstant* (F.N. Robinson 1957, 865–66; Wimsatt 1978, 66 and 83–84; Wimsatt 1991b, 144–47).

EDITIONS OF MUSIC. Ludwig 1926–54, 1:44–45; Schrade 1956b, 3:130–31 (critical notes 1956c, 119); Wilkins 1980b, 3–4 (Chaucer, *Madame, for your newe-fangelnesse* underlaid). Aspects of syncopation discussed in Günther 1962–63, 24.

DISCUSSION (musical). Schering 1931a, 18 (removes diminutions to obtain skeletal melody); Preston 1951, 617 (word-painting); Machabey 1955b, 2:50–51; Dömling 1970, 44 (analysis, criticized in Kühn 1973, 260 n. 440); Salop 1971, 70 (melodic planning); Dömling 1972, 304, 305–6 (text setting; refrain); Reaney 1982, 298 (mode); Leech-Wilkinson 1993a, 59–60 (word-painting).

The pervasive use of certain melodic formulas in *tempus imperfectum, prolatio major* links *Donnez, signeurs* (B26), *Une vipere* (B27), and *Je puis trop* (B28) as one group, and *Plourez, dames* (B32), *Nes qu'on* (B33), and *Se pour ce muir* (B36) as another; the same formulas are seen to a lesser extent in *En amer* (RF4), *Cinc, un* (R6), and *Douce dame, tant* (R20) (cf. Reaney 1955, 47; Günther 1957, 80–84; Hirshberg 1971, 120–33; Little 1980, 49; Leech-Wilkinson 1993a, 59 n. 38). On melodic formulae in B32–33 and B36, see also Reaney 1971, 42; Mulder 1978, 99–114 (the theme of despair common to the three ballades is mirrored in their similar musical material); Little 1980, 57–59; Leech-Wilkinson 1993a, 59–60).

Se quanque amours puet donner a ami (ballade B21)

Refrain: *Contre le bien et la joie que j'ay*

MANUSCRIPTS WITH TEXT AND MUSIC.

[1]	**C**	fols. 200v–201r	no. 22	4v (tr, ca, ten, ct)
[3]	**V g**	fol. 307r	no. 21	4v (tr, ca, ten, ct)
[4]	**B**	fol. 305r	no. 21	4v (tr, ca, ten, ct)
[5]	**A**	fol. 474v	no. 38	3v (ca, ten, ct)[88]
[6]	**G**	fols. 141r–141v	no. 21	4v (tr, ca, ten, ct)
[7]	**E**	fol. 151v	no. 16	4v (tr, ca, ten, ct)

TEXT MANUSCRIPTS.

[10]	**M**	fol. 240v	no. 21		[50]	**Pa**	fols. 52v–53r	no. 166
[40]	**Wm**	fol. 20r	no. 17					

FACSIMILE. Bofill Soliguer 1991, 23 (MS **C**).

EDITION OF TEXT. Chichmaref 1909, 2:552–53 no. 23.

TRANSLATION. See discography (chap. 8.3 and 8.8).

TEXT STRUCTURE. 3 strophes: $\begin{smallmatrix} a & b & a & b & c & c & d\,D \\ 10 & 10 & 10 & 10 & 7 & 10 & 10\,10 \end{smallmatrix}$ a:-*i*, b:-*er*, c:-*ent*, d:-*ay*

EDITIONS OF MUSIC. Ludwig 1926–54, 1:22; Schrade 1956b, 3:96–97 (critical notes 1956c, 110). Brief mention of Schrade's notational errors in Hoppin 1960, 19 n. 25.

MUSICAL LEGACY. Matheus de Sancte Johanne, ballade *Science n'a nul annemi* (ed. Apel 1970–72, 1:137–38 no. 73; Greene 1981–89, 19:149–51 no. 94); cited in Hirshberg 1971, 207.

DISCUSSION (musical). Machabey 1955b, 2:34; Wykes 1956, 76–81 and diagrams in appendix C (analysis); Hirshberg 1971, 138–41 (motivic analysis of B21 and *Il m'est avis* [B22]); Lühmann 1978, 69–85, 136–37 (harmonic structure, rhythm and declamation); Mulder 1978, 79 (motivic analysis).

Se quanque Diex en monde a fait. [*Le Lay du Mirouer Amoureux*] (lai L11)

TEXT MANUSCRIPTS.

[1]	**C**	fols. 191r–192v	no. 12		[6]	**G**	fols. 86v–87v	no. 11
[3]	**V g**	fols. 239v–240v	no. 11		[7]	**E**	fols. 109v–110v	no. 4 (has title)
[4]	**B**	fols. 237v–238v	no. 11		[10]	**M**	fols. 224r–225v	no. 13
[5]	**A**	fols. 386r–387v	no. 11		[28]	**Ars**	fols. 12r–13v	no. 2

EDITION OF TEXT. Chichmaref 1909, 2:362–70 no. 11.

TRANSLATION. Wimsatt 1991b, 160 (ll. 15–20 only).

TEXT STRUCTURE. 12 strophes, 242 lines:

1a. $\frac{a\,a\,a\,b}{8\,8\,8\,8}$ | $\frac{a\,a\,a\,b}{8\,8\,8\,8}$ ‖ 1b. same ‖

4a. $\frac{g\,g\,g\,g\,g\,g\,h}{7'5'7'5'7'5'7}$ | $\frac{g\,g\,g\,g\,g\,g\,h}{7'5'7'5'7'5'7}$ ‖ 4b. same ‖

2a. $\frac{c\,c\,c\,d}{3\,3\,7\,7}$ | $\frac{c\,c\,c\,d}{3\,3\,7\,7}$ ‖ 2b. same ‖

5a. $\frac{i\,j\,j\,k\,k\,i\,i\,j\,j\,k\,k\,k\,i}{7\,3\,4\,4\,7\,4\,3\,4\,4\,7\,4\,3\,4\,4}$ ‖ 5b. same ‖

3a. $\frac{e\,f\,e\,f\,f\,e\,f\,f\,e\,f}{7'3\,7'3\,77'7\,37'3}$ ‖ 3b. same ‖

6a. $\frac{l\,l\,m\,m\,l\,l\,m\,m\,l}{7\,7\,4\,7\,4\,7\,4\,7\,4}$ ‖ 6b. same ‖

---

[88] Added later; the reduced voices are due to a problem in page layout (Earp 1983, 68–69).

7a. $\frac{nnno}{5557}$ | $\frac{nnno}{5557}$ || 7b. same || 10a. $\frac{uuuv}{7775}$ | $\frac{uuuv}{7775}$ || 10b. same ||

8a. $\frac{p\ p\ p\ q\ r}{3'3'7'3'3}$ | $\frac{p\ p\ p\ q\ r}{3'3'7'3'3}$ || 8b. same || 11a. $\frac{w\ x\ w\ x\ w\ x\ w}{33'33'33'7}$ | $\frac{w\ x\ w\ x\ w\ x\ w}{33'33'33'7}$ || 11b. same ||

9a. $\frac{s\ s\ s\ s\ t}{8'8'8'8'8}$ | $\frac{s\ s\ s\ s\ t}{8'8'8'8'8}$ || 9b. same || 12a–b. = 1a–b.

a:-*ait*, b:-*ance*, c:-*our*, d:-*oie*, e:-*ure*, f:-*é*, g:-*ée*, h:-*a*, i:-*ours*, j:-*oir*, k:-*i*, l:-*ir*, m:-*ay*, n:-*ui*, o:-*ort*, p:-*ie*, q:-*ame*, r:-*oy*, s:-*ue*, t:-*eus*, u:-*ueil*, v:-*ement*, w:-*is*, x:-*ise*

DISCUSSION (literary). Luttrell 1965, 172 (vocabulary); Huot 1987, 266–68, 272–73 (feminine voice; pairing of *Lay de l'Ymage, Ne say comment* (L14/9) and L11 in MS C).

TEXTUAL LEGACY (Catalonia). Pere Torroella, *Tant mon voler* (ll. 147–51; ed. Bach y Rita 1930).

TEXTUAL LEGACY (England). Chaucer, *Troilus* (Wimsatt 1976, 288–89; 291; 1991b, 159–60; Windeatt 1992, 120–21).

Se vous n'estes pour mon guerredon nee (rondeau R7)

MANUSCRIPTS WITH TEXT AND MUSIC.

[1] **C**	fol. 202r	no. 2	2v (ca, ten; with empty staves for tr)
[3] **V g**	fol. 318r	no. 7	2v (ca, ten)
[4] **B**	fol. 317r	no. 7	2v (ca, ten)
[5] **A**	fol. 477v	no. 7	2v (ca, ten)
[6] **G**	fol. 151r	no. 7	2v (ca, ten)
[7] **E**	fol. 134r	no. 4	3v (ca, ten, ct)
[18] **P m**	fol. 214v	no. 3	2v (ca, ten)
[56] **C a B**	fol. 6v	no. 29	4v (tr, ca, ten, ct)
[61] **F P**	fol. 60r	no. 110	3v (ca, ten, ct)
[65] **S L**	fol. 77r		
[66] **Mod**	fol. 34r	no. 66	2v (ca, ten)
[66] **Mod**	fol. 5v	no. 7a	new ct only
[68] **Gr 3360**	fol. 3r	no. 7	frag. (ten, ct)[89]
[72] **P g**	fol. 257v	no. 25	2v no text
[73] **Str**	fol. 73v [73r?]	no. 119	(index only).

TEXT MANUSCRIPTS.

[10] **M**	fol. 244r	no. 7	[50] **Pa** fols. 57r–57v	no. 181
[49] **Jp**	fol. 69v	no. 80		

TREATISE. Anonymous Pennsylvania/Schloss Harburg treatise (Staehelin 1974, 239).

FACSIMILE. *Jardin* 1910–25, vol. 1, fol. 69v (**Jp**); Apel 1953, 411 facs. 82 (MS **Mod**, fol. 34r); Pirrotta 1955, 405–6 (**FP**, fol. 60r); Gallo 1981, fol. 60r (**FP**).

EDITIONS OF TEXT. Chichmaref 1909, 2:571 no. 7; Bertoni 1917b, 44 (**Mod**).

TRANSLATION. Hoppin 1978a, 145.

TEXT STRUCTURE. $\frac{A\ B}{10'10}\ \frac{a}{10}\ \frac{A}{10'10'}\ \frac{a\ b}{10'10}\ \frac{A\ B}{10'10}$ a:-*guerredonnée*,[90] b:-*iant*

EDITIONS OF MUSIC. Ludwig 1926–54, 1:56–57 (includes the fragmentary triplum of **CaB**, the contratenor in MSS **E**, **CaB**, and **FP**, and the different contratenor in **Mod**; Schrade 1956b, 3:146–47 (critical notes 1956c, 126–28, with fragmentary triplum of **CaB**); Hoppin 1978a, 143–45 no. 63 (includes the alternative contratenors in MSS **E** and **Mod**); Stolba 1991, 71–72 no. 48.

DISCUSSION (musical). Ludwig 1926–54, 3:57 ("isorhythm" at the beginnings of the A- and B-sections); Machabey 1955b, 1:157; Günther 1957, 105–6 (motivic analysis); Lühmann 1978, 106 (declamation); Hirshberg 1980, 30 (comparison of the contratenor in E with that of **Mod**); Snizkova 1982, 72 (relates R7 to *Soyés lies*, an anonymous rondeau in **Pg**; ed.

---

[89] On the filial relationship of this MS to E and the Italian anthologies, see the commentary on date and provenance of MS E [7], chap. 3.

[90] On such *rimes équivoquées*, see Poirion 1965, 435.

Kammerer 1931, 131–32; Apel 1970–72, 3:141 no. 279; Greene 1981–89, 22:133 no. 73; Earp 1991b, 130–31).

MUSICAL LEGACY. Christopher Page (personal communication) has noted that the refrain of the anonymous ballade *S'espoir n'estoit* (ed. Apel 1970–72, 2:97–99 no. 175; Greene 1981–89, 20:204–6 no. 62) quotes the cantus and tenor of the B-section of R7.

Speravi. See *De Bon Espoir / Puis que* (M4).

Super omnes speciosa. See *Quant vraie amour / O series* (M17).

Suspiro. See *Tous / De* (M2).

Tant doucement m'ont / Eins que ma dame / Ruina (motet M13)

MANUSCRIPTS WITH TEXT AND MUSIC (all 3v: tr, mot, ten).

[1]	**C**	fols. 217v–218r	no. 12		[5]	**A**	fols. 426v–427r	no. 13
[3]	**V g**	fols. 272v–273r	no. 13		[6]	**G**	fols. 114v–115r	no. 13
[4]	**B**	fols. 270v–271r	no. 13		[7]	**E**	fol. 142v	no. 16

EDITION OF TEXT. Chichmaref 1909, 2:507–8 no. 13.

TEXT STRUCTURE AND RELATIONSHIP TO ISORHYTHM. Both triplum and motetus exhibit regular correlation between text and *talea* structure (Besseler 1927, 224; Reichert 1956, 201; ex. 3 after p. 204, discussed pp. 206–7, 213); See also Reichert 1956, 207, 209 table (irregular strophic structure at end of triplum); Clarkson 1971, 263 (three different quatrain patterns in motetus); Ziino 1978, 444–45 (strophic structure of triplum).

Triplum: $\frac{\text{aab aaab b}}{775'7775'7'} \frac{\text{ccb cccb b}}{775'7775'7'} \frac{\text{ddb dddb b}}{775'7775'7'} \frac{\text{eeb eeeb b}}{775'7775'7'}$ a:-*ait*, b:-*aire*, c:-*i*, d:-*oit*, e:-*é*

Motetus: $\frac{\text{abab baba abba aba}}{7575 \ 7575 \ 7575 \ 757}$ a:-*our*, b:-*is*

TENOR SOURCE. Unidentified, but also appears in the 3v motet *Super cathedram / Presidentes* (Ludwig 1926–54, 2:60b*; ed. Schrade 1956a, 5–7 no. 4[4]); comparison of the two motets in Dobrzańska 1979a, 13–15 (English summary, p. 18).

EDITIONS OF MUSIC. Ludwig 1926–54, 3:49–51; Schrade 1956b, 2:151–53 (critical notes 1956c, 83). Barring discussed in Hoppin 1960, 25.

DISCUSSION (musical). Unipartite, almost pan-isorhythmic (the few deviations are given in Günther 1958, 31 n. 18). M. Schneider 1931, ex. 1 (isorhythm in motetus); Machabey 1955b, 2:89–90; Pelinski 1975, 68 (the pitch *a* recurs in the tenor at same place in each *talea*, and thus the work is "isoharmonic"). On recurrence of similar musical phrases in each *talea*, see Reichert 1956, 213; Ziino 1978, 447, 449.

Tant doucement me sens emprisonnés (rondeau R9)

MANUSCRIPTS WITH TEXT AND MUSIC.

[1]	**C**	fols. 202v–203r	no. 4	4v (tr, ca, ten, ct)
[3]	**V g**	fol. 318v	no. 9	4v (tr, ca, ten, ct)
[4]	**B**	fol. 317v	no. 9	4v (tr, ca, ten, ct)
[5]	**A**	fol. 475r	no. 1	4v (tr, ca, ten, ct) (added later)
[5]	**A**	fol. 477v	no. 10	2v (ca, ten)[91]
[6]	**G**	fols. 151r–151v	no. 8	4v (tr, ca, ten, ct)
[7]	**E**	fol. 134r	no. 3	4v (tr, ca, ten, ct)
[18]	**P m**	fol. 214v	no. 4	2v (ca, ten)
[20]	**P e**	fol. 35r	*Remede* [92]	4v (tr, ca, ten, ct)
[58]	**Trém**	fol. xxxii	no. 76	(index only)

TEXT MANUSCRIPTS.

[10] **M**   fol. 244v   no. 8   [50] **Pa** fol. 56v   no. 177

EDITIONS OF TEXT. Chichmaref 1909, 2:571–72 no. 8; Lucas 1957.

TRANSLATIONS. Marrocco/Sandon 1977, 160; see also discography (chap. 8.3 and 8.8).

---

[91] See Dömling 1970, 80 n. 22; Earp 1983, 69–80.

[92] In MS **Pe**, the musically more modern rondeau *Tant doucement* (R9) was substituted for *Dame, mon cuer* (RF7).

TEXT STRUCTURE. 10AB aa ab AB a:-*prisonnés*, b:-*prison* [93]

TEXTUAL LEGACY. A Cypriot rondeau, *Amour me tient en sa douce prison* uses the same rhymes in reverse order (ed. Hoppin 1960–63, 4:75–76 no. 63 [texts laid out for comparison, pp. xxiv–xxv; discussed pp. viii–ix]; cited in Günther 1972, 60). There is no musical relationship.

EDITIONS OF MUSIC. Ludwig 1926–54, 1:58–59; Schrade 1956b, 3:150–51 (critical notes 1956c, 128–29); Marrocco/Sandon 1977, 159–60 no. 71.

DISCUSSION (musical). Machabey 1955b, 1:160 (motivic analysis); Günther 1957, 106 (motivic analysis); 1958, 35 n. 27 (*tempus* changes); 1962–63, 17 (notation of long followed by minim); Saponov 1978, 30, 39–40 (palindromic rhythmic motive in tenor; rhythmic analysis); Powell 1979, 253–57 (numerological analysis); Hughes 1989, 116–17 (dissonance); Kügle 1991, 376–77 (represents style of the very late 1340s).

Tels rit au main qui au soir pleure (*complainte* RF2)

MANUSCRIPTS WITH TEXT AND MUSIC (all monophonic).

[1] **C**   fols. 30r–35r   [6] **F**   fols. 45r–48r
[3] **V g** fols. 96v–100v   [7] **E**   fols. 25r–26v
[4] **B**   fols. 96v–100v (new 113v–117v)   [20] **Pe**   fol. 8r–12v
[5] **A**   fols. 55v–59v

TEXT MANUSCRIPTS.

[10] **M**   fols. 55v–59r
[15] **K**   fols. 49v–51r (strophes 1–3; 24–36)
[16] **J**   fols. 52v–56v   *Une complainte selonc l'ymage de Fortune*
[18] **Pm** fols. 53r–56v

FACSIMILES (refer to chap. 4.4e). Miniatures C14–19.

EDITIONS OF TEXT (*Remede*, ll. 905–1480). Hoepffner 1908–21, 3:33–54; Wimsatt/Kibler 1988, 219–49.

TRANSLATIONS. J. Stevens 1973, 202–3 (strophe 1); Switten 1988c, 32–44; Wimsatt/Kibler 1988, 218–48; Boulton 1993, 190 (strophe 33, excerpt); see also discography (chap. 8.3 and 8.8).

TEXT STRUCTURE. Thirty-six six-line strophes, 576 lines.[94]

$$1. \quad \begin{matrix} a\,a\,a\,b \\ 8'8'8'4' \end{matrix} \Big|\; \begin{matrix} a\,a\,a\,b \\ 8'8'8'4' \end{matrix} \;\|\; \begin{matrix} b\,b\,b\,a \\ 8'8'8'4' \end{matrix} \Big|\; \begin{matrix} b\,b\,b\,a \\ 8'8'8'4' \end{matrix} \;\| \quad \text{a:-}eure, \text{ b:-}ourne$$

Rhymes for the remaining strophes (may be masculine or feminine):

2. -*able*, -*ere*	9. -*esse*, -*ance*	16. -*euse*, -*é*	23. -*eil*, -*ist*	30. -*oint*, -*eille*
3. -*oing*, -*onde*	10. -*ent*, -*oe*	17. -*ie*, -*orte*	24. -*é*, -*aire*	31. -*ue*, -*ur*
4. -*une*, -*einne*	11. -*ain*, -*ange*	18. -*ois*, -*at*	25. -*eingne*, -*ort*	32. -*ace*, -*er*
5. -*uis*, -*onte*	12. -*ise*, -*ole*	19. -*is*, -*oie*	26. -*estre*, -*ir*	33. -*oir*, -*a*
6. -*ique*, -*ant*	13. -*aut*, -*age*	20. -*ait*, -*ire*	27. -*endre*, -*ant*	34. -*eindre*, -*aint*
7. -*ure*, -*oit*	14. -*iens*, -*ui*[*s*]*t*	21. -*u*, -*as*	28. -*aie*, -*ente*	35. -*ée*, -*mi*
8. -*ose*, -*our*	15. -*euse*, -*é*	22. -*oy*, -*ez*	29. -*on*, -*iez*	36. -*ame*, -*ine*

DISCUSSION (literary). Poirion 1965, 406–9; B. and J. Cerquiglini 1976, 368 (begins with a proverb); Kelly 1978, 132; Cerquiglini 1985b, 71; Wimsatt 1985, 28; Huot 1987, 252–54; Imbs 1991, 119–20. For some literary studies that deal with all of the inserted lyrics, see chap. 5.7.

LITERARY ANTECEDENT. Mulder (1978, 38–39) compares the passage on Fortune to the passage on Amour in the *Roman de la Rose*.

EDITIONS OF MUSIC. Ludwig 1911, 9–10 (appendix); Quittard 1917–19, after p. 138; Ludwig 1926–54, 1:96; Schrade 1956b, 2:106 (critical notes 1956c, 73); Binkley 1977, 28–29 (performing edition of strophe 1 with lute and fiddle accompaniment); Switten 1988c, 31–32 (after Schrade); Wimsatt/Kibler 1988, 423, critical notes pp. 437–38 (ed. Baltzer).

DISCUSSION (musical). Ludwig 1911, 410; Machabey 1931, 333–34; 1955b, 1:131–33 (antecedents); Hoppin 1978b, 409–10; Mulder 1978, 74–75 (image of Wheel of Fortune in

---

[93] A comparable use of the *rime équivoquée* is seen in *Confort*, ll. 1421–24.

[94] On the form, see chap. 5.5, introduction to *Jugement Behaingne*.

textual and musical structure), 97–98 (rhythmic materials of *Qui n'aroit* [RF1], *Tels rit* [RF2] and *Joie, plaisence* [RF3] are similar); Malizia 1984, 25–28 (general); J. Stevens 1984, 115–17 (musical motives). For some musical studies that deal with all of the inserted lyrics, see chap. 5.7.

Tous corps / De souspirant cuer / Suspiro (motet M2)

MANUSCRIPTS WITH TEXT AND MUSIC (all 3v: tr, mot, ten).

[1]	**C**	fols. 207v–208r	no. 2	[5]	**A**	fols. 415v–416r	no. 2
[3]	**V g**	fols. 261v–262r	no. 2	[6]	**G**	fols. 103v–104r	no. 2
[4]	**B**	fols. 259v–260r	no. 2	[7]	**E**	fols. 132v–133r	no. 3

FACSIMILE. Machabey 1966, 216 (MS **A**, fol. 415v).

EDITION OF TEXT. Chichmaref 1909, 2:485–86 no. 2.

TEXT STRUCTURE AND RELATIONSHIP TO ISORHYTHM. No correlation between strophe and *talea* (Machabey 1955b, 2:69; Reichert 1956, 200–201; Leech-Wilkinson 1982–83, 13; Koehler 1990, 1:106). See also Reichert 1956, 209 table (irregular strophic structure at end of triplum); Clarkson 1971, 268, 271 (compares the form of the triplum—three strophes plus an *envoi*—to the form of the ballade).

Triplum: ab ab ccb ddb eb eb ffb ggb hb hb iib jjb cc kk
$\frac{ab}{75}$, $\frac{ab}{75}$, $\frac{ccb}{775}$, $\frac{ddb}{775}$, $\frac{eb}{75}$, $\frac{eb}{75}$, $\frac{ffb}{775}$, $\frac{ggb}{775}$, $\frac{hb}{75}$, $\frac{hb}{75}$, $\frac{iib}{775}$, $\frac{jjb}{775}$, $\frac{cc}{77}$ $\frac{kk}{77}$

a:-*er*, b:-*ure*, c:-*oir*, d:-*és*, e:-*oint*, f:-*ant*, g:-*is*, h:-*ait*, i:-*ours*, j:-*i*, k:-*ir*

Motetus: abab baab ba ba ba
$\frac{abab}{77\,77}$, $\frac{baab}{7\,777}$, $\frac{ba}{7\,7}$ $\frac{ba}{7\,7}$ $\frac{ba}{7\,7}$ a:-*ent*, b:-*aire*

DISCUSSION (literary). Poirion 1965, 508 (Nature and love); Huot 1994 (paired with *He! Mors / Fine* [M3], analogue to the pair *Jugement Behaingne* and *Jugement Navarre*, analogue to Boethius's *Consolation of Philosophy*).

TENOR SOURCE. See Huot 1994, 225. *Suspiro* is the third word of the respond of *Antequam comedam suspiro* (Job 3:24–26, 23:6); only the first seven notes of Machaut's tenor correspond to the Responsory (Huot 1994, 236–37 n. 13).

EDITIONS OF MUSIC. Wolf 1926; Ludwig 1926–54, 3:6–8; Schrade 1956b, 2:112–14 (critical notes 1956c, 75). Harmonic problems in tenor, m. 53; harmonic augmented second in m. 29 (Ludwig 1926–54, 3:8, with a listing of similar instances in other motets). On the ambiguous tenor notation, see Boogaart, forthcoming study.

DISCUSSION (musical). Bipartite, with irregular diminution. Diminution section involves a conflict of *tempus*. Ficker 1925, 530–31 (isorhythm); Machabey 1955b, 2:68–71; Dobrzańska 1979b, 56–59 (figure vertically aligning four *taleae* of the *integer valor* section, mm. 1–96); Boogaart, forthcoming study. Machabey 1955b, 2:70, n. 520 and Günther 1958, 32 (melodic correspondences between *taleae*).

MUSICAL ANTECEDENTS. Possibly related to *Almifonis / Rosa* (ed. F.Ll. Harrison 1968, 46–49 no. 8), ascribed to Philippe de Vitry by Leech-Wilkinson (1982–83, 13, 16 ex. 9) and Kügle (1993, 223–33).

Tres bonne et belle, mi oueil (virelai V26; Schrade virelai 23)

MANUSCRIPTS WITH TEXT AND MUSIC (all 3v: ca, ten, ct).

[3]	**V g**	fol. 330v	no. 26	[6]	**G**	fols. 160r–160v	no. 26
[4]	**B**	fol. 328v	no. 26	[7]	**E**	fols. 161v–162r	no. 17
[5]	**A**	fols. 489v–490r	no. 26				

TEXT MANUSCRIPTS.

[10]	**M**	fols. 251v–252r	no. 26	Lo205 **VgBMAD**
[50]	**Pa**	fols. 69r–69v	no. 220	

EDITIONS OF TEXT. Chichmaref 1909, 1:185 no. 205; Wilkins 1972, 118 no. 281.

TRANSLATIONS. See discography (chap. 8.3 and 8.8).

TEXT STRUCTURE. 3 strophes:

ABBAAB ‖ b ba b ba ǀ ab b aab ‖ ABBAAB a:-*ueil*, b:-*ure*
$\frac{ABBAAB}{75'7'5\,77}$ ‖ $\frac{b\,ba\,b\,ba}{7'5'7\,7'5'7}$ ǀ $\frac{ab\,b\,aab}{75'7'577}$ ‖ $\frac{ABBAAB}{75'7'5\,77}$.

EDITIONS OF MUSIC. Ludwig 1926–54, 1:82–83; Schrade 1956b, 3:182 (critical notes 1956c, 143–44).

DISCUSSION (musical). Machabey 1955b, 1:188–89.

Tres douce dame que j'aour (ballade B24)
Refrain: *Tant com je vivray, sans meffaire*
MANUSCRIPTS WITH TEXT AND MUSIC (all 2v: ca, ten).

[1] **C**	fols. 201v–202r	no. 23		[5] **A**	fol. 466r		no. 23
[3] **V g**	fol. 309r	no. 24		[6] **G**	fol. 142v		no. 24
[4] **B**	fol. 307r	no. 24		[7] **E**	fol. 156v		no. 34

TEXT MANUSCRIPT.
   [10] **M**   fol. 241r   no. 24

FACSIMILES. Paulsmeier 1986, 81 (MS A); Bofill Soliguer 1991, 24 (MS A).

EDITION OF TEXT. Chichmaref 1909, 2:553–54 no. 26.

TRANSLATIONS. Heitmann 1978, 358–59 (strophes 1–2; German); A. Pulido 1991, 47 (strophes 1–2); see also discography (chap. 8.3 and 8.8).

TEXT STRUCTURE. 3 strophes: $\frac{ab\ ab\ b\ cC}{88\ 88\ 88'8'}$, a:-*our*, b:-*er*, c:-*aire*

EDITIONS OF MUSIC. Ludwig 1926–54, 1:27; Schrade 1956b, 3:104–5 (critical notes 1956c, 112); A. Pulido 1991, 46.

DISCUSSION (musical). Machabey 1955b, 2:37–38; Reichert 1962 (harmony); Reaney 1971, 45 ("displacement technique" and underlying structure); Salop 1971, 58 (melodic direction in the cantus); Kühn 1973, 90, 245 n. 262 (tonal aspect); Lühmann 1978, 230–31 (declamation); Cogan/Escot 1981, 64–66 (approaches to analysis); A. Pulido 1991 (detailed analysis).

ANTECEDENT (text and music). On the refrain, see *N'en fait* (B11). B24 bears a slight resemblance to the tenor of Adam de la Halle's rondeau; Günther (1972, 54), employs the term *balade entée*; Frobenius (1986, 11 col. b) finds the relationship questionable.

Tribulatio proxima est. See *Christe / Veni* (M21).

Trop plus est bele / Biauté paree / Je ne sui mie certains d'avoir amie (motet M20)
MANUSCRIPTS WITH TEXT AND MUSIC.

[1] **C**	fols. 224v–225r	no. 19	3v (tr, mot, ten)
[3] **V g**	fols. 279v–280r	no. 20	3v (tr, mot, ten)
[4] **B**	fols. 277v–278r	no. 20	3v (tr, mot, ten)
[5] **A**	fols. 433v–434r	no. 20	3v (tr, mot, ten)
[6] **G**	fols. 121v–122r	no. 20	3v (tr, mot, ten)
[7] **E**	fol. 131r	no. 1	3v (tr, mot, ten)
[58] **Trém**	fol. xii	no. 23	(index only)

FACSIMILES. Wolf 1913, facing p. 360 (MS E); 1923, plate 23 (MS E); Bank 1972, 40 ex. 13 (diplomatic facs. in score of beginning).

EDITION OF TEXT. Chichmaref 1909, 2:524–25 no. 20.

TRANSLATIONS. L. Wright 1985–86, 12 (complete); Wilkins 1989, 138 (complete); see also discography (chap. 8.3 and 8.8).

DATE AND OCCASION. This is the only motet of Machaut that employs syncopation in major prolation at the semibreve level. It was certainly the latest motet at the time of the production of MS C (ca. 1350). Just as this manuscript may be a memorial offering to Bonne of Luxembourg, M20, with its final "Amen" in triplum and motetus, may be considered a kind of benediction. The content of the texts respond ironically to this speculative occasion (see chap. 1.9).

TEXT STRUCTURE AND RELATIONSHIP TO MUSICAL STRUCTURE. There are three upper-voice isorhythmic periods, but they are not defined by the rondeau tenor (Günther 1958, 29; Sanders 1973, 564; 1980, 352); each sets four lines of the motetus, with a hocket on line 3 of each stanza (Clarkson 1971, 317). Clarkson (1971, 315–18) employs the term "phasic motet" for this work. See also Clarkson 1971, 245 n. 74 (text structure of triplum).

Triplum: 8aabb ccdd eeff gghh iijj + Amen
   a:-*té*, b:-*oir*, c:-*desir*, d:-*uis*, e:-*on*, f:-*chiés*, g:-*ien*, h:-*ient*, i:-*ort*, j:-*i*

Motetus: 8aaaa aaaa aaaa + Amen a:-*our*

Tenor (rondeau refrain): $\frac{a\dagger b}{10'7}$ or $\frac{a\ a\ b}{4'6'7}$ a:-*ie*, b:-*is* (†: epic caesura)

DISCUSSION (literary). Sonnemann 1969, 62; L. Wright 1985–86; Boogaard 1993b, 32–33.

TENOR SOURCE. *Je ne sui mie certeins d'avoir amie,* / *Mais je suis loyaus amis* is a rondeau refrain, not cited in Van den Boogaard 1969. Machabey (1955b, 2:103–4) notes a vague similarity to the refrain *Cis a cui je sui amie* (Van den Boogaard 1969, 125 no. 366). None of Machaut's rondeaux are heterometric, strengthening the possibility that the tenor is an older, borrowed work (L. Wright 1985–86, 3); Wright also discusses the structural significance of m. 6 in the tenor, ambiguous with regard to poetic versification.

EDITIONS OF MUSIC. Wolf 1913, 361–62 (partial; errors); Ludwig 1926–54, 3:71–72 (errors); Schering 1931b, 18–20 no. 27; Schrade 1956b, 3:11–12 (errors; 1956c, 88); Hüschen 1975. Errors in editions discussed and corrected in Hoppin 1960, 15–16; see also Günther 1962–63, 23.

DISCUSSION (musical). The tenor is structured as a rondeau, thus the two musical sections repeat in the irregular pattern ABAAABAB, making a *talea* structure supported by the tenor impossible. M. Schneider 1931, ex. 2 (isorhythm in triplum); Machabey 1955b, 2:103–4; Günther 1958, 35, n. 28 (no *modus*); Bank 1972, 39, 43 (tempo); Sanders 1973, 564 (phrase-structure analysis); Covington 1978; L. Wright 1985–86 (thorough analysis); Boogaard 1993b, 28 (relation to *Dame, je sui* / *Fins cuers* [M11]).

Tu qui gregem / *Plange, regni respublica!* / *Apprehende arma et scutum et exurge* (motet M22)

MANUSCRIPTS WITH TEXT AND MUSIC (all 4v: tr, mot, ten, ct).

[3] **Vg** fols. 281v–282r no. 22	[6] **G** fols. 123v–124r no. 22
[4] **B** fols. 279v–280r no. 22	[7] **E** fol. 145r no. 21
[5] **A** fols. 435v–436r no. 22	

EDITIONS OF TEXT. Lebeuf 1743, 432 (motetus only); Chichmaref 1909, 2:529–30 no. 22.

TRANSLATIONS. Kühn 1983, 1:32 (German); Markstrom 1989, 37–38 (trans. by Anna Kirkwood); see also discography (chap. 8.3 and 8.8).

DATE. (a) 1356, after the Battle of Poitiers (Reaney 1967, 93); (b) 10 April 1358, for the Estates of Provins (Markstrom 1989, 27–29, 34; but see chap. 1.13.1); (c) December 1361 (Leech-Wilkinson 1989, 1:106–7); see chap. 1.15.1a.

TEXT STRUCTURE AND RELATIONSHIP TO ISORHYTHM. The motetus exhibits correlation between text structure and *talea* (Reichert 1956, 201). Machabey (1955b, 2:108) noted a recurring pattern of five lines of triplum text in each period with enjambment (i.e., phrase overlap) at the end. See also Ziino 1978, 444 (hymn-like structure of triplum text), 440, 443 (sequence-like structure of the motetus text); Leech-Wilkinson 1989, 1:120 n. 31 (layout of the motetus suggests a "Grosstalea" made up of two tenor *taleae*).

Triplum: $\frac{aabb\ ccdd\ eeff\ gghh\ i\ i\ j\ j}{8888\ 8888\ 8888\ 8888\ 8888}$ a:-*ducis*, b:-*duci*, c:-*io*, d:-*ire*, e:-*iter*, f:-*uce*,

g:-*ucem*, h:-*duciter*, i:-*ores*, j:-*ducas*

Motetus: $\frac{aabaab\ bbcbbc\ ccdccd}{884884\ 884884\ 884888}$ a:-*ica*, b:-*atur*, c:-*enter*, d:-*ari*

DISCUSSION (literary). Chichmaref 1909, 1:lxi (the lament on current conditions seen in motetus l. 21 and following recalls the tirade of *A toi, Hanri* [Cp3], as well as the complaint of the narrator to the "Roi qui ne ment" in the *Voir Dit* and the triplum of *Christe* / *Veni* [M21]); Clarkson 1971, 222 (on the word root "duc"); Leech-Wilkinson 1989, 1:138 (Machaut possibly not the author of the texts).

TENOR SOURCE. *Apprehende arma et scutum et exurge* (Psalm 35 [34]:2) is from the end of the verse *Judica Domine nocentes me,* from the mode 2 Responsory *Posuit coronam capiti meo,* for the birth of a single martyr (Anderson 1976, 122, 126).

EDITIONS OF MUSIC. Ficker 1929, 503–4 (partial); Ludwig 1926–54, 3:79–81; Schrade 1956b, 3:22–25 (critical notes 1956c, 89–90); Kühn 1983, 2:11–16; Leech-Wilkinson 1989, 2:71–73 (critical notes 1989, 1:245).

DISCUSSION (musical). Unipartite with *introitus*. Ficker 1929, 502–5 (rhythm, performance practice); M. Schneider 1931, ex. 4 (isorhythm in tenor); Gombosi 1950, 222 (rhythmic structure of lower voices); Machabey 1955b, 2:107–8 (ABB rhythmic structure of each *talea*); Günther 1958, 32 (melodic rhyme at end of each *talea*); Kühn 1973, 91–92 (harmonic organization), 138–44 (see pp. 143–44 on possible word-painting); Pelinski 1975, 70 table 3 (harmonic layout); Wernli 1977, 21–23 (means that make the isorhythmic structure perceptible to the listener are inconsistent and variable); Kühn 1983 (detailed analysis); Leech-Wilkinson 1989, 1:119–28 (texts, isoperiodic structure, lower-voice *taleae*, phrase-lengths, upper-voice isorhythm, harmony, *introitus*), Markstrom 1989, 35 (old and new stylistic characteristics).

Leech-Wilkinson 1982–83, 3–4 (summary of related features among *Christe / Veni* [M21], M22, and *Felix virgo / Inviolata* [M23]); Newes 1987, 205–10 (comparison of complementary tenor-contratenor pair in *Aucune gent / Qui plus* [M5], M21–23); Leech-Wilkinson 1989, 1:105–7, 135–36, 138–41 (summary comparison of M21–23); 1:165 n. 45 (rate of harmonic change compared to several other motets).

MUSICAL LEGACY. Anonymous 4v motet *Altissonis / Hjn* (ed. F.Ll. Harrison 1968, 7–12 no. 2; Leech-Wilkinson 1989, 2:77–79; discussed in 1989, 1:149–51; relationships down-played in Leech-Wilkinson 1982–83, 18 n. 31).

Tuit mi penser (virelai V28; Schrade virelai 25)
MANUSCRIPTS WITH TEXT AND MUSIC (all monophonic).

[1] **C**	fol. 198r	no. 25	[5] **A**	fols. 490r–490v	no. 27
[3] **V g**	fol. 331v	no. 28	[6] **G**	fols. 160v–161r	no. 28
[4] **B**	fol. 329v	no. 28	[7] **E**	fol. 161r	no. 12

TEXT MANUSCRIPT.
[10] **M**   fols. 252r–252v   no. 28

FACSIMILES. Parrish 1957, plate xlvii (MS E), discussed pp. 149–52; Ultan 1977a, 67 (diplomatic facs.).

EDITION OF TEXT. Chichmaref 1909, 2:615–16 no. 28.

TRANSLATION. See discography (chap. 8.3 and 8.8).

TEXT STRUCTURE. 3 strophes: $\frac{AAAAB}{44446}$ ‖ $\frac{aaab}{7446}, \frac{aaab}{7446}$ | $\frac{aaaab}{44446}$ ‖ $\frac{AAAAB}{44446}$, a:-*er*, b:-*ure*

DISCUSSION (literary). Hassell (1982, no. P51) indexes a proverb.

EDITIONS OF MUSIC. Ludwig 1926–54, 1:84; Schrade 1956b, 3:184 (critical notes 1956c, 144–45); Kohn 1981, 45 (differently barred and beamed; discussed pp. 45–46).

DISCUSSION (musical). Machabey 1955b, 1:190–91; Weber-Bockholdt 1992, 274–75 (rhyme does not contribute to melodic structure).

Un mortel lay vueil commencier. Le Lay Mortel (lai L12; Schrade lai 8)
MANUSCRIPTS WITH TEXT AND MUSIC (all monophonic).

[1] **C**	fols. 184r–186v	no. 9	[6] **G**	fols. 87v–89r	no. 12 (has title)
[3] **V g**	fols. 241r–243v	no. 12	[7] **E**	fols. 117r–118r	no. 10
[4] **B**	fols. 239r–241v	no. 12	[27] **Maggs**		
[5] **A**	fols. 387v–389v	no. 12 (has title)	[28] **Ars**	fol. 13v	no. 3 (frag.)

TEXT MANUSCRIPTS.
[10] **M**	fols. 220r–221v	no. 10
[15] **K**	fols. 127r–127v	no. 1 (strophes 6–12 only)
[16] **J**	fols. 139v–141r	no. 1 (has title)
[40] **I**	fol. 1r	no. 1 (strophes 1–6 only)

FACSIMILES (refer to chap. 4.4s). Miniature C101. Maggs 1928 (MS **Maggs**).

EDITION OF TEXT. Chichmaref 1909, 2:371–79 no. 12.

TRANSLATION. Heinrichs 1989a, 595 (strophe 12, ll. 229–36).

DATE. Schrade (1958–61, 849) suggested that this work's date of composition was "not too distant" from the time of the *F:Pn 146* redaction of the *Roman de Fauvel* (ca. 1316) owing to the dependence of Machaut's lai on a lai in that collection, yet there seems no logical necessity for this extraordinarily early date.

TEXT STRUCTURE. 12 strophes, 236 lines:

1a. $\frac{aaab}{8888}$, $|$ $\frac{aaab}{8888}$, $\|$ 1b. same $\|$

7a. $\frac{111m}{8486}$, $|$ $\frac{111m}{8486}$, $\|$ 7b. same $\|$

2a. 7ccd $|$ ccd $\|$ 2b. same $\|$

8a. $\frac{nnnno\,nnnno}{33336\ 33336}$ $|$ $\frac{nnnno\,nnnno}{33336\ 33336}$ $\|$ 8b. same $\|$

3a. $\frac{eeee\,f}{75757}$, $|$ $\frac{eeee\,f}{75757}$, $\|$ 3b. same $\|$

9a. $\frac{p\,qp\,qqrr}{5\,55\,5747}$ $\|$ 9b. same $\|$

4a. $\frac{ggh}{557}$, $|$ $\frac{ggh}{557}$, $\|$ 4b. same $\|$

10a. $\frac{s\,s\,s\,s\,s\,s\,s\,s\,s}{5\,5\,5\,7\,5\,5\,5\,5\,7}$, $\|$ 10b. same $\|$

5a. $\frac{iiiii\ iiiii}{45335\ 45335}$ $\|$ 5b. same $\|$

11a. $\frac{ttttttu}{44444486}$, $|$ $\frac{ttttttu}{44444486}$, $\|$ 11b. same $\|$

6a. $\frac{jjkjjkkjjk}{7377373777}$ $\|$ 6b. same $\|$

12a–b. = 1a–b.

a:-*ier*, b:-*ère*, c:-*ors*, d:-*i*, e:-*ent*, f:-*ame*, g:-*is*, h:-*ière*, i:-*as*, j:-*eint*, k:-*our*,
l:-*ort*, m:-*euse*, n:-*ir*, o:-*er*, p:-*age*, q:-*ay*, r:-*art*, s:-*ence*, t:-*é*, u:-*ie*

DISCUSSION (literary). Patch 1927, 119 n. 1 (theme of Fortune); Huot 1987, 265; Heinrichs 1989a, 594–95. On the grouping of L12 and the *Lay de Plour, Qui bien aimme* (L22/16), see Huot 1987, 266 n. 22.

EDITIONS OF MUSIC. Gérold 1932, 327 (strophe 5); Prunières 1943, 64 (=1934 ed., 1:118) (strophe 5); Gérold 1936, 370 (strophe 5); Ludwig 1926–54, 4:38–40 (ed. Besseler); Schrade 1956b, 2:26–29 (critical notes 1956c, 61–62). Hoppin (1960, 19 n. 23) indicates that strophe 2 calls for triple subdivision of the breve in a prevailing duple context. The music of strophes 1 and 12 is the same, without transposition.

LITERARY AND MUSICAL ANTECEDENT. Schrade (1958–61, 848–49) indicates that L12 is metrically, semantically, and melodically very close to the *Roman de Fauvel* lai *Pour recouvrer alegiance* (ed. Rosenberg/Tischler 1991, 106–14 no. 48). L12 (ll. 27–28, strophe 2) quotes part of strophe 9 of *Pour recouvrer*; the crucial words quoted by Machaut, "Venés au corps," are even found on a banderole held by Fauvel in a miniature in the unique source, *F:Pn 146*, fol. 28*ter*, col. b.

DISCUSSION (musical). Machabey 1955b, 1:117–18 ("isorhythmic" formulas); Günther 1957, 123–24 (relationship between text and musical motives); Dömling 1970, 25–26, 29–30 (verse declamation, rhythmic motive); Bellamy 1978 (strophic structure). Schrade (1958–61, 848) indicates that the *Lay de Plour, Malgré Fortune* (L19/14) is modeled on L12.

Une vipere en cuer ma dame maint (ballade B27)
Refrain: *Cil troy m'ont mort et elle que Dieus gart*

MANUSCRIPTS WITH TEXT AND MUSIC.

[3] **V g**	fol. 310v	no. 27	2v (ca, ten)	[6] **G**	fol. 143v	no. 27	2v (ca, ten)
[4] **B**	fol. 308v	no. 27	2v (ca, ten)	[7] **E**	fol. 148r	no. 5	3v (ca, ten, ct)
[5] **A**	fol. 467v	no. 26	2v (ca, ten)				

TEXT MANUSCRIPT.

[10] **M**	fol. 241v	no. 27			
[41] **Wm**	fol. 23r	no. 23	[50] **Pa**	fol. 49v	no. 151
			Lo204 **VgBMAD** (see chap. 6.4)		

EDITIONS OF TEXT. Chichmaref 1909, 1:184 no. 204; Wilkins 1972, 67 no. 69.

TRANSLATION. Wilkins 1989, 156 (strophe 1); Wilson 1990a, 247.

TEXT STRUCTURE. 3 strophes: $\frac{a\ b}{1010}$, $\frac{a\ b\ c\ c\ dD}{1010\ 7101010}$ a:-*aint*, b:-*eille*, c:-*ort*, d:-*art*

EDITIONS OF MUSIC. Ludwig 1926–54, 1:30–31; Schrade 1956b, 3:110–11 (critical notes 1956c, 114); Wilson 1990a, 245–46 no. 73. See mention of syncopation problems in Hoppin 1960, 16 n. 16. The added contratenor in MS E is more skillfully composed than other added contratenors in E, with its musical rhyme, its recurring hocket sections, and even a touch of imitation with the tenor; Machabey (1955b, 2:41) considers it authentic; Dömling (1970, 75) also praises it.

DISCUSSION (musical). Machabey 1955b, 2:40–41; Dömling 1972, 304, 306 (text setting, refrain); Kühn 1973, 212–13 (melodic design); Reaney 1982, 297 (mode). The pervasive use of certain melodic formulas in *tempus imperfectum, prolatio major* links *Donnez, signeurs* (B26), *Une vipere* (B27), and *Je puis trop* (B28) as one group, and *Plourez, dames* (B32), *Nes qu'on* (B33), and *Se pour ce muir* (B36) as another; the same formulas are seen to a lesser extent in *En amer* (RF4), *Cinc, un* (R6), and *Douce dame, tant* (R20) (cf. Reaney 1955, 47; Günther 1957, 80–84; Hirshberg 1971, 120–33; Little 1980, 49; Arlt 1993, 63).

Veni Creator Spiritus. See *Christe / Veni* (M21).

Vidi Dominum. See *Amours qui a / Faus Samblant* (M15).

Vo dous regars, douce dame, m'a mort (rondeau R8)
MANUSCRIPTS WITH TEXT AND MUSIC (all 3v: ca, ten, ct).

[3]	**V g**	fol. 318r	no. 8	[6] **G**	fols. 151v–152r	no. 10
[4]	**B**	fol. 317r	no. 8	[7] **E**	fol. 138r	no. 11
[5]	**A**	fol. 479v	no. 15			

TEXT MANUSCRIPT.
[10] **M** fol. 244v no. 10

TREATISES. Deschamps, *Art de Dictier* (*F:Pn 840*, fol. 399r and [40] **I**, fol. 32r); see chap. 2.1.1m.

EDITIONS OF TEXT. Queux de Saint-Hilaire/Raynaud 1878–1903, 7:286; Chichmaref 1909, 2:572 no. 10; Sinnreich 1987, 114.

TRANSLATION. Sinnreich 1987, 139.

TEXT STRUCTURE. 10AB aA ab AB a:-*ort*, b:-*eint*

DISCUSSION (literary). Hoepffner 1908–21, 3:255, note to l. 340 of *Fonteinne*.

TEXTUAL LEGACY (England). Chaucer, *Merciles Beaute* (Benson 1987, 1091).

EDITIONS OF MUSIC. Ludwig 1926–54, 1:57–58; Schrade 1956b, 3:148–49 (critical notes 1956c, 128); Dömling 1970, 37 (diplomatic facs. in score). Barring discussed in Hoppin 1960, 24.

DISCUSSION (musical). Machabey 1955b, 1:157–59 (relates the tight structure of rhythmic blocks to the concept of *talea*); Günther 1957, 106–7 (motivic analysis); Dömling 1970, 37–47 (rhythmic and tonal structure; contratenor is essential, not added successively); Salop 1971, 77 (rhythmic procedure not successful); Kühn 1973, 260 n. 440 (criticism of Dömling 1970).

Voir Dit. See *Cilz ha bien* (VD18=V24); *Dame, se vous* (VD14=R13); *Dix et sept* (VD56=R17); *Je ne me puis* (VD11=V33); *L'ueil, qui est* (VD9=V34); *Longuement* (VD47=L18/13); *Nes qu'on* (VD16=B33); *Plourez, dames* (VD5=B32); *Plus belle* (VD10=V35); *Quant Theseüs / Ne quier* (VD57–58=B34); *Sans cuer, dolens* (VD31=R4); *Se pour ce muir* (VD61=B36).

4. Some related fourteenth-century musical works

Armes, Amours, Dames, Chevalerie / O fleur des fleurs de toute melodie (double ballade *déploration* on the death of Machaut; music by F. Andrieu, text by Eustache Deschamps).[95]
Refrain: *La mort Machaut, le noble rethorique*
MANUSCRIPT WITH TEXT AND MUSIC.
[59] **Ch** fol. 52r no. 84 4v (ca1, ca2, ten, ct)
TEXT MANUSCRIPTS.
F:Pn 840 fols. 28r–28v [40] **I** fol. 16v (*Armes, Amours*)
FACSIMILE. Gennrich 1948, plate 16 (**Ch**)

---

[95] Possibly the same composer as the Magister Franciscus who composed *Phiton Phiton* (Reaney 1960b, 27; Wilkins 1968, 55–56); see above on Machaut's *Phyton* (B38). Günther (1964, 186) suggests Franciscus de Goano as the composer of *Phiton* (bibliography in Tomasello 1983, 226–27).

EDITIONS OF TEXT. P. Paris 1875, x–xi (*O fleur*); Queux de Saint-Hilaire/Raynaud 1878–1903, 1:243–46 nos. 123–24 (notes, 1:375–76 with list of other editions); Patterson 1935, 2:66 (*Armes*); Wilkins 1969a, 67–68 nos. 50–51 (notes p. 132); Wilkins 1987, 60; Mühlethaler 1989, 389–90.

TRANSLATIONS. Cerquiglini/Berthelot 1987, 123–24 (*Armes, Amours* in modern French trans.); Wilkins 1987, 61 (complete); 1989, 105 (*O fleur*, strophe 1); L.W. Johnson 1990, 59–60 (strophe 1 of each ballade); Wimsatt 1991b, 246–47 (excerpts from each ballade); Palmer 1992, xxv (*O fleur*, strophe 1); see also discography (chap. 8.3 and 8.8).

TEXT STRUCTURE. 2 x 3 strophes, double ballade: $\frac{a}{10}'\frac{b}{10}\ \frac{a}{10}'\frac{b}{10}\ \frac{b}{1010}'\frac{c}{1010}\frac{b}{}\frac{C}{}$, a:-*ie*, b:-*ois*, c:-*ique*

DISCUSSION (literary). Caylus 1753a, 404; Zumthor 1972, 277 (=Eng. ed., 223); Brownlee 1978a, 219–20; Rubin 1978; G. Olson 1979; Kooijman 1982, 44; Brownlee 1984, 7–9; Cerquiglini 1985b, 88; Wilkins 1987, 61–62; Mühlethaler 1989; L.W. Johnson 1990, 59–60; Wimsatt 1991b, 246–47, 251; Walters 1992, 65; Cerquiglini-Toulet 1993b, 41, 42, 146, 151 (with text emendation); 1993c, 39–40; Magnan 1993; Planche 1993, 1138.

LITERARY ANTECEDENTS. Wilkins (1972, 176 n. 162; 1987, 62) and Wimsatt (1978, 74; 1991b, 246–47) note that *Armes, Amours* especially recalls Machaut's *Plourez, dames* (Lo229=B32=VD5); Wimsatt further notes (1984, 169–70; 1991b, 65, 82, 253, esp. n. 36) that Deschamps's pair of ballades imitates the ballade exchange of Jean de le Mote and Philippe de Vitry (see also Mühlethaler 1989, 400–401). Cerquiglini/Berthelot (1987, 123) note an allusion recalling Machaut's *Je preing congié* (Lo223).

TEXTUAL LEGACY (France). Jean Lebègue, letter of ca. 1395 (see chap. 2 n. 20). Martin Le Franc, *Champion des Dames* (see chap. 2.3.2d). For further on the theme "armes, amours," see, for instance, Wilkins 1969a, 129–30 (notes to nos. 38–39), 132 (notes to nos. 50–51); Günther 1972, 58; Cerquiglini 1985b, 124.

TEXTUAL LEGACY (England). John Gower, ballade *D'entier voloir sanz jammes departir*, with the *envoy, Au flour des flours, u toute ma creance* (ed. Macaulay 1899, 340–41; cited in Wilkins 1984, 166–67, without insisting upon a direct link). For further works in this tradition (Froissart, Deschamps, Chaucer, Gower), see Lowes 1904, 614–15 n. 3, 629 n. 2.

EDITIONS OF MUSIC. Droz/Thibault 1924, 13–20 (erroneously edited as two 2v works); Ludwig 1926–54, 1:49–51; Wooldridge 1932, 310–11 (ed. by Westrup after Droz/Thibault); Wilkins 1969a, 152–55 no. 6; Apel 1970–72, 1:2–3 no. 2; Wilkins 1980, 19–21 (Chaucer, *This wrecched worldes transmutacion* and *No man is wrecched* underlaid); Wilkins 1987, 57–62 no. 11; Greene 1981–89, 19:114–16 no. 84.

DISCUSSION (musical). Günther 1957, 167, 174–76 (analysis).

MUSICAL ANTECEDENT. Machaut, *Quant Theseüs / Ne quier* (B34) (Günther 1957, 176; Newes 1991a, 70).

MUSICAL LEGACY. Ciconia, virelai *Aler m'en veus* (cited in Günther 1972, 62; ed. Apel 1970–72, 1:23–24 no. 13; Bent/Hallmark 1985, 167–69 no. 44). The line "Armez, Amors, Damez, Chevalerie" was borrowed by Trebor for the refrain of his ballade *En seumeillant m'avint une vision* (ed. Apel 1970–72, 1:209–10 no. 108; Greene 1981–89, 18:53–55 no. 20), composed in 1389 for King John I of Aragon (Günther 1961–62, 45; 1972, 58). For a twentieth-century composition inspired by *Armes, amours / O fleur*, see chap. 2.5 (Thiele).

L[i] enseignement de Chaton / De touz les biens / Ecce tu pulchra et [sic] amica mea

SOURCES FOR TEXT AND MUSIC.

[57] **Iv**	fols. 26v–27r		no. 44	3v (tr, mot, ten)
[58] **Trém**	fol. xxviii		no. 63	(index only)
[70] **Frib**	fol. 86r *Guillermus de Mascandio*			3v (tr, mot, ten)

EDITION OF TEXT. Zwick 1948, 48–49.

ASCRIPTION. Besseler, in Ludwig 1926–54, 4:[82] (argues against attribution to Machaut); S.J. Williams 1952, 352–53 (against); Machabey 1955b, 2:111–12; Schrade 1956c, 44–46, 91–92 (against); Günther 1957, 143 n. 112 and 1958, 32 n. 23 (argues against attribution on the grounds that the regular cadences at the end of each *talea* are a very rare occurrence in authentic motets of Machaut).

TEXT STRUCTURE AND RELATIONSHIP TO ISORHYTHM.

Triplum: $\frac{\text{aa b b cc aa dd ee ff gg hh i i}}{88\ 8'8'\ 7'8\ 88\ 88\ 88\ 88\ 88\ 88\ 88}$ a:-*on*, b:-*ie*, c:-*ée*, -*té*, d:-*onne*, -*aye*,

e:-*ose*, f:-*iée*, -*ie*, g:-*aine*, h:-*ine*, i:-*er* (d- and f-rhymes are corrupt)

Motetus: $\frac{\text{a b a b a b a b b a}}{1010'\ 1010'\ 1010'\ 1010'\ 10'10}$ a:-*er*, b:-*ie*

TENOR SOURCE. *Ecce tu pulchra es amica mea* (Song of Songs, 1:14; see brief discussion in Burstyn 1976, 71) is a Matins antiphon for the Feast of the Annunciation (Zwick 1948, 50; Schrade 1956c, 91).

EDITIONS OF MUSIC. Zwick 1948, 53–57; Schrade 1956b, 3:34–36 (critical notes 1956c, 91–92); Burkhart 1972, 3–7.

DISCUSSION (musical). Zwick 1948, 47–52.

VIII

Discography

1. Introduction

The discography is organized in two complementary parts. After an introduction, the first part provides a listing of recordings of Machaut's music
arranged alphabetically by title (chap. 8.3), with a separate section for the Mass
(chap. 8.4). Chap. 8.5 comprises some medieval musical works related to
Machaut, including the *déploration* of Eustache Deschamps, a recording of the
anonymous ballade *Phiton, Phiton, beste tres venimeuse*, Anthonello da
Caserta's musical setting of Machaut's ballade *Biauté parfaite* (Lo140), and the
motet *Li enseignement de Chaton / De touz*, ascribed to Machaut in one
peripheral source. Finally I include two summaries, one for readers seeking
recordings of *Remede* and *Voir Dit* lyrics set to music (chap. 8.6), and the other
listing recommended recordings of works representative of each genre (chap.
8.7).

Unless specifically noted, I have heard and evaluated all performances.
Recordings are listed for each individual work, by director or name of
ensemble, record company, record number, and date of recording (if known or
inferable). Following this is a list of performance forces, with names of singers
when available, and the timing of the selection. For ballades, virelais, and lais, I
indicate how many strophes of the poem are performed, or, if the performance
is instrumental, repetition schemes. Finally, I have included some comments
and recommendations on the recordings available for each work, based not on
the entertainment or historical value of a given performance, but rather on recent
notions of performance practice in Machaut's time, or on a performance's utility
for instruction.

The second large part of the discography (chap. 8.8) is an index arranged
alphabetically by record label, providing a full bibliographical reference for each
recording, and a list of the works of Machaut performed on each recording
arranged alphabetically by title. This index also includes a few references to
reviews of the individual recordings. Many recordings have been re-released,
either by the original company under a new number or by another company;
such re-issues are listed in parentheses after the main number, or in a footnote. I
have avoided an elaborate cross-index of the re-issues, except in the case of re-
issues by the Musical Heritage Society.

A number of recordings remain that I have been unable to examine; for these,
printed discographies have provided the bibliographical citation (Jahiel 1960–
61; Coover/Colvig 1964; 1973; Croucher 1981; and most especially J.F. Weber
1979, an indispensable and reliable source of information). I am indebted
especially to Jerome F. Weber and John W. Barker for discographical
information and for the opportunity to hear recordings from their personal
collections. In addition, Weber has heard a number of the recordings that I have
not examined and has kindly supplied me with information on timings and
instrumentation.

2. Performance practice

Chansons. Recent research has greatly influenced our views of the performance
of the polyphonic fixed forms. The works notated in parts in the manuscripts
probably present versions to be sung, although skilled chamber instrumentalists

of the time would doubtless have been able to construct suitable instrumental arrangements. In any case, a typical manner of performance involved the participation of solo voices exclusively.[1] The recordings of Christopher Page's Gothic Voices on the Hyperion label provide us with beautiful realizations of this manner of performance, both in monophonic and polyphonic music. In earlier issues (Hyperion A66087, recorded in 1983), text was applied to parts that in the original sources remain textless (tenor, and, when present, triplum and contratenor), while the most recent releases (Hyperion CDA66463, CDA66588, CDA66619, and CDA66739) employ textless vocalization for these parts.[2] This newer practice seems to be the correct one. Scribes in the manuscripts exercised great care in clearly indicating the relationship between words and music in texted voices, scrupulously correcting copying errors (Earp 1983, chap. 3; 1991c). That performers should then haphazardly apply the text to parts left textless in such sources—breaking ligatures and splitting up long values as needed—seems unreasonable to me. It gives a false impression of the texture of the songs that have only one texted voice and also dulls the effect of those songs that actually were conceived—and notated explicitly in the manuscripts—with more than one texted part.

In the remarks below, I occasionally criticize all-instrumental performances of chansons. I certainly believe that the fixed forms were performed on instruments, but in such cases an arrangement was probably concocted, perhaps something similar to the arrangements seen in the Faenza codex [67]. The two Machaut arrangements in this manuscript, *Hont paur* (based on B25) and *De tout flors* (based on B31), have been recorded several times.

Probably the best we can do to get some impression of Machaut's songs today is to have solo voices perform the manuscript version, with only one voice declaiming the text, unless the manuscript calls for more than one texted voice, as in *Sans cuer m'en / Amis / Dame* (B17), *De triste / Quant / Certes* (B29), and *Quant Theseüs / Ne quier* (B34). Otherwise, all untexted parts ought to be vocalized.

Occasionally anonymous later composers supplied additional voices for some of Machaut's most widely-transmitted songs, and modern performers have tended to perform and record these unauthentic versions instead of the text Machaut left.[3] This problem arises for *On ne porroit* (B3), *Biauté qui* (B4), *De petit po* (B18), *De Fortune* (B23), and *De toutes flours* (B31).[4] I do not object

---

[1] See Page 1977; C. Wright 1981; Page 1982. The practice of singing untexted accompanying voices in chansons was recognized as a possibility quite a while ago. For instance, Reaney (1954c, 245; 1956, 8, 95–96; 1977, 7–9) suggests that lower voices could either be vocalized, or sung with the text of the cantus voice adapted. He maintains nevertheless that instrumental performance was the norm. J.R. White (1969) provides a brief conspectus of performance practices of the late 1960s. Another facet of this issue is text underlay (see Ludwig 1926–54, 3:1; Earp 1983, chap. 3; Bent 1984; Brown 1987; Earp 1991c; Welker 1992, 184–89). Earp demonstrates that the text placement in the manuscripts of Machaut is quite exact, indeed more exact and trustworthy than for many genres of music written between 1440 and 1540.

[2] See especially Page 1992.

[3] To be fair, it is often difficult to determine from the presentation of such works in the modern editions what is authentic and what is not.

[4] Two further works have not yet been recorded, *Une vipere* (B27), and *Se vous n'estes* (R7). *Rose, lis* (R10) has an unauthentic extra contratenor maladroitly scratched into MS C, a manuscript that lacks the triplum. The vocal scoring of the chansons is discussed in Ludwig 1902–3, 37–38; 1911, 409; Lowinsky 1954, 200; Reaney 1955, 48–49; Apfel 1960; 1961; Fischer 1961; Apfel 1964–65, 54–56; Reaney 1968, 65–66; S.J. Williams 1968; Dömling

to the performance of these later versions, but since we know Machaut's intentions in this regard, it would be valuable to hear those versions as well. Of the works listed above, only two recent recordings of *De toutes flours* give us the work as Machaut conceived it (see the recordings listed in chap. 8.3 by Vellard and Pérès).

Two other problems are peculiar to the virelais. First is the monophonic character of most of the works. Solo performers are tempted to present the works with rhythmic flexibility, especially employing rests of variable or indeterminate length at the ends of sections. I believe instead that the dance character of these works calls for an inflexible rhythm, not necessarily a fast tempo, but solid rhythm. Second, there is an unfortunate error in the printing of the text residua in the Schrade edition, implying that the refrain is to be repeated twice between strophes. This erroneous performance practice has spoiled many recordings that are otherwise competent (for examples, see *Douce dame jolie* [V4], *Dou mal* [V8], *Dame, vostre* [V17], *Foy porter* [V25/22], *Dame, mon cuer emportez* [V32/29], and *Se je souspir* [V36/30]).

Finally, recent recordings show a concern for authentic pronunciation of the French texts. Alton/Jeffery (1976) provides some guidance, including a cassette recording of a reading of Machaut's virelai *Plus dure* (V31/28), followed by a musical performance of the same work.

Motets. The considerations discussed above with regard to the performance of voices textless in the sources—tenor and contratenor—apply also to the motets. Most recordings use instruments on the untexted tenors and contratenors; fortunately, the formerly common practice of playing the tenor on a crumhorn seems largely to have gone out of fashion. Page's beautiful recording of *Felix virgo / Inviolata* (M23) uses voices only. In addition, the motet *Lasse! comment / Se j' aim* (M16) and *Trop plus / Biauté* (M20) have texted tenors, and thus the listener may sample several all-vocal performances.

Mass. The requirements for an ideal recording of the Mass embodying the most recent research can be boiled down to a single factor: a scoring involving only one voice to a part, with no instruments.[5]

Recordings vary greatly in the way the Kyrie is treated, from a single performance of each movement without any repetitions (Safford Cape), to repetitions of the polyphony in different scorings (Konrad Ruhland) to an *alternatim* treatment, the polyphony alternating either with plainchant (Alfred Deller and Andrew Parrott), or the polyphony alternating with an organ elaboration of the chant (Grayston Burgess). The manuscripts indicate a different solution. The repetition mark ".iii." is placed after the Kyrie I and Christe, and ".ii." is placed after the Kyrie II. Surely this indicates a threefold repetition of the polyphony as written for Kyrie I and Christe, a twofold repetition of the Kyrie II, with the Kyrie III rounding out the full ninefold invocation. Of the recordings I have heard, only August Wenzinger, doubtless

---

1969; 1970, 74–76; Hirshberg 1971, 76–90; Apfel 1974; Hoppin 1978b, 422–24; Reaney 1980a, 430, 435; Harden 1983, 163–68, 169–209; Leech-Wilkinson 1984, 21.

[5] Parrott (1977) provides an excellent overview of problems to be considered in a performance of the Mass. See also Fallows 1977a; for some views no longer current, see, for instance, Ficker 1929, 505; Cape 1959–60; Cramer 1975. The vast array of instrumental forces advocated by Ficker resulted in such recordings as that directed by Boepple in 1951 (see chap. 8.8, Concert Hall Society CHS 1107). Fallows (1977a, 290) notes that the researches of Roger Bowers and James McKinnon prove that the only instrument admissible in the Mass in the fourteenth century was the organ. See also Monnidendam 1953 (scoring); Reaney 1966, 719–21 and 1977, 10 (example of heterophonic instrumental doubling in the Credo, mm. 82–89); Dömling 1971, 26 n. 11 (tempo of Kyrie movements).

on the advice of Wolfgang Dömling, chooses this solution.[6]

The tenor-contratenor linking passages in the Gloria and Credo are clearly textless in the manuscripts and should be vocalized without carrying a syllable of text. All recordings give these passages to instruments except those by Burgess, Parrott, and Hillier. Parrott's version, employing textless vocalization, seems to me to be the correct one. The evidence of the manuscripts does not support texting this linking passage with the first syllable of the upcoming phrase of text, as is done in Burgess's version, supervised by Frank Harrison, and in Hillier's recent performance.

With regard to the fourteenth-century French pronunciation of Latin, Laurence Wright has supplied a transcription in the International Phonetic Alphabet of the text of the Mass Ordinary reflecting a medieval French pronunciation (Leech-Wilkinson 1990c, 110–14).

Some recordings have presented the Mass with Mass Propers, sometimes even including recitations and prayers. J.F. Weber (1991), and A.W. Robertson (1992, 110–11) discuss such liturgical reconstructions (items 11, 20 and 23 in the Mass discography, chap. 8.4).

3. The recordings in alphabetical series by title

Amis, t'amour me contreint [Le Lay des Dames] (L10/7)
Not recorded.

Amours doucement me tente (L7/6)
Not recorded.

Amours me fait desirer (B19)
1. George Hunter, Westminster XWN 18166 (1956). Lute, two vielles (1'35").
2. Ancient Instrument Ensemble of Zurich, Odyssey 32 160178 (1966). Bill Austin Miskell, tenor; Baroque oboe, bass viol (5'00"). Strophes 1 and 3 only.
3. Pierre Pernoux, Guilde Internationale du Disque SMS 2423 (1968?). Not heard.
4. Grayston Burgess, L'Oiseau-Lyre SOL 310 (1969). John Buttrey, tenor; tenor recorder, harp (4'11"). Strophes 1–3.
5. Symposium "Pro Musica Antiqua" de Prague, Charlin CL 39 (1970). Two recorders, vielle (2'03").
6. Dietrich Knothe, Philips 6580 026 (1971). Wolf Reinhard, tenor; alto recorder, tenor fiddle (4'48"). Strophes 1–3.
7. David Munrow, Seraphim SIC 6092 (1973). Martyn Hill, tenor; fiddle, bass rebec (2'36"). Strophes 1–2 only.
8. Christopher Page, Hyperion A66087 (1983). Margaret Philpot, contralto; Rogers Covey-Crump, tenor; Peter McCrae, baritone (4'07"). Strophes 1–3.
9. Paul Hillier, Schirmer Books ISBN 0-02-872953-6 (1990). Rogers Covey-Crump, John Potter, and Mark Padmore, tenors (4'44"). Strophes 1–3.
10. Alba Musica Kyo, Channel Classics CCS 7094 (1994). Chiyomi Yamanda, soprano; recorder, citole (4'43"). Strophes 1–3.

The Zurich group gives the work at a very slow tempo. The triplum in the Burgess and Knothe recordings is an octave too high. Munrow's performance is lively and well done.

---

[6] Parrott (1977, 493) acknowledges the manuscript evidence for this interpretation but implies that it is less practical for a modern presentation of the work than the alternation of plainsong and polyphony. If one must alternate plainsong, one must at least adopt the melody of Machaut's tenor. See also Cape 1959–60, 49–50.

Except for the erroneous texting of triplum and tenor, the performance by Page would be hard to surpass. Hillier almost does so—triplum and tenor are vocalized—but his recording is rhythmically too reserved.

Amours qui a / Faus Semblant / Vidi Dominum (M15)
1. Dominique Vellard, Harmonic Records H/CD 8825 (1988). Anne-Marie Lablaude, Brigitte Lesne, and Emmanuel Bonnardot, voices (2'28").

A fine recording, the best recorded example of one of the unipartite isorhythmic motets.

Armes, Amours / O fleur des fleurs (ballade, Deschamps/Andrieu)
See chap. 8.5.

Aucune gent / Qui plus aimme / Fiat voluntas tua (M5)
1. Dietrich Knothe, Philips 6580 026 (1971). Roswitha Trexler, contralto; Wolf Reinhold, tenor; tenor fiddle, tenor crumhorn (2'32").

One can gain at least something of an idea of the work from this recording.

Aymi! dame de valour (V3)
1. Thomas Binkley, EMI Reflexe 1C 063-30 106 (1972). Richard Levitt, countertenor; lira, lute, harp, bells (3'05"). Strophes 1–3.
2. Ensemble Tre Fontane, Scalen disc TRFC 0389 (1989). Shawm, hurdy-gurdy, percussion (2'50").
3. Christopher Page, Hyperion CDA66739 (1994). Andrew Tusa, tenor (2'49").

Binkley's performance is far too free, with an ornate prelude and postlude for lira, lute and bells. Drastic tempo variances at the *piedi* destroy the dance song character of the work. Tempo in Tusa's performance for Page is also too variable for the dance. The instrumental version of the Ensemble Tre Fontane includes newly-composed interludes.

Biauté qui toutes autres pere (B4)
1. Dietrich Knothe, Philips 6580 026 (1971). Hans-Joachim Rotzsch, tenor; alto lute, tenor fiddle (5'58"). Strophes 1–3.
2. Music for a While, 1750 Arch S 1773 (1977). Sheila Schonbrun and Christopher Kenny, voices; vielle (2'32"). Strophe 1 only.
3. Lukáš Matoušek, Panton 8111 0056 (1978). Zuzana Matoušková, mezzo-soprano; alto fiddle, dulcimer, bass recorder (1'35"). Strophe 1 only.
4. Helga Weber, I.H.W. 66.22371 (1980). Two recorders, transverse flute (1'40").
5. Christopher Page, Hyperion A66087 (1983). Margaret Philpot, contralto; Rogers Covey-Crump and Andrew King, tenors (4'46"). Strophes 1–3.
6. Ensemble Tre Fontane, Alba musica MU 244882 (1993). Not examined.

All five recordings examined utilize the unauthentic contratenor given only in MS E. In the rather slow recording by Music for a While, cantus and tenor are sung, with the text unfortunately applied to the tenor. In Page's recording, all voices are sung to beautiful effect, but text is applied to both tenor and contratenor, with long notes freely split in both lower voices to accommodate it.

Bone pastor Guillerme / Bone pastor qui / Bone pastor (M18)
1. Konrad Ruhland, Telefunken 6.41125 AS (1970). James Bowman, countertenor; Tom Sutcliffe, countertenor; organetto, recorder, two fiddles, crumhorn (2'25").
2. Guy Robert, Adès 7078–7080 (1977). Jean Belliard and Alain Zoepffel, countertenors; crumhorn, vielle, organetto (2'05").
3. Helga Weber, I.H.W. CD3.108 (1993). Kai Wessel, countertenor; Wilfried Jochens, tenor; two alto bombards, trombone, drum, bells (2'33").

The voices in Ruhland's recording are excellent, but the crumhorn on the tenor is regrettable. Robert's performance is well done but too fast for a clear articulation of the hockets in the diminution section. The tenor line in Weber's recording, already heavily scored, is unfortunately further emphasized by a drum and bell.

C'est force, faire le vueil (V16)
1. Ensemble Tre Fontane, Scalen disc TRFC 0187 (1987). Maurice Moncozet, voice; hurdy-gurdy (5'09"). Strophes 1–3 (lacks final refrain).
2. Christopher Page, Hyperion CDA66463 (1990–91). Andrew Tusa, tenor solo (3'27"). Strophes 1–3.

The performance by the Ensemble Tre Fontane is extroverted, with extensive interludes on the hurdy-gurdy. Page's performance is not rhythmically vital enough for dance.

Ce qui soustient moy, m'onneur et ma vie (R12)
1. Michel Sanvoisin, Arion ARN 38252 (1974). Soprano recorder, viol (1'18").
2. Ensemble Tre Fontane, Scalen disc TRFC 0187 (1987). Shawm, hurdy-gurdy (4'39").
3. Dominique Vellard, Harmonic Records H/CD 8825 (1988). Dominique Vellard and Emmanuel Bonnardot, voices (2'56").
4. Michel Sanvoisin, Edelweiss ED 1021 (1990). Soprano recorder, lute (1'29").

Both of Sanvoisin's instrumental recordings are overly fast. Vellard's all-vocal version is excellent, although unfortunately the text has been applied to the tenor. The instrumental rendition of the Ensemble Tre Fontane includes a prelude and very developed interlude on the hurdy-gurdy.

Certes mon oueil richement visa bel (R15)
Not recorded.

Christe qui lux es / Veni creator spiritus / Tribulatio proxima est et (M21)
1. Konrad Ruhland, Telefunken 6.41125 AS (1970). James Bowman, countertenor; Tom Sutcliffe, countertenor; recorders, crumhorn, fiddles, sackbut (3'44").
2. David Munrow, Archiv 2723 045 (1975). James Bowman and Charles Brett, countertenors; slide trumpet, tenor shawm (4'13").
3. Bernard Gagnepain, Erato EFM 18041 (1977). Recorder, vielle (*introitus*); two voices, vielle, lute, organ (6'04").
4. Les Ménestrels, Mirror Music 00006–00009 (1979). René Jacobs, countertenor; Yoshiharu Matsuura, tenor; Herbert Vogel and Manfred Weidmann, voices; organetto (3'43").
5. Dominique Vellard, Harmonic Records H/CD 8825 (1988). Anne-Marie Lablaude, Brigitte Lesne, Dominique Vellard, and Emmanuel Bonnardot, voices (4'28").
6. Helga Weber, I.H.W. CD3.108 (1993). Paul Gerhardt Adam and Kai Wessel, countertenors; two fiddles, two flutes, two tenor bombards, bass flute, drum (4'22").

For the textless *Introitus*, Ruhland uses viols, Les Ménestrels use an organ, Gagnepain uses recorder and vielle, while Munrow, Vellard, and Weber have the singers vocalize, the preferred solution. The tenor and contratenor in Les Ménestrels's recording are provided by a strangely distant doubling of voices and organ. Gagnepain is too slow. Munrow's recording is musically fine, but Vellard's unaccompanied performance is superb. The curious accentuation of the combined rhythms of the tenor and contratenor by a drum in Weber's performance renders it useless except as a curiosity to underline a single analytical point.

Cinc, un, trese, wit, neuf d'amour fine (R6)
1. Music for a While, 1750 Arch S 1773 (1977). Sheila Schonbrun, voice; recorder, vielle, finger cymbals (2'20").
2. Zoltán Majó, Electrecord ST-ECE 01929 (1981). Two recorders; viol (1'25").

Music for a While gives this important work a sprightly performance, but the text is left incomplete. The italicized portions of the following scheme (i.e., the crucial initial and internal statements of the refrain) are performed by instruments alone: A*Ba*A*ab*AB.

Comment puet on miex ses maus dire (R11)
1. Dietrich Knothe, Philips 6580 026 (1971). Hans-Joachim Rotzsch, tenor; alto lute, tenor fiddle (3'41").
2. Thomas Binkley, EMI Reflexe 1C 063-30 109 (1973). Andrea von Ramm, mezzo-soprano; lute, fiddle (3'51").
I prefer Binkley's very effective recording.

Comment qu'a moy lonteinne (V5)
1. Studio S.M. 45-71 (1961). Joseph Sage, countertenor solo (1'17"). Not heard.
2. Alfred Deller, Bach Guild 70656 (1961). Alfred Deller, countertenor; fiddle, recorder, tambourine (1'45"). Strophe 1 only.
3. Howard Brown, Pleiades P 250 (1968?). Judith Nelson, soprano solo (1'13"). Strophe 1 only.
4. Denis Stevens, Musical Heritage Society MHS 830437 (1969). Edgar Fleet, tenor solo (0'36"). Strophe 1 only.
5. Dietrich Knothe, Philips 6580 026 (1971). Hans-Joachim Rotzsch, tenor solo (3'28"). Strophes 1–3.
6. Thomas Binkley, EMI Reflexe 1C 063-30 106 (1972). Richard Levitt, countertenor; organetto, lute, harp (3'02"). Strophes 1–3.
7. Michel Jaffee, Vanguard VSD 71179 (1973). Joan Summers, soprano; psaltery, harp, oud (2'52"). Strophes 1–3.
8. David Munrow, Angel SBZ 3810 (1976). Bowed lyre solo (1'29").
9. Guy Robert, Adès 7078–7080 (1977). Jean Belliard, countertenor; recorder, Arabian lute, vielle, drums, tambourine (5'15"). Strophes 1–3.
10. Electrecord ST-ECE 01601 (1977?). Martha Kessler, mezzo-soprano solo (1'04"). Strophe 1 only, lacking final refrain.
11. Joel Cohen, Harmonia Mundi HMC 5122 (1985). Mark Kagan, tenor solo (3'50"). Strophes 1–3.
12. Christopher Page, Hyperion CDA66463 (1990–91). Margaret Philpot, alto solo (2'53"). Strophes 1–3.
13. Sonus, Dorian DIS 80109 (1993). Hazel Ketchum, soprano; saz, recorder, percussion (3'26"). Strophe 1, irregular repetitions.
Another popular work. Binkley indicates rather cryptically that he is aware that the work is a contrafact (the situation is fully explained in Arlt 1982, 268–71). Robert includes an instrumental prelude, interludes, and a very extended postlude; Sonus has a similar plan, without the postlude. Of the unaccompanied performances—which I prefer to those that add instrumental accompaniment—Knothe's recording is good, while Page's is ideal.

Contre ce dous mois de may. Le Lay de Nostre Dame (L15/10)
Not recorded.

Dame, a qui (V12)
1. Christopher Page, Hyperion A66087 (1983). Colin Scott Mason, baritone solo (5'38"). Strophes 1–3.
Too slow and not danceable.

Dame, a vous sans retollir (virelai RF6/V33)
1. Studio S.M. 45-71 (1961). Joseph Sage, countertenor solo (1'26"). Not heard.
2. Thomas Binkley, EMI Reflexe 1C 063-30 106 (1972). Andrea von Ramm, mezzo-soprano; women's chorus, tambourine (2'51"). Strophes 1–3.
3. Michel Sanvoisin, Arion ARN 38252 (1974). Joseph Sage, countertenor solo (2'52"). Strophes 1–2, lacking the final refrain.
4. Guy Robert, Adès 7078–7080 (1975). Jean Belliard, countertenor; transverse flute, vielle, Moorish guitar, bells (3'13"). Strophes 1–2 only.

5. Odhecaton, Carus 63205 (1979). Instrumental. Not heard.
6. Christopher Page, Hyperion A66087 (1983). Emma Kirkby, soprano solo (2'51"). Strophes 1–3.
7. Joel Cohen, Harmonia Mundi HMC 5122 (1985). Vielle, tambourine, recorder (1'43"). 2 repetitions.
8. Margaret Switten and Robert Eisenstein, The Medieval Lyric (1987). Peter Becker, baritone solo (2'18"). Strophes 1–3.
9. Ensemble P.A.N., New Albion Records NA068 CD (1994). John Fleagle, tenor; Laurie Monahan, mezzo-soprano; Michael Collver, countertenor; lute, two vielles (3'16"). Strophes 1–3.

The context of this work in the *Remede* makes the manner of performance clear. The narrator returns to his lady's château to find her and several courtiers outside, singing unaccompanied dance songs and doing a round dance. The only recording that allows such a scenario is Binkley's rhythmically vital rendition (although the verses from the *Remede* that immediately precede the virelai are recited in a badly garbled order [cf. *Tels rit*]). All three strophes are performed: first by the soloist, then subsequent refrains are sung by the ensemble, as if they had been taught the refrain by the soloist, a performance practice that is conceivable in such a dance. Sanvoisin's version is too mournfully slow and the rests too rhythmically free to be danceable (the *musica ficta* applied is also perverse). Robert's very slow rendition with drone is totally inappropriate to this genre. Emma Kirkby's performance for Page is not rhythmically insistent enough for dance music. Cohen's all-instrumental performance includes a recorder in heterophony. The version sung by Peter Becker for Margaret Switten is nicely done (the context of the poem makes it clear that the singer is a male) but again is marred by a delivery that is rhythmically too free. An enormous "danse balladée" for two vielles provides a prelude to the version by the Ensemble P.A.N., sung by a tenor with (heterophonic) vielle for the strophes and tutti refrains. Machaut's carefully calculated rhythms are altered in many places.

Dame, comment qu' amez de vous ne soie (B16)
1. August Wenzinger, Archiv 2533 054 (1969). Ernst Haefliger, tenor; harp (1'52"). Strophe 1 only.
2. Solveig Faringer, etc., BIS LP 2 (1974). Not heard (1'25").
3. Ensemble Tre Fontane, Scalen disc TRFC 0389 (1989). Hurdy-gurdy, recorder, percussion (4'44").

Wenzinger's presentation is rhythmically too free, and Haefliger's sliding attacks are irritating. Neither recording delivers the very lively performance suggested by this composition's notation in augmentation (see Günther 1960b, 296; 1982, 112).

Dame, de qui toute ma joie vient (ballade RF5/B42)
1. Michel Sanvoisin, Arion ARN 38252 (1974). Joseph Sage, countertenor, harp, two viols (3'27"). Strophes 1–2 only.
2. Guy Robert, Adès 7078–7080 (1975). Jean Belliard, countertenor; soprano lute, crumhorn, recorder, lute, rebec (4'41"). Strophes 1–2 only.
3. Christopher Page, Hyperion A66087 (1983). Emily van Evera, soprano; Margaret Philpot, contralto; Rogers Covey-Crump and Andrew King, tenors (5'24"). Strophes 1–3.
4a. Margaret Switten and Robert Eisenstein, The Medieval Lyric (1987). Mark Bleeke, tenor; William Sharp, baritone (4'16"). Strophes 1–3.
4b. Margaret Switten and Robert Eisenstein, The Medieval Lyric (1987) Mark Bleeke, tenor; lute, two vielles (4'25"). Strophes 1–3.
5. Ensemble P.A.N., New Albion Records NA068 CD (1994). Michael Collver, countertenor; two vielles (5'20"). Strophes 1–3.

Sanvoisin's recording is useable, though his singer curiously swallows the *-oie* syllables. Instrumentation changes between sections in Robert's version. Christopher Page offers a stunningly beautiful performance marred by the texting of voices untexted in the sources. Particularly in a four-voice texture as here, the texted triplum unduly obscures the cantus voice. The first version recorded for Margaret Switten is the two-voice version found in MS C, beautifully performed here by two soloists. Unfortunately, the tenor line has been texted. Since none of the longer note values are split up, the two voices are sometimes several measures apart in the text they are declaiming. The second version recorded for Margaret Switten is the four-voice version for voice and instruments, and this must be counted as the most successful recorded performance of the work to date. The Ensemble P.A.N. performs three lines, omitting the triplum.

Dame, je sui cilz / Fins cuers doulz / Fins cuers doulz (M11)
1. George Hunter, Westminster XWN 18166 (1956). Jantina Noorman, contralto; Richard Krause, tenor; vielle (3'13").
2. Dietrich Knothe, Philips 6580 026 (1971). Roswitha Trexler, contralto; Hans-Joachim Rotzsch, tenor; alto lute (1'35").
3. Thomas Binkley, EMI Reflexe 1C 063-30 109 (1973). Andrea von Ramm, mezzo-soprano; Richard Levitt, countertenor; lira (1'57").
4. Music for a While, 1750 Arch S 1773 (1977). Sheila Schonbrun and Christopher Kenny, voices; vielle (2'06").
5. Christopher Page, Hyperion A66087 (1983). Margaret Philpot, contralto; Rogers Covey-Crump, tenor; Peter McCrae, baritone (2'54").
6. Christopher Page, Hyperion CDA66619 (1992). Margaret Philpot, alto; Rogers Covey-Crump and Leigh Nixon, tenors (2'21").

The notation in augmentation (see Günther 1960b, 296) calls for a very lively performance. No recording is satisfactory in this regard, although Knothe comes closest.

Dame, je vueil endurer (V9)
1. Miroslav Klement, Supraphon 1112 2451-2 G (1977). Zdeněk Jankovský, tenor; fiddle (2'30"). Strophes 1–3, incomplete.
2. Ensemble Tre Fontane, Scalen disc TRFC 0187 (1987). Maurice Moncozet, voice; hurdy-gurdy (3'20"). Strophes 1–3.
3. Christopher Page, Hyperion CDA66619 (1992). Margaret Philpot, alto solo (2'28"). Strophes 1–3.

In Klement's version, the fiddle plays the refrain as an introduction, then the tenor and fiddle perform in unison. The refrain is omitted between strophes and at the end. The performance by the Ensemble Tre Fontane includes a very developed accompaniment on the hurdy-gurdy. Page's performance is nearly ideal.

Dame, mon cuer emportez (V32/29)
1. Pierre Hudrisier, Ariane ARI 148 (1988). Jean-Yves Guerry, countertenor; lute, rebec (4'30"). Strophes 1–2 only.

Instruments play through both sections before the voice enters. A superfluous repetition of the refrain follows the incorrect printing of the text residuum in Schrade's edition. Otherwise, the performance is quite useable.

Dame, mon cuer en vous remaint (rondeau RF7/R22)
1. Guy Robert, Adès 7078–7080 (1975). Jean Belliard, countertenor; vielle, recorder, lute, crumhorn (3'51").
2. Christopher Page, Hyperion A66087 (1983). Margaret Philpot, contralto; Rogers Covey-Crump and Andrew King, tenors (4'22").
3. Margaret Switten and Robert Eisenstein, The Medieval Lyric (1987). Peter Becker, countertenor; Mark Bleeke, tenor; William Sharp, baritone (3'55").
4. Ensemble P.A.N., New Albion Records NA068 CD (1994). Laurie Monahan, mezzo-soprano; Michael Collver, countertenor; John Fleagle, tenor (4'30").

Instrumentation changes in the course of Robert's performance. The other two recordings employ voices with no instrumental doubling, but with text applied to the originally untexted triplum and tenor. This practice, while still unjustified, is not too objectionable for a highly melismatic rondeau such as this one, since it is usually possible for all three voices to set a syllable in the same place, and thus to declaim at the same rate. Of the three choices, I prefer Page's recording.

Dame, ne regardez pas (B9)

1. Lukáš Matoušek, Panton 8111 0056 (1978). Vladimír Doležal, counter-tenor; ala bohemica, alto fiddle, alto crumhorn, alto recorder, lute, tenor cornemuse, alto cornett, triangle (1'40"). Strophe 1 only.
2. Early Music Consort, JRC 970 (1979). Two recorders, lute, viol, with guitar part newly composed (1'56").
3. Dominique Vellard, Harmonic Records H/CD 8825 (1988). Two vielles (3'30").
4. Ensemble Tre Fontane, Scalen disc TRFC 0389 (1989). Shawm, hurdy-gurdy, percussion (3'52").
5. Michel Sanvoisin, Edelweiss ED 1021 (1990). Tenor recorder, vielle (1'51").
6. Sonus, Dorian DIS 80109 (1993). Lute, chitarra (3'15").
7. Alba Musica Kyo, Channel Classics CCS 7094 (1994). Shawm, vielle (2'02").

Matoušek's performance is sung; he confines his imposing instrumentarium to the refrain. The instrumental version of the Ensemble Tre Fontane is quite unorthodox in its repetition scheme and use of prelude and interlude.

Dame, se vous m'estes lointeinne (B37)

1. David Munrow, Seraphim SIC 6092 (1973). Bagpipes solo (2'02").
2. Dominique Vellard, Harmonic Records H/CD 8825 (1988). Recorder, harp, lute, two vielles (2'02"). Three repetitions.
3. Michel Sanvoisin, Edelweiss ED 1021 (1990). Marc Guillard, baritone; organ, vielle, cornett (2'55").

Munrow treats the work as virtuoso bagpipes music. The refrain, which also serves as an introduction, is always repeated twice (three times at the very end). Two fiddles provide drones for Vellard's instrumental version. Sanvoisin's sung version, which is accompanied by a drone *C* in the organ throughout, is the simplest presentation yet.

Dame, se vous n'avez aperceü (R13)

1. Les Ménestrels, Mirror Music 00006–00009 (1979). René Jacobs, countertenor; douçaine, cornett (3'22").

This recording is useable, despite Jacobs's unappealing vocal mannerisms.

Dame, vostre dous viaire (V17)

1. August Wenzinger, Archiv 2533 054 (1969). Ernst Haefliger, tenor; hurdy-gurdy (2'56"). Strophe 1 only.
2. Aliénor AL 1019 (1987). Esther Lamandier, soprano and organetto (5'20"). Strophes 1 and 3 only.
3. Dominique Vellard, Harmonic Records H/CD 8825 (1988). Dominique Vellard, voice; flute, vielle (6'02"). Strophes 1–3.
4. Paul Hillier, Schirmer Books ISBN 0-02-872953-6 (1990). Rogers Covey-Crump, tenor solo (5'25"). Strophes 1–3.

Wenzinger's lugubrious and rhythmically free approach obscures the dance-like quality of the work. Lamandier plays a prelude and interlude on the organetto and accompanies herself with drones and unison playing. A superfluous repetition of the refrain follows the incorrect printing of the text residuum in Schrade's edition. Vellard begins with an instrumental statement of the refrain on recorder with drones in the fiddle. The drones are retained throughout the vocal number, and the recorder returns for the refrains. Rogers Covey-Crump gives a nice solo performance for Hillier, but the interpretation is not rhythmically vital enough for dance.

David Hoquetus. See *Hoquetus David.*

De Bon Espoir / Puis que la douce / Speravi (M4)
1. David Munrow, Seraphim SIC 6092 (1973). James Bowman and Charles Brett, countertenors; alto cornemuse (2'58").
2. Zoltán Majó, Electrecord ST-ECE 01929 (1981). Three recorders; viol; drum (3'28").
3. Paul Hillier, Schirmer Books ISBN 0-02-872953-6 (1990). Rogers Covey-Crump and John Potter, tenors; organ (2'52").
4. Egbert Schimmelpfennig, Fono FCD 97736 (1990). Anita Weltzien, Lucia Laake, and Kai Roterberg, voices; organetto (2'34").

Musically Munrow's recording is superb, although the tenor, played on a cornemuse, is too reedy for my taste. Hillier's reading is more reserved, although beautifully done. The voices in Schimmelpfennig's performance are badly overbalanced by the organetto. Majó's instrumental version begins with the second *talea* of the diminution section, eventually running through the complete work.

De bonté, de valour (V10)
1. Sonus, Dorian DIS 80123 (1993). Hazel Ketchum, soprano; oud, saz, percussion (4'35"). Strophes 1–3.

Includes instrumental prelude and interludes. As in other recordings of this singer, the French pronunciation is notably poor.

De desconfort, de martyre amoureus (B8)
Not recorded.

De Fortune me doy pleindre et loer (B23)
1. John White, Decca DL 79431 (1967). Earnest Murphy, countertenor; soprano recorder, bass viol, alto crumhorn, organetto (2'53"). Strophes 1–2 only.

B23 was almost as popular in the fourteenth century as *De petit po* (B18), and again manuscripts of the late fourteenth century provide a contratenor (in this case there are three different versions) for a work that Machaut had left in a scoring for three voices (triplum, cantus, tenor). Both Ludwig and Schrade print two versions of the contratenor, and White gives us everything in the edition, an improbable five-voice version with adjustments for the many places when the contratenor(s) as written are incompatible with the triplum.

De petit po, de niant volenté (B18)
1. Ancient Instrument Ensemble of Zurich, Odyssey 32 160178 (1966). Bill Austin Miskell, tenor; fiddle, soprano recorder, crumhorn, viol (4'00"). Strophes 1–2 only.
2. John White, Decca DL 79431 (1967). Flute, harpsichord, crumhorn, bass viol, organetto (1'28").
3. August Wenzinger, Archiv 2533 054 (1969). Ernst Haefliger, tenor; lute, positive organ (1'45"). Strophe 1 only.

The first two recordings present the unauthentic four-voice version transmitted only in manuscripts of the late fourteenth century. The contratenor should be suppressed; Machaut left the work in three voices with triplum. The tempo is snappy and the performance attractive in White's instrumental recording. The instrumental accompaniment in the Zurich recording changes in the course of the piece, and the quality of this performance is not high. Wenzinger's recording omits the unauthentic contratenor and is useable but a bit slow. It is unfortunate that Machaut's most popular work has not yet received a recording worthy of it.

De tout flors (intabulation in **Fa** [67]). See *De toutes flours* (B31).

De tout sui si confortee (V38/32)
1. Safford Cape, Anthologie Sonore AS 3 (1940). H.H. Guermant, soprano; medieval harp (1'46"). Strophe 1 only, incomplete.
2. Safford Cape, Archive ARC 3032 (1956). Elisabeth Verlooy, soprano; recorder (1'40"). Strophe 1 only.

3. Studio für alte Musik, Da Camera SM 91702 (1969). Helge Eicke, soprano solo (2'16"). Not heard.
4. Marin Constantin, Electrecord STM-ECE 0899 (1967?). Women's chorus (1'39"). Strophe 1 only, incomplete.
5. Lukáš Matoušek, Panton 8111 0056 (1978). Zuzana Matoušková, mezzosoprano; Vladimír Doležal, countertenor; Josef Života, baritone; alto recorder, tenor crumhorn, shawm, soprano cornett, two fiddles, lute, tambourine, triangle (1'38"). Strophe 1 only.

No recording examined is useable. The recording with chorus by Constantin provides an early example of vocalization of the textless tenor line.

De toutes flours n' avoit et de tous fruis (B31)
1. George Hunter, Westminster XWN 18166 (1956). Jantina Noorman, contralto; recorder, lute, vielle (2'39"). Strophe 1 only.
2. J.J. Lesnour, Ducretet Thompson 320 C 081 (1960?). Not heard.
3. Lawrence Selman, Musical Heritage Society MHS 1141 (1969). Two bass recorders, lute, two bass viols (1'43").
4. Thomas Binkley, EMI Reflexe 1C 063-30 109 (1973). Andrea von Ramm, harp; Richard Levitt, countertenor; lute, fiddle (6'16"). Strophes 1–3.
5. David Munrow, Seraphim SIC 6092 (1973). Martyn Hill, tenor; treble recorder, lute, fiddle, bass rebec (3'14"). Strophes 1–2 only.
6. Kees Otten, Telefunken, 6.42357 AW (1979). Marius van Altena, tenor; bass recorder, lute, tenor fiddle, sackbut (8'03"). Strophes 1–3
7. Ensemble Super Librum, Sonclair Records CD JB128836 (1988). Susanne Norin, mezzo-soprano; recorder, organetto (5'27"). Strophes 1–2 only.
8. Dominique Vellard, Harmonic Records H/CD 8825 (1988). Dominique Vellard, tenor; harp, vielle (6'36"). Strophes 1–3.
9. Paul Hillier, Schirmer Books ISBN 0-02-872953-6 (1990). David James, countertenor; John Potter and Rogers Covey-Crump, tenors; Paul Hillier, bass (5'56"). Strophes 1–3.
10. Marcel Pérès, Harmonia Mundi HMC 901354 (1990). Gérard Lesne, countertenor; Josep Benet, tenor; Josep Cabré, baritone (5'03"). Strophes 1 and 3 only.

Recordings of the Faenza intabulation:
1. Aimée Van de Wiele, Critère CRD 130 (1959). Harpsichord. Not heard.
2. August Wenzinger, Archiv 2533 054 (1969). Positive organ solo (3'00").
3. Thomas Binkley, EMI Reflexe 1C 063-30 109 (1973). Gittern, harp (2'18").
4. David Munrow, Seraphim SIC 6092 (1973). Organ solo (2'47").
5. Guy Robert, Adès 7078–7080 (1975). Soprano lute, rebec, tenor lute, crumhorn (2'05").
6. Ensemble Super Librum, Sonclair Records CD JB128836 (1988). Recorder, organetto (2'52").
7. Michel Sanvoisin, Edelweiss ED 1021 (1990). Organ, vielle (3'31").
8. Marcel Pérès, Harmonia Mundi HMC 901354 (1990). Clavicytherium solo (5'55").
9. Ensemble Tre Fontane, Alba musica MU 244882 (1993). Not examined (5'53").
10. Ensemble P.A.N., New Albion Records NA068 CD (1994). Vielle, lute (2'45").

All recordings of the chanson except Vellard's and Pérès's include an unauthentic fourth part, not a contratenor, as in the earlier *De petit po* (B18), but a triplum. Of these, I like

Munrow's bright tempo the best. Binkley's performance is very tasteful, and in some ways preferable to Munrow, who seems to force things along a bit too squarely. The instrumentation of Otten's recording provides for a very strong cantus/tenor projection.

There are three strong choices of recordings, the authentic three-voice version of Vellard, the all-vocal three-voice performance of Pérès, and the four-voice performance of Hillier, in which untexted voices vocalize. The recording by the Ensemble Super Librum stands apart; after an improvisatory prelude on the organetto, it too omits the triplum but has a very curious scoring, placing the vocalist on the tenor, to which text is applied.

The Binkley, Munrow, Sanvoisin, Pérès and Ensemble P.A.N. recordings of the Faenza instrumental arrangement are well done. Robert's recording is too heavily scored, and he composes an additional part. Again, the performance by the Ensemble Super Librum is unusual; after an improvisatory introduction on the recorder, it proceeds in a highly embellished version of the already florid Faenza music.

De triste cuer faire joyeusement / Quant vrais amans aimme amoureusement / Certes, je di et s'en quier jugement (B29)
1. Safford Cape, Archive ARC 3032 (1956). René Letroye and Franz Mertens, tenors; Willy Pourtois, bass (2'24"). Strophe 1 only.
2. John White, Decca DL 79431 (1967). Sheila Schonbrun, soprano; Ray De Voll, tenor; Anthony Tamburello, bass; flute, bass flute, bass viol, psaltery (3'47"). Strophe 1 only.
Both recordings are too ponderously slow to be useful.

Diex, Biauté, Douceur, Nature (V19)
Not recorded.

Dix et sept, .v., .xiii., .xiiii. et quinse (R17)
1. Guy Robert, Adès 7078–7080 (1977). Jean Belliard, countertenor; crumhorn, transverse flute, rebec, organetto, lute (3'41").
2. Les Ménestrels, Mirror Music 00006–00009 (1979). René Jacobs, countertenor; lute, fiddle (3'54").
Instrumentation changes in Robert's performance, which is introduced and followed by spoken text from the *Voir Dit*. Jacobs's recording for Les Ménestrels, also framed by *Voir Dit* readings, is useable, with fewer vocal mannerisms than in his recording of *Dame, se vous n'avez* (R13).

Donnez, signeurs, donnez a toutes mains (B26)
1. August Wenzinger, Archiv 2533 054 (1969). Ernst Haefliger, tenor; alto fiddle, tenor fiddle, dulcian (3'15"). Strophes 1 and 3 only.
2. Christopher Page, Hyperion CDA66588 (1991). Margaret Philpot, alto; Charles Daniels and Leigh Nixon, tenors (4'21"). Strophes 1–3.
Page's all-vocal version now supersedes Wenzinger's recording.

Dou mal qui m'a longuement (V8)
1. Joel Cohen, Harmonia Mundi HMC 5122 (1985). Nancy Armstrong, soprano solo (2'50"). Strophes 1–2 only.
2. Aliénor AL 1019 (1987). Esther Lamandier, soprano and organetto (1'45"). Strophes 1–3
Cohen's performance is far too slow. Lamandier's performance is nice, though marred by the double repeat between strophes of the refrain, one of which is always played on the organetto alone.

Douce dame jolie (V4)
1. Victor 45083 (1915). Lambert Murphy, tenor; harp, lute (1'12"). Not heard.
2. Lumen 33405 (1947). Pierre Deniau, tenor; ensemble. Not heard.
3. Boite à Musique LD 306 (1954). Jacques Douai, tenor; guitar (1'26"). Not heard.
4. Vanguard VRS 448 (1954). Roland Hayes, tenor; piano (1'30"). Strophe 1 only, arr. Weckerlin.

5. George Hunter, Westminster XWN 18166 (1956). Richard Krause, tenor solo (2'25"). Strophes 1–3.
6. Club Français du Disque CFD set 230 (1960?). Yves Tessier, tenor; lute. Not heard.
7. Studio S.M. 45-71 (1961). Joseph Sage, countertenor (1'38"). Not heard.
8. John White, Decca DL 79431 (1967). Sheila Schonbrun and Elizabeth Humes, sopranos; Anthony Tamburello, bass; soprano recorder, viols, rauschpfeife, finger cymbals, tambourine, drum (2'02"). Strophes 1–3.
9. Grayston Burgess, L'Oiseau-Lyre SOL 310 (1969). Geoffrey Shaw, baritone solo (1'24"). Part of strophe 1, then strophe 3.
10. David Munrow, Seraphim SIC 6092 (1973). Martyn Hill, tenor; James Bowman, Charles Brett, Martyn Hill, and Geoffrey Shaw, chorus; sopranino recorder, two cornetts, two rebecs, citole, tabor (2'13"). Strophes 1–3.
11. Les Musiciens de Provence, Arion ARN 34217 (1973). Maurice Guis, psaltery; harp (1'48").
12. Michel Jaffee, Vanguard VSD 71179 (1973). Joan Summers, soprano; Jan DeGaetani, mezzo-soprano; Constantine Cassolas, tenor; Alan Baker, baritone; recorder, lute, fiddle (4'19"). Strophes 1–3, then strophe 1 repeated.
13. Michel Sanvoisin, Arion ARN 38252 (1974). Joseph Sage, countertenor solo (1'54"). Strophes 1–2 only, lacking the final refrain.
14. Guy Robert, Adès 7078–7080 (1977). Lute solo (0'52").
15. John Sothcott, Enigma VAR 1046 (1977). Soprano, recorder, hurdy-gurdy, dulcimer, drum (2'35"). Strophes 1–3, incomplete.
16. John Renbourn, Kicking Mule Records KM312 (1980). John Molineux, tenor; dulcimer, guitar, soprano and tenor recorders, glockenspiel, tabla, spoons, finger cymbals (3'10"). Strophes 1–3 in English translation, lacking final refrain.
17. Guy Robert, Arion 36554 (1981). Arabian lute, recorder, fiddle, chalumeau, jew's harp, soprano and bass tamburas (3'55").
18. Sphemusations IMI 1002 (1982?). Andree Back, soprano; harp. Not heard.
19. Christopher Page, Hyperion A66087 (1983). Margaret Philpot, contralto solo (2'45"). Strophes 1–3.
20. Joel Cohen, Harmonia Mundi HMC 5122 (1985). Lute; Mark Kagan, tenor; Nancy Armstrong, soprano; vielle, transverse flute (5'26"). Strophes 1–3.
21. Michel Sanvoisin, Edelweiss ED 1021 (1990). Joseph Sage, countertenor solo (3'54"). Strophes 1–3.
22. Alba Musica Kyo, Channel Classics CCS 7094 (1994). Citole, lute, transverse flute, shawm, vielle (4'35").

Perhaps it is the folk-like simplicity of this song that has contributed to its popularity. It is the most recorded chanson of Machaut. The work is best presented as a simple unaccompanied dance song. White, Munrow, Jaffee, and Sothcott all employ whole orchestras full of special instruments, and often free heterophonic lines are mixed in. Cohen's recording, which begins with a fanciful lute solo, is only slightly more modest. Munrow observes Schrade's incorrect indication of the internal refrains in the virelai form, repeating the refrain twice between each strophe. Robert's lute solo is short (Abb), and near the end provides background music to a recited text from the *Voir Dit* as an introduction to the recording of *Plourez, dames* (B32) that follows. The same director's 1980 instrumental rendition is a wild fantasia. Hunter, Burgess, Sanvoisin (two recordings), and Page adopt the prudent monophonic route. But Burgess is not useable because the *cauda* of the first strophe is omitted. Sanvoisin and Page are too free with the length of rests. This leaves Hunter's early recording, still the best in all respects. Two of the recordings are quite unusual. The folksong-like arrangement by the John Renbourn Group is quite attractive, giving the work in free translation by Ann Lister (refrain: "My sweet and fair lady, never believe of me that I have bent my knee to anyone but you"). Finally, Roland Hayes sings the nineteenth-century arrangement for voice and piano by Jean-Baptiste Théodore Weckerlin (see chap. 2.5).

Douce dame, tant com vivray (R20)
1. George Hunter, Westminster XWN 18166 (1956). Recorder, lute (1'23").
2. Michel Sanvoisin, Arion ARN 38252 (1974). Joseph Sage, countertenor; recorder (2'48").

Sanvoisin's recording is useable, though the text underlay has been altered for some reason.

Dous amis, oy mon complaint (B6)
1. Joel Cohen, Harmonia Mundi HMC 5122 (1985). Nancy Armstrong, soprano; vielle (3'42"). Strophes 1–2 only.
2. Dominique Vellard, Harmonic Records H/CD 8825 (1988). Dominique Vellard and Emmanuel Bonnardot, voices (6'28"). Strophes 1–3.
3. Ensemble Tre Fontane, Alba musica MU 244882 (1993). Not examined (5'46").

Cohen provides a fluid delivery, but uses the erroneous Schrade transcription.[7] The solo voices in the Vellard performance provide an excellent impression of this early work, although the tenor has been texted.

Dous viaire gracieus (R1)
1. August Wenzinger, Archiv 2533 054 (1969). Ernst Haefliger, tenor; alto recorder, tenor fiddle (1'31").
2. Thomas Binkley, EMI Reflexe 1C 063-30 109 (1973). Richard Levitt, countertenor; lute, harp (1'37").
3. Lukáš Matoušek, Panton 8111 0056 (1978). Vladimír Doležal, countertenor; alto fiddle, alto crumhorn (1'10").
4. Les Ménestrels, Mirror Music 00006–00009 (1979). René Jacobs, countertenor; fiddle, cornett (1'55").
5. Alba Musica Kyo, Hungaroton SLPD 12589 (1986). Not heard.
6. Dominique Vellard, Harmonic Records H/CD 8825 (1988). Anne-Marie Lablaude and Brigitte Lesne, voices; recorder (1'45").
7. Alba Musica Kyo, Channel Classics CCS 7094 (1994). Chiyomi Yamanda, soprano; citole, recorder (2'00").

All recordings I have heard are useable. In Wenzinger's recording, the triplum is played an octave too high. It would be interesting to hear this short but highly dissonant work with voices on all three parts. The version of Vellard is closest to the ideal, with two parts sung (the text has been applied to the tenor, however).

En amer a douce vie (ballade RF4/B41)
1. Lawrence Selman, Musical Heritage Society MHS 1141 (1969). Alto recorder, two tenor recorders, bass recorder (1'29").
2. Guy Robert, Adès 7078–7080 (1975). Jean Belliard, countertenor; rebec, Moorish guitar, lute, transverse flute (3'15"). Strophes 1–2 only.
3. Margaret Switten and Robert Eisenstein, The Medieval Lyric (1987). Laurie Monahan, mezzo-soprano; rebec, lute, fiddle (3'52"). Strophes 1–3.
4. Ensemble P.A.N., New Albion Records NA068 CD (1994). Laurie Monahan, mezzo-soprano; two vielles, lute (4'00"). Strophes 1–3.

The instrumentation employed in Robert's and in Switten's performance is less than ideal; Switten's version is quite fast, with the instruments lightly played. The version by the Ensemble P.A.N. is currently the best available.

---

7 See Hoppin 1960, 24 and the corrected transcription in Hoppin 1978a, no. 62 (Ludwig's correct underlay should be adapted to this edition).

En demantant (L24/18)
Not recorded.
En mon cuer ha un descort (V27/24)
Not recorded.
Esperance qui m'asseüre (B13)
1. Sequentia, University of Texas Press ISBN 0-292-78520-8 (1988). Barbara Thornton, soprano; fiddle (3'46"). Strophes 1–3. This performance is rhythmically too free for my taste.

Felix virgo mater / Inviolata genitrix / Ad te suspiramus gementes (M23)
1. Jeanne Rambert, Lumen 3.22.015 (1949?). Jeanne Rambert, alto; M. Husson, tenor; two trombones (3'21"). Not heard.
2. Jacques Chailley, Erato LDE 3377 (1968). Rémy Corazza, tenor; José van Dam, bass; viol, trombone (5'19").
3. Bernard Gagnepain, Erato EFM 18041 (1977). Recorder, three viols, lute (2'18"). Introitus and one *talea* only.
4. Guy Robert, Adès 7078–7080 (1977). Jean Belliard and Alain Zoepffel, countertenors; crumhorn, bombard, organetto, lute, rebec (3'00").
5. Christopher Page, Hyperion A66087 (1983). Margaret Philpot, contralto; Rogers Covey-Crump, tenor; Colin Scott Mason and Peter McCrae, baritones (3'41").
6. Dominique Vellard, Harmonic Records H/CD 8825 (1988). Anne-Marie Lablaude, Brigitte Lesne, Dominique Vellard, and Emmanuel Bonnardot, voices (4'35").
7. Helga Weber, I.H.W. CD3.108 (1993). David Cordier, countertenor; Wilfried Jochens, tenor; fiddle, flute, tenor bombard, drum (4'16").

Chailley's performance is very slow and dated. Robert's recording is very fast, but well done, although the lower voices have an overly full instrumentation. The drum tapping out combined rhythms of tenor and contratenor, apparently to serve an analytical point, spoils Weber's recording. Two excellent performances with solo voices are available, by Page and Vellard. Page has underlaid the chant text to both tenor and contratenor, surely an unsupportable performance practice, nevertheless his is perhaps the best available recording of any Machaut motet.

Fons tocius superbie / O livoris feritas / Fera pessima (M9)
1. Konrad Ruhland, Telefunken 6.41125 AS (1970). James Bowman and Tom Sutcliffe, countertenors; recorder, cornett, crumhorn, fiddle (2'30").
2. Thomas Binkley, EMI Reflexe 1C 063-30 109 (1973). Andrea von Ramm, mezzo-soprano; Richard Levitt, countertenor; douçaine (1'52").
3. Bernard Gagnepain, Erato EFM 18041 (1977). Male chorus, sackbut (3'45").
4. Lukáš Matoušek, Panton 8111 0056 (1978). Zuzana Matoušková, mezzo-soprano; Vladimír Doležal, countertenor; alto fiddle, tenor fiddle, bass recorder, lute, chime bells, dulcimer (2'20").
5. Helga Weber, I.H.W. CD3.108 (1993). Paul Gerhardt Adam, counter-tenor; Gerd Türk, tenor; crumhorn, woodblock (2'06").

The rhythmic freedom so exciting in Binkley's recording of *Quant en moy / Amour* (M1) is rather irritating here; the tempo is far too fast for comfortable declamation of the text. Ruhland's recording is preferable, even with its heavily scored tenor line. Matoušek tries a varied scoring of the motetus, partially sung with text, and partially performed on instruments. The result is unsatisfactory. Gagnepain's version is very slow, and the vocal lines are an octave too low in relation to the tenor. In Weber's recording, a woodblock perversely taps out combined rhythms of triplum and motetus.

Foy porter (V25/22)
1. Grayston Burgess, L'Oiseau-Lyre SOL 310 (1969). Ian Partridge, tenor; sopranino recorder, tabor (2'46"). Strophes 1 and 3 only.

2. Michel Jaffee, Vanguard VSD 71179 (1973). Alan Baker, baritone; lute, oud, kemençe (2'38"). Strophes 1–2 only.
3. Music for a While, 1750 Arch S 1773 (1977). Sheila Schonbrun and Christopher Kenny, voices; kemençe, vielle, percussion (3'42"). Strophes 1–3.
4. Christopher Page, Hyperion A66087 (1983). Emma Kirkby, soprano solo (3'13"). Strophes 1–3.
5. Aliénor AL 1019 (1987). Esther Lamandier, soprano and organetto (3'52"). Strophes 1–3.

Burgess begins with a highly decorated recorder solo, which continues to accompany the voice heterophonically. Lamandier's version is again spoiled by observing Schrade's double repetition of the refrain between strophes. The version sung by Emma Kirkby for Page ought to be definitive, but small unmeasured pauses between sections mar the rhythmic vitality.

Gais et jolis, liés, chantans et joieus (B35)
1. Robert Eisenstein, Delos D/CD 1003 (1979). Peter Becker, countertenor; psaltery, lute, harp (3'47"). Strophes 1 and 3 only.
2. Kees Otten, Telefunken 6.42357 AW (1979). Rita Dams, mezzo-soprano; two bass recorders (4'38"). Strophes 1–3.
3. Joel Cohen, Harmonia Mundi HMC 5122 (1985). Transverse flute, lute, vielle (3'00"). Two repetitions.
4. Alba Musica Kyo, Hungaroton SLPD 12589 (1986). Not heard.
5. Alba Musica Kyo, Channel Classics CCS 7094 (1994). Chiyomi Yamanda, soprano; citole, recorder (4'56"). Strophes 1–3.

The choice of instruments for the lower voices is unfortunate in Otten and Alba Musica Kyo, but both recordings are nicely sung, and complete. Eisenstein's recording includes an instrumental introduction. The flute in Cohen's recording heavily embellishes the repeats, in a style completely unattested for the fourteenth century.

Hareu! hareu! le feu / Helas! ou sera / Obediens usque ad mortem (M10)
1. David Munrow, Seraphim SIC 6092 (1973). James Bowman and Charles Brett, countertenors; slide trumpet (1'58").

A lively recording, beautifully done.

Hé! dame de vaillance (V1)
1. Lumen 33405 (1947). Pierre Deniau, tenor; ensemble. Not heard.

Hé! dame de valour (V11)
Not recorded.

Hé! Mors com tu / Fine Amour / Quare non sum mortuus (M3)
1. Dietrich Knothe, Philips 6580 026 (1971). Roswitha Trexler, contralto; Wolf Reinhold, tenor; tenor crumhorn (2'07").

One can gain at least something of an idea of the work from this recording.

Helas! et comment aroie (V18)
Not recorded.

Helas! pour quoy se demente et complaint (R2)
1. Monique Rollin, London International W91116 (1955). Mathilde Siderer, soprano; flute, vielle, lute (1'11"). Not heard.
2. Ensemble Guillaume de Machaut, Adès 14040 (1983). Jean Belliard, countertenor; oud (2'40").

The Ensemble Guillaume de Machaut provides an excellent recording of this early song.

Helas! pour quoy virent / Corde mesto cantando / Libera me (M12)
Not recorded.

Helas! tant ay doleur et peinne (B2)
Not recorded.

Hont paur (intabulation in **Fa** [67]). See *Honte, paour* (B25).

Honte, paour, doubtance de meffaire (B25)
1. Thomas Binkley, EMI Reflexe 1C 063-30 109 (1973). Andrea von Ramm, mezzo-soprano; lute, fiddle (5'47"). Strophes 1–3.
2. Marcel Pérès, Harmonia Mundi HMC 901354 (1990). Josep Benet, tenor; Josep Cabré, baritone; and Malcolm Bothwell, bass (2'59"). Strophe 1 only.

Recordings of the Faenza intabulation:
1. Thomas Binkley, EMI Reflexe 1C 063-30 109 (1973). Lute, gamba (2'52").
2. Guy Robert, Adès 7078–7080 (1977). Arabic lute, lute, rubebe, transverse flute (3'35").
3. Marcel Pérès, Harmonia Mundi HMC 901354 (1990). Clavicytherium solo (3'18").
4. Ensemble Tre Fontane, Alba musica MU 244882 (1993). Not examined (5'33").

Binkley provides an excellent performance of Machaut's ballade, although the effect of the highly dissonant contratenor is attenuated by its realization on the lute. Pérès's all-vocal performance is a disappointment—too slow. All versions of the Faenza instrumental arrangement are well done, though Robert's performance is surely too heavily scored.

Hoquetus David
1. Guillaume de Van, L'Oiseau-Lyre OL 3 (1939). Trumpet, bass trumpet, trombone (3'30"). Not heard.
2. René Clemenčić, Supraphon GSST 50598 (1964). Cornet, recorder, shawm, drum (3'08").
3. Roger Cotte, Arion 30 A 070 (1969). Three recorders. Incomplete (0'51"). Not heard.
4. Richard Taruskin, Collegium Stereo JE 104 (1970). Not heard.
5. Konrad Ruhland, Telefunken 6.41125 AS (1970). Three fiddles, organ (2'38").
6. Thomas Binkley, EMI Reflexe 1C 063-30 109 (1973). Rebec, organetto, recorder (1'59").
7. Michel Sanvoisin, Arion ARN 38252 (1974). Recorder, harp, fiddle (2'13").
8. David Munrow, Archiv 2723 045 (1975). Two cornetts, alto shawm, bells (3'17").
9. Music for a While, 1750 Arch S 1773 (1977). Recorder, organ, vielle, bells (2'48").
10. Guy Robert, Adès 7078–7080 (1977). Crumhorn, vielle, bombard, lute, organetto (2'33").
11. Miroslav Klement, Supraphon 1112 2451-2 G (1977). Two fiddles, organetto, triangle (2'20").
12. Michel Sanvoisin, Edelweiss ED 1021 (1990). Vielle, lute, organ (2'16").
13. Helga Weber, I.H.W. CD3.108 (1993). Two alto bombards, tenor trombone, drum (2'57").
14. Alba Musica Kyo, Channel Classics CCS 7094 (1994). Two lutes, citole (3'55").
15. Consort Fontegara, Bongiovanni GB 5532 2 (1994). Not heard.

The performances by Ruhland, Binkley, Sanvoisin, and Music for a While are overly fast. Munrow takes a slow enough tempo (although it could stand to be slower) that the archaic Franconian triple rhythms at the prolation level are audible. So does Clemenčić, but unfortunately a drum accompanies throughout; the drum in Weber's recording taps out combined rhythms of triplum and hoquetus voices. Robert transforms the Franconian short-long rhythm into long-short. Chiyomi Yamanda (soprano) sings "alleluia" to the *David* melisma to introduce the performance by Alba Musica Kyo. The *Hoquetus David* seems to be Machaut's most popular work for arrangement and recomposition by twentieth-century composers; see chap. 2.5 (compositions by Bedford, Birtwistle, A. Gilbert, Holt, Matoušek, and Muldowney)

Il m'est avis qu'il n'est dons de Nature (B22)
Not recorded.

J'ai tant mon / Lasse! je sui / Ego moriar pro te (M7)
1. Dietrich Knothe, Philips 6580 026 (1971). Roswitha Trexler, contralto; Hans-Joachim Rotzsch, tenor; tenor crumhorn (3'46").
Not recommended.

J'aim la flour (L2)
1. St. George's Canzona, Enigma K53571 (1978). Not heard.
2. Aliénor AL 1019 (1987). Esther Lamandier, soprano and harp (6'50").
Lamandier's quick tempo makes the play of rhymes especially palpable, and the simple accompaniment is not too obtrusive. This lai has but seven strophes and is well-suited as an example for teaching purposes.

J'aim miex languir en ma dure dolour (B7)
Not recorded.

J'aim sans penser laidure (V14)
Not recorded.

Je ne cesse de prier. Le Lay de la Fonteinne (L16/11)
1. Thomas Binkley, EMI Reflexe 1C 063-30 106 (1972). Andrea von Ramm, mezzo-soprano; lute; women's chorus (24'09").
2. Music for a While, 1750 Arch S 1773 (1977). Sheila Schonbrun, voice; fiddle, bell, recorder, rebec, organetto, psaltery, saz, and harp, variously used in different strophes (22'17").
3. Peter and Timothy Davies, L'Oiseau-Lyre DSDL 705 (1983). Rogers Covey-Crump, Paul Elliott, Andrew King, tenors (27'25").
4. Paul Hillier, Hyperion CDA66358 (1989). Mark Padmore, Rogers Covey-Crump, and John Potter, tenors (23'20").

L16 alternates monophonic strophes with three-voice *chaces*. Based on the number symbolism in the text, Günther (1983, 264; 1984a, 263–64) suggests that three soloists singing the *chaces* without instruments should sing the monophonic strophes in unison. This interesting performance suggestion has yet to be tried. Binkley invents a lute accompaniment for the monophonic strophes—beautifully sung by Andrea von Ramm—while the *chaces* are sung by an unaccompanied women's chorus. Both the Binkley and Davies recordings are good up to the very last strophe (a restatement of the first strophe a fifth higher, this time as a *chace*), which is given an octave too low, an error traceable to the Schrade edition. The recording by Davies is otherwise excellent. The singer of the monophonic strophes, presumably Rogers Covey-Crump, is the lead singer of the *chaces*, a logical performance practice. He is the only singer in the *chaces* to declaim the text (the others vocalize). The tempo between strophes is kept constant, a conservative practice not heard in other recordings, and one that deserves consideration. The performance by Music for a While has the pitch of the final strophe correct, but it hardly matters, since so many other unfortunate things have happened before this point. Strophes 1 and 3 are presented an octave too high, and strophe 4 up a fourth. Strophes 7, 8, and 10 are instrumental; most of the *chaces* are presented with two instruments and one vocalist. Almost every strophe is introduced by a spoken recitation that freely evokes the text of the strophe to come, destroying the forward direction of the music.

The several recordings give us two different manners of ending the *chaces*, neither of which can be proven as the correct treatment. The Ludwig edition (edited by Besseler) would have them end as they began, in staggered fashion, with one voice at a time finishing its complete text. This treatment is heard in the Music for a While recording, as well as in the performance directed by Hillier. Both Binkley and Davies end each *chace* with all three voices together, at the point when the leading voice finishes its text (this makes sense especially in the Davies' recording, since the other two voices are not declaiming text). Although it would seem desirable for all voices to finish their text, it is true that the final phrases of music are much less melodic than the initial phrases, and sometimes rather strange rests and incomplete hocket effects are heard at the end of the *chaces* in the version of Music for a While and Hillier. Overall, the most satisfying recording is that of Hillier. Incidentally, the compact disc is marked with a new track for each strophe, which makes access very convenient.

Je ne cuit pas qu' onques a creature (B14)

1. Guy Robert, Adès 7078–7080 (1977). Annie Bartelloni, contralto; organetto, lute; recorder for interlude and postlude (4'10"). Strophes 1 and 3 only.
2. Dominique Vellard, Harmonic Records H/CD 8825 (1988). Anne-Marie Lablaude, voice; lute (5'59"). Strophes 1–3.
3. Ensemble Tre Fontane, Scalen disc TRFC 0389 (1989). Recorder, hurdy-gurdy (2'05").
4. Alba Musica Kyo, Channel Classics CCS 7094 (1994). Shawm, vielle, lute (3'05").

Robert's recording includes an instrumental interlude and postlude. In Vellard's recording, after a lute introduction, a free lute paraphrase of the tenor line accompanies the soprano.

Je puis trop bien ma dame comparer (B28)

1. Safford Cape, Anthologie Sonore AS 3 (1940). Franz Mertens, tenor; soprano recorder, lute, tenor viol (1'27"). Strophe 1 only.
2. Safford Cape, Archive ARC 3032 (1956). Jeanne Deroubaix, alto; alto recorder, lute, tenor fiddle (1'34"). Strophe 1 only.
3. Wesley K. Morgan, Pleiades P 250 (1968?). Kathryn Grimmer, alto; viola, cello (1'27"). Strophe 1 only.
4. Denis Stevens, Musical Heritage Society MHS 830437 (1969). Mark Deller, countertenor; bassoon, cello (1'09"). Strophe 1 only.
5. Electrecord ST-ECE 01601 (1977?). Martha Kessler, mezzo-soprano; harmonium, alto and tenor gambas, recorder (1'50"). Strophe 1 only.
6. Sonus, Dorian DIS 80123 (1993). Chitarra, vihuela (2'20").

All of these recordings utilize the old transcriptions; Hoppin's corrections (1960, 16–17 n. 16) have yet to make their effect.[8] Cape's two recordings provide us with the only example I have found among Machaut recordings of the performance of vocal melismas on instruments, a performance practice that dates back to Hugo Riemann and Arnold Schering, and still heard in some recent recordings of fifteenth-century music. Here, a recorder plays the nine-note melisma near the end of the A-section. Kessler's performance includes harmonium doubling the tenor an octave below at times. None of the recordings can be recommended.

Je suis aussi com cils qui est ravis (B20)

1. Monique Rollin, Club National du Disque CND 9 (1955). Flute, lute (2'08").
2. Ancient Instrument Ensemble of Zurich, Odyssey 32 160178 (1966). Baroque oboe, harp, fiddle (2'30").
3. John White, Decca DL 79431 (1967). Sheila Schonbrun, soprano; bass recorder, bass flute, bass viol (2'49"). Strophe 1 only.
4. Michael Jaffee, Vanguard VSD 71179 (1973). Joan Summers, soprano; vielle, organetto (3'04"). Strophe 1 only.
5. Sequentia, University of Texas Press ISBN 0-292-78520-8 (1988). Barbara Thornton, soprano; fiddle, lute (5'30"). Strophes 1–3.
6. Ensemble Tre Fontane, Alba musica MU 244882 (1993). Not examined (3'15").

---

[8] T. Campbell (1989–90, 280–81) prints a practical edition by Earp.

Except for the effective recording by Sequentia, these performances are mournfully slow. As was the case with *Biauté qui* (B4), all recordings—except Monique Rollin's instrumental version—present the unauthentic contratenor given only in MS **E**. In addition, White's version has some ill-conceived and inconsistent octave displacements.

Je vivroie liement (V23/21)
1. Music for a While, 1750 Arch S 1773 (1977). Recorder, saz, vielle, percussion (1'17").
2. Christopher Page, Hyperion A66087 (1983). Emily van Evera, soprano solo (2'17"). Strophes 1–2 only.
3. Dominique Vellard, Harmonic Records H/CD 8825 (1988). Bagpipes, rek (3'05"). Two repetitions: bagpipes; bagpipes plus rek.
Page's recording is well done.

Joie, plaisance, et douce nourriture (*chant royal* RF3)
1. Thomas Binkley, EMI Reflexe 1C 063-30 106 (1972). Richard Levitt, countertenor; fiddle (6'04"). Strophes 1–5 and *envoy*.
2a. Michel Sanvoisin, Arion ARN 38252 (1974). Soprano recorder solo (0'43").
2b. Michel Sanvoisin, Arion ARN 38252 (1974). Musette solo (0'43").
3. Guy Robert, Adès 7078–7080 (1975). Jean Belliard, countertenor; vielle, recorder, Arabian lute, Moorish guitar, percussion (3'45"). Strophes 1, 5, and envoy.
4. Music for a While, 1750 Arch S 1773 (1977). Sheila Schonbrun and Christopher Kenny, voices; vielle, kemençe, percussion (2'25"). Strophes 1, 2, 4, and *envoy*.
5. Toronto Consort, Collegium COL 83-03 (1983). Garry Crighton, countertenor; vielle (7'12"). Strophes 1–5 and *envoy*.
6. Margaret Switten and Robert Eisenstein, The Medieval Lyric (1987). Laurie Monahan, mezzo-soprano solo (4'33"). Strophes 1–5 and *envoy*.
7. Ensemble P.A.N., New Albion Records NA068 CD (1994). Laurie Monahan, mezzo-soprano; vielle (4'45"). Strophes 1–5 and *envoy*.

Binkley's recording begins with a recitation of *l'amant*'s speech introducing the *chant royal*, but the order of verses is garbled, apparently due to a misunderstanding of the layout of these lines in the Ludwig edition. The introductory fiddle fantasy is far too ornate, as is the accompaniment throughout. Each succeeding strophe is embellished to an extent that the performance becomes hair-raising by strophe 5. *L'amant* surely could not have dozed through such an onslaught. The version by Music for a While was made for stage presentation: Sheila Schonbrun sings strophe 1 and Christopher Kenny strophe 2; strophe 3 is played on a vielle; the voices sing together in the course of strophe 4 and for the *envoy*, omitting strophe 5. The performances of Robert and the Toronto Consort include instrumental prelude, interludes, and postlude. Although the versions of the Toronto Consort and the Ensemble P.A.N. are nicely sung, in each case the vielle accompaniment is more developed than most recordings of Machaut's monophony. Switten's is the only version that can be recommended without qualification.

Lasse! comment oublieray / Se j'aim / Pour quoy me bat mes maris? (M16)
1. Vielle Trio, Allegro AL 14 (1949). Du Bose Robertson, tenor; three fiddles (3'28").
2. George Hunter, Westminster XWN 18166 (1956). Jantina Noorman, contralto; Richard Krause, tenor; tenor (1'36").
3. David Munrow, Archiv 2723 045 (1975). Paul Elliott and Martyn Hill, tenors; Geoffrey Shaw, bass (4'06").
4. Guy Robert, Adès 7078–7080 (1977). Annie Bartelloni, contralto; Jean Belliard, countertenor; Bernard Huneau, baritone; rebec (3'42").
5. Estampie, Christophorus CD 74583 (1989). Sigrid Hausen, soprano, recorder, organ (1'52").

The recording by the Vielle Trio ranks among the worst recordings of early music ever made. Hunter's recording is excellent—even though the sound engineering is not good—since his lively tempo makes better sense than Munrow's very slow performance. Robert's recording includes a performance of the monophonic dance song tenor (contralto, rebec, Moorish guitar), followed by a lively rendition of the motet. The Estampie recording also includes a lusty performance of the motet tenor (soprano, hurdy-gurdy, tār, tambourine), which then becomes the only sung voice in the motet, not a possible scoring for a motet, one would think.[9]

Lay de Nostre Dame, Le. See *Contre ce dous mois de may* (L15/10)

Lay de Bonne Esperance, Le. See *Longuement me sui tenus* (L18/13)

Lay de Confort, Le. See *S'onques dolereusement* (L17/12)

Lay de Consolation, Un. See *Pour ce que plus proprement* (L23/17)

Lay de l'Ymage, Le. See *Ne say comment commencier* (L14/9)

Lay de la Fonteinne, Le. See *Je ne cesse de prier* (L16/11)

Lay de la Rose, Le. See *Pour vivre joliement* (L21/15)

Lay de Plour, Le. See *Malgré Fortune et son tour* (L19/14); *Qui bien aimme a tart oublie* (L22/16)

Lay des Dames, Le. See *Amis, t'amour me contreint* (L10/7)

Lay Mortel, Le. See *Un mortel lay vueil commencier* (L12/8)

Liement me deport (V30/27)
1. Dominique Vellard, Harmonic Records H/CD 8825 (1988). Anne-Marie Lablaude and Brigitte Lesne, sopranos; rek (5'29").
2. Ensemble P.A.N., New Albion Records NA068 CD (1994). Vielle, lute (2'10").

Would that there were a way to filter out the percussion in Vellard's recording; at least it forces strict adherence to the pulse. Ensemble P.A.N. performs a fantasy on the virelai.

Longuement me sui tenus. Le Lay de Bonne Esperance (L18/13=VD47)
1. Guy Robert, Adès 7078–7080 (1977). Jean Belliard, countertenor; vielle, transverse flute, recorder, lute, Moorish guitar, drum, tambourine (16'36").
2. Les Ménestrels, Mirror Music 00006–00009 (1979). René Jacobs, countertenor; harp (20'39").

One can get only an incomplete idea of the work from Robert's recording. After a heavily scored instrumental prelude, only strophes 1, 10, and 12 are given with their full text; the others are cut in half. Many instrumental interludes disrupt the work, often repeating material either from strophe 1 or from part of strophe 7 combined with part of strophe 1, so that Machaut's carefully calculated rise in tessitura is obscured. The performance ends with a long instrumental postlude. Jacob's performance for Les Ménestrels is complete, although a rather too fancy harp accompaniment is supplied throughout, and the tempo between strophes varies widely.

Loyauté, que point ne delay (L1)
1. George Hunter, Westminster XWN 18166 (1956). Jantina Noorman, contralto; lute (2'35"). Strophe 1 only.
2. Thomas Binkley, EMI Reflexe 1C 063-30 106 (1972). Andrea von Ramm, mezzo-soprano; lute (6'39"). Strophes 1, 9, 12, and 24 only.
3. Gregorio Paniagua, Hispavox HHS 10-459 (1976). Instrumental, with percussion (0'56").

---

[9] For another recording of the dance song (although with obtrusive percussion) see Hyperion CDA 66625 (CD), *Lo douz esgart e l'amoros semblan*; *"The sweet look and the loving manner"*; *Trobairitz Love Lyrics and Chansons de femme from Medieval France*; Sinfonye, directed by Stevie Wishart, recorded 7–9 July 1992 (1'34"); includes texts and translations.

4. Isaak-Ensemble-Heidelberg, Bayer 100 164 (1992). Not heard.

L1 is exceptional in that it uses the same music for all twelve strophes. However, the pattern of phrase-endings, whether masculine or feminine, changes freely throughout the work. The manuscripts copied during Machaut's lifetime do not supply a solution to the problems encountered in adapting the masculine and feminine end rhymes even for the first strophe. A complete setting of strophe 1 is provided only in the late MS **E**. This then should serve as the key for the changing patterns in the remaining strophes. Hunter's recording is useable for the one strophe sung. Binkley's recording gives four of the twelve strophes. Here strophe 9 employs only the high-range phrase of music (mm. 14–26), while the treatment of strophe 24 employs only the low-range phrase (mm. 1–14), suggesting that the singer is free to choose from the phrases given for strophe 1 to fashion succeeding strophes, an interesting but speculative solution. The performance difficulties of accommodating the constantly changing patterns of masculine and feminine rhymes are brought out when von Ramm treats *-ine* as a masculine rhyme in strophe 12. In my view, the lute accompaniment throughout is too highly developed.[10]

Loyauté vueil tous jours maintenir (V2)
Not recorded.

Ma chiere dame, a vous mon cuer envoy (B40)
1. Robert Haas, Anthologie Sonore LD 3012 (1956). Erika Metzer-Ulrich, soprano; instrumental ensemble. Not heard.
2. George Hunter, Westminster XWN 18166 (1956). Recorder, lute, vielle (1'57").
3. Westminster XWN 18683 (1958). Hugues Cuénod, tenor; lute (2'56"). Not heard.
4. Studio für alte Musik, Da Camera SM 91702 (1969). Instrumental (2'00"). Not heard.
5. René Clemenčić, Harmonia Mundi France HMU 939 (1973). Zeger Vandersteene, countertenor; rebec, medieval harp (2'31"). Not heard.
6. Les Ménestrels, Mirror Music 00005 (1977). Marie-Thérèse Escribano, soprano; lute, discant fiddle (3'04"). Strophes 1–2.
7. Lukáš Matoušek, Panton 8111 0056 (1978). Zuzana Matoušková, mezzo-soprano; bass recorder, alto fiddle (1'48"). Strophe 1 only.
8. Michel Sanvoisin, Edelweiss ED 1021 (1990). Joseph Sage, countertenor; tenor recorder, vielle, lute (1'48"). Strophe 1 only.

The sung performance of Matoušek is useable, but Sanvoisin's now supplants it. The version of Les Ménestrels presents the work very facilely, with a rhythmic flexibility rarely heard in this music, and it has the advantage of presenting two strophes.

Ma fin est mon commencement (R14)
1. Bernard Rose, RCA Victor LM 6016 (1951?). Lemuel Hughes and Clarence Roberts, tenors; oboes, low strings (2'36"). Refrain only.
2. Dietrich Knothe, Philips 6580 026 (1971). Hans-Joachim Rotzsch, tenor; alto recorder, alto lute (4'59").
3. David Munrow, Seraphim SIC 6092 (1973). Two cornetts, soprano cornemuse (1'38").
4. Michel Sanvoisin, Arion ARN 38252 (1974). Joseph Sage, countertenor; two viols; then varied instrumentation, with recorder, harp (5'29").
5. Guy Robert, Adès 7078–7080 (1977). Jean Belliard, countertenor; rebec, transverse flute, lute, organetto (6'00").
6. Lukáš Matoušek, Panton 8111 0056 (1978). Vladimír Doležal, countertenor; bass recorder, alto crumhorn, alto fiddle (1'25"). Refrain only.
7. Paul Hillier, Hyperion CDA66358 (1989). Rogers Covey-Crump and John Potter, tenors; Paul Hillier, bass (5'38").

---

[10] Binkley (1977, 27) gives the arrangement for lute used in strophe 1 of this recording.

8. Michel Sanvoisin, Edelweiss ED 1021 (1990). Joseph Sage, counter-tenor; recorder, lute (6'14").
9. Sonus, Dorian DIS 80123 (1993). Chitarra, oud, vihuela (2'49").
10. Consort Fontegara, Bongiovanni GB 5532 2 (1994). Not heard.

Rose's old recording is too slow. Sanvoisin's two recordings are useable, as is Knothe's. Munrow's instrumental rendition is beautifully articulated and well illustrates the compositional structure of the work. Robert's performance, formerly the best recording of the full rondeau (although the instrumentation changes frequently), is now superseded by Hillier's all-vocal version.

Malgré Fortune et son tour. Le Lay de Plour (L19/14)
Not recorded.

Martyrum gemma latria / Diligenter inquiramus / A Christo honoratus (M19)
1. Olaf Raitzig, VEB Deutsche Schallplatten 8 27 956 (1984). Ute Schimmel-pfennig, soprano; Werner Marschall, countertenor; recorder, discant gamba, dulcian (3'08").
2. Helga Weber, I.H.W. CD3.108 (1993). Paul Gerhardt Adam and Kai Wessel, countertenors; fiddle, flute, tenor bombard, drum (2'59").

I prefer Raitzig's recording, despite the instrumental doublings.

Maugré mon cuer / De ma dolour / Quia amore langueo (M14)
1. Johannes Rahe, Carus 83.123 (1991). Mixed chorus (2'05").

The Cathedral at Osnabrück is too resonant a venue for a satisfactory performance.

Merci vous pri, ma douce dame chiere (R3)
Not recorded.

Mes esperis se combat a Nature (B39)
1. Recorder Consort of the Musician's Workshop, Classic Editions CE 1018 (1953). Three alto recorders (2'11").
2. George Hunter, Westminster XWN 18166 (1956). Richard Krause, tenor; two vielles (2'22"). Strophe 1 only.
3. August Wenzinger, Archiv 2533 054 (1969). Ernst Haefliger, tenor; tenor fiddle, positive organ (2'07"). Strophe 1 only.
4. David Munrow, Seraphim SIC 6092 (1973). James Bowman, countertenor; alto shawm, tenor cornett (3'51"). Strophes 1–2 only.
5. Michel Sanvoisin, Arion ARN 38252 (1974). Joseph Sage, countertenor, lute, viol, bass recorder (2'08"). Strophe 1 only.
6. Zoltán Majó, Electrecord ST-ECE 01929 (1981). Barbara Rónai, soprano; recorder; viol (2'45"). Strophe 1 only.
7. Ensemble Tre Fontane, Alba musica MU 244882 (1993). Not examined (3'14").

There are two versions, that of MS G, printed by Ludwig and performed by Hunter, Wenzinger, Sanvoisin, Majó, and instrumentally by the Recorder Consort, and the corrupt version of MS E, printed by Schrade and performed by Munrow.[11] Munrow's forceful approach—inspired by the military imagery of the poem—is the most musical presentation. Wenzinger's reading is useable but not as exciting.

Messe de Nostre Dame. See chap. 8.4.

Mors sui, se je ne vous voy (V29/26)
Not recorded.

Moult sui de bonne heure nee (V37/31)
1. Thomas Binkley, EMI Reflexe 1C 063-30 109 (1973). Andrea von Ramm, mezzo-soprano; lute (3'47"). Strophes 1–3.
2. Jean-Claude Malgoire, CBS Masterworks 76534 (1976). Two vielles (2'45"). Strophe 1 only.

---

[11] Hirshberg (1971, 143–47) shows that the version of MS G is superior.

3. Guy Robert, Adès 7078–7080 (1977). Annie Bartelloni, contralto; vielle, two lutes, flute (3'10"). Refrain and strophe 2 only.
4. Estampie, Christophorus CD 74583 (1989). Sigrid Hausen, soprano; organetto, lute (5'27"). Strophes 1–3.

Binkley treats the tenor rather too freely as the work unfolds, but I find his an exciting and danceable performance. Estampie provides a nice performance of the first strophe, similar in style to Binkley's but rhythmically more strict; unfortunately, improvised interludes come between superfluous extra statements of the refrain.

N' en fait n' en dit n' en pensee (B11)
Not recorded.

Ne pensez pas, dame, que je recroie (B10)
Not recorded.

Ne say comment commencier. Le Lay de l'Ymage (L14/9)
Not recorded.

Nes qu' on porroit les estoilles nombrer (B33)
1. Safford Cape, Archive ARC 3032 (1956). Recorder, lute, treble fiddle (2'06").
2. Ancient Instrument Ensemble of Zurich, Odyssey 32 160178 (1966). Baroque oboe, fiddle, viol (1'46").
3. John White, Decca DL 79431 (1967). Ray DeVoll, tenor; organetto, bass viol (3'00"). Strophe 1 only.
4a. Guy Robert, Adès 7078–7080 (1977). Jean Belliard, countertenor; Poitouvian oboe, lute, crumhorn, rebec, organetto (3'33"). Strophes 1–2 only.
4b. Guy Robert, Adès 7078–7080 (1977). Poitouvian oboe, lute, crumhorn, rebec, organetto, drum (1'38").
5. Les Ménestrels, Mirror Music 00006–00009 (1979). Two fiddles, bass recorder (2'12").

White's recording is slow and uses Schrade's faulty text underlay, as does Robert. Robert's sung version is very lively, but the instrumentation is full and changes between strophes. The four instrumental renditions are all fairly well done, especially that by Les Ménestrels.

Nuls ne doit avoir merveille (L5/4)
1. Grayston Burgess, L'Oiseau-Lyre SOL 310 (1969). Nigel Rogers, tenor; harp (3'35").

Burgess was the first to attempt to market a recording of a larger portion of one of the lais, but his recording of L5 gives a very misleading representation of the work. Nigel Rogers's performance is beautifully done, but only the first half of each strophe is sung, and strophes 8 and 9 are skipped entirely (the music of strophe 10 is heard twice, both times to the first text). The harp accompaniment devised by Frank Harrison seems too elaborate, and long harp solos have been inserted between strophes 3 and 4 and between strophes 11 and 12.

On ne porroit penser ne souhaidier (B3)
1. Ensemble Guillaume de Machaut, Adès 14040 (1983). Jean Belliard, countertenor, lute, vielle, recorder, sackbut, with positive organ in interludes (3'20"). Strophes 1–2 only.

The editions are followed literally in this performance: 8 measures for two voices, after which the spurious and corrupt contratenor found only in MS E is added. After the refrain, the B-section is repeated instrumentally. This performance at least gives one an impression of this early ballade.

Par trois raisons me vueil deffendre (L6/5)
Not recorded.

Pas de tor en thies païs (B30)
1. John White, Decca DL 79431 (1967). Bass and tenor viols, organetto, bass recorder (3'34").

2. Christopher Page, Hyperion CDA66588 (1991). Rogers Covey-Crump, Charles Daniels, and Leigh Nixon, tenors (4'22"). Strophes 1–2 only.

White's all-instrumental recording is unusably slow, and now completely superseded by Page's all-vocal performance, which employs the edition of Keitel (1977b).

Phyton, le mervilleus serpent (B38)
1. David Munrow, Seraphim SIC 6092 (1973). Martyn Hill, tenor; two tenor crumhorns (4'46"). Strophes 1–2 only.

The performance is well done, despite the buzz of the reeds on the lower voices.

Plourez, dames, plourez vostre servant (B32)
1. Columbia 70701D (1940). Yves Tinayre, baritone; strings (3'51"). Strophe 1 only.
2. Michel Sanvoisin, Arion ARN 38252 (1974). Joseph Sage, countertenor; viol, lute (3'16"). Strophe 1 only.
3a. Guy Robert, Adès 7078–7080 (1977). Rebecs, transverse flute, organetto (1'54").
3b. Guy Robert, Adès 7078–7080 (1977). Jean Belliard, countertenor; rebec, bass recorder, organetto (5'31"). Strophes 1–2 only.
4. Lukáš Matoušek, Panton 8111 0056 (1978). Zuzana Matoušková, mezzo-soprano, occasionally with gemshorn, alto fiddle, tenor fiddle (2'10"). Strophe 1 only.
5. Les Ménestrels, Mirror Music 00006–00009 (1979). Taina Kataja, soprano; bass recorder, fiddle (7'49"). Strophes 1–3.

Tinayre's and Sanvoisin's recordings are painfully slow, while both Robert (sung version) and Matoušek change the instrumentation in the course of the piece. Les Ménestrels's recording is useable, valuable for its presentation of the complete ballade.

Plus dure qu'un dyamant (V31/28)
1. Roger Blanchard, Philips N 00993 R (1955?). Jean Archimbaud, countertenor; instrumental ensemble. Not heard.
2. George Hunter, Westminster XWN 18166 (1956). Jantina Noorman, contralto; lute, vielle (2'28"). Strophe 1 only.
3. Wesley K. Morgan, Pleiades P 250 (1968?). Barbara Boedges, alto; viola (2'52"). Strophe 1 only.
4. Denis Stevens, Musical Heritage Society MHS 830437 (1969). Mark Deller, countertenor; fiddle (4'03"). Strophe 1 only.
5. Studio für alte Musik, Da Camera SM 91702 (1969). Instrumental (3'02"). Not heard.
6a. Michel Sanvoisin, Arion ARN 38252 (1974). Harp solo (2'01").
6b. Michel Sanvoisin, Arion ARN 38252 (1974). Lute solo (1'55").
7. Solveig Faringer, BIS LP 2 (1974). Not heard (1'43").
8. Alton/Jeffery 1976. Countertenor; fiddle (2'33"). Strophe 1 only.
9. Electrecord ST-ECE 01601 (1977?). Martha Kessler, mezzo-soprano; harmonium, tenor gamba, lute (1'40"). Incomplete strophe.
10. Jean-Patrice Brosse, Arion ARN 38771 (1983). Organ solo. Not heard.
11. Michel Sanvoisin, Edelweiss ED 1021 (1990). Lute solo (1'59").

Of the recordings I have heard, I recommend both Hunter and Alton/Jeffery, which includes recitation of all three strophes in medieval French pronunciation; Stevens's version remains useable. Kessler occasionally doubles the tenor an octave below with harmonium.

Pour ce qu'on puist miex retraire (L3)
Not recorded.

Pour ce que plus proprement. Un Lay de Consolation (L23/17)
1. Peter and Timothy Davies, L'Oiseau-Lyre DSDL 705 (1983). Rogers Covey-Crump, tenor; fiddle, rebec, psaltery, harp, gittern, and lute used variously (21'18").

This lai was first edited as a polyphonic work in Hoppin 1958. The directors of this recording have apparently taken a cue from Fallows (1980, 371) and have a solo voice projecting the text while a plucked or bowed string instrument plays the contrapuntal voice.

Pour ce que tous mes chans fais (B12)
Not recorded.

Pour vivre joliement. Le Lay de la Rose (L21/15)
1. Jecklin-Disco JD 622-2 (1988). Conrad Steinmann, recorder solo (13'45").

Toneless breathing into the recorder, whistling, humming, multiphonics and other weird effects render this version useless except as a curiosity. Steinmann does perform the work from beginning to end, though usually without the repeats that would be required in a texted performance.

Puis qu' en oubli sui de vous, dous amis (R18)
1. Safford Cape, Archive ARC 3032 (1956). Willy Pourtois, bass; lute, treble and tenor fiddles, recorder (2'12").
2. Roger Cotte, Arion 30 A 096 (1970). Ana Maria Miranda, soprano; instrumental ensemble (1'30"). Not heard.
3. Dominique Vellard, Harmonic Records H/CD 8825 (1988). Brigitte Lesne, voice; two vielles (1'31").
4. Paul Hillier, Schirmer Books ISBN 0-02-872953-6 (1990). Rogers Covey-Crump and Mark Padmore, tenors; Paul Hillier, bass (4'11").

Cape performs the version in MS E at an excruciatingly slow tempo, with occasional doublings of the tenor at the octave by a recorder. Vellard's performance, giving the version of MSS A and G transposed up a major seventh, is very satisfying. Hillier's recording of the A and G version, transposed up a major third, is also excellent, using a lower range to good effect (unfortunately, tenor and contratenor have been texted).

Puis que ma dolour agree (V7)
1. Ensemble Tre Fontane, Scalen disc TRFC 0389 (1989). Shawm, saz (2'37").
The shawm is quite crudely played here.

Quant en moy / Amour et biauté / Amara valde (M1)
1. Dietrich Knothe, Philips 6580 026 (1971). Roswitha Trexler, contralto; Hans-Joachim Rotzsch, tenor; tenor fiddle (3'29").
2. Thomas Binkley, EMI Reflexe 1C 063-30 109 (1973). Andrea von Ramm, mezzo-soprano; Richard Levitt, countertenor; lira (2'16").
3. Guy Robert, Adès 7078–7080 (1977). Annie Bartelloni, contralto; Jean Belliard, countertenor; rebec, crumhorn, organetto (2'20").
4. Paul Hillier, Schirmer Books ISBN 0-02-872953-6 (1990). David James, countertenor; John Potter, tenor; organ (3'34").

Knothe's performance is tame and square beside Binkley's very exciting recording, which is unfortunately too free rhythmically and overly fast for clear text declamation. The work becomes an engaging love song, attractive, but one wonders, should not an isorhythmic motet be very strict rhythmically? Robert's recording is rhythmically tighter, although very fast; it seems influenced by Binkley in the rushed hocket sections. Hillier's performance is superb, although musically a bit reserved.

Quant j' ay l' espart (R5)
1. David Munrow, Seraphim SIC 6092 (1973). James Bowman, countertenor; tenor cornett (3'16").
Useable.

Quant je ne voy ma dame n' oy (R21)
1. August Wenzinger, Archiv 2533 054 (1969). Ernst Haefliger, tenor; harp, tenor fiddle (5'14").
2. Pierre Hudrisier, Ariane ARI 148 (1988). Jean-Yves Guerry, countertenor; lute, rebec (4'51").

3. Paul Hillier, Schirmer Books ISBN 0-02-872953-6 (1990). Rogers Covey-Crump, John Potter, and Mark Padmore, tenors (5'44").
4. Christopher Page, Hyperion CDA66588 (1991). Rogers Covey-Crump, tenor; medieval harp, medieval lute (5'20").

Wenzinger's recording is still useable. Hillier employs the ideal combination, with the lower voices vocalizing. Hudrisier's delightful recording is rhythmically more lively than Hillier. I find the modest ornaments introduced in Page's recording annoying on repeated listening.

Quant je sui mis au retour (V13)
1. John White, Decca DL 79431 (1967). Anthony Tamburello, bass; male vocal ensemble; rauschpfeife, drum (1'38"). Strophes 1–3.
2. Dietrich Knothe, Philips 6580 026 (1971). Hans-Joachim Rotzsch, tenor solo (1'20"). Strophes 1–3.
3. Thomas Binkley, EMI Reflexe 1C 063-30 106 (1972). Three solo voices, choir (1'34"). Strophes 1–3.
4. David Munrow, Seraphim SIC 6092 (1973). Martyn Hill, tenor; James Bowman, Charles Brett, Martyn Hill, and Geoffrey Shaw, chorus; bass rebec, lute (2'41"). Strophes 1–3.
5. David Munrow, Angel SBZ 3810 (1976). Gittern solo (0'56").
6. Guy Robert, Adès 7078–7080 (1977). Jean Belliard, countertenor; Arabian lute (2'40"). Strophes 1–3.
7. Miroslav Klement, Supraphon 1112 2451-2 G (1977). Zdeněk Jankovský, tenor; fiddle (1'45"). Strophes 1–3.
8. František Pok, Supraphon 1119 3419 G (1982). Hurdy-gurdy, dulcimer, bombard, fiddle, drum (1'27").
9. Joel Cohen, Harmonia Mundi HMC 5122 (1985). Nancy Armstrong, soprano; Mark Kagan, tenor; vielle, recorder, lute (2'48"). Strophes 1–3.
10. Hilliard Ensemble, Hyperion CDA66370 (1987). Rogers Covey-Crump, tenor solo (1'36"). Strophes 1–3.
11. Sonus, Dorian DIS 80123 (1993). Hazel Ketchum, soprano; chitarra, psaltery (3'52"). Strophes 1–3.

Although formally not a virelai, Machaut ranges this and the following work in the manuscripts, *J'aim sans* (V14), among his dance songs. The text—the lover returning perhaps from the crusades to his lady—has elicited different scenarios among the recorded performances. White puts us among the returning pilgrims, with bagpipes chanter, drum and bass voice. The full chorus enters on each repetition of the refrain. Munrow's 1973 recording adopts a melancholy tempo, with two levels of drones; a fanciful viol solo introduces the work. Binkley's version is effective, with a monophonic presentation of the strophe (perhaps nonsensically, a woman sings), followed by a unison women's chorus on the refrain. Robert includes an instrumental introduction and interludes, as does Sonus. Cohen introduces the work with a fanciful solo on the fiddle; a tenor sings the strophes with instrumental doubling, and a soprano joins in for the refrain and a final repetition of the first strophe with refrain. The best performances are those of Knothe and the Hilliard Ensemble.

Quant ma dame les maus d'amer m'aprent (R19)
1. Grayston Burgess, L'Oiseau-Lyre SOL 310 (1969). John Buttrey, tenor; viola, alto clarinet (5'54").

With nice tempo and articulation, this recording sounds well despite the unusual instrumentation.

Quant Theseüs, Hercules et Jason / Ne quier veoir la biauté d'Absalon (B34)
1. Safford Cape, Anthologie Sonore AS 3 (1940). E. Jacquier and Franz Mertens, tenors; tenor rebec, lute, tenor viol (3'32"). Strophe 1 only.
2. Safford Cape, Archive ARC 3032 (1956). René Letroye and Franz Mertens, tenors; lute, treble and tenor fiddle, recorder (3'28"). Strophe 1 only.

3. Dietrich Knothe, Philips 6580 026 (1971). Roswitha Trexler, contralto; Hans-Joachim Rotzsch, tenor; tenor fiddle, tenor crumhorn (8'26"). Strophes 1–3.
4. Thomas Binkley, EMI Reflexe 1C 063-30 109 (1973). Andrea von Ramm, mezzo-soprano; Richard Levitt, countertenor; douçaine, fiddle, lute (7'05"). Strophes 1–3
5. David Munrow, Seraphim SIC 6092 (1973). James Bowman and Charles Brett, countertenors; fiddle, tenor kortholt (2'17"). Strophe 1 only.
6. Guy Robert, Adès 7078–7080 (1977). Annie Bartelloni, contralto; Jean Belliard, countertenor; rebec, soprano crumhorn, crumhorn, organetto, bombard, lute (4'14"). Strophes 1–2 only.
7. Les Ménestrels, Mirror Music 00006–00009 (1979). Taina Kataja, soprano; René Jacobs, countertenor; lute, fiddle (6'31"). Strophes 1–3.
8. Kees Otten, Telefunken 6.42357 AW (1979). Rita Dams, mezzo-soprano; Marius van Altena, tenor; lute, tenor fiddle (6'29"). Strophes 1–3.
9. Helga Weber, I.H.W. 66.22371 (1980). Wilfried Jochens and Martin Nitz, tenors; two recorders, two gambas (3'35"). Strophe 1 only.
10. Ensemble P.A.N., New Albion Records NA021 CD (1987). Laurie Monahan, mezzo-soprano; Michael Collver, countertenor; two fiddles (6'06"). Strophes 1–3.
11. Michel Sanvoisin, Edelweiss ED 1021 (1990). Hugues Primard and Pierre Eyssartier, tenors; vielle, organ, lute (4'44"). Strophes 1–2 only.

Cape's mournful performances make for painful listening today. A crumhorn on the tenor spoils Knothe's performance. Binkley adopts a nice tempo, although the cantus II, structurally the principal text-bearing voice, is overpowered by the cantus I; accompanying instruments change for strophe 2 and then return to the initial instrumentation for strophe 3. The balance between the voices is perfect in the Munrow recording, though unfortunately he presents only one strophe. Octave doublings make for a bad effect in Robert's recording, which changes instrumentation for strophe 2. Les Ménestrels's recording is complete and well done. Weber's performance is slow but nicely sung. The Ensemble P.A.N. adopts a fast tempo and is also well done. The new recording of Sanvoisin uses two perfectly matched voices, but now an organ on the tenor overbalances the contratenor. Otten's version is quick, nicely balanced, and complete, though a little forceful in approach: it may nevertheless be regarded as the best recording available of the complete ballade.

Quant vraie amour / O series summe / Super omnes speciosa (M17)
Not recorded.

Qui bien aimme a tart oublie. Le Lay de Plour (L22/16)
Not recorded.

Qui es promesses / Ha! Fortune / Et non est qui adjuvet (M8)
1. Safford Cape, Archive ARC 3032 (1956). Elisabeth Verlooy, soprano; Jeanne Deroubaix, alto; tenor fiddle (2'00").
2. David Munrow, Archiv 2723 045 (1975). James Bowman and Charles Brett, countertenors; tenor shawm (1'54").

Munrow's recording is musically very effective.

Qui n'aroit autre deport (lai RF1/L19)
1. Guy Robert, Adès 7078–7080 (1975). Jean Belliard, countertenor; Arabian lute, Moorish guitar, vielle, transverse flute, recorder, percussion (14'15").
2. Margaret Switten and Robert Eisenstein, The Medieval Lyric (1987). Mark Bleeke, tenor solo (19'36"). Strophes 1–12.
3. Ensemble P.A.N., New Albion Records NA068 CD (1994). John Fleagle, tenor; harp (11'20").

The use of instruments is too fanciful in Robert's performance. Ensemble P.A.N. avoids the rise tessitura by performing the last five strophes a fifth lower than notated; in addition, only strophes 1, 8, and 12 are given complete. Switten's is the only recording of any of the monophonic lais that can be recommended virtually without qualification. One small quibble: instead of following Schrade's editorial accidentals in the final strophe, one should perform it as an exact transposition up a fifth of the first strophe.[12]

Riches d'amour et mendians d'amie (B5)

1. Christopher Page, Hyperion CDA66588 (1991). Rogers Covey-Crump, tenor; medieval harp (5'00"). Strophes 1–3.

Beautifully done.

Rose, lis, printemps, verdure (R10)

1. Boite à Musique 44 (1947). Simone Gebelin, soprano; flute, clarinet (2'35"). Not heard.
2. George Hunter, Westminster XWN 18166 (1956). Jantina Noorman, contralto; recorder, two vielles (4'47").
3. August Wenzinger, Archiv 2533 054 (1969). Ernst Haefliger, tenor; lute, alto recorder, tenor fiddle, positive organ (4'40").
4. Michael Jaffee, Vanguard VSD 71179 (1973). Constantine Cassolas, tenor; psaltery, two lutes, vielle (4'36").
5. Michel Sanvoisin, Arion ARN 38252 (1974). Joseph Sage, countertenor; lute, recorder, two viols (4'22").
6. Robert Eisenstein, Delos D/CD 1003 (1979). David Gordon, tenor; recorder, three vielles (3'29").
7. Christopher Page, Hyperion A66087 (1983). Emily van Evera, soprano; Margaret Philpot, contralto; Rogers Covey-Crump and Andrew King, tenors (4'31").
8. Michel Sanvoisin, Edelweiss ED 1021 (1990). Hugues Primard, tenor; Marc Guillard, baritone; vielle, organ, cornett (4'16").
9. Ensemble P.A.N., New Albion Records NA068 CD (1994). Laurie Monahan, mezzo-soprano; Michael Collver, countertenor; John Fleagle, tenor; lute, vielle (5'00").
10. Alba Musica Kyo, Channel Classics CCS 7094 (1994). Chiyomi Yamanda, soprano; two recorders, lute, vielle (4'23").

The instrumentation changes in the course of Jaffee's recording, as it does in Eisenstein's overly fast reading. Sanvoisin's 1975 performance embarrassingly combines all five voices given in the editions, even including the faulty and corrupt contratenor added to MS C (cf. J.R. White 1969, 89). His 1990 recording returns to the authentic four-part version, but the very weak triplum and very powerfully reinforced contratenor (the sung tenor line has been texted) makes for a strange sound. Wenzinger's recording is rather slow but useable. This leaves us with the nice recording of Hunter with Jantina Noorman, and the newer recordings by Page and the Ensemble P.A.N. Page's strikingly beautiful performance is the only one besides Wenzinger's that takes into account the corrections to the editions discussed by Hoppin (1960, 20–23). Unfortunately, Page's performance is marred by the application of text to all four voices, especially destructive in works with tripla, as here. Machaut's carefully fashioned cantus voice is buried by the text syllables of the other voices. See also chap. 2.5 for a jazz arrangement of R10 by Frederic Hand.

S'Amours ne fait par sa grace adoucir (B1)

1. Lukáš Matoušek, Panton 8111 0056 (1978). Zuzana Matoušková, mezzo-soprano; alto crumhorn (1'50"). Strophe 1 only.
2. Joel Cohen, Harmonia Mundi HMC 5122 (1985). Nancy Armstrong, soprano; Mark Kagan, tenor (3'39"). Strophes 1–2 only.

---

[12] See the commentary in chap. 7.3 to *Qui bien aimme* (L22/16), which suggests that the written-out transposition of the final strophe may normally have been left to the scribe in the earliest stages of transmission.

Matoušek's performance is useable, but the all-vocal performance by Cohen gives a much better representation of this curious work. Unfortunately, Cohen has adapted the text to the tenor line.

S'il estoit nulz / S'Amours / Et gaudebit cor vestrum (M6)
1. Alfred Deller, Bach Guild BGS 70656 (1961). Alfred Deller, countertenor; Robert Tear, tenor; treble viol, tenor viol, recorder, organ, trombone, tambourine (1'51").
2. Miroslav Klement, Supraphon GSST 50598 (1964). Milada Boublíková, soprano; Franz Lukasovsky, countertenor; recorder, viol, organ (1'35").
3. Alejandro Planchart, Expériences Anonymes EAS 83 (1966). Janet Steele, soprano; Lorraine Gorrell, alto; recorder, lute, viol, bassoon (1'44").
4. Howard Brown, Pleiades P 250 (1968?). Judith Nelson, soprano; Steven Crockett, countertenor; bass viol (1'39").
5. Denis Stevens, Musical Heritage Society MHS 830437 (1969). Ursula Connors, soprano; Shirley Minty, mezzo-soprano; Peter Vel, countertenor; fiddle (1'57").

No recordings can be recommended; any is adequate to gain an impression of the work.

S'onques dolereusement. Le Lay de Confort (L17/12)
1. Kees Boeke, Channel Classics CCS 0390 (1988). Lucia Meeuwsen, soprano; three tenor recorders with occasional vielle, psaltery, zither, lute (39'04").

All twelve strophes of this lay are three-voice *chaces*, with texts in two segments. Boeke, however, presents each strophe in four segments, effectively doubling the length of the work (unfortunately, it occupies but a single track on the compact disc). Most strophes begin instrumentally, with a full statement by the recorders, followed by a statement of the first half-strophe by the soprano; this pattern then repeats for the second half-strophe. Schrade's transcription is used, an unfortunate choice because of the syncopation errors in strophes 10 and 11 (see Hoppin 1960, 17).[13] Even with these problems, one does at least gain some impression of this vast work, Machaut's "Art of the *Chace*."

Sans cuer, dolens, de vous departirai (R4)
1. Michel Sanvoisin, Arion ARN 38252 (1974). Joseph Sage, countertenor; lute, viol (5'00").
2. Lukáš Matoušek, Panton 8111 0056 (1978). Zuzana Matoušková, mezzo-soprano; alto fiddle, bass recorder (2'40").
3. Les Ménestrels, Mirror Music 00006–00009 (1979). René Jacobs, countertenor; fiddle (5'21").

Sanvoisin and Les Ménestrels respond to the text by giving overly slow, mournful readings. Matoušek provides a bright tempo but is equally unstylish.

Sans cuer m'en vois, dolens et esplourez / Amis, dolens, maz et desconfortez / Dame, par vous me sens reconfortez (B17)
1. Safford Cape, Archive ARC 3032 (1956). Tenor fiddle, lute, recorder (2'08").
2. Sandy Bull, Vanguard VSD 79191 (1965). Guitar, oud, banjo (3'11").
3. John White, Decca DL 79431 (1967). Earnest Murphy, countertenor; Elizabeth Humes and Sheila Schonbrun, sopranos; bells (3'01"). Strophe 1 only.
4. John Renbourn, Transatlantic ORL 8654 (1970). Guitar, violin, flute (2'00").
5. Guy Robert, Adès 7078–7080 (1977). Annie Bartelloni, contralto; Jean Belliard and Alain Zoepffel, countertenors; recorder, fiddle, organetto, lute (4'40"). Strophes 1–3.

---

13 Günther (1962–63, 21–22) discusses further syncopation errors—ignored in both editions—in strophes 3, 4, and 9.

6. Lukáš Matoušek, Panton 8111 0056 (1978). Zuzana Matoušková, mezzo-soprano; Vladimír Doležal and Josef Života, countertenors (1'55"). Strophe 1 (incomplete) only.

Cape, Bull, and Renbourn use the erroneous transcription found in both the Ludwig and Schrade editions (see chap. 7.3). White uses the corrected transcription (ed. Reaney 1955, 57–58) in an all-vocal performance, but at such a slow tempo and with such vibrato (further, there is an unwritten octave displacement between voices) as to render the recording useless. Robert's recording is nicely sung but also unfortunately utilizes the erroneous transcription. Matoušek's performance is a curious amalgam, going once through in the correct transcription but taking the *clos* ending, and once through again, this time singing the incorrect transcription, again taking the *clos* ending, and repeating the words of the first strophe.

Se d'amer me repentoie (V20)
Not recorded.

Se je me pleing, je n'en puis mais (B15)
Not recorded.

Se je souspir parfondement (V36/30)
1. Lumen 33405 (1947). Pierre Deniau, tenor; instrumental ensemble. Not heard.
2. Safford Cape, Archive ARC 3032 (1956). René Letroye, tenor; tenor fiddle, recorder, lute (1'30"). Strophe 1 only.
3. George Hunter, Westminster XWN 18166 (1956). Richard Krause, tenor; lute (2'46"). Strophes 1–2 only.
4. Westminster XWN 18683 (1958). Hugues Cuénod, tenor; lute (2'31"). Not heard.
5. René Clemenčić, Supraphon GSST 50598 (1964). Franz Lukasovsky, tenor; recorder, viol (1'27"). Strophe 1 only.
6. Electrecord EXE 0234 (1965?). Valentin Teodorian, tenor; viol (2'21"). Not heard.
7. John White, Decca DL 79431 (1967). Arthur Burrows, baritone; bass viol (2'46"). Strophes 1–2 only.
8. David Munrow, Seraphim SIC 6092 (1973). Martyn Hill, tenor; descant recorder, citole, bass rebec, harp (2'22"). Strophes 1–2 only.
9. St. George's Canzona, Enigma K53571 (1978). Not heard.
10. Opus Musicum OM 122–124 (1979). Karl Markus, tenor; cello (1'50"). Strophe 1 only.
11. Paul Hillier, Schirmer Books ISBN 0-02-872953-6 (1990). John Potter, tenor; organ (4'11"). Strophes 1–3.

The doublings in Cape's performance are annoying, the tempo much too slow. Both Hunter, who employs a simple and effective scoring, and White, are also a bit too slow to be useful. Clemenčić's tempo is better, but the recording itself is very distant and reverberant. It is too bad that Munrow, doubtless working from Schrade's edition, repeats the refrain twice in the middle; his forceful rhythmic approach is excellent. In contrast, I find Hillier's performance rhythmically too reserved.

Se ma dame m'a guerpi (V6)
Not recorded.

Se mesdisans en acort (V15)
1. Guy Robert, Adès 7078–7080 (1977). Sopranino recorder, transverse flute, lute, vielle, drums, tambourine (1'52").
2. Christopher Page, Hyperion CDA66619 (1992). Rogers Covey-Crump, tenor solo (4'37"). Strophes 1–3.

In Robert's instrumental rendition, the refrain is repeated twice at the beginning and twice at the end; the recorder supplies heterophony. Page's performance is nearly ideal, although the text underlay has been oddly readjusted.

Se pour ce muir qu' Amours ai bien servi (B36)
1. Les Ménestrels, Mirror Music 00006–00009 (1979). Taina Kataja, soprano; fiddle, bass recorder (7'21"). Strophes 1–3.
   This recording is useable.

Se quanque amours puet donner a ami (B21)
1. Alejandro Planchart, Expériences Anonymes EAS 83 (1966). Janet Steele, soprano; lute, two recorders, viol, viola (2'14").
   This recording, slow and dull, is not recommended.

Se vous n'estes pour mon guerredon nee (R7)
   Not recorded.

Tant doucement m'ont / Eins que ma dame / Ruina (M13)
   Not recorded.

Tant doucement me sens emprisonnés (R9)
1. Grayston Burgess, L'Oiseau-Lyre SOL 310 (1969). Ian Partridge, tenor; tenor recorder, harp, viola (4'09").
2. Christopher Page, Hyperion CDA66463 (1990–91). Rogers Covey-Crump and Leigh Nixon, tenors (4'22").
   The Burgess recording is well done. Page employs textless vocalization of the tenor, but unfortunately the four-voice work is presented here with only two voices.

Tels rit au main qui au soir pleure (*complainte* RF2)
1. Safford Cape, Archive ARC 3032 (1956). Jeanne Deroubaix, alto solo (2'08"). Strophe 1 only.
2. Thomas Binkley, EMI Reflexe 1C 063-30 106 (1972). Andrea von Ramm, mezzo-soprano; fiddle, lute (8'36"). Strophes 1, 2, 9, 15, and 30 only.
3. Guy Robert, Adès 7078–7080 (1975). Jean Belliard, countertenor; Moorish guitar, lute, vielle, recorder (6'30"). Strophes 1, 15, and 36 only.
4. Michel Sanvoisin, Arion ARN 90814 (1975). Joseph Sage, countertenor, bass viol (2'42"). Strophe 1 only.
5. Music for a While, 1750 Arch S 1773 (1977). Voice, psaltery, saz; later: voice, fiddle (3'24"). Strophes 1 and 36 only.
6. Les Ménestrels, Mirror Music 00006–00009 (1979). René Jacobs, countertenor; vielle, psaltery (4'05"). Strophes 1–2 only.
7. Margaret Switten and Robert Eisenstein, The Medieval Lyric (1987). Peter Becker, baritone; hurdy-gurdy (14'33"). Strophes 1, 2, 15, 18, 19, 20, 21, 29, 30, and 36 only.
8. Dominique Vellard, Harmonic Records H/CD 8825 (1988). Recorder solo (2'15").
9. Ensemble P.A.N., New Albion Records NA068 CD (1994). Michael Collver, countertenor; vielle, sinfonia (10'30"). Strophes 1, 2, 18, and 19 only.
   Cape's presentation is still useable. Binkley makes a large production of the *complainte*: the work begins with a recitation of the verses in the *Remede* that introduce the *complainte*, followed by a fanciful and extended fiddle and lute prelude (and later interlude).[14] Strophes 2 and 15 are recited over lute and fiddle. Robert also begins with recitation of the verses that introduce the *complainte*, followed by strophe 1 with accompaniment, an interlude, recitation of strophe 15, and strophe 36 sung. Sanvoisin's performer is doubled an octave below by a bass viol. The first strophe in the Music for a While recording is accompanied at pitch by a psaltery, then after a recited paraphrase of strophe 20, an incomplete performance of the last strophe is given with drone and psaltery. Jacobs's recording for Les Ménestrels is useable. The performance by Ensemble P.A.N. is notable for the very free but slow tempo,

---

[14] Binkley (1977, 28–29) prints the arrangement for lute and fiddle used in strophe 1 of this recording.

requiring nearly three minutes for the first strophe; a complete performance at that tempo would last more than one hour and forty-five minutes. Again, Switten's project has supplied the best performance available, presenting ten of the thirty-six strophes accompanied only by a discreet drone on a hurdy-gurdy.

Tous corps / De souspirant cuer / Suspiro (M2)
Not recorded.

Tres bonne et belle, mi oueil (V26/23)
1. George Hunter, Westminster XWN 18166 (1956). Richard Krause, tenor; lute, vielle (2'24"). Strophe 1 only.
2. Ancient Instrument Ensemble of Zurich, Odyssey 32 160178 (1966). Baroque oboe, fiddle, viol (2'31").
3. Les Ménestrels, Mirror Music 00006–00009 (1979). René Jacobs, countertenor; lute, fiddle (6'21"). Strophes 1–3.
4. Ensemble Guillaume de Machaut, Adès 14040 (1983). Jean Belliard, countertenor; sackbut, flute, lute (3'50"). Strophe 1 only.
5. Christopher Page, Hyperion CDA66619 (1992). Rogers Covey-Crump, Julian Podger, and Leigh Nixon, tenors (2'22"). Strophe 1 only.

The Ensemble Guillaume de Machaut begins with a solo lute. On the repeat of the refrain, the singer tries some embellishments, perhaps inspired by the Baroque oboe's embellishments in the old recording by the Zurich group. Hunter's performance is useable, as is that of Les Ménestrels, which moreover has the advantage of giving the complete text. Page's is the ideal performance; unfortunately, he presents only one strophe.

Tres douce dame que j' aour (B24)
1. George Hunter, Westminster XWN 18166 (1956). Jantina Noorman, contralto; vielle (1'34"). Strophe 1 only.
2. Grayston Burgess, L'Oiseau-Lyre SOL 310 (1969). Grayston Burgess, countertenor; psaltery (2'27"). Strophes 1 and 3 only.
3. Lukáš Matoušek, Panton 8111 0056 (1978). Alto recorder, alto crumhorn, tenor crumhorn, soprano shawm, alto fiddle, tenor fiddle, lute, tabor (0'50").
4. Zoltán Majó, Electrecord ST-ECE 01929 (1981). Alexandru Nagy, countertenor; viol (1'17"). Strophe 1 only.

Hunter's recording is still satisfying. I find the sympathetic vibrations of the psaltery used in Burgess's recording annoying. Majó's more recent recording is unremarkable.

Trop plus est bele / Biauté paree / Je ne sui mie certains d' avoir amie (M20)
1. Kees Otten, Seraphim SIC 6052 (1969). Will Kippersluys, contralto; Marius van Altena, tenor with recorder; cornett, portative organ, fiddle pizzicato. (1'40").
2. David Munrow, Seraphim SIC 6092 (1973). James Bowman and Charles Brett, countertenors; Martyn Hill, tenor (2'28").
3. Ensemble Guillaume de Machaut, Adès 14040 (1983). Jean Belliard, countertenor; Jean-François Barrès, tenor; lute, recorder, positive organ, two vielles (2'45").
4a. Michel Sanvoisin, Edelweiss ED 1021 (1990). Fiddle, organ (1'26").
4b. Michel Sanvoisin, Edelweiss ED 1021 (1990). Joseph Sage, counter-tenor; Hugues Primard, tenor; Pierre Eyssartier, tenor; Marc Guillard, baritone; organ, cornett (1'32").
5. Christopher Page, Hyperion CDA66619 (1992). Margaret Philpot, alto; Rogers Covey-Crump and Leigh Nixon, tenors (1'25").
6. Ensemble P.A.N., New Albion Records NA068 CD (1994). Two vielles, harp, lute (2'00").

Only Page's fast recording incorporates the important corrections to the transcription given by Hoppin (1960, 15–16). Otten begins with a tenor solo performance of the rondeau refrain tenor alone, followed by an overly fast rendition of the motet. The Ensemble Guillaume de

Machaut builds the piece up gradually, beginning with an instrumental presentation of the tenor's rondeau refrain (mm. 1–11), then repeating this segment, adding motetus (organ) and finally triplum (recorder). We then begin again, adding the voices for a performance of the complete motet. Sanvoisin provides an all-instrumental performance followed by an overly full ensemble performance. Ensemble P.A.N.'s instrumental rendition opens with a fantasy on the tenor rondeau theme. Munrow's unaccompanied performance is superb, but for the errors in the transcription.

Tu qui gregem / Plange regni / Apprehende arma et scutum et exurge (M22)
1. John Beckett, Philips SAL 3722 (1969). Jantina Noorman, mezzo-soprano; Nigel Rogers, tenor; tenor shawm, sackbut (2'28").
2. Konrad Ruhland, Telefunken 6.41125 AS (1970). James Bowman and Tom Sutcliffe, countertenors; fiddle, organ, crumhorn (2'33").
3. Helga Weber, I.H.W. CD3.108 (1993). David Cordier, countertenor; Wilfried Jochens, tenor; flute, alto bombard, tenor bombard, trombone, drum (3'01").

I prefer by a hair Ruhland's straight-laced and dependable recording (despite the crumhorns) to the rhythmically less clear recording by Beckett (with Jantina Noorman employing one of the more barbaric of her many voices). The drum tapping out the combined rhythms of tenor and contratenor in Weber's version supports an analytical point but otherwise renders it unusable.

Tuit mi penser (V28/25)
1. Michel Sanvoisin, Arion ARN 38252 (1974). Joseph Sage, countertenor solo (2'13"). Strophes 1–2 only, lacking final refrain.
2. Christopher Page, Hyperion A66087 (1983). Rogers Covey-Crump, tenor solo (3'01"). Strophes 1–3.

Sanvoisin's recording is far too slow, while Page's is not rhythmically vital enough for dance.

Un mortel lay vueil commencier. Le Lay Mortel (L12/8)
Not recorded.

Une vipere en cuer ma dame maint (B27)
Not recorded.

Vo dous regars, douce dame, m'a mort (R8)
Not recorded.

4. Recordings of the *Messe de Nostre Dame*

For the discussion below, the many recordings of the Mass are separated by decade.[15] Of the twenty-nine recordings listed, nine include only excerpts. No. 16 may never have been released; thus, nineteen recordings of the complete Mass are known to me.

1950s and earlier:
1. Guillaume de Van, Anthologie Sonore AS 3 (1936). Chorus; two trombones sometimes added (15'30"). Credo, Sanctus, Agnus I–II, Ite only.
2. Jacques Chailley, Voix de son Maître DB 5118 (1939). Kyrie I, incomplete Credo only. Not heard.
3. Paul Boepple, Concert Hall Society CHS 1107 (1951). Large chorus, instrumental ensemble (35'15").

---

[15] Apparently the first modern performance of the Mass (Kyrie, fragments of Credo, Agnus Dei) took place in Paris, 26 March 1918 (Gastoué 1922, 67 n. 1; see the critical comments in Ludwig 1922–23, 436, 441 n. 1). The Paraphonistes de Saint-Jean-des-Matines, directed by Guillaume de Van, performed the Mass complete on 2 Feb. 1936, 18 March 1936, and 1 June 1942 (de Van 1949, iii). Levarie (1954, 106–7) and Chailley (1982, 304) mention some later performances.

4. Henry Washington, RCA Victor LM 6016 (1951?). Chorus, instrumental ensemble (1'38"). Benedictus and Osanna II only.
5. Niels Møller, Haydn Society HSL 2071 (1953). Chorus, positive organ (1'09"). Agnus I only.
6. Roger Blanchard, Ducretet Thompson 270 C 085 (1955). Jean Archimbaud, countertenor; Pierre Deniau, countertenor; Georges Cathelat, tenor; Eugène Bousquet, baritone; Marcel Vigneron, bass; vocal and instrumental ensemble (33'53"). Not heard.
7. Safford Cape, Archive ARC 3032 (1956). Elisabeth Verlooy, soprano; Jeanne Deroubaix, alto; René Letroye, tenor; Franz Mertens, tenor; Willy Pourtois, bass; recorders, three fiddles, lute (28'44").
8. Alexander Peloquin, Gregorian Institute EL 17 (1959). Vocal ensemble, organ (1'16"). Et incarnatus only. Not heard.

The recording for the Anthologie Sonore is interesting today only as an historical curiosity, yet it is far superior to the ugly performance directed by Boepple, aptly dubbed a "mastodonic misadventure" by Barker (1988, 128 n. 53). The recording of the Benedictus and Osanna II, made for the *History of Music in Sound*, is not useable, nor is Møller's recording of the Agnus I, made for the records to accompany Parrish/Ohl 1951. Although the performance is slow for today's listeners, Safford Cape's 1956 recording must have been a revelation in its day. Solo voices are used throughout, with discreet instrumental accompaniment added in a few sections (only the Sanctus is marred by constant changes of scoring). The textless passages in the tenor and contratenor of the Gloria and Credo are played on fiddles, which seem always to enter a measure before the passage and play the measure after the voices re-enter. The sudden tempo changes in the Amen of the Gloria and Credo are explained rather elliptically in the "Musicological Note" found on the sleeve notes (see also Cape 1959–60, 46, 56–57).

1960s:
9. Alfred Deller, Bach Guild BGS 5045 (1961). Alfred Deller, countertenor; Wilfried Brown, tenor; Maurice Bevan baritone; Gerald English, tenor; fiddle, cornett, recorder, regal, tenor bombard, trombone (25'30").
10. Ensti Pohjola, Ylioppilaskunnan Laulajat YLLP 1 and 2 (1965?). Risto Juvonen, Pertti Saurola, Markku Johansson, Antti Mäkelä, voices; strings (25'20").
11. John McCarthy, Nonesuch H 71184 (1966). Chorus with large instrumental ensemble (24'22").
12. Grayston Burgess, L'Oiseau-Lyre SOL 310 (1969). Small choir; organ in Kyrie only (24'14").
13. August Wenzinger, Archiv 2533 054 (1969). Friedrich Melzer and Ernst Haefliger, tenors; Jakob Stämpfli and Kurt Widmer, basses; with a variety of instrumental doublings: alto fiddle with alto recorder, harp with regal, lute with dulcian, organ with tenor fiddle (28'13").
14. Richard Taruskin, Collegium Stereo JE 101 (1969–70). Ite, missa est only. Not heard.

1970s:
15. Konrad Ruhland, Telefunken 6.41125 AS (1970). James Bowman and Tom Sutcliffe, countertenors; Leopold Fendt, Konrad Ruhland, Norbert Regul, Hans Bichler, and Frieder Neunhoeffer, tenors; with two recorders, three fiddles, organ, sackbut, in a variety of instrumental doublings (25'27").
16. Martin Behrmann, Da Camera SM 94033 (1971). Not heard; apparently not released.
17. Charles Ravier, Inédits ORTF 995 010 (1971). Jocelyne Chamonin, soprano; Amelia Salvetti, mezzo-soprano; Joseph Sage, countertenor;

Pierre-Michel Pégaud, tenor; André Meurant, tenor; Jean Boulay, baritone; Georges Abdoun, bass; instrumental ensemble (29'44").
18. Bernard Gagnepain, Erato EFM 18041 (1977). Mixed chorus, instrumental ensemble (27'30").
19. Kurt Weinhöppel, Calig CAL 30451 (1977). Erika Rüggeberg, soprano; Renate Freyer, alto; Anton Rosner, tenor; Erwin Buchbauer, bass; instrumental ensemble (2'35"). Sanctus, Pleni, Osanna I only.
20. Les Ménestrels, Mirror Music 00006–00009 (1978). John Patrick Thomas, countertenor; Meiczyslav Antoniak, tenor; Yoshiharu Matsuura, tenor; Laszlo Kunz, bass; chorus, instrumental ensemble (25'05").
21. Arsène Bedois, Erato STU 71303 (1979). Esther Lamandier, Christopher Wells, Jean-Louis Bouillat, Mario Hacquard, and Jacques Bona, voices; two cornetts, two sackbuts, organ (23'21").

Several recordings of the 1960s and 1970s present constant changes of scoring and instrumentation in various movements, perhaps in an effort to highlight the supposed "coronation" function of the Mass.[16] All of these sound very unsatisfactory today, including the 1966 recording by McCarthy, the 1970 recording by Ruhland, the 1971 recording by Ravier made by the Office de Radiodiffusion-Télévision Française (in a number of movements, the tenor and bass are doubled at the octave below),[17] the 1977 Gagnepain recording, and the 1978 recording by Les Ménestrels, the Mozartsängerknaben-Wien, "und viele andere." Of these, Ruhland employs excellent singers and effective tempos and is still quite a satisfying experience for the Gloria and Credo. McCarthy's performance, recorded in the Cathedral of Reims, may have some use for its inclusion of the Proper chants for the Assumption of the Blessed Virgin Mary; for Machaut's Mass it is useless. Les Ménestrels include Propers for the Common of Apostles in Paschal Time, a Mass cycle that was first collected in the 1974 Graduale Romanum.[18] The 1961 recording by the Deller Consort has been reissued in compact disc format, and at the time of this writing it remains available for purchase. In spirit and tempo it compares with Ruhland's recording, scored throughout for full voices with instruments, for the most part without the annoying changes of scoring that mar Ruhland's version. Curiously, Deller himself sings a kind of "*solus triplum*" in the Credo, put together from whichever voice—triplum or motetus—is sounding higher at a given moment. For the Kyrie movement alone, a bell ringer has absurdly marked the beginning of (almost) all of the isorhythmic periods. Wenzinger's performance is fairly discreet in its use of instruments, but the vibrato of the chorus is unpleasant today. The 1965 Finnish recording, pitched a tritone low, alternates a solo quartet with chorus and strings; parts of this recording—notably the Amen of the Gloria and Credo—are fine. Bedois's 1979 recording has some changes in instrumentation but is usually full. The voices in this version are excellent; the instrumentation is unfortunate. In 1969, Grayston Burgess, under the supervision of Frank Harrison, supplied one of the best recordings of the Mass yet made, employing a small chorus of excellent singers without accompanying instruments. Tempos are fast and virtuosic, and the authentic medieval French pronunciation of the Latin is delightful. I have only two quibbles. First, *alternatim* practice is adopted for the Kyrie, but instead of alternating phrases of plainchant, organ elaborations of the Kyrie Cunctipotens from the Faenza codex are inserted. It is of course useful to have recordings of these, but they are out of place in a performance of Machaut's Mass. Second, the linking passages in tenor and contratenor in the Gloria and Credo, now for the first time performed by voices, are unfortunately and I believe wrongly supplied each time with a syllable of text.

1980s–1990:
22. Günther Andergassen, Koch H 320 901 (1983). Mixed chorus (1'54"). Benedictus only.

---

[16] Reaney (1966, 719–21; 1977, 10) describes a 1958 performance score he prepared with instrumental doubling and simplification of the vocal parts, resulting in heterophony.

[17] Some comments on the nonsensical instrumentation employed in Ravier's recording are given in Parrott 1977, 493.

[18] I thank J.F. Weber for this information.

23. Andrew Parrott, Angel/EMI S 38044 (1983). Rogers Covey-Crump and Andrew Parrott, tenors; Paul Hillier and Simon Grant, basses (23'33").
24. Joel Cohen, Harmonia Mundi HMC 5122 (1985). Kenneth Fitch, Jeffrey Gall, Fred Raffensberger, Larry Zukof, countertenors; Mark Kagan, Reed Boland, John Clarke, tenors; David Ripley, Gilbert High, basses; two vielles, rebec, sackbut, douçaine (21'15").
25. Paul Hillier, Hyperion CDA66358 (1987). David James and Ashley Stafford, countertenors; Rogers Covey-Crump, John Potter, Mark Padmore, and Leigh Nixon, tenors; Paul Hillier and Michael George, basses (24'06").
26. Svatopluk Jányš, Panton 81 0771 (1988). Two countertenors, five tenors, four basses, boys' choir, instrumental ensemble (22'24").
27. Michel Sanvoisin, Edelweiss ED 1021 (1990). Joseph Sage, countertenor; Hugues Primard, tenor; Pierre Eyssartier, tenor; Marc Guillard, baritone; guitar, cornett, organ (28'36").
28. Egbert Schimmelpfennig, Fono FCD 97736 (1990). Anita Weltzien, voice; Lucia Laake, voice; Kai Roterberg, voice; fiddle, hurdy-gurdy, flute [Agnus III only] (3'31"). Agnus Dei only.
29. Dominique Vellard, Harmonic Records H/CD 8931 (1990). Andreas School, Gerd Türk, Emmanuel Bonnardot, and Jacques Bona, voices (29'04").

Cohen's recording has effective bright tempos but reverts to the practice of a constantly changing vocal and instrumental scoring, as does the poor performance of Jányš. The timing of Jányš's recording is short because it eschews any bow to liturgical propriety: the four segments of the Kyrie are simply presented in a series, and the intonations of the Gloria and Credo are omitted. At least Cohen's vocal renditions of the repeat of the Kyrie 1, the Amen of the Gloria, and the Agnus 2, are superb. In certain teaching contexts, this might be the best version of the Mass to present. The recent recording of the Mass by Sanvoisin also employs some instrumental doublings, but again it is the occasional unaccompanied passages in the Gloria and Credo that are most beautiful. Andergassen presents the Benedictus in reverberant surroundings at a slow tempo with large chorus. We can only be grateful that Schimmelpfennig recorded only a single movement in the instrumentation he employs. Three excellent recent recordings are those directed by Parrott, Hillier, and Vellard. Of these, Vellard is markedly slow, and lacks the authentically French-influenced pronunciation of the Latin heard in Parrott and Hillier. Parrott's is the most exciting performance of the three, although his transposition by a perfect fourth downwards seems too extreme; I would prefer a brighter sound. The overly pretty sound of the Hilliard Ensemble is also not apt for Machaut's style, for it leaves the hockets too muddy. We are getting closer, but there is still room for the ideal recording of Machaut's Mass.

5. Recordings of some related fourteenth-century musical works

Armes, Amours, Dames, Chevalerie / O fleur des fleurs de toute melodie (double ballade *déploration* on the death of Machaut, music by F. Andrieu, text by Eustache Deschamps).[19]

1. David Munrow, Seraphim SIC 6092 (1973). James Bowman and Charles Brett, countertenors; fiddle, bass rebec, organ (2'47"). Strophe 1 only.
2. Kees Otten, Telefunken 6.35257 ER (1974). René Jacobs, countertenor; Marius van Altena, tenor; two gambas, two bass recorders (6'30"). Strophe 1; strophes 2 and 3 of *O fleur des fleurs* are performed simultaneously in the second repetition, an error.
3. Jean-Claude Malgoire, CBS Masterworks 76534 (1976). Mary Criswick, mezzo-soprano; Charles Brett, countertenor; two vielles, lute, bass flute (8'27"). Strophes 1–3.

---

[19] For editions, see chap. 7.4.

4. Guy Robert, Adès 7078–7080 (1977). Jean Belliard and Alain Zoepffel, countertenors; vielle, organetto, crumhorn, tenor lute, bass flute (6'25"). Strophes 1–3.
5. Bernard Gagnepain, Erato EFM 18041 (1977). Mixed chorus, instrumental ensemble (5'55"). Strophes 1 and 3 only.
6. Lukáš Matoušek, Panton 8111 0056 (1978). Zuzana Matoušková, mezzo-soprano; Vladimír Doležal, countertenor; alto fiddle, ala bohemica, tenor fiddle pizzicato (2'30"). Strophe 1 only.
7. Robert Eisenstein, Delos D/CD 1003 (1979). Peter Becker, countertenor; David Gordon, tenor; lute, fiddle (2'37"). Strophe 1 only.
8. Marcel Pérès, Harmonia Mundi France HMC 901252 (1986). Instrumental introduction on vielle and clavicytherium; Gérard Lesne, countertenor; Josep Benet, tenor; François Fauché, bass; vielle, clavicytherium (5'59"). Strophes 1 and 3 only.
9. Ensemble P.A.N., New Albion Records NA021 CD (1987). Laurie Monahan, mezzo-soprano; Michael Collver, countertenor; Peter Becker, tenor; vielle, lute (6'29"). Strophes 1–3.

Gagnepain's recording is poor, alternating men, women, and then all together; most of the other performances are useable, though Robert and Matoušek are less good. Both Pérès and the Ensemble P.A.N. effectively employ vocalized tenor parts. I prefer the Ensemble P.A.N.'s performance of the complete text.

Biauté parfaite et bonté souvereinne (Lo140). Set to music by Anthonello da Caserta (fl. late fourteenth-early fifteenth century).[20]
1. Kees Otten, Telefunken 6.42357 AW (1979). Rita Daws, mezzo-soprano; bass recorder, tenor fiddle (6'02"). Strophes 1–2 only.
2. Thomas Binkley, Focus 883-4S, cassette 2 (1988). Wendy Gillespie, soprano; lute, fiddle (5'36"). Strophes 1 and 3 only.
3. Alba Musica Kyo, Channel Classics CCS 7094 (1994). Chiyomi Yamanda, soprano; recorder, vielle, citole (8'54"). Strophes 1–3.

Anthonello's musical style, so unlike Machaut's, provides interesting material for comparison. This is the only known example of one of Machaut's texts set to music by another composer. All three performances are sensitively done.

Li enseignement de Chaton / De touz les biens / Ecce
1. Ensemble Guillaume de Machaut, Adès 14040 (1983). Jean Belliard, countertenor; Jean-François Barrès, tenor; two vielles, sackbut (3'20").

This motet counts as an *opus dubium*, ascribed to Machaut in a single peripheral manuscript, but lacking in the central Machaut manuscripts (see chap. 7.4). The recording is valuable for presenting an example of a rare mensuration for the fourteenth-century isorhythmic motet, *tempus perfectum minor*. Hocket sections in the upper voices are performed by the vielles alone.

Phiton, Phiton, beste tres venimeuse (Refrain: *Tu qui contes gaster la flour du monde*), by Magister Franciscus.[21] Ballade related to *Phyton, le mervilleus serpent* (B38).
1. David Munrow, Seraphim SIC 6092 (1973). Martyn Hill, tenor; two tenor crumhorns (2'13"). Strophe 1 only.

Of the fourteenth-century chansons imitating Machaut chansons (see chap. 7.3, commentaries to *De Fortune* [B23], *Phyton* [B38], *Se je me pleing* [B15], and *Se vous n'estes* [R7]), this is the only one recorded.

---

[20] Ed. Apel 1950, No. 23; 1970–72, 1:5–1 no. 4; Greene 1981–89, 20:7–10 no. 3.
[21] For editions, see chap. 7.3, commentary to *Phyton* (B38).

6. Musical insertions in the *Remede* and *Voir Dit*

Each of the inserted lyrics set to music in the *Remede* has been recorded at least three times. They are listed here in the order of their appearance in the *Remede*. For recordings, find the title in the above alphabetical list, chap. 8.3. In addition, the famous passage (ll. 3957–4006/3959–4008) naming several kinds of instruments is recited on the LPs Adès 7078–7080 and Mirror Music 00006–00009, followed by a performance of one or more estampies. The same passage is recited on the compact disc Harmonic Records H/CD 8825.

RF1   *Qui n'aroit autre deport* (lay)
RF2   *Tels rit au main qui au soir pleure* (*complainte*)
RF3   *Joie, plaisance, et douce nourriture* (*chant royal*)
RF4   *En amer a douce vie* (duplex ballade)
RF5   *Dame, de qui toute ma joie vient* (ballade)
RF6   *Dame, a vous sans retollir* (virelai)
RF7   *Dame, mon cuer en vous remaint* (rondeau)

Each of the inserted lyrics set to music in the *Voir Dit* has been recorded at least once. They are listed here in the order of their appearance in the *Voir Dit* (see chap. 5.13 table 5.3). For recordings, find the title in the above alphabetical list, chap. 8.3. In addition, several passages from the *Voir Dit* are read on the LPs Adès 7078–7080, Mirror Music 00006–00009, and the compact disc Harmonic Records H/CD 8825.

VD5   *Plourez, dames, plourez vostre servant* (B32)
VD14   *Dame, se vous n'avez aperceü* (R13)
VD16   *Nes qu'on porroit les estoilles nombrer* (B33)
VD31   *Sans cuer, dolens, de vous departirai* (R4)
VD47   *Longuement me sui tenus* (L18/13)
VD56   *Dix et sept, .v., .xiii., .xiiii. et quinse* (R17)
VD57–58 *Quant Theseüs, Hercules et Jason / Ne quier veoir la biauté d'Absalon* (B34)
VD61   *Se pour ce muir qu'Amours ai bien servi* (B36)

7. Recommended recordings

For those interested specifically in examples of Machaut's music that are superior for musical or musicological reasons—at least by current standards—the following suggestions are offered. All may be located in the above alphabetical series of recordings, chap. 8.3.

For a lai: *J'aim la flour* (L2; Lamandier); *Lay de la Fonteinne, Je ne cesse* (L16/11; Hillier); *Qui n'aroit* (RF1; Switten).

For a motet: *Amours qui a / Faus Semblant* (M15; Vellard); *Christe / Veni* (M21; Munrow or Vellard); *De Bon Espoir / Puis que* (M4; Hillier); *Felix virgo / Inviolata* (M23; Page or Vellard); *Hareu! / Helas!* (M10; Munrow); *Lasse! comment / Se j'aim* (M16; Robert); *Quant en moy / Amour* (M1; Hillier); *Qui es / Ha! Fortune* (M8; Munrow); *Trop plus / Biauté* (M20; Munrow or Page).

For the Mass (chap. 8.4): Burgess; Parrott; Hillier; Vellard.

For the *Hoquetus David*: Munrow.

For a ballade: *Amours me fait* (B19; Munrow, Page, or Hillier); *Dame, de qui* (RF5; Page or Switten [four-voice version]); *De toutes flours* (B31; Vellard, Hillier, or Pérès); *Honte, paour* (B25; Binkley); *Ma chiere* (B40; Sanvoisin); *Mes esperis* (B39; Munrow); *Phyton* (B38; Munrow); *Quant Theseüs / Ne quier* (B34; Binkley, Munrow, Robert, or Otten); *Riches d'amour* (B5; Page); *S'Amours ne fait* (B1; Cohen); *Se pour ce muir* (B36; Les Ménestrels).

For a rondeau: *Ce qui soustient* (R12; Vellard); *Dame, mon cuer en vous* (RF7; Page or Ensemble P.A.N.); *Dous viaire* (R1; Vellard); *Helas! pour quoy se demente* (R2; Ensemble Guillaume de Machaut); *Ma fin* (R14; Hillier); *Puis qu'en oubli* (R18; Vellard or Hillier); *Quant je ne voy* (R21; Hudrisier or Hillier); *Rose, lis* (R10; Page).

For a virelai: *Comment qu'a moy* (V5; Page); *Dame, a vous* (RF6; Binkley); *Dame, je vueil* (V9; Page); *Dame, vostre* (V17; Hillier); *Douce dame jolie* (V4; Hunter); *Foy porter* (V25/22; Page); *Moult sui* (V37/31; Binkley); *Tres bonne* (V26/23; Page).

8. Index of recordings by record label

1750 Arch Records.

S 1773 (LP). *La Fontaine Amoureuse*. Music for a While. Recorded Aug. 1977. Texts; English translations by Meg Bogin.

Biauté qui (B4), *Cinc, un* (R6), *Dame, je sui / Fins* (M11), *Foy porter* (V25/22), *Hoquetus David, Je ne cesse* (L16/11), *Je vivroie* (V23/21), *Joie, plaisance* (RF3), *Tels rit* (RF2). Review: J.F. Weber 1979.

Adès.

7078–7080 (3 LPs; 2 CDs as 13294-2 [no texts]; selections on ACD 14077-2 with M18, M23, V5 and all *Remede* selections; *Remede* selections first released on a single LP, Alvarès C 499, recorded 1975). *L'art musical et poétique de Guillaume de Machaut*. Motets, ballades, virelays. *Le Remede de Fortune. Le Veoir Dit.* Ensemble Guillaume de Machaut de Paris. Guy Robert, director. 1977. French texts only.

F. Andrieu, *Armes, Amours / O fleur* (Deschamps's *déploration*), *Bone paster / Bone pastor* (M18), *Comment qu'a moy* (V5), *Dame, a vous* (RF6), *Dame, de qui* (RF5), *Dame, mon cuer en vous* (RF7), *De toutes flours* (B31 [Faenza intabulation]), *Dix et sept* (R17), *Douce dame jolie* (V4), *En amer* (RF4), *Felix virgo / Inviolata* (M23), *Hoquetus David, Honte, paour* (B25 [Faenza intabulation]), *Je ne cuit* (B14), *Joie, plaisance* (RF3), *Lasse! comment / Se j'aim* (M16), *Longuement* (L18/13), *Ma fin* (R14), *Moult sui* (V37/31), *Nes qu'on* (B33), *Plourez, dames* (B32), *Quant en moy / Amour* (M1), *Quant je sui* (V13), *Quant Theseüs / Ne quier* (B34), *Qui n'aroit* (RF1), *Sans cuer m'en / Amis / Dame* (B17), *Se mesdisans* (V15), *Tels rit* (RF2). Also includes some spoken texts from the *Remede* and *Voir Dit*. Review: J.F. Weber 1979.

14040 (LP). *L'Ars nova française: Guillaume de Machaut (1300–1377) et son temps*. Ensemble Guillaume de Machaut de Paris. 1983. French texts only.

Helas! pour quoy se demente (R2), *Li enseignement / De touz* (*opus dubium*, see chap. 7.4), *On ne porroit* (B3), *Tres bonne* (V26/23), *Trop plus / Biauté* (M20).

Alba musica.

MU 244882 (CD). *Guillaume de Machaut & Le Codex Faenza*. Ensemble Tre Fontane. Recorded Sept. 1993. Not heard.

Biauté qui (B4), *Dous amis* (B6), *Honte, paour* (B25 [Faenza intabulation]), *De toutes flours* (B31 [Faenza intabulation]), *Je suis aussi* (B20), *Mes esperis* (B39).

Aliénor.

AL 1019 (CD; LP as AL 19, with L2 and V17 only). *Domna*. Esther Lamandier, voice and instruments (harp, organetto). Recorded 1987. Released 1987. Texts; modern French translations by Gaston Zinc.

Dame, vostre (V17), *Dou mal* (V8), *Foy porter* (V25/22), *J'aim la flour* (L2). Reviews: David Fallows, *Gramophone* 65 (1987–88): 1232, 1235; P. Miller, *American Record Guide* 51/5 (Sept.–Oct. 1988): 105.

Allegro.
Al 14 (2 LPs; reissued as Concord CRD 4006). *Music of the Gothic Period and the Early Renaissance.* Vielle Trio with Du Bose Robertson, tenor. 1949.

Lasse! comment / Se j'aim (M16).

Alton/Jeffery 1976.

Plus dure (V31/28). See main bibliography.

Angel.
SBZ 3810 (2 LPs; also EMI SLS 988). *Instruments of the Middle Ages and Renaissance.* Early Music Consort of London. David Munrow, director. 1976.

Comment qu'a moy (V5), *Dame, se vous m'estes* (B37),[22] *Quant je sui* (V13).

S 38044 (LP; CD as CDC 7479492 [released 1989]; LP released in England as HMV Reflexe ASD 143576 1, in Germany as EMI Reflexe 1C 067-1435761). *Guillaume de Machaut. Messe de Nostre Dame.* Taverner Consort and Taverner Choir. Andrew Parrott, director. Recorded Jan.–Feb. 1983. Released 1984. Texts; English translations by Father David Evans.

Mass (liturgical reconstruction of the Mass for the Nativity of Our Lady with chant from a Reims manuscript). Reviews: Mary Berry, *Gramophone* 66 (1988–89): 325; J. Blezzard, *Musical Times* 125 (1984): 601; J. Blume, *Neue Zeitschrift für Musik* 146/2 (Feb. 1985): 39; D. Fallows, *Gramophone* 61 (1983–84): 1094; J.F. Weber 1990, 1:303 and 1991, 31–32 (on the liturgical reconstruction). Parrott 1977 provides introductory remarks.

Anthologie Sonore (France).
LD 3012 (LP; reissued as Adès ADE 13 003). *Musique du Moyen Age et début Renaissance.* Collegium Musicum Krefeld. Robert Haas, director. 1956. Not heard.

Ma chiere (B40).

Anthologie Sonore (Haydn Society).
AS 3 (LP; Mass movements originally on two 78 rpm discs, Anthologie Sonore 31 and 32, Album 4, matrix: AS 74, 75, 77, 76; reissued as 7" LP 1803 LD; 45 rpm as Adès 532; secular songs originally on one 78 rpm disc, Anthologie Sonore 67, Album 7, matrix: 135-1, 140-1). *The 14th and 15th Centuries (Machault and Dufay).* Vol. 1, record 3. Les Paraphonistes de St-Jean des Matines; Brass Ensemble. Guillaume de Van, director. Curt Sachs, musicological director (Mass). La Société Pro Musica Antiqua, Brussels. Safford Cape, director. Curt Sachs, musicological director (chansons). Recorded 1936 (Mass)[23]; 1940 (chansons). LP released May 1954.

De tout sui (V38/32), *Je puis trop* (B28), Mass (Credo, Sanctus, Agnus I–II, Ite only), *Quant Theseüs / Ne quier* (B34).

Archiv (Deutsche Grammophon Gesellschaft); Archive (American Decca).
ARC 3032 (LP; also APM 14063; Sanctus only in 136 306 IMS). *The Central Middle Ages (1100–1350). Series D, The Ars Nova in France. Guillaume de Machaut: La Messe de Nostre Dame. Ten Secular Works.* Pro Musica Antiqua, Brussels. Safford Cape, director. Recorded 31 Jan. and 2–3 Feb. 1956. Texts, no translations.

De tout sui (V38/32), *De triste / Quant / Certes* (B29), *Je puis trop* (B28),[24] Mass,[25] *Nes*

---

[22] The recording of B37 also appears on Seraphim SIC 6092.

[23] The performance was based in part on photographs of Ludwig's transcription, sent to de Van by Besseler (de Van 1949, iii).

[24] B28 was reissued in Eterna 820 347 (LP), *1000 Jahre Musikgeschichte in klingenden Beispielen*, Vol. 1, *1000–1580* (1967).

qu'on (B33), *Puis qu'en oubli* (R18), *Quant Theseüs / Ne quier* (B34), *Qui es / Ha! Fortune* (M8), *Sans cuer m'en / Amis / Dame* (B17), *Se je souspir* (V36/30), *Tels rit* (RF2). Reviews: Gunden 1974–75; Reaney 1957, 182, 184–85.

2533 054 (LP). *Guillaume de Machaut. La Messe de Nostre Dame. Nine Secular Works.* Schola Cantorum Basiliensis. August Wenzinger, director. Editions revised by Wolfgang Dömling. Recorded 5–7 and 17–20 Oct. 1969. Texts; English and German translations.

Dame, comment qu'amez (B16), *Dame, vostre* (V17), *De petit po* (B18), *De toutes flours* (B31 [Faenza intabulation]), *Donnez, signeurs* (B26), *Dous viaire* (R1), Mass, *Mes esperis* (B39), *Quant je ne voy* (R21), *Rose, lis* (R10). Reviews: Denis Arnold, *Gramophone* 49 (1971–72): 876; Margaret Bent, *Musical Times* 113 (1972): 163.

2723 045 (3 LPs; also 2710 019; CD reissue of *Hoquetus David*, M8 and M16 as 415 292-2). *Music of the Gothic Era.* Early Music Consort of London, David Munrow, director. Recorded April and Oct. 1975. Released 1976. Texts; English translations by Hans Heimler and Michael Freeman.

Christe / Veni (M21), *Hoquetus David, Lasse! comment / Se j'aim* (M16), *Qui es / Ha! Fortune* (M8). Reviews: Hugh Keyte, *Gramophone* 54 (1976–77): 862; J. Milsom, *Gramophone* 63 (1985–86): 266.

Ariane.

ARI 148 (CD; SCA 500). *Musique liturgique et profane du XIVe siècle: La Messe de Barcelone; La Messe de Toulouse; chansons-motets-danses.* Ensemble Médiéval de Toulouse. Pierre Hudrisier, director. Recorded June 1988. No texts.

Dame mon cuer emportez (V32/29), *Quant je ne voy* (R21).

Arion (Peters International).

30 A 070 (LP; reissued as Musical Heritage Society MHS 3071). *L'art de la flûte*, Vol. 1. Groupe des Instruments Anciens de Paris. Roger Cotte, director. 1969. Not heard.

Hoquetus David.

30 A 096 (LP; also ARN 90808). *Chants à la cour de France.* Groupe des Instruments Anciens de Paris. Roger Cotte, director. 1970. Not heard.

Puis qu'en oubli (R18).

ARN 34217 (LP; also ARN 413; ARN 90413; ARN 36613; record 1 of three-record set as ARN 334 022; reissued as Musical Heritage Society MHS 3987; CD reissue as Arion ARN 68064). *Musique des trouvères et troubadours.* Les Musiciens de Provence. Released 1973.

Douce dame jolie (V4).

ARN 36554 (LP; reissued as Musical Heritage Society MHS 4391). *L'art du luth au Moyen-Age.* L'Ensemble Perceval. Guy Robert, director. 1981.

Douce dame jolie (V4).

ARN 38252 (LP; also ARN 90814; reissued as Musical Heritage Society MHS 3198). *The Art of Guillaume de Machaut.* The Ars Antiqua Group of Paris. Michel Sanvoisin, director. 1974. No texts.

Ce qui soustient (R12), *Dame, a vous* (RF6), *Dame, de qui* (RF5), *Douce dame jolie* (V4), *Douce dame, tant* (R20), *Hoquetus David, Joie, plaisance* (RF3, 2 versions),[26] *Ma fin* (R14), *Mes esperis* (B39), *Plourez, dames* (B32), *Plus dure* (V31/28, 2 versions), *Rose, lis* (R10), *Sans cuer, dolens* (R4), *Tels rit* (RF2), *Tuit mi penser* (V28/25).

---

[25] The Agnus of the Mass was reissued in Deutsche Grammophon Gesellschaft 136306 (LP), *Musik des Mittelalters und der Renaissance.*

[26] One version of RF3 was reissued in Arion ARN 36337.

ARN 38771 (LP). *Les premiers chefs-d'œuvre de l'orgue français.* Jean-Patrice Brosse, organ. Recorded March 1983. Not heard.

Plus dure (V31/28). Review: Michel Roubinet, *Diapason* no. 306 (June 1985): 80–81.

Bach Guild (Vanguard Records).

BGS 5045 (LP; also BG 622; HM 1SD; HM 3 SD; issued variously as Angelicum 5951; BASF 25 29377 7; BASF 68 20323 9; EA 293777; Deutsche Harmonia Mundi 1C 065 99718; Harmonia Mundi HM 450; HM 29377; 30898; 34917 and HMO 30917 with the Ancient Instrument Ensemble of Zurich recording of chansons, see Odyssey 32 160178; Sine Qua Non MS 5001; Lumen AMS 5005 [10" LP]; OPUS 6 [10" LP]; Harmonia Mundi HM 25148; Kyrie only in Opus Musicum OM 101–103 and 201–203; CD reissue as EMI CDM 7 69479 2 [released 1988]; later CD reissue as Deutsche Harmonia Mundi 77064-2-RG). *Music at Notre Dame, 1200–1375. Guillaume de Machaut. Notre Dame Mass and Works of Perotin.* Deller Consort, with members of the Collegium Aureum. Alfred Deller, director. Recorded Jan. 1961.

Mass. Reviews: Denis Arnold, *Gramophone* 51 (1973–74): 85–86; Gunden 1974–75; Janet Knapp, *Musical Quarterly* 48 (1962): 543–46.

BGS 70656 (LP; also BG 656). *Music of Medieval France, 1200–1400: Sacred and Secular.* Deller Consort and Concentus Musicus Wien. Alfred Deller, director. 1961. Texts; English translations by Charles Harmon.

Comment qu'a moy (V5), *S'il estoit / S'Amours* (M6).[27]

Bayer.

100 164 (CD). Isaak-Ensemble-Heidelberg. Lebherz-Valentin. Issued 1992. Not heard.

Loyauté, que (L1).

BIS.

LP 2 (LP). *Musica Intima.* Solveig Faringer, soprano; Clas Pehrsson, recorder; Jürgen Rörby, guitar. Recorded 1974. Not heard.

Dame, comment qu'amez (B16), *Plus dure* (V31/28).

Boite à Musique.

44 (78 rpm, matrix: PARTX 4519-1). Simone Gebelin, soprano; H. Akoka, clarinet; Georges Boo, flute. 1947. Not heard.

Rose, lis (R10).

LD 306 (10" LP). *Chansons poétiques anciennes et modernes.* Jacques Douai, tenor; J. Liebrard, guitar. 1954. Not heard.

Douce dame jolie (V4).

Bongiovanni.

GB 5532 2 (CD). *Il giardino dell'amore. Musiche strumentale nell'Europa fra Medioevo e Rinascimento.* Consort Fontegara. 1994. Not heard.

Hoquetus David, Ma fin (R14).

CBS Masterworks (France).

76534 (LP). *Music from the Time of the Popes at Avignon.* Florilegium Musicum de Paris. Jean-Claude Malgoire, director. 1976.

F. Andrieu, *Armes, Amours / O fleur* (Deschamps's *déploration*), *Moult sui* (V37/31). Review: J.F. Weber 1982.

---

[27] V5 was reissued in Vanguard SRV 298-SD (LP), *Songs of Birds, Battles, and Love, and the Flowering of the French Chanson,* Deller Consort, Alfred Deller, director (1968).

Calig.
CAL 30451 (LP). *Musik der Gotik und der Renaissance.* Capella Monacensis. Kurt Weinhöppel, director. 1977. Texts; German translations. Mass (Sanctus, Pleni, Osanna I only). Review: J.F. Weber 1982.

Carus.
FSM 63205 EB (LP). *La danza: Tanzmusik aus vier Jahrhunderten.* Odhecaton: Ensemble für alte Musik Köln. Recorded 1979. Not heard.
Dame, a vous (RF6).
83.123 (CD). *Canticum Canticorum. Das Hohelied der Liebe in Motetten alter Meister.* Vokalensemble Cantos, Osnabrück. Johannes Rahe, director. Recorded April 1991. Texts; German translations.
Maugré mon cuer / De ma dolour (M14). Review: J.F. Weber, *Fanfare* 15:6 (Jul.–Aug. 1992): 336.

Channel Classics.
CCS 0390 (CD). *Guillaume de Machault. Le Lay de Confort.* Little Consort & Frans Brüggen. Kees Boeke, director. Recorded June 1988. Released 1990. French text; summary in English.
Le Lay de Confort, S'onques (L17/12).
CCS 7094 (CD). *Machaut and His Time. 14th Century French Ars Nova.* Ensemble Alba Musica Kyo. Toyohiko Satoh, director. Recorded 21–23 June 1994. Released 1994. Texts; English translations.
Amours me fait (B19), *Biauté parfaite* (Lo140; music by Anthonello da Caserta), *Dame, ne regardez* (B9), *Douce dame jolie* (V4), *Dous viaire* (R1), *Gais et jolis* (B35), *Hoquetus David, Je ne cuit* (B14), *Rose, lis* (R10).

Charlin.
CL 39 (LP; also Schwann Musica Mundi VMS 1011). *Musique à la cour de Prague.* Symposium "Pro Musica Antiqua" de Prague. Recorded April 1970.
Amours me fait (B19).

Christophorus.
CD 74583 (CD). *"A chantar:" Lieder der Frauen-Minne.* Estampie: Münchner Ensemble für frühe Musik. Recorded 24–26 May 1989. Released 1990. Texts; German and English summaries.
Lasse! comment / Se j'aim (M16), *Moult sui* (V37/31).

Classic Editions.
CE 1018 (LP). *Recorder Music of Six Centuries.* The Recorder Consort of the Musician's Workshop. 1953.
Mes esperis (B39).

Club Français du Disque.
CFD set 230 (45 rpm). 1960? Not heard.
Douce dame jolie (V4).

Club National du Disque.
CND 9 (LP). *La musique et la poésie au Moyen-Age et à l'époque de la Renaissance.* Le Trio Monique Rollin and La Chorale Sine Nomine. Monique Rollin, director. 1955. French texts only.
Je suis aussi (B20). Includes also a reading of *Ne cuidiez pas* (Lo176).

Collegium Records.
COL 83-03 (LP). *La chanson française. Songs of Medieval and Renaissance France.* The Toronto Consort. Recorded May 1983. Released 1985. Texts; English translations by Guy Sauvé.
Joie, plaisance (RF3).

Collegium Stereo.
JE 101 (LP). *Music of the Ars Nova. A Composite Fourteenth-Century Mass.* The Columbia University Collegium Musicum. Richard Taruskin, director. Recorded 1969–70. Not heard.
Mass (Ite only).
JE 104 (LP). *The French Ars Antiqua.* The Columbia University Collegium Musicum. Richard Taruskin, director. Recorded Dec. 1970. Not heard.
Hoquetus David.

Columbia.
70701D in set M 431 (78 rpm, matrix: XCO 27379; LP: The Record Hunter TRH-2). *An Yves Tinayre Recital: Sacred and Secular Music from the XII thru the XVII Centuries.* Yves Tinayre, baritone; Dvonch Ensemble. Recorded 1940.
Plourez, dames (B32).

Concert Hall Society.
CHS 1107 (LP; also Classic 6193). *Guillaume de Machaut: Notre Dame Mass.* Dessoff Choirs, New York Brass Ensemble. Paul Boepple, director. 1951.[28]
Mass. Review: Kerr 1951.

Critère.
CRD 130 (LP). *La ligne d'or du clavecin français.* Aimée Van de Wiele, harpsichord. 1959. Not heard.
De toutes flours (B31 [Faenza intabulation]). Review: H. Halbreich, *Disques* no. 113 (Nov. 1959): 666.

Da Camera.
SM 91702 (LP; reissued as Musical Heritage Society MHS 1442). *Französische Musik aus Mittelalter und Renaissance.* Studio für alte Musik, Düsseldorf. 1969. Not heard.
De tout sui (V38/32), *Ma chiere* (B40), *Plus dure* (V31/28).

SM 94033 (LP). Capella Vocale and Instrumentale. Martin Behrmann, director. 1971. Not heard (see J.F. Weber 1979, 14: "apparently not released").
Mass.

Decca.
DL 79431 (LP; also 9431; reissued by MCA Records as MCA 2516). *Ah Sweet Lady: The Romance of Medieval France.* New York Pro Musica. John White, director. 1967. Texts; English translations by Wm. Earle Nettles.
De Fortune (B23), *De petit po* (B18), *De triste / Quant / Certes* (B29), *Douce dame jolie* (V4), *Je sui aussi* (B20), *Nes qu'on* (B33), *Pas de tor* (B30), *Quant je sui* (V13), *Sans cuer m'en / Amis / Dame* (B17), *Se je souspir* (V36/30).[29] Review: J.R. White (1969, 88–89) provides commentary on performance practices adopted for B17 and B29.

Delos.
D/CD 1003 (CD). *A Distant Mirror. Music from the Fourteenth Century. Shakespeare's Music.* Folger Consort. Robert Eisenstein, director.

---

[28] The booklet accompanying the recording, commemorating the performance of the Mass and the companion recording of Perotin's *Viderunt* (CHS-1122), was written by Gustave Reese.

[29] B18 and V4 were reissued in DL 79438 and MCA 2519; B29 and V4 were reissued in Horizon DL 34541 (LP), *Music for a Medieval Day*, New York Pro Musica, Noah Greenberg and John Reeves White, directors (1968).

Recorded Sept.–Oct. 1979. Released 1986. Texts; English translations.

F. Andrieu, *Armes, Amours / O fleur* (Deschamps's *déploration*), *Gais et jolis* (B35), *Rose, lis* (R10).

Dorian.

DIS 80109 (CD). *Songs and Dances of the Middle Ages*. Sonus. 1993. Texts; English translations.

Comment qu'a moy (V5), *Dame, ne regardez* (B9).

DIS 80123 (CD). *Chanterai: Music of Medieval France*. Sonus. Recorded Sept. 1993. Released 1994. Texts; English translations.

De bonté (V10), *Je puis trop* (B28), *Ma fin* (R14), *Quant je sui* (V13).

Ducretet Thompson.

270 C 085 (10" LP). Ensemble Vocal Blanchard. Roger Blanchard, director. Recorded 28–29 March 1955. Not heard.

Mass.

320 C 081 (5 LPs). *L'encyclopédie sonore. Record 1. Trésor de la poésie lyrique française, I. Moyen Age*. J.J. Lesnour, French Vocal Trio. 1960? Not heard.

De toutes flours (B31).

EMI Reflexe (Electrola).

1C 063-30 106 (LP; also 1C 063-30 101/6; CD as EMI CDM 7631422). *Guillaume de Machaut. Chansons 1*. Studio der frühen Musik. Thomas Binkley, director. 1972. Texts; German translations.

Aymi! (V3), *Comment qu'a moy* (V5), *Dame, a vous* (RF6), *Je ne cesse* (L16/11), *Joie, plaisance* (RF3), *Loyauté, que* (L1), *Quant je sui* (V13), *Tels rit* (RF2). Review: see the following entry.

1C 063-30 109 (LP; also 1C 063-30 107/12; CD as EMI CDM 7634242 [released 1990]). *Guillaume de Machaut. Chansons 2*. Studio der frühen Musik. Thomas Binkley, director. Released 1973. Texts; German translations.

Comment puet (R11), *Dame, je sui / Fins* (M11), *De toutes flours* (B31, 2 versions, including Faenza intabulation), *Dous viaire* (R1), *Fons tocius / O livoris* (M9), *Hoquetus David, Honte, paour* (B25, 2 versions, including Faenza intabulation), *Moult sui* (V37/31), *Quant en moy / Amour* (M1), *Quant Theseüs / Ne quier* (B34). Review: Robert Craft, "Guillaume de Machaut Chansons 1 and Chansons 2," *New York Review of Books* 23 (10) (12 July 1976): 39–41.

The Early Music Consort.

JRC 970 (LP). *The Age of Chivalry: Court Music of the Middle Ages and Renaissance*. Released 1979.

Dame, ne regardez (B9).

Edelweiss.

ED 1021 (CD). *Guillaume de Machaut: La Messe Nostre-Dame; L'Amour courtois*. Ars Antiqua de Paris. Michel Sanvoisin, director. Recorded 1990. Released 1990. French texts only.

Ce qui soustient (R12), *Dame, ne regardez* (B9), *Dame, se vous m'estes* (B37), *De toutes flours* (B31), *Douce dame jolie* (V4), *Hoquetus David, Ma chiere* (B40), *Ma fin* (R14), Mass, *Plus dure* (V31/28), *Quant Theseüs / Ne quier* (B34), *Rose, lis* (R10), *Trop plus / Biauté* (M20).

Electrecord (Romania).

EXE 0234 (LP). 1965? Not heard.

Se je souspir (V36/30).

STM-ECE 0899 (LP; also ECE 0611 and ST-ECE 0625). Corul de camera "Madrigal" al Conservatorului diu Bucuresti. Marin Constantin, director. 1967?

De tout sui (V38/32).

ST-ECE 01601 (LP). *De la trubaduri la "Ars Nova." Pagini vocale din Evul Mediu și Renaștere.* Martha Kessler, mezzo-soprano; instrumental ensemble. 1977?

Comment qu'a moy (V5), Je puis trop (B28), Plus dure (V31/28)

ST-ECE 01929 (LP). *Musica antiqua.* Musica Antiqua Cluj-Napoca. Zoltán Majó. director. Recorded April 1981.

Cinc, un (R6), *De Bon Espoir / Puis que* (M4), *Mes esperis* (B39), *Tres douce dame que* (B24).

Enigma.

VAR 1046 (LP; also K53552; Hispavox S90 241 in Spain; reissued as Musical Heritage Society MHS 4440). *A Tapestry of Music for King Wenceslas and His Page.* St. George's Canzona. John Sothcott, director. 1977.

Douce dame jolie (V4).

K53571 (LP; reissued as Musical Heritage Society MHS 4485). *A Tapestry of Music for the Black Prince and his Knights.* St. George's Canzona. John Sothcott, director. Released 1978. Not heard.

J'aim la flour (L2), *Se je souspir* (V36/30).

Erato.

LDE 3377 (LP; also STE 50277, STU 70277; reissued as Musical Heritage Society MHS 894). *Cinq siècles de musique dans la Cathédrale de Reims.* Maîtrise de la Cathédrale de Reims. Paillard Chamber Orchestra. Jean-François Paillard and Jacques Chailley, directors. 1968.

Felix virgo / Inviolata (M23).

EFM 18041 (LP). *Guillaume de Machault. Messe de Nostre Dame. Trois motets latins.* Séminaire Européen de Musique Ancienne. Bernard Gagnepain, director. Recorded July 1977. Released 1979. No texts.

F. Andrieu, *Armes, Amours / O fleur* (Deschamps's *déploration*), *Christe / Veni* (M21), *Felix virgo / Inviolata* (M23), *Fons / O livoris* (M9), Mass.

STU 71303 (LP). *Anonyme du XIVe siècle. Messe de Tournai. Guillaume de Machault. Messe de Nostre-Dame.* Ensemble Vocal Guillaume Dufay, Les Saqueboutiers de Toulouse. Arsène Bedois, director. Recorded Aug. 1979. Released 1981. Notes by Jacques Chailley. No texts.

Mass. Review: Denis Arnold, *Gramophone* 58 (1980–81): 1217.

Eterna.

826 077 (LP; see Philips 6580 026).

Expériences Anonymes (Lyrichord).

EAS 83 (LP; also EA 83; reissued as Musical Heritage Society MHS 899). *Music of the Middle Ages.* Vol. 9, *The Fourteenth Century. The Ars Nova.* Capella Cordina. Alejandro Planchart, director. 1966. Texts; English translations by Lorna Brodtkorb and Alejandro Planchart.

S'il estoit / S'Amours (M6), *Se quanque amours* (B21).

Focus Recordings (Indiana University Press).

883-4S (cassette). ISBN 0-13-608621-7. Recordings to accompany Jeremy Yudkin, *Music in Medieval Europe II.* Studio der frühen Musik; Early Music Institute. Thomas Binkley, director. 1988. The setting of Anthonello da Caserta is a new recording; the Machaut works are reissued from

EMI/Electrola 1C 063-30 106 or 1C 063-30 109. No texts; see Yudkin 1989 for texts and translations.

Biauté parfaite (Lo140; music by Anthonello da Caserta), *Comment puet* (R11), *Dous viaire* (R1), *Honte, paour* (B25), *Je ne cesse* (L16/11; stanzas 1 and 12 only), *Moult sui* (V37/31).

Fono Schallplattengesellschaft mbH.

FCD 97736 (CD; LP as FSM 68736). *Frese nouvele! Motetten in Ars Antiqua und Ars Nova. Vielfältigste Kunstform Gotischer Polyphonie.* Musica mensurata. Egbert Schimmelpfennig, director. Recorded March 1990. Released 1990. No texts.

De Bon Espoir / Puis que (M4), Mass (Agnus Dei only).

Gregorian Institute of America.

EL 17 (LP; set EL 100). *Thirteen Centuries of Christian Choral Art.* Peloquin Chorale. C. Alexander Peloquin, director. 1959. Not heard.

Mass (Et incarnatus only).

Guilde Internationale du Disque.

SMS 2423 (LP). Capella Instrumentalis et Psallette de Genève, Pierre Pernoux, director. 1968? Not heard.

Amours me fait (B19).

Harmonia Mundi (French import).

HMU 939 (LP; HM 939; set HMU 2472 with Ancient Instrument Ensemble of Zurich recording of chansons, see Odyssey 32 160178; reissued as Musical Heritage Society MHS 3496; CD as HMC 90610; also reissued in HMF 445 [3 LPs]). *Guillaume Dufay: Missa sine nomine. Danses médiévales, Livre de danses de Marguerite d'Autriche.* Clemenčić Consort, René Clemenčić, director. 1973. Not heard.

Ma chiere (B40).

HMC 5122 (LP). *Guillaume de Machaut (1300–1377). Messe de Nostre Dame. Chansons.* The Boston Camerata. Joel Cohen, director. 1985. French texts only.

Comment qu'a moy (V5), *Dame, a vous* (RF6), *Dou mal* (V8), *Douce dame jolie* (V4), *Dous amis, oy* (B6), *Gais et jolis* (B35), Mass, *Quant je sui* (V13), *S'Amours ne fait* (B1). Review: Josef Wieland, *Neue Zeitschrift für Musik* 147/2 (Feb. 1986): 50.

HMC 901252 (CD). *Codex Chantilly: Airs de Cour du XIVe siècle.* Ensemble Organum. Marcel Pérès, director. Recorded Sept. 1986. Released 1987. French texts only.

F. Andrieu, *Armes, amours / O fleur* (Deschamps's *déploration*).

HMC 901354 (CD). *Codex Faenza: Italie, XVe siècle.* Ensemble Organum. Marcel Pérès, director. Recorded Oct. 1990. Released 1991. Texts; modern French, English, and German translations by Viviane Scarpellini, James O. Wootton, and Liesel B. Sayre.

De toutes flours (B31, 2 versions, including Faenza intabulation), *Honte, paour* (B25, 2 versions, including Faenza intabulation). Review: Jerome F. Weber, *Fanfare* 15/3 (Jan.–Feb. 1992): 399.

Harmonic Records.

H/CD 8825 (CD). *Guillaume de Machaut: Ballades, rondeaux, virelais, motets.* Ensemble Gilles Binchois. Dominique Vellard, director. Recorded Oct. 1988. Released 1988. French texts with modern French glossary; Latin texts with French translations.

Amours qui a / Faus Samblant (M15), *Ce qui soustient* (R12), *Christe / Veni* (M21), *Dame, ne regardez* (B9), *Dame, se vous m'estes* (B37), *Dame, vostre* (V17), *De toutes flours* (B31), *Dous amis, oy* (B6), *Dous viaire* (R1), *Felix virgo / Inviolata* (M23), *Je ne cuit* (B14), *Je vivroie* (V23/21), *Liement* (V30/27), *Puis qu'en oubli* (R18), *Tels rit* (RF2). Review: Tess Knighton, *Gramophone* 69 (1991–92): 73–74.

H/CD 8931 (CD). *Messe de Notre-Dame de Guillaume de Machaut (1300–1377). Propre grégorien de la messe de l'Assomption de la Bienheureuse Vierge Marie.* Ensemble Gilles Binchois. Dominique Vellard, director. Recorded Sept. 1990. Released 1990.
Mass (liturgical reconstruction of the Mass for the Assumption with chant Propers from *F:Pn 17311*). Review: Jerome F. Weber, *Fanfare* 16/3 (Jan.–Feb. 1993): 182.

Haydn Society.
HSL 2071 in set HSL-B (LP; reissued as HSE 9038; French issues: Club National du Disque CND 4; Erato LDE 3018/3019; CD as HSCD 9038; reissued by W.W. Norton as ISBN 0-393-99161-X). *Masterpieces of Music before 1750. An Anthology of Musical Examples from Gregorian Chant to J. S. Bach. Record 1: Gregorian Chant to the 16th Century.* Danish Soloists and Ensembles. Mogens Wöldike, director. The Copenhagen Boy's and Men's Choir. Niels Møller, director. 1953.
Mass (Agnus I only)

Hispavox.
HHS 10-459 (LP; also Erato STU 71098; EFM 18047). *L'Europe joyeuse des XIIe au XVIIe siècles.* Atrium Musicae de Madrid. Gregorio Paniagua, director. Released 1976.
Loyauté, que (L1).

S90 241 (LP; see Enigma K53552).

Hungaroton.
SLPD 12589 (LP). *Mihályi Zenei Tábor. Early and New Music in Early and New Style: The Best of the Mihályi Festival.* Various groups; Machaut performed by Alba Musica Kyo, Holland. Released 1986. Not heard.
Dous viaire (R1), *Gais et jolis* (B35).

Hyperion.
A66087 (LP; CD as CDA66087). *The Mirror of Narcissus.* Gothic Voices. Christopher Page, director. Recorded 1983. Texts; English translations by Stephen Haynes.
Amours me fait (B19), *Biauté qui* (B4), *Dame, a qui* (V12), *Dame, a vous* (RF6), *Dame, de qui* (RF5), *Dame, je sui / Fins* (M11), *Dame, mon cuer en vous* (RF7), *Douce dame jolie* (V4), *Felix virgo / Inviolata* (M23), *Foy porter* (V25/22), *Je vivroie* (V23/21), *Rose, lis* (R10), *Tuit mi penser* (V28/25).[30] Reviews: David Fallows, *Gramophone* 61 (1983–84): 898; Daniel Leech-Wilkinson, *Early Music* 12 (1984): 411–13.

CDA66358 (CD). *Guillaume de Machaut. Messe de Notre Dame. Le Lai de la fonteinne. Ma fin est mon commencement.* The Hilliard Ensemble. Paul Hillier, director. Recorded March 1987 (Mass), Feb. 1989 (lai and rondeau). Released 1989. Texts; English translations by Nigel Wilkins.
Je ne cesse (L16/11), *Ma fin* (R14), Mass. Reviews: Mary Berry, *Gramophone* 67 (1989–90): 1504–6; Roger Bowers, *Early Music* 18 (1990): 489–90.

CDA66370 (CD). *Sacred and Secular Music from Six Centuries.* Hilliard Ensemble. Recorded 1987 and 1989. Released 1990. Texts; English translations by Marianne Fernée.
Quant je sui (V13). Reviews: D. Fallows, *Gramophone* 69 (1991–92): 82; Jerome F. Weber, *Fanfare* 14/5 (May–June 1991): 351.

---

[30] V25 was reissued in Hyperion A66227 (LP; CD as CDA66227), *The Emma Kirkby Collection,* Emma Kirkby, soprano. Reviewed by John B. Steane, *Gramophone* 65 (1987–88): 477.

CDA66463 (CD). *The Medieval Romantics. French Songs and Motets, 1340–1440*. Gothic Voices. Christopher Page, director. Recorded Oct. 1990, May 1991. Released 1991. Texts; English translations.

C'est force (V16), *Comment qu'a moy* (V5), *Tant doucement me sens* (R9). Reviews: Lawrence Earp, *Early Music* 21 (1993): 289–95; Jerome F. Weber, *Fanfare* 15/4 (Mar.– April 1992): 393–94.

CDA66588 (CD). *Lancaster and Valois. French and English Music, 1350– 1420*. Gothic Voices. Christopher Page, director. Recorded Dec. 1991. Released 1992. Texts; English translations by Stephen Haynes.

Donnez, signeurs (B26), *Pas de tor* (B30), *Quant je ne voy* (R21), *Riches d'amour* (B5). Reviews: Lawrence Earp, *Early Music* 21 (1993): 289–95; Tom Moore, Fanfare 16/1 (Sept.–Oct. 1992): 412–13; Jerome F. Weber, *Fanfare* 16/3 (Jan.–Feb. 1993): 287–88.

CDA66619 (CD). *The Study of Love. French Songs and Motets of the 14th Century*. Gothic Voices. Christopher Page, director. Recorded April–May 1992. Released 1992. Texts; English translations.

Dame, je suis / Fins / Ne vueil (V9), *Se mesdisans* (V15), *Tres bonne* (V26/23), *Trop plus / Biauté* (M20). Reviews: Lawrence Earp, *Early Music* 21 (1993): 289–95; Tom Moore, *Fanfare* 16/5 (May–June 1993): 373–74; Jerome F. Weber, *Fanfare* 17/1 (Sept.–Oct. 1993): 352–53.

CDA66739 (CD). *The Spirits of England and France—I. Music for Court and Church from the Later Middle Ages*. Gothic Voices. Christopher Page, director. Recorded March 1994. Released 1994. Texts; English translations.

Aymi! (V3).

I.H.W. Plattenverstand.

66.22371 (LP; CD as Christophorus CHE 0042-2). *Pour l'amour. Liebeslieder des 14. und 15. Jahrhunderts*. Instrumentalkreis Helga Weber. Helga Weber, director. Recorded May and July 1980. Texts; German translations by Rudolf Harneit.

Biauté qui (B4), *Quant Theseüs / Ne quier* (B34). Reviews: Ludolf Lützen, *Musica* 37 (1983): 292; Jerome F. Weber, *Fanfare* 7/1 (Sept.–Oct. 1983): 312–13.

CD3.108 (CD). *Guillaume de Machaut (ca. 1300–1377). 7 isorhythmische geistliche Motetten / Guillaume Dufay (ca. 1400–1474). Sämtliche isorhythmischen Motetten, 7 Cantilenen-Motetten*. Helga Weber, director. Marianne Richert Pfau, musicological consultant. Recorded Oct. 1990 and Jan. 1991. Issued 1993. Texts; English translations by Eliot Wirshbo.

Bone paster / Bone pastor (M18), *Christe / Veni* (M21), *Felix virgo / Inviolata* (M23), *Fons / O livoris* (M9), *Hoquetus David, Martyrum / Diligenter* (M19), *Tu qui gregem / Plange* (M22).

Inédits ORTF.

995 010 (LP). *Chefs d'Œuvre de la Polyphonie française*. Ensemble Polyphonique de l'ORTF. Charles Ravier, director. 1971.

Mass. Review: Denis Arnold, *Gramophone* 49 (1971–72): 1247; Parrott 1977, 493.

Jecklin-Disco.

JD 622-2 (CD). *Melpo*. Conrad Steinmann, flutes. Recorded 1988.

Pour vivre joliement (L21/15).

Kicking Mule Records.

KM312 (LP; CD as Shanachie Records 79074, released 1990). *The Enchanted Garden*. John Renbourn Group. 1980.

Douce dame jolie (V4) Arranged by John Renbourn, John Roberts, Keshav Sathe, and John Molineux.

Koch.

H 320 901 (CD; LP as E 120 901). *1000 Jahre Chormusik. Vom Gregorian-*

ischen Choral bis zur Gegenwart. Kammerchor des Konservatoriums der Stadt Innsbruck. Günther Andergassen, director. Recorded July 1983. Text; German translation.
Mass (Benedictus only).

London International.

W 91116 (10" LP; French Decca FS 123632). *Music from the Middle Ages to the Renaissance.* Monique Rollin Ensemble. Monique Rollin, director. 1955. Not heard.
Helas! pour quoy se demente (R2).

Lumen.

33405 (78 rpm, also 2.50.001). *Recorded History of French Song.* Vol. 1. Pierre Deniau, tenor, and ensemble. 1947. Not heard.
Douce dame jolie (V4), *He! dame de vaillance* (V1), *Se je souspir* (V36/30).

3.22.015 (78 rpm, matrix: YEV41-1). Jeanne Ramber, alto; M. Husson, tenor; Henri Arqué and … Royer, trombones. 1949? Not heard.
Felix virgo / Inviolata (M23).

The Medieval Lyric.

Cassette 4 (cassette tape). *The Medieval Lyric: A Project Supported by the National Endowment for the Humanities and Mount Holyoke College.* Margaret Switten and Robert Eisenstein, directors. (Mt. Holyoke College, with The National Endowment for the Humanities, 1987). Texts and translations in Switten 1988c.
Dame, a vous (RF6), *Dame, de qui* (RF5, 2 versions), *Dame, mon cuer en vous* (RF7), *En amer* (RF4), *Joie, plaisance* (RF3), *Qui n'aroit* (RF1), *Tels rit* (RF2).

Mirror Music.

00005 (LP). *Liebe und Minne.* Les Ménestrels. Recorded 1977.
Ma chiere (B40).

00006–00009 (4 LPs; Mass also released separately as 00007a). *Guillaume de Machaut. Le Livre Du Voir Dit—La Messe de Nostre Dame.* Les Ménestrels. Mozartsängerknaben, Wien. Klaus Walter, Michel Walter, and Eva Brunner, directors. Mass recorded Oct. 1978. 1979. Texts; German and English translations. Booklet 69 p.
Christe / Veni (M21), *Dame, se vous n'avez* (R13), *Dix et sept* (R17), *Dous viaire* (R1), *Longuement* (L18/13), Mass, *Nes qu'on* (B33), *Plourez, dames* (B32), *Quant Theseüs / Ne quier* (B34), *Sans cuer, dolens* (R4), *Se pour ce muir* (B36), *Tels rit* (RF2), *Tres bonne* (V26/23). The recording also includes readings of texts cobbled together from *Voir Dit* and *Remede*; see L. Wright's review. Reviews: Ludolf Lützen, *Musica* 36 (1982): 377; Jerome F. Weber, *Fanfare* 5/2 (Nov.–Dec. 1981): 187–89; 1990, 1:28 and 1991, 30 (with comments on liturgical reconstruction); Laurence Wright, *Early Music* 8 (1980): 408–11.

Musical Heritage Society.

MHS 894 (LP; see Erato LDE 3377).

MHS 899 (LP; see Expériences Anonymes EAS 83).

MHS 1141 (LP). *Music of the Late Middle Ages and Renaissance.* The Festival Consort (San Diego). Lawrence Selman, director. 1969.
De toutes flours (B31), *En amer* (RF4).

MHS 1442 (LP; see Da Camera SM 91702).

MHS 3071 (LP; see Arion 30 A 070).

MHS 3198 (LP; see Arion ARN 90814).

MHS 3496 (LP; see Harmonia Mundi France HMU 939).

MHS 3987 (LP; see Arion ARN 34217).

MHS 4391 (LP; see Arion 36554). *The Art of the Lute in the Middle Ages.*

MHS 4440 (LP; see Enigma VAR 1046).

MHS 4485 (LP; see Enigma K53571).

MHS 830437 (3 LPs, MHS 0437/0438/0439, Nos. 42–75 of Davison/Apel 1949; Orpheus OR 437). *History of European Music.* Schola Cantorum Londiniensis, Ambrosian Singers, etc. Denis Stevens, director. Recorded June–July 1969.

Comment qu'a moy (V5), *Je puis trop* (B28), *Plus dure* (V31/28), *S'il estoit / S'Amours* (M6).

New Albion Records.

NA021 CD (CD). *Ars magis subtiliter: Secular Music of the Chantilly Codex.* Ensemble P[roject].A[rs].N[ova]. Recorded 20–22 July 1987. Released 1989. Texts; English translations.

F. Andrieu, *Armes, Amours / O fleur* (Deschamps's *déploration*), *Quant Theseüs / Ne quier* (B34). Reviews: Daniel Leech-Wilkinson, *Early Music* 22 (1994): 337–38; Jerome F. Weber, *Fanfare* 13/4 (March–April 1990): 359.

NA068 CD (CD). *Remede de Fortune.* Ensemble P[roject].A[rs].N[ova]. Recorded Nov. 1993. Released 1994. Texts; English translations.

Dame, a vous (RF6), *Dame, de qui* (RF5), *Dame, mon cuer en vous* (RF7), *De toutes flours* (B31 [Faenza intabulation]), *En amer* (RF4), *Joie, plaisance* (RF3), *Liement* (V30/27), *Qui n'aroit* (RF1), *Rose, lis* (R10), *Tels rit* (RF2), *Trop plus / Biauté* (M20).

Nonesuch.

H 71184 (LP; also Belvedere [Centrocord] ELY 0430; Tudor TUD 0430; Harmonia Mundi France HM 10071). *Guillaume de Machaut. Notre Dame Mass and Gregorian Proper for the Feast of the Assumption.* The London Ambrosian Singers and The Vienna Renaissance Players. John McCarthy, director. Recorded 1966.

Mass. Reviews: Denis Arnold, *Gramophone* 46 (1968): 698; Gunden 1974–75; J.F. Weber 1990, 1:97 (on liturgical reconstruction).

Odyssey (Columbia/CBS).

32 160178 (LP; also 32 160177; Harmonia Mundi 30592; HM 592; HMA 592; HMF 592; HMU 592; set HMU 2472 with Clemenčić Consort recording of B40, see HMU 939; 34917 and HMO 30917 with Deller Consort recording of the Mass, see Bach Guild BGS 5045). *Ballades, Rondeaux and Virelais from the 14th and 15th Centuries.* The Ancient Instrument Ensemble of Zurich [Ensemble Ricercare de Zurich]. Bill Austin Miskell, tenor. 1966. No texts.

Amours me fait (B19), *De petit po* (B18), *Je sui aussi* (B20), *Nes qu'on* (B33), *Tres bonne* (V26/23).

L'Oiseau-Lyre.

OL 3 (78 rpm, matrix: PART 1059). E. Foveau, trumpet; A. Lafosse, bass trumpet; R. Tudesq, trombone. Guillaume de Van, director. 1939. Not heard.

Hoquetus David. Review: Reaney 1957, 187.

SOL 310 (LP). *Guillaume de Machaut. La Messe de Notre Dame, virelais, rondeaux, ballades, lai.* The Purcell Choir, with instrumental ensemble. Grayston Burgess, director. Frank Harrison, artistic director. 1969. Pronunciation of Latin and French supervised by Daffyd Evans. Texts; English translations (often abridged) by C.A. Robson.

Amours me fait (B19), *Douce dame jolie* (V4), *Foy porter* (V25/22), Mass, *Nuls ne doit*

(L5/4), *Quant ma dame les maus* (R19), *Tant doucement me sens* (R9), *Tres douce dame que* (B24). Review: Denis Arnold, *Gramophone* 47 (1969–70): 69.

DSDL 705 (LP). *Guillaume de Machaut. Le Lay de la Fonteinne. Un Lay de Consolation.* Medieval Ensemble of London. Peter and Timothy Davies, directors. 1983. Texts; English translations by Nigel Wilkins.
Je ne cesse (L16/11), *Pour ce que plus* (L23/17). Reviews: David Fallows, *Musical Times* 124 (1983): 620–21; Iain Fenlon, *Gramophone* 60 (1982–83): 1288.

Opus Musicum (Arno Volk Verlag).
OM 122–124 (LP; also OM 222–224). *Chanson, Madrigal, Chorlied.* 1979.
Se je souspir (V36/30).

Orpheus.
OR 437 (LP; see Musical Heritage Society MHS 830437).

Panton.
8111 0056 (LP). *Hommage à Machaut.* Ars Cameralis, Prague. Lukáš Matoušek. Released 1978. Summary of texts in Czech.
F. Andrieu, *Armes, Amours / O fleur* (Deschamps's *déploration*), *Biauté qui* (B4), *Dame, ne regardez* (B9), *De tout sui* (V38/32), *Dous viaire* (R1), *Fons / O livoris* (M9), *Ma chiere* (B40), *Ma fin* (R14), *Plourez, dames* (B32), *S'Amours ne fait* (B1), *Sans cuer, dolens* (R4), *Sans cuer m'en / Amis / Dame* (B17), *Tres douce dame que* (B24). In addition, the record contains two modern works inspired by Machaut. See chap. 2.5 (compositions by Matoušek and Štědroň). Review: J.F. Weber 1982.

81 0771 (LP). *Dialogues.* Symposium Musicum. Svatopluk Jányš, director; Miroslav Klement, artistic leader. Recorded 29 Nov. 1987 and 11 Sept. 1988. Released 1989. Texts; English translations by Till Gottheinerová.
Mass. In addition to the Machaut Mass, the record contains a modern work inspired by Machaut; see chap. 2.5 (composition by Fišer).

Philips.
N 00993–0094 R (2 10" LPs). *French Chansons.* Vols. 1–2, *La fleur des chansons d'amour. Chansons polyphoniques françaises.* Ensemble Vocal Blanchard. Roger Blanchard, director. 1955? Not heard.
Plus dure (V31/28).

SAL 3722 (LP; also 839 753LY; as disc 2 of 5 LP set 6747 004). *Music of the Hundred Years War.* Musica reservata. John Beckett, director. 1969.
Tu qui gregem / Plange (M22).

6580 026 (LP; also Eterna 826 077). *Guillaume de Machault: Secular Works.* Capella Lipsiensis. Dietrich Knothe, director. 1970.
Amours me fait (B19), *Aucune gent / Qui plus* (M5), *Biauté qui* (B4), *Comment puet* (R11), *Comment qu'a moy* (V5), *Dame, je sui / Fins* (M11), *He! Mors / Fine* (M3), *J'ay tant / Lasse!* (M7), *Ma fin* (R14), *Quant en moy / Amour* (M1), *Quant je sui* (V13), *Quant Theseüs / Ne quier* (B34). Reviews: Denis Arnold, *Gramophone* 49 (1971): 876; Margaret Bent, *Musical Times* 113 (1972): 163.

Pleiades (University of Southern Illinois Press).
P 250 (LP). *Historical Anthology of Music in Performance. Late Medieval Music.* University of Chicago Collegium Musicum. Howard M. Brown, director. Southern Illinois University Collegium Musicum. Wesley K. Morgan, director. 1968? English translations.
Comment qu'a moy (V5), *Je puis trop* (B28), *Plus dure* (V31/28), *S'il estoit / S'Amours* (M6).

RCA Victor.
LM 6016 (2 LPs; 78 rpm His Master's Voice HMS 21, matrix: 2EA 15609-1B; reissued as LP, H.M.V. HLP 5). *The History of Music in Sound. Edited by Gerald Abraham.* Vol. 3, *Ars Nova and the Renaissance.* Various

performers. The booklet, ed. Dom Anselm Hughes, includes a score of the rondeau and a score of the Benedictus and Osanna 2 of the Mass on two staves, ed. by Denis Stevens. 1951?

Mass (Benedictus and Osanna 2 only) (Brompton Oratory Choir with Instrumental Ensemble. Henry Washington, director), *Ma fin* (R14) (Lemuel Hughes and Clarence Roberts with Instrumental Ensemble. Bernard Rose, director). Reviews: Denis Stevens, *Musical Times* 95 (1954): 82–83; Reaney 1957, 181–82.

Scalen disc.

    TRFC 0187 (CD). *L'art des jongleurs. Musiques du XIVe siècle.* Vol. 1. Ensemble Tre Fontane. Recorded Sept. 1987. No texts.

    Ce qui soustient (R12), *C'est force* (V16), *Dame, je vueil* (V9).

    TRFC 0389 (CD). *L'art des jongleurs.* Vol. 2. Ensemble Tre Fontane. Recorded May 1989. No texts.

    Instrumental arrangements based on the following works: *Aymi!* (V3), *Dame, comment qu'amez* (B16), *Dame, ne regardez* (B9), *Je ne cuit* (B14), *Puis que ma dolour* (V7).

Schirmer Books (A Division of Macmillan, Inc.).

    ISBN 0-02-872953-6 (Cassette 2). Recording to Accompany *Music of the Middle Ages*, by David Fenwick Wilson. The Western Wind. Paul Hillier, director. Recorded Jan. 1990.

    Amours me fait (B19), *Dame, vostre* (V17), *De Bon Espoir / Puis que* (M4), *De toutes flours* (B31), *Puis qu'en oubli* (R18), *Quant en moy / Amour* (M1), *Quant je ne voy* (R21), *Se je souspir* (V36/30).

Seraphim.

    SIC 6052 (3 LPs; also His Master's Voice HQS 1195; Voix de son Maître SME 191761-2). *The Seraphim Guide to Renaissance Music.* Syntagma musicum of Amsterdam. Kees Otten, director. 1969. French texts only.

    Trop plus / Biauté (M20).

    SIC 6092 (3 LPs; released in England as His Master's Voice set SLS 863; Electrola 1C 167 05410-2; released in France as EMI 2C167-05410/2; Machaut record issued separately as His Master's Voice ASD 3454). *The Art of Courtly Love.* Early Music Consort of London. David Munrow, director. Released 1973. Texts; translations by Michael Freeman.

    Amours me fait (B19), F. Andrieu, *Armes, Amours / O fleur* (Deschamps's *déploration*), *Dame, se vous m'estes* (B37),[31] *De Bon Espoir / Puis que* (M4), *De toutes flours* (B31, 2 versions), *Douce dame jolie* (V4), *Hareu! / Helas!* (M10), *Ma fin* (R14), *Mes esperis* (B39), *Phiton, Phiton* (ballade related to Machaut B38), *Phyton* (B38), *Quant j'ay l'espart* (R5), *Quant je sui* (V13), *Quant Theseüs / Ne quier* (B34), *Se je souspir* (V36/30), *Trop plus / Biauté* (M20). Reviews: David Fallows, *Gramophone* 56 (1978–79): 366 (review of the separately released Machaut record only); Jeremy Noble, *Gramophone* 51 (1973–74): 1238–39.

Sonclair Records.

    CD JB128836 (CD). *Intabulation and Improvisation in the 14th Century.* Ensemble Super Librum. 1988.

    De toutes flours (B31, 2 versions, including Faenza intabulation).

Sphemusations.

    IMI 1002 (cassette). *The Magic of Harp and Voice.* Andree Back, soprano; Phyllis Schlomovitz, harp. 1982? Not heard.

    Douce dame jolie (V4).

Studio S.M.

    45-71 (45 rpm). Joseph Sage, countertenor. 1961. Not heard.

    Comment qu'a moy (V5), *Dame, a vous* (RF6), *Douce dame jolie* (V4), *Tant comme*

---

[31] The recording of B37 also appears on Angel SBZ 3810.

vivray [*sic*. Not Machaut?]. The second side includes various texts recited by Nathalie Nerval, among them *Tant doucement me sens* (R9), *Rose, lis* (R10), and *Ma fin* (R14).

Supraphon.
1112 2451-2 G (2 LPs). *Musica in Bohemia in tempore Caroli IV*. Soloists, Symposium Musicum. Miroslav Klement, director. 1977. French texts only.
Dame, je vueil (V9), *Hoquetus David, Quant je sui* (V13). Review: J.F. Weber 1982.

1119 3419 G (LP). *Music in the Reign of Czech Kings*. Rožmberk Ensemble. František Pok, director. 1982.
Quant je sui (V13).

GSST 50598 (LP; also SUAST 50598; GS 10598). *Medieval Music at the Prague Royal Court. Gothical and Renaissance Period*. Musica Antiqua Vienna. René Clemenčić, director. Pro Arte Antiqua Ensemble, Quartet of Recorders. Miroslav Klement, director. Prague Madrigal Singers. Miroslav Venhoda, director. Recorded 1964.
Hoquetus David, S'il estoit / S'Amours (M6), *Se je souspir* (V36/30).

Telefunken/Teldec.
6.35257 ER (LP set). *Guillaume Dufay und seine Zeit*. Syntagma Musicum. Kees Otten, director. 1974. Texts; no translations. Notes by L. Finscher.
F. Andrieu, *Armes, Amours / O fleur* (Deschamps's *déploration*).

6.41125 AS (LP; also SAWT 9566). *Guillaume de Machault Messe de Nostre Dame und Motetten*. Capella Antiqua München, Konrad Ruhland, director. Recorded July 1970. Texts; English and German translations.
Bone paster / Bone pastor (M18),[32] *Christe / Veni* (M21), *Fons / O livoris* (M9), *Hoquetus David*, Mass, *Tu qui gregem / Plange* (M22). Review: Denis Arnold, *Gramophone* 48 (1970–71): 1503.

6.42357 AW (LP). *Denkmäler alter Musik aus dem Codex Reina (14./15. Jh.)*. Syntagma Musicum. Kees Otten, director. 1979.
Biauté parfaite (Lo140, musical setting composed by Anthonello da Caserta), *De toutes flours* (B31), *Gais et jolis* (B35), *Quant Theseüs / Ne quier* (B34).

Transatlantic.
ORL 8654 (LP; also Reprise 6407 and RS 6407; CD as TRACD 224; also Lost Lake Arts LL087 and Shanachie 97022). *The Lady and the Unicorn*. John Renbourn, guitar and sitar. Released 1970.
Sans cuer m'en / Amis / Dame (B17).

University of Texas Press.
Baltzer 1991b (see main bibliography). Recorded May and July 1988.
Esperance (B13), *Je sui aussi* (B20). See comments in Baltzer 1991a, 154–55.

Vanguard (see also Bach Guild).
VRS 448 (LP). *The Art of Roland Hayes; Six Centuries of Song*. Vol. 1. Roland Hayes, tenor; Reginald Boardman, piano. Recorded 1954.
Douce dame jolie (V4). Arranged by Jean-Baptiste Théodore Weckerlin (see chap. 2.5).

VSD 71179 (LP). *Douce dame. Music of Courtly Love from Medieval France and Italy*. The Waverly Consort. Michael Jaffee, director. Recorded June 1973. No texts.
Comment qu'a moy (V5), *Douce dame jolie* (V4), *Foy porter* (V25/22), *Je sui aussi* (B20), *Rose, lis* (R10). Review: Denis Arnold, *Gramophone* 53 (1975–76): 356, 359.

---

[32] M18 was reissued in Argo (American Heritage Pub. Co.) CSL 1000 (2 LPs), *Great Music of Europe's Courts and Cathedrals* (1974).

VSD 79191 (LP; also VRS 9191). *Inventions*. Sandy Bull, guitar, oud, and banjo. 1965.
Sans cuer m'en / Amis / Dame (B17).

VEB Deutsche Schallplatten.
8 27 956 (LP). *Gotische Polyphonie*. Musica mensurata. Olaf Raitzig, director. Recorded 1984.
Martyrum / Diligenter (M19).

Victor.
45083 (78 rpm, matrix: B15594-4). Lambert Murphy, tenor; Francis Lapitino, harp; ... Carline, lute. 1915. Not heard.
Douce dame jolie (V4).

Voix de son Maître.
DB 5118 (78 rpm: matrix: 2LA 2447 I). *Les maîtres français du Moyen Age*. Psallette Notre-Dame. Jacques Chailley, director. 1939. Not heard.
Mass (Kyrie I, incomplete Credo).

Westminster.
XWN 18166 (LP; France: Véga C 30 A 80). *Guillaume de Machaut: Motets, Ballades, Virelais, Rondeaux*. Collegium musicum of the University of Illinois, George Hunter, director. 1956. Texts; English summaries by Dragan Plamenac.
Amours me fait (B19), *Dame, je sui / Fins* (M11), *De toutes flours* (B31), *Douce dame jolie* (V4), *Douce dame, tant* (R20), *Lasse! comment / Se j'aim* (M16), *Loyauté, que* (L1), *Ma chiere* (B40), *Mes esperis* (B39), *Plus dure* (V31/28), *Rose, lis* (R10), *Se je souspir* (V36/30), *Tres bonne* (V26/23), *Tres douce dame que* (B24).

XWN 18683 (LP; reissued as W 9610). *French Troubadour Songs*. Hugues Cuénod, tenor; Günther Leeb, lute. 1958. Not heard.
Ma chiere (B40), *Se je souspir* (V36/30).

Ylioppilaskunnan Laulajat.
(LP; matrix YLLP-1 and YLLP-2). Ylioppilaskunnan Laulajat [Helsinki University Male Chorus]. Ensti Pohjola, director. 1965?
Mass.

Bibliography

Due to the nature of the topical chapters in this book, the bibliography includes many works that are not exclusively concerned with Machaut; in such cases the annotation addresses only the item's connection with Machaut. For books of direct relevance to Machaut, I include references to reviews. A few book reviews containing especially important material specifically referenced in the topical chapters above have been given separate entries in the bibliography, e.g., Guesnon 1912. Numbers in square brackets that follow manuscript *sigla* are keyed to the through-numbered manuscript descriptions in chapter 3.

Abert, Hermann.
1904–5. "Die Musikästhetik der *Echecs Amoureux.*" *Sammelbände der Internationalen Musikgesellschaft* 6:346–55.

Discussion of the conception of music in a long passage from the anonymous *Echecs Amoureux*, published elsewhere by Abert. An additional passage (354–55, l. 17) includes mention of the "rés d'Allemaigne"; see chap. 7.3, commentary to *Nes qu'on* (B33). For a new edition of the *Echecs Amoureux*, see Kraft 1977.

Aboshi, Tsuyoshi.
1981. "Machaut no ongaku no nezasumono" (On the foundation of Machaut's music; in Japanese; summary in English). *Bigaku* (Aesthetics) 125 (summer): 39–50.

Not examined. According to the abstract, seems to be trying to prove that Machaut is a medieval, not a Renaissance, composer. Abstract: *RILM* 15 (1981), no. 2354.

Allaire, Gaston G.
1972. *The Theory of Hexachords, Solmization and the Modal System. A Practical Application.* Musicological Studies and Documents 24. [Rome]: American Institute of Musicology.

Example 26 (112–14) interprets source accidentals in terms of Allaire's theory of hexachords and solmization. Abstract: *RILM* 6 (1972), no. 201.

1980. "Les énigmes de l'Antefana et du double hoquet de Machault: une tentative de solution" (summary in English). *Revue de musicologie* 66:27–56.

A new solution to problems of *musica ficta* in the *Hoquetus David* (43–56). Abstracts: *RILM* 14 (1980), no. 360; Michel Huglo, *Scriptorium* 35 (1981): 3* no. 6.

Allen, Mark, and John H. Fisher.
1987. *The Essential Chaucer: An Annotated Bibliography of Major Modern Studies.* Reference Publication in Literature. Boston: G.K. Hall.

Excellent annotated bibliography of twentieth-century scholarship.

Allorto, Riccardo, ed.
1983. *Antologia storica della musica (dai Greci al Rinascimento).* E.R. 2815. Milan: Ricordi.

Historical anthology of music, with commentary and Italian translation of texts, including Machaut's *De tout sui* (V38/32), *Je puis trop* (B28), *Qui es / Ha! Fortune* (M8), and the Kyrie and Gloria from the Mass.

Alós-Moner, Ramón d'.
1924. "Documenti per la storia della biblioteca d'Alfonso il Magnanimo." In *Miscellanea Francesco Ehrle: Scritti di storia e paleografia.* Vol. 5, *Biblioteca ed Archivio Vaticano. Biblioteche diverse*, 390–422. Studi e testi 41. Rome: Biblioteca Apostolica Vaticana.

Publication of the 1417 inventory of the library of Alfonso the Magnanimous. Earp (1989, 478–79) notes that the description of the Machaut manuscript matches MS **Vg** [3].

Altmann, Barbara K.

1987. "Diversity and Coherence in Christine de Pizan's *Dit de Poissy*." *French Forum* 12:251–71.

Includes brief mention of *Jugement Behaingne* and *Jugement Navarre* as models for Christine's *Dit de Poissy* (262).

1988. "Christine de Pizan's *Livre du Dit de Poissy*: An Analysis and Critical Edition." Ph.D. diss. University of Toronto. Ann Arbor: University Microfilms. Order no. 59958.

Not examined; publication forthcoming. Part I contains an analysis of Christine's *Dit de Poissy*, with discussion of Machaut's *Jugement Behaingne* and *Jugement Navarre* as models. Abstracts: *DAI* A 50/1 (July 1989): 134–35; 52/11 (May 1991): 3951–52; *Dalhousie French Studies* 14 (spring–summer 1989): 113–14.

1992. "Reopening the Case: Machaut's *Jugement* Poems as a Source in Christine de Pizan." In *Reinterpreting Christine de Pizan*, ed. Earl Jeffrey Richards et al., 137–56. Athens and London: University of Georgia Press.

Excellent discussion of Christine's literary debt to Machaut's debate poems, emphasizing the critical and ironic aspects of her reworkings. Review: J.C. Laidlaw, *French Studies* 48 (1994): 191–92.

Alton, Jeannine, and Brian Jeffery.

1976. *Bele buche e bele parleure: A Guide to the Pronunciation of Medieval and Renaissance French for Singers and Others*. London: Tecla. Includes audio cassette.

A useful guide to historical French pronunciation, including a taped recitation of Machaut's *Plus dure* (V31/28), followed by a sung performance of the first strophe. Reviews: C.A. Robson, *Music and Letters* 62 (1981): 417; Laurence Wright, *Early Music* 6 (1978): 599.

Ambros, August Wilhelm.

1891. *Geschichte der Musik*. Vol. 2, *Die Anfänge der europäisch-abendländischen Musik. Die Entwicklung des geregelten mehrstimmigen Gesanges*. Breslau: Leuckart, 1864. 2nd ed., revised by Otto Kade. Leipzig: Leuckart, 1880. 3rd ed., revised by Heinrich Riemann. Leipzig: Leuckart, 1891. Reprint. Hildesheim: Georg Olms, 1968.

Ambros first mentions Machaut in connection with Adam de la Halle: "He and Machault form the connecting transition from the trouvères to the actual schooled musicians. As the former, they briskly invented words and tunes for their poems, just as their inner compulsions drove them, and in this they succeeded with charming productions" [examples from *Dame, a vous* (RF6) and *J'aim la fleur* (L2), both from Bottée de Toulmon 1836] (251). "As learned musicians they set polyphonic vocal pieces that we will get to know later, which however appear to us as highly crude, almost barbaric attempts" (254). Ambros's view of Machaut and others as transitional figures is first stated in the "Vorrede" to the volume (vi). Later, Ambros gives Kiesewetter's example from the opening of the Gloria of the Mass, indicating that "the entire piece belongs to the childhood of harmonic art" (370). Finally, Ambros contrasts Machaut's previously discussed grace as a melodist in his monophonic works with his failure as a contrapuntist, based on *Dous viaire* (R1), again published after Kiesewetter (374–75).

Amon, N[icole] (see also Jordan, Nicole Amon).

1976. "Le vert: Guillaume de Machaut, poète de l'affirmation et de la joie." *Revue du Pacifique* 2:3–11.

Aspects of color symbolism in the *Voir Dit*.

Anderson, Gordon A.

1976. "Responsory Chants in the Tenors of Some Fourteenth-Century Continental Motets." *Journal of the American Musicological Society* 29: 119–27.

Identifies the sources of five motet tenors not identified by Ludwig, including *Hé! Mors / Fine* (M3), *S'il estoit / S'Amours* (M6), *Helas! pour quoy virent / Corde* (M12), *Maugré mon cuer* / *De ma dolour* (M14), and *Tu qui gregem* / *Plange* (M22). For the tenor of *Martyrum* / *Diligenter* (M19), see Fuller (1990, 231 n. 43) and A.W. Robertson's forthcoming study of music at Reims cathedral. Abstract: *RILM* 10 (1976), no. 2384.

Anderson, J.J.
1991. "Criseyde's Assured Manner." *Notes and Queries* n.s. 38:160–61.
Chaucer's adaptation of some passages in *Jugement Behaingne* and *Remede* for his *Troilus and Criseyde*.

1992. "The Man in Black, Machaut's Knight, and Their Ladies." *English Studies* 73:417–30.
Chaucer's use of Machaut's *Jugement Behaingne* and *Remede* for the Man in Black's description of Blanche in *The Book of the Duchess*.

Angiolini, Giuliano d'.
1987. "Le son du sens: Machaut, Stockhausen. La ballade 34 et le Chant des Adolescents." *Voix et instrument, parole et musique dans le répertoire musical du Moyen-Age à nos jours*. *Analyse Musicale* 9 (Oct.): 43–51.
Besides revealing certain correspondences between the musical conceptions of Machaut and Stockhausen, Angiolini provides some interesting strategies for the analysis of poetical and musical aspects of polytextuality in Machaut, strategies also suggestive for the analysis of motets. Abstract: *RILM* 21 (1987), no. 8298.

Anglès, Higinio.
1970. *Historia de la música medieval en Navarra (obra postuma)*. Pamplona: Diputación Foral de Navarra; Institución Principe de Viana.
Includes discussion of Machaut and King Charles II of Navarre (191–98), especially concerning a horse given by Charles to Machaut (see chap. 1.12. 2).

Anton, Herbert.
1967. *Der Raub der Proserpina. Literarische Traditionen eines erotischen Sinnbildes und mythischen Symbols*. Heidelberger Forschungen 11. Heidelberg: Winter.
Machaut's treatment of the Rape of Proserpina in *Confort*; includes reproductions of miniatures A74–75 (see chap. 4.4h).

Apel, Willi.
1938. "The Partial Signatures in the Sources up to 1450." *Acta musicologica* 10:1–13. Reprint. Apel 1986, 31–43.
Partial signatures in thirteenth- and fourteenth-century music express "a kind of 'bitonality'" (5). Machaut discussed pp. 9–10, esp. *De Bon Espoir* / *Puis que* (M4). Summary in Lowinsky 1945, 228–34.

1946–47. "The French Secular Music of the Late Fourteenth Century." *Acta musicologica* 18–19:17–29. Reprint. Apel 1986, 47–59.
Introduction to the music and notational idiosyncrasies of the post-Machaut generation of composers. The style of Machaut's chansons provides the point of departure for Apel's remarks on the style of the later works; many musical examples.

1950 (ed.). *French Secular Music of the Late Fourteenth Century*. Texts ed. Robert W. Linker and Urban T. Holmes, Jr., with a foreword by Paul Hindemith. Mediaeval Academy of America Publication 55. Cambridge, Mass.: Mediaeval Academy of America.
The introduction, expanded from Apel 1946–47, is still worth consulting for its survey of fixed-form genres. Criticisms in Günther 1957, 14–15. Reviews: Heinrich Besseler, "Hat Matheus de Perusio Epoche gemacht?", *Musikforschung* 8 (1955): 19–23; Thurston Dart, *Galpin Society Journal* 4 (1951): 49; Leonard Ellinwood, *Journal of the American Musicological Society* 4 (1951): 59–60; Otto Gombosi, *Musical Quarterly* 36 (1950): 603–10; Glen Haydon, *Speculum* 26 (1951): 145–48; François Lesure, *Romania* 74 (1951): 277; Walter H. Rubsamen, *Notes* 8 (1950–51): 695–97.

1953. *The Notation of Polyphonic Music 900–1600*. 1st ed. Mediaeval Academy of America Publication 38. Cambridge, Mass.: Medieval Academy of America, 1942. 3rd rev. ed. 1945. 5th rev. ed. 1953. *Die Notation der polyphonen Musik, 900–1600*. German trans. by the author, with corrections. Leipzig: VEB Breitkopf & Härtel, 1970.

Standard textbook on the notation of medieval polyphony. Includes a discussion of Machaut's notational practices, with facsimiles of *Biauté qui* (B4; MS **E**), *Dous amis, oy* (B6; MS **A**), *Ne pensez pas* (B10; MS **A**), *Se vous n'estes* (R7; MS **Mod** [66]), and small excerpts from a few other works. Reviews of 1st ed.: Manfred F. Bukofzer, *Musical Quarterly* 30 (1944): 112–18; J.A. Westrup, *Music and Letters* 24 (1943): 245–46. Review of 3rd. ed.: Eric Blom, *Music and Letters* 27 (1946): 127–28. Review of 4th ed.: Otto Gombosi, *Notes* 7 (1949–50): 283–85. Reviews of 5th ed.: *Mens en melodie* 6 (1951): 319; Heinrich Husmann, *Musikforschung* 6 (1953): 372–74.

1955. "French Music of the Fourteenth Century." *Journal of the American Musicological Society* 8:70–71.

Abstract of a conference paper finding Machaut a "romantic' individualist." Apel's chronology of the music is not acceptable: for the most part, motets are early works (ca. 1330–50?), chansons are late (ca. 1350–70?), and the Mass—"a rather tedious work and one that is not representative of Machaut at his best and at his greatest"—is very early.

1957. "Imitation in the Thirteenth and Fourteenth Centuries." In *Essays on Music in Honor of Archibald Thompson Davison by His Associates*, 25–38. Cambridge, Mass.: Harvard University Department of Music. Reprint. Apel 1986, 1–14.

Brief mention of some "intentional" imitation in *Dame, mon cuer en vous* (RF7) (p. 31).

1959. "Remarks about the Isorhythmic Motet." In Wégimont 1959, 139–44 (discussion, 144–48). Reprint. Apel 1986, 15–20.

On terminology, with introduction of the term "pan-isorhythmic"; brief analysis of *S'il estoit / S'Amours* (M6) (pp. 141, 143).

1970–72 (ed.). *French Secular Compositions of the Fourteenth Century*. Texts ed. Samuel N. Rosenberg. 3 vols. Corpus Mensurabilis Musicae 53. [Rome]: American Institute of Musicology, 1970, 1971, 1972. Vol. 1, *Ascribed Compositions*. Vol. 2, *Anonymous Ballades*. Vol. 3, *Anonymous Virelais, Rondeaux, Chansons, Canons. Appendix: Compositions with Latin Texts*.

Standard edition of fourteenth-century chansons (omitting works of Machaut and the Turin codex). Includes notes on source concordances and a useful Middle French glossary. See also Greene 1981–89.

1973. "The Development of French Secular Music During the Fourteenth Century." *Musica disciplina* 27:41–59.

A chronology of fourteenth-century secular music, unfortunately based on erroneous datings (criticism in Günther 1975). Distinguishes seven stylistic characteristics of Machaut's music (47–48).

1978. "French, Italian and Latin Poems in 14th-Century Music." *Journal of the Plainsong & Mediæval Music Society* 1:39–56. Reprint. Apel 1986, 162–79.

Includes brief consideration of themes treated in Machaut's chansons set to music (39–41); all are on love themes except *Donnez, signeurs* (B26) and *Ma fin* (R14). Poems set to music later in the fourteenth century are more varied in theme, including many interesting topical works. Abstract: *RILM* 12 (1978), no. 1981.

1986. *Medieval Music: Collected Articles and Reviews*. Foreword by Thomas E. Binkley. Stuttgart: Steiner.

Collection of reprints. Review: John Caldwell, *Music and Letters* 68 (1987): 256.

Apfel, Ernst.
1960. "Zur Entstehung des realen vierstimmigen Satzes in England." *Archiv für Musikwissenschaft* 17:81–99.
Alternative versions of fourteenth-century chansons suggest that contratenor and triplum were added to a two-voice cantus-tenor framework (92–93).

1961. "Über den vierstimmigen Satz im 14. und 15. Jahrhundert." *Archiv für Musikwissenschaft* 18:34–51.
Untexted contratenors were added to a two-voice cantus-tenor structure. Four-voice versions of *De petit po* (B18) provide two different three-voice performance alternatives, one with triplum and the other with contratenor. The description of alternative transmissions of various Machaut chansons is flawed. See comments in Kühn 1973, 27.

1964–65. *Beiträge zu einer Geschichte der Satztechnik von der frühen Motette bis Bach.* 2 vols. Munich: Fink.
Slightly revised presentation of Apfel's earlier work. Harmonic structure of Machaut motets (39–41); vocal scoring in chansons (54–56); the Mass (77, 80). Vol. 2 not examined. Reviews: J.D. Bergsagel, *Music and Letters* 48 (1967): 80–82; Wolfgang Marggraf, *Musikforschung* 19 (1966): 217–19; reply in Apfel 1974, 180–82.

1974. *Grundlagen einer Geschichte der Satztechnik vom 13. bis zum 16. Jahrhundert.* [vol. 1.] Saarbrücken: Selbstverlag Ernst Apfel.
Includes brief discussion of harmonic structure in Machaut (esp. with attention to the treatment of harmonic fourths), with additional discussion of the material in Apfel 1960 and 1961 (236–37). Abstract: *RILM* 10 (1976), no. 306.

1982. *Diskant und Kontrapunkt in der Musiktheorie des 12. bis 15. Jahrhunderts.* Taschenbücher zur Musikwissenschaft 82. Wilhelmshaven: Heinrichshofen.
Includes harmonic reductions of *S'Amours ne fait* (B1) and *Helas! tant* (B2), and a reduction and analysis of part of Kyrie I. Abstract: *RILM* 16 (1982), no. 1489.

Arlt, Wulf.
1980. "Musik, Schrift und Interpretation: zwei Studien zum Umgang mit Aufzeichnungen ein- und mehrstimmiger Musik aus dem 14. und 15. Jahrhundert." *Basler Jahrbuch für historische Musikpraxis* 4:91–132.
In the second study, "Zur Frage nach Gruppierung, Mensur und Iktus im französischen Liedsatz des 14. und 15. Jahrhunderts" (115–32), Arlt discusses problems of phrasing in late fourteenth and early fifteenth-century music, considering mensuration, rhythmic motives, ligatures, and texting. In early Machaut chansons, phrasing often fits the mensuration; beginning with middle-period works, melody is more complex and conflicts with mensuration. In the Ars Subtilior, mensuration sometimes clearly indicates grouping, while in other works the complex tendencies of late Machaut are extended even further.

1982. "Aspekte der Chronologie und des Stilwandels im französischen Lied des 14. Jahrhunderts." In *Aktuelle Fragen der musikbezogenen Mittelalterforschung: Texte zu einem Basler Kolloquium des Jahres 1975*, 193–280. Forum Musicologicum: Basler Beiträge zur Musikgeschichte 3. Winterthur: Amadeus.
The most important recent study of musical style in the early-to-mid fourteenth-century chanson (pp. 208–9 has an overview of the contents of the essay). The historiographical survey of theories of the development of the polyphonic chanson from Ludwig (1902–3) to Hasselman (1970) is marred by an acceptance of the views of Keitel (1976). Addresses the question of simultaneous versus successive composition, emphasizing the poor state of the source situation. Discusses aspects of the songs of Lescurel, Machaut's early ballades (with a corrected transcription of *Esperance* [B13]), and Machaut's monophonic virelais. Arlt's work ought to be consulted by literary scholars.

1983. "Musik und Text: Verstellte Perspektiven einer Grundlageneinheit." *Musica* [Kassel] 37:497–503.

Argues against the view that attention to text setting is a characteristic that began in the Renaissance; the medieval concern for text setting goes well beyond a merely formal coordination between music and text. Word-painting in *Dous amis, oy* (B6) and *Amours me fait* (B19). Abstract: *RILM* 17 (1983), no. 4675.

1984. "Musik und Text." *Musikforschung* 37:272–80.

Further reflections on sensitive text setting before the Renaissance, with a consideration of word-painting in *Dous amis, oy* (B6).

1993. *"Donnez signeurs*—Zum Brückenschlag zwischen Ästhetik und Analyse bei Guillaume de Machaut." *Tradition und Innovation in der Musik. Festschrift für Ernst Lichtenhahn zum 60. Geburtstag*, ed. Christoph Ballmer and Thomas Gartmann, 39–64. Winterthur: Amadeus.

Machaut's polyphonic chansons distinguish themselves from those of his contemporaries by their extreme individuality and by their musical style, the result of meticulous effort and reflection. What Machaut says of his artistic conceptions—the qualities of *nouveauté, subtilité*, and his discussion of *Scens, Retorique et Musique* in the *Prologue*—can also inform an analysis of his music. An instance of revision in Machaut, the two distinct versions of the opening of *Donnez signeurs* (B26), one earlier and one later (MSS **VgBE: AG**), allows a rare glimpse into Machaut's workshop. Arlt demonstrates that the second version is intentionally better, a careful authorial reworking of the first version. B26 exhibits a compositional process that proceeds from a comparatively simple melodic idea that was suggested by the text of the first verse. Machaut emphasizes the striking musical idea of the opening, the descending interval of a perfect fourth setting the word "Donnez"—an insistent exhortation to "give"—in the setting of the remaining verses. Machaut's close work with the musical material raised his sensitivity to its further potentialities and led to a revision of the ballade's beginning, sharpening its focus in anticipation of later musical events. The musical thought processes at work are comparable to those of later composers, such as Haydn and Beethoven. Concerning the historical context of the ballade, Arlt discusses unpublished research of Dominik Sackmann that associates B26, Machaut's only political ballade set to music, with the treaty of Brétigny of 1360, placing it at St-Omer for the 20 October 1360 confirmation of the treaty.

In press. "Machauts Pygmalion-Ballade." In *Das Paradox musikalischer Interpretation. Bericht über ein Symposium zum 80. Geburtstag von Kurt von Fischer*, ed. Dorothea Baumann, Roman Brotbeck, and Joseph Willimann.

Analysis of *Je puis trop bien* (B28).

Aubry, Pierre.

1905 (ed.). *Les plus anciens monuments de la musique française.* Mélanges de Musicologie Critique. Paris: Welter. Reprint. New York: Broude Bros., 1969. Reprint. *Mélanges de musicologie critique.* Introduction by Pierre Féruselle. Geneva: Minkoff, 1980.

Includes facsimiles of *Hé! dame de vaillance* (V1) and *Loyauté vueil* (V2) from MS **A**.

1907. Recherches sur les "Tenors" français dans les motets du treizième siècle. Paris: Champion.

Includes a study of the tenor of *Lasse! comment / Se j'aim* (M16) (pp. 35–40).

Audbourg-Popin, Marie-Danielle.

1986. "'Riches d'amours et mendians d'amie...': La rhétorique de Machaut." *Revue de musicologie* 72:97–104.

A close study of text and music in B5, concluding that the music does not realize the subtleties of the text. The carefully chiseled antitheses and semantic correspondences of the first four lines are not, and cannot be, mirrored in the musical setting. Although Machaut's careful underlay has a musical sense, it does not make for sensible prosody. Certain cadence types and vocal extensions of syllables detract from the intelligibility of the text, and yet proceed with perfect musical sense. The various structural elements of the ballade—meter, mode, melody, disposition of text—play a separate role. The "rhetoric" of the music consists of the cumulative effect of contrasting elements: ascent vs. descent; leap vs. conjunct motion; long vs. short. Abstract: Michel Zink, *Encomia* 10 (1988): 41 no. 133.

Aust, Rudolph.

1890. *Beiträge zur französischen Laut- und Formenlehre nach den Dichtungen des Guillaume de Machault, Eustache Deschamps und der Christine de Pisan.* Vol. 1, *Der Vocalismus.* Breslau: Buchdruckerei zum Gutenberg Anton Schreiber.

Publication of a University of Breslau doctoral dissertation on vocalism in Machaut, based on the antiquated editions of Tarbé (1849), P. Paris (1875), and Mas Latrie (1877b).

Avril, François.

1969. "Trois manuscrits napolitans." *Bibliothèque de l'Ecole des Chartes* 127:291–328.

Includes information on Remiet and an assistant, artists Avril identifies in Machaut MSS **F-G** [6] and **Bk** [21].

1973. "Un Chef-d'œuvre de l'enluminure sous le règne de Jean le Bon: La Bible Moralisée manuscrit français 167 de la Bibliothèque Nationale." In *Monuments et Mémoires de la Fondation Eugène Piot*, 91–125. Publications de l'Académie des Inscriptions et Belles-Lettres 58. Paris: Presses Universitaires de France.

A path-breaking art-historical study of illuminators in mid-fourteenth-century Paris; Avril proves that MS C dates from the early 1350s.

1978. *L'enluminure à la cour de France au XIVe siècle.* Paris: Chêne. *Manuscript Painting at the Court of France: The Fourteenth Century (1310–1380)*, trans. Ursula Molinaro and Bruce Benderson. New York: Braziller; London: Chatto and Windus, 1978. *Buchmalerei am Hofe Frankreichs 1310–1380*, trans. Brigitte Sauerländer. Munich: Prestel, 1978.

Includes color facsimiles of miniatures from MSS C and A. The commentary provides detailed descriptions of the achievements of the illustrators of the two Machaut manuscripts that are the most important from the art-historical perspective.

1982a. "Les manuscrits enluminés de Guillaume de Machaut: Essai de chronologie." In Guillaume de Machaut 1982, 117–33.

The most important study of the art-historical aspects of MSS C [1], **Vg** [3], **A** [5], **E** [7], **F-G** [6], **Pm** [18], and **D** [11], also providing a chronology of these manuscripts.

1982b. "Un Moment méconnu de l'enluminure française." *Archéologia* 162 (Jan.): 24–31.

The crucial importance of the principal artist of MS C—the Master of the *Remede de Fortune*—for the history of manuscript illumination in fourteenth-century France.

Avril, François, and Jean Lafaurie.

1968. *La librairie de Charles V.* Paris: Bibliothèque Nationale.

Includes descriptions of the stylistic characteristics of the illuminators who contributed to the decoration of MSS A [5], **Vg** [3], **F-G** [6], and **E** [7].

Bach y Rita, Pedro, ed.

1930. *The Works of Pere Torroella: A Catalan Writer of the Fifteenth Century.* New York: Instituto de las Españas en los Estados Unidos.

Torroella's *Tant mon voler* (ll. 147–51) quotes from Machaut's *Se quanque Diex* (L11; strophe 1, ll. 12–16) (pp. 105, 125n.).

Badel, Pierre-Yves.

1980. *Le Roman de la Rose au XIVe siècle: Etude de la réception de l'œuvre.* Publications romanes et françaises 153. Geneva: Droz.

Reception history of the *Roman de la Rose* in the fourteenth century; see especially chap. 2, "Lecteurs du XIVe siècle; Machaut et la poésie de cour" (82–94). Abstract: Peck 1988, no. 78. Reviews: Charles R. Dahlberg, *Speculum* 56 (1981): 844–47; Jean Dufournet,

Revue des langues romanes 86 (1982): 150–58; Albert Gier, *Vox romanica* 41 (1982): 361–62; Marion Schnerb-Lièvre, *Bibliothèque de l'Ecole des Chartes* 140 (1982): 106–7; Gianni Mombello, *Studi francesi* 27 (1983): 122–23; Giuseppe Porta, *Studi medievali* 21 (1980): 783–88; Paul Verhuyck, *Rapports—Het Franse Boek* 51 (1981): 126–28; Nigel Wilkins, *Modern Language Review* 76 (1981): 957.

1985. Review of Cerquiglini 1985b. *Romania* 106:550–61.

A very detailed review, useful in its own right.

1986. *"Par un tout seul escondire:* Sur un virelai du *Buisson de Jeunesse."* *Romania* 107:369–79.

Fascinating account of various versions of an anonymous virelai that appears in six places: Froissart's *Joli Buisson de Jonece,* the anonymous *Roman de Cardenois* [43], the anthologies **Pa** [50] and **Bc** [55], and cited by Evrart de Conty, doctor of King Charles V, both in his gloss of the *Echecs Amoureux* and in his translation of Aristotle. Most important for Machaut is the material on the relationships between the *Roman de Cardenois,* **Bc,** and **Pa,** and on possible connections to Oton de Granson.

1988. "Le débat." In Poirion 1988b, 95–110.

Study of fourteenth- and fifteenth-century French debate and judgment poems, with bibliography.

Baird, Lorrayne Y.

1977. *A Bibliography of Chaucer, 1964–1973.* Reference Guides in Literature. Boston: G.K. Hall.

Standard Chaucer bibliography. See also Griffith 1955; Crawford 1967; Baird-Lange/ Schnuttgen 1988.

Baird-Lange, Lorrayne Y., and Hildegard Schnuttgen.

1988. *A Bibliography of Chaucer 1974–1985,* ed. Stephen G. Smyczynski. Hamden, Conn.: Archon.

Standard Chaucer bibliography; lists reviews but lacks annotations. The introductory section "Critical Theories and Critical Controversies" (xx–lii) by Baird-Lange provides an excellent historiography of literary criticism. See also Griffith 1955; Crawford 1967; Baird 1977.

Balasch, Rose. See Lühmann.

Balensuela, C. Matthew, ed. and trans.

1994. *Ars cantus mensurabilis mensurata per modos iuris. The Art of Mensurable Song Measured by the Modes of Law.* Greek and Latin Music Theory 10. Lincoln, Nebr. and London: University of Nebraska Press.

New critical edition and translation of an anonymous music theory treatise, perhaps Florentine, of the last quarter of the fourteenth century. The extensive introduction discusses the relationship of the treatise to the influential *Libellus cantus mensurabilis,* attributed to Johannes de Muris. Coussemaker (1864–76, 3:379–98) incompletely published the treatise as Anonymous V in vol. 3 of the *Scriptores.* Reviews: Christian Meyer, *Revue de musicologie* 81 (1995): 126–27; Roger Wibberley, *Music and Letters* 76 (1995): 406–8.

Balayé, Simone.

1988. *La Bibliothèque Nationale des origines à 1800.* Preface by André Miquel. Histoire des Idées et Critique Littéraire 262. Geneva: Droz.

Includes information on sixteenth- and seventeenth-century owners of Machaut MS **B** [4].

Ballif, Claude.

1969. "XIVe siècle: L'*Ars nova* et Guillaume de Machaut." In *Encyclopédie des musiques sacrées.* Vol. 2, ed. Jacques Porte, 250–74. Paris: Labergerie.

Includes a survey of Machaut's sacred music (esp. 267–71).

Baltzer, Rebecca A.

1991a. "Notes on the Accompanying Tape by Sequentia." In Baltzer 1991b, 151–55.

Comments on performances by Sequentia that illustrate Earp 1991b, Guthrie 1991, and Wimsatt 1991a. Baltzer also edited *Esperance* (B13) (pp. 149–50) and *Je suis aussi* (B20) (pp. 98–99).

1991b (ed.). *The Union of Words and Music in Medieval Poetry*, ed. Rebecca A. Baltzer, Thomas Cable, and James I. Wimsatt, tape recorded by Sequentia. Austin: University of Texas Press. Includes audio cassette.

See Baltzer 1991a; Earp 1991b; Guthrie 1991; Wimsatt 1991a; Wimsatt/Cable 1991. Review: Beverly J. Evans, *Studies in the Age of Chaucer* 16 (1994): 145–49.

Bank, J[oannes] A[ntonius].

1972. *Tactus, Tempo and Notation in Mensural Music from the 13th to the 17th Century*. Amsterdam: Annie Bank.

Publication of author's 1972 University of Amsterdam dissertation, presenting a theory of tempo relationships. Includes excerpts from *Bone pastor / Bone pastor* (M18), *Trop plus / Biauté* (M20), *Felix virgo / Inviolata* (M23), Christe, Gloria, *Biauté qui* (B4), *Plourez, dames* (B32), and *Quant ma dame les maus* (R19), all in diplomatic facsimiles (38–46). On the question of note values and declamatory rhythm, see Lühmann 1978, 75–140, 211–15. Abstract: *RILM* 6 (1972), no. 2437. Reviews: Elena Ferrari Barassi, *Nuova rivista musicale italiana* 8 (1974): 637–39; Howard Mayer Brown, *Musical Times* 115 (1974): 847; Carl Dahlhaus, *Tijdschrift van de Vereniging voor Nederlandse Muziekgeschiedenis* 23 (1973): 44–48; K.G. Fellerer, *Kirchenmusikalisches Jahrbuch* 56 (1972): 105; Alejandro Enrique Planchart, *Journal of Music Theory* 19 (1975): 154–60; Wilhelm Seidel, *Musikforschung* 30 (1977): 530–31.

Barker, John W.

1988. *The Use of Music and Recordings for Teaching About the Middle Ages: A Practical Guide, with Comprehensive Discography and Selective Bibliography*. Produced by TEAMS (Consortium for the Teaching of the Middle Ages, Inc.) in cooperation with Medieval Institute Publications. Kalamazoo, Mich.: Medieval Institute Publications.

Useful survey of recorded materials for medieval music (through Dufay). For recordings of Machaut, see pp. 70–71, 128–31 nn. 53–54, and the index of record labels (151–89). Reviews: Daniel Leech-Wilkinson, *Early Music* 17 (1989): 573–75; J.F. Weber, *Fanfare* 12/5 (May–June 1989): 535–36.

Barksdale, A. Beverly.

1953a. *Medieval and Renaissance Music Manuscripts*. Toledo, Oh.: The Toledo Museum of Art, January and February 1953.

Catalogue no. 57 describes MS **Vg** [3], with a plate of the opening of the Gloria (fol. 285v).

1953b. "On the Planning and Arranging of Music Exhibitions." *Notes* 10: 561–69.

Includes a plate of the opening of the Mass from MS **Vg** [3] (fols. 283v–284r), the only manuscript with the rubric *Ci commence la Messe de Nostre Dame*.

Baron, Françoise, François Avril, et al.

1981. *Les Fastes du Gothique: Le siècle de Charles V (Galéries nationales du Grand Palais 9 oct. 1981–1 fév. 1982)*. Paris: Editions de la Réunion des Musées Nationaux.

The chapter on manuscripts by François Avril includes further discussion of the artists that illustrated MSS C and A, with bibliography. See pp. 318–19, §271 (MS C); 328–29 §283 (A); color plate 38 (C); plate 271 (C), and plate 283 (A).

Barraque, Jean.

1954. "Rythme et développement." *Polyphonie* 9–10:47–73.

A rhythmic analysis of parts of the Mass (49–52).

Barrois, J[ean Baptiste Joseph].
    1830. *Bibliothéque protypographique, ou librairies des fils du roi Jean,
        Charles V, Jean de Berri, Philippe de Bourgogne et les siens.* Paris:
        Crapelet.
    Publication of library inventories of the French Royal Court and the Court of Burgundy;
    this work is superseded for some of the inventories by Doutrepont 1906, Delisle 1907,
    and De Winter 1985, but remains the only publication of the important Burgundian
    inventory of 1467.

Bartsch, Karl.
    1880. *Chrestomatie de l'ancien français (VIIIe–XVe siècles). Accompagnée
        d'une grammaire et d'un glossaire.* [1st ed. 1866.] 4th rev. ed. Leipzig:
        Vogel, 1880. With summary grammar and glossary. 9th ed., revised by
        Leo Wiese. Leipzig, Vogel, 1908. 12th ed. Leipzig, Vogel, 1919. Reprint.
        New York: Hafner, 1958.
    Served as a standard textbook of readings for many generations. Includes excerpts from
    Lyon (ll. 1587–698) and *Harpe* (ll. 1–92).

Baudouin, Rae S., ed.
    1978. *Jean Froissart: Ballades et rondeaux. Edition avec introduction, notes et
        glossaire.* Textes Littéraires Français 252. Geneva: Droz.
    A critical edition of Froissart's ballades and rondeaux, based on the author's 1973 Paris-IV
    thesis; see also McGregor 1975. Reviews: Rudolf Besthorn, *Beiträge zur romanischen
    Philologie* 18 (1979): 340–41; Hans Helmut Christmann, *Romanische Forschungen* 92
    (1980): 398–99; Marie-Claire Gérard-Zai, *Vox romanica* 38 (1979): 341–42; Geneviève
    Hasenohr, *Bibliothèque de l'Ecole des Chartes* 137 (1979): 104–6 (corrections); Brigitte
    Horiot, *Revue de littératures romanes* 43 (1979): 199–200; Jacques Lemaire, *Scriptorium*
    35 (1981): 167–68; Aldo Menichetti, *Studi medievali* 20 (1979): 424–25; Nathaniel B.
    Smith, *Speculum* 54 (1979): 592–93; P. Verhuyck, *Revue belge de philologie et
    d'histoire* 62 (1984): 643–44.

Baumann, Dorothea.
    1979. *Die dreistimmige italienische Lied-Satztechnik im Trecento.* Collection
        d'Etudes musicologiques / Sammlung musikwissenschaftlicher Abhand-
        lungen 64. Baden-Baden: Koerner.
    Study of the musical structure of Italian trecento songs; includes a summary of points of
    similarity and contrast with chansons of Machaut (18–21), summarizing Dömling 1970.
    Tables summarize cadences in two-voice chansons of Machaut (108–9). Abstract: *RILM*
    13 (1979), no. 273.

Baumgartner[-Danchaud], Emmanuèle.
    1988. *Moyen Age, 1050–1486.* Histoire de la Littérature Française 1. Paris:
        Bordas.
    Brief survey of the period from 1340 to 1480 (165–99), with bibliography.

Bec, Pierre.
    1992. *Vièles ou violes? Variations philologiques et musicales autour des
        instruments à archet du Moyen Age (XIe–XVe siècle).* Collection Sapience.
        Paris: Klincksieck.
    Philological and iconographical study of medieval French lists of instruments, including
    those in *Remede* and *Prise*, with a large bibliography. Review: Max Pfister, *Zeitschrift
    für romanische Philologie* 110 (1984): 212–13.

    1993. "Note musico-philologique sur l'orgue et l'*aile* chez Guillaume de
        Machaut." In *Et c'est la fin pour quoy sommes ensemble. Hommage à Jean
        Dufournet, Professeur à la Sorbonne Nouvelle. Littérature, histoire et
        langue du Moyen Age,* 1:149–61. Nouvelle Bibliothèque du Moyen Age
        25. 3 vols. Paris: Champion.
    Catalogues of instruments found in many medieval texts are to be understood as rhetorical
    tours de force, with only contingent relationship to musical practice. Bec discusses the

passages in *Prise* and *Remede* in this light, focusing on the *orgue* (organ) and *ele / elles*. Contrary to what we frequently read in survey books, Machaut did not name the organ the "king of instruments." The term *Ele / elles* does not indicate an instrument; Bec emends to *et le / e[l] les*.

Becker, Georges.

1964. "Guillaume de Machaut (1300?–1377)." In *Dictionnaire des lettres françaises: Le Moyen Age*, ed. Robert Bossuat et al., 353–58. Paris: Fayard.

Dictionary article. A good, even-handed survey of the life and especially of the literary works of Machaut.

Beer, Jeanette M.A.

1980. "The Ambiguity of Guillaume de Machaut." *Parergon* 27:27–31.

The ambiguous interplay between truth and fiction in Machaut, with examples from *Remede, Lyon, Alerion, Voir Dit*, and *Prise*.

1981. *Narrative Conventions of Truth in the Middle Ages*. Etudes de Philologie et d'Histoire 38. Geneva: Droz.

Chap. 6, "The Game of Truth," discusses Machaut's *Lyon, Alerion*, and especially *Voir Dit*. Reviews: Norris J. Lacy, *French Review* 57 (1983–84): 103–4; J.C. Laidlaw, *Modern Language Review* 79 (1984): 928–29; Peter S. Noble, *Medium Ævum* 52 (1983): 320.

Bellamy, Sister Laurette.

1978. "Some Comments on the Lais of Guillaume de Machaut." *Indiana Theory Review* 2:41–53.

General account of the lais, with some particulars on *Un mortel lay* (L12/8) (pp. 44–47).

Bennett, Philip E.

1991. "The Mirage of Fiction: Narration, Narrator, and Narrative in Froissart's Lyrico-Narrative *Dits*." *Modern Language Review* 86:285–97.

Study of Froissart's *Paradis d'Amour, Prison Amoureuse*, and *Joli Buisson de Jonece*; considers influence of Machaut's *Jugement Behaingne, Jugement Navarre*, and *Voir Dit*.

Benson, Larry D., gen. ed.

1987. *The Riverside Chaucer*. 3rd edition. Boston, Mass.: Houghton Mifflin. Oxford: Oxford University Press, 1988.

Standard edition of Chaucer's works, based on F.N. Robinson 1957, revised by a team of editors.

Bent, Margaret.

1972. "Musica Recta and Musica Ficta." *Musica disciplina* 26:73–100.

Although this study does not mention Machaut directly, it is of importance for musical performance practice. Comments on the works of Lowinsky (1945; 1954) and Hoppin (1953; 1956). Hughes 1972 is a complementary study; Harden (1983) applies the work of Bent and Hughes to Machaut.

1981. "Some Criteria for Establishing Relationships between Sources of Late Medieval Polyphony." In *Music in Medieval and Early Modern Europe*, ed. Ian Fenlon, 295–317. Cambridge: Cambridge University Press.

Emphasizes the unique aspects of musical transmission when compared to text transmission. Brief discussion of the relationship between MSS B and E (see also Bent 1983).

1983. "The Machaut Manuscripts *Vg, B* and *E*." *Musica disciplina* 37:53–82.

The most important recent study of relationships between the Machaut manuscripts. Rejecting the arguments of Keitel (1976), Bent reconfirms Ludwig's discovery that MS B was copied from **Vg**, but with the interesting twist that the *Prise* in **Vg** was copied from **B**. Further, much of the music in MS E was copied directly from **B**. Abstract: *RILM* 17 (1983), no. 4636.

1984. "Text Setting in Sacred Music of the Early 15th Century: Evidence and Implications." In Günther/Finscher 1984, 291–326.

Texting practices in motet and Mass music of the late fourteenth and early fifteenth centuries, covering both scribal practice and compositional procedures. Brief discussion of planning exerted by Machaut in *Bone pastor / Bone pastor* (M18) (pp. 316–17).

1990a. "Manuscripts as Répertoires, Scribal Performance and the Performing Scribe." In *Atti del XIV congresso della Società Internazionale di Musicologia: Trasmissione e recezione delle forme di cultura musicale. Bologna, 27 agosto–1° settembre 1987; Ferrara-Parma, 30 agosto 1987*. Vol. 1, *Round Tables*, ed. Angelo Pompilio et al., 138–48 (discussion, 148–51; abstract by Reinhard Strohm, 96). Turin: Edizioni di Torino.

The relationship between surviving manuscripts and actual "living repertories" of the Middle Ages (on the Machaut manuscripts, see 138–39, 145, 149).

1990b. "A Note on the Dating of the Trémoïlle Manuscript." In *Beyond the Moon: Festschrift Luther Dittmer*, ed. Bryan Gillingham and Paul Merkley, 217–42. Musicological Studies 53. Ottawa: Institute of Mediaeval Music, 1990.

Bent distinguishes different scribal layers among the entries in the original index of MS Trém [58]. Since the heading, with its 1376 date, was written at the same time as the first layer of index entries, the *terminus* applies only to musical works included in that layer of copying; subsequent entries may postdate 1376, extending possibly into the fifteenth century. The dating affects one of the main pillars in current chronologies of late fourteenth-century music (cf. Günther 1963b, 113–14). Review: Mark Everist, *Notes* 48 (1991–92): 475–77.

1991. "Deception, Exegesis and Sounding Number in Machaut's Motet 15." *Early Music History* 10:15–27.

Possible instances of number symbolism in *Amours qui a / Faus Samblant* (M15), considering *talea* structure, text structure, and word count as constituent elements. Bent discovers intentional programmatic strategies in many parameters of the motet, particularly with the "false-seeming" (*Faus Samblant*) of the motetus, although some features typical of Machaut's motets in general are interpreted here in isolation as significant for this motet alone. The analysis is brilliant, but some speculations seem pushed too far; for instance, reliance on the Golden Section needs supporting evidence (cf. Busse Berger 1990). Includes an analytical edition of the motet (16–19) with a suggested emendation of the ending of the triplum.

Bent, Margaret, and Anne Hallmark, eds.
1985. *The Works of Johannes Ciconia*. Latin texts ed. M.J. Connolly. Polyphonic Music of the Fourteenth Century 24. Les Remparts, Monaco: L'Oiseau-Lyre.

Standard critical edition of Ciconia's works

Berger, Christian.
1987. "Tonsystem und Textvortrag: Ein Vergleich zweier Balladen des 14. Jahrhunderts." In *Alte Musik als ästhetische Gegenwart* 2:202–11. Internationaler musikwissenschaftlicher Kongress 1985, Stuttgart. Kassel: Bärenreiter.

Analysis of *De Fortune* (B23), compared with the related anonymous ballade *Dame qui fust*. Abstract: *RILM* 21 (1987), no. 1334.

1990. "Die melodische Floskel im Liedsatz des 14. Jahrhunderts: Magister Franciscus' Ballade 'Phiton.'" In *Atti del XIV congresso della Società Internazionale di Musicologia: Trasmissione e recezione delle forme di cultura musicale. Bologna, 27 agosto–1° settembre 1987; Ferrara-Parma, 30 agosto 1987*. Vol. 3, *Free Papers*, ed. Angelo Pompilio et al., 673–79. Turin: Edizioni di Torino.

Analysis of *Phiton Phiton*, a ballade based on Machaut's *Phyton* (B38) (cf. also Hirschberg 1973–74, 57–59). Proposes emendations to the published edition of *Phiton Phiton*.

1992. *Hexachord, Mensur und Textstruktur: Studien zum französischen Lied des 14. Jahrhunderts.* Beihefte zum Archiv für Musikwissenschaft 35. Stuttgart: Steiner.

Analytical study of fourteenth-century French chansons. Although Machaut is not neglected entirely, Berger focuses primarily on his contemporaries and immediate followers. Includes chapters on mensuration (*mutatio qualitatis*, syncopation, ligatures and mensuration, melodic sequences), text underlay, and tonal system. Description of the characteristics of each "polyphonic mode," based on counterpoint treatises, the system of hexachords, and modal theory. Focusing on the repertory of eighty chansons in the old part of the *Reina* Codex (**PR** [63]), Berger interprets many of the manuscript accidentals as hexachordal signs or cautionary accidentals. Review: Nigel Wilkins, *Medium Ævum* 64 (1995): 145.

Bergeron, Réjean.

1992. "Examen d'une œuvre vouée à l'oubli: Les *Jeux a Vendre* de Christine de Pizan." In *Préludes à la renaissance: Aspects de la vie intellectuelle en France au XVe siècle,* ed. Carla Bozzolo and Ezio Ornato, 163–89. Centre Régional de Publication de Paris. Paris: Editions du Centre National de la Recherche Scientifique.

The first examples of a literary genre cultivated by Christine de Pizan appear in MS **K** [15]. Such *Ventes d'Amour* circulated from the fourteenth until the nineteenth centuries. Cf. Klein 1911.

Berlière, Ursmer.

1906. *Suppliques de Clément VI (1342–1352). Textes et analyses.* Analecta Vaticano-Belgica 1. Rome: Institut Historique Belge; Bruges: Desclée, de Brouwer; Paris: Champion.

Papal documents.

1911. *Suppliques d'Innocent VI (1352–1362). Textes et analyses.* Analecta Vaticano-Belgica 5. Rome: Bretschneider; Brussels: Dewit; Paris: Champion.

Papal documents.

1924. *Lettres de Clément VI (1342–1352). Tome 1 (1342–1346). Textes et analyses,* ed. Philippe van Isacker. Analecta Vaticano-Belgica 6. Rome: Institut Historique Belge; Brussels: Imbreghts; Paris: Champion.

Papal documents.

Bertoni, Giulio.

1917. "Il 'Chastel d'Amours' del manoscritto di Berna 218." *Archivum romanicum* 1:237–39.

Describes miniature **K**11 (see chap. 4.4x). Useful material on works in the manuscript not by Machaut.

1932. "Lyriche di Oton de Grandson, Guillaume de Machaut e di altri poeti in un nuovo canzoniere." *Archivum romanicum* 16:1–20.

First mention of MS **Pa** [50], with an inventory; superseded by Mudge 1972 and Wimsatt 1982.

Besseler, Heinrich.

1924–25. "Musik des Mittelalters in der Hamburger Musikhalle 1.–8. April 1924." *Zeitschrift für Musikwissenschaft* 7:42–54.

Interesting views on an early music concert that included performances of *Christe / Veni* (M21), *De toutes flours* (B31), and *Dix et sept* (R17). See also comments in Haas 1931, 94–98.

1925. "Studien zur Musik des Mittelalters: I. Neue Quellen des 14. und beginnenden 15. Jahrhunderts." *Archiv für Musikwissenschaft* 7:167–252.

Includes the first inventories of the MSS **CaB** [56], **Iv** [57], and **Trém** [58].

1927. "Studien zur Musik des Mittelalters: II. Die Motette von Franko von Köln bis Philipp von Vitry." *Archiv für Musikwissenschaft* 8:137–258.

A path-breaking study of the medieval motet; includes consideration of Machaut's isorhythmic motets.

1931. *Die Musik des Mittelalters und der Renaissance.* Handbuch der Musikwissenschaft 1. Potsdam: Athenaion. Reprint. Laaber: Laaber, 1979.

Survey (on Machaut, see pp. 136–43, 148–50); emphasizes Machaut's very different, more "romantic" personality as compared to that of Philippe de Vitry. Examples include *Longuement* (L18/13), *Mes esperis* (B39), *Rose, lis* (R10), and Agnus I.

1949–51. "Ars nova." *MGG* 1:702–29.

Dictionary article.

Besseler, Heinrich, and Peter Gülke.
1973. *Schriftbild der mehrstimmigen Musik.* Musikgeschichte in Bildern 3/5. Leipzig: VEB Deutscher Verlag für Musik.

Includes facsimiles and discussions of Kyrie and Gloria (MS **G**), and *Donnez, signeurs* (B26; MS **A**). Abstract: *RILM* 9 (1975), no. 471.

Bessen, David M.
1985. "The Jacquerie: Class War or Co-Opted Rebellion?" *Journal of Medieval History* 11:43–59.

The 1358 anti-royalist revolt and the involvement of supporters of Charles of Navarre.

Bibliothèque Impériale.
1868. *Département des manuscrits. Catalogue des manuscrits français.* Vol. 1, *Ancien fonds.* Paris: Firmin-Didot, 1868.

Remains the standard inventory of the *ancien fonds français.*

Bibliothèque Nationale.
1975. *Catalogue général des manuscrits latins.* Vol. 6, *Nos 3536 à 3775ᴮ.* Paris: Bibliothèque Nationale.

Includes useful bibliographical information on historical catalogues of manuscripts held at the Bibliothèque Nationale (815).

1981. *Catalogue général des manuscrits latins. Tables des tomes III à VI (Nos 2693 à 3775ᴮ).* Vol. 1, *Table analytique.* Paris: Bibliothèque Nationale.

Includes useful plates identifying historical bindings and shelfmarks found in manuscripts at the Bibliothèque Nationale.

Biezen, J. van, and J.P. Gumbert.
1985 (ed.). *Two Chansonniers from the Low Countries: French and Dutch Polyphonic Songs from the Leiden and Utrecht Fragments [Early 15th Century].* Monumenta Musica Neerlandica 15. Amsterdam: Vereniging voor Nederlandse Muziekgeschiedenis.

Detailed inventory, description, and edition of two fragments of music, one of which—Utr [69]—contains fragments of *Biauté qui* (B4), *Plourez, dames* (B32), and the anonymous *S'espoir n'estoit,* a ballade related to *Se vous n'estes* (R7).

Binkley, Thomas.
1977. "Zur Aufführungspraxis der einstimmigen Musik des Mittelalters—Ein Werkstattbericht. *Basler Jahrbuch für historische Musikpraxis* 1:19–76.

A report from a practicing musician on performing medieval monophony. Brief discussion of the arrangements used in Binkley's 1972 recording of *Loyauté, que* (L1) and *Tels rit* (RF2), including editions utilized for strophe 1 of each song (26–29).

Blanchard, Roger.
1956. "Une grande œuvre musicale française: La messe 'Nostre Dame' de Guillaume de Machaut." *Cerf-volant* 12:18–22.

Survey of the Mass; not examined.

Bockholdt, Rudolf.
1971. "Französische und niederländische Musik des 14. und 15. Jahrhunderts." In *Musikalische Edition im Wandel des historischen Bewusstseins*, ed. Thrasybulos G. Georgiades, 149–73. Kassel: Bärenreiter.
Includes a discussion of the late eighteenth- and early nineteenth-century rediscovery of Machaut as a composer (149–50). Interesting historiographical study of editorial principles for fourteenth- and fifteenth-century music and how they have changed since the eighteenth century. Some discussion of the editorial principles behind the Machaut editions of Ludwig and Schrade (154–55), with an example from *Tous corps / De* (M2). Abstract: *RILM* 6 (1972), no. 3948.

Bofill Soliguer, Joan.
1991. "Cuestiones de notación consideradas en la ballade 'De Fortune' (n.º 21) de Guillaume de Machaut." *Anuario musical* 46:5–25.
Questions arising from the original notation of *De Fortune* (B23) in MSS C, A, G, and, to a lesser extent, Ch [59]. Considers texting and especially accidentals. Valuable for the facsimiles of B23 in MSS C, A, and G.

Böker-Heil, Norbert.
1989. "Ein Lieblingsmotiv der ars subtilior?" In *Festschrift Wolfgang Rehm zum 60. Geburtstag am 3. September 1989*, ed. Dietrich Berke and Harald Heckmann, 9–14. Kassel: Bärenreiter.
Computer-aided study of 147 compositions by a variety of composers from the period ca. 1350 to ca. 1430, seeking a four-note motive frequent in Machaut, here designated by the notes *CBCA*. Böker-Heil compares the motive's frequency with a measure of the degree of "subtlety" in compositions, based on the variety of note values used, the use of polyrhythms, number of attacks, etc. A summary table reveals that *CBCA* was not much used in Ars Subtilior compositions, but remained in use in simpler works. Abstract: *RILM* 23 (1989), no. 1810.

Boogaart, Jacques.
1990. "Armes, Amours: een onderzoek naar de relatie tussen tekst en muziek in de motetten van Machaut." M.A. Thesis, University of Amsterdam.
Analyses of all of Machaut's French and French-Latin motets, with a study of the literary context of the *Roman de la Rose*. Not examined.

1993a. "Love's Unstable Balance. Part I: Analogy of Ideas in Text and Music of Machaut's Motet 6." *Muziek & Wetenschap* 3:1–23.
The rhythmic irregularity in the isorhythmic layout of *S'il estoit / S'Amours* (M6) can be explained through a careful analysis of the text (in the context of the *Roman de la Rose*) and music.

1993b. "Love's Unstable Balance. Part II: More Balance Problems and the Order of Machaut's Motets." *Muziek & Wetenschap* 3:24–33.
An analysis of *Hareu! / Helas!* (M10), with careful attention to the text as well as music. Machaut seems to have utilized proportional relationships and number symbolism as a principle of ordering in the motet collection of the manuscripts. Mentions several motets.

Boorman, Stanley.
1977a. "A New Edition of Machaut." *Early Music* 5:495–98.
A very critical review of Leguy 1977. Includes a general discussion of editorial principles and considerations for an edition of Machaut. See also *Early Music* 6 (1978): 307 (letter of Leguy), 483–85 (response of Boorman). Abstract: *RILM* 11 (1977), no. 4410.

1977b. "Guillaume de Machaut—Introduction." *Early Music* 5:458–59.
A good survey of Machaut's importance, introducing an issue of *Early Music* devoted to studies of Machaut.

1980. "Sources, MS. §I, Introduction." *New Grove* 17:590–609.
Dictionary article, discussing problems that concern musical manuscripts.

1983 (ed.). *Studies in the Performance of Late Mediaeval Music*. Cambridge: Cambridge University Press.

Collection of essays, including Fallows 1983; Günther 1983; Hallmark 1983. Reviews: Daniel Leech-Wilkinson, *Early Music History* 4 (1984): 347–55; Christopher Page, *Early Music* 13 (1985): 82–85; Dennis Slavin, *Notes* 42 (1985–86): 56–58; Peter Williams, *Organ Yearbook* 16 (1985): 178–79.

Borghezio, Gino.

1921. "Poesie musicali latine e francesi in un codice ignorato della Biblioteca capitolare d'Ivrea (Torino)." *Archivum romanicum* 5:173–86.

First modern study and description of MS **Iv** [57].

Borren, Charles van den.

1923–27. "Le manuscrit musical M 222 C 22 de la Bibliothèque de Strasbourg (XVe siècle) brûlé en 1870, et reconstitué d'après une copie partielle d'Edmond de Coussemaker." *Annales de l'Académie Royale d'Archéologie de Belgique* 71 (1923): 343–74; 72 (1924): 272–303; 73 (1925): 128–96; 74 (1927): 71–152. Reprint. Antwerp: Secelle, 1924.

Classic study of the destroyed MS **Str** [73].

1946. "L'école et le temps de Guillaume de Machaut et de Francesco Landini." In *La musique des origines à nos jours*, ed. Norbert Dufourcq, 114–16. Paris: Larousse.

Brief biography of Machaut with some interesting comments on the musical works. Includes reproductions of miniatures C40 (chap. 4.4e) and A2 (chap. 4.4a).

Bossuat, Robert (see also Vielliard/Monfrin 1991).

1931. *Histoire de la littérature française*, ed. J. Calvet. Vol. 1, *Le Moyen Age*. Paris: de Gigord. 2nd ed. Paris: del Duca-de Giord 1955.

Includes a discussion of Machaut (360–61), with facsimiles of four miniatures from MS **J** (plate xxi).

1951. *Manuel bibliographique de la littérature française du Moyen Age*. Bibliothèque Elzévirienne, n.s., Etudes et documents. Melun: Librairie d'Argences. Reprint in one vol. (Bossuat 1951; 1955; 1961). Nendeln, Liechtenstein: Kraus, 1970.

Annotated bibliography; nos. 4351–74 pertain to Machaut.

1955. *Manuel bibliographique de la littérature française du Moyen Age. Supplément (1949–1953)*. With Jacques Monfrin. Bibliothèque Elzévirienne, n.s., Etudes et documents. Melun: Librairie d'Argences. Reprint in one vol. (Bossuat 1951; 1955; 1961). Nendeln, Liechtenstein: Kraus, 1970.

Nos. 6817–20 pertain to Machaut.

1961. *Manuel bibliographique de la littérature française du Moyen Age. Second supplément (1954–1960)*. Bibliothèque Elzévirienne, n.s., Etudes et documents. Melun: Librairie d'Argences. Reprint in one vol. (Bossuat 1951; 1955; 1961). Nendeln, Liechtenstein: Kraus, 1970.

Nos. 7881–82 pertain to Machaut.

Bottée de Toulmon, Auguste.

1836. "De la chanson musicale en France, au Moyen Age." In *Annuaire historique pour l'année 1837*, 214–20; supplement of 7 pp. with musical examples after p. 334. Société de l'Histoire de France. Paris: Renouard.

Brief survey of the chanson, including a discussion of Machaut's *J'aim la flour* (L2) and *Dame, a vous* (RF6), with diplomatic facsimiles and transcriptions of brief musical examples from MS **A**.

1838. "Instruments de musique en usage dans le Moyen Age." In *Annuaire historique pour l'année 1839*, 186–200. Société de l'Histoire de France. Paris: Renouard.

Discussion of instruments by types, including the instruments listed in the *Prise* (198–99); reprints most of Roquefort-Flaméricourt's list from the *Remede* (199–200).

[1846]a (ed.). *Archives curieuses de la musique.* Part 1, *Musique religieuse. Publications de la Revue et Gazette Musicale.*
Includes transcription of Et in terra (up to "Gloriam tuam") as "In terra pax. Par Guillaume de Machaut. Fragment de la Messe executée au Sacre de Charles V en 1367" [*sic*]. With modern clefs, reduced note values, and lacking underlay for the linking passages in tenor and contratenor, this has the appearance of a very modern edition.

[1846]b (ed.). *Archives curieuses de la musique.* Part 2, *Musique de chambre. Publications de la Revue et Gazette Musicale.*
Includes transcriptions of *S'Amours ne fait* (B1) as "Ballade de Guillaume de Machault. Vers 1320. Samans ne fait"; and *J'aim la flour* (L2): "Lays. Par Guillaume de Machault" (strophe 1 texted, strophes 2–7 textless).

Boulez, Pierre.
1991. *Stocktakings from an Apprenticeship,* ed. Paul Thévenin, trans. Stephen Walsh, with an introduction by Robert Piencikowski. Oxford: Clarendon.
Under "Counterpoint" in his "Entries for a Musical Encyclopaedia," Boulez sketches a history of counterpoint that includes high praise for Machaut, "one of the greatest composers of all time" (229).

Boulton, Maureen Barry McCann.
1981. "Lyric Insertions in French Narrative Fiction in the Thirteenth and Fourteenth Centuries." B. Litt. diss. Oxford University.
Not examined; revised as Boulton 1993. Cf. *Index to Theses* 31/2 (1982), no. 4530.

1989. "The Dialogical Imagination in the Middle Ages: The Example of Guillaume de Machaut's *Voir Dit.*" *Allegorica* 10:85–94.
The *Voir Dit* in the context of medieval grammatical and rhetorical theory: the prose letters correspond to the low style, the narrative to the middle style, and the lyrics to the high style, although Machaut undermines these distinctions on occasion (see also Calin 1974, 177; Cerquiglini 1985b, 131–32). The story is thus told three times in these different forms. Boulton calls on the literary theories of Mikhail Bakhtin (polyphonic narrative) in discussing the variety of voices in the work, operating on five levels: the narrative, letters, and lyrics of the narrator, and the letters and lyrics of Toute Belle, all reacting differently to each other.

1990. "Guillaume de Machaut's *Voir Dit:* The Ideology of Form." In *Courtly Literature: Culture and Context. Selected papers from the 5th Triennial Congress of the International Courtly Literature Society, Dalfsen, The Netherlands, 9–16 August, 1986,* ed. Keith Busby and Erik Kooper, 39–47. Utrecht Publications in General and Comparative Literature 25. Amsterdam and Philadelphia: Benjamins.
The *Voir Dit* is a combination of two types of narrative with lyrical insertions: the biographical romance and the erotic allegory. Study of three different styles (letter, narrative, and lyric) and how they are incorporated into the work.

1993. *The Song in the Story: Lyric Insertions in French Narrative Fiction, 1200–1400.* Philadelphia: University of Pennsylvania Press.
Analysis of the literary functions of lyrical insertions in narratives, with a chapter devoted to each function. Machaut figures mostly in chap. 5, "The Song as Message," and in chap. 6, "The Song and the *Dit:* the Poet as Hero." Discussion of *Remede, Fonteinne,* and *Voir Dit.* Appendix i provides a comprehensive "List of Narrative Works Containing Lyric Insertions." Review: Philip E. Bennett, *Medium Ævum* 64 (1995): 134–35.

Bouteron, M., and J. Tremblot.
  1928. *Catalogue général des manuscrits des bibliothèques publiques de France. Paris, Bibliothèque de l'Institut, ancien et nouveau fonds.* Ministère de l'Instruction Publique et des Beaux-Arts. Paris: Plon.
  Standard manuscript catalogue for the Bibliothèque de l'Institut.

Bowers, Roger.
  1975–76. "Some Observations on the Life and Career of Lionel Power." *Proceedings of the Royal Musical Association* 102:103–27.
  Lionel Power, who was in the household chapel of the duke of Clarence, may have examined MS E when it was in the duke's possession, and thus Power's knowledge of Machaut's Mass could have influenced development of the unified cyclic Mass (107, esp. n. 23).

Braddy, Haldeen.
  1935. "The Two Petros in the 'Monkes Tale.'" *PMLA* 50:69–80.
  Machaut's *Prise* was a source for a passage on the assassination of Pierre de Lusignan in Chaucer's *Monk's Tale* (78–80).

  1947. "Two Chaucer Notes." *Modern Language Notes* 62:173–79.
  Part 1, "Chaucer on Murder: *De Petro Rege de Cipro*" (173–75) includes discussion of Machaut's *Prise* as a source for a passage on the assassination of Pierre de Lusignan in Chaucer's *Monk's Tale*.

  1968. "The French Influence on Chaucer." In *Companion to Chaucer Studies*, ed. Beryl Rowland, 123–38. Toronto: Oxford University Press. 2nd ed. New York: Oxford University Press, 1979.
  General survey article.

Brandt, William, et al., eds.
  1980. *The Comprehensive Study of Music.* Vol. 1, *Anthology of Music from Plainsong through Gabrieli.* New York: Harper's College Press.
  Includes musical editions of *Douce dame* (V4), *Honte* (B25), *Qui es / Ha! Fortune* (M8), and *Rose, lis* (R10).

Brejon de Lavergnée, Marie-Edith.
  1982. "Note sur la maison de Guillaume de Machaut à Reims." In Guillaume de Machaut 1982, 149–52, 2 plates (facing p. 152).
  Includes a map of the location of Machaut's house at Reims, as well as a floor plan.

Brewer, D[erek] S.
  1966. "The Relationship of Chaucer to the English and European Traditions." In *Chaucer and Chaucerians: Critical Studies in Middle English Literature*, ed. D.S. Brewer, 1–38. London and Edinburgh: Nelson.
  Includes a discussion of Machaut's *Prologue* (21–22), and *Jugement Behaingne* (22–24).

Bridgman, Nanie.
  1973. "France and Burgundy: 1300–1500." In *Music from the Middle Ages to the Renaissance*, ed. F.W. Sternfeld, 145–73. A History of Western Music 1. London: Weidenfeld & Nicolson.
  Survey; for Machaut, see esp. 157–60. Review: Alejandro Enrique Planchart, *Musical Quarterly* 60 (1974): 646–54.

Briner, Andres.
  1960. "Guillaume de Machaut 1958/59 oder Strawinskys 'Movements for Piano and Orchestra.'" *Melos* 27:184–86.
  Isorhythm in movement 4 of the *Movements for Piano and Orchestra.* See also H. Weber 1987.

Brink, Bernhard ten.
  1870. *Chaucer. Studien zur Geschichte seiner Entwicklung und zur Chronologie seiner Schriften. Erster Theil.* Münster: Russell.

Includes discussion of the relationship between Chaucer's *Book of the Duchess* and Machaut's *Fonteinne* (7–12), with an edition of excerpts from the *Fonteinne* (197–205). Cf. Sandras 1859.

Brosnahan, Leger.
1974. "Now (This), Now (That) and *BD* 646." In *The Learned and the Lewed: Studies in Chaucer and Medieval Literature*, ed. Larry D. Benson, 11–18. Harvard English Studies 5. Cambridge, Mass.: Harvard University Press.

Chaucer borrowed a proverb on the inconstancy of Fortune from *Jugement Behaingne* for his *Book of the Duchess*.

Brown, Howard Mayer.
1987. "A Ballade for Mathieu de Foix: Style and Structure in a Composition by Trebor." *Musica disciplina* 41:75–107.

Close analysis of Trebor's ballade *Se Alixandre et Hector fussent en vie*, with ideas for an analytical approach to the musical structure of fourteenth-century chansons. Discusses text underlay, suggesting that Machaut ballades are not texted properly in the sources and should be re-edited; cadences; hexachord structure, with important comments on Hirshberg 1971 and 1980 (86–88); modal structure; and counterpoint. Brown sees a gradual imposition of modality on French and Italian music in the course of the fourteenth century (that fifteenth-century music is modally organized seems to be a given). Brown finds it "impossible to see how modal criteria can be applied to Machaut's ballades" (91 n. 38), but concludes that modality does control the ballades of Trebor (contrast this view with Fuller 1990, 213). Abstract: *RILM* 21 (1987), no. 7324.

Brownlee, Kevin.
1978a. "The Poetic *Œuvre* of Guillaume de Machaut: The Identity of Discourse and the Discourse of Identity." In Cosman 1978, 219–33.

A study of the first-person poet-narrator in Machaut's *Prologue* and *Voir Dit*. The *Roman de la Rose* is the ultimate source of Machaut's poetic identity. The term "poète" was first applied to contemporary vernacular poets by Deschamps in two of his ballades on Machaut (see chap. 2.1.1g and j). See also G. Olson 1979.

1978b. "Transformations of the Lyric 'Je': The Example of Guillaume de Machaut." *Esprit créateur* 18:5–18.

Machaut's first-person poet-narrator persona derives especially from the *Roman de la Rose*, combining the clerkly narrator of Old French romance, the first-person lyric voice, and his own view of himself as a professional writer. Study of the poetic persona in Machaut's *Prologue*, the poet-narrator as "lover-protagonist"—seen in *Vergier, Remede, Alerion, Jugement Navarre*, and *Voir Dit*—and the poet-narrator as "witness-participant"—seen in *Jugement Behaingne, Lyon*, and *Fonteinne. Confort* and *Prise* stand apart.

1984. *Poetic Identity in Guillaume de Machaut*. Madison: University of Wisconsin Press.

Publication of author's 1979 Princeton dissertation. The development of Machaut's poetic voice, with extensive analyses of Machaut's narrative poems (except *Jugement Navarre, Confort*, and *Prise*), analyzed according to the diverse transformations and permutations of the narrator figure (see annotations to Brownlee 1978a and 1978b). Machaut foreshadows the modern concepts of "author" and "book." Abstract: *Forum for Modern Language Studies* 20 (1984): 368. Reviews: C.R. Attwood, *Medium Ævum* 55 (1986): 321–22; Pierre-Yves Badel, *Romania* 107 (1986): 430–31; David A. Fein, *French Review* 59 (1985–86): 124–25; John Hare, *Renaissance and Reformation* 21 (1985): 286–88; Sylvia Huot, *Modern Philology* 84 (1986–87): 63–64; Douglas Kelly, *French Forum* 11 (1986): 95–96; David G. Lanoue, *Philological Quarterly* 65 (1986): 539–40; Ricarda Liver, *Vox romanica* 47 (1988): 274–75; Nadia Margolis, *Speculum* 62 (1987): 388–89; Emanuel J. Mickel, *Romance Quarterly* 34 (1987): 237–39; Don A. Monson, *Modern Language Review* 81 (1986): 477–78; Nigel Wilkins, *French Studies* 40 (1986): 60–61; see also Sturges 1992, 145–46.

1988. "Discourses of the Self: Christine de Pizan and the *Romance of the Rose.*" *Romanic Review* 79:199–221. Also published in *Rethinking the Romance of the Rose: Image, Text, Reception,* ed. Kevin Brownlee and Sylvia Huot, 234–61. University of Pennsylvania Press Middle Ages Series. Philadelphia: University of Pennsylvania Press, 1992.

Christine's modification of courtly and clerkly discourse—both derived from the *Roman de la Rose*—to create a new poetic voice. Studies her *Epistre au Dieu d'Amours, Dit de la Rose,* and *Epistre sur le Débat du "Roman de la Rose."* Brief mention of Machaut's *Rose* and *Voir Dit.*

1989a. "Lyricism in the Age of Allegory." In *A New History of French Literature,* ed. Denis Hollier et al., 109–14. Cambridge, Mass. and London: Harvard University Press.

A concise summary of many of Brownlee's critical concerns with Machaut. Many works surveyed, with special emphasis on *Remede.* Concludes with a brief treatment of Machaut's literary influence.

1989b. "Metaphoric Love Experience and Poetic Craft: Guillaume de Machaut's *Fonteinne Amoureuse.*" In *Poetics of Love in the Middle Ages: Texts and Contexts,* ed. Moshe Lazar and Norris J. Lacy, 147–55. Fairfax, Va.: George Mason University Press.

As the chapter on *Fonteinne* in Brownlee 1984, with some updated references.

1991a. "Guillaume de Machaut's *Remede de Fortune:* The Lyric Anthology as Narrative Progression." In *The Ladder of High Designs: Structure and Interpretation of the French Lyric Sequence,* ed. Doranne Fenoaltea and David Lee Rubin, 1–25. Charlottesville and London: University Press of Virginia.

Important discussion of lyric insertions in the *Remede,* especially concerned with how they fit into the narrative structure. Appendix provides a table showing interlocking relationships among the lyrical insertions (21). Review: Jerry C. Nash, *French Forum* 18 (1993): 80–81.

1991b. "Machaut's Motet 15 and the *Roman de la Rose*: The Literary Context of *Amours qui a le pouoir / Faus Semblant m'a deceü / Vidi Dominum.*" *Early Music History* 10:1–14.

The literary context of M15, relating the texts of the upper voices to the *Roman de la Rose*; close literary analysis of the dialogue between *Faus Samblant* and *Amour,* using Mikhail Bakhtin's literary theory of "dialogic opposition" (polyphonic narrative). Also considers the context of the Biblical citation in the tenor, with brief mention of the literary importance of the tenor texts of *De Bon Espoir / Puis que* (M4), *Qui es / Ha! Fortune* (M8), and *Felix / Inviolata* (M23).

Bryan, William Frank, and Germaine Dempster, eds.
1941. *Sources and Analogues of Chaucer's "Canterbury Tales."* Chicago: University of Chicago Press. Reprint. New York: Humanities Press; London: Routledge and Kegan Paul, 1958.

See R.K. Root 1941 and Work 1941.

Bukofzer, Manfred.
1960. "La musique de danse et la musique instrumentale: La musique des tablatures d'orgue." In *Histoire de la musique.* Vol. 1, *Des origines à Jean-Sébastien Bach,* ed. Roland-Manuel, 856–63. Encyclopédie de la Pléiade 9. [Paris]: Gallimard.

Brief survey of instrumental intabulations, such as those in MS **Fa** [67] (pp. 858–59).

Burke, Mary Ann.
1980. "A Medieval Experiment in Adaptation: Typology and Courtly Love. Poetry in the Second Rhetoric." *Res Publica Litterarum* 3:165–75.

Discussion of Ovidian *exempla* listed in Second Rhetoric treatises, and Machaut's use of mythological references in *Jugement Navarre* (the "figures have a concrete, even historical reality" [166]). Also considers Machaut's adaptation of the mythological figures for particular purposes.

Burkhart, Charles, ed.

1972. *Anthology for Musical Analysis*. 2nd ed. New York: Holt, Rinehart and Winston.
Includes editions of *En mon cuer* (V27/24), and the anonymous *Li enseignement / De touz* (*opus dubium*).

1979. *Anthology for Musical Analysis*. 3rd ed. New York: Holt, Rinehart and Winston. 4th ed. 1986. 5th ed. New York: Harcourt, Brace, 1994.
Includes an edition of *De Bon Espoir / Puis que* (M4) (pp. 12–17).

Burney, Charles.

1776–89. *A General History of Music from the Earliest Ages to the Present Period*. 4 vols. London: Printed for the author. Rev. ed. by Frank Mercer. 2 vols. London, Foulis; New York: Harcourt, Brace, 1935. Reprint. New York: Dover, 1957. London: Folio Society, 1969. London: Eulenberg, 1974.
Includes some mention of Machaut (2:303–5 = rev. ed. 1:614–16), in which Burney notes the inability of his contemporaries to transcribe a single sample of Machaut's music.

Burnley, David.

1986. "Some Terminology of Perception in the *Book of the Duchess*." *English Language Notes* 23/3 (Mar.): 15–22.
Chaucer's *Book of the Duchess* and Machaut's *Remede*.

Burrow, J[ohn] A[nthony].

1971. *Ricardian Poetry: Chaucer, Gower, Langland and the* Gawain *Poet*. London: Routledge and Kegan Paul; New Haven: Yale University Press. Reprint. London: Penguin, 1992.
This brief history of fourteenth-century English poetry includes some interesting remarks on the *Voir Dit*.

1983. "The Portrayal of Amans in *Confessio Amantis*." In *Gower's* Confessio Amantis: *Responses and Reassessments*, ed. A.J. Minnis, 5–24. Cambridge: Brewer.
Mention of *Voir Dit* as an antecedent of John Gower's *Confessio Amantis*.

1988. "The Poet and the Book." In *Genres, Themes, and Images in English Literature: From the Fourteenth to the Fifteenth Century. The J.A.W. Bennett Memorial Lectures, Perugia, 1986*, ed. Piero Boitani and Anna Torti, 230–45. Tübinger Beiträge zur Anglistik 11. Tübingen: Narr.
Study of several examples of late medieval authorial compilations, here termed a "sequence." Considers works by Dante, Petrarch, Machaut, Charles d'Orléans, Juan Ruiz, and Thomas Hoccleve. The *Voir Dit* concerns itself with its own composition and transcription as a book (238–41, 243–44). Hoccleve's *Series* is even more self-referential in this respect; such works are symptomatic of the period of greatest efficiency in manuscript book production, 1300 to 1450.

Burstyn, Shai.

1976. "Power's *Anima mea* and Binchois' *De plus en plus*: A Study in Musical Relationships." *Musica disciplina* 30:55–72.
The motets *Maugré mon cuer / De ma dolour* (M14) and *Li enseignement / De touz* (*opus dubium*, see chap. 7.4) have tenors on texts from the Song of Songs (71).

Busse Berger, Anna Maria.

1990. "Musical Proportions and Arithmetic in the Late Middle Ages and Renaissance." *Musica disciplina* 44:89–118.

Although Euclid and Boethius were required texts in universities and cathedral schools for the instruction of mathematics in the fifteenth century, they were neglected. Instead, treatises of commercial arithmetic became influential in the course of the fifteenth century; there is no evidence that composers knew of the Fibonacci series or the Golden Section at that time. While this article does not engage Machaut directly, it mentions Gombosi 1950 (90 n. 6) and Powell 1979 (91 n. 13); further, it may bear on the analysis of *Amours qui a / Faus Samblant* (M15) proposed by Bent (1991).

Butterfield, Ardis.

1988. "Interpolated Lyric in Medieval Narrative Poetry." Ph.D. diss. Cambridge University.

Not examined. Abstract: *Index to Theses* 38/1 (1988): 25 no. 38-0124.

1991. "Lyric and Elegy in *The Book of the Duchess.*" *Medium Ævum* 60:33–60.

Unusual aspects in Chaucer's borrowings from French models for *The Book of the Duchess*. Includes interesting discussion of the role of *sentement* in Machaut's *Remede, Fonteinne*, and *Voir Dit*.

1994. "Pastoral and the Politics of Plague in Machaut and Chaucer." *Studies in the Age of Chaucer* 16:3–27.

The pastoral tradition in France and England in the fourteenth century, focusing especially on Machaut and Chaucer. Characteristics of the pastoral, encounter, debate, and complaint are also characteristic of the *dit*, although the *dit* is concerned not with shepherdesses and knights, but with the relationship between the clerk poet and his aristocratic patron. After brief discussion of how this operates in *Jugement Behaingne, Remede, Lyon*, and especially *Fonteinne*, Butterfield focuses on the historical prologue to *Navarre* as a "counter-pastoral." In this sense, *Navarre* is much more important to Chaucer's *Book of the Duchess* than has been previously thought. The examples show the interaction between historical event and literary tradition.

Byrne, Donal.

1984. "A Fourteenth-Century French Drawing in Berlin and the *Livre du Voir-Dit* of Guillaume de Machaut." *Zeitschrift für Kunstgeschichte* 47:70–81.

Byrne analyzes a courtly scene in a parchment fragment from the Berlin Kupferstichkabinett (mentioned in Avril 1978, 23 and 28) as a further example of the work of Avril's Master of the *Remede de Fortune*. The activity of this artist is thereby advanced far beyond the chronological bounds laid down by Avril. Byrne's thesis has not met with general acceptance. Review: Léon Gillissen, *Scriptorium* 39 (1985): 13* no. 46.

CCMS.

1979–88. *Census-Catalogue of Manuscript Sources of Polyphonic Music 1400–1550*. Compiled by the University of Illinois Musicological Archives for Renaissance Manuscript Studies. Renaissance Manuscript Studies 1. Neuhausen-Stuttgart: American Institute of Musicology, Hänssler. Vol. 1 (A–J), 1979. Vol. 2 (K–O), 1982. Vol. 3 (P–U), 1984. Vol. 4 (V–Z and Supplement), 1988. Vol. 5 (Cumulative Bibliography and Indices), 1988.

Essential bibliographical tool for information on musical manuscripts, although the time period covered eliminates most of the Machaut manuscripts. Reviews of vol. 1: John Caldwell, *Music and Letters* 61 (1980): 394–95; Giulio Cattin, *Rivista italiana di musicologia* 15 (1980): 276–85; David Fallows, *Early Music* 7 (1979): 535–39; James Haar, *Journal of the American Musicological Society* 33 (1980): 384–89; Martin Just, *Musikforschung* 34 (1981): 344–46; Thomas Noblitt, *Tijdschrift van de Vereniging voor Nederlandse Muziekgeschiedenis* 32 (1982): 156–65.

Caldwell, John.

1978. *Medieval Music*. London: Hutchinson. Bloomington and London: Indiana University Press.

Survey history of medieval music. Machaut is discussed on pp. 170–81.

1980. "Sources of Keyboard Music to 1600." *New Grove* 17:717–33.
Dictionary article; includes a description of MS **Fa** [67] (p. 718).

Calin, Françoise and William.
1974. "Medieval Fiction and New Novel: Some Polemical Remarks on the Subject of Narrative." *Yale French Studies* 51:235–50.
Similarities between medieval and modern fiction, with many comparative examples. Includes consideration of Machaut's *Jugement Navarre, Fonteinne,* and *Voir Dit.*

Calin, William.
1971. "A Reading of Machaut's *Jugement dou Roy de Navarre.*" *Modern Language Review* 66:294–97.
The accepted view is that *Jugement Navarre* reverses the decision of *Jugement Behaingne.* Calin maintains that although Machaut gives this impression, he actually defends the original judgment, and the punishment, that the poet must write more poetry, is ironic. Expanded in Calin 1974, chap. 6.

1974. *A Poet at the Fountain: Essays on the Narrative Verse of Guillaume de Machaut.* Studies in Romance Languages 9. Lexington: The University Press of Kentucky.
With Poirion 1965 and Wimsatt 1968, this work restored Machaut's position as an important and influential figure in French literature. It remains the most broadly-based introductory study to Machaut's entire corpus of narrative poetry, path breaking in its serious treatment of Machaut's poetry as literary works of art. Reviews: Rae S. Baudoin, *Revue des langues romanes* 82 (1976): 283–85; M.-A. Bossy, *Romanic Review* 70 (1979): 187; Alice M. Colby-Hall, *Modern Language Notes* 93 (1978): 765–67; Gerhard Damblemont, *Vox romanica* 41 (1982): 362–63; Robert Deschaux, *Romance Philology* 34 (1980–81): 113–22 (very detailed); Marie-Claire Gérard-Zai, *Studi medievali* 18 (1977): 467–68; Norma L. Goodrich, *Bibliothèque d'Humanisme et Renaissance* 38 (1976): 208–9; John L. Grigsby, *Comparative Literature* 29 (1977): 185–88; William W. Kibler, *Speculum* 52 (1977): 633–34; Reine Mantou, *Revue belge de philologie et d'histoire* 58 (1980): 472; Alice Planche, *Moyen Age* 83 (1977): 375–77; B. Vadin, *Studi francesi* 59 (1976): 330; Colin Wilcockson, *Medium Ævum* 46 (1977): 325–27; Nigel Wilkins, *French Studies* 29 (1975): 314–15; see also Brownlee 1984, 5–6.

1978. "The Poet at the Fountain: Machaut as Narrative Poet." In Cosman 1978, 177–87.
Study of the narrator figure in the *Roman de la Rose* of both Guillaume de Lorris and Jean de Meun, and the development of the comic, naive, maladroit narrator figure in Machaut's *Vergier, Jugement Behaingne,* and *Voir Dit.* See also Calin 1979; 1982.

1979. "Problèmes de technique narrative au Moyen Age: Le *Roman de la Rose* et Guillaume de Machaut." In *Mélanges de langue et de littérature françaises du Moyen Age offerts à Pierre Jonin,* 125–38. Senefiance 7. Aix-en-Provence: C.U.E.R. M.A.
French version of Calin 1978. See also Calin 1982.

1982. "Le *moi* chez Guillaume de Machaut." In Guillaume de Machaut 1982, 241–52.
Reprint of Calin 1979, with additional material on the question of truth and the identity of Toute Belle in the *Voir Dit* (248–50). For Calin, the *Voir Dit* is a work of pure fiction.

1983a. *"La Fonteinne Amoureuse* de Machaut: son or, ses œuvres-d'art, ses mises en abyme." In *L'or au Moyen Age: monnaie-métal-objets-symbole,* 75–87. Senefiance 12. Aix-en-Provence: C.U.E.R. M.A.
An analysis and appreciation of *Fonteinne* from the perspective of the work of art as *mise en abyme.*

1983b. *A Muse for Heroes: Nine Centuries of the Epic in France.* University of Toronto Romance Series 46. Toronto, Buffalo, and London: University of Toronto Press.

Chap. 6 provides an excellent study of Machaut, focusing on the *Jugement Navarre* and *Voir Dit* (141–64). Reviews: Philip E. Bennett, *Modern Language Review* 80 (1985): 926–28; Robert Francis Cook, *Speculum* 60 (1985): 662–64; Larry S. Crist, *Romance Philology* 42 (1988–89): 375–81; Peter F. Dembowski, *Olifant* 9 (1981–82): 151–59; W.G. van Emden, *French Studies* 40 (1986): 368–69; William W. Kibler, *Romance Quarterly* 33 (1986): 491–92; Ruth Morse, *Medium Ævum* 55 (1986): 306–8; Patricia Harris Stablein, *French Review* 60 (1986–87): 112; Karl D. Uitti, *Modern Philology* 83 (1985–86): 416–19.

1987a. *In Defense of French Poetry: An Essay in Revaluation.* University Park and London: Pennsylvania State University Press.

Machaut is given his due as an influential poet in the history of French literature in this wide-ranging appreciation of French poetry. In particular, Calin treats the "biographical fallacy" and Machaut's narrator figure (chap. 2). Reviews: Patrice Bouysse, *Revue de l'histoire littéraire de la France* 89 (1989): 1084–85; Peter Broome, *French Studies* 42 (1988): 375–76; Sarah Kay, *Medium Ævum* 59 (1990): 146–47; Janice L. Pallister, *Seventeenth-Century News* 46 (1988): 78; Roger Pensom, *Modern Language Review* 84 (1989): 972–73; François Rigolot, *Continuum* 2 (1990): 157–58.

1987b. "Machaut's Legacy: The Chaucerian Inheritance Reconsidered." *Studies in the Literary Imagination* 20:9–22.

Excellent summary of the most important Chaucer criticism that concerns French influence, with a defense of Chaucer's French sources. Abstract: Palmer 1987a, 1–3.

1988–89. "Medieval Intertextuality: Lyrical Inserts and Narrative in Guillaume de Machaut." *French Review* 62:1–10.

An analysis of *Remede* using the terminology of intertextual theory.

1990. "Contre la *fin'amor?* Contre la femme? Une relecture de textes du Moyen Age." In *Courtly Literature: Culture and Context. Selected papers from the 5th Triennial Congress of the International Courtly Literature Society, Dalfsen, The Netherlands, 9–16 August, 1986,* ed. Keith Busby and Erik Kooper, 61–82. Utrecht Publications in General and Comparative Literature 25. Amsterdam and Philadelphia: Benjamins.

Texts both for and against *fin'amor*, texts both celebrating and attacking women, and texts in high and low styles were all written for the enjoyment of a noble and courtly audience. Considers a twelfth-century romance, the *pastourelle* genre, the *Roman de la Rose* of Jean de Meun, and Machaut's *Jugement Behaingne* and *Jugement Navarre.*

1993. "Narrative Technique in Fourteenth-Century France: Froissart and His *Chroniques.*" In *Studies in Honor of Hans-Erich Keller: Medieval French and Occitan Literature and Romance Linguistics,* ed. Rupert T. Pickens, 227–236. Kalamazoo, Mich.: The Medieval Institute.

The emergence of the self-conscious artist in the fourteenth century brings with it a sophisticated use of narrative technique. Calin finds that hitherto puzzling aspects of Froissart's narrative in the *Chroniques* are comparable to what is found in Machaut's and Froissart's amorous *dits.*

1994. *The French Tradition and the Literature of Medieval England.* Toronto, Buffalo, and London: University of Toronto Press.

The cultivation of the French language and literature in medieval England, and the influence of the French literary tradition on English vernacular writers (style, rhetoric, rhyme and meter, genre). Calin's study reasserts the importance of the French literary tradition to medieval English literature. Romance scholars of the nineteenth and early twentieth century notoriously neglected middle French literature, and this historiography still colors many modern English literary scholars' views of French influence. For Machaut, Calin focuses on *Remede, Jugement Navarre, Fonteinne,* and *Voir Dit* (198–

229). He traces Machaut's presence in Chaucer, Gower, and Hoccleve. "No one, not even Jean de Meun, had a greater impact shaping the Ricardian poets and their sensibility" (228). Review: R. O'Gorman, *Choice* 32 (1995): 1591–92.

Calvez, Daniel.
1981–82. "La structure du rondeau: mise au point." *French Review* 55:461–70.
Structural flexibility of the fourteenth- and fifteenth-century rondeau, especially when it is not set to music.

Campbell, P[ercy] G[erald] C[adogan].
1924. L'Epître d'Othéa: Etude sur les sources de Christine de Pisan. Paris: Champion.
Christine's sources for the story of Troy and some Ovidian myths include Machaut's *Jugement Navarre* and *Fonteinne*.

Campbell, Thomas P.
1989–90. "Machaut and Chaucer: *Ars nova* and the Art of Narrative." *Chaucer Review* 24:275–89.
Some characteristics of Chaucerian narrative are analogous to contemporary procedures of polyphony; analysis of *Je puis trop* (B28). Includes a corrected practical edition of B28 by Lawrence Earp (280–81). Abstract: Jean E. Jost, *Encomia* 14 (1992): 46–47 no. 162.

Cape, Safford.
1959–60. "The Machaut Mass and its Performance." *Score* 25 (1959): 38–57; and 26 (1960): 20–29.
Detailed movement-by-movement discussion of tempo, voices and instruments, and text underlay by a pioneer among modern conductors of the Mass. Many of Cape's performance suggestions are not supported by more recent studies of performance practice.

Carapetyan, Armen.
1961. *An Early Fifteenth-Century Italian Source of Keyboard Music: The Codex Faenza, Biblioteca Comunale, 117: A Facsimile Edition Presented by Armen Carapetyan.* Musicological Studies and Documents 10. [Rome]: American Institute of Musicology. Also published as: "The Codex Faenza, Biblioteca Comunale, 117 [*Fa*]: A Facsimile Edition Presented by Armen Carapetyan." *Musica disciplina* 13 (1959): 79–107; 14 (1960): 65–104; 15 (1961): 63–104.
Facsimile of the music in MS **Fa** [67], including intabulations of *Hont paur* (B25; fols. 37r–37v) and *De tout flors* (B31; fols. 37v–38v).

Caron.
1860. *Catalogue des manuscrits de la Bibliothèque de la ville d'Arras.* Arras: Courtin.
Catalogue description of MS **Ar** [32] (pp. 458–59, 698).

1861. *Mémoires de l'Académie d'Arras* 33:307–66.
Edition of *Jugement Behaingne* after MS **Ar** [32], ascribed not to Machaut, but to Jehan Désirés, the scribe of MS **Ar**.

Cartier, Normand R.
1966. "Le Bleu Chevalier." *Romania* 87:289–314.
Several quotations demonstrate the dependence of Froissart's *Bleu Chevalier* on Machaut's *Fonteinne*. See Cartier 1967.

1967. "Le *Bleu Chevalier* de Froissart et le *Livre de la Duchesse* de Chaucer." *Romania* 88:232–52.
Discusses the dependence of Chaucer's *Book of the Duchess* on Froissart's *Bleu Chevalier*. (Wimsatt [1972a] finds that the true relationship is the opposite.) Includes further discussion of Machaut's *Fonteinne* as Froissart's model (see Cartier 1966).

Castil-Blaze [François Henri Joseph Blaze].

1832. *Chapelle-musique des rois de France*. Paris: Paulin.

"Philippe-le-Bon, duc de Bourgogne, fonda en sa chapelle de Dijon et collége de l'ordre de la Toison-d'Or, une messe quotidienne et perpétuelle pour être chantée solennellement à haute voix, à chant et à déchant. Une messe de ce genre, composée à quatre parties par Guillaume de Machault, fut exécutée par la Chapelle de Charles V, au sacre de ce prince. Le manuscrit de cette messe est à la Bibliothèque du Roi" (42).

Castro, José Ramón.

1953. *Catálogo del Archivio General de Navarra. Catálogo de la seccion de comptos documentos.* Vol. 3, *Años 1358–1361.* Diputacion foral de Navarra. Archivio General de Navarra. Pamplona: Editorial Aramburu.

Includes abstract of a document of 16 October 1361 concerning a horse given by King Charles of Navarre to Machaut (404 no. 1025).

1956. *Catálogo del Archivio General de Navarra. Catálogo de la seccion de comptos documentos.* Vol. 15, *Años 1384–1385.* Diputacion foral de Navarra. Archivio General de Navarra. Pamplona: Editorial Aramburu.

Includes abstract of a document of 21 January 1384 concerning King Charles of Navarre's purchase of a manuscript of Machaut's *Confort* (19–20 no. 35).

Catalogue générale.

1928. *Catalogue générale des manuscrits des bibliothèques publiques de France. Paris. Bibliothèques de l'Institut. Musée Condé à Chantilly. Bibliothèque Thiers. Musées Jacquemart-André à Paris et à Chaalis.* Paris: Plon.

Standard catalogue description of *F:CH 485* [33] (p. 105) and **Ch** [59] (p. 122).

Caylus [Anne-Claude-Philippe de Tubières de Grimoard de Pestels de Lévy, Comte de].

1753a. "Premier mémoire sur Guillaume de Machaut, poëte et musicien dans le XIVe siècle: Contenant des recherches sur sa vie, avec une notice de ses principaux ouvrages." *Mémoires de littérature, tirés des registres de l'Académie Royale des Inscriptions et Belles-Lettres* 20:399–414.

An early study of Machaut's works, read to the Academy in January 1747.

1753b. "Second mémoire sur les ouvrages de Guillaume de Machaut: Contenant l'histoire de la prise d'Alexandrie, et des principaux évènements de la vie de Pierre de Lusignan, roi de Chypre et de Jérusalem; tirée d'un poëme de cet ecrivain." *Mémoires de littérature, tirés des registres de l'Académie Royale des Inscriptions et Belles-Lettres* 20:415–39.

Second installment of an early study of Machaut's works, read to the Academy in January 1747.

Cazelles, Brigitte

1984. "Souvenez-vous." *Poétique* 60:395–410.

Concerns devotional poetry of the trouvères; mentions Machaut's *Plourez, dames* (B32) (pp. 401–5).

Cazelles, Raymond.

1947. *Jean l'Aveugle: Comte de Luxembourg roi de Bohême.* Bourges: Tardy.

A biography of Machaut's first patron.

1958. *La société politique et la crise de la royauté sous Philippe de Valois.* Bibliothèque Elzévirienne. Nouvelle série. Etudes et documents. Paris: Librairie d'Argences.

A political history of France, 1328–50. Reviews: John le Patourel, *English Historical Review* 76 (1961): 93–96; J.R. Strayer, *Speculum* 34 (1959): 656–58.

1982. *Société politique, noblesse et couronne sous Jean le Bon et Charles V.* Mémoires et documents publiés par la Société de l'Ecole des Chartes 28. Geneva: Droz.

A political history of France, 1350–80. Review: John Bell Henneman, *Speculum* 59 (1984): 127–29.

Černy, Václav.
1982. "Guillaume de Machaut au service du roi de Bohême." In Guillaume de Machaut 1982, 67–68.

Interesting summary of the period of Machaut's direct service to John of Luxembourg.

Cerquiglini, Bernard and Jacqueline.
1976. "L'écriture proverbiale." *Revue des sciences humaines* 163:359–75.

Analysis of proverbs in selected texts of Machaut (*Remede, Fonteinne, Voir Dit*), Froissart, and Deschamps. For the *Voir Dit*, the discussion focuses especially on the articulative function of proverbs in the story of Apollo and Coronis.

1984. "Le Moyen Age." In *Histoire de la littérature française*, ed. Bernard Lecherbonnier, 9–39. Paris: Nathan.

Machaut discussed on pp. 27–34; the approach is similar to Cerquiglini 1983.

Cerquiglini[-Toulet], Jacqueline.
1972–73. "Le 'Voir-Dit' de Guillaume de Machaut et les langues poétiques du Moyen Age." Thèse d'Etat Paris-IV.

Not examined.

1977a. "Le montage des formes: L'exemple de Guillaume de Machaut." *Perspectives médiévales* 3:23–26.

Detailed discussion of the technique of *montage* (see Cerquiglini 1977b) in Machaut's narratives with lyrical insertions, including *Remede* and *Voir Dit*. The narrative frame serves to guarantee the truth of the lyrics and the genuineness of the feeling (*sentement*). Briefly touches upon many ideas that Cerquiglini develops more fully subsequently. See Cerquiglini 1978a and 1985b, chap. 1.2, "Le montage des formes dans le 'Voir Dit.'"

1977b. "Pour une typologie de l'insertion." *Perspectives médiévales* 3:9–14.

Distinguishes three types of narrative with lyrical insertion: *collage* or anthology (thirteenth century), in which miscellaneous lyrics or refrains not by the author of the narrative are included as divertissements and performance pieces; *montage* or *art poétique* (fourteenth century), in which the inserted lyrics, entire poems composed by the author of the narrative, form the pseudo-autobiographical point of departure for the story; and the edition, a mixture of the previous two types, represented uniquely by Froissart's *Meliador*, in which the narrative is designed to incorporate a corpus of lyrics by a different author. A table lays out the characteristics of each type. See also Cerquiglini 1985b, chap. 1.1 "Typologie de l'insertion lyrique." English summary in J.H.M. Taylor 1990, 541–42.

1978a. "Syntaxe et syncope: Le langage du corps et écriture chez Guillaume de Machaut." *Langue française* 40 (Dec.): 60–74.

In the *Voir Dit*, language of the body—concerning heart, eyes, etc.—is one means of authenticating truth; there is a distinction between the truth of lyrics and the truth of the letters. What is true about the *Voir Dit* is the textuality (*écriture*). Includes citations from *Remede* and *Lyon*. Much of this material is revised in Cerquiglini 1985b, part 3, chap. 2, "Ecrire le vrai"; for an English summary of some of the main points and terminology, see Peckham's review of Cerquiglini 1985b (916).

1978b. "Tension sociale et tension d'écriture au XIVème siècle: Les dits de Guillaume de Machaut." In *Littérature et société au Moyen Age*, ed. Danielle Buschinger, 111–29. Actes du colloque d'Amiens des 5 et 6 mai 1978. Paris: Champion.

Concerns the relation between clerk and chevalier in the narrative *dits* of Machaut, especially the *Fonteinne* and *Voir Dit*, but also mentions *Jugement Behaingne, Jugement*

Navarre, Alerion, and *Remede.* Revised in Cerquiglini 1985b, part 2, chap. 1, "Le clerc-écrivain."

1980a. "Le clerc et l'écriture: Le *Voir dit* de Guillaume de Machaut et la définition du *dit.*" In *Literatur in der Gesellschaft des Spätmittelalters,* ed. Hans Ulrich Gumbrecht et al., 151–68. Grundriss der romanischen Literaturen des Mittelalters. Begleitreihe zum GRLMA 1. Heidelberg: Winter.

Machaut's *Voir Dit* is the focus for a wide-ranging study of the definition of the term *dit.* Cerquiglini considers titles, the discontinuity of lyrical insertions, and the stance of the I-narrator as defining characteristics of a new form in the fourteenth century. Cerquiglini pursues the question further in 1988a; see also comments in Huot 1987, 212–13.

1980b. "Le lyrisme en mouvement." *Perspectives médiévales* 6:75–86.

Discusses the fourteenth-century tendency towards a narrative aspect of lyrics, seen in collections (*Cent Ballades*) and in groups of lyrics that treat a similar theme (Machaut's *Loange*). Cerquiglini links this tendency to the new attention to time in literature and life. Consideration of twelfth- and thirteenth-century lyricism compared to late medieval lyricism, with the example the *Cent Ballades* of Jean le Seneschal et al.

1981. "Guillaume de Machaut et l'écriture: L'énigme du 'Voir Dit.'" Thèse de doctorat d'Etat, Paris, Université de Paris-Sorbonne. 3 vols. Microfilm: Lille, Atelier des thèses, no. 12.83.1271.

Revised and much abridged as Cerquiglini 1985b. Abstract: *Perspectives médiévales* 8 (June 1982): 84–88.

1982. "Ethique de la totalisation et esthétique de la rupture dans le *Voir-Dit* de Guillaume de Machaut." In Guillaume de Machaut 1982, 253–62.

Machaut's works exhibit *totalisation*—the urge to collect diverse elements together (the complete-works manuscripts, the *Prologue,* the *Voir Dit* itself), but also *rupture*—discontinuity, by presenting different types of writing at once. Narrative portions comment on the lyric texts, while the Ovidian *exempla* are digressions, forming a kind of verbal polyphony.

1983. "Le nouveau lyrisme (XIVe–XVe siècle)." In Poirion 1983, 275–92.

Rehabilitation of the fourteenth and fifteenth centuries as a time of creative tendencies in literature. Discusses the narrative aspect of the lyrics, textuality, and narratives with lyrical insertions.

1984. "Le clerc et le louche: Sociology of an Esthetic," trans. Monique Briand-Walker. *Poetics Today* 5:479–91.

The literary physical attributes of a clerk, and the change to the more writerly poetics of the fourteenth and fifteenth centuries. Develops ideas also presented in Cerquiglini 1985b, part 2.

1985a. "L'écriture louche. La voie oblique chez les Grands Rhétoriqueurs." In *Les Grands Rhétoriqueurs. Actes du Ve Colloque International sur le Moyen Français. Milan, 6–8 mai 1985,* 1:21–31. Centro Studi sulla Letteratura Medio-Francese 3. Scienze Filologiche e Letteratura 29. Milan: Università Cattolica del Sacro Cuore.

Further development of Cerquiglini 1984, concerning the literary attributes of the writer in the fourteenth and fifteenth centuries.

1985b. *"Un Engin si soutil" : Guillaume de Machaut et l'écriture au XIVe siècle.* Bibliothèque du XVe Siècle 47. Geneva: Slatkine; Paris: Champion.

The most important recent literary analysis of Machaut's narrative poetry, an abridged publication of Cerquiglini 1981. Although focused on the *Voir Dit,* Cerquiglini ranges far beyond this single work. Cerquiglini had access to the unpublished complete edition of the poem by Paul Imbs, and references are freely made to portions of the poem omitted in the Paris 1875 edition. Abstract: *Encomia* 9 (1987): 36 no. 105. Reviews: Badel 1985; Anne Berthelot, *Médiévales* 10 (spring 1986): 130–33; Joël Blanchard, *Moyen français* 17 (1985): 151–52; Frederick Goldin, *Romance Philology* 44 (1990–91): 497–503; Dieter Ingenschay, *Romanische Forschungen* 98 (1986): 423–26; Monique Léonard, *Revue des sciences humaines* 202/2 (1986): 180–81; Löfstedt 1987 (with new material on the title *Voir Dit*, 231); Robert D. Peckham, *Speculum* 62 (1987): 914–16 (corrections); Bernard Ribémont, *Revue des langues romanes* 89 (1985): 287–91; see also abstracts above to Cerquiglini 1978a, 1978b, and 1981; R. Liver review of Brownlee 1984; and Sturges 1992, 146–47.

1986a. "Ecrire le temps. Le lyrisme de la durée aux XIVe et XVe siècles." In *Le temps et la durée dans la littérature au Moyen Age et à la Renaissance. Actes du colloque organisé par le Centre de Recherche sur la Littérature du Moyen Age et de la Renaissance de l'Université de Reims (novembre 1984)*, ed. Yvonne Bellenger, 103–14. Journées rémois 1984 sur le Moyen Age et la Renaissance. Paris: Nizet.

New to lyrics in the fourteenth century is a narrative aspect; also new is an attention to time: viewing the past and the passage of time. The lyrics scattered throughout the *Voir Dit* depict the principal moments of the love affair, similar to scenes in miniatures. Discusses the term *souvenir*. Considers many works and poets, but especially Machaut's *Voir Dit*. Abstract: Gilles Roussineau, *Encomia* 10 (1988): 43 no. 146.

1986b. "Guillaume de Machaut, poète de la subtilité." *Etudes Champenoises* 5:19–25.

Consideration of Machaut's reputation and fame, with an excellent summary of important points in Cerquiglini 1985b.

1987a (ed.). *Guillaume de Machaut. Lob der Frauen. Gedichte altfranzösisch und deutsch. Mit 21 Miniaturen und einer Notenseite aus einer Handschrift des 14. Jahrhunderts*, trans. René Pérennec and Uwe Grüning. Leipzig: Reclam.

New editions, with German translations, of fifty poems of the *Loange des Dames*, including (in this order): *Gent corps* (Lo5=VD42), *Or voy je bien* (Lo11), *On dist souvent* (Lo14), *Ou païs* (Lo17), *Se je me fusse* (Lo24), *Dame plaisant* (Lo26), *Gentils cuers* (Lo27), *Souvent me fait* (Lo32), *Tenus me sui* (Lo36), *Grant merveille* (Lo44), *Trop me seroit* (Lo50), *Trop est crueus* (Lo51), *Helas! pour quoy* (Lo53), *Se faire sçay* (Lo55), *Helas! je sui* (Lo56), *Dame, merci* (Lo66), *Las! j'ai failli* (Lo70), *Douce dame, vous* (Lo73), *Aucunes gens* (Lo75), *Puis que j'empris* (Lo77), *Blanche com lis* (Lo82), *N'est pas doleur* (Lo83), *Loing de mon cuer* (Lo86), *Certes mes dous* (Lo90), *Vo dous gracieus* (Lo92), *D'uns dous ueil* (Lo94), *Un dous regart* (Lo95), *Nulz homs ne puet* (Lo97), *La grant ardeur* (Lo99), *Li cuers me tramble* (Lo104), *Hé! mesdisans* (Lo127), *Se pleins fusse* (Lo145), *Peines, doleurs* (Lo147), *Trop se peinne* (Lo164), *Ne pensés pas* (Lo174), *Li plus grans biens* (Lo180=VD30), *Pour Dieu* (Lo183), *Il m'est avis* (Lo188=B22), *Helas! pour ce que* (Lo189), *On ne puet riens* (Lo192), *Je puis trop* (Lo203=B28), *Une vipere* (B27; cf. Lo204), *Je maudi l'eure* (Lo213), *Helas! dolens* (Lo215), *Je preing congié* (Lo223), *Se je vous aim* (Lo231), *Dire scens* (Lo233), *Certes mon oueil* (Lo234=R15), *Je di qu'il n'a* (Lo242), and *Quant je commençay* (Lo246). The publication contains several color facsimiles of miniatures from MS **F-G**, as well as G fol. 153r, containing *Ma fin* (R14) and *Certes, mon oueil* (R15). The afterword by Cerquiglini (123–44) has a brief biography and introduction to the *Loange*, comments on poems included in the edition, and notes on language by René Pérennec (145–48).

1987b. "Guillaume de Machaut ou de Machault (v. 1300–1377)." In *Dictionnaire des littératures de langue française*, ed. J.-P. de Beaumarchais, Daniel Couty, and Alain Rey, 1068–69. 4 vols., continuous pagination. Paris: Bordas.

Dictionary article; includes a succinct treatment of the innovative narrator persona in Machaut's *dits*.

1987c. "Quand la voix s'est tue: La mise en recueil de la poésie lyrique au XIVe et XVe siècles." In *La présentation du livre. Actes du colloque de Paris X-Nanterre (4, 5, 6 décembre 1985)*, ed. Emmanuèle Baumgartner and Nicole Boulestreau, 313–27. Littérales 2. Cahiers du Département de Français, Paris X-Nanterre. Paris: Centre de Recherches du Département de

Français de Paris X-Nanterre. Also appears in *Der Ursprung von Literatur: Medien, Rollen, Kommunikationssituationen zwischen 1450 und 1650*, ed. Gisela Smolka-Koerdt et al., 136–48. Materialität der Zeichen. Munich: Fink, 1988.

A principal difference between lyricism of the twelfth and thirteenth centuries compared to the fourteenth and fifteenth centuries is the immediate organization of the latter into collections. Three different kinds of lyric compilations are seen in the fourteenth and fifteenth centuries, (1) lyrics organized into a larger work, as Machaut's *Voir Dit*; (2) the lyric collection as an album; and (3) the collection as an anthology, a selection of lyrics without a single theme, as in the *Jardin de Plaisance*. Considers Froissart, Oton de Granson, and Machaut's *Voir Dit* especially; aspects are revisited in Cerquiglini 1991a.

1988a. "Le dit." In Poirion 1988b, 86–94.

Develops Cerquiglini 1980a, with further discussion of elements of fragmentation and textuality in the *dit*. Examples from many authors, including Machaut.

1988b. "Le rondeau." In Poirion 1988b, 45–58.

Survey of the history, structure, aesthetic, and function of the rondeau.

1991a. "Fullness and Emptiness: Shortages and Storehouses of Lyric Treasure in the Fourteenth and Fifteenth Centuries," trans. Christine Cano and John Jay Thompson. *Yale French Studies Special Edition; Contexts: Style and Values in Medieval Art and Literature*, ed. Daniel Poirion and Nancy Freeman Regalado, 224–39.

Two images in Froissart, making garlands of flowers, and enclosing lyrical poems in boxes, are related to the emergence of the professional writer, who was concerned with anxieties over poetic composition, demands of the patron, and maintaining his works. The discussion of the "aesthetic of the book" (236–39) further develops aspects of Cerquiglini 1987c. Mentions Machaut's *Prologue*, *Fonteinne*, and *Voir Dit*.

1991b. "Le *Voir Dit* mis à nu par ses éditeurs, même. Etude de la réception d'un texte à travers ses éditions." In *Mittelalter-Rezeption. Zur Rezeptionsgeschichte der romanischen Literaturen des Mittelalters in der Neuzeit*, ed. Reinhold R. Grimm, 337–80. Grundriss der romanischen Literaturen des Mittelalters. Begleitreihe zum GRLMA 2. Heidelberg: Winter.

Fascinating account of the history of the *Voir Dit* in its editions of Tarbé (1849; 1856) and P. Paris (1875). Consideration of order of letters and lines omitted by Paris, which reveal his own view of the work, one which badly misrepresents Machaut's *dit*.

1993a. "Cadmus ou Carmenta: Réflexion sur le concept d'invention à la fin du Moyen Age." In *What is Literature? France 1100–1600*, ed. François Cornilliat, Ullrich Langer, and Douglas Kelly, 211–30. The Edward C. Armstrong Monographs on Medieval Literature 7. Lexington, Ky.: French Forum.

Discussion of the medieval concept of invention; includes consideration of the "Roi qui ne ment" episode in the *Voir Dit* (216–18).

1993b. *La couleur de la mélancolie. La fréquentation des livres au XIVe siècle, 1300–1415*. Collection Brèves Littérature. Paris: Hatier.

Characterization of the fourteenth century in French literature, extending approximately from the accession of the Valois (1328) to the Battle of Agincourt (1415). For Cerquiglini-Toulet, themes of melancholy confirm Huizinga's metaphor of an "autumn" (Huizinga 1924). Cerquiglini-Toulet develops a number of topics: the supplanting of Latin by French; the concern for genealogical hierarchy (paternity) represented in literature by questions of authority and heritage; the clerkly writer and his patrons and *auctoritates* (predecessors, models); the *Cour d'Amour*; new subject matters besides the traditional *armes et amours*; images of poetic creation and the book. Machaut cited passim, esp. *Fonteinne* and *Voir Dit*. Parts of Cerquiglini-Toulet 1991a reappear in chap. 4. Reviews: Pierre-Yves Badel, *Romania* 112 (1991): 564; Renate Blumenfeld-Kosinski, *Romance Philology* 48 (1995): 300–302; M.J. Freeman, *French Studies* 49 (1995): 186–87.

1993c. "*Fama* et les preux: Nom et renom à la fin du Moyen Age." *Médiévales* 24 (spring): 35–44.

Authors utilized lists of renowned names in fourteenth-century poetry, such as the *Neuf Preux*, the *Neuf Preuses*, or the nine muses, to include the name of a patron or even to introduce the poet's own name. Poets guaranteed themselves undying renown through their writings. Mentions *Prologue*, *Voir Dit*, *Prise*, and Deschamps's *déploration*.

1993d (ed. and trans.). *Guillaume de Machaut. La Fontaine Amoureuse*. Moyen Age. Paris: Stock.

Introductory essay on the *Fonteinne*, with a new edition and translation into modern French. Review: Adrian Armstrong, *French Studies* 49 (1995): 183–84.

Cerquiglini, Jacqueline and Anne Berthelot, eds. and trans.
1987. *Poètes du Moyen Age. Chants de guerre, d'amour et de mort*. Preface by Jacques Roubaud. Paris: Librairie Générale Française.

Anthology of medieval French poetry in modern French translations, with brief biographies of the poets and commentary. Includes eight works of Machaut, cited here by the original titles: *A toi, Hanri* (Cp3), *Je puis trop* (Lo203=B28), *Se pour ce muir* (Lo238= VD60=B36), *Plourez, dames* (Lo229= VD5=B32), *Dou memoire* (Lo253), *Blanche com lis* (Lo82), *Quant Colette* (Lo237), and *Ma fin* (R14).

Chailley, Jacques.
1948 (ed.). *Guillaume de Machaut (1300–1377): Messe Nostre Dame dite du Sacre de Charles V (1364) à 4 voix égales*. La Musique Française au Moyen-Age. Répertoire de la Psallette Notre-Dame. Paris: Rouart & Lerolle.

One of the earliest editions of the complete Machaut Mass, transposed down a fourth and edited for practical performance. Reviews: Willi Apel, *Speculum* 26 (1951): 187–90 (reprinted in Apel 1986, 193–96); Leonard Ellinwood, *Notes* 7 (1949–50): 130–31.

1950. *Histoire musicale du Moyen Age: Les genèses, les monuments*. Paris: Presses Universitaires de France. 2nd ed. *Histoire musicale du Moyen Age*. Collection Hier. Paris: Presses Universitaires de France, 1969. 3rd ed. Quadrige 55. Paris: Presses Universitaires de France, 1984.

On Machaut, see esp. 240–49 (1st ed.); 247–57 (2nd ed.). Abstract: *RILM* 3 (1969), no. 488.

1960. "La musique post-Grégorienne: L'Ars nova." In *Histoire de la musique*. Vol. 1, *Des origines à Jean-Sébastien Bach*, ed. Roland-Manuel, 765–80. Encyclopédie de la Pléiade 9. [Paris]: Gallimard.

Survey of music of the Ars Nova.

1972. "Machault (Machau, Machaut) Guillaume de." In *Rizzoli Ricordi Enciclopedia della musica*, ed. Angelo Solmi, 4:77–79. Milan: Rizzoli.

Dictionary article. Includes reproductions of miniatures C36 (see chap. 4.4e), D1 (in color; see chap. 4.4p), and A2 (in color; see chap. 4.4a).

1973. "Du cheval de Guillaume de Machaut à Charles II de Navarre." *Romania* 94:251–58.

Includes summary publication and discussion of a 1361 document concerning a horse given by King Charles of Navarre to Machaut (see chap. 1.12.2).

1982. "La composition dans la *Messe* de Guillaume de Machaut." In Guillaume de Machaut 1982, 281–88.

An attempt to establish a step-by-step compositional procedure for the Mass, especially the Kyrie, which would have been carried out presumably on a slate. Leech-Wilkinson (1989; 1990c) has a better treatment of the question of compositional procedure.

Champion, Pierre.
1910. "Un 'liber amicorum' du XVe siècle: Notice d'un manuscrit d'Alain Chartier ayant appartenu à Marie de Clèves, femme de Charles d'Orléans (Bibl. Nat., ms. français 20026)." *Revue des bibliothèques* 20:320–26.

Study of **Ra** [44], a fifteenth-century manuscript containing *Jugement Behaingne*.

Chevalier, Cyr Ulisse Joseph.

1905. *Répertoire des sources historiques du Moyen Age. Bio-bibliographie*, Vol. 1. Rev. ed. Paris: Picard. Reprint. New York: Kraus, 1960.

Bibliography, still valuable for nineteenth-century items. For Machaut, see pp. 1956–57.

Chichmaref, Vladimir F.

1909 (ed.). *Guillaume de Machaut: Poésies lyriques. Edition complète en deux parties, avec introduction, glossaire et fac-similés publiée sous les auspices de la Faculté d'Histoire et de Philologie de Saint-Pétersbourg.* 2 vols., continuous pagination. Paris: Champion, [1909]. Reprint in one volume. Geneva: Slatkine, 1973.

Standard edition of the lyrical works of Machaut. Based on **F-G**, and not a critical edition. An appendix gives some works that appear in MS **J** that are doubtless unauthentic. Wilkins (1972) provides a more recent edition of most of the works in Chichmaref 1909, arranged by genre in alphabetical order. Chichmaref 1909 has the advantage of presenting the lyrics in an authoritative manuscript order, and thus retains its utility, with readings corrected after the reviews. Reviews: Guesnon 1912 (corrections); E. Hoepffner, *Literaturblatt für germanische und romanische Philologie* 31 (1910): 22–26 (many corrections); A. Jeanroy, *Revue critique d'histoire et de littérature* 68 (1909): 405–7 (corrections); A. Jeanroy, *Journal des Savants* (1911): 187–88; Leo Jordan, *Zeitschrift für französische Sprache und Literatur* 35/2 (1909): 198–200; Ernest Langlois, *Bibliothèque de l'Ecole des Chartes* 71 (1910): 94–96; Raynaud 1909 (corrections); further, Ludwig 1926–54, 2:7b*– 8a* n. 3 and 2:45b* has some important corrections.

1911. *Lirika i Liriki pozdnyago srednevekovya. Ocherki po istorii poezii Franzii i Provansa* (Lyrical poetry and lyrical poets of the late Middle Ages. Studies on the history of French and Provençal poetry). Paris: Danzig.

The reviews give summaries of the contents; the book is apparently far ahead of its time (Cerquiglini 1985b, 125 n. 32). Reviews: Myrrha Borodine, *Romania* 41 (1912): 127–31; Guesnon 1912.

Clarkson, G[eorge] Austin E.

1971. "On the Nature of Medieval Song: The Declamation of Plainchant and the Lyric Structure of the Fourteenth-Century Motet." Ph.D. diss. Columbia University, 1970. Ann Arbor: University Microfilms. Order no. 7117475.

Includes a study of versification and declamation in fourteenth-century motet poetry, comprising a repertory of 141 works. Concerning Machaut's French motets, see also Lühmann 1978, 141–72. Abstract: *DAI* A 32/1 (July 1971): 473–74.

Clemen, Wolfgang.

1963. *Chaucer's Early Poetry*, trans. C.A.M. Sym. London: Methuen. New York: Barnes and Noble, 1964. Originally published as *Chaucers frühe Dichtung*. Göttingen and Zurich: Vandenhoeck & Ruprecht, 1963. Based on *Der junge Chaucer: Grundlagen und Entwicklung seiner Dichtung.* Kölner anglistische Arbeiten 33. Bochum-Langendreer: Pöpinghaus, 1938.

Includes discussion of Machaut's influence on Chaucer, especially concerning *Jugement Behaingne* and *Fonteinne*.

Cocco, Marcello.

1971. "L'inedito *Roman de Cardenois* et la fortuna di Guillaume de Machaut." *Cultura neolatina* 31:125–53.

The *Roman de Cardenois* (MS [43]) is an anonymous fifteenth-century prose romance with insertions from Machaut's *Jugement Behaingne*, *Mon cuer, m'amour* (Cp6), *Hé! gentilz cuers* (Lo37), *Douce dame, vous ociés* (Lo73), *Quant vrais amans* (Lo216), *Amis, mon cuer* (Lo220), *Qui n'aroit* (RF1), *Riches d'amour* (B5), *Diex, Biauté* (V19), and *Je ne me puis* (V33).

1975 (ed.). *Roman de Cardenois*. Testi e Saggi di Letterature Moderne. Testi 6. Bologna: Pàtron.
See description of Cocco 1971; this edition has not been well received critically.
Reviews: Kurt Baldinger, *Zeitschrift für romanische Philologie* 93 (1977): 396–97 (corrections); Roberto Crespo, *Studi medievali* 16 (1975): 450; Philippe Ménard, *Romance Philology* 39 (1985–86): 121–23 (many corrections); Speroni 1977 (many corrections).

Coen Pirani, Emma.
1966. *La miniatura gotica*. Milan: Fratelli Fabbri. Translation as Emma Pirani. *Gothic Illuminated Manuscripts*, trans. Margaret Crosland. London: Hamlyn, 1970.
Color reproduction of *Remede* miniature C41 (p. 131 plate 58, discussed p. 136).

Cogan, Robert, and Pozzi Escot.
1976. *Sonic Design: The Nature of Sound and Music*. Englewood Cliffs, N.J.: Prentice Hall. Reprint. Cambridge, Mass.: Publication Contact International, 1985.
Chapters 2–3 include extensive analyses of *Plus dure* (V31/28) and portions of the Mass.

1981. *Sonic Design: Practice and Problems*. Englewood Cliffs, N.J.: Prentice Hall. Reprint. Cambridge, Mass.: Publication Contact International, 1984.
Editions of *Hé! dame de valour* (V11) and *Tres douce dame que* (B24), with questions for analysis.

Cohen, Gustave.
1947. "Le *Voir Dit* de Guillaume de Machaut (vers 1365)." *Lettres romanes* 1: 99–111.
A partial plot summary, with excerpts. Cohen accepts the work as a literal account of a love affair.

1949. *La vie littéraire en France au Moyen Age*. Histoire de la Vie Littéraire. Paris: Tallandier.
Includes discussion and excerpts from *Voir Dit* (esp. 273–88).

1951. *Littérature française du Moyen Age*. Collection "J'apprends à loisir." Lausanne: Payot.
Includes discussion and excerpts from *Voir Dit* (esp. 81–84). Not useful.

1952. *La poésie en France au Moyen Age*. Bibliothèque d'Etudes Historiques. Paris: Richard-Masse.
See chap. 7 (87–101), "Un grand compositeur en notes et en vers au XIVe siècle: Guillaume de Machaut." After a brief biography, Cohen concentrates on the *Voir Dit*.

Collin, Simone.
1977. "A l'occasion d'un sixième centenaire: La vie et l'œuvre de Guillaume de Machaut." *Revue Historique Ardennaise* 12:41–52.
A brief overview of Machaut's life and works, for popular consumption.

Combarieu, J[ules].
1913. *Histoire de la musique des origines au début du XXe siècle*. Vol. 1, *Des origines à la fin du XVIe siècle*. Paris: Colin.
Brief mention of *Dous viaire* (R1) and *Ma fin* (R14); interesting discussion of *Rose, lis* (R10) (pp. 391–99).

Connery, William Joseph.
1974. "The Poet and the Clerk: A Study of the Narrative Poetry of Guillaume de Machaut." Ph.D. diss. Yale University. Ann Arbor: University Microfilms. Order no. 7425728.
Discussion of *Vergier, Jugement Behaingne, Jugement Navarre, Remede, Confort, Fonteinne*, and *Voir Dit*. The learned, clerical aspect is dominant in early and middle-period works, while the poet becomes increasingly important for the *Fonteinne* and *Voir Dit*. Abstract: *DAI* A 35/5 (Nov. 1974): 2933.

Constans, Léopold.
1904. "Le Songe vert." *Romania* 33:490–539.
Includes a description of *F:CF 249* [42] (pp. 491–94).

Coover, James, and Richard Colvig.
1964. *Medieval and Renaissance Music on Long-Playing Records*. Detroit Studies in Music Bibliography 6. Detroit, Mich.: Information Service.
Discography.

1973. *Medieval and Renaissance Music on Long-Playing Records: Supplement, 1962–1971*. Detroit Studies in Music Bibliography 26. Detroit, Mich.: Information Coordinators.
Discography.

Cordey, Jean.
1911. *Les comtes de Savoie et les rois de France pendant la guerre de cent ans (1329-1391)*. Bibliothèque de l'Ecole des Hautes Etudes... Sciences Historiques et Philologiques 189. Paris: Champion.
Includes mention of a 1368 document concerning Machaut and the Green Count of Savoy.

Cosman, Madeleine Pelner, and Bruce Chandler, eds.
1978. *Machaut's World: Science and Art in the Fourteenth Century*. Annals of the New York Academy of Sciences 314. New York: New York Academy of Sciences.
Report of the 1977 New York Machaut conference. Not all of the articles pertain to Machaut directly; six are indexed here: Brownlee 1978a, Calin 1978, Poirion 1978, M. Thomas 1978, Williams 1978, and Uitti 1978. Reviews: Dorothy Koenigsberger, *Technology and Culture* 25 (1984): 328–32; Claudia Kren, *Isis* 71 (1980): 508–9; Robert S. Sturges, *Romanic Review* 72 (1981): 496–98; Nicholas H. Steneck, *Annals of Science* 39 (1982): 611–12; Claude Thiry, *Moyen Age* 91 (1985): 130–32.

Couderc, Camille, et al.
1890. *Catalogue général des manuscrits des bibliothèques publiques de France. Départements*. Vol. 14, *Clermont-Ferrand, Caen, Toulon, Draguignan, Fréjus, Grasse, Nice, Tarascon*. Ministère de l'Instruction Publique et des Beaux-Arts. Paris: Plon.
Catalogue of the manuscripts at Clermont-Ferrand, including *F:CF 249* [42] (pp. 82–88).

Couderc, Camille.
1889. "Notice du ms. 249 de la bibliothèque de Clermont-Ferrand." *Bulletin de la Société des Anciens Textes Français* 15:98–114.
A description and inventory of *F:CF 249* [42].

1910. *Album de portraits d'après les collections du département des manuscrits [de la Bibliothèque Nationale]*. Paris: Berthaud Frères.
Black-and-white reproduction of *Prologue* miniature A1 (plate 18; description p. 8).

Coussemaker, Charles Edmond de.
1864–76 (ed.). *Scriptorum de musica medii aevi novam seriem a Gerbertina alteram*. 4 vols. Paris: Durand, 1864–76. Reprint. Hildesheim: Olms, 1963.
For abstract and list of contents, see Hughes 1980, 127–29 no. 925.

Coville, Alfred.
1938. "Ecrits contemporains sur la peste de 1348 à 1350." In *Histoire littéraire de la France* 37:325–90. Paris: Imprimerie Nationale.
Includes discussion of *Jugement Navarre* (326).

1949. "Poèmes historiques de l'avènement de Philippe VI de Valois au traité de Calais (1328–1360)." In *Histoire littéraire de la France* 38:259–333. Paris: Imprimerie Nationale.
Includes brief survey of Machaut's narrative poems as historical sources (328–31), esp. *Jugement Navarre* (329–30).

Covington, Kate.
  1978. "A Theory of Dissonance in the Fourteenth Century." *Indiana Theory
    Review* 2:29–40.
    A traditional and anachronistic analysis of dissonance treatment in *Plus dure* (V31/28), *Se
    je souspir* (V36), *Ma chiere* (B40), and *Trop plus / Biauté* (M20), along with some Italian
    trecento works.

Cox, Eugene L.
  1967. The Green Count of Savoy: Amadeus VI and Transalpine Savoy in the
    Fourteenth Century. Princeton, N.J.: Princeton University Press.
    Includes material on a 1368 document concerning Machaut and the Green Count.

Cramer, Eugen Casjen.
  1975. "Guillaume de Machaut, *La Messe de Notre Dame.*" *Adagio* 1/5
    (Sept.): 17–21.
    Examination of performance practice in four recordings of the Mass. Not examined.
    Abstract: *RILM* 10 (1976), no. 15176.

Crawford, William R.
  1967. *Bibliography of Chaucer 1954–63*. Seattle: University of Washington
    Press.
    Standard bibliography. See also Griffith 1955; Baird 1977; Baird-Lange/Schnuttgen 1988.

Crocker, Richard L.
  1966. *A History of Musical Style*. McGraw-Hill Series in Music. New York:
    McGraw-Hill. Reprint. New York: Dover, 1986.
    Insightful survey of music, with a brief discussion of Machaut (121–26), and some ana-
    lytical comments on *Mes esperis* (B39). Crocker's interesting theory of the development
    of the polyphonic song (116–19, 123–29) is thoroughly worked out in Hasselman 1970.
    Abstract: Hughes 1980, 13 no. 27. Reviews: Martin Chusid, *Notes* 23 (1966–67): 732–
    33; Henry Leland Clark, *Journal of the American Musicological Society* 21 (1968): 103–
    5; Gwynn S. McPeek, *Journal of Research in Music Education* 15 (1967): 333–36; James
    Pruett, *Journal of Music Theory* 11 (1967): 144–49; Leo Treitler, *Perspectives of New
    Music* 7/2 (spring-summer 1969): 1–58 (esp. 36–44).
  1967. "A New Source for Medieval Music Theory." *Acta musicologica* 39:
    161–71. [See also Margaret Bent, "A Postscript on the Berkeley Theory
    Manuscript,"*Acta musicologica* 40 (1968): 175.]
    First description of the Berkeley treatise, which includes a ballade resembling Machaut's
    Je puis trop (B28) (discussed p. 166; ed. pp. 169–71 by Thomas Walker). Abstract:
    RILM 1 (1967), no. 1178.

Cropp, Glynnis M.
  1982–83. "Les manuscrits du 'Livre de Boece de Consolacion.'" *Revue
    d'histoire des textes* 12–13:263–352.
    Includes a description of MS **Pm** [18].

Cross, Lucy E.
  1990. "Chromatic Alteration and Extrahexachordal Intervals in Fourteenth-
    Century Polyphonic Repertories." Ph.D. diss. Columbia University. Ann
    Arbor: University Microfilms. Order no. 9118548.
    In the fourteenth century, chromatic alterations were not part of the performance practice;
    chromatic "extrahexachordal" intervals were either directly specified or implied by the
    counterpoint, and composers had one version of a given work's intervallic content in
    mind. Includes a thorough examination of evidence from the theorists concerning *musica
    ficta*. Cross considers several examples from Machaut mainly in her discussions of
    extrahexachordal intervals, such as the tritone, major seventh, augmented second, and
    diminished fourth. Cited by Fuller (1992b, 255 n. 28, 256 n. 42). Abstract: *DAI* A 52/2
    (Aug. 1991): 336.

Croucher, Trevor.
   1981. *Early Music Discography: From Plainsong to the Sons of Bach.* 2 vols.
   Phoenix, Ariz.: Oryx; London: Library Association.
   Discography. Includes a useful "international guide to record label distribution" that charts
   the names that companies use in different countries (1:ix–xvi).

Crow, Martin M., and Clair C. Olson.
   1966. *Chaucer Life-Records.* Austin: University of Texas Press. Oxford:
   Clarendon.
   Documentary material on Chaucer's life. See pp. 23–28 on Chaucer's capture during the
   Siege of Reims.

Cyrus, Cynthia J.
   1991–92. "Musical Distinctions between Descorts and Lais: Non-Strophic
   Genres in the Troubadour and Trouvère Repertory." *Ars Musica Denver*
   4:3–19.
   Useful discussion of musical distinctions in the Old French repertory of lais and descorts.
   Generic distinctions—clear in the music—coalesce late in the thirteenth century.
   Machaut's strictly-defined works fall outside the period of development covered here,
   although Cyrus discusses the immediate predecessors of Machaut's lais in the *Roman de
   Fauvel* (MS *F:Pn 146*) (pp. 13–16).

DA.
   1952–June 1969. *Dissertation Abstracts.* Vols. 12–29. Ann Arbor: University
   Microfilms.
   Standard index of American dissertations.

DAI.
   July 1969–. *Dissertation Abstracts International.* Vols. 30–. Ann Arbor: Uni-
   versity Microfilms (from July 1976: University Microfilms International).
   Standard index, primarily of American dissertations.

DDC.
   1935–65. *Dictionnaire de droit canonique,* ed. R. Naz. 6 vols. Paris:
   Letouzey et ané.
   Important dictionary for liturgical matters.

D'Accone, Frank.
   1984. "Una nuova fonte dell'*ars nova* italiana: Il codice di San Lorenzo,
   2211." *Studi musicali* 13:3–31.
   First description of MS **SL** [65].

Dahlhaus, Carl.
   1982. "'Zentrale' und 'periphere' Züge in der Dissonanztechnik Machauts."
   In *Aktuelle Fragen der musikbezogenen Mittelalterforschung: Texte zu
   einem Basler Kolloquium des Jahres 1975,* 281–299 (discussion, 300–
   305). Forum Musicologicum: Basler Beiträge zur Musikgeschichte 3.
   Winterthur: Amadeus.
   Syncopated dissonances at the beginning of *S'Amours ne fait* (B1) resolve according to
   sixteenth-century principles of counterpoint, while a chain of syncopated dissonances in
   Biauté qui (B4) does not. Is the dissonance practice of B1 therefore "central" and that of B4
   "peripheral" for the fourteenth century? Dahlhaus ruminates on this point, considering
   what questions one may fairly pose about such a situation. One cannot use sixteenth-
   century terminology (as in Reaney 1968) to describe Machaut's practice. The article poses
   interesting questions for the application of discant theory to Machaut's music. See also
   Kühn (1973, 74–75) on this question. Abstract: *RILM* 16 (1982), no. 1514.

Damerini, Adelmo.
   1960. "Guglielmo de Machaut e l'Ars Nova' italiana." In *Scritti vari dedicati
   a Marino Parenti per il suo sessantesimo anniversario,* ed. Giovanni
   Semerano, 157–66. Contributi alla Biblioteca Bibliografica italica diretta da

Marino Parenti 23. Florence: Sansoni. Reprint. Biblioteca degli eruditi e dei bibliofili, Scritti di bibliografia e di erudizione raccolti da Marino Parenti 51. Florence: Sansoni, 1960.

A very general look at Machaut's life and works. Damerini sees an Italian stamp in the embellished melodic style of some Machaut lais and chansons. Critical summary in Connery 1974, 15.

Danckwardt, Marianne.
1993. "Möglichkeiten dreistimmigen Komponierens bei Guillaume de Machaut." In *De musica et cantu: Studien zur Geschichte der Kirchenmusik und der Oper; Helmut Hucke zum 60. Geburtstag*, ed. Peter Cahn and Ann-Katrin Heimer, 372–83. Musikwissenschaftliche Publikationen. Hochschule für Musik und darstellende Kunst Frankfurt/Main 2. Hildesheim, Zurich, and New York: Olms.

Distinguishes basically two compositional procedures in 3-voice works. In the motet, static sonorities (cf. Pelinski 1975) provide rhythmic articulation (*talea*), while the recurrence of perfect sonorities provide the articulation of pitch (*color*); text, rhythm, and pitch are independent layers of structure. In the chanson, the point of departure is the rhythm and melody of the cantus, regulated by the text, and all parameters of the polyphonic structure work together. *Dame, je sui / Fins cuers* (M11) operates less like a motet than a chanson and is possibly an early example of the new style of 3-voice composition.

Davenport, W[illiam] A[nthony].
1988. *Chaucer: Complaint and Narrative*. Chaucer Studies 14. Cambridge: Brewer.

Chaucer's use of complaint—passages of lament—with discussion of French models.

David, Alfred.
1992. "Chaucer's Edwardian Poetry." In *The Idea of Medieval Literature: New Essays on Chaucer and Medieval Culture in Honor of Donald R. Howard*, ed. James M. Dean and Christian K. Zacher, 35–54. Newark: University of Delaware Press; London and Toronto: Associated University Press.

Study of Chaucer's early poetry. Machaut is discussed on pp. 37–41, especially *Jugement Behaingne* as a source for the *Book of the Duchess*.

Davis, Steven B.
1991. "The Mediating Vision: Patronage and Literary Tradition in Guillaume de Machaut and Chaucer's *Book of the Duchess*." Ph.D. diss. Yale University. Ann Arbor: University Microfilms. Order no. 9224335.

Develops a reading of Chaucer's *Book of the Duchess* that takes Machaut's *dits* as a point of departure. "It appears that in his first narrative poem, Chaucer was responding to the problematic relationship of poet and patron as depicted by Machaut" (author's abstract). Abstract: *DAI* A 53/4 (Oct. 1992): 1154.

Davison, Archibald T., and Willi Apel.
1949. *Historical Anthology of Music*. Vol. 1, *Oriental, Medieval and Renaissance Music*. Cambridge, Mass.: Harvard University Press; London: Cumberlege, Oxford University Press, 1946. Rev. ed. Cambridge, Mass.: Harvard University Press, 1949.

Includes editions, commentary, and translations of *S'il estoit / S'Amours* (M6), *Je puis trop* (B28), *Comment qu'a moy* (V5), and *Plus dure* (V31/28).

Dean, James.
1985. "Chaucer's *Book of the Duchess*: A Non-Boethian Interpretation." *Modern Language Quarterly* 46:235–49.

The theme of consolation in the *Book of the Duchess* does not derive directly from Boethius, but from Chaucer's reading of French courtly poems such as the *Remede*.

Dear, F.M.
1938. "Chaucer's *Book of the Lion.*" *Medium Ævum* 7:105–12.
Speculations concerning Chaucer's lost *Book of the Lion* and its relationship to Machaut's *Lyon*. Includes an English plot summary of *Lyon* (111–12).

De Boer, Cornelis.
1913. "Een Frans 'classicus' uit de veertiende eeuw." In *Handelingen van het zevende Nederlandse Filologen-Kongres*, 81–92. Groningen, The Netherlands, 27 March 1913. Groningen: Wolters.
Summary of a conference report on the importance of the *Ovide Moralisé* for fourteenth- and fifteenth-century French poets, with consideration of Machaut's *Voir Dit* and *Jugement Navarre* (88–90).

1914. "Guillaume de Machaut et l'*Ovide Moralisé*." *Romania* 43:335–52. Reprint. De Boer 1915–38, 1:28–43.
Machaut's use of the moralized French translation of Ovid's *Metamorphoses* in lieu of the original Latin for *exempla* in *Voir Dit, Jugement Navarre, Fonteinne,* and *Confort.*

1915–38 (ed.). *Ovide Moralisé. Poème du commencement du quatorzième siècle, publié d'après tous les manuscrits connus.* Vol. 1 (books 1–3). Verhandelingen der Koninklijke Akademie van Wetenschappen te Amsterdam. Afdeeling Letterkunde n.s. 15. Amsterdam: Müller, 1915. Vol. 2 (books 4–6). Verhandelingen...n.s. 21. Amsterdam: Müller, 1920. Vol. 3 (books 7–9), ed. C. de Boer, M.G. de Boer, and J.Th.M. Van't Sant. Verhandelingen...n.s. 30/3. Amsterdam: Noord-Hollandsche Uitgeversmaatschappij, 1931. Vol. 4 (books 10–13), ed. C. de Boer, M.G. de Boer, and J.Th.M. Van't Sant. Verhandelingen...n.s. 37. Amsterdam: Noord-Hollandsche Uitgeversmaatschappij, 1936. Vol. 5 (books 14–15). Verhandelingen...n.s. 43. Amsterdam: Noord-Hollandsche Uitgeversmaatschappij, 1938. Reprint. 5 vols. Wiesbaden: Sändig, 1966–68.
The anonymous moralized French translation of Ovid's *Metamorphoses* (before 1328) is an important source for *exempla* in Machaut's *dits.* See 1:28–43 for a reprint of De Boer 1914.

De Bure, Guillaume François.
1769. *Bibliographie instructive, ou Traité de la connoissance des livres rares et singuliers....* Vol. 8, *Supplément à la Bibliographie instructive, ou, Catalogue des livres du cabinet de feu M. Louis Jean Gaignat.* Paris: De Bure le jeune.
Includes material on the eighteenth-century provenance of MS **F-G** [6].

1783. *Catalogue des livres de la bibliothèque de feu M. le duc de la Vallière.* Part 1/2. Paris: De Bure.
Includes material on the eighteenth-century provenance of MS **F-G** [6].

Delachenal, R[oland].
1909–31. *Histoire de Charles V.* Vol. 1, *1338–1358.* Paris: Picard, 1909. Vol. 2, *1358–1364.* Paris: Picard, 1909. Vol. 3, *1364–1368.* Paris: Picard, 1916. Vol. 4, *1368–1377.* Paris: Picard, 1928. Vol. 5, *1377–1380.* Paris: Picard, 1931.
The most authoritative political history of the period of the lifetime of Charles V (1338–80), which includes most of the active period of Machaut's life. Delachenal died in 1923; vols. 4 and 5 were published posthumously.

Delaissé, L.J.M.
1957. "Enluminure et peinture dans les Pays-bas: A propos du livre de E. Panofsky, 'Early Netherlandish Painting.'" *Scriptorium* 11:109–18.
Important review that clarifies issues concerning some miniaturists involved in manuscripts of Machaut.

Delisle, Léopold.
1866. "Observations sur l'origine de plusieurs manuscrits de la collection de M. Barrois." *Bibliothèque de l'Ecole des Chartes* 27:193–264.
Information on the modern history of MS I [40].

1868–81. *Le Cabinet des manuscrits de la Bibliothèque Impériale / Nationale.* Histoire générale de Paris. Vol. 1. Paris: Imprimerie Impériale, 1868. Vol. 2. Paris: Imprimerie Nationale, 1874. Vol. 3. Paris: Imprimerie Nationale, 1881. Vol. 4, *Planches.* Paris: Imprimerie Nationale, 1881. Reprint of vols. 1–4. Amsterdam: van Heusden, 1969. Vol. 3 (*supplément*), *Index des manuscrits cités*, by Emmanuel Poulle. Paris: Imprimerie Municipale, 1977.
On MS E [7], see 1:58 no. 2; 1:66 no. 3; 3:193 nos. 282–83.

1888. *Bibliothèque Nationale. Catalogue des manuscrits des fonds Libri et Barrois.* Paris: Champion.
On MS I [40], see p. 124.

1900. *Chantilly. Le Cabinet des livres. Manuscrits.* Vol. 2, *Belles lettres.* Paris: Plon, 1900.
See 71–75 on *F:CH 485* [33]; 277–303 on **Ch** [59].

1907. *Recherches sur la librairie de Charles V.* 2 vols. Paris: Champion. Reprint. Amsterdam: van Heudsen, 1967.
Important study of the library of Charles V and Jean, Duke of Berry. Includes material on the early history of MS E [7].

Della Seta, Fabrizio.
1975. "I motetti di Guillaume de Machaut—loro relazione con le teoriche del suo tempo." Laurea, Music History, Università degli Studi di Roma.
Not examined. Abstract: *RILM* 10 (1976), no. 426.

DeLone, R.P.
1978. "Machaut and the Ballade Style." *Indiana Theory Review* 2:15–28.
Includes a four-voice reduction of *De toutes flours* (B31) (p. 26), providing one sonority for each breve of music. Too general to be useful.

De Looze, Laurence.
1984. "Guillaume de Machaut and the Writerly Process." *French Forum* 9: 145–61.
Fascinating analysis of textual self-consciousness and narrative structure in *Voir Dit*, and especially in *Fonteinne*. See comments in Huot 1987, 294 n. 41.

1987. "The *Mise en scène* of the Poetic Process in Fourteenth-Century Pseudo-Biographical and -Autobiographical Narratives." Ph.D. diss. University of Toronto. Ann Arbor: University Microfilms, 1988.
"Detailed studies of the most important fourteenth-century poets, Guillaume de Machaut and Jean Froissart, reveal a conception of the poet as both a reader and a writer and a depiction of the poetic process as the elaboration of an ordered, microcosmic world—the codex—which not only mirrors the poet's life but also creates a kind of secular (textual) afterlife" (author's abstract). Not examined. Abstract: *DAI* A 48/11 (May 1988): 2868.

1988a. "Masquage et démasquage de l'auteur dans les *Jugements* de Guillaume de Machaut." In *Masques et déguisements dans la littérature médiévale*, ed. Marie-Louise Ollier, 203–9. Etudes Médiévales. Montreal: Presses de l'Université de Montréal; Paris: Vrin.
Stimulating discussion of the hidden author motif in *Jugement Behaingne*, proceeding to the very prominent author figure in *Jugement Navarre*, who judges the earlier text. Concludes with a discussion of anagrams in Machaut. Reviews: Helen Solterer, *Speculum* 65 (1990): 472–75 (esp. 474).

1988b. "'Mon nom trouveras': A New Look at the Anagrams of Guillaume de Machaut: the Enigmas, Responses, and Solutions." *Romanic Review* 79: 537–57.

Modern critical reassessment of Machaut's *dits* through their anagrams, with comments on the work of previous scholars. The identity of the narrator persona as Machaut is guaranteed by self-naming in *Navarre* and *Prise*, and by an anagram in *Jugement Behaingne*, *Remede*, *Alerion*, *Confort*, and *Fonteinne*. The anagram is insoluble in *Lyon*, *Harpe*, and *Voir Dit*; *Vergier* lacks an anagram. Finding the name in the anagram is not really a search, since the reader knows the solution in advance.

1991. "Signing Off in the Middle Ages: Medieval Textuality and Strategies of Authorial Self-Naming." In *Vox intexta: Orality and Textuality in the Middle Ages*, ed. A.N. Doane and Carol Braun Pasternack, 162–78. Madison: University of Wisconsin Press.

Changing strategies of authorial naming in texts of the twelfth, thirteenth, fourteenth, and fifteenth centuries, with particular attention to the *Roman de la Rose*, and anagrams in Machaut and Christine de Pizan.

1993a. "From Text to Text and From Tale to Tale: Jean Froissart's *Prison Amoureuse*. In *The Centre and Its Compass: Studies in Medieval Literature in Honor of Professor John Leyerle*, ed. Robert A. Taylor et al., 87–110. Studies in Medieval Culture 33. Kalamazoo: Western Michigan University.

Machaut's clerkly narrator is reworked in Froissart. De Looze focuses on bookmaking, writing, glossing, and *exempla* in Froissart's *Prison Amoureuse*. Includes some discussion of Machaut's *Voir Dit* as a model for Froissart (88–93, 109).

1993b. "'Pseudo-Autobiography' and the Body of Poetry in Guillaume de Machaut's *Remede de Fortune*." *Esprit créateur* 33/4 (winter): 73–86.

Typology of the genre "pseudo-autobiography"; discussion of the pseudo-autobiographical *Remede*.

Dembowski, Peter F.

1978. "La position de Froissart-poète dans l'histoire littéraire: bilan provisoire." *Travaux de linguistique et de littérature* 16/1:131–47. *Mélanges d'études romanes du Moyen Age et de la Renaissance offerts à monsieur Jean Rychner.*

Excellent overview of Froissart's poetical works, with a summary of Froissart reception and major studies of Froissart.

1983. *Jean Froissart and His* Meliador: *Context, Craft, and Sense.* The Edward C. Armstrong Monographs on Medieval Literature 2. Lexington, Ky.: French Forum.

Critical study of a much unappreciated work. The material on fourteenth-century crusading sensibilities provides a useful context for Machaut's treatment of John of Luxembourg.

1986 (ed.). *Jean Froissart: Le Paradis d'Amour; L'Orloge Amoureus. Edition avec notes, introduction et glossaire.* Textes Littéraires Français 339. Geneva: Droz.

Critical edition of two *dits* of Froissart. The introduction notes some influence of Machaut's *Fonteinne* on Froissart's *Paradis d'Amour.*

1987a. "Metrics and Textual Criticism: The Example of Froissart's Decasyllables." *Esprit créateur* 27/1 (spring): 90–100.

This study of the metrics of Froissart's *L'Orloge amoureus* is applicable to Machaut; see esp. 100 n. 18 on the *Complainte d'Amant* in *Fonteinne.*

1987b. "Tradition, Dream Literature, and Poetic Craft in *Le Paradis d'Amour* of Jean Froissart." *Studies in the Literary Imagination* 20:99–109.

Critical study of Froissart's *Paradis d'Amour.* The *Complainte de l'Amant* imitates Machaut's *complainte* in *Fonteinne* (101–2 n. 13). Abstract: Palmer 1987a, 6–7.

Deschaux, Robert.
1975 (ed.). *Un poète bourguignon du XVe siècle: Michault Taillevent (Edition et étude)*. Publications Romanes et Françaises 132. Geneva: Droz.
Publication of the author's 1973 Sorbonne thesis, a critical edition of the works of Michault de Caron dit Taillevent (1395–1477). Taillevent mentions Machaut in his *Dialogue fait par Michault de son voiage de Saint Glaude*. Abstract of original dissertation: *Information littéraire* 26 (1974): 151–54.

1978a. "Consolateur d'illustres exclus: Guillaume de Machaut." In *Exclus et systèmes d'exclusion dans la littérature et la civilisation médiévales*, 59–67. Actes du colloque organisé par le C.U.E.R. M.A. à Aix-en-Provence, les 4–5–6 mars 1977. Senefiance 5. Aix-en-Provence: C.U.E.R. M.A.; Paris: Champion.
Study of *Confort* and *Fonteinne*, two poems of comfort directed at illustrious prisoners.

1978b. "Etude comparée de trois ballades amoureuses. *Recherches et Travaux* (Université de Grenoble. U.E.R. de Lettres). *Bulletin*, 17:2–9.
A comparative literary study of Machaut's *On ne porroit* (B3), a ballade by Deschamps, and a ballade by Christine de Pizan.

1979. "Le bestaire de Guillaume de Machaut d'après les dits." *Cahiers de l'Association Internationale des Etudes Françaises* 31:7–16 (discussion, 251–52).
Animals, real and mythological, in Machaut's *dits*, esp. birds in *Alerion* and the lion and his torturers in *Lyon*.

1988. "Le lai et la complainte." In Poirion 1988b, 70–85.
Survey of two lyric genres of the fourteenth and fifteenth centuries.

Desportes, Pierre.
1975 "L'enseignement à Reims aux XIIIe et XIVe siècles." In *Enseignement et vie intellectuelle (IXe–XVIe siècle). Actes du 95e Congrès National des Sociétés Savantes (Reims, 1970)*, 1:107–22. Section de Philologie et d'histoire jusqu'à 1610 1. Paris: Bibliothèque Nationale.
This study of education at Reims is possibly relevant to Machaut's early formation.

1979. *Reims et les Rémois au XIIIe et XIVe siècles*. Paris: Picard.
An important historical study of Reims, publication of the author's 1976 Paris-I thesis. For material relevant to Machaut, see esp. 537–94.

Despy, Georges.
1953. *Lettres d'Innocent VI (1352–1362)*. Vol. 1, *1352–55*. Analecta Vaticano-Belgica 17. Brussels and Rome: Institut Historique Belge de Rome.
Papal documents.

De Van, Guillaume.
1938 (ed.). *Les monuments de l'Ars Nova. Double hoquet. Guillaume de Machaut (XIVe siècle)*. Paris: L'Oiseau-Lyre.
The earliest edition of the *Hoquetus David*.

1943. "La prolation mineure chez Guillaume de Machaut." *Sources* 1:24–35.
Based on a discussion of theorists, de Van concludes that minor prolation was of Italian origin. Thus, according to de Van, 75 of Machaut's 142 musical works utilize rhythm originally foreign to the French tradition (33). See criticisms in Günther 1957, 22–23; 1958, 35; 1962–63, 10, 16–17, 27.

1949 (ed.). *Guglielmi de Mascaudio: Opera I, La Messe de Nostre Dame*. Corpus Mensurabilis Musicae 2. Rome: American Institute of Musicology.
The best of the early editions of the Mass. Reviews: Gerald Abraham, *Music Review* 11 (1950): 325; Willi Apel, *Speculum* 26 (1951): 187–90 (reprint in Apel 1986, 193–96); Leonard Ellinwood, *Notes* 7 (1949–50): 130–31; see also comments in Gombosi 1950, 204–8.

Devillers, Léopold.
1896. *Cartulaire des comtes de Hainaut de l'avènement de Guillaume II à la mort de Jacqueline de Bavière.* Vol. 6/1. Brussels: Hayez.
Includes a document for a lost MS [60] containing Machaut's Mass (p. 630).

De Winter, Patrick M.
1978. "Copistes, éditeurs et enlumineurs de la fin du XIVe siècle: La production à Paris de manuscrits à miniatures." In *Archéologie urbaine. Actes du 100e Congrès National des Sociétés Savantes (1975),* 173–98. Section d'Archéologie et d'Histoire et l'Art. Paris: Bibliothèque Nationale.
Interesting material on manuscript production, with material on specific miniaturists involved with Machaut manuscripts.

1980. "French Gothic and Renaissance Illuminated Manuscripts in Vienna." *Scriptorium* 34:289–94.
Includes information on Remiet, the artist of MS F-G [6] (p. 291).

1982. "The *Grandes Heures* of Philip the Bold, Duke of Burgundy: The Copyist Jean L'Avenant and His Patrons at the French Court." *Speculum* 57:786–842.
Includes material on specific miniaturists involved with Machaut manuscripts.

1985. *La bibliothèque de Philippe Le Hardi, duc de Bourgogne (1364–1404): Etude sur les manuscrits à peintures d'une collection princière à l'époque du "style gothique international."* Documents, Etudes et Répertoires publiés par l'Institut de Recherche et d'Histoire des Textes. Paris: Editions du Centre National de la Recherche Scientifique.
Excellent study of the late medieval Burgundian library, in particular the library of Duke Philip the Bold. Critical edition of the inventories of 1404 and 1405, a critical study of extant manuscripts belonging to the ducal library, and art historical studies. Includes material on lost MSS [8] and [19], and the music MS **Trém** [58]; touches upon several of the artists that illuminated Machaut manuscripts. Reviews: Albert Châtelet, *Zeitschrift für Kunstgeschichte* 51 (1988): 147–48; Catherine Reynolds, *Burlington Magazine* 130 (1988): 231–33; Françoise Robin, *Bulletin monumental* 144 (1986): 374–76; Anne Hagopian Van Buren, *Art Bulletin* 70 (1988): 699–705; Daniel Williman, *Speculum* 62 (1987): 925–27.

Diekstra, F.N.M.
1983. "Chaucer's Digressive Mode and the Moral of *The Manciple's Tale.*" *Neophilologus* 67:131–48.
Chaucer's *Manciple's Tale* and the story of Apollo and Coronis in the *Ovide Moralisé* and in Machaut's *Voir Dit.*

Dillon, Bert.
1974. *A Chaucer Dictionary: Proper Names and Allusions Excluding Place Names.* Boston: G.K. Hall.
Includes a tabular summary of lines from Machaut works that inspired lines in Chaucer works.

Dobrzańska, Zofia.
1978. "Technika izorytmiczna w twórczości Guillaume'a de Machaut" (Isorhythmic technique in the creative works of Guillaume de Machaut). Thesis, Jagiellonian University, Krakow.
Not examined.

1979a. "Kształtowanie tenoru w motetach Guillaume'a de Machaut" (The composition of tenor parts in Guillaume de Machaut's motets; in Polish, summary in English). *Muzyka* 24/2:3–18.
Tenor structure in Machaut's isorhythmic motets, with examples from *J'ay tant / Lasse! (M7), Qui es / Ha! Fortune (M8), Fons / O livoris (M9), Tant doucement m'ont / Eins*

(M13), *Maugré mon cuer* / *De ma dolour* (M14), *Martyrum* / *Diligenter* (M19), and *Tu qui gregem* / *Plange* (M22). Abstract: *RILM* 13 (1979), no. 278.

1979b. "Rola tenoru w kształtowaniu motetu izorytmicznego" (The role of the tenor in the composition of the isorhythmic motet; in Polish, summary in English). *Muzyka* 24/3:45–75.
Comparative examples and voice-leading reductions for *Tous corps* / *De* (M2), *De Bon Espoir* / *Puis que* (M4), *J'ay tant* / *Lasse!* (M7), *Qui es* / *Ha! Fortune* (M8), and *Hareu!* / *Helas!* (M10) are of use even without a knowledge of Polish. Abstract: *RILM* 13 (1979), no. 3698.

Dolidze, Dali.
1975. "Svetskaja mngogolosnaja pesnja èpohi ars nova vo Francii" (Secular part songs from the period of the French Ars Nova; in Russian). Ph.D. diss. Leningradskij inst. teatra, muzyki i kinematografii, Leningrad.
Not examined. Abstract: *RILM* 10 (1976), no. 9124.

Domínguez Bordona, J[esus].
1931. *Catálogo de los manuscritos catalanes de la Biblioteca Nacional.* Madrid: Blass.
Description and inventory of **Mn** [43] (p. 78).

Dömling, Wolfgang.
1969. "Zur Überlieferung der musikalischen Werke Guillaume de Machauts." *Musikforschung* 22:189–95.
Study of the filiation of the musical works of Machaut that are transmitted outside the Machaut manuscripts, with discussion of what constitutes a significant variant in music. Machaut works in the musical anthologies descend from E's exemplar. Rarely lists specific variants upon which the conclusions are based. Abstract: *RILM* 3 (1969), no. 496.

1970. *Die mehrstimmigen Balladen, Rondeaux und Virelais von Guillaume de Machaut: Untersuchungen zum musikalischen Satz.* Münchner Veröffentlichungen zur Musikgeschichte 16. Tutzing: Schneider.
Publication of author's 1966 Munich dissertation. Several examples support the thesis of simultaneous conception of voices. Important analyses of compositional procedure, and consideration of vocal scoring. Examples include *Helas! tant* (B2), *Pour ce que tous* (B12), *Se je me pleing* (B15), *De toutes flours* (B31), *Gais et jolis* (B35), *Se pour ce muir* (B36), *Mes esperis* (B39), *Ma chiere* (B40), *Vo dous regars* (R8), *Rose, lis* (R10), and *Ce qui soustient* (R12). Abstracts: *RILM* 2 (1968), no. 3075; *RILM* 3 (1969), no. 495; abstract of original dissertation: *Musikforschung* 20 (1967): 455–56; see also Sonnemann 1969, 21–22. Review: Sarah Jane Williams, *Notes* 27 (1970–71): 711–12. See also comments in Kühn 1973, 260 n. 440; Apfel 1974, 175–77; summary in Baumann 1979, 18–21.

1971. "Isorhythmie und Variation: über Kompositionstechniken in der Messe Guillaume de Machauts." *Archiv für Musikwissenschaft* 28:24–32.
Important analysis of isorhythm in the Mass (Kyrie, Agnus, and Amen of the Credo). The rhythmic structure of tenor and contratenor in the Kyrie shows a gradual increase of rhythmic complication, continuous variation that by the Kyrie II forms a palindrome. Emphasis on how the use of isorhythm in the Mass is different from the procedures of the isorhythmic motets. Abstract: *RILM* 5 (1971), no. 234.

1972. "Aspekte der Sprachvertonung in den Balladen Guillaume de Machauts." *Musikforschung* 25:301–7.
Discussion of rhetoric and music in the ballades; musical emphasis of individual words or important parts of the text and relationships between textual and musical structure. Short but excellent article, with examples from *On ne porroit* (B3), *Biauté qui* (B4), *Dous amis, oy* (B6), *De desconfort* (B8), *Pour ce que tous* (B12), *Esperance* (B13), *Je ne cuit* (B14), *Se je me pleing* (B15), *De petit po* (B18), *Je suis aussi* (B20), *Donnez, signeurs* (B26), *Une vipere* (B27), *Je puis trop* (B28), *De triste* / *Quant* / *Certes* (B29), *De toutes flours* (B31), *Plourez, dames* (B32), *Quant Theseüs* / *Ne quier* (B34), *Se pour se muir* (B36),

Phyton (B38), *Mes esperis* (B39), and *Sans cuer, dolens* (R4). Abstract: *RILM* 7 (1973), no. 219.

Donnelly, Colleen.
  1987. "Challenging the Conventions of Dream Vision in *The Book of the Duchess.*" *Philological Quarterly* 66:421–35.
  Chaucer skillfully provides the reader of the *Book of the Duchess* with multiple perspectives and interpretations. Some mention of *Jugement Behaingne* and *Remede.*

Douce, André.
  1948. *Guillaume de Machaut: Musicien et poète rémois.* Reims: Matot-Braine.
  Douce admits his is a "histoire romancée" of Machaut, especially concerning the *Voir Dit* and the coronation of Charles V. Useful for some facsimiles of miniatures.

Douët-d'Arcq, L[ouis].
  1867. *Inventaire de la Bibliothèque du Roi Charles VI fait au Louvre en 1423 par ordre du régent duc de Bedford.* Paris: Société des Bibliophiles.
  Library inventories of 1411 and 1423 include MS [29], a lost manuscript of lais.

Doutrepont, Georges.
  1906. *Inventaire de la "librairie" de Philippe le Bon (1420).* Commission Royale d'Histoire. Brussels: Kiessling. Reprint. Geneva: Slatkine, 1977.
  Excellent edition of the 1420 inventory of the Burgundian library, which lists two Machaut manuscripts no longer extant, as well as **Trém** [58].

Dragonetti, Roger.
  1960. *La technique poétique des trouvères dans la chanson courtoise. Contribution à l'étude de la rhétorique médiévale.* Rijksuniversiteit te Gent, Werken uitgegeven door de Faculteit van de Letteren en Wijsbegeerte 127. Bruges: De Tempel. Reprint. Paris: Gex, 1979.
  Important study of themes, figures, and technical formal aspects of trouvère poetry.

  1961. "'La poésie... ceste musique naturele.' Essai d'exégèse d'un passage de l'*Art de Dictier* d'Eustache Deschamps." In *Fin du Moyen Age et Renaissance: Mélanges de Philologie française offerts à Robert Guiette,* 49–64. Antwerp: Nederlandsche Boekhandel. Reprint. *La musique et les lettres. Etudes de littérature médiévale,* 27–46. Publications Romanes et Françaises 171. Geneva: Droz, 1986.
  The background of Deschamps's distinction between "artificial" and "natural" music in Boethius and Garlandia; the importance of number to natural music. Review: Daniel Poirion, *Revue belge de philologie et d'histoire* 41 (1963): 867–71; comments in Lühmann 1978, 38–39 n. 13.

Dricot, Michel.
  1982. "Note sur la formation de Guillaume de Machaut." In Guillaume de Machaut 1982, 143–47.
  On Machaut's education.

Droz, Eugénie, and Geneviève Thibault.
  1924. *Poètes et musiciens du XVe siècle.* Documents Artistiques du XVe Siècle 1. Paris, n.p. Reprint. Geneva: Slatkine, 1976.
  Reproductions (all facing p. 13) of miniatures E6 (see chap. 4.4r), E7 (see chap. 4.4b), E30 (see chap. 4.4j), and E31 (see chap. 4.4s).

  1926. "Un Chansonnier de Philippe le bon." *Revue de musicologie* 7:1–8.
  First study of the fragment **Trém** [58]; includes a complete facsimile.

  1927. "Un Manuscrit de Guillaume de Machaut." *Revue de musicologie* 8:44.
  Discussion of MS **Maggs** [27].

Duhamel, [Léopold], et al.
1901. *Catalogue général des manuscrits des bibliothèques publiques de France. Départements.* Vol. 34, *Carpentras.* Vol. 1. Ministère de l'Instruction Publique et des Beaux-Arts. Paris: Plon.
Some unpublished notes by the abbé Rive in the MS Carpentras 1259 may bear on the eighteenth-century history of MSS **F-G** [6] and **Bk** [21] (pp. 650–51).

Duval, Amaury.
1824. "Discours sur l'etat des beaux-arts en France au XIIIe siècle." In *Histoire littéraire de la France* 16:255–335.
Includes material on the description of instruments in *Remede* (274–75).

Du Verdier, Antoine.
1585. *La bibliotheque d'Antoine du Verdier....* Lyon: Honorat.
Brief mention of Machaut (498). See also Rigoley de Juvigny 1773.

Dzelzainis, Angela D.
1985. "An Edition and Study of Guillaume de Machaut's *La Prise d'Alixandre.*" Ph.D. diss. Cambridge University.
The first new edition of the *Prise* since Mas Latrie 1877b. Abstract: *Index to Theses* 35/1 (1986): 59 no. 35-0296.

Earp, Lawrence.
1983. "Scribal Practice, Manuscript Production and the Transmission of Music in Late Medieval France: The Manuscripts of Guillaume de Machaut." Ph.D. diss. Princeton University. Ann Arbor: University Microfilms. Order no. 8318466.
Study of the manuscripts of Machaut's music and issues of music manuscript copying and transmission in late medieval France. Includes charts of the gathering structure of the principal manuscripts; the appended tables of miniatures are superseded by chap. 4 above. Abstracts: *DAI* A 44/4 (Oct. 1983): 904; *RILM* 17 (1983), no. 3863.

1986. "Guillaume de Machaut." In *Dictionnaire d'histoire et de géographie ecclésiastiques,* ed. R. Aubert, 22:947–49. Paris: Editions Letouzey et Ané.
Dictionary article.

1989. "Machaut's Role in the Production of Manuscripts of His Works." *Journal of the American Musicological Society* 42:461–503.
The current state of knowledge of Machaut's role in the copying of his manuscripts. Includes a facsimile of the original index of MS **A** (fols. Av–Bv). Abstract: *RILM* 23 (1989), no. 1828.

1991a. "Genre in the Fourteenth-Century French Chanson: The Virelai and the Dance Song." *Musica disciplina* 45:123–41.
Further development of Earp 1991b. Machaut seems to have created a refined fourteenth-century dance song in his earlier virelais. These works exhibit a style quite unlike that of the polyphonic ballades and rondeaux, which served as successors to the old *grand chant courtois.* Traces of the traditional quasi-improvised, unaccompanied dance songs may survive in the handful of anonymous fourteenth-century virelais that incorporate popular melodies as their tenor voices. This issue of *Musica disciplina* appeared in 1995.

1991b. "Lyrics for Reading and Lyrics for Singing in Late Medieval France: The Development of the Dance Lyric from Adam de la Halle to Guillaume de Machaut." In Baltzer 1991b, 101–31.
The development and consolidation of the fixed forms in the first half of the fourteenth century, emphasizing Machaut's key role. See also Hoepffner 1910; 1911, 162–66; 1920a; 1920b; Reaney 1962; Frobenius 1986, 11.

1991c. "Texting in 15th-Century French Chansons: A Look Ahead from the 14th Century." *Early Music* 19:194–210.
As in the fourteenth century, chansons in the early fifteenth century were texted by entering music over words ("music overlay"). The procedure was reversed in the middle of the

fifteenth century, when text was copied after the music ("text underlay"), a much less accurate practice. A variety of texing options have been masked in many modern editions and performances. Includes brief discussion of texting practices in Machaut chansons. See comments in Welker 1992, 187.

Eberlein, Roland.
1992. "The Faenza Codex: Music for Organ or for Lute Duet?" *Early Music* 20:461–66.
On performance practice in MS Fa [67]; see McGee 1992.

Edbury, P[eter W.].
1980. "The Murder of Peter I of Cyprus (1359–1369)." *Journal of Medieval History* 6:219–33.
Concerns political events recounted in *Prise*.

Edmunds, Sheila.
1971. "The Library of Savoy (II): Documents." *Scriptorium* 25:253–84.
Includes a document concerning Machaut and the Green Count of Savoy (257 no. 19).

Edwards, Robert R.
1982. "The *Book of the Duchess* and the Beginnings of Chaucer Narrative." *New Literary History* 13:189–204.
Includes a discussion of Chaucer's use of the story of Ceyx and Alcyone from Machaut's *Fonteinne* (192–94).

1989. *The Dream of Chaucer: Representation and Reflection in the Early Narratives*. Durham, N.C. and London: Duke University Press.
Includes discussion of the influence of Machaut's *Prologue, Jugement Behaingne, Remede*, and *Fonteinne* on Chaucer's *Book of the Duchess*.

Eggebrecht, Hans Heinrich.
1961. "Musik als Tonsprache." *Archiv für Musikwissenschaft* 18:73–100. Reprint. *Musikalisches Denken. Aufsätze zur Theorie und Ästhetik der Musik*, 7–53. Taschenbücher zur Musikwissenschaft 46. Wilhelmshaven: Heinrichshofen, 1976.
Includes brief discussion of harmony in *Quant en moy / Amour* (M1) (pp. 84–85).

1962–63. "Machauts Motette Nr. 9." *Archiv für Musikwissenschaft* 19–20:281–93. Reprint: see Eggebrecht 1968.
See Eggebrecht 1968.

1968. "Machauts Motette Nr. 9." *Archiv für Musikwissenschaft* 25:173–95. Reprint. *Sinn und Gehalt. Aufsätze zur musikalischen Analyse*. Taschenbücher zur Musikwissenschaft 57. Wilhelmshaven: Heinrichshofen, 1979.
A model analysis of text and music of *Fons / O livoris* (M9). Abstract: *RILM* 2 (1968), no. 3076. See criticisms and comments in Clarkson 1971, 155–56; Kühn 1973, 104–10; Lühmann 1978, 170–71; Fuller 1986, 36–37; Leech-Wilkinson 1989, 12; Fuller 1990, 204.

1991. *Musik im Abendland: Prozesse und Stationen vom Mittelalter bis zur Gegenwart*. Munich: Piper.
Survey of music history; on Machaut, see 232–40.

Ehrhart, Margaret.
1974. "Chaucer's Contemporary, Guillaume de Machaut: A Critical Study of Four *Dits amoureux*." Ph.D. diss. University of Illinois at Urbana-Champaign. Ann Arbor: University Microfilms, 1975. Order no. 7511705.
After an introductory chapter on Chaucer, considers *Lyon, Alerion, Jugement Navarre*, and *Fonteinne*, emphasizing Machaut's handling of the narrator and mythological materials. "That human love, rightly directed, mirrors divine love and creates on earth a model of the City of God is [Machaut's] constant theme" (206). Abstracts: *DAI* A 35/11 (May 1975): 7299–300; Peck 1983, no. 97.

1979. "Guillaume de Machaut's *Jugement dou Roy de Navarre* and Medieval Treatments of the Virtues." *Annuale Mediævale* 19:46–67.

> The intellectual background—especially the influence of the *Nicomachean Ethics*—of the twelve personified virtues in *Jugement Navarre*, combined from the four cardinal virtues and the seven virtues connected with gifts of the Holy Spirit. See comment in Heinrichs 1990, 190 n. 42.

1980a. "The 'Esprueve de fines amours' in Machaut's *Dit dou Lyon* and Medieval Interpretations of Circe and Her Island." *Neophilologus* 64:38–41.

> The island in *Lyon* derives from the Circe myth, known from Boethius's *Consolation of Philosophy* and from the *Ovide Moralisé*. Machaut thereby intends a critique of *fin'amors*.

1980b. "Machaut's *Dit de la Fonteinne Amoureuse*, the Choice of Paris, and the Duties of Rulers." *Philological Quarterly* 59:119–39.

> Problems with the anagram in *Fonteinne*; *Fonteinne*'s connection to the advice to rulers tradition. "Machaut intends the poem to show the effects of a ruler's abdication of his responsibility for the common good to pursue the private pleasures of *fin'amors*" (120). Ehrhart interprets *Fonteinne* as an admonition to the ruler—the regent Charles—to more effective rule, a significant commentary in the France of ca. 1360.

1980c. "Machaut's *Jugement dou Roy de Navarre* and the Book of Ecclesiastes." *Neuphilologische Mitteilungen* 81:318–25.

> Borrowings from the book of Ecclesiastes in *Navarre*, suggesting that there is a link between the prologue and the body of the poem.

1987. *The Judgment of the Trojan Prince Paris in Medieval Literature*. University of Pennsylvania Press Middle Ages Series. Philadelphia: University of Pennsylvania Press.

> Adaptations of the myth of the Judgment of Paris in medieval literature. Detailed discussion of the story in Machaut's *Confort* and *Fonteinne*. Reviews: Renate Blumenfeld-Kosinski, *Speculum* 64 (1989): 409–12; Steven Justice, *Journal of English and Germanic Philology* 88 (1989): 391–93; J.B. Trapp, *Notes and Queries* n.s. 36 (1989): 214–15; Kenneth Varty, *Medium Ævum* 58 (1989): 138–39.

1990. "Christine de Pizan and the Judgment of Paris: A Court Poet's Use of Mythographic Tradition." In *The Mythographic Art: Classical Fable and the Rise of the Vernacular in Early France and England*, ed. Jane Chance, 125–56. Gainesville: University of Florida Press.

> Extended treatment of three works of Christine de Pizan and their use of the myth of the Judgment of Paris, derived from the *Ovide Moralisé* and Machaut's *Fonteinne*. Both Machaut and Christine use the myth to admonish their princely patrons to choose wisdom, carefully concealing their counsel so as not to endanger the poet's social position.

1992. "Machaut and the Duties of Rulers Tradition." *French Forum* 17:5–22.

> Interesting analysis of *Jugement Navarre* and *Fonteinne* in light of the duties of rulers tradition.

Eichelberg, Walter.

1935. *Dichtung und Wahrheit in Machauts "Voir Dit."* Frankfurt: Düren.

> Publication of the author's Frankfurt dissertation. Extended discussion of the *Voir Dit*, arguing for the priority of the letters in the composition of the work. For the most part, they may be regarded as authentic letters. Argues forcefully for a largely truthful foundation to the events behind the *Voir Dit*. Comments in S.J. Williams 1952, 73–78; Sonnemann 1969, 19; Calin 1974, 170–71. The work has often been dismissed without examination by recent literary critics; it is supported in Leech-Wilkinson 1993b.

Einstein, Alfred.

1927 (ed.). *Beispielsammlung zur älteren Musikgeschichte*. Aus Natur und Geisteswelt 439. 3rd ed. Leipzig and Berlin: Teubner.

> Includes an edition of *De toutes flours* (B31), ed. R. Ficker (4–6 no. 3). The example is lacking in the the first two editions (1917 and 1924). The collection of examples is included in Einstein 1947.

1947. *A Short History of Music.* Trans. Eric Blom et al. 3rd rev. American ed. New York: Knopf. [Originally published as *Geschichte der Musik.* Leiden: Sijthoff, 1934. 1st British ed. London: Cassell, 1936. 1st American ed. New York: Knopf, 1937. Illustrated ed. by A. Hyatt King. London: Cassell, 1953. 4th rev. American ed. New York: Vintage Books, 1954.] Includes an edition of *De toutes flours* (B31) (pp. 267–71 no. 11).

Ellsworth, Oliver B.
   1969. "The Berkeley Manuscript (*olim* Phillipps 4450): A Compendium of Fourteenth-Century Music Theory." 2 vols. Ph.D. diss. University of California at Berkeley. Ann Arbor: University Microfilms. Order no. 7013044.
   Edition and study of a music theory treatise related to the *Libellus* of Johannes de Muris. The discussion of musical notation concerns Machaut. Abstract: *DAI* A 31/2 (Aug. 1970): 783.

   1984. *The Berkeley Manuscript: University of California Music Library, MS. 744* (olim *Phillipps 4450): A New Critical Text and Translation on Facing Pages, with an Introduction, Annotations, and indices verborum and nominum et rerum.* Greek and Latin Music Theory 2. Lincoln, Nebr. and London: University of Nebraska Press.
   Edition and study based on Ellsworth 1969. Abstract: *RILM* 18 (1984), no. 1031.

Elwert, W[ilhelm] Theodor.
   1965. *Traité de versification française des origines à nos jours.* Bibliothèque Française et Romane A8. Paris: Klincksieck. French trans. of *Französische Metrik.* Munich: Hueber, 1961. 3rd ed. 1970.
   Handbook on French versification.

Emerson, Oliver Farrar.
   1912. "Chaucer's First Military Service—A Study of Edward Third's Invasion of France in 1359–60." *Romanic Review* 3:321–61.
   The course of the English armies in the invasion of 1359–60, with special attention to the Siege of Reims. A document of October 1360 shows that Chaucer was at Calais, perhaps at the same time that Machaut saw the duke of Berry off into exile, as described at the end of *Fonteinne.*

Enders, Jody.
   1992. "Music, Delivery, and Rhetoric of Memory in Guillaume de Machaut's *Remede de Fortune.*" *PMLA* 107:450–64.
   Poetry, music, and rhetoric are not separate genres but fluid ones in the memory. The emphasis on memory can explain some otherwise puzzling aspects of performance in *Remede*, such as the inclusion of polyphonic songs for a single performer, and the *prière.*

Escot, Pozzi.
   1991. "Earth, Heaven and Music's Universal Quest—Machaut's Ballade *Dame, se vous m'estes lonteinne;* Zuni *Buffalo Dance.*" *Sonus* 12:32–44. Also published as "Earth, Heaven and Music's Universal Quest—Machaut, Zuni," *Interface* 20 (1991): 143–52.
   Includes a curious analysis of *Dame, se vous m'estes* (B37).

Esteve Barba, Francisco.
   1942. *Biblioteca publica de Toledo. Catálogo de la colección de manuscritos Borbón-Lorenzana.* Cuerpo Facultativo de Archiveros, Bibliotecarios y Arqueologos. Madrid: Góngora.
   Library catalogue describing MS *E:Tp 329*, containing the *Reglas de canto plano* (1410) of Fernando Estevan (242–43 no. 329), with a facsimile plate. See chap. 2.4.1f.

Estrich, Robert M.
   1939. "Chaucer's Prologue to the *Legend of Good Women* and Machaut's *Le Jugement dou Roy de Navarre.*" *Studies in Philology* 36:20–39.

Develops a relationship noted by Kittredge.

Fabin, Madeleine.

1919. "On Chaucer's *Anelida and Arcite*." *Modern Language Notes* 34:266–72.

On *Je ne me say* (L20) as a source for Chaucer's *Anelida and Arcite*. Includes a detailed description of L20. Abstract: Peck 1983, no. 238.

Falke, Anne.

1986. "The 'Marguerite' and the 'Margarita' in Thomas Lodge's *A Margarite of America*." *Neophilologus* 70:142–54.

The *Marguerite* image in English literature of the fourteenth, fifteenth, and sixteenth centuries; see 146–47 on *Marguerite* poetry of Machaut, especially *Lis et Marguerite*.

Fallows, David.

1976. "L'origine du ms. 1328 de Cambrai." *Revue de musicologie* 62:275–80.

New fragments belonging with the MS **CaB** [56]. See also Lerch 1987. Abstract: *RILM* 10 (1976), no. 2398. Review: M. Huglo, *Scriptorium* 34 (1980): 39* no. 156.

1977a. "Guillaume de Machaut and His Mass, a Commemoration and a Review." *Musical Times* 118:288–91.

An interesting assessment of the state of research on Machaut biography and Machaut's influence on his contemporaries; review of Stevens 1973, with a discussion of editorial problems in the Mass. Stevens replies, followed by Fallows's further comments, in *Musical Times* 118 (1977): 641–42. Abstract: *RILM* 11 (1977), no. 308.

1977b. "Guillaume de Machaut and the Lai: A New Source." *Early Music* 5:477–83.

First study of Lille, Archives du Nord, MS 134 [26], a new source for *Pour ce qu'on puist* (L3). An analysis of rhyme scheme and rhythm in L3, with some general guidelines for the musical analysis of lais. Abstract: *RILM* 11 (1977), no. 4419.

1980. "Lai." In *New Grove Dictionary of Music and Musicians*, ed. Stanley Sadie, 10:364–76.

Excellent brief yet comprehensive discussion of the history of the lai and related forms, with full bibliography and checklist of the repertory. Lais of the *Roman de Fauvel* (MS *F:Pn 146*) and Machaut discussed (369–72).

1983. "Specific Information on the Ensembles for Composed Polyphony, 1400–1474." In Boorman 1983, 109–59.

This extremely rich article concerns Machaut only peripherally. Fallows notes that the mention of the "rés d'Alemaigne" in letter 10 of the *Voir Dit* may be the earliest evidence for a work for soloist and instrumental ensemble based on a polyphonic model (133 n. 54). Abstract: *RILM* 18 (1984), no. 5484.

1990. "Busnoys and the Early Fifteenth Century: A Note on 'L'Ardant desir' and 'Faictes de moy.'" *Music and Letters* 71:20–24.

Reconstruction of the late fourteenth-century virelai *L'ardant desir* reveals a work similar in style to the late two-voice virelais of Machaut (*Se je souspir* [V36/30], *Moult sui* [V37/31], and *De tout sui* [V38/32]). Includes a table of ten fourteenth-century works that have stylistic characteristics comparable to the three late Machaut virelais.

Fansler, Dean Spruill.

1914. *Chaucer and the* Roman de la Rose. New York: Columbia University Press. Reprint. Gloucester, Mass.: Smith, 1965.

Machaut's *Vergier* as a source for Chaucer's Prologue to the *Legend of Good Women* (69–72).

Fässler, Ewald.

1973. "Die Kadenzen der französischen Chansons von Machaut bis Dufay." Diss. Innsbruck. Ann Arbor: University Microfilms. Order no. 7429223.

Examination of 714 cadences in 315 three- and four-voice French chansons attributed to 52 composers from Machaut to Dufay. Musical exx. 1–54 cover the works of Machaut.

Faulhaber, Charles B., et al.

1984. *Bibliography of Old Spanish Texts*. 3rd ed. The Hispanic Seminary of Medieval Studies Bibliographic Series 4. Madison, Wis.: The Hispanic Seminary of Medieval Studies.

See no. 3159 (with unnumbered appended facsimile) for a bibliographical citation, with additional bibliography, on MS *E:Tp 329*, containing the *Reglas de canto plano* (1410) of Fernando Estevan, a music theory treatise mentioning Machaut. See chap. 2.4.1f.

Faye, C.U., and W.H. Bond.

1962. *Supplement to the Census of Medieval and Renaissance Manuscripts in the United States and Canada*. New York: Bibliographical Society of America.

Description of MS **Pa** [50] (pp. 480–81); additions to the Ricci/Wilson 1937 description of MS **Pm** [18] (p. 344).

Fayen, Arnold.

1912. *Lettres de Jean XXII (1316–1334)*. Vol. 2, *1325–34*. Analecta Vaticano-Belgica 3. Rome: Bretschneider; Brussels: Dewit; Paris: Champion.

Papal documents.

Feil, Patricia Ann.

1985. "Chaucer's *Parlement of Foules* Considered in Relation to the Medieval *Demande d'Amour* and the Debate Genre." Ph.D. diss. Lehigh University. Ann Arbor: University Microfilms. Order no. 8516250.

Includes some discussion of *Jugement Behaingne* and *Jugement Navarre* in the context of the *demandes d'amour* (62–71). Abstract: *DAI* A 46/6 (Dec. 1985): 1620. Cf. Klein 1911.

Feininger, Laurence K.

1937. *Die Frühgeschichte des Kanons bis Josquin des Prez (um 1500)*. Emsdetten: Lechte.

Publication of author's 1937 Heidelberg dissertation. Signals a correction (p. 13n.) in Ludwig's transcription of *Sans cuer m'en / Amis / Dame* (B17), first transcribed after Feininger in Reaney 1955, 57–58. Discusses Machaut's nineteen canonic works, including *Je ne cesse* (L16/11), with six canons; *S'onques* (L17/12), with twelve canons; and B17.

Ferrand, Françoise.

1982. "Regards sur le *Prologue* de Guillaume de Machaut." In Guillaume de Machaut 1982, 235–39.

Especially concerns the images of Orpheus and David in the *Prologue*.

1987. "Les portraits de Guillaume de Machaut à l'entrée du Prologue à ses œuvres, signes iconiques de la nouvelle fonction de l'artiste, en France, à la fin du XIVè siècle." In *Le portrait*, ed. Joseph-Marc Bailbé with a preface by Madeleine Ambrière, 11–20. Publications de l'Université de Rouen 128. Rouen: Publications de l'Université de Rouen.

Excellent iconographical study of the two *Prologue* miniatures in MS A. In the *Prologue* portraits, the artist, Guillaume de Machaut, has taken the place of the patron, a reversal of the usual social order.

1988. "Aux frontières de l'écriture de la narration et du lyrisme, la complainte." In *Sammlung—Deutung—Wertung. Ergebnisse, Probleme, Tendenzen und Perspektiven philologischer Arbeit. Mélanges de littérature médiévale et de linguistique allemande offerts à Wolfgang Spiewok à l'occasion de son soixantième anniversaire par ses collèges et amis*, ed. Danielle Buschinger, 101–17. Université de Picardie, Centre d'études médiévales.

Not examined.

1994. "Œuvres lyriques, de Guillaume de Machaut (1300?–1377)." In *Dictionnaire des œuvres littéraires de langue française*, ed. Jean-Pierre de Beaumarchais and Daniel Couty, 1419–20. 4 vols., continuous pagination. Paris: Bordas.

Survey article.

Fétis, François-Joseph.
1860–65. "Guillaume de Machau ou de Machaut." In *Biographie universelle des musiciens et bibliographie générale de la musique*. 8 vols. Paris: Fournier, 1835–44. Brussels: Méline, 1837–44. 2nd rev. ed. Paris: Didot; Brussels: Méline, 1860–65, 4:158–59.

Dictionary article.

Ficker, Rudolf.
1920. "Die Kolorierungstechnik der Trienter Messen." *Studien zur Musikwissenschaft* 7:5–47.

Brief mention of plainchant paraphrase in the Mass (23).

1924–25. "Formprobleme der mittelalterlichen Musik." *Zeitschrift für Musikwissenschaft* 7:195–213.

Includes an analytical study of Machaut's isorhythmic motets (210–13), considering *Quant en moy / Amour* (M1), *Hé! Mors / Fine* (M3), *De Bon Espoir / Puis que* (M4), *Felix virgo / Inviolata* (M23).

1925. "Die Musik des Mittelalters und ihre Beziehungen zum Geistesleben." *Deutsche Vierteljahrsschrift für Literaturwissenschaft und Geistesgeschichte* 3:501–35.

Includes example from *Tous corps / De* (M2), a foil for general comments on isorhythm (530–31).

1929. "Polyphonic Music of the Gothic Period," trans. Theodore Baker. *Musical Quarterly* 15:483–505.

A history of medieval polyphony from a time when aesthetic interest in such music was at the beginning stages. Machaut's music is illustrated with excerpts from *De Fortune* (B23) and *Tu qui gregem / Plange* (M22).

Figg, Kristen Mossler.
1994a. "Critiquing Courtly Convention: Jean Froissart's Playful Lyric Persona." *French Studies* 48:129–42.

Analysis of Froissart's poetic persona in his lyrics, with consideration of two lyrics in the series, a rondeau and a ballade, that undercut his traditional poetic persona. Includes an analysis of *Sur toutes fleurs tient on la rose a belle*, related to Machaut's *De toutes flours* (B31).

1994b. *The Short Lyric Poems of Jean Froissart: Fixed Forms and the Expression of the Courtly Ideal*. Garland Studies in Medieval Literature 10; Garland Reference Library of the Humanities 1749. New York and London: Garland.

Revised publication of author's 1988 Kent State dissertation. Translations and useful analyses of selected Froissart lais, *chansons royales*, *pastourelles*, ballades, virelais, and rondeaux, including works related to Machaut's *De toutes flours* (B31), *Je puis trop* (B28), and *Quant Theseüs / Ne quier* (B34).

Finlayson, John.
1963–64. "Rhetorical 'Descriptio' of Place in the Alliterative *Morte Arthure*." *Modern Philology* 61:1–11.

A descriptive passage in Arthur's second dream in an anonymous fourteenth-century English poem, the alliterative *Morte Arthure*, resembles a passage near the opening of *Lyon* (9).

1973. "The *Book of the Duchess*: Sources for Lines 174, 203–205, 249–253." *English Language Notes* 10:170–72.
Some borrowings from Machaut's *Fonteinne* in Chaucer's *Book of the Duchess*.

Finscher, Ludwig.

1975. "Die 'Entstehung des Komponisten': zum Problem Komponisten-Individualität und Individualstil in der Musik des 14. Jahrhunderts" (summary in English and Croatian). *International Review of the Aesthetics and Sociology of Music* 6:29–45.
Discusses the earliest composer ascriptions and the development of an individual musical style associated with a specific composer. Italian trecento composers are especially important in this development. Philippe de Vitry and Machaut, for their part, were never primarily known as composers. See also Hoffmann-Axthelm 1991, 341. Abstract: *RILM* 9 (1975), no. 482.

Fischer, Kurt von.

1957. "The Manuscript Paris, Bibl. Nat., Nouv. Acq. Frç. 6771 (Codex *Reina = PR*)." *Musica disciplina* 11:38–78.
Description and inventory of MS **PR** [63].

1961. "On the Technique, Origin, and Evolution of Italian Trecento Music," trans. Joel Newman. *Musical Quarterly* 47:41–57. Reprint. *Medieval Music*. Vol. 2, *Polyphony*, ed. Ellen Rosand, 51–68. Garland Library of the History of Western Music 2. London and New York: Garland, 1985. Earlier French version: "Les compositions à trois voix chez les compositeurs du Trecento." In *L'Ars Nova italiana del Trecento I*, ed. Bianca Becherini, 418–31. Certaldo: Centro Studi sull'Ars Nova italiana del Trecento, 1962.
Older trecento compositions lack the voice-crossing common in two- and three-voice works of Machaut. Examples of essential contratenors in Machaut (*Plourez, dames* [B32], and *Phyton* [B38]); it is typical that the number of voices can vary in Italian music, but not in French music (Hirshberg [1971, 80–82] disagrees). Some Machaut three-voice works can be understood as two-voice works with an added voice, others were conceived as three-voice works from the beginning.

1980. "Sources, MS, §VIII. Italian Polyphony *c*1325–*c*1430." *New Grove* 17:665–68.
Includes descriptions of MSS **FP** [61], **PR** [63], and **Pit** [64]. See also Günther 1980b; Reaney 1980b.

1990. "Remarks on Some Trecento and Early Quattrocento Fragments." In *Atti del XIV congresso della Società Internazionale di Musicologia: Trasmissione e recezione delle forme di cultura musicale. Bologna, 27 agosto–1° settembre 1987; Ferrara-Parma, 30 agosto 1987*. Vol. 1, *Round Tables*, ed. Angelo Pompilio et al., 160–62 (discussion, 162–67). Turin: Edizioni di Torino.
Includes remarks on the Paduan fragments, MS [62] (p. 161).

Flores, Angel, ed.

1962. *An Anthology of Medieval Lyrics*. The Modern Library of the World's Best Books. New York: Modern Library.
Includes translations of *Amis, bien* (VD32), *Amis, se Dieus* (VD38), *Blanche com lis* (Lo82), *De morir sui* (Lo163), *Douce dame, cointe* (Lo226), *Faites mon cuer* (Lo125), *Je maudi l'eure* (Lo213), *Partués moy* (Lo118), *Riches d'amour* (B5), and *Se vos courrous* (Lo247).

Flügel, Ewald.

1901. "Chaucers kleinere Gedichte." *Anglia* 23:195–224.
Influence of Machaut's *Vergier* on Chaucer's *Complaint unto Pity* (197–98).

Flutre, Louis-Fernand, and Gilbert Reaney.

1967. "Guillaume de Machaut." In *Encyclopaedia Britannica.* 1967 revision.
Encyclopedia article.

Ford, Terence, Andrew Green, et al.

1988. *The Pierpont Morgan Library; Medieval and Renaissance Manuscripts.*
RIdM/RCMI Inventory of Music Iconography 3. New York: The Graduate
School and University Center of the City University of New York,
Research Center for Musical Iconography.
MS **Pm** [18], fol. 118 (200–208 no. 640).

Foulet, Lucien.

1923. "Le Moyen Age." Part 3, "Du début de la guerre de cent ans (1337) à la
fin du XVe siècle." *Histoire de la littérature française illustrée.* Vol. 1, ed.
Joseph Bédier and Paul Hazard, 86–125. Paris: Larousse. Rev. ed. by
Pierre Martino, 113–63. Paris: Larousse, 1948.
Influential treatment of the fourteenth and fifteenth centuries as an unfortunate period for
French letters, one which built upon the past without any original contributions of its
own. Machaut is discussed on pp. 87–88 (unaltered reprint in the 1948 ed., 114–15).

Fourrier, Anthime, ed.

1963. *Jean Froissart: L'Espinette Amoureuse. Edition avec introduction,
notes et glossaire.* Bibliothèque Française et Romane B2. Paris: Klincksieck. 2nd rev. ed. Paris: Klincksieck, 1972.
Standard critical edition. Reviews of 1st ed.: Kurt Baldinger, *Zeitschrift für romanische
Philologie* 82 (1966): 221–22 (corrections); Sergio Cigada, *Studi francesi* 10 (1966): 536;
John L. Grigsby, *Romance Philology* 19 (1965–66): 510–12 (corrections); Félix Lecoy,
Romania 85 (1964): 132–34 (corrections); Marilina Luz, *Revista portuguesa de filologia*
13 (1964–65): 499–500; Jean Rossbach, *Revue belge de philologie et d'histoire* 43
(1965): 729–30; Margaret L. Switten, *Romanic Review* 56 (1965): 206–7. Reviews of
rev. ed.: Kurt Baldinger, *Zeitschrift für romanische Philologie* 88 (1972): 691–92; John
L. Grigsby, *Romance Philology* 30 (1976–77): 687; Omer Jodogne, *Revue belge de
philologie et d'histoire* 56 (1978): 215; Ruggero M. Ruggieri, *Studi medievali* 14 (1973):
1180 (corrections); *Bulletin critique du livre français* 27 (1972): 1555 no. 86202.

1974. *Jean Froissart: La Prison Amoureuse. Edition avec introduction, notes
et glossaire.* Bibliothèque Française et Romane B13. Paris: Klincksieck.
Standard critical edition. Reviews: Edoardo Esposito, *Medioevo romanzo* 2 (1975): 454–
56; Enzo Giudici, *Francia* 19–20 (Sept.–Dec. 1976): 166–67; Anne Iker-Gittleman,
Romance Philology 31 (1977–78): 171–73; J.C. Laidlaw, *French Studies* 33 (1979):
573; Félix Lecoy, *Romania* 96 (1975): 429–30 (corrections); Aldo Menichetti, *Studi
medievali* 19 (1978): 748–52 (corrections); Gert Pinkernell, *Zeitschrift für romanische
Philologie* 92 (1976): 207–8; Claude Thiry, *Moyen Age* 82 (1976): 618–20 (corrections).

1975. *Jean Froissart: Le Joli Buisson de Jonece. Edition avec introduction,
notes et glossaire.* Textes Littéraires Français 222. Geneva: Droz.
Standard critical edition. Reviews: Kurt Baldinger, *Zeitschrift für romanische Philologie*
93 (1977): 394–95 (corrections); A.H. Diverres, *French Studies* 33 (1979): 574–75;
Michelle A. Freeman, *Romance Philology* 34 (1980–81): 366–69; Ruggero M. Ruggieri,
Studi medievali 20 (1979): 449.

1979. *Jean Froissart: "Dits" et "Débats." Introduction, édition, notes, glossaire. Avec en appendice quelques poèmes de Guillaume de Machaut.*
Textes Littéraires Français 274. Geneva: Droz.
Standard critical edition. Contains *Marguerite, Rose, Lis et Marguerite,* and *Cerf Blanc*
(*opus dubium,* see chap. 5.19), *Sire, a vous fais ceste clamour* (Cp7) and *Tu qui vues
avoir mon cheval* (Cp8). Fourrier was unaware that Wimsatt (1970) had already edited *Lis
et Marguerite.* The edition of *Rose* is the first since Tarbé 1849. The two *complaintes*
also appear in Chichmaref 1909, although Fourrier's commentary is useful. Reviews:
Nelly Andrieux, *Bibliothèque de l'Ecole des Chartes* 138 (1980): 255–56; Hans Helmut

Christmann, *Romanische Forschungen* 92 (1980): 398–99; Alfred Foulet, *Romance Philology* 36 (1982–83): 628–30; Jacques Lemaire, *Scriptorium* 35 (1981): 168–69 (corrections); Gianni Mombello, *Studi francesi* 25 (1981): 529–30; J. Monfrin, *Romania* 101 (1980): 429; Gilles Roques, *Zeitschrift für romanische Philologie* 96 (1981): 685 (corrections); W. Van Hoecke, *Archives et Bibliothèques de Belgique* 52 (1981): 403 no. 2199; Nigel Wilkins, *French Studies* 36 (1982): 186–87.

Fowler, Maria Vedder.
  1979. "Musical Interpolations in Thirteenth- and Fourteenth-Century French Narratives." 2 vols. Ph.D. diss. Yale University. Ann Arbor: University Microfilms. Order no. 7927625.
    Includes brief consideration of the *Remede* and the *Voir Dit* (120–24), with catalogues of lyrical insertions in *Remede* (288), *Fonteinne* (308), and *Voir Dit* (289–93). Abstracts: *DAI* A 40/6 (Dec. 1979): 2968–69; *RILM* 13 (1979), no. 2398.

Fox, John.
  1974. *A Literary History of France: The Middle Ages*, ed. P.E. Charvet. London: Benn; New York: Barnes and Noble.
    General introduction. On Machaut, see pp. 293–97.

Françon, Marcel.
  1947. "Note on the Use of the Guidonian Nomenclature by Machaut and Rabelais." *Speculum* 22:249–50.
    Concerns wordplay on solmization syllables in *Confort*, ll. 3993–94.

Frank, Grace.
  1961. "French Literature in the Fourteenth Century." In *The Forward Movement of the Fourteenth Century*, ed. Francis Lee Utley, 61–77. Columbus: Ohio State University Press.
    An early reappraisal of fourteenth-century French literature, though not kind to Machaut (64–66). Frank sees progress in drama, not in narrative and lyrical forms; see summary in Knight 1982, 56–57.

Frappier, Jean.
  1946. "*La Chastelaine de Vergi*; Marguerite de Navarre et Bandello." In *Mélanges 1945*. Vol. 2, *Etudes littéraires*, 89–150. Publications de la Faculté des Lettres de l'Université de Strasbourg 105. Paris: Les Belles Lettres.
    Some details of *Jugement Behaingne* and *Jugement Navarre* derived from the *Chastelaine de Vergi* (106–8).

  1973. "Orphée et Proserpine ou la lyre et la harpe." In *Mélanges de langue et de littérature médiévales offerts à Pierre Le Gentil, par ses collègues, ses élèves et ses amis*, 277–94. Paris: S.E.D.E.S.
    Discusses the *exempla* of Orpheus and Eurydice and the rape of Proserpina in *Confort* (282–83, 292).

Frémiot, Marcel.
  1981. "La musique du XIVe siècle est à votre portée: La Messe Notre-Dame de Guillaume de Machaut." *Musique ancienne* 12:12–30.
    Not examined.

Frese, Dolores Warwick.
  1981–82. "The *Nun's Priest's Tale*: Chaucer's Identified Master Piece?" *Chaucer Review* 16:330–43.
    Includes a discussion of the anagram at the end of *Jugement Behaingne* (335–36, 341 n. 33).

Frobenius, Wolf.
  1985. "Virelai." *Handwörterbuch der musikalischen Terminologie*, ed. Hans Heinrich Eggebrecht. Wiesbaden: Steiner, 1971–. 10 pp.

Detailed study of the history and meaning of the term "virelai" from the second half of the thirteenth until the late sixteenth century. Many quotations from primary witnesses (including Machaut's *Jugement Navarre*, *Remede*, *Voir Dit*, and *Prologue*) and a large bibliography.

1986. "Ballade (Mittelalter)." *Handwörterbuch der musikalischen Terminologie*, ed. Hans Heinrich Eggebrecht. Wiesbaden: Steiner, 1971–. 18 pp.

Detailed study of the history and meaning of the term "ballade" from the thirteenth to the fifteenth century, including Chaucer and Lydgate. Many quotations from primary witnesses (with an important discussion of the *balade entée*, 11) and a large bibliography.

1988. "Hoquetus." *Handwörterbuch der musikalischen Terminologie*, ed. Hans Heinrich Eggebrecht. Wiesbaden: Steiner, 1971–. 13 pp.

Detailed study of the history and meaning of the term "hoquetus" in the thirteenth and fourteenth century. Many quotations from primary witnesses (including Machaut's *Prologue*) and a large bibliography.

Fuller, Sarah.

1971. "Hidden Polyphony—A Reappraisal." *Journal of the American Musicological Society* 24:169–92.

Includes consideration of successive notation in *Pour ce que plus* (L23/17) and *En demantant* (L24/18), 188–90. Abstract: *RILM* 5 (1971), no. 2065.

1985–86. "A Phantom Treatise of the Fourteenth Century? The *Ars nova*." *Journal of Musicology* 4:23–50.

Reappraisal of the shadowy evidence for Philippe de Vitry's contribution as a music theorist, with broad ramifications for our view of musical developments in the early fourteenth century. Abstract: *RILM* 20 (1986), no. 1040.

1986. "On Sonority in Fourteenth-Century Polyphony: Some Preliminary Reflections." *Journal of Music Theory* 30:35–70.

New directions in the analysis of the harmony and tonal system of Machaut's motets, including specific examples from *Fons / O livoris* (M9), *Amours qui a / Faus Samblant* (M15), *Quant vraie amour / O series* (M17), *Bone pastor / Bone pastor* (M18), as well as *Comment puet* (R11). Fuller builds on Kühn 1973 and Pelinski 1975, with a more refined terminology and more sensitive musical insight, establishing a powerful yet historically-based theory for the classification of sonorities and progressions. See further Fuller 1992b. Abstract: *RILM* 20 (1986), no. 5363.

1987a. "Line, *Contrapunctus* and Structure in a Machaut Song." *Music Analysis* 6:37–58.

A highly detailed analysis of *J' aim miex* (B7), showing it to be a very polished, multi-faceted work, operating on many levels, "a sort of cubist construct with intersecting planes of reference, association, process" (54). Abstract: *RILM* 21 (1987), no. 7368.

1987b (comp.). *The European Musical Heritage 800–1750*. With Allan W. Schindler, consulting editor. New York: Knopf.

Contains editions, translations, and analytical commentary of four Machaut works: *Bone pastor / Bone pastor* (M18), *Nes qu' on* (B33), *Quant j' ay l' espart* (R5), and *Dame, a vous* (RF6).

1990. "Modal Tenors and Tonal Orientation in Motets of Guillaume de Machaut." *Studies in Medieval Music: Festschrift for Ernest H. Sanders*, ed. Peter M. Lefferts and Brian Seirup. *Current Musicology* 45–47:199–245.

Strategies of tonal control in fourteenth-century polyphony, based on analyses of the motets of Machaut. Tonal structure depends not on pre-existing conventions, but on the individual characteristics of the tenor chosen. The polyphonic context shapes the *cantus firmus* by emphasizing certain pitches and sonorities in new and inventive ways. Fuller's focus on tonal structure is corrective of the prevailing view of the isorhythmic motet as primarily a rhythmic structure. The composer considered pitch aspects as he planned the rhythm. Motets discussed include *Bone pastor / Bone pastor* (M18), and especially *Fons /*

O livoris (M9), *Quant vraie amour / O series* (M17), *J'ay tant / Lasse!* (M7), and *Martyrum / Diligenter* (M19). Fuller also discusses "mode" in fourteenth-century polyphony, with theoretical citations from Grocheio and others, concluding that at most "mode" can be invoked only insofar as the finals of the motet tenors are treated as stable; mode does not govern the polyphony, rather, counterpoint does.

1991. "Machaut and the Definition of Musical Space." *Sonus* 12:1–15.

The "definition of musical space" refers to the manner in which the opening of a song sets out the parameters of rhythm and pitch. Analysis of both monophonic and polyphonic versions of *Mors sui* (V29/26) reveals essentially two different works; analysis of *Donnez, signeurs* (B26) demonstrates a dual focus on the pitches *F* and *C* with metrical ambiguity in the first half of the work.

1992a. "Guillaume de Machaut: *De toutes flours.*" In *Music Before 1600,* ed. Mark Everist, 41–65. Models of Musical Analysis. Oxford: Blackwell.

Exhaustive analysis of B31, considering the text and its articulation by the musical setting, rhythm, melodic design, harmony, and tonal aspects. Includes voice-leading reductions and editions of both the three-voice and four-voice versions. Reviews: Annie Cœurdevey, *Revue de musicologie* 79 (1993): 383–86; David Fallows, *Early Music* 22 (1994): 321–22; Anthony Pryer, *Musical Times* 134 (1993): 396–97.

1992b. "Tendencies and Resolutions: The Directed Progression in *Ars Nova* Music." *Journal of Music Theory* 36:229–58.

Further development of the analytical system of Fuller 1986, with illustrations of the variety of uses of directed progressions (i.e., unstable sonorities that resolve by step into stable sonorities). Many directed progressions relate to the syntactic or semantic setting of the text. Examples from *Hé! Mors / Fine* (M3), *De Bon Espoir / Puis que* (M4), *Dame, je sui / Fins cuers* (M11), the Credo of the Mass, *Honte, Paour* (B25), *De toutes flours* (B31), *Mes esperis* (B39), and *Dous viaire* (R1).

Gafori, Franchino.

1496. *Practica musice.* Milan: Guilermus Signerre. Facsimile reprint. Farnborough: Gregg Press, 1967.

Music theory treatise that cites Machaut. For translations, see Miller 1968 and I. Young 1969.

Gagnepain, Bernard.

1961. *La musique française du Moyen Age et de la Renaissance.* Que sais-je? 931. Paris: Presses Universitaires de France. 2nd ed. 1968. 3rd ed. 1977. 4th ed. 1984.

Survey of musical genres cultivated by Machaut (59–68).

1982. "La musique en France a l'arrivée de Guillaume de Machaut." In Guillaume de Machaut 1982, 273–80.

A brief look for precursors—such as Adam de la Halle, Lescurel, and *Roman de Fauvel* compositions—for the genres cultivated by Machaut.

Gallo, F. Alberto.

1966 (ed.). *Prosdocimus de Beldemandis: Opera.* Vol. 1, *Expositiones tractatus practice cantus mensurabilis magistri Johannes de Muris.* Antiquae Musicae Italicae Scriptores 3. Bologna: Antiquae Musicae Italicae Studiosi; Università degli Studi di Bologna; Istituto di Studi Musicali e Teatrali, Sez. Musicologia.

Critical edition of a music theory treatise that glosses Johannes de Muris, including the passage on Machaut.

1968. "Alcune fonti poco note di musica teorica e pratica." In *L'Ars Nova italiana del Trecento II,* ed. F. Alberto Gallo, 49–76, 4 plates. Certaldo: Centro Studi sull'Ars Nova italiana del Trecento.

Includes discussion of an anonymous Seville treatise that cites Machaut (59–73). Abstract: *RILM* 2 (1968), no. 3080.

1981 (ed.). *Il Codice musicale Panciatichi 26 della Biblioteca Nazionale de Firenze*. Comune di Certaldo. Centro di Studi sull'Ars Nova musicale italiana del Trecento. Studi e Testi per la storia della musica 3. Florence: Olschki.

Facsimile edition of an Italian anthology manuscript containing music for *En amer* (RF4), *De petit po* (B18), *Honte, paour* (B25), *De toutes flours* (B31), and *Se vous n'estes* (R7). Abstract: *RILM* 15 (1981), no. 330. Review: Fabrizio Della Seta, *Nuova rivista musicale italiana* 17 (1983): 593–94.

1984. "Die Notationslehre im 14. und 15. Jahrhundert." In *Die mittelalterliche Lehre von der Mehrstimmigkeit*, ed. Frieder Zaminer, 257–356. Geschichte der Musiktheorie 5. Darmstadt: Wissenschaftliche Buchgesellschaft.

Includes a discussion of the *Libellus cantus mensurabilis* of Johannes de Muris (298–303). Reviews: Mark Everist, *Music and Letters* 69 (1988): 57–60; Erich Reimer, *Musikforschung* 40 (1987): 380–82.

1985. *Il medioevo II*. Storia della musica a cura della Società Italiana di Musicologia 2. Turin: Edizioni di Torino, 1977. *Music of the Middle Ages II*, trans. Karen Eales. Cambridge: Cambridge University Press, 1985.

Survey of medieval music. Chap. 10 (39–44) on Machaut is good, with summaries of the *Remede* and *Voir Dit*. Reading 6.2 (132–33) gives excerpts from the *Remede*, including the scene surrounding the virelai *Dame, a vous* (RF6), and some scenes of life in the castle. Abstract: *RILM* 11 (1977), no. 2357; 19 (1985), no. 1172. Reviews of Italian original: Howard Mayer Brown, *Early Music* 9 (1981): 100–103; Fabrizio Della Seta, *Nuova rivista musicale italiana* 14 (1980): 628–31. Reviews of English trans.: John Caldwell, *Music and Letters* 67 (1986): 308–9; Gareth R.K. Curtis, *Early Music* 14 (1986): 96–97.

Garci-Gómez, Miguel, ed.

1984. *Marqués de Santillana. Prohemios y cartas literarias*. Madrid: Editora Nacional.

An edition of the famous letter that indicates knowledge of Machaut works and manuscripts (see the comments of the reviewer). Review: Ángel Gómez Moreno, *Romance Philology* 41 (1987–88): 244–49.

Gastoué, Amédée.

1921. *L'orgue en France: de l'antiquité au début de la période classique*. Paris: Bureau d'Edition de la "Schola."

Includes consideration of *Hoquetus David* as a work for organ, with a transcription of the beginning (56–57).

1922. *Les primitifs de la musique française*. Les Musiciens Célèbres. Paris: Laurens.

Includes a general introduction to the musical works of Machaut and his influence (57–74). Considers the *Hoquetus David* a conclusion to Perotin's Alleluia *Nativitas*, and thus an all-vocal work (62–63), an idea later taken up by Reaney. Facsimile of Sanctus (triplum and motetus) in MS G (65). Mention of a 26 March 1918 performance of parts of the Mass at the conservatoire by the *Amis des cathédrales* under H. Letocart. Criticism in Ludwig 1922–23, 441 n. 1.

Gaudet, Minnette.

1993. "Machaut's *Dit de l'Alerion* and the Sexual Politics of Courtly Love." *Romance Languages Annual* 4 (1992): 55–63.

Feminist analysis of *Alerion*.

Gaudet, Minnette, and Constance B. Hieatt, eds. and trans.

1994. *Guillaume de Machaut. The Tale of the Alerion*. Toronto Medieval Texts and Translations 10. Toronto, Buffalo, and London: University of Toronto Press.

Verse translation of *Alerion*, with introduction and notes; an appendix discusses numerology.

Gauvard, Claude.
1982. "Portrait du prince d'après l'œuvre de Guillaume de Machaut: Etude sur les idées politiques du poète." In Guillaume de Machaut 1982, 23–39 (comments, 61–65).
An important revisionist picture of Machaut's biography, particularly concerning his interest in politics.

Geiselhardt, Jakob.
1914. *Machaut und Froissart: Ihre literarischen Beziehungen.* Ph.D. diss. Jena. Weida i.Th.: Thomas & Hubert.
A study of Machaut's influence on Froissart, including his manuscripts (12–16), lyrical forms (including the *pastourelles,* a genre not cultivated by Machaut, 16–27), *dits* (form and contents, 27–29; sources and use of *exempla,* 29–37), and the narrator persona, with specific examples of influence (38–57). Criticisms in Sonnemann 1969, 20–21.

Genevois, A.-M., J.F. Genest, and A. Chalandon.
1987. *Bibliothèques de manuscrits médiévaux en France. Relevé des inventaires du VIIIe au XVIIIe siècle.* Centre Régional de Publication de Paris. Paris: Centre National de la Recherche Scientifique.
Computer catalogue of medieval library inventories. See chap. 3, lost MSS [9] and [14].

Gennrich, Friedrich.
1921–27. *Rondeaux, Virelais und Balladen aus dem Ende des XII., des XIII. und dem ersten Drittel des XIV. Jahrhunderts mit den überlieferten Melodien.* Vol. 1, *Texte.* Gesellschaft für romanische Literatur 43. Dresden: Gesellschaft für romanische Literatur, 1921. Vol. 2, *Materalien, Literaturnachweise, Refrainverzeichnis.* Gesellschaft für romanische Literatur 47. Göttingen: Gesellschaft für romanische Literatur, 1927. Vol. 3, *Das altfranzösische Rondeau und Virelai im 12. und 13. Jahrhundert.* Summa Musica Medii Aevi 10. Langen bei Frankfurt: n.p., 1963.
Standard catalogue of *refrains.* For texts, supplanted by van den Boogaard 1969; for music, however, Gennrich remains indispensable. Reviews: Hans Spanke, *Zeitschrift für französische Sprache und Literatur* 52 (1929): 187–88 (vol. 2); A. Wallensköld, *Literaturblatt für germanische und romanische Philologie* 50 (1929): 34–40 (corrections).

1926–27. "Zur Instrumentenkunde der Machaut-Zeit." *Zeitschrift für Musikwissenschaft* 9:513–17.
As part of a plea for the reconstruction of medieval instruments for modern performance, Gennrich prints some lists of instruments from a French translation of Ovid in MS H [17], from the *Meditations* of Gilles li Muisis, and from the *Parfait du Paon* of Jean de le Mote.

1930. "Zur Machaut-Forschung." *Zeitschrift für romanische Philologie* 50: 351–57.
Mainly a review, intended for philologists, of Ludwig 1926–54 (vol. 2), focusing on sources.

1948. *Abriss der Mensuralnotation des XIV. und der ersten Hälfte des XV. Jahrhunderts.* Musikwissenschaftliche Studien-Bibliothek 3–4. Nieder-Modau: n.p., 1948. 2nd rev. ed. Langen bei Frankfurt: n.p., 1965.
Includes a facsimile of *Lasse! / Se j'aim* (M16) from MS A, and *Armes, Amours* (Deschamps's *déploration*) from MS Ch [59].

1957 (ed.). *Guillaume de Machaut: Messe de Nostre Dame.* Summa musicae medii aevi 1. Darmstadt: n.p.
Facsimile edition of Machaut MS B [4], fols. 281v–294r.

Gerlich, Alois.
1973. "König Johann von Böhmen: Aspekte luxemburgischer Reichspolitik von 1310 bis 1346." *Geschichtliche Landeskunde* 9:131–46.

Political history concerning King John of Luxembourg; includes important additional bibliography.

Gérold, Théodore.
1932. *La musique au Moyen Age*. Les Classiques Français du Moyen Age 73. Paris: Champion.

Includes a good survey of Machaut's music (317–40).

1933. "Le réveil en France, au XVIIIe siècle, de l'intérêt pour la musique profane du Moyen Age." In *Mélanges de musicologie offerts à M. Lionel de la Laurencie*, 223–34. Publications de la Société Française de Musicologie, sér. 2, t. 3–4. Paris: Droz.

Historiographical review. Machaut mentioned on pp. 228–29.

1936. *Histoire de la musique des origines à la fin du XIVe siècle*. Manuels d'Histoire de l'Art. Paris: Renouard.

Includes a survey of Machaut's music (366–76).

Gieber, Robert L.
1982. "Poetic Elements of Rhythm in the Ballades, Rondeaux and Virelais of Guillaume de Machaut." *Romanic Review* 73:1–12.

Meter, stanzaic structure, caesura, rhyme, and enjambment in chansons set to music, illustrated with many examples. Abstract: *RILM* 16 (1982), no. 3805.

Girard, René.
1986. *The Scapegoat*, trans. Yvonne Freccero. Baltimore, Md.: Johns Hopkins University Press.

Machaut's naive account of the persecution of the Jews in *Jugement Navarre* is the sort of text that reflects real persecution, yet Machaut would not have been able to recognize the Jews as scapegoats: that is a modern interpretation. Thus, the modern interpretation of the text is radically different from Machaut's purpose. Girard uncovers structural similarities in his analyses of other "persecution texts" (e.g., the myth of Oedipus, the Gospels). On Machaut, see 1–11 ("Guillaume de Machaut and the Jews"), 117–24 et passim; includes a translation of *Jugement Navarre*, ll. 212–40 (2) and ll. 341–46 (4). Reviews: Lee Worth Bailey, *Journal of the American Academy of Religion* 55 (1987): 832–33; David B. Burrell, *Cross Currents* 38 (1988–89): 443–47; Gerald Gillespie, *Comparative Literature* 38 (1986): 289–97; Phillip G. Williams, *Journal of Religion* 68 (1988): 155–57.

Gleason, Harold, ed.
1945. *Examples of Music Before 1400*. Eastman School of Music Series. New York: Appleton-Century-Crofts, 1942. 2nd corrected printing, 1945.

Editions of *Dame, mon cuer emportez* (V32/29), *Ma fin* (R14), *Mes esperis* (B39), *De Bon Espoir / Puis que* (M4), and Agnus I. Some works are transposed; all include keyboard reductions.

Godwin, Joscelyn.
1975 (ed.). *Schirmer Scores. A Repertory of Western Music*. New York: Schirmer Books (Macmillan).

Anthology; includes editions of Agnus Dei and Ite (45–49 no. 6b), with the Agnus Dei plainsong used as *cantus firmus* in Machaut's setting (44 no. 6a), and *Se je souspir* (V36/30) (pp. 143–44 no. 19).

1977. "'Mains divers acors': Some Instrument Collections of the *Ars nova* Period." *Early Music* 5:148–59.

Discussion of lists of instruments in Machaut's *Remede* and *Prise*, with glossary (156–59). Abstract: *RILM* 11 (1977), no. 137; *Encomia* 6 (1984): 103 no. 624.

Göllner, Marie Louise [see also Martinez, Marie Louise].
1989. "Musical and Poetic Structure in the Refrain Forms of Machaut." In *Liedstudien. Wolfgang Osthoff zum 60. Geburtstag*, ed. Martin Just and Reinhard Wiesend, 61–76. Tutzing: Schneider.

Musical and textual elements are combined in unique and different ways in Machaut's chansons. "The musical fabric does not, however, serve simply to reinforce features of the poetry, but rather sets up a structure of its own to counterbalance that of the text" (75). Brief but insightful analyses of *Aymi!* (V3), *Dou mal* (V8), *Diex, Biauté* (V19), *J'aim miex* (B7), *Honte, Paour* (B25), and *Je puis trop* (B28). Abstract: *RILM* 23 (1989), no. 1852.

1993. "'Un Res d'Alemaigne.'" In *Festschrift für Horst Leuchtmann zum 65. Geburtstag*, ed. Stephan Hörner and Bernhold Schmid, 147–60. Tutzing: Schneider.

Analysis of *Nes qu'on* (B33). Göllner identifies a German melody possibly related to Machaut's cantus and proposes that Machaut tried out a new compositional technique in his ballade by paraphrasing the German melody.

Göllner, Theodor.

1981. "Das *Kyrie cunctipotens*: zwischen Organum und Komposition." In *Musik in Bayern* 22:37–57.

A history of the *cantus firmus* Machaut used in the Kyrie of the Mass (53–57). Göllner traces the use of the *Kyrie cunctipotens* in two-voice compositions from the twelfth to the late fifteenth century; the tenor-contratenor pair in Machaut's Mass relates to this tradition. Abstract: *RILM* 15 (1981), no. 275.

Gombosi, Otto.

1950. "Machaut's *Messe Notre-Dame*." *Musical Quarterly* 36:204–24 (*errata*, 466).

Important analysis of the Mass, particularly the Gloria and Credo. Reviews Machabey (1948) and de Van (1949), providing emendations (207 n. 6). Discussion of *Quant en moy / Amour* (M1), *De Bon Espoir / Puis que* (M4), *Aucune gent / Qui plus* (M5), *S'il estoit / S'Amours* (M6), *J'ay tant / Lasse!* (M7), *Tu qui gregem / Plange* (M22), and *Felix virgo / Inviolata* (M23), with some general comments on architectural structures in motets. Günther (1958, 30 n. 16) and Dömling (1971, 26 n. 9) criticize Gombosi's charts analyzing rhythmic structures in the motets, but Powell (1979) pushes the analysis to greater lengths. Hughes (1989, 165) criticizes the "stanzaic" analyses of Gloria and Credo.

Gómez Muntané, María del Carmen [María Carmen Gómez; Maricarmen Gómez].

1979. *La música en la casa real catalano-aragonesa durante los años 1336–1432*. Vol. 1, *Historia y documentos*. Barcelona: Bosch.

Documentary study of music and musicians in service of the Court of Aragon. Includes a comparative table of instruments, organized by type, incorporating Machaut's lists in *Remede* and *Prise* (79–82).

1985a. "Quelques remarques sur le répertoire sacré de l'Ars nova provenant de l'ancien royaume d'Aragon." *Acta musicologica* 57:166–79.

Includes a comparison of the Gloria and Credo movements of both the Machaut Mass and the Mass of Tournai (173–75). Abstract: *RILM* 19 (1985), no. 1177.

1985b. "Une version à cinq voix du motet *Apollinis eclipsatur / Zodiacum signis* dans le manuscrit *E-BCEN 853*." *Musica disciplina* 39:5–44.

Includes a new reference, dated 1391, to a Machaut manuscript of the infante Martin (r. 1396–1410); see chap. 2.2.1g. Abstract: *RILM* 19 (1985), no. 1178.

1987. "La musique à la maison royale de Navarre à la fin du Moyen-Age et le chantre Johan Robert." *Musica disciplina* 41:109–51.

Includes mention of a manuscript of Machaut's *Confort* that Charles of Navarre had made in 1384 (115). See chap. 3, lost MS [24]. Abstract: *RILM* 21 (1987), no. 1371.

Gorcy, Gérard.

1961. "'Courtois' et 'courtoisie' d'après quelques textes du Moyen Français." *Bulletin des jeunes romanistes* 4 (Dec.): 15–25.

Study of the terms "courtois" and "courtoisie" in fourteenth- and fifteenth-century French texts, including *dits* of Machaut.

Gourmont, Remy de.
1913. "Le roman de Guillaume de Machaut et de Peronne d'Armentières."
Promenades littéraires, 5ème série, 5–35. Paris: Mercure de France.
Entertaining discussion of the *Voir Dit* by an author fully convinced of the truth of the
love affair and the importance and beauty of Peronne's poetry and letters. Includes some
criticism of Machaut: "c'était le moment d'être moins poète et plus amoureux" (58). Cf.
Cerquiglini 1985b, 102 n. 28.

Goy, Jean.
1982. "Note sur la tombe de Guillaume de Machaut en la cathédrale de
Reims." In Guillaume de Machaut 1982, 153–55, 2 plates.
Summary references to Machaut in Reims cathedral archives.

Greckel, Wilbert C.
1981. "The *Ballades notées* of Guillaume de Machaut." *Music Review* 42:91–
102.
General discussion of musical aspects of the ballades. Abstract: *RILM* 15 (1981), no.
2366.

Green, Richard Firth.
1990. *"Le Roi qui ne ment* and Aristocratic Courtship." In *Courtly Literature:
Culture and Context. Selected papers from the 5th Triennial Congress of the
International Courtly Literature Society, Dalfsen, The Netherlands, 9–16
August, 1986,* ed. Keith Busby and Erik Kooper, 211–25. Utrecht Publications in General and Comparative Literature 25. Amsterdam and Philadelphia: Benjamins.
Does not mention Machaut, but provides an ample bibliography and discussion of the
game played in *Remede* and *Voir Dit.* Cf. Klein 1911.

Greene, Gordon K., ed.
1981–89. *French Secular Music: Manuscript Chantilly, Musée Condé 564,
First Part.* Texts ed. Terence Scully. Polyphonic Music of the Fourteenth
Century 18. Les Remparts, Monaco: L'Oiseau-Lyre, 1981.
Standard critical edition of fourteenth-century chansons (omitting works of Machaut and
the Turin codex). See also Apel 1970–72. Reviews: Laurie Koehler, *Journal of the
American Musicological Society* 39 (1986): 633–41; Christopher Page, *Early Music* 11
(1983): 381–83; Andrew Tomasello, *Notes* 41 (1984–85): 150–51.

*French Secular Music: Manuscript Chantilly, Musée Condé 564, Second
Part.* Texts ed. Terence Scully. Polyphonic Music of the Fourteenth
Century 19. Les Remparts, Monaco: Monaco: L'Oiseau-Lyre, 1982.
Reviews: Laurie Koehler, *Journal of the American Musicological Society* 39 (1986):
633–41; Andrew Tomasello, *Notes* 41 (1984–85): 150–51.

French Secular Music: Ballades and Canons. Texts ed. Terence Scully.
Polyphonic Music of the Fourteenth Century 20. Les Remparts, Monaco:
L'Oiseau-Lyre, 1982.
Review: Laurie Koehler, *Journal of the American Musicological Society* 39 (1986): 633–
41.

French Secular Music: Virelais. Texts ed. Terence Scully. Polyphonic
Music of the Fourteenth Century 21. Les Remparts, Monaco: L'Oiseau-
Lyre, 1987.
Reviews: Lawrence Earp, *Notes* 46 (1989–90): 218–20; David Fallows, *Early Music* 16
(1988): 437–41.

French Secular Music: Rondeaux and Miscellaneous Pieces. Texts ed.
Terence Scully. Polyphonic Music of the Fourteenth Century 22. Les
Remparts, Monaco: L'Oiseau-Lyre, 1989.
Reviews: Daniel Leech-Wilkinson, *Music and Letters* 71 (1990): 460–61; Luigi Lera,
Nuova rivista musicale italiana 26 (1992): 610–15.

Griffith, Dudley David.
  1955. *Bibliography of Chaucer 1908–1953*. University of Washington Publications in Language and Literature 13. Seattle: University of Washington Press.
  Standard Chaucer bibliography. See also Crawford 1967; Baird 1977; Baird-Lange/ Schnuttgen 1988.

Grimm, Jürgen.
  1965. *Die literarische Darstellung der Pest in der Antike und in der Romania.* Freiburger Schriften zur romanischen Philologie 6. Munich: Fink.
  A study of the tradition of plague literature, with some mention of the *Jugement Navarre* (143–54).

Gröber, Gustav, et al.
  1902 (ed.). *Grundriss der romanischen Philologie*. Vol. 2/1. Strasbourg: Trübner.
  Excellent introduction to the period (1037–42); the account of Machaut, however (1042–47), is based largely on the works published in Tarbé 1849. The discussion of *Voir Dit* remains interesting (1046–47).

Gröber, Gustav, and Stefan Hofer.
  1933. *Geschichte der mittelfranzösischen Literatur*. Vol. 1, *Vers- und Prosadichtung des 14. Jahrhunderts, Drama des 14. und 15. Jahrhunderts*. 2nd. ed., revised by Stefan Hofer. Vol. 1 of 2 vols. Grundriss der romanischen Philologie, begründet von Gustav Gröber, Geschichte der französischen Literatur 1. Berlin and Leipzig: de Gruyter.
  Revision and expansion of Gröber 1902. Introduction, pp. 1–13; Machaut discussed, pp. 14–29. Literary works are described fully, based on the editions of Hoepffner and Chichmaref. On the other hand, the discussion of the *Voir Dit* is shorter and less colorful than that of Gröber 1902. The discussion of the lyrics provides an extensive treatment of themes.

Guelliot, Octave.
  1914. "Guillaume de Machaut." *Revue historique ardennaise* 21:297–316.
  Wide-ranging review of Machaut's biography, including biographical material in the literary works, with a description of the principal manuscripts, and a bibliography.

Guesnon, A.
  1912. Review of Chichmaref 1909 and 1911. *Moyen Age* 25:89–99.
  First modern mention of MS **Pm** [18]. Full of interesting biographical information and corrections, including corrections to Hoepffner's review of Chichmaref 1909 (96–97).

Guiette, Robert.
  1949. "D'une poésie formelle en France au Moyen Age." *Revue des sciences humaines*, 61–68. Reprint, with additions. In *Questions de Littérature. Romanica Gandensia* 8 (1960): 9–18 (two supplementary notes, 19–23). Reprint, with further additions. *D'une poésie formelle en France au Moyen Age*. Paris: Nizet, 1972. Reprint. *Forme et senefiance: Etudes médiévales recueillies*, ed. J. Dufournet et al., 1–15. Publications Romanes et Françaises 148. Geneva: Droz, 1978.
  Publication of a 1946 lecture. The play of form is primary in the *chanson courtoise*. See also Guiette 1960.

  1960. "Aventure de la poésie formelle." In *Questions de littérature. Romanica Gandensia* 8:24–32. Reprint. *Forme et senefiance: Etudes médiévales recueillies*, ed. J. Dufournet et al., 16–24. Publications Romanes et Françaises 148. Geneva: Droz, 1978.
  Publication of a 1946 lecture, complementing Guiette 1949. Influential early reappraisal of the historical development of lyrics from the late thirteenth century through Villon. Discusses the crystallization of the fixed forms, the more personal and realistic subject

matter, and the complex formal acrobatics of the second rhetoric. On Machaut's lyrics, see pp. 28–31. Reviews of *Questions de littérature:* A.H. Diverres, *French Studies* 16 (1962): 389–90; Poirion 1963. Reviews of *Forme et senefiance:* B.N. Sargent-Baur, *Langues romanes* 34 (1980): 391–93; A.H. Diverres, *French Studies* 33 (1979): 321; Francis Dubost, *Moyen Age* 86 (1980): 332–35; Tony Hunt, *Modern Language Review* 75 (1980): 878–79; Sebastian Neumeister, *Romanische Forschungen* 92 (1980): 286–88; Daniel Poirion, *Informations littéraires* 32 (1980): 31; J.C. Rivière, *Bibliothèque d'Humanisme et Renaissance* 42 (1980): 270–73; Jean Subrenat, *Revue des langues romanes* 83 (1978): 528–30.

Guiffrey, Jules.
1894–96. *Inventaires de Jean, duc de Berry (1401–1416).* 2 vols. Paris: Leroux.
One document concerns the loan of MS E [7] to the Duke of Clarence in 1412 (1:226 no. 860). See Ludwig 1926–54, 11a* n. 1; Bowers 1975–76; Wathey 1988.

Guigard, Joannis.
1890. *Nouvel armorial du bibliophile. Guide de l'amateur des livres amoriés.* 2 vols. Paris: Rondeau.
Information on the modern bindings of MSS E [7] and M [10] (1:32).

Guillaume de Machaut.
1982. *Guillaume de Machaut: Poète et compositeur. Colloque-table ronde organisé par l'Université de Reims (19–22 avril 1978).* Actes et Colloques 23. Paris: Klincksieck.
Important collection of papers from a Machaut conference. See Avril 1982a; Brejon de Lavergnée 1982; Calin 1982; Cerquiglini 1982; Chailley 1982; Dricot 1982; Ferrand 1982; Gagnepain 1982; Gauvard 1982; Goy 1982; Günther 1982; Holzbacher 1982; Israel-Meyer 1982; Keitel 1982a; Leguy 1982; Musso 1982; Planche 1982; Poirion 1982; Reaney 1982; Roques 1982; Snizkova 1982; Vachulka 1982; Voisé 1982; Wozna 1982; Ziino 1982b. Reviews: Pascale Bourgain, *Romania* 104 (1983): 150–53; Giuseppe Di Stefano, *Zeitschrift für romanische Philologie* 101 (1985): 463–64; Angela Dzelzainis, *French Studies* 38 (1984): 324–25; J. Everett, *Moyen français* 13 (1983): 108–9; Louise Gnädinger, *Vox romanica* 47 (1988): 271–73; Dieter Ingenschay, *Romanische Forschungen* 97 (1985): 302–5; E.R. Sienaert, *Lettres romanes* 37 (1983): 236–38; Nigel Wilkins, *Medium Ævum* 54 (1985): 142–43.

Guillemain, Bernard.
1952. *La politique bénéficiale du pape Benoît XII 1334–1342.* Bibliothèque de l'Ecole des Hautes Etudes 299. Paris: Champion.
Useful study of benefices in the period of Pope Benedict XII.

1962. *La cour pontificale d'Avignon (1309–1376): Etude d'une société.* Bibliothèque des Ecoles Françaises d'Athènes et de Rome 201. Paris: Boccard.
Utilized here for material on papal politics and Machaut's princely patrons.

Günther, Ursula.
1957. "Der musikalische Stilwandel der französischen Liedkunst in der zweiten Hälfte des 14. Jahrhunderts, dargestellt an Virelais, Balladen und Rondeaux von Machaut sowie datierbaren Kantilenensätzen seiner Zeitgenossen und direkten Nachfolger." Ph.D. diss. Hamburg.
Important stylistic study (Machaut discussed esp. 45–163). Thorough review of research on the Ars Nova up to 1957; discussion of problems in editing fourteenth-century music. The chapter on mensural notation was revised and expanded as Günther 1962–63. A long chapter on Machaut chronology and chanson genres was partially expanded, but with the musical analyses much reduced, in Günther 1963a; the discussion of motets was thoroughly reworked as Günther 1958. The chapter on twelve chansons that Günther dates before 1380, which include Deschamps's *déploration, Armes amours / O flour* and the anonymous ballade *Ma dame m'a congié donné* (related to *Se je me pleing* [B15]),

remains unpublished. The study of ten works that Günther dates after 1380 was published as Günther 1961–62, and the edition of ten datable songs was published as Günther 1959.

1958. "The 14th Century Motet and its Development." *Musica disciplina* 12: 27–47.

Survey of the stylistic development of the fourteenth-century motet. Provides points of comparison between Machaut motets and fourteenth-century isorhythmic motets in the MSS **Iv** [57] and **Ch** [59] (pp. 28–35). Emphasis on the stylistic distinctions between chanson and motet.

1959 (ed.). *Zehn datierbare Kompositionen der ars nova.* Schriftenreihe des musikwissenschaftlichen Instituts der Universität Hamburg 2. Hamburg: Musikwissenschaftliches Institut der Universität.

Includes an edition of the anonymous ballade *Ma dame m'a congié donné,* related to Machaut's *Se je me pleing* (B15). Review: Kurt von Fischer, *Musikforschung* 13 (1960): 499–500.

1960a. "Die Anwendung der Diminution in der Handschrift Chantilly 1047." *Archiv für Musikwissenschaft* 17:1–21.

Included here for the remarks on the versions of *Quant Theseüs / Ne quier* (B34) transmitted in MSS **Ch** [59] and **PR** [63] (p. 7).

1960b. "Der Gebrauch des tempus perfectum diminutum in der Handschrift Chantilly 1047." *Archiv für Musikwissenschaft* 17:277–97.

On the notation of difficult rhythms of the Ars Subtilior in augmented note values (pp. 295–97). The practice extends back to Machaut, and is seen in a number of monophonic lais, in the *complainte Tels rit* (RF2) and *chant royal Joie, plaisence* (RF3), as well as in *Hoquetus David, Dame, je sui / Fins cuers* (M11), and *Dame, comment qu'amez* (B16).

1961. "Das Wort-Ton-Problem bei Motetten des 14. Jahrhunderts." *Festschrift Heinrich Besseler zum sechzigsten Geburtstag,* 163–78. Institut für Musikwissenschaft der Karl-Marx-Universität. Leipzig: VEB Deutscher Verlag für Musik.

Günther applies principles of Reichert (1956) to ten motets of the late fourteenth century transmitted in **Ch** [59]. Four of the ten exhibit good-to-excellent correspondence of textual and musical structure. Comments in Clarkson 1971, 155.

1961–62. "Datierbare Balladen des späten 14. Jahrhunderts, I." *Musica disciplina* 15 (1961): 39–61; "Datierbare Balladen des späten 14. Jahrhunderts, II." *Musica disciplina* 16 (1962): 151–74.

Critical reports and studies of ten ballades dating from between 1378 and 1394, with a discussion of stylistic elements and a comparison with the chanson style of the Machaut generation of composers. Contributes towards a refinement of Machaut's style characteristics by tracing the evolution of the styles of younger composers. Besides scattered comments on individual works, see especially the "summary and comparison with the chanson style of the Machaut period" (pt. 2, 165–74).

1962–63. "Die Mensuralnotation der Ars nova in Theorie und Praxis." *Archiv für Musikwissenschaft* 19–20:9–28.

A survey of problems in the four *tempus/prolatio* combinations of the Ars Nova; discusses the development of syncopation. Considers *Plourez, dames* (B32), *Ma fin* (R14), and *Quant ma dame les maus* (R19). Builds on Hoppin 1960, finding further unrecognized examples of syncopation in several works, especially *S'onques* (L17/12).

1963a. "Chronologie und Stil der Kompositionen Guillaume de Machauts." *Acta Musicologia* 35:96–114.

Still the best overall account of the style characteristics of Machaut's musical works, related to an overall chronological development. Considerations on chronology are expanded from Günther 1957, but the analyses of individual genres are vastly reduced.

1963b. "Das Ende der *ars nova*." *Musikforschung* 16:105–21, 1 plate.
Includes a discussion of musical style in chansons in the years after Machaut's death.
Introduction and chronological delimitation of the term Ars Subtilior, applied to the style
period corresponding more or less to the period of the Schism (1378–1417).

1963c. "Die Musiker des Herzogs von Berry." *Musica disciplina* 17:79–95.
Information on several contemporaries of Machaut: Jean Vaillant, Pierre des Molins, and
Solage.

1964. "Zur Biographie einiger Komponisten der Ars subtilior." *Archiv für
Musikwissenschaft* 21:172–99.
Discusses King John I of Aragon as a patron of music and Avignonese musicians in his
service, with new material on the biographies of several late fourteenth-century composers
from account books of popes Clement VII (1378–1394) and Benedict XIII (1394–deposed
1409). Includes mention of a possible candidate for the "M. Franciscus" who composed
Deschamps's double ballade *déploration* on Machaut's death (186), and discusses the 1361
document reporting Charles of Navarre's gift of a hackney to Machaut (195 n. 160). See
chap. 1.12.2.

1965 (ed.). *The Motets of the Manuscripts Chantilly, musée condé, 564* (olim
1047) and Modena, Biblioteca estense, α.M.5,24 (olim *lat. 568*). Corpus
Mensurabilis Musicae 39. [Rome]: American Institute of Musicology.
Edition of motets in MSS **Ch** [59] and **Mod** [66], with valuable historical and textual
notes.

1966. "Die Rolle Englands, Spaniens, Deutschlands und Polens in der Musik
des 14. Jahrhunderts." *Bericht über der neunten internationalen Kongress
Salzburg 1964.* Vol. 2, *Protokolle von den Symposia und Round Tables;
Vorträge und Kongressprogramm,* 188–200. Kassel: Bärenreiter.
Summary of reports by Gilbert Reaney, Theodor Göllner, Frank Harrison, and Ursula
Günther. The summary of Günther's paper on musical life at the court of Navarre includes
mention of the 1361 document reporting Charles of Navarre's gift of a hackney to
Machaut (196–97). See chap. 1.12.2.

1967. "Bemerkungen zum älteren französischen Repertoire des Codex Reina
(PR)." *Archiv für Musikwissenschaft* 24:237–52.
An extended critical review of Wilkins 1966. Includes emendations (249–51) for *Phiton,
Phiton*, a ballade based on Machaut's *Phyton* (B38). Abstract: *RILM* 2 (1968), no. 1641.

1970. "Das Manuskript Modena, Biblioteca estense, α.M.5,24 (*olim lat. 568
= Mod*)." *Musica disciplina* 24:17–67.
Inventory and study of the manuscript **Mod** [66]. Abstract: *RILM* 6 (1972), no. 218.

1972. "Zitate in französischen Liedsätzen der Ars Nova und Ars Subtilior."
Musica disciplina 26:53–68.
Survey of textual and musical quotations in fourteenth-century chansons. Many of these
cases of imitation or borrowing relate to Machaut works, and Günther employs Machaut's
term *balade entée* from the *Prologue* in this regard. Includes mention of works related to
Machaut's *On ne porroit* (B3), *N'en fait* (B11), *Pour ce que tous* (B12), *Se je me pleing*
(B15), *De Fortune* (B23), *Tres douce dame que* (B24), *Quant Theseüs / Ne quier* (B34),
Phyton (B38), *Tant doucement me sens* (R9), *Ma fin* (R14), and *Puis qu'on oubli* (R18).
Abstract: *RILM* 6 (1972), no. 219.

1975. "Problems of Dating in Ars Nova and Ars Subtilior." In *L'Ars Nova
italiana del Trecento IV,* ed. Agostino Ziino, 289–301. Certaldo: Centro
Studi sull'Ars Nova italiana del Trecento.
A critical response to the stylistic chronology of fourteenth century music given in Apel
1973; Günther's account of the dating and provenance of the MS **Iv** [57].

1980a. "Matteo de Perusio." *New Grove* 11:830.
Includes mention of a relationship—noted by Lucy Cross—between Matteo da Perugia's ballade *Se je me plaing de Fortune* and two of Machaut's ballades, *Se je me pleing* (B15) and *De Fortune* (B23).

1980b. "Sources, MS, §VII, 1." "Sources, MS, §VII, 3." *New Grove* 17: 661, 663–65.
A brief description of the principal musical collections of fourteenth-century French polyphony other than the Machaut manuscripts, including **Iv** [57], **Ch** [59], **FP** [61], **Mod** [66], and **Str** [73]; see also Fischer 1980. For the main Machaut manuscripts, see Reaney 1980b.

1982. "Contribution de la musicologie à la biographie et à la chronologie de Guillaume de Machaut." In Guillaume de Machaut 1982, 95–116.
An extended critique of the chronology of Keitel (1976), with a review of the theories of chronology proposed by Günther (1957; 1963), Reaney (1952; 1967), and Swartz (1974). Also contains some important speculation concerning the provenance of MS C [1], as well as a new interpretation of the document concerning a gift of a hackney from Charles of Navarre to Machaut discussed in Anglès 1970 and Chailley 1973 (see chap. 1.12.2).

1983. "Fourteenth-Century Music with Texts Revealing Performance Practice." In Boorman 1983, 253–70.
Problems of transcription and interpretation of an anonymous retrograde rondeau—similar to Machaut's *Ma fin* (R14)—and of *Sans cuer m'en / Amis / Dame* (B17), *Je ne cesse* (L16/11), and other works not by Machaut. Abstract: *RILM* 18 (1984), no. 5486.

1984a. "Sinnbezüge zwischen Text und Musik in ars nova und ars subtilior." In Günther/Finscher 1984, 229–68.
A contribution to the growing number of studies that demonstrate close connections between text meaning and musical expression in fourteenth-century music. Large repertory discussed; for Machaut, see 231–32, 256, 263–65, and 267, discussing *Je ne cesse* (L16/11), *S'onques* (L17/12), *Martyrum / Diligenter* (M19), *Sans cuer m'en / Amis / Dame* (B17), *De Fortune* (B23), and *Ma fin* (R14).

1984b. "Unusual Phenomena in the Transmission of Late 14th Century Polyphonic Music," trans. Gilbert Reaney. *Musica disciplina* 38:87–117.
Includes new material on the date and provenance of **Ch** [59] (pp. 88–107). Abstract: *RILM* 18 (1984), no. 1043.

1990. "Polymetric Rondeaux from Machaut to Dufay: Some Style-Analytical Observations." *Studies in Musical Sources and Style: Essays in Honor of Jan La Rue*, ed. Eugene K. Wolf and Edward H. Roesner, 75–108. Madison, Wis.: A-R Editions.
Discussion of polyrhythm in *Quant ma dame les maus* (R19) and in a large number of later works possibly modeled on R19.

Günther, Ursula, and Ludwig Finscher, eds.
1984. *Musik und Text in der Mehrstimmigkeit des 14. und 15. Jahrhunderts: Vorträge des Gastsymposions in der Herzog August Bibliothek Wolfenbüttel, 8. bis 12. September 1980.* Göttinger musikwissenschaftliche Arbeiten 10. Kassel: Bärenreiter.
Collection of conference papers. See Bent 1984; Günther 1984a; Newes 1984; Reaney 1984; Wilkins 1984.

Gunden, Heidi von.
1974–75. "Tête-à-tête." *Composer* 6, no. 15, 33–37.
A contemporary composer of a Mass carries on an imaginary dialogue with Guillaume de Machaut. Machaut's comments on some recordings (Alfred Deller, Bach Guild BGS 70656 [1961]; Safford Cape, Archiv ARC 3032 [1956]; and John McCarthy, Nonesuch H 71184 [1966]) are not in line with recent scholarship on performance practice (36).

Gushee, Lawrence.
1980. "Two Central Places: Paris and the French Court in the Early Four-teenth Century." In *Bericht über den internationalen musikwissenschaft-lichen Kongress Berlin 1974*, ed. Hellmut Kühn and Peter Nitsche, 135–51 (discussion, 151–57). Gesellschaft für Musikwissenschaft. Kassel: Bären-reiter.

Documents from early fourteenth-century Paris indicate that minstrels worked for both city and court, and thus their styles of improvisation could have influenced high-level court composers of written polyphony. Unfortunately largely lacking in the written pre-sentation is Gushee's theory of the development of the polyphonic chanson, as "the syn-thesis of monophonic song (manifested in the Cantus) with the ensemble practices of urban minstrelsy (in Tenor and Contratenor), rather than as the product of a more or less continuous historical development (say, from the motet) for which much of the manuscript evidence has vexingly disappeared, or as the highly original and daring discov-ery of a musical genius" (147; cf. Earp 1991b, 105–6). Some of the flavor of Gushee's presentation can be gleaned from the discussion (153–57). See also Arlt 1982 and Gushee 1982. A supplementary note contains new documents from the period of Machaut's service to the king of Bohemia (see chap. 1.5.4).

1982. "Analytical Method and Compositional Process in Some Thirteenth and Fourteenth-Century Music." In *Aktuelle Fragen der musikbezogenen Mittel-alterforschung: Texte zu einem Basler Kolloquium des Jahres 1975*, 165–91. Forum Musicologicum: Basler Beiträge zur Musikgeschichte 3. Winter-thur: Amadeus.

Questions on compositional procedure in the early fourteenth century. Provides a few more details of Gushee's theory of the interaction of improvising instrumentalists and composers of art polyphony (cf. Gushee 1980), and some interesting comments on problems of early music analysis.

Guthrie, Steven R.
1985. "Chaucer's French Pentameter." Ph.D. diss. Brown University. Ann Arbor: University Microfilms. Order no. 8519842.

Metrical study of Chaucer's *Troilus and Criseyde*, including consideration of decasyllabic lines in Machaut's *Jugement Behaingne* (ll. 1–833). "Chaucer's metrical practice... seems to suggest an affinity with Machaut which goes deeper than youthful influence or the incidental plunder of source material, and at the same time it seems to suggest that Boccaccio's influence on Chaucer has been overstated" (2). Abstract: *DAI* A 46/8 (Feb. 1986): 2289.

1987. "Machaut and the *Octosyllable*." *Studies in the Literary Imagination* 20: 55–75.

A study of the rhythmic structures of several narrative and lyrical texts. Concerning Machaut, Guthrie finds distinctions between ballades not set to music and those set to music: "the meter of the *Ballades Notées* is more complex than that of the ballades without music.... Machaut's mature intuition apparently tells him that he can get away with greater variation in a song than in a spoken lyric..." (68–69).

1988–89. "Prosody and the Study of Chaucer: A Generative Reply to Halle-Keyser." *Chaucer Review* 23:30–49.

Generative analysis of metrical stress in Chaucer demonstrates that his lines are strongly influenced by Machaut's decasyllabic line (*Jugement Behaingne* provides the sample).

1991. "Meter and Performance in Machaut and Chaucer." In Baltzer 1991b, 72–100.

Analysis of caesura and stress in octosyllabic and decasyllabic narrative and lyric verse. By the time of Machaut, an evolution is evident from a fixed caesura towards greater rhyth-mic variety of forms. Poetic rhythm is not mirrored in musical settings; there are rhyth-mic differences between lyrics composed with music and lyrics composed only as poetry. Includes a transcription of *Je sui aussi* (B20) from MS A, ed. Rebecca A. Baltzer (98–99).

Gybbon-Monypenny, G.B.
1957. "Autobiography in the *Libro de Buen Amor* in Light of Some Literary Comparisons." *Bulletin of Hispanic Studies* 34:63–78.

Isolates the genre "erotic pseudo-autobiography," which includes Machaut's *Voir Dit* (esp. 70–74). "The poet writes a story—a *roman*—presenting himself as the hero of a great love affair" (70).

1973. "Guillaume de Machaut's Erotic 'Autobiography': Precedents for the Form of the *Voir-Dit*." In *Studies in Medieval Literature and Languages in Memory of Frederick Whitehead*, ed. W. Rothwell et al., 133–52. Manchester: Manchester University Press.

Study of the subgenre identified in Gybbon-Monypenny 1957, with an important study of the larger genre, the narrative with lyrical insertions. Cf. De Looze 1993b.

Haas, Robert.
1931. *Aufführungspraxis der Musik*. Handbuch der Musikwissenschaft. Potsdam: Athenaion.

History of performance practice, with some discussion of early performances by Gurlitt (see Ludwig 1922–23 and Besseler 1924–25).

Hagen, Hermann, ed.
1875. *Catalogus Codicum Bernensium (Bibliotheca Bongarsiana)*. Part 1. Bern: Haller.

Catalogue description of MSS **K** [15] and **L** [34] by Gustav Gröber.

Haggh, Barbara.
1988. "Music, Liturgy, and Ceremony in Brussels, 1350–1500." 2 vols. Ph.D. diss. University of Illinois at Urbana-Champaign. Ann Arbor: University Microfilms. Order no. 8908694.

Music in medieval Brussels from the period of the earliest documented performances of polyphony, which were established by systems of endowments and incorporations of wealthy parishioners. Such endowments are comparable to those that supported performances of Machaut's Mass. Abstracts: *DAI* A 50/2 (Aug. 1989): 293; *RILM* 22 (1988), no. 1622.

Hallmark, Anne.
1983. "Some Evidence for French Influence in Northern Italy, *c.* 1400." In Boorman 1983, 193–225.

Includes a discussion of the Paduan fragments (196–97), and mention of *Ma fin* (R14) (p. 215). Abstract: *RILM* 18 (1984), no. 1046.

Hamburg, Otto, and Margaretha Landwehr von Pragenau, eds.
1976. *Musikgeschichte in Beispielen, von der Antike bis Johann Sebastian Bach*. Taschenbücher zur Musikwissenschaft 39. Wilhelmshaven: Heinrichshofen. Original Dutch ed. Utrecht: Spectrum, 1973. *Music History in Examples: From Antiquity to Johann Sebastian Bach*. New York: Peters, 1978.

Includes editions of *Comment qu'a moy* (V5) (pp. 19–20 no. 24); *Je puis trop* (B28) (p. 19 no. 23); and *S'il estoit / S'Amours* (M6) (pp. 17–19 no. 22).

Hamm, Charles.
1962. "Manuscript Structure in the Dufay Era." *Acta musicologica* 34:166–84.

An influential theory concerning manuscript transmission of music in the fifteenth century, unsuccessfully applied to the Machaut manuscripts in Keitel 1976. Useful application in Kügle 1993, 33–73, 84–94.

Hamzaoui, Sylvie.
1981. *Guillaume de Machault. Sélection de références bibliographiques*. 2nd rev. ed. Reims: Bibliothèque de l'Université (Lettres). 1st ed., no author, 1977.

Includes many items of general interest, which are not repeated in the present bibliography.

Handlist.
1951. *Handlist of Manuscripts in the National Library of Wales. The National Library of Wales Journal. Supplement.* Series 2/2. Aberystwyth: Council of the National Library of Wales.
Standard catalogue of MS **W** [2].

Handschin, Jacques.
1923. "Die ältesten Denkmäler mensural notierter Musik in der Schweiz." *Archiv für Musikwissenschaft* 5:1–10.
Includes a discussion of MS **K** [15] (pp. 1–2).

1927–28. "Zur Frage der melodischen Paraphrasierung im Mittelalter." *Zeitschrift für Musikwissenschaft* 10:513–59; 12 (1929–30): 192.
Includes a discussion of chant paraphrase in fourteenth-century Mass movements, with an analysis of Machaut's Credo that demonstrates how the melody of Gregorian Credo I appears in different voices (542–43). Handschin does not insist that Machaut consciously paraphrased the chant; rather, he approaches Leech-Wilkinson's view (1990c, 39) that Machaut's setting shows the extent to which he had internalized the melody. Handschin further presages Leech-Wilkinson in his conclusion that "it goes without saying that to a high degree all voices must have been planned at the same time" (543).

1929–30. "Über Estampie und Sequence I." *Zeitschrift für Musikwissenschaft* 12:1–20.
On the "rés d'Alemaigne" and *Nes qu'on* (B33), see pp. 9–10 n. 4.

1931. "Die Rolle der Nationen in der Musikgeschichte." *Schweizerisches Jahrbuch für Musikwissenschaft* 5:1–42.
On the "rés d'Alemaigne" and *Nes qu'on* (B33), see pp. 38–39.

1948. *Musikgeschichte im Überblick.* Aulos-Bücher. Lucerne: Räber. 2nd ed., revised by Franz Brenn. Lucerne: Räber, 1964. Reprint. Wilhelmshaven: Heinrichshofen, 1981. Reprint. Wilhelmshaven: Noetzel, 1990.
Survey of music history. The fourteenth century is covered on pp. 200–216, including the Machaut motets (203–4); chansons (204–6); Mass (210–11); and *Hoquetus David* (216).

1949. "The Sumer Canon and Its Background." *Musica disciplina* 3:55–94.
On the "rés d'Alemaigne" and *Nes qu'on* (B33), see p. 85.

Hanf, Georg.
1898. "Über Guillaume de Machauts *Voir Dit.*" *Zeitschrift für romanische Philologie* 22:145–96.
Publication of the author's 1898 Halle dissertation. Considers earlier writings on the question of truth and the identity of Toute Belle, with an excellent plot summary (149–53). Information on people and places mentioned in the poem, style of letters, various inconsistencies, dates of letters, and the possibility of lost letters. Hanf believes that the order of letters 40 and 41 should be exchanged, but determines finally that the internal contradictions cannot be resolved, and that the *Voir Dit* is a free invention of the author. The first half of the work was much more worthwhile and carefully worked out that the second half; Machaut's interest flagged, and he padded the second half with ready-made material from Ovid, quickly finished the work and did not revise it (but see Calin 1974, 201–2). Summary in Calin 1974, 169–71. Review: Gaston Paris, *Romania* 27 (1898): 509–13, esp. 509.

Hanning, Robert W.
1986. "Chaucer's First Ovid: Metamorphosis and Poetic Tradition in *The Book of the Duchess* and *The House of Fame.*" In *Chaucer and the Craft of Fiction*, ed. Leigh A. Arrathoon, 121–63. Rochester, Mich.: Solaris.
Includes material on Machaut's *Fonteinne*, which influenced Chaucer's use of the story of Ceyx and Alcyone in the *Book of the Duchess* (125–26, 130–37, and notes 159–60).

Harden, Jean.
  1977. "'Musica ficta' in Machaut." *Early Music* 5:473–77.
    Advocates retaining mainly the accidentals written in the manuscripts, although some
    ambiguities and alternatives remain. Abstracts: *RILM* 11 (1977), no. 4426; Karin
    Paulsmeier, *Basler Jahrbuch für historische Musikpraxis* 2 (1978): 224 no. 144.
  1983. "Sharps, Flats, and Scribes: Musica ficta in the Machaut Manuscripts."
    Ph.D. diss. Cornell University. 2 vols. Ann Arbor: University Microfilms.
    Order no. 8328707.
    Applies the work of Hughes (1972) and Bent (1972) to Machaut. Argues for as literal as
    possible an interpretation of source accidentals, taking into account problems of copying
    from exemplars of different line length and format. Essentially, the sources have all the
    accidentals needed. Scribal practice and manuscript families discussed in chaps. 3–4. On
    alternative scorings, see chap. 7. Includes a new edition of Machaut's polyphonic
    ballades, rondeaux, and polyphonic virelais. Abstracts: *DAI* A 44/11 (May 1984): 3199–
    200; *RILM* 17 (1983), no. 326.

Harman, Alec.
  1958. *Mediaeval and Early Renaissance Music (up to c. 1525)*. Man and His
    Music 1. Fair Lawn, N.J.: Essential Books.
    Includes a survey of Machaut's music (129–53, 172, 179–80). The explanation of partial
    signatures in *De Bon Espoir / Puis que* (M4) summarizes the position of Hoppin (1953;
    1956).

Harrison, Benjamin S.
  1934. "Medieval Rhetoric in the *Book of the Duchesse*." *PMLA* 49:428–42.
    Based on the author's 1932 Yale dissertation. Chaucer derived rhetorical techniques (e.g.,
    dream elements, use of *exempla*, description) from the *Roman de la Rose* and Machaut,
    not from twelfth- and thirteenth-century Latin manuals.

Harrison, Frank Ll., ed.
  1968. *Motets of French Provenance*. Texts ed. Elizabeth Rutson and A.G.
    Rigg. Polyphonic Music of the Fourteenth Century 5. Monaco: L'Oiseau-
    Lyre.
    Standard critical edition of motets by Machaut's contemporaries (excluding the French-
    Cypriot repertory of the Turin codex). Abstract: *RILM* 2 (1968), no. 3087.

Hasenohr-Esnos, Geneviève.
  1969. *Le Respit de la Mort par Jean le Fèvre*. Société des Anciens Textes
    Français. Paris: Picard.
    Includes an excellent description of MS *F:Pn 994* [35].

Hassell, James Woodrow, Jr.
  1982. *Middle French Proverbs, Sentences, and Proverbial Phrases*. Subsidia
    Mediaevalia 12. Toronto: Pontifical Institute of Mediaeval Studies. Leiden:
    Brill.
    Standard catalogue of proverbs. Reviews: Kurt Baldinger, *Zeitschrift für romanische
    Philologie* 99 (1983): 416–17; P. Bourgain, *Revue historique* 269 (1983): 494–96;
    Giuseppe Di Stefano, *Studi francesi* 28 (1984): 131–32; J. Everett, *Moyen français* 11
    (1982): 138–47 (corrections); Jean-Claude Mühlethaler, *Vox romanica* 44 (1985): 339–
    40; Nathaniel B. Smith, *Speculum* 58 (1983): 756–58.

Hasselman, Margaret Paine.
  1970. "The French Chanson in the Fourteenth Century." Ph.D. diss.
    University of California at Berkeley. 2 vols. Ann Arbor: University Micro-
    films. Order no. 719830.
    An important study—developing some ideas in Crocker 1966—of style and chronology in
    fourteenth-century chansons, focusing mainly on works by composers other than
    Machaut. Machaut is specifically discussed in the conclusion, 241–43 (see comments in
    Earp 1983, 169–70 n. 327). Contains transcriptions of some fragments unavailable else-
    where, inventories of the sources, and important material on **CaB** [56]. Some criticisms

and praise in Arlt 1982, 202–7, 253. Abstracts: *DAI* A 31/10 (Apr. 1971): 5446; *RILM* 10 (1976), no. 9138.

Hasselman, Margaret, and Thomas Walker.
1970. "More Hidden Polyphony in a Machaut Manuscript." *Musica disciplina* 24:7–16.
The first correct edition with commentary of *En demantant* (L24/18). Abstract: *RILM* 6 (1972), no. 221.

Hatten, R.S.
1978. "Towards a Unified Theory: The Music of Machaut." *Indiana Theory Review* 2:4–14.
Dissonance treatment, rhythm, and melody in the secular works of Machaut, with examples focusing on *Dous viaire* (R1), *Douce dame jolie* (V4), and *Loyauté, que* (L1). Builds in a fruitful way on the work of Reaney.

Hayez, Michel and Anne-Marie.
1983. *Urbain V (1362–1370)*. Bibliothèque des Ecoles Françaises d'Athènes et de Rome 3/5 bis. Lettres communes des papes du XIVe siècle. Rome: Ecole Française de Rome.
Papal documents.

Heger, Henrik.
1967. *Die Melancholie bei den französischen Lyrikern des Spätmittelalters.* Romanistische Versuche und Vorarbeiten 21. Bonn: Romanisches Seminar der Universität Bonn.
Publication of author's 1965 Bonn thesis. On Machaut's treatment of *merencolie* in the lyrics, see 75–81; for the *Jugement Navarre*, see 81–91. Reviews: William Calin, *Romance Philology* 24 (1970–71): 527–29; Jean Charles Payen, *Moyen Age* 76 (1970): 600–602; Daniel Poirion, *Bibliothèque d'Humanisme et Renaissance* 30 (1968): 383–85; Hans Rheinfelder, *Die neueren Sprachen* n.s. 16 (1967): 512; John H. Watkins, *French Studies* 23 (1969): 169–70; Werner Ziltener, *Zeitschrift für romanische Philologie* 88 (1972): 548–54.

1988. "La ballade et le chant royal." In Poirion 1988b, 59–69.
Although ballade and *chant royal* were closely related in the fourteenth and fifteenth centuries, their origins are quite different. Considers varieties and functions, formal patterns, contributions of various poets, and the disappearance of the form in the sixteenth century.

Heinrichs, Katherine.
1989a. "Love and Hell: The Denizens of Hades in the Love Poems of the Middle Ages." *Neophilologus* 73:593–604.
The use of images from Hades in late medieval love poems. For Machaut, Heinrichs discusses the Tantalus image in *Un mortel lay* (L12/8, ll. 229–36), and in *Voir Dit* (ed. P. Paris 1875, 264 letter 35).

1989b. "'Lovers' Consolations of Philosophy' in Boccaccio, Machaut, and Chaucer." *Studies in the Age of Chaucer* 11:93–115.
Includes discussion of Boethius's *Consolation of Philosophy* in *Jugement Behaingne* and *Remede*; and the influence of *Jugement Behaingne* and *Remede* on Chaucer's *Troilus*.

1990. *The Myths of Love: Classical Lovers in Medieval Literature.* University Park and London: Pennsylvania State University Press.
A close look at Ovidian *exempla* and mythological materials and how they are interpreted by the characters in medieval narratives of Boccaccio, Machaut, Froissart, and Chaucer. Also considers narrative voice and the relationship between "love and learning." Actively engages previous scholarship but lacks a bibliography. Reviews: Ardis Butterfield, *Medium Ævum* 61 (1992): 147–48 (on Robertsonian approach); Christine Ferlampin, *Information littéraire* 43/2 (Mar.-Apr. 1991): 44; Elaine Tuttle Hansen, *Modern Language Quarterly* 52 (1991): 100–102; Regina Psaki, *Comparative Literature* 46 (1994): 101–4; Karla Taylor, *Speculum* 68 (1993): 1130–32.

1994. "The Language of Love: Overstatement and Ironic Humor in Machaut's *Voir dit.*" *Philological Quarterly* 73:1–9.

The contrast seen between the conventional love language of *Voir Dit* lyrics and letters on the one hand, and the genuinely felt account of the narrative on the other, is meant ironically; the work is "a witty meditation on the power of self-deluding vanity" (5).

Heinz, Rudolf.
1976. *Interpretationsvorschläge: Paul Klee, Henri Matisse, Caspar David Friedrich, Johann Wolfgang von Goethe, Gustav Mahler, Antonio Vivaldi, Franz Liszt, Maurice Ravel, Guillaume de Machaut,* ed. Heide Heinz. Herrenberg: Döring.

Includes an analysis of traditional and progressive tendencies in the A-section of *Mes esperis* (B39) (pp. 35–51). The musical terminology, emphasizing harmonic aspects, is anachronistic. Review: Peter Rummenhöller, *Zeitschrift für Musiktheorie* 7/2 (1976): 49.

Heitmann, Klaus.
1978. "Französische Lyrik von Guillaume de Machaut bis Jean Marot." In *Europäisches Spätmittelalter,* ed. Willi Erzgräber, 355–72. Neues Handbuch der Literaturwissenschaft 8. Wiesbaden: Athenaion.

Overview of fourteenth- and fifteenth-century French lyrical poetry, with bibliography. On Machaut, see esp. 358–60.

Henneman, John Bell.
1971. *Royal Taxation in Fourteenth Century France: The Development of War Financing 1322–1356.* Princeton: Princeton University Press.

See Henneman 1976.

1976. *Royal Taxation in Fourteenth-Century France: The Captivity and Ransom of John II, 1356–1370.* Memoirs of the American Philosophical Society, 116. Philadelphia: American Philosophical Society.

With Henneman 1971 the most important book in English on the historical situation in France in the mid-fourteenth century, particularly during the critical period following the defeat at Poitiers. Well documented, with full bibliography.

Hervieux, Léopold.
1893. *Les fabulistes latins. Depuis le siècle d'Auguste jusqu'à la fin du Moyen Age.* Vol. 1/1, *Phèdre et ses anciens imitateurs directs et indirects.* 2nd rev. ed. Paris: Firmin-Didot. Reprint. Hildesheim and New York: Olms, 1970.

Contains a brief description of MS **Ys** [37] (pp. 528–30).

Hieatt, Constance B.
1979–80. "*Un autre fourme*: Guillaume de Machaut and the Dream Vision Form." *Chaucer Review* 14:97–115.

A very sympathetic view of Machaut's narratives, especially considering *Alerion* (111–13). The views on form are applicable to all of the *dits.* Includes a chart of a generalized formal structure of the dream vision (157). Discussed in Davis 1991, 52–53.

Higgins, Paula.
1991. "Parisian Nobles, a Scottish Princess, and the Woman's Voice in Late Medieval Song." *Early Music History* 10:145–200.

A study of the context of Antoine Busnoys's songs to Jacqueline de Hacqueville. In the course of a brilliant rehabilitation of the participation of women in late medieval literary and musical culture, Higgins discusses Toute Belle's poetic production in the *Voir Dit.*

1993a. "From the Ivory Tower to the Marketplace: Early Music, Musicology, and the Mass Media." *Current Musicology* 53:109–23.

Fascinating historiography of the uses of early music in contemporary popular culture; mentions Machaut and modern works inspired by his music (115, 117).

1993b. "The 'Other Minervas': Creative Women at the Court of Margaret of Scotland." In *Rediscovering the Muses: Women's Musical Traditions*, ed. Kimberly Marshall, 169–85. Boston: Northeastern University Press.

Further development of parts of Higgins 1991, with further discussion of Toute Belle's poetic production in the *Voir Dit*.

Hindemith, Paul.

1968. *The Craft of Musical Composition*. Book 1 (4th ed.), *Theoretical Part*, trans. Arthur Mendel. New York: Associated, 1942. Reprint. London, New York, and Mainz: Schott, 1968. Originally *Unterweisung im Tonsatz*. Part 1, *Theoretischer Teil*. Mainz: Schott, 1937. 2nd rev. ed. 1940.

Includes a sympathetic analysis of *Il m'est avis* (B22) (pp. 204–6). "We see in this music a true counterpart of the Gothic style of architecture of the same period, in which the great, central features of the structure are of elementary simplicity, corresponding to the harmony of this Ballade, while the fullness of decorative detail, here represented by the non-chord tones, is almost oppressive" (206).

Hindman, Sandra L.

1986. *Christine de Pizan's "Epistre Othéa": Painting and Politics at the Court of Charles VI*. Studies and Texts 77. Toronto: Pontifical Institute of Mediaeval Studies.

An interpretation of the *Epistre Othea* based on the miniatures. Christine's role in the planning of the iconography may be relevant for the Machaut manuscripts.

Hirshberg, Jehoash.

1971. "The Music of the Late Fourteenth Century: A Study in Musical Style." Ph.D. diss. University of Pennsylvania. Ann Arbor: University Microfilms. Order no. 7126031.

Includes a detailed study of musical style in Machaut's ballades (43–163). See the discussion in Brown 1987, 86–88, 91–92. Abstract: *DAI* A 32/4 (Oct. 1971): 2121.

1973–74. "The Relationship of Text and Music in Machaut's Ballades." *Orbis Musicae: Studies in Musicology* 2:53–66.

This statistical study covers all of the ballades, discussing patterns of melismas, correspondence of text line and musical phrase, etc.

1980. "Hexachordal and Modal Structure in Machaut's Polyphonic Chansons." In *Studies in Musicology in Honor of Otto E. Albrecht: A Collection of Essays by His Colleagues and Former Students at the University of Pennsylvania*, ed. John Walter Hill, 19–42. Kassel: Bärenreiter.

A hexachordal study of *musica ficta* in Machaut's chansons, especially focusing on the ballades. Criticizes the application of modal theory to fourteenth-century polyphony, yet attempts to reconcile modal theory with the music. See discussions in Berger 1992, 108; Brown 1987, 86–88, 91–92. Abstract: *RILM* 14 (1980), no. 2568.

Hoepffner, Ernest.

1906. "Anagramme und Rätselgedichte bei Guillaume de Machaut." *Zeitschrift für romanische Philologie* 30:401–13.

Solves several anagrams in Machaut's narrative poems. Hoepffner also discusses ten anagrams at the end of MS K [15] (see Guesnon 1912, 93 n. 1 for some different solutions).

1908–21 (ed.). *Œuvres de Guillaume de Machaut*. 3 vols. Société des Anciens Textes Français 57. Vol. 1. Paris: Firmin-Didot, 1908. Vol. 2. Paris: Firmin-Didot, 1911. Vol. 3. Paris: Champion, 1921. Reprint. New York: Johnson, 1965.

The standard critical edition for most of the narrative *dits* of Machaut. Vol. 1 includes *Vergier*, *Jugement Behaingne*, and *Jugement Navarre*; vol. 2, *Remede*, *Lyon*, and *Alerion*; vol. 3, *Confort* and *Fonteinne*. The introductions remain excellent starting places for study of the *dits*. The introduction to vol. 1 provides a readable and accurate biography.

Hoepffner's discussion of the manuscripts is the foundation for the most widely accepted chronology of Machaut's *dits*. Review of vol. 3: A. Långfors, *Romania* 49 (1923): 628–29 (corrections).

1909 (ed.). "Frage- und Antwortspiele in der französischen Literatur des 14. Jahrhunderts." *Zeitschrift für romanische Philologie* 33:695–710.

Edition of the *Chastel d'Amours* after MSS **K** [15] and **J** [16] (pp. 702–10).

1910 (ed.). *La Prise Amoureuse von Jehan Acart de Hesdin: Allegorische Dichtung aus dem XIV. Jahrhundert.* Gesellschaft für romanische Literatur 22. Dresden: Gesellschaft für romanische Literatur.

The introduction provides a detailed study of the metrics and rhymes of the rondeaux and ballades inserted in the *Prise Amoureuse*, with an important discussion of the development of these forms by later fourteenth-century poets. See also Hoepffner 1911, 1920a, 1920b.

1911. "Die Balladen des Dichters Jehan de le Mote." *Zeitschrift für romanische Philologie* 35:153–66.

A detailed study of the metrics and rhymes of the thirty ballades inserted into *Li Regret Guillaume, Comte de Hainaut* (1339) is the point of departure for an important discussion of the chronological and stylistic development of the ballade in the early fourteenth century, from Jean Acart to Jean de le Mote. Also considers the literary relationship between Jean de le Mote and Machaut. See also Hoepffner 1910, 1920a, 1920b.

1913. "La chronologie des 'Pastourelles' de Froissart." In *Mélanges offerts à M. Emile Picot.* Vol. 2 of 2 vols., 27–42. Paris: Morgand.

The chronological arrangement of works in the Machaut manuscripts influenced the organization of Froissart's works.

1917–19. "Crestien de Troyes und Guillaume de Machaut." *Zeitschrift für romanische Philologie* 39:627–29.

Machaut's use of *Yvain* in *Lyon*.

1920a. "Les Poésies lyriques du *Dit de la Panthère* de Nicole de Margival." *Romania* 53:204–30.

A detailed study of the metrics and rhymes of the lyrics inserted in the *Dit de la Panthere*, followed by an important discussion of the early development of the fixed forms. Nicole's *Dit de la Panthere* served as a model for Machaut's *Remede*. See also Hoepffner 1910, 1911, 1920b.

1920b. "Virelais et ballades dans le Chansonnier d'Oxford (Douce 308)." *Archivum romanicum* 4:20–40.

Discusses the early development of the fixed forms and the formal separation of the virelai from the ballade, based on a systematic study of the formal aspects of the *ballettes* in MS *GB:Ob 308*. Machaut was the first to make a clear distinction between ballades and virelais. See also Hoepffner 1910, 1911, 1920a.

Hoffmann, Rolf.
1943. "Form und Gestalt in der frühen mehrstimmigen Kunstmusik. Beiträge zur ästhetischen Wertung der gotischen Musik in Form von Analysen ausgewählter Beispiele der Epoche Leonin bis Machaut." Diss. Marburg.
Not examined.

Hoffmann-Axthelm, Dagmar.
1991. "Die Musik des 14. Jahrhunderts: Musikleben und Musikanschauung." In *Die Musik des Mittelalters*, ed. Hartmut Möller and Rudolf Stephan, 335–51 (notes, 430–32). Neues Handbuch der Musikwissenschaft 2. Laaber: Laaber.

Overview of the sociological context for fourteenth-century music—music for the bourgeois, the intellectuals, and the church. Reviews: *Concerto* 9 (Feb. 1992): 9–10; Kurt von Fischer, *Musikforschung* 46 (1993): 202–4; Hermann Moeck, *Tibia* 15–16 (1990–91): 645; John Stevens, *Plainsong and Medieval Music* 1 (1992): 197–200.

Holmes, Urban T., Jr.
1952. *A Critical Bibliography of French Literature*, ed. David C. Cabeen. Vol. 1, *The Mediaeval Period*. Syracuse, New York: Syracuse University Press, 1947. Enlarged ed., 1952.
Annotated bibliography (see pp. 152–53 for Machaut; 153–54 for Machaut and Chaucer).

Holzbacher, Ana-María.
1973–74. [Valero, Ana María.] "Rehabilitando la memoria de Guillaume de Machaut." *Boletín de la Real Academia de Buenas Letras de Barcelona* 35:157–66.
Discussion of two controversial points concerning the interpretation of the *Voir Dit*. Includes a citation from the *Roman de Cardenois* (see chap. 3, MS [43]), a work dependent on Machaut. See Holzbacher-Valero 1982.

1982. [Holzbacher-Valero, Anne-Marie.] "En réhabilitant la mémoire de Guillaume de Machaut." In Guillaume de Machaut 1982, 41–48.
French translation of Holzbacher 1973–74.

1983–84. "Elementos histórico-geográficos en el 'Roman de Passebeauté et Cardenois': Un ejemplo más de la presencia de Cataluña en la novela francesa de los siglos XIV y XV." *Boletín de la Real Academia de Buenas Letras de Barcelona* 39:177–90.
As a further example of French influence on Catalan literature of the fourteenth and fifteenth centuries, Holzbacher links the story of the French *Roman de Cardenois* geographically and historically to Catalonia. She tries to support the thesis that Machaut was the author of the *Roman de Cardenois*, but the argument remains unconvincing. Includes a discussion of Machaut's influence on Andreu Febrer.

Homburger, Otto.
1953. "Über die kunstgeschichtliche Bedeutung der Handschriften der Burgerbibliothek." In *Schätze der Burgerbibliothek Bern*. Bern: Lang.
Art-historical description of MS **K** [15] (pp. 124–25, 135), with a facsimile (172) of fol. 46v, including *Remede* miniature K4.

Hoppin, Richard H.
1953. "Partial Signatures and Musica Ficta in Some Early 15th-Century Sources." *Journal of the American Musicological Society* 6:197–215.
Argues that cadences do not explain conflicting key signatures in late medieval music (against Lowinsky 1945). Instead, they signal voices with pitch levels a fifth apart. Modal terminology is anachronistic. Criticized in Lowinsky 1954.

1956. "Conflicting Signatures Reviewed." *Journal of the American Musicological Society* 9:97–117.
Reply to Lowinsky 1954, with examples from Apel 1950 and discussion of Machaut's *De desconfort* (B8) (pp. 109–10). The modal aspect is considered anachronistic today, but Hoppin's analysis is important and should be consulted. See also Hoppin 1989.

1957. "The Cypriot-French Repertory of the Manuscript Torino, Biblioteca Nazionale, J. II. 9." *Musica disciplina* 11:79–125.
Includes discussion of some relationships between Machaut's works and the anonymous repertory of the Turin codex.

1958. "An Unrecognized Polyphonic Lai of Machaut." *Musica disciplina* 12:93–104.
The first correct edition with commentary of *Pour ce que plus* (L23/17).

1960. "Notational Licences of Guillaume de Machaut." *Musica disciplina* 14:13–27.
Essential revision of some errors in the musical transcriptions of Wolf, Ludwig and Schrade. Includes emendations in *Un mortel lay* (L12/8), *Trop plus / Biauté* (M20), *Dous amis, oy* (B6), *Une vipere* (B27), *Je puis trop* (B28), *Rose, lis* (R10), and discussion of how *modus* and *tempus* affect barring.

1960–63 (ed.). *The Cypriot-French Repertory of the Manuscript Torino, Biblioteca Nazionale, J.II.9.* 4 vols. Corpus Mensurabilis Musicae 21. Vol. 1, *Polyphonic Mass Movements.* Rome: American Institute of Musicology, 1960. Vol. 2, *Motets.* Rome: American Institute of Musicology, 1961. Vol. 3, *Ballades.* Rome: American Institute of Musicology, 1963. Vol. 4, *Virelais and Rondeaux.* Rome: American Institute of Musicology, 1963.

Edition of the polyphony of the MS *I:Tn 9*, which includes some motets, ballades, and rondeaux related to lais and rondeaux of Machaut. See chap. 7, commentary to *Contre ce dous* (L15/10), *Je ne cesse* (L16/11), and *Tant doucement* (R9).

1966. "Tonal Organization in Music Before the Renaissance." In *Paul A. Pisk: Essays in His Honor*, ed. John Glowacki, 25–37. Austin: College of Fine Arts, The University of Texas.

Notes a growing tendency in the fourteenth century to establish a tonal center at the beginning of a composition. Studies several opening phrases from the polyphonic secular songs of Machaut and other fourteenth- and early fifteenth-century composers. Notes almost exclusive use of Dorian and Lydian (with *B*-flat) modes, and their transpositions. Anachronistic in its use of modal theory and related terminology. Criticism in Hirshberg 1971, 383–84; Fuller 1987a, 57–58 n. 22.

1978a (ed.). *Anthology of Medieval Music.* Norton Introduction to Music History 1. New York: Norton.

Editions of *Qui es / Ha! Fortune* (M8), *Dous amis* (B6), *Se vous n'estes* (R7; with two optional contratenors from **E** and **Mod**), and *De bonté* (V10), all after MS **A**. Abstract: *RILM* 12 (1978), no. 2533. Reviews: *Church Music* (1979): 53; Courtney Adams, *Diapason* 72/11 (Nov. 1981): 11; Rebecca A. Baltzer, *Notes* 35 (1978–79): 869–70; John Caldwell, *Music and Letters* 61 (1980): 89–92; Michel Huglo, *Revue de musicologie* 64 (1978): 285–86; Elizabeth A. Keitel, *Music Educator's Journal* 65/9 (May 1979): 79–81; Charlotte Roederer, *Musical Quarterly* 65 (1979): 447–51.

1978b. *Medieval Music.* The Norton Introduction to Music History 1. New York: Norton.

Chap. 17, "Guillaume de Machaut" (396–432) is the best short survey of Machaut's music in English. Includes comparison and contrast of the biographies of Vitry and Machaut; discussion of chronology and literary works; and considers all genres of music. Abstract: *RILM* 12 (1978), no. 300. Reviews: *Church Music* (1979): 53; Courtney Adams, *Diapason* 72:11 (Nov. 1981): 11; Rebecca A. Baltzer, *Notes* 35 (1978–79): 869–70; Gwilym Beechey, *Consort* 43 (1987): 40; John Caldwell, *Music and Letters* 61 (1980): 89–92; Elizabeth A. Keitel, *Music Educator's Journal* 65/9 (May 1979): 79–81; Charlotte Roederer, *Musical Quarterly* 65 (1979): 447–51.

1989. "Conflicting Views in Retrospect." In Lowinsky 1989, 2:678–80.

Review of a musicological controversy (see Lowinsky 1945, Hoppin 1953, Lowinsky 1954, and Hoppin 1956). On Machaut's *De desconfort* (B8), see pp. 679–80.

Housley, Norman.

1986. *The Avignon Papacy and the Crusades, 1305–1378.* Oxford: Clarendon.

Political history bearing on King Pierre de Lusignan and Machaut's *Prise.*

Hübsch, Hanns, ed.

1953. *Guillaume de Machault: La Messe de Nostre Dame.* Heidelberg: Süddeutscher Musikverlag Willy Müller.

A practical edition of the Mass in modern clefs, based on the edition of De Van (1949). Text added editorially to the contratenor in Sanctus and Agnus; interludes in Gloria and Credo are considered instrumental. See commentary in Fallows 1977a, 290.

Hughes, Andrew.

1972. *Manuscript Accidentals: Ficta in Focus, 1350–1450.* Musicological Studies and Documents 27. Rome: American Institute of Musicology.

Although this study does not mention Machaut directly, it is of importance for musical performance practice. Bent 1972 is a complementary study; Harden (1983) applies the work of Bent and Hughes to Machaut. Abstract: *RILM* 6 (1972), no. 223. Reviews: Richard H. Hoppin, *Journal of the American Musicological Society* 27 (1974): 338–43; Alejandro Enrique Planchart, *Journal of Music Theory* 17 (1973): 326–29.

1980. *Medieval Music: The Sixth Liberal Art.* 2nd rev. ed. Toronto: University of Toronto Press.
Bibliography of medieval music, with brief annotations.

1989. *Style and Symbol. Medieval Music: 800–1453.* Musicological Studies 51. Ottawa: Institute of Mediaeval Music.
Survey of medieval music.

Hughes, Andrew, and Margaret Bent, eds.
1969. *The Old Hall Manuscript.* Corpus Mensurabilis Musicae 46. Vol. 1/2. [Rome]: American Institute of Musicology, 1969. Vol. 3, *Commentary.* [Rome]: American Institute of Musicology, 1973.
Leech-Wilkinson (1990c, 17) relates a Sanctus-Agnus pair by Lionel Power (ed. 1/2:357–60 no. 118; 1/2:402–4 no. 141) to the Machaut Mass.

Huizinga, Johann.
1924. *The Waning of the Middle Ages: A Study of the Forms of Life, Thought and Art in France and the Netherlands in the XIVth and XVth Centuries,* trans. F. Hopman. London: Arnold. Reprint. New York: Doubleday Anchor, 1954.
English translation of of *Herfstij der middeleeuwen* (1919), a very influential history of the fourteenth and fifteenth centuries. See the critique in Page 1993, chap. 5.

1953. *Herbst des Mittelalters: Studien über Lebens- und Geistesformen des 14. und 15. Jahrhunderts in Frankreich und in den Niederlanden.* 7th ed., revised by Kurt Köster, trans. T. Wolff-Mönckeberg and Kurt Köster. Stuttgart: Kröner.
German translation of *Herfstij der middeleeuwen,* based on the last Dutch edition revised by the author; valuable also because the 1924 English translation lacks notes.

Huot, Sylvia.
1987. *From Song to Book: The Poetics of Writing in Old French Lyric and Lyrical Narrative Poetry.* Ithaca: Cornell University Press.
A study of medieval French poetry that focuses on the presentation of works in extant books or compilations, considering rubrics, decoration, the role of the scribe, etc. Documents the progression from oral performance of texts in the early thirteenth century to texts conceived as written artifacts by the late fourteenth century. Machaut's collections, organized presentations of the complete range of works by a single author, are of course extremely important in this approach (see esp. 232–38). Includes studies of the evolution of the iconography of MSS C and A, as well as Machaut's role in establishing it. Reviews: Emmanuèle Baumgartner, *Revue des langues romanes* 93 (1989): 464–67; Ardis Butterfield, *Medium Ævum* 58 (1989): 165–66; Peter F. Dembowski, *French Forum* 14 (1989): 85–88; David F. Hult, *Style* 23 (1989): 316–22; Sarah Kay, *Comparative Literature* 43 (1991): 88–90; Douglas Kelly, *Speculum* 65 (1990): 177–78; Francisco Marcos-Marín, *Revue belge de philologie et d'histoire* 68 (1990): 773–79; Rupert T. Pickens, *Romance Quarterly* 37 (1990): 357–58; Elizabeth W. Poe, *Romance Philology* 45 (1992): 532–35; Angelica Rieger, *Zeitschrift für romanische Philologie* 110 (1994): 232–40; G. Matteo Roccati, *Studi francesi* 33 (1989): 122–23; J.-C. Seigneuret, *Choice* 25 (1988): 1561; Helen Solterer, *Romanic Review* 79 (1988): 517–20; John Stevens, *Music and Letters* 71 (1990): 528–29; Françoise Vielliard, *Bibliothèque de l'Ecole des Chartes* 149 (1991): 169–72.

1991. "The Daisy and the Laurel: Myths of Desire and Creativity in the Poetry of Jean Froissart." *Yale French Studies Special Edition; Contexts: Style and*

Values in Medieval Art and Literature, ed. Daniel Poirion and Nancy Freeman Regalado, 240–51.

Froissart's adaptations of Ovidian myths in his intellectualized love poetry; the god Apollo as a literary figure; and Froissart's reworkings of his own myth of the daisy (*marguerite*) throughout his career. "Froissart created a new myth of love and creativity, one appropriate to the social context in which he wrote. It responded to his audience's taste for secular amorous readings of myths" (251). Relevant to Machaut as well, with interesting comments on the tension between poet and patron in late fourteenth-century literature. Brief mention of *Voir Dit*.

1993. *The* Romance of the Rose *and its Medieval Readers*. Cambridge Studies in Medieval Literature 16. Cambridge: Cambridge University Press.

This wide-ranging study of the textual tradition and medieval reception of the *Roman de la Rose* includes a chapter on Machaut, focusing on his knowledge of a variety of interpolated versions of the *Roman de la Rose*, and how these several versions influenced his *Fonteinne, Remede*, and *Voir Dit*. Review: Leslie C. Brook, *Modern Language Review* 89 (1994): 995–96.

1994. "Patience in Adversity: The Courtly Lover and Job in Machaut's Motets 2 and 3." *Medium Ævum* 63:222–38.

The French motet incorporates the literary juxtaposition of the themes of courtly love lyric—the secular discourse of motetus and triplum—with the rhetorical tradition of scripture and liturgy—the devotional discourse of the tenor. The interplay between these two registers provides two contexts for interpretation. In a pair of Machaut motets, *Tous corps / De* (M2) and *Hé! Mors / Fine* (M3), with tenors derived from Responsories based on the Book of Job, the sufferings of Job mirror the sufferings of the courtly lover. (In the case of M2, Huot identifies the hitherto unrecognized tenor source.) In M2, the juxtaposition of the courtly and devotional places the sublimated love characteristic of *Remede*— "independent of sexual desire or gratification" (227)—in a broader context of human suffering. In M3, a man laments the death of his lady, but faith in God gives him the strength to resist despair. Huot goes on to consider *Jugement Behaingne* and *Jugement Navarre* as literary analogues to M2-3: "the *Jugement Behaingne*, like motet 2, is dominated by the topos of male desire in conflict with female resistance; the *Jugement Navarre*, like motet 3, is dominated by the theme of death and of the power of true love to survive beyond the grave" (230). The historical prologue to *Jugement Navarre* functions in a way analogous to the tenors of the motets, placing love in a universal context of tragedy. A second literary analogue to the motets is Boethius's *Consolation of Philosophy*. The new perspective afforded by the motet tenor recalls the discourse of Philosophy, which serves to broaden the context of Boethius's misfortune. Finally, Huot analyses the macaronic *Helas! pour quoy virent / Corde* (M12), showing that both the Latin motetus and tenor recast the courtly love-longing of the French triplum, providing a critique of the courtly tradition.

Hüschen, Heinrich, comp.

1975. *The Motet*. Trans. A.C. Howie. Anthology of Music 47. Cologne: Volk.

Includes an edition of *Trop plus / Biauté* (M20) (pp. 31–32 no. 6).

Imbs, Paul.

1991. *Le* Voir-Dit *de Guillaume de Machaut: etude littéraire*. Centre National de la Recherche Scientifique. Institut National de la Langue Française. Paris: Klincksieck.

Posthumous publication of Imbs's literary study of the *Voir Dit*. (His critical edition has been taken over by Jacqueline Cerquiglini-Toulet for the Société des Anciens Textes Français; the translation into modern French is to appear from Champion-Slatkine.) Part one characterizes Hoepffner's edition of the Machaut *dits*, and introduces the problem of making an edition of the *Voir Dit*; part two is an analysis of the work from the point of view of a late fourteenth-century reader; part three provides analyses of earlier narratives— *Vergier, Jugement Behaingne, Remede, Lyon, Alerion, Jugement Navarre, Confort*, and *Fonteinne*—focusing especially on aspects that prepare the way for the *Voir Dit*; part four provides comparisons across all of these works; and part five approaches the problem of truth in the *Voir Dit*. Imbs takes the work more literally than most contemporary literary critics; the present study provides almost no critical response to those opposing views. Reviews: Aloysia R. Berens, *Romanische Forschungen* 104 (1992): 440–42; Laurence de Looze, *Speculum* 69 (1994): 179–81; Jane H.M. Taylor, *Medium Ævum* 63 (1994): 149–51.

International Style.
    1962. *The International Style: The Arts in Europe around 1400. October 23–December 2, 1962.* Baltimore: The Walters Art Gallery.
    US:NYpm Glazier 52, a manuscript closely related to Machaut MS C, is discussed as no. 38 (plate xlii).

Israel-Meyer, Pierre.
    1982. "De artibus novis." In Guillaume de Machaut 1982, 337–38.
    Draws lines of comparison between the music of the fourteenth and twentieth centuries.

Jahiel, Edwin.
    1960–61. "French and Provencal Poet-Musicians of the Middle Ages: A Biblio-Discography." *Romance Philology* 14:200–207.
    Discography.

James, M[ontague] R[hodes].
    1923. *Biblioteca Pepysiana. A Descriptive Catalogue of the Library of Samuel Pepys.* Part 3, *Mediaeval Manuscripts.* London: Sidgwick and Jackson.
    Description of MS **Pe** [20] (pp. 24–26).

Jameux, Dominique.
    1991. *Pierre Boulez.* Trans. Susan Bradshaw. Cambridge, Mass.: Harvard University Press.
    Includes description of a 1954 concert series organized by Boulez that included works of Machaut (61–62).

Jankowski, Bogdan M.
    1983. *Rozmyślania nad pięcioliniq* (Reflections on the staff; in Polish). Warsaw: Centralny Ośrodek Metodyki Upowszechniania Kultury.
    See "Pięć wieków zapomnienia" (Five centuries of oblivion) (84–85). On Machaut's legacy.

Jardin.
    1910–25. *Le Jardin de Plaisance et Fleur de Rhétorique. Reproduction en facsimilé de l'édition publiée par Antoine Vérard vers 1501*, by L'Infortuné. Société des Anciens Textes Français 59. Vol. 1, *Facsimile.* Paris: Champion, 1910. Vol. 2, *Introduction et Notes*, by E[ugénie] Droz and A[rthur] Piaget. Paris: Champion, 1925.
    A facsimile edition (see chap. 3 [49]) containing a few works of Machaut, none attributed: *Certes, mon oueil* (R15), *Dame, de qui* (RF5), *De Fortune* (B23), *De petit po* (B18), *Je puis trop* (B28), *Phyton* (B38), *Se vous n'estes* (R7), as well as two ballades (*opera dubia*), that appear in MS J [16]: *S'il n'est d'argent* (LoA5) and *Jugez, amans* (LoA20).

Jeanroy, Alfred.
    1921. "La littérature de langue française des origines à Ronsard." In *Histoire des lettres.* Vol. 12/1, *Des origines à Ronsard*, by Joseph Bédier, Alfred Jeanroy, and F. Picavet. *Histoire de la nation française*, ed. Gabriel Hanotaux. 15 vols. Paris: Société de l'Histoire Nationale; Plon-Nourrit, 1920–29.
    Includes an unsympathetic survey of Machaut's lyrics (465–66) and *dits* (466 n. 2).

Jireček, Konst[antin].
1878. "Guillaume de Machaut, sekretář krále Jana Lucemburského" (Guillaume de Machaut, secretary of King John of Luxembourg). *Časopis musea královstvi Českého* (Prague) 52:78–93.
Discussion of Machaut's relations with Bohemia, based on quotations in his literary works.

Johnson, Glenn Pierr.
1991. "Aspects of Late Medieval Music at the Cathedral of Amiens." 2 vols. Ph.D. diss. Yale University. Ann Arbor: University Microfilms. Order no. 9315192.
Study of liturgy at Amiens in the thirteenth and fourteenth centuries. Includes some new biographical information on Machaut. Abstract: *DAI* A 54/1 (July 1993): 21.

Johnson, Leonard W.
1979. "'Nouviaus dis amoureux plaisans': Variation as Innovation in Guillaume de Machaut." In *Musique naturelle et musique artificielle: In memoriam Gustave Reese*, ed. Mary Beth Winn, 11–28. Le Moyen Français 5. Montreal: Ceres.
An excellent close literary analysis of five ballades on Fortune, including *Il m'est avis* (B22), *De Fortune* (B23), *Amours, ma dame* (Lo227=VD6), and *De toutes flours* (B31); see the revised version in L.W. Johnson 1990, 41–58. Abstract: *RILM* 13 (1979), no. 2403.

1990. *Poets as Players: Theme and Variation in Late Medieval French Poetry.* Stanford, Calif.: Stanford University Press.
Emphasis on the structure of the lyrics and constant renewal in the fixed forms. See especially chap. 1, *"Les règles du jeu*: Guillaume de Machaut and Poetic Practice," which includes a revised version of L.W. Johnson 1979, adding translations of all the texts quoted. Reviews: Cynthia J. Brown, *French Review* 65 (1991–92): 1060–61; M.J. Freeman, *French Studies* 46 (1992): 310–11; Sylvia Huot, *Speculum* 68 (1993): 183–85; Douglas Kelly, *Modern Language Quarterly* 52 (1991): 102–4; Jan A. Nelson, *Romance Quarterly* 41 (1994): 186–87.

Jonen, Gerda Anita.
1974. *Allegorie und späthöfische Dichtung in Frankreich.* Beiträge zur romanischen Philologie des Mittelalters 9. Munich: Fink.
Publication of the author's 1972 Tübingen thesis, a study of the works of Alain Chartier, with consideration of his debt to Machaut.

Jordan, Nicole Amon (see also Amon).
1976. "Des couleurs et des signes: Essai sur la symbolique des couleurs chez quelques auteurs du Moyen Age et de la Renaissance." Ph.D. diss. University of California at Berkeley, 1975. Ann Arbor: University Microfilms. Order no. 7615244.
Includes material on color symbolism in the *Voir Dit.* Not examined. Abstract: *DAI* A 37/1 (July 1976): 361.

Joukovsky-Micha, Françoise.
1968. "La notion de 'vaine gloire' de Simund de Freine à Martin Le Franc." *Romania* 89:1–30, 210–39.
Includes discussion of Machaut's view of glory, centered on a mistrust of Fortune (*Remede*). Although *souffisance* frees man from the tyranny of Fortune (*Jugement Navarre*), the best solution is to sing to the glory of God (*Confort*) (pp. 11–13).

Jung, Marc-René.
1971. "Poetria: Zur Dichtungstheorie des ausgehenden Mittelalters in Frankreich." *Vox romanica* 30:44–64.
On late medieval poetics, including the Second Rhetoric, the *Ovide Moralisé,* and the *Echecs Amoureuses,* with mention of Machaut's *Prologue* (esp. 45–47, 54). Concerning

the first application of the term *poète* to a late medieval poet, which Jung places at ca. 1400, see Brownlee 1978a, 219–20 (=1984, 7–8), noting Deschamps's application of the term ca. 1377 to Machaut.

Junger, Erwin.
1967. "Aspecte cromatice în stilul armonic modal al secolelor XIV–XVI" (Chromatic aspects in the modal harmonic style of the fourteenth to sixteenth centuries; in Rumanian; summary in French, Russian, and German). *Lucrări de Muzicologie* 3:171–82.
Study of direct chromatic steps in practical and theoretical sources, including examples from Machaut's Mass and *Je puis trop* (B28). Abstract: *RILM* 1 (1967), no. 1503.

Jurgens, Madeleine.
1982. *Archives Nationales. Documents du Minutier central des notaires de Paris: Inventaires après décès.* Vol. 1, *1483–1547.* Introduction by Jean Favier. Paris: Archives Nationales.
Catalogue listing the 1519 inventory of the library of Jean Turquam, with lost MS [9].

Kaiser, Ulrike.
1981. "Die 'Schwurszene' in Chaucer's *Book of the Duchess.*" *Euphorion* 75:110–17.
Close comparison of a scene from Chaucer's *Book of the Duchess* with its source, Machaut's *Jugement Behaingne* (113–16).

Kalas, B.-E.
1921. *La vie Rémoise à travers les ages.* Reims: La Dépêche.
Includes a chapter on Machaut (97–198), heavily romanticized.

Kalkbrenner, C[hristian].
1802. *Histoire de la musique.* 2 vols. in 1. Paris and Strasbourg: Kœnig.
Joie, plaisance (RF3) (plate 4) and beginning of the Gloria (plate 5), in diplomatic facsimile and transcription. See Bockholdt 1971, 150.

Kamien, Roger, comp.
1970. *The Norton Scores. An Anthology for Listening.* Vol. 1, *Gregorian Chant to Beethoven.* New York: Norton.
Includes edition of Agnus I (3–4 no. 1).

1972. *The Norton Scores. An Anthology for Listening.* 3rd rev. ed. New York: Norton.
Includes edition of Kyrie (5–9 no. 2). See also the 3rd rev. ed., expanded (1977), vol. 1, *Gregorian Chant to Beethoven* (7–11 no. 3).

1984. *The Norton Scores. An Anthology for Listening.* Vol. 1, *Gregorian Chant to Beethoven.* 4th rev. ed., expanded. New York and London: Norton.
Includes an edition of *Hareu!* / *Helas!* (M10) (pp. 6–9 no. 4), and *Rose, lis* (R10) (pp. 10–11 no. 5). M10 also appears in the 1984 single-vol. ed. and vol. 1 of the 5th rev. ed. (1990)

Kammerer, Friedrich.
1931. *Die Musikstücke des Prager Kodex XI E 9.* Veröfflichungen des musikwissenschaftlichen Institutes der deutschen Universität in Prag 1. Augsburg: Filser and Brünn: Rohrer. Reprint. 4 vols. in 1 (1931–34). Nendeln, Liechtenstein: Kraus, 1975.
Edition and study of works in Pg [72], including *Se vous n'estes* (R7) and *De petit po* (B18).

Kämper, Dietrich.
1971. "'Fortunae rota volvitur': Das Symbol des Schicksalsrades in der spätmittelalterlichen Musik." In *Der Begriff der Repraesentatio im Mittelalter: Stellvertretung, Symbol, Zeichen, Bild,* ed. Albert Zimmermann, 357–71.

Miscellanea medievalia: Veröffentlichungen des Thomas-Instituts der Universität zu Köln 8. Berlin and New York: de Gruyter.

Images of the wheel of Fortune from the fourteenth to the sixteenth centuries. Kämper considers Machaut's *De Fortune* (B23) to be the first known example for the musical symbolism of the wheel of Fortune. Unfortunately, for Kämper the symbolism lies uniquely in the unauthentic contratenors of MSS **E** and **Ch**; see Günther 1984a, 265. Abstract: *RILM* 6 (1972), no. 225.

Karp, Theodore

1988. "Compositional Process in Machaut's Ballades." *Music from the Middle Ages through the Twentieth Century: Essays in Honor of Gwynn S. McPeek*, ed. Carmelo P. Comberiati and Matthew C. Steel, 64–78. Musicology: A Book Series 7. New York: Gordon and Breach.

Argues for successive composition in some ballades, though the order of composition of the voices varies depending on the work. If a voice is tonally more cogent, and secondarily if it is thematically more coherent, that voice was created first. Considers Gloria, *Cinq, un* (R6), *De desconfort* (B8), *Dous amis, oy* (B6), *Honte, paour* (B25), *N'en fait* (B11), *Puis qu'en oubli* (R18) (this group composed tenor first); *Biauté qui* (B4), *Je puis trop* (B28), *Mes esperis* (B39), *Phyton* (B38), *Quant Theseüs / Ne quier* (B34) (this group composed cantus first). Also brief mention of *Je ne cesse* (L16/11), *Ma chiere* (B40), *Ne pensez pas* (B10), and *Sans cuer m'en / Amis / Dame* (B17). The analysis does not mention text, although many of the striking irregularities in the shape of the cantus in the examples are text motivated. For further discussion of the hypothesis of successive composition, see Dömling (1970), Arlt (1982, 200–202, 253–58, 279), Leech-Wilkinson (1984, 9–11), and Fuller (1987a, 44, 56 n. 10).

Kastner, L.E.

1905. "A Neglected French Poetic Form." *Zeitschrift für französische Sprache und Literatur* 28/1:288–97.

Discussion of the rhyme pattern aab bbc ccd, etc., or aaab bbbc cccd, etc. Considers the verse structure of the *Jugement Behaingne* (291–92).

Katz, Daniel Seth.

1989. "The Earliest Sources for the *Libellus cantus mensurabilis secundum Johannem de Muris*." Ph.D. diss. Duke University. Ann Arbor: University Microfilms. Order no. 9010364.

Preliminary study to a projected critical edition of this important treatise. Includes a new provisional text of the *Libellus*. Abstract: *DAI* A 50/11 (May 1990): 3407.

Kehler, Robert.

1984. "Historical Sketch of the Rondeau: The Widening Gap between Music and Poetry." *Proceedings of the Annual Meeting of the Western Society for French History* 10:41–53.

A useful quick survey of the development of the rondeau from the thirteenth to the sixteenth century, considering both changing text forms and changing musical forms; emphasizes the treatment of the refrain. Considers works by Guillaume d'Amiens, Adam de la Halle, Lescurel, Machaut, Deschamps, Froissart, Christine de Pizan, Charles d'Orléans, Marot, Dufay, Binchois, Josquin, and Claudin de Sermisy.

Keitel, Elizabeth A.

1976. "A Chronology of the Compositions of Guillaume de Machaut Based on a Study of Fascicle-Manuscript Structure in the Larger Manuscripts." Ph.D. diss. Cornell University. Ann Arbor: University Microfilms. Order no. 7615885.

A study that applies insights drawn from Hamm (1962) to a new chronology of Machaut's music. The principal basis of the chronology is a breakdown of MS **B** into segments copied separately ("first-generation fascicle manuscripts") and assembled later into the manuscript. The physical divisions posited for MS **B**, however, are illusory. Some criticism in Günther 1982, passim. Earp (1983, 102–9) shows that the uneven appearance of **B** derives not from the assemblage of parts originally separate, but due to the activity of several scribes copying from MS **Vg** (see also Bent 1983). Many scholars have not recognized the weaknesses of this work, e.g., Arlt (1982, 229, 247–48); Markstrom (1989); Roesner (1990, 38 n. 187); Tomasello (1990); Wilson (1990, 290); Berger (1987, 207 n. 8; 1992, 14); and Danckwardt (1993, 383n.). The demonstration of the dating of MS **B** remains useful. Abstract: *DAI* A 37/1 (July 1976): 26–27.

1977a. "The Musical Manuscripts of Guillaume de Machaut." *Early Music* 5: 469–72.

A brief overview of various problems of the main Machaut manuscripts. The argument that the *Qui bien aimme* (L22/16) was a later addition to *Jugement Navarre* is misleading. Abstracts: *RILM* 11 (1977), no. 4429; Karin Paulsmeier, *Basler Jahrbuch für historische Musikpraxis* 2 (1978): 224 no. 145.

1977b (ed.). "Seur Toute Creature Humeinne." Early Music Series EM31. Supplement to *Early Music* 5.

Useful edition of *Pas de tor* (B30), with a solution to the corrupt tenor, a translation, and commentary on the text. Some text references remain unsolved (see also the translation by Stephen Haynes for the compact disc Hyperion CDA 66588 [chap. 8.8], which includes a performance by Christopher Page's Gothic Voices after this edition).

1982a. "Les problèmes rencontrés pour dater la *Messe*." In Guillaume de Machaut 1982, 289–94.

Largely a French version of the first half of Keitel 1982b. The attempt to prove that there are different layers of composition of the Mass still ascertainable from the evidence of extant manuscripts is misleading. The material on changes of scribes in MS **B** was eliminated in 1982b.

1982b. "The So-Called Cyclic Mass of Guillaume de Machaut: New Evidence for an Old Debate." *Musical Quarterly* 68:307–23.

Attempts to prove that the Mass was compiled from originally disparate parts. The presentation of manuscript evidence lacks some of the erroneous statements about MS **B** found in the French version (1982a), probably eliminated in light of a paper read in 1978 by Margaret Bent at a meeting of the American Musicological Society, later published as Bent 1983; even so, what remains proves little. Much is made of changes of manuscript format, but since these concern sections of the Mass that move between syllabic and melismatic style, or have to do with the overall size of a given manuscript, the different formats tell us nothing about questions of compositional process or separate layers of composition. A.W. Robertson corrects the observations on liturgical sources, proving that the Mass was composed for Reims (1992, 103, 104 n. 15, 105 n. 19, 108 n. 22 and 27, 110 n. 34); there is no liturgical evidence that the Mass was not conceived of as a unit. Abstract: *RILM* 16 (1982), no. 2212.

1982c. "La tradition manuscrite de Guillaume de Machaut." In Guillaume de Machaut 1982, 75–94.

Expanded French version of Keitel 1977a.

Kelly, Douglas.
1978. *Medieval Imagination. Rhetoric and the Poetry of Courtly Love.* Madison: University of Wisconsin Press.

A study of late medieval French love poetry, from the *Roman de la Rose* to the fifteenth-century *Rhétoriqueurs*. This is a poetry of imagination, of the perception and retention of images in the mind. The poet (more accurately a *trouvère*) imitates creation in the reinterpretation and variation of images through rhetorical means such as *descriptio* and *amplificatio*. Chap. 6, "Guillaume de Machaut and the Sublimation of Courtly Love in Imagination" (121–54) demonstrates a transformation in Machaut's treatment of *fin' amors* beginning with the *Remede*, when the desire for *merci* becomes a secondary consideration, and Hope alone is sufficient for the perfect lover. Abstract: *Cultura neolatina* 41 (1981): 262; Peck 1988, no. 123. Reviews: Mechthild Albert, *Vox romanica* 42 (1983): 266–68; Judson Boyce Allen, *Clio* 11 (1981–82): 213–15; Gerard J. Brault, *French Review* 53 (1979–80): 287–88; R.T. Davies, *Modern Language Review* 76 (1981): 149–50; Boyd Davis, *Style* 15 (1981): 39–40; Ingeborg Glier, *Beiträge zur Geschichte der deutschen*

Sprache und Literatur 103 (1981): 459–64; Norris J. Lacy, *Esprit créateur* 19/4 (winter 1979): 120–21; Christiane Leube, *Zeitschrift für romanische Philologie* 99 (1983): 166–67; Nadia Margolis, *Modern Language Notes* 95 (1980): 1101–3; Marie-Louise Ollier, *SubStance* 23–24 (1979): 211–13; Lee W. Patterson, *Modern Language Notes* 94 (1979): 1237–41; Jean-Charles Payen, *Encomia* 2/2 (fall 1979): 17–19; *idem, Studi francesi* 25 (1981): 280–85; A.R. Press, *French Studies* 33 (1979): 432–33; Barbara Nelson Sargent-Baur, *Romance Philology* 34 (1980–81), Special Issue Feb. 1981, *219–22; John Stevens, *Comparative Literature* 33 (1981): 90–91; Sara Sturm-Maddox, *Degré second* 5 (July 1981): 131–32; Karl D. Uitti, *French Forum* 5 (1980): 179–81; see also comments in Brownlee 1984, 6–7, 128, 231 n. 26.

1981. "Les inventions ovidiennes de Froissart: réflexions intertextuelles comme imagination." *Littérature* 41 (Feb.): 82–92.

Discusses Froissart's *exempla*, freely adapted—a product of imagination—from Ovid, and their use in his *dits*. Froissart's transformations of Ovid are not marks of ineptitude, but an expression of creative imagination—"intertextual reflections"—to adapt the material to new contexts. Some mention of Machaut's use of Ovidian *exempla* in *Jugement Navarre* and *Confort*.

1983. "La spécialité dans l'invention des topiques." In *Archéologie du signe*, ed. Lucie Brind'Amour and Eugène Vance, 101–25. Recueils d'Etudes Médiévales / Papers in Mediaeval Studies 3. Toronto: Pontifical Institute of Mediaeval Studies.

Study of what twelfth- and thirteenth-century medieval arts of poetry say about invention, the identification of source material, and the adaptation and arrangement of that material to do something new. Machaut figures only as a small part of a much larger demonstration; the treatises are used to illuminate passages in *Prologue, Remede*, and *Confort*.

1985. "Assimilation et montage dans l'amplification descriptive: La démarche du poète dans le dit du XIVe siècle." In *Mittelalterbilder aus neuer Perspektive. Diskussionsanstösse zu amour courtois, Subjektivität in der Dichtung und Strategien des Erzählens. Kolloquium Würzburg, 1984*, ed. Ernstpeter Ruhe and Rudolf Behrens, 289–301 (discussion, 301–2). Beiträge zur romanischen Philologie des Mittelalters, Editionen und Abhandlungen 14. Munich: Fink.

Discusses the incorporation of Ovidian *exempla* (*montage*) in the fourteenth-century *dit* or *traité* as well as medieval conceptions of form and poetic creation (*forma tractatus* and *forma tractandi*). Kelly discusses *Fonteinne* in particular, but also mentions *Vergier, Jugement Behaingne, Jugement Navarre, Remede, Lyon, Alerion, Voir Dit*, and works of Froissart.

1987. "The Genius of the Patron: The Prince, the Poet, and Fourteenth-Century Invention." *Studies in the Literary Imagination* 20:77–97.

Important discussion of the roles the patron can take in the creation of a literary work.

1989. "Medieval Rhetoric." In *A New History of French Literature*, ed. Denis Hollier et al., 93–97. Cambridge, Mass. and London: Harvard University Press.

Includes a discussion of Machaut's *Prologue* (96).

1992. "Image et imagination dans les inventions des poètes: miroir et réceptivité dans les dits allégoriques." In *L'image au Moyen Age. Actes du Colloque Amiens, 19–23 mars 1986*, ed. Danielle Buschinger and Wolfgang Spiewok, 137–49. WODAN: Recherches en littérature médiévale 15; Serie 3/5. Göppingen: Kümmerle.

Topical invention in medieval French poetry. In Machaut's *Prologue, Scens* provides the creative faculty—imagination—with the ability to invent and fashion amorous images. In the fourteenth century, poets transform images known from the *Ovide Moralisé*. A master writer is adept at finding common threads in different materials susceptible to multiple significations and contexts, and various conceptions of love proposed by various authors (e.g., Guillaume de Lorris, Jean de Meun, Guillaume de Machaut) are expressed by the formation and adaptation of images appropriate to the several conceptions. Machaut's *Jugement Behaingne* and *Jugement Navarre* treat the same question, but do so according to two different conceptions of love and thus have two different outcomes.

Kendrick, Laura.
1992. "The Art of Mastering Servitude: Eustache Deschamps's Deployment of Courtly Love." *Romanistische Zeitschrift für Literaturgeschichte / Cahiers d'Histoire des Littératures Romanes* 16:30–45.
Deschamps's love poetry—a conventional mask—provides political commentary and exhorts his patrons to proper behavior; the lady in a poem is a metaphor for the princely patron. Includes brief consideration of Machaut, who assumes the role of both lover and lady in *Voir Dit* lyrics. Toute Belle is a cover for the real patron, Charles V, and may also cover other patrons (39–40 n. 7).

Kennedy, Angus J.
1984. *Christine de Pizan: A Bibliographical Guide*. Research Bibliographies and Checklists 42. London: Grant and Cutler.
Annotated bibliography; cf. Yenal 1989.

Kervyn de Lettenhove, [Joseph Marie Bruno Constantin], Baron, ed.
1882. *Poésies de Gilles Li Muisis*. Vol. 1. Louvain: Lefever.
The *Méditations* of 1350 mention Machaut (88).

Kibler, William W.
1978. "Poet and Patron—Froissart's *Prison Amoureuse*." *Esprit créateur* 18: 32–46.
Interesting account of the literary production of Wenceslas of Brabant and his role in determining the form of the completed *Prison Amoureuse*. Also mentions Machaut's *Remede* and *Voir Dit*. Criticism in De Looze 1993a, 108–9 n. 30.

Kibler, William W., and James I. Wimsatt.
1983. "The Development of the Pastourelle in the Fourteenth Century: An Edition of Fifteen Poems with an Analysis." *Mediaeval Studies* 45:22–78.
Edition of *pastourelles* from MS Pa [50], included here for the information on the manuscript. On the importance of the group of *pastourelles*, see also Wimsatt 1984.

1987. "Machaut's Text and the Question of His Personal Supervision." *Studies in the Literary Imagination* 20:41–53.
An earlier presentation of some of the material in the Preface to Wimsatt/Kibler 1988. Demonstrates an "early" and "late" text tradition for both *Jugement Behaingne* and *Remede* and indicates that careful proofreading was not part of Machaut's authorial supervision. The analysis of the manuscript tradition provides a view different from that implied by Hoepffner's stemma (1908–21, 1:xlviii).

Kibler, William W., Grover A. Zinn, Lawrence Earp, and John Bell Henneman, Jr., eds.
1995. *Medieval France: An Encyclopedia*. New York and London: Garland.
A one-volume interdisciplinary reference encyclopedia. Includes many articles of interest to scholars and students of Machaut.

Kiesewetter, R[aphael] G[eorg].
1831. *Allgemeine musikalische Zeitung* 33, no. 23, *Beilage* no. 4.
Diplomatic facsimile of the opening of the Gloria after Kalkbrenner 1802, with an attempted transcription (*Beilage*, p. 4). See Kiesewetter 1846.

1838. "Ueber den weltlichen und volksmässigen Gesang im Mittelalter." *Allgemeine musikalische Zeitung* 40:233–47, and *Beilage* no. 15.
Includes two examples of monophonic works by Machaut, *J'aim la flour* (L2, strophe 1a; ed. in *Beilage*, no. 12, in modern edition and in diplomatic facsimile, after Bottée de Toulmon 1836), and *Dame, a vous* (RF6, refrain only; ed. in *Beilage*, no. 13, in modern

edition and in diplomatic facsimile, after Bottée de Toulmon 1836), with some discussion (244, 246–47).

1841. *Schicksale und Beschaffenheit des weltlichen Gesanges vom frühen Mittelalter bis zu der Erfindung des dramatischen Styles und den Anfängen der Oper.* Leipzig: Breitkopf & Härtel. Reprint. Osnabrück: Biblio, 1970.

Includes two examples of monophonic works by Machaut, *J'aim la flour* (L2, strophe 1a; ed. in *Beilagen*, p. 3 no. 8 after Bottée de Toulmon 1836), and *Dame, a vous* (RF6, refrain only; ed. in *Beilagen*, p. 3 no. 9 after Bottée de Toulmon 1836), discussing them as examples of simple songs by "Contrapunctisten von *métier*" after Adam de la Halle (9). Machaut's polyphony is represented by *Dous viaire* (R1; ed. by Kiesewetter in *Beilagen*, p. 7 no. 14), which Kiesewetter finds extremely crude; Ambros (1891, 374–75) reprints the example.

1843. "Ueber die musikalischen Instrumente und die Instrumental-Musik im Mittelalter und bis zu der Gestaltung unserer dermaligen Kammer- und Orchester-Musik." *Caecilia* 22:187–238.

Includes the list of instruments from the *Prise* after Bottée de Toulmon 1839 (200–202). Kiesewetter notes that "the poet Guillaume de Machault flourished in the middle of the fourteenth century; he is praised in the musical literature not only as inventor of very beautiful melodies to his lais, ballades, and songs of various genres, but also as a daring, though not correct contrapuntist" (202).

1846. *Geschichte der europaeisch-abendlaendischen oder unsrer heutigen Musik. Darstellung ihres Ursprunges, ihres Wachsthumes und ihrer stufenweisen Entwickelung; von dem ersten Jahrhundert des Christenthums bis auf unsre Zeit.* Leipzig: Breitkopf & Härtel, 1834. 2nd rev. ed. Leipzig: Breitkopf & Härtel, 1846. Reprint. Wiesbaden: Sändig, 1972. *History of the Modern Music of Western Europe, from the First Century of the Christian Era to the Present Day, with Examples, and an Appendix, Explanatory of the Theory of the Ancient Greek Music*, trans. Robert Müller. London: Newby, 1848. Reprint, with an Introduction by Frank Ll. Harrison. New York: Da Capo, 1973.

A history of music with some discussion of Machaut (41=Eng. ed., 100–101). *Beilagen*, p. iii no. 2 (Eng. ed., 4–5) gives a diplomatic facsimile of the opening of the Gloria after Kalkbrenner 1802, with a transcription (discussed in Bockholdt 1971, 150; Vellekoop 1990, 173).

1847. *Galerie der alten Contrapunctisten; eine Auswahl aus ihren Werken, nach der Zeitfolge geordnet zu deutlicher Anschauung des Fortschreitens der Kunst; von den frühesten Versuchen harmonischer Verbindungen bis zum Anfang des achtzehnten Jahrhunderts und dem Aufblühen der neapolitanischen Schule, als der Periode der neueren Musik. Alles in verständlichen Partituren aus dem Archiv alter Musik des k.k. Hofrathes R.G. Kiesewetter Edl. von Wiesenbrunn von ihm eigens zusammengestellt. Eine Zugabe zu seinem Haupt-Catalog.* Vienna: Mechitharisten.

Composers from Hucbald up to the eighteenth century—Kiesewetter's plan for a history of early music in examples—are listed in tabular format with a few of their works, grouped into "galleries." Machaut appears in the *Vorsaal* (vestibule), among the "first attempts at joining different voices harmonically; then a long period of low level contrapuntal art" (1). For Machaut (characterized as a "dilettante"), Kiesewetter listed only the Mass, "performed 1364 at the coronation of Charles V at Paris…composition anything but correct; often bizarre and loathsome" (1).

Kirsch, Johann Peter.

1894. *Die päpstlichen Kollektorien in Deutschland während des XIV. Jahrhunderts.* Quellen und Forschungen aus dem Gebiete der Geschichte. Görres-Gesellschaft 3. Paderborn: Schöningh.

Includes material relating to a canonicate at Verdun obtained by Jean de Machaut (171, 228, 233).

Kitchel, Anna Theresa.
1923. "Chaucer and Machaut's *Dit de la Fontaine Amoureuse.*" In *Vassar Mediæval Studies*, ed. Christabel Forsyth Fiske, 217–31. New Haven: Yale University Press.
Includes a detailed summary of *Fonteinne* in outline form, written without the benefit of Hoepffner's edition.

Kittredge, George Lyman.
1909–10. "Chauceriana." *Modern Philology* 7:465–83.
Two of the eleven sections are relevant here: "I. The *Book of the Duchess* and Guillaume de Machaut" (465–71); and "II. 'Make the metres of hem as thee leste'" (471–74), which concerns Machaut's *Jugement Navarre* and the Prologue to the *Legend of Good Women*.

1910. "Antigone's Song of Love. " *Modern Language Notes* 25:158.
A note on Chaucer's use of Machaut's *Amours, se plus* (L9) in *Troilus*.

1915a. *Chaucer and His Poetry.* Cambridge, Mass.: Harvard University Press. 2nd ed., 1946.
Publication of a series of lectures. The lecture on the *Book of the Duchess* considers Machaut (54–58, 60–66), emphasizing Chaucer's originality in his adaptation of material borrowed from Machaut's *Jugement Behaingne, Remede*, and *Fonteinne*.

1915b. "Chaucer's *Troilus* and Guillaume de Machaut." *Modern Language Notes* 30:69.
Borrowings from *Remede*.

1915c. "Guillaume de Machaut and the *Book of the Duchess.*" *PMLA* 30:1–24.
Discusses Chaucer's borrowings from *Jugement Behaingne, Remede, Lyon, Fonteinne*, and several lyrics and motets: *Amours, tu* (Cp1), *S'onques* (L17/12), *Hé! Mors / Fine* (M3), *J'ay tant / Lasse!* (M7), *Qui es / Ha! Fortune* (M8), and *Fons / O livoris* (M9).

Klapp, Otto, ed., continued since 1986 by Astrid Klapp-Lehrmann.
1956–. *Bibliographie der französischen Literaturwissenschaft / Bibliographie d'histoire littéraire française.* Frankfurt a.M.: Klostermann. 32 vols. to date.
Excellent annual bibliography of scholarship on French literature; includes reviews.

Klein, Alexander.
1911. *Die altfranzösischen Minnefragen.* Part 1, *Ausgabe der Texte und Geschichte der Gattung.* Marburger Beiträge zur romanischen Philologie 1. Marburg a.L.: Ebel.
Includes editions of the anonymous *Chastel d'Amours* after MSS K [15] and J [16] (pp. 153–56), and the *Demandes d'Amours* in MSS J and Wm [41], as well as a study of the game of "Le roi qui ne ment" (211–31); cf. Green 1990.

Klicman, Ladislaus.
1903. *Acta Clementis VI. Pontificis romani. 1342–1352.* Monumenta Vaticana res gestas Bohemicas illustrantia 1. Prague: Gregerianis.
Papal documents.

Knight, Alan E.
1982. "French Literature." In *The Present State of Scholarship in Fourteenth-Century Literature*, ed. Thomas D. Cooke, 55–93. Columbia and London: University of Missouri Press.
A brief bibliographical essay on scholarship of fourteenth-century French literature.

Kneif, Tibor.
1964. "Die Erforschung mittelalterlicher Musik in der Romantik und ihr geistesgeschichtlicher Hintergrund." *Acta musicologica* 36:123–36.

Interesting historiographical study that bears on the reception of Machaut in the nineteenth century.

Knopp, Sherron E.

1992. "Augustinian Poetic Theory and the Chaucerian Imagination." In *The Idea of Medieval Literature: New Essays on Chaucer and Medieval Culture in Honor of Donald R. Howard*, ed. James M. Dean and Christian K. Zacher, 91–107. Newark: University of Delaware Press; London and Toronto: Associated University Press.

Includes consideration of Machaut's *Fonteinne* and Chaucer's *Book of the Duchess* (96–102).

Knowlton, E.C.

1922–23. "Nature in Old French." *Modern Philology* 20:309–29.

A study of the allegorical figure Nature, with mention of Machaut's *Prologue, Remede, Alerion*, and *Jugement Navarre*.

Koehler, Laurie.

1990. *Pythagoreisch-platonische Proportionen in Werken der ars nova und ars subtilior*. Göttinger musikwissenschaftliche Arbeiten 12. 2 vols. Kassel: Bärenreiter.

Studies the extent to which simple Pythagorean proportions (2:1, 3:1, 4:1, 3:2, 4:3) were utilized for rhythmic and formal proportions, principally in fourteenth-century music. In isorhythmic motets, Koehler investigates tenor structure, the relationship between *color* and *talea*, and text disposition, finding a direct relation between proportion and parameters of musical structure in many works. In chansons, the emphasis is on rhythmic proportions brought about by coloration. Analytically the work does not go very far, but the comparative material on large numbers of works is useful. For Machaut, Koehler investigates the ten Machaut motets with diminution sections, *Quant en moy / Amour* (M1), *Tous corps / De* (M2), *Hé! Mors / Fine / (M3), De Bon Espoir / Puis que* (M4), *Aucune gent / Qui plus* (M5), *J'ay tant / Lasse!* (M7), *Hareu! / Helas!* (M10), *Bone pastor / Bone pastor* (M18), *Christe / Veni* (M21), and *Felix virgo / Inviolata* (M23) (1:93–95, 102–9, 2:21, 25–28), and the single chanson with coloration, *Biauté qui* (B4) (1:102–3, 110–13). For the motets, Koehler concludes that Machaut was more apt to use simple proportions in all aspects of motet structure than Vitry (1:108).

Kohn, Karl.

1981. "The Renotation of Polyphonic Music." *Musical Quarterly* 67:29–49.

Argues for rebarring early music according to phrasing. For Machaut, Kohn offers renotated versions of *Biauté qui* (B4) and *Tuit mi penser* (V28/25). Abstract: *RILM* 15 (1981), no. 1627.

Komma, Karl Michael.

1961. *Musikgeschichte in Bildern*. Stuttgart: Kröner.

Contains some reproductions of miniatures in Machaut manuscripts.

Kooijman, Jacques.

1982. "Une étrange duplicité: La double ballade au bas Moyen Age." In *Le génie de la forme. Mélanges de langue et littérature offerts à Jean Mourot*, 41–49. Nancy: Presses universitaires de Nancy.

Machaut's place in the history of the double ballade; mentions *Quant Theseüs / Ne quier* (B34) and Deschamps's *déploration, Armes, Amours / O flour*.

Kooper, Erik Simon.

1985. *Love, Marriage and Salvation in Chaucer's* Book of the Duchess *and* Parlement of Foules. Diss. Rijksuniversiteit te Utrecht. Utrecht: Elinkwijk. Ann Arbor: University Microfilms. Order no. 8817730.

Includes consideration of Chaucer's literary sources, among them Machaut's *Jugement Behaingne, Remede*, and *Fonteinne*. Abstract: *DAI* A 49/9 (Mar. 1989): 2651.

Kornmüller, Utto.
  1895. "Die Musiklehre des Ugolino von Orvieto." *Kirchenmusikalisches Jahrbuch* 10:19–40.
  Includes a German translation of the passage in Ugolino on Machaut (33).

Kovarik, Edward.
  1973. "Mid Fifteenth-Century Polyphonic Elaborations of the Plainchant *Ordinarium missae*." Ph.D. diss. Harvard University. 2 vols.
  Includes discussion of plainsong *cantus firmi* in Machaut's Kyrie, Sanctus, and Agnus (148–51). Not examined (cited in A.W. Robertson 1992, 112 n. 40).

Kraft, Christine (ed.).
  1977. *Die Liebesgarten-Allegorie der "Echecs Amoureux." Kritische Ausgabe und Kommentar*. Europäische Hochschulschriften 13/48. Frankfurt a.M.: Lang.
  Publication of author's 1975 Giessen thesis, a critical edition of a poem that includes mention of a "rés d'Alemaigne"; see chap. 7.3, commentary to *Nes qu'on* (B33).

Kraus, H[ans] P[eter].
  1968? *Medieval and Renaissance Manuscripts Selected for the Beauty of Their Illumination and the Significance of Their Text*. Catalogue 117. New York: H.P. Kraus.
  Catalogue description of MS **Kr** [36].

Kuckertz, Josef.
  1968. "Die Satztechnik in den mehrstimmigen Messordinarien des 14. Jahrhunderts." *Kirchenmusikalisches Jahrbuch* 52:45–70.
  Melodic correspondences in several fourteenth-century polyphonic Mass Ordinaries. Includes a musical example vertically aligning many sections of Machaut's Mass for comparative purposes, based on the "generating cell" of Gastoué. Mentioned in Dömling 1971, 25 n. 7. Abstract: *RILM* 2 (1968), no. 1653.

Kügle, Karl.
  1990. "Codex Ivrea, Bibl. cap. 115: A French Source 'Made in Italy.'" *Revista de musicología* 13:527–61.
  Study of the compilation, repertory, scribes, and provenance of MS **Iv** [57].

  1991. "Die Musik des 14. Jahrhunderts: Frankreich und sein direkter Einflussbereich." In *Die Musik des Mittelalters*, ed. Hartmut Möller and Rudolf Stephan, 352–84. Neues Handbuch der Musikwissenschaft 2. Laaber: Laaber.
  Survey of French fourteenth-century music, considering the term Ars Nova, chronology, and sources, with a detailed chronology of developments in motet composition, and brief consideration of secular songs, especially the *chace*. Large bibliography. Reviews: *Concerto* 9 (Feb. 1992): 9–10; Kurt von Fischer, *Musikforschung* 46 (1993): 202–4; Hermann Moeck, *Tibia* 15–16 (1990–91): 645; John Stevens, *Plainsong and Medieval Music* 1 (1992): 197–200.

  1993. "The Manuscript Ivrea, Biblioteca capitolare 115: Studies in the Transmission and Composition of Ars Nova Polyphony." Ph.D. diss. New York University. Ann Arbor: University Microfilms. Order no. 9333648.
  Comprehensive study of the structure, provenance, and repertory of MS **Iv** [57]. Includes a valuable new account of fourteenth-century motets, *chaces*, and liturgical music, all of which is relevant to Machaut.

Kugler, Michael.
  1972. *Die Tastenmusik im Codex Faenza*. Münchner Veröffentlichungen zur Musikgeschichte 21. Tutzing: Schneider.
  Publication of author's 1970 Munich dissertation, a study of intabulation techniques in MS **Fa** [67], with diplomatic facsimile edition. Abstracts: *RILM* 7 (1973), no. 3210; abstract of original dissertation: *Musikforschung* 26 (1973): 104. Reviews: John

Caldwell, *Music and Letters* 54 (1973): 227–28; Robert Huestis, *Journal of the American Musicological Society* 27 (1974): 522–25 (corrections).

1975. *Die Musik für Tasteninstrumente im 15. und 16. Jahrhundert.* Taschenbücher zur Musikwissenschaft 41. Wilhelmshaven: Heinrichshofen. Material on MS **Fa** [67] (pp. 31–50). Abstract: *RILM* 10 (1976), no. 2477.

Kuhn, David.
  1967. *La poétique de François Villon.* Paris: Colin.
    Publication of author's 1967 Paris thesis. See 469–73 for a literary analysis of *De toutes flours* (B31) (strophes 2 and 3 are inverted, as in the edition of Woledge [1961]).

Kühn, Hellmut.
  1973. *Die Harmonik der Ars Nova. Zur Theorie der isorhythmischen Motette.* Berliner musikwissenschaftliche Arbeiten 5. Munich: Katzbichler.
    Not credited as much as it should be, this work includes an important discussion of harmonic structure and compositional practice in the fourteenth-century motet and chanson, especially in Machaut. Emphasizes priority of the *Gerüstsatz,* or compositional framework. Varying degrees of perfection of intervals allows a ranking of interval successions (Fuller 1986 provides a more refined development of this theory). Analyses consider especially the motets *Fons / O livoris* (M9), *Dame, je sui / Fins cuers* (M11), *Bone pastor / Bone pastor* (M18), and *Tu qui gregem / Plange* (M22), and the chansons *Je puis trop* (B28), *Quant Theseüs / Ne quier* (B34), and *Puis qu'en oubli* (R18). For subsequent comments and critiques, see Apfel 1974, 182–84, 364; Stenzl 1975, 122; Wernli 1977, 14, 20 n. 15; Fuller 1986, 67 n. 25, 68 n. 37 and 39, 69 n. 46; Leech-Wilkinson 1989, 1:122 n. 37. Abstract: *RILM* 10 (1976), no. 334; abstract of original dissertation: *Musikforschung* 23 (1970): 461–62. Reviews: Wolfgang Dömling, *Musikforschung* 29 (1976): 352–54; Jürg Stenzl, *Neue Zeitschrift für Musik* 135 (1974): 467.

  1983. "Guillaume de Machaut, Motette Nr. 22." In *Chormusik und Analyse: Beiträge zur Formanalyse und Interpretation mehrstimmiger Vokalmusik.* Vol. 1, *Texte,* ed. Heinrich Poos, 29–41; Vol. 2, *Noten,* ed. Heinrich Poos, 11–16. Mainz: Schott.
    Edition of *Tu qui gregem / Plange* (M22), with an analysis that accords differing degrees of perfection to a variety of parameters (pitch level, duration, sonority, text). Any given moment in the motet shows differing degrees of perfection among these parameters; overall perfection is reached only at the end of the work. Abstract: *RILM* 17 (1983), no. 1672.

Kurose, Tamotsu.
  1977. *Miniatures of Goddess Fortune in Mediaeval Manuscripts.* Tokyo: Sanseido, 1977.
    A study of various attributes of Lady Fortune in medieval manuscripts, including facsimiles of miniatures in MSS **K** (plates 112 and 140), **C** (plate 137), and **Pm** (plates 139 and 148). Introduction and commentary in Japanese, with bibliography in English, French, German, and Italian (341–42), and table of miniatures in English.

Kurtzman, Jeffrey Gordon.
  1967. "The Development of the Isorhythmic Motet in Fourteenth-Century France." M.M. diss. University of Illinois.
    Periodicity in all parameters of motet composition. Not examined. Abstract: *RILM* 1 (1967), no. 1444.

La Fage, Adrien de.
  1864. *Essais de diphthérographie musicale, ou notices, descriptions, analyses, extraits et reproductions de manuscrits relatifs à la pratique, à la théorie et à l'histoire de la musique.* Paris: Legouix. Reprint. Amsterdam: Knuf, 1964.
    Includes an excerpt from Ugolino commenting on Johannes de Muris's criticism of Machaut's notational practice (162–63, 539).

Laidlaw, J[ames] C[ameron].
1968. "André du Chesne's Edition of Alain Chartier." *Modern Language Review* 63:569–74.
Discussion of the Le Caron 1489 edition of Alain Chartier (569–70) (see chap. 3, item [47]).
1974 (ed.). *The Poetical Works of Alain Chartier.* Cambridge: Cambridge University Press.
Standard critical edition of Chartier's poetry. Includes excellent descriptions of MSS **Pm** [18], **I** [40], **Wm** [41], *F:CF 249* [42], **Ra** [44], **R** [45], St [46], *F:Pn 833* [48], *F:Pn 24440* [53], **La** [54], and the incunabulum *Chartier* [47].
1987. "Christine de Pizan—A Publisher's Progress." *Modern Language Review* 82:35–75.
Christine's role in the planning and preparation of manuscripts of her works.

La Monte, John L.
1932. "The 'Roy de Chippre' in François Villon's 'Ballade des Seigneurs du Temps Jadis.'" *Romanic Review* 23:48–53.
The king of Cyprus referred to by Villon was Pierre de Lusignan, whom Villon knew through Machaut's *Prise* (52).

Långfors, Arthur.
1917. *Les incipit des poèmes français antérieurs au XVIe siècle: Répertoire bibliographique établi à l'aide de notes de M. Paul Meyer.* Paris: Champion. Reprint. New York: Franklin, 1970.
Signals four manuscripts of the *Jugement Behaingne* not known to Hoepffner (also mentioned in Långfors's review of Langlois 1910).

Langhans, Victor.
1928. "Chaucer's Book of the Leoun." *Anglia* 52:113–22.
Upholds the idea that Chaucer's lost *Book of the Leoun* was a translation of Machaut's *Lyon.*

Langlois, Ernest.
1902 (ed.). *Recueil d'arts de seconde rhéthorique.* Collection de documents inédits sur l'histoire de France 85. Paris: Imprimerie nationale. Reprint. Geneva: Slatkine, 1974.
Standard edition of the important rhetorical treatises of the early fifteenth century. The anonymous *Regles de la Seconde Rettorique* (between ca. 1404 and 1432; ed. pp. 11–103) places Machaut historically after Philippe de Vitry, and cites *Jugement Behaingne*, while the *Doctrinal de la Secunde Retorique* of Baudet Herenc (ed. pp. 104–98) cites the first strophe of *Par trois raisons* (L6/5), *Amours doucement* (L7/6), and *Qui bien aimme* (L22/16), respectively.
1910. *Les manuscrits du Roman de la Rose; description et classement.* Travaux et mémoires de l'Université de Lille n.s. 1/7. Lille: Tallandier; Paris: Champion. Reprint. Geneva: Slatkine, 1974.
Includes a description of MS **Ar** [32] (pp. 110–16).

Langner, Johannes.
1982. "Figur und Saiteninstrument bei Picasso." *Pantheon—Internationale Zeitschrift für Kunst* 40:98–113.
Includes a discussion of several literary references to string instruments, including ll. 1–11 of *Harpe* (104). Abstract: *RILM* 18 (1984), no. 6905.

Lanoue, David G.
1981a. "History as Apocalypse: The 'Prologue' of Machaut's *Jugement dou Roy de Navarre.*" *Philological Quarterly* 60:1–12.
Argues that the 458-line Prologue to *Jugement Navarre* is integrally linked with the rest of the poem.

1981b. "Musical Imagery in the Poetry of Juan Ruiz, Guillaume de Machaut, and Chaucer: A Comparative Study." Ph.D. diss. University of Nebraska-Lincoln. Ann Arbor: University Microfilms. Order no. 8118170.

The descriptions of musical practice in poems of Ruiz, Machaut, and Chaucer serve different functions in the works discussed. For Machaut, Lanoue considers *Jugement Behaingne*, *Jugement Navarre*, and *Remede*. Abstracts: *DAI* A 42/3 (Sept. 1981): 1141–42; *RILM* 15 (1981), no. 3889.

1984. "Music Therapy and Guillaume de Machaut: Hope's *Chanson royal* in the *Remede de Fortune*." *Kentucky Romance Quarterly* 31:363–70.

Literary analysis of the *Remede* demonstrates the healing powers of the music of *Joie, plaisance* (RF3). Discussion of speculative musical aspects: "music was thought to be a remedy for despair or melancholy, since this condition derives from dissonance in the *musica humana* of the individual" (366).

1985. "*La Prise d'Alexandrie*. Guillaume de Machaut's Epic." *Nottingham Medieval Studies* 29:99–108.

Machaut intended the *Prise* less as a historical chronicle and more as a medieval epic poem with political ramifications for the 1370s. The theme of a knight seeking Christian unity against the common enemy would not have been lost on contemporaries at a time when war with the English had once again broken out. Abstract: *Encomia* 9 (1987): 63 no. 390.

Lanson, Gustave.

1894. *Histoire de la littérature française*. Paris: Hachette. 4th rev. ed. 1896.

A standard and influential survey of French literature, reprinted in many editions. The segment on Machaut (144–45) remained unchanged well into the twentieth century. For instance, the revised edition by Paul Truffrau (Hachette, 1959, 148–49), gives exactly the same text on Machaut as the original edition; only a footnote listing the editions of Chichmaref and Hoepffner (with the wrong dates) replace the old footnote to the editions of Tarbé and P. Paris.

1923. *Histoire illustrée de la littérature française*. Vol. 1. 2nd ed. Paris and London: Hachette.

The literary history of the fourteenth century is unsympathetic (107–24); included here for the facsimile of *Prologue* miniature F4, and of the ornate *Ex-libris* in MS E [7].

Laurie, I.S.

1964. "Deschamps and the Lyric as Natural Music." *Modern Language Review* 59:561–70.

Examination of Deschamps's works for the application of the poetical prescriptions laid out in the *Art de Dictier*.

Lawlor, John.

1956. "The Pattern of Consolation in *The Book of the Duchess*." *Speculum* 31:626–48. Reprint (with abbreviations). *Chaucer Criticism*. Vol. 2, *Troilus and Criseyde and the Minor Poems*, ed. Richard J. Schoek and Jerome Taylor, 232–60. Notre Dame, Ind.: Notre Dame University Press, 1961.

A literary study of Chaucer's *Book of the Duchess*, with comments on Machaut's *Jugement Navarre* (636).

Lebedev, Sergej.

1988. *Problema modal' noj garmonii v muzyke rannego Vozroždenija* (The problem of modal harmonies in the music of the early Renaissance). Ph.D. diss. Moskovskaja Gosudarstvennaja Konservatorija.

A dissertation that includes analyses of Machaut works. Not examined. Abstract: *RILM* 22 (1988), no. 8539.

Lebeuf, l'abbé [Jean].

1743. *Dissertations sur l'histoire ecclésiastique et civile de Paris, suivies de plusieurs eclaircissemens sur l'histoire de France.* Vol. 3. Paris: Durand.

Includes an extract from the *Prise* (413–14), the motetus text of *Tu qui gregem / Plange* (M22) and the triplum text of *Felix virgo / Inviolata* (M23) (pp. 431–33); also reference to MSS **A** [5] and **G** [6].

1751. "Mémoire sur la vie de Philippe de Mezières, Conseiller du roi Charles V, et chancelier du royaume de Chypre." *Mémoires de l'Académie Royale des Inscriptions et Belles-Lettres* 17:491–514.

Includes the first modern mention of Machaut MS **F-G** [6]; read 25 June 1743.

1753. "Notice sommaire de deux volumes de poësies françoises et latines, conservés dans la bibliothèque des Carmes-Déchaux de Paris; Avec une indication du genre de musique qui s'y trouve." *Mémoires de littérature, tirés des registres de l'Académie royale des Inscriptions et Belles-Lettres* 20:377–98.

The first modern study of Machaut's writings, based on the rediscovery of MS **F-G**; read December 1746.

Leech-Wilkinson, Daniel.

1980. "Compositional Procedure in Machaut's *Hoquetus David.*" *RMA Research Chronicle* 16:99–109.

A convincing analysis of the procedure likely employed by Machaut in the composition of *Hoquetus David*. Abstract: *RILM* 14 (1980), no. 3758.

1982. *Cambridge Music Manuscripts, 900–1700*, ed. Iain Fenlon, 100–103. Cambridge: Cambridge University Press.

Excellent description of MS **Pe** [20], with a facsimile of *En amer* (RF4).

1982–83. "Related Motets from Fourteenth-Century France." *Proceedings of the Royal Musical Association* 109:1–22.

Based on close structural relationships and cross-references between many fourteenth-century isorhythmic motets, argues that the repertory stems from a restricted circle of composers. Ascribes several anonymous motets to Philippe de Vitry or to his immediate followers. Machaut's imitations of Vitry have features atypical of Machaut's usual procedures, arguing for self-conscious modeling on Machaut's part. Mention of *Tous corps / De* (M2), *Aucune gent / Qui plus* (M5), *Qui es / Ha! Fortune* (M8), *Fons / O livoris* (M9), *Hareu! / Helas!* (M10), *Amours qui a / Faus Samblant* (M15), *Quant vraie amour / O series* (M17), *Bone pastor / Bone pastor* (M18), *Christe / Veni* (M21), *Tu qui gregem / Plange* (M22), and *Felix virgo / Inviolata* (M23). Abstract: *RILM* 17 (1983), no. 2450.

1983. "Compositional Procedure in the Four-Part Isorhythmic Works of Philippe de Vitry and His Contemporaries." Ph.D. diss. Cambridge University. 3 vols.

See Leech-Wilkinson 1989; 1990b; 1990c. Still useful for some of the analytical examples not retained in Leech-Wilkinson 1990c. Abstract: *RILM* 17 (1983), no. 1694.

1984. "Machaut's *Rose, lis* and the Problem of Early Music Analysis." *Music Analysis* 3:9–28.

The introduction discusses the question of the application of modern analytical techniques to the analysis of medieval music (cf. Kühn 1973, 30–33; for a literary viewpoint, see Palmer 1987b). Several approaches to the analysis of R10, including hexachordal areas, melodic motives, cadences and directed progressions, prolongation, harmonic structure, and discussion of views of successive vs. simultaneous composition. Includes voice-leading diagrams of middleground and background levels. The song consists of a melodic and contrapuntal structure decorated through prolongation, the overall harmonic structure reducible to four descending sequences in octaves, with a surface structure permeated with descending hexachords. Text is not much taken into account. Abstract: *RILM* 18 (1984), no. 5955.

1989. *Compositional Techniques in the Four-Part Isorhythmic Motets of Philippe de Vitry and His Contemporaries.* 2 vols. Outstanding Dissertations in Music from British Universities. New York and London: Garland.
Publication of Leech-Wilkinson 1983, omitting chapters on the Mass (revised and expanded in Leech-Wilkinson 1990b and 1990c), and adding a brief bibliography of studies published since 1983. Includes a study of Machaut's isorhythmic motets, with particular emphasis on the four-voice works: *Aucune gent / Qui plus* (M5), *Christe / Veni* (M21), *Tu qui gregem / Plange* (M22), and *Felix virgo / Inviolata* (M23). The emphasis is on a composer's procedures of composition, and Leech-Wilkinson touches upon questions of the projection of text structure in the musical structure, and the problem of successive vs. simultaneous conception of the parts. Certain infelicities in motets stem from pre-compositional problems. Reviews: Lawrence Earp, *Journal of the American Musicological Society* 46 (1993): 295–305; Sarah Fuller, *Notes* 48 (1991–92): 473–75.

1990a. "Ars Antiqua—Ars Nova—Ars Subtilior." *Man and Music I: Antiquity and the Middle Ages,* ed. James McKinnon, 218–40. London: Macmillan-Granada. Published in the United States as *Antiquity and the Middle Ages: From Ancient Greece to the 15th Century,* ed. James McKinnon. Music and Society. Englewood Cliffs, N.J.: Prentice Hall.
Excellent overview of music in fourteenth-century France. Survey of Machaut (224–31), and discussion of his musical influence (237–38). Includes a brief annotated bibliography.

1990b (ed.). *Guillaume de Machaut: La Messe de Nostre Dame.* Oxford Choral Music. Oxford: Clarendon Press.
Edition of the Mass for performance, with a one-page introductory note. Reviews: see Leech-Wilkinson 1990c.

1990c. *Machaut's Mass: An Introduction.* Oxford: Clarendon Press. Paperback ed. 1992.
A brief biography of Machaut and an analytical study, with a new edition of the Mass. The biography is important for its careful citation of documents that Machabey (1955b) only vaguely identifies, and for fleshing out the problem of the destination of the Mass (see further A.W. Robertson 1992). The analytical section forms the core of the work, approaching the Mass from the point of view of pre-compositional constraints on the composer. The discussion of the Gloria and Credo offers the first compelling alternative to Gombosi's analysis (1950) and finds evidence for a loose paraphrase of a plainsong Gloria. Leech-Wilkinson further engages the problem of successive vs. simultaneous conception, arguing forcefully in favor of the latter view. Specific similarities to the Mass in compositions datable to a narrow chronological span, including *Christe / Veni* (M21), *Felix virgo / Inviolata* (M23), *Plourez, dames* (B32), *Nes qu'on* (B33), and *Quant Theseüs / Ne quier* (B34), argue for placing the Mass in the early 1360s (see further Leech-Wilkinson 1993a). The edition is accompanied by an extensive critical report and material on performance. The paperback edition has some corrections to the biography. Reviews: Christian Berger, *Musiktheorie* 7 (1992): 273–76; Roger Bowers, *Music and Letters* 74 (1993): 54–59; Lawrence Earp, *Journal of the American Musicological Society* 46 (1993): 295–305; Cristle Collins Judd, *Music Analysis* 11 (1992): 120–28; Olga E. Malyshko, *Notes* 48 (1991–92): 1231–33; Anthony Milner, *Musical Times* 132 (1991): 300–301; Christopher Page, *Early Music* 19 (1991): 107–8; Marielle Popin, *Revue de musicologie* 77 (1991): 128–29; Edward H. Roesner, *Speculum* 68 (1993): 196–97; Nigel Wilkins, *Medium Ævum* 60 (1991): 319–20; Ronald Woodley, *TLS* no. 4571 (9–15 Nov. 1990): 1210.

1991. "Not Just a Pretty Tune: Structuring Devices in Four Machaut Virelais." *Sonus* 12:16–31.
Voice-leading analyses of *Douce dame jolie* (V4), *Dame, a qui* (V12), *Je vivroie* (V23/21), and *Dame, a vous* (RF6).

1993a. "*Le Voir Dit* and *La Messe de Nostre Dame*: Aspects of Genre and Style in Late Works of Machaut." *Plainsong and Medieval Music* 2:43–73.

Through an analysis of interpolated chansons new to the *Voir Dit*, which were composed as work on the narrative proceeded, and thus presumably products of the early 1360s, Leech-Wilkinson isolates some musical ideas that inform several works of diverse genres. Musical parallels extend to the Mass, which can now be placed in the early 1360s with reasonable assurance. The relationships between works of different tonal centers, different mensurations, different genres—as between ballade and rondeau, or even Mass and ballade—imply a common "sound world." "It follows that Machaut's musical ideas were conceived at a level below that of form, mensuration or tonal type. Depending upon his choices about those three, the musical ideas were of course realized differently. And the different characters of each realization... were settled at a higher level still, as Machaut began to think about how to set a particular text. But text is not the first factor to be considered: the music already has some existence before the text is composed" (61). For musicians, the article provides important corroboration of Leech-Wilkinson's argument (already begun in 1990c) of simultaneous rather than successive conception of the parts. The view of abstract "musical ideas" that reappear in several contexts parallels one of Machaut's primary compositional procedures for the text of the *Voir Dit*, in which a single textual idea appears in several guises—in the prose of a letter, in the rhyming couplets of the narrative, or in the more abstract verse structure of a lyric. Just so, a single musical idea can appear across several genres.

1993b. *"Le Voir Dit*: A Reconstruction and a Guide for Musicians." *Plainsong and Medieval Music* 2:103–40.

A detailed annotated outline of the entire *Voir Dit*, with extensive footnotes that explain internal dates and historical references. Leech-Wilkinson has restored the letters to the order in the manuscripts, except that he reorders letters 2–7 and 40–41, thus arriving (independently) at the results of Eichelberg's 1935 study. The whole makes for fascinating reading for those familiar with the *dit*, and provides an invaluable outline for those just getting started. An appendix includes a newly-edited collection of excerpts that are relevant to music. This is a serious attempt to make sense of the ordering of Machaut's material.

Lefferts, Peter, and Sylvia Huot, eds.

1989. *Five Ballades for the House of Foix*. Antico Edition AE 27. Newton Abbot: Antico.

Includes an edition, with textual notes and translation, of *Phiton Phiton* by Magister Franciscus, a ballade related to Machaut's *Phyton* (B38).

Le Gentil, Pierre.

1963. *La littérature française du Moyen Age*. Collection Armand Colin, Section de langues et littératures 369. Paris: Colin. 2nd ed. Collection U2. Paris: Colin, 1968.

A small book full of insight and understanding, with an early rehabilitation of Machaut (158–63).

Leguy, Sylvette.

1977 (ed.). *Guillaume de Machault 1300–1377: Œuvres complètes*. Edition commémorative établie par S. Leguy. Vol. 1, *Les virelais*. Vol. 2, *Les rondeaux*. Vol. 3, *Les ballades*. Vol. 4, *Les lais*. Vol. 5, *Les motets*. Vol. 6, *La Messe de Notre Dame*. Vol. 7, *La Remède de Fortune*. Paris: Le Droict Chemin de Musique.

An uncritical edition after MS **F-G**; only vols. 1, 2, and 4 were published, all in 1977. The review of Boorman contains important caveats. Reviews: Boorman 1977a; Jean Maillard, *Revue de musicologie* 66 (1980): 247–48.

1982. "Les procédés de composition dans l'œuvre de Machaut (à l'exclusion de la *Messe*)." In Guillaume de Machaut 1982, 307–20.

General discussion of motets, rondeaux (especially *Dame, se vous n'avez* [R13]), ballades, and lais.

Lehoux, Françoise.
1966–68. *Jean de France, duc de Berri. Sa vie. Son action politique (1340–1416).* Vol. 1, *De la naissance de Jean de France à la mort de Charles V.* Paris: Picard, 1966. Vol. 3, *De l' «avènement» de Jean sans Peur à la mort du duc de Berri.* Paris: Picard, 1968.
The standard biography of John of Berry, with full documentation and bibliography. Vol. 3 contains a complete itinerary of the duke.

Lemm, Siegfried, and Martin Löpelmann, eds.
1918. *Kurzes Verzeichnis der romanischen Handschriften.* Mitteilungen aus der Königlichen Bibliothek 4. Berlin: Wiedmannsche Buchhandlung.
Standard catalogue of MS **Bk** [21] (p. 27, MS *Hamilton 214).

Lenneberg, Hans.
1988. *Witnesses and Scholars: Studies in Musical Biography.* Musicology: A Book Series 5. New York: Gordon and Breach.
Includes interesting historiographical material bearing on the rediscovery of Machaut's works in the eighteenth and nineteenth centuries.

Lerch[-Calavrytinos], Irmgard.
1987. *Fragmente aus Cambrai: Ein Beitrag zur Rekonstruktion einer Handschrift mit spätmittelalterlicher Polyphonie.* Göttinger musikwissenschaftliche Arbeiten 11. 2 vols. Kassel: Bärenreiter.
Incorporating new fragments of the MS **CaB** [56] (see Fallows 1976), Lerch reconstructs two gatherings of a motet manuscript [Lerch's *siglum* for the reconstructed manuscript is *F:CA(n)*] and confirms the results of Hasselman (1970) for the chanson manuscript (nevertheless, the new fragments of chansons await a thorough study). Provides a complete study of *F:CA(n)*, with critical editions of the motets, Mass sections, and fragments, and a complete facsimile. The only Machaut work in the motet section is *Qui es / Ha! Fortune* (M8). Abstract: *RILM* 21 (1987), no. 1391. Reviews: Jürgen Appell, *Neue Zeitschrift für Musik* 149 (1988): 56; Christian Berger, *Musikforschung* 42 (1989): 278–81; David Hiley, *Musiktheorie* 4 (1989): 92–94; Marielle Popin, *Revue de musicologie* 75 (1989): 291–92.

Lerner, Edward R., comp.
1968. *Study Scores of Musical Styles.* New York: McGraw-Hill.
Includes an edition of *Qui es / Ha! Fortune* (M8), with commentary and text translation (45–48 no. 27).

Leube, Eberhard.
1969. *Fortuna in Karthago: Die Aeneas-Dido-Mythe Vergils in den romanischen Literaturen vom 14. bis zum 16. Jahrhundert.* Studien zum Fortwirken der Antike 1. Heidelberg: Winter.
Considers the treatment of the Dido myth in the *Ovide Moralisé* (41–54), and Machaut's use of it in *Jugement Navarre* (48–54).

Leuchter, Erwin, comp.
1964. *Florilegium musicum. History of Music in 180 Examples from Antiquity to the 18th Century.* 2 vols. Buenos Aires: Ricordi Americana.
Includes musical editions of the Agnus Dei (23–26 no. 32) and *Ma fin* (R14) (pp. 26–27 no. 33). Vol. 2 includes brief commentary (44–45).

Leupin, Alexandre.
1986. "The Powerlessness of Writing: Guillaume de Machaut, the Gorgon, and *Ordenance*," trans. Peggy McCracken. *Yale French Studies* 70:127–49.
Poetic language and the relationship between poet and prince in selected narratives, especially *Alerion, Confort, Voir Dit,* and *Prise.*

Levarie, Siegmund.
1954. *Guillaume de Machaut.* Great Religious Composers. New York: Sheed and Ward. Reprint. New York: Da Capo, 1969, 1973.

Very general, and little concerns Machaut directly. Includes some useful information on mid-twentieth-century performances of the Mass, and on the rediscovery of MS **Vg** [3]. Reviews: *Catholic Choirmaster* 40 (1954): 189; James Ringo, *American Record Guide* 37 (1971): 622–23; A.F. Leighton Thomas, *Music Review* 32 (1971): 190–91; Harold Schonberg, *Musical Courier* 150/7 (1 Dec. 1954): 44.

Levi, Ezio.
1908. Chapter 8, Francesco di Vannozzo e la leteratura francese, §II.7, "Guglielmo di Machaut e la sua influenza su Francesco di Vannozzo." In Ezio Levi, *Francesco di Vannozzo e la lirica nelle corte lombarde durante la seconda metà del secolo XIV*, 297–300. Pubblicazioni del R. Istituto di Studi superiori prattici e di perfezionamento in Firenze. Sezione di filosofia e filologia. Pubblicazioni 23. Florence: Galletti e Cocci.
Possible influence of Machaut, especially *Harpe*, on Francesco di Vannozzo.

Levine, Robert.
1985. "Myth and Antimyth in *La vie vaillante* de Bertrand du Guesclin." *Viator* 16:259–75.
Poetry and history, with mention of Machaut's *Prise* (259–60), "a bizarre amalgamation of allegory, epic, patristic exegesis, panegyric, and discontinuous bursts of reality" (260).

Levy, Claude.
1935. "Guillaume de Machaut, 'Le Livre du Voir Dit.'" *Diplôme d'études supérieurs (lettres)*. Paris.
Not examined.

Lewis, P.S.
1985. "Une devise de chevalerie inconnue, créée par un comte de Foix?" and "Le dragon de Mauvezin et Jean I comte de Foix (1412–36)." In *Essays in Later Medieval French History*, 29–36 and 37–40, respectively. History series 29. London: Hambledon.
Includes material possibly relevant to the provenance of MS **Vg** [3].

Liborio, Mariantonia.
1973. "Una versione piccarda inedita della 'Visio Philiberti.'" *Cultura neo-latina* 33:105–45.
Includes a description of MS **Ar** [32].

Lincoln, Harry B., and Stephen Bonta, eds. and comps.
1986. *Study Scores of Historical Styles*. Vol. 1. Englewood Cliffs, N.J.: Prentice Hall.
Includes editions of *Douce dame jolie* (V4), *Mes esperis* (B39), and *Rose, lis* (R10).

Little, Patrick.
1980. "Three Ballades in Machaut's *Livre du Voir-Dit*." *Studies in Music* (Australia) 14:45–60.
Context in the *Voir Dit* of *Plourez, dames* (B32), *Nes qu'on* (B33), and *Se pour ce muir* (B36), with some musical comparisons. Abstract: *RILM* 14 (1980), no. 344.

1983. "The Poet and the Duke." *Early Music* 11:217–20.
Comparison of Machaut's *Aymi!* (V3) with Duke Ellington's "I got it bad and that ain't good," showing some surprising similarities with the aid of a "courtly" translation of the Ellington text. Abstract: *RILM* 17 (1983), no. 1928.

Löfstedt, Leena.
1987. Review of Cerquiglini 1985b. *Neuphilologische Mitteilungen* 88:230–32.
Includes new material on the title of the *Voir Dit* (231).

Long, Michael.
1981. "Musical Tastes in Fourteenth-Century Italy: Notational Styles, Scholarly Traditions, and Historical Circumstances." Ph.D. diss. Princeton University. Ann Arbor: University Microfilms. Order no. 8108092.

Includes a discussion of the theoretical background of *mutatio qualitatis*—the equivalency of *tempus perfectum prolatio minor* and *tempus imperfectum prolatio maior*—a question of musical notation that involves Machaut. Abstracts: *DAI* A 41/10 (Apr. 1981): 4208; *RILM* 15 (1981), nos. 283, 4491.

1992. "*Ita se n'era a star nel paradiso*: The Metamorphoses of an Ovidian Madrigal in Trecento Italy." In *L'Ars Nova italiana del Trecento VI*, ed. Giulio Cattin and Patrizia Dalla Vecchia, 257–67. Certaldo: Polis.

A madrigal set by both Vincenzo da Rimini and Lorenzo Masini treats the Ovidian myth of Pluto and Proserpina. Long traces a change in the fourteenth-century treatment of the myth, from a "parable for uncontained desire and loss of innocence," seen in the *Ovide Moralisé*, to the transformation of the protagonists by Boccaccio and Petrarch "into a classical love pair" (259). Machaut's treatment of the myth in *Confort*, though based on the *Ovide Moralisé*, introduces Proserpina's beauty, rather than Cupid's arrow, as the source of Pluto's desire, and thus establishes a contemporary courtly love relationship. Long goes on to treat biographical aspects of the composers and musical aspects of the two madrigals.

Longo, John Duane.
1982. "Literary Appropriation as *Translatio* in Chaucer and the *Roman de la Rose*." Ph.D. diss. Princeton University, 1981. Ann Arbor: University Microfilms. Order no. 8206940.

Considers Chaucer's use of the *Roman de la Rose* through Machaut, with discussion especially of *Jugement Navarre*, *Remede*, and *Fonteinne*. Abstract: *DAI* A 42/10 (Apr. 1982): 4444.

Longnon, Auguste.
1908. *Pouillés de la province de Reims*. Recueil des Historiens de la France; Pouillés 6/1. 2 vols. Paris: Imprimerie Nationale.

Includes an account of clerical tenths levied in 1362 for the diocese of Noyon, chapter of St-Quentin. *G. de Machau* is taxed for an income of 40 *livres* (1:196 E).

Loomis, Roger Sherman.
1944. "Chaucer's Eight Years' Sickness." *Modern Language Notes* 59:178–80.

The reference in Chaucer's *Book of the Duchess* to a sickness of eight years is not autobiographical, but simply borrowed from Machaut's *Jugement Behaingne*. For more bibliography on this question, see Heinrichs 1990, 214 n. 7; Nolan 1981, 211n.

1965. *A Mirror of Chaucer's World*. Princeton: Princeton University Press.

Includes facsimiles of miniatures C14 (see chap. 4.4e), A1 (see chap. 4.4a), A81–87 (see chap. 4.4i), and A149 (see chap. 4.4o).

Lord, Carla.
1975. "Three Manuscripts of the *Ovide Moralisé*." *Art Bulletin* 57:161–75.

Includes a concordance of miniatures for three *Ovide Moralisé* manuscripts with scenes that may have influenced programs of illustrations in Machaut manuscripts.

Lote, Georges.
1949. "Quelques Remarques sur l'*Art de Dictier* d'Eustache Deschamps." In *Mélanges de philologie romane et de littérature médiévale offerts à Ernest Hœpffner...par ses élèves et ses amis*, 361–67. Publications de la Faculté des Lettres de l'Université de Strasbourg 113. Paris: Les Belles Lettres.

Machaut's *Remede* provides models of lyrical forms, but no commentary; it was Deschamps who wrote the first French poetic treatise. Lote focuses on insufficiencies in Deschamps's descriptions of forms. Criticism in Varty 1965, 164.

1949–51. *Histoire du vers français*. Vol. 1/1, *Le Moyen Age i: Les origines du vers français; Les éléments constitutifs du vers: La césure; La rime; Le numérisme et le rythme*. Paris: Boivin, 1949. Vol. 1/2, *Le Moyen Age ii: La déclamation; Art et versification; Les formes lyriques*. Paris: Boivin, 1951.

Study of French versification, including the aspects of caesura, rhyme, syllable count, strophic structures, and a typology of the various lyrical forms, from the earliest beginnings through the fifteenth century. On Machaut, see esp. 1/2:242–44, and the discussions of the lyrical forms cultivated by Machaut, including the lai, virelai, ballade, *chant royal*, and rondeau; among "autres poèmes," Lote discusses the motet and *complainte*.

Lowes, John Livingston.
1904. "The Prologue to the *Legend of Good Women* as Related to the French *Marguerite* Poems, and the *Filostrato*." *PMLA* 19:593–683.

A major study of the complex of *Marguerite* poems as sources for Chaucer's Prologue to the *Legend of Good Women*. Lowes considers Machaut's *Marguerite* only; for *Lis et Marguerite*, see Wimsatt 1970. Commentary in Wimsatt 1991b, 165.

1910. "Simple and Coy: A Note on Fourteenth Century Poetic Diction." *Anglia* 33:440–51.

The use of the phrase "simple et coie" in Machaut and his contemporaries.

1918. "Chaucer and the *Ovide Moralisé*." *PMLA* 33:302–25.

Examples from *Jugement Navarre* in Chaucer's *Legend of Good Women* and *House of Fame*. Criticized in Shannon 1929, 67–68 and 229–49; upheld in Meech 1931.

Lowinsky, Edward.
1945. "The Function of Conflicting Signatures in Early Polyphonic Music." *Musical Quarterly* 31:227–60. Reprint. Lowinsky 1989, 2:647–64.

Conflicting "key" signatures in fourteenth- and fifteenth-century musical sources depend on the pitches needed for the formation of cadences. The change in signatures seen in the course of the fifteenth-century is due to a new type of cadence. Examples include *Dame, comment qu'amez* (B16) (pp. 238–39) and *De desconfort* (B8) (p. 241). See Apel 1938, Hoppin 1953, Lowinsky 1954, Hoppin 1956 and 1989.

1954. "Conflicting Views on Conflicting Signatures." *Journal of the American Musicological Society* 7:181–204. Reprint. Lowinsky 1989, 2:665–78.

Reply to Hoppin 1953. Further discussion of *De desconfort* (B8) (p. 186), and four-part writing and vocal scoring in Machaut (199–200).

1989. *Music in the Culture of the Renaissance and Other Essays*, ed. Bonnie J. Blackburn. Forewords by Howard Mayer Brown and Ellen T. Harris. 2 vols. Chicago and London: University of Chicago Press.

Collection of essays, reprinting the above articles and including the first publication of Hoppin 1989.

Lubienski-Bodenham, H.
1979. "The Origins of the Fifteenth Century View of Poetry as 'Seconde Rhétorique.'" *Modern Language Review* 74:26–38.

Medieval views of poetry; includes discussion of Deschamps's "natural music" and Machaut's *Prologue*.

Lucas, St. John.
1957. *The Oxford Book of French Verse, xiiith Century—xxth Century*. 2nd ed., revised by P. Mansell Jones. Oxford: Clarendon.

Includes four lyrics of Machaut, the ballade *Je pren congié* (Lo223), and the rondeaux *Blanche com lis* (Lo82), *Tant doucement* (R9), and *Ce qui soustient* (R12) (pp. 15–17, with notes, 597–98).

Ludwig, Friedrich.
1902–3. "Die mehrstimmige Musik des 14. Jahrhunderts." *Sammelbände der Internationalen Musikgesellschaft* 4:16–69. Reprinted in *Studien über die*

Geschichte der mehrstimmigen Musik im Mittelalter, ed. Friedrich Gennrich, 1–54. Langen bei Frankfurt: n.p., 1966.

The earliest comprehensive overview of fourteenth-century music, light-years ahead of anything published previously. Discusses sacred liturgical works, Latin and French motets, French chansons, and Italian music. Discussion of Machaut's Mass (21), motets (26–27, 29–30), and chansons (33–42).

1904–5. Review of Wolf 1904. *Sammelbände der Internationalen Musikgesellschaft* 6:597–641. Wolf's reply in *Sammelbände der Internationalen Musikgesellschaft* 7 (1905–6): 131–38.

Essential and detailed corrections to Wolf 1904. Machaut is discussed on pp. 604, 606, 608, 610–11, 620–22, 627–28, 629–31 (this last segment gives corrections for Wolf's musical transcriptions of Machaut, Wolf 1904, vols. 2–3 nos. 13–26).

1911. "La musique des intermèdes lyriques dans le *Remede de Fortune*," trans. Ernest Hoepffner. In Hoepffner 1908–21, 2:405–13, with appendix of musical transcriptions and facsimiles after p. 413).

The first publication of the music of the lyrical interpolations to the *Remede* (RF1–7), with full critical notes. Includes facsimiles from MSS **A** and **E** of the beginning of *Qui n'aroit* (RF1) and *Dame, a vous* (RF6). The introductory essay provides new material on MS **Vg**, on the copy of **B** from **Vg**, and comments especially on the monophonic works among the *Remede* insertions.

1922–23. "Musik des Mittelalters in der Badischen Kunsthalle Karlsruhe, 24.–26. September 1922." *Zeitschrift für Musikwissenschaft* 5:434–60.

A fascinating sketch of medieval music historiography beginning in the eighteenth century, with details on some early twentieth-century performances of Machaut's Mass. Discussion of the Machaut Mass, especially the Kyrie (440–41). Provides the first published transcription of Kyrie III (457–58), omitted from the edition of the Kyrie movements in Wolf 1904. See also comments in Haas 1931, 94–98.

1923. "Die Quellen der Motetten ältesten Stils." *Archiv für Musikwissenschaft* 5:185–222, 273–315.

This enormously detailed and wide-ranging article stood as a substitute for Ludwig's unpublished *Repertorium* vol. 1/2 until the publication of Ludwig 1978. Includes what is still the most complete list of thirteenth- and fourteenth-century narrative poems with lyrical insertions (216–19), including Machaut's *Remede* and *Voir Dit* (cf. Boulton 1993, appendix i), a study of the MS **Iv** [57] (pp. 281–82), and **CaB** [56] (pp. 283–87).

1925. "Die mehrstimmige Messe des 14. Jahrhunderts." *Archiv für Musikwissenschaft* 7:417–35 (*errata*, 8 [1926]: 130).

Brief sketch of the development of the motet and secular forms in France and Italy (417–20), followed by a more detailed study of the sacred repertory (on the Machaut Mass, see 420–21). Mention of several newly discovered sources, and final consideration of two questions, the change in the fourteenth century from polyphonic settings of Proper items to polyphonic settings of Ordinary items, and the relationship of fourteenth-century sacred music to contemporary secular music.

1926–54 (ed.). *Guillaume de Machaut: Musikalische Werke*. Vol. 1, *Balladen, Rondeaux und Virelais*. Publikationen älterer Musik 1/1. Leipzig: Breitkopf & Härtel, 1926. Vol. 2, *Einleitung*. Publikationen älterer Musik 3/1. Leipzig: Breitkopf & Härtel, 1928. Vol. 3, *Motetten*. Publikationen älterer Musik 4/2. Leipzig: Breitkopf & Härtel, 1929. Vol. 4, *Messe und Lais*, ed. Heinrich Besseler from the *Nachlass Ludwig*. Leipzig: Breitkopf & Härtel, 1943 (destroyed). Reprint. 4 vols. Leipzig: VEB Breitkopf & Härtel; Wiesbaden: Breitkopf & Härtel, 1954.

Remains an important and useful edition of the musical works. Variants are given for MSS **Vg**, **A**, **F-G**, and peripheral manuscripts, with only occasional variants from the other central Machaut manuscripts. The edition of Schrade is more sympathetic for modern performance purposes, although Ludwig's edition is to be preferred with regard to text underlay. Notably inaccurate editions are given for the lais *Pour ce que plus* (L23/17) and *En demantant* (L24/18); for the motet *Trop plus / Biauté* (M20); for the ballades *Dous amis, oy* (B6), *Esperance* (B13), *Sans cuer m'en / Amis / Dame* (B17), *Je puis trop* (B28), and *Pas de tor* (B30); and for the rondeau *Rose, lis* (R10); for corrected editions, see the discussions of individual works in chap. 7.3. On editorial principles, see Bockholdt 1971, 154–55; on barring and notation, Günther 1957, 26–29, 92 n. 54; and Hoppin 1960; on accidentals, Hirshberg 1980, 23–24; on text underlay, Earp 1983, 222–27. Reviews: Maurice Cauchie, *Revue de musicologie* 8 (1927): 172–73 (vol. 1) and 11 (1930): 224 (vol. 3); Gennrich 1930 (vols. 1–3); Spanke 1929 (vols. 1–2); Rudolf Stephan, *Musikforschung* 9 (1956): 341 (vol. 4).

1930. "Die geistliche nichtliturgische/weltliche einstimmige und die mehrstimmige Musik des Mittelalters bis zum Anfang des 15. Jahrhunderts." In *Handbuch der Musikgeschichte*, ed. Guido Adler, 127–250. Frankfurt a.M.: Frankfurter Verlags-Anstalt, 1924. 2nd rev. ed. Vol. 1 of 2 vols, 265–95. Berlin-Wilmersdorf: Keller, 1930. Reprint in 3 vols. Tutzing: Schneider, 1961. Paperback reprint. Munich: Deutscher Taschenbuch Verlag, 1975.

Survey of medieval music. Machaut is discussed on pp. 267–73 (2nd ed.), with an edition of *Quant Theseüs / Ne quier* (B34). Review of 1st ed.: *Musikerziehung* 6 (1929): 13–20.

1978. *Repertorium organorum recentioris et motetorum vetustissimi stili.* Vol. 1, *Catalogue raisonné der Quellen.* Part 2, *Handschriften in Mensural-Notation.* Musicological Studies 26. Institute of Mediaeval Music. Assen: Van Gorcum.

The completion of Ludwig's catalogue of Notre-Dame organum and motet manuscripts. Pages 345–456 were already in proof when publication broke off in 1910; transcription by Max and Sylvie Lütolf of Ludwig's manuscript has allowed posthumous completion of the volume. Useful here for the catalogues of MSS *F:Pn 146* and **CaB** [56].

Lühmann, Rose.

1978. "Versdeklamation bei Guillaume de Machaut. Ph.D. diss. Ludwig-Maximilians-Universität, Munich, 1975.

Discusses the rhythmic declamation of the poetry in Machaut's music, especially in the ballades. Most ballades and rondeaux employ ten-syllable verse with caesura. Comparison of motet poetry and lyrical poetry (with conclusions different from Clarkson 1971), and notational considerations in monophonic works. Many examples are cited, esp. *Amours me fait* (B19), *Aucune gent / Qui plus* (M5), *Dame, comment qu'amez* (B16), *De Fortune* (B23), *De toutes flours* (B31), *Esperance* (B13), *Helas! tant* (B2), *J'aim miex* (B7), *N'en fait* (B11), *Pour ce qu'on puist* (L3), and *Se quanque amours* (B21).

Lukitsch, Shirley.

1983. "The Poetics of the *Prologue:* Machaut's Conception of the Purpose of His Art." *Medium Ævum* 52:258–71.

Analysis of the *Prologue* for Machaut's view of music and poetry. Considers Boethius, Augustine, Dante, and Deschamps.

Luttrell, Claude A.

1965. "*Pearl*: Symbolism in a Garden Setting." *Neophilologus* 49:160–76. Reprint. Sir Gawain *and* Pearl: *Critical Essays*, ed. Robert J. Blanch, 60–85. Bloomington and London: Indiana University Press, 1966. Reprint with revisions. *The Middle English* Pearl: *Critical Essays*, ed. John Conley, 297–324. Notre Dame, Ind. and London: University of Notre Dame Press, 1970.

Includes discussion of the allegory of the garden setting in *Alerion* (169, 171–76).

1978. "The Introduction to the Dream in *Pearl.*" *Medium Ævum* 47:274–91.

Includes examples of the phrases "dous dangier" and "amoureus dangier" in Machaut's *Jugement Behaingne* and the lyrics *Dame, pour vous ma joie* (Lo69), *Douce dame, savoir ne puis* (Lo187), *Douce dame, soiés* (Lo41), *Loyauté, que* (L1), *Ne say comment* (L14/9), and *On ne porroit* (Lo7=B3) (p. 276). There is also brief mention of *Alerion* as a "love allegory of loss" (280, 286).

MGG.
> 1949–86. *Die Musik in Geschichte und Gegenwart. Allgemeine Enzyklopädie der Musik.* 17 vols., ed. Friedrich Blume. Kassel: Bärenreiter.
>> Encyclopedia of music.

Macaulay, G[eorge] C[ampbell], ed.
> 1899. *The Complete Works of John Gower.* Vol. 1, *The French Works.* Oxford: Clarendon. Reprint. Grosse Pointe, Michigan: Scholarly Press, 1968.
>> Standard edition.

McGee, Timothy J.
> 1986. "Instruments in the Faenza Codex." *Early Music* 14:480–90.
>> Concerns performance practice of intabulations in MS **Fa** [67], arguing that works are to be performed on two lutes. Abstract: *RILM* 20 (1986), no. 5012.

> 1987. "Ornamentation, National Styles, and the Faenza Codex." *Early Music New Zealand* 3/2 (June): 3–14.
>> Not examined. Abstract: *RILM* 21 (1987), no. 6583.

> 1992. "Once Again, the Faenza Codex: A Reply to Roland Eberlein." *Early Music* 20:466–68.
>> See Eberlein 1992.

McGregor, Rob Roy, Jr., ed.
> 1975. *The Lyric Poems of Jehan Froissart: A Critical Edition.* University of North Carolina Studies in the Romance Languages and Literatures 143. Chapel Hill: University of North Carolina Department of Romance Languages.
>> Standard critical edition of Froissart's lyric poetry (lais, *pastourelles*, *chants royaux*, ballades, virelais, and rondeaux); for the ballades and rondeaux, see also Baudouin 1978. Review: A.H. Diverres, *French Studies* 33 (1979): 574–75.

Machabey, Armand.
> 1928. *Histoire et évolution des formules musicales du Ier au XVe siècles de l'ère chrétienne.* Bibliothèque Musicale. Paris: Payot.
>> Includes a discussion of cadences and harmony in Machaut (207–18), in highly anachronistic terms. Machaut plays a key role because of the final cadence of *Il m'est avis* (B22), in which Machabey finds a "perfect cadence" with third in the final sonority. New edition in Machabey 1955a. Review: J. Marnold, *Mercure de France* 208 (1928): 207–16.

> 1930. "Guillaume de Machault: La vie et l'homme." *Revue musicale* 11:424–52.
>> Biography of Machaut, with a study of Machaut's physiognomy based on miniatures. Bibliography in Machabey 1931.

> 1931. "Guillaume de Machault: L'œuvre." *Revue musicale* 12:320–44, 402–16.
>> Survey of Machaut's music by genre, with a few musical examples. The conclusion discusses Machaut's influence. Bibliography (415–16).

> 1948 (ed.). *Messe Notre-Dame à quatre voix de Guillaume de Machault (130?–1377) transcrite en notation moderne.* Liège: Aelberts.
>> With Chailley 1948 the earliest edition of the complete Mass. Reviews: Willi Apel, *Speculum* 26 (1951): 187–90 (reprinted in Apel 1986, 193–96); Leonard Ellinwood, *Notes* 7 (1949–50): 130–31; see also comments in Gombosi 1950, 204–7.

> 1953–54. "La musique religieuse au XIVe siècle." *Revue musicale* 222:30–43.
>> Brief survey of religious music in fourteenth-century France. Discussion of Machaut (36–42) considers the *Lay de Nostre Dame* (L15/10), the Latin motets, and the Mass.

1954. "Guillaume de Machault." *Musica* 4:35–39.
Brief popular survey of Machaut's life and music. Includes a large-format reproduction of miniature D11 (see chap. 4.4d).

1955a. *Genèse de la tonalité musicale classique, des origines au XVe siècle.* Bibliothèque d'Etudes Musicales. Paris: Richard-Masse.
New edition of Machabey 1928; includes a study of cadence types and "tonality" in Machaut (220–30 [=1928, 207–18 with a few additions]), in highly anachronistic terms. Strongly criticized in Hoppin 1966, 36 n. 1.

1955b. *Guillaume de Machault 130?–1377: La vie et l' œuvre musical.* 2 vols. Bibliothèque d'Etudes Musicales. Paris: Richard-Masse.
Currently the most complete biography of Machaut, especially thorough for its study of potential relatives of Machaut. The brief analyses of the musical works are much less useful. Reviews: Jan Maegaard, *Nordisk Musikkulter* 7 (1958): 61–62; Massimo Mila, *Rassegna musicale* 26 (1956): 162–65; Gilbert Reaney, *Music and Letters* 37 (1956): 294–98; Mario Roques, *Romania* 77 (1956): 556–57; "Voir Dit," *Musical Times* 97 (1956): 304–5. See also critical comments in Günther 1957, 19–22 et passim.

1955c. "Le Manuscrit Weyen et Guillaume de Machault." *Romania* 76:247–53.
Description and discussion of the key documents concerning the date of Machaut's death.

1957. "Guillaume de Machault." *Larousse de la musique*, ed. Norbert Dufourcq, 1:420–21. Paris: Larousse.
Dictionary article; includes a map of "Voyages de Guillaume de Machault."

1958. "La polyphonie occidentale du IXe au XIVe siècle." Chap. 11 of *Précis de musicologie*, ed. Jacques Chailley, 126–51. Institut de Musicologie de l'Université de Paris. Paris: Presses Universitaires de France.
Includes brief discussion of Machaut (129–31, 141–45).

1960. "Guillaume de Machault." *MGG* 8:1392–99.
Dictionary article.

1964. "Machault (Machaut) Guillaume." In *Enciclopedia della musica*, ed. Claudio Sartori, 61. Milan: Ricordi.
Dictionary article.

1966. "Guillaume de Machault." In *La musica*. Part 1, *Enciclopedia storica*, ed. Guido M. Gatti and Alberto Basso, 3:213–26. Turin: Unione Tipografico.
Dictionary article. Includes small reproductions of miniatures C36 and C40 (see chap. 4.4e), and A1 (see chap. 4.4a), and the opening of *Tous corps / De* (M2) in MS **A**.

1970. "Machault, Guillaume de (Machaut)." In *Dictionnaire de la musique*. Vol. 2, *Les hommes et leurs œuvres, L–Z*, ed. Marc Honegger, 663–64. [Paris]: Bordas.
Dictionary article. Includes reproduction of miniature D11 (see chap. 4.4d).

Machabey, Armand, and Claudio Capriolo.
1986. "Machault, Guillaume de (Machaut, Michault)." In *Dizionario enciclopedico universale della musica e dei musicisti*, ed. Alberto Basso, *Le Biografie*, 4:549–56. Turin: UTET.
Dictionary article with extensive work list, revised from Machabey 1966, but lacking the illustrations.

McKitterick, Rosamond, and Richard Beadle, comps.
1992. *Catalogue of the Pepys Library at Magdalene College Cambridge*, ed. Robert Latham. Vol. 5/1, *Manuscripts (Medieval)*. Cambridge: Brewer.
Description of MS **Pe** [20] (p. 23). See also J. Stevens et al. 1989.

Maekawa, Kumiko.
   1985. "Recherches iconographiques sur les manuscrits des poésies de
   Guillaume de Machaut: Les décorations des premiers 'recueils personnels.'"
   Ph.D. diss. Sorbonne, Paris.
   Thorough description and study of the miniatures in the main Machaut manuscripts.
   1987. "Guillaume de Machaut to 'Sakuhinshu'" (Guillaume de Machaut and
   the Manuscripts of His Collected Works). *Bunmei* (Culture) 49:13–28.
   Not examined.
   1988. "La présentation des Œuvres de Guillaume de Machaut." *Mémoires de
   la Société d'agriculture, commerce, science et arts du département de la
   Marne*, 103:139–54 and plates i–ix.
   Reproductions and analyses of miniatures from MSS C, Vg, A, and F.
   1989a. "Les Illustrations des Œuvres de Guillaume de Machaut: Formation et
   évolution." *Matrix* 7:20–31.
   Not examined.
   1989b. "New Analytical Methods for Study of Secular Illuminated
   Manuscripts—in the Case of Guillaume de Machaut's *Collected Works*."
   Dokkyō Daigaku Furansu Bunka Kenkyū (Studies on French Culture at
   Dokkyō University) 20:69–92.
   Includes reproductions and analyses of several miniatures from MSS C, Vg, A, and F.
Maggs Bros.
   1926. *Music: Books, Manuscripts, Autographs and Engravings*. No. 476.
   London: Maggs Bros.
   Catalogue description of the untraced *rotulus* MS Maggs [27], with a facsimile.
   1928. *Music: Early Books, Manuscripts, Portraits and Autographs*. No. 512.
   London: Maggs Bros.
   Catalogue description of the untraced *rotulus* MS Maggs [27], with a facsimile.
Magnan, Robert.
   1993. "Eustache Deschamps and His Double: *musique naturele* and *musique
   artificiele*." *Ars Lyrica* 7:47–64.
   F. Andrieu's musical setting of Deschamps's work obscures the poet's intended *ballade
   double* (six-strophe ballade) that begins with the text *O fleur des fleurs de toute melodie*.
Magnin, [Charles].
   1851. "Guillaume de Machaut." *Journal des savants* (July): 399–410; (Aug.):
   475–91.
   A long review of Tarbé 1849. Magnin is mainly concerned with the *Voir Dit*; he
   publishes and discusses several excerpts lacking in Tarbé (406–10, 475–91).
Maillard, Jean.
   1954. "Autour de Guillaume de Machaut." *Education musicale* 10, no. 13, 3–
   5, 8, 18.
   Good brief survey of Machaut's life and works, particularly rich in historiographical
   information, including quotations from a manuscript address by François Louis Perne to
   the French *Institut*. Maillard proposes that the Mass was composed for Rouen, ca. 1350,
   while Machaut was in the service of Bonne of Luxembourg (5). Another focus is a
   proposal suggesting how to utilize Machaut's music in the French program of education.
   1957. "Chronologie sommaire des événements contemporains de Vitry et
   Guillaume de Machaut." *Education musicale* 12, no. 36, 10–12.
   Chronological listing of the major events in the lives Vitry and Machaut, and the major
   events in political history, 1291–1377. Some corrections are listed in Maillard 1963, 337
   n. 754.

1963. *Evolution et esthétique du lai lyrique. Des origines à la fin du XIVe siècle.* Paris: Centre de documentation universitaire, 1952–61.

For Machaut, a catalogue of editions of the lais with brief commentary on verse and music (339–56).

1973. "Lai, Leich." In *Gattungen der Musik in Einzeldarstellungen. Gedenkschrift Leo Schrade, I*, ed. Wulf Arlt et al., 323–45. Bern: Franke.

Survey of the lai genre; little on Machaut (343). Abstract: *RILM* 10 (1976), no. 5128.

1984. "Un Diptyque marial chez Guillaume de Machaut: Les lais XV et XVI." In *Mélanges de langue et de littérature médiévales offerts à Alice Planche*, ed. Maurice Accarie and Ambroise Queffelec, vol. 2 of 2 vols., 327–37. Annales de la Faculté des Lettres et Sciences Humaines de Nice 48. Centre d'Etudes Médiévales. Paris: Les Belles Lettres.

General comments about rhythm and polyphony, followed by a consideration of two Marian lais, *Contre ce dous* (L15/10) and *Je ne cesse* (L16/11).

Malizia, Uberto.

1984. "Guillaume de Machaut: Le sette *chansons* del *Remede de Fortune*." *Quaderni di filologia e lingue romanze* 6:11–48.

Brief discussion of the seven *Remede* lyrics, followed by a general consideration of the music for each.

Marchal, J[oseph].

1842. *Catalogue des manuscrits de la bibliothèque royale des ducs de Bourgogne.* Vol. 1 of 3 vols. Brussels and Leipzig: Muquardt.

Catalogue that gives an overview of all of the inventories of the Burgundian library from the fifteenth century to the nineteenth-century Bibliothèque Royale.

Marggraf, Wolfgang.

1964. "Tonalität und Harmonik in der französischen Chanson vom Tode Machauts bis zum frühen Dufay." Ph.D. diss. Leipzig.

Not examined. For criticisms, see Hirshberg 1971, 92, 94–98, chap. 9 *passim*; 1980, 19, 40. Abstract: *Musikforschung* 19 (1966): 62.

1966. "Tonalität und Harmonik in der französischen Chanson zwischen Machaut und Dufay." *Archiv für Musikwissenschaft* 23:11–31.

An examination of cadences and tonal plans in three-voice chansons with contratenor, composed in the period between Machaut and Dufay, looking for dominant-tonic relationships (on Machaut, see esp. 14–15). Summary in Kühn 1973, 24–26, 245 n. 259a; criticized in Apfel 1974, 195–98.

Margolis, Nadia.

1992. "Christine de Pizan and the Jews: Political and Poetic Implications." In *Politics, Gender, and Genre: The Political Thought of Christine de Pizan*, ed. Margaret Brabant, 53–73. Boulder, Colo. and Oxford: Westview Press.

Includes consideration of Machaut's *Navarre* in weighing Christine's various references to the Jews.

Marks, Diane R.

1984. "The English Poems of Charles of Orleans." Ph.D. diss. City University of New York. Ann Arbor: University Microfilms. Order no. 8423088.

See chap. 3, "Petrarch, Machaut and Chaucer" (on Machaut, 81–130, 103–11). Abstract: *DAI* A 45/7 (Jan. 1985): 2096.

Markstrom, Kurt.

1989. "Machaut and the Wild Beast." *Acta musicologica* 61:12–39.

Discusses possible historical occasions for the motets *Fons / O livoris* (M9), *Christe / Veni* (M21) *Tu qui gregem / Plange* (M22), and *Felix virgo / Inviolata* (M23), as well as for the Mass, with translations of M9 and M22 by Anna Kirkwood. Abstract: *RILM* 23 (1989), no. 1889.

Marrocco, W. Thomas, and Nicholas Sandon, eds.
  1977. *Medieval Music*. The Oxford Anthology of Music. London and New York: Oxford University Press.
  Useful musical anthology with text translations; includes Machaut's *J'aim la flour* (L2), a corrected edition of *Sans cuer m'en / Amis / Dame* (B17), *Tant doucement me sens* (R9), and *Se je souspir* (V36/30).

Martin, Henry.
  1886–89. *Catalogue des manuscrits de la Bibliothèque de l'Arsenal*. Vols. 2, 3, and 5. Paris: Plon.
  Standard manuscript inventories.

  1923. *La miniature française du XIIIe au XVe siècle*. Librairie nationale d'art et d'histoire. Paris and Brussels: Van Oest, 1923. 2nd rev. ed. 1924.
  Includes discussion, with reproductions, of *Prologue* miniatures A2 and A1 (44–48, 94–95; plates 47 and 48). Discussion of the *Maître aux boqueteaux* (48–51 and fig. lxiii on p. 105).

  1928. *Les joyaux de l'enluminure à la Bibliothèque Nationale*. Introduction by Count A. de Laborde. Paris and Brussels: Van Oest.
  Includes discussion, with reproduction, of *Prologue* miniature A1 (127; plate 49). Discussion of the *Maître aux boqueteaux* (48–52).

Martinez, Marie Louise [see also Göllner, Marie Louise].
  1963. *Die Musik des frühen Trecento*. Münchner Veröffentlichungen zur Musikgeschichte 9. Tutzing: Schneider.
  See chap. 6, "Die weltliche Mehrstimmigkeit bei Guillaume de Machaut: Die Ballade und das italienische Madrigale" (99–116). Discusses the treatment of caesura and repeated words, musical rhyme and texting, and recurring musical segments in *Biauté* (B4), *Je ne cuit* (B14), *Donnez* (B26), *Je puis* (B28), *Plourez, dames* (B32), and *Nes qu'on* (B33). Comparison of Machaut's treatment with the more uniform musical and texting style of the madrigal. Martinez's work seems especially influential on the subsequent work of Dömling. See comments in Kühn 1973, 259–60 n. 439; and Apfel 1974, 172–75. Review: Andreas Wernli, *Musikforschung* 23 (1970): 365–67.

Mas Latrie, [Jacques Marie Joseph] Louis de.
  1844–45. "Des Relations politiques et commerciales de l'Asie mineure avec l'île de Chypre, sous le règne des princes de la maison de Lusignan." *Bibliothèque de l'Ecole des Chartes* 6:301–30, 485–521.
  The first article mentions the *Prise* (323 and n. 2); the second article has many references to the *Prise* in MS A. La Société de l'histoire de France had rejected a proposal "il y a quelques années" from F[rancisque] Michel, Bordeaux, to publish a modern edition of the *Prise* (491 n.1).

  1852. *Histoire de l'Ile de Chypre sous le règne des princes de la maison de Lusignan*. Vol. 2, *Documents et mémoires servant de preuves à l'histoire de l'île de Chypre sous les Lusignans*. Part 1, *Documents*. Paris: Imprimerie Impériale.
  Includes many excerpts from the *Prise*, with extensive commentary (206–8, 237–45, 273–80, 309–31, 333–37, 342–45).

  1876. "Guillaume de Machaut et *La Prise d'Alexandrie*." *Bibliothèque de l'Ecole des Chartes* 37:445–70.
  Prior publication of most of the introductory material to the edition Mas Latrie 1877b (viii–xxvi, and documents, xxx–xxxvii). Corrections in Mas Latrie 1877a, 188. Review: G. Paris 1877.

  1877a. "Additions et corrections concernant Guillaume de Machaut et les assises d'Antioche." *Bibliothèque de l'Ecole des Chartes* 38:188–90.
  Includes corrections to Mas Latrie 1876 and a response to G. Paris 1877.

1877b (ed.). *La Prise d'Alexandrie ou chronique du roi Pierre Ier de Lusignan par Guillaume de Machaut.* Publications de la Société de l'Orient latin, série historique 1. Geneva: Fick. Reprint. Osnabrück: Zeller, 1968.

The standard edition of the *Prise*, awaiting publication of the critical edition by Dzelzainis (1985; a new edition and translation by R. Barton Palmer is currently in press). The introductory study and the documents also appeared separately as Mas Latrie 1876. Errors in Machaut's biography were corrected in G. Paris 1877. Reviews: C. Desimoni, *Académie des Inscriptions et Belles-Lettres: Comptes rendus des séances de l'année 1877,* ser. 4, vol. 5 (1878): 45–46; Pasquale Fazio, *Giornale Ligustico di archeologia, storia et belle arti* 5 (1878): 79–80.

Mathews, Harry.
1982. "The Monkey at the Wheel." *Parnassus: Poetry in Review* 10:20–44.

Examples of problems in setting words to music throughout music history. Compares Machaut's *Qui es / Ha! Fortune* (M8) to the trio at the end of Strauss's *Rosenkavalier:* in both, the verbal counterpoint renders the poetry unintelligible, although the result is nevertheless aesthetically satisfying (29–34). Abstract: *RILM* 16 (1982), no. 5979.

Medeiros, M.-T. de.
1994. "Dit de la Fontaine Amoureuse (le)." In *Dictionnaire des œuvres littéraires de langue française,* ed. Jean-Pierre de Beaumarchais and Daniel Couty, 558–59. 4 vols., continuous pagination. Paris: Bordas.

Excellent survey article.

Meech, Sanford Brown.
1931. "Chaucer and the *Ovide Moralisé*—A Further Study." *PMLA* 46:182–204.

A study corrective of Lowes (1918) and Shannon (1929) concerning Chaucer's use of *Jugement Navarre* in his *House of Fame* (182–85, 203, 204 n. 106) and *Legend of Good Women* (187, 192 n. 58, 196, 200).

Meiss, Millard.
1956. "The Exhibition of French Manuscripts of the XIII–XVI Centuries at the Bibliothèque Nationale." *Art Bulletin* 38:187–96.

Exhibition review with material relevant to an artist of miniatures in MSS **Vg** and **A**, identified here as Jean Bondol (John of Bruges) (190). See chap. 4.2, table 4.2 no. 2.

1969. *French Painting in the Time of Jean de Berry.* Part 1, *The Late Fourteenth Century and the Patronage of the Duke.* 2 vols. National Gallery of Art: Kress Foundation Studies in the History of European Art. London: Phaidon, 1967. 2nd ed. 1969.

Includes discussion of the Master of the Bible of Jean de Sy, here identified with John Bondol. Reviews: L.J.M. Delaissé, *Art Bulletin* 52 (1970): 206–12; Mojmír S. Frinta, *Art Journal* 30 (1970): 106, 110; F. Salet, *Bulletin monumental* 127 (1969): 60–62; Eleanor P. Spencer, *Burlington Magazine* 111 (1969): 226–27; Marcel Thomas, *Gazette des Beaux Arts* 71 (1968): 353–54; P. Verdier, *Œil* 167 (Nov. 1968): 36–37; *Apollo* 86 (Oct. 1967): 250–53.

Mémoires.
1756. "Description historique et topographique de l'hôtel de Soissons." *Mémoires de l'Académie des Inscriptions et Belles-Lettres* 23:262–71.

A description of John of Luxembourg's Parisian hôtel and its subsequent history.

Meyer, Paul.
1875. "Notice d'un recueil manuscrit de poésies françaises du XIIIe au XVe siècle, appartenant à Westminster Abbey." *Bulletin de la Société des Anciens Textes Français* 1:25–36.

Description of MS **Wm** [41].

1891. "Nouvelles Catalanes inédites. V, Histoire de Frondino et de Brisona." *Romania* 20:599–613.

Publication of an anonymous Catalan poem of the late fourteenth or early fifteenth century that imitates the *Voir Dit*. It contains five prose letters in Catalan and six interpolated lyrics (one virelai and five rondeaux) in French.

Michels, Ulrich.

1970. *Die Musiktraktate des Johannes de Muris*. Beihefte zum Archiv für Musikwissenschaft 8. Wiesbaden: Steiner.

Publication of author's 1968 Freiburg i.Br. dissertation, a study of the life and music treatises of Johannes de Muris, whose *Libellus cantus mensurabilis* mentions notational practices in Machaut's music. Abstract of original dissertation: *RILM* 3 (1969), no. 533. Reviews: G.A. Trumpff, *Neue Zeitschrift für Musik* 132 (1971): 458–59; Agostino Ziino, *Nuova rivista musicale italiana* 6 (1972): 286–87.

1972 (ed.). *Johannes de Muris: Notitia artis musicae et Compendium musicae practicae; Petrus de Sancto Dionysio: Tractatus de musica*. Corpus Scriptorum de Musica 17. [Rome]: American Institute of Musicology.

Edition of a music theory treatise with early speculation about the possibility of *mutatio qualitatis* (84). Abstract: *RILM* 10 (1976), no. 9149.

Miller, Clement A., trans.

1968. *The* Practica musicae *of Franchinus Gafurius*. Musicological Studies and Documents 20. Dallas, Tex.: American Institute of Musicology.

Translation; for the original Latin treatise, see Gafori 1496. Another translation is in I. Young 1969. Reviews: Peter Bergquist, *Journal of the American Musicological Society* 23 (1970): 144–50; Lawrence Gushee, *Journal of Music Theory* 14 (1970): 127–32; Albert Seay, *Notes* 26 (1969–70): 264–66.

Millet, Hélène.

1982. *Les chanoines du chapitre cathédral de Laon 1272–1412*. Collection de l'Ecole Française de Rome 56. Rome: Ecole Française de Rome.

A model study of the cathedral chapter and canons at Laon, useful in lieu of a similar study of the cathedral of Reims. See also Pycke 1986.

Mirot, L., and H. Jassemin.

1935. *Lettres secrètes et curiales du pape Grégoire XI (1370–1378) relatives à la France*. Bibliothèque des Ecoles Françaises d'Athènes et de Rome 3/VII-1. Paris: Boccard.

Summary of a document that mentions Jean de Machaut (256–57 no. 765).

Mollat, Guillaume.

1921. *Lettres communes de Jean XXII (1316–1334). Introduction: La collation des bénéfices ecclésiastiques à l'époque des papes d'Agivnon (1305–1378)*. Bibliothèque des Ecoles Françaises d'Athènes et de Rome 3. Paris: Boccard.

Detailed study of the mechanism of granting benefices in the early fourteenth century.

1928. *Jean XXII (1316–1334): Lettres communes analysées d'après les registres dits d'Avignon et du Vatican*. Vol. 9. Bibliothèque des Ecoles Françaises d'Athènes et de Rome 3/1 bis. Paris: Boccard.

Summary of a document that mentions Machaut (392 no. 50428).

1930. *Jean XXII (1316–1334): Lettres communes analysées d'après les registres dits d'Avignon et du Vatican*. Fasc. 25. Bibliothèque des Ecoles Françaises d'Athènes et de Rome 3. Paris: Boccard.

Summary of a document that mentions Machaut (176 no. 56947).

1932. *Jean XXII (1316–1334): Lettres communes analysées d'après les registres dits d'Avignon et du Vatican*. Fasc. 25. Bibliothèque des Ecoles Françaises d'Athènes et de Rome 3. Paris: Boccard.

Summary of documents that mention Jean de Machaut (73 no. 59242) and Guillaume de Machaut (73 no. 59243).

1963. *The Popes at Avignon 1305–1378*, trans. Janet Love from 9th French ed., 1949. London: Nelson and Sons.
Includes material on the papal politics of King John of Luxembourg.

Monnidendam, M.
1953. "De Machauts 'Messe Notre-Dame.' Oudste mannenkoormis?" *Mens en melodie* 8:344–46.
Not examined.

Monod, Bernard, ed.
1903. *Quinze poésies inédites de Guillaume de Machault, poète champenois du XIVe siècle, publiées d'après les manuscrits 843, 1584 et 1586 du fonds français de la Bibliothèque Nationale.* Versailles: Cerf.
Edition of eight ballades, six rondeaux, and one fragment, including (in this order): *Amis, je t'aporte* (Lo212), *D'un cuer si fin* (Lo172), *Loing de mon cuer* (Lo86), *Il n'est confors* (Lo74), *Amours me fait* (Lo177=B19), *De vous servir* (Lo78), *Vo dous gracieus* (Lo92), *Douce dame, cointe* (Lo226), *Biauté, douceur* (Lo240), *Ne qu'on porroit* (Lo232=B33), *Onques dame* (Lo221), *Dame, de moy* (Lo168), *Le bien de vous* (Lo179), *Vueillés avoir* (Lo116), and *De vraie amour* (Lo85). Published for the marriage of L[ily] Lévy and J[ean] Javal, 8 October 1903.

Montfaucon, Bernard de.
1739. *Bibliotheca bibliothecarum manuscriptorum nova: ubi, quæ innumeris pene manuscriptorum bibliothecis continentur, ad quodvis literaturæ genus spectantia & notatu digna, discribuntur & indicantur.* 2 vols. Paris: Briasson.
Includes a catalogue of the Parisian Bibliothèque Royale, "Bibliotheca Regia Parisiensis, Omnium Bibliothecarum præstantissima" (2:709–1040), with a separate listing of the manuscripts of Colbert acquired in 1732 by King Louis XIII (2:922–1014).

Moore, Arthur K.
1951. "Chaucer's Use of Lyric as an Ornament of Style." *Comparative Literature* 3:32–46.
Discussion of narrative works with lyrical insertions, including Machaut's *Remede* and *Voir Dit.*

Morel, Octave.
1900. *La grande chancellerie royale et l'expédition des lettres royaux de d'avènement de Philippe de Valois à la fin du XIVe siècle (1328–1400).* Mémoires et documents publiés par la Société de l'Ecole des Chartes 3. Paris: Picard.
Study of the officers of the "great" chancellery, including interesting material on the distinction between clerks, notaries, and secretaries.

Morel-Fatio, A.
1893. "Sur Guillaume de Machaut." *Romania* 22:275–76.
A Catalan document citing a Machaut manuscript; corrections in Ludwig 1926–54, 2:32b* n. 1.

Moreton, Rebecca Larche.
1963. "Literary Convention in *The Book of the Duchess.*" *University of Mississippi Studies in English* 4:69–78.
Discusses French sources of Chaucer's *Book of the Duchess*, comparing the views of previous scholars. Many passages from Machaut are quoted, especially *Jugement Behaingne.*

Morgan, Glen Edward.
1963. "Stylistic Features of the Music of Guillaume de Machaut." Ph.D. diss. Indiana University. Ann Arbor: University Microfilms. Order no. 6405474.
A statistical survey of individual parameters of Machaut's musical compositions, presented in eighty tables, often with counts of frequency and percentages. A few of the

statistics may be useful, for instance the "Frequency of Scale Degrees at Internal Cadences in the Monophonic Lais" (9 table 3). Abstract: *DA* 25/1 (July 1964): 523–24.

Morris, Lynn King.
1985. *Chaucer Source and Analogue Criticism. A Cross-Referenced Guide.* Garland Reference Library of the Humanities 454. New York and London: Garland.
Bibliography of works published before January 1981. Indexes Machaut works used by Chaucer (285–89).

Morris, Rosemary.
1988. "Machaut, Froissart, and the Fictionalization of the Self." *Modern Language Review* 83:545–55.
Similarities and differences between fourteenth-century *dits amoureux* of Machaut and Froissart and the tradition of the Arthurian romance, with a negative judgment for Machaut and Froissart.

Mudge, Charles R.
1972. "The Pennsylvania *Chansonnier*, a Critical Edition of Ninety-Five Anonymous Ballades from the Fourteenth Century with Introduction, Notes and Glossary." Ph.D. diss. Indiana University. Ann Arbor: University Microfilms. Order no. 7219498.
An important study of a late fifteenth-century text manuscript containing many works of Machaut. After Mudge's death, Wimsatt (1982) built upon his work. Abstract: *DAI* A 33/1 (July 1972): 282.

Mühlethaler, Jean-Claude.
1989. "Un Poète et son art face à la postérité: Lecture des deux ballades de Deschamps pour la mort de Machaut." *Studi Francesi* 33:387–410.
Detailed analysis of Deschamps's two ballades of *déploration*. Includes an appendix of passages from fourteenth- and fifteenth-century poets who cite Machaut as a love poet.

1992 (ed.). *Charles d'Orléans. Ballades et rondeaux. Edition du manuscrit 25458 du fonds français de la Bibliothèque Nationale de Paris.* Lettres Gothiques. Paris: Livre de Poche.
Standard edition.

Mulder, Etty Martha.
1974. "Guillaume de Machaut." *Mens en melodie* 29:48–50.
Brief popular survey of Machaut's life and works, with some considerations concerning modern performances. In Dutch.

1978. *Guillaume de Machaut, een grensbewoner: Samenhang van allegorie en muziek bij een laat-Middeleeuws dichter-componist. Guillaume de Machaut entre deux mondes: Les rapports d'allégorie et musique chez un poète-compositeur de la fin du Moyen Age (avec un résumé en français).* Amsterdam: Stichting Musicater.
In Dutch (French résumé lacking in the exemplar examined); publication of author's 1978 Utrecht dissertation. Interdisciplinary study that draws upon semiotics. Older analyses of Machaut's music have focused on details of motive and rhythm, neglecting the symbolic and allegorical relationship between text and music. Discussion of the allegorical symbols of Fortune's wheel, and how it is expressed in the music of *Tels rit* (RF1), *Il m'est avis* (B22), *De Fortune* (B23), and *De toutes flours* (B31). Study of the *Prologue* and the nature of Machaut's *fine amour*. The *Prologue* is central because the personification figures provide textual images that receive emphasis through musical means. Analysis of "Machaut motive" (Böker-Heil's "*CBCA*"), a motive that seems to be associated with the central image of the *dame*, in *Ne say comment* (L14/9), *Quant en moy / Amour* (M1), *On ne porroit* (B3), *Se quanque amours* (B21), *Honte, paour* (B25), *Cinq, un* (R6), *Rose, lis* (R10), and *Diex, Biauté* (V19). An image of despair is mirrored in the similar musical material of *Plourez, dames* (B32), *Nes qu'on* (B33), and *Se pour ce muir* (B36). Number

and Marian symbolism in *Ne say comment* (L14/9), *Contre ce dous* (L15/10), and *Qui n'aroit* (RF1). Includes Dutch translations of all of Machaut's ballades set to music.

1979. "Einige Bemerkungen zu Machauts 'Lay de l'Ymage.'" *Musikforschung* 32:58–62.

Analysis of *Le Lay de l'Ymage*, *Ne say comment* (L14/9), relating images in the text with musical techniques. Discusses number symbolism, Marian symbolism, the variety of means by which strophe 6 (the first to mention *bon Amour*) is set off, and musical motives that connect widely separated images in the text. The attributes of Love given in strophe 4 are compared to a similar list in *Lyon*, and both are related to a list in the *Roman de la Rose*. An anagram found near the end of the lai is similar to the anagram of the *Voir Dit* (62). Based on Mulder 1978, 81–82 and 118–22, which is slightly fuller in its treatment, including mention of the lai *Qui n'aroit* (RF1). Abstract: *RILM* 13 (1979), no. 286.

1990. "Uit de sluimering van het individu: Beeldvorming en 'de middeleeuwen'" In *Terugstrevend naar ginds: de wereld van Helene Nolthenius*, ed. Etty Mulder, 195–213. Nijmegen, The Netherlands: SUN.

The development of the individual is a central moment in Western civilization. Using Freudian psychoanalytical theory, Mulder contrasts the representation of the individual in the *Roman de la Rose*, in which *Amant* is the sum of the many personifications and allegorical figures—not yet an individual in the modern sense—with the representation of Machaut—more of a modern individual—in the miniatures of the *Prologue* in MS A. Just as the *Prologue* miniatures show a new direction towards perspective, so too does Machaut's Ars Nova music show a greater feeling for sonority, increasing rhythmic subtlety, and a growing consciousness of self-standing motives. Abstract: *Encomia* 14 (1992): 73 no. 393.

Mullally, Robert.

1986. "Cançon de carole." *Acta musicologica* 58:224–31.

The virelai is the song associated with the carole in Machaut and Froissart. An example from Machaut is *Dame, a vous* (RF6). Abstract: *RILM* 20 (1986), no. 1067.

1990. "Dance Terminology in Machaut and Froissart." *Medium Ævum* 59: 248–59.

In Machaut and Froissart, the term *carole* indicates a circular dance, accompanied vocally by virelais, while *danse* indicates dancing to instruments and serves as a generic term. In the course of the fourteenth century, use of the term *carole* declines in poetry, and *danse* becomes more frequent. The decline of the sung dance in favor of the instrumental dance in the fourteenth century parallels the separation between poets and composers. Includes a table comparing frequency of the terms *bal*, *carole*, *danse*, and *tresche* in fourteenth- and early fifteenth-century poetry.

Muscatine, Charles.

1957. *Chaucer and the French Tradition: A Study in Style and Meaning*. Berkeley and Los Angeles: University of California Press. Reprint. 1964.

Influential critical study emphasizing the importance of French literature for Chaucer's formation as a poet. Muscatine focuses on the *Roman de la Rose* and the tradition of romance, de-emphasizing the influence of fourteenth-century French poets (the work of Wimsatt and Calin [1994] is corrective). For unflattering commentary on Machaut, see especially pp. 99–101.

Musso, Noël (see also Roques, Gilles).

1982. "Comparaison statistique des lettres de Guillaume de Machaut et de Peronne d'Armentière dans le *Voir-Dit*." In Guillaume de Machaut 1982, 175–93 (discussion, 215–21, 264–67).

Quantitative statistics on vocabulary in the *Voir Dit* letters suggest that Machaut was not the author of Toute Belle's letters. For further commentary, see the Di Stefano review of Guillaume de Machaut 1982; and Higgins 1991, 166 n. 69.

Muzerelle, Denis.
1985. *Vocabulaire codicologique: Répertoire méthodique des termes français relatifs aux manuscrits.* Comité International de Paléographie. Rubricae: histoire du livre et des textes 1. Paris: Editions CEMI.
Very useful glossary of French terms concerning all aspects of manuscripts, manuscript production, and decoration, richly illustrated and with a full bibliography. Review: Jacques Lemaire, *Scriptorium* 42 (1989): 270–76 (corrections).

Nádas, John L.
1981. "The Structure of Panciatichi 26 and the Transmission of Trecento Polyphony." *Journal of the American Musicological Society* 34:393–427.
Thorough study of the MS **FP** [61]. Abstract: *RILM* 15 (1981), no. 4496.

1985. "The Transmission of Trecento Secular Polyphony: Manuscript Production and Scribal Practices in Italy at the End of the Middle Ages." Ph.D. diss. New York University. Ann Arbor: University Microfilms, 1986. Order no. 8604074.
An excellent bibliographical overview of studies on musical manuscripts and codicology (chap. 1). Manuscripts investigated in detail include **FP** [61], **PR** [63], and **Pit** [64]. Abstracts: *DAI* A 46/12 (June 1986): 3530; *RILM* 19 (1985), no. 1208.

1987. "The Reina Codex Revisited." In *Essays in Paper Analysis,* ed. Stephen Spector, 69–114. Folger Books. Washington, D.C.: Folger Shakespeare Library; London: Associated University Presses.
Study of MS **PR** [63]. Abstract: *RILM* 23 (1989), no. 1896.

1989. "The Songs of Don Paolo Tenorista: The Manuscript Tradition." In *In cantu et in sermone: For Nino Pirrotta on His 80th Birthday,* ed. Fabrizio Della Seta and Franco Piperno, 41–64. Italian Medieval and Renaissance Studies, The University of Western Australia 2. Florence: Olschki; n.p.: University of Western Australia Press.
Includes new material, with a full bibliography, on the MS **Pit** [64] (pp. 43–57).

1992. "Manuscript San Lorenzo 2211: Some Further Observations." In *L'Ars Nova italiana del Trecento VI,* ed. Giulio Cattin and Patrizia Dalla Vecchia, 145–68. Certaldo: Polis.
Study of MS **SL** [65].

Nejedlý, Zdeněk.
1904. *Dějiny zpěvu předhusitského v Čechách* (History of song in Bohemia before the Hussites). Prague. Later incorporated into *Dějiny husitského zpěvu.* Book 1, *Zpěv předhusitský.* Sebrané Spisy Zdeňka Nejedlého 40 (Collected works of Zdeněk Nejedlý 40). Prague: Nakladatelství Československé adademie věd, 1954.
In Czech. Includes material on the supposed influence of Machaut on Bohemian song.

1905–6. "Magister Záviše und seine Schule. Zur Musikgeschichte Böhmens im 14. Jahrhundert." *Sammelbände der Internationalen Musikgesellschaft* 7: 41–69.
Brief consideration of Machaut's influence on Czech music in the fourteenth century (54–55). See remarks in Gastoué 1922, 68.

Nelson, Alan H.
1980. "Mechanical Wheels of Fortune, 1100–1547." *Journal of the Warburg and Courtauld Institutes* 43:227–33, plates 28–29.
Mechanical aspects of illustrated wheels of fortune; includes a reproduction and discussion of *Remede* miniature C14b , which "reveals particularly astonishing mechanical sophistication" (227).

Nelson, Jan A.
1982–83. "Guillaume de Machaut as Job: Access to the Poet as Individual Through His Source." *Romance Notes* 23:185–90.
A literary study of the ballade *Dou memoire des hommes degradés* (Lo253) as an adaptation of Job 3:1–10.

New Grove.
1980. *The New Grove Dictionary of Music and Musicians,* ed. Stanley Sadie. 20 vols. London: Macmillan.
Encyclopedia of music.

Newels, Margarete.
1989. "Natur in der spätmittelalterlichen Poesie." In *Kontinuität und Transformation der Antike im Mittelalter. Veröffentlichung der Kongressakten zum Freiburger Symposion des Mediävistenverbandes,* ed. Willi Erzgräber, 193–204. Sigmaringen: Thorbecke.
Wide-ranging consideration of nature in late medieval poetry. The conception of the relation between Love and Nature in the *Roman de la Rose* influenced poetic themes from Machaut to the sixteenth century. Discusses the rhetorical basis for late medieval love poetry and realism in late medieval poetry. Study of the poetics of Machaut's *Prologue,* with particular consideration of the meaning behind the six personification figures. Brief discussion of *Vergier, Jugement Behaingne, Jugement Navarre, Lyon, Alerion, Fonteinne* (200–201), and *Remede* (201–3). Examples of feelings (*sentement*), as expressed through nature figurations of wind, water, turtle doves, and in May poems.

Newes, Virginia.
1977. "Imitation in the Ars Nova and Ars Subtilior." *Revue belge de musicologie* 31:38–59.
Survey; mentions several examples of melodic imitation in Machaut. Abstract: *RILM* 11 (1977), no. 2368.

1984. "The Relationship of Text to Imitative Techniques in 14th Century Polyphony." In Günther/Finscher 1984, 121–54.
Mentions declamation in the hocket section of *Quant en moy / Amour* (M1) (pp. 136–37). Abstract: *RILM* 18 (1984), no. 6105.

1987. "Fuga and Related Contrapuntal Procedures in European Polyphony ca. 1350–ca. 1420." Ph.D. diss. Brandeis University. Ann Arbor: University Microfilms. Order no. 8715753.
After a consideration of contemporary terminology and citations in music theory, the main part of this work is a study of canonic works of the fourteenth and early fifteenth centuries arranged by structural type. Discusses works of Machaut with unaccompanied canons at the unison, including *Je ne cesse* (L16/11), *S'onques* (L17/12), and *Sans cuer m'en / Amis / Dame* (B17) (pp. 70–72, 109–69); and with retrograde canons, namely, *Ma fin* (R14) (pp. 282–97). Abstract: *DAI* A 48/5 (Nov. 1987): 1051.

1990. "Writing, Reading and Memorizing: The Transmission and Resolution of Retrograde Canons from the 14th and Early 15th Centuries." *Early Music* 18:218–34.
Includes a discussion of *Ma fin* (R14) (pp. 224–34).

1991a. "Dialogue and Dispute in Some Polytextual Songs by Machaut and His Successors." *Sonus* 12:66–86.
Study of a group of polytextual songs not based on pre-existent material. The point of departure is provided by the many paired lyrics in Machaut's *Voir Dit,* which Newes relates to the provençal *tenso* (debate song). Includes brief consideration of literary and musical aspects of *Sans cuer m'en / Amis / Dame* (B17), *De triste / Quant / Certes* (B29), and *Quant Theseüs / Ne quier* (B34).

1991b. "Turning Fortune's Wheel: Musical and Textual Design in Machaut's Canonic Lais." *Musica disciplina* 45:95–121.

A study of canonic writing in *Je ne cesse* (L16/11) and *S'onques* (L17/12), demonstrating the problems of text setting that this compositional procedure entailed. Nevertheless, the three-voice canon provides an effective metaphor for the image of the Trinity in L16, and for Fortune's wheel in L17. This issue of *Musica disciplina* appeared in 1995.

Nikžentaitis, Alvydas.
  1988. "Del čekų feodalų vaidmens 1329 m. Vokeičių ordino žygyje į Lietuvą" (On the role of the Czech feudal lords in the Teutonic Order's crusade to Lithuania in 1329; in Lithuanian; summary in Russian, 57–58). *Lietuvos TSR Mokslų* Akademijos Darbai, A Serija 3/104:52–57.
    Includes mention of the place names Machaut cites in *Confort* (52).

Nolan, Barbara.
  1981. "The Art of Expropriation: Chaucer's Narrator in *The Book of the Duchess.*" In *New Perspectives in Chaucer Criticism*, ed. Donald M. Rose, 203–22. Norman, Ok.: Pilgrim Books.
    French materials are "deliberately subverted" by Chaucer. See especially the discussion of Chaucer's use of the story of Ceyx and Alcyone from *Fonteinne* (213–17, 219–20).

Nolan, Robert J.
  1974. "The Roman de Mélusine: Evidence for an Early Missing Version." *Fabula* 15:53–58.
    Argues that Machaut was possibly the author of a lost early version of *Mélusine* (written 1349 or 1350), a view first suggested by Leo Hoffrichter (see Nolan's reference, 53 n. 1).

Nouvet, Claire.
  1986. "Pour une économie de la dé-limitation: La *Prison Amoureuse* de Jean Froissart." *Neophilologus* 70:341–56.
    On the professional poet, the patron, and the notion of oeuvre, mainly discussing Froissart's *Prison amoureuse*. Includes brief consideration of Machaut's *Prologue*, *Confort*, and *Voir Dit*.

Oana-Pop, Rodica.
  1966. "Elemente ale gîndirii funcționale prezente în creația lui Guillaume de Machault (1300–1377)" (Elements of functional harmony in the works of Guillaume de Machaut; in Rumanian; summary in French, Russian, and German). *Lucrari de Muzicologie* 2:1–11.
    Anachronistic study finding progressive elements in Machaut's harmony that can be explained in terms of functional tonality (cf. Machabey 1955a). Several musical examples. Abstract: *RILM* 1 (1967), no. 1454.

Obniska, Ewa.
  1977. "Piewca miłości dwornej" (Poet of courtly love; in Polish). *Ruch muzyczny* 17:3–6.
    Introduction to the life and works of Machaut. Abstract: *RILM* 11 (1977), no. 4438.

  1983. "Guillaume de Machaut—poeta wieku niepokoju" (Guillaume de Machaut—poet in a troubled century; in Polish). *Ruch muzyczny* 27:9–12.
    Life and musical works: motets, Mass, virelais, rondeaux, ballades.

Oliver, Dennis.
  1972. "Guillaume de Machaut: Art poétique / art d'amour." *SubStance* 4 (autumn): 45–50.
    Discusses Machaut's poetics, based primarily on the first 400 lines of *Remede*, and on the *Prologue*.

Olschki, Leonardo.
  1932. Manuscrits français à peintures des bibliothèques d'Allemagne. Geneva: Olschki.
    Description of MS **Bk** [21].

Olson, Clair C. (see also Crow/Olson).
   1941. "Chaucer and the Music of the Fourteenth Century." *Speculum* 16:64–91.
   Discussion of fourteenth-century poems naming instruments; passages in Chaucer that discuss instruments and music. Very dated, due to the very rudimentary state of knowledge on music in fourteenth-century England in 1941.

Olson, Glending.
   1973. "Deschamps' *Art de Dictier* and Chaucer's Literary Environment." *Speculum* 48:714–23.
   Deschamps's theory of lyric poetry as laid out in the *Art de Dictier*, its context in the French tradition, and its influence on Chaucer.

   1979. "Making and Poetry in the Age of Chaucer." *Comparative Literature* 31:272–90.
   The poetics of court writers in the period of Chaucer as revealed in their own terminology on poetry, focusing on the distinction between "poete" and "makere" (Fr. "faiseur"). On Deschamps's characterization of Machaut in the double ballade *déploration*, see 277–78. "The implication is that Machaut is a 'faiseur' as composer-lyricist and a 'poete' as user of classical material" (278). See also Brownlee 1978a.

   1982. *Literature as Recreation in the Later Middle Ages.* Ithaca and London: Cornell University Press.
   Includes a consideration of *Jugement Navarre* in conjunction with Boccaccio's *Decameron* as a "response" to the Plague (183–204).

Olsson, Kurt.
   1992. *John Gower and the Structures of Conversion: A Reading of the* Confessio Amantis. Publications of the John Gower Society 4. Cambridge: Brewer.
   Includes material on Gower and Machaut, considering *Remede, Fonteinne,* and *Voir Dit.*

Omont, Henri.
   1895. *Bibliothèque Nationale. Catalogue général des manuscrits français. Ancien supplément français.* Vol. 1, *Nos. 6171–9560 du fonds français.* Paris: Leroux.
   Standard catalogue; includes MS **E** [7] (p. 326).

   1898. *Bibliothèque Nationale. Catalogue général des manuscrits français. Ancien petits fonds français.* Vol. 1, *Nos. 20065–22884 du fonds français,* by Ch. de la Roncière. Paris: Leroux.
   Standard catalogue; includes MS **F-G** [6] (pp. 520–21).

   1900a. *Bibliothèque Nationale. Catalogue général des manuscrits français. Ancien Saint-Germain français.* Vol. 3, *Nos. 18677–20064 du fonds français,* by L. Auvray and H. Omont. Paris: Leroux.
   Standard catalogue; includes MS **Ra** [44] (pp. 463–64).

   1900b. *Bibliothèque Nationale. Catalogue général des manuscrits français. Nouvelles acquisitions français.* Vol. 2, *Nos. 3061–6500.* Paris: Leroux.
   Standard catalogue; includes **I** [40] (pp. 419–20).

   1902. *Bibliothèque Nationale. Catalogue général des manuscrits français. Ancien petits fonds français.* Vol. 2, *Nos. 22885–25696 du fonds français,* by C. Couderc and Ch. de la Roncière. Paris: Leroux.
   Standard catalogue; includes MS *F:Pn 24440* [53] (pp. 379–80).

   1908–21. *Anciens inventaires et catalogues de la Bibliothèque nationale.* 5 vols. Paris: Leroux, 1908–21.
   Publication of sixteenth- and seventeenth-century catalogues of the French royal library, including the 1518 and 1544 inventories of the royal library at the château de Blois, the

Nicolas Rigault catalogue of 1622, the brothers Dupuy catalogue of 1645, and the Nicolas Clément catalogue of 1682.

1918. *Bibliothèque Nationale. Catalogue général des manuscrits français. Nouvelles acquisitions français.* Vol. 4, *Nos. 10001–11353 et 20001– 22811.* Paris: Leroux.

Standard catalogue; includes MS *F:Pn 11198* [5a].

Ouy, Gilbert.
1967. "Le songe et les ambitions d'un jeune humaniste Parisien vers 1395. (Une épître latine inconnue de Jean Lebègue à Pierre Lorfèvre, chancelier de Louis d'Orléans, lui demandant la main de sa fille Catherine. — Ms. Paris, B.N. lat. 10400, f. 30–35)." In *Miscellanea di studi e ricerche sul quattrocento francese,* ed. Franco Simone, 357–407. Università degli Studi di Torino; Fondazione Parini Chirio. Turin: Giappichelli.

The young humanist's letter mentions Machaut.

Ouy, Gilbert, et al.
1983. *Le catalogue de la bibliothèque de l'abbaye de Saint-Victor de Paris de Claude de Grandrue 1514.* Introduction by Gilbert Ouy and Véronika Gerzvon Buren. Text and Index by Véronika Gerz-von Buren with Raymonde Hubschmid and Catherine Regnier. Concordances by Gilbert Ouy. Paris: Editions du Centre Nationale de la Recherche Scientifique.

Material on the early provenance of MS **I** [40]; see item TT 23 (284).

Owens, Jessie Ann.
1990–91. "Music Historiography and the Definition of 'Renaissance.'" *Notes* 47:305–30.

Includes material on the historiography of Machaut and fourteenth-century music (325–29).

Page, Christopher.
1977. "Machaut's 'Pupil' Deschamps on the Performance of Music: Voices or Instruments in the 14th century *Chanson?*" *Early Music* 5:484–91.

A pioneering study suggesting that the most typical scoring for performances of fourteenth-century chansons was all-vocal. Abstract: *RILM* 11 (1977), no. 5657.

1979. "The Myth of the Chekker." *Early Music* 7:482–89.

Different authors at different times mean different things by the term "chekker." Abstract: *RILM* 13 (1979), no. 5502.

1982. "The Performance of Songs in Late Medieval France: A New Source." *Early Music* 10:441–50.

Further support for the all-vocal thesis of chanson performance (see Page 1977) from the fifteenth-century romance *Cleriadus et Meliadice.* Abstract: *RILM* 16 (1982), no. 5692.

1990. "Polyphony before 1400." In *Performance Practice: Music before 1600,* ed. Howard Mayer Brown and Stanley Sadie, 79–104. The Norton/Grove Handbooks in Music. New York and London: Norton.

Excellent overview of the most recent concerns regarding performance practice in medieval polyphony. Discusses tuning, rhythm, ornamentation, instrumentation, and vocalization. Reviews: Stanley Boorman, *Early Music* 18 (1990): 641–45; Ross W. Duffin, *Historical Performance* 4 (1991): 61–64; Timothy J. McGee, *Performance Practice Review* 4 (1991): 64–70; Howard Schott, *American Recorder* 32/1 (Mar. 1991): 31–32; Denis Stevens, *Musical Times* 131 (1990): 368; Richard Turbet, *Brio* 27 (1990): 84–85; J.F. Weber, *Association for Recorded Sound Collections Journal* 21 (1990): 277–78.

1992. "Going Beyond the Limits: Experiments with Vocalization in the French Chanson, 1340–1440." *Early Music* 20:446–59.

Practical experiments in vocalizing textless tripla, tenors, and contratenors. The results can be heard in several recordings of Page's Gothic Voices: see Hyperion CDA66463, CDA66588, CDA66619, and CDA66739 in chap. 8.8.

1993. *Discarding Images: Reflections on Music and Culture in Medieval France*. Oxford: Clarendon.

Stimulating reconsideration of some common generalizations concerning music and poetry in France from the thirteenth to the fifteenth century. Among the paradigms Page attacks are the emphasis on a medieval music as number (the Pythagorean model), architectural metaphors for music, the notion of a cultural elite who cultivated the motet, and the persistent view (after Huizinga 1924) that the culture of the fifteenth century represents a period of decline. For Machaut, the book has relevant material on the question of successive vs. simultaneous conception of voices, performance practice, and the analysis of motets. Reviews: Margaret Bent, "Reflections of Christopher Page's *Reflections*," *Early Music* 21 (1993): 625–33 (responses by Christopher Page, *Early Music* 22 [1994]: 127–32; and Reinhard Strohm, *Early Music* 22 [1994]: 715–19); R. Freedman, *Choice* 31 (1994): 946; Richard J. Schuler, *Sacred Music* 121/2 (summer 1994): 30; Ruth Steiner, *Catholic Historical Review* 80 (1994): 346–47; Margaret Switten, *Speculum* 70 (1995): 186–87; Rob C. Wegman, *Music and Letters* 76 (1995): 265–73.

Pagès, Amédée.

1936. *La poésie française en Catalogne du XIIIe siècle à la fin du XVe*. Bibliothèque méridionale 1/23. Toulouse: Privat; Paris: Didier.

Influence of French poetry on Catalan courts in the late Middle Ages. Machaut, Oton de Granson, and Alain Chartier exerted the most influence. Study of MS **Bc** [55].

Palisca, Claude V., comp.

1980. *Norton Anthology of Western Music*. Vol. 1. New York: Norton, 1980. 2nd ed. New York: Norton, 1988. Shorter Version. New York: Norton, 1980.

Includes editions of Agnus and *Quant Theseüs / Ne quier* (B34) by Elizabeth Keitel.

Palmer, R. Barton.

1980. *"The Book of the Duchess* and *Fonteinne amoureuse*: Chaucer and Machaut Reconsidered." *Canadian Review of Comparative Literature / Revue Canadienne de Littérature Comparée* 7:380–93.

Chaucer's transformation of material from Machaut's *Fonteinne*, especially the myth of Ceyx and Alcyone, in the *Book of the Duchess*; the incorporation of dream into the narrative frame; and the persona of the narrator.

1981. "Vision and Experience in Machaut's *Fonteinne amoureuse*." *Journal of the Rocky Mountain Medieval and Renaissance Association* 2:79–86.

Boethius provides the model of sorrow and consolation for Machaut's successful reconciliation of idealistic courtly convention and the fourteenth-century trend to realism. The reality ("experience") of the duke of Berry's impending exile is the frame for a dream vision which in turn informs a new reality.

1984 (ed. and trans.). *Guillaume de Machaut*: The Judgment of the King of Bohemia (Le Jugement dou Roy de Behaingne). Garland Library of Medieval Literature 9A. New York and London: Garland.

An edition and translation of *Jugement Behaingne*, with notes and an appendix of borrowings in Chaucer's *Book of the Duchess* (97–104). Introduction provides a brief biography, an overview of scholarship, an essay on narrative *dits*, and an introduction to *Jugement Behaingne*, with discussion of sources and influences, and an annotated bibliography. See also Windeatt 1982; Wimsatt/Kibler 1988. Reviews: Keith Busby, *Encomia* 7 (1985): 9–11 (corrections); Giuseppe Di Stefano, *Moyen français* (1990): 294 (corrections); Angela Dzelzainis, *Medium Ævum* 55 (1986): 322–23 (corrections); Howard B. Garey, *Speculum* 61 (1986): 153–55; Gilles Roques, *Zeitschrift für romanische Philologie* 101 (1985): 536–37; Nigel Wilkins, *French Studies* 40 (1986): 313–15.

1987a. "Editor's Comment." *Studies in the Literary Imagination* 20:1–7.
Introductory essay to the volume provides useful summaries of Calin 1987, Dembowski 1987, Guthrie 1987, Kelly 1987, Kibler/Wimsatt 1987, and Palmer 1987.

1987b. "The Metafictional Machaut: Self-Reflexivity and Self-Mediation in the Two Judgment Poems." *Studies in the Literary Imagination* 20:23–39.
In a prologue to the essay, Palmer argues for the application of modern analytical techniques, rather than attempting to read a medieval text as it was then read (23–26). (Provides interesting reading for musicologists; note the similarity to Leech-Wilkinson [1984] on *Rose, lis*). Analysis of *Jugement Behaingne*, especially concerning the clerkly narrator. In *Jugement Navarre*, the poet's self-consciousness concerning his own literary creation, the "poetics of authorship" (38) is paramount. Abstract: Palmer 1987a, 3–4; criticized in Heinrichs 1989, 107–8 n. 38.

1988 (ed. and trans.). *Guillaume de Machaut*: The Judgment of the King of Navarre. Garland Library of Medieval Literature 45A. New York and London: Garland.
Edition and translation of *Navarre*, with notes. Includes a brief biography of Machaut and an essay on *Jugement Navarre* as a response to *Jugement Behaingne*, and how both fit with the poetics of the *Prologue*. Summary of *Jugement Navarre*, discussion of sources and influences (though unaware of De Boer 1914). Reviews: Jody Enders, *Speculum* 65 (1990): 414–16; Giuseppe Di Stefano, *Moyen français* (1990): 294 (corrections); Jane H. M. Taylor, *Medium Ævum* 61 (1992): 341–42 (corrections).

1992 (ed. and trans.). *Guillaume de Machaut*: Le Confort d'Ami. (Comfort for a Friend). Garland Library of Medieval Literature 67A. New York and London: Garland.
Edition and translation of *Confort*. The introduction includes material on Charles of Navarre and material in *Confort* that relates to historical circumstances. Thorough discussion of *exempla* in *Confort* and their sources in the Bible and *Ovide Moralisé*. Reviews: Ardis Butterfield, *Medium Ævum* 63 (1994): 343–44 (corrections); Philip E. Bennett, *French Studies* 48 (1994): 190–91 (corrections).

1993a (ed. and trans.). *Guillaume de Machaut*: The Fountain of Love (La Fonteinne Amoureuse) *and Two Other Love Vision Poems*. Garland Library of Medieval Literature 54A. New York and London: Garland.
New editions and translations of *Prologue*, *Vergier*, and *Fonteinne*. Review: J.E. Parker Jr, *Choice* 31 (1994): 1728

1993b. "Transtextuality and the Producing-I in Guillaume de Machaut's Judgment Series." *Exemplaria* 5:283–304.
Considers *Jugement Behaingne*, *Jugement Navarre*, and the *Lay de Plour* (L22/16), three works tied to each other in a series, a step towards the collective conception of the oeuvre ultimately seen in the *Prologue* to the late manuscripts. The "producing-I," characteristic of the judgment series, is a new poetic *je* ("narrating-I") concerned with textuality and authorship, a result of the ambiguous position of a poet required to celebrate the loves of the noble patron.

In press. *Chaucer's French Contemporaries: The Poetry/Poetics of Self and Tradition*. Georgia State Literary Studies 10. New York: AMS Press.
Will include new essays by Ehrhart, Hieatt, Huot, and Palmer; and reprints of Calin 1987, Guthrie 1987, Kelly 1987, Palmer 1987b, and Wimsatt/Kibler 1987.

Panofsky, Erwin.
1939. *Studies in Iconology*. New York: Harper and Row. 2nd ed. 1962.
Includes material on the depiction of the god of Love (95–128); *Vergier* cited (101 n. 18).

1953. *Early Netherlandish Painting: The Origins and Character*. Vol. 1. Cambridge, Mass.: Harvard University Press. London: Cumberledge.
Includes material on the miniaturists of MSS **A** and **D**.

Paris, Gaston.
   1877. Review of Mas Latrie 1876. *Revue historique* 4:215–17.
   Includes important corrections to Machaut's biography. Response in Mas Latrie 1877a, 189–90.
   1887. "Un poème inédit de Martin Le Franc." *Romania* 16:383–437.
   Paris cites two passages in the *Champion des Dames* that mention Machaut: (1) Le Franc declares himself against the judgment in *Behaingne (F:Pn 12476*, fol. 44c; edition of Galiot du Pré [Paris, 1530], 48) (p. 409); and (2) Le Franc puts Machaut among the greatest *rethoriques (F:Pn 12476*, fol. 114b; edition of Galiot du Pré [Paris, 1530], 318) (pp. 415–16).
   1895. *La poésie du Moyen Age: Leçons et lectures.* Deuxième série. Paris: Hachette. 2nd ed. 1903.
   The lecture "La littérature française au XIVe siècle" (185–211) includes brief mention of Machaut (199–201, 208). Paris's main interest in fourteenth-century French literature is the useful information on real-life customs it provides (202–3).
   1898. Review of Suchier 1897. *Romania* 27:162–63.
   Includes additional material on the anagram in *Voir Dit.*
   1907. *Esquisse historique de la littérature française au Moyen Age (depuis les origines jusqu'à la fin du XVe siècle).* Paris: Colin.
   See chap. 6, "Periode de la guerre de cent ans (1328–1436) (pp. 207–40). Concerning Machaut, "Ses ballades... ont peu de relief.... Mais l'ouvrage le plus original de Machaut est son *Voir Dit*... il est très vraisemblablement l'auteur du tout" (223).

Paris, Paulin.
   1836–48. *Les manuscrits françois de la Bibliothèque du roi, leur histoire et celle des textes allemands, anglois, hollandois, italiens, espagnols de la même collection.* 7 vols. Paris: Techner.
   Manuscript catalogue for the French royal library.
   1875 (ed.). *Le Livre du Voir-Dit de Guillaume de Machaut où sont contées les amours de Messire Guillaume de Machaut et de Péronnelle, Dame d'Armentières, avec les lettres et les réponses, les ballades, lais et rondeaux dudit Guillaume et de la dite Péronnelle, publié sur trois manuscrits du XIVe siècle, pour la Société des Bibliophiles françois.* Paris: Société des Bibliophiles françois. Reprint. Geneva: Slatkine, 1969.
   Introduction on the identity of Toute Belle includes a new view of Machaut's biography, revising Tarbé 1849, but still not definitive. This is the only published edition of the *Voir Dit,* notorious among literary critics for its shortcomings. A. Thomas (1912) printed a large segment left out by Paris; several other missing lines are quoted as needed in the studies of Cerquiglini, who has had access to the completed but still unpublished edition of Paul Imbs. Includes a transcription of *Dix et sept* (R17) by Marie Colas (many errors). Review: Tamizey de Larroque, *Revue critique d'histoire et de littérature* 17 (1875): 394–96 no. 121; see also Cerquiglini 1991b.

Parrish, Carl.
   1957. *The Notation of Medieval Music.* New York: Norton, 1957; London: Faber and Faber, 1958; New York: Norton, 1959. Reprint, with a new introduction by J.W. McKinnon. New York: Pendragon, 1978.
   Contains facsimiles of *Dame, de qui* (RF5), *Hareu! / Helas!* (M10) (partial), *Felix virgo / Inviolata* (M23), Sanctus, *Dame, se vous n'avez* (R13), *Quant je ne voy* (R21), *Tuit mi penser* (V28/25), *Mors sui* (V29/26), and *Liement* (V30/27), with a description of the notation of each.

Parrish, Carl, and John F. Ohl, eds.
   1951. *Masterpieces of Music Before 1750. An Anthology of Musical Examples from Gregorian Chant to J.S. Bach.* New York: Norton.
   Includes commentary and edition of Agnus I (36–39 no. 13).

Parrott, Andrew.
  1977. "Performing Machaut's Mass on Record." *Early Music* 5:492–95.
  Performance problems and how they have been handled in seven recordings of the Mass.
  Discusses presentation of the Kyrie, liturgical context, and instrumental participation.
  Abstracts: *RILM* 11 (1977), no. 5658; Karin Paulsmeier, *Basler Jahrbuch für historische
  Musikpraxis* 2 (1978): 224 no. 146.

Patch, Howard Rollin.
  1923. "Fortuna in Old French Literature." In *Smith College Studies in
  Modern Languages* 4/4 (July): 1–45.
  Discusses passages in Machaut that mention Fortune (21–23), esp. *Remede*, with numer-
  ous references (23 n. 91) to *Jugement Behaingne*, *Jugement Navarre*, *Alerion*, *Voir Dit*,
  and many lyrics of the *Loange*. The citations, in the following order, include *On verroit
  meint amant* (Lo38), *Se trestuit cil* (Lo48), *Helas! je sui de si* (Lo56), *Las! j'ai failli*
  (Lo70), *Douce dame, prenés temps* (Lo76), *Puis qu'Eürs* (Lo113), *Trop se peinne*
  (Lo164), *Il m'est avis* (Lo188=B22), *Helas! pour ce que Fortune* (Lo189), *De Fortune*
  (Lo195=B23), *Tant ay perdu confort* (Lo202), *Je maudi l'eure* (Lo213), *Amours, ma dame*
  (Lo227), *Nes qu'on* (Lo232=B33), *Amours qui m'a* (Lo243), *Se vo grandeur* (Lo263), *On
  ne doit pas* (Lo264), *Aus amans* (L4, strophe 9), *Amis, t'amour* (L10/7, strophes 4 and
  7), *Un mortel lay* (L12/8, strophe 1), *S'onques* (L17/12, strophes 1, 3, 5, and 6), *Malgré
  Fortune* (L19/14, strophes 1 and 2), *Je ne me say* (L20, strophe 5), *En demantant*
  (L24/18, strophes 5, 6, 7, 10, and 12), *Hé! Mors / Fine* (M3, motetus), *Qui es / Ha!
  Fortune* (M8, triplum and motetus), *Helas! pour quoy virent / Corde* (M12, motetus),
  Maugré mon cuer / De ma dolour (M14, motetus), *De toutes flours* (B31), *De triste /
  Quant / Certes* (B29, *De triste* only), *Cuer qui se sent jeune* (LoA3; see also Patch 1927,
  72 n. 4), and *Folle largesse* (LoA10; see also Patch 1927, 96n.).

  1927. *The Goddess Fortuna in Mediaeval Literature*. Cambridge, Mass.:
  Harvard University Press. Reprint. New York: Octagon Books, 1967.
  Facsimile of miniatures C14b (see chap. 4.4e) and A147 (see chap. 4.4k). Besides the
  many references to Fortune in *Remede* (separately indexed by Patch), the following works
  are cited: *Jugement Behaingne* (92 n. 1, 96n.), *Jugement Navarre* (41 n. 3, 64 n. 2, 76 n.
  1), *Alerion* (40 n. 2, 63 n. 2, 75 n. 3, 76 n. 1, 91 n. 1, 100 n. 2, 104 n. 2), *Amis,
  t'amour* (L10/7; 94 n. 1), *Amours, ma dame* (Lo227; 92 n. 1), *Amours qui m'a* (Lo243;
  91 n. 1), *Aus amans* (L4; 156 n. 1), *De Fortune* (Lo195=B23; 96n.), *De toutes flours* (64
  n. 2), *De triste* (Bn32=B29[1]; 96n.), *En demantant* (L24/18; 68 n. 3, 80 n. 2, 119 n. 1),
  He! Mors / Fine (M3; 108 n. 4), *Helas! pour ce que* (Lo189; 96n.), *Helas! pour quoy
  virent / Corde* (M12; 81 n. 2), *Il m'est avis* (Lo188=B22; 75 n. 3, 84 n. 1), *Malgré
  Fortune* (L19/14; 92 n. 1), *Maugré mon cuer / De ma dolour* (M14; 94 n. 1), *Puis que
  j'empris* (Lo77; 96n.), *Quant Ecuba* (Cp4; 83 n. 3), *Qui es / Ha! Fortune* (M8; 50 n. 2,
  56 n. 2, 65n., 101 n. 4, 119 n. 1), *S'onques* (L17/12; 77 n. 1, 96n., 134 n. 2), *Se
  trestuit cil* (Lo48; 42n.), *Se vo grandeur* (Lo263; 91 n. 1), *Tant ay perdu confort* (Lo202;
  96n.), and *Un mortel lay* (L12/8; 119 n. 1); Patch cites the following *opera dubia* as
  works of Machaut: *Cuer qui se sent* (LoA3; 96n.), and *Folle largesse* (LoA10; 72 n. 4).

  1935. *The Tradition of Boethius: A Study of His Importance in Medieval
  Culture*. New York: Oxford University Press. Reprint. New York: Russell
  and Russell, 1970.
  Includes brief discussion of Boethius's influence on *Remede*, *Confort*, and *Voir Dit*.

  1950. *The Other World, According to Descriptions in Medieval Literature*.
  Smith College Studies in Modern Languages, New Series 1. Cambridge,
  Mass.: Harvard University Press.
  Mention of visions of the Earthly Paradise in *Vergier*, *Jugement Behaingne*, *Lyon*, and
  Fonteinne.

Patterson, Warner Forrest.
  1935. *Three Centuries of French Poetic Theory: A Critical History of the
  Chief Arts of Poetry in France (1328–1630)*. University of Michigan Publi-

cations; Language and Literature 14–15. 2 vols. in 3. Ann Arbor: University of Michigan Press. Reprint. New York: Russel and Russel, 1966.

Discussion of Machaut's *Prologue,* Deschamps's *Art de Dictier,* the anonymous *Regles de la Seconde Rettorique,* and Baudet Herenc's *Doctrinal de la Secunde Retorique.* Vol. 2 includes editions of *En haut penser* (Lo1; ed. 2:63–64), *Blanche com lis* (Lo82; ed. 2:121), *Se je vous aim* (Lo231; ed. 2:75), *Douce, plaisant* (VD25; ed. 2:149–51), *Onques si bonne* (VD45; ed. 2:156–57), *Prologue* ballades 1 and 3 (ed. 2:72–74, *Harpe* (excerpt; ed. 2:197–99), and *Lyon* (excerpt; ed. 2:199–200).

Paulsmeier, Karin.

1986. "Aspekte der Beziehung zwischen Notation und Stil." *Basler Jahrbuch für historische Musikpraxis* 10:63–90.

Includes a facsimile of MS A, fol. 466r, with *Tres douce dame* (B24).

Pearcy, Roy. J.

1980. "The Genre of William Dunbar's *Tretis of the Tua Mariit Wemen and the Wedo.*" *Speculum* 55:58–74.

The poet as hidden observer in Dunbar's *Tretis* has a parallel in Machaut's *Jugement Behaingne* (72 n. 21).

Pearsall, Derek, and Elizabeth Salter. See also Salter and Pearsall.

1973. *Landscapes and Seasons of the Medieval World.* London: Elek.

Includes consideration of Machaut's garden landscapes in *Vergier, Jugement Behaingne, Remede, Lyon,* and *Fonteinne* (172–73 and notes, 224).

Peck, Russel A.

1983. *Chaucer's Lyrics and* Anelida and Arcite: *An Annotated Bibliography, 1900 to 1980.* The Chaucer Bibliographies. Toronto, Buffalo, and London: University of Toronto Press.

Annotated Chaucer bibliography.

1988. *Chaucer's* Romaunt of the Rose *and* Boece, Treatise on the Astrolabe, Equatorie of the Planetis, *Lost Works, and Chaucerian Apocrypha: An Annotated Bibliography, 1900 to 1985.* The Chaucer Bibliographies. Toronto, Buffalo, and London: University of Toronto Press.

Annotated Chaucer bibliography.

Peignot, G[abriel].

1841. *Catalogue d'une partie des livres composant la bibliothèque des ducs de Bourgogne, au XVe siècle.* 2nd rev. ed. Dijon: Lagier.

A Machaut manuscript is listed in inventories of 1405 and 1477, but the description is too vague to identify (67, 97). Lost MS [8], [12], or [19] may have been the manuscript in question.

Pelen, Marc. M.

1973. "The Marriage Journey: Dream Vision, Romance Structures and Epithalamic Conventions in Medieval Latin and French Poems and in Middle English Dream Poems." Ph.D. diss. Princeton University. Ann Arbor: University Microfilms. Order no. 7409711.

Not examined. Abstract: *DAI* A 34/11 (May 1974): 7242.

1976–77. "Machaut's Court of Love Narratives and Chaucer's *Book of the Duchess.*" *Chaucer Review* 11:128–55.

Analyzes Machaut's *Jugement Behaingne, Jugement Navarre, Remede,* and *Fonteinne* in light of the literary tradition for love debate poems, which Pelen traces to late antiquity. A three-part structure is evident in the tradition: (1) dream vision; (2) debate; and (3) resolution. Pelen also treats the influence of these works on Chaucer's *Book of the Duchess.* Ehrhart (1980b, 129, 138 n. 21 and 1987, 266 n. 45) takes issue with Pelen's interpretation of *Fonteinne.* Abstract: *Encomia* 2/1 (1978): 78 no. 164.

1979. "Form and Meaning of the Old French Love Vision: The *Fableau dou Dieu d'Amors* and Chaucer's *Parliament of Fowls.*" *Journal of Medieval and Renaissance Studies* 9:277–305.

Includes valuable material on the Medieval Latin erotic debate (286–97), esp. the *Altercatio Phyllidis et Florae*, with further discussion of the tradition and structure studied in Pelen 1976–77. Only peripheral mention of Machaut (296–97).

Pelicier, P[aul].

1899. *Inventaire-Sommaire des Archives départementales antérieurs à 1790.* Marne. Archives Ecclésiastiques. Série G4. Châlons.

Publication of a document that mentions Jean de Machaut (124, G. 471 no. 4).

Pelinski, Ramòn A.

1963. "Die Motetten Machauts." Master's thesis, Munich, 1963.

Not examined.

1975. "Zusammenklang und Aufbau in den Motetten Machauts." *Musikforschung* 28: 62–71.

Begins with a selection of nineteenth-century critical views of Machaut as a composer. Mainly concerned with *Ruheklänge* (static sonorities), which have an articulating function for the rhythmic, harmonic, and textual structure of a motet. Examples are drawn from several motets, especially *Quant en moy / Amour* (M1), *De Bon Espoir / Puis que* (M4), *Tant doucement m'ont / Eins* (M13), *Amours qui a / Faus Samblant* (M15), *Quant vraie amour / O series* (M17), *Bone pastor / Bone pastor* (M18), and *Tu qui gregem / Plange* (M22). Cf. also Zipay 1983. Abstract: *RILM* 1976, 5136.

Pellegrin, Elisabeth.

1955. *La bibliothèque des Visconti et des Sforza, ducs de Milan, au XVe siècle.* Publications de l'Institut de Recherche et d'Histoire des Textes 5. Paris: Centre National de Recherche Scientifique.

Includes a library inventory description of a lost manuscript that began with *Lyon* [39].

Perle, George.

1948. "Integrative Devices in the Music of Machaut." *Musical Quarterly* 34: 169–76.

A respected twentieth-century composer finds analogies between the motivic, harmonic, and rhythmic unifying elements in the music of Machaut and those in the music of Schoenberg. Appreciation of medieval music is only possible in a century that has overthrown traditional tonal harmony. (For some general thoughts on this issue, see Israel-Meyer 1982.) Many examples are cited, including *Quant Theseüs / Ne quier* (B34), the Credo, and several isorhythmic motets.

Petersen, Nils Holger.

1987. *Kristendom i musikken: Sammenhaeng og splittelse i den vestlige musikkultur—Den europaeiske musik belyst i forhold til kristendom gennem centrale historiske perioder* (Christianity in music: coherence and disunion in Western musical culture—European music in the light of Christianity in the major historical periods). Copenhagen: Schønberg.

Machaut's Mass considered in a wide-ranging history of music and theology. Not examined. Abstract: *RILM* 21 (1987), no. 9811.

Petit de Julleville, Louis.

1892–93. "La poésie lyrique au XIVe siècle. Guillaume de Machaut." *Revue des cours et conférences* 1:194–200, 289–96, 330–37, 429–34.

Actually concerns narrative, not lyric, poetry. The first installment has a biography of Machaut up to the time of his service to John of Bohemia; the second continues the biography, with a discussion of *Jugement Behaingne*, *Jugement Navarre*, and *Confort*; the third concerns the *Voir Dit*; the fourth concerns the *Prise*. Displays very little sympathy for Machaut's poetry.

1896. "Les derniers poètes du Moyen Age." Chap. 7 of *Histoire de la langue et de la littérature française des origines à 1900*, ed. L. Petit de Julleville. Vol. 2, *Moyen Age (des origines à 1500), deuxième partie*. Paris: Colin. Reprint. Nendeln, Liechtenstein: Kraus, 1975.

Based on Petit de Julleville 1892–93. Discussion of *Jugement Navarre, Confort, Prise*, and especially *Voir Dit*, with some interesting comments on the lack of appeal of Machaut's poetry for the late nineteenth century (338–43); short bibliography (397–98).

Phillips, Helen, ed.
1982. *Chaucer: The Book of the Duchess*. Durham and St. Andrews Medieval Texts 3. Durham: Department of English Language and Medieval Literature; St. Andrews: Department of English.

The edition includes a general introduction to the Machaut *dits* (19–27). An appendix gives comparative passages with translations from *Jugement Behaingne* (170–76), *Remede* (176–80), *Lyon* (180–81), and *Fonteinne* (181–84).

Phillipps.
1968. *The Phillipps Manuscripts: Catalogus librorum manuscriptorum in bibliotheca D. Thomæ Phillipps, bt. Impressum typis medio-montanis 1837–1871*. With an introduction by A.N.L. Munby. London: Holland.

Includes mention of MS **Kr** [36] (p. 100).

Piaget, Arthur.
1892. "Michaut pour Machaut." *Romania* 21:616–17.

Clears up confusion concerning some references to Michault Taillevent (1390/95–ca. 1458) that had been taken as references to Machaut.

1905. "La *Belle Dame Sans Merci* et ses imitations." *Romania* 34:559–602.

A rondeau on the last flyleaf of a Chartier manuscript described here recalls the language of a bergerette inscribed in Machaut MS **W** [2].

1941 (ed.). *Oton de Grandson. Sa vie et ses poésies*. Mémoires et Documents publiés par la Société d'Histoire de la Suisse Romande 3/1. Lausanne: Payot.

Includes editions of *Fueille ne flour* (Lo18; ed. 288), *Gent corps, faitis* (Lo5=VD42; ed. 290–91), *Hé! gentilz cuers* (Lo37; ed. 289), *Je ne fine nuit* (Lo40; ed. 294), *Je ne sui pas* (Lo11; ed. 292–93), *Las! amours* (Lo52; ed. 297–98), *Loing de vous* (Lo30; ed. 299), *Riens ne me puet* (Lo29; ed. 330), *Se faire sçay* (Lo55; ed. 332), *Se je ne say* (Lo6; ed. 331), all from MS **La** [54].

1968 (ed.). *Martin Le Franc, Le Champion des Dames*. Part I. Mémoires et Documents publiés par la Société d'Histoire de la Suisse Romande 3/8. Lausanne: Payot.

Partial edition; includes one of the passages mentioning Machaut.

Piaget, Arthur, and Eugénie Droz.
1932. "Recherches sur la tradition manuscrite de Villon. I. Le manuscrit de Stockholm." *Romania* 58:238–54.

Inventory and description of MS **Sk** [46].

Picherit, Jean-Louis.
1982. "Les *exemples* dans le *Jugement dou Roy de Navarre* de Guillaume de Machaut." *Lettres romanes* 36:103–16.

Close analysis of *Jugement Navarre* in the context of the examples cited by the debaters.

Pierpont Morgan Library.
1957. *Treasures from the Pierpont Morgan Library. Fiftieth Anniversary Exhibition 1957*. [New York]: Pierpont Morgan Library.

Includes a description of MS **Pm** [18] (p. 20 no. 28).

Pirani, Emma. See Coen Pirani, Emma.

Pirro, André.

1930. "Musiciens allemands et auditeurs français au temps des rois Charles V et Charles VI." *Studien zur Musikgeschichte, Festschrift für Guido Adler zum 75. Geburtstag*, 71–77. Vienna: Universal. Reprint. 1971.

Documents concerning German musicians in the French-speaking orbit. The list of instruments in the *Remede* includes some German instruments (71); discussion of the "rés d'Allemagne" in the *Voir Dit* (71–72).

1940. *Histoire de la musique de la fin du XIVe siècle à la fin du XVIe.* Manuels d'Histoire de l'Art. Paris: Renouard.

The panorama of musical practice offered in the chapter "La musique et la société mondaine" (5–44) mentions Machaut in a variety of contexts.

Pirrotta, Nino.

1955. "Florenz. C. Codex Palatino Panciatichiano 26 (FP)." *MGG* 4:401–5.

Study of MS **FP** [61], with a facsimile of Machaut's *Se vous n'estes* (R7).

1966. "Ars nova." *La musica*. Part 1, *Enciclopedia storica*, ed. Guido M. Gatti and Alberto Basso, 1:188–97. Turin: Unione Tipografico.

Dictionary article, with discussion of Machaut's music (191–93). See Pirrotta 1983.

1983. "Ars nova." *Dizionario enciclopedico universale della musica e dei musicisti*, ed. Alberto Basso, *Il Lessico*, 1:190–96. Turin: UTET.

Dictionary article, mostly reprinted from Pirrotta 1966 (without illustrations).

Plamenac, Dragan.

1951. "Keyboard Music of the 14th Century in Codex Faenza 117." *Journal of the American Musicological Society* 4:179–201, 3 facsimiles.

The first scientific description of the MS **Fa** [67], which includes instrumental arrangements of *Honte, paour* (B25) and *De toutes flours* (B31). Includes a facsimile and edition of the arrangement of B31 (p. 188, ed. 189–90, notes 194).

1972 (ed.). *Keyboard Music of the Late Middle Ages in Codex Faenza 117.* Corpus Mensurabilis Musicae 57. [Rome]: American Institute of Musicology.

Edition of the instrumental arrangements in MS **Fa** [67].

Planche, Alice.

1980. "*Est vrais amans li drois oisiaus de proie...* Sur une image de Guillaume de Machaut." In *Etudes de philologie romane et d'histoire littéraire offertes à Jules Horrent à l'occasion de sa 60e anniversaire*, ed. Jean Marie D'Heur and Nicoletta Cherubini, 351–60. Tournai and Liège: Gedit.

Close study of the image of the true lover as a bird of prey in *Jugement Behaingne*, l. 1097. Includes discussion of passages in *Remede, Alerion, Jugement Navarre*, and *Confort*.

1982. "Le langage poétique de Guillaume de Machaut." In Guillaume de Machaut 1982, 195–214 (discussion, 215–22).

On the qualities of Machaut's poetic language: rich rhymes, long enumerations, the word *rosée* (dew), metaphors; illustrated with many examples.

1990a. "*Une approche de l'infini*: Sur un passage du *Voir Dit* de Guillaume de Machaut. In *Ecrire pour dire: Etudes sur le Dit médiéval*, ed. Bernard Ribémont, 93–108. Sapience 3. Paris: Klincksieck.

Close explication of a long passage in the *Voir Dit*, ll. 8898–977 (ed. P. Paris 1875, 363–66).

1990b. "*Eür, Bon Eür et Bonheur* dans un corpus lyrique du Moyen Age tardif." *L'idée de bonheur au Moyen Age: Actes du Colloque d'Amiens de mars 1984*, ed. Danielle Buschinger, 355–68. Göppinger Arbeiten zur Germanistik 414. Göppingen: Kümmerle.

Vocabulary study; mentions *Esperance* (B13), *On verroit meint* (Lo38), and *Trop se peinne* (Lo164). *Eür* and *Bon Eür* are associated with Fortune in the *Roman de la Rose*, Machaut, Deschamps, and Charles d'Orléans. The modern concept of happiness was expressed by *joie, plaisance, plaisir*, or *liesse*. On "Bonneürté" see also Patch 1927, 40–42.

1990c. "Les neuf soleils." *Razo. Cahiers du Centre d'Etudes Médiévales de Nice* 11: 25–33.

Planche seeks literary sources for a passage in *Fonteinne*.

1993. "Larmes du cœur, larmes du corps, dans quelques textes français en vers des XIVe et XVe siècles." In *Et c'est la fin pour quoy sommes ensemble. Hommage à Jean Dufournet, Professeur à la Sorbonne Nouvelle. Littérature, histoire et langue du Moyen Age*, 3:1133–42. Nouvelle Bibliothèque du Moyen Age 25. 3 vols. Paris: Champion.

Tears and crying in late medieval French poetry, including Machaut's.

Plumley, Yolanda M.

1990. "Style and Structure in the Late Fourteenth-Century Century Chanson." Ph.D. diss. University of Exeter.

Not examined. Abstract: *Index to Theses* 40/4 (1991): 1601 no. 40-7366.

Plummer, John.

1959. *Manuscripts from the William S. Glazier Collection*. New York: Pierpont Morgan Library.

Description of *US:NYpm Glazier G.52*, a manuscript related to Machaut MS C (21–22 no. 29 and plate 25). See Avril 1973, 99 n. 1, 100 n. 2.

Poirion, Daniel.

1963. Review of Guiette 1960 (*Questions de littérature*). *Revue belge de philologie et d'histoire* 41:537–40.

Discussion of the development of poetry in the fourteenth and fifteenth centuries.

1965. *Le poète et le prince. L'évolution du lyrisme courtois de Guillaume de Machaut à Charles d'Orléans*. Université de Grenoble, Publications de la Faculté des lettres et sciences humaines 35. Paris: Presses Universitaires de France. Reprint. Geneva: Slatkine, 1978.

Important study of lyric poetry in the fourteenth and early fifteenth century in the context of the French courts. Machaut, Froissart, Deschamps, Christine, Chartier, and Charles d'Orléans are treated in detail, as well as several lesser figures such as Jean de Garencières and Oton de Granson. Analyses of forms, metrics, and poetics. Wide-ranging bibliography, but lacks an index. Abstract: *Annales de l'Université de Paris* 36 (1966): 394–96. Reviews: Joan Crow, *French Studies* 20 (1966): 285–87; Alfred Foulet, *Romanic Review* 59 (1968): 123–25; Lionel J. Friedman, *Romance Philology* 24 (1970–71): 230–36 (corrections); P. Le Gentil, *Romania* 88 (1967): 548–57; Robert Guiette, *Revue belge de philologie et d'histoire* 46 (1968): 533–35; Pierre Jodogne, *Studi francesi* 10 (1966): 296–99; A. Micha, *Information littéraire* 18 (1966): 75–76; J.C. Payen, *Moyen Age* 74 (1968): 133–42; Matthias Waltz, *Deutsche Literaturzeitung* 91 (1970): 594–97.

1971. *Le Moyen Age. II: 1300–1480*. Littérature française 2. Paris: Arthaud.

A survey of French literature in the late Middle Ages. Machaut discussed on pp. 49–51, 55, 60–63, 191–96; includes facsimiles of *S'Amours ne fait* (B1; MS A), and miniatures A2 (see chap. 4.4a), A83–85 (chap. 4.4i), and A150 (chap. 4.4m). Reviews: K. Baldinger, *Zeitschrift für romanische Philologie* 87 (1971): 653–54; Robert Deschaux, *Recherches et Travaux* 5 (Mar. 1972): 76–81; Robert Guiette, *Revue belge de philologie et d'histoire* 50 (1972): 1249–50; Luigi Losito, *Cultura française* 19 (1972): 111; M. Marnat, *Magazine littéraire* 60 (Jan. 1972): 45; René Rancœur, *Bulletin des bibliothèques de France / Bulletin de documentation bibliographique* 17 (1972): *357–*358; A. Slerca, *Studi francesi* 20 (1976): 588; H. Sonneville, *Lettres romanes* 33 (1979): 214–15; J. Wathelet-Willem, *Marche romane* 20/4 (1970): 144–45.

1978. "The Imaginary Universe of Guillaume de Machaut." In Cosman 1978, 199–206.

Relationships and analogies between music, poetry, and the fourteenth-century view of the universe. Machaut's poetic language is illustrated with many examples from lyrical and narrative texts. French version in Poirion 1982.

1980. "Traditions et fonctions du *dit poétique* au XIVe et au XVe siècle." In *Literatur in der Gesellschaft des Spätmittelalters,* ed. Hans Ulrich Gumbrecht, 147–50. Grundriss der romanischen Literaturen des Mittelalters. Begleitreihe zum GRLMA 1. Heidelberg: Winter.

Typology and definition of the *dit.*

1982. "Le monde imaginaire de Guillaume de Machaut." In Guillaume de Machaut 1982, 223–34.

French version of Poirion 1978, with a new introduction and ending.

1983 (ed.). *Précis de littérature française du Moyen Age.* Paris: Presses Universitaires de France.

Survey. See Cerquiglini 1983.

1988a. "L'épanouissement d'un style: Le gothique littéraire à la fin du Moyen Age." In Poirion 1988b, 29–44.

Broad consideration of the context of literary history in the fourteenth and fifteenth centuries, with discussion of political history, centers of activity, rhetoric, the new poetics of lyrics without music, the textuality of citation and compilation, and realism.

1988b (ed.). *La littérature française aux XIVe et XVe siècles.* Vol. 1, *Partie historique.* Grundriss der romanischen Literatur des Mittelalters, 8/1. Heidelberg: Winter.

See Badel 1988; Cerquiglini 1988a; 1988b; Deschaux 1988; Heger 1988; Poirion 1988a.

1990. "Les tombeaux allégoriques et la poétique de l'inscription dans le *Livre du Cuer d'Amours Espris,* de René d'Anjou (1457)." *Académie des Inscriptions et Belles-Lettres. Comptes rendus des séances de l'année 1990,* fasc. 2, 321–34.

Includes some remarks on René d'Anjou's description of the tomb of Machaut.

Porcher, Jean.

1959. *L'enluminure française.* Paris: Arts et métiers graphiques. *French Miniatures from Illuminated Manuscripts,* trans. Julian Brown. London: Collins, 1960. *Medieval French Miniatures,* trans. Julian Brown. New York: Abrams, [1960]. *Französische Buchmalerei,* trans. Peter Ronge. Recklinghausen: Bongers, 1959.

Includes reproduction of *Prologue* miniature A2 (plate 56, discussed p. 56 in English editions).

Powell, Newman W.

1979. "Fibonacci and the Gold Mean: Rabbits, Rumbas, and Rondeaux." *Journal of Music Theory* 23:227–73.

Includes a study of numerological relationships and symmetry in *S'il estoit / S'Amours* (M6), building on the analysis of Gombosi (1950, 220–21); briefly considers *Tant doucement me sens* (R9). See comments in Koehler 1990, 73.

Preston, Raymond.

1951. "Chaucer and the *Ballades notées* of Guillaume de Machaut." *Speculum* 26:615–23.

Musical elements of Machaut's poetry, with some discussion of Machaut songs, especially *De toutes flours* (B31) and *Se pour ce muir* (B36).

1952. *Chaucer.* London and New York: Sheed and Ward. Reprint. New York: Greenwood, 1969.

Includes an edition in piano score of *De toutes flours* (B31) (facing p. 18).

Prioult, A.
   1950. "Un Poète voyageur: Guillaume de Machaut et la *Reise* de Jean
   l'Aveugle, roi de Bohême, en 1328–1329." *Lettres romanes* 4:3–29.
   Machaut's description of John of Luxembourg's Lithuanian campaign.

Prisor, Lothar.
   1971. "Die Motette in der Frühzeit der Ars Nova." Inaugural-dissertation,
   Albert-Ludwig-Universität, Freiburg im Briesgau. Freiburg: n.p.
   Detailed analyses of the fourteen motets attributed by Schrade (1956a) to Vitry. Comparative material drawn from Machaut in the discussion of combining binary and ternary
   rhythms (97–110, 143–47); discussion of Machaut's four-voice motets (197–210).

Professione, Alfonso.
   1967. *Inventario dei manoscritti della Biblioteca Capitolare di Ivrea*. Rev. ed.
   by Ilo Vignono. Alba: Domenicale.
   Includes facsimiles of MS **Iv** [57] (plates 4–5, discussed p. 86).

Prunières, Henry.
   1943. *A New History of Music: The Middle Ages to Mozart*, trans. Edward
   Lockspeiser with an introduction by Romain Rolland. London: Dent; New
   York: Macmillan. Reprint in two vols. New York: Vienna House, 1972.
   Originally *Nouvelle histoire de la musique*. Paris: Rieder, 1934–36.
   Includes an edition and discussion of an excerpt from *Un mortel lay* (L12/8) (1:118).

Pryer, Anthony.
   1977. "Guillaume de Machaut, circa 1300–1377." *Music and Musicians* 25/9
   (May): 26–30.
   Good popular survey of Machaut's life and music.

   1983. "Machaut [Machault], Guillaume de." *The New Oxford Companion to
   Music*, ed. Denis Arnold. Vol. 2, *K–Z*. Oxford and New York: Oxford
   University Press.
   Dictionary article.

Pugh, Annie Reese.
   1894. *"Le Jugement du Roy de Behaigne* de Guillaume de Machaut et le *Dit
   de Poissy* de Christine de Pisan." *Romania* 23:581–86.
   Pioneering study of the literary relationship between *Jugement Behaingne* and Christine's
   Dit de Poissy. Also suggests a relationship between Christine's *Livre du Duc des Vrais
   Amans* and Machaut's *Voir Dit*.

Pulido, Alejandro.
   1991. "Machaut's Ballade *Tres douce dame*: An Interdisciplinary Approach."
   Sonus 12: 45–65.
   Thorough analysis of B24, with voice leading reduction. Engages in various manipu-
   lations in an attempt to give some significance to the Fibonacci series and Golden
   Section in relation to this work.

Pulido, Esperanza.
   1978a. "Guillaume de Machault." *Heterofonia* 11/1 (Jan.–Feb., no. 58): 19–
   22, 27–29.
   Brief overview of Machaut's biography and literary works, based on Machabey 1955b.

   1978b. "Guillaume de Machault, fuentes de su obra musical." *Heterofonia*
   11/2 (Mar.–Apr., no. 59): 10–15 (summary in English, 47).
   Very basic introduction to Machaut's musical works, based on Machabey 1955b.

Pustejovsky, Otfrid.
   1975. *Schlesiens Übergang an die bömische Krone: Machtpolitik Böhmens
   im Zeichen von Herrschaft und Frieden*. Forschungen und Quellen zur
   Kirchen- und Kulturgeschichte Ostdeutschlands 13. Cologne: Böhlau.
   Political history relevant to John of Luxembourg.

Puymaigre, Comte de.

1887. "Une campagne de Jean de Luxembourg, roi de Bohême." *Revue des questions historiques* 42:168–80.

A study of a military campaign of John of Luxembourg during which Machaut was present.

1892. "Jean l'Aveugle en France." *Revue des questions historiques* 52:391–452.

Historical study of John of Luxembourg; includes mention of Machaut's *Jugement Behaingne*.

Pycke, Jacques.

1986. *Le chapitre cathédral Notre-Dame de Tournai de la fin du XIe à la fin du XIIIe siècle: Son organisation, sa vie, ses membres.* Université de Louvain Recueil de Travaux d'Histoire et de Philologie 6/30. Louvain-la-Neuve: Collège Erasme; Brussels: Nauwelaerts.

A model study of the cathedral chapter and canons at Tournai, useful in lieu of a similar study of the cathedral of Reims. See also Millet 1982.

Queux de Saint-Hillaire, A[uguste Henry Edouard, marquis de], and Gaston Raynaud, eds.

1878–1903. *Œuvres complètes d'Eustache Deschamps.* Vols. 1–5 ed. Le Marquis de Queux de Saint-Hillaire. Vols. 6–11 ed. Gaston Raynaud. Société des Anciens Textes Français 10. Paris: Firmin-Didot. Reprint. New York: Johnson, 1966.

Standard edition of the works of Deschamps. Vol. 10 includes editions of Machaut's *Douce dame, vo maniere* (Lo65), *Plourez, dames* (Lo229=B32), *Mes esperis* (Lo258= B39), and *Jugez, amans* (LoA20); on Raynaud's misattribution of these works to Machaut, see Arthur Piaget, "Note sur le tome X des œuvres complètes d'Eustache Deschamps," *Bulletin de la Société des Anciens Textes Français* 28 (1902): 64–67.

Quicherat, Jules, et al.

1872. *Catalogue général des manuscrits des bibliothèques publiques des départements.* Vol. 4, *Arras, Avranches, Boulogne.* Paris: Imprimerie Nationale.

Catalogue description of MS **Ar** [32] (pp. 235–36).

Quittard, Henri.

1917–19. "Notes sur Guillaume de Machaut et son œuvre." *Revue de musicologie* 1:91–105, 123–38.

Discussion of extracts of the *Voir Dit* that are important for music. Also includes an interesting early discussion of instruments, the *carole*, Boccaccio and music, and performance practices. Ludwig (1926–54, 1:39, 92, 96) mentions editions of *Tels rit* (RF2), *Nes qu'on* (B33), and *De tout sui* (V38/32) after p. 138; these were lacking in the exemplar examined.

RILM.

1967–. *RILM Abstracts of Music Literature,* ed. Barry S. Brook. Répertoire Internationale de la Littérature Musicale. International Repertory of Music Literature. New York: RILM Abstracts.

Standard bibliography and abstract service for music history.

RISM.

1969. *Manuscripts of Polyphonic Music (c. 1320–1400),* ed. Gilbert Reaney. Répertoire Internationale des Sources Musicales. International Inventory of Musical Sources, Ser. B IV². Munich: Henle.

Standard manuscript inventory, with musical incipits and bibliography. This volume includes the main Machaut manuscripts and many of the anthology manuscripts. Review: Ernest Sanders, *Music and Letters* 51 (1970): 458–59.

1972. *Handschriften mit mehrstimmiger Musik des 14., 15. und 16. Jahrhunderts*, ed. Kurt von Fischer and Max Lütolf. 2 vols. Répertoire Internationale des Sources Musicales. International Inventory of Musical Sources, Ser. B IV3–4. Munich and Duisberg: Henle.

Standard manuscript inventory, with musical incipits and bibliography. These volumes include many anthology manuscripts that contain works of Machaut. Reviews: Charles Hamm, *Journal of the American Musicological Society* 27 (1974): 518–22; Jaromír Černý, *Hudebni Veda* 11 (1974): 293–97.

1992. *The Theory of Music*. Vol. 4, *Manuscripts from the Carolingian Era up to ca. 1500 in Great Britain and in the United States of America: Descriptive Catalogue*, ed. Christian Meyer, Michel Huglo, and Nancy C. Phillips. Répertoire Internationale des Sources Musicales. International Inventory of Musical Sources. Munich: Henle.

Includes a description of the anonymous Pennsylvania/Schloss Harburg treatise (174–75).

1993. *Manuscripts of Polyphonic Music. Supplement 1 to RISM B IV1–2. The British Isles, 1100–1400*, ed. Andrew Wathey. Répertoire Internationale des Sources Musicales. International Inventory of Musical Sources, Ser. B IV1–2 Suppl. 1. Munich: Henle.

Includes a description of Machaut MS **W** [2] and a facsimile of the one surviving fragment of music, the first verso of the motet section (4–6, 101 plate 1).

Raynaud, Gaston.

1903. *"Le Dit du Hardi Cheval." Romania* 32:586–87.

Edition of a 60-line work that Raynaud relates to Machaut's *Tu qui vues* (Cp8). Review: P. Meyer, *Romania* 41 (1912): 90–94.

1909. Review of Chichmaref 1909. *Romania* 38:461–62.

Includes important corrections and some additional material on *Pas de tor* (B30).

Reaney, Gilbert. Reaney's many writings on Machaut call for an orientation by subject matter. Surveys and dictionary articles include 1952a, 1960a, 1960b, 1960d, 1961, 1971 (monograph), 1980a, and 1980c. On chronology, see 1952b and 1967. On the general development of the fixed forms, see 1952c, 1958a, and 1962. On Machaut's chansons in particular, see 1955, 1955–56, 1958b, and 1959b. On Machaut's contrapuntal practice ("harmony"), see 1953 and 1968. On *musica ficta*, see 1955 and 1959a. On mode, see 1963 and 1982. On performance practice, see 1954c, 1956, 1957, 1966, and 1977.

1951–52. "The Ballades, Rondeaux and Virelais Set to Music by Guillaume de Machaut." M.A. thesis, University of Sheffield.

Not examined.

1952a. *Chanson*. Part 1, *Die Chanson, mehrst., von den Anfängen bis etwa 1420*. In *MGG* 2:1034–46.

Survey; on Machaut's chansons, see esp. 1039–41.

1952b. "A Chronology of the Ballades, Rondeaux and Virelais Set to Music by Guillaume de Machaut." *Musica disciplina* 6:33–38.

An early look at Hoepffner's chronology of the *dits* and what this suggests for a chronology of the musical works. The dates of the *Remede* (before 1349), *Voir Dit* (ca. 1365), and the corpus of MS **Vg** (1365–69) are the pillars of Reaney's chronology.

1952c. "Concerning the Origins of the Rondeau, Virelai and Ballade Forms." *Musica disciplina* 6:155–66.

This article deals with the earliest development of the fixed forms, reviewing several theories of origin (Jeanroy, Gennrich, Verrier, Spanke, and theories of Arabic origin). Only peripheral mention of Machaut.

1953. "Fourteenth Century Harmony and the Ballades, Rondeaux and Virelais of Guillaume de Machaut." *Musica disciplina* 7:129–46.

"Harmony" here means dissonance treatment and counterpoint. The basic structure of Machaut's songs is consonant, although the surface may exhibit dissonances in *cantus fractabilis* or in "displacement technique." Cites many examples, with discussion of cadences, dissonances produced by Machaut's typical melodic figures, and citations of theorists. Mentioned in Hirshberg 1971, 91–98.

1954a. "Franciscus." In *MGG* 3:634–36.

Discussion of an important musical follower of Machaut, whose compositions show "the most exact imitations of Machaut's style that we know." Includes a motivic analysis of *Phiton Phiton*, a ballade that takes Machaut's *Phyton* (B38) as its point of departure.

1954b. "The Manuscript Chantilly, Musée Condé 1047." *Musica disciplina* 8:59–113 (*errata* on unnumbered page preceding 59). "A Postscript to 'The Manuscript Chantilly, Musée Condé 1047.'" *Musica disciplina* 10 (1956): 55–59.

Inventory and study of the MS **Ch** [59]. Correction in Günther 1957, 11 n. 55 from notes in the Nachlass Ludwig.

1954c. "Voices and Instruments in the Music of Guillaume de Machaut." *Bericht über den internationalen Musikwissenschaftlichen Kongress Bamberg 1953*, ed. Wilfried Brennecke et al., 245–48. Gesellschaft für Musikforschung. Kassel: Bärenreiter.

Considers evidence for performance with voices or instruments.

1955. "The Ballades, Rondeaux and Virelais of Guillaume de Machaut: Melody, Rhythm and Form." *Acta musicologica* 27:40–58.

Discusses melodic and rhythmic motives, and *musica ficta* in Machaut's songs. Many examples are cited, especially *Quant Theseüs / Ne quier* (B34) and *Plus dure* (V31/28), with the first correct edition of *Sans cuer m'en / Amis / Dame* (B17).

1955–56. "The *Lais* of Guillaume de Machaut and Their Background." *Proceedings of the Royal Musical Association* 82:15–31 (discussion, 31–32).

Consideration of the lai and descort before the fourteenth century, the four *Roman de Fauvel* lais, and the Machaut lais. Discusses poetry, musical meter, melody and motives, tonality, and "modulation." Cites many examples from Machaut's lais (23–31).

1956. "Voices and Instruments in the Music of Guillaume de Machaut." *Revue belge de musicologie* 10:3–17, 93–104.

Review of the evidence for performance with voices or instruments, discussion of instruments, and suggestions for scoring, including experimentation with heterophonic instrumental doubling of the cantus voice, a practice heard in some recordings of Machaut's music. Reaney's principle of contrasting timbres demands realization with a variety of instruments, and was until recently the rule in performances of chansons. "It seems unlikely that much 14th century music was for voices only..." (99) is a conclusion quite the opposite of current views. See discussion in Page 1990, 92.

1957. "Medieval Music on the Gramophone." *Music and Letters* 38:180–90.

A survey of all recordings of medieval music available in England in 1957. For Machaut, see 181–82, 184–85, 187.

1958a. "Concerning the Origins of the Medieval Lai." *Music and Letters* 39:343–46.

Summary of literature on origins of the lai, with brief mention of Machaut (346).

1958b. "Guillaume de Machaut: Lyric Poet." *Music and Letters* 39:38–51.

Early consideration of themes and style in Machaut's lyric poetry. The examples are drawn mostly from those poems set to music. Includes a typology of themes in the lyrics, citing many works.

1958c. "Machaut's Influence on Late Medieval Music. I. France and Burgundy. II. The non-Gallic Countries." *Monthly Musical Record* 88:50–58, 96–101.

Influence of Machaut on composers in France, Burgundy, Poland, Cyprus, Spain, Italy, England, and Germany.

1959a. "Musica ficta in the Works of Guillaume de Machaut." In Wégimont 1959, 196–203 (discussion, 203–13).

Remarks on *musica ficta* in Machaut, citing several examples. Reaney assumes that mode operates in polyphony, and that it is not masked by the application of *ficta*, a view questioned in the discussion especially by Pirrotta, whose comments anticipate the most recent views on the issue of mode and polyphony.

1959b. "The Poetic Form of Machaut's Musical Works: I. The Ballades, Rondeaux and Virelais." *Musica disciplina* 13:25–41.

Analysis of literary aspects—form and rhyme—of the ballades, rondeaux, and virelais set to music, citing many examples. The analytical table of syllable count does not distinguish feminine endings.

1960a. "Ars Nova." In *The Pelican History of Music.* Vol. 1, *Ancient Forms to Polyphony*, ed. Alec Robertson and Denis Stevens, 259–319. Harmondsworth (Middlesex); Baltimore: Penguin Books.

General historical comments, an introduction to important sources, and a survey of music in France, Italy, England, and other countries. On the Ars Nova in France, see esp. 261–90; Machaut discussed esp. 269–70, 276–83, and 285–88.

1960b. "Ars Nova in France." In *The New Oxford History of Music.* Vol. 3, *Ars Nova and the Renaissance, 1300–1540,* ed. Dom Anselm Hughes and Gerald Abraham, 1–30. London: Oxford University Press.

An excellent survey of Ars Nova styles and composers, with a discussion of Machaut (15–29).

1960c. "The Manuscript Paris, Bibliothèque Nationale, fonds italien 568 (*Pit*)." *Musica disciplina* 14:33–63.

Description and inventory of MS Pit [64].

1960d. "The Middle Ages." In *A History of Song,* ed. Denis Stevens, 15–64. London: Hutchinson, 1960; New York: Norton, 1961.

Survey of monophonic music (Latin secular song, troubadours and trouvères, Minnesinger, and Spanish, Italian, and English song), and polyphony (thirteenth-century motet, fourteenth-century France and Italy). Discusses Machaut's monophonic works (31–33); and his polyphonic works (46–50).

1961. "Machaut (Machault) Guillaume de." In *Encyclopédie de la musique,* ed. François Michel, François Lesure, and Vladimir Fédorov, 3:122–26. Paris: Fasquelle.

Dictionary article with biography and survey of music. Includes reproductions of miniatures A2 (see chap. 4.4a) and E31 (chap. 4.4s), and MS G fol. 131v (Sanctus tr. and mot.).

1962. "The Development of the Rondeau, Virelai and Ballade Forms from Adam de la Hale to Guillaume de Machaut." In *Festgabe Karl Gustav Fellerer zum sechzigsten Geburtstag am 7. Juli 1962,* ed. Heinrich Hüschen, 421–27. Regensberg: Bosse.

A summary of the important work of Hoepffner (1910, 1911, 1920a, 1920b) on the development of the fixed forms.

1963. "Modes in the Fourteenth Century, in Particular in the Music of Guillaume de Machaut." In *Organicae voces: Festschrift Joseph Smits van Waesberghe,* ed. Pieter Fischer, 137–43. Amsterdam, Institute for Medieval Music.

An account of modality in Machaut's polyphony; accepts without question the application of modal theory—including Ionian mode—to Machaut. All is described in anachronistic terminology, and the concept of "mode" is reduced essentially to major and minor keys. Cites many examples. See criticisms in Hirshberg 1971, chap. 9 passim; 1980, 19–20; Fuller 1986, 69–70 n. 54; 1987a, 57–58 n. 22.

1965. "New Sources of *Ars Nova* Music." *Musica disciplina* 19:53–67.
Includes descriptions of MSS **Utr** [69] and **Nur** [71].

1966. "The Performance of Medieval Music." *Aspects of Medieval and Renaissance Music: A Birthday Offering to Gustave Reese*, ed. Jan LaRue, 704–22. New York: Norton. Corrected reprint. New York: Pendragon, 1978.
Musical performance practice with voices and instruments, covering a much wider chronological span than Reaney 1956. Also considers heterophonic treatment of voices, with discussion of a curious performance score of the Mass employing heterophony, prepared by Reaney in 1958 (719–21).

1967. "Towards a Chronology of Machaut's Musical Works." *Musica disciplina* 21:87–96.
A complement to Günther 1963a; includes specific dates for individual works interpolated in the *Voir Dit* (after Machabey 1955b), and a discussion of some stylistic features that bear on chronology. The largest difficulty with the chronological table (95; also reproduced in Reaney 1971, 74) is the placement of the first twenty motets in the range 1349–63, due to a misunderstanding of Günther 1963a.

1968. "Notes on the Harmonic Technique of Guillaume de Machaut." In *Essays in Musicology: A Birthday Offering for Willi Apel*, ed. Hans Tischler, 63–68. Bloomington: Indiana University School of Music.
Analysis of counterpoint and dissonance technique in *Biauté qui* (B4), *De petit po* (B18), and *Quant Theseüs / Ne quier* (B34). Criticism in Dahlhaus 1982, 289. Abstract: *RILM* 2 (1968), no. 194.

1971. *Guillaume de Machaut*. Oxford Studies of Composers 9. London: Oxford University Press.
Summary biography, and a survey of Machaut's music, with many musical examples. After a survey of genres and musical techniques—melody and harmony—chapters are devoted to forms: lais and virelais, ballades and rondeaux, motets, Mass and *Hoquetus David*. The conclusion considers Adam de la Halle and Philippe de Vitry. Abstract: *RILM* 8 (1974), no. 1865. Reviews: *Church Music* (London) 3 (1972): 26; *Music Teacher and Piano Student* 51 (1972): 27; *TLS* no. 3653 (3 Mar. 1972): 253; Luigi Bellingardi, *Nuova rivista musicale italiana* 8 (1974): 313–14; Margaret Bent, *Musical Times* 113 (1972): 155; Wolfgang Dömling, *Musikforschung* 27 (1974): 264–65; David Epps, *Music in Education* 36 (1972): 140; Hans Eppstein, *Svensk tidskrift för musikforskning* 54 (1972): 142; Ursula Günther, *Revue de musicologie* 59 (1973): 128–29; John Hind, *Australian Journal of Music Education* 10 (Apr. 1972): 59; Hans Hollander, *Neue Zeitschrift für Musik* 133 (1972): 483–84; David G. Hughes, *Speculum* 49 (1974): 142–43; Nicholas Sandon, *Music and Musicians* 20/5 (Jan. 1972): 45; Sarah Jane Williams, *Notes* 29 (1972–73): 244–45.

1977. "The Part Played by Instruments in the Music of Guillaume de Machaut." *Studi musicali* 6:3–11.
Urges a variety of performance options in realizing medieval music, including instruments, instrumental arrangements, and all-vocal performance with text adapted to the lower voices.

1980a. "Machaut [Machau, Machaud, Machault], Guillaume de [Guillelmus de Machaudio]." *New Grove*, 11:428–36.
Survey, with brief biography; especially useful for Machaut's musical style.

1980b. "Philippus de Caserta." *New Grove* 14:653–54.
Includes material on textual borrowings from Machaut.

1980c. "Sources, MS, §VII, 2." *New Grove* 17:661–63.
A brief description of the main Machaut manuscripts. Does not incorporate Avril's revisions in their chronology (Avril 1973 and 1978).

1982. "La tonalité des ballades et des rondeaux de Guillaume de Machaut." In Guillaume de Machaut 1982, 295–300.
Begins by applying the Berkeley theory treatise—a witness to mode in secular polyphony—to Machaut but soon returns to the modal classification of Reaney 1963.

1984. "A Consideration of the Relative Importance of Words and Music in Composition from the 13th to the 15th Century." In Günther/Finscher 1984, 175–95.
Importance of text as opposed to music in several medieval genres, including *estampie* (*ductia, note*), lai, conductus, and in *contrafacta*. Discusses formal musical procedures such as canon, and compositional procedures in the motet, including secular tenors in Machaut. Abstract: *RILM* 18 (1984), no. 1287.

Reaney, Gilbert, André Gilles and Jean Maillard, eds.
1964. *Philippi de Vitriaco: Ars nova.* Corpus Scriptorum de Musica 8. [Rome]: American Institute of Musicology.
The version of the *Ars nova* treatise in *F:Pn 14741* cites *Qui es / Ha! Fortune* (M8).

Reckow, Fritz.
1972. "Rondellus / rondeau, rota." *Handwörterbuch der musikalischen Terminologie*, ed. Hans Heinrich Eggebrecht. Wiesbaden: Steiner, 1971–. 7 pp.
Detailed study of the history and meaning of the term "rondeau" from the thirteenth until the fifteenth century. Many quotations from primary witnesses and a large bibliography. Does not directly address Machaut.

Reese, Gustave.
1940. *Music in the Middle Ages.* New York: Norton; London: Dent.
Excellent survey of medieval music, with extensive bibliography, though now far out of date. Machaut discussed on pp. 347–58.

Reichert, Georg.
1956. "Das Verhältnis zwischen musikalischer und textlicher Struktur in den Motetten Machauts." *Archiv für Musikwissenschaft* 13:197–216.
A study of the fundamental importance of the text for the analysis of Machaut's motets, with ramifications for the isorhythmic motets of Vitry and the *anonymi* of the fourteenth century (see Günther 1961 and Leech-Wilkinson 1989). Most Machaut motets exhibit a systematic relationship between the formal structure of the text and isorhythmic articulation (*talea*). Fourteen of twenty isorhythmic motets show parallelism between strophe and *talea* in both voices; only three motets show no correlation in either voice (*Tous corps / De* [M2], *Hé! Mors / Fine* [M3], and *Aucune gent / Qui plus* [M5]). Discusses three complications: (1) "Phasendifferenz" ("staggered phrasing" in Sanders 1973, 562; "phrase overlap" in Leech-Wilkinson 1989), in which text strophes or groups of lines in triplum or motetus fall a little before or after the boundary of the *talea* (a textual mirror of the overlapping musical phrases); (2) the effect of diminution sections on the correspondence of text and *talea* structure; and (3) the shortening of the final *talea*. Also considers hocket passages and melodic parallels, and gives text forms for all triplum and motetus voices. Comments and criticism in Clarkson 1971, 155; Sanders 1973, 562–63; Leech-Wilkinson 1989, 11; Koehler 1990, 1:105–6.

1962. "Tonart und Tonalität in der älteren Musik." In *Die Natur der Musik als Problem der Wissenschaft*, 97–104. Musikalische Zeitfragen 10. Kassel and Basel: Bärenreiter.
Thoughts on the many applications of "tonality" and tonal organization in Gregorian chant, Machaut ballades, Dufay songs, and in music of the sixteenth century. The variety is partly due to the personal idiosyncrasies of composers, and one should not try to seek dogmatically a single "correct" system. Provides an interesting viewpoint from a time

when scholars often sought precursors of dominant-tonic tonality in Machaut, or anachronistically applied aspects of the church modes to his music.

Ribémont, Bernard.

1990. "Avant-propos." In *Ecrire pour dire: Etudes sur le dit médiéval,* ed. Bernard Ribémont. Sapience 3. Paris: Klincksieck.

On the definition of *dit.*

1992. "Le cheval et le poète. Hippiatrie et écriture: L'exemple de Guillaume de Machaut, de Jean Froissart et du *Dit du hardi cheval.*" In *Le cheval dans le monde médiévale,* 511–25. Senefiance 32. Aix-en-Provence: C.U.E.R. M.A.

Includes discussion of *Tu qui vues* (Cp8) and related works.

Ricci, Seymour de, and W.J. Wilson.

1937. *Census of Medieval and Renaissance Manuscripts in the United States and Canada.* Vol. 2, *Michigan to Canada.* New York: Wilson. Reprint. New York: Kraus, 1961.

Description of MS **Pm** [18] (p. 1440 no. 396). See also Faye/Bond 1962.

Riemann, Hugo.

1905. *Handbuch der Musikgeschichte.* Vol. 1/2, *Die Musik des Mittelalters (bis 1450).* Leipzig: Breitkopf & Härtel. 2nd ed., revised by Alfred Einstein. Leipzig: Breitkopf & Härtel, 1920–23. 2 vols. in 4. Reprint. New York: Johnson Reprint, 1972.

Discusses proportions in *Felix virgo / Inviolata* (M23), with an edition and discussion of *S'amours ne fait* (B1) and *Ma fin* (R14) after Wolf 1904 (336–41). "One must be warned against overestimating Machault as a composer. Nor is Machault a representative of the Ars Nova (in the sense of a contrapuntal compositional technique cleaned of the dross of organal style). Wolf has thankfully incorporated a rather large number of musical pieces by him in his *Geschichte der Mensuralnotation....* The majority of these pieces, however, teem with parallel voice leading of the worst sort as well as from all sorts of other archaisms" (336–37).

1906. *Hausmusik aus alter Zeit. Intime Gesänge mit Instrumental-Begleitung aus dem 14. bis 15. Jahrh. in ihrer Originalgestalt.* 3 vols. in 1. Leipzig: Breitkopf & Härtel.

Includes an edition of *De toutes flours* (B31) (no. 3).

1912 (ed.). *Musikgeschichte in Beispielen. Eine Auswahl von 150 Tonsätzen, geistliche und weltliche Gesänge und Instrumentalkompositionen zur Veranschaulichung der Entwicklung der Musik im 13.–18. Jahrhundert. In Notierung auf 2 Systemen von Dr. Hugo Riemann. Mit Erläuterungen von Dr. Arnold Schering.* Leipzig: Seemann.

Includes an edition of *Plourez, dames* (B32) (pp. 4–5 no. 4; commentary, p. 2).

Rigoley de Juvigny, [Jean Antoine], ed.

1773. *Les bibliothéques françoises de La Croix du Maine et de Du Verdier, sieur de Vauprivas. Nouvelle Edition, dediée au Roi....* 6 vols. Paris: Saillant & Nyon.

Eighteenth-century revision of the sixteenth-century reference books of La Croix du Maine and Du Verdier. Repeats Du Verdier's brief notice on Machaut (4:106), with an additional note by Bernard de la Monnoye reporting that among the epitaphs in the cemetery of the *ospital d'Amours* in the *Livre du Cuer d'Amours Espris* is that of Machaut, and giving the first two verses: "Guillaume de Machault, ainsi avoie nom. / Né en Champagne fus, et si eus grand renom" (see chap. 2.3.2e). He also reports mention of a Machaut manuscript in Philippe Labbe, *Nova bibliotheca mss. librorum* (Paris, 1653), 312 and 314.

Ripin, Edwin M.
  1975. "Towards an Identification of the Chekker." *Galpin Society Journal* 28: 11–25.
  Identifies the chekker as a clavichord. An appendix gives thirty-one references to the term from the fourteenth through the sixteenth centuries, including Machaut's *Prise* (15). Abstract: *RILM* 9 (1975), no. 2441. See Page 1979

Riquer, Martí de.
  1951 (ed.). *Andreu Febrer: Poesies*. Els Nostres Clàssics. Obres completes dels escriptors Catalans medievals. Col·lecció A68. Barcelona: Barcino.
  Life and works of Andreu Febrer (ca. 1375–ca. 1444), including an edition with critical notes for *Amors, qui tost fér, quant li play*, based on Machaut's *Loyauté, que* (L1).

Ritter, Otto.
  1914. *Die Geschichte der französischen Balladenformen, von ihren Anfängen bis zur Mitte des XV. Jahrhunderts*. Halle: Niemeyer.
  Discussion of the metrical structure of Machaut's ballades (91–105).

Rive, l'abbé [Joseph-Jean].
  1780. "Notice d'un manuscrit de la bibliothèque de M. le Duc de la Vallière, contenant les poésies de Guillaume de Machau, accompagnée de recherches historiques et critiques, pour servir à la vie de ce poëte." In Jean-Benjamin de La Borde and l'abbé Roussier, *Essai sur la musique ancienne et moderne*. Vol. 4, p. 475 and Appendix [I], 1–27. Paris: Pierres. Reprint. *Music and Theatre in France in the 17th and 18th Centuries*. New York: AMS Press, 1978.
  Early description of MS F-G [6], with a review of all bibliography up to 1780, by the irascible librarian of the duke of La Vallière.

Robertson, Anne W.
  1992. "The Mass of Guillaume de Machaut in the Cathedral of Reims." In *Plainsong in the Age of Polyphony*, ed. Thomas Forrest Kelly, 100–39. Cambridge Studies in Performance Practice 2. Cambridge: Cambridge University Press.
  New transcription and translation of the brass epitaph commemorating Guillaume and Jean de Machaut, and an examination of the chants used as *cantus firmi* in the Mass, demonstrating that readings in regional chant manuscripts correspond to peculiarities of Machaut's *cantus firmi*. A foundation of 1352 may have provided singers suitable for the performance of polyphony at Reims cathedral. Reconstruction of Machaut's will, based on the epitaph and comparable foundations, suggests that Machaut's Mass was originally written to be performed as a Saturday Marian Mass. After the death of the two brothers, it became a Requiem Mass to their memory. Reviews: David Hiley, *Music and Letters* 74 (1993): 414–17; Rob C. Wegman, *Early Music* 21 (1993): 273–74; Isobel Preece, *Journal of the Royal Music Association* 118 (1993): 300–307.

Robertson, D.W., Jr.
  1962. *A Preface to Chaucer: Studies in Medieval Perspectives*. Princeton: Princeton University Press; London: Oxford University Press.
  Influential work of exegetical criticism. Machaut briefly mentioned (233–36).

Robinson, F.N., ed.
  1957. *The Works of Geoffrey Chaucer*. 2nd ed. New Cambridge Edition. Boston: Houghton Mifflin; London: Oxford University Press.
  Standard edition of Chaucer, now revised as Benson 1987.

Robinson, Ray, comp.
  1978. *Choral Music: A Norton Historical Anthology*. New York: Norton.
  Includes edition of the Kyrie (7–15 no. 4).

Robinson, J[oseph] Armitage, and Montague Rhodes James.
  1909. *The Manuscripts of Westminster Abbey*. Notes and Documents
  Relating to Westminster Abbey 1. Cambridge: Cambridge University Press.
  Standard library catalogue, includes description of MS **Wm** [41].

Roesner, Edward H., et al.
  1990. *Le Roman de Fauvel in the Edition of Mesire Chaillou de Pesstain: A*
  Reproduction in Facsimile of the Complete Manuscript Paris, Bibliothèque
  Nationale, Fonds Français 146. With an introduction by Edward H.
  Roesner, François Avril, and Nancy Freeman Regalado. New York:
  Broude Bros.
  Facsimile edition of *F:Pn 146*. The introduction includes important material on Philippe
  de Vitry.

Root, Jerry.
  1990. "'Space to Speke': Confessional Practice and the Construction of
  Character in the Works of Geoffrey Chaucer, Guillaume de Machaut, and
  Juan Ruiz. Ph.D. diss. University of Michigan. Ann Arbor: University
  Microfilms. Order no. 9034501.
  "Machaut's *Livre du Voir Dit* is central to the 'metamorphosis in literature' and the new
  'relation to the true' that confessional practice makes possible. The *Livre du Voir Dit*
  shifts away from the love debates and the judgment trials of Machaut's earlier poems to
  an inner trial. It shifts from questions of authority and proof, to the familiar terms of the
  discourse of confession: intention, sincerity, experience" (12). Abstract: *DAI* A 51/7 (Jan.
  1991): 2373–74.

Root, Robert K.
  1941. "The Monk's Tale." In Bryan/Dempster 1941, 615–44.
  Discusses Machaut's *Prise* (636–37). Excerpt from Mas Latrie ed. (ll. 8631–703), with
  English glosses. Since Chaucer's mention of Pierre de Lusignan shares Machaut's
  historical inaccuracies, his account was possibly taken from Machaut.

Roquefort-Flaméricourt, B. de. [Roquefort, Jean-Baptiste Bonaventure de].
  1815. *De l'état de la poésie françoise dans les XIIe et XIIIe siècles. Mémoire*
  qui a remporté le Prix dans le Concours proposé en 1810, par la Classe
  d'histoire et de littérature ancienne de l'Institut de France, sur cette question:
  Déterminer quel fut l'état de poésie françoise dans les XIIe et XIIIe siècles:
  quels genres de poésie furent les plus cultivés? Paris: Fournier.
  Includes a discussion of the list of instruments in the *Remede* (erroneously entitled *Tems*
  pastour) (104–31).

Roques, Gilles.
  1982. "Tradition et innovation dans le vocabulaire de Guillaume de Machaut."
  In Guillaume de Machaut 1982, 157–73.
  Study of relationships among Machaut's lyrics, with examples of sources in thirteenth-
  century chansons. Discusses peculiarities of Machaut's vocabulary, including his use of
  set phrases borrowed from the *Roman de la Rose* and Gautier de Coinci, his use of
  regional vocabulary (some of which is found only in Machaut and Deschamps), new
  words in Machaut, and exotic vocabulary. In an aside, Roques notes that Machaut was the
  first author to mention paper. Promises a glossary of Machaut by Roques and Noël
  Musso, at the Institut de la Langue Française, Nancy.

  1986. "Les noms de bateaux dans la Prise d'Alexandrie de Guillaume de
  Machaut." *Actes du IIe colloque de langues et de littérature dialectale d'oïl*
  de l'ouest de la France sur le thème de l'eau. Nantes 16–17–18 février
  1984. Textes et Langages 13:269–79.
  Study of specialized nautical nomenclature in the *Prise*, including a concordance for the
  names of boats in other *dits*.

Roques, Gilles, and Noël Musso.
1978. "Etude du vocabulaire de Guillaume de Machaut: Projet d'un lexique de ses œuvres." In *Etudes de Syntaxe du Moyen Français. Colloque organizé par le Centre d'Analyse Syntaxique de l'Université de Metz et par le Centre de Recherche pour un Trésor de la langue française*, ed. Robert Martin, 189–92. Recherches linguistiques 4. Paris: Klincksieck.
Not examined.

Rosenberg, Samuel N., and Hans Tischler, eds.
1991. *The Monophonic Songs in the Roman de Fauvel*. Lincoln and London: University of Nebraska Press.
Edition of texts and music, with commentary. Reviews: Ardis Butterfield, *Plainsong & Medieval Music* 2 (1993): 193–95; Daniel Leech-Wilkinson, *Early Music* 20 (1992): 489–91 (strongly critical of the musical transcriptions); Gilles Roques, *Revue de linguistique romane* 56 (1992): 625; Nigel Wilkins, *Medium Ævum* 62 (1993): 148–49; Carol Williams, *Australian Journal of French Studies* 28 (1991): 315–19.

Roussel, Henri.
1967. "En quête d'un humanisme: XIVe et XVe siècle." In *Littérature française*. Vol. 1, *Des origines à la fin du XVIIIe siècle*, ed. Antoine Adam, Georges Lerminier, and Edouard Morot-Sir, 42–73. Paris: Larousse.
Sympathetic and modern survey of Machaut as a poet (54–56).

Roy, Bruno.
1974 (ed.). *L'Art d'Amours: Traduction et commentaire de l'Ars amatoria d'Ovide*. Leiden: Brill.
Includes an excellent description of MS **H** [17].

Roy, Maurice, ed.
1886–91. *Œuvres poétiques de Christine de Pisan*. Vols 1–2. Société des Anciens Textes Français. Paris: Firmin-Didot, 1886, 1891.
Standard critical edition.

Rubin, Frances Anne.
1978. "'Car Atropos...': A Study of the Renaissance *déploration*." M.A. diss. University of North Carolina.
Includes discussion of Deschamps's *déploration* on the death of Machaut. Abstract: *RILM* 13 (1979), no. 336.

Rubió y Lluch, Antoni.
1908–21. *Documents per l'historia de la cultura Catalana mig-eval*. 2 vols. Barcelona: Institut d'Estudis Catalans, 1908, 1921.
Includes documents on Machaut manuscripts at the court of Aragon in the late fourteenth and early fifteenth century.

Rudt de Collenberg, Wipertus.
1980. "Le choix des exécuteurs dans les bulles de provision au XIVe siècle (d'après les bulles accordées à Chypre par les papes d'Avignon)." *Mélanges de l'Ecole Française de Rome: Moyen Age–temps modernes* 92:393–440.
The three executors named in bulls of provision of benefices where indicated by the supplicant beneficiary, and usually included—the order is not fixed—(a) a high ecclesiastical dignitary of the province, but not of the diocese in which the benefice was situated; (b) a member of the papal Curia; and (c) a personal choice of the beneficiary, usually a prelate known by the beneficiary either from his diocese of origin or from a diocese in which the beneficiary had attachments. When one can determine which of the three executors item (c) represents, it can provide important information concerning the origins or career of the beneficiary.

Ruhe, Ernstpeter.
  1975. De Amasio ad Amasiam: *Zur Gattungsgeschichte des mittelalterlichen Liebesbriefes*. Beiträge zur romanischen Philologie des Mittelalters 10. Munich: Fink.

   Discussion of the *complainte* genre and its use as letters (274–75); innovative aspects of Machaut's *Voir Dit*, discussed in terms of its love letters (275–85). Reviews: A. Keith Bate, *French Studies* 33 (1979): 595–96; Tore Janson, *Romance Philology* 32 (1978–79): 440–44; Ewald Könsgen, *Romanische Forschungen* 88 (1976): 447–49; Massimo Oldoni, *Studi medievali* 17 (1976): 724–27; W. Rothwell, *Erasmus* 27 (1975): 795–98; Dieter Schaller, *Arcadia* 12 (1977): 307–13; Arnulf Stefenelli, *Zeitschrift für romanische Philologie* 93 (1977): 116–18; L.T. Topsfield, *Cahiers de civilisation médiévale* 20 (1977): 68–69.

Rychner, Jean.
  1981. "La flèche et l'anneau." *Revue des sciences humaines* 55 no. 183 (July-Sept.), 55–69. Reprint. *Du "Saint-Alexis" à François Villon: Etudes de littérature médiévale*, with a preface by Jacques Monfrin, 321–35. Publications Romanes et Françaises 169. Geneva: Droz, 1985.

   Influence of the *Roman de la Rose* on *dits* of Machaut, including *Vergier, Jugement Navarre, Remede, Lyon*, and especially *Fonteinne*.

Sabbé, Herman.
  1980–81. "Techniques médiévales en musique contemporaine: histoire de la musique et sens culturel." *Revue belge de musicologie* 34–35:220–33.

   Isorhythm in the Mass resembles similar procedures in the modern composer Goeyvaerts (226–28); cf. Zenck 1990. The vertical comparison of the rhythms of the tenor and contratenor of the Kyrie, with commentary, resembles the analysis of Dömling 1971. Abstract: *RILM* 15 (1981), no. 3955.

Sachs, Klaus-Jürgen.
  1974. *Der Contrapunctus im 14. und 15. Jahrhundert: Untersuchungen zum Terminus, zur Lehre und zu den Quellen*. Beihefte zum Archiv für Musikwissenschaft 13. Wiesbaden: Steiner.

   Publication of author's 1966 Freiburg dissertation, a study of medieval contrapuntal theory, the basis of Machaut's polyphony. Abstracts: *RILM* 9 (1975), no. 3418; 12 (1978), no. 313; abstract of original dissertation: *Musikforschung* 21 (1968): 499–500. Reviews: Carl Dahlhaus, *Melos/NZ* 2 (1976): 504; Karl Gustav Fellerer, *Kirchenmusikalisches Jahrbuch* 58–59 (1974–75): 152; Martin Just, *Musikforschung* 31 (1978): 211–12; Alexander Hyatt King, *Erasmus* 29 (1977): 33–34; Albert Seay, *Journal of Music Theory* 20 (1976): 301–6; Edward Stam, *Tijdschrift van de Vereniging voor Nederlandse Muziekgeschiedenis* 26 (1976): 45–46.

Salop, Arnold.
  1971. *Studies on the History of Musical Style*. With a Foreword by John W. Grubbs. Detroit: Wayne State University Press.

   See chap. 2, "The Secular Polyphony of Guillaume de Machaut" (39–80). Considers long-range dramatic possibilities of the ballade structure, as determined by melodic characteristics that produce tension and direction, and groups ballades according to criteria of musical narrative. Attention exclusively to music; the many examples include no text. Abstract: *RILM* 7 (1973), no. 1677.

Salter, Elizabeth, and Derek Pearsall. See also Pearsall and Salter.
  1980. "Pictorial Illustration of Late Medieval Poetic Texts: The Role of the Frontispiece or Prefatory Picture." In *Medieval Iconography and Narrative: A Symposium*, ed. Flemming G. Andersen et al., 100–123. Proceedings of the Fourth International Symposium organized by the Centre for the Study of Vernacular Literature in the Middle Ages. Held at Odense University on 19–20 November, 1979. Odense: Odense University Press.

Includes a list of iconographic models for the portrayal of an author in a frontispiece, with brief discussion of *Remede* miniature **F**14 (115–16).

Salzer, Felix.

1952. *Structural Hearing: Tonal Coherence in Music.* With a foreword by Leopold Mannes. 2 vols. New York: Charles Boni. *Strukturelles Hören. Der tonale Zusammenhang in der Musik.* Ed. and trans. by Hans Wolf and Felix Salzer, with a foreword by Saul Novak. 2 vols. Wilhelmshaven: Noetzl, 1960. Reprint. Taschenbücher zur Musikwissenschaft 10–11. Wilhelmshaven: Heinrichshofen, 1977.

Voice-leading reductions inspired by the theory of Heinrich Schenker purport to demonstrate the increasing "harmonic thinking" in Machaut (1:275–78, 2:328–36). Examples analyzed include *Dame, mon cuer* (V32/29), *Dame, se vous n'avez* (R13), *De tout sui* (V38/32), *Donnez, signeurs* (B26), *On ne porroit* (B3), and *Plus dure* (V31/28). Criticism of the reduction of R13 in Kühn 1973, 33.

Samaran, Charles, and Robert Marichal.

1959. *Catalogue des manuscrits en écriture latine portant des indications de date, de lieu ou de copiste.* Vol. 1 (in 2), *Musée Condé et Bibliothèques parisiennes.* Comité International de Paléographie. Paris: Centre National de la Recherche Scientifique.

Description of MS **J** [16], with a facsimile of one folio.

Samaran, Ch[arles], and G[uillaume] Mollat.

1905. *La fiscalité pontificale en France au XIVe siècle (période d'Avignon et grand schisme d'occident).* Paris: Fontemoing.

Includes historical material on *décimes* (tenths), a tax imposed on ecclesiastical revenues in the fourteenth century (12–22).

Sanada, Fusako.

1961. "Guillaume de Machaut." *Ongaku-Geijutsu* (The Art of Music) 19 (July): 22–31.

Not examined.

Sanders, Ernest.

1973. "The Medieval Motet." In *Gattungen der Musik in Einzeldarstellungen: Gedenkschrift Leo Schrade, I,* ed. Wulf Arlt, Ernst Lichtenhahn, Hans Oesch, and Max Haas, 497–573. Bern: Franke.

Important survey of the motet; discusses Vitry and Machaut (554–65). Abstract: *RILM* 10 (1976), no. 5146. Review: Michel Huglo, *Revue de musicologie* 61 (1975): 333–37.

1980a. "Isorhythm." *New Grove* 9:351–54.

Dictionary article.

1980b. "Motet, §I, 3: Medieval—Ars Nova." *New Grove* 12:625–28.

Dictionary article; includes brief discussion of tenors *Fera pessima* (to *Fons / O livoris* [M9]) and *Quia amore langueo* (to *Maugré mon cuer / De ma dolour* [M14]).

1980c. "Vitry, Philippe de." *New Grove* 20:22–28.

Dictionary article.

Sandras, E.-G.

1859. *Etude sur G. Chaucer, considéré comme imitateur des trouvères.* Paris: Durand.

First study to remark Chaucer's borrowings of Machaut. Sandras recognizes Machaut's importance without according him much merit as a poet (75–81). Discussion of the *Book of the Duchess* emphasizes Chaucer's dependence on *Remede* and *Fonteinne* (89–95). Sandras's conclusion, "Ce poëme qui, dans son ensemble et souvent dans ses détails, n'offre qu'une imitation servile de Machault, est certainement une des plus faibles productions de Chaucer" (95), has been a bone of contention for later studies more favorable to Chaucer (see, for instance, criticism in ten Brink 1870, 7–8). The appendix contains some excerpts for comparative purposes, especially from *Remede* (289–94).

Saponov, Mikhail A.
    1978. "Menzural'naya ritmika i ea apogee v tvorchestve Guillauma de
    Machaut" (Mensural rhythm and its apogee in the works of Guillaume de
    Machaut). In *Problemy muzykal' nogo ritma* (Problems in musical rhythm;
    in Russian). Compiled by Valentine Holopova. Moscow: Muzyka.
    Draws on a wide range of examples, and has fairly up-to-date scholarly references.

Sasaki, Shigemi.
    1978. "*Le Dit de l'Alérion*" (in Japanese). *Tategoto* (Harp) 12 (Mar.): 59–69.
    Not examined.

    1982. "Le jardin et son *estre* dans le *Roman de la Rose* et dans le *Dit dou
    Lyon.*" In *Les jardins et la littérature française jusqu'à la Révolution.
    Cahiers de l'Association Internationale des Etudes Françaises* 34:25–37.
    The idea of the closure of a garden is emphasized in *Lyon*, because the garden is sur-
    rounded by a river (29–30); comparison of the garden in *Lyon* with that in the *Roman de
    la Rose* (34–37).

Schaar, Claes.
    1954. *Some Types of Narrative in Chaucer's Poetry.* Lund Studies in English
    25. Lund: Gleerup; Copenhagen: Munksgaard.
    Early study of narrative techniques in Chaucer and his literary sources, including discus-
    sion of *Jugement Navarre, Lyon,* and *Fonteinne.* Abstracts: Allen/Fischer 1987, no. 161.

    1955. *The Golden Mirror: Studies in Chaucer's Descriptive Technique and Its
    Literary Background.* Kungl. Humanistiska Vetenskapssamfundet i Lund,
    Skrifter 54. Lund: Gleerup.
    Language describing emotions in *Jugement Behaingne, Jugement Navarre, Remede,
    Lyon, Confort,* and *Fonteinne.* Language describing appearance of characters in *Vergier,
    Jugement Behaingne, Jugement Navarre, Remede, Lyon, Alerion,* and *Fonteinne.*

Schalz, Nicolas.
    1980. *Studien zur Komposition des Gloria. Musikalische Formgestaltung von
    der Gregorianik bis zu Monteverdi.* Frankfurter Beiträge zur Musikwissen-
    schaft 3. Tutzing: Schneider.
    Publication of author's 1974 Frankfurt a.M. dissertation. Comparative analyses of
    settings of the Gloria of the Mass, from Machaut to Monteverdi. Abstract: *RILM* 14
    (1980), no. 295; abstract of original dissertation: *RILM* 9 (1975), no. 3382.

Scheler, August, ed.
    1882. *Li Regret Guillaume, comte de Hainaut. Poëme inédit du XIVe siècle
    par Jehan de le Mote.* Louvain: Lefever.
    The first inserted ballade in *Li Regret Guillaume* is the model for Machaut's *On ne
    porroit* (B3).

Schering, Arnold.
    1911–12. "Die kolorierte Orgelmadrigal des Trecento." *Sammelbände der
    Internationalen Musikgesellschaft* 13:172–204.
    A marvelously absurd theory that all manuscripts of fourteenth- and fifteenth-century
    French and Italian music transmit purely instrumental music, especially organ music,
    based on simple folk songs that have been paraphrased. If and when anyone ever sang
    these works, they sang the simplified versions. For Machaut, examples include *S'Amours
    ne fait* (B1) and *Comment puet* (R11).

    1914. *Studien zur Musikgeschichte der Frührenaissance.* Studien zur Musik-
    geschichte 2. Leipzig: Kahut Nachfolger.
    More on the instrumental basis of Ars Nova compositions, showing that the chanson is
    an "accompanied solo song." Examples include *De Bon Espoir* (M4 triplum) (pp. 135–
    36), *S'Amours ne fait* (B1) (pp. 79–80), and *Se pour se muir* (B36) (p. 85). See Reaney
    1956, 99; 1966, 719–21.

1931a. *Aufführungspraxis alter Musik*. Musikpädagogische Bibliothek 10. Leipzig: Quelle & Meyer. Reprint. Wiesbaden: Sändig, 1969. Reprint, with introduction by Siegfried Goslich. Taschenbücher zur Musikwissenschaft 35. Wilhelmshaven: Heinrichshofen, 1975.

Further discussion of the performance practice discussed in Schering 1911–12 and 1914: "A time that scarcely had the lyrics of the troubadours (also known in Italy) behind it, that possessed an abundance of natural, singable songs, cannot possibly have overlooked its past and misunderstood the essence of song to the extent that is expressed in these compositions. Therefore the hypothesis has been advanced that this music was perhaps pure instrumental music, and that its connection to the text is to be understood as a coloratura-like paraphrase of a simple core-melody that is no longer known to us" (16–17). On Machaut in particular, see 18–20.

1931b. *Musikgeschichte in Beispielen: Dreihundertfünfzig Tonsätze aus neun Jahrhunderten*. Leipzig: Breitkopf & Härtel. American ed. New York: Broude Bros., 1950.

Includes editions of *Ma chiere* (B40), *Se je souspir* (V36/30), and *Trop plus / Biauté* (M20).

Schiff, Mario Lodovico.

1905. *La bibliothèque du Marquis de Santillane: Etude historique et bibliographique de la collection de livres manuscrits de Don Iñigo López de Mendoza, 1398-1458, Marqués de Santillana, Conde del real de Manzanares, humaniste et auteur espagnol célèbre*. Bibliothèque de l'Ecole des Hautes Etudes. Sciences historiques et philologiques 153. Paris: Bouillon. Reprint. Amsterdam: van Heusden, 1970.

Includes a description of MS **Mn** [43], the *Roman de Cardenois*.

Schilperoort, Johanna Catharina.

1936. *Guillaume de Machaut et Christine de Pisan (étude comparative)*. The Hague: de Swart & zoon, [1936].

Publication of author's 1936 Leiden dissertation, a discussion of the relationship between the lyrical and narrative poetry of Machaut and Christine. *Jugement Behaingne* is related to Christine's *Livre du Dit de Poissy*, while *Jugement Navarre* is related to Christine's *Livre des Trois Jugemens* and *Debat de Deux Amans*. Includes an important early comparative literary study of sources, and a discussion of themes and aspects of local color in the poetry of both Machaut and Christine. Summary, 126–30.

Schlumbohm, Christa.

1974. *Jocus und Amor: Liebesdiskussionen vom mittelalterlichen "joc partit" bis zu den preziösen "questions d'amour."* Hamburger romanistische Dissertationen 14. Hamburg: Romanisches Seminar der Universität Hamburg.

Publication of author's 1974 Hamburg dissertation. Includes an analysis of how *Jugement Behaingne* fits into the tradition of the love-debate (236–62). Reviews: Glynnis M. Cropp, *Bibliothèque d'Humanisme et Renaissance* 38 (1976): 205–8; J.H. Marshall, *French Studies* 33 (1979): 593–95; Hugo Sonneville, *Langues romanes* 31 (1977): 275; Manfred Tietz, *Arcadia* 11 (1976): 300–302.

Schmidt, Gerhard.

1975. "Zur Datierung des 'kleinen' Bargello-Diptychons und der Verkündigungstafel in Cleveland." *Etudes d'art français offertes à Charles Sterling*, ed. Albert Châtelet and Nicole Reynaud, 47–63. Paris: Presses Universitaires de France.

Includes material relevant to the Master of the *Remede de Fortune*, the most important artist of MS C [1].

1977–78. "Die Wiener 'Herzogswerkstatt' und die Kunst Nordeuropas." *Wiener Jahrbuch für Kunstgeschichte* 30–31:179–206.

Includes material relevant to the Master of the *Remede de Fortune*, the most important artist of MS C [1].

Schmidt-Görg, Joseph, comp.
  1968. *History of the Mass*. Trans. Robert Kolben. Anthology of Music 30.
  Cologne: Volk.
  Includes edition of the complete Kyrie (33–37 no. 15).

Schneider, Jean.
  1990. "Yolande de Flandre (1326–1395) comtesse de Bar, dame de Cassel et
  les pouvoirs de son temps." In *La femme au Moyen-Age*, ed. Michel
  Rouche and Jean Heuclin, 353–63. Maubeuge: Ville de Maubeuge.
  Historical study of Yolande of Flanders, patron of Jean de Machaut. Includes further bibliographical references.

Schneider, Marius.
  1931. *Die Ars nova des XIV. Jahrhunderts in Frankreich und Italien*.
  Potsdam: Hayn's Erben; Wolfenbüttel and Berlin: Kallmeyer.
  Publication of author's 1930 Berlin dissertation. Schneider, a loyal student of Johannes
  Wolf, paid little attention to the work of Ludwig and Besseler, who had already far
  surpassed his work. Appended musical examples from *Fiat voluntas* (M5 tenor), *Eins que*
  (M13 motetus), *A Christo* (M19 tenor), *Trop plus* (M20 triplum), *Apprehende arma*
  (M22 tenor), *Ma fin* (R14), and *Hoquetus David*. Criticism in Apel 1946–47, 26 n. 7.
  Review: Gerhard Peitzsch, *Acta musicologica* 4 (1932): 28.

Schofield, William Henry.
  1901. "Chaucer's Franklin's Tale." *PMLA* 16:405–49.
  Influence of Machaut's *Vergier* and *Voir Dit* on Chaucer's Franklin's Tale.

Schrade, Leo.
  1956a (ed.). *The* Roman de Fauvel; *The Works of Philippe de Vitry; French
  Cycles of the* Ordinarium Missae. Polyphonic Music of the Fourteenth
  Century 1. Les Remparts, Monaco: L'Oiseau-Lyre.
  Standard edition. Reviews: Willi Apel, *Speculum* 32 (1957): 863–66 (reprinted in Apel
  1986, 209–12); David G. Hughes, *Journal of the American Musicological Society* 9
  (1956): 221–25; Jeremy Noble, *Musical Times* 100 (1959): 22.

  1956b (ed.). *The Works of Guillaume de Machaut*. 2 vols. Polyphonic Music
  of the Fourteenth Century 2–3. Les Remparts, Monaco: L'Oiseau-Lyre.
  Reprint. *Guillaume de Machaut, Œuvres complètes*. Uncorrected reprint
  with introductions by Stanley Boorman. Vol. 1, *Les lays. Complainte.
  Chanson royale*. Vol. 2, *Les motets*. Vol. 3, *La Messe de Nostre-Dame.
  Double hoquet. Remède de Fortune*. Vol. 4, *Les ballades*. Vol. 5, *Les
  rondeaux. Les virelais*. Les Remparts, Monaco: L'Oiseau-Lyre, 1977.
  The most-used edition of Machaut's music, although it is not a fully critical edition.
  Notably inaccurate editions are given for the lais *S'onques* (L17/12), *Pour ce que plus*
  (L23/17), and *En demantant* (L24/18); for the motet *Trop plus / Biauté* (M20); for the
  ballades *Dous amis, oy* (B6), *Esperance* (B13), *Sans cuer m'en / Amis / Dame* (B17), and
  Je puis trop (B28); and for the rondeau *Rose, lis* (R10); for corrected editions, see the
  discussions of individual works in chap. 7.3. A supplementary volume containing a
  revised critical apparatus by Gordon K. Greene has been promised, but recent
  advertisements from the publisher indicate curiously that it "has proved impractical and
  will not be published for purely scholarly reasons." On barring and notation, see Hoppin
  1960. Reviews: Willi Apel, *Speculum* 33 (1958): 433–34 (reprinted in Apel 1986, 212–
  13); Richard H. Hoppin, *Notes* 15 (1957–58): 472–74; David G. Hughes, *Journal of the
  American Musicological Society* 11 (1958): 240–43; Jeremy Noble, *Musical Times* 100
  (1959): 22.

  1956c (ed.). *The Works of Guillaume de Machaut. Commentary Notes to
  Volumes II and III*. Monaco: L'Oiseau-Lyre (typescript).
  Critical notes to Schrade 1956b.

1958–61. "Guillaume de Machaut and the 'Roman de Fauvel.'" In *Miscelánea en homenaje a Monseñor Higinio Anglés*, vol. 2 of 2 vols., 843–50. Barcelona: Consejo superior de investigaciones cientificas.

Machaut was familiar with the monophonic lais inserted into the *Roman de Fauvel* (MS *F:Pn 146*). Schrade distinguishes two musical groups among the lais, those in *modus* and those in *tempus*. A few have some strophes of each type. Four lais of Machaut in the long-breve group have affinities with *Fauvel* lais, namely *Nuls ne doit* (L5), *Lay Mortel, Un mortel lay* (L12/8), *Lay de Nostre Dame, Contre ce dous* (L15/10), *Lay de Plour, Malgré Fortune* (L19/14) (Schrade confuses the two *Lays de Plour*, L19 and L22; his remarks refer to L19, despite what he says). The relation to *Fauvel* (and possibly also to the lais of the *Roman de Perceforest*) proves that Machaut was not a "romantic," harkening back to a thirteenth-century form, but that he was in touch with his generation (here Schrade rejects the views of Besseler 1931).

1959. "The Chronology of the Ars Nova in France." In Wégimont 1959, 37–59 (discussion, 59–62).

Chronological and geographical limits of the term Ars Nova; gaps in the sources; the chronological development of the genres motet, chanson, and Mass movement, emphasizing gaps in our knowledge; chronologies of composers (Vitry, Machaut, post-Machaut generation). In the ensuing discussion, Nino Pirrotta asserts that Ars Nova treatises only codify a musical transformation that had already occurred, while Schrade reaffirmed that the rhythmic characteristics of early fourteenth-century really are new; Pope John XXII speaks of a *schola nova*, and Jacob of Liège speaks of the *moderni*.

1960. "La musique de Machaut à Dufay." In *Histoire de la musique*. Vol. 1, *Des origines à Jean-Sébastien Bach*, ed. Roland-Manuel, 868–89. Encyclopédie de la Pléiade 9. [Paris]: Gallimard.

Survey of music after Machaut. The introductory remarks provide an encomium of Machaut's musical influence (868–69).

1967. "Tragische Gestalten in der Musik." *Melos* 34:281–89.

Includes brief discussion of Machaut's "autobiography," the first autobiography of a musician, the *Voir Dit* (283). The tone of melancholy present in all his compositions is an expression not of personal tragedy, but of the atmosphere of the late Middle Ages.

Schwob, Marcel, ed.

1905. *Le Petit et le Grand Testament de François Villon. Les cinq ballades en jargon et des poésies du cercle de Villon, etc. Reproduction fac-simile du manuscrit de Stockholm*. Paris: Champion. Reprint. Geneva: Slatkine, 1977.

Concerns MS **St** [46].

Schutz, A[lexander] H[erman].

1951. "Gleanings from Parisian Private Libraries of the Early Renaissance (1494–1558)." *Romance Philology* 5:25–34.

A study of the literary importance of several library inventories made after the deaths of their owners. A manuscript of Machaut's *Prise* was in the library of one Turquan (or Turquam), a bourgeois of Paris who died in 1519.

1955. *Vernacular Books in Parisian Private Libraries of the Sixteenth Century According to The Notarial Inventories*. University of North Carolina Studies in the Romance Languages and Literatures 25. Chapel Hill: University of North Carolina Press.

Expanded and more systematic version of Schutz 1951.

Scully, Terence Peter.

1966. "The Love Debate in Mediæval French Literature with Special Reference to Guillaume de Machaut." Ph.D. diss. University of Toronto. Order microfilm from National Library of Canada, Ottawa.

Not examined. History of the love debate genre from the late twelfth to the mid-fifteenth century. Machaut's *Jugement Behaingne* and *Jugement Navarre* determined the subsequent treatment of the genre. On Machaut and Christine's *Livre dou Dit de Poissy*, see 159–61 (cited in Altmann 1987, 270 n. 7). Abstract: *DAI* A 29/9 (Mar. 1969): 3109.

1980. "'Douce dame d'onour': Late Fourteenth Century Qualifications of the Lady." *Medioevo romanzo* 7:37–47.

A survey of epithets attached to the word "dame" in 261 late fourteenth-century polyphonic chansons with music, including 69 rondeaux, virelais, and ballades of Machaut. Not surprisingly, the combination "douce dame" is the most popular. Unlike modern French, an adjective in Middle French has greater stress when placed after its noun.

1990. "French Songs in Aragon: The Place of Origin of the *Chansonnier* Chantilly, Musée Condé 564." In *Courtly Literature: Culture and Context.* *Selected papers from the 5th Triennial Congress of the International Courtly Literature Society, Dalfsen, The Netherlands, 9–16 August, 1986*, ed. Keith Busby and Erik Kooper, 509–21. Utrecht Publications in General and Comparative Literature 25. Amsterdam and Philadelphia: Benjamins.

Argues that MS **Ch** [59] originated at the court of John I, king of Aragon (r. 1387–96), copied by a Catalan scribe between 1392 and 1396. Scully's work is oddly isolated from the ample bibliography on this manuscript.

Seay, Albert.

1960 (ed.). *Ugolino of Orvieto. Declaratio musicae disciplinae.* Corpus Scriptorum de Musica 7/2. Rome: American Institute of Musicology.

Ugolino's treatise of 1431 glosses Johannes de Muris's criticism of Machaut's notational practice (see Hoppin 1960).

1965. *Music in the Medieval World.* Prentice Hall History of Music Series. Englewood Cliffs, N.J.: Prentice Hall. 2nd ed. 1975. Reprint. Prospect Heights, Ill.: Waveland Press, 1991.

Includes a survey of Machaut (143–47). Facsimile of opening of Gloria of the Mass from MS **B** (146).

Seibt, Ferdinand.

1967. "Die böhmischen Länder in der europäischen Politik 1306 bis 1346." In *Handbuch der Geschichte der böhmischen Länder.* Vol. 1, *Die böhmischen Länder von der archaischen Zeit bis zum Ausgang der hussitischen Revolution*, ed. Karl Bosl, 351–84. Stuttgart: Hiersemann.

Excellent overview, with full bibliography, of the political situation in Bohemia under John of Luxembourg.

1974. "Johann von Böhmen, König von Böhmen." In *Neue deutsche Biographie*, 10:469–70. Berlin: Duncker & Humblot.

Brief biography of John of Luxembourg.

Seronde, Joseph.

1915. "A Study of the Relations of Some Leading French Poets of the XIVth and the XVth Centuries to the Marqués de Santillana." *Romanic Review* 6: 60–86.

An early literary study of the famous letter of the Marqués de Santillana to the constable of Portugal.

Severs, J[onathan] Burke.

1952. "Is the *Manciple's Tale* a Success?" *Journal of English and Germanic Philology* 51:1–16.

Includes a discussion of Machaut's *Voir Dit* as a source for the story of Apollo and Coronis in Chaucer's *Manciple's Tale* (2 n. 8, 3, 6–7 nn. 13–14). Abstracts: Allen/Fisher 1987, no. 672.

1963. "The Sources of 'The Book of the Duchess.'" *Mediæval Studies* 25: 355–62.

A passage in Chaucer's *Book of the Duchess* is from *Vergier* (355–57).

Shannon, Edgar Finley.
  1929. *Chaucer and the Roman Poets.* Harvard Studies in Comparative Literature 7. Cambridge, Mass.: Harvard University Press. Reprint. New York: Russell & Russell, 1957, 1964.
  Includes some discussion of Machaut sources for Chaucer's *House of Fame* and the Prologue to the *Legend of Good Women*, mainly in critical response to Lowes 1918. See Meech 1931.

Siciliano, Italo.
  1934. *François Villon et les thèmes poétiques du Moyen Age.* Paris: Colin.
  Study of the historical circumstances, milieu, and sources that influenced and informed Villon's poetry. Literary influence is treated in a series of themes, including the Virgin, death, Fortune, etc. Machaut's *Remede* and *Voir Dit* figure in the study of Fortune. Siciliano criticizes Machaut's poetry (325–26).

Silver, Isidore.
  1975. "The Marriage of Poetry and Music in France: Ronsard's Predecessors and Contemporaries." In *Poetry and Poetics from Ancient Greece to the Renaissance: Studies in Honor of James Hutton,* ed. G.M. Kirkwood, 152–84. Ithaca and London: Cornell University Press.
  Brief survey of the union of poetry and music from the trouvères to Du Bellay. Machaut discussed on pp. 155–57.

Sinnreich, Deborah Margaret.
  1987. "Eustache Deschamps' *L'Art de Dictier.*" Ph.D. diss. City University of New York. Ann Arbor: University Microfilms. Order no. 8713799.
  Provides an introduction, a critical edition after *F:Pn 840,* translation, notes, and glossary to Deschamps's *Art de Dictier.* Abstract: *DAI* A 48/3 (Sept. 1987): 646.

Snizkova, Jitka.
  1982. "Les traces de Guillaume de Machaut dans les sources musicales de Prague." In Guillaume de Machaut 1982, 69–74.
  The musical milieu with which Machaut as a servant of John of Luxembourg may have come in contact. The discussion of MS **Pg** [72] is not up to current scholarly standards. Attributes an additional rondeau and virelai in this manuscript to Machaut.

Sonnemann, Günter.
  1969. *Die Ditdichtung des Guillaume de Machaut.* Ph.D. diss. Göttingen. Göttingen: Funke
  Definition of the term *dit,* a brief biography of Machaut, discussion of Machaut's influence, historiographical overview of research, and discussion of each of the larger narrative works (*Prologue, Vergier, Jugement Behaingne, Remede, Lyon, Alerion, Jugement Navarre, Confort, Fonteinne,* and *Voir Dit*). Sonnemann goes on to discuss a variety of topics such as the mixing of sacred and secular aspects (61–64); lyrics in *Voir Dit* that also appear in the *Loange* of MS C (151–56); rhetorical aspects such as asyndeton, rhyme, anaphora, "adoublement," hyperbole, and adynaton; the use of proverbs and dreams (173–184); finally returning to the question of the meaning of the term *dit.* It is unfortunate that Sonnemann's work seems to have remained unread for the most part.

Sorrento, Luigi.
  1922. "Il Proemio del Marchese di Santillana." *Revue hispanique* 55:1–49.
  A literary study and edition of the famous letter of the Marqués de Santillana to the constable of Portugal.

Sotheby and Co.
  1882. *Catalogue of the Magnificent Collection of Manuscripts from Hamilton Palace.* London: Sotheby and Co., [1882].
  Includes a description of MS **Bk** [21] (p. 33 no. 214).

1966. *Bibliotheca Phillippica. Medieval Manuscripts: New Series.* Part 2, *Catalogue of Forty-Four Manuscripts of the 9th to the 17th Century. Day of Sale: Tuesday 29 November 1966.* London: Sotheby and Co.
An auction catalogue describing the manuscript now identified as **Kr** [36].

Spanke, Hans.
1929. Review of Ludwig 1926–54, vols. 1–2. *Zeitschrift für französische Sprache und Literatur* 52:183–87.
This review is useful in its own right.

Spearing, A[nthony] C[olin].
1976. *Medieval Dream-Poetry.* Cambridge: Cambridge University Press.
Includes brief discussion of a few Machaut *dits*, especially *Vergier* and *Jugement Navarre* (41–47).

Speroni, Gian Battista.
1977. "Una rilettura del 'Roman de Cardenois' (a proposito di una recente edizione)." *Medioevo Romanzo* 4:110–34.
An essential corrective study of Cocco 1975.

Stäblein-Harder, Hanna.
1962. *Fourteenth-Century Mass Music in France.* Corpus Mensurabilis Musicae 29. [Rome]: American Institute of Musicology.
Standard edition of fourteenth-century Mass music (omitting the Machaut Mass).

Staehelin, Martin.
1974. "Beschreibungen und Beispiele musikalischer Formen in einem unbeachteten Traktat des frühen 15. Jahrhunderts." *Archiv für Musikwissenschaft* 31:237–42.
Edition of an early fifteenth-century South German or Austrian music theory treatise. Cites *De petit po* (B18), *De toutes flours* (B31), *Se vous n'estes* (R7), and possibly *De Fortune* (B23). Abstract: *RILM* 10 (1976), no. 354.

1989. "Bemerkungen zum verbrannten Manuskript Strassburg M.222 C.22." *Musikforschung* 42:2–20.
Concerns the date and provenance of **Str** [73], destroyed in 1870. The treatises and main musical corpus of **Str**, written by one scribe in Zofingen (60 km SE of Basel), were finished in 1411. By the 1430s, **Str** was in Basel, then, perhaps much later, it found its way to Strasbourg. An extant manuscript with concordances to music theory treatises in the destroyed MS **Str** is a direct copy of the Strasbourg source, made in Basel in 1442.

Starr, Pamela.
1987. "Music and Music Patronage at the Papal Court, 1447–1484." Ph.D. diss. Yale University. Ann Arbor: University Microfilms, 1988. Order no. 8810283.
Includes a clear and thorough discussion of the system of the provision of papal benefices, with ample bibliography. Abstracts: *DAI* A 49/4 (Oct. 1988): 655; *RILM* 21 (1987), no. 1640.

1992. "Rome as the Centre of the Universe: Papal Grace and Music Patronage." *Early Music History* 11:223–62.
Useful material on ecclesiastical benefices, based on Starr 1987.

Starr, William J., and George F. Devine, comps.
1964. *Music Scores Omnibus. Part 1, Earliest Music Through the Works of Beethoven.* Englewood Cliffs, N.J.: Prentice Hall.
Includes editions of Kyrie (complete), and *Ma fin* (R14).

1974. *Music Scores Omnibus. Part 1, Earliest Music Through the Works of Beethoven.* 2nd ed. Englewood Cliffs, N.J.: Prentice Hall.
Includes editions of Kyrie (complete), *Ma fin* (R14), and *Se je souspir* (V36/30).

Steinle, Eric M.
1984. "The Medieval Lyric Romance." Ph.D. diss. University of California at Berkeley. Ann Arbor: University Microfilms. Order no. 8427108.
Consideration of poetic voice in *Remede, Fonteinne*, and *Voir Dit* (chap. 3) and Chaucer's *Book of the Duchess* as a reaction to the French tradition. Not examined. Abstract: *DAI* A 45/9 (Mar. 1985): 2869.
1989. "'Car tu as scens, retorique et musique': Machaut's Musical Narrative of the *Remede de Fortune*." *Mediaevalia* 11 (1985): 63–82.
Description of the lyric insertions in the *Remede*, and the complex role they play in the organization of the work. Discussion of the poetics of music vs. the poetics of rhetoric, based on the *Prologue*, and applied here to the *Remede*.

Stenzl, Jürg.
1975. "Bewahrende und verändernde musikalische Überlieferung." *Archiv für Musikwissenschaft* 32:117–23.
For Machaut, includes a discussion of ramifications of the two different versions of tenor and contratenor in *Puis qu'en oubli* (R18), which separate MSS A and G from MS E (122). R18 is an example of a work illustrating the illusory nature of a fixed, perfected composition in this period: we are not dealing with a stable tradition (*bewahrende Überlieferung*), but rather with a changing tradition (*verändernde Überlieferung*). It is not possible to find a single authentic, original version. Abstract: *RILM* 10 (1976), no. 7096.

Stephens, George.
1847. *Förteckning öfver de förnämsta brittiska och fransyska handskrifterna, uti kongl. bibliotheket i Stockholm*. Stockholm: Norstedt & söner, 1847.
Inventory of MS St [46] (pp. 155–80).

Sterling, Charles.
1987. *La peinture médiévale à Paris: 1300–1500*. Vol. 1. Paris: Bibliothèque des Arts (Fondation Wildenstein).
Comprehensive survey of Parisian miniaturists, including many that illuminated Machaut manuscripts. Includes plates (color or black-and-white), and bibliography for each item.

Stevens, Denis, ed.
1973. *Guillaume de Machaut. La Messe de Nostre Dame*. London: Oxford University Press.
Stevens indicates that his edition is based on Ludwig's collation of the manuscripts, but his application of *ficta* is very different; apparently Stevens suppresses some manuscript accidentals to avoid problems. Scoring calls for choir, soloists, and instruments, with changing combinations of instruments and vocal soloists in each movement. A brief analysis is provided. Reviews: Fallows 1977a; Gilbert Reaney, *Early Music* 3 (1975): 93.

Stevens, John.
1973. *Medieval Romance: Themes and Approaches*. London: Hutchinson.
Discussion of *Remede*, especially the *complaint Tels rit* (RF2) (pp. 201–3).
1984. "The 'Music' of the Lyric. Machaut, Deschamps, Chaucer." In *Medieval and Pseudo-Medieval Literature. The J.A.W. Bennett Memorial Lectures (Perugia, 1982–1983)*, ed. Piero Boitani and Anna Torti, 109–29. Tübinger Beiträge zur Anglistik 6. Tübingen: Narr; Cambridge: Brewer.
Music and poetry in Machaut's *Remede* lyrics, with special consideration of *Qui n'aroit* (RF1) and *Tels rit* (RF2); Machaut's *Prologue*, Deschamps's "artificial" and "natural" music, and the rhythm of Chaucer's poetry.

Stevens, John, et al., comps.
1989. *Catalogue of the Pepys Library at Magdalene College Cambridge*, ed. Robert Latham. Vol. 4, *Music, Maps and Calligraphy*. Cambridge: Brewer.
Brief description of musical items in MS Pe [20] by John Stevens (4). See also McKitterick 1992.

Stevenson, Kay Gilliland.
    1989–90. "Readers, Poets, and Poems within the Poem." *Chaucer Review*
    24:1–19.
    A study of how Chaucer changed materials borrowed from *Jugement Behaingne*, and
    especially from *Fonteinne*, in his *Book of the Duchess*.

Stewart, L.
    1973. "The Chant-Royal, A Study of the Evolution of a Genre." *Romania* 96:
    431–96.
    Origins of the *chant royal* and its mention by contemporary theorists.

Stillwell, Gardiner.
    1940. "Analogues to Chaucer's *Manciple's Tale* in the *Ovide Moralisé* and
    Machaut's *Voir-Dit*." *Philological Quarterly* 19:133–38.
    The story of Apollo and Coronis.

Stolba, K. Marie, comp.
    1991. *The Development of Western Music: An Anthology*. Vol. 1, *Ancient,
    Medieval, Renaissance, Baroque*. Dubuque, Iowa: Brown.
    Includes musical editions of *Ma fin* (R14), and *Se vous n'estes* (R7).

Stravinsky, Igor.
    1985. *Stravinsky: Selected Correspondence*, ed. Robert Craft. Vol. 3 of 3
    vols. New York: Knopf.
    Stravinsky apparently ordered the reprint of Ludwig's Machaut edition in 1954 (382).

Stravinsky, Igor, and Robert Craft.
    1962. *Expositions and Developments*. Garden City, N.Y.: Doubleday.
    Stravinsky denies that his Mass of 1944–48 was influenced by Machaut's Mass, which he
    first heard a year after the completion of his Mass (65).

Strohm, Reinhard.
    1984a. "The *ars nova* Fragments of Ghent." *Tijdschrift van de Vereniging
    voor Nederlandse Muziekgeschiedenis* 34:109–31.
    Description of two fragments of music, one of which—**Gr 3360** [68]—contains
    Machaut's *De petit po* (B18) and *Se vous n'estes* (R7). Includes a brilliant analysis of an
    "international repertory" of French/Flemish Ars Nova chansons that circulated from the
    Flemish-Burgundian court to Germany and Italy, a tradition distinct from the musically
    complex works of the Ars Subtilior that were cultivated in the south of France. Abstract:
    RILM 18 (1984), no. 1109.

    1984b. "Native and Foreign Polyphony in Late Medieval Austria." *Musica
    disciplina* 38: 205–30.
    Includes further material on the "international repertory" described in Strohm 1984a, and
    information on the MS **Nur** [71]. Abstract: *RILM* 18 (1984), no. 1108.

    1985. *Music in Late Medieval Bruges*. Oxford: Clarendon Press.
    Institutions that cultivated music—churches, convents, confraternities, city, and court—
    the sacred and secular repertories they performed, and extant sources for music at Bruges, a
    principal city in the Low Countries in the Middle Ages. For the most part, the period
    considered falls later than Machaut's period of activity. Abstract: *RILM* 19 (1985), no.
    1405. Reviews: Margaret Bent, *Musical Times* 128 (1987): 87–89; Peter Cahn, *Neue
    Zeitschrift für Musik* 147/11 (Nov. 1986): 77; Willem Elders, *Tijdschrift van de
    Vereniging voor Nederlandse Muziekgeschiedenis* 37 (1987): 213–19; David Fallows,
    Early Music History 6 (1986): 279–90; Iain Fenlon, *Early Music* 14 (1986): 263–65;
    Paula Higgins, *Journal of the American Musicological Society* 42 (1989): 150–61;
    Sophie Le Castel, *Nuova rivista musicale italiana* 20 (1986): 443–44; Agnieszka
    Leszczyńska, *Muzyka* 33/1 (1988): 123–26; Claire Maître, *Revue de musicologie* 72
    (1986): 143–44; Karen E. Manley, *Brio* 22 (1985): 59–60; Martin Staehelin,
    Musikforschung 43 (1990): 282–84; Andrew Wathey, *Music and Letters* 70 (1989): 79–

82; Edith Weber, *Revue historique* 557 (1986): 261–62; Isobel Woods, *Journal of the Royal Musical Association* 112 (1987): 323–26.

1989. "Filippotto da Caserta, ovvero i francesi in Lombardia." In *In cantu et in sermone: For Nino Pirrotta on His 80th Birthday*, ed. Fabrizio Della Seta and Franco Piperno, 65–74. Italian Medieval and Renaissance Studies 2. Florence: Olschki; n.p.: University of Western Australia Press.
The principal center of the cultivation of the Ars Subtilior in Italy was the Visconti court, especially the court of Giangaleazzo Visconti (r. 1385–1402). Filippotto da Caserta was attached to this circle. Some of the works Strohm discusses contain textual allusions to works of Machaut. Abstract: *RILM* 23 (1989), no. 1943.

1993. *The Rise of European Music, 1380–1500*. Cambridge: Cambridge University Press.
An enormously wide-ranging study of music and institutions in the Ars Subtilior and fifteenth century in France, the Low Countries, Britain, Italy, Spain, and Central Europe. Although Machaut is not addressed directly, Strohm's study of the Ars Subtilior and early fifteenth century is essential reading for any attempt to come to terms with Machaut's position in the musical tradition and with his legacy. Reviews: Michael Eckert, *Antioch Review* 53 (1995): 114; Lewis Lockwood, *Proceedings of the Royal Musical Association* 120 (1995): 151–62; Alejandro Planchart, *Early Music* 22 (1994): 677–79.

Sturges, Robert S.
1986. "Speculation and Interpretation in Machaut's *Voir-Dit*." *Romance Quarterly* 33:23–33.
Analysis of the narrator's and the reader's response to the texts he reads; what the reader and narrator learn, and what is hidden from the reader. Revised as 1991a, 100–124.

1991a. *Medieval Interpretation: Models of Reading in Literary Narrative, 1100–1500*. Carbondale and Edwardsville: Southern Illinois University Press.
See especially chap. 3, "Marie de France and Guillaume de Machaut: Love and Reading in the Twelfth and Fourteenth Centuries," which discusses the self-conscious textuality in Marie de France's lais and Machaut's *Voir Dit*. The section on Machaut is a much revised version of Sturges 1986, actively engaging the scholarship of S.J. Williams, Calin, Brownlee, and J. Cerquiglini. Machaut's *Voir Dit* reflects the questioning of knowledge seen in the philosophy of William of Ockham: "Guillaume de Machaut's *Livre du Voir-Dit*, with its playful destabilization of all meaning, including its own claims to truth, is the most sophisticated literary response to the indeterminate, post-neoplatonic *mentalité* yet to appear" (221). Reviews: Mark Amsler, *Studies in the Age of Chaucer* 14 (1992): 212–16; Norris J. Lacy, *Speculum* 69 (1994): 569–71; Paul Zumthor, *Canadian Review of Comparative Literature* 19 (1992): 640–42.

1991b. "Textual Scholarship: Ideologies of Literary Production." *Exemplaria* 3:109–31.
Authority, stability, and intention in medieval literary works, and the methodologies of modern edition-making. Machaut is mentioned on p. 115; the *Voir Dit* anagram is discussed on pp. 120–21.

1992. "The Critical Reception of Machaut's *Voir-Dit* and the History of Literary History." *French Forum* 17:133–51.
The historiography of medieval literary criticism of the last hundred years falls into three periods, the scholarly, the critical, and the metacritical. Machaut's works, demonstrated here with the *Voir Dit*, have only been of interest to the first and last of these periods. Highly informative.

Suard, F.
1994. "Voir Dit (le Livre du)." In *Dictionnaire des œuvres littéraires de langue française*, ed. Jean-Pierre de Beaumarchais and Daniel Couty, 2052–53. 4 vols., continuous pagination. Paris: Bordas.
Survey article.

Suchier, Hermann.
  1897. "Das Anagramm in Machauts *Voir Dit.*" *Zeitschrift für romanische Philologie* 21:541–45.
  Discussion of anagrams in *Confort*, *Prise*, *Harpe*, and *Voir Dit*. See comments in Cerquiglini 1985b, 238–39. Review: G. Paris 1898.

Suchier, Hermann, and Adolf Birch-Hirschfeld.
  1900. *Geschichte der französischen Literatur von den ältesten Zeiten bis zur Gegenwart.* Leipzig and Vienna: Bibliographisches Institut. 2nd rev. ed. Vol. 1 of 2 vols. Leipzig and Vienna: Bibliographisches Institut, 1913.
  Discussion of *Jugement Navarre*, *Confort*, *Voir Dit*, and *Prise*; lyrics discussed, with German translations, include *Blanche* (Lo82), *Celle qui unques* (VD1), *Donnez, seigneurs* (B26), *Dou memoire* (Lo253), *Onques mes cuers* (Lo218), and *Se vos courrous* (Lo247) (pp. 234–39; no changes in 2nd edition, pp. 241–46).

Swartz, Anne.
  1974. "A New Chronology of the *Ballades* of Machaut." *Acta musicologica* 46:192–207.
  This work apparently attacks the thesis—proposed by no one—that Machaut wrote all of his ballades within a five-year period at the end of his life. Full of errors; should not be consulted. Some criticism in Günther 1982, 106–8. Abstract: *RILM* 8 (1974), no. 1880.

Switten, Margaret L.
  1988a. "Manuscript Sources and Presentation of Materials." In *The Medieval Lyric: A Project Supported by The National Endowment for the Humanities and Mount Holyoke College. Commentary Volume,* 76–84. South Hadley, Mass.: The Medieval Lyric, Margaret Switten, director, 1988.
  Includes a brief discussion of the manuscript tradition of *Remede*.

  1988b. *The Medieval Lyric: A Project Supported by The National Endowment for the Humanities and Mount Holyoke College. Anthology I: Monastic Song, Troubadour Song, German Song, Trouvère Song.* Rev. ed. South Hadley, Mass.: The Medieval Lyric, Margaret Switten, director, 1988.
  Includes a verse translation of the ballade *Dame de qui* (RF5) by Walter A. Blue (173).

  1988c. *The Medieval Lyric: A Project Supported by The National Endowment for the Humanities and Mount Holyoke College. Anthology II: Guillaume de Machaut,* Remede de Fortune. Rev. ed. South Hadley, Mass.: The Medieval Lyric, Margaret Switten, director, 1988.
  Essay on *Remede,* especially on the lyrical insertions, with presentation of the argument of Switten 1989. Translation of large excerpts from *Remede,* including all of the lyrical insertions, by Margaret Switten, adapted from William W. Kibler's translation in Wimsatt/Kibler 1988. Xerox facsimiles of *Remede* lyrics from MS C.

  1989. "Guillaume de Machaut: Le *Remede de Fortune* au carrefour d'un art nouveau." *Cahiers de l'Association Internationale des Etudes Françaises* 41:101–16, plates (discussion, 310).
  A reading of the *Remede* based on the transformation of the musical notation employed for the lyrical insertions, from the archaic Ars Antiqua notation of *Qui n'aroit* (RF1), *Tels rit* (RF2), and *Joie, plaisence* (RF3), to the most up-to-date Ars Nova notation of *En amer* (RF4), *Dame, de qui* (RF5), *Dame, a vous* (RF6), and *Dame, mon cuer en vous* (RF7).

  1995. *Music and Poetry in the Middle Ages. A Guide to Research on French and Occitan Song, 1100–1400.* Garland Medieval Bibliographies 19; Garland Reference Library of the Humanities 1102. New York and London: Garland, 1995.
  Useful annotated bibliography. Includes an important historiographical essay.

Tarbé, [Louis Hardouin] Prosper, ed.
  1849. *Les Œuvres de Guillaume de Machault*. Collection des Poëtes Champenois Antérieurs au XVIe Siècle 3. Reims and Paris: Techener. Reprint. Geneva: Slatkine, 1977.

Biographical study and editions of excerpts from a number of narrative works, and including the following lyrics: *Amis, je t'aporte* (Lo212), *Blanche com lis* (Lo82), *Ce qui soustient* (R12), *Celle qui unques* (VD1), *Cinc, .vii.,* (VD63), *Cinc, un* (R6), *Dame, qui vuet* (R16), *Dix et sept* (R17), *Donnez, signeurs* (B26), *Dou memoire* (Lo253), *Douce dame, quant* (Lo64), *Douce dame, tant* (Lo235=R20), *Gentils cuers* (Lo27), *Je ne suis pas* (Lo11), *Je puis trop* (Lo203=B28), *Las! amours* (Lo52), *Ma fin* (R14), *On ne puet riens* (Lo192), *Onques mes cuers* (Lo218), *Plourez, dames* (Lo229=B32), *Pour Dieu, dame* (Lo208), *Quant Theseüs / Ne quier* (B34), *Qui sert se faire* (Lo262), *Riches d'amour* (B5), *Sans cuer* (Lo148=R4), *Se je vous aim* (Lo231), *Se li espoirs* (Lo257), *Se par amours* (Lo207), *Se pour ce muir* (Lo248=B36), *Se vos courrous* (Lo247), *Se vos regars* (Lo9), *Trop est crueus* (Lo51).Tarbé's work has been completely superseded by other, more complete and more correct editions and studies. See the historiographical discussion in Cerquiglini 1991b. Review: Magnin 1851 (with additional excerpts from the *Voir Dit*). Review of reprint ed.: Waldemar Voisé, "Guillaume de Machaut Seven [*sic*] Centuries Later," *Kwartalnik historii nauki i techniki* 24 (1979): 154–55.

  1856. *Poésies d'Agnès de Navarre-Champagne, dame de Foix*. Collection des Poëtes Champenois Antérieurs au XVIe Siècle 16. Paris: Aubry; Reims: Brissart-Binet.

Tarbé fancifully attributed the lady's lyrics in the *Voir-Dit*, as well as other of Machaut's lyrics in a feminine voice, to Agnes of Navarre, sister of Charles of Navarre and wife of Gaston Fébus. Tarbé had uncritically accepted her as the dedicatee of the *Voir Dit*, following Caylus 1753a. Editions of *Amis, bien voy* (VD36), *Amis, comment que* (Lo224), *Amis, dolens* (Bn10=B17), *Amis, je t'ay* (Lo254), *Amis, mon cuer* (Lo220), *Amis, se Dieus* (VD38), *Amis si parfaitement* (VD50=Lo199), *Amis, venés* (VD24), *Amis, vostre* (Lo137), *Amours, se plus* (L9), *Autre de vous* (VD43), *Celle qui unques* (VD1), *Certes mes dous* (Lo90), *Certes moult* (Lo169), *Cilz ha bien* (VD18=V24), *Cinc, .vii.,* (VD63), *Des que premiers* (VD26), *Deus choses* (Cp2), *Douce dame, tant* (Lo235=R20), *Dous amis* (B6), *Il n'est dolour* (VD48=Lo194), *L'amour de vous* (VD22), *Merveille fu* (VD46), *Mes dous amis* (Cp5), *Moult sui* (V37), *Ne soiez* (VD54), *Ne vous estuet* (VD12), *Nes qu'on* (VD16=Lo232=B33), *On parle* (L8), *Pour vivre* (VD3), *Puis qu'en oubli* (R18), *Quant Ecuba* (Cp4), *Sans cuer* (VD31=Lo148=R4, attributed to Machaut), *Se bons* (Lo198), *Se damer* (V20), *Se mes dous* (Lo181), *Se mesdisans* (V15), *Toute Belle* (VD33, attributed to Machaut), *Tresdoulz amis quant* (VD28), *Tresdoulz amis, j'ay* (VD34), *Trop ne me puis* (Lo225), and *Vostre langueur* (VD40).

Tavani, Giuseppe.
  1985. "Musica e poesia in Guillaume de Machaut." In *L'Ars Nova italiana del Trecento V*, ed. Agostino Ziino, 245–56. Palermo: Enchiridion.

Unlike the well-regulated relationship between poetry and music in the Ars Antiqua, the Ars Nova displays a bizarre and capricious relation between text and music, with total subordination of text to music. Machaut's works are exceptions that exhibit a concern for poetry not seen elsewhere. The demonstration is based on an analysis of passages from the *Prologue, Remede,* and *Voir Dit*.

Taylor, Ann.
  1987. "Epic Motifs in Chaucer's 'Tale of Ceyx and Alcyone.'" *Helios* n.s. 14/1 (spring): 39–45.

Chaucer's use of the myth of Ceyx and Alcyone in the *Book of the Duchess*. Many references to literary studies of the myth, with consideration of structural analogies in other literature, including Machaut's *Fonteinne*.

Taylor, Jane H.M.
  1990. "The Lyric Insertion: Towards a Functional Model." In *Courtly Literature: Culture and Context. Selected Papers from the 5th Triennial Congress*

of the International Courtly Literature Society, Dalfsen, The Netherlands, 9–16 August, 1986, ed. Keith Busby and Erik Kooper, 539–48. Utrecht Publications in General and Comparative Literature 25. Amsterdam and Philadelphia: Benjamins.

Concerned mainly with Froissart's *Meliador,* this article mentions Machaut only briefly (548 n. 26, concerning the *Voir Dit*); but the discussion of the lyric insertion is important and worth consulting. Includes a summary of Cerquiglini 1977b (541–42).

1993. "Machaut's *Livre du Voir-Dit* and the Poetics of the Title." In *Et c'est la fin pour quoy sommes ensemble. Hommage à Jean Dufournet, Professeur à la Sorbonne Nouvelle. Littérature, histoire et langue du Moyen Age,* 3:1351–62 Nouvelle Bibliothèque du Moyen Age 25. 3 vols. Paris: Champion.

The analysis of medieval titles for literary works. "Machaut's *Livre du Voir-Dit* [is] a supreme example of the title in its most complex and most sophisticated relationship with both text and reader" (1355).

Taylor, Steven M.
1980. "Portraits of Pestilence: The Plague in the Work of Machaut and Boccaccio." *Allegorica* 5:105–18.

Close analysis of Machaut's portrayal of the plague in *Jugement Navarre,* with some points of comparison to Boccaccio's *Decameron.* Contains an appendix of analogous passages, translated into English (115–18).

Tesnière, Marie-Hélène.
1986. "Les manuscrits copiés par Raoul Tainguy: un aspect de la culture des grands officiers royaux au début du XVe siècle." *Romania* 107:282–368.

Exhaustive study of the manuscripts copied by Raoul Tainguy, best known as a copyist of the manuscript of the complete works of Eustache Deschamps (*F:Pn 840*), but also copyist of Machaut MS H [17]. Tainguy was retained by Arnaud de Corbie (ca. 1325–1414), first President of Parlement (1373) and Chancellor of France (1388–1413). MS H was probably in his library.

Thiébaux, Marcelle.
1974. *The Stag of Love: The Chase in Medieval Literature.* Ithaca and London: Cornell University Press.

Includes a discussion of the *Dit du Cerf Blanc,* ascribed by Fourrier (1979) to Machaut (145–49, 161–66). Includes translations of a few passages, and black-and-white reproductions of miniatures J28 and 32 (see chap. 4.4x).

Thiry-Stassin, Martine.
1970. "Quelques allusions médiévales au thème de Narcisse." *Marche Romane* 20/4:47–58.

Mention of Narcissus in *Fonteinne* and *J'ay tant / Lasse!* (M7).

Thomas, Antoine.
1881. "Extraits des archives du Vatican pour servir à l'histoire littéraire. I. Luchetto Gattilusio. II. Jaufré de Foixa. III. Guillaume de Machaut." *Romania* 10:321–33.

Includes papal documents concerning Guillaume and Jean de Machaut (325–33). Thomas was the first to distinguish which documents refer to our Machaut, thereby clearing up confusion over Machaut's date of birth. This publication of the material is slightly more complete than A. Thomas 1884.

1882. "Extraits des archives du Vatican pour servir à l'histoire littéraire (*Suite*). IV. Philippe de Vitri. V. Gace de la Bigne. VI. Pierre Bersuire." *Romania* 11:177–87.

Includes papal documents concerning Philippe de Vitry (177–79).

1884. "Extraits des archives du Vatican pour servir à l'histoire littéraire du Moyen-Age." *Mélanges d'archéologie et d'histoire de l'Ecole française de Rome* 4:9–52.
Includes papal documents concerning Philippe de Vitry (16–19) and Guillaume and Jean de Machaut (36–46). See A. Thomas 1881; 1882.

1912. "Guillaume de Machaut et l'*Ovide Moralisé*." *Romania* 41:382–400.
Critical edition of the 265-line sequence of Polyphemus's song to Galatea from the *Voir Dit*, omitted in P. Paris 1875, where it would follow l. 7215. Machaut copied ll. 29–256 directly from the *Ovide Moralisé*. This is the longest, but by no means the only, text omission in the Paris edition. See the commentary in Cerquiglini 1991b, 365.

Thomas, Heinz.
1973. *Zwischen Regnum und Imperium: Die Fürstentümer Bar und Lothringen zur Zeit Kaiser Karls IV.* Bonner historische Forschungen 40. Bonn: Röhrscheid.
Political history of a region important to Jean and Guillaume de Machaut.

Thomas, Madelaine Cottet.
1977. "L'Art d'écrire de Guillaume de Machaut dans ses *Dits*." Ph.D. diss. Université de Grenoble-III.
Not examined.

Thomas, Marcel.
1978. "French Illumination in the Time of Guillaume de Machaut." In Cosman 1978, 145–65.
An overview of the art of French manuscript illumination during Machaut's lifetime. Includes a reproduction of *Prologue* miniature A1 (160 fig. 9).

Tihon, Camille.
1962. *Lettres de Grégoire XI (1371–1378).* Vol. II. Analecta Vaticano-Belgica 20. Brussels and Rome: Institut Historique Belge de Rome.
Papal documents.

Tischler, Hans.
1988. "The Lyric Lai before Machaut." In *Music from the Middle Ages through the Twentieth Century: Essays in Honor of Gwynn S. McPeek*, ed. Carmelo P. Comberiati and Matthew C. Steel, 56–63. New York: Gordon and Breach.
Study of nine lais (including five Latin works) in the *Roman de Fauvel* (MS *F:Pn 146*), a repertory with characteristics that distinguish it from earlier lais and from the lais of Machaut. Abstract: *RILM* 23 (1989), no. 1949.

Tomasello, Andrew.
1983. *Music and Ritual at Papal Avignon 1309–1403.* Studies in Musicology 75. Ann Arbor: UMI Research Press.
Publication of the author's 1982 Yale dissertation. Includes a biography of Johannes Lehoudain, who obtained Machaut's canonicate after his death (59–61, 174 n. 81, 244).

1988. "Scribal Design in the Compilation of Ivrea MS. 115." *Musica disciplina* 42:73–100.
Study of MS **Iv** [57]. Abstract: *RILM* 22 (1988), no. 1721.

Torrents, Jaume Massó.
1913–14. "Bibliografía dels antics poetes catalans." *Institut d'Estudis Catalans. Anuari.* 5:3–205.
Includes a catalogue of MS **Bc** [55] (pp. 72–76).

Travers, Emile.
1881. *Les Instruments de musique au XIVe siècle d'après Guillaume de Machaut. Réunion des sociétés des beaux-arts des départements à la*

Sorbonne 5:189–225. Offprint. Paris: Plon.

Systematic discussion of the twenty-two wind instruments, thirteen string instruments, and eight percussion instruments listed in the *Remede* and *Prise*.

Tuchman, Barbara W.

1978. *A Distant Mirror: The Calamitous 14th Century*. New York: Knopf.

Mentions *Voir Dit*, but based only on Tarbé 1849 (209).

Turek, Ralph, comp.

1984. *Analytical Anthology of Music*. New York: Knopf.

Includes edition of *J'ay tant / Lasse!* (M7) (pp. 33–41).

Tyson, Diana B.

1975 (ed.). *La Vie du Prince Noir by Chandos Herald. Edited from the Manuscript in the University of London Library*. Beihefte zur Zeitschrift für romanische Philologie 147. Tübingen: Niemeyer.

A French biographical poem of the late fourteenth century, probably influenced by Machaut's *Prise*.

1981. "King Arthur as a Literary Device in French Vernacular History Writing of the Fourteenth Century." *Bulletin Bibliographique de la Société Internationale Arthurienne* 33:237–57.

Includes material on the *Neuf Preux* (Nine Worthies), relevant to passages in *Lyon*, *Confort*, and the *Prise* (242–43).

1986. "French Vernacular History Writers and Their Patrons in the Fourteenth Century." *Medievalia et Humanistica* n.s. 14:103–24.

Machaut's *Prise* could have been requested by Charles V (105).

Uitti, Karl D.

1978. "From *Clerc* to *Poète*: The Relevance of the *Romance of the Rose* to Machaut's World." In Cosman 1978, 209–16.

The learned clerkly narrator of twelfth-century romance and the first-person lover of trouvère chansons combine to form the "Poet-Lover" in the portion of the *Roman de la Rose* by Guillaume de Lorris. Yet Jean de Meun, who continued the work, retained Guillaume as lover and protagonist, maintaining the first person for both narrator and protagonist. Such a narrator figure—a true poet singing someone else's love—is the model for the narrator in Machaut. See the summary of the argument in Brownlee 1984, 12–14.

Ultan, Lloyd.

1977a. *Music Theory: Problems and Practices in the Middle Ages and Renaissance*. Minneapolis: University of Minnesota Press.

Includes diplomatic facsimiles of *Dame, comment qu'amez* (B16), *En mon cuer* (V27/24), and *Tuit mi penser* (V28/25), and a discussion of musical aspects of the Mass.

1977b. *Workbook / Anthology for Music Theory: Problems and Practices in the Middle Ages and Renaissance*. Minneapolis: University of Minnesota Press.

Includes diplomatic facsimiles of *C'est force* (V16), *Hé! dame de vaillance* (V1), *Ma fin* (R14), *Martyrum / Diligenter* (M19), *Quant je sui* (V13), and *Sans cuer m'en / Amis / Dame* (B17); and editions of Agnus, *Cinc, un* (R6), and *N'en fait* (B11).

Vachulka, Ladislav.

1982. "Guillaume de Machaut et la vie musicale de Prague." In Guillaume de Machaut 1982, 321–27.

Information on Prague under Emperor Charles IV. Concludes incredibly that Machaut returned to Prague, where he remained almost to the end of his life.

Valero, Ana María. See Holzbacher, Ana-María.

Vallet de Viriville, Auguste.
1858. "La bibliothèque d'Isabeau de Bavière, reine de France." *Bulletin du bibliophile* 13:663–87.
A document mentioning gold clasps for "le livre des *Balades*, Messire Othes de Grantson" may relate to MS **Pa** [50] (p. 684).

Van Buren, Ann Hagopian.
1986a. "Reality and Literary Romance in the Park of Hesdin." *Medieval Gardens*, ed. Elisabeth Blair MacDougall, 117–34. Dumbarton Oaks Colloquium on the History of Landscape Architecture 9. Washington, D.C.: Dumbarton Oaks Research Library and Collection; Trustees of Harvard University.
Detailed description of the garden described in *Remede*.
1986b. "Thoughts, Old and New, on the Sources of Early Netherlandish Painting." *Simiolus—Netherlands Quarterly for the History of Art* 16:93–112.
Miniatures of Toute Belle's *image* in the *Voir Dit* may provide evidence of portrait painting in France earlier than hitherto known.

Van den Abeele, Baudouin.
1990. *La fauconnerie dans les lettres françaises du XIIe au XIVe siècle.* Mediaevalia Lovaniensia 1/18. Katholieke Universiteit Leuven, Instituut voor Middeleeuwse Studies. Leuven: Leuven University Press.
Includes a study of *Alerion* (229–38). Reviews: Jean-Olivier Benoist, *Cahiers de civilisation médiévale* 36 (1993): 331–33; Paola Cifarelli, *Studi francesi* 36 (1992): 324; Constance B. Hieatt, *Romance Philology* 47 (1993–94): 252–54.

Van den Boogaard, Nico H.J.
1969. *Rondeaux et refrains du XIIe siècle au début du XIVe. Collationnement, introduction et notes.* Bibliothèque Française et Romane D3. Paris: Klincksieck.
Standard catalogue of *refrains*.

Vander Linden, Albert, ed.
1972. *Le manuscrit musical M 222 C 22 de la Bibliothèque de Strasbourg, XVe siècle.* Thesaurus Musicus 2. Brussels: Office International de Librairie.
Facsimile of Edmond de Coussemaker's incipit catalogue and partial copy of **Str** [73], a manuscript destroyed in 1870.

van der Werf, Hendrik, and Wolf Frobenius.
1983. "Cantus coronatus." *Handwörterbuch der musikalischen Terminologie*, ed. Hans Heinrich Eggebrecht. Wiesbaden: Steiner, 1971–. 12 pp.
Detailed study of the history and meaning of the term "cantus coronatus" (thirteenth to sixteenth century). Considers the *chant royal*; brief mention of Machaut's *Joie, plaisance* (RF3) (pp. 2–6). Many quotations from primary sources, and a large bibliography.

van Uytven, R.
1984. "Rood-wit-zwart: kleurensymboliek en kleursignalen in de Middeleeuwen." *Tijdschrift voor Geschiedenis* 97:447–69.
Machaut's *Remede* and *Voir Dit* mentioned, with a comparative chart of courtly color codes from the fourteenth to the seventeenth century (448–49).

Varin, Pierre.
1843–48. *Archives administratives de la ville de Reims. Collection de pièces inédites pouvant servir à l'histoire des institutions dans l'intérieur de la cité.* Collection de documents inédits sur l'histoire de France. 1er sér. Histoire politique. Vols. 2/1–2. Paris: Crapelet, 1843. Vol. 3. Paris: Crapelet, 1848.
Archival documents.

1844. *Archives législatives de la ville de Reims. Collection de pièces inédites pouvant servir à l'histoire des institutions dans l'intérieur de la cité. Seconde partie. Statuts.* Collection de documents inédits sur l'histoire de France. 1er sér. Histoire politique. Vol. 1. Paris: Crapelet.
Archival documents.

1853. *Archives administratives et législatives de la ville de Reims. Collection de pièces inédites pouvant servir à l'histoire des institutions dans l'intérieur de la cité. Table générale des matières,* by L. Amiel. Paris: Lahure.
Index to the archival documents published in Varin 1844 and elsewhere.

Varty, Kenneth.
1965. "Deschamps's *Art de Dictier.*" *French Studies* 19:164–67.
Emphasizes Deschamps's new definition of lyrical poetry, one divorced from a consideration of music. Comments on earlier studies of the *Art de Dictier.*

Vaughan, Richard.
1962. *Philip the Bold: The Formation of the Burgundian State.* Cambridge, Mass.: Harvard University Press.
Biography of Duke Philip the Bold of Burgundy.

Vecchi, Giuseppe.
1977. "'Alcune memorie intorno all musica figurata' di Padre Giambattista Martini (dalla *Storia della musica,* Vol. 4)." In *Festschrift Ferdinand Haberl zum 70. Geburtstag. Sacerdos et cantus Gregoriani magister,* ed. Franz A. Stein, 303–10. Regensburg: Bosse.
Only three of the five planned volumes of Padre Martini's history of music appeared during his lifetime (1706–84). Notes preserved at the Accademia Philarmonica in Bologna give the plan for the rest of the work, which would have included a discussion of Johannes de Muris's passage on Machaut and imperfect breves (305, 308). Abstract: *RILM* 11 (1977), no. 289.

Vellekoop, Kees.
1984. "Die Estampie: ihre Besetzung und Funktion." *Basler Jahrbuch für historische Musikpraxis* 8:51–65.
Review of extant *estampies* and the literary evidence for their performance practice. Concludes that until ca. 1350, the vielle was preferred for performance of the *estampie* at court. After this, the term *estampie* may simply imply instrumental music in general. Machaut's extensive list of instruments in *Remede* in the context of dance is a kind of vision: such a large and varied ensemble is unimaginable in a practical context. Nevertheless, modern performances of *estampies,* which employ large instrumental ensembles, seem inspired by the passage in Machaut (62–63).

1990. "De ontdekking van de middeleeuwse muziek: Een historiografische studie." In *Terugstrevend naar ginds: de wereld van Helene Nolthenius,* ed. Etty Mulder, 161–86. Nijmegen, The Netherlands: SUN.
A readable overview of figures important for the rediscovery of medieval music in the period 1775–1900, from Gerbert to Ambros. Especially valuable for the overview of the accomplishments of Kiesewetter and Fétis. Review: Martin van Schaik, *Tijdschrift van de Vereniging voor Nederlandse Muziekgeschiedenis* 42 (1992): 63–66.

Verger, Jacques.
1973. *Les Universités au Moyen Age.* L'Historien 14. Collection SUP. Paris: Presses Universitaires de France.
Helpful survey of medieval universities.

Vesce, Thomas, E.
1969–70. "Love as Found in Machaut's *Dit dou Lion.*" *Romance Notes* 11: 174–80.
Literary study of *Lyon.*

Vidal, J.-M.
1903. *Benoît XII (1334–1342). Lettres communes analysées d'après les registres dits d'Avignon et de Vatican.* Vol. 1, *Années I, II et III.* Bibliothèque des Ecoles Françaises d'Athènes et de Rome 3. Registres et lettres des papes du XIVe siècle. Paris: Fontemoing.
Papal documents.

Vielliard, Françoise, and Jacques Monfrin (see also Bossuat 1951; 1955; 1961).
1991. *Manuel bibliographique de la littérature française du Moyen Age de Robert Bossuat. Troisième supplément (1960–1980).* Vol. 2, *L'ancien français (chapitres IV à IX); Le Moyen Français.* Paris: Editions du CNRS.
Nos. 6826–901 pertain to Machaut.

Vielliard, Jeanne.
1930. "Nouveaux documents sur la Culture Catalane au Moyen Age." *Estudis Universitaris Catalans* 15:21–40.
Contains some documents on the diffusion of Machaut manuscripts in Aragon in the late fourteenth century.

1935. "Yolande de Bar, reine d'Aragon." *Revue des questions historiques* 122:39–55.
Brief biography of an enthusiastic connoisseur of Machaut's poetry, and possibly an early owner of MS **Vg** [3].

Vitale-Brovarone, Alessandro, ed.
1980. *Recueil de galanteries (Torino, Archivio di Stato, J.b.IX.10).* Le Moyen Français 6. Montreal: Ceres.
A collection of poetry transmitting some lyrics of Machaut, including *Avec raison l'Escripture est d'acord* [*opus dubium*; ed. no. 11], *Helas! pour quoy virent* (Lo53; ed. no. 14), *De petit po* (B18; ed. no. 16), *Se pour ce muir* (B36; ed. no. 20), *En oil estrange* (MS **J** no. 101, LoA9; ed. no. 166), *J'ay mon bec jaune* (MS **J** no. 99, LoA7; ed. no. 169). Reviews: James W. Hassel III, *Speculum* 59 (1984): 963–64; Martijn Rus, *Rapports—Het Franse Boek* 54 (1984): 137–38.

Voisé, Waldemar.
1965. "Guillaume de Machaut w Polsce i o Polsce" (Guillaume de Machaut in Poland and on Poland). *Muzyka* 10:52–62.
Historical references to areas of Poland mentioned in *Confort* and *Prise*. Includes several excerpts from *Confort* and *Prise* translated into Polish.

1982. "Guillaume de Machaut en Pologne." In Guillaume de Machaut 1982, 49–54.
Voisé 1965 provides a more detailed treatment of the same material.

Wagner, Peter.
1913. *Geschichte der Messe.* Part 1, *Bis 1600.* Kleine Handbücher der Musikgeschichte nach Gattungen 11/1. Leipzig: Breitkopf & Härtel.
Includes a discussion of those segments of the Mass that had been published by 1913 (43–46).

Wallen, Martha.
1980. "Biblical and Mythological Typology in Machaut's *Confort d'Ami.*" *Res Publica Litterarum* 3:191–206.
An excellent literary analysis of *Confort* based on iconographical material in the miniatures in **A** and **F**, with a facsimile of miniature F54 (chap. 4.4h). Wallen's use of the iconography of the *Ovide Moralisé* opens a significant area for future research. Unfortunately, Wallen did not take account of MS **Vg**, which, with 39 miniatures, has the most developed cycle of miniatures for *Confort*.

Walravens, Cornelis J.H.
1971. *Alain Chartier: Etudes biographiques, suivies de pièces justificatives, d'une description des éditions et d'une édition des ouvrages inédits.* Amsterdam: Meulenhoff-Didier.

Publication of author's 1971 Utrecht dissertation, a bibliographical study of printed editions from 1489 to 1617 of works of Chartier (see *Chartier* [47]) which include the text of Machaut's lai *Amis t'amour* (L10).

Walters, Lori.
1992. "Fathers and Daughters: Christine de Pizan as Reader of the Male Tradition of *Clergie* in the *Dit de la Rose*." In *Reinterpreting Christine de Pizan*, ed. Earl Jeffrey Richards et al., 63–76. Athens and London: University of Georgia Press.

Primarily addresses Christine's literary relationship to Eustache Deschamps, but includes a discussion of the ballades Deschamps composed in Machaut's honor.

Wathey, Andrew (see also *RISM* 1993).
1988. "Lost Books of Polyphony in England: A List to 1500." *RMA Research Chronicle* 21:1–19.

Prints a document from Guiffrey 1894–96, concerning a Machaut manuscript loaned in 1412 by the duke of Berry to the duke of Clarence, presumably MS **E** [7] (p. 17 no. 173).

1989. "The Production of Books of Liturgical Polyphony." In *Book Production and Publishing in Britain 1375–1475*, ed. Jeremy Griffiths and Derek Pearsall, 143–61. Cambridge Studies in Publishing and Printing History. Cambridge: Cambridge University Press.

Although not directly concerned with Machaut, this study is important for any consideration of manuscripts of polyphony. Considers the peculiar nature of musical texts, the manners in which repertories were collected into manuscripts, and manuscript copying.

1994. "Musicology, Archives and Historiography." In *Archives et bibliothèques de Belgique / Archief- en bibliotheekwezen in België*. Extranummer 46, *Musicology and Archival Research*, ed. Barbara Haggh, Frank Daelemans, and André Vanrie. Colloquium Proceedings Brussels, 22–23.4.1993. Brussels: Algemeen Rijksarchief.

Historiography of the use of archival documents in history writing, and a discussion of pitfalls of their proper interpretation for musicological research. Wathey provides particular examples of problems associated with administrative records, including documents relating to benefices, payments, land holdings, and wills. Among the documents discussed is a warrant of Charles of Navarre regulating payment for a hackney given to Machaut (see chap. 1.12.2).

Weber, Horst.
1987. "Zu Strawinskys Machaut-Rezeption." In *Alte Musik als ästhetische Gegenwart* 2:317–24. Internationaler musikwissenschaftlicher Kongress 1985, Stuttgart. Kassel: Bärenreiter.

The influence of Machaut's Mass on Stravinsky's Mass of 1944–48, with special attention to the Agnus Dei movements; the influence of Machaut's musical techniques (harmony and isorhythm) on the *Canticum sacrum* of 1955; and the influence of Machaut's isorhythm on the *Movements for Piano and Orchestra* of 1959 (see also Briner 1960).

Weber, Jerome F.
1979. "The Greatest Composer of His Century." *Fanfare* 3/1 (Sept.–Oct.): 10–16, 206–10.

A review of the sound recordings Adès 7078–80 and 1750 Arch Records S-1773 (see chap. 8.8), with an excellent discography of recordings of Machaut up to 1979.

1982. "Vitry and Machaut in the 14th Century of Kaiser Karl." *Fanfare* 5/3 (Jan.–Feb.): 34–37.

A review of the sound recordings Supraphon 1112 2451-2, Panton 8111 0056, Calig CAL 30451, and CBS Masterworks 76534 (see chap. 8.8), with a discography of recordings of Philippe de Vitry up to 1982.

1990. *A Gregorian Chant Discography.* Discography Series, 20. 2 vols. Utica, New York: J.F. Weber.

A superb discography of plainchant, used here to identify plainchant in recordings of the Machaut Mass that include Mass Propers. Reviews: Joseph Dyer, *Notes* 47 (1990–91): 1174–76; Martin Elste, *Musikforschung* 45 (1992): 375–76; Keith Falconer, *Early Music* 19 (1991): 287–88.

1991. "Liturgical Reconstruction as Reflected in Recordings." *Historical Performance* 4:29–37.

Commentary on the practice of placing the movements of medieval Masses in reconstructed liturgical context, a practice seen in many recent recordings.

1992. "Recent Releases of Plainchant." *Plainsong and Medieval Music* 1:203–13.

Brings J.F. Weber 1990 up to date; item 18 concerns Machaut.

Weber-Bockholdt, Petra.

1992. "Beobachtungen zu den Virelais von Guillaume de Machaut." *Archiv für Musikwissenschaft* 49:263–81.

Strophic structure, text rhythm, and musical setting in Machaut's virelais. Text accents are sometimes mirrored in the music. Concerning the relationship between strophe and refrain, Weber-Bockholdt notes that the opening melody is often not solid tonally because of its function as an interior verse.

Wégimont.

1959. *Les Colloques de Wégimont. II. 1955. L'Ars Nova: Recueil d'études sur la musique du XIVe siècle.* Bibliothèque de la Faculté de Philosophie et Lettres de l'Université de Liège 149. Paris: Les Belles Lettres.

An important collection of papers from a conference on the Ars Nova. See Apel 1959; Reaney 1959a; Schrade 1959. Reviews: Samuel E. Brown, Jr., *Notes* 17 (1959–60): 567; Ursula Günther, "Les colloques de Wégimont 1955," *Musikforschung* 14 (1961): 210–13.

Weiss, Piero, ed. and comp.

1967. *Letters of Composers Through Six Centuries.* Philadelphia: Chilton.

Includes a translation of letter 10 of the *Voir Dit* (1–2).

Weiss, Piero, and Richard Taruskin, eds. and comps.

1984. *Music in the Western World: A History in Documents.* New York: Schirmer Books; London: Collier Macmillan.

Includes a translation of letter 10 of the *Voir Dit* (76–77).

Welker, Lorenz.

1992. "Die Musik der Renaissance." In *Musikalische Interpretation,* ed. Hermann Danuser, 139–215. Neues Handbuch der Musikwissenschaft 11. Laaber: Laaber.

Treats a variety of questions of performance practice in the years ca. 1300 to 1600, including performing forces, tuning, *musica ficta,* tempo, texting, improvisation, and ornamentation, with a large bibliography. Review: Stephen Blum, *Notes* 51 (1994–95): 173–75.

Wennerstrom, Mary H., ed.

1983. *Anthology of Musical Structure and Style.* Englewood Cliffs, N.J.: Prentice Hall.

Includes editions of *Bone pastor / Bone pastor* (M18) (pp. 13–18), and *Foy porter* (V25/22) (pp. 12–13).

Wernli, Andreas.
   1977. "La percettibilità delle strutture isoritmiche. Osservazioni sui Motetti di
   Guillaume de Machaut." *Studi musicali* 6:13–25.
   Some scholars—Besseler, Reichert, and Günther—have viewed isorhythmic structure as
   imperceptible to the listener, while others—Eggebrecht, Sanders, and Kühn (we can now
   add Leech-Wilkinson [1989, 1:37, 126–27])—have argued that the structure can be perceptible. Wernli discusses examples showing various means by which the structure is rendered perceptible, especially in the motets *S'il estoit / S'Amours* (M6), *Bone pastor /
   Bone pastor* (M18), *Christe / Veni* (M21), and *Tu qui gregem / Plange* (M22). The degree
   of perceptibility is different for each work. A looser attitude seems to characterize
   Machaut's late motets.

Wescher, Paul.
   1931. *Beschreibendes Verzeichnis der Miniaturen—Handschriften und
   Einzelblätter—des Kupferstichkabinetts der Staatlichen Museen Berlin.*
   Leipzig: Weber.
   Includes a description of MS Bk [21], with a description of each miniature, and a fac-
   simile of *Lyon* miniature **Bk5**.

Westervelt, L.A.
   1981. "The Mediaeval Notion of Janglery and Chaucer's *Manciple's Tale.*"
   Southern Review 14:107–15.
   Chaucer's use of the story of Apollo and Coronis, with a consideration of the version in
   Machaut's *Voir Dit* (108, 109, 112). Includes a summary of earlier scholarship on this
   question.

Wharton, Susan.
   1980 (ed.). *René d'Anjou: Le Livre du Cuer d'Amours Espris.* 10/18 Bibliothèque médiévale 1385. Paris: Union Générale d'Editions.
   Publication of author's 1979 Cambridge dissertation. King René d'Anjou (1409–80)
   places Machaut among the great poets in his *Livre du Cuer d'Amours Espris* of 1457.
   Reviews: Kurt Baldinger, *Zeitschrift für romanische Philologie* 97 (1981): 648; Ruth
   Morse, *Modern Language Review* 76 (1981): 960.

White, John.
   1957. *The Birth and Rebirth of Pictorial Space.* London: Faber and Faber.
   2nd ed. 1967. 3rd ed. Cambridge, Mass.: Belknap Press of Harvard University Press, 1987.
   Includes discussion of some of the miniaturists of the Machaut manuscripts.

White, John Reeves.
   1969. "Performing Fourteenth-Century Music." *College Music Symposium*
   9:85–90.
   The leader of the New York Pro Musica on performance practice. Abstract: *RILM* 3
   (1969), no. 2665.

Whiting, B[artlett] J.
   1946. "Froissart as Poet." *Mediaeval Studies* 8:189–216.
   Remains an important survey of Froissart's narrative and lyrical poetry. Whiting notes
   many instances of Machaut's influence on Froissart.

Wild, Gerhard.
   1990. "Guillaume de Machaut." In *Kindlers Neues Literatur Lexikon*, ed.
   Walter Jens, 7:44–46. Munich: Kindler. Vol. 7 of 20 vols.
   Dictionary article; brief but current bibliography.

Wilheim, F. András, ed.
   1974. *Guillaume de Machaut, Missa für zwei Frauen- und zwei Männer-
   stimmen.* Budapest: Editio Musica; Zurich, Edition Eulenberg; New York:
   Edition Eulenberg.
   Preface in German and English. Text added to the contratenor in the Sanctus and Agnus.

Recommends performance by two female and two male voices, with instruments especially on the tenor and contratenor. Modern clefs.

Wilkins, Nigel.

1966 (ed.). *A Fourteenth-Century Repertory from the Codex Reina.* Corpus Mensurabilis Musicae 36. American Institute of Musicology.
Edition of selected musical works from MS **PR** [63]. Review: Günther 1967 (corrections).

1967 (ed.). *The Lyric Works of Adam de la Hale (Chansons, Jeux-Partis, Rondeaux, Motets).* Corpus Mensurabilis Musicae, 44. [Rome]: American Institute of Musicology.
Standard edition of the musical works of Adam de la Halle. Abstract: *RILM* 5 (1971), no. 3581.

1968. "The Post-Machaut Generation of Poet-Musicians." *Nottingham Mediaeval Studies* 12:40–84.
Archival references and capsule biographies of minstrels and composers, showing the importance of southern courts and patrons for musicians who were mainly northerners. Includes a concordance list of secular works by twenty-three composers, with editions. Discussion of the three fixed forms and their post-Machaut characteristics, including subjects treated by the poetry, and the relationship between poet and composer. Abstract: *RILM* 5 (1971), no. 3599. ·

1969a (ed.). *One Hundred Ballades, Rondeaux and Virelais from the Late Middle Ages.* Cambridge: Cambridge University Press.
A valuable introduction to forms and themes of the fixed-form lyrics in the fourteenth and fifteenth centuries, with examples from Lescurel to Charles d'Orléans. Editions of *Amours me fait* (B19), *Dame, a qui* (V12), *Dame plaisant* (Lo26), *De toutes flours* (B31), *Dix et sept* (R17), *Dou memoire* (Lo253), *Dous amis, oy* (B6), *Onques mais nuls* (Lo19), *Ou loyauté* (Lo54), *Phyton* (B38), *Plus dure* (V31/28), *Quant Theseüs / Ne quier* (B34), *Qui des couleurs* (Lo272), *Rose, lis* (R10), with notes on each poem, a glossary, and fifteen musical examples, including B6 (without the essential corrections of Hoppin 1960), B31, B34, R17, and V31. Reviews: Margaret Bent, *Music and Letters* 50 (1969): 527–28; Sergio Cigada, *Studi francesi* 13 (1969): 324–25; Henrik Heger, *Zeitschrift für romanische Philologie* 88 (1972): 554–56 (corrections); Brian Jeffery, *Early Music* 1 (1973): 243–45; Norris J. Lacy, *Modern Language Journal* 54 (1970): 460; Ian Laurie, *AUMLA* 33 (1970): 146–49 (corrections); Gilbert Reaney, *Notes* 28 (1971–72): 684–85; Judith Rice Rothschild, *French Review* 43 (1969–70): 942–43; John Stevens, *Medium Ævum* 48 (1979): 167–68; Alberto Várvaro, *Romance Philology* 28 (1974–75): 152–53; John H. Watkins, *French Studies* 24 (1970): 45–46; Agostino Ziino, *Nuova rivista musicale italiana* 4 (1970): 958–59. See also Zumthor 1972, 273–79 (Eng. ed., 219–25).

1969b. "The Structure of Ballades, Rondeaux and Virelais in Froissart and in Christine de Pisan." *French Studies* 23:337–48.
Introduction to the formal structures of fixed-form lyrics in the fourteenth and fifteenth centuries. Brief history of the forms from Adam de la Halle to Villon. Emphasis on the musical basis of the forms, taking some text editors to task for misrepresenting the forms of rondeaux and virelais.

1972 (ed.). *Guillaume de Machaut. La Louange des dames.* Edinburgh: Scottish Academic Press; London: Chatto and Windus, 1972. New York: Barnes and Noble, 1973.
A new edition, based on MS **Vg** [3], of the lyrical poems of Machaut, less complete with regard to the poems set to music than Chichmaref 1909. The works are organized by genre, in alphabetical order by first line. The concordance table, which gives the location of each lyric in the manuscripts, is more complete than Chichmaref's, but makes it difficult to reconstruct the order of poems in the manuscripts. The introduction notes poems that are thematically related. Notes, but no glossary or translations. Abstract: *RILM* 6 (1972), no. 241. Reviews: *Musart* 26/1 (fall 1973): 35; *TLS* no. 3703 (23 Feb. 1973): 217; F.R.P. Akehurst, *French Review* 47 (1973–74): 1175–76; Frank Dobbins, *Music*

and Letters 54 (1973): 365; Dafydd Evans, *Notes and Queries* n.s. 20 (1973): 200; J.H. Marshall, *French Studies* 30 (1976): 187–88 (corrections); John Stevens, *Medium Ævum* 48 (1979): 167–68; Sarah Jane Williams, *Notes* 30 (1973–74): 525–26.

1977. "Guillaume de Machaut, 1300–1377." *Consort* 33:213–21.

Survey, especially of the musical genres, with comments on Machaut's influence. A few short musical examples have ideas for accompaniments for monophonic works. Includes reproduction of miniature D2 (see chap. 4.4q); the cover of this issue features a reproduction of MS **Pe** [20], fols. 25v–26r (with *Dame de qui* [RF5]). Abstract: *RILM* 11 (1977), no. 334.

1979. *Music in the Age of Chaucer*. Chaucer Studies 1. Cambridge: Brewer; Totowa, N.J.: Rowman and Littlefield. 2nd ed., with *Chaucer Songs*. Cambridge: Brewer, 1995.

Chap. 1, "France," includes a survey of Machaut and music (9–23). Chap. 4, "Chaucer," gives a large number of citations from Chaucer that pertain to music. Chap. 5, "Minstrels," is particularly rich in references. Abstracts: Allen/Fisher 1987, no. 231; *RILM* 13 (1979), no. 4523. Reviews: John Caldwell, *Music and Letters* 61 (1980): 410–11; F.N.M. Diekstra, *English Studies* 65 (1984): 555; David Fallows, *Musical Times* 124 (1983): 679–80; Barbara R. Hanning, *Musical Quarterly* 67 (1981): 285–89; Peter Phillips, *Music and Musicians* 28/12 (Aug. 1980): 41; Richard Rastall, *Early Music* 8 (1980): 531–33; Karl Reichl, *Anglia* 100 (1982): 501–4; Nick Sandon, *Consort* 37 (1981): 422–23.

1980a. "Ballade (i)." *New Grove* 2:76–78.

Dictionary article; includes brief discussion of *De toutes flours* (B31), *Dous amis, oy* (B6), and *Quant Theseüs / Ne quier* (B34) (p. 77).

1980b (ed.). *Chaucer Songs*. Chaucer Studies 4. Cambridge: Brewer; Totowa, N.J.: Rowman and Littlefield. 2nd ed. *Music in the Age of Chaucer*, with *Chaucer Songs*. Cambridge: Brewer, 1995.

This edition provides music for Chaucer lyrics by means of *contrafacta*, a curious undertaking not justified in the introductory note (but see Wilkins 1977, 218–19). Includes ten *contrafacta* of Machaut chansons, adapting lyrics of Chaucer to music of Machaut and others (no. 1 on *Nes qu'on* [B33], no. 2 on *Se pour ce muir* [B36], no. 3 on *S'Amours ne fait* [B1], no. 4 on *Mes esperis* [B39], no. 5 on *Gais et jolis* [B35], no. 6 on *On ne porroit* [B3], no. 11 on *J'aim miex* [B7], no. 12 on *De desconfort* [B8], no. 13 on *Riches d'amour* [B5], no. 14 on *Dame, se vous n'avez* [R13]). In addition, no. 9 utilizes F. Andrieu's setting of Deschamps's two ballades of *déploration, Armes, Amours / O flour*. Reviews: David Fallows, *Notes and Queries* n.s. 28 (1981): 255–56; David Fallows, *Musical Times* 124 (1983): 679–80; Richard Rastall, *Early Music* 8 (1980): 547–48.

1980c. "Rondeau (i)." *New Grove* 16:166–70.

Dictionary article; includes brief discussion of Machaut's rondeaux, especially *Ma fin* (R14) (pp. 168–69), with a facsimile from MS **G** (167).

1980d. "Virelai." *New Grove* 20:1–3.

Dictionary article; includes an edition and brief discussion of *Mors sui* (V29/26).

1983a. "Music and Poetry at Court: England and France in the Late Middle Ages." In *English Court Culture in the Later Middle Ages*, ed. V.J. Scattergood and J.W. Sherborne, 183–204. London: Duckworth.

A study of contacts in music and in poetry between England and France in the fourteenth and fifteenth centuries, rich in references to contemporary musical practice. Includes material on the court of Queen Philippa, especially the activities of Jean de le Mote, an important precursor of Machaut; musical activities of King John II during his captivity in England; musical interests of the Charles d'Orléans circle; and English musicians working on the continent in the fifteenth century. Valuable bibliographical references.

1983b. "A Pattern of Patronage: Machaut, Froissart and the Houses of Luxembourg and Bohemia in the Fourteenth Century." *French Studies* 37: 257–84.

Sketch of the broad influence of the House of Luxembourg-Bohemia on fourteenth-century literary and musical history (Machaut discussed on pp. 258–62). In addition, Wilkins provides material on Emperor Charles IV at Prague and Duke Wenceslas of Brabant at Brussels, and passages relevant to music in Froissart. Contains references to important published collections of documents.

1984. "The Late Mediaeval French Lyric: With Music and Without." In Günther/Finscher 1984, 155–74.

A wide-ranging overview of problems of poetry and music in the fourteenth and fifteenth centuries, including lyrics without music, lyrics commemorating patrons or historical circumstances, religious lyrics, lyrics in the secular theater, narratives with lyric insertions, *contrafacta*, double ballades, acrostics, formal innovations, etc. Abstract: *RILM* 18 (1984), no. 6725.

1987 (ed.). *Armes, Amours, Dames, Chevalerie: An Anthology of French Song from the Fourteenth Century.* Cambridge: New Press.

Transcriptions, texts, translations, and notes for a large selection of chansons from the thirteenth to the early fifteenth centuries. Works of Machaut include *Dame, de qui* (RF5), *Helas! / Hareu!* (M10), *Ma fin* (R14), *Mors sui* (V29/26), and *Sans cuer m'en / Amis / Dame* (B17); in addition, the collection includes F. Andrieu's setting of Deschamps's two ballades of *déploration, Armes, Amours / O flour.* Review: M.J. Freeman, *French Studies* 44 (1990): 446–47.

1989. *The Lyric Art of Medieval France.* Fulbourn: New Press, 1988. 2nd rev. ed. 1989.

Comprehensive survey of medieval French lyrical poetry, from the trouvères through the fifteenth century, considering social context of the poet-musicians, poetic themes, music, dissemination of works outside France, manuscript sources, and poetic treatises. Machaut treated passim.

Willard, Charity Cannon.

1985. "Concepts of Love According to Guillaume de Machaut, Christine de Pizan and Pietro Bembo." In *The Spirit of the Court. Selected Proceedings of the Fourth Congress of the International Courtly Literature Society, Toronto 1983,* ed. Glyn S. Burgess and Robert A. Taylor, 386–92. Cambridge: Brewer.

Christine's use of Machaut's *Jugement Behaingne* and *Jugement Navarre* in her *Livre des Trois Jugemens* and *Debat de Deux Amans* (384–89).

Williams, Harry F.

1987. "Martin Le Franc as Literary Critic." *Fifteenth-Century Studies* 12: 187–94.

Brief account of Le Franc's citations of medieval French literature and authors in his *Champion des Dames,* including citations of Machaut (190–91).

Williams, Sarah Jane.

1952. *The Music of Guillaume de Machaut.* Ph.D. diss. Yale University. Ann Arbor: University Microfilms, 1964. Order no. 6411892.

Pioneering study of Machaut's music, considering the *Prologue,* biography, and chronology, with chapters devoted to each of the musical genres, and consideration of questions such as the shift in emphasis from motet to ballade. Mulder (1978, 33–34) criticizes her discussion of the relationship of text and music. Abstract: *DA* 25/6 (Dec. 1964): 3613.

1968. "Vocal Scoring in the Chansons of Machaut." *Journal of the American Musicological Society* 21:251–57.

Chansons transmitted in more than one version—in differing numbers of voices—in Machaut manuscripts and in the musical anthologies. The different versions coexist as alternatives; the chansons may be performed in a variety of vocal scorings. The same question is considered in more detail by Dömling (1970, 74–80), with the conclusion that a contratenor is often essential, while a triplum is not. Earp (1983, chap. 2) shows that some of the variant versions in the Machaut manuscripts arose because of technical problems of manuscript copying. Abstract: *RILM* 2 (1968), no. 3111.

1969. "An Author's Role in Fourteenth-Century Book Production: Guillaume de Machaut's 'livre où je met toutes mes choses.'" *Romania* 90:433–54.

An excellent study of references in the *Voir Dit* to book making and the transmission of manuscripts, and to the dictation, writing, and copying of individual lyrics, letters, *dits*, and manuscripts. The second part, on problems with Hoepffner's chronology, particularly in relation to MS C [1], has been superseded. Corrections in Cerquiglini 1985b, 217 n. 5, 218 n. 7. Abstract: *RILM* 3 (1969), no. 3483.

1977. "The Lady, the Lyrics and the Letters." *Early Music* 5:462–68.

Considers the *Voir Dit* essentially true, but Toute Belle's actual lyrics make up only a small part of what is ascribed to her. Technical problems give some clues as to which poems are hers. Williams attributes *Celle qui unques ne vous vid* (VD1), *Pour vivre en joieuse vie* (VD3), *Celle qui nuit et jou* (VD7), *Ne vous estuet* (VD12), *Des que premiers* (VD26), *Nuit et jour* (VD52), and *Cent mille fois* (VD62) to Toute Belle; on this question, see also Sonnemann 1969, 148–51. Also discusses the reuse of old lyrics (see Sonnemann 1969, 151–56), paired lyrics, and practical information from letters on the performance practice of music. Abstracts: *RILM* 11 (1977), no. 4451; Dagmar Hoffmann-Axthelm, *Basler Jahrbuch für historische Musikpraxis* 2 (1978): 224–25 no. 148.

1978. "Machaut's Self-Awareness as Author and Producer." In Cosman 1978, 189–97.

Discussion of the *Prologue, Voir Dit*, and the original index to MS A [5].

1987. "Machaut, Guillaume de." In *Dictionary of the Middle Ages*, ed. Joseph R. Strayer, 8:2–8. 13 vols. New York: Scribner's Sons, 1982–89.

Dictionary article, with brief biography, introduction to the literary and musical works, and a brief bibliography; includes a facsimile of miniature **Pm**110 (see chap. 4.4k).

1993. "The Lyrics of Machaut's *Voir Dit:* 'Voir' and 'Veoir.'" *Ars Lyrica* 7: 5–15.

Reuse of old lyrics (see S.J. Williams 1977); images of *vie, cuer, veoir,* and *voir.* Includes an appendix (though incomplete) of inserted lyrics.

Wilson, David Fenwick.

1990a. *Music of the Middle Ages: An Anthology for Performance and Study.* Text translations by Robert Crouse and Hans T. Runte. New York: Schirmer Books.

Includes editions of *Amours me fait* (B19), *Dame, vostre* (V17), *De Bon Espoir / Puis que* (M4), *De toutes flours* (B31), *Puis qu'en oubli* (R18), *Quant en moy / Amour* (M1), *Quant je ne voy* (R21), *Se je souspir* (V36/30), and *Une vipere* (B27).

1990b. *Music of the Middle Ages: Style and Structure.* New York: Schirmer Books.

Textbook survey. Machaut discussed on pp. 292–94, 296–306, 308–13, 322–23, 327, 330–32, 336–44, 351–55; includes a reproduction of MS A fol. 414v, with beginning of *Quant en moy / Amour* (M1) and miniature A153 (see chap. 4.4t) (p. 294).

Wimsatt, James I.

1967a. "The Apotheosis of Blanche in *The Book of the Duchess.*" *Journal of English and Germanic Philology* 66:26–44.

The description of Lady White in Chaucer's *Book of the Duchess* and its sources, especially Machaut's *Jugement Behaingne* and *Remede.* Chaucer's description also evokes the Blessed Virgin Mary. Some criticism in Donnelly 1987, 433–34 n. 8. Abstract: Allen/Fisher 1987, no. 842.

1967b. "The Sources of Chaucer's 'Seys and Alcyone.'" *Medium Ævum* 36: 231–41.

Discussion of Chaucer's use of *Fonteinne* in his *Book of the Duchess.* Abstract: Allen/Fisher 1987, no. 845.

1968. *Chaucer and the French Love Poets: The Literary Background of the* Book of the Duchess. University of North Carolina Studies in Comparative Literature 43. Chapel Hill: University of North Carolina Press. Reprint. New York: Johnson, 1972.

Revision of the author's 1963 Duke dissertation; includes the first larger study of Machaut's narrative poems in English (70–117). An appendix gives a line-by-line listing of major and minor sources for Chaucer's *Book of the Duchess*. Works of Machaut that served as major sources for Chaucer include *Jugement Behaingne*, *Remede*, and *Fonteinne*; minor sources include *Lyon*, *Jugement Navarre*, *Voir Dit*, and several lyrics, *Amours, tu m'as* (Cp1), *S'onques* (L17/12), *Hé! Mors / Fine* (M3), *Qui es / Ha! Fortune* (M8), *Fons / O livoris* (M9), and *Phyton* (B38). Abstracts: Allen/Fisher 1987, no. 844; Peck 1983, no. 276. Reviews: D.S. Brewer, *Review of English Studies* 22 (1971): 66–67; Christopher Brookhouse, *Speculum* 45 (1970): 186; J.R. Collins, *Medium Ævum* 43 (1974): 80–83 (with new material on Ceyx and Alcyone); Alan T. Gaylord, *Journal of English and Germanic Philology* 69 (1970): 667–71; Albert E. Hartung, *Romanic Review* 61 (1970): 219–20; Robert M. Jordan, *Comparative Literature Studies* 8 (1971): 160–63; Helaine Newstead, *Romance Philology* 24 (1970–71): 351–52; R.M. Wilson, *Yale English Studies* 1 (1971): 216–18.

1970 (ed.). *The Marguerite Poetry of Guillaume de Machaut.* University of North Carolina Studies in the Romance Languages and Literatures 87. Chapel Hill: University of North Carolina Press.

The first edition of *Lis et Marguerite*, with a study of the destinations of Machaut's "marguerite" poems. Machaut originated the "marguerite" imagery used by his French and English followers. See Fourrier 1979 for a later edition, prepared without knowledge of Wimsatt's prior work. Reviews: F.R.P. Akehurst, *French Review* 45 (1971–72): 537–38 (with new material on Marguerite of Flanders); N. Mann, *Studi francesi* 16 (1972): 127; Steven Smith, *Modern Language Journal* 56 (1972): 192–93; Nigel Wilkins, *French Studies* 26 (1972): 441–43 (with two additional "Marguerite" ballades).

1970–71. "*Anelida and Arcite*: A Narrative of Complaint and Comfort." *Chaucer Review* 5:1–8.

Precedents for the long complaint with difficult metrical form, interpolated into a framing narrative, are found in Machaut and Froissart. Mention of *Jugement Behaingne*, *Remede*, and *Fonteinne*. Abstracts: Allen/Fisher 1987, no. 922; Peck 1983, no. 277.

1972a. "The *Dit dou Bleu Chevalier:* Froissart's Imitation of Chaucer." *Mediæval Studies* 34:388–400.

Machaut's *Jugement Behaingne*, *Remede*, and *Fonteinne* influenced Chaucer's *Book of the Duchess*, which in its turn influenced Froissart's *Dit dou Bleu Chevalier*. This last relationship argues against Cartier 1967. Calin (1994, 523 n. 20, to p. 277) disagrees.

1972b. "Guillaume de Machaut (1300?–1377). *Dizionario critico della letteratura francese*, ed. Franco Simone, 1:511–12. Turin: Unione Tipografico. Dictionary article.

1974. "Chaucer and French Poetry." In *Geoffery Chaucer. Writers and Their Backgrounds*, ed. Derek S. Brewer, 109–36. London: Bell. Reprint. Athens: Ohio University Press, 1976. Reprint. *Geoffrey Chaucer: The Writer and His Background*. Cambridge: Brewer, 1990.

Excellent short summary of some of the most important debts of Chaucer to Machaut and the French tradition. On Machaut, see esp. 118–30.

1975. "Machaut's *Lay de Confort* and Chaucer's *Book of the Duchess*." In *Chaucer at Albany*, ed. Rossell Hope Robbins, 11–26. Middle English Texts & Contexts 2. New York: Franklin.

Discussion of a literary structure borrowed by Chaucer in the *Book of the Duchess*, whereby a complaint is followed by comfort, as seen in Machaut's *Remede*, the *Lay de Confort* (L17/12), and *Fonteinne*. Other Chaucer contemporaries borrow the same plan. Includes a close study of L17, with translation of many passages.

1976. "Guillaume de Machaut and Chaucer's *Troilus and Criseyde.*" *Medium Ævum* 45:277–93.

Discussion of Chaucer's use of the *Jugement Behaingne, Remede*, and several lyrics in his *Troilus and Criseyde*. Abstract: Allen/Fisher 1987, no. 703.

1977. "Medieval and Modern in Chaucer's *Troilus and Criseyde.*" *PMLA* 92: 203–16.

The analysis includes consideration of the influence of Machaut's narrative *dits*, especially *Remede*, on the aspect of love romance in Chaucer's *Troilus* (206–9). Abstract: Allen/Fisher 1987, no. 720.

1978. "Guillaume de Machaut and Chaucer's Love Lyrics." *Medium Ævum* 47:66–87.

Chaucer's dependence on Machaut models for his independent love lyrics. Many works are cited. Abstract: Allen/Fisher 1987, no. 188.

1979. "Chaucer, Fortune, and Machaut's 'Il m'est avis.'" In *Chaucerian Problems and Perspectives: Essays Presented to Paul E. Beichner C.S.C.*, ed. Edward Vasta and Zacharias P. Thundy, 119–31. Notre Dame, Ind.: University of Notre Dame Press.

Traces the influence of Machaut's B22 on five Chaucer works that range over his entire career as a poet, including the *Book of the Duchess*, the Boethius translation, the Merchant's Tale, the triple ballade *Fortune* (see also Preston 1951, 616), and the late ballade *Lak of Stedfastnesse*. Abstract: Allen/Fisher 1987, no. 187.

1981. *"The Book of the Duchess:* Secular Elegy or Religious Vision?" In *Signs and Symbols in Chaucer's Poetry*, ed. John P. Hermann and John J. Burke, Jr., 113–29 (notes, 230–33). University, Ala.: University of Alabama Press.

Interprets the *Book of the Duchess* as an artistically successful work in each of two genres, both as a love poem and as a spiritual vision. Machaut's *dits* are the forerunners for the secular interpretation. Abstract: Allen/Fisher 1987, no. 843.

1982. *Chaucer and the Poems of 'Ch' in University of Pennsylvania MS French 15.* Chaucer Studies 9. Cambridge: Brewer; Woodbridge and Totowa, N.J.: Boydell & Brewer.

Analysis, inventory, and discussion of MS **Pa** [50]. Poets represented include Philippe de Vitry, Jean de le Mote, Machaut, Oton de Granson, and others. Abstracts: Allen/Fisher 1987, no. 41; Peck 1988, no. 485. Reviews: Susan Dannenbaum, *Studies in the Age of Chaucer* 6 (1984): 226–28; F.N.M. Diekstra, *English Studies* 65 (1984): 562–64; Bernard O'Donoghue, *TLS* no. 4233 (18 May 1984): 555; Karl Reichl, *Anglia* 103 (1984): 187–89; Claude Thiry, *Moyen Age* 91 (1985): 149–51.

1983. See Kibler/Wimsatt 1983.

1984. "Froissart, Chaucer, and the Pastourelles of the Pennsylvania Manuscript." In *Studies in the Age of Chaucer. Proceedings, No. 1, 1984: Reconstructing Chaucer*, ed. Paul Strohm and Thomas J. Heffernan, 69–79. Knoxville: New Chaucer Society, University of Tennessee.

The *pastourelles* in MS **Pa** [50] (see Kibler/Wimsatt 1983 for an edition) provide a source for a strain of French realism centered at northern *puys* that may have influenced Chaucer. Subsequently, the *pastourelle* genre was transformed and regularized by Froissart according to the Machaut tradition. Historical occasions alluded to in a number of the Pennsylvania *pastorelles* include the fateful years 1357–58 and 1359–60.

1985. "The French Lyric Element in *Troilus and Criseyde.*" *Yearbook of English Studies* 15:18–32.

Discusses non-narrative, lyric-like passages in *Troilus*, especially those that derive from *Remede*; some discussion of *Jugement Behaingne* as well. See commentary in Guthrie 1991, 91–93.

1991a. "Chaucer and Deschamps' 'Natural Music.'" In Baltzer 1991b, 132–50.

On Deschamps's conception of natural music, with a close analysis of Machaut's *Tout ensement* (Lo190). The technical aspects of such French poetry inform Chaucer's short poems. Lo190 probably was the model for Chaucer's *To Rosemounde*; native Middle English lyrics, with alliterative lines, are a very different type of poetry. Includes an edition of *Esperance* (B13) from MS A by Rebecca A. Baltzer (149–50).

1991b. *Chaucer and His French Contemporaries: Natural Music in the Four-teenth Century.* Toronto, Buffalo, and London: University of Toronto Press.

The "natural music" of French poetry in the fourteenth century, its metrical structure and themes, and its influence on Chaucer. Machaut's most important immediate forerunner, Jean de le Mote, receives rehabilitating treatment. Three central chapters are devoted to Machaut and his influence on Chaucer. Froissart, Oton de Granson, and Deschamps also receive full treatment. Illustrations from manuscript miniatures, many from Machaut manuscripts, provide several scenes of the poet presenting his book to the patron, the poet and his audience performing or reading the text. Reviews: Robert Boenig, *Speculum* 69 (1994): 273–75; Julia Boffey, *Modern Language Review* 89 (1994): 187–88; L.L. Bronson, *Choice* 29 (1992): 1683; Ardis Butterfield, *Medium Ævum* 63 (1994): 133–35; Jane H.M. Taylor, *Review of English Studies* 45 (1994): 551–52.

1991c. "Reason, Machaut, and the Franklin." *The Olde Daunce: Love, Friendship, Sex, and Marriage in the Medieval World*, ed. Robert R. Edwards and Stephen Spector, 201–10 (notes, 287–89). SUNY Series in Medieval Studies. Albany: State University of New York Press.

Influence of Boethius's *Consolation of Philosophy*, the *Roman de la Rose*, and Machaut's *Remede* on Chaucer's *Troilus*; influence of *Roman de la Rose* and *Remede* on the Franklin's Tale.

1993. "Machaut's *Voir Dit* as Game." *Ars Lyrica* 7:17–24.

Interesting argument that the *Voir Dit* is a fiction, "a literary game in which friends or patrons of the poet are behind the girl's communications" (19).

1994. "Rhyme/Reason, Chaucer/Pope, Icon/Symbol." *Modern Language Quarterly* 55:17–46.

Here Wimsatt substantially broadens his arguments on the musical nature of poetry—Deschamps's "natural music"—discussed in a medieval context in 1991a and 1991b. Pope argued that to be effective, rhyme had to reinforce meaning. Chaucer's rhymes are less striking than Pope's, yet they create an organized sound, independent of verbal sense, that can be considered a kind of music. Wimsatt illustrates Machaut's versification, an important influence on Chaucer's, with *Nes qu'on* (B33) (pp. 32–34).

Wimsatt, James I., and Thomas Cable.

1991. "Introduction." In Baltzer 1991b, 1–14.

Introductory essay to the volume, provides useful summaries of Earp 1991b, Guthrie 1991, and Wimsatt 1991a.

Wimsatt, James I., and William W. Kibler, eds. and trans.; music ed. Rebecca A. Baltzer.

1988. *Le Jugement du Roy de Behaigne and Remede de Fortune.* The Chaucer Library. Athens: University of Georgia Press.

Editions and translations of *Jugement Behaingne* and *Remede*. The introduction contains important new information on the text tradition of Machaut's poetry. The base manuscripts for the edition, chosen as the best individual representatives of the "early" Machaut tradition known to Chaucer (MS P [30] for *Jugement Behaingne*; MS C [1] for *Remede*) provide texts superior to those of Hoepffner 1908–21. Reviews: Josette Britte-Ashford, *Journal of the Rocky Mountain Medieval and Renaissance Association* 11 (1990): 170–71; Ardis Butterfield, *Review of English Studies* 42 (1991): 246–48; Leo Carruthers, *Etudes Anglaises* 44 (1991): 331–32; Larry S. Crist, *Studies in the Age of Chaucer* 12 (1990): 285–87; Margaret J. Ehrhart, *South Central Review* 8/1 (spring

1991): 96–98; Louis Gemenne, *Moyen Age* 98 (1992): 134–36 (corrections); Sylvia Huot, *Romance Quarterly* 37 (1990): 482–83; Norris J. Lacy, *French Review* 64 (1990–91): 842; Daniel Leech-Wilkinson, *Music and Letters* 71 (1990): 379–80; Rosemary Morris, *Modern Language Review* 85 (1990): 948–49; Charles Muscatine, *Speculum* 66 (1991): 879–81; Christopher Page, *Early Music* 18 (1990): 654–55; Gilles Roques, *Revue de linguistique romane* 55 (1991): 278–80 (corrections); Hans R. Runte, *Zeitschrift für romanische Philologie* 108 (1992): 354–55; Claude Thiry, *Scriptorium* 44 (1990): 174* no. 553; Nigel Wilkins, *Medium Ævum* 60 (1991): 133–34.

Windeatt, Barry A.
  1982. *Chaucer's Dream Poetry: Sources and Analogues.* Chaucer Studies 7. Cambridge: Brewer; Totowa, N.J.: Rowman and Littlefield.
    General discussion of Chaucer's borrowings, with English prose translations of *Jugement Behaingne* (complete) and *Marguerite* (complete). Also gives an extensive excerpt from *Fonteinne*; and excerpts from *Remede, Lyon, Jugement Navarre,* and *Lis et Marguerite.* Reviews: F.N.M. Diekstra, *English Studies* 65 (1984): 558–59; Nicholas Jacobs, *Medium Ævum* 57 (1988): 104–6 (corrections); Derek Pearsall, *Notes & Queries* 30 (1983): 248–50; David Staines, *Speculum* 58 (1983): 1143–44; James I. Wimsatt, *Studies in the Age of Chaucer* 5 (1983): 210–12.

  1992. *Troilus and Criseyde.* Oxford Guides to Chaucer. Oxford: Clarendon.
    This exhaustive guide to Chaucer's *Troilus* includes consideration of Machaut's influence, especially *Jugement Behaingne* and *Remede* (118–21).

Winn, James Anderson.
  1981. *Unsuspected Eloquence: A History of the Relations between Poetry and Music.* New Haven and London: Yale University Press.
    For the Ars Nova, Winn stresses the general contrast between the "constructive" techniques of the motet and the "expressive" techniques of the chanson, although the two principles are both present in true works of art (see esp. 101–21). Abstracts: *RILM* 15 (1981), no. 1871. Reviews: Nan Cooke Carpenter, *Comparative Literature* 36 (1984): 75–77; Jean-Louis Cupers, *Revue belge de philologie et d'histoire* 61 (1983): 778–79; John T. Dzieglewicz, *Modern Philology* 80 (1982–83): 449–52; Mortimer H. Frank, *Journal of English and Germanic Philology* 83 (1984): 547–49; Hans Hollander, *Neue Zeitschrift für Musik* 143/5 (May 1982): 92; 547–49; Jerome Mazzaro, *Journal of Music Theory* 27 (1983): 290–93; James Parakilas, *Notes* 40 (1983–84): 49–51; Henry Raynor, *Music Review* 44 (1983): 143–45; Francis Routh, *Composer* 76–77 (summer-winter 1982): 36–39; Erik Ryding, *Current Musicology* 37–38 (1984): 228–32; Gregory Sandow, *Village Voice* 28 (4 Jan. 1983): 34; John Stevens, *Modern Language Review* 78 (1983): 397–400; Seth Weiner, *Philological Quarterly* 63 (1984): 273–77.

Wixom, William D.
  1963. "A Missal for a King: A First Exhibition. An Introduction to the Gotha *Missal* and a Catalogue to the Exhibition *Gothic Art 1360–1440* Held at The Cleveland Museum of Art, August 8 through September 15, 1963." *Bulletin of the Cleveland Museum of Art* 50:158–73, 24 figures.
    Based on work of Harry Bober, this study is relevant to an artist of some miniatures in MSS **Vg** and **A**, identified here as Jean Bondol (John of Bruges). See chap. 4.2, table 4.2 no. 2.

  1964. "Twelve Masterpieces of Medieval and Renaissance Book Illumination. A Catalogue to the Exhibition: March 17–May 17, 1964." *Bulletin of the Cleveland Museum of Art* 51:42–64.
    Includes a brief summary of Wixom 1963 (52–53 no. 7).

Woledge, Brian, ed.
  1961. *The Penguin Book of French Verse.* Vol. 1, *To the Fifteenth Century.* Harmondsworth (Middlesex): Penguin Books.
    Includes editions and translations of *De toutes flours* (B31; strophes 2 and 3 are reversed), *Nes qu'on* (B33), *J'aim miex* (B7), *Se je vous aim* (Lo231), *Se vo grandeur* (Lo263), and

extracts from *Lyon* (ll. 1248–1300; 1311–30). The single-volume edition of 1975 contains only Lo263 (96–97).

Wolf, Johannes.
1904. *Geschichte der Mensural-Notation von 1250–1460.* 3 vols. Part 1, *Geschichtliche Darstellung.* Part 2, *Musikalische Schriftproben des 13. bis 15. Jahrhunderts.* Part 3, *Übertragungen.* Leipzig: Breitkopf & Härtel. Reprint. Hildesheim: Olms; Wiesbaden: Breitkopf & Härtel, 1965.
Vol. 1 has a historical discussion of notation and sources, including an early study of Machaut's notational practices. Vol. 2 gives diplomatic facsimiles of a number of works, with transcriptions in vol. 3. The corrections of Ludwig 1904–5 (629–30 on motets, 630–31 on Mass, 631 on chansons) are essential. Review: Ludwig 1904–5 (response by Wolf in *Sammelbände der Internationalen Musikgesellschaft* 7 [1905–6]: 131–38).

1913. *Handbuch der Notationskunde.* Part 1, *Tonschriften des Altertums und des Mittelalters; Choral- und Mensuralnotation.* Kleine Handbücher der Musikgeschichte nach Gattungen 8/1. Leipzig: Breitkopf & Härtel. Reprint. Hildesheim: Olms; Wiesbaden: Breitkopf & Härtel, 1963.
Includes a facsimile of MS E, fol. 131r (*Trop plus / Biauté* [M20]) (facing p. 360).

1923. *Musikalische Schrifttafeln, für den Unterricht in der Notationskunde.* Veröffentlichungen des Fürstlichen Instituts für musikwissenschaftliche Forschung zu Bückeburg 2/2. Bückeburg and Leipzig: Kistner & Siegel. 2nd ed. 1927.
Collection of facsimiles. Plates 41–42 give Machaut MS A, fols. 429v–430r (*Lasse! comment / Se j'aim* [M16]) and plate 23 gives MS E, fol. 131r (*Trop plus / Biauté* [M20]).

1926 (ed.). *Sing- und Spielmusik aus älterer Zeit.* Wissenschaft und Bildung 218. Leipzig: Quelle & Meyer. Reprint (American ed.). *Music of Earlier Times. Vocal and Instrumental Examples (13th Century to Bach).* New York: Broude Bros., 1947.
Includes an edition of *Tous corps / De* (M2) (pp. 9–13).

Wolfzettel, Friedrich.
1980. "La poésie lyrique en France comme mode d'appréhension de la réalité: remarques sur l'invention du sens visuel chez Machaut, Froissart, Deschamps et Charles d'Orléans." In *Mélanges de langue et littérature françaises du Moyen Age et de la Renaissance offerts à monsieur Charles Foulon*, vol. 1 of 2 vols., 409–19. Rennes: Institut de Français, Université de Haute-Bretagne.
A subjective perspective is seen in fourteenth- and fifteenth-century lyrics that emphasize the aspect of seeing ("voir"), evidence of personal experience. Includes an analysis of *Ne quier* (B34) (pp. 413–14). Abstract: *Encomia* 4 (1982): 75 no. 340.

Wooldridge, H.E.
1905. *The Oxford History of Music.* Vol. 2, *The Polyphonic Period.* Part 2, *Method of Musical Art, 1300–1600.* Oxford: Clarendon.
Survey, with discussion of Machaut (22–40).

1929. *The Oxford History of Music.* Vol. 1, *The Polyphonic Period.* Part 1, *Method of Musical Art, 330–1400.* 2nd. ed., revised by Percy C. Buck. London: Oxford University Press.
Survey, with editions of Agnus II, *De toutes flours* (B31), and *De tout sui* (V38/32).

1932. *The Oxford History of Music.* Vol. 2, *The Polyphonic Period.* Part 2, *Method of Musical Art, 1400–c. 1600.* 2nd. ed., revised by Percy C. Buck. London: Oxford University Press.
Added chapter "Song," by J.A. Westrup, discusses Machaut (307–11). Review: Scott Goddard, *Music and Letters* 14 (1933): 68–69.

Work, James A.
  1941. "The Manciple's Tale." In Bryan/Dempster 1941, 699–722.
  Edition of the story of Apollo and Coronis from the *Voir Dit* (ll. 7773–826, 7969–8110
  in P. Paris 1875), with English glosses (711–16).

Wozna, Malgorzata.
  1982. "L'accueil de Guillaume de Machaut en Pologne." In Guillaume de
  Machaut 1982, 55–60.
  Includes some nineteenth- and twentieth-century Polish bibliographical items on
  Machaut. There was a performance of *J'aim la fleur* (L2) in Prague in 1904 (57).

Wright, Craig.
  1974. "A Fragmentary Manuscript of Early 15th-Century Music in Dijon."
  Journal of the American Musicological Society 27:306–15.
  The last known musical transmission of a lai. Abstract: *RILM* 8 (1974), no. 2026.

  1979. *Music at the Court of Burgundy, 1364–1419: A Documentary History.*
  Musicological Studies 28. Henryville Penn., Ottawa, and Binningen:
  Institute of Mediæval Music.
  Study of the musical establishment at the court of Burgundy under the first two Valois
  dukes. Includes an inventory of the MS **Trém** [58]. Reviews: Nanie Bridgman, *Revue de
  musicologie* 69 (1983): 230–32; David Fallows, *Journal of the American Musicological
  Society* 34 (1981): 545–52.

  1981. "Voices and Instruments in the Art Music of Northern France during
  the 15th Century: A Conspectus." *International Musicological Society:
  Congress Report Berkeley, 1977*, ed. D. Heartz and B. Wade, 643–49.
  Kassel: Bärenreiter.
  Documentary evidence for the instrumental participation in the performance of fifteenth-
  century chansons and Mass music.

  1989. *Music and Ceremony at Notre Dame of Paris 500–1550.* Cambridge
  Studies in Music. Cambridge: Cambridge University Press.
  Includes important material on ecclesiastical institutions and liturgical practices in late
  medieval France. Abstract: *RILM* 23 (1989), no. 1957.

Wright, Laurence.
  1977. "The Medieval Gittern and Citole: A Case of Mistaken Identity." *Galpin
  Society Journal* 30:8–42.
  Includes discussion of the musical instruments *guiterne* and *morache*, mentioned in
  Remede and *Prise* (10–11); gives the excerpt from *Remede* (41). Abstract: *RILM* 11
  (1977), no. 3598.

  1985–86. "Verbal Counterpoint in Machaut's Motet *Trop plus est belle-Biauté
  parée de valour-Je ne suis mie.*" *Romance Studies* 7 (winter): 1–12.
  "Verbal counterpoint" refers to the several levels that work together and complement each
  other when the separate voices and texts are performed. Considers versification, especially
  irregularities in the tenor, syntax, and text meaning. A diagram (11) explores the relationships between *Dame* and *Amours* or *Dieus*, and *Moi* (the poet's mind). Concerning "syn-
  chronisation," or "verbal counterpoint," considers sounds that occur simultaneously (e.g.
  ami—Amen at the end of the motet); line endings that occur simultaneously (the diagram
  is inaccurate); and juxtapositions of themes between the three voices, giving the effect of
  a dramatic dialogue, but all in the mind of one person. Since all activity is in the poet's
  mind, without jealous *losengiers*, and without reference to Nature or pastoral themes,
  Wright describes the work as "egocentric" (6)

  1986. "Attitudes to Minstrels and Musical Instruments in Old French Narrative Poetry, 1100–1400." Ph.D. diss. Bangor, Wales.
  Survey of instruments, terminology, minstrels, fêtes, knowledge of instrumental playing
  among the nobility, etc., based on a comprehensive study of 154 texts, c. 1100–c. 1400,
  including all of the Machaut *dits*. Abstract: *Index to Theses* 39/2 (1990), no. 39-0230.

Wright, Steven Alan.
1986. "Literary Influence in Medieval Literature: Chaucer and the *Roman de la Rose*." Ph.D. diss. Indiana University. Ann Arbor: University Microfilms. Order no. 8707831.
See chap. 3, "Chaucer's Use of the *Roman* in the *Book of the Duchess*: Rewriting Machaut" (97–169). Wright focuses especially on *Jugement Behaingne* and *Fonteinne*. Abstract: *DAI* A 47/12 (June 1987): 4400.

Wykes, Robert Arthur.
1956. "Tonal Movement in the Polyphonic Ballades, Rondeaux, and Virelais of Guillaume de Machaut." D.M.A. diss. University of Illinois. Ann Arbor: University Microfilms. Order no. 16440.
An approach to analysis that borrows much from Salzer (1952), with a distinction between "structural" and "prolonging" sonorities. Appended diagrams of *Ne pensez pas* (B10), *Se quanque amours* (B21), and *Quant je ne voy* (R21) present the compositions at three analytical levels. The analyses are marred by anachronistic terminology and tonal expectations, with too little attention to contrapuntal structure and cadential formulas. Wykes defines "tonal movement" in Machaut's polyphonic works in terms of stepwise descending tetrachords, which account for the tonal movement of the individual phrase and of the overall work, a helpful concept. Abstract: *DA* 16/5 (May 1956): 969–70.

Yenal, Edith.
1989. *Christine de Pizan: A Bibliography*. 2nd ed. Scarecrow Author Bibliographies 63. Metuchen, N.J., and London: Scarecrow Press.
Annotated bibliography; cf. Kennedy 1984. Reviews of 1st ed. (1982): John B. Beston, *Speculum* 59 (1984): 462–64; Jacqueline Cerquiglini, *Moyen Age* 90 (1984): 565–68; Gianni Mombello, *Romance Philology* 38 (1984–85): 104–5; Marvin J. Ward, *French Review* 57 (1983–84): 550. Reviews of 2nd ed.: Angus J. Kennedy, *Medium Ævum* 61 (1992): 345; J.C. Laidlaw, *French Studies* 46 (1992): 56–57; Nadia Margolis, *Speculum* 67 (1992): 761–64 (corrections); Gianni Mombello, *Studi francesi* 36 (1992): 117.

Young, Irwin, trans.
1969. *The Practica musicae of Franchinus Gafurius*. Madison: The University of Wisconsin Press.
Translation; for the original Latin treatise, see Gafori 1496. Another translation is in Miller 1968. Reviews: Peter Bergquist, *Journal of the American Musicological Society* 23 (1970): 144–50; Lawrence Gushee, *Journal of Music Theory* 14 (1970): 127–32; Michel Huglo, *Revue de musicologie* 56 (1970): 95–96; Katarzyna Morawska, *Muzyka* 15/1 (1970): 98–103; Albert Seay, *Notes* 26 (1969–70): 264–66; Lavern Wagner, *Music Educator's Journal* 56/3 (Nov. 1969): 97–98; David Wulstan, *Music and Letters* 51 (1970): 194–95.

Young, Karl, ed.
1943. "The *Dit de la Harpe* of Guillaume de Machaut." In *Essays in Honor of Albert Feuillerat*, ed. Henri M. Peyre, 1–20. New Haven: Yale University Press.
A critical edition of *Harpe*.

Yudkin, Jeremy.
1989. *Music in Medieval Europe*. Prentice Hall History of Music Series. Englewood Cliffs, N.J.: Prentice Hall.
Textbook survey. On Machaut, see esp. 474–508.

Zacour, Norman P. and Rudolf Hirsch, comps.
1965. *Catalog of Manuscripts in the Libraries of the University of Pennsylvania to 1800*. Philadelphia: University of Pennsylvania Press.
Catalogue description of MS **Pa** [50] (p. 57).

Zajączkowski, Stanisław.
1929. "Wilhelm de Machaut i jego wiadomości do dziejów Polski i Litwy w XIV w." (Guillaume de Machaut and his knowledge of Poland and Lithuania in the fourteenth century). *Kwartalnik historyczny* 43/1:217–28.
Citations in Machaut that mention Poland and Lithuania.

Zeeman, Nicolette.
1988. "The Lover-Poet and Love as the Most Pleasing 'Matere' in Medieval French Love Poetry." *Modern Language Review* 83:820–42.
In the thirteenth century love was the most pleasing subject for lyrical poetry, while non-lyric poets stressed the desire to delight an audience. Machaut is more explicit, and for all genres insists both that love is the most pleasing subject for poetry, and that a sincere love experience (*sentement*) is necessary to inspire poetry. Excellent discussion of the poetics of the *Prologue* and *Voir Dit* (832–37). Also considers the positions of Deschamps, Froissart, Charles d'Orléans, Christine de Pizan, and Chaucer on this question.

1991. "The Verse of Courtly Love in the Framing Narrative of the *Confessio Amantis*." *Medium Ævum* 60:222–40.
The debt of John Gower's *Confessio Amantis* to fourteenth-century French Courtly Love poetry. Considers Machaut's *Jugement Behaingne, Jugement Navarre, Remede, Voir Dit,* and the ballade *Trop ne me puis* (Lo225).

Zenck, Martin.
1990. "Karel Goeyvaerts und Guillaume de Machaut: Zum mittelalterlichen Konstruktivismus in der seriellen Musik der fünfziger Jahre." *Musikforschung* 43:336–51.
Fascinating account of an avant-garde serial composer of the early 1950s who found authority for contemporary musical experiments in Machaut's isorhythmic techniques; cf. Sabbé 1980–81.

Ziino, Agostino.
1978. "Isoritmia musicale e tradizione metrica mediolatina nei mottetti di Guillaume de Machaut." *Medioevo Romanzo* 5:438–65.
Poetic and metrical traits and traditions, especially in Machaut's Latin motets. Eight texts have sequence-like paired half-strophes, including the motetus voices *O livoris* (M9), *Corde mesto* (M12), *Diligenter inquiramus* (M19), *Plange regni* (M22), *Inviolata genitrix* (M23); and the triplum voices *J'ay tant* (M7), *Christe qui* (M21), and *Felix virgo* (M23). Ziino also considers *Hé! Mors / Fine* (M3), *S'il estoit / S'Amours* (M6), and *Lasse! comment / Se j'aim* (M16). In general, motets with sequence-like texts are more rigorously and systematically treated and the correspondence between *talea* and verse is more precise than in the other motets (451). Commentary in Bent 1984, 316–17.

1982a. "*Balade* e *baladelle*: osservazioni sul rapporto tra poesia e musica in alcune composizioni di Guillaume de Machaut." *Prospettive musicali* 1/1: 10–16.
Not examined; see revised and expanded version in Ziino 1990.

1982b. "Guillaume de Machaut fondateur d'école?" In Guillaume de Machaut 1982, 329–35.
Considers the question of Machaut's influence on subsequent composers, summarizing the work of previous scholars. Provides an important list of "omaggi" to Machaut.

1982c. "Guillaume de Machaut fondateur d'école?" In *Scritti offerti a Gino Raya dalla Facoltà di Magistero dell' Università di Messina*, ed. Antonio Mazzarino, 499–509. Rome: Herder.
A slightly expanded version of Ziino 1982b.

1990. "*Balade* e *baladelle*: osservazioni sul rapporto tra poesia e musica in alcune composizioni di Guillaume de Machaut." In *Studi in onore di Giulio Cattin*, ed. Francesco Luisi, 15–27. Istituto di Paleografia Musicale 3/1. Rome: Torre d'Orfeo.

Revised and expanded version of Ziino 1982a. Discussion of the duplex ballades *Amours me fait* (B19), *Dous amis, oy* (B6), *En amer* (RF4), *Phyton* (B38), as well as the *complainte*-like *Ma chiere* (B40). The poetic structures of these works resemble those seen in medieval Latin sequences (cf. Ziino 1978). Ziino finds only three examples of fourteenth-century duplex ballades not by Machaut.

Zillhardt, Rainer.
1986. "Zur Problematik einer historisch übergeordneten Strukturanalyse der Tonhöhen." In *Mikrotöne: Bericht über das internationale Symposium Mikrotonforschung, Musik mit Microtönen, Ekmelische Musik, 10.–12. Mai 1985 in Salzburg*, ed. Franz Richter Herf, 69–105. Veröffentlichungen der Gesellschaft für Ekmelische Musik 3. Innsbruck: Helbling.

Analysis of pitch content according to three different historical tonal systems. Machaut's Kyrie I provides the example for medieval Pythagorean tuning. Abstract: *RILM* 20 (1986), no. 748.

Zink, Michel.
1982. "Musique et subjectivité: Le passage de la chanson d'amour à la poésie personnelle au XIIIe siècle." *Cahiers de civilisation médiévale* 25:225–32.

An important discussion of the disassociation of poetry and music in the thirteenth and fourteenth centuries. "Personal" poetry, which claims to reveal biographical aspects of the poet, is not poetry to be set to music. In Adam de la Halle and Machaut, personal poetry is not lyrical poetry, but the *dit*. Some discussion of *Voir Dit* (231) and Deschamps's artificial and natural music (232). Abstract: *RILM* 16 (1982), no. 5990.

1990. *Le Moyen Age: Littérature française*. Collection Phares. Nancy: Presses Universitaires de Nancy.

Survey; Machaut is discussed on pp. 122–27.

1991. "The Time of the Plague and the Order of Writing: Jean le Bel, Froissart, Machaut," trans. Katherine Lydon. *Yale French Studies Special Edition; Contexts: Style and Values in Medieval Art and Literature*, ed. Daniel Poirion and Nancy Freeman Regalado, 269–80.

Comparison of descriptions of the Black Death in Jean le Bel, Froissart, and the prologue to Machaut's *Jugement Navarre*. Machaut upsets the sequence of historical events because he follows a poetic logic. Ironically, the chroniclers—interested mainly in writing political history—say little of the plague, while Machaut's more complete poetic description is more satisfying to us as history.

1992. *Littérature française du Moyen Age*. Collection Premier Cycle. Paris: Presses Universitaires de France.

Excellent survey; the late Middle Ages (fourteenth and fifteenth centuries) are treated in part 4 (265–301); Machaut is discussed on pp. 278–81. Reviews: Micheline de Combarieu du Gres, *Revue des langues romanes* 97 (1993): 415–19; Stewart Gregory, *French Studies* 48 (1994): 86–87.

Zink, Michel, with Pierre-Yves Badel.
1991. "Histoire littéraire." In *L'histoire médiévale en France: Bilan et perspectives*. Preface by Georges Duby, ed. Michel Balard, 199–218. Société des Historiens Médiévistes de l'Enseignement Supérieur. L'Univers Historique. Paris: Seuil.

Interesting résumé of the achievements of the period 1965 to 1985 in French literary criticism, treating manuals, editions, socio-historical approaches, formalist approaches, psychoanalytical approaches, linguistics, and new paths.

Zipay, Terry Lee.
1983. "Closure in the Motets of Machaut." Ph.D. diss. State University of New York at Buffalo. Ann Arbor: University Microfilms. Order no. 8312465.

"Closure refers to the perception of points of relative repose which articulate patterns and complete events" (iv). For each of Machaut's motets, five appended graphs explore the contribution of melody, poetry, harmony, and rhythm towards the articulation of structure; a composite of the four parameters indicates its relative strength. Abstracts: *DAI* A 44/1 (July 1983): 12–13; *RILM* 17 (1983), no. 4031.

Zumthor, Paul.

1972. *Essai de poétique médiévale.* Collection Poétique. Paris: Seuil. *Toward a Medieval Poetics,* trans. Philip Bennett. Minneapolis and Oxford: University of Minnesota Press, 1992.

Zumthor's discussion of new critical strategies for approaching medieval French poetry strongly influenced the critical reorientation of the 1970s. Zumthor emphasizes considerations that bear on our modern act of "reading" and "interpreting" a medieval text. For many medieval works, the question arises of who is the "author," and what is the "work." The relationship of poet and text ranges from the performative recreation of works, characteristic of much early medieval literature that was primarily orally transmitted (e.g., epic), to the more modern concept of "author" and "work" seen in Machaut. Besides facing questions of orality head on, Zumthor's concept of *mouvance,* a term describing the fluidity of the manuscript tradition for much medieval literature, has remained influential. His analyses of courtly love lyrics eschew the concept of genre, and utilize instead linguistic criteria he calls "registers." Although Zumthor does not often address Machaut directly, his ideas contributed to the remarkable renewal of interest in the fourteenth century seen in the last thirty years. Reviews of French ed.: Pierre-Yves Badel, *Poétique* 5 (1974): 246–64; Morton W. Bloomfield, *Speculum* 49 (1974): 388–90; Al. Călinescu, *Cahiers roumains d'études littéraires,* fasc. 4 (1976): 110–13; Costanzo Di Girolamo, *Cultura neolatina* 32 (1972): 261–64; Robert Guiette, *Revue belge de philologie et d'histoire* 52 (1974): 92–94; Peter Haidu, *Diacritics* 4/2 (summer 1974): 2–11; Marcel Lobet, *Revue générale* 108/7 (Sept. 1972): 109; Francisco López Estrada, *Anuario de estudios medievales* 9 (1974–79): 733–86; Jean-Claude Margolin, *Etudes philosophiques* 28 (1973): 425–26; W. Noomen, *Rapports—Het Franse Boek* 43 (1973): 97–99; Jean-Marcel Paquette, *Etudes littéraires* 7 (1974): 193–94; J.C. Payen, *Moyen Age* 80 (1974): 563–66; Damnjan Petrović, *Filološki pregled* 22 (1974): 111–14; Daniel Poirion, *Le Monde* (17 Nov. 1972); Elżbieta Sarnowska-Temeriusz, *Pamiętnik literacki* 66/1 (1975): 400–407; Jean Rychner, *Zeitschrift für romanische Philologie* 89 (1973): 552–55; Wolf-Dieter Stempel, *Archiv für das Studium der neueren Sprachen und Literaturen* 210 (1973): 445–52; Lewis A.M. Sumberg, *French Review* 47 (1973–74): 817–18; G. Turquin, *Le langage et l'homme* 22 (May 1973): 76; Eugene Vance, *Romanic Review* 64 (19-): 140–51; Harald Weinrich, *Romanische Forschungen* 85 (1973): 356–58; Friedrich Wolfzettel, *Germanisch-romanisch Monatsschrift* n.s. 26 (1976): 237–41; Alicia Yllera, *Filología moderna* 13 (1972–73): 171–72. Review of English trans.: Roger Pensom, "Zumthor and After: A Survey of Some Current Trends in the Reading of Old French Literature," *Medium Ævum* 62 (1993): 294–306.

1973. "Autobiography in the Middle Ages?" trans. Sherry Simon. *Genre* 6: 29–48.

Typology based on the use of the pronoun "I" in medieval French poetry; mention of *Voir Dit,* 45–46.

Zwick, Gabriel.

1948. "Deux motets inédits de Philippe de Vitry et de Guillaume de Machaut." *Revue de musicologie* 30:28–57, facsimile.

Description of the fragment **Frib** [70] and its two motets, with transcriptions. The motet attributed to Machaut (*Li enseignement* / *De touz*) has a concordance in **Iv** [57], but does not appear in the main Machaut tradition. Zwick takes it as a work of Machaut, but it is surely not authentic.

Index of manuscripts

(Numbers in square brackets following MS *sigla* are keyed to the through-numbered descriptions in chapter 3; these main descriptions are listed in boldface.)

A. *See* Paris, Bibliothèque Nationale, MS fr. 1584

Aberystwyth, National Library of Wales
MS 5010 C: **W** [2]: 75, **79–84**, 96, 97, 102, 185 n. 210, 190, 191, 193, 206; *Loange* in, 247–52; music section in, 292, 338, 340, 360; narrative *dits* in, 206, 207, 212, 217

AMR. *See* Reims, Archives départementales de la Marne, Annexe de Reims

Apt, Basilique Sainte-Anne, Trésor
MS 16*bis*: 346

Ar. *See* Arras, Bibliothèque Municipale, MS 897

Aragon. *See* lost manuscripts: Aragon

Arras, Bibliothèque Municipale
MS 897: **Ar** [32]: **107**, 138, 149, 207

Ars. *See* Paris, Bibliothèque de l'Arsenal, MS 683

Autun, Bibliothèque Municipale
MS 152: 346

B. *See* Paris, Bibliothèque Nationale, MS fr. 1585

Barcelona, Biblioteca de Catalunya
MS 8: **Bc** [55]: 75, 106 and n. 58, 112 and n. 68, 113, **120–21**, 253, 266
MS M 971: 65 n. 48

Bayeux chansonnier. *See* Paris, Bibliothèque Nationale, MS fr. 9346

Bc. *See* Barcelona, Biblioteca de Catalunya, MS 8

Berkeley, University of California, Music Library
MS 744: 68, 334

Berlin, Staatliche Museen Preussischer Kulturbesitz, Kupferstichkabinett
Court scenes (parchment strip), 133
MS 78 C 2: **Bk** [21]: **103–4**, 109, 131, 215; miniatures in, 138, 140–41, 158–63

Bern, Burgerbibliothek
MS A 95 (10): **L** [34]: 8, **107–8**, 218
MS 218: **K** [15]: 46, 57, 76 n. 13, **97–99**, 102, 116, 219, 243, 289, 292, 303, 317, 365, 371, 384; *Loange* in, 240 n. 9, 247–51, 255; miniatures in, 129, 135, 139–45, 147–50, 152–63, 165–75, 181–82, 184–85, 187–88; narrative *dits* in, 206–7, 212, 215, 218, 220, 223;

works not by Machaut in, 98, 111, 125 n. 94, 240 n. 9

Besançon, Bibliothèque Municipale
MS 434: 135

Bk. *See* Berlin, Staatliche Museen Preussischer Kulturbesitz, Kupferstichkabinett, MS 78 C 2

Bruges. *See* lost manuscripts: Bruges

Brussels. *See* lost manuscripts: Brussels

C. *See* Paris, Bibliothèque Nationale, MS fr. 1586

CaB. *See* Cambrai, Bibliothèque Municipale, MS B.1328

Cambrai, Bibliothèque Municipale
Inc. B 144: 121 n. 89
Inc. B 447: 121 n. 90
MS B.1328: **CaB** [56]: 118 n. 83, **121**, 310, 367, 378

Cambridge, Magdalene College, Pepysian Library
MS 1594: **Pe** [20]: **103**, 117 n. 81, 138, 154, 212, 302, 303, 317, 335, 368, 379, 380

Ch. *See* Chantilly, Bibliothèque du Musée Condé, MS 564

Chantilly, Bibliothèque du Musée Condé
MS 485: [33]: **107**, 218
MS 564: **Ch** [59]: 65 and n. 45, 67, 74, 117 n. 79, 118 n. 82, 121, **123**, 309, 310, 363, 386

Chambéry. *See* lost manuscripts: Chambéry

Chartier. See Paris, Pierre Le Caron

Châteaudun. *See* lost manuscripts: Châteaudun

Clermont-Ferrand, Bibliothèque Municipale
MS 249: [42]: 106, **111**, 223

Cleveland, Cleveland Museum of Art
no. 62.287 (Gotha Missal): 134

D. *See* Paris, Bibliothèque Nationale, MS fr. 1587

E. *See* Paris, Bibliothèque Nationale, MS fr. 9221

E:Bc. *See* Barcelona, Biblioteca de Catalunya

E:Sco. *See* Seville, Biblioteca Colombina

General Index

Index of titles, first lines, and refrains

(Principal discussions are listed in boldface.)